Contributors

Graeme J. Milne is Senior Lecturer in Modern History at the University of Liverpool, United Kingdom

Anders Monrad Møller is a former lecturer at the University of Copenhagen, Denmark

Leos Müller is Professor of History at Stockholm University, Sweden

Martin N. Murphy is a Visiting Fellow at the Corbett Centre for Maritime Policy Studies, Kings' College London

Phillips Payson O'Brien is Emeritus Professor of Economic History at the London School of Economics, London, United Kingdom

Avner Offer is Chichele Professor Emeritus of Economic History at the University of Oxford, and a Fellow of All Souls College, Oxford, United Kingdom

Kevin Hjortshøj O'Rourke is Chichele Professor of Economic History at the University of Oxford, and a Fellow of All Souls College, Oxford, United Kingdom

S.C.M. Paine is William S. Sims Professor of History and Grand Strategy at the US Naval War College, United States

Sarah Palmer is Emeritus Professor of Maritime History at the University of Greenwich, United Kingdom

Andrew Preston is Professor of American History at the University of Cambridge, and a Fellow of Clare College, Cambridge, United Kingdom

Werner Rahn is a Captain (ret.) of the German Navy and freelance researcher and lecturer in Military and Naval History, Germany

N.A.M. Rodger is a Senior Research Fellow, All Souls College, Oxford, United Kingdom

Nicholas Evan Sarantakes is an Associate Professor of Strategy at the US Naval War College, United States

Norman Saul is Professor Emeritus of History at the University of Kansas, United States

Lawrence Sondhaus is Professor in History and Director of the Graduate Program in History at the University of Indianapolis, United States

David Stevens is Director of Strategic and Historical Studies at the Department of Defence, Canberra, Australia

Jon T. Sumida is Professor in the Department of History, University of Maryland, United States

Craig L. Symonds is Professor Emeritus, US Naval Academy, United States

Geoffrey Till is Professor of Maritime Studies at King's College London, United Kingdom

Jesús M. Valdaliso is Professor of Economic History and Institutions at the University of the Basque Country, Spain

Brian Vale is an independent researcher, United Kingdom

Anita M.C. van Dissel is a Lecturer at Leiden University, the Netherlands

Philippe Vial is Research Director of the Centre d'Etudes d'Histoire de la Défense, France

Johanna von Grafenstein is Professor in Latin American Studies at the Instituto Mora, Mexico

Francesco Zampieri is a lecturer at the Naval Staff College, Italy

Abbreviations

AB	Able seaman
ADEME	Agence de l'Environnement et de la Maîtrise de l'énergie
AIFM	Autorité internationale des fonds marins [=ISA]
APEC	Asia Pacific Economic Cooperation group
ASEAN	Association of South-East Asian Nations
ASL	Archipelagic sea lanes
ASW	Anti-Submarine Warfare
ATS	Amphetamine-type stimulants
BATRAL	Bâtiments de transports légers
BMW	Bayerische Motoren Werke
BP	British Petroleum
BPF	British Pacific Fleet
CEE	Communauté économique européenne
CCP	Chinese Communist Party
CEP	Centre d'expérimentation du Pacifique
CESA	Community of European Shipyards Associations
CFM	Cluster maritime français
CGM	Compagnie Générale Maritime
CGT	Compagnie Générale Transatlantique
CIMer	Comité interministériel de la mer
CLCS	Commission on the Limits of the Continental Shelf
CMA	Compagnie Maritime d'Affrètement
CNEXO	Centre national pour l'exploitation des océans
CNG	Compressed natural gas
CNRS	Centre national de la recherche scientifique
CSS	Confederate States Ship
CTO	Caribbean Tourist Organization
DATAR	Délégation à l'aménagement du territoire et à l'action régionale
DCNS	Direction des constructions navales
DEA	Drug Enforcement Agency
DFDS	Det Forenede Dampskibs Selskab
DGA	Délégation Générale pour l'Armement
DIP	Drug Interdiction Program
dwt	Deadweight tonnage

Abbreviations

EDF	Eléctricité de France
EEZ	Exclusive Economic Zone [=ZEE]
ERDF	European Regional Development Fund [=FEDER]
EROI	Energy return on investment
ESCO	Expertise scientifique collective [=Joint Scientific Appraisal]
EU	European Union
FPU	Floating Production Unit
FANu	Force aéronavale nucléaire
FAO	Food and Agriculture Organization
FARC	Fuerzas Armadas Revolucionárias de Colombia
FBI	Federal Bureau of Investigation
FEDER	Fonds européen de développement régional [=ERDF]
FOC	Flag of convenience
FOST	Force océanique stratégique
FPSO	Floating Production, Storage and Off-Landing
FPU	Floating Production Unit
GAM	Gerakan Aceh Merdeka
GDP	Gross Domestic Product
gf	gold francs
GHG	Greenhouse gas
GICAN	Groupement des industries de construction et activités navales
GIUK	Greenland-Iceland-UK Gap
GNP	Gross National Product
GoG	Gulf of Guinea
GRT	Gross Register Tons
HAL	Holland-America Line
Hapag	Hamburg-Amerikanische Packetfahrt Actiengesellschaft
HMAS	His Majesty's Australian Ship
HMCS	Her Majesty's Canadian Ship
HMS	Her/His Majesty's Ship
HSDG	Hamburg Südamerikanische Dampfschifffahrts-Gesellschaft
HSF	High Seas Fleet
ICJ	International Court of Justice
IEA	International Energy Agency
IFM	l'Institut français de la Mer
IFREMER	Institut Français de Recherche pour l'Exploitation de la Mer
ILO	International Labour Organization
IMB	International Maritime Bureau
IMO	International Maritime Organization
IOC	International oil companies
IPCC	Intergovernmental Panel on Climate Change
ISA	International Seabed Authority [=AIFM]
ISF	International Shipping Federation
ITF	International Transport Workers' Federation

ITLOS	International Tribunal for the Law of the Sea
JMSDF	Japanese Maritime Self-Defence Force
KuK	Kaiserlich und Königlich
LEA	Law enforcement agencies
LEDET	Law enforcement detachment
LeT	Lashkar-e-Taiba
LNG	Liquefied natural gas
LPG	Liquefied petroleum gas
LST	Landing Ship, Tank
LTTE	Liberation Tigers of Tamil Eelam
MARPOL	Convention against Marine Pollution
MCF	Maritime Contingency Forces
MEND	Movement for the Emancipation of the Niger Delta
MISMer	Mission interministérielle de la mer
MP	Member of Parliament
MT	Metric tons
MW	Megawatts
NATO	North Atlantic Treaty Organization [=OTAN]
NDA	Naval Defence Act
NGH	Natural gas hydrate
NGI	Navigazione Generale Italiana
NGO	Non-governmental organization
NHM	Nederlandsche Handel Maatschappij
NID	Naval Intelligence Department/Division
NLF	National Liberation Front (of Vietnam)
NSC	National Security Cutter
NYK	Nippon Yusen Kaisha
OAS	Organización de los Estados Americanos [=Organization of American States]
OBO	Oil and bulk ore carrier
OCS	Outer Continental shelf
OECD	Organization for Economic Co-operation and Development
O/O	Oil or ore carrier
OPEC	Organization of the Petroleum-Exporting Countries [=OPEP]
OPEP	Organisation des pays exportateurs de pétrole [=OPEC]
OSK	Osaka Shosen Kaisha
OTAN	Organisation du Traité de l'Atlantique Nord [=NATO]
OTEC	Ocean Thermal Energy Conversion
P&I	Protection and Indemnity
P&O	Peninsular and Oriental Steam Navigation Company
PLA	People's Liberation Army (of China)
PLAN	People's Liberation Army Navy
PNG	Pressurised natural gas
POA	Pacific Ocean Areas

Abbreviations

PRC	People's Republic of China; Piracy Reporting Centre
RAF	Royal Air Force
R&D	Research and development
RAN	Royal Australian Navy
RCN	Royal Canadian Navy
RCP	Representative Concentration Pathways
RIM	Royal Indian Marine
RL	Rotterdamsche Lloyd
RMS	Royal Mail Ship
RN	Royal Navy
RNN	Royal Netherlands Navy
ROC	Republic of China
SACEUR	Supreme Allied Commander Europe
SACLANT	Supreme Allied Commander Atlantic
SGMer	Secrétariat général de la mer
SHOM	Service hydrographique et océanographique de la marine
SLBM	Submarine-launched ballistic missile
SMN	Stoomvaart Maatschappij 'Nederland'
SNA	Sous-marin nucléaire d'attaque
SNLE	Sous-marin nucléaire lanceur d'engins
SNML	Stratégie nationale pour la mer et le littoral
SOLAS	(Convention on) Safety of Life at Sea
SPSS	Self-propelled semi-submersibles
SSBN	Ballistic-missile carrying nuclear submarine
SSN	Nuclear attack submarine
SWPA	South-West Pacific Area
TAAF	Terres australes et antarctiques françaises
TEU	Twenty-foot equivalent units
tjb	tonnage de jauge brute [=GRT]
TNI	Tentara Nasional Indonesia
TZ	Transit zone
UAV	Unmanned aerial vehicle
UBC	Universal bulk carriers
UE	Union Européenne
UK	United Kingdom
UN	United Nations
UNCLOS	United Nations Conference/Convention on the Law of the Sea
UNCTAD	United Nations Conference on Trade and Development
UNSC	United Nations Security Council
URSS	Union des Républiques Socialistes Soviétiques [=USSR]
USA	United States of America
USAAF	United States Army Air Force
US	United States [of America]
USCG	United States Coast Guard

Abbreviations

USN	United States Navy
USS	United States Ship
USSR	Union of Soviet Socialist Republics [=URSS]
VLCC	Very large crude (oil) carrier
WTO	World Trade Organization
ZEE	Zone exclusive économique [=EEZ]

General Introduction

'History is not a fishing expedition, historians do not cast their net at random to see what (if any) fish they may catch. We will never find answers to questions that have not been asked', wrote Antoine Prost in his remarkable book *Douze Leçons sur l'Histoire*.[1] This is the very spirit, the sum and substance of Océanides.

This international research programme, unprecedented in the breadth of its approach since the publication of the first Encyclopædia, does not aim to write a maritime history of the world; indeed, diverse teams have already done so within various academic initiatives. Rather, building on the proliferation of research into maritime history, particularly over the past 15 years, the goal is to answer the following question: *is the sea the differentiating factor in the overall development of populations?* What developments can be attributed to the sea, both in general history and in the history of specific entities, particularly political entities? How did the sea modify the course of history for the populations in question? In what ways do maritime activities make it possible to consolidate strength and development by enabling actors to take full advantage of demographic potential and scientific knowledge, as well as geographic, political and financial situations? Is the sea a factor in success, development and/or influence? For the purposes of this study, the 'sea' is more than the water and the beach. It also encompasses all activities linked with maritime pursuits, be they on the shore, on riverbanks or even far inland.

This research programme is organized around simple questions that apply everywhere and throughout history:

- Is the sea the differentiating factor in world history, part and parcel of the most distinguished accomplishments?
- What additional advantages did the sea provide to the groups that engaged in maritime activities (regardless of the nature of the populations in question: social groups, tribes, peoples, cultural entities, regions, cities, states, etc.) compared to other groups that remained firmly on dry land? How did the sea influence development and leadership, however these phenomena may be manifested in relation to economy, culture, forms of political organization, technical progress, etc., and how have these contributions continued to the present day?

---

[1] Prost A., *Douze Leçons sur l'Histoire*, Paris : Éditions du Seuil (1996).

- What resources (natural, human, financial, etc.) did these groups have at their disposal before taking to the sea? What were their needs?
- What was the structure and hierarchy of these groups when they turned toward the sea? Are some systems of political or social organization more likely than others to engender a pronounced interest in the sea?
- What benefits did the sea provide to these groups? Did it feed and supply them generally? Did it furnish the means to trade, pillage, explore, and to dominate by controlling maritime traffic or deploying overwhelming force by sea?
- What are the respective developmental paths for fishing fleets, trade fleets, war fleets and even scientific fleets, and how might they intersect with each other?

The number and diversity of questions to be addressed demonstrates the scope of the investigation.

- The identities and organizational structures of the different players are highly diverse in nature and are not necessarily linked to the political arena (when an overarching political entity has yet to emerge, is challenged, or supplanted, or simply not involved);
- Resources: what financial or natural resources are required for a population to turn toward the sea? What needs is the group in question looking to meet?
- Contexts, also highly diverse, that serve to shed light on motivations for taking to the sea, ranging from subsistence to world domination;
- Indispensable tools to navigate at sea: which ships are suited to which activities? What is the relationship between quantity and quality? How can equipment be adapted to meet the desired objectives? What infrastructure is necessary? What activities are related to this infrastructure?
- Trajectories of development associated with maritime activities and with variations of such activities, the areas of development to which they contribute.

Assessing the importance of the sea in World History requires nothing less than a re-examination of Universal History through that particular lens. This analytical inquiry could not be conducted solely by historians specialized in the Western world. We had to bring together historians from every region of the globe. One of the principal achievements of this Research Programme is its contribution to the breaking down of barriers between academic communities which, with their excessive focus on their respective areas of research, find themselves isolated from one another.

With one small stroke after another, through encounters between different communities, and with the support of an international scientific council that explored beyond the Western world, we gradually succeeded in weighing anchor with a crew of 260 researchers from 40 countries,[2] ensuring that all major geographic areas were truly represented.

We were able to consider the extent to which visions of Universal History vary from one region to another, always strongly influenced by a terrestrial focus. The phases of Western history that underpin the most widely used chronological structure, with its four periods (Antiquity, Medieval, Early Modern and Modern), are undoubtedly ill-suited to many parts of the world, such as Asia, Oceania, etc.

We realized very early on that the sea, as a vector of communication between peoples, could serve to balance historical temporality and enable us to attain a universal structuration. Nonetheless, we first had to assess the significance of maritime activities in each area and for each period, and to make connections in order to allow a new division of World History into periods to emerge, to be verified and to be validated scientifically. Thus, out of a desire for absolute rigour, we have worked within the framework of four historical periods, ancient, medieval, early modern and modern, and devoted a volume to each one. As a conclusion, we presented the benefits that viewing World History through a maritime lens can provide for Universal History and for people today, whether they are from the worlds of politics, economics or geopolitics.

Indeed, by demonstrating that the sea has governed a grand equilibrium, Océanides makes it possible to move forward from intuition, which Alfred Mahan was among the first to exhibit,[3] to a verified assessment, indeed, more even than that, to a vision of History laden with meaning, sure to provide insights for any decision-maker and to demonstrate to any and all that the sea is the key to History. Based on this assessment, the sea is evidently the catalyst of our future.

CHRISTIAN BUCHET
from the Académie de Marine,
Professor of Maritime History, Catholic University of Paris,
Océanides Scientific Director

---

[2] Australia, Belgium, Brazil, Canada, China, Ivory Coast, Croatia, Cyprus, Denmark, Egypt, Estonia, Finland, France, Germany, Greece, India, Ireland, Israel, Italy, Japan, Mexico, The Netherlands, Norway, Peru, Philippines, Portugal, Russia, Senegal, Singapore, Spain, Sweden, Switzerland, Taiwan, Tanzania, Togo, Tunisia, Turkey, Ukraine, United Kingdom, United States.
[3] MAHAN A.T., *The Influence of Sea Power Upon History, 1660-1783*, Paris and London: s.n. (1890).

Acknowledgements

On behalf of the 260 scientists involved in Océanides, it is a gratifying duty to recognize the companies and institutions cited at the end of the volume for their support, which made this ambitious research programme possible.

Thanks are also in order for Mrs Anne-Marie Idrac, Chair of the Board of Directors, Mrs Claudie Haigneré, Chair of the Committee of Honour, and the members of these two bodies, for their consistent support and encouragement.

Maxime Petiet, Treasurer of Océanides, and Managing Director Sabine Marie Decup-Provost also contributed to making this work possible thanks to their daily and ebullient commitment. They deserve our gratitude.

I would also like to thank the 260 Océanides researchers who were willing to reorganize their own research programmes and other commitments to accommodate our requests with enthusiasm, as well as the members of the Scientific Committee for their insights and vigilance, and I convey my sincere gratitude to the Period Directors, Pascal Arnaud, Michel Balard, Philip de Souza, Gérard Le Bouédec and Nicholas Rodger, for the extensive and extraordinary work they have accomplished.

Finally, special thanks go out to Patrick Boissier, as Océanides was born from our cordial encounters. Patrick, thank you for entrusting me with a feasibility study back in 2010 as Chairman of DCNS, and for leading this wonderful project to the success embodied by these four initial volumes.

Christian Buchet
from the Académie de Marine,
Océanides Scientific Director

Introduction générale

« L'histoire n'est pas une pêche au filet, l'historien ne lance pas son chalut au hasard, pour voir s'il prendra des poissons et lesquels. On ne trouvera jamais la réponse à des questions qu'on ne s'est pas posées » écrivait Antoine Prost dans son remarquable ouvrage *Douze Leçons sur l'Histoire*[1]. Là est précisément tout l'esprit, tout l'objet d'Océanides.

L'ambition de ce programme international de recherches qui n'a pas de précédent par son ampleur, en Sciences humaines, depuis l'Encyclopédie n'est pas d'écrire une histoire maritime mondiale, que différents travaux menés par diverses équipes ont déjà édifiée. Il s'agit, fort du développement qu'ont connu les recherches en histoire maritime, notamment depuis une quinzaine d'années, de répondre à la question suivante : *est-ce le fait maritime qui fait la différence dans l'évolution générale des peuples ?* Quelles sont les évolutions imputables à la mer dans l'histoire générale comme dans l'histoire particulière des entités, notamment politiques ? Comment la mer a-t-elle changé la trajectoire des ensembles considérés ? Comment le fait de se tourner vers la mer permet-il d'exploiter au mieux le potentiel démographique, la situation géographique, politique, financière, les connaissances scientifiques... pour constituer un puissant moteur de développement et de puissance ? La mer est-elle un facteur de réussite, de développement, de rayonnement ? En parlant de mer, nous désignons non seulement les flots et l'estran mais aussi tout ce qui vit d'elle sur le rivage, le long des fleuves et jusque loin dans l'intérieur des terres.

Ce programme de recherche se décline en questions simples, valables en tous lieux et toute époque :

- Est-ce que la mer est le facteur discriminant dans l'histoire du monde, inséparable de toutes les réussites les plus accomplies ?
- Qu'est-ce que la mer a apporté en plus aux groupes humains (quelle que soit leur nature : groupes sociaux, tribus, peuples, ensembles culturels, régions, villes, États...) qui se sont tournés vers elle si nous les comparons avec d'autres qui, eux, se sont désintéressés des flots ? Économie, culture, formes d'organisation politique, progrès techniques... en quoi fut-elle hier, et est-elle aujourd'hui encore, cause de développement et de rayonnement (quelles que soient les formes prises par ceux-ci) ?

---

[1] PROST A., *Douze Leçons sur l'Histoire*, Paris: Éditions du Seuil (1996).

- De quelles ressources (naturelles, humaines, financières...) ces groupes disposaient-ils avant de se lancer sur la mer ? Quels étaient leurs besoins ?
- Comment ces groupes étaient-ils structurés ou dirigés au moment où ils se sont tournés vers la mer ? Certaines formes d'organisation politique ou sociale sont-elles plus propices que d'autres à un intérêt marqué pour la mer ?
- Quels usages de la mer ? Se nourrir et plus largement s'approvisionner, commercer ou razzier, explorer, imposer sa domination (soit en contrôlant les circulations maritimes, soit en franchissant la mer en force) ...
- Quelles sont les logiques respectives de développement des marines de pêche, de commerce, de guerre, voire scientifique, et les interactions qui peuvent exister entre elles ?

La richesse du questionnement permet de mesurer l'ampleur du champ d'investigation.

- Les acteurs qui sont très variés et ne relèvent pas nécessairement du niveau politique (lorsque celui-ci n'existe pas encore, se trouve dépassé ou contesté, ou bien n'est tout simplement pas concerné), leurs formes d'organisation ;
- Les ressources : de quelles ressources financières ou naturelles est-il nécessaire de disposer pour qu'un groupe humain se tourne vers la mer ? Quels besoins cherche-t-on à satisfaire ?
- Les contextes, eux aussi très divers, qui éclairent les motivations portant à choisir la mer, de la subsistance à l'aspiration à la domination universelle ;
- Les instruments indispensables aux usages de la mer : quels navires et pour quelles utilisations ? Quels rapports entre le nombre et la qualité ? Quelle adéquation entre le matériel et les objectifs recherchés ? Quelles infrastructures ? Quelles activités liées à celles-ci ?
- Les trajectoires de développement liées aux usages de la mer et aux variations de ceux-ci, les domaines de développement concernés par eux.

Évaluer le poids de la mer dans l'Histoire mondiale n'est rien moins que de revisiter l'Histoire Universelle sous ce prisme particulier. Ce questionnement analytique ne pouvait faire l'objet de la seule appréhension par les historiens spécialisés du monde occidental. Il nous fallait faire travailler ensemble des historiens de toutes les régions du monde, et ce n'est pas l'un des moindres mérites de ce Programme de recherches que d'avoir contribué à décloisonner des communautés universitaires par trop centrées sur leurs zones de recherches respectives et sans liens les unes avec les autres.

Par petites touches successives, par les contacts des uns et des autres, en nous appuyant sur un conseil scientifique international et dépassant le seul cadre occidental, nous sommes progressivement parvenus à appareiller avec un

Introduction générale

équipage de 260 chercheurs issus de 40 pays[2], en veillant à ce que toutes les grandes zones géographiques soient véritablement et non marginalement représentées.

Nous avons pu mesurer combien les découpes de l'Histoire Universelle varient d'un espace géographique à l'autre, toujours sous l'emprise du tropisme terrien. Les temps de l'histoire de l'Occident qui constituent la structuration la plus communément utilisée avec ses quatre Temps (Antiquité, Moyen Âge, Moderne et Contemporaine) n'est assurément pas opérante dans bien des espaces, à commencer par l'Asie, l'Océanie ...

Très tôt, nous avons senti que la mer, vecteur de communication entre les peuples pouvait être le balancier de la temporalité historique et permettre d'aboutir à une structuration universelle. Mais il nous fallait peser préalablement la part du maritime dans chaque espace et à chaque période, opérer des rapprochements pour pouvoir laisser scientifiquement émerger, vérifier, valider une nouvelle segmentation des Temps de l'Histoire mondiale. C'est ainsi que dans un souci de rigueur absolue, nous avons œuvré dans le cadre des quatre temps de l'histoire que sont les périodes antique, médiévale, moderne et contemporaine, et consacré un volume à chacun d'eux, avant de présenter en conclusion ce que l'Histoire du monde sous le prisme du maritime peut apporter à l'Histoire Universelle et à la réflexion des hommes d'aujourd'hui, qu'elle soit d'ordre politique, économique ou géopolitique.

En effet, en montrant que la mer a présidé aux grands équilibres, Océanides permet de passer d'une intuition, qu'Alfred Mahan a été l'un des tout premiers à porter[3], à un constat. Bien plus, à une vision de l'Histoire qui lui donne sens et qui ne manquera pas d'être éclairante pour tout décideur, et qui peut montrer à tout un chacun que la mer est la clef de l'Histoire et, partant de ce constat, à l'évidence le catalyseur de notre avenir.

Christian Buchet
de l'Académie de Marine,
Professeur d'Histoire maritime, Institut catholique de Paris,
Directeur scientifique d'Océanides

---

[2] Allemagne, Australie, Belgique, Brésil, Canada, Chine, Chypre, Côte d'Ivoire, Croatie, Danemark, Égypte, Espagne, Estonie, États-Unis, Finlande, France, Grèce, Inde, Irlande, Israël, Italie, Japon, Mexique, Norvège, Pays-Bas, Pérou, Philippines, Portugal, Royaume-Uni, Russie, Sénégal, Singapour, Suède, Suisse, Taïwan, Tanzanie, Togo, Tunisie, Turquie, Ukraine.

[3] MAHAN A.T., *L'Influence de la puissance maritime sur l'Histoire, 1660-1783*, Paris et Londres: s.n. (1890).

Remerciements

Il m'est un bien agréable devoir de remercier, au nom de l'ensemble des 260 scientifiques d'Océanides, les entreprises et institutions, citées à la fin de ce volume, qui ont soutenues et donc permis la réalisation de cet ambitieux programme de recherches.

Que Madame Anne-Marie Idrac, Présidente du Conseil d'Administration, Madame Claudie Haigneré, Présidente du Comité d'Honneur trouvent également l'expression de notre gratitude pour leurs encouragements et leurs soutiens constants, et à travers leurs personnes à chacun des membres du Conseil d'Administration et du Comité d'Honneur.

Rien n'eut été aussi possible sans l'implication souriante de tous les jours de Maxime Petiet, Trésorier d'Océanides, et de notre Déléguée générale Sabine Marie Decup-Provost, qu'ils trouvent ici le témoignage de notre reconnaissance.

Je remercie les 260 chercheurs d'Océanides qui n'ont pas hésité à bousculer leurs propres programmes de recherches et autres engagements pour répondre avec enthousiasme à notre sollicitation, les membres du Conseil scientifique pour leur éclairage et leur vigilance de tous les instants, et remercie, avec chaleur, les directeurs de périodes, Pascal Arnaud, Michel Balard, Philip de Souza, Gérard Le Bouédec, Nicholas Rodger, pour le long et magnifique travail accompli.

Enfin, je voudrais remercier de manière particulière Patrick Boissier. C'est de nos rencontres amicales qu'est née l'idée d'Océanides. Merci cher Patrick de m'avoir confié, en 2010, en tant que Président de DCNS, une étude de faisabilité et d'avoir porté ce formidable projet dont ces quatre volumes en sont les premiers fruits.

Christian Buchet
de l'Académie de Marine,
Directeur scientifique d'Océanides

Introduction

There are many ways of thinking and writing about history, but the usual practice of scholars with new research to report is to concentrate on subjects sufficiently limited and precise to be thoroughly explored within the limits of a single article or book. This means that such writing is typically detailed and sometimes technical, addressed to fellow-scholars, or at least assuming some knowledge of the subject and its background. It will invariably be supported by a full apparatus of notes indicating the sources, and often by statistics, documents and other evidence. For general readers or undergraduates, historians will adopt a different style, covering a broader sweep of the past by summing-up their own and others' research. Such writing is designed to be more accessible, but it too will be supported by references to the published works on which it is based. Both sorts of history are firmly based on the most and best available evidence. This is fundamentally factual history, of what is known for certain or can be confidently inferred. The conventions intended to ensure intellectual rigour provide it with a formal structure which deliberately limits the scope for speculation. The deeper meaning of the history, its significance for modern society, is likely to be left for other writings, if not other writers.

The scholars who have written for the Océanides project are all authorities on their subjects, but they were not asked to write conventional scholarly articles, to undertake fresh research, nor to summarize all that is known on a particular subject in the style of an encyclopaedia. Their brief was to write interpretative essays exploring the significance of a particular subject and period of history through the lens of a single basic question. In its simplest form, the question was 'was it the sea which made the difference?', or 'what difference did the sea make?' These are simple questions, even simplistic, but they are meant to force authors and readers to reconsider the broad significance of their subjects in a way which conventional detailed scholarship does not usually do. Though the range of subjects and the styles of treatment vary a good deal, the fact that the same basic question is being put to each gives the whole work a common theme and unity.

Using this basic question of course exposes the editors' basic assumption. The project assumes that the sea exists – a fact not obviously known to all historians – and takes it as at least a plausible hypothesis that the sea was important. It might be objected that the subjects are all ones in which the sea was evidently involved; that they have been chosen to elicit the answer 'yes', the sea did make

1

a difference. There is no study in this volume of the importance of the sea to, say, the Sahara Desert (though such a one could have been written, the trans-Sahara trade routes being both extensions and competitors of seaborne trades). The point of asking the big, simple question, however, was not to get the big, simple answer 'yes', but to encourage authors and readers to reflect on how and why, when and where it mattered. The authors believe that the importance of the sea in history has not been fully appreciated, and intend these studies to demonstrate the many ways and circumstances in which the sea has made a difference. In that sense these essays test a hypothesis; they may be regarded as so many 'thought-experiments' applied to a range of real situations in the past, stretching in some cases up to the present day and even somewhat into the future. It is in the nature of history that such studies cannot be regarded as definite proofs, since we do not have an alternative history of a world without sea with which to make comparisons. In the hands of good scholars, however, causes and effects can be connected with a high degree of probability. In the case of this, the last of four volumes, whose period ranges from the nineteenth century well into the twenty-first, it is explicit as well as implicit that history connects the past with the present and the future. The significance of the sea in the past is laden with meaning for our own time, and our children's.

These are short essays by experts who were invited to reflect on the significance of their subjects, but not to deploy detailed new research. They are united by a common theme, but no attempt has been made to enforce a completely standard style. Different scholars, handling a range of subjects and periods with different approaches and materials, have naturally adopted varied styles. The influence of national schools of history can be discerned: many nationalities are represented here, though all the sections are written in either French or English. Readers will also observe, if they do not already know, that maritime historians tend to divide between those who write about war and strategy, and those who specialise in trade and economics. The contributors to this volume were encouraged to integrate the two approaches as far as possible, in the hope of making clear how closely they are in fact linked.

Contributors were encouraged to keep their notes to a minimum and rely as far as possible on a short bibliography. Some, however, who draw on little-known or unpublished research, have had good reason to provide a fuller apparatus of references.

Introduction

S'il existe de nombreuses façons de penser et d'écrire l'Histoire, de se concentrer sur des sujets suffisamment restreints et précis pour être explorés de manière exhaustive au sein d'un seul article ou ouvrage est maintenant devenu la pratique courante des chercheurs qui doivent rendre compte d'une nouvelle recherche. Cela veut dire qu'un tel texte est généralement détaillé, parfois technique, et qu'il s'adresse à des collègues chercheurs, ou du moins suppose quelques connaissances préalables du sujet et de son contexte. Il s'appuiera systématiquement sur un appareil complet de notes indiquant les sources, et souvent sur des statistiques, des documents et d'autres preuves. Pour les lecteurs profanes ou les étudiants de premier cycle, les historiens adopteront un style différent, en balayant un spectre plus large du passé et en résumant leurs propres recherches et celles des autres. De tels textes sont conçus pour être plus faciles d'accès, mais s'appuient également sur leurs ouvrages de référence. Ces deux types de discours sur l'Histoire s'appuient solidement sur les preuves les plus sûres et les plus pertinentes qu'il soit. Il s'agit essentiellement d'une Histoire factuelle, de ce qui est connu avec certitude ou peut être déduit en toute confiance. Les conventions visant à garantir la rigueur intellectuelle des publications fournissent d'ailleurs un cadre formel qui limite délibérément les possibilités de spéculation. La signification profonde de l'Histoire, sa portée dans la société moderne, sont des réflexions laissées d'ordinaire à d'autre types d'écrits, voire à d'autres écrivains.

Les chercheurs (et les chercheuses) qui ont écrit pour le projet Océanides sont tous des autorités dans leur domaine. Mais il ne leur a pas été demandé de rédiger des articles universitaires, d'entreprendre de nouvelles recherches, ni de résumer l'état des connaissances sur un sujet particulier à la manière d'une encyclopédie. Leur mission a consisté à écrire des essais d'interprétation qui permettent d'explorer l'importance d'un sujet spécifique et d'une période historique donnée par le prisme d'une question simple. Dans son expression la plus claire, la question était la suivante : « Est-ce la mer qui a fait la différence ? », ou « En quoi la mer a-t-elle changé les choses ? » Ces questions sont simples, voire simplistes, mais elles ont pour but d'inciter les auteurs et les lecteurs à réexaminer la vaste portée des sujets proposés sur un mode que l'érudition académique et exhaustive ne permet généralement pas. Bien que l'éventail des sujets et leur traitement aient beaucoup varié, le fait que cette question élémentaire ait été posée à tous a donné à l'ensemble un thème commun et une unité.

Le recours à cette question essentielle révèle bien entendu les hypothèses de départ sur lesquelles se sont fondés les instigateurs du projet. On suppose que la mer existe – un fait qui n'est pas forcément connu de tous les historiens – et envisage au moins comme une hypothèse vraisemblable que la mer avait son importance. On pourrait objecter que la mer était clairement impliquée dans tous les sujets abordés, et que ces derniers ont justement été choisis pour obtenir la réponse suivante: « oui, la mer a fait la différence. » Il n'y a, par exemple, pas d'étude dans ce volume consacrée à l'importance du rôle de la mer par rapport au désert du Sahara (bien qu'une telle étude soit envisageable, les routes commerciales trans-sahariennes étant à la fois des prolongements et des concurrentes des routes commerciales maritimes). Toutefois, en posant cette question simple et générale, le but n'était pas d'obtenir la réponse simple et générale « oui », mais d'inciter les auteurs et les lecteurs à se demander pourquoi, comment, où et quand cela importait. Les auteurs ont estimé que l'importance du rôle de la mer dans l'Histoire n'a pas été appréciée à sa juste valeur, et ont voulu démontrer avec ces études les multiples façons et circonstances au cours desquelles la mer a fait la différence. En ce sens, ces essais vérifient une hypothèse; ils peuvent être considérés comme autant « d'expériences théoriques » appliquées à un éventail de situations réelles du passé, s'étendant dans certains cas jusque dans le présent, et même dans une certaine mesure dans le futur. De par la nature de l'Histoire, de telles études ne peuvent être considérées comme des preuves définitives, puisque nous ne disposons pas d'une Histoire alternative d'un monde sans mer pour établir des comparaisons. Cela dit, entre les mains de chercheurs éminents, les causes et les conséquences peuvent être reliées avec un haut degré de probabilité. Dans le cas qui nous intéresse, le dernier des quatre volumes, dont la période d'étude s'étend du XIXe siècle et s'avance dans le XXIe, il est à la fois explicite et implicite que l'Histoire relie le passé au présent et au futur. L'importance de la mer dans le passé est chargée de signification pour notre époque, et pour celle des générations futures.

Il s'agit ici de courts essais écrits par des spécialistes invités à réfléchir sur la portée de leurs sujets d'étude, sans mettre en œuvre une nouvelle recherche exhaustive. Ils sont unis par une thématique commune, mais il n'a pas été convenu d'un style standard. Des chercheurs différents, traitant un vaste éventail de sujets à des périodes différentes, avec des approches et des sources diverses, ont naturellement adopté des styles variés. On peut déceler l'influence des écoles nationales d'Histoire: de nombreuses nationalités sont ici représentées bien que tous les articles aient été rédigés en français ou en anglais. Les lecteurs remarqueront également, s'ils ne le savent pas déjà, que les historiens de la mer ont tendance à se diviser entre ceux qui écrivent sur la guerre et la stratégie, et ceux qui se spécialisent dans les échanges commerciaux et l'économie. Les contributeurs de ce volume ont été invités à incorporer autant que possible ces deux approches, dans le but de souligner combien elles sont en fait liées.

Les contributeurs ont également été incités à restreindre au minimum leur appareil de notes et à s'appuyer dans la mesure du possible sur une bibliographie succincte. Certains cependant, qui ont dessiné les contours d'une recherche méconnue ou inédite, ont eu de bonnes raisons de fournir un ensemble plus complet de références.

The sea and seapower within the international system

Paul Kennedy is Professor in History at Yale University, United States

Abstract. *The 19th century was dominated by naval power and seaborne trade, which allowed Britain to reproduce afloat something like the political and economic dominance of the Roman Empire. The Industrial Revolution reinforced British power for a short time, but quickly generated rival naval powers, while the strategic dangers of dependence on overseas markets and raw materials became clearer by the end of the century. An international naval arms race ensued in which Britain was challenged first by France and Russia, then the United States and Germany, but before and during the First World War Britain outspent all of them except the U.S.A., which was glad to get out of the race in 1922 with a nominal equality. The Washington Treaties "froze" the battle-fleets of the major powers, and diverted international competition towards the new technology of aircraft. Aircraft in turn, and submarines, were to change the nature of naval war, but the Second World War only confirmed the dominant role of navies in a world war. Post-war economic growth and the container revolution helped to shift the centre of gravity of world trade to the Pacific, and the centre of effort of the U.S. Navy from the Atlantic to the Pacific, but the sea and sea power remain today at the heart of international affairs.*

Résumé. *Le XIXe siècle fut dominé par la puissance navale et le commerce maritime, permettant à la Grande-Bretagne de reproduire sur l'eau une domination économique et politique proche de celle de l'Empire romain. La Révolution industrielle renforça l'autorité britannique pendant une courte période mais suscita rapidement la montée de puissances maritimes rivales. En outre, les dangers stratégiques d'une dépendance aux marchés et matières premières extérieurs devinrent plus clairs à la fin du siècle. Une course à l'armement naval internationale s'ensuivit, pour laquelle la Grande-Bretagne dut tout d'abord faire face à la France et la Russie, puis aux États-Unis et à l'Allemagne. Avant et pendant la première guerre mondiale, elle les surpassa tous, excepté les États-Unis qui se réjouit de sortir de la course en 1922 par une égalité symbolique. Le traité de Washington « gela » les flottes de combat des principales puissances et dispersa la compétition internationale vers la nouvelle technologie aérienne. L'avion et les sous-marins changèrent à leur tour la nature de la guerre navale, mais la seconde guerre mondiale ne fit que confirmer le rôle fondamental que revêtaient les marines en cas de conflit mondial. La croissance économique d'après-guerre et la révolution des conteneurs participèrent au déplacement du centre de gravité du commerce mondial vers le Pacifique et celui de l'effort de l'U.S. Navy de l'Atlantique au Pacifique. La mer et la puissance maritime demeurent néanmoins aujourd'hui au cœur des affaires internationales.*

.•.

Fig. 1. *HMS Ark Royal in Grand Harbour, Malta, c. 1937.* © Ian Marshall

By the time the riflemen, cuirassiers, and artillery troops left the fields of Waterloo in 1815, sea power had already established itself as a force in world affairs, especially Western affairs. With a few historical exceptions like the Greeks and the Vikings, the deployment of force at sea to effect major political change had been very rare in earlier times. This began to change after 1500, when the newer nation-states of Western Europe, aided by improvements in marine architecture and gunnery and navigation, began to exert their power and extend their rivalries upon the sea. The result was over three hundred years of naval struggles that ranged from the Baltic seas to the coasts of India and had by 1815 left one of the European powers, Great Britain, in almost absolute command of the maritime routes and commerce of much of the globe. Pax Britannica might have sounded boastful to those who knew the story of the Roman Empire; it did not sound so silly in, say, 1870 were one a resident of Malta or Cape Town.

Later theorists of empires and navies had no difficulty in explaining why this had come about, or at least of explaining the parts that made up it all. At the end of his magnificent studies on the sixteenth-century world, Braudel described how the Mediterranean was giving place to the Atlantic in terms of trade and power. The Indian author K.M. Panikkar symbolically termed the world after 1494 as "the Vasco da Gama era". The Italian economic historian Carlo Cipolla showed how much of this came about because of Europe's technological breakthroughs in "guns and sails" that abetted the explorations and imperial conquests. In the geopolitician Halford J. Mackinder's description, Western sailors had after 1500 outflanked the land power of those Central Asian horsemen and camelmen that had dominated the "world island" for so long. And it was left to the American navalist Captain A.T. Mahan to show, in a series of books, how it was that Britain, with the superior advantages of geographical position, supportive government, good resources, abundant seamen, and "national character", had come to be the predominant maritime nation by 1815. This situation did not change over the next seventy years, which therefore stood in remarkable contrast to the seven or so decades of conflict and change prior to the French Revolution.

The next great feature of the post-1815 decades was the coming of the Industrial Revolution with its many consequences, some rather swift, others longer-term in their appearance, and many of them unintended. The West went even further ahead of "the Rest" in economic productivity, per capita wealth, military-technological power, and organized force. And, in that same time, Great Britain went even further ahead of the other occidental states; catch-up did not really begin until the 1880s, when Germany and America's economies surged forward, while Russia, Japan, and Italy began moving too. After about 1830 warships at first became hybrid things, with funnels sprouting amidst their masts, before moving fully into the ironclad age. In the 1860s the American Civil War saw, briefly, fighting between armoured vessels; and the first submarine. The first torpedo was produced, by Whitehead. The undersea cable, and the wireless, were at hand; the first transatlantic cable was laid as early as 1858. On land, railways were opening vast continental areas of settlement, production, supply, and military advantage. At sea, commerce, populations, technology, seemed to flow everywhere, from Queensland to Shanghai. The world seemed to settle into a long peace, with naval clashes (as at Lissa in 1866) few and far between. Mid-Victorian liberals exulted in the coming of a newer, more enlightened age in which navies protected and guaranteed commerce, and thus played a welcome cosmopolitan role – so different from the large standing armies with which autocratic European regimes often crushed civil liberties.

Both the distribution of naval power enjoyed by the major nations, and the physical and technical size and shape of navies, changed dramatically, once, then twice, in the three decades after 1885. Sea power, as represented by a large surface fleet, commercial activity, naval bases at home and abroad, remained still the best indicator of the relative national power of all those nations who wished to play on the world stage. This certainly was true of France and Russia, who, after their necessary focus on army re-building (France after 1871, Russia after the Crimea defeat), now began to lay down many newer, more heavily armed, and much faster warships, including enormous armored cruisers designed to challenge Britain's command of the sea. This, and the coming together of Paris and St Petersburg into a political alliance by the early 1890s, alarmed the British public and galvanized the government into ever larger naval estimates, successive defence reviews, and a heavy investment also in overseas bases and cable communications.

But by end of that decade, a frenzied battleship-building was also being undertaken in Italy and Austria-Hungary and, much more importantly, in two rising and powerful extra-European great powers, Japan and the United States. Here, now, were not only potential challengers to existing British naval predominance but also, and for the first time in half a millennium (since the Chinese fleets of the early 15th century) newer centres of power – industrial-technological power, naval power, geopolitical power – *outside* the confines of Europe. This was even more important than the fact that now, in the era of the Second Industrial Revolution, ironclads were becoming steel-clads, vastly larger, stronger, with far greater main batteries (10-inch, 12-inch, 15-inch guns), and much faster, the later types driven by oil-fuelled turbine engines – all horribly more expensive. This was a strain upon every nation's budget, producing a general "crisis of the tax state" in the 1900s, and causing the British in particular to seek for all sorts of devices (new, computerized fire-control, for example) to maintain their edge. Novel forms of weapons-systems such as the submarine, the torpedo-boat, the larger torpedo-boat-destroyers, and more powerful naval mines, threatened the safety of even the strongest Dreadnought battleship.

The scary, twenty-year-long Franco-Russian naval threat to Britain's naval predominance (1885–1905) gave way after 1900 to a challenge closer to home caused by Kaiser Wilhelm II's High Seas Fleet. Steadily, the Royal Navy's newer flotillas were based in North Sea ports. Everywhere, it seemed, there were frenzied naval races, with each Admiralty requesting further ships as it learned of another's newest building plans. The American and Japanese navies were still steadily building, and increasingly against each other, when, in 1914, the European naval situation changed from peace to war following Archduke Ferdinand's assassination. Here, after the long peace, was a new Great-Power war for which (to many) sea power never seemed more valued – ironically, just before it was about to be de-valued.

Because of geography the European navies of 1914 were more fixed in place than ever before in history. The Russian fleets could get out of neither the Baltic nor the Black seas, although limited engagements (against Germany and Turkey, respectively) occurred in both. The Austro-Hungarian Navy was bottled up in the Adriatic by Italian, French and British forces. Otherwise, the French Navy had little to do. The Kaiser's hugely expensive battle-squadrons were similarly "bottled up" in the North Sea; the important battles of the Dogger Bank (1915) and Jutland (1916) simply confirmed that fate. Only one alternative weapon of attack lay at hand, the submarine, which could not be contained by any superior surface navy, and was a threat to all. The war at sea after 1916 was an odd one: a slow, grinding Allied blockade of Germany's shipping (plus financial sanctions and other forms of economic warfare), answered by Tirpitz's dire and dangerous counter-blockade through unrestricted U-boat attacks upon Allied merchantmen, especially in the vital Atlantic routes.

Those unrestricted attacks upon neutral shipping soon brought America into the war in April 1917, with its own large navy and its almost unlimited financial and productive power. This meant (with Japan already in the war since August 1914), an enormous Allied advantage at sea; and when the U-boat threat was eventually contained, through convoys, counter-attacks, depth charges, the only hope for Berlin and Vienna was victory on land. That did not come. When

Ludendorff's massive final assaults were broken in June–August 1918, the First World War was over.

Sea power had played a great role in this struggle, certainly, albeit a negative one. It had helped, distantly, in the elimination of the German, Austro-Hungarian, and Turkish empires and had, more importantly, contained the German Navy's surface and undersea threats to British naval predominance. But there were no new battles of the Nile or Trafalgar. Once the Central Powers' navies were surrendered and scrapped in 1919, the victorious Allied leaders could focus instead upon such matters as Germany's new borders, reparations, the Middle East situation, the Bolshevik Revolution, the League of Nations. There was an important naval matter to be settled, to be sure, but that was to settle fleet ratios *between the victors*, which was eventually done at Washington in 1921-1922. Overall, the Great-Power landscape of (say) 1923 was amazingly different from that of 1910, and navies struggled hard to fit in, especially when their governments assumed a long peace ahead and ordered savage budget cuts accordingly.

In the two decades that followed 1919, sea power was very much an Anglo-American affair, with a distant though significant Japanese component to it in the Far East. The German High Seas Fleet was no more. The Russian fleet was gone, in revolution and self-destruction. The French Navy remained much the same, the fourth in the world in numbers although constricted by geography and the nation's obsession with the German land (and later air) threat. The only other navy of note was that of Italy, nicely modernized under Mussolini but possessing only a Mediterranean field of play. This was an era when the West's domination of the world seemed to have reached its peak. Its cruisers occasionally paid courtesy visits to the ports of a sleepy Latin America. Its gunboats patrolled up the great rivers of a fully colonised Africa. The Persian Gulf, the Indian sub-continent, Southeast Asia, the Pacific islands, were all under European sway. Western warships anchored without dispute in China's treaty ports.

The one exception to this story of Occidental dominance was provided by Japan. Somehow, and for the first time since before 1500, sea power had been recovered by a non-Western nation, through Tokyo's most ruthless imitation. The Washington naval treaties of 1921-1922 recognized her navy as the third-largest in the world, and the treaties' territorial restrictions made a special place for Japan in the Far East. But throughout the 1920s Japan's real power was restrained by its more liberal domestic conditions. Even its later takeover of Manchuria in 1931-1934 could probably have been accepted by the West through vague compromise.

Perhaps, then, the general international scene and the arrangements of navies could have been for sea power just another long nineteenth-century story but for two quite distinct interrupters: Adolf Hitler, and airpower. The first's ruthless organization of German industrial might and revisionist will meant that the Versailles order in Central and Eastern Europe was going to be overthrown as soon as he could manage it, even if it meant another conflict with France, possibly also (though unwillingly) with Britain. And the existence of the new German navy, along with a parallel revisionism in the Mediterranean of Mussolini's Italy – and a further Japanese advance, into China, after 1937 – shattered the British Admiralty's planning regarding future war scenarios, fleet allocations, and budget requests. The British and French navies went into hasty rearmament after 1936 (there were no more treaty restrictions after that date), and the U.S. Navy, keeping its distance, began an even greater build-up.

At the same time, the rapid growth in the size and power of air forces was also forcing change upon existing navies. This was seen, within the American, British, and Japanese fleets, in the introduction of ever-larger aircraft carriers with ever-greater capacities. But what was also happening here was the emergence of very threatening land-based air forces like the Luftwaffe, with the future potential to make it impossible for traditional surface warships to operate close to the shore, at least not without severe loss. At sea, the next Great-Power war was not going to be a repetition of the last one. Splendid new classes of battleships were being laid down (*Bismarck, Vittorio Veneto, King George V*), but it was not clear in which fighting circumstances they would find themselves.

That said, it was remarkable how broadly and intensively sea power manifested itself between 1939 and 1945. There were other huge campaigns taking place in this greatest of all wars – the Sino-Japanese struggle across mainland China, the Nazi–Soviet War, the strategic bombing campaign – but in the Atlantic, Mediterranean, and Pacific realms it was the contest for command of the sea routes that counted. Even in the early years (1939–1941), air power swiftly entered and became a dominant new factor, and in many cases *the* dominant factor, in the fight off Norway, in attacks upon the convoys, in the bludgeoning of the Royal Navy off Crete. The German Navy might be small and the Italian fleet cautious, but Axis air power considerably reduced the superiority which the British possessed in the more traditional forms of sea power, and its bombers often negated the possession of key naval harbours like Dover and Malta. When Japan entered the conflict, it was with a naval air power that wrecked the American battle fleet in Hawaii, assisted the conquest of the Philippines, Dutch East India, and Malaya/Singapore, and even ravaged Britain's main bases at Ceylon.

Along with these aerial and surface upsets to Allied naval dominance there were the early, then unrelenting attacks by U-boats upon their vital sea lanes, in particular against the greatest supply route of all, that from the United States and Caribbean to the United Kingdom. If that campaign succeeded, and Britain were crippled, and the build-up for an eventual invasion of France made impossible, then Allied grand strategy would be in shreds; this was, as Churchill kept repeating, the greatest issue. And if there were no invasion from the west, or the south, or strategic bombing campaign (without oil shipping, B-17s and Lancasters in their East Anglian bases were grounded), then the Wehrmacht's attack upon Russia might be overwhelming. Simply put, the Allies had (a) to beat the U-boat, (b) contain and defeat Axis air over the sea, and (c) crush Japanese naval and air power, and bring the war back to Toyko. The first two were achieved in the grinding air–sea campaigns over the Atlantic and Mediterranean between

1941 and 1943, especially in the smashing of the German submarines in the North Atlantic in May–June 1943. Then came the Pacific War.

There could be no greater example of the role of sea power in determining the fate of empires than in the relentless march of the carrier task forces and amphibian armies of Admiral Nimitz's Central Pacific Fleet from November 1943 (Gilbert Islands landings) onwards. Japan's carrier forces were greatly reduced in size at Midway in June 1942, and its Army's advances were pushed back in New Guinea and the Solomons later that year. Then American power seemed to take a breather in the Pacific, coincidentally while it was expressing itself, with its British ally, in the campaigns to occupy North Africa, Sicily, and Italy. But by the winter of 1943/44 it had achieved an amazing productivity burst at home, allowing streams of carriers and light fleet carriers, fast battleships, newer cruisers and destroyers, above all, landing-ships and fleet supply trains, to arrive at Pearl Harbor, with a lesser supply to MacArthur's Southwest Pacific Command for its slower, parallel advances from New Guinea to the southern Philippines.

Japanese air power was then broken in the course of 1944, irrevocably, by the massive aerial attacks upon its main base at Rabaul, and by the loss of so many of its planes and aircraft in the so-called "Great Marianas Turkey Shoot", before the advance upon the Philippines. By then Nimitz's flotillas had turned their attention further north, to the important island groups of Iwo Jima (taken April 1945) and Okinawa (taken June 1945), which stood in the way of the invasion of the Japanese home islands themselves. Meanwhile, the seizure of the Marianas and construction of giant B-29 airbases there had permitted the massive aerial destruction of Japan's defences, its industry and infrastructure, its cities and towns. More quietly, the U.S. Navy's submarine arm totally eliminated its enemy's merchant shipping. Japan was already beleaguered, starving, desperate, beaten (even if it would not surrender) before the two atomic bombs were dropped in August and the surrender negotiations commenced.

The apotheosis of Western sea power thus took place in Tokyo Bay, on the deck of the giant battleship USS *Missouri* (President Truman's home state), with rows and rows of American and Allied warships anchored in parallel across the extensive harbor, witnesses to the collapse of Japan's imperial bid. The historical trajectory – back to Drake, the Armada, the eighteenth-century wars, Trafalgar, Jutland – was eagerly seized upon by American navalist apologists, describing how the nation's Manifest Destiny had unfolded so well, and unerringly, at sea. Off Normandy, off Leyte Gulf, but especially off Tokyo's beaches, naval force had shown itself to be irresistible.

What must have seemed remarkable to the observer, therefore, was the apparent retreat of sea power's significance in international power politics in the decades after 1945. Overall, in any case, changes were occurring in so many ways. As after 1815, there was only one really great naval nation, this time America rather than Britain. As had happened earlier, its own fleet size was reduced to its proper needs rather than being held at an artificial high. But the U.S. Navy's size was still mighty. Now it was the flotillas of its warships, rather than those of the

Royal Navy, that were to be seen in the Mediterranean, off the Persian Gulf, in East Asian waters.

It was noteworthy, too, that the types of warships preferred in the American fleet had changed from those of the mid-1930s. Battleships had lost their importance, and were scrapped in large numbers, as were many older heavy cruisers. The escort fleet shrank as the U-boat menace passed into history. Fleet carriers, with an adequate cover of destroyers and like vessels, were at the centre of American naval power. Fast attack submarines (increasingly with nuclear propulsion) remained in being, although after 1945 there were no targets around to think of attacking, and thus the submarine branch eagerly embraced arming itself with missiles, with an ever-longer range to hit inland targets, and now with nuclear warheads, to add to the West's deterrent force against the newer Soviet threat.

And the U.S. Navy under Admiral Rickover and his successors had raced to re-structure itself because it seemed that this historic service, like the Army and much of the conventional fixed-wing Air Force, might have been made utterly redundant by the destructive power of a single atomic (hydrogen) bomb, soon capable of being delivered deep into the Soviet heartland by missiles sited in Nebraska, far away from the sea. Of what purpose was a modern version of Mahan's main battle fleet, or of what value Corbett's theories about sea lines of communication, if a Superpower war could end in mass mutual destruction within the first week? Of what merit, and attractiveness, the Nelsonic tradition?

Yet sea power was surviving, in interesting forms. The first was the transformation of maritime commerce in the decades following 1945, a shift that showed itself most significantly in the coming of the "container revolution" for international trade. This revolution, first really getting under way in the 1960s, was devised by a group of American businessmen as an exercise in standardization and cost-cutting: what, after all, if the greater part of the goods transported across the oceans (though obviously not petroleum, coal, grain) could be placed in identical-sized boxes which could be hauled individually by lorries and in their hundreds by rail, then also placed onto giant container-ships which would carry the contents from Hamburg and Harbin through the English Channel, across the Atlantic, across the Pacific? Commerce, then, would surely be quickened up, though the implications, for older ports, for stevedore trade-unions, their jobs and ways of life, their closely clustered portside housing, were immense. Newer container ports like Felixstowe were built, distinct from an older trading city like Ipswich or Hull. Rotterdam, closer to the oceans, was favoured over Amsterdam and Antwerp. Imports and exports were now out of sight to the next generation, whisked onto trucks that sped the containers along super-highways to the industrial midlands. London docks moved down-river, if only to survive. Most children, while growing up not far from the seas, would rarely see a ship in movement. Maritime museums took the place of reality.

Lots of older, familiar shipping lines disappeared in this change – the Elder Dempster line, the Blue Funnel line, the British-India Steam Navigation Company, all folded their doors, leaving their closed-up headquarter buildings near the

City of London or along the water-front at Liverpool. Ironically, their ships and their crews had survived the attacks of Hitler's U-boats more robustly than they did the advances of modern technology and capitalism.

Another change was the erosion of human beings' travel by sea, at least in the older forms of it: service families en route through the Suez Canal to their colonial jobs, elite passengers (and many less wealthy ones, including emigrants) on fast liners across the Atlantic. The turning point was the arrival of Boeing jetliners as early as the 1960s, taking over all of those categories of passengers even as the liners were being scrapped – first-class travel across the Atlantic by air became a brief and pale imitation of a first-class trip at sea – and introducing the era of mass aerial tourism, on both long- and medium-distance flights. Thus ended the century-long tale of ocean-liner travel begun with Brunel's Great Eastern. Now there was mass cruise-ship travel by sea, usually short-range and often circuitous, through the Greek islands or from one Caribbean tax-free port to another.

Thus the largest shipping companies (with their giant, varied vessels) of the world were now of three sorts: the few enormous container-shipping companies, such as Maersk, engaged essentially in a huge ship–land–air conveyance of most of the world's goods – a full 85 percent of which travels by sea, nearly out of sight; an array of energy companies, large and small, like Exxon or BP, that transfer liquid fuels from regions of extraction and refining to their mass consumer destinations in huge tankers; and then the towering palaces of tourism at sea, taking millions to scenic harbors and beaches which their grandparents would have had little chance of enjoying.

Much of this has involved a giant turn to the East, two centuries after the original turn by the British Empire in the 1770s. The English Channel and the Straits of Gibraltar remain as busy as ever, but it is the ports along the Chinese coast, and the traffic coming through the Straits of Malacca, that are now the most crowded in the world; and it would be for observers at Vancouver and Long Beach, Ca., to observe where the greatest import harbors of the world now lie.

A great deal of the world's shipbuilding industry also shifted to the East in the decades after 1950. The American shipbuilding industry, cramped by protectionism and extremely high wages, was never much. It was artificially boosted by the high demands of the Second World War into building millions of tons of Liberty ships and landing ships, then fell off very swiftly. The war also destroyed the shipbuilding firms of continental Western Europe, though it did resuscitate the older-fashioned British yards – until they were destroyed by the competition of the lower-wage, faster-assembling shipbuilding industries of, first Japan, and then South Korea and neighbouring states. Now China is intent on being the largest producer. Some specialized shipbuilders in the West survive, in France, for example, building ocean liners and cruise-ships – but in many older centres of shipbuilding and port commerce like the Clyde there is total collapse. By a different though parallel "modernization" of the fishing industry, there has also been a swing to the East, to Japan's massive catching ships, and thus a further decline of older, smaller ports.

Perhaps these collapses of industry and jobs were less seen along America's shores as the 20th century gave way to the next one. The export by ship of vast amounts of grain and oil from the Gulf ports was larger than ever. The import of Oriental container traffic onto New Jersey and Californian rail-heads and lorry parks just grew and grew. And hugely expensive United States Navy contracts allowed the subsidy of a few specialized yards to build warships such as *Nimitz*-class carriers and *Ticonderoga*-class cruisers that no other country could match. Navalist U.S. senators and congressmen, well conscious of the benefits to their states of such contracts, keep an awareness of sea power alive where it has faded in many other political constituencies.

What has also kept that awareness alive has been another completely new development, that is, the rise of Eastern navies in recent decades, with almost explosive growth: the number of destroyers and frigates in the present Japanese Navy, for example, is more than in the British and French navies combined. The South Korean and Indian navies are also growing fast, and yet no naval power in these waters is growing faster than that of the People's Republic of China, its newer surface fleet being buttressed by naval air squadrons, medium-range sea-skimming missiles, ultra-quiet submarines, even a moored carrier.

While it is true, then, that the traditional ports and navies of Europe may be much shriveled compared with 1900, and that its maritime power has ebbed since the Second World War, this may not mean the erosion of sea power itself but simply its metamorphosis towards Asia and the Pacific. Were today's observer to look out from Singapore, would the view be much different from that which existed in the West in the 1920s or 1860s? Here would be a big mercantile port, lots of bustle; lots of employment; busy shipping lines handling the entrepôt trades; foreign navies' warships passing offshore, from the South China Sea through the Straits of Malacca, with occasional port visits, including perhaps by a giant U.S. carrier.

In respect of the sea and sea power as dimensions of international power, then, perhaps there is less change than might have been assumed just by thinking of this as a Western story. There is no doubt also that the display of power *on land* continues in its large, Mackinder-ite significance, with the contest for Ukraine, power ripples along the Silk Road, giant Middle East struggles for control of Iraq, Afghanistan, and Syria, Iran re-emerging as a large regional player, and the future of Saudi Arabia, even Israel, uncertain by 2050. But it is also true that, after seeming perhaps to wither away in the 1970s and 1980s, sea power is re-affirming itself as having a very large role in international politics, economics and strategy. With the U.S. Navy still so strong and far ahead in conventional surface measures, and until the Chinese Navy is so much bigger, there is not at present a Mahanian narrative, which would anticipate great fleet encounters if a future war broke out. But there is a Corbettian one, were that theorist of the importance of sea routes to come back and observe all the maritime activities presently on the Indian Ocean and across the Pacific.

Sea power was always an affirmation of the strong, and therefore always showed up the weak in world affairs, since only a few nations could ever possess great warships. This has not changed today; for example, Africa and Latin America still play no role here. But the locus of power has definitely shifted, from the Western European nations, and from Russia (which was never very strong), to the Far Eastern national powers. It has not yet shifted from the U.S., though, which remains the Number One naval power. Four hundred years ago, English navalists like Bacon and Bolingbroke extolled the importance of the sea in world politics. Even now, since maritime power continues to be a critical instrument of policy to those possessing it, so it will always be striven for. For better or worse, therefore, the 21st century will be a century in which navies still count.

FURTHER READING

The books referred to in the second paragraph of the text above are BRAUDEL F., *The Mediterranean and the Mediterranean World in the Age of Philip II* (New York, 1972; 1st edn, 1949); PANIKKAR K.M., *Asia and Western Dominance: A Survey of the Vasco da Gama Epoch of Asian History, 1498-1945* (London, 1953); CIPOLLA C., *Guns, Sails, and Empires: Technological Innovation and the Early Phases of European Expansion, 1400-1700* (New York, 1965); MACKINDER H., 'The Geographical Pivot of History', *The Geographical Journal* 23.4 (1904), 421-37; and MAHAN A.T., *The Influence of Sea Power Upon History, 1660-1783* (London: Methuen, 1965; 1st edn, 1890).

For an American navalist account of this story, see POTTER E.B. and NIMITZ C.W., *Sea Power: A Naval History* (Englewood Cliffs, 1960). For the 19th-century global transformation, see OSTERHAMMEL J., *The Transformation of the World: A Global History of the Nineteenth Century* (Princeton, 2014). For the slightly later changes in Britain's naval position, see MARDER A.J., *The Anatomy of British Sea Power: A History of British Naval Policy in the Pre-Dreadnought Era, 1880-1905* (New York, 1940). The best single volume for World War I is HALPERN P., *A Naval History of World War I* (Annapolis, MD, 1994); there is no equivalent good single-volume study of World War II.

For general background, see MCNEILL W., *The Pursuit of Power: Technology, Armed Force, and Society since A.D. 1000* (Chicago, 1984) and KENNEDY P., *The Rise and Fall of British Naval Mastery* (London, 1976).

Germany, 1870–1914: A Military Empire Turns to the Sea

Michael Epkenhans is Director of Research of the Centre for Military History and Social Sciences of the Bundeswehr, Germany

Abstract. *The navy of newly united Germany fulfilled a minor strategic role as a coast-defence force, and a political role as the Reich's only national armed service. Under Wilhelm II (1888-1918) the navy and merchant fleet grew to become symbols as well as instruments of Germany's status as a world power. Germany's naval threat to Britain - its obvious ally in the European power system - isolated it and provoked a 'naval race' which it could not win.*

Résumé. *Dans l'Allemagne tout juste unifiée, la marine joua un rôle stratégique mineur en tant que force de défense des côtes mais un rôle politique important car elle constituait le seul service national armé du Reich. Sous le règne de Wilhelm II (1888-1918), la marine et la flotte marchande s'agrandirent jusqu'à devenir les symboles ainsi que les instruments de la puissance allemande. La menace navale que l'Allemagne exerçait sur la Grande-Bretagne - son alliée évidente dans le système de pouvoir européen - l'isola et provoqua « une course à l'armement naval » qu'elle ne pouvait gagner.*

.•.

Germany and the Sea from the Middle Ages until the 19th Century

Although Germany was an empire with a long history dating back into the 10th century, it had never aspired to become a sea power until the mid-19th century. Its rulers had concentrated all their efforts upon defending Germany's borders, or conquering new territories in Europe. Building a fleet like the kings of Britain, France, or Spain in order to found colonies overseas had never been a viable political option. The Hanseatic League founded in the 13th century was nothing but a commercial association. Powerful and rich in the 14th and 15th centuries, its influence started to decline in the 16th century due to economic crises, the rise of rival powers in the Baltic and the impact of globalization on trade after the discovery of the New World in 1492. The small fleet built up by Frederick William, the Great Elector of Brandenburg, at the end of the 17th century and the colony founded on the west coast of Africa were only a short interval. His successors were neither able to provide sufficient financial resources nor willing to turn Prussia into a maritime power. Their interests lay in Eastern Europe, not overseas.

Modest Beginnings, 1848–1870

The revolution of 1848 proved a remarkable change in Germany's attitude towards the sea. Though the German states, loosely connected in a confederation, had begun to industrialize very slowly compared to Britain or France, the Danish blockade of the German coasts in the Baltic and the North Sea, which seriously affected trade with other countries, revealed the necessity of a fleet. As a result, in June 1848 the revolutionary National Assembly passed a law which established Germany's first navy. Although the ships, bought in Britain or even in the United States, were soon sold after the revolution failed, it is this navy to which Germany's navy today dates its origins.

However, even though most ships had been sold, Prussia began to realize that a navy was necessary in a changing world. Subsequently, the Prussian government bought a strip of land on the North Sea coast to establish a naval base in 1853. This base and the town surrounding it were eventually called Wilhelmshaven in honour of the king of Prussia, Wilhelm I. Only a naval base that was close enough to the most important sea-lanes of the world in the Atlantic Ocean seemed able to support German commerce in the case of conflict. In this respect, Danzig, Prussia's only naval base, was of no use, owing to its position in the Baltic. In 1865, after victory over Denmark in the war of 1864, Prussia also established a naval base at Kiel, thus transferring its small fleet closer to the strategically important entrances into the Baltic.

The Imperial German Navy, 1871–1897

In the Wars of Unification against Denmark, Austria and France the Prussian Navy had played no role. Minor encounters in 1864 and 1866 off Heligoland or in the Baltic had no impact upon the outcome of the wars. French attempts at blockading German ports after the outbreak of the Franco-Prussian War in 1870 had to be given up after France's armies had been defeated. Nevertheless, the government of the newly founded German Empire was convinced that it should possess a navy. Most importantly, the navy was to be the only nationwide imperial institution, unlike the army, which consisted of contingents provided by the different states which now had been united under Prussia's leadership. In peacetime (and not only in wartime, as was the case with the armies) the German Emperor was commander-in-chief of the Imperial Navy. Wilhelmshaven and Kiel became Imperial Naval bases (*Reichskriegshafen*), where the bulk of the fleet was to be stationed.

Another peculiarity of the Imperial Navy was the fact that generals and not admirals were responsible for its build-up in the 1870s and 1880s: Generals Albrecht von Stosch (1872–1883) and Leo von Caprivi (1883–1888). Obviously, no naval officer seemed either suitable or willing. However, both were highly distinguished generals and experienced organizers. Stosch in particular dedicated himself systematically to the task of building up a navy. In 1873, a first fleet development plan, *Flottengründungsplan*, was passed by the Reichstag, which aimed at building up a navy consisting of six armoured frigates, eighteen corvettes and six gunboats. There were to be two overseas stations, an overseas squadron and a substantial reserve as well. Unlike the High Seas Fleet in the Wilhelmine era, this fleet aimed only to defend the coast, protect commerce and support the army.[1]

Though Stosch and Caprivi were later blamed for many deficiencies in the build-up of the navy, they were only partly responsible for them. Rather, technological progress was so fast and had revolutionized naval warfare in such a short time in its transition from the age of sail to the age of the iron-clad that all navies had difficulties in solving the problems they were now facing on the level of strategy, tactics and shipbuilding. Accordingly, the Imperial Navy lived "from hand to mouth", not the least because "the views that prevailed in the naval officer corps were far too vague to allow a definite shipbuilding policy to crystallize".[2]

However, even if the navy had developed plans for naval expansion in the 1880s, it is very unlikely that these would have led to a more far-reaching change in Germany's attitude towards the sea. Under the chancellorship of the "Iron Chancellor", Otto von Bismarck, it was rather unlikely that the navy would play a more decisive role in political and military planning. In Bismarck's eyes only a cautious policy towards its neighbours, and a powerful army to support it if need be, could preserve the nation's position on the European continent. Bismarck's land-oriented thinking left no room for expansion overseas, which, in his opinion, would lead only to conflicts with other great powers that would eventually prove disastrous for the Empire's existence. However, after Bismarck's dismissal by the young German emperor, Kaiser Wilhelm II, in 1890, German foreign and naval policy underwent a fundamental change within a few years.

NEW AIMS, NAVAL EXPANSION, AND ANGLO-GERMAN RIVALRY: THE WILHELMINE NAVY, 1890–1914

The Kaiser's naval passion

German naval expansion is, no doubt, difficult to explain without the influence of the new emperor, Wilhelm II, who had succeeded to the throne in 1888. In contrast to his predecessors the Kaiser was the first member of the Imperial

---

[1] Cf. LAMBI I.N., *The Navy and German Power Politics, 1862-1914* (London, 1984), pp. 3–5.
[2] VON TIRPITZ A., *My Memoirs* (London, 1919), vol. 1, p. 30.

family who was both really interested in naval affairs and willing to acknowledge the need for a powerful navy. In the course of his reign the navy was to benefit greatly from this Imperial favour. In 1888, the victorious German army consisted of 19,294 officers and 468,409 non-commissioned officers and men in peacetime,[3] whereas the navy's total strength amounted to only 15,480 men, including 534 executive officers. The fleet itself consisted of eighteen iron-clads, eight large and ten small cruisers.[4] By 1913, when Wilhelm II celebrated his silver jubilee, the navy's strength had risen to 2,196 officers and 59,991 non-commissioned officers and men.[5] Moreover, the *Novelle* (amended Navy Law) of 1912 had stipulated that the fleet was to consist of 61 capital ships, 40 small cruisers, 144 torpedo boats and 72 submarines. In comparison to 1888, this was indeed a powerful military instrument, capable of both offensive and defensive warfare.

"A place in the sun"

One of the reasons for this huge expansion of the navy was the intention to become a real world power. In the eyes of the Kaiser as well as of many contemporaries this meant the acquisition of a colonial empire overseas equal to that of the British Empire. Whereas many European powers had begun to build up colonial empires since the 16th century, Germany was a late-comer in this respect. Although Bismarck eventually established colonies in Africa and in the Pacific in the mid-1880s, he was always a very reluctant imperialist.

The new Kaiser was one of the most important protagonists of a more offensive colonial policy, aimed at turning Germany into a world power, but he was not alone. Like him, many contemporaries felt that Imperial Germany had to become more imperialist in order to preserve the nation's status and its future. Looking back in the 1920s, one of Germany's leading liberal historians, Friedrich Meinecke, described this public perception quite rightly: "Given how the world looked at that time, a nation like Germany, in its confined and (as it expanded) increasingly cramped situation, was forced to the conclusion that a larger colonial empire was indispensable."[6] This conviction was further strengthened by the attempts of other powers to enlarge their spheres of influence in the Middle and in the Far East in the mid-1890s. The situation seemed favourable. Tensions between Germany's most important rivals – Britain and France in Africa as well as Britain and Russia in Asia – seemed to allow Germany the opportunity to play the *tertius gaudens* among the great powers.

---

[3] REICHSARCHIV (ed.), *Der Weltkrieg. Kriegsrüstung und Kriegswirtschaft*, Supplement vol. 1 (Berlin, 1930), p. 460.
[4] HERWIG H.H., *'Luxury' Fleet. The Imperial German Navy 1888-1918* (reprinted Atlantic Highlands, NJ, 1987), p. 15.
[5] 'Nauticus', *Jahrbuch für deutsche Seeinteressen* (Berlin) 16 (1914), 27-8.
[6] Cited in CANIS K., *Von Bismarck zur Weltpolitik. Deutsche Außenpolitik 1890-1900* (Berlin, 1997), p. 225.

Germany's sea interests

However, traditional motives of power politics and power projection, the defence of Germany's coastlines or the emperor's naval enthusiasm only partly explain the expansion of the navy. Since the late 1840s Germany had changed from an agrarian to a modern industrial country. German gross domestic product rose from 9.4 million marks in 1850 and 17.6 million marks in 1875 to 33.1 million marks in 1900. In 1913 it amounted to 48.4 million marks. Similarly, the output of "classical" industries like the coal and iron-ore industries increased enormously. The production of iron-ore, for example, rose from 0.2 million tons in 1850 to 2.2 million tons in 1873, 5.4 million tons in 1895 and eventually 19.3 million tons in 1913.[7] Soon the industrial late-comer began to catch up with or even overtake the mother-country of the industrial revolution, Great Britain, in old industries like iron-ore and steel, not to speak of the new optical, chemical, machine-building or electrical industries.

These industries needed markets, as well as raw materials from many regions of the world. Shipping companies like the Norddeutscher Lloyd, the Hamburg-Amerikanische Packetfahrt Actiengesellschaft (Hapag), or the Hamburg Südamerikanische Dampfschifffahrts-Gesellschaft (HSDG) transported these goods and materials over the oceans of the world. After modest beginnings in the 1880s, they helped to build up a considerable merchant fleet. Although most of its vessels were still built in Britain, the share of those built in German yards slowly increased, and so did the number and the size of Germany's shipbuilding industries, which included thousands of bigger or smaller suppliers scattered all over the country. Lagging behind Britain in the 1870s and 1880s, this industry had also made a great leap forward. Shipyards in Hamburg, Bremen and Kiel, Stettin and Danzig had eventually acquired the necessary skills to compete with their rivals in Britain. Orders for warships as well as mail-steamers had greatly supported this development; however, many engineers had spent years in Britain to learn how to construct and build a ship.

Most importantly, Germany's population had risen from 33.7 million in 1850 and 39.2 million in 1870 to 56.3 million in 1900. In 1910, Germany, with its 64.9 million inhabitants, had the second-largest population in Europe.

This population needed food. Whereas Germany had been an agrarian, self-sufficient country until the mid-19th century, it had increasingly begun to import food in later years. Though figures vary, these imports made up between 20 and 25 per cent of food consumption on the eve of war in 1914. Most of these imports – meat as well as grain – were transported by ship. The same applies to raw materials. Although Germany was able to export iron-ore and coal, it had to import other materials to keep its industry running. Most important were palm-seeds, later oil, and metals like nickel and tin, cotton for the textiles industry and saltpetre for the chemical industry. In an era of rival

---

[7] All figures from WEHLER H.-U., *Deutsche Gesellschafsgeschichte*, vol. 3: *Von der 'Deutschen Doppelrevolution' bis zum Ersten Weltkrieg* (Munich, 1995), pp. 44, 75, 597, 601.

imperialist powers, safe trade-routes were a prerequisite for the provision of food for a growing population and the continuous flow of imports and exports of a prospering and dynamically expanding industrial nation. Unlike in earlier centuries, when German states had more or less left the protection of their merchant vessels against pirates or of its citizens overseas to the Royal Navy, a powerful nation-state like Imperial Germany now had to protect its interests itself. As a result, German cruisers protected German merchant vessels from the 1870s in Chinese waters, in South America, in Africa or in the Mediterranean. Moreover, as the conflicts with Denmark in the 1840s and 1860s had shown, only a navy could break a blockade and thus protect industry and commerce from serious economic consequences, as well as the people from starving.

World politics, naval build-up and domestic politics

A prospering economy was not only an aim in itself. In an era of rapid political and social change, economic wealth seemed the best means of guaranteeing domestic stability. In the late 19th century economic crises repeatedly shattered European countries. These crises had caused political upheavals which threatened the existing political and social order, for they endorsed the conviction of socialist parties that only revolutions could improve the lives of the great majority of the population. Imperial Germany was no exception in this respect. However, unlike its neighbours in Western Europe, Germany was still partly pre-modern. During the Wars of Unification between 1864 and 1871, the monarch and the old elites, which had ruled the country for centuries, had been able to defend many of their prerogatives in politics, in the army and within the society. Although they had increasingly come under pressure from the middle as well as the working classes, they were still unwilling to yield. Instead, a successful social-imperialist policy, generating economic prosperity and political prestige, offered a solution that made political and social reforms unnecessary.

World politics, sea interests and sea power

In the eyes of the Kaiser as well as of many contemporaries "more ships" were the only means to becoming a world and colonial power, to securing political stability at home and to safeguarding German sea interests. Having "devoured" the "Bible" of all naval enthusiasts at the turn of the century, Captain Alfred T. Mahan on "The Influence of Sea-Power upon History", he was deeply convinced of the interrelationship between naval power and world power.[8] The Sino-Japanese War of 1894/95 and the obviously impending collapse of the Chinese Empire were a new spur to his ambitions

However, although the Kaiser was a naval enthusiast full of ideas, he would

---

[8] WILHELM II to Poultney Bigelow, Mai 1894, quoted in WINZEN P., 'Zur Genesis von Weltmachtkonzept und Weltpolitik', in *Der Ort Kaiser Wilhelms II in der deutschen Geschichte*, ed. J.C.G. RÖHL (Munich, 1991), p. 207, fn. 82.

hardly have succeeded if he had not had a young naval officer at his side who was able to develop these ideas systematically: Admiral Alfred Tirpitz. Belonging to a generation of naval officers who had been educated in the Prussian and the Imperial Navies, Tirpitz had soon demonstrated exceptional qualities both as an organizer and as a political and strategic thinker. These qualities attracted the Kaiser's attention in the early 1890s. He fully shared Tirpitz's conviction that Germany had to further develop and protect its maritime interests unless it was willing to inevitably decline to the status of a pre-industrial, "poor farming country" as he later described the only alternative in his eyes. Moreover, the Kaiser was deeply impressed by Tirpitz's reflections upon naval strategy and tactics as well as the latter's proposals of a systematic build-up of a powerful battle-fleet.

Political success, public support and navy laws

After the setbacks of the early 1890s the Kaiser, with the support of Tirpitz, who was appointed Secretary of the Imperial Navy Office, and the ambitious young diplomat Bernhard von Bülow, who became foreign secretary in 1897 and chancellor in 1900, eventually succeeded in re-orientating German foreign, naval and domestic policy. For almost two decades world politics and naval building dominated German policy. The demand for equal entitlement (*Gleichberechtigung*) and a larger "place in the sun", which Bülow presented in a famous first speech in the Reichstag in December 1897, appealed to many contemporaries. The occupation of an outpost in distant China – Kiachow – at the same time and the purchase of a number of islands in the Pacific from Spain only a year later obviously proved that the government was on the right road.

Success overseas, however, can only partly explain the fact that the Imperial Navy became popular very quickly. In order to achieve this aim in a country with a long history of land-power thinking, Tirpitz, supported by a Navy League, which soon had almost one million members, organized a modern propaganda campaign when taking office in 1897. Naval officers, professors and teachers began travelling all over the country explaining the "dire need of a navy" as the Kaiser phrased it. At the same time, the navy itself began organizing all kinds of public events which excited the imagination of an increasing number of people: public ship launches, visits of naval manoeuvres and mock naval battles in specially built basins.

Within two years (1898 and 1900) the Reichstag passed two laws which greatly increased the strength of the navy. Three more were to follow in 1906, 1908 and 1912, accelerating the pace of naval building. These laws were by no means unique at that time, for many countries influenced by Mahanian ideas had began to build up navies as well. However, no government did so as systematically and energetically as Germany. Moreover, nowhere else did the government bind parliament by stipulating that the navy would in time renew itself automatically at a building rate of three capital ships a year.

A navy against Great Britain

In 1899 Tirpitz assured the Kaiser that after completion of the High Seas Fleet Britain would lose "every inclination to attack us, and as a result concede to Your Majesty such a measure of naval influence and enable Your Majesty to carry out a great overseas policy".[9] At first sight, these assurances seemed reasonable. Considering Britain's commitments all over the world, a navy in the North Sea seemed to promise success. Britain, Tirpitz argued, would neither be able to deploy its whole fleet in home waters nor have enough funds and men to out-build Germany by more than one third. The ratio of 3:2 between the two fleets would give the German fleet a fair chance in a war against the Royal Navy, especially if (as Tirpitz anticipated) the battle were fought under the guns of Heligoland. This conviction that it would be possible to hold the dagger to Britain's throat not only generated increasing tensions between Germany and its neighbours but also upset the fragile European power system. Instead of becoming a *tertius gaudens* free to choose the most attractive ally, Germany soon became isolated.

ANGLO-GERMAN NAVAL RACE

At the turn of the century Great Britain's naval superiority was such that it had no reason to worry about Germany's naval build-up, but worries about Germany's aims, and its naval build-up in particular, steadily increased. When the Royal Navy started to build a new type of battleship, the *Dreadnought*, in 1905 and Germany not only followed suit in 1906, but even accelerated the building tempo in 1908, a naval race began with disastrous consequences for Anglo-German relations. Eventually, Germany lost this race, which reached its peak in the years 1908–1912. The Imperial government proved unable to keep up financially with the pace of British naval building. More importantly, however, Germany's chancellors, Bülow, who was replaced in 1909, and then Theobald von Bethmann Hollweg, were increasingly convinced that a re-orientation of both German foreign and naval policy was inevitable. Instead of achieving the desired "place in the sun", Germany had suffered a series of diplomatic setbacks, leaving the country isolated on the Continent. An open conflict had to be avoided. Whereas Germany's army seemed strong enough to fight both France and Russia, an open conflict with Great Britain could only end in disaster. Despite all efforts, the Imperial Navy was still inferior to the Royal Navy, as Tirpitz secretly had to admit.

Attempts at negotiating an agreement with Britain failed. Whereas Germany had much to demand from Britain politically, but nothing substantial to offer as

---

[9] TIRPITZ's report to the Kaiser, 28 September 1899, cited in *Rüstung im Zeichen der wilhelminischen Weltpolitik. Grundlegende Dokumente 1890-1914*, ed. V.R. BERGHAHN and W. DEIST (Düsseldorf, 1988), p. 161.

far as the naval question was concerned, the government in London was only interested in naval concessions, but had nothing to offer politically. For the German government, naval concessions, if not accompanied by an agreement securing Britain's neutrality in a continental war, would shatter its foundations after the huge costs and great expectations of the naval building programme. For the British government, any political concessions would leave Britain isolated in a continental war which Germany was likely to win, thus establishing a full hegemony on the continent – a nightmare for every British politician.

Moreover, it was more than doubtful that any chancellor would have got the consent of both the Kaiser and Tirpitz to a naval agreement. Again and again Tirpitz told the Kaiser in the years of crisis not to yield to the mounting pressure upon him to exchange a political agreement against an arms limitations agreement which did not provide the necessary measure of security: "Because it is the backbone of Your Majesty's naval policy that the German fleet must be so strong that a British attack becomes a risky undertaking. The position of the German Empire as a world power rests on this risk, as does the effect our fleet has in maintaining the peace," he argued during an interview with the Emperor in October 1910.[10]

Similarly, he summarized his social-Darwinistic view of the course of world history, which had always been one of his driving motives, in a secret speech to the officers of the Imperial Navy Office in October 1913: "Generally speaking the question whether Germany should fight for its place in the world against England [...] or whether it should be content with the status of a second-rate power on the continent is a question of one's political faith. For a great nation, however, it seems more honourable to fight for the most important aim and to go under honourably, rather than accept a future without glory."[11]

Failure

These were indeed bold aims and assertions, but they could hardly conceal that Germany's turn to the sea had failed on the eve of war, in spite of Tirpitz's success in introducing another *novelle* in 1912. Soon he had to admit that he did not have the financial resources to build the ships stipulated by the navy law. More importantly, the deterioration of Germany's position on the Continent had strengthened the conviction of Germany's leadership that the nation's fate did not depend upon the navy but upon the army as before. In 1912, and again in 1913, the army was increased twice, whereas the navy in vain asked for new funds. Even the Kaiser, Germany's most important naval enthusiast, had begun to lose interest in his navy. Most importantly, the navy realized on the eve of war that its strategic assumptions had also proved wrong. Reports from manoeuvres

---

[10] Notes for a Report to the Sovereign, Concerning the Naval Relation to England by ADMIRAL VON TIRPITZ on 24 October 1910; Bundesarchiv (Federal Archives), Tirpitz papers, N 253/24.
[11] Speech by TIRPITZ, 9 October 1913, in Bundesarchiv, Tirpitz papers, N 253/423.

of the Royal Navy left no doubt that it would not seek battle right after the outbreak of war. Instead, it would establish a distant blockade, which the High Seas Fleet would be unable to break, unless it was willing to risk self-destruction.

Détente

However, although the future seemed bleak from Tirpitz's point of view, it was an open question if the road Germany had taken at the turn of the century would lead into the abyss. The two years following the Haldane mission of 1912, during which the German chancellor and the British secretary of war had tried in vain to find a solution to the naval question, were in fact years of some kind of détente. Neither Grey nor Bethmann Hollweg thought it wise to touch the naval question again. Both of them were convinced that negotiations would do more harm than good. Moreover, they had realized that more confidence was necessary to deal with such difficult matters as the reduction of naval expenditure or the conclusion of some kind of political agreement. As a sign of confidence, in June 1914, a British squadron took part in Kiel Week for the first time in ten years. When the squadron left Kiel, Admiral Warrender signalled to the ships of the High Seas Fleet lying in harbour: "Friends today, friends in future, friends for ever!" This was a very astonishing signal after years of severe conflicts.

War

Against this background, it was an irony of fate that only four weeks later this message proved an illusion: both fleets, the Royal Navy and the High Seas Fleet, waited for a battle which would decide their rivalry in the preceding decade. After four years of fighting both on land and at sea, however, Imperial Germany collapsed and had to surrender. While Tirpitz, who had desperately tried to save his life's work, had been dismissed in 1916, the Kaiser had no choice but to go into exile in 1918. And the High Seas Fleet? Without success at sea and after a humiliating internment at Scapa Flow, it scuttled itself in June 1919 in the hope that this would pave the way for a new attempt to turn Germany into a world and sea power.

What difference did the sea make for Germany at the turn of the last century? No doubt, after unification in 1871 Germany had quickly become a highly industrialized country and it was only natural that it wanted to protect its steadily increasing maritime interests in a globalizing world. However, instead of peacefully developing these interests and defending them by pursuing a careful and moderate foreign policy, Germany's rulers decided to challenge Britain's status as the leading sea and world power. As a result, an arms race followed which Germany could not win and which, moreover, soon isolated her in Europe. This isolation eventually caused Germany's political leadership to pursue a course of political brinkmanship in July 1914, hoping to loosen the iron ring around its neck. Instead of achieving a political success, this course resulted in the outbreak of the Great War. For Germany's maritime interests this war proved a disaster.

Select Bibliography

ASSMANN K., *Deutsche Seestrategie in zwei Weltkriegen* [German Naval Strategy in two World wars] (Heidelberg, 1957).
BERGHAHN V.R., *Der Tirpitz-Plan. Genesis und Verfall einer innenpolitischen Krisenstrategie unter Wilhelm II* [The Tirpitz-Plan. Rise and Fall of a Domestic-Political Crisis-Strategy under Wilhelm II], (Düsseldorf, 1971).
BERGHAHN V.R., *Germany and the Approach of War in 1914* (New York, 1973).
BERGHAHN V.R., *Imperial Germany 1871-1914. Economy, Society, Culture, and Politics* (Providence, RI and Oxford, 1994).
BERGHAHN V.R. and DEIST W., eds, *Rüstung im Zeichen der wilhelminischen Weltpolitik. Grundlegende Dokumente 1890-1914* [Armaments in the Era of German World Policy. Basic Documents, 1890-1914] (Düsseldorf, 1988).
DEIST W., *Flottenpolitik und Flottenpropaganda. Das Nachrichtenbureau des Reichsmarineamtes 1897-1914*, [Naval Policy and Naval Propaganda. The News Bureau of the Imperial Navy Office, 1897-1914] (Stuttgart, 1976).
DUPPLER J., *Der Juniorpartner. England und die Entwicklung der Deutschen Marine 1848-1890* [The Junior Partner. England and the Development of the German Navy, 1848-1890] (Herford, 1985).
EPKENHANS M., *Tirpitz. Architect of the German High Seas Fleet* (Washington. DC, 2008).
EPKENHANS M., *Die wilhelminische Flottenrüstung 1908-1914. Weltmachtstreben, industrieller Fortschritt, soziale Integration* [Naval Policy in the Wilhelmine Era, 1908-1914. The Grasp for World Power, indsutrial Progress, and social Integration] (Munich, 1991).
HERWIG H.H., *'Luxury' Fleet: The Imperial German Navy 1888-1918* (London, 1980).
HOBSON R., *Imperialism at Sea. Naval Strategic Thought, the Ideology of Sea Power and the Tirpitz Plan, 1875-1914* (Boston, MA and Leiden, 2002).
KENNEDY P.M., *The Rise of the Anglo-German Antagonism, 1860-1914* (London, 1980).
LAMBI I.N., *The Navy and German Power Politics 1862-1914* (London, 1984).
SALEWSKI M., *Tirpitz: Aufstieg, Macht, Scheitern* [Tirpitz. Rise, Power, and Failure] (Göttingen, 1979).
SELIGMANN M., NÄGLER F. and EPKENHANS M., eds, *The Naval Route to the Abyss: The Anglo-German Naval Race 1895-1914*, Navy Records Society, vol. 161 (London, 2014).
STEINBERG J., *Yesterday's Deterrent: Tirpitz and the Birth of the German Battle Fleet* (London, 1968).
TIRPITZ A. VON, *My Memoirs*, 2 vols (London, 1919).

The Imperial Japanese Navy, 1937–1942

RICHARD B. FRANK is an independent scholar, United States

ABSTRACT. *From 1937 Japan fought a war of conquest in China. In support of that war Japanese leaders allowed themselves to be drawn into war with Britain and the Netherlands, and hence the United States – though they knew they were not likely to win it. In the initial phase the tactics and equipment of the Naval Air Force, developed in the war in China, yielded stunning success. There was a possibility of linking up with Germany and driving China and Russia out of the war, but the leadership instead chose to fight the U.S. Navy, and at Midway it lost.*

RÉSUMÉ. *En 1937, le Japon lança la conquête de la Chine, suite à laquelle les dirigeants japonais se laissèrent entraîner dans une guerre contre la Grande-Bretagne et les Pays-Bas, puis les États-Unis – et ce alors qu'il était peu probable qu'il la gagne. Les tactiques et équipements de la Marine impériale japonaise, développés pendant la guerre en Chine, lui permirent tout d'abord de connaître d'incroyables succès. Bien qu'il lui eût été possible de s'allier avec l'Allemagne et de sortir la Chine et la Russie de la guerre, le gouvernement préféra combattre l'US Navy et perdit finalement à mi-parcours.*

•:•

Introduction

The Imperial Navy (*Kaigun*) entered 1937 planning war with the U.S.; it ended the year making war in China. While the massive clashes in China held center stage, the far less conspicuous role of the Imperial Navy produced a very malign echo. Japan immediately installed a blockade of the China coast, enhanced by the capture of major ports and inland waterways. For months the Chinese still managed to obtain large quantities of supplies, particularly through the port of Guangdong (then Canton) until it fell to the Japanese in November 1938. Japanese seizure of Northern Indochina in 1940 severed another important link via Haiphong in French Indochina and hence by rail to southern China.

Some supplies and weapons still leaked past the blockade through British Hong Kong, from the Soviet Union, or across the Burma Road, but the long-term consequence of the blockade played an outsized role in China's history. After the war's first two years the blockade starved Chiang Kai-shek's Nationalist-led coalition of supplies and munitions. But the evisceration of China's foreign trade administered a further and perhaps even more devastating blow. For decades,

Chinese national governments depended on customs duties for nearly half of their revenue. Thus, the blockade severely undermined the Chinese national fiscal base just as war vastly boosted financial demands. This left but one recourse: to print money. This unleashed the demon of inflation that in turn wrought havoc on the classes of individuals the Nationalist-led coalition relied upon, such as state workers and those working primarily for wages. In the long term, the inability of the Nationalist government to provide services and control inflation administered a grave wound to its legitimacy and played a key role in the triumph of the Chinese Communists.

The second notable dimension of the Imperial Navy's role in the China War involved aerial warfare, where it hefted by far the heaviest burden. Navy aviators established air dominance and exploited it with wide-scale bombing of Chinese targets, particularly cities. Experience in China accelerated development of aircraft, most notably the Mitsubishi A6M Type 0 fighter with unmatched range, in order to escort bombers in attacks on the distant Chinese wartime capital at Chongqing (then Chungking). Air operations in China also fostered advanced operational concepts stressing mass and the importance of fighters.

The year 1937 carried significance for the Imperial Navy for reasons beyond conflict with China. The Washington Naval treaties (1922) abruptly halted a nascent post-World War I warship-building race. It also established a ratio of "5-5-3" between the United Kingdom, United States, and Japan of permitted tonnage of capital ships. The "Fleet Faction" within the navy seethed at both the insulting inequality inflicted upon Japan at Washington and the fact that it was not remedied in a subsequent London agreement (1931). This faction focused narrowly on ship numbers and capabilities. Their rivals, the "Treaty Faction" found merit in the treaty system because it forbade the U.S. and U.K. to establish naval bases close enough to Japan to support effective projection of sea power into the Western Pacific, thus making the Imperial Navy supreme in that region.

After the London agreement, the "Fleet Faction" secured ascendancy and drove Japan to abandon the treaty system at the end of 1936. Japan then embarked on an ambitious building program emphasizing quality over quantity, a principle installed in the hearts of Japanese naval officers by victory over Russia in 1905. Its most notable progeny was the *Yamato* class super battleships that melded unmatched 46cm (18.1 inch) guns and ultra-heavy armor on a displacement of 72,809 tons, becoming the largest battleships ever put into service.

THE ROAD TO PEARL HARBOR

Confounding worldwide, not to mention Japanese, expectations, and despite many battlefield defeats and loss of vast swathes of territory, Chiang's coalition refused to bow to the Japanese. Chiang vested his long-term strategy in the conviction that ultimately hostilities in China would merge into a world war in which China would gain allies who could defeat Japan. From late 1938, senior

Japanese soldiers admitted the war could not be settled by military means. Then, after Hitler's startling conquest of Western Europe in 1940, Imperial Navy opposition to an alliance with Germany and Italy collapsed. While it appeared at the time that Japan had enlisted with the victorious side, Japan turned down a disastrous path.

Then, in a second episode of short-sighted opportunism, Japanese leaders reacted to Hitler's invasion of the Soviet Union in June 1941 by rejecting a "Strike North" against the Soviets for a "Strike South" to obtain resource areas that would render Japan self-sufficient and sever the last outside support for China to drive her out of the war. Japan's tiny group of top leaders recognized that "Strike South" meant certain war with Britain and the Netherlands, and unavoidable war with the U.S. When Japan moved to implement the "Strike South" by occupying Southern Indochina in July 1941, the U.S. responded with what effectively became an embargo on trade with Japan. Since Japan derived 80 percent of her oil imports from the U.S., her leaders faced the choice of retreat or war.

Thus came to pass the most fraught moment in the history of the Imperial Navy. War with the U.S. meant a naval war across the Pacific. All eyes turned to a handful of admirals to answer the question: could Japan prevail in such a conflict? All these elite flag officers recognized that Japan faced scant prospects of success. Indeed, they acknowledged that Japan could not win a Pacific War, both in private conversations among themselves and even with newly appointed Prime Minister Tojo Hideki. But in formal governmental councils, none of the key admirals mustered the moral courage to admit they entertained no confidence in the successful outcome of the war. So it would be war.

With the die cast, the navy turned to the Combined Fleet commander, Admiral Yamamoto Isoroku for operational execution. Yamamoto's reasoned that: (1) Japan had no chance of success in a long war; (2) the standard Imperial Navy short war plan never worked in war games; and (3) Japan lacked the means to attack the United States and impose a peace by arms. Therefore, Yamamoto identified just one conceivable Japanese strategy: collapse the American will to prosecute the conflict from the outset. He ordered an attack on Pearl Harbor emphasizing the American battleships (not aircraft carriers), reasoning that destruction of these symbols of naval mastery would strike the most devastating blow at American public morale. This daring scheme completely reversed the shared conventional template for war in both navies that the "correct" Japanese stance was to wait defensively in the Western Pacific to confront the U.S. fleet.

Working independently but in synergy with Yamamoto's overall vision emerged as a revolutionary step in naval warfare. Far from being captives of outmoded thinking, many officers in both the Imperial Japanese and U.S. Navies recognized the superior offensive striking power of aircraft carriers over battleships. But carriers remained far more vulnerable than battleships, especially to air attack. Before radar, exercises and war games repeatedly demonstrated that opposing aircraft could locate carriers and then deliver seriously damaging or fatal blows. Therefore, prior to 1941, the Japanese and Americans practiced passive defense: carriers must be dispersed. But in April 1941, the Imperial Navy formed the 1st Air Fleet, eventually comprised of Japan's six largest carriers – and massed them in one formation. The Imperial Navy seized upon the much greater potency on offense of massed carriers without addressing the issue of enhanced vulnerability.

Advancing the 1st Air Fleet (also known as the *Kido Butai*) to Hawaii constituted the third unprecedented element in the Japanese plan. The conventional expectation that the Imperial Navy would only fight a "decisive battle" in the Western Pacific resulted in construction of relatively short-ranged ships. Three of the six fleet carriers assembled for the attack lacked the inherent range for the Hawaii mission, as did many consorts. Only development of underway refueling and bulk storage of extra fuel outfitted the *Kido Butai* with the capability of hitting Pearl Harbor. Thus, the inability of any senior American official to anticipate the Pearl Harbor attack stemmed fundamentally from the triple level of surprise the Japanese packed into their plan: strategic, operational, and tactical.

Opening Operations

At dawn, 7 December (West Longitude date), the 1st Air Fleet launched two attack waves totaling 350 aircraft. Owing to strictures imposed by Tokyo, Japanese diplomats failed to deliver a declaration of war before the attack. Japanese aviators sank four battleships, damaged to varying degrees four more and inflicted other loss and damage to ships and planes. All three U.S. Pacific Fleet carriers were away: two at sea and one on the West Coast. A total of 2,403 Americans died; in terms of battle deaths, probably the worst single day of the war for the U.S. The cost to the *Kido Butai* was twenty-nine aircraft with fifty-five crew members. The five midget submarines participating in the attack obtained no success. All were lost with nine crewmen.

Tactically and operationally the attack achieved success. Strategically it negated the only Allied force in the Pacific that might have challenged Japan's opening operations. But strategically the attack was a disaster – for Japan. If Yamamoto identified American will as the singular American vulnerability, then the surprise attack without prior declaration of war succeeded in uniting and enraging the heretofore divided American public behind relentless prosecution of the war.

Immediately following the spectacular Pearl Harbor attack, the Imperial Navy landed two more stunning blows. Both the Imperial Army and Navy identified air superiority as an essential prerequisite to success. The American air concentration in the Philippines formed the most potent single land-based aerial array facing the Japanese. Thanks to a combination of careful Japanese planning, American ineptitude and just plain good fortune, a major strike of twin-engine land-attack planes (Mitsubishi G3M and G4M) escorted by Mitsubishi A6Ms knocked out about a third of the B-17s and a still larger share of defending fighters in the Philippines on 8 December. Japan immediately gained air control over the Philippines.

Then, on 10 December, Mitsubishi G3Ms and G4Ms armed with bombs and torpedoes sank the British battleship *Prince of Wales* and battle cruiser *Repulse*. This epochal event marked the first time that aircraft sank freely maneuvering capital ships. Decades later, divers would reveal that a single Japanese torpedo hit on *Prince of Wales* had unleashed a chain of freakish events that inflicted catastrophic damage. Thus, the symbolism of the episode considerably exceeded the actual technical achievement in terms of the vulnerability of modern capital ships to torpedo attack.

Over the next six months, the Japanese armed forces surged out across seven time zones to create one of the greatest empires in history at an unexcelled velocity. The Imperial Navy stood in the vanguard of this triumph. In Malaya and Burma Imperial Army aviators generally played the dominant role in securing air superiority, while Japanese naval aviators handled that task over the Pacific. Concentrating their forces against their numerically superior but widely dispersed Allied counterparts, the Japanese defeated their adversaries in detail. Combat experience in China also gave the Japanese airmen an edge in these early months.

With air superiority in hand, the Imperial Navy and Army executed a brilliant series of amphibious operations. In an explosive surge from December 1941 to May 1942 a Japanese tide rolled over the Western Pacific and to the borders of India. The intricate choreography of the sequence of landings as well as the economy of force employed have not been exceeded, and perhaps not equaled. Allied airmen inflicted only pinprick damage. Allied submariners, particularly the small Dutch contingent, inflicted at least some small war- and merchant-ship damage. Next to the abysmal failure of British Commonwealth forces in Malaya and Singapore, the U.S. Asiatic Fleet submarine force (twenty-nine boats) contributed the next most egregious failure of Allied arms. Landings were executed with skill. Only the initial effort to land on Wake Island was defeated. Coordination between the Imperial Army and Navy – never a forte of the Japanese armed forces – peaked during these months. By May, Japan had secured the vital resource areas to the south with essential raw materials, especially oil, to sustain theoretically at least a protracted war.

THE HINGE

By March 1942, with initial objectives secured or about to be secured, Japanese strategists inspected options for the war's next stage. Imperial Navy officers, heady with success, surveyed three basic choices: strike west towards the Indian Ocean; strike south against Australia to neuter it before it formed a platform for a counterattack; or strike east against the Hawaiian-based U.S. main fleet. Japan would attempt all three lunges, an inherently unsound dissipation of effort.

In April 1942, the Imperial Navy conducted its one major foray west into the India Ocean. Nagumo's *Kido Butai* with five powerfully escorted fleet carriers attacked British bases on Sri Lanka (then Ceylon), sinking a British carrier, two heavy cruisers, and several other vessels. Another raiding force and a submarine contingent slaughtered about 125,000 tons of Allied shipping. This event dramatically underscored the global overstretch of Britain. A smattering of mostly old battleships and the outnumbered carriers with small and inferior-quality air groups of the Royal Navy's Eastern Fleet ventured a near-foolhardy and fortunately abortive effort to confront the Japanese.

The Japanese rampage triggered alarm in London and kindled fond hopes in Tokyo. It seemed to preview Japan's strategic convergence with her German ally at the west coast of Africa. Such a stroke might have been the one great combined Axis strategy that could win or at least substantially protract the war, for it would have collapsed the British position in the Middle East and India, thereby completing the isolation and likely collapse of China (as well as the probable fall of Churchill's government). Freed from the China morass, Japan could have joined the attack on the Soviets, with consequences including the severing of the routes across the North Pacific and via the Persian Gulf that moved 70 percent of U.S. Lend Lease aid to the Soviet Union. This whole tapestry underscores the fact that Japan's only realistic hope of prevailing in a war with the U.S. depended upon joint action with Germany. Hitler recognized this promising strategy, but in early 1942 he deferred it to finish the Soviet war. With that goal seemingly in sight in September 1942, Hitler sent word to Japan that he was "considering ways of bringing the war to a favorable conclusion ... [and he was] putting special emphasis on a German-Japanese junction across the Indian Ocean".[1] Besides Hitler's endorsement, however, the strike west also required Japan's continued devotion. If any component of Japan's leadership should have grasped this point and advocated it relentlessly, it was the Imperial Navy. But Japan's sailors proved incapable of holding to a single strategy.

As for a strike south, after the Imperial Army emphatically ruled out any invasion of Australia for want of troops or shipping, the Naval General Staff advocated a southerly thrust to cut off lines of communication to Australia and New Zealand. In other words, use the seas against the Antipodes the way they were used against China. Early May brought the first phase of this move as the Japanese occupied Tulagi in the southern Solomons and readied an invasion force to seize Port Moresby on New Guinea. Allied code breakers, however, extracted from the Japanese naval communications forewarning of the move. This resulted in the Battle of the Coral Sea, history's first naval action where the opposing fleets never came within sight of each other and traded blows solely by air. Tactically, the Japanese won, sinking the American fleet carrier *Lexington* and seriously damaging the *Yorktown* in exchange for loss of the light carrier *Shoho*.

---

[1] Summary of Radio Intercept Intelligence 30 September 1942, Record Group 38, Inactive Stations, Box 62, file 3222/6, F-20 Summaries of Radio intercept Intelligence–Japanese–20 February to 30 September 1942, National Archives and Records Administration.

But damage and aircraft losses removed the two Japanese fleet carriers, *Shokaku* and *Zuikaku*, from the lineup for the next major battle. Strategically, Coral Sea represented at least a temporary Allied success as the Japanese Port Moresby invasion force turned back.

As noted, the action in the Coral Sea stemmed from only the initial phase of the southern thrust, for the main effort had been postponed pending Yamamoto's favored eastern thrust designed to achieve a knockout blow to American will before the U.S. fully mobilized. Yamamoto's vision comprised two parts: lure the remaining American carriers into a battle off Midway Island and destroy them. Then Japan would seize the Hawaiian Islands. Those islands plus their nearly half a million inhabitants would become bargaining chips for a negotiated peace. Whether this scheme could have worked is doubtful, but at least Yamamoto grasped the urgency of Japan's situation and devised a strategy to address it.

The central premise of Yamamoto's hideously complex Midway plan was that the Japanese would have surprise. A significant part of the fleet would first seize Attu and Kiska in the Aleutian Islands to block that as a potential future American avenue of attack. The plan rested further on the misconception that the demoralized American sailors would have to be provoked to fight. This in part explains the dispersion of the huge fleet Yamamoto deployed. After Midway was captured, the American carriers and battleships hurrying to its defense would be crushed. Hawaii would then be invaded. The Naval General Staff's favored southern thrust to isolate Australia and New Zealand would follow.

American radio intelligence (assisted by Allied units) presented the U.S. Pacific Fleet commander, Admiral Chester W. Nimitz, with the essential elements of Yamamoto's plan. Nimitz boldly and brilliantly exploited this treasure, securing the incredibly fast repair of carrier *Yorktown* damaged at Coral Sea, and stationing his three available carriers in an ambush position northeast of Midway. In the ensuring battle on 3–7 June, all four Japanese fleet carriers were sunk in exchange for *Yorktown*. The destruction of the four Japanese carriers related directly to the decision to concentrate carriers for maximum offensive potential in a single formation without dealing with defensive vulnerability – thus there is a direct link between success at Pearl Harbor and disaster at Midway. The outcome represented a calamity for Japan, but the reality was that American production would have still overmatched the Japanese fleet by 1944.

With the Midway victory, Admiral Ernest J. King, Commander in Chief, U.S. Fleet, willed the American effort in the Pacific into a counteroffensive to take the island of Guadalcanal in the Solomons to block further Japanese South Pacific advances. Although the initial landing on 7 August achieved success, an Imperial Navy counterattack inflicted the worst loss at sea the U.S. Navy ever sustained, at the Battle of Savo Island. This marked the first of seven major naval battles (two featuring carriers), an enormous air attrition campaign, and repeated clashes ashore as the Japanese sought to wrest back Guadalcanal.

Excellent design and equipment of its warships and the superb level of crew training characterized the Imperial Navy's surface-ship operations. All of this stemmed from pre-war concepts. Prior to an expected "Decisive Battle" in the

Western Pacific, Japanese officers aimed to unleash massive torpedo attacks by destroyer flotillas supported by cruisers and fast battleships on the numerically superior U.S. battle fleet. The survivors would then be crushed by the Japanese battle line. The key weapon of the attrition phase was the giant Type 93 61cm (24-inch) torpedo, the finest such weapon in the world. For the first thirteen months of the war, the Imperial Navy dazzled at surface-ship combat, particularly at night. One stunning metric of that superiority is that during that time, Imperial Navy surface warships sank eleven Allied cruisers against one loss.

Despite its high quality in many spheres, the Imperial Navy exhibited debilitating weaknesses. Japanese research and development proved very deficient, particularly in regard to electronics (especially radar). Japan commenced the war with parity or better almost across the spectrum of aircraft but never matched the tempo of her adversaries in aircraft development. Japan's seamen also neglected logistics, notably the importance of fleet oilers. And any list of deficiencies must award a high place to the insecurity of Imperial Navy codes and ciphers.

Yet another weakness stabbed at the heart of Japan's Pacific War prospects. Japan required about ten million tons of shipping to sustain her economy but counted only six million tons under her own flag. The four-million-ton deficit was made up overwhelmingly by the nations that she chose to attack: the U.S. and the U.K. Even with captured tonnage at the start of the war, her shortfall still totaled about 2.75 million tons. Japan's limited shipyard capacity and the diversion of available repair resources towards warships aggravated the fundamental ship shortage. Further, rather than gathering all tonnage in a common pool subject to rationalization, the Japanese chopped their resources into three: one share for each armed service and one for civilian users. The shipping mathematics argued vehemently for a short war. They undermined the concept entertained by some Japanese leaders that they could sustain a protracted war and exhaust their materially more powerful adversary.

Conclusion

Institutionally, the Imperial Navy between 1937 and 1942 proved that it could match or exceed the technical achievements of its Western adversaries in the excellence of warship, aircraft, and weapon design. It innovated in the newly dominant field of naval aviation, proved adept at amphibious warfare and ruled supreme in night surface combat. At a tactical level the Imperial Navy could tender a strong claim to be the worlds' best navy in 1942.

But brilliance at the tactical level gleaned only ephemeral triumphs for the Imperial Navy's deficiencies in the higher realms of war making and within its leadership produced catastrophe. Neither the Imperial Navy nor the Imperial Army could restrain their rivalries in the national interest. Both sets of uniformed Japanese leaders failed to pursue vigorously the admittedly difficult challenge of coordinating a global strategy with Japan's German ally.

The oceans played a paradoxical role in this last phase of the Imperial Japanese Navy's history. Japan exploited its sea control to inflict devastating wounds on the reigning government of China and contributed materially to a great pivot in the history of that huge continental power. But that pivot proved the diametric opposite of the Japanese strategic goal of preventing communist rule in its neighbor. Japan then turned the water highways of the Pacific into pathways of audacious advance to create an enormous empire and undermine Western colonialism. But, as seamen, Japanese sailors knew from the outset that water highways could be traversed in both directions. As Japan's soldiers learned from 1942, the enemy-dominated oceans also served as prison walls. More Japanese soldiers perished from hunger and lack of medicine than in battle in the archipelago of isolated garrisons across the Pacific.

But the greatest importance of the oceans in the history of the Imperial Navy rests more in intangible than tangible facets. Like their British and American counterparts, Imperial Navy officers as a class viewed themselves as more far sighted and sophisticated than their military or civilian counterparts. With firsthand knowledge of the world lacking among other leaders, Japanese admirals in 1941 comprehended far better than other components of the elite leadership just how dim Japan's prospects were in an expanded war. The seas had instilled this breath of knowledge. Their violent moods had provided stern tests of mental toughness and physical courage. But what the oceans did not and could not do was fashion moral courage within a handful of admirals to stop the march to war with the U.S. The lack of moral courage among its highest leaders ultimately destroyed the state they served.

Bibliography

ARAKAWA K., 'Japanese Naval Blockade of China in the Second Sino-Japanese War, 1937–41', in *Naval Blockades and Seapower, Strategies and Counter-Strategies*, ed. B. ELLEMAN and S. PAINE (London, 2006).
ASADA S., *From Mahan to Pearl Harbor: The Imperial Japanese Navy and the United States* (Annapolis, 2006).
BARTSCH W., *December 8, 1941: MacArthur's Pearl Harbor* (College Station, TX, 2003).
BOOG H., RAHN W. and STUMPF R., *Germany and the Second World War, vol. VI, The Global War* (Oxford, 2001).
CALLAHAN R., *The Worst Disaster: The Fall of Singapore* (Cranbury, 1977).
CAMPBELL J., *Naval Weapons of World War II* (Annapolis, 1985).
combinedfleet.com, Tabular Record of Movement carriers *Akagi* and *Ryujo* [Last accessed 22 September 2014].
DREA E., *Japan's Imperial Army: Its Rise and Fall, 1853–1945* (Lawrence, KS, 2009).

EVANS D. and PEATTIE M., *Kaigun: Strategy, Tactics and Technology of the Imperial Japanese Navy, 1887-1941* (Annapolis, 1997).

FRANK R., *Guadalcanal: The Definitive Account of the Landmark Battle* (New York, 1989).

GARKZE W., DULIN R. and DENLAY K., *Death of a Battleship: The Loss of HMS Prince of Wales December 10, 1941, A Marine Forensics Analysis of the Sinking* (2012 revision) at rina.org.uk [Last accessed 11 November 2014).

HAGIWARA M., 'The Japanese Air Campaigns in China, 1937-1941', in *The Battle for China: Essays on the Military History of the Sino-Japanese War 1937-47*, ed. M. PEATTIE, E. DREA and H. VAN DE VEN (Stanford, 2010).

HEINDRICHS W., *Threshold of War: Franklin D. Roosevelt & American Entry into World War II* (New York, 1988).

HOSOYA C., 'The Tripartite Pact, 1939-1940', in *Japan's Road to the Pacific War, Deterrent Diplomacy: Japan, Germany, and the USSR 1935-1940*, ed. J. MORLEY (New York, 1976).

HOTTA E., *Japan, 1941: Countdown to Infamy* (New York, 2013).

IKE N., *Japan's Decision for War: Records of the 1941 Policy Conferences* (Stanford, 1967).

IRIYE A., *Power and Culture: The Japanese American War, 1941-1945* (Cambridge, MA, 1982).

KIMBALL W., *Churchill and Roosevelt: The Complete Correspondence, vol. I, Alliance Emerging, October 1933-November 1942* (Princeton, 1984).

LACROIX E. and WELLS L., *Japanese Cruisers of the Pacific War* (Annapolis, MD, 1997).

LARY D., *The Chinese People at War: Human Suffering and Social Transformation, 1937-45* (Cambridge, 2010).

LU D., *The Agony of Choice: Matsuoka Yosuke and the Rise and Fall of the Japanese Empire, 1880-1946* (Lanham, MD, 2003).

LUNDSTROM J., *The First South Pacific Campaign: Pacific Fleet Strategy December 1941-June 1942* (Annapolis, MD, 1976).

LUNDSTROM J., *The First Team: Pacific Naval Air Combat from Pearl Harbor to Midway* (Annapolis, MD, 1984).

MARCI F., *Clash of Empires in South China: The Allied Nations' Proxy War with Japan, 1935-1941* (Lawrence, KS, 2012).

MILLER T., *The Persian Corridor and Aid to Russia* (Washington, DC, 1952).

MORLEY J., ed., *Japan's Road to the Pacific War, The Final Confrontation, Japan's Negotiations with the United States, 1941* (New York, 1994).

NICHOLSON A., *Hostages to Fortune: Winston Churchill and the Loss of the Prince of Wales and Repulse* (Stroud, 2005).

PAINE S., *The Wars for Asia 1911-1949* (New York, 2012).

PARILLO M., *The Japanese Merchant Marine in World War II* (Annapolis, MD, 1993).

PARSHALL J. and TULLY A., *Shattered Sword: The Untold Story of the Battle of Midway* (Washington, DC, 2005).

PEATTIE M., *Sunburst: The Rise of Japanese Naval Air Power, 1909-1941* (Annapolis, MD, 2001).

ROSKILL S., *The War at Sea 1939-1945. Vol. II, The Period of Balance* (London, 1956).

SHORES C., CULL B. and IZAWA Y., *Bloody Shambles, vol. 1, The Drift to War to the Fall* of Singapore (London, 1992); vol. 2, *The Defense of Sumatra to the Fall of Burma* (London, 1993).

SKULSKI J., *The Battleship Yamato* (Annapolis, MD, 1988).

STEPHAN J., *Hawaii Under the Rising Sun: Japan's Plans for Conquest After Pearl Harbor* (Honolulu, 1984).

TAYLOR J., *The Generalissimo: Chiang Kai-shek and the Struggle for Modern China* (Cambridge, MA, 2009).

VAN DE VEN H., 'Overview of Major Military Operations', in *The Battle for China: Essays on the Military History of the Sino-Japanese War of 1937-1945*, ed. M. PEATTIE, E. DREA and H. VAN DE VEN (Stanford, 2011).

VAN DE VEN H., *War and Nationalism in China 1925-1945* (London, 2003).

WILLMOTT H., *Empires in the Balance: Japanese and Allied Pacific Strategies to April 1942* (Annapolis, MD, 1982).

WILLMOTT H., *Pearl Harbor* (London, 2001).

WILLMOTT H., *The Second World War in the East* (London, 1999).

YOUNG A., *China's Wartime Finance and Inflation, 1937-1945* (Cambridge, MA, 1965).

ZIMM A., *Attack on Pearl Harbor: Strategy, Combat, Myths, Deceptions* (Havertown, PA, 2011).

THE US AS A NEW NAVAL POWER, 1890–1919

KENNETH J. HAGAN is Professor Emeritus of History at the U.S. Naval Academy, United States

ABSTRACT. *The American admiral Mahan effectively invented the modern concept of "sea power", but when his countrymen were persuaded to adopt it, they found that it was not quite the simple formula for world power which they had been promised. The new U.S. battle fleet expressed America's new authority, but naval victory did not come quickly and clearly, and the battleships were only indirectly involved.*

RÉSUMÉ. *Bien que l'amiral américain Mahan inventât le concept moderne de « puissance maritime », lorsque ses concitoyens se décidèrent à l'adopter, ils n'y retrouvèrent pas exactement la recette simple d'une puissance mondiale qui leur avait été promise. Cette flotte de guerre inédite exprima la nouvelle autorité américaine mais les victoires navales ne vinrent ni rapidement ni clairement et les navires de guerres n'y étaient que peu impliqués.*

.•.

"SEA POWER" IN THE AMERICAN MIND

Throughout the 20th century, and well into the 21st, the term "sea power" defined the overarching strategy of the United States Navy. The phrase first entered the U.S. naval lexicon with the publication in May 1890 of Captain Alfred Thayer Mahan's epochal book, *The Influence of Sea Power upon History, 1660-1783*.[1] In this extraordinary treatise the captain conceived of "sea power" in broad terms, as consisting of "contests between nations, of mutual rivalries, of violence frequently culminating in war."[2] Mahan's purpose was to advance the thesis of the indispensability of "sea power" to national greatness. Only through pursuing a strategy of gaining victory in fleet engagements could a navy insure that greatness. His model was the Royal Navy of Great Britain before and during the age of Horatio Nelson.

Mahan had written a book for the ages, but his classic work was spawned by the unique American naval conditions of the 1880s. American officers and

---
[1] MAHAN A.T., *The Influence of Sea Power upon History 1660-1783* (Boston, MA, 1890).
[2] *Ibid.*, p. 1.

civilian officials were reluctantly coming to recognize the obsolescence of the navy's wooden-hulled sailing warships featuring auxiliary steam engines and muzzle-loading guns. Beginning in 1883, Congress authorized a new generation of steel-hulled, steam-driven cruisers mounting modern breech-loading rifled guns. With each subsequent congressional appropriation, the cruisers grew in hull displacement and size of guns, but there was no corresponding reconsideration of how to use the new warships. The navy remained wedded to a wartime strategy of coastal defense and commerce raiding, or *guerre de course*. This orthodoxy had prevailed since the navy's founding in October 1775, and it remained dominant throughout the 1880s. At decade's end, however, publication of Mahan's book and unanticipated events in the far-distant Pacific Ocean archipelago of Samoa would cause its collapse.

SAMOA AS CATALYST: THE HURRICANE OF 1889

In the 1870s the great powers of Europe were laying claim to independent island groups throughout the Pacific. The United States stumbled into the Western devastation of native cultures in 1872, when Commander Richard W. Meade of the 2nd-class screw sloop USS *Narragansett* signed a treaty with a Samoan high chief granting the U.S. Navy the right to deposit coal for the auxiliary engines of the sail-powered warships that occasionally dipped in for replenishment while on peacetime patrols of the vast southwest Pacific. Meade's unsanctioned handiwork was never ratified by the United States, but in 1878 a Samoan-American treaty of amity and commerce was negotiated and ratified. Based on these tentative authorizations, the U.S. Navy established a coaling and repair station in the superb harbor of Pago Pago, on the island of Tutuila.

The U.S. government and navy thereafter largely ignored Samoa, until in 1885 German Chancellor Otto von Bismarck concluded that to insure good order in the islands eventual "German control of Samoa was both desirable and necessary ...."[3] Germany's establishment of a protectorate over Samoa seemed a foregone conclusion, but the Americans were not compliant. Late in 1887, Secretary of State Thomas F. Bayard warned Berlin that the goal of the United States was "the preservation of native independence and autonomy."[4] To put teeth into Bayard's protest, the U.S. Senate in January 1889 authorized $100,000 for construction of a naval base in Pago Pago, and the navy ordered the commander of the Pacific Station to neutral Apia to protect Americans and "to protest against German misdeeds."[5] The pitiful force at Rear Admiral Lewis A. Kimberley's command consisted of three antediluvian veterans of the "old navy."

The Americans were saved from battle by a most surreal climax. On 15–16

---

[3] KENNEDY P.M., *The Samoan Tangle: A Study in Anglo-German-American Relations, 1878-1900* (New York, 1974), p. 45. Kennedy's words.
[4] Bayard quoted in KENNEDY, *Samoan Tangle*, p. 73.
[5] KENNEDY, *Samoan Tangle*, p. 79. Kennedy's words.

March a very destructive hurricane hit Samoa, devastating Apia harbor, where there were anchored one British warship, three small German warships, six merchantmen, and three American naval relics: the screw steamer *Trenton*, the screw sloop *Vandalia* and the gunboat *Nipsic*. Only the British HMS *Calliope* managed to claw her way to safety at sea; the American and German naval ships were lost, as were the six merchantmen. One hundred and fifty seamen died, including forty-nine Americans. The disaster sobered statesmen in Washington, London, and Berlin. An international conference of Great Britain, Germany, and the United States was hastily convened in Berlin, and a system of tripartite supervision of the Samoan islands was agreed upon. The arrangement would function for ten years, until the United States and Germany divided the islands between themselves in the wake of the Spanish–American War.

THE BIRTH OF THE BATTLESHIP NAVY, 1890–1898

The German–American confrontation over Samoa fed directly into the annual report of Republican Secretary of the Navy Benjamin F. Tracy, which was published in 1890, as was Mahan's book. A navalist and imperialist, Tracy echoed Mahan and called for the construction of no fewer than twenty battleships: "We must have a fleet of battleships that will beat off the enemy's fleet on its approach ...." The new-age men-of-war "also must be able to divert an enemy's force from our coast by threatening his own ...."[6] The Naval Affairs Committee of the House of Representatives tempered Tracy's vociferous offensiveness and shrank his numbers to "three seagoing coastline battleships."[7] On 30 June 1890, Congress approved construction of the battleships *Indiana*, *Massachusetts*, and *Oregon*. Each armor-plated, steam-driven leviathan displaced more than 10,000 tons and mounted centerline batteries of large-bore breech-loading rifled cannon. To deter an attack by Germany or another European sea power, the new battleships would be stationed mostly on the East Coast of the United States, the heartland of America's industry and the center of its population. But the real naval action of the new age was to come first in the Pacific, where battleships were notable for their absence.

The irrelevance of battleships to the inchoate American strategy and policy in the Pacific became obvious in January 1893, when the expansionistic American minister to Hawai'i, John L. Stevens, helped to precipitate a revolution by white planters against Queen Liliuokalani. He was abetted by sailors and Marines from the protected steam cruiser *Boston*, one of the three original steel-hulled cruisers authorized by Congress in 1883, just prior to the Mahanian sea-power revolution. Captain Gilbert C. Wiltse, commanding officer of the *Boston*, tersely reported his action of 16 January: "At 4:30 p.m. landed force in accordance with request

[6] Secretary of the Navy Benjamin F. Tracy's annual report for 1889, quoted in HAGAN K.J., *This People's Navy: The Making of American Sea Power* (New York, 1991), p. 195.
[7] Chairman of House Naval Affairs Committee quoted in HAGAN, *This People's Navy*, p. 197.

of U.S. Minister Plenipotentiary [Stevens]. Tuesday afternoon the Provisional Government was established, the Queen dethroned, without loss of life."[8] The incoming anti-expansionistic Democratic administration of Grover Cleveland (1893–1897) repudiated the resulting treaty of annexation, but the president's proud retreat to continentalism would be permanently aborted during the diplomatic climax of the Spanish–American War.

In February 1898 an ongoing uprising of Cuban nationals against brutal Spanish overlordship led Republican President William McKinley (1897–1901) to dispatch the battleship *Maine* to Havana for the classic purpose of guaranteeing the safety of American residents in the capital city. Instead, the *Maine* mysteriously blew up on 15 February, with the loss of 266 sailors. The United States declared war against Spain. In one of the many ironies of what Secretary of State John Hay would call "the splendid little war," the first major naval action took place in the Philippine Islands, at that time a Spanish colony.[9]

Encouraged by Assistant Secretary of the Navy Theodore Roosevelt, the Asiatic Squadron commander, Commodore George Dewey, hunted for the aged Spanish fleet with his new protected cruisers *Olympia*, *Boston*, *Raleigh*, and *Baltimore*. He caught the anchored Spaniards in Manila Bay, and on 1 May he annihilated their obsolete ships at a cost of 371 Spanish casualties and six wounded Americans. Elements of the U.S. Army were rushed to Dewey's aid, and on 13 August the Americans captured the Spanish colonial capital of Manila. Spain ceded the Philippines, Guam, and Puerto Rico to the United States in the peace treaty of 10 December 1898. Cuba was granted its independence. Dewey's victory in Manila Bay can be interpreted as quintessentially Mahanian in that it was a decisive fleet engagement, an annihilation. Yet, it was fought in a harbor, not on the high seas. Moreover, Dewey did not command a single battleship.

The means to Dewey's victory may not have been Mahanian, but the results clearly were. As a direct consequence of the navy's Pacific operations during the Spanish–American War, President McKinley persuaded the two houses of Congress to pass a joint resolution annexing Hawai'i on 7 July 1898. Acquisition of the mid-ocean archipelago established the physical foundations of American empire deep in the Pacific, complete with a naval base at Pearl Harbor. The United States now stood in direct geopolitical opposition to the rising sea power of Japan, where Mahan's book was widely read in naval circles.

If Dewey's triumph belched only a whiff of Mahanian sea power, the U.S. naval victory over Spain in Cuba on 3 July 1898 was pure Mahan. The United States had declared war on 25 April with the express purpose of eliminating Spanish sovereignty over Cuba. Virtually the entire U.S. Navy – excepting Dewey's Far Eastern command – was rushed to the island to intercept and defeat the Spanish fleet coming from Europe. Admiral Pascual Cervera y Topete understandably thought

---

[8] Wiltse quoted in HAGAN, *This People's Navy*, p. 202.
[9] John Hay quoted in U.S. DEPARTMENT OF STATE, OFFICE OF THE HISTORIAN, *Milestones: 1866–1898, The Spanish-American War, 1898*. Online: www.history.state.gov/milestones/1866-1898/spanish-american-war [Accessed 19 December 2013].

he was steaming towards his doom as he sought refuge in the harbor of Santiago de Cuba, which the Americans promptly blockaded.

On 3 July 1898, Cervera valiantly sortied with his four cruisers and two destroyers, straight into the gaping jaws of an American fleet of three cruisers and four battleships: *Indiana, Iowa, Oregon,* and *Texas*. It was all over in about four hours; the Spanish lost 323 dead, the Americans one officer. Coming on the heels of Dewey's triumph in Manila Bay, this battle vindicated Mahan's strategy of sea power in the eyes of the U.S. Navy. That unassailable doctrine would be given life by battleship construction, fleet concentration, and strategic planning in the administration of the nation's greatest navalist, President Theodore Roosevelt (1901–1909).

Mr. Roosevelt's Battleship Navy: 1901–1917

An assassin's bullet felled President William McKinley on 14 September 1901, elevating Vice President Roosevelt to the presidency. In the 1890s, Roosevelt's association with Mahan and his experience as assistant secretary of the navy had made him an ardent proponent of sea power as defined by the naval captain and his adherents. Once he became president, Roosevelt used his office to transform the United States and its navy from a regionally preponderant presence in North America and the Caribbean Sea into a formidable global sea power: "by 1906 (by a British reckoning) or by 1908 (by Congress's count) the United States stood second among naval powers in the index of capital ships."[10]

President Roosevelt's first geopolitical initiative was negotiation and ratification of the Hay-Pauncefote Treaty in December 1901, a mere three months after becoming president. Bowing to his insistence, London agreed that the United States could build, fortify, and control an interoceanic canal across the Central American isthmus. Such a major waterway would permit rapid transfer of the U.S. battle fleet from the Atlantic to the Pacific, where in times of acute tension it could shield the continental West Coast and Hawai'i from hostile moves by Imperial Japan, and failing that it could engage the Japanese battle fleet in an apocalyptic Mahanian clash. This concept formed the core of War Plan ORANGE, the U.S. Navy's prevailing operational dogma for war in the Pacific from its formulation in 1911 until the Japanese attack on Pearl Harbor in 1941.

Armed with carte blanche from the world's premier sea power, Roosevelt schemed to build an American canal across Panama, a component state of Colombia. When the Colombian congress proudly rejected a treaty granting the U.S. a century of dominion over the proposed canal, the American president encouraged a group of Panamanian revolutionaries to seize power. They did so in November 1903, with the backing of the 1,300-ton gunboat USS *Nashville*. Minuscule though she was, *Nashville* symbolized the formidable naval power

---

[10] BAER G.W., *One Hundred Years of Sea Power: The U.S. Navy, 1890–1990* (Stanford, CA, 1994), p. 40.

undergirding Roosevelt's aggressive statecraft. One Colombian diplomat wailed, "The Americans are against us. What can we do against the American Navy?"[11]

Perfunctory diplomacy quickly closed the deal. On 23 February 1904, the U.S. Senate approved a treaty with the freshly created nation of Panama granting the United States governing authority over the newly defined Canal Zone, as "if it were the sovereign of the territory."[12] Construction began that year. A technological and industrial masterwork, the canal was completed ten years later, in August 1914. Thanks to Roosevelt's robust determination, a nation with a one-ocean navy had become a two-ocean sea power.

London acceded to American hegemony in the Caribbean because it was busily redeploying its naval forces and concentrating them in European waters, where the capital ships of the Royal Navy faced the swelling menace of the German High Seas Fleet. Washington and its navy, by contrast, would never quarrel dangerously with Great Britain. In the words of Admiral Sir John Fisher, the United States was "a kindred spirit with whom we shall never have a parricidal war."[13]

Roosevelt capitalized on Britain's goodwill by deft use of his favorite gunnery specialist and future naval aide, Lieutenant Commander William S. Sims. The outspoken naval officer was a vociferous supporter of the "all big gun" battleship, the naval weapons system of the future, which Roosevelt and Sims believed in but which Mahan uncomprehendingly opposed.[14] The inexorable march of naval technology had bewildered the prophet of sea power and opened the field to his disciples. Late in 1906 Roosevelt ordered Sims to England to make an ostensibly unofficial inspection of the recently completed HMS *Dreadnought*, whose heavy displacement, high speed, armor, and large-caliber guns would instantly render obsolescent all of the world's existing battleships, including those of the U.S. Navy. Personally acquainted from previous tours of duty with leading British ordnance officers, including Captain John Jellicoe, Sims hit pay dirt.

The climax of his visit came in two parts. On Christmas Eve, in civilian clothes, he boarded HMS *Dreadnought*, where the ship's captain showed him the entire vessel, including "the inside of one of the turrets, etc." The result, he wrote to his undoubtedly enthralled wife, "was that I got a great deal of information about the ship and will be able to make an interesting report."[15] The next day, Christmas 1906, the American lieutenant commander had lunch with the family of Admiral Sir John Fisher, the First Sea Lord, who admired Sims's criticism of Mahan. Sims later quoted Fisher as saying, "It is clear to me that we want to put

---

[11] Diplomat quoted in PATERSON T.G. et al., *American Foreign Relations: A History, Volume 1: To 1920*, 8th edn (Stamford, CT, 2015), p. 249.

[12] Treaty quoted in *Ibid.*, pp. 249–250.

[13] Fisher quoted in *Ibid.*, p. 271.

[14] SIMS W.S., LIEUTENANT-COMMANDER, U.S. NAVY, INSPECTOR OF TARGET PRACTICE, 'The Inherent Tactical Qualities of All-Big-Gun, One-Caliber Battleships of High Speed, Large Displacement and Gun-Power', *Proceedings of the United States Naval Institute*, December 1906, pp. 1337–66.

[15] WILLIAM S. SIMS to Anne H. Sims, undated, but 24 December 1906, William S. Sims Collection, No. 168, Box 6, Folder 31, U.S. Naval War College.

as many heavy guns as possible on the same ship so as to have as heavy a concentration of fire as possible."[16]

With an understandably inflated ego, Sims returned to the United States, where President Roosevelt used his description of HMS *Dreadnought* to help ram through Congress an authorization for the battleships *Delaware* and *North Dakota*. The two 22,000-ton sister ships were among America's first dreadnoughts. Soon thereafter, in November 1907, the month *Delaware* was laid down, Roosevelt appointed Sims, now a commander, to be his naval aide. In March 1909 he further rewarded Sims by naming him commanding officer of the pre-dreadnought battleship *Minnesota*, just home from the globe-circling cruise of the "Great White Fleet."

So-named because of their gleaming white hulls, the fleet of sixteen American pre-dreadnoughts had departed Hampton Roads, Virginia, on 16 December 1907, outbound on a 46,000-mile circumnavigation of the globe. It would be completed with the return of the warships on 22 February 1909, symbolically and significantly the birthday of George Washington. Theodore Roosevelt had conceived and ordered the unprecedented cruise, one never subsequently equaled by an American fleet of surface ships, in order to demonstrate unquestionably that under his tutelage the United States Navy had matured into a world-class sea power.

The primary object of the President's attention was Japan. In the Russo-Japanese War of 1904–1905, Japan had fought and resoundingly defeated Tsarist Russia on land, and at sea in the historic fleet battle of Tsushima Strait. Japan had exhibited truly formidable power, which the United States feared could be directed against its new possession in the western Pacific, the Philippines. For Roosevelt, a statesman who saw force and diplomacy as two faces of the same coin, it seemed logical to send his battle fleet into Tokyo Bay for a non-hostile but admonitory port call. The ploy worked. The Japanese were hospitable and the fleet continued westward, passing through the Suez Canal and Mediterranean before steaming back into Hampton Roads. Roosevelt welcomed the armada home from the deck of the presidential yacht *Mayflower*.

Early the next year, 1910, Roosevelt's chosen successor, William Howard Taft (1909–1913), employed sixteen battleships of the Atlantic Fleet to demonstrate to Europe the arrival of the United States as a modern naval power. The purpose of the battle fleet's voyage, according to the *Times* of London, "was primarily educational" and a means of familiarizing the officers and men with the handling of squadrons and fleets through "strategical manoeuvres, tactical evolutions, battle practice and training cruises."[17]

While in the eastern Atlantic the fleet served not so subtly as a bellwether of U.S. foreign policy. It showed favor to Britain and France, not to Germany, a signatory to the Triple Alliance locked in a major naval race with England, a

---

[16] WILLIAM S. SIMS to Anne H. Sims, 25 December 1906, *ibid*.
[17] 'The American Naval Visit', *Times* [of London], 15 November, 1910, William S. Sims Collection, Cont. 115, Folder 'Clippings 1910', Manuscript Division, Library of Congress.

member of the Triple Entente. All sixteen of the American battleships visited England and France; not one of them called at a German port.

Maturation as a Mahanian sea power characterized the U.S. Navy in the four-year period from the visit of the Atlantic Fleet to England and the outbreak of World War I. Battleship construction continued unabated; the navy's dominant strategic plans were ORANGE and BLACK, each of which envisioned fighting a major fleet engagement with the most likely enemy, Japan in the one case and Germany in the other. With the opening of the Panama Canal in October 1914, the American battleships could speed between the Atlantic and Pacific to engage whichever was the more threatening of the two enemies.

SOMETHING OLD, SOMETHING NEW: NAVAL WAR IN THE ATLANTIC

The outbreak of the military conflagration in Europe in July 1914 immediately demonstrated that the Atlantic was the ocean that should preoccupy the U.S. Navy's strategists. War with Britain was unthinkable; war with Germany must be anticipated. Democratic President Woodrow Wilson (1913–1921) believed it must be avoided if at all possible. To evade American belligerency, he proclaimed a policy of neutrality that tolerated the loss of 124 American lives when a German U-boat sank the British ocean liner *Lusitania* in May 1915. Not until early 1917, when U-boats resumed attacking neutral merchant vessels without warning in an announced German policy of unrestricted submarine warfare, did Wilson concede that the U.S. must join the conflict. The officer he chose to command all U.S. naval forces in Europe was Rear Admiral William S. Sims, the former naval aide to President Roosevelt.

Sims arrived in England on 9 April 1917, three days after the United States declared war. In London the next day he conferred with the First Sea Lord, Admiral John Jellicoe, who somberly informed him that German submarines were ravaging British and neutral shipping at such a rate that the Allied Powers would unquestionably lose the war for want of food and matériel, possibly as early as August, certainly by October. Dumbfounded and alarmed, Sims joined with creative staff officers in the Admiralty to devise a solution to the looming disaster. By 30 April, the sea lords had agreed to experiment with destroyer escorts of convoys "as the general plan of campaign."[18]

Besotted by Mahanian battle-fleet strategy, Washington resisted the wholesale allocation of naval resources to convoys. Several months elapsed before President Wilson and the secretary of the navy were finally won over by the gradual but unfaltering reduction in the monthly rate of U-boat sinkings of merchant ships as the convoy system was expanded by the Admiralty and the U.S. Navy's man

---

[18] John V. Babcock, quoted in MORISON E.E., *Admiral Sims and the Modern American Navy* (Boston, MA, 1942), p. 351.

in London. In the summer of 1917 the Navy Department at last agreed to curtail capital ship construction and to put the full weight of the U.S. naval shipbuilding industry behind construction of convoy escorts.

When Sims first arrived in London, Admiral Jellicoe had predicted that in April 1917 the U-boats would sink 900,000 tons of merchant transports. By December 1917 the Allies were losing 350,000 tons per month. In October 1918, the month before the war ended, the U-boats could sink no more than 112,427 tons. This massive reduction in loss, with the corollary monthly increase in tonnage of matériel being shipped from the United States, was accomplished between May 1917 and November 1918 by fifteen hundred convoys of eighteen thousand ships. The U.S. Navy provided about 27 percent of the escorting ships in British waters, the Royal Navy 70 percent.[19] Simultaneously, the United States initiated a separate category of shipments: troops and their equipment that were routed to Brest, France, on a more southerly track around the British Isles. The destroyer escorts jointly commanded by Sims and British Vice Admiral Sir Lewis Bayly protected the convoys of this balance-tipping force of two million American soldiers "without losing a single man."[20]

The Anglo-American sailors had painstakingly defeated the U-boats of Imperial Germany, the deadly modern practitioners of the ancient art of *guerre de course*, a type of warfare erroneously dismissed by Mahan as strategically inconsequential in the modern age. No less a "naval person" than Winston S. Churchill said that "the harmony and success of this cooperation form a new precedent, and one which is of the highest value to the future in which such vast issues hang on unity between our two countries in ideals and in action."[21]

A COLLABORATION OF BATTLE FLEET COMMANDERS

Such glowing retrospective praise cannot detract from the fact that for several months the Navy Department in Washington had resisted Sims's heretical strategy of convoying cargo and troopships in order to win the war. At the same time it had rejected his proposal to deploy a group of battleships to the war zone. In July 1917, after first obtaining the endorsement of Admiral Sims, Admiral John Jellicoe, the First Sea Lord, and the Admiralty requested a detachment of four American coal-burning dreadnoughts. The American battlewagons would strengthen the Grand Fleet in its blockade of the German High Seas Fleet in the North Sea. They also would permit the British to retire some of their pre-dreadnoughts, thereby freeing up crewmen to man 119 new antisubmarine destroyers under construction in British yards.[22]

---

[19] *Ibid.*, p. 412.
[20] SIMS W.S., *The Victory at Sea* (Garden City, New York, 1920), p. 357.
[21] CHURCHILL to Sims, 19 March 1919. Online: www.loc.gov/exhibits/churchill/wc-affairs.html [Accessed 19 December 2013].
[22] JONES J.W., *U.S. Battleship Operations in World War I* (Annapolis, MD, 1998), p. 12.

Admiral Henry T. Mayo, commander in chief of the U.S. Atlantic Fleet, and Chief of Naval Operations William S. Benson would have none of it. The two most senior officers in the U.S. Navy remained adamant in their Mahanian conviction that they must not fragment the battle fleet by detaching a quarter of its ships. To do so would emasculate the force should the U.S. find itself in a war with Japan, always a feared outcome of the perpetual tensions over the American political and territorial presence in the Philippine Islands.

It took Benson and Mayo four months and two trips to London to change their minds. Finally, on 10 November 1917, the chief of naval operations capitulated. He advised Secretary of the Navy Josephus Daniels to divide the American battle fleet – heresy in Mahanian terms – and deploy one division to the war zone. Daniels immediately ordered Rear Admiral Hugh Rodman, commander of the U.S. Atlantic Fleet's Battleship Division Nine, to join up with the Royal Navy's Grand Fleet in the North Sea. The other three divisions would remain as national sentries on the American East Coast.

An 1880 Naval Academy classmate of Sims, and a thoroughbred fighting admiral, Rodman wasted no time. On 25 November he led his four coal-burning dreadnoughts to sea. After an extremely rough passage across the gale-swept wintry Atlantic, flagship *New York*, *Florida*, *Delaware*, and *Wyoming* steamed into the massive base of the British Grand Fleet in the basin of Scapa Flow in the Orkney Islands. The date was 7 December 1917; that day's marriage of American and British capital fleets lasted until the end of World War I in November 1918.

As soon as he arrived, Rodman called upon British Admiral Sir David Beatty, commander in chief of the Grand Fleet, aboard his flagship *Queen Elizabeth*. The American's intent was to place his four dreadnoughts under the operational command of the Royal Navy. The U.S. Navy's battleship division became the Sixth Battle Squadron of the Grand Fleet, a component constituting about 12 percent of the fleet's capital ships.[23] The chain of command was clear and direct: Beatty was Rodman's operational commander and would remain so until the war's end.

Rodman always kept in sight what he correctly considered to be the crucial importance of the Grand Fleet: to maintain its station in the North Sea until "the surrender of the whole German fleet ...."[24] When the capitulation came in November 1918, Rodman's ships formed part of Beatty's Grand Fleet as it escorted the entire German High Seas Fleet to Scapa Flow for internment. The curtain had descended on Imperial Germany's sea power without the prescribed battle of annihilation.

Despite the absence of Armageddon, the Americans in World War I had achieved their ultimate naval strategic goal: the elimination of the German navy as the existential "threat" feared by U.S. policy makers and strategists since the time of the Samoan Crisis of 1889, the year before Mahan published his misconceived masterpiece.

---

[23] *Ibid.*, pp. 27–28.
[24] RODMAN H., *Yarns of a Kentucky Admiral* (Indianapolis, IN, 1928), p. 266.

Mahan at Bay

In the end, sea power did prove to be a critical factor underlying the Allied defeat of the German armies in 1918, but its configuration differed fundamentally from the concept of Mahanians who sought a maritime cataclysm of massed fleets. Instead, victorious American sea power consisted of remorselessly nibbling away at the enemy's raiders until the men and matériel shipped across the sea made the Allies invincible on land. It was a formula for victory that would be repeated on a gargantuan scale a generation later.

World War Suspended and Resumed: Russia, 1919–1940

Gunnar Åselius is Professor in Military History at the Swedish Defence University, Sweden

Abstract. *Soviet governments initially regarded their navy with suspicion and could hardly foresee a use for it. By the 1930s Russian strategists were moving from revolutionary enthusiasm towards great-power realism and planning to build a battle-fleet able to dominate the Baltic and Black Sea. In reality this expressed Soviet aspirations to great-power status rather than any realistic strategy. Like the army, the navy lost many of its senior officers to Stalin's purges, it had always suffered from the low educational level of Russian society and in 1940 it was completely outfought by the Finns, after which the battleship programme was quietly abandoned.*

Résumé. *Les gouvernements soviétiques ont dans un premier temps été très méfiants à l'égard de leur marine qui ne revêtait pour eux que peu d'utilité. À partir des années 1930, les stratèges russes quittèrent leur enthousiasme révolutionnaire pour un réalisme propre aux grandes puissances, et projetèrent de construire une flotte de guerre capable de dominer la mer Baltique et la mer Noire. En réalité, ces plans étaient plus le reflet des velléités soviétiques à devenir une grande puissance, qu'une stratégie réaliste. Tout comme l'armée, la marine perdit un grand nombre de ses hauts gradés suite aux purges menées par Staline, et a toujours pâti de la faiblesse du niveau d'éducation de la société russe. Après avoir subi une cuisante défaite face aux Finlandais en 1940, le programme fut discrètement abandonné.*

. • .

What role did the sea play for the young Soviet regime before the Second World War? The economic system the Bolsheviks introduced in Russia did not assign much importance to economic exchange with the surrounding world, and throughout the inter-war period Soviet seaborne trade remained limited. Already before the First World War the bulk of Russian foreign trade had gone either by rail or in foreign ships, and the dissolution of the Tsarist Empire in 1917–1920 reinforced this pattern. Suddenly, most of Russia's Baltic Sea coastline belonged to other countries, together with most of the Russian merchant fleet. In 1928, when the world's seaborne commerce finally had begun to return to pre-war levels, the Soviet merchant marine (*Sovtorgflot*) totalled less than 256,000 register tons (including sailing ships and tugs). As a comparison, the world's total merchant tonnage at the time amounted to some 61.6 million tons (excluding sailing ships and vessels under 100 gross tons). In January 1928, the steam-shipping tonnage lying idle in Italian ports was actually much larger than the entire Soviet merchant fleet![1] Hence, arguments that Russia must look to the sea to further her economic interests would carry limited weight with Soviet leaders.

The maritime dimensions of national security were more difficult to ignore, and the Bolsheviks were aware of the sea as a potential gateway for foreign invasion. In 1918, they had moved Russia's capital away from Saint Petersburg on the Gulf of Finland – where it had been situated for two hundred years – back to Moscow in the inner parts of the country, This, however, did not mean that they were willing to invest in their own naval forces. In March 1921, when the sailors in Kronstadt were rebelling against the regime and the Kremlin's appreciation of the navy sank to its lowest, Lenin wrote to Trotsky, People's Commissar of Defence:

> Should we not close down the Navy completely for a year? What is its purpose? And give the coal to the railways or textile factories, to provide the peasants with cloth? I think that here we should be prepared to take decisive measures. Let the Navy suffer. The Soviet regime will benefit.[2]

An ocean-going fleet under construction had been inherited from the old regime. The 1912 naval construction program had planned a navy consisting of twenty-four battleships and twelve battle cruisers by 1930. Only three of those battleships had been completed by 1917, and none of the battle cruisers.[3] The new regime left the gigantic hulls rusting in the dockyards and eventually sold them off as scrap to Germany.

From the mid-1930s, however, when the Soviet Union had entered a period of intense industrialization and upheaval, there was a renewed will to join the competition. In the eyes of the Soviets, naval power had now become associated with advanced military technology and great-power prestige. Mahanian rhetoric, similar to that which had been prevalent in Tsarist Russia, could be heard in a speech by Premier Minister Vyatcheslav Molotov in January 1938: "The powerful Soviet State must have a sea-going and ocean-going fleet, consistent with its interests, worthy of our great task."[4] Regardless of what the Soviet interests at sea really were, the navy as a national symbol remained important. This is not

---

[1] THE SOVIET INFORMATION BUREAU, *The Soviet Union: Facts, Description, Statistics* (Washington DC, 1929), p. 122; GREGG E.S., 'Transportation II: Shipping', in *Recent Economic Changes in the United States* I–II, NBER, ed. COMMITTEE ON RECENT ECONOMIC CHANGES OF THE PRESIDENT'S CONFERENCE ON UNEMPLOYMENT (Washington DC, 1929), pp. 309–10.
[2] MEIJER J.M., ed., *The Trotsky Papers 2: 1917–1922* (The Hague, 1971), p. 414.
[3] WESTWOOD J.N., *Russian Naval Construction, 1905-1945* (London, 1993), pp. 73–5; BREYER S., *Soviet Warship Development*, vol. I: *1917-1937* (London, 1992), pp. 33–5, 114–15.
[4] Quoted from ERICSON J., *The Soviet High Command, 1918–1941: A Military-Political History* (London, 1962), p. 475.

least demonstrated by the naming of Soviet warships, which – as we shall see – like Soviet national identity, went through significant changes.

What remained of the Russian Navy in the early 1920s were three rusting battleships and about a dozen destroyers and submarines in the Baltic. Very few of these ships were in fact operational. In 1919, the British Royal Navy had sailed unopposed into the Gulf of Finland and even raided the main Soviet naval base in Kronstadt. There were also a few destroyers and patrol craft left in the Caspian Sea and in the Arctic Sea, but in the Black Sea and the Pacific almost all the remaining warships had fled to the West during the Civil War.[5] If the navy was to be put back on its feet, the Soviet leaders knew it would cost enormous sums and tie up scarce industrial capacity for years to come.

Although the navy managed to rehabilitate itself politically after the Kronstadt Rebellion, its strategic role remained subordinated to the Red Army. In wartime, it was to support the ground forces in coastal areas, but unlike the army it could not be deployed against domestic unrest, at least not outside the coastal zones. In addition, the conscripts who served in the navy were too few for the service to have a significant impact on the ideological education of the nation's youth. It is therefore no surprise that a person like Lenin was unable to understand the "purpose" of the navy.

And even if the Bolsheviks had been more positively inclined towards the navy and prepared to invest huge sums in it, they still had to deal with their country's awkward maritime geography. Although Russia has the longest coastline in the world, its access to the high seas is limited and Soviet ships could nowhere reach the oceans without passing through sounds and archipelagos controlled by other powers. Nor were the vast distances that separated the maritime theaters in the Baltic, the Black Sea, the Arctic, and the Pacific easy to overcome. Even if the sea lane along the Arctic Coast could be used for redeploying ships from the Arctic to the Pacific, the distance to cover was gigantic. Not until 1936 did Soviet warships travel this route successfully. It took two destroyers (*Voykov* and *Stalin*) more than three months to cover the distance from Kronstadt to Vladivostok, needing continuous support from icebreakers, supply ships, and reconnaissance aircraft. Part of the crews did not even travel aboard the ships but were sent by railroad through Siberia. Nonetheless, the passage of *Voykov* and *Stalin* was celebrated as an extraordinary achievement, with plenty of decorations bestowed upon the participants. Although the Soviet Communist Party in its congratulatory telegram assured the expedition that its "victory in the Arctic" would be of great importance to the country's defense, it was hard to see how this long and cumbersome route could be perceived as a strategic asset. Even within Europe, between the Baltic Sea and the Black Sea, the peacetime transfer of warships seemed an extraordinary achievement to the Soviets. In 1929, the redeployment of the battleship *Parizhkaya Kommuna* and the cruiser *Profintern* from Kronstadt to Sevastopol (in order to restart the Black Sea Fleet) took almost two months

---

[5] BEREZOVKSY N.Y., BEREZHNOY S.S. and NIKOLAYEVA Z.V., *Boevaya letopis sovetskogo voenno-morskogo flota 1917–1941* (Moscow, 1993), p. 499.

to complete. There were few ports along the route where Soviet warships were welcome to bunker, and the stormy Bay of Biscay put the crews to a severe trial.[6]

An additional route between European theaters was created in 1933 (at frightful human cost!), when the White Sea Canal – or "Stalin Canal" – was inaugurated between the Baltic and Arctic Seas. However, the canal was shallow, narrow, and blocked by ice for six months a year. The first ships to sail from Kronstadt to Murmansk this way were upon arrival constituted into the Soviet Northern Fleet – two submarines, two destroyers, and two patrol craft – but they had to travel partly dismantled, by barge, and took more than three months to complete their journey. In 1937, the submarine *Dekabrist* set a record by making the trip in "only" three weeks, which was really not very impressive.[7]

Clearly, the Soviet Union could have no such thing as a global naval strategy, nor even articulate plans for how fleets in the different theaters were to support each other in the event of war.

The doctrine that the navy proposed during the 1920s for the main theater in the Baltic suggested that an attacking enemy fleet, advancing towards Leningrad through the Gulf of Finland, should be confronted by the old battleships of pre-war design.[8] Supported by minefields, coastal artillery, aircraft, torpedo-boats and submarines, these three old battleships would grind the enemy to a halt and eventually roll it back. There were more confident voices which called for a doctrine aimed at securing command of the sea in the Baltic at the outbreak of hostilities, so that the western great powers could be prevented from entering the region with their warships. The Revolutionary Military Council even claimed in a resolution passed in June 1924 that the Soviet Navy should be made strong enough to defend "world revolution" – a proposal which suggested a navy with global reach.[9] In spite of this naval assertiveness, the navy was disbanded as an independent service in 1926 and reorganized as "The Red Army's Naval Forces." At the same time, all plans for constructing new warships were cancelled.

The naval officer-corps was regarded with suspicion by the Communist Party. Already after the Kronstadt Rebellion, about half of the officers and officials in the Baltic Fleet had been purged, but there were still a large number of naval commanders who had served as officers in the Imperial Navy. Even in the mid-1930s, about a fifth of the submarine commanders in the Baltic Fleet came from aristocratic families. Only some 10% of navy personnel were party members, which was markedly lower than in the more proletarian Red Army. The system of political commissars, who supervised the officers and gave political

---

[6] BEREZOVSKY N.Y., BEREZHNOY S.S. and NIKOLAYEVA Z.V., *Boevaya letopis sovetskogo voenno-morskogo flota 1917-1941* (Moscow, 1993), pp. 604, 571–2.

[7] BEREZOVSKY N.Y., *Boevaya letopis*, pp. 587–8; Monakov M., 'Sudba doktrin i teoriy. 8: Flot dlya "maloy voyny", *Morskoy Sbornik* 147.3 (1994), 39–40; ÅSELIUS G., *The Rise and Fall of the Soviet Navy in the Baltic, 1921-1941* (London and New York, 2005), p. 22; on the construction of the White Sea Canal, see APPELBAUM A., *Gulag: A History* (London, 2004), Ch. 4.

[8] ÅSELIUS, *Rise and Fall*, pp. 73–9.

[9] BEREZOVSKY et al., *Boevaya letopis*, p. 535.

lectures to the crews, was not sufficient to strengthen ideological control. The navy's traditions also had to be challenged.

One way of doing this was to change the names of warships. The three remaining battleships of the Gangut class (*Gangut*, *Sevastopol*, and *Petropavlovsk*) were renamed after a French revolutionary journalist (*Marat*), after the October Revolution (*Oktyabrskaya Revolutiya*), and after the Paris Commune (*Parizhkaya Kommuna*). The cruiser *Svetlana* was first renamed after the German socialist heroine *Klara Zetkin*. Later, it carried the name 'Red Crimea' (*Krasny Krim*), and finally *Profintern* (abbreviation for the trade union international). The destroyers, whose names in the Imperial Navy had been related to military, heroic and masculine adjectives (*Bdetelny* = watchful, *Storozhevoy* = guard-, *Voyskovoy* = troop-, *Vnushitelny* = impressive, *Vynoslivy* = endurable), were renamed after various revolutionary leaders: *Karl Marx*, *Friedrich Engels*, *Lenin*, *Stalin*, *Trotsky*, *Frunze*, *Zinovyev*, *Rykov*, and *Kalinin*. The submarines, which in the Imperial Navy had been named after various predators (*Tigr*, *Leopard*, *Jaguar*, *Smeya* = snake) were given names that represented radical political or social groups: 'the Communard' (*Kommunar*), 'the Red Army Man' (*Krasnoarmets*), 'the Red Navy Man' (*Krasnoflotets*), 'the Proletarian' (*Proletary*), 'the Worker' (*Rabochy*), 'the Bolshevik' (*Bolshevik*), 'the Comrade' (*Tovarishch*). The British submarine *L 55*, which had been sunk by the Soviet destroyer *Azard* in July 1919 and then raised and repaired, joined the Soviet Navy as 'the Atheist' (*Bezbozhnik*).[10]

As can be gathered from these examples, the naming of Soviet warships in the 1920s was unique, in that the historical figures and events which the new ship names alluded to were not exclusively national. Soviet Russia named two of its three mightiest warships after a French revolutionary and a French revolutionary regime.

In 1928, the first five-year plan and the collectivization of agriculture started in the Soviet Union. This brought about purges among "bourgeois specialists" like engineers and scientists, who had been academically trained in pre-revolutionary society and were now suspected of delaying the realization of the five-year plan through exaggerated formalism and theorizing. Soon enough, those suspicions turned into formal accusations of sabotage and treason, with tens of thousands of people being arrested. In a similar way, former tsarist naval officers who had advocated the use of battleships came under attack as representatives of an "Old School" in naval thinking and as spokesmen for "bourgeois concepts" like command of the sea.[11] They were publicly criticized, removed from key positions, and eventually sent to labor camps in Siberia. Among the latter were four professors at the Naval War College in Leningrad, five out of eight squadron commanders in the Baltic Fleet, one out of two battleship commanders, ten out of twelve commanders of destroyers and five out of nine submarine commanders.

The new naval doctrine, which replaced the battleship-centered "Old School,"

---

[10] ÅSELIUS, *Rise and Fall*, pp. 94–107.
[11] HERRICK R.W., *Soviet Naval Theory and Policy: Fifty Years of Theory and Practice* (Annapolis, MD, 1968), pp. 19–64.

was referred to as the "Young School." It emphasized coastal defense and support of the Red Army as the navy's primary missions. Battleships could still have a role to play, but only as second-line platforms for artillery support. The main defense against an enemy fleet should rely on a dynamic cooperation between minefields, coastal artillery, aircraft, fast torpedo boats, and submarines. The navy should also develop an offensive capability in coastal waters with amphibious forces, as it was expected to support the Red Army, which during the 1930s experimented with a highly offensive ground-warfare doctrine based on joint air and armored operations. The protagonists of the Young School as a rule came from a proletarian background (some were former petty officers of the Imperial Navy). They had joined the Bolshevik Party during the Civil War and served as political commissars in the red naval forces. They identified heavy artillery and battleships with an old and dying civilization and saw their own way of warfare as progressive and modern, expecting that future technological developments would enhance the defensive potential of naval weapon systems even more.

The first warships to be produced domestically in the Soviet Union were submarines. Initially, the principles which had directed the earlier naming of Soviet warships were applied. The first series of submarines launched in 1928–1932 were named after revolutionary archetypes. "The Revolutionary" (*Revolutioner*), "The Komsomol Member" (*Komsomolets*), and "The Red Guard Man" (*Krasnogvardets*) were honored, as were the disciples of various Soviet leaders: "The Leninist" (*Leninets*), "The Stalinist" (*Stalinets*), and even "The Frunzeist" (*Frunzovets* – after Mikhail Frunze, People's Commissar of Defence 1924–1925). Submarines were also named after nineteenth-century revolutionary groups, like "The Decembrist" (*Dekabrist*) and "The Supporter of the People's Will" (*Narodvolets*). Nor was the Soviet Union's responsibility as leader of the world revolutionary movement forgotten. Submarines were named after the German Spartakist (*Spartakovets*), French Jacobin (*Yacobinets*), British Chartist (*Khartist*), as well as after the Italian Carbonari (*Karbonariy*) and Garibaldi Supporter (*Garibaldisets*).

Warships that were built later, however, were given more conventional names. The long series of submarines that went into production in 1932 – later abbreviated as the Shch-class – was named after a fish, the pike (*Shchuka*). Other submarines were named after perches (*Okun, Yorzh*) or the burbot (*Nalim*). The class of midget submarines which was launched in 1933 were called M-submarines, simply due to the fact that they were small (*Malyutka* = baby). The famous class that went into production in 1936 and became the Soviet standard submarine in the Baltic during the Second World War was designated as the S-class, simply because of its middle size (*sredny* = middle). The series of large destroyers – flotilla leaders – which began appearing in 1933 were named after major Soviet cities: *Leningrad, Moskva, Kharkov, Minsk, Baku*. In this, the Soviet Navy did not differ much from other navies. Concrete realism had begun to overcome revolutionary romanticism as a cultural ideal.[12]

---

[12] ÅSELIUS, *Rise and Fall*, pp. 137–44.

In the mid-1930s, then, Russia finally resumed her great-power aspirations and started to plan for an ocean-going navy. The drafting of a new naval construction program began towards the end of 1935, so that the commissions of new warships could be included in the third five-year plan, which would be launched two years later. The first official version of this naval construction program, approved by the Soviet government in June 1936, contained 533 ships of 1.307 million tons, including twenty-four battleships. Later, the number of battleships was reduced as new categories of major warships were added, including aircraft carriers, heavy cruisers and ocean-going submarines. However, the scheduled total tonnage continued to grow, as did the size of the battleships. A third version of the program, from 1938, contained a total tonnage of 2.3 million tons, more than either the British or the US navies at the time. Each of the fifteen battleships that were now scheduled was to weigh 59,000 tons. Most of the new warships were to be deployed with the North and Pacific Fleets and operate in the open oceans.[13]

While the naval forces had received less than 10% of defense spending in 1930, nine years later their proportion had risen to 18.5% – or nearly 5% of total Soviet government expenditure. With growing resources being allotted to the naval sector, the navy's organizational subjugation under the Red Army no longer seemed practical. In January 1935, naval forces in the Arctic, Baltic and Black Seas, and the Pacific Ocean ceased being mere support units to the regional military districts and were elevated to the rank of independent fleets with their own permanent headquarters. During 1937, the navy was fully resurrected as an independent service when it was endowed with a central headquarters and a People's Commissariat of its own. In 1939 a People's Commissariat for Naval Construction was added. This third stage in Russian naval doctrinal development during the inter-war period has been referred to as the "Soviet School" era. How the Soviets planned to fight under this new doctrine remains vague, as everything was decided in great haste and secrecy, and hardly any of the warships planned in the grandiose construction program were ever completed. To understand the motives behind the doctrinal shift, the changed strategic situation in the mid-1930s has to be considered. In June 1935, Britain and Nazi Germany had signed a naval agreement which allowed Germany to construct up to 35% of the Royal Navy's surface tonnage. This, the Soviets concluded, would enhance German influence over smaller states in the Baltic Sea region and increase the likelihood that countries like Latvia, Estonia, and Finland would allow Germany to base military forces on their territories. In order to "influence not only the political orientation of the Border States [= Finland and the Baltic states], but also that of the Scandinavian states and especially the military conduct of those states", the revised naval construction plan of 1937 stated, the Soviet Union must acquire strong naval forces in the Baltic Sea. If they were capable of operating outside the Gulf of Finland, they could cut off Germany's sea lines of communications not only with Finland and the Baltic republics, but also with

---

[13] ROHWER J. and MONAKOV M., *Stalin's Ocean-Going Fleet: Soviet Naval Strategy and Shipbuilding Programmes, 1935-1953* (London, 2001), pp. 62-4.

Sweden, whence the Germans imported strategic raw materials like iron ore.[14] In the Black Sea, a powerful Soviet fleet would probably be useful to prevent Rumanians and Turks from leaning too far towards Germany. In the Far East, where Japan could threaten the Soviet Union only overland, strong Soviet naval forces would nonetheless make it possible to cut off the sea lines of communications between the Japanese Islands and the Asian mainland, and greatly improve the prospects for the Red Army of resisting a Japanese invasion across the border. To acquire convincing offensive capabilities, however, the Soviet Navy needed heavy artillery ships rather than a coastal navy equipped with torpedoes and mines. As Russian naval historian Mikhail Monakov has argued, Stalin's bid for an oceangoing fleet was probably also a gesture towards the Western Powers. It was humiliating that the Soviet Union – unlike France, Germany, Italy, Japan, or the USA – had not been invited to sign the London Naval Treaty in 1936. To count in the eyes of the British and make them willing to enter into serious talks on cooperation against Nazi Germany, the Soviet Union would need a serious navy.[15]

For various reasons, an agreement with the Western Powers concerning the German threat was never accomplished. Stalin made a deal with Hitler instead, according to which Finland and the Baltic States were recognized as part of the Soviet sphere of influence. With German non-intervention secured, the Baltic States were forced in September–October 1939 to allow the stationing of Soviet forces on their territories. Even if huge sums had to be invested in new port facilities, coastal fortifications, and airstrips for the Soviet Navy in Estonia and Latvia, its twenty-year-long confinement to the inner part of the Gulf of Finland was now over. Finally, the entire Baltic Sea lay within reach.

When similar demands for base rights were made on Finland, the Finns refused. During the winter of 1939–1940, the Soviet Union therefore had to fight a humiliating war against Finland, losing much of its international credibility by attacking a small neighbor, and demonstrating surprising military incompetence at that. The performance of the Soviet naval forces was no more impressive than that of the Red Army. Before the vastly inferior neighbor was finally defeated in March 1940, the navy had lost one submarine and twelve aircraft but failed to sink any Finnish warships or to cut off Finland's sea lines of communications (although the ice situation in the Baltic eventually terminated Finnish imports). Nine cargo ships were sunk in Finnish waters during the war by Soviet submarines and aircraft, while no fewer than 425 ships cleared in or out of Finnish ports in the period. When put to the test, the equipment, training, and tactics of the Soviet naval forces proved inadequate for the missions they were expected to solve.[16]

These military setbacks have often been explained by the decimation of the officer-corps during the Great Terror of 1937–1938, when the navy alone lost

---

[14] Quoted in ÅSELIUS, *Rise and Fall*, p. 158.
[15] MONAKOV M., 'Sudba doktrin i teory 8: K bolshomu morskomu i okeanskomu flotu (1936–1939 gg.)', *Morskoy Sbornik* 147.5 (1994), 37.
[16] PETROV P., *Baltiskiy flot. Finskiy gambit* (Saint Petersburg, 2005).

some 3,000 officers. Most of those people simply lost their jobs, but a considerable number of them were also imprisoned or shot as spies and saboteurs. Among those executed were two People's Commissars and one Deputy People's Commissar, two Naval Commanders and one deputy Naval Commander, six fleet and flotilla commanders, five chiefs of fleet staffs or deputy chiefs of fleet staffs, six heads of sections in the central naval apparatus, fifteen heads or chief-specialists in fleet staffs, thirty-two subordinate commanders or chiefs of staff of subordinate commanders, twenty-two commanders of 1st and 2nd class warships (battleships, cruisers, destroyers), as well as one commandant of the Naval War College.[17] Just as important as the purges for explaining the navy's poor performance, however, was the low level of education in Russian society at large. The people with technical training were too few to go around in the rapidly industrializing Soviet Union. In December 1940, when the navy's official strength was given at 35,977, the deputy People's Commissar responsible for naval personnel reported some 11,000 vacancies in the service. Because of the oceanic program the naval organization had almost quadrupled since the summer of 1936, so quite a few people were probably promoted far above their level of incompetence. At a conference in Moscow with the naval command in late 1940, the Navy Chief Commissar, Ivan Rogov, stated with surprising frankness:

> I must say that the basic fault in our management is weak organization and very weak culture. The level of our military and political training, I would even say our general level, is still suffering. In this, we have little to be proud of.[18]

In October 1940, the great oceanic construction program was discreetly halted. It had become apparent that Soviet industry lacked construction materials, machinery, and expertise, and Soviet admirals were no longer convinced that battleships had a role to play in future naval wars. Moreover, none of those battleships commissioned would be operational before 1943, and there were signs that the Soviet Union would have to go to war earlier than that.

To understand the temptation of the oceanic naval program to Stalin's Russia, however, it is necessary to look at the cultural context of the late 1930s, when the Soviet Union was busy adapting to European "normality." Battleship construction, a "normal activity" for the group of states in the international system with which the Soviet Union wished to identify, was in tune with other developments in Soviet society at the time which all signaled a new conceptualization of national identity: the introduction of school uniforms and school fees for secondary education, patriotic history teaching, the return of neoclassical ideals in art and architecture, a more conservative family legislation, etc.

The introduction of admirals' ranks in the Soviet Navy in June 1940 (they

---

[17] MONAKOV, 'Sudba doktrin i teory 8', 42.
[18] BARSUKOV A.I. and ZOLOTAREV V.A., eds, *Russky arkhiv: Velikaya Otechestvennaya Voyna 1 (2): nakanune voyny: Materialy soveshchany vyshego rukovodyastyego sostava VMF SSSR v kontse 1940 goda* (Moscow, 1997), pp. 375-7, 443.

had been abolished in 1917) was a further sign of this development, as were the new directives for the naming of warships which the Soviet government issued in September that same year. Battleships, regarded as the most prestigious warships, were to be named after the union republics (*Sovetskaya Rossiya, Sovetskaya Ukraina, Sovetskaya Gruziya*), a practice identical to that of the US Navy. The new class of heavy cruisers were to have names after the main naval bases (*Kronshtadt, Sevastopol, Vladivostok*, etc.) and large destroyers/flotilla-leaders after major cities and the capitals of the republics (*Moskva, Leningrad, Tashkent*). Soviet destroyers were to be named after masculine adjectives (*Gnevny* = furious, *Stremitelny* = energetic, *Opytny* = experienced), a practice identical to that of the Imperial Navy. Like the submarines in the Imperial Navy, patrol ships were to be named after predators (*Tigr, Leopard, Oryol* = eagle).

The only major warships which were to be named after revolutionary heroes in the future were light cruisers (the *Kirov* class and its successors) and minesweepers, a category of ships for which were to be reserved the names of sailors fallen during the Civil War. Thus, *Russian* revolutionary heroes were to be commemorated, whereas persons like Marat or Klara Zetkin no longer seemed suitable sources of inspiration to Soviet sailors. As long as they were properly Russian, historical memories did not even need to have a revolutionary significance. When an annual "Soviet Navy Day" was proclaimed in the summer of 1939, the date chosen was the last Sunday in July – in commemoration of Tsar Peter's and Admiral Apraxin's victory over the Swedes at the battle of Gangut in 1714. In a comment, the commander of the Baltic Fleet pointed out this battle as the first heroic deed in the annals of his fleet.[19] He did not mention the storming of the Winter Palace in 1917 or any of the battles of the Civil War, which only a few years before would have been the proper point of departure for historical reflections by a Soviet naval commander.

The significance of the sea to the Soviet regime, then, was not so much linked to the concrete economic or strategic benefits that could be reaped from the sea, but to questions of national identity and to the perception of Russia's role in the international system. In the immediate aftermath of the First World War, when the Bolsheviks aimed at overthrowing the existing world order, they suspended Russia's participation in the global great-power race by downgrading the navy to a mere coastal force. On the way to becoming one of the world's leading industrial producers in the late 1930s, with a new world war in sight and in need of impressing on potential allies, it was likewise natural to resume Russia's age-old struggle to become a leading maritime nation.

---

[19] TRIBUTS V., 'Krasnoznamenny baltflot na strazhe rodiny', *Morskoy Sbornik* 92.12 (1939), pp. 12–18.

FREEDOM AND CONTROL OF THE SEAS, 1856-1919

GABRIELA A. FREI is a British Academy Postdoctoral Research Fellow, University of Oxford, United Kingdom

ABSTRACT. *In wartime, belligerent naval powers always exercised their power by restricting neutrals' freedom to trade. Britain and France reached a compromise position during the Crimean War, and afterwards offered it as a model international treaty, the 1856 Declaration of Paris, which abolished privateering, guaranteed neutral trade and restricted the right of blockade. This became the basis of a new international law of naval warfare. The Declaration of London of 1909 was meant to extend and refine it, but it was not ratified in 1914, and few of its provisions survived the war.*

RÉSUMÉ. *En temps de guerre, les puissances navales belligérantes ont toujours exercé leur pouvoir en réduisant la liberté commerciale des pays neutres. La France et la Grande-Bretagne parvinrent à établir un compromis pendant la guerre de Crimée, qu'ils proposèrent par la suite comme modèle de traité international. La Déclaration de Paris, signée en 1856, abolit la guerre de course, garantit le commerce neutre et restreignit le droit au blocus. Ceci devint la base d'un nouveau droit international relatif à la guerre maritime que la déclaration de Londres de 1909 avait pour intention d'étendre et de préciser. Cette dernière n'ayant toujours pas été ratifiée en 1914, peu de ses propositions survécurent à la guerre.*

.•.

The birth of modern international law was a result of one of the most famous legal disputes, namely the controversy over the principle of freedom of the seas. In the early 17th century, the Dutch philosopher and lawyer Hugo Grotius argued in a pamphlet, *Mare Liberum*, defending a case for the Dutch East India Company, that

> [t]he sea is common to all, because it is so limitless that it cannot become a possession of any one, and because it is adapted for the use of all, whether we consider it from the point of view of navigation or of fisheries.[1]

Grotius' claims were directed against the Portuguese, who had proclaimed sovereignty of the seas, and thus a monopoly in the East India trade. The Dutch

---

[1] GROTIUS H., *The Freedom of the Seas or, The Right which belongs to the Dutch to take part in the East Indian Trade*, ed. J.B. SCOTT, trans. R.VAN DEMAN MAGOFFIN (New York, 1916), p. 28.

East India Company, on the other hand, desired access to those markets, which was the underlying reason for the dispute. At the same time, other lawyers (among them John Selden) disagreed with Grotius and defended the concept of the sovereignty of the seas. However, Selden's claims were not as absolute as those of the Portuguese. For the Englishman, claims were legitimate only as long as the area could be controlled and defended by force, thus applying the concept of territoriality onto the seas. Since the ability to control the seas was limited, so were the claims for the sovereignty of the seas. The claims of Grotius and Selden were not mutually exclusive but, rather, complemented one another. Lawyers would later develop the term territorial sea and the status of the high seas.

Freedom of the Seas in the 19th Century

Ideas of freedom of the seas resurfaced again in the 19th century with the rise of liberalism in Great Britain, and Liberals demanding the opening of markets worldwide. The repeal of the Corn Laws in 1846 and the Navigation Laws in 1849 were crucial steps in reducing trade barriers, allowing the import of corn and goods from other countries, as well as allowing transport of these goods in foreign ships. Throughout the 19th century, British foreign policy advocated free trade over protectionism, and thus endorsed the principle of the freedom of the seas. Similarly to Grotius' understanding some two centuries earlier, the Liberals hoped with the adoption of a free trade policy to gain access to new markets and to benefit generally from a more open world economy.

Control of the Seas in the 19th Century

Challenges to the principle of the freedom of the seas, however, arose in time of war, when belligerents claimed control of the seas and curtailed enemies' and neutrals' free navigation on the open seas. Neutrals insisted on the principle of freedom of the seas and their right as neutrals to freely trade in time of war. Belligerents, though, exercised the means to control the sea, by which they meant blockade and the right of search and capture. While the blockade operated in close proximity to the enemy's coastline or ports, the right of search and capture was exercised anywhere on the open seas. The aim of both means was to deny the enemy the use of the sea, and so undermine his war effort. Consequently, belligerents were allowed to stop neutral ships, either when they sailed towards a blockaded port or when they carried contraband goods. Legal disputes over the rightful capture of neutral ships often resulted. There were no agreed rules upon which belligerents operated; rather, they themselves defined the terms of blockade and contraband. The various state practices of belligerents unavoidably clashed with the interests of neutrals, and the principle of the freedom of the seas was severely compromised in time of war.

Declaration of Paris

The Crimean War, 1853–1856, marked a turning point for the development of international law. For the first time, the two major sea powers at the time, Great Britain and France, abandoned their different state practices in a war at sea and adopted new rules during the war. After the war, they agreed on the Declaration of Paris of 1856, which summarised their adopted practices. To this day, lawyers see the Declaration as a significant step towards the codification of international law and, more precisely, the laws of naval warfare. Moreover, the Declaration was novel in the sense that it formed a multilateral treaty, which states could join anytime. The Declaration attempted to regulate the relationship between belligerents and neutrals at sea in time of war. It consisted of four main principles:

1. Privateering is, and remains, abolished;
2. The neutral flag covers enemy's goods, with the exception of contraband of war;
3. Neutral goods, with the exception of contraband of war, are not liable to capture under enemy's flag;
4. Blockades, in order to be binding, must be effective, that is to say, maintained by a force sufficient really to prevent access to the coast of the enemy.[2]

The abolition of privateering, as referred to in point 1, was advocated by Great Britain, whose interest it was to protect its trade from interference. In return, Great Britain was willing to strengthen neutral rights, which were dealt with in points 2 and 3. Granting neutrals to freely trade in time of war with the exception of contraband trade, and thus endorsing the principle of 'free ship, free goods', was a major concession from the perspective of a major sea power. Contraband goods described goods such as arms and ammunition which directly aided the enemy's war effort and could legitimately be seized in time of war. Conditional contraband described goods which could be used for civilian or military purposes, such as food or timber. Depending on the usage of the goods, they could be considered as contraband. Finally, the law of blockade was more strictly defined under point 4. Overall, the Declaration restrained belligerent rights while reaffirming the principle of freedom of the seas claimed by neutrals.

Although the adoption of the Declaration at first met with considerable political resistance in Great Britain, the British government adhered to the principles of the Declaration in every conflict after 1856. In fact, British foreign policy embraced the Declaration and even adhered to strict neutrality throughout the latter half of the 19th century and until the outbreak of the First World War. The experience of the American Civil War, 1861–1865, in which the United States had accused Great Britain of unneutral behaviour, led to a major change of British domestic legislation to enforce neutrality more effectively.

---

[2] Declaration respecting Maritime Law, Paris, 16 April 1856, in *British State Papers*, vol. LXI, pp. 155–8.

Great Britain's neutrality policy went hand in hand with its free trade policy, endorsing the principle of freedom of the seas. The powerful Royal Navy acted as a reassurance for Great Britain's claims as a neutral.

Codification of the Laws of Naval Warfare

By the end of the 19th century, as peace societies and internationalist movements gained ground, the process of the codification of the laws of war was resumed. An earlier attempt at the Brussels Conference in 1874 had failed because the great powers were then not seriously committed to restraining the laws of war. When, in 1899, the Russian Tsar Nicholas II invited major and minor states to meet in The Hague to discuss the regulation of the laws of war, his initiative was met with great enthusiasm from many sides. At the First Hague Peace Conference in 1899 the delegates mainly dealt with the laws of land warfare. The only agreement concerning the laws of naval warfare was *Convention (X) for the Adaption to Maritime Warfare of the Principles of the Geneva Convention*. The convention regulated the status of the shipwrecked, wounded or sick of a belligerent party, and declared hospital ships as neutral and not subject to capture.

At the Second Hague Peace Conference, in 1907, the regulation of war at sea was the main subject of the negotiations. After the Russo-Japanese War of 1904–5, which had increased tensions between belligerents and neutrals over freedom of the seas, the atmosphere was particularly strained. On the list of topics to be discussed at The Hague were neutrality, contraband, conversion of merchant ships into warships, creation of an international prize court and the right of search and capture. Notably, the question of the law of blockade was left aside out of fear that it could compromise the overall outcome of the conference. In essence, the conference dealt with the ideas of freedom versus control of the seas in time of war. In the light of recent war experience where neutrals had seen the sinking of their merchant ships and the expansion of contraband lists by belligerents, these issues seemed particularly urgent. Several conventions were adopted at the conference, among them *Convention (XI) relative to Certain Restrictions with regard to the Exercise of the Right of Capture in Naval War*, or *Convention (XIII) concerning the Rights and Duties of Neutral Powers in Naval War*. Both conventions reaffirmed the principle of freedom of the seas and strengthened neutral rights. While the British were the major architects of the neutrality convention, and accepted the limitation of the right of search and capture, they were not willing to discuss the more contentious issue of blockade. Their initial proposal of abolishing contraband altogether, to avoid endless disputes over contraband lists, met with severe resistance and was not further pursued.

The American proposal of immunity of private property at sea, with the exception of contraband and blockade, was met with equal opposition. Intended to severely restrict the right of search and capture, the American proposal expressed one of the core values of US foreign policy, namely freedom of the seas. American neutrality brought economic prosperity, but while the American economy grew steadily, the US Navy was too small to effectively protect American trade. Therefore, the proposal of immunity was aimed at ensuring American trade interests. Similar ideas had already been advocated during negotiations with Great Britain in 1783, then at the negotiations at Paris in 1856 and again at the First Hague Peace Conference in 1899.

Opposition to the proposal came from two prominent naval strategists at the time, the American Captain Alfred T. Mahan and the British naval historian Julian S. Corbett. Mahan rose to fame in 1890 as the author of *The Influence of Sea Power upon History, 1688-1783* – a book which had a huge impact on the understanding of sea power. It was aimed at ordinary American citizens and tried to explain why the United States should aspire to become a major sea power and invest in the building of a big navy. The book was also a success abroad, and politicians worldwide celebrated Mahan as a visionary. In many countries, his ideas gave an impetus to pursuing naval policies more vigorously. Mahan, who had been a member of the American delegation at The Hague in 1899, opposed immunity of private property at sea for the reason that control of the seas was essential for a sea power in order to undermine the enemy's war efforts. He argued that war affected not only those fighting but also those at home. With the dramatic increase of international trade in the latter half of the 19th century, people's dependence on the import of goods made them more vulnerable in times of war. Therefore, waging economic warfare would be crucial in shortening wars – not least because the effects would be felt instantly on the home front. The interception of neutral trade was a logical consequence. In fact, Mahan was critical of the role of neutrals in war. In his opinion, trading with belligerents was a form of taking part in war. He thus suggested defining neutral duties more carefully, rather than focusing on neutral rights. Mahan's view diametrically opposed the official American position towards freedom of the seas. Corbett argued similarly to Mahan in his writing on the subject:

> The value of the sea internationally is as a means of communication between States and parts of States, and the use and enjoyment of these communications is the actual life of a nation at sea. [...] All, then, that we can possibly gain from our enemy upon the sea is to deny him its use and enjoyment as a means of communication. Command of the sea means nothing more nor less than control of communications. It occupies exactly the same place and discharges the same function in maritime warfare that conquest and occupation of territory does in land warfare. If one is lawful and necessary, so is the other; if both are lawful and necessary, then each connotes the legality and necessity of the means by which alone the condition of stagnation can be brought about.[3]

Corbett understood the sea as a space of communication. Denying the enemy

---

[3] CORBETT J.S., 'The Capture of Private Property at Sea', in *Some Neglected Aspects of War*, ed. A.T. MAHAN (London, 1907; reprinted from *The Nineteenth Century*, June 1907), pp. 131-2.

access to the open sea was the primary goal in naval warfare. Only major naval powers could effectively exercise control of the seas.

Mahan's and Corbett's considerations resonated in the arguments of the British delegation at The Hague in 1907 when the issue of immunity of private property was discussed. For Great Britain, as the major sea power, the proposal undermined the very basis upon which a sea power operated. Without the right to intercept neutral and enemy trade, sea powers were deprived of their primary weapon in war, namely blockade and the right of search and capture as a means to control the seas. Unsurprisingly, the British delegates at The Hague vehemently opposed the American proposal, which was later withdrawn. Its supporters were mainly smaller sea powers, which were not able to protect their trade on their own and thus had a vested interest in the proposal.

The result of the Second Peace Conference of 1907 was meagre in terms of actual achievements in the codification of the laws of naval warfare. While the conference seemingly strengthened the rights of neutrals, belligerent rights were hardly discussed, which was a major shortcoming. The British celebrated *Convention (XII) relative to the Creation of an International Prize Court*, in which the signatories agreed on a prize court of appeal, where disputes over the legitimate capture of neutral ships should be settled. Yet, soon after the conference, the operability of such a future court was questioned because of the unclear legal basis upon which the court was to function.

The London Conference in 1909 intended to rectify the situation and agree upon a code of naval warfare for a future international prize court. Previous conferences had illustrated the opposing interests of prospective belligerents and neutrals, which was why the British government invited only the ten major sea powers to the conference. When they adopted the Declaration of London, more than half of whose seventy-one articles dealt with the two prominent issues, blockade and contraband. For the first time, contraband lists were agreed to. The Declaration also stated when the lists could be amended, and how to communicate this to neutrals in time of war. The law of blockade was further specified, limiting the radius of operation for a blockading fleet to pursue ships which had breached the blockade. The London Declaration expanded on the existing principles of the Declaration of Paris, while other issues, such as the conversion of merchant ships into warships, remained unresolved.

None of the signatory states ratified the Declaration before the outbreak of the First World War. The fate of the Declaration of London of 1909 was symptomatic for the period in which it was created. While some believed in the restraining force of the law, others were sceptical as to how practicable the rules would be in time of war. The agreed rules seemed to reaffirm neutral rights, even though it was doubtful to what extent the principle of freedom of the seas would be respected in time of war. Belligerent rights and, thus, the exercise of control of the seas were hardly curtailed. The discussion on the immunity of private property at sea revealed that major sea powers were not willing to compromise on their main weapon in time of war.

Overall, the process of the codification of the laws of naval warfare had achieved little in clarifying the relationship between belligerents and neutrals. And yet, the series of international conferences opened up a platform where major and minor states could voice their differing opinions. While major sea powers influenced the creation of the laws of naval warfare substantially, minor powers at least gained small concessions.

Freedom of the Seas in the First World War

The outbreak of the First World War in August 1914 led to a rapid deterioration of the principle of freedom of the seas. Many of the rules so carefully negotiated at the Hague and London Conferences were broken in the name of military necessity. Although all major belligerents professed at the outbreak of war to adhere to the rules of the Declaration of London, they had all withdrawn from it by 1916.

The United States, a neutral power for the first three years of the war, had the most substantive claims on freedom of the seas. The President of the United States, Woodrow Wilson, explained this in an address to the Senate on 22 January 1917:

> [T]he paths of the sea must alike in law and in fact be free. The freedom of the seas is the *sine qua non* of peace, equality, and cooperation. No doubt a somewhat radical reconsideration of many of the rules of international practice hitherto thought to be established may be necessary in order to make the seas indeed free and common in practically all circumstances for the use of mankind, but the motive for such changes is convincing and compelling. There can be no trust or intimacy between the peoples of the world without them. The free, constant, unthreatened intercourse of nations is an essential part of the process of peace and of development. It need not be difficult either to define or to secure the freedom of the seas if the governments of the world sincerely desire to come to an agreement concerning it.[4]

Germany's launch of unrestricted submarine warfare was only the last straw in a long list of violations of neutral rights, which led the United States to enter the war on 6 April 1917. After the outbreak of war, the British government swiftly expanded its contraband lists, which undermined the principle of "free ship, free goods". Great Britain's blockade policy further aggravated the relationship between neutrals and belligerents. By Orders in Council, the British government operated a *quasi* blockade, establishing a distant blockade from the North Sea to the Atlantic. Mines on the open seas added to the danger of crossing the seas safely. By November 1914, the British declared a large area of the North Sea to be a war zone, which ships entered at their own risk. Essentially, this practice closed

---

[4] Woodrow Wilson's Address to the Senate on Peace without Victory, Washington, 22 January 1917.

neutral ports on the continent, e.g. the port of Rotterdam in the Netherlands. The British further increased their grip on neutral trade by summoning neutral ships into British ports without capture but requesting them to clear their cargo before heading to a neutral port within the war zone. The British government also expanded the doctrine of continuous voyage and stopped ships which were destined for neutral ports, contesting that this would be the final destination for the goods. Instead, the British feared that these goods were further transported to Germany. As a reaction to the British blockade policy, the German government announced a war zone around the British Isles in March 1915. Any ship which entered that area was subject to destruction by submarines without warning. All these measures by belligerent states challenged the principle of freedom of the seas and strained the relationship between belligerents and neutrals.

Control of the Seas in the First World War

The British government explained its wartime measures with regard to the treatment of neutrals. Justifying the decision for the creation of a war zone, the Prime Minister, Herbert H. Asquith, addressed the House of Commons on 17 November 1914:

> His Majesty's Government are fully aware of the anxiety prevailing in the United States and other neutral countries on these subjects, and they trust that their policy will be fully understood. They are confident that public opinion in neutral countries will appreciate their earnest desire that there should be no interference with neutral trade provided the vital interests of Great Britain, which are at stake in the present conflict, are adequately maintained.[5]

Neutral rights were respected only on British terms as blockade and the right of search and capture were key assets for a sea power to control the seas. Despite the violation of the principle of freedom of the seas, Great Britain understood itself as the guardian of the very principle it violated. A temporary suspension, so the British government argued, was no disregard for the principle as such. On the contrary, the Royal Navy acted as its defender.

After four and half years of war, there was not much left of the principle of freedom of the seas. Throughout the war, President Wilson had advocated the foundation of a League of Nations, which should ensure freedom of the seas in time of peace and war. His demand, though, for absolute freedom of the seas was not tenable at the time. When President Wilson announced his peace plan (also known as the Fourteen Points) in January 1918, he used a more moderate formulation of freedom of the seas:

---

[5] Speech of Herbert Asquith, Hansard, 5th series, *House of Commons Debates*, 17 November 1914, vol. 68, c. 317.

II. Absolute freedom of navigation upon the seas, outside territorial water, alike in peace and in war, except as the seas may be closed in whole or in part by international action for the enforcement of international covenants.[6]

By accepting a certain degree of interference, Wilson acknowledged the blockade and the right of search and capture as the means to control the seas in times of war.

Epilogue

The end of the First World War did not bring the desired changes President Wilson had envisaged. Great Britain opposed any debate on freedom of the seas at the Paris Peace Conference in 1919. The newly created League of Nations, so it was hoped, would continue the process of the codification of the laws of naval warfare, and also discuss freedom of the seas. Throughout the interwar years, naval conferences, organised by different states or the League, focused on a variety of issues, among them arms limitation and the prohibition of certain weapons. However, freedom of the seas was not discussed, due to Great Britain's refusal to enter any negotiations on this topic. During the Second World War, the President of the United States, Franklin D. Roosevelt, and the British Prime Minister, Winston Churchill, outlined the post-war order in the Atlantic Charter of 1941. Freedom of the seas was again among the principles upon which an international order should be based. After 1945, the newly established United Nations was more successful than its predecessor in the codification of the law of the sea. No longer were the means to control the seas the focus of the negotiations at various conferences, but, rather, freedom of the seas in time of peace. Following technological innovations and the detection of resources below the seabed, states started to claim larger areas of the sea as territorial waters. The sea continues to be an important factor in the making of international law, and claims for freedom and control of the seas in time of peace and war will always be at the heart of the debates.

Select Bibliography

ANAND R.P., 'Freedom of the Seas. Past, Present and Future', in *New Directions in International Law. Essays in Honour of Wolfgang Abendroth-Festschrift zu seinem 75. Geburtstag*, ed. R. GUTIÉRREZ GIRARDOT, H. RIDDER, M. LAL SARIN and T. SCHILLER (Frankfurt a.M., 1982), pp. 215-33.

---

[6] Woodrow Wilson's Address to the Joint Session of the two Houses of Congress, Washington, 8 January 1918.

BEST G., *Humanity in Warfare. The Modern History of the International Law of Armed Conflicts* (London, 1980).

BUTLER W.E., 'Grotius and the Law of the Sea', in *Hugo Grotius and International Relations*, ed. H. BULL, B. KINGSBURY and A. ROBERTS (Oxford, 1990), pp. 209-20.

COOGAN J.W., *The End of Neutrality. The United States, Britain, and Maritime Rights, 1899-1915* (Ithaca, NY, 1981).

CORBETT J.S., *The League of Nations and Freedom of the Seas* (Oxford, 1918).

CORBETT J.S., *Some Principles of Maritime Strategy* (London, 1911).

DÜLFFER J., *Regeln gegen den Krieg? Die Haager Friedenskonferenzen von 1899 und 1907 in der internationalen Politik* (Frankfurt a.M., 1981).

DUPUIS C., *Le droit de la guerre maritime d'après les conférences de La Haye et de Londres* (Paris, 1911).

FREI G.A., *Britain, International Law, and the Evolution of Maritime Strategic Thought, 1856-1914*, Oxford Historical Monographs (Oxford, forthcoming).

FULTON T.W., *The Sovereignty of the Sea: An Historical Account of the Claims of England to the Dominion of the British Seas, and of the Evolution of the Territorial Waters, with special Reference to the Rights of Fishing and the Naval Salute* (Edinburgh, 1911).

HALL W.E., *A Treatise on International Law*, ed. J.B. ATLAY, 5th edn (Oxford, 1904).

HAMILTON C.I., 'Anglo-French Seapower and the Declaration of Paris', *International History Review* 4.2 (1982), 166-90.

HATTENDORF J.B., 'Maritime Conflict', in *The Laws of War. Constraints on Warfare in the Western World*, ed. M. HOWARD, G.J. ANDREOPOULOS and M.R. SHULMAN (New Haven, 1994), pp. 98-115.

HATTENDORF J.B., 'The US Navy and the "Freedom of the Seas", 1775-1917', in *Navies in Northern Waters 1721-2000*, ed. R. HOBSON and T. KRISTIANSEN (London, 2004), pp. 151-74.

HOWE A., *Free Trade and Liberal England, 1846-1946* (Oxford, 1998).

HULL I.V., *A Scrap of Paper. Breaking and Making International Law during the Great War* (Ithaca, NY, 2014).

KNOCK T.J., *To End all Wars. Woodrow Wilson and the Quest for a New World Order* (New York, 1992).

KRASKA J., *Maritime Power and the Law of the Sea. Expeditionary Operations in World Politics* (Oxford, 2011).

LEMNITZER J.M., '"That moral league of nations against the United States": The Origins of the 1856 Declaration of Paris', *International History Review* 35.5 (2013), 1068-88.

MAHAN A.T., 'The Hague Conference: The Question of Immunity for Belligerent Merchant Shipping', in *Some Neglected Aspects of War*, ed. A.T. MAHAN (London, 1907; repr. from *National Review*, July 1907), pp. 157-92.

MAHAN A.T., *The Influence of Sea Power upon History, 1660-1783* (Boston, MA, 1890).

O'CONNELL D.P., *The Influence of Law on Sea Power* (Manchester, 1975).

RANFT B., 'Restraints on War at Sea before 1945', in *Restraints on War. Studies in the Limitation of Armed Conflict*, ed. M. HOWARD (Oxford, 1979), pp. 39-56.

RONZITTI N., 'Naval Warfare', in *Max Planck Encyclopedia of Public International Law*, ed. R. WOLFRUM (Oxford, 2009); opil.ouplaw.com/home/ORIL [Last accessed 21 January 2015].

SCHINDLER D. and TOMAN J., *The Laws of Armed Conflicts. A Collection of Conventions, Resolutions and other Documents*, 4th edn (Dordrecht, 2004).

SEMMEL B., *Liberalism and Naval Strategy. Ideology, Interest, and Sea Power during the Pax Britannica* (Boston, MA, 1986).

STOCKTON C.H., 'The International Naval Conference of London, 1908–1909', *American Journal of International Law* 3.3 (1909), 596–618.

UNCLOS AND THE MODERN LAW OF THE SEA

SAM BATEMAN is a Professorial Research Fellow at the Australian National Centre for Ocean Resources and Security (ANCORS), University of Wollongong, Australia

ABSTRACT. *Since the 1960s a new framework of international law has been developed under the auspices of the United Nations. This defines "Exclusive Economic Zones", "Continental Shelf Regimes", "Archipelagic Waters" and other areas in which the traditional "freedoms of the seas" are restricted. The tendency is to limit the "freedoms of the seas" traditionally enjoyed by the maritime powers in favour of the interests of other coastal states, but much uncertainty still surrounds both the definition and the enforcement of these new legal rights.*

RÉSUMÉ. *Depuis les années 60, un nouveau cadre juridique international a été développé sous l'égide des Nations Unies. Il définit les « zones économiques exclusives », les « régimes du plateau continental », les « eaux archipélagiques » et autres zones dans lesquelles la traditionnelle « liberté des mers » est restreinte. Visant principalement à limiter la « liberté des mers » dont jouissent généralement les puissances maritimes au profit d'autres États côtiers, il demeure néanmoins beaucoup d'incertitudes quant à la définition et la mise en application de ces nouveaux droits juridiques.*

.•.

The *law of the sea* provides the legal framework for managing the 71% of the earth's surface covered by water. The modern law of the sea is derived from the 1982 UN Convention on the Law of the Sea (UNCLOS)[1] and other international instruments; the custom and practice of states; the judgments of international courts and tribunals; and the opinions of eminent international jurists. It may be either the "hard law" of binding international treaties, or the "soft law" of non-binding guidelines or codes of conduct.

The law of the sea is the part of public international law that deals with human uses of the oceans and seas of the world, exploiting their resources and preserving their utility for future generations. It covers regimes for navigation, fishing, offshore mining, marine scientific research, the laying of cables and pipelines, sea dumping, resolving maritime disputes and the preservation

---

[1] United Nations Convention on the Law of the Sea, 10 December 11982, U.N. A/CONF.62/122, 1982, reprinted in *The Law of the Sea Official Text of the United Nations Convention on the Law of the Sea with Annexes and Index* (1982), UN Sales No. E.83.V.5, 1983 and 21 I.L.M. 1261.

and protection of the marine environment. A particularly important aspect is the extent and nature of the jurisdiction and sovereignty exercised by coastal states over their adjacent waters. The law of the sea has evolved over the years in response to changing political circumstances, demands posed by new and wider uses of the sea, technological developments and increasing concern for the health of the world's oceans and their living resources. Following the 9/11 terrorist attacks in New York, new law was also introduced to deal with the threat of maritime terrorism.

Evolution of the law of the sea

There was little change in the international law of the sea from the times of Grotius in the early 17th century until the 1950s and 1960s. The freedom of the seas was the dominant paradigm with only a narrow belt of territorial sea under the jurisdiction of coastal states. All this started changing, however, following World War II, with increased interest in the exploitability of offshore oil resources and the greater number of independent states following decolonisation. The influence of these states on the law of the sea in seeking wider control over their adjacent waters is evident in UNCLOS, particularly with its introduction of a twelve-nautical-mile limit to the territorial sea and the regimes of the exclusive economic zone (EEZ) and archipelagic state.

The pace of evolution of the law of the sea has continued in recent decades with increased awareness of the importance of the global oceans to the future of the planet and of the need for new legal frameworks to underpin oceans' management and preserve and protect the marine environment. The new paradigm has seen increased coastal state control over adjacent waters and new limitations on the freedoms of the high seas, especially freedoms of fishing, with new regulations preventing indiscriminate fishing on the high seas. These trends with the evolution of the international law of the sea have coincided with the shift of economic and maritime power from the West towards the East.

International regulation of the oceans and seas has widened significantly in recent decades. These new regimes have involved the development of much international law and the establishment of new international organizations. Greater concern for the protection of the marine environment is a driving force for this development, while the major Asian countries, China, India and Japan, seek increased control due to their security concerns.

In the 1960s, the mariner did not have to worry much about the law of the sea or how he used the sea. If his vessel was more than three miles offshore, he could largely go wherever he pleased and do whatever he liked, including disposing of any type of waste into the sea. He was not concerned about laws that the nearby coastal state might have in force about marine pollution (and in the 1960s few states had such laws), or indeed about any international conventions his country might or might not have ratified. Even in port, raw sewage could be discharged directly into the harbour. Then, if the mariner was also a naval officer, his ship could fire its weapons, launch its aircraft and generally conduct whatever naval operation or exercise that he chose, content in the knowledge that he was simply exercising one of the freedoms of the high seas.

All this has changed. The evolution of international law has had a marked impact on what can be done at sea. Numerous major conventions now exist regulating shipping and seafarers, marine safety and marine environmental protection. The contemporary mariner faces a strict regulatory environment with laws and regulations emanating from a range of international and regional agreements, as well as national legislation from his flag state. These cover what he must not dump at sea, and, in many areas of sea, they dictate the shipping lanes to use and when he is obliged to report the position of his vessel. The naval officer must also consider the type of passage he is exercising, and what his ship can and cannot do when he passes off the coast of a foreign country.

UNCLOS

All maritime regimes are based on the framework provided by UNCLOS. UNCLOS itself is an international regime but there are a host of other maritime regimes for shipping, fishing, seabed mining, marine environmental protection, sea dumping, preventing ship-sourced pollution, search and rescue and so on that together provide the modern law of the sea. UNCLOS is a large and complex convention that provides the constitution for the oceans and the basis for the types of jurisdiction that a country may exercise at sea in its various roles as a coastal, port or flag State.

UNCLOS sets out the rights and duties of a state with regard to the various uses of the oceans and prescribes the regime of maritime zones that establish the nature of State sovereignty and sovereign rights over ocean space and resources. UNCLOS also provides the principles and norms for navigational rights and freedoms, flag State responsibility, countering piracy, rights of visit, hot pursuit and regional cooperation, all of which are relevant to the maintenance of good order at sea. Other achievements of UNCLOS include the legal frameworks for preserving and protecting the marine environment, the sustainable development of marine living resources, marine scientific research and dispute resolution. UNCLOS also established three new international bodies: an international judicial body, the International Tribunal for the Law of the Sea, which has jurisdiction with regard to maritime disputes; the Commission on the Limits of the Continental Shelf (CLCS) established to assess continental-shelf claims that extend beyond two hundred miles; and the International Seabed Authority (ISA) to manage the deep seabed mining regime.

UNCLOS now has a great many State parties but its effectiveness is still open to question in several areas. Many examples can be found of apparent non-compliance with UNCLOS. These include the uses and abuses of straight territorial sea baselines, a reluctance to acknowledge the rights and duties of other States in the EEZ, and the failure of flag States to observe the "genuine link" requirement in UNCLOS Article 91 and to fulfil their duties as flag States under Article 94. It is a major limitation of UNCLOS as a foundation for good order at sea that the United States remains outside the Convention.

UNCLOS was formulated in a period when there was less concern for the health of the marine environment than there is at present. Norms and principles for preserving and protecting the marine environment have multiplied exponentially over the last thirty years or so. It is not surprising therefore that many of the apparent "gaps" in UNCLOS arise in the area of environmental protection. The navigational regimes in UNCLOS provide an example of the underdeveloped level of concern for the marine environment evident in the 1970s. The regimes of straits transit passage and archipelagic sea lanes (ASL) passage apply to "all ships and aircraft" and there is no direct right of the coastal or archipelagic State to prevent the passage of vessels that could threaten the marine environment.

The Third UN Conference on the Law of the Sea (UNCLOS III), leading to UNCLOS, was the first international conference on the law of the sea that reflected coastal State interests. The views of major user states had prevailed at the earlier conferences, UNCLOS I in 1958 and UNCLOS II in 1960, but at UNCLOS III, developing countries lobbied together to ensure that they shared equitably in the exploitation of marine resources. A major interest was the deep seabed beyond the limit of national jurisdiction. The developing countries considered that the deep seabed should be regarded as the "common heritage of mankind". They were concerned that rapid development of marine technology by developed countries would promote national claims to the seabed by those countries, the exploitation of seabed resources by a few developed countries and the use of the ocean floor for military purposes.

Although UNCLOS has entered into force, many of its provisions lack the clarity to remove all uncertainties in the law of the sea. There are still "grey areas" with the law of the sea which require negotiation between interested parties. This is particularly so with provisions relating to the EEZ regime, which was new with UNCLOS. Problems arise because jurisdictional aspects of the regime are either uncertain or not universally accepted and because it requires countries to delimit new maritime boundaries with each other – in many instances where sovereign interests had not previously overlapped. Under pressure from environmental concerns and non-governmental organizations (NGOs), coastal states around the world are introducing tighter regulations over their adjacent waters.

The United States remains outside UNCLOS despite the active support for the Convention by defence and foreign policy interests. A naval concern of the United States is that new maritime regulations pose a threat to the freedom of the seas, a core American interest with the possibility that the introduction of marine protected areas, incorporating a variety of navigational restrictions, such as mandatory ship reporting, pilotage requirements and routing measures, may increase in the future.

Paradoxically, new regulations are often being introduced by some of

America's closest allies: Canada with mandatory ship reporting in the Arctic, Australia with compulsory pilotage in Torres Strait, and the European Union with restrictive policies over vessels entering the EEZ. Even the United States itself is torn between its historical interest in freedom of navigation and the need for measures to protect the marine environment, including mandatory ship reporting in parts of the United States' EEZ and the creation of marine sanctuaries that exclude international shipping.

Maritime Zones

Prior to UNCLOS, the only maritime zones recognised under international law were internal waters, territorial sea, contiguous zone, continental shelf and the high seas. UNCLOS further defined the regimes for these zones, including rules for determining the territorial sea baselines from which all maritime zones are measured, and introduced two new types of zone: the EEZ and archipelagic waters.

Exclusive Economic Zone

The EEZ is an area adjacent to the territorial sea subject to the regime in UNCLOS Part V. It cannot extend more than two hundred nautical miles measured from territorial sea baselines. Coastal States do not have sovereignty over the EEZ but, rather, have sovereign rights over natural resources in their EEZs, both living and non-living, and other economic activities, such as the production of energy from tides and winds. Coastal States also have jurisdiction under UNCLOS Article 56(1)(b) with regard to the establishment and use of artificial islands, installations and structures; marine scientific research; and the protection and preservation of the marine environment (including the conservation of species). All other states have freedom of navigation and overflight in the EEZ, as well as the freedom to lay submarine cables and pipelines.

The EEZ was introduced to satisfy the perceived need for coastal states to have rights over the resources of their adjacent waters. The precise nature of its jurisdictional regime is still evolving. This is especially so with marine scientific research, the prevention of marine pollution and the measures which can be adopted by coastal States. An important area of disagreement relates to the ability of a coastal State to introduce regulations that have the effect of denying freedoms of navigation and overflight in all or part of its EEZ. Maritime powers believe that, subject to the resource-related rights and environmental-protection obligations of a coastal state, the freedoms of navigation and overflight in the EEZ are the same as those on the high seas.

Negotiation of the EEZ regime at UNCLOS III was difficult and complex, with widely divergent points of view about the status of the new zone. One major group, the "territorialists", mainly comprising developing countries, saw the

EEZ as an extension of national jurisdiction in which coastal states would enjoy sovereignty subject to certain limitations. However, this position was sharply disputed by the maritime powers, led by the United States and the then Soviet Union, who saw the zone as a part of the high seas where coastal States had some rights over offshore resources. The compromise reached was that the EEZ should be regarded as a separate zone in its own right ("*sui generis*"), neither high seas nor territorial sea, and subject in accordance with UNCLOS Article 55 to its own specific legal regime,

Now, over thirty years since UNCLOS was agreed in 1982, the political debate over the nature of the EEZ continues to surface. American political leaders have referred to the South China Sea as "international waters" when in reality they are the EEZs of littoral states where such states have significant rights and duties. To refer to EEZs as "international waters" amounts to turning the clock back to UNCLOS III and arguing the position of the maritime powers that the EEZ was part of the high seas where coastal states had certain resource rights. It denies the *sui generis* nature of the EEZ.

Continental shelf

The continental shelf regime has its origins in the Truman Proclamation by the United States in 1945, proclaiming that the resources on the continental shelf contiguous to the United States belonged to the United States. This was in response to heavy demand for fuels during World War II and awareness that there were rich hydrocarbon resources offshore in the Gulf of Mexico in particular. Other nations quickly followed the American precedent.

The continental shelf occurs physically where the seabed slopes gently away from the coast for a long distance before it plunges steeply down to the ocean depths. Under certain conditions set out in UNCLOS Article 76, the outer limits of the continental shelf may extend to a maximum of 350 nautical miles from territorial sea baselines. The *legal* continental shelf is defined by this article as the seabed and subsoil of the submarine areas adjacent to the territorial sea of a coastal State. The coastal State has sovereign rights over the non-living resources of the seabed and subsoil of the continental shelf, as well as over living resources of a sedentary nature, such as clams and pearl-shell, on its continental shelf. It must share with the international community part of the revenue derived from exploiting resources from any part of its continental shelf beyond the two-hundred-mile limit.

Ordinarily, the continental shelf cannot extend beyond two hundred nautical miles measured from the territorial sea baseline, but in cases where the coastal State has a wide continental margin, the continental shelf may extend further – the outer continental shelf (OCS). Coastal States wishing to establish an OCS are required to submit information on their proposed outer limits to the CLCS. The CLCS then assesses such submissions and provides recommendations based on which coastal States may finalize the outer limits to their continental shelf rights. A UN commission was required for this purpose to protect the interests of the international community as the limits of the OCS constitute the boundary between a state's continental shelf and the deep seabed, which is the common heritage of mankind.

As of December 2014, the CLCS had received seventy-seven submissions and finalized nineteen of them. However, it will not address many of the submissions it has received because they relate to areas in dispute. The Commission is a scientific rather than legal body and lacks the mandate to consider areas subject to a sovereignty dispute or overlapping maritime claims. The Commission's recommendations are without prejudice to the delimitation of maritime boundaries.

Greater interest is being shown in the potential of OCS. Recent years have witnessed great advances in technologies applicable to seabed resource exploration and exploitation. These developments permit oil and gas exploration and development further offshore, in more hostile conditions and in ever deeper waters. Underpinning these technological developments is the realisation that on- and near-shore reserves are reaching a limit while demand continues to escalate. This has reinforced the case for undertaking oil and gas exploration activities in hitherto under-explored areas such as those of the OCS.

Archipelagic waters

Archipelagic waters are the waters within archipelagic baselines drawn in accordance with UNCLOS Article 47 and joining the outermost points of the outermost islands and drying reefs of an archipelagic State. They are under full sovereignty of the archipelagic State, with the exceptions of the rights of innocent passage and archipelagic sea lanes (ASL) passage allowed to foreign ships and aircraft. Following years of lobbying by archipelagic countries, particularly Indonesia, UNCLOS III accepted the concept of the archipelagic State. UNCLOS Articles 46 and 47 set out the main criteria that should be met before a country can claim the status of an archipelagic State. Several tests are involved. First, the country must be constituted wholly by one or more archipelagos or islands. Thus in the Asia-Pacific, New Caledonia and the Hawaiian Islands, for example, cannot exploit the benefits of archipelagic status as they are parts of larger continental States (France and the United States, respectively), although they otherwise meet the criteria for an archipelagic State.

Secondly, the islands and groups of islands should form an intrinsic geographical, economic and political entity, or have been historically regarded as such. The third test involves maximum and minimum limits to the area of water that can be included within the archipelago. When legitimate archipelagic baselines are drawn around the outer limits of the islands and drying reefs comprising the archipelago, UNCLOS Article 47(1) requires that the ratio of the area of the water to the area of land, including atolls, must lie between 1 to 1 and 9 to 1. Hence Japan, for example, cannot claim to be an archipelagic State because, no matter how it draws its archipelagic baselines, its land to water ratio will always be too high.

Navigational regimes

Innocent passage was the only passage regime that existed prior to UNCLOS but the extension of the width of the territorial sea and acceptance of the regime of the archipelagic State led to two new regimes being introduced: transit passage through straits used for international navigation, and ASL passage through archipelagic waters. Transit and ASL passage are liberal regimes that include overflight and cannot be suspended by a coastal State. They provide maximum rights to ships and aircraft to travel in their normal modes (e.g. submarines may transit submerged) without the restrictions of innocent passage. These reflect the consideration implicit in these regimes that the international community should continue to enjoy the same rights and freedoms as before the extension of the territorial sea to 12 nautical miles and agreement on the regime of the archipelagic State.

Innocent passage

Innocent passage applying to the territorial sea and to archipelagic waters outside of ASLs is the most restrictive passage regime. Under provisions of UNCLOS Articles 19 and 20, it may be suspended by the coastal State; it restricts ships from a range of activities, including exercises and operating aircraft; and requires submarines to travel on the surface and show their flag.

Transit passage

The regime of straits' transit passage in Section 2 of Part III of the UNCLOS gives all ships and aircraft the right to travel through straits used for international navigation in their normal operational mode on, under or over the water. Introduction of this regime overcame the difficulty that many straits, parts of which had previously been high seas, became territorial seas when the legal territorial sea of a coastal State was extended to 12 nautical miles. It has been estimated that there were 153 straits around the world, including such key waterways as the Malacca, Dover, Gibraltar and Hormuz straits, with least breadths of between 6 and 24 miles that had previously included high seas "corridors" but became enclosed within the territorial sea of one or more coastal States with acceptance of the 12-mile limit. Without this regime, only the innocent passage regime would have been available through these straits.

Archipelagic sea lanes passage

In accordance with UNCLOS Part IV, the archipelagic State must allow ships and aircraft of all nations the right of "continuous, expeditious and unobstructed transit" through archipelagic waters along and over sea lanes which it may designate. If sea lanes are not designated, then the right of ASL passage may be exercised through the routes normally used for international navigation. Outside these sea lanes, ships of all nations have the right of innocent passage only, and there is no right of overflight.

Dispute resolution

Modern international law requires States to settle their disputes by peaceful means without the use of force. A dispute settlement regime for maritime disputes is provided in Part XV of UNCLOS. Section 2 of Part XV deals with compulsory procedures entailing binding decisions on disputes related to the Convention. States have a choice to settle disputes through International Tribunal for the Law of the Sea, the International Court of Justice (ICJ) or an arbitral tribunal, but under Article 298 they may opt out of mandatory dispute settlement for maritime boundary delimitations and military activities.

States may settle their maritime sovereignty disputes by negotiation, by one of the procedures prescribed in UNCLOS Part XV, or in an interim way by some form of joint development or joint management. Pending agreement on a boundary between overlapping EEZs or continental shelves, States under UNCLOS Articles 74(3) and 83(3), respectively, are obligated to "make every effort to enter into provisional arrangements of a practical nature and, during this transitional period, not to jeopardize or hamper the reaching of the final agreement".

Despite general exhortations to take sovereignty disputes to international arbitration, States are often reluctant to do so, due to uncertainty over the outcome – a "lose-lose" situation could result. Other reasons why states are reluctant to unilaterally invoke dispute settlement procedures include the costs of doing so; whether a state feels it has enough at stake; and the possible negative impact on the relations between the two states in other areas.

Ongoing developments

There is a tendency for states to increase their jurisdiction over their adjacent waters contrary to what others regard as UNCLOS or customary international law. Indeed there is something about the modern law of the sea and international oceans governance that breeds hypocrisy. Nations can sign up for global programmes of action on the marine environment but then have little capacity for, or intention of, implementing such programmes at the national level. These programmes are rather like motherhood. They are unquestionably worthy of support and praiseworthy in a general sense but sometimes unwanted and difficult for an individual.

In another example of hypocrisy, countries may preach the virtues of something at the international level (say, the freedoms of fishing, navigation or marine scientific research or the importance of the marine environment) while pursing contrary practices in their own waters. Australia, for example, while being a strong supporter of freedoms of navigation, with a particular concern for navigational rights in the archipelagos to its north, has acted to restrict these freedoms in its own waters in ways that are disputed by other countries. It has introduced compulsory pilotage in the Torres Strait, despite strong opposition from the United States in particular; declared prohibited anchorage areas around undersea cables in the EEZ; introduced mandatory ship reporting in parts of the EEZ adjacent to the Great Barrier Reef; and declared the entire Australian EEZ as a submarine exercise area.

Tensions over law of the sea issues may become more significant in the future. Major Western navies are structuring their forces for littoral operations and power projection, while regional navies, in East Asia in particular, continue to focus on sea-denial operations to deny their littoral waters to the forces of a possible adversary. Expeditionary operations in the littoral waters of other states require maximum freedoms of navigation and overflight, while sea denial is supported by applying restrictions on those freedoms.

As the years have gone by since UNCLOS was opened for signature, it has become clear that navigational rights and freedoms in the *new* law of the sea are not quite as clear as the drafters of the Convention intended. Despite the long history of the freedom of navigation and the efforts made in UNCLOS to ensure the preservation of traditional freedoms, coastal states are introducing new regulations that amount to restrictions on navigational rights and freedoms in their adjacent waters. Concern for the preservation and protection of the marine environment is the usual imperative for these new regulations.

Uncertainty in the law of sea may grow, and the United States, in particular, may find increasing difficulty in maintaining its strict interpretation of navigational regimes and coastal State jurisdiction. East Asian waters will be critical in shaping developments with the future law of the sea. In doing so, State practice in this theatre, under the influence of nationalistic domestic politics and regional tensions, may well diverge from the orthodox, largely Western view of the customary law of the sea. There are important implications here for the modern law of the sea and how it might evolve in the future. Where differences are evident at present between Western, primarily American, views of the law of the sea, and those of the rising powers of Asia, there can be no certainty that the Western views will prevail. A key causal factor is the long-standing tension between maritime powers seeking maximum freedoms to use the sea and coastal States seeking to restrict these freedoms in their adjacent waters. Unfortunately UNCLOS, with its many "grey areas" and built-in ambiguities, allows these opposing views to sit side by side.

The modern law of the sea is a dynamic phenomenon but the changes occur through new conventions and evolving customary law rather than through amendments to UNCLOS. Amendment is possible under UNCLOS Article 312, but one half of the States Parties are required to agree to convene a conference to consider possible amendments, and getting that agreement in the contemporary world would be difficult. UNCLOS was a magnificent achievement for the 1970s and 1980s and it remains a careful balance of the rights and duties of the different categories of State. However, its limitations must also be appreciated.

The evolution of the law of the sea is shaped by changing uses of the sea and greater awareness of its environmental significance and the need to conserve its living resources. Requirements for new law continue to emerge. Examples of emerging issues include the need for regimes to manage the living resources of the deep sea-bed and to provide for marine sanctuaries on the high seas.

The law of the sea has come to play an important part in international and regional relations and the development of national maritime strategies. It has had a marked influence on how we think about the sea both as a resource and as central to the future of the planet and ensuring the way of life of future generations. In this context, developing new law of the sea has not just been a matter for international lawyers but has required inputs from marine scientists, political scientists and economists, as well as other disciplines, who in most instances set the agenda for change. As the eminent international relations scholar Ken Booth once famously observed, "The record suggests that the changing law of the sea is too serious to be left to international lawyers".[2]

---

[2] BOOTH K., *Law, Force and Diplomacy at Sea* (London, 1985), p. 5.

New Navies and Maritime Powers

STEVEN HAINES is Professor of Public International Law in the University of Greenwich, United Kingdom

ABSTRACT. *In the century from 1914 the number of navies increased more than four-fold. In the same period the legal, cultural, political and economic environment has massively changed. With one exception (China) large merchant fleets are no longer flagged to major naval powers. The seas are subject to varying degrees of national and international legal jurisdiction, but piracy and other seaborne crime is increasing. Navies have essential "constabulary" functions, with "war-fighting" held in reserve.*

RÉSUMÉ. *Depuis 1914, le nombre de marines a plus que quadruplé. L'environnement juridique, culturel, politique et économique s'est dans le même temps fortement transformé. À une exception près - la Chine -, les flottes marchandes importantes n'appartiennent plus aux principales puissances navales. Les mers sont sujettes à des degrés changeants de juridiction nationale et internationale mais la piraterie et autres formes de criminalité maritime sont en augmentation. Les marines ont des fonctions policières fondamentales et gardent en réserve des navires de guerre.*

．•．

Broad and traditional interpretations of "maritime power" include both naval forces and, as Mahan noted, "the peaceful commerce and shipping from which alone a military fleet naturally and healthfully springs, and on which it securely rests". Mention will certainly be made of commerce and shipping in what follows, but this essay's focus is on navies, with "maritime power" implying a concentration of "military strength afloat".[1]

The past century has probably been the most intense period of naval development in history.[2] Today, there are over four times as many navies as there were at the beginning of the First World War, when the principal defining feature of all was their war-fighting capability. Today, war-fighting is not of such importance, with a great many navies having little, if any, capacity for it. Before concentrating on what navies do, however, we should explain why so many new ones have appeared since the Second World War.

---

[1] MAHAN A.T., *The Influence of Sea Power Upon History 1660-1783* (London, 1889), p. 28.
[2] The early-modern period of naval development, which launched the expansion of the European maritime-based empires, was arguably more profound in its consequences.

A CENTURY OF NAVAL PROLIFERATION

When the Great War broke out in 1914, there were thirty-nine navies included in *Jane's Fighting Ships*. By 1950, they had increased slightly, to 56, but by 1970 they had almost doubled, to 106. In 1990 there were 149 and today there are just over 160.[3] Overall, an increase of over a hundred since 1950.

The rate of increase in navies has reflected the increase in sovereign states.[4] Since 1945, states have trebled, to about two hundred, most new states resulting from de-colonisation between the 1950s and the 1970s, and the break-up of the Soviet Union and Yugoslavia in the 1990s.[5] A further significant increase in navies would require an equally significant increase in coastal states.[6] Since this would most likely require the break-up of one or more of the larger states (e.g. China, India or the US), it seems improbable. Naval proliferation may have peaked.[7]

More likely (though not probable) is a reduction in navies by the creation of regional forces serving the interests of groups of states. This would need more than mere cooperation like that achieved through the North Atlantic Treaty Organisation (NATO). While other aspects of state sovereignty seem amenable to a degree of integration (as within the European Union), it remains politically problematic. Armed forces are especially symbolic of sovereignty and, even in Europe, integration has never been a realistic possibility.

With navies neither increasing nor decreasing, any significant change in the pattern of maritime power will be about existing navies either growing or reducing in size, and shifting noticeably in terms of their capability relative to others. Much will depend on changes in the maritime strategic environment.

THE CHANGING CHARACTERISTICS OF THE MARITIME ENVIRONMENT

The ever-changing character of the maritime environment shapes the development and employment of navies. That environment is multi-dimensional: physical, political, economic, social and cultural, scientific and technical, military

---

[3] *Jane's Fighting Ships* for the years 1914, 1950, 1970–71, 1990–91, and 2014–15. The figures are for navies belonging to sovereign states (other forces listed are excluded from these figures).
[4] Non-state entities rarely develop navies. The most notable recent exception was the Tamil Tigers during their armed struggle in Sri Lanka.
[5] Statehood is now virtually synonymous with membership of the UN (now 193), although a few small states remain outside the organisation.
[6] A quarter of states are land locked, although some do have naval forces for use on inland lakes and rivers. Examples include Switzerland, Azerbaijan, Kazakhstan, Turkmenistan, Bolivia and Paraguay.
[7] Smaller states can also divide, of course, with both Scottish and Catalonian independence movements having the potential to add additional navies to the global count. Significant increase in numbers would, however, require the sort of break-up that the end of the Soviet Union precipitated.

and normative. While minor changes to the physical have not greatly affected maritime strategic decisions, other dimensions have been notably dynamic, and especially so since the Second World War. Traditional assumptions about ocean governance are arguably no longer tenable and we may even be experiencing the end of one era and the beginning of another.

The modern international political system is referred to as "Westphalian" because of the effects of the 1648 Peace of Westphalia on evolving notions of sovereignty. This has been relevant to the 30 per cent of the earth's surface covered by land, where sovereignty underpins governance. In stark contrast, the governance of the 70 per cent of our planet covered by sea has been underpinned by the absence of sovereignty, resulting in what Grotius referred to as *Mare Liberum*.[8] The "Freedom of the Seas" became the defining feature of ocean governance during the Grotian era of maritime imperialism, which lasted for three centuries, from the 17th to the middle of the 20th.

The Grotian era

Grotian *Mare Liberum* was predicated on the belief that the oceans were non-appropriable *res nullius* – owned by nobody, with none able to lay claim to them. They remained free for all to use for whatever purpose they wished, consistent only with the need not to interfere with legitimate use by others. A bare minimum of regulation was required, but simply to ensure that the oceans remained free. Singled out as uniquely illegitimate was piracy, with pirates declared outlaws subject to universal jurisdiction.[9] Piracy interfered with the free and secure movement of goods. It was suppressed by the major maritime powers because their interests were best served by free seas. Great-power navies and merchant fleets sailed the oceans at will, their peacetime right to do so limited only by their obligations to respect the integrity of other states' territorial seas and the shipping they encountered on the high seas. A bare minimum of ocean regulation, the outlawing of piracy, and respect for exclusive flag-state jurisdiction became the three main pillars of *Mare Liberum*.

All powers could use the oceans for transportation and communications, linking imperial centres with distant colonial possessions. This freedom was essential for ease of trade and assumed to be a major factor supporting the process of globalisation. The main merchant fleets were owned by commercial interests in the major maritime powers and sailed under their flags. The same powers deployed the principal naval forces to protect trade. A symbiotic relationship existed between navies and merchant fleets. *Guerre de course* and blockade operations, to disrupt the enemy's trade and undermine his ability to sustain war-fighting effort, were core naval missions.

It was entirely legitimate to use the oceans as a theatre for naval war in an

---

[8] Hugo de Groot ("Grotius") produced two works, *Mare Liberum* (1609) and *De Jure Belli ac Pacis* (1625), that did much to define the governance of the oceans and to develop international law.
[9] COLOMBOS C.J., *The International Law of the Sea* (London, 6th edn, 1967), p. 444.

international system in which conflict between great powers was a routine occurrence. War could be conducted wherever on the high seas an enemy's naval forces or merchant ships were encountered. The rights of neutrals to continue to use the oceans for legitimate trading activities had to be respected. In return, neutrals were obliged to respect belligerent rights and refrain from trading in contraband. The resultant pattern of belligerent and neutral rights and obligations was eventually codified in the 1856 Paris Declaration.[10]

Until the middle of the 20th century, exploitation of ocean resources was a marginal activity. Few fish stocks were under existential threat, exceptions being mainly local and inshore. The mineral resources of the sea were largely unknown, awaiting the technology to both discover and recover them. Navies were not generally needed to protect resource interests, except in inshore areas within their territorial jurisdiction.

Four factors determined the character of maritime power in the Grotian era, therefore: the function of navies as agents of imperial interest; the prevalence of great-power conflict; the relationship between naval power and merchant shipping; and, finally, the complete freedom navies enjoyed to manoeuvre across 70 percent of the earth's surface.

The post-Grotian era

The Second World War signalled the beginning of the end of the European-based maritime empires. Within three decades they had all dissolved, with numerous new states emerging from colonial rule. The imperial purpose of navies in the creation, maintenance and security of formal colonial empires had all but disappeared.

Coincidentally, great powers have avoided the use of force in their relations with each other; there has been no great-power war since 1945. Nuclear weapons and the substantial development of international organisation (especially the United Nations) have transformed international relations. During the Grotian era, state-on-state aggression was routinely legitimate. Now, it is unlawful. Current rivalries and tensions between powers like India, China and Japan are certainly of concern, but have not seemed imminently likely to result in general war. Russian belligerence on the very edge of Europe is deeply worrying, but seems less likely to result in active hostilities between great powers than once it might. It is seventy years since navies last fought a sustained and general naval campaign involving economic warfare at sea.

The symbiotic relationship between navies and merchant fleets has broken down completely, perhaps through the absence of naval war. Most merchant ship tonnage is now flagged to open registries, the largest being those of Panama, Liberia and the Marshall Islands. Panama has a small collection of naval vessels but Liberia has no navy at all, and the Marshall Islands' navy consists of a single

---

[10] This is still extant and reflected in a recent reassessment of the laws of war at sea. See *The San Remo Manual on International Law Applicable to Armed Conflicts at Sea* (Cambridge, 1995).

inshore patrol craft. China is the only "top ten" merchant ship registry with significant naval power. While beneficial ownership of shipping and the origins and destinations of goods shipped by sea may suggest a connection between naval power and trade, in practice there is no longer an essential link between navies and merchant shipping fleets.

Technology has transformed the exploitation of ocean resources. Enhanced fishing techniques have put fish stocks under pressure as demand has been driven up by population growth (in 1945 there were two and a half billion mouths to feed globally; today there are seven billion). The global sea-fish catch has quadrupled, from 20 to 80 million tonnes. Offshore oil and gas exploitation became feasible in the 1940s. Pressure on resources and the wealth they represent fuelled coastal-state demands for ownership and regulation of offshore resources. Previously non-appropriable sea areas became subject to sovereign claims.

Today, coastal-state jurisdiction extends to the limit of the continental shelf (over three hundred miles in some instances). The Law of the Sea was transformed through the series of UN conferences, in particular the third between 1974 and 1982. Non-appropriable *res nullius* was abandoned with respect to the continental shelf. Beyond that, the oceans changed, from *res nullius* to *res communis* – from the principle of no ownership to one of communal possession. That led to an "international community" desire to regulate maritime activity, consistent with the global trend towards the regulation of all human activity.

World seaborne trade has risen dramatically since the 1940s, but especially so in the last fifty years, over the course of which it has increased from less than ten billion tonne-miles in the late 1960s to almost forty billion tonne-miles today.[11] Bulk carriers and tankers have grown ever larger, but the greatest change has been in the carriage of general cargo, now carried mostly in containers. Introduced in the mid-1950s, these are a post-Grotian phenomenon. The largest container ship today has a capacity of almost 20,000 TEUs.[12] They can be serviced only in specialist container ports with adequate berths and approaches. If there were to be another naval war involving economic warfare, its characteristics would be markedly different from those fought in the past. Traditional visit and search and the seizure of ships and cargoes as prize long pre-dated containerisation; they will not have survived it.[13]

The oceans are not the legal vacuum they once were. Treaties are proliferating, defying the minimalist Grotian-era approach to ocean regulation. The normative framework is the 1982 UN Convention on the Law of the Sea, and a growing body of international law is emerging within it, covering issues from

---

[11] The estimation of "tonne-miles" is the recognised means of combining weight of cargo and the distance shipped.
[12] Twenty-foot Equivalent Units – or TEUs – is the standard means of expressing container capacity, with the bulk of the world's containers consisting of either 20-foot or 40-foot-long containers.
[13] While visit and search may not be feasible, capture may be, although the multi-national character of most of today's ships and cargoes renders the simple capture of enemy shipping potentially problematic.

fishing and recovery of seabed minerals to marine pollution, and from vessel safety and navigation to the suppression of maritime crime. International Maritime Organisation treaties are especially important in this respect.

Crime is increasing and is not confined to piracy. It includes the illicit trades in drugs, arms and people. Maritime terrorism has never risen to oft-predicted levels, but contingencies are needed in case it does. Maritime crime causes concerns for states, especially those with vulnerable coastal communities. Combating it requires the extension of the rule of law to the oceans, and effective policing both ashore and at sea.

An important Grotian-era principle is now creating difficulties for peacetime law enforcement on the high seas. Exclusive flag-state jurisdiction renders vessels free from interference from all but their own flag state's warships. Open registries have few, if any, warships capable of exercising jurisdiction, leaving a potential law enforcement vacuum. While there has been no serious attempt to dispense with exclusive flag-state jurisdiction, one wonders how long it can survive in the new, increasingly regulated era.

Regulations now include international human rights law, a post-Grotian phenomenon that did not exist before the 1940s. Applying in all circumstances, at sea as well as on land, it has significant influence on the conduct of constabulary operations. Three hundred years ago pirates could be hanged from their ships' yardarms after cursory legal process. Today their detention and prosecution must be compliant with human rights standards, the death penalty is not an option and, on release from prison in the jurisdiction that prosecuted them, they may seek and obtain asylum to avoid repatriation.

The seas are no longer as free as once they were. Traditional *Mare Liberum* no longer exists and demands for it to be preserved are like appeals to King Canute to stem the incoming tide. Ocean governance is going through an irresistible transition from *Mare Liberum* to something fundamentally different.

All four factors influencing the character of maritime power in the Grotian era (imperial purpose, great-power conflict, the symbiosis between naval and merchant fleets, and *Mare Liberum*) are now absent from the maritime strategic environment. Maritime power has been affected by the changes, with the roles and functions of navies differing from those of a century ago.

The Purpose of Navies and the Application of Maritime Power

Grotian-era navies were principally to do with great-power competition and imperial rivalry. They had three defining functions, each about applying force in war.

First, they had to achieve sea control in order to use the sea for their own purposes. This involved navies in combat with other navies, success depending on more, bigger and faster warships, with better armament and greater resilience, with superior commanders employing better tactics for strategic effect. Once sea control was achieved, navies could conduct economic warfare and project power from sea to shore. Economic warfare involved the interdiction of enemy trading activity. Power projection consisted of either the landing of a force, bombardment of enemy positions ashore or the provision of fire support and logistics to friendly forces already operating on land. Despite the importance attached to maintaining order at sea, the enforcement of regulations within territorial seas and the suppression of piracy on the high seas were relatively minor functions for navies in the Grotian era. Constabulary tasking was secondary to their primary war-fighting purpose.

Today, sea control remains essential but, even before the end of the Grotian era, achieving it became more difficult. Technology rendered sea denial more potent, with sea mines and submarines denying surface warships the freedom to use the sea. Potential asymmetries were introduced into naval warfare, with even the most powerful navies vulnerable to attack. Additionally, the influence of air power has made obtaining sea control even more challenging.

Power projection remains a major naval function, but there have been two profoundly significant developments in relation to the application of maritime power. First, offensive economic warfare has virtually disappeared from discussions of naval utility.[14] Second, previously secondary constabulary functions have become the principal employment for most navies globally.

The utility of navies has undergone significant change, although the consequences for force development are not entirely clear. If great-power tensions were to result in open conflict once more, economic warfare could conceivably re-emerge, albeit in a different form in response to changes in the global shipping industry. Great-power navies need to remain armed for naval war-fighting, for deterrence purposes as much as for actual combat. Nevertheless, the meaning of "maritime power" may require review, with naval force development taking account of the shift from combat to constabulary tasking.

"MARITIME POWER" AND THE HIERARCHY OF NAVIES

The mere possession of a navy never turned a state into a true maritime power. As Herbert Richmond noted, maritime power in the Grotian era was:

> that form of national strength which enables its possessor to send his armies and commerce across stretches of sea and ocean which lie between his country or the country of his allies, and to those territories to which he needs access in war; and to prevent his enemy from doing the same."[15]

---

[14] Although such as the Israeli use of blockade off Gaza, Iranian threats to the free movement of shipping through the Straits of Hormuz and occasional discussion of the possibility of major naval war involving China and the US do keep the subject alive.

[15] RICHMOND H., *Statesmen and Sea Power* (Oxford, 1974), p. ix.

Maritime power suggests the ability to project force as an instrument of coercion and to dominate an ocean or more. There have been very few navies in history capable of this. Major navies are expensive and few can afford them. During the whole of the Grotian era, only eight states became maritime powers. Initially these were Spain, the Netherlands and Britain, with France also competing for a time. Later, Britain was on its own, subsequently to be joined by the US, but with strong bids from Germany, Japan and the Soviet Union. Their navies were routinely used both aggressively and defensively, their ability to do so sitting as a backdrop to diplomacy. Grotian-era maritime powers were imperial and assertive, with the ambition to dominate.

Hardly any navies today are true instruments of maritime power. Most are essentially coastguards, their function being almost exclusively constabulary. That is not to downplay their importance; law enforcement is essential for good governance. All coastal states need constabulary forces and international society needs a collective ability to ensure the rule of law at sea. Indeed, a post-Grotian definition of maritime power must include both combat potential and a sophisticated constabulary capability – but constabulary competence alone does not suggest maritime power.

Identifying maritime powers involves placing navies in a hierarchy based on capability and reach, only the upper levels signifying "maritime power". The best hierarchy available has evolved through academic exchanges since 1987. The most recent version uses eight ranks.[16] These are now further refined, as follows:

1. *Major global force projection navies:* with a full range of naval capabilities in depth, able to operate independently across the full combat spectrum in all oceans without allied support. Capable of conducting sophisticated constabulary operations globally.
2. *Medium global force projection navies:* with a full range of naval capabilities, able to deploy independently in all oceans but benefiting from allied support when operating across the full combat spectrum. Capable of leading sophisticated constabulary operations globally.
3. *Medium regional force projection navies:* with a full range of naval capabilities, able to deploy independently across the adjacent ocean and to a limited degree beyond, but needing support from allies to operate effectively across the full combat spectrum. Capable of effective constabulary operations within their maritime domains and of contributing to wider rule-of-law operations.
4. *Adjacent force projection navies:* with most naval capabilities and able to deploy across the adjacent ocean. Can project force well offshore but only engage in the full combat spectrum as an element of a larger force. Capable of effective constabulary operations within their maritime domains and of contributing to coalition operations, but essentially within their own region.

---

[16] GROVE E., 'The Ranking of Smaller Navies Revisited', in *Small Navies: Strategy and Policy for Small Navies in War and Peace*, ed. M. MULQUEEN, D. SANDERS and I. SPELLER (Farnham, 2014), pp. 15–20.

5. *Offshore territorial defence navies:* with sufficient combat capabilities adequately to defend their offshore interests and capable of effective constabulary operations within their maritime domains. Can play a minor role in larger coalition operations within their own region.
6. *Inshore territorial defence navies:* with sufficient combat capabilities to mount an adequate coastal defence and capable of effective constabulary operations within their maritime domains.
7. *Constabulary navies:* capable of efficient constabulary operations within their maritime domains.
8. *Token navies:* with a rudimentary naval capability but no effective capacity for combat and a very limited ability to conduct constabulary operations in adjacent waters.

Navies able to project force (Ranks 1 to 4) can certainly conduct sea control/denial operations and apply appropriate levels and types of force, in either combat or constabulary terms. Nevertheless, only states with navies in Ranks 1 and 2 are maritime powers, with those at Rank 3 representing a capable supporting cast.

Navies in Ranks 4 to 7 may well be eminently suited to the purposes for which they were procured, and fully professional, efficient and effective in that sense. Without either the capability to project force over oceanic distances or the national desire to do so, however, they will not be effective instruments of influence. (Power is relative, however. A lower-ranking navy may be in a local position of superiority, able to apply considerable pressure on its neighbours.)

Maritime powers in the post-Grotian era

Fewer than ten states were maritime powers in the Grotian era. A similar number have achieved that status in the seven decades of the post-Grotian era. Caution is necessary, however, in making assumptions about maritime power today based on its character in the past. The maritime strategic environment has changed fundamentally and the principal naval function today is not what it was. The transition from the Grotian era is not yet complete, although the new characteristics of maritime power are beginning to clarify. Combat potential remains vital but a new essential feature of maritime power is the ability to conduct constabulary operations consistent with the rule of law at the global level.

Rank 1 navies

There have been three Rank 1 navies since 1945. Two have since declined, leaving just one at that level.

In 1945, British naval power and the US Navy were both at Rank 1, but the US Navy was already pre-eminent. The sheer scale of American naval power during the later stages of the Pacific campaign in 1944 and 1945 has never been matched. In terms of size, the US Navy is today smaller than during the Korean and Viet Nam wars, but it remains the ultimate war-fighting navy. This has had the unfortunate effect of leaving it culturally disinclined to accept constabulary responsibility. This would be a serious shortcoming, except that the US Coastguard (USCG) is itself one of the largest and most capable navies in the world. When the US Navy and USCG are combined, there is no doubt that US naval power is uniquely capable.

The first navy to lose Rank 1 status was the British. It is important to distinguish between "British naval power" and the Royal Navy (RN). The former means British imperial naval power and included the navies of Australia, New Zealand, South Africa, Canada and India as well as the RN itself. The disintegration of the British Empire also ended Britain's naval mastery – if the US Navy's rise had not already done so. The core of Britain's former naval power (the RN) has been in a steady but inexorable decline ever since. During the Cold War, it remained securely in Rank 2, but since then it has declined further, now barely managing to remain at that level. It will require the maintenance of its current capability and the expected regeneration of its organic air capability to secure Rank 2 status.

The other Rank 1 navy was the Soviet Union's, which rose to that level under Admiral Gorshkov's leadership from the 1950s. When the Soviet Union disintegrated in the 1990s, however, so too did the Soviet Navy. A dire lack of funding in the following two decades reduced the Russian Federation Navy to a shadow of its former Soviet self. Indeed, it may even have declined to Rank 4 because of lack of funding. It has since recovered, as the Russian economy has improved and funding has increased. If its rise continues, it will be securely at Rank 2. Funding is crucial, however, and recent drops in oil revenue coupled with Western economic sanctions threaten to undermine its status.

Rank 2 navies

By the end of the Cold War, only two navies were in Rank 2: the RN and the French Navy. Both remain at this level, notwithstanding the RN's temporary lack of organic air power. The Russian Navy is also probably now at Rank 2, although its ability to conduct effective rule-of-law operations is not clear. The same might also be said of the Chinese Navy, which is either already at Rank 2 or about to achieve it. The Indian Navy is similarly moving up from Rank 3 to Rank 2. Based on its capability, the Japanese Maritime Self Defence Force would undoubtedly be at Rank 2, but Japan's continuing reluctance to use armed forces proactively as instruments of policy undermines its status as a maritime power. As intentions can change overnight, it makes sense to regard Japan as a Rank 2 maritime power, despite its reluctance to act like one.

Rank 3 navies

States with Rank 3 navies are not "maritime powers". They do, of course, have some maritime power and not insignificant regional maritime influence, but fall just short of the degree of power and influence necessary to have global effect. Several very capable navies are at Rank 3, with the clear potential to rise beyond that level. Australia, Brazil, South Korea, Singapore, Canada, Italy, Spain and Germany are certainly at Rank 3. Less clearly so are the navies of Denmark, Norway and Sweden. An attribute these navies have is a clear ability to make substantial contributions to multi-national naval operations, including of a constabulary nature (such as that mounted in the Indian Ocean to counter Somali piracy).

CONCLUDING COMMENTS

There are today up to eight maritime powers, with one (the US) clearly pre-eminent. Significantly, all five Permanent Members of the UN Security Council – the recognised great powers with the remit to maintain international peace and security – have this status. Only one maritime power (Japan) lacks a nuclear capability. Interestingly, India (both a maritime and a nuclear power) has been regarded as a potential UN Security Council Permanent Member. Maritime power is clearly an important ingredient of great-power status.

Contemporary great powers cannot have imperial objectives as Grotian-era powers most certainly did. While we are not yet fully in the post-Grotian age, the transition to it is well advanced, with the high seas having shifted from a state of non-appropriable *res nullius* to one of *res communis*. Nevertheless, the oceans retain many of the characteristics of an anarchic space. Effective governance has not yet fully materialised. For it to do so, change needs to continue along the lines and at the rate it has done since the 1940s. Maritime power needs to be more to do with collective action to secure the oceans and maintain the rule of law at sea and less about great-power rivalry.

If this happens – and it is clearly possible – the new ocean governance will be about all coastal states ensuring the rule of law within their zones of jurisdiction, while the more capable maritime powers increasingly cooperate to maintain good order across the high seas. The maritime powers, together with the states with Rank 3 navies, could become the guarantors of global maritime security, acting for the international community to protect and secure the ocean commons. Instead of the free seas of *Mare Liberum*, the need is for seas to be well regulated. This view is not driven by idealism. Indeed, it is the notion of *Mare Liberum* that is looking increasingly idealistic and impractical. The perceived need for effective government reflects the more pragmatic approach to ensuring security for trade and responsible resource exploitation – and ultimately, to be effective, it will need to be driven by great-power interest.

BRITAIN, 1815–1850:
NAVAL POWER OR SEA POWER?

ANDREW LAMBERT is Laughton Professor of Naval History, King's College London, United Kingdom

ABSTRACT. *In the 1815 settlement Britain was able to achieve a stable Europe in which minimal naval intervention sufficed to keep the great military powers in balance, while Britain herself concentrated on rebuilding her economic strength and reducing the debts inherited from the war years. After the loss of America, British statesmen aimed for economic influence rather than direct rule of overseas territory.*

RÉSUMÉ. *Avec le traité de 1815, la Grande-Bretagne sut parvenir à l'établissement d'une Europe stable, dans laquelle une intervention navale réduite suffisait à maintenir l'équilibre entre les grandes puissances militaires. Cela lui permit de se concentrer, quant à elle, sur la reconstruction de sa force économique et sur la réduction des dettes engendrées par ces années de guerre. Suite à la perte de l'Amérique, les citoyens britanniques préférèrent s'attacher à l'influence économique plutôt qu'au contrôle direct de territoires étrangers.*

．•．

The days of England's glory have their number, and the period of her decline will at length arrive.[1]

Between 1815 and 1850 Britain was a sea power, an imperial state in which the sea dominated national security, economic development and political culture. Yet this distinctive form of power, in which communications, capital and cruisers were the key instruments, was a response to weakness and defeat. Lacking the population to operate as a major European power, chastened by the experience of the American Revolution, British statesmen chose to depend on a limited war strategy of sea control, only engaging the Continent at critical maritime locations: Flanders, Lisbon, Copenhagen and Cadiz. Sea power and insularity enabled Britain to evolve strategic concepts and cultural forms that harnessed the asymmetric advantage of sea control to outmanoeuvre far stronger

---

[1] EUSTACE J.C., *A Classical Tour through Italy* (Paris, 6th edn, 1837), pp. 6–7.

continental powers, primarily through maritime economic war.[2] Ultimately, British security depended on a peaceful, balanced and stable European system.

SUSTAINING SEA POWER CONSTRUCTING STABILITY.

Britain celebrated her role in the downfall of Bonaparte as "The Sheet Anchor of Europe", the powerful external agency that prevented the Continent from running onto the rocks of revolution or the shoals of imperial hegemony.[3] Maritime power enabled Britain to rebalance and reinforce but not dominate. After the defeat of Napoleon British statesmen, anxious to reduce peace-time defence expenditure, used the peace conferences at Paris, Ghent and Vienna to create the diplomatic context for a unique sea-power empire. They began by removing France from the Scheldt estuary, the only viable invasion base. Continued French occupation of Belgium would mean "imposing upon Great Britain the charge of a perpetual war establishment". Instead, Foreign Secretary Lord Castlereagh combined Belgium and the Dutch Republic as the Kingdom of the Netherlands.[4] This strategic barrier was upheld by Wellington's victory at Waterloo. Castlereagh defended Britain's controversial maritime belligerent rights regime, the key to economic warfare, by refusing to discuss the subject with Russia, France or the United States at Ghent or Vienna.[5] Maritime economic warfare, which had bankrupted the United States in 1814, required similar levels of sea control to the defence of British floating trade, including vital food and strategic raw material imports. Finally, the Vienna settlement blocked the hegemonic ambitions of other Great Powers. Having secured these core aims, Britain was able to open major European rivers to international commerce, but restricted its own European acquisitions to Heligoland, Malta and the Ionian Islands, emphasising the maritime insular agenda. As the undisputed maritime hegemon, Britain quietly abandoned the ceremonial requirement that ships transiting the English Channel lower their topsails to British warships as irrelevant.[6]

The Vienna process created a balanced, stable European state system which, by reducing the need for British intervention, cut defence costs and increased trade, reducing domestic taxation, while releasing British capital and commerce to exploit new markets in the former Spanish colonies and China. As Castlereagh

---

[2] The underlying assumption of CORBETT J., *Some Principles of Maritime Strategy* (London, 1911).
[3] LAMBERT A.D., *The Last Sailing Battlefleet: Maintaining Naval Mastery 1815-1850* (London, 1991), p. 6.
[4] CASTLEREAGH to Aberdeen, 13 November 1813 and CASTLEREAGH to Earl Clancarty 1 February 1814, in *Castlereagh Correspondence*, ed. MARQUESS OF LONDONDERRY, 3rd Series (London, 1850) vol. 1, pp. 73-5, 223-4.
[5] LAMBERT A.D., *The Challenge: Britain versus America in the Naval War of 1812* (London, 2012), pp. 383-401.
[6] BARTLETT C.J., *Great Britain and Sea Power 1815-1853* (Oxford, 1963).

observed, the only serious threat to Britain would come from a Franco-Russian alliance, consequently a "Two Power Standard" of naval power was adopted to reduce the risk. While sea power retained its economic bite, Belgium remained independent of France and Britain maintained a "Two Power" fleet, Pitt's fiscal-military warfare state could be dismantled, returning to the economically driven naval/mercantile policy of the late 1780s. Force levels were constantly compared with those of 1792.

Across the next 35 years Britain supported the Vienna settlement as the key to European stability, maintained naval superiority, improved global communications, extended capital exports and shipping services and opened new commercial opportunities by diplomacy, coercion and war. The creation of an independent and neutral Belgium, through the 1839 Treaty of London, enabled the strategic system of 1815 to survive the division of the Netherlands. Belgium and Lisbon often required British action, because they posed fundamental threats to insular security and oceanic commerce. However, Britain never sought, let alone acquired, the power to defeat another great power single handed. Instead it waged small wars to open new markets and protect old ones, used the threat of naval force to deter more serious threats, while attending to the fundamental issue of rebuilding the economic sinews of war and reducing the national debt. Liberal economic reforms enhanced national power; free trade made food imports cheaper, while increasing trade and the spread of British capital.

The new Carthaginians: British identity and Grand Strategy

Both the United Kingdom and British identity were shaped by the threat of Napoleon's neo-Roman "Universal Monarchy", and Napoleon's dismissive insult that the islanders were "Carthaginians" and therefore doomed to defeat.[7] The new identity helped to sustain Britain through a long, often unsuccessful war, and dominated nineteenth-century attitudes toward Europe. Napoleon's insult followed Montesquieu, who had explained British success against Louis XIV by observing that Britain was a modern Carthage, a commercial republic, combining a great navy, a political system controlled by the merchant class (which gave the state access to the economic resources needed to sustain long wars) and an empowered citizen class.[8] By 1812 British statesmen and cultural leaders, including George Canning and J.M.W. Turner, owned the insult as a badge of honour and a guide to the future of their own empire.[9]

---

[7] COLLEY L., *Britons: Forging the Nation, 1707-1837* (New Haven, 1992).
[8] RAHE P., *Montesquieu and the Logic of Liberty* (New Haven, 2009), pp. 3-61, esp. p. 59.
[9] WALSH R., ed., *Select Speeches of George Canning* (Philadelphia, 1842), pp. 483-7; EUSTACE, *A Classical Tour through Italy*, pp. 6-7; Lambert A.D., '"Now Is Come a Darker Day": Britain, Venice and the Meaning of Sea Power', in *The Victorian Empire and Britain's Maritime World, 1837-1901: The Sea and Global History*, ed. M. TAYLOR (Basingstoke, 2013), pp. 19-42.

The economy

The bases of British power were economic, rather than human or territorial. To secure stable long-term finances and low interest rates on the national debt, Britain needed a peaceful world, open to trade, connected by seas that were safe for British shipping. International trade was the basis of British power, and the security of that trade, rather than of the formal empire, provided the Navy's core mission. Trade with the empire complicated the picture, but it did not affect the fundamentals.[10] The empire was a mechanism to stabilise the international capital market for the City, not an object to be defended. In this context "Imperial Defence" takes on an entirely different meaning: much naval effort was expended securing "informal" control over developing export economies like Argentina and Brazil, and ensuring they paid interest on their loans. Although Britain led global industrialisation, manufacturing was never the primary driver of the economy.

Economic success had a domestic dimension. It undermined reform agitation, and this became a key argument for "Free Trade". Limited political reform, domestic prosperity and opportunities for emigration defused the unrest of the 1840s.[11] As Liberal Foreign Secretary between 1830 and 1851, Palmerston responded to domestic economic distress by opening new markets, notably in China. The link between expanding trade and naval power was obvious: the import duty on Chinese tea more than covered the cost of the Royal Navy in 1850. A student of Adam Smith's "political economy", Palmerston recognised that British imperialism was both complex and economically driven.[12] Furthermore, ministers understood that the only serious threat to British prosperity was a Europe war.

The connection between economic and strategic interests was shifting. After 1815 the percentage of British investment going to Europe fell as new, more profitable markets opened in the Americas. By 1850 only 50% of total capital exports went to the Continent. City interests were global; they were not restricted to formal and informal empire, and could be secured only by naval mastery, preferably achieved through arms races rather than war. Unsurprisingly, trade followed the same pattern, although the decline was less marked. As European and United States protectionism cut British markets, the rest of the world took up the slack and the British economy continued to grow strongly. European stability allowed British economic interests to prosper.

Palmerston's 1839 Treaty of London ensured that the only threat that could compel Britain to act in Europe, a dominant power occupying the Rhine/Scheldt

---

[10] CAIN P.J., 'Economics and Empire: The Metropolitan Context', in *The Oxford History of the British Empire: Vol. III The Nineteenth Century*, ed. A. PORTER (Oxford, 1999), pp. 42-50.
[11] CAIN P.J. and HOPKINS A.G., *British Imperialism: Innovation and Expansion 1688-1914* (London, 1993), pp. 125-77.
[12] WONG J.Y., *Deadly Dreams: Opium and the Arrow War (1856-1860) in China* (Cambridge, 1998), pp. 350-5, 470-8.

region, would be met by a treaty-based coalition. Elsewhere in Europe, Britain carefully retained a diplomatic "free hand", responding to events as they arose. At the same time the ideology of "Free Trade" was used to reposition the Royal Navy as a "world-policeman", curbing pirates and slavers, rather than as the cutting edge of a national strategy. This image, actively fostered by contemporary publicists, continues to confuse the unwary.

Repealing the Corn Laws, an autarkic measure designed to limit Britain's wartime dependence on imported grain, broke the Conservative Party and the bi-partisan understanding of the centrality of City finance to the economy. Appalled by the destruction of old certainties, the Tory party adopted a "Protectionist" agricultural agenda, while the Whig government of 1846-52 opened the flood gates to full-blown free trade, ending imperial tariff preferences, before sweeping away the mercantilist Navigation Laws in 1848-49, a central pillar of eighteenth-century British maritime economic power. British power was not affected.

Rebuilding the fleet, reducing the army

Defence spending, the only significant budget variable, dominated British political debate. In 1815 the House of Commons voted down Pitt's Income or War Tax, obliging Lord Liverpool's government to cut the defence estimates. In 1828 Prime Minister Wellington imposed double-entry book-keeping on the Admiralty to control spending.[13] After a decade of Whig deficit budgets and unsustainably low defence spending, Sir Robert Peel reintroduced Income Tax in 1843, stabilising government expenditure and funding significant increases in naval and fortress construction.

Despite these problems, the battle fleet was rebuilt to a "Two Power" standard by 1830. Battleships projected British identity: *Royal George* and *Britannia*, *Royal Sovereign* and *Victory*, *Nelson* and *Trafalgar*, *Neptune* and *Waterloo*, represented a unique state, while the "captured" names *Temeraire* and *President* reminded recent foes that resistance was futile. British statesmen recognised the that reserve battle fleet was the deterrent and enabled the Navy to operate as a gunboat force in peace time.[14]

After 1815 the wartime Army was rapidly reduced and dispersed to support the civil power at home and abroad. Garrisons dominated colonial budgets, accounting for 90% of the cost of governing Canada in the 1840s.[15] With the empire secured by the Navy, the Whig government of 1846-52 removed British troops from the self-governing colonies to cut costs and create an expeditionary

---

[13] LAMBERT A.D., 'Politics, administration and decision-making: Wellington and the Navy 1828-1830', in *Wellington Studies IV*, ed. C. WOOLGAR (Southampton, 2008), pp. 185-243.

[14] Canning's speech 28 October 1823 in *The Foreign Policy of Canning: 1822-1827*, ed. H. TEMPERLEY (London, 1925), pp. 119-20.

[15] STACEY C.P., *Canada and the British Army 1846-1871* (Toronto, 1963), p. 59.

capability at Aldershot. In 1854 this force deployed, with a French army, to destroy the Russian naval base at Sevastopol.[16]

EMPIRE AND COMMUNICATIONS

The British synergy of men, politics, ideas and money generated a unique world view, one in which the Navy and the merchant marine connected an interdependent constellation of ports and hinterlands. Britain relied on making money through trade and capital investment, using naval power and sea control to defend interests and, if necessary, defeat enemies. British statesmen consistently opposed the economic burden of adding new territory to the empire, with the exception of India. The French occupation of Tahiti was not opposed, but Britain did acquire a series of strategic offshore islands and port towns from the Falkland Islands and Aden to Karachi and Hong Kong, extending the chain of defended harbours and communication nodes through which British commerce flowed. Extensive overseas capital investments added "invisible" earnings, while the movement of goods and raw materials sustained expanding shipping, investment, insurance and shipbuilding industries.

Obliged to respond to unexpected events across the globe with limited resources, Britain was uniquely dependent on information dominance and strategic mobility. In the late 1830s the government subsidised the latest communication system, the oceanic steam ship, through mail contracts.[17] These contracts secured information dominance, for war, diplomacy and commerce, and drove globalization, enabling high-risk commercial projects using cutting-edge technology to be capitalised by the City of London. Improved communications were the key to the effective use of British power.

Subsidised mail steamship services were a classic British response to political, economic and, above all, strategic problems; the model would be applied to submarine telegraph cables and wireless. It sustained British communication dominance into the age of steam and guided naval commanders on distant stations. The steamship enabled Britain to control the periphery from the centre, to move forces from the centre or other parts of the periphery, and to control commercial information flows. The process was synergistic and self-reinforcing. The steamship companies depended on government subsidies, but the government relied on them to sustain the empire across vast ocean spaces, as symbols of prestige and vital reinforcements in a maritime war.[18]

---

[16] LAMBERT A.D., *The Crimean War: British Grand Strategy against Russia 1853-1856* (Aldershot, 2011).
[17] ROBINSON H., *Carrying British Mails Overseas* (London, 1964).
[18] PALMER S., 'Afterword', in *Flagships of Imperialism: The P&O Company and the Politics of Empire from its origins to 1867*, ed. F. HARCOURT (Manchester, 2006), p. 229.

War

Although British governments had no plans to begin a major war, being content with the *status quo* in Europe and North America, they recognised that war might be imposed upon them – by French ambition, Russian aggression or an American "Manifest Destiny". These threats had shaped the diplomatic strategy of 1814–15, which tried to reduce threats and sustain the strategic impact of Britain's limited maritime approach to conflict. British war plans remained essentially unchanged after 1815: build coalitions to resist dominant powers, defend the home islands, floating trade and colonies. These measures were linked to rigorous economic blockade, overseas expeditions and, if possible, the destruction of hostile ships and bases by coastal offensives or amphibious power. Questions were raised about the impact of technology, economic interdependence and international law, but the only major conflict of the century after Waterloo, the Crimean War of 1854–56, was waged as a limited reprise of the Napoleonic conflict – tempered by the absence of any threat to Britain or her empire. That said, the war followed a major failure of British policy. It is probable British aims could have been secured by diplomacy backed, if necessary, by a deterrent naval mobilisation. The failure to deter occurred at the political level. Service leaders and statesmen knew what to do, but on this occasion the statesmen, paralysed by a coalition government more focused on French bluster than Russian action, allowed the country to drift into war.

Deterrence

The standard signal of British determination had long been the public order for a large-scale naval mobilisation, expressly linked to a specific diplomatic issue. The language of sea power could not be misunderstood. It reminded potentially hostile states that they could not hope to defeat Britain, however successful they might be on land, and would suffer long-term economic damage, the loss of outlying territory and possibly attacks by other continental powers. After 1815 the long-term threat of sea power was given sharper focus by the development of a dynamic coastal offensive capability – designed to render sea control more complete by destroying enemy resources in harbour.

The primary focus of the new strategy would be the French naval base at Cherbourg, begun by Louis XVI, resumed by Napoleon and brought to fruition by successive post-war regimes. Cherbourg demanded attention as an invasion base and, more significantly, a station for cruisers raiding British commerce in the Western Approaches. Although historians have viewed the response through a military paradigm of a steam-powered invasion,[19] British planners were primarily

---

[19] PARTRIDGE M.S., *Military Planning for the Defence of the United Kingdom 1814-1870* (London, 1989) reflects contemporary army literature, rather than strategic reality, while STRACHAN H.,

concerned by the threat to oceanic commerce.[20] The Admiralty responded by developing the highly aggressive "attack at source" doctrine of the post-Trafalgar period, using naval and amphibious assaults to reinforce battle-fleet sea control and economic blockade. When Anglo-French relations deteriorated in the 1840s Cherbourg became the focal point for strategic solutions, including enhanced cruiser strength, new forward bases, specialist bombardment forces and the Corps of Royal Engineers, specially trained to capture and destroy hostile naval bases.[21] The need to forestall French steam operations prompted the shift of wartime manpower mobilisation from impressment to continuous service.[22] Coastal operations dominated nineteenth-century naval warfare, driving hydrographic survey work and fundamental research on tides.[23] The synergy between national scientific activity and sea power, established in the 17th century, was reinforced and refined as naval expeditions took science to the furthest reaches of the globe.[24]

Nor was invasion taken seriously; Lord Melville had warned of the danger of steam-powered raids on exposed dockyards in 1824, but dismissed invasions from practical consideration.[25] In the 1840s Palmerston said steam had "bridged the Channel", and Wellington claimed that Britain was largely defenceless if the Royal Navy could not defend it. Prime Minister Sir Robert Peel responded to these alarmist texts with a Commission to consider "Harbours of Refuge", both to shelter merchant ships from bad weather and to facilitate attack and defence in war. Four of the six sites were chosen to blockade Cherbourg and funded "as deep water harbours for steamers ... for the purpose of guarding the Channel".[26] The defence of floating trade was paramount.[27]

New harbours at Alderney, twenty-five miles from Cherbourg, and Portland, the nearest point on the mainland, only sixty miles from the French base, enabled

---

Wellington's Legacy: The Reform of the British Army 1830-1854 (Manchester, 1985) and From Waterloo to Balaclava: Tactics, Technology, and the British Army, 1815-1854 (Cambridge, 1985) underplays the primacy of naval defence.

[20] BARROW J., An Autobiographical Memoir of Sir John Barrow (London, 1847), pp. 363-4.
[21] CRICK T., Ramparts of Empire: The Fortifications of Sir William Jervois Royal Engineer, 1821-1897 (Exeter, 2012) and KENDALL P., The Royal Engineers at Chatham 1750-2012 (English Heritage, 2013).
[22] BEELER J.F., 'Ploughshares into Swords: The Royal Navy and Merchant Marine Auxiliaries in the late 19th Century', in The Merchant Marine in International Affairs, ed. G. KENNEDY (London, 2000), pp. 5-18.
[23] REIDY M.S., Tides of History: Ocean Science and Her Majesty's Navy (Chicago, 2008) and DAY A., The Admiralty Hydrographic Service 1795-1919 (London, 1967) for tidal research and survey work.
[24] LAMBERT A.D., Franklin: Tragic Hero of Polar Navigation (London, 2009) for magnetic science and navigational research.
[25] LORD MELVILLE to Wellington 3 July 1824, British Library Add.MSS 38,291, ff. 36-7.
[26] SIR CHARLES WOOD to Lord John Russell (Prime Minister) 21 March 1847, UK National Archives, PRO 30/22/6B.
[27] JAMIESON A.G., A People of the Sea: A Maritime History of the Channel Islands (London, 1986), p. 235.

the Royal Navy to control the Western Channel in the steam age.[28] Wellington applauded, observing that Alderney would "separate St Malo, Brest and the southern ports from Cherbourg. This would insulate, castrate, Cherbourg, which for anything of a large operation would be worth nothing without St Malo and Brest." As any French ships trying to enter the Channel would have to pass north of Alderney, bringing them into contact with British forces, "the safety of the country in case of a French war depends on these islands".[29] After 1843 increased taxes enabled British policy makers to counter the challenge posed by steam warships at Cherbourg and maintain naval dominance.

The threat had been diplomatic rather than strategic. After the Syrian Crisis of 1840 a forty-four-million franc extraordinary credit funded extra work at Cherbourg.[30] While some French commentators hoped paddle steam warships and shell-firing guns would undermine British sea control, command of the sea still required a battle fleet, and Britain consistently out-built France in steam warships and sailing battleships.[31] In reality, French security concerns were dominated by the German armies, not British warships.[32]

In 1847-48 the invasion bubble burst. The entire French steam marine, about one hundred small vessels, could not lift thirty thousand men with guns and horses: twenty British war steamers could destroy any such force. The primary threat, cruisers attacking floating commerce, could be stopped by blockading Cherbourg.[33] By 1850 a superior steam fleet and new bases meant the Royal Navy could maintain an effective blockade, secure commerce and prepare for an assault.[34] British countermeasures had obliged France to shift defence spending from ships to forts. With floating commerce and the British Isles secure France, lost her ability to deflect British policy. An invasion of Belgium, which would be met by German as well as British bayonets, was unlikely, because France remained a continental state, anxiously watching her German neighbours. British coastal offensive power could be used against any power, and although no great power would be mortally damaged by the loss of a naval base or a fleet, Russia and America constructed massive coastal fortresses. Unable to invade

---

[28] CARTER G.H., 'The Rise and Fall of Portland Naval Base, 1845-1995' (PhD thesis, University of Exeter, 1998); D. EVANS *Building the Steam Navy: Dockyards, Technology and the Creation of the Victorian Battle Fleet, 1830-1906* (London, 2004).

[29] Notes by JAMES WALKER (Engineer of the Alderney Breakwater) on a conversation with Wellington 27 August 1847, Northumberland MSS E/4/482; WELLINGTON to Sir John Burgoyne 9 January 1847, in W. BOWLES *Pamphlets on Naval Subjects* (London, 1854), p. 198.

[30] THIN E., *Cherbourg Bastion Maritime du Cotentin* (Condé-sur-Noireau, 1990), pp. 157-8; *Pierres de Mer: Le Patrimoine Immobilier de la Marine Nationale* (Paris 1996), p. 25.

[31] ROBERTS S., 'The Introduction of Steam Technology into the French Navy 1818-1852.' (PhD thesis, University of Chicago, 1976).

[32] COX G.P., *The Halt in the Mud: French Strategic Planning from Waterloo to Sedan* (Oxford, 1994), pp. 28, 45, 82, 100, 129 and Ch.8; HAMILTON C.I., *Anglo-French Naval Rivalry 1840-1870* (Oxford, 1993), pp. 30, 119. 127.

[33] LAMBERT, *Last Sailing Battlefleet*, pp. 53-4.

[34] VICE ADMIRAL SIR JAMES W.D. DUNDAS to Henry Drummond nd. (early 1852), Drummond of Allbury MSS, Alnwick Castle, C4 f.1.

Britain or contest command of the sea, they could only fortify themselves in case their actions in Canada, Cuba, Ottoman Turkey or Afghanistan prompted a British response.

INSTRUMENTS

The new technologies of iron and steam that fascinated Turner in the 1820s enabled Britain to sustain her global power. By 1850 British commercial shipping was moving into iron-hulled, screw-propelled steamships, prompted by I.K. Brunel's epochal SS *Great Britain* of 1845. Neither the United States nor France possessed the industrial capacity, investment capital or national commitment to follow the British lead. France, America and Russia all had far more pressing issues to resolve on land. By 1850 the Royal Navy had comprehensively out-built rival fleets in steam warships.[35] In addition, a new propulsion system, the screw propeller, enabled British warships to mount full broadside armaments and cruise for long periods under sail, without foregoing tactical steam power.[36] This changed the strategic balance in the Channel. By 1850 work had begun on a screw-propelled battle fleet to ensure insular security, global commerce and international influence. The full application of iron technology to naval forces, adding iron armour and rifled artillery, took another decade.

CONCLUSION

Secured by the Navy, Britain depended on the commercial and industrial sectors to address the massive debt burden generated by the Revolutionary and Napoleonic Wars and preserve domestic stability through rising prosperity. In 1814–15 Britain used the peace process to improve long-term security, reduce the risk of a hegemonic European state, remove France from Northern Flanders and ensure that British economic warfare strategy remained unrestricted. In exchange Britain carefully avoided European entanglements, while adding to the national portfolio of offshore insular bases. Malta, the Ionian Islands and Heligoland, together with the Cape and Mauritius, emphasised the global economic dimension of policy. These choices enabled Britain to operate as a dynamic global maritime empire on very low levels of defence spending. While the maintenance of the Vienna system dominated post-1815 British diplomacy, economic expansion determined the direction of British policy. Consequently, new strategic hubs were acquired in the Falkland Islands, Aden, Karachi, Fernando Po, Hong Kong and Sydney, while existing bases were upgraded, both

---

[35] ROBERTS, 'The Introduction of Steam Technology', pp. 314–15.
[36] LAMBERT A.D., 'Responding to the Nineteenth Century: The Royal Navy and the Introduction of the Screw Propeller', *History of Technology* 21 (2000), 1–28.

at home and abroad, notably at Bermuda, the key to an Anglo-American conflict. The ability to threaten major naval and commercial ports enabled Britain to signal intent, as the leading edge of a limited strategy of economic warfare, capable of outlasting, if not overpowering, most rivals. However, Britain had no ambitions which required war with any other major power, and worked actively for the maintenance of peace in Europe and North America. While the conflicts of 1793 to 1815 remained the worst-case scenario for defence planning, peace enabled Britain to prosper and pursue a dynamic policy outside Europe, opening markets in Latin and South America, Asia and Africa. Petty tyrants, pirates and slave traders were effectively overawed by naval patrols or subdued by force.[37] However, Britain, a small, relatively weak state, could not control the world, and never essayed a "Pax Britannica".

Like Athens, Carthage, Venice and the Dutch Republic, Britain had evolved into a sea state, largely free from the costly toils of European politics, which owned its oceanic identity with pride. Past precedents prompted deeper reflections. While most Britons revelled in the millennial bombast of the Great Exhibition of 1851, John Ruskin raised a very different vision, one that placed his country in a mental world shaped by the Bible, sea power and the circular rhythm of history.

> Since first the dominion of men was asserted over the ocean, three thrones, of mark beyond all others, have been set upon its sands: the thrones of Tyre, Venice, and England. Of the First of these great powers only the memory remains; of the Second the ruin; the Third which inherits their greatness, if it forget their example, may be led through prouder eminence to less pitied destruction.[38]

---

[37] BETHELL L., *The Abolition of the Brazilian Slave Trade: Britain, Brazil and the Slave Trade Question 1807-1869* (Cambridge, 1970) esp. pp. 257-307.
[38] RUSKIN J., *The Stones of Venice: The Foundations* (London, 1851), p. 1.

FREE TRADE, INDUSTRIALIZATION AND THE GLOBAL ECONOMY, 1815–1914

KEVIN HJORTSHØJ O'ROURKE is Chichele Professor of Economic History at the University of Oxford, and a Fellow of All Souls College, Oxford, United Kingdom

ABSTRACT. *The nineteenth-century industrialization of some countries but not others, and the spread of free trade, opened up a world of massive trade flows, with manufactured goods exchanged for food and raw materials. Steamships and railways rapidly forced down transport costs. Urban consumers benefited from cheaper food, but European landowners suffered, and in France and Germany were able to re-impose tariffs to force up food prices.*

RÉSUMÉ. *Au XIX*ᵉ *siècle, l'industrialisation de certains pays au contraire d'autres, et la propagation du libre-échange ouvrirent les portes d'un monde aux mouvements commerciaux massifs, grâce auxquels produits manufacturés, matières premières et nourriture purent s'échanger. Le développement du chemin de fer et des navires à vapeur fit rapidement chuter les coûts de transport. Les consommateurs urbains bénéficièrent d'une nourriture moins chère mais les propriétaires terriens européens en souffrirent, si bien que la France et l'Allemagne parvinrent à réimposer des droits de douane entraînant une hausse des prix alimentaires.*

. • .

For economic historians, the period between 1815 and 1914 (for the sake of brevity "the 19th century"), is defined above all by the consequences of the first Industrial Revolution. This ultimately led to more and more countries enjoying rising living standards, even as population grew at unprecedented rates. The process of industrialization was uneven, however. It began in Britain, and quickly spread to Northwest Europe and North America. By the end of the 19th century there were clear signs of modern industrialization in countries all around the world.[1] But the delayed diffusion of modern industry meant that an enormous gap in living standards opened up: a "Great Divergence" that is only now being slowly unwound.[2]

This Great Divergence implied that the world became increasingly asymmetric,

---

[1] BÉNÉTRIX A.S., O'ROURKE K.H. and WILLIAMSON J.G., 'The spread of manufacturing to the poor periphery 1870–2007', in *Open Economies Review* (2014), 1–37.

[2] POMERANZ K., *The Great Divergence: China, Europe, and the Making of the Modern World Economy* (Princeton, 2000).

divided between an industrializing "core" and an as yet non-industrial (or even de-industrializing) "periphery". This opened up the possibility of large-scale trade, with the core exchanging manufactured goods for the food and raw materials produced by the periphery. Since the core and the periphery were located in different continents, trans-oceanic trade would necessarily be at the heart of such a development, which required lower trade costs. And trade costs did eventually fall, massively, as a result of two consequences of the Industrial Revolution.

The first was technological: steamships, railroads and the telegraph combined to lower transport costs across the oceans of the world, and to make the oceans more accessible from continental interiors. The second was geopolitical: the Great Divergence in incomes and technological prowess inevitably produced an equally lop-sided international system, which was dominated both militarily and politically by the industrial core. By and large, Europeans and Americans used the power thus acquired to impose the benefits of free trade upon the rest of the world (although it should be said that nineteenth-century Americans were not nearly so keen to embrace free trade themselves).

The combination of rapidly falling trade costs and geographically uneven industrialization led to a radical shift in the international division of labour in the 19th century. To a greater and greater extent, the industrial core, particularly in Northwest Europe, exported manufactured goods in exchange for primary products produced in the poor periphery and the land-abundant "regions of recent settlement". This "Great Specialization"[3] had implications in many domains. It allowed countries like Britain to become far more industrial than they could ever have been in a more autarkic world. As the pioneer economist David Ricardo pointed out, this was a source of immense benefit to Britain, since it allowed her to specialize in those sectors of the economy where productivity had advanced the most. By exporting manufactures, Britain could obtain primary products from other continents, via trans-oceanic trade, far more cheaply than she could ever have done by producing them at home. According to Ricardian theory, primary producers should also have gained by specializing in those goods in which they had a comparative advantage. Even in the 19th century, however, there were those who argued that primary producers would lose in the long run by not industrializing. The argument makes sense *if* industry promoted growth in ways that other sectors of the economy, such as agriculture and mining, did not. Thus were set some of the key battle lines in twentieth-century debates about trade and development. It was only towards the very end of the late 20th century that "southern" economies began to export increasing quantities of manufactured goods to the "north", a trend that is set to continue into the 21st century.

Mass trans-oceanic trade was one of the major features of nineteenth-century globalization, which was different from anything that had gone before, and it had major effects both on national economies and individual people. The Voyages of

---

[3] ROBERTSON D.H., 'The future of international trade', *Economic Journal* 48.189 (1938), 1–14.

Discovery had in principle made vast amounts of land available for Europeans to exploit; according to one well-known estimate they increased the European endowment of land per capita by a factor of six.[4] The potential implications for European living standards were obvious, but in order for this potential to be realized, the oceans of the world had to shrink, economically speaking. This happened in spectacular fashion during the 19th century as the full economic implications of Christopher Columbus were, finally, realized.

NINETEENTH-CENTURY GLOBALIZATION WAS DIFFERENT

Long-distance trade is an ancient activity, and the answer to the question "When did globalization begin?" depends entirely on how you define the term "globalization". A possible date is 1571, since with the foundation of Manila in that year America and Asia started directly trading with each other.[5] Others have dated the origins of globalization far earlier.[6] It is certainly safe to say that the globalization of the 19th century was, quantitatively speaking, at least one order of magnitude more advanced than previous globalizations; and that it was qualitatively different as well.

A good indication that international markets are becoming better integrated is when prices in exporting and importing regions are pulled closer together, reflecting declining trade costs. Figure 1 shows the price of cloves and pepper in Amsterdam as a multiple of the purchase price of these spices in Southeast Asia. Pepper prices were generally between three and six times higher in Amsterdam than in Southeast Asia between the late 16th and early 19th centuries, while clove prices were more than thirteen times higher in Amsterdam for most of the period. These price gaps fell very sharply in the 19th century, to less than 100 per cent in the case of cloves, and in the case of pepper to 113 per cent by the 1880s.

Figure 2 plots Anglo-American wheat price gaps for the 19th and 20th centuries, as well as the quantity of wheat shipped between the two countries. As can be seen, the wheat price gap fluctuated sharply around an average of around 100 per cent until 1840 or so, when it commenced a sharp decline that saw these price gaps being almost eliminated by the early 20th century. This decline in price gaps was matched by a huge increase in American wheat exports. The timing coincides with the growing importance of steamships on the trans-Atlantic

---

[4] JONES E.L., *The European Miracle: Environments, Economies, and Geopolitics in the History of Europe and Asia* (Cambridge, 1981), p. 82.
[5] FLYNN D.O. and GIRÁLDEZ A., 'Born with a "silver spoon": the origin of world trade in 1571', *Journal of World History* 6.2 (1995), 201-21.
[6] ABU-LUGHOD J.L., *Before European Hegemony: The World System A.D. 1250-1350* (New York and Oxford, 1989); FRANK A.G. and GILLS B.K., *The World System: Five Hundred Years or Five Thousand?* (London, 1993).

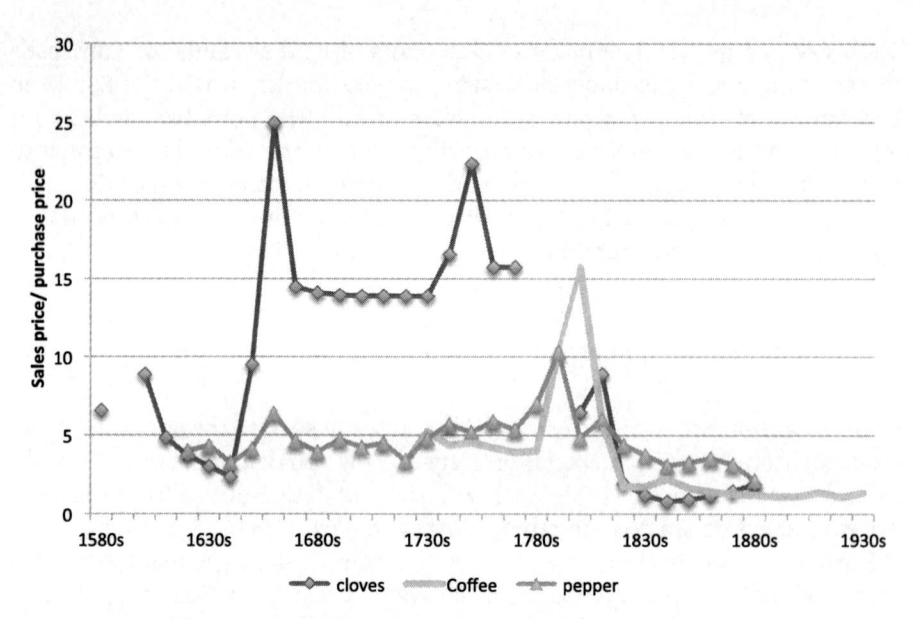

Fig. 1. *Price gaps (Amsterdam-Southeast Asia, 1585-1935) (O'ROURKE K.H. and WILLIAMSON J.G., 'When did globalisation begin?', European Review of Economic History, 6.1 (2002), 23-50)*

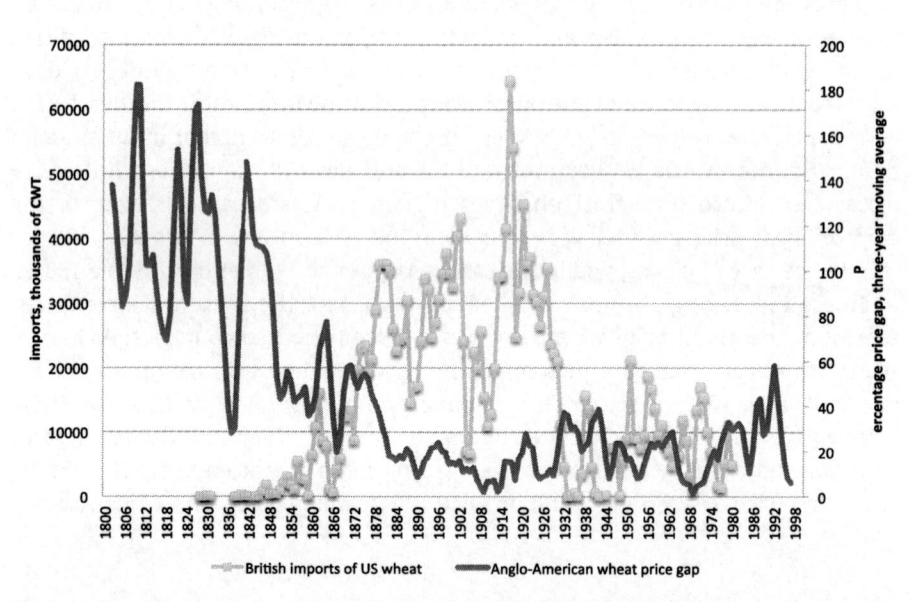

Fig. 2. *The Anglo-American wheat trade, 1800-2000 (O'ROURKE K.H. and WILLIAMSON J.G., 'From Malthus to Ohlin: trade, industrialisation and distribution since 1500', Journal of Economic Growth, 10.1 (2005), 5-34)*

route, and with the many technological improvements that successively lowered freight rates over the remainder of the 19th century.[7]

However, the steamship revolution – and the associated railway revolution which played just as important a role, by linking the interiors of continents to coastal ports – were not the only factors dramatically increasing the integration of markets in different continents over the course of the 19th century. They built on a long period of slow and steady improvements in shipping technology, associated for example with the introduction of copper sheathing.[8] Furthermore, the establishment of British naval supremacy meant an end to constant mercantilist wars, which had regularly impeded international trade, and permitted a switch to smaller, less heavily armed and more economical ships.[9] The century between Waterloo and the Great War was unusually peaceful by European standards, and created conditions within which the new transport technologies of the Industrial Revolution could have their full impact. It helped that the dominant nineteenth-century power had a vital strategic interest in maintaining open international markets, and that the *pax Britannica* was one in which the dominant naval force helped to maintain free trading conditions generally. Britain gradually liberalized its trade policies from the 1820s onwards, and in 1846 moved to a unilateral free trade policy; several other European countries followed suit, especially during the 1860s and early 1870s.

Geopolitics, domestic politics and technological change thus all had a role in shrinking the oceans of the world during the 19th century. To be sure, Figure 2 exaggerates the novelty of the nineteenth-century experience, since the data series plotted there begin during the French and Napoleonic Wars, when international trade was severely disrupted.[10] Grain was exported from North America to Britain during the 1700s,[11] and there is evidence that wheat prices in London and Philadelphia were correlated with each other during that century.[12] However, it does not take a lot of direct trade to produce price correlations – British imports in years of particular scarcity could do the trick, as could trade with a third market. The volume of grain traded across the Atlantic in the 18th century was tiny by nineteenth-century standards. And the market integration

[7] HARLEY C.K., 'Ocean freight rates and productivity, 1740-1913 – the primacy of mechanical invention reaffirmed', *Journal of Economic History* 48.4 (1988), 851-76; O'ROURKE K.H. and WILLIAMSON J.G., *Globalization and History: The Evolution of a Nineteenth-Century Atlantic Economy* (Cambridge, MA, 1999).
[8] SOLAR P.M., 'Opening to the East: shipping between Europe and Asia, 1770-1830', *Journal of Economic History* 73.3 (2013), 625-61.
[9] Ibid. The late 18th and early 19th centuries also saw the end of the great mercantilist trade monopolies.
[10] O'ROURKE K.H., 'The worldwide economic impact of the French Revolutionary and Napoleonic Wars, 1793-1815', *Journal of Global History* 1.1 (2006), 123-49.
[11] SHARP P. and WEISDORF J., 'Globalization revisited: market integration and the wheat trade between North America and Britain from the eighteenth century', *Explorations in Economic History* 50.1 (2013), 88-98.
[12] ALLEN R.C., *Global Economic History: A Very Short Introduction* (Oxford and New York, 2011), pp. 68-9.

of the 18th century, such as it was, was not sufficient to produce the collapse in grain prices that Europe experienced in the late 19th century.

The volume of international trade increased dramatically during the 19th century, both in absolute terms and relative to the size of the world economy as a whole. Between 1500 and 1800, intercontinental trade probably grew at an average rate of slightly more than 1 per cent per annum: a respectable performance in a world where overall economic growth rates were perhaps of the order of 0.1 to 0.2 per cent per annum. After 1815, average annual growth of international trade jumped to around 3.7 per cent per annum, an unprecedented rate. Indeed, trade grew at about this speed during both 1815-1913 and 1913-1992, which is striking, since the growth rate of the overall world economy was roughly twice as high in the latter period as in the former. It follows that trade growth as a share of GDP was much more rapid in the 19th century than in the 20th (although the pace of globalization has clearly accelerated in dramatic fashion since the 1990s).[13] According to one estimate, while merchandise exports accounted for just 1 per cent of world GDP in 1820, they accounted for roughly 8 per cent in 1913.[14]

The globalization of the 19th century was something quite different from what had gone before. It led to large-scale trans-oceanic trade in bulky, low-value commodities produced in different continents with very different relative endowments of land and labour. Peasants in land-abundant regions of the world, such as the American mid-west, the Argentinian pampas, the Punjab, Burma, Russia or Australia were now in direct competition with farmers in comparatively land-scarce regions such as Western Europe or Japan. This would have major economic and political implications.

GLOBALIZATION AND INCOME DISTRIBUTION

Between 1870 and 1913, land rents in Britain fell by slightly more than 50 per cent in real terms (i.e. corrected for the cost of living), while the real wages of unskilled urban labourers rose by more than 40 per cent.[15] The net effect was a big shift in the distribution of British income, away from landowners who tended to be near the top of the income distribution, towards unskilled workers who tended to be near the bottom. In sharp contrast, while real wages in the United States rose by a similar amount over the same period, land rents rose there by over 250 per cent in real terms. Thus, while the ratio of wages to land rents rose

---

[13] O'ROURKE K.H. and WILLIAMSON J.G., 'After Columbus: explaining Europe's overseas trade boom, 1500-1800', *Journal of Economic History* 62.2 (2002), 418-22.

[14] MADDISON A., *Monitoring the World Economy 1820-1992* (Paris, 1995), p. 38; MADDISON, A., *The World Economy: A Millennial Perspective* (Paris, 2001), p. 127.

[15] O'ROURKE K.H. and WILLIAMSON J.G., 'Erratum: late nineteenth-century Anglo-American factor-price convergence: were Heckscher and Ohlin right?', *Journal of Economic History* 55.4 (1995), 921-2.

sharply in Britain (by more than 200 per cent), it fell sharply in the United States, by more than 50 per cent.[16] While Britain was becoming a more equal society, along this dimension, over the course of the late 19th century, the United States was becoming less so.

This sharp distinction between British and American distributional trends during the late 19th century is not an Anglo-American anomaly, but part of a much broader pattern. Within Europe, the ratio of wages to land rents more than doubled in Denmark and Sweden between the early 1870s and World War I; it rose by roughly 50 per cent in France and Spain; and it rose by roughly a fifth in Germany. Meanwhile, the same ratio *fell* in Australia by more than 75 per cent. In Europe, late-nineteenth-century workers were gaining relative to landowners, and it seems as though the size of this gain was higher in countries such as Britain and Denmark that maintained relatively open trading policies than in countries such as France or Germany that erected tariff barriers.[17]

There were similar contrasts between countries outside Europe and North America. The ratio of wages to land rents rose sharply in Japan, Korea and Taiwan during the late 19th century – for example, it rose by about a third in Japan between the late 1880s and World War I. On the other hand, the wage-rental ratio *fell* very sharply in Argentina, Uruguay, Burma, Siam, Egypt and the Punjab during the same period.

What, if anything, did late-nineteenth-century Western Europe have in common with Japan and its colonies during this period? And what, if anything, did Australia and the United States have in common with such apparently distinct countries as Burma, Thailand, Egypt or Argentina? The answer was provided by two Swedish economists, Eli Heckscher and Bertil Ohlin, writing in the early 20th century, who came to believe that these differing distributional trends in different parts of the world were the product of the globalization of the late 19th century; and that the key difference between those regions such as Europe, where wages were rising relative to land rents during this period, and those regions such as the New World, where they were falling, had to do with these regions' endowments of land relative to labour.

In Western Europe or Japan, population pressed hard against a land endowment that was relatively limited. Wages in these economies were relatively low and land was expensive; food was expensive too. What the shipping revolution of the late 19th century did was to bring these parts of the world much closer to the land-abundant regions of the New World and elsewhere, economically speaking. In the frontier societies of the late 19th century, workers were relatively scarce and expensive, and land was abundant and relatively cheap; food was cheap too. And thus the scene was set for the massive trade flows alluded to earlier, in which regions like Europe exported their labour, embodied in manufactured

---

[16] *Ibid.*
[17] WILLIAMSON J.G., 'Land, labor, and globalization in the third world, 1870–1940', *Journal of Economic History* 62 (2002), 55–85.

goods, in return for imports of New World land, embodied in food and agricultural raw materials such as cotton.

As we have seen, those trade flows set in motion a process of convergence, whereby agricultural prices in land-scarce regions like Europe fell to something close to the levels prevailing in countries like the United States. And what was true for agricultural prices was also true for the prices of manufactured goods, although here it was relatively expensive New World manufactured goods whose prices gradually fell closer to European levels, as local manufacturers found themselves exposed to British and German competition.[18] The insight of Heckscher and Ohlin was that as prices of wheat and iron bars converged between continents, thanks to improvements in maritime technology, so the prices of the land and labour embodied in those goods would also tend to converge, other things being equal. Low European wages would tend to converge on high frontier wages; low frontier-land rents would tend to converge on expensive European rents. To a remarkable extent, given that this period saw so many other economic and political changes that influenced income distribution, this is what seems to have happened. According to one calculation, if in 1870 ocean freight rates and other transport costs had instantly fallen to their 1913 levels, *and nothing else had changed*, this one shock to the international economic system would, on its own, have sufficed to bring about a reduction in British land rents of more than 50 per cent, and an increase in British real wages of more than 20 per cent. While landlords saw their rental incomes fall sharply as a result of an invasion of cheap New World grain, workers benefited from cheap food and the extra employment opportunities which the growing division of labour afforded.[19]

We earlier encountered the estimate that the Voyages of Discovery increased the land endowment available to Europeans by a factor of six. It should be obvious that if the land endowment within Europe had miraculously increased six-fold, this would lead to cheaper land and better-off workers. In effect this happened indirectly during the 19th century, as ocean transport brought Europe and her "ghost acres" sufficiently close together in economic terms.

It is hardly surprising that contemporaries noticed these distributional trends, and that they made the connection with globalization, even though it had not yet been theorized by Heckscher and Ohlin. Nor is it surprising that globalization's losers (in this instance, European landowners) tried to stem the tide, by substituting "artificial oceans" for the real thing.[20] It is to this political backlash against globalization that I now turn.

---

[18] O'ROURKE K.H. and WILLIAMSON J.G., 'Late nineteenth-century Anglo-American factor-price convergence: were Heckscher and Ohlin right?', *Journal of Economic History* 54.4 (1994), 892-916.
[19] O'ROURKE and WILLIAMSON, 'Erratum'.
[20] BAIROCH P., 'European Trade Policy, 1815-1914', in *The Cambridge Economic History of Europe from the Decline of the Roman Empire*, ed. P. MATHIAS and S. POLLARD (Cambridge, 1989), pp. 55-8.

GLOBALIZATION AND DOMESTIC POLITICS

Between Waterloo and the mid-1870s, European trade policy moved steadily in a more liberal direction, slowly at first and then more rapidly. Britain had adopted what virtually amounted to unilateral free trade in 1846, and a plethora of bilateral trade treaties after 1860 lowered tariffs and institutionalized the principle of non-discrimination in trade policy. By 1877, "Germany had virtually become a free trade country", according to Paul Bairoch.[21]

The backlash against free trade began soon after, as cheaper trans-oceanic transport led to cheaper food and lower agricultural rents: in this sense, globalization undermined itself. In 1879, Bismarck imposed tariffs on both agricultural and manufactured imports. The policy reflected what is often referred to as a marriage of iron and rye, the powerful protectionist coalition of large landowners and heavy industry. Other countries soon followed suit: France and Sweden introduced tariffs in the 1880s, while traditionally liberal Italy, which had already introduced modest tariffs as early as 1878, raised them again in 1887, in the process sparking a trade war with France.[22] Notable exceptions to the protectionist trend within Europe include the United Kingdom and Denmark. Britain's exceptionalism can perhaps be explained by the fact that, by the 1870s, its agriculture accounted for only a small share of output and employment, a legacy of the country's precocious industrialization. It was easier for a country where agriculture employed less than a quarter of the labour force to cope with a further downturn in the sector than for a country such as France, where a half of all employment was still in farming.[23] As for Denmark, its farmers did extremely well during the late 19th century, importing grains and feedstuffs and exporting processed animal products to Britain: no need for protection there.[24]

It is perhaps not surprising that constituencies whose interests were damaged by free trade lobbied for protection, and that where they were sufficiently powerful they were successful. More interestingly, the distributional effects of trans-oceanic trade were important in shaping political cleavages, and political coalitions, in many countries throughout this period.[25] In Europe, as we have seen, landowners tended to be protectionist, while workers, who benefited from free trade, supported it. European socialists were thus generally in favour of free trade, while conservatives were protectionist. As for capitalists and the liberals who represented them, it depended on whether the country in question was advanced and abundant in capital, or relatively backward and capital scarce. In

---

[21] Ibid., p. 41.
[22] BAIROCH, 'European trade policy', provides a good discussion of the trade politics of the period.
[23] Neither this argument nor those that follow seek to deny the independent role of ideology in the British case.
[24] O'ROURKE K.H., 'The European grain invasion, 1870-1913', *Journal of Economic History* 57.4 (1997), 775-801.
[25] ROGOWSKI R., *Commerce and Coalitions: How Trade Affects Domestic Political Alignments* (Princeton, 1989).

more advanced economies, capitalists and liberal parties tended to support free trade, while they tended to be protectionist in economies whose industries were not yet competitive on international markets. Thus, in countries like Britain or Belgium, liberals and socialists were on the same side as regards trade policy, in an era when trade policy was a highly 'salient' political issue: politics fractured along rural–urban lines. In a country like Spain, on the other hand, protectionist landowners could make common cause with equally protectionist capitalists, against free-trading workers.

In land-abundant regions, on the other hand, land was in favour of free trade, while labour was protectionist. As long as capital was relatively scarce, and manufacturing relatively uncompetitive, capital could make common cause with labour against land. In the Northern United States workers and capitalists came together in the protectionist Republican Party, opposing the free-trading Democratic Party with its traditional land-owning Southern support; similar coalitions were to be found elsewhere in the regions of recent settlement and Latin America.

The long-run implications of these different types of political coalitions could be radically different. In countries where liberals and socialists were on the same side of the trade divide, deals could be struck according greater rights for workers and their families.[26] On the other hand, coalitions in which capital and land (liberals and conservatives) combined to exclude socialists from power had much darker implications for the future of the political system and for its capacity to absorb the working classes in a relatively consensual manner.

GLOBALIZATION AND THE EUROPEAN MIRACLE

In 2000, Kenneth Pomeranz published a book that transformed the economic history landscape.[27] *The Great Divergence* made two big claims. The first was that when comparing like with like – relatively advanced parts of China, like the Yangzi Delta, with relatively advanced parts of Europe, like England – the similarities in terms of the level of economic development were more striking than the differences, until 1750 or so. The Great Divergence thus emerged only in the late 18th and 19th centuries. More recent work prompted by Pomeranz's book has nuanced this claim considerably.[28]

The second claim, which has stood the test of time better, was that the causes of the British, and later European, take-off were a series of fortuitous and historically contingent circumstances. In particular, Britain, and later Europe, were able

---

[26] HUBERMAN M., 'Ticket to trade: Belgian labour and globalization before 1914', *Economic History Review* 61.2 (2008), 326–59.

[27] POMERANZ K., *The Great Divergence: China, Europe, and the Making of the Modern World Economy* (Princeton, 2000).

[28] BROADBERRY S.N., 'Accounting for the Great Divergence', in *LSE Department of Economic History Working Paper* 184 (2013).

to escape the Malthusian constraints that had previously limited income growth by drawing on hitherto under-used resources. The first of these was coal, which in Europe was located in the right place (northern England) at the right time, unlike in the case of China, whose coal deposits were situated in the northwest, far from the most dynamic regions of the country. The second was the vast land endowment of the New World, which as this essay has emphasized became more effectively available for use by Europeans during the 19th century as a result of improved shipping (and railroad) technology that brought Europe, the Americas and Oceania closer together.

This land endowment helped Britain and Western Europe to escape from Malthusian constraints in two ways. First, there were the food imports that have been stressed thus far. These were not sufficient to stop food prices from rising in Britain during the early 19th century, and food was scarce and expensive in many European economies during this period. But from the mid-century onwards the upward pressure on agricultural prices was gradually relieved, and eventually prices started falling. Second, the New World acted as a demographic safety valve during this period. Some sixty million Europeans left the continent between Waterloo and the Great War; emigration was significantly higher in those countries where the excess of births over deaths was higher.[29] This was a very direct way in which access to the oceans helped Europe to escape from Malthusian pressures.

The timing was highly fortuitous from a European point of view, since the 19th century saw an acceleration of population growth, consistent with the standard Malthusian prediction that birth rates should rise with income. It was only in the latter half of the century (France being a notorious exception to the rule) that the demographic transition produced declining birth rates. As two well-known economic theorists say, "By easing the land constraint at a crucial point – when income per capita had begun to rise rapidly, but before the demographic transition had gotten under way – the 'ghost acres' of the New World provided a window of time, which allowed Europe to pull decisively away from the Malthusian equilibrium" (of stagnant living standards for the masses).[30] The 19th century was a time of falling passenger and freight rates, open frontiers and generally open borders, which smoothed Europe's economic and demographic path during a potentially dangerous period of population growth: Africa would not be so lucky a century later. In peripheral European economies such as Ireland, Italy and Norway, emigration raised real wages far above what they would otherwise have been.[31]

---

[29] HATTON T.J. and WILLIAMSON J.G., *Global Migration and the World Economy: Two Centuries of Policy and Performance* (Cambridge, MA, 2005).
[30] GALOR O. and WEIL D.N., 'Population, technology, and growth: from Malthusian stagnation to the demographic transition and beyond', *American Economic Review* 90.4 (2000), 826.
[31] HATTON and WILLIAMSON, *Global Migration and the World Economy*.

Conclusions

This essay has concentrated on just some of the economic implications of the falling transportation costs of the 19th century, which shrank the oceans of the world economically speaking and allowed Western Europe to reap the full economic potential of the New World. The consequences were enormous. Maritime transport allowed an economy like Britain to specialize far more in manufacturing than would have been the case otherwise, and to rely on trade to provide it with the food and raw materials required to feed her people and factories. The growing international division of labour of the period led to huge gains from trade for economies such as Britain or Germany, as well as for Argentinian ranchers, Ghanaian cocoa producers and rice-producing Burmese peasants. Both intercontinental trade and intercontinental emigration helped to relieve Malthusian pressures in Europe by bringing European workers closer to the resources of the New World.

But 19th century trans-oceanic trade, like today's globalization, produced losers as well as winners. This led to a widespread protectionist backlash, while in some countries governments started to put in place the bare rudiments of what would later become the welfare state.[32] The politics of trans-oceanic trade helped to shape the nature of party politics in more than one country during this period, for good or for ill. And there would eventually be implications for the international political system as well as for domestic systems. Britain had been heavily dependent on imports of food and raw materials since the beginning of the century; policy makers there saw naval hegemony as essential for her economic wellbeing and security. By the end of the century Germany was well down the same path, becoming increasingly reliant on imports of food and raw materials, especially from overseas sources such as Latin America. This would have consequences for naval strategy, war planning and the stability of the international system that go well beyond the scope of this chapter.[33]

---

[32] HUBERMAN M., *Odd Couple: International Trade and Labor Standards in History* (New Haven, CT, 2012).

[33] LAMBERT N.A., *Planning Armageddon: British Economic Warfare and the First World War* (Cambridge, MA, 2012); OFFER A., *The First World War: An Agrarian Interpretation* (Oxford, 1989).

COAL AND THE SEA

SARAH PALMER is Emeritus Professor of Maritime History at the University of Greenwich, United Kingdom

ABSTRACT. *Coal was integral to the industrial revolution at sea in two ways: as a fuel it made international trade far cheaper and more extensive than before; as an export it went far to cement British dominance of seaborne trade. Its significance declined in both respects after 1918, but as a cargo it once more rose to international importance in the late 20th century as a result of China's industrialization.*

RÉSUMÉ. *Le charbon fit partie intégrante de la révolution industrielle en mer de deux manières. En tant que carburant, il permit d'étendre le commerce international et de réduire son coût; tandis que son exportation massive offrit à l'empire britannique les moyens de consolider sa domination sur le commerce maritime. Son importance à ces deux égards diminua après 1918, mais l'industrialisation de la Chine à la fin du XXe siècle lui rendit sa portée internationale en tant que marchandise de base.*

.•.

Coal profoundly shaped the later-nineteenth- and early-twentieth-century maritime world. As a fuel it was the basis of the transition from wind to steam power on the oceans; as a seaborne cargo it contributed to Britain's maritime dominance. In the interwar years, although coal remained the world's main source of energy, economic depression, together with the adoption of oil for marine propulsion, reduced international demand for coal shipment and had a severe impact on tramp shipping. After the Second World War, oil and gas captured most of coal's markets and by the early 1960s large-scale oceanic coal shipment appeared to be a thing of the past. The situation then changed remarkably. In the later 20th century oil-supply crises and Asian industrialisation not only gave coal renewed importance as an energy source, but also created a new global market dependent on sea transport. The link between coal and shipping was re-established and, along with this, the connection between coal supplies and the spread of industrialisation which had been a key feature of the world economy as it had existed a century earlier.

COAL AND THE MARITIME WORLD OF THE LATE 19TH AND EARLY 20TH CENTURIES

Transport of coal by sea, at least within Northern Europe, has a long history, but as long as the main use of coal was as a domestic fuel, trade was limited, as was also the incentive to find new coal deposits. The stimulus to discovery and exploitation of world coal reserves came in the later 19th century, with the spread of the use of steam power accompanying industrialisation.[1] By 1913 output had reached about 1,130 million tons. Of this total the United States accounted for approximately 39%, Britain 22% and Germany 21%. When we add the contribution of other European coal-producing regions, it is clear that the industrialised or industrialising West dominated the coal industry in the early 20th century. Although Japan, Australia and South Africa were increasingly exploiting their coal reserves, this was on a far smaller scale (Table 1).[2]

Coal still had a near monopoly as a source of power, so those regions with insufficient local supplies of coal to serve the needs of their industries, railways and growing populations had to meet the deficit from elsewhere. Conversely, those with output surplus to their domestic requirements sought other markets. Before the development of railways, coal's bulk made terrestrial transport costly, so inland coalfields in Europe and North America were at a disadvantage. Britain, a maritime nation with an advanced mining industry and most of its coalfields close to the coast, was in the best position to grasp the opportunities offered by the growth in external demand. Furthermore the high calorific value of much British coal made this well suited for steam generation. In the 1860s just 10% of Britain's coal output was exported. By 1913 a third of its output went overseas.[3]

Britain's major markets were geographically close; in 1913, 86% of its coal was shipped to European destinations, in particular France. Brazil and Argentina, with economies dominated by British interests, were the only significant distant importers. Canada took the largest share of United States' coal, with most of the remainder going to the West Indies and Central America. German coal exports before the First World War were likewise mostly confined to neighbouring countries. There was a comparable regional focus to the relatively limited tonnages of coal exported by sea from other countries with developing

---

[1] Coal is organically complex, but the basic distinction is between hard coal and soft or brown coal, which is very combustible and so not generally transported. Hard coal is classified as steam or thermal coal, used for power generation, and coking coal, which because of its chemical properties is used in the production of iron and steel. Available coal statistics do not always distinguish the two types of hard coal. Coal can be measured by Imperial or British ton of 2,240 pounds, United States ton of 2,000 pounds or by metric tonne, where one metric tonne = 1,000 kilograms or approximately 2,000 pounds. Unless otherwise indicated, 'ton' in this paper refers to the Imperial measure.

[2] Imperial Mineral Resources Bureau, *The Mineral Industry of the British Empire and Foreign Countries, War Period, Coal, Coke and By-Products (1913-1919), Part I* (London, 1921).

[3] PALMER S., 'The British Coal Export Trade, 1850–1913', in *Volumes Not Values: Canadian Sailing Ships and World Trade*, eds. D. ALEXANDER and R. OMMER (St John's, Newfoundland, 1979), p. 333.

Table 1. *World coal production, national exports and imports in 1913 (millions of tons)*

	Output	% World output	Exports	% Output exported	Imports
United States	508.9	38.5	26.6	5.2	1.4
United Kingdom	287.4	21.9	94.4	32.8	0.0
Germany	274.3	20.8	34.0	2.4	10.4
Austria-Hungary	53.2	4.0	0.7	1.3	13.5
France	40.2	3.0	1.2	3.0	18.4
Russia	31.7	2.4	0.0	0.0	7.6
Belgium	22.5	1.7	4.9	21.8	8.7
Japan	21.0	1.6	3.8	18.1	0.6
India	16.2	1.2	0.8	4.9	0.5
Australia, N. Zealand	14.3	1.1	3.7	25.9	0.5
China	13.6	1.0	1.5	11.0	0.0
Canada	13.4	1.0	1.4	10.4	16.2
South Africa	9.8	0.7	1.8	18.4	0.0
Other countries	14.2	1.1	0.0	0.0	0.0
Total	1,320.7	100.0			

Note: Coal output includes brown coal and lignite. Export figures for United States, United Kingdom Australia and New Zealand, South Africa include coal for bunkers.
Source: IMPERIAL MINERAL RESOURCES BUREAU, *The Mineral Industry of the British Empire and Foreign Countries, War Period, Coal, Coke and By-Products (1913-1919), Part I* (London, 1921), p. 46.

coal industries. In the late 19th and early 20th centuries, Australia exported New South Wales coal to New Zealand, Asia, Chile, the West Coast of the United States and Pacific islands. Japanese coal went to China and Singapore, Indian coal to Ceylon, the Straits Settlements, Sumatra and Aden, South African coal to Aden and Bombay.[4]

How was shipping affected by the emergence of demand for transport of what was effectively a new bulk cargo? In the Northern European trades British-built specialised steam colliers came to predominate. These took coal out from Britain and returned in ballast. On short-sea routes coal was a profitable cargo for the shipowner in its own right. On other routes coal transport was generally interconnected with the carriage of other bulk cargoes. Hence the shipment of coal to the Baltic was associated with the region's timber exports; to the Black Sea and Eastern Mediterranean with grain imports; to French Atlantic ports with Spanish ore exports; to South America with grain, nitrates exports and other bulky regional products; to North America with grain exports. Round voyages were not always possible, so such connections were not necessarily direct. New

---

[4] British Parliamentary Papers [BPP] [Cd 6960], East India (trade), 1912-13, 1913; BPP 1914-16 [Cd 7766] East India (trade). Review of the trade of India in 1913-14; BPP 1924-25 (168) Coal Tables; BPP 1919 [Cmd 360], Report of the Coal Commission.

South Wales coal, for example, met the need of British vessels bringing imports for Australia for an intermediate cargo for the onward voyage to San Francisco to load grain for the return to Europe. Since the effect of the transportation of coal as an outward or intermediate cargo was to depress homeward cargo rates, arguably, shippers rather than shipowners benefited most from these trading patterns, which were underpinned by commercial experience, expertise and information flows, with the hub being London's Baltic Exchange.

Ultimately, though, it was the European consumer on the other side of the world who gained from the access to food and raw materials facilitated by "the outward flow of trampers lugging coal", with a global reach which exceeded that in the liner trades.[5]

Coal's contribution to the growing integration of world commodity markets was not only as a cargo but also as a fuel. The late-nineteenth-century international economy was forged by falling transport costs on land and sea; without coal, neither the railway nor the steamship could have existed. On some tramping routes sail persisted: traditional sailing vessels continued late in the century in the Baltic coal-out/timber-back business and technically advanced new-built large iron and steel square-rigged ships carried coal to American Pacific ports and elsewhere in the 1880s and 1890s. But in most cases progressive improvements in engine efficiency from the 1860s meant that sailing vessels rapidly became the exception, as first liner services and then the cargo-seeking "tramp" sector adopted the newer technology. The steam tramp, wherever owned and registered, was typically built in a British yard and characterised by relatively low power, medium capacity and size, though there evolved a large variety of types. These were adaptable carriers, as suited to ore, nitrates or grain cargoes as they were to coal. Only on certain short sea or coastal routes was it economic to employ specialist steam colliers.

Of course, the steamship was itself a consumer of coal. As a 1925 report pointed out, in the British case, "for every million tons of coal sold abroad about 270,000 tons are needed as bunkers by the ships that convey it".[6] But the maritime market for coal extended beyond the commercial sector; navies also switched from sail to steam. Once steam became viable on oceanic routes, with links to the East aided by the opening of the Suez Canal in 1869, a world-wide network of coaling stations, the majority of these located where they sustained Britain's imperial connections, was established. Coaling stations had strategic significance. So many bunkering agents and coal merchants in foreign ports were British, or sold British coal, that Britain was able to impose "bunker control" on foreign ships during the First World War. The impact went, however, beyond commerce and defence. Just as the need to shovel coal into boiler furnaces created a new maritime labour force on board ship, so also it did ashore. And

---

[5] MILLER M.B., *Europe and the Maritime World: A Twentieth-Century History* (Cambridge, 2012), pp. 71–2.
[6] BPP 1926 [Cmd 2600] Royal Commission on the Coal Industry (1925) with minutes of evidence and appendices. Volume I. Report, p. 13.

the foreign coaling station itself had cultural and social significance as a site for interaction between sailors and locals.

Internationally, British shipping benefited the most from the coal trade. In 1913 an estimated 5 million tons of tramp shipping carried Britain's coal exports, of which 3 million tons were British owned.[7] In 1913 British ships carried less than half of coal shipments to European destinations, but practically all British coal exports going beyond Europe. By now British coal had lost out to Indian, Japanese and Australian coal in the Far East, so South America took by far the largest share of Britain's oceanic business. Since serving distant markets required more tonnage, there was a disproportionate impact on the size of the British tramp fleet. A British government report considering the historical reasons for Britain's dominance of world ocean carriage before the First World War identified three factors: "the strong industrial position", "a world-wide Empire with well-distributed coaling stations and ports of call" and "a large coal trade which provided ships with outward freights which would otherwise have been lacking".[8]

Even so, while coal resources gave Britain an initial advantage in developing steam shipping, it is questionable whether coal exports provided British shipping with a substantial and lasting competitive advantage. Other national fleets also benefited from British-established coaling stations and could, as happened in Europe, compete successfully with British tramp ships. As an outward cargo, depressing round-trip freight rates, coal did not contribute sufficiently to the earnings of British shipowners to give them a competitive edge. In any case, by the 1900s coal's "ballast" role was diminishing. Other factors therefore need also to be taken into account in explaining the nineteenth-century success of British shipping. To point this out is not to suggest that coal was unimportant. Certainly the post-war collapse of coal exports had serious consequences for British tramp shipping.

A DIMINISHED MARKET – THE SEABORNE COAL TRADE 1913–C. 1960

In 1913 seaborne coal was a key element of the globalised economy which had emerged in the later 19th century, but there were some signs of change affecting the world's coal markets.[9] These included economies in coal consumption resulting from improvements in steam technology; the growing use of electricity generated by water power or by burning lignite or soft coal; the substitution of oil for coal. The effect of the First World War was to hasten these developments

---

[7] STURMEY S.G., *British Shipping and World Competition* (London, 1962), pp. 73–4.
[8] BPP 1918 [Cd 9092], Report of the Departmental Committee on Shipping and Shipbuilding. Final Report, p. 71.
[9] FREMDLING R., 'Historical Precedents of Global Markets', Groningen Growth and Development Centre Research Memorandum, 43, October 1996, http://irs.ub.rug.nl/ppn/242560326 [Accessed 20 January 2015].

and to seriously disrupt the coal trade. During the war itself, to meet the fuel demands of wartime industries, Britain deliberately reduced coal exports, largely restricting these to its allies France and Italy, though Italy was also supplied by United States producers. Its markets outside Europe were starved of supplies – shipments to South America stopped almost completely. Coaling stations also lacked bunkers. In response to the opportunity, United States coal exports to South America rose substantially and railways in the region also turned to oil for fuel. India, South Africa, Japan and China responded to scarcity and rising export prices by increasing domestic output.[10]

War and its immediate aftermath almost halved total world coal exports, and expectations that in due course there would be a return to pre-war levels of trade proved unfounded.[11] Instead, disintegration of the international economy over the following two decades further undermined coal's role as a globally traded fuel. Within Europe British coal was displaced by local and newer sources of supply. Although it remained Britain's best customer, France benefited from German reparation coal, Spain increased its domestic output, Germany made greater use of its lignite reserves, and Britain's previous dominance of the Scandinavian market was undermined by Poland.[12]

Since British tramps carried just 40% of European coal shipments, a fall in coal exports to more distant destinations was of greater significance for their owners. Coal still fulfilled 95% of Europe's fuel and power needs in 1925, but, thanks to the development of Caribbean oil fields, in South America already coal accounted for only 38% of the region's energy and by 1938 its share was less than a quarter.[13] Competition from oil extended beyond the loss of particular markets, to the maritime sector itself. Overseas coaling-station demand was reduced as a result of the adoption of the diesel engine; motorships accounted for 2.6% of world merchant shipping tonnage in 1923, but 24.4% by 1939.[14] The overall effect of these factors, together with improving industrial efficiency in the use of fuel, was a reduction in demand for coal shipment, and increased international oceanic competition between tramp-ship owners, with lower-cost operators, in particular the Greeks, at an advantage in the contest for cargo. Indeed in 1933 it was reported by Britain's Chamber of Shipping that, whereas the number and tonnage of British tramps had more than halved since 1913, the number of foreign tramps had increased by as much as a third.

While the interwar depression reduced coal output internationally and coal exports also fell, particularly for Britain, coal remained the main source

---

[10] IMPERIAL WAR RESOURCES BUREAU, *The Mineral Industry of the British Empire and Foreign Countries – War Period – Coal, Coke and By-Products (1913-1919) Part I* (London, 1921).
[11] BPP, 1924-25 (168), Coal Tables, 1924, pp. 31-2.
[12] BPP 1926 [Cmd 2600], Report of the Royal Commission on the Coal Industry (1925), pp. 3-10; BPP 1930-31 [Cmd 3702], Report of the British Coal Delegation to Sweden, Norway and Denmark, pp. 4-5.
[13] DARMSTADTER J., *Energy in the World Economy. A Statistical Review of Trends in Output, Trade and Consumption since 1925* (Baltimore and London, 1971), pp. 14-15.
[14] STURMEY, *British Shipping*, pp. 82-4.

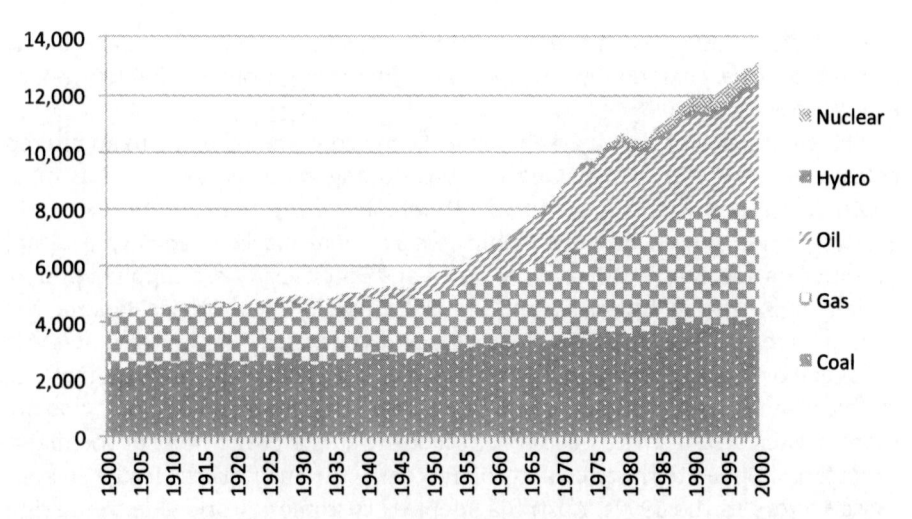

Fig. 1. *World primary energy production, 1900–2000 (million tonnes oil equivalent) (The Shift Project Data Project, Historical Energy Production Statistics)*

of energy, despite some inroads from alternative types of power, including oil. This situation changed dramatically and very swiftly after the Second World War. Although coal shared in the general energy boom fuelled by the world's economic growth and output grew, its contribution became small in comparison with that of gas and oil.

The war itself had severely disrupted the already reduced international coal trade, and seaborne exports failed to revive for almost two decades, with a particularly adverse impact on the British tramp shipping sector. In 1960 half of the world's international coal trade was within Europe, where Germany was the main supplier to Western Europe and Russia to Eastern Europe. The United States sold to Canada and exported to Europe and Japan, but there was no significant seaborne export trade.

THE NEW GLOBAL COAL TRADE OF THE LATER 20TH CENTURY

The oceanic trade in coal then revived to such an extent that by 2000 85% of all coal traded internationally was carried in ships, although exports still represented a small share of total coal output. In the 1960s developments in the international steel industry increased the demand for coking coal. Industrialising South Korea, China, Japan and Brazil became major importers, with Australia the main supplier. The next spur to the re-emergence of coal as a seaborne cargo was the use of steam coal in the generation of electricity. The oil price rises of 1973 and 1979 led to the conversion of power stations to coal and the construction of new coal-fired power stations. Rapid Asian industrialisation, together with continued growth in world demand for electricity, then further compounded the attraction of coal as an energy source. In response, the tonnage of seaborne steam coal more than doubled in the 1990s, increasing from 183 million tonnes in 1990 to 356 in 2000.[15]

The emergence of new markets for seaborne coal was reflected in an altered pattern of supply. In 1973 Poland was the leading exporter, by 1990 Australia, South Africa and the USA dominated.[16] Demonstrating that distance was still a factor, trade flowed broadly within two regional markets: Pacific/Asia and Atlantic/Europe. By the 21st century North and South Asia were supplied preferentially by Australia, Indonesia and China; Europe by South Africa, Poland, the United States and new exporters Colombia and Venezuela. The United States was a residual or "swing" supplier, moving between the Asian and European markets in response to changes in prices and so ensuring that, in terms of price, globally there now existed a single market for seaborne steam coal.[17] Most of the major exporters supplied both steam and coking coal, with Australia the leader in both these sectors in the 1990s. Australia supplied customers worldwide, rendering the coking market more global than that for steam coal. Coking demand was also more volatile because of its dependence on the vagaries of the steel industry.[18]

Shipping services were key to the creation and operation of the global seaborne coal trade in the later 20th century. The supply of cargo-space for dry bulk commodities, through its impact on ocean freight rates and hence delivered costs, influenced the international coal market. Demand for sea transportation of coal, together with the other major internationally traded bulk commodities – iron ore, grain, bauxite, alumina and phosphate rock – resulted in expansion of the world's dry bulk shipping fleet from 181.8 million dead weight (dwt) in 1980 to 274.6 million dwt by 2000.[19] Coal contributed to the growth of dry bulk business in the 1980s and 1990s and, because of the distances involved, together with iron ore, also gave the most employment to this sector's shipping (Table 2).[20] The length of haul also meant that shipping demand tended to grow faster than the volumes of coal transported.

Economies of scale in shipping and cargo handling underpinned the growth of the coal trade. A new generation of vessel, the Dry Bulk Cargo Carrier, emerged in response to the demand for large shipments over longer distances. Under these conditions, the traditional multi-deck tramp ship, many of which in the 1950s and 1960s were former Liberty Ships, were replaced by more efficient single-deck bulkers. These varied in size and type. Those specialist bulk carriers destined to carry ore and coking coal in the trade with Japan had small holds strengthened for the high-density ore cargo, whereas the general-purpose bulk

---

[15] International Energy Agency (IEA), *Coal Information 2012*.
[16] UNCTAD, *Review of Maritime Transport 1993*.
[17] IEA, *International Coal Trade, the Evolution of a Global Market* (Paris, 1997), p. 25.
[18] IEA, *Coal Information 2012*.
[19] UNCTAD, Merchant Fleet by Flag of Registration and by Type of Ship, annual series, 1980–2014, http://unctadstat.unctad.org/wds/TableViewer/tableView.aspx?ReportId=93 [Accessed 19 April 2015]. Dwt = deadweight tonnage.
[20] UNCTAD, *Review of Maritime Transport 1998*.

Table 2. *World shipping performance by types of dry cargo, selected years (billions of metric tonne-miles)*

Year	Coal	Iron Ore	Grain	Other dry cargoes
1970	481	1093	475	2118
1980	952	1613	1087	3720
1990	1849	1978	1073	4400
2000	2500	2515	1210	6295

Source: UNCTAD, *Review of Maritime Transport 2001*, Table 5 world shipping performance by types of cargo, selected years, p. 15.

carrier needed large holds suitable for stowing several different types of bulk cargoes. Coal's stowage was forty cubic feet to the ton, in contrast to fifteen cubic feet for iron ore, which made some carriers with small holds unsuitable because these would be full before loaded to the vessel's maximum capacity. In the 1990s the world's bulk carrier fleet consisted of vessels categorised as Cape Size (at more than 80,000dwt, too large for the Panama and Suez Canals); Panamax (not too large for the Panama Canal); Handymax (35,000–50,000dwt) and Handysize (10,000–30,000dwt).

Where demand for shipment was stable and predictable, multinational commodity owners and corporate customers for ore and coal, such as Japanese steel mills, themselves ran fleets of large bulk carriers or placed long-term charters. There remained, however, the more traditional competitive and fragmented spot and term shipping market served by smaller participants, including many Greek owners, utilising medium-size bulk cargo vessels. Perhaps for this reason, some commentators continued to refer to "tramp" shipping, while others abandoned the expression. Given the commercial pressures, the dry bulk sector found open registers attractive; almost a quarter of ships in open registers in the mid-1990s were bulk carriers.

Port infrastructure investment accompanied the growth of dry bulk shipping. Coal terminals opened in the major coal-exporting ports. Introduction of new facilities mechanising waterfront coal handling began in New South Wales and Queensland in the 1960s, and South Africa's Richards Bay, with direct rail access to the coalfields, opened in 1976. The impact of such industrial-scale maritime-related facilities on the local environment proved controversial in some countries, as increasingly, once climate change became a global issue, did the use of coal itself.

Conclusion

Coal's later-twentieth-century renaissance as an energy source, albeit one of several others including oil, invites comparison with its role a century or so earlier. The commodity itself remained basically the same, though the share of coking coal was higher than previously, but, in contrast to the situation at the beginning of the century, steam coal competed with other sources of power supply. Problems with the security of oil supply were in part responsible for coal's revival but, as in the 19th century, it was the spread of industrialisation – this time in Eastern rather than Western economies – that underpinned increased demand. Coal's characteristic high volume/low value per ton remained the prime factor affecting transport and, without the cost-effective shipping services provided by bulk carriers, Asian economic development, and with this the growth of the global economy, would have faltered.

However, while it is tempting to treat the renewed seaborne coal trade as a revival of the earlier business; both the trade itself and its impact on the wider maritime sector were different in a number of respects, not least the countries participating. In 1900 the seaborne coal trade was to only a limited extent oceanic and dominated on deep sea passages by one nation's coal and shipping. In 2000, within a globalised shipping industry, it was truly global in its reach and connections and, although Atlantic or Pacific focused, operated as a single world market. Even so, coal's status as a bulk trade was lower than it had been in the later 19th century; it did not affect the general carrying trade in the way that it had in its role as a ballast cargo. Crucially, despite the importance of bulk carriers in ensuring the flow of coal across the oceans, no twentieth-century developments associated with coal could rival the economic and political impact of the transition from sail to steam in shipping.

BIBLIOGRAPHY

BURLEY K.H., 'The overseas trade in New South Wales coal and the British shipping industry, 1860–1914', *Economic Record* 36 (1960), 371–81.

CHAMBERLAIN A., '"Stokers – the Lowest of the Low?" A Social History of Royal Navy Stokers 1850–1950' (PhD thesis, University of Exeter, 2013).

CLARK M., 'Bound out for Callao: the Pacific coal trade 1876 to 1896; selling coal or selling lives? Part 1', *The Great Circle: Journal of the Australian Association for Maritime History* 28 (2006), 26–45.

DARMSTADTER J., *Energy in the World Economy. A Statistical Review of Trends in Output, Trade and Consumption since 1925* (Baltimore, MD and London, 1971).

FENTON R., *Tramp Ship: An Illustrated History* (Barnsley, 2013).

GORDON R.L., *World Coal, Economics, Policies and Prospects* (Cambridge, 1989).

GRAY S., 'Black Diamonds: Coal, the Royal Navy, and British Imperial Coaling Stations, circa 1870–1914' (University of Warwick PhD Thesis, 2014).

GREENHILL B., *The Ship: The Life and Death of the Merchant Sailing Ship 1815-1965* (London, 1980).

HARLAFTIS G., *A History of Greek-Owned Shipping: The Making of an International Tramp Fleet 1830 to the Present Day* (London, 1996).

HARLEY C.K., 'Coal exports and British shipping 1850-1913', *Explorations in Maritime History* 26 (1989), 311-38.

HOAR H.M., *The Coal Industry of the World, with Special Reference to the Trade in Coal*, US Department of Commerce, Trade Promotion Series (Washington, DC, 1930).

INTERNATIONAL ENERGY AGENCY (IEA), *International Coal Trade, The Evolution of a Global Market* (Paris, 1997).

JAMIESON A.G., *Ebb Tide in the British Maritime Industries. Change and Adaptation, 1918-1990* (Exeter, 2003).

JEVONS H.S., *The British Coal Trade* (London, 1920).

KIRKALDY A.W., *British Shipping. Its History, Organisation and Importance* (London, 1914).

MARTIN D., *Seaborne Steam Coal Trade - Demand Prospects to 2000*. IEA Coal Research (London, 1992).

METAXAS B.N., *The Economics of Tramp Shipping* (London, 1971).

MILLER M.B., *Europe and the Maritime World: A Twentieth-Century History* (Cambridge, 2012).

NOTZ W., 'The world's coal situation during the war', *Journal of Political Economy* 26 (1918), 567-611.

PALMER S., 'The British Coal Export Trade, 1850-1913', in *Volumes Not Values: Canadian Sailing Ships and World Trade*, ed. D. ALEXANDER and R. OMMER (St John's, Newfoundland, 1979), 333-54.

PALMER S., 'The British Shipping Industry 1850-1914', in *Change and Adaptation in Maritime History: The North Atlantic Fleets in the Nineteenth Century*, ed. L.R. FISCHER and G.E. PANTING (St John's Newfoundland, 1985).

PLATT D.C.M., *Latin America and British Trade* (London, 1972).

POLLARD S. and ROBERTSON P., *The British Shipbuilding Industry 1870-1914* (Cambridge, MA, 1979).

ROGERS P., STRANGE J. and STUDD B., *Coal Carriage by Sea* (London, 1991).

ROWLINSON M.P. and LEEK B.M., 'The decline of the regionally based UK deepsea tramp shipping industry', *Journal of Transport Geography* 5 (1997), 277-90.

SARGENT A.J., *Coal in International Trade* (London, 1922).

SCHERNIKAU L., *Economics of the International Coal Trade. The Renaissance of Steam Coal* (Dordrecht, 2010).

STOPFORD M., *Maritime Economics*, 3rd edn (Abingdon, 2009).

STURMEY S.G., *British Shipping and World Competition* (London, 1962).

SUPPLE B., *The History of the British Coal Industry, Vol. 4, 1913-1946: The Political Economy of Decline* (Oxford, 1987).

THEOTOKAS I. and HARLAFTIS G., *Greek Family Firms in International Business* (Basingstoke, 2009).

Shipbuilding and power: some reflections

Alan Lemmers is a Research Fellow at the Netherlands Institute of Military History, the Netherlands

ABSTRACT. *Shipbuilding and state power were more closely associated in the case of Britain than any other major naval power. Elsewhere naval or commercial domination was not necessarily built on a dominant shipbuilding industry, and few of the leading modern shipbuilding nations are also naval powers. Weapons and systems rather than hull and engines constitute the high technology of a modern warship.*

RÉSUMÉ. *La Grande-Bretagne plus qu'aucune autre puissance navale de taille constitue l'exemple le plus significatif de l'association de la construction navale et de la puissance étatique. Partout ailleurs, la domination maritime ou commerciale ne se construisit pas nécessairement sur l'industrie nautique, et aujourd'hui, peu de nations leader en construction de navires sont en parallèle des puissances maritimes. Ce sont désormais les armements et les systèmes plus que les coques et les moteurs qui témoignent d'une technologie avancée en matière de bâtiment de guerre.*

.•.

In *The Tragical History of Doctor Faustus* (1604) Christopher Marlowe coined the image of Helen of Troy as "the face that launched a thousand ships". Its poetical power aside, the image implies that a lot of shipbuilders were employed in the preparation of the Trojan campaign. The fleet they knocked together in no time was a splendid display of power. Even if it were to be proved untrue in this particular instance, the possibility of such a building effort is supported by other historical examples of sudden, sometimes miraculous, maritime development. So one observation in considering the relationship between shipbuilding and power is that a nation or society can acquire the ability and start building ships in a surprisingly short time and virtually from scratch. Think of the huge building programmes accomplished by the USA in both world wars. Other telling examples are the fluctuating state of the Russian fleet in the 19th century, Germany's naval and commercial rise after 1870 and recently South Korea's and China's industrial rise. These examples also show that continuity is a problem. Besides its birth, we need also to consider the industry's growth and decline.

The Trojan myth goes on to relate that ships alone were not sufficient for the campaign to go ahead. The Greeks still required permission from the forces above, the UN council on Mount Olympus so to speak, before the Trojan War could begin. Then (as with many such ventures – there are plenty of recent analogies) the execution of the plan was a lot tougher than had been foreseen. After ten years of battle still no outcome was in sight and the war was forced to a conclusion by cunning and deceit, not by naval superiority. Naval – and in the much broader sense military – superiority is not a guarantee for power or victory. We consider this angle, with its many examples of vast naval deployment ending in failure or stalemate, as belonging to the domain of military rather than maritime history. However, the relation between naval power and other forms of national success – economic, commercial or in shipbuilding – needs to be examined.

POWER

Ships are manifestations of transport technology specific to certain periods and cultures. As such they are comparable to other transport technologies that play a pivotal role in a society, culture or civilisation, like the horse, railway or car. Western trade and colonisation from the 15th century onwards were definitely a maritime affair, peaking in the 19th and early 20th centuries. After the Second World War decolonisation and globalisation set in, causing an even more explosive growth of sea trade. Although from the 1930s aviation encroached on shipping (first international mail and then passenger transport), sea transport maintained its competitive edge in most areas, thanks to its cost-effectiveness.

Shipping requires ships to be built (or bought), maintained and regularly replaced. That requires a manufacturing (leastways a maintenance) industry. But shipbuilding can also be exercised for its own worth. It is, for instance, a capital-intensive but attractive economic choice for countries aiming for industrial development. Besides its obvious use for shipping, it functions as the backbone for the development of downstream and upstream industries of suppliers and subcontractors such as the steel, machine and electrical industries. It is technology- and labour-intensive, with huge effects on employment, education, national wealth and income. Finally, it can become a major foreign currency earner when operating in the international market.

The ability to build ships is not the same as the acquisition of naval power. Some nations with a great merchant fleet or a great shipbuilding industry have (had) insufficient access to military technology or lack(ed) the ambition to become a naval power. For the sake of our argument we will confine our interpretation of the concept of power to "hard power" as seen in international relations, as the coercive means (violence, threat, sanctions) available to a nation to influence/deter unfriendly behaviour of other nations. In the end, such power is always founded in wealth, but a country can be wealthy and forego the acquisition of hard power, e.g. modern Japan, or a country may be economically unsuccessful but concentrate all its available resources on national security, e.g. North Korea. Economic success, moreover, is subject to global economic versatility and therefore unpredictable in the long run, less manageable by political means: where the acquisition of power is a political act of will, economic success – certainly in a free market economy – is far more uncertain and complicated to achieve.

Cultural and ideological factors furthermore determine how keen a nation is to participate in the global community and to exercise power with respect to other nations. On the one hand, there are sheer isolationist countries (societies) such as North Korea, Burma, Albania and Cambodia in recent history – going back in time the list grows. There are examples both of landlocked isolationist societies, e.g. Paraguay 1814–1840, and of isolationist coastal or island societies, such as Japan during its seclusion (*sakoku*, 1633–1868) or North Sentinel Island in the Andamans (from prehistory to today). Opposite to isolationist societies we find thalassocracies (Venice, Portugal, Spain, the Dutch Republic, post-war Greece), maritime empires (with Great Britain and pre-1945 Japan as the most prominent examples) and finally land empires (e.g. Russia). For communities with a maritime geographic setting isolationism impedes maritime activity and therefore shipbuilding. However, isolationism should not been seen as an absolute, nor as a constant. The example of the nineteenth-century United States illustrates that it need not be all-encompassing and can manifest itself in various degrees.

Modern shipbuilding was largely an invention of nineteenth-century British industrialisation. Where naval and maritime technology before had been almost equal for all rivalling (western) maritime nations, from 1850 Britain's industrial might offered the nation a material lead to any potential adversary with a coastline. Its success was fuelled by high economic growth, an enormous expansion of seaborne trade and by British shipbuilding itself, which became the world's leading supplier by far. Never were shipbuilding and state power as closely related as with the British Empire. In contrast the (very much naval) super powers USA and USSR during the Cold War were also economic giants, but not in the maritime sense: neither in commercial shipbuilding nor in shipping. In that same period Japan (for the second time) and South Korea rose as shipbuilding giants without becoming naval powers, while elsewhere shipping empires were founded without the help of a domestic shipbuilding industry (e.g. post-war Greece – we'll ignore flags of convenience). So we'll need to keep in mind the distinction between naval power and maritime success in other ways. Meanwhile, sea trade no doubt contributes to a nation's wealth, but examples like Switzerland illustrate that it is not vital.

One can consequently ask oneself how far the Mahanian contention that sea power is an indivisible force of industrial, commercial and military elements can be upheld. As Todd and Lindberg argue, only the US today is capable of globally providing adequate naval protection to its merchant navy and in fact protects much of the rest of the world's commercial shipping as well – naval involvement from other maritime states occurs largely in formal and informal alliances, as none is capable of global deployment. Robert Rubel in 2012 pursued this line of thought to analyse "the relationship between navies and the economic prospects of their parent nations". Meanwhile the American share in global shipbuilding exports remains under 3%, hardly more than the Netherlands. So naval power, although it requires a strong naval shipbuilding industry, need not go together with a strong commercial shipbuilding sector. On the other hand, in times of crisis the availability of non-naval shipping is crucial to the success of the military effort for supply, troop transport etc., as both world wars clearly demonstrated.

Technology

Let us return to the observation that a shipbuilding industry can be founded relatively quickly. That implies that shipbuilding technology can be acquired in a relatively short time. Traditionally, shipbuilding is classed as an assembly industry, with on the one hand the pre-fabrication, assembly and erection of the hull and on the other the installation of systems, equipment and fittings. Today the industry is closely entwined with other sectors, ranging from steel (in all its forms) to electronics. Modern shipbuilding is furthermore supported by a sound and extensive theoretical engineering framework. Now, one could consider shipbuilding technology, even for commercial shipbuilding, to be of strategic value and therefore expect it to be jealously guarded. But such has seldom been the case. The international spreading of shipbuilding skills and theory in the course of history has never ceased to amaze me, this nearly free flow of information across national borders. From the 17th century onward examples of expatriate shipbuilders abound, and in the 18th and 19th centuries we can observe a steady growth in the number of shipbuilding intelligence missions, some covert but many quite open. Skilled labour also moved freely across borders. Combined with the international openness of the scientific academies and the organisations of naval architects since the 18th century, also reflected in the global accessibility of their journals, we get the not unfounded impression that naval architecture and shipbuilding are for a large part technologies freely shared around the world.

There are counter-examples, of course. At times certain information, such as the actual hull lines, are considered too important to share. The many feuds between shipbuilders at the national level, in which the guarding of trade secrets or the refusal to adopt innovations often played a role, also stand in contrast to the apparent free flow of information at the international level. But in those cases there were other things at stake, such as position and income. In fact the history of shipbuilding is rife with this curious mixture of free technology transfer and jealous, often secretive competition. But I think we can voice the tentative conclusion that in shipbuilding and naval architecture nothing remains monopolistic knowledge for very long. Today most of naval architectural expertise is simply a commercial product: engineering and testing stations provide design support to clients all over the world, technical universities generally have an international student programme and sophisticated designing programmes can simply be bought on the internet. Britain's Royal Institution of Naval Architects today has members in industry, education and maritime organisations in over ninety countries, while the American Society of Naval Architects and Marine Engineers considers itself global.

How can we explain this free flow of information? For one, a ship is first and foremost a floating dirigible supporting a variety of human activities: from transport to fishing, to leisure, to warfare. Many of the basic aspects of the platform, such as stability, construction, propulsion and building techniques, are equivalent, whatever the purpose of the vessel. They are concerned mainly with safety and economics, while other aspects are equally applied in other industries, such as engineering, aviation or telecommunication. Classified technologies are mostly limited to the military aspects of war vessels, such as armament and sensor technology, or to very special hydrodynamic or material properties. Meanwhile most shipbuilding industries across the globe are focused on the civic sector, as commercial shipping always vastly outnumbers naval shipping. Risk management has of old played an important role in commercial shipping, whether for humanitarian reasons or insurance, with ship owners, insurance companies, classification societies and governments laying down regulations for all shipyards and shipping to follow. Combined with the freedom of information, education and employment, the free flow of much of the technological expertise involved is easily understood. Finally there are other ways of acquiring technological expertise and skills, whether in shipbuilding or other occupations: by hiring experts, buying information, participating in multinational projects, foreign education, one's own scientific research etc. However, as we shall see, recently the protection of intellectual property has been mentioned as a competitive measure by the European shipbuilding industry.

Rise, shine and decline

Apart from technological expertise, what other favourable circumstances contribute to the emergence of a shipbuilding industry? Good access to the sea? It is indeed unlikely that Switzerland, unless it acquires a colony with a coastline, will become a major shipbuilding nation, although with today's global corporate climate nothing is impossible. Meanwhile many countries with ample access to navigable waters have never or only poorly turned to shipbuilding. We will come back to this.

So, what other favourable conditions can we consider? Access to raw materials? Yes, but examples such as the seventeenth-century Dutch Republic and South Korea today demonstrate that this need not be from domestic sources, as raw materials can be acquired elsewhere. Naval (and other strategic) stores have of course played an important role in naval conflicts, but as far as can be assessed they have never been decisive. As for skilled labour, this, as we have seen, can be bought, hired or acquired by training, while social organisation seems irrelevant. This last aspect can differ locally from free employment to guild and union organisations, to forced labour.

So what does characterise shipbuilding in its broadest sense? Apart from war situations, shipbuilding generally is an economic activity foremost, taking place in a specific socio-economic, political and cultural climate and influenced by factors ranging from the local labour market to entrepreneurship, to the global economy. Together they define the success of a shipbuilding industry and in turn its influence on the success of a nation – commercial, military or both. Limiting and backfiring mechanisms manifest themselves along the way, as both shipbuilding industries and power peaks of states generally have finite lifecycles.

Shipbuilding above all is a business. A shipbuilder typically builds for money, so that he can build more ships and earn more money. Generally domestic shipping will be targeted to begin with, but with the increase in size a yard will inevitably look for a share in the global shipbuilding market. In its quest for political, economic and military power the state can also become a stakeholder in the shipbuilding industry: it can erect state-owned building yards, acquire an interest in existing yards or provide subsidies. In some countries the state-owned yards are the only ones of importance, other countries have a strong state-owned sector next to a strong commercial sector, and in still other countries shipbuilding (even naval) is left entirely to privately owned yards or even to foreign production.

It has been observed that the shipbuilding industry in a nation "without exception" follows a particular pattern from its emergence to its decline. Typically this pattern begins with a dependence on foreign shipping and the purchase of foreign-built ships, necessitating the creation of repair facilities and initialising the importation of foreign technology. As the shipping sector grows, the demand for ships increases, so domestic building yards are erected. This stage practically always requires active government support. As the industry grows, the steel and supply industries grow alongside. The rise in production at some stage makes it possible to build for foreign clients as well and thus to acquire a share in the world market. Low wages at this stage grant cost leadership, but they rise due to the increase of national wealth. To reduce the production costs, notably in labour, high-level production technology is then acquired. This involves high investment and fans inflation, reducing the competitive edge. Now salvage strategies need to be devised, such as product differentiation, company segmentation and specialisation. Sliding down, the industry looks out for financial (government) support, until it starts losing its footing in the global shipbuilding market and is forced to reduce its capacity and return to domestic production. Finally the country reverts to the acquisition of ships from foreign shipbuilders.

I would like to add some observations on the model presented above. For one, it skips naval shipbuilding or exceptional conditions. Yet these can have great (temporary) impact on the industry. The 1956 Suez crisis, for instance, was a window of opportunity for Japanese shipbuilding – and for the Greek shipping tycoons. Another telling illustration is the 1982 Elvis Costello song *Shipbuilding*, chanting with great irony the industrial reawakening of shipbuilding areas in Great Britain as a result of the outbreak of the Falklands War.

The extent in which shipbuilding is a national undertaking is illustrated by the numerous national salvage operations for the industry – when government support falls away, the industry generally succumbs. Naval shipbuilding generally reflects the maritime military ambitions of a nation, but governments also use naval building programmes to rescue an ailing industry, so as an economic measure. Although it is then often argued that the loss of industrial potential and technological skills would lead to an unacceptable dependence of national defence on foreign supply, fears of unemployment and economic decline of course are the underlying reasons. The success of such salvage operations varies. The main building yards in the Netherlands from 1823 onwards were regularly saved by government orders, but the extensive government effort to rescue the shipbuilding and steel industry in the 1970s and 1980s ended in financial disaster, with 80 per cent of the industry wiped out and what was left state owned. That the same occurred in Great Britain, West Germany and Sweden was hardly a comfort. The Royal Netherlands Navy, on the other hand, ended up with a brand new fleet, thanks to all the efforts to save the yards.

What is furthermore striking in the business cycle mentioned above is the inevitability of the downward trend after the peak. Until now history confirms this. The fate of British shipbuilding in the 19th and 20th centuries, for instance, can be understood in broad lines as rising to great height until the First World War, after which decline set in, ending in almost non-existence by the year 2000. The first period is marked by important protectionist politics and then, with the onset of global liberalisation around 1850, by the advantages provided by Britain's technological and industrial lead, plus the worldwide British shipping network, that had been built on entrepreneurship, the geographic omnipresence of the Empire and the absence of alternative technological networks (e.g. aviation). The high living standards emanating from its success encouraged foreign low-cost competition, which ultimately sealed the industry's fate. This process is not always acknowledged by the shipbuilding world itself. In a 1985 course for the improvement of assembly techniques in US shipbuilding for instance, it was stated that "there is a need to improve and become more competitive. Being more competitive by improving manufacturing techniques will result in more jobs, better wages, job security, and many other benefits". However, no account is taken of the dialectics of lead and the backfiring mechanisms of economic and technological progress, such as overinvestment, overproduction and wage inflation, which ultimately undermine the lead a shipbuilding industry may have over (foreign) competition. Furthermore, national shipbuilding and shipping can be endangered by competing technological systems, such as air transport, land transport (including pipelines) and telecommunication, but also by production outsourcing to low-wage areas and, finally, by technology transfer to competing countries. Needless to add, the engineering course quoted above did not turn the tide for American commercial shipbuilding, which like many other western shipbuilding industries from 1973 onwards was hit hard by competition and crisis.

Industrialisation

When we cast an eye over the world map to identify the leading shipbuilding nations of the last two centuries, we see modern history reflected in it. Not so very long ago the western colonial powers dominated world commerce and transport. During the colonial era global transport was dominated by shipping and the military and commercial infrastructures of the colonies were provided for by the mother nations. There was little or no incentive to address such matters locally. Harbours, maintenance yards and supply stations were laid out, and railroad tracks leading into the interior, but the ships, trains, engines and later on cars and aeroplanes – in fact all the capital goods – were produced in the mother countries. Industrial production capacity was kept at home. The colonies provided raw materials and agricultural produce and served as retail markets for domestic production, while the local economies could continue regional maritime activities in traditional ways. When decolonisation set in, therefore, these areas were left devoid of industrial infrastructure with which to acquire a share in the global industrial and shipbuilding market. Furthermore, many of the new countries lacked a stable state or structured society suited for industrialisation. For such countries the backlog in these areas first has to be overtaken before they can enter the industrial market.

This picture applies to most of Africa, Asia and South America up to the 1970s. As settler colonies the United States, Canada and Australia had strong cultural and commercial ties with industrial Europe, which together with their early decolonisation gave these countries distinct advantages in starting industrialisation at an early stage – which is not saying that they immediately developed great shipbuilding industries. The US had its periods of boom in commercial shipping and shipbuilding, notably 1830-1860 and around 1900, but first the Civil War and later unfavourable economic conditions and trade legislation seriously handicapped the industry. True, Central and South America were decolonised early as well, and have a likewise Europe-centred culture, but their European collocutors (Spain and Portugal) were not industrial forerunners. Latin America therefore was less subject to industrial influence and largely continued to be a source of agricultural produce and raw materials.

In Asia Japan is an obvious exception, as it never had been a colony but a coloniser, and had a vast pre-war industrial experience of its own. After the war the restoration of its merchant navy was given priority, which resulted in a rapid recovery of the shipyards. How did today's other shipbuilding countries in the region find their way? South Korea in the 1970s purposefully chose shipbuilding as a core development industry, profiting greatly from US help and guidance, as later did Taiwan. Singapore and Hong Kong, which together with South Korea and Taiwan today make up the Four Asian Tigers, profited from British influence, their free trade policy and foreign investment. China, like Japan, was never truly colonised, but had long been subdued in many other ways. Shanghai meanwhile developed through several regimes to become the industrial centre of China. With massive government support it has in recent times become global leader in shipbuilding and shipping. Although perhaps late, Chinese shipbuilding seems to have completely overcome its arrears. Likewise Turkey, Russia and former colonies such as India, Vietnam, the Philippines, Brazil and Chile today are on the rise in the shipbuilding market.

The era of the great western thalassocracies and empires ended with the abolition of colonialism after the Second World War. Seaborne trade and consequently the demand for ships soared to unexpected heights, reinforced by factors such as world population growth, increased urbanisation and industrialisation and rising living standards. Although decolonisation did not automatically entail the transfer of technology and industrial potential to the former colonies, the more liberal climate enabled the aforementioned Asian shipbuilding countries to compete and to seize a share of the global shipbuilding market. The shipbuilding industries of the former colonial powers well-nigh collapsed.

However, since the 2008 economic crash it looks as though Asia's leading shipbuilding countries are heading towards massive overproduction, as the global demand for shipping space is expected to grow much more slowly than their output. Meanwhile western shipbuilding organisations like CESA (the Community of European Shipyards Associations) are devising survival strategies (some clearly protectionist) such as stimulating and pooling R&D efforts, intensifying safety and environmental standards both in shipping and shipbuilding, introducing more sustainable industrial structures, improving cooperation in naval shipbuilding programmes, protecting intellectual property rights (curtailing the free technology transfer noted above) and insisting on the application of World Trade Organisation rules to level the playing field in the shipbuilding market, notably by restricting government support. Needless to say that giants like China, which profit from low wages and low-tech production, at present are not inclined to support such measures.

Back to naval power

In the above we have investigated shipbuilding and its relation to power from several perspectives: by looking at industry-inherent aspects, such as the transfer of technology and the lifecycle of shipbuilding industries, as well as at external conditions, such as cultural and economic conditions. I'd like to end, however, with some remarks on naval power.

While the United States and the USSR dominated the global naval theatre during the Cold War, American commercial shipbuilding plummeted from the 1970s, victim to the same crisis as the rest of western shipbuilding. Concentrating naval shipbuilding to a limited number of state-owned yards, the US managed to preserve its naval dominance, which Russia as the foremost inheritor of the USSR largely lost – although, judging from its latest naval programmes, it is very hard trying to regain this. Today new naval contenders have entered the global arena, such as India and China.

These are players, but we can also look at the rules of the game. Since the transition from wood and sail to iron and mechanical propulsion the evolution of naval power has increasingly concentrated on armament and other military technology rather than naval architecture. As of old, a warship is designed as a platform for weapons systems, but in the last century the systems have evolved way faster than the platforms themselves (with the exception of submarines, nuclear propulsion, stealth, new materials, assembly techniques and such). Illustrative is the range of fire power, which over the last 150 years has increased from 1000m to intercontinental distances (ballistic and guided missiles or carrier aircraft), while the speed of the platform has increased five-fold at the utmost. Recently also naval strategy has tended to shift from the high seas to land-oriented operations and competing (technological) environments, such as (cyber-)space. Furthermore the politics of alliance today play a larger role than domestic industrial and technological potential, except for the super powers maybe: the average country finds itself not only faced with the prohibitive costs of independent military development, but also with the requirement to operate in a shared technological environment to enable allied deployment. Even for relatively wealthy nations, allied naval shipbuilding programmes have therefore become inescapable; the rest buy off-the-shelf commercial naval technology or second-hand matériel.

The distribution of naval power across the globe today depends on military technological superiority combined with industrial potential, often in an allied context. With the speeding-up of information transfer and the globalisation of industrial potential, newcomers will announce themselves more easily. But, once again, naval power need not have a bearing on the outcome of a conflict, as the First World War clearly illustrated, nor on the economic success of a nation.

BIBLIOGRAPHY

Many works and websites have been researched for this article. The following, eclectic list (in alphabetical order) contains only studies from which quotes/paraphrases have been used or which had a direct bearing on the argumentation.

BRUIJN J.R. et al., eds., *Strategy and Response in the Twentieth Century Maritime World. Papers presented to the Fourth British-Dutch Maritime History Conference* (Amsterdam 2001).

EPKENHANS M., *Die wilhelminische Flottenrüstung 1908-1914* (Munich, 1991).

FERREIRO L.D., 'Shipbuilders to the world. Evolution and revolution in Spanish and Chilean shipbuilding from the Cold War to the 21st century: a study in international technology transfer in the naval industries', *International Journal of Naval History* 8.3 (2010).

HATTENDORF J., ed., *Oxford Encyclopaedia of Maritime History*, 4 vols (Oxford, 2007).

INSTITUTE OF INDUSTRIAL ENGINEERS, *Methods Engineering Workshop for the Shipbuilding Industry* (Norcross, GA, 1985).

JOHNMAN L. and MURPHY H., *British Shipbuilding and the State since 1918. A Political Economy of Decline* (Exeter, 2002).

KING R.W., ed., *Naval Engineering and American Sea Power* (Baltimore, [1989]).

MICKEVICIENE R., 'Global Competition in Shipbuilding: Trends and Challenges for Europe', in *The Economic Geography of Globalization* ed. P. PACHURA (Open Access Book, Intech 2011, www.intechopen.com [Accessed December 2014]).

PORTER M.E., *Competition in Global Industries* (Cambridge, MA, 1986).

RUBEL R.C., *Navies and Economic Prosperity - the New Logic of Sea Power*, Corbett Paper No. 11, King's College, University of London (London, 2012).

RÜGER J., *The Great Naval Game. Britain and Germany in the Age of Empire* (Cambridge, 2007).

SONDHAUS L., *Navies in Modern World History* (London, 2004).

SPROUT H. and M., *The Rise of American Naval Power* (Princeton, 1939).

TODD D. and LINDBERG M., *Navies and Shipbuilding Industries: The Strained Symbiosis* (Westport, CT, 1996).

UN COMTRADE, *International Merchandise Trade Statistics 1992-2013* (http://comtrade.un.org/pb/first.aspx [Accessed December 2014]).

WILLUMSEN T. and TUTTUREN J-T., 'Why the Sun Has Yet to Set on Japanese Shipbuilding' (Seatrade Communications Limited 2014) http://www.seatrade-global.com/news/asia [Accessed December 2014]).

WON D.H., *A Study of Korean Shipbuilders' Strategy for Sustainable Growth* (Seoul, 2010).

Maintaining naval hegemony in the industrial age: Britain, 1850–1889

John F. Beeler is Professor in History at the University of Alabama, United States

Abstract. *It is a paradox that Britain came to feel under threat from foreign navies in an age when the Royal Navy outmatched all its potential enemies together, in numbers and even more in quality. The coming of the iron, armoured warship greatly advantaged the country whose engineering and shipbuilding industries dominated the world. Nevertheless, the British did not feel as confident in their naval superiority as they pretended, because they were beginning to experience the long-term consequences of abandoning the Corn Laws and the Navigation Acts. Now dependent on imported food and raw materials to feed and give work to the new mass electorate, Britain found herself reliant on command of the sea in a new and radical sense. In reaction, Britain started in 1889 what was to become a multi-national naval arms race lasting almost forty years.*

Résumé. *Le fait que la Grande-Bretagne se soit sentie menacée par les marines étrangères à une époque où la Royal Navy surpassait, par son nombre et plus encore par sa qualité, tous ses ennemis potentiels est paradoxal. La création d'un cuirassé blindé en fer avantagea particulièrement le pays, dont les industries de construction navale et d'ingénierie dominaient le monde. Néanmoins, les britanniques n'étaient pas aussi confiants de leur supériorité maritime qu'ils ne le prétendaient. L'abandon des « Corn Laws » et des « Actes de Navigation », dont ils commençaient à ressentir les conséquences à long terme, rendit le pays tributaire de l'importation de nourriture et de matières premières pour nourrir et faire travailler son nouvel électorat de masse. La Grande-Bretagne se retrouva dépendante du contrôle de la mer, dans un sens radical et nouveau. En réaction, elle débuta en 1889 ce qui devint une course à l'armement naval internationale qui dura plus de quarante ans.*

⁂

The economic and political context, 1850–70

This period opened with the government's adoption of free trade, symbolized less in this context by the repeal of the Corn Laws (1846) than by that of the Navigation Acts (1849). The latter had been a foundation stone of British imperial policy since first enacted in 1651 and were a key factor, in more ways than one, in the Royal Navy's rise to global dominance. The abandonment of mercantilism, therefore, put the navy's relationship to the government and the economy on a different footing than that which had existed for the past two centuries.

Despite the Navigation Acts' demise, however, no contemporary politician entertained doubts as to the navy's ongoing centrality to national and imperial security, on the one hand, and economic health, on the other. Between the 1820s and 1860s the value of Britain's total exports grew from an annual average of £43.9 million to £127.16 million. The value of imports climbed similarly from a yearly average of £54.35 million during the 1820s to £157.85 million during the 1860s.[1] As of 1860, Britain was producing 53 percent of the world's iron, half of the world's coal, and consuming almost half of the world's raw cotton.[2]

Moreover, that predominance extended to other sectors of the economy, among them machine tools, steam engineering, and shipbuilding, and it, along with concurrent British dominance in the financial services and marine insurance sectors, meant that not only was it was the "workshop of the world": its goods were also carried to overseas destinations, usually in British bottoms, insured by British underwriters.[3] Finally, the rapid growth of Britain's population meant growing demand for food, a demand that was by mid-century exceeding Britain's domestic productive capacity. The sea, long important to Britain's prosperity, was, as a consequence of population growth and industrialization, more essential than ever, and so too was the Royal Navy.

Yet paradoxically, this era of economic and industrial dominance witnessed an episodic challenge to British naval hegemony, courtesy of France, which rashly attempted to employ technology as a means of negating Britain's unassailable lead in wooden, sailing warships. Hence, in 1847 it was France, rather than Britain, that pioneered the steam line-of-battle ship; it was France that first employed armour plate on floating batteries destined for service in the Crimean War, and in 1858 it was France that laid down the first seagoing ironclad warship. In all three instances, however, the British response was swift and unequivocal: naval supremacy was to be upheld, no matter the cost.

The long-term outcome was never in doubt. Britain's superior shipbuilding capacity and vastly superior steam engineering sector ensured that the French challenge would be beaten back as long as the funding was forthcoming, and Britain's more advanced and wealthier economy ensured there was no shortage of money. Likewise, although some politicians, like Richard Cobden, denounced the sums spent on shipbuilding in 1847–1863 as extravagant, few agreed with them, and both Parliament and government opened the purse wide enough to win the naval arms race narrowly, but nonetheless decisively. Britain's technological and shipbuilding superiority meant that any such challenge was futile as long as the political will to meet it existed.

French efforts in the 1840s, 1850s, and 1860s to surmount Britain's quantitative superiority by obtaining a qualitative edge announced the arrival of the

---

[1] IMLAH A.H., *Economic Elements in the* Pax Britannica: *Studies in British Foreign Trade in the Nineteenth Century* (Cambridge, MA, 1958), 37–8; MITCHELL B.R., *British Historical Statistics* (Cambridge, 1988), 451–3. The figure for exports includes both domestic production and re-exports. For explanation of how these figures were calculated, see IMLAH, pp. 20–41.
[2] KENNEDY P., *The Rise and Fall of the Great Powers* (New York, 1987), p. 151.
[3] Ibid. As of 1860 more than a third of the world's merchant marine was British.

machine age, and with it the phenomenon of continuous technological change. The consequences for British naval policy were portentous, for with the rapid pace of technological advance in steam engineering, weaponry, armour, and electric and hydraulic power, came the need continuously to modernize the battlefleet on which national, imperial, and oceanic security depended.

ECONOMICS, TECHNOLOGY, AND STRATEGY, 1850-1870

Contemporaries routinely lamented the expense of "reconstructing" the fleet every few years, yet for the whole of the period Britain had critical advantages over all of its would-be or might-be naval rivals. The decisiveness of Britain's triumph in the ironclad race of 1858-1863 owed to more than quantitative superiority over France, for, as the latter's ongoing partiality to British steam technology and reliance chiefly on wooden-hulled ironclads suggests, Britain enjoyed an equally decisive qualitative advantage over its challenger, as the decision to construct HMS *Warrior* and most other first-generation ironclads of iron rather than wood suggests. The backward state of France's iron industry ruled out its competing head-to-head with Britain in that medium, and with it the advantages accruing from iron hulls, beginning with durability and longevity (as *Warrior* continues to demonstrate), and extending to less obvious areas such as rigidity and watertight compartmentalization below decks. These features gave the Royal Navy's ironclad battlefleet a decisive edge in battle-worthiness, as well as in numbers.

Critics, both then and later, alleged that the navy's administration was conservative and adverse to technological or design innovation, but these charges generally lack foundation. The Admiralty's overall receptivity to novel technology and designs was cautious but progressive.[4] That said, the Royal Navy did not enjoy the level of political and financial support that some contemporaries – naval officers chief among them – sought, and it certainly was not lavished with funds to indulge in large-scale technological experimentation.

The result of this situation was a building policy in which large classes of identical ships were generally eschewed in favor of individual or pairs of vessels, often openly imitative of foreign designs, leading to what some deride as the "fleet of samples." The drawbacks of the policy were obvious, beginning with the lack of uniformity of speed and maneuverability, which in turn led to tactical liabilities when operating in squadrons. But, given the technological flux that engulfed capital warship design from the late 1850s through the late 1880s, it is impossible to conceive of a sound alternative policy.

As was and sometimes still is the case regarding its receptivity to technological innovation, the Admiralty has also been widely criticized on strategic

---

[4] See LAMBERT A., ed., *Steam, Steel, and Shellfire: The Steam Warship, 1815-1905* (London, 1992) and BEELER J., *The Birth of the Battleship: British Capital Ship Design, 1870-1881* (London, 2001).

grounds, some detractors maintaining that it failed to develop a coherent strategy suitable for a steam-powered navy. To be sure, the application of steam to capital warships cast into doubt Britain's existing naval strategy, which centered on blockade to prevent the egress of enemy warships and thus stymie would-be invaders. "Steam ha[d] bridged the Channel," alleged many contemporaries, and this outcry figured largely into the "Navy scares" that accompanied France's challenge, 1847–1863. The upshot, according to many scholars, was that Britain's traditional reliance on the navy as the first line of defense (the "Blue Water" school) was supplanted from about 1850 to the late 1880s by land-based strategic views (the "Bricks and Mortar" school).

Much superficial evidence can be found to support this interpretation, beginning with the construction of elaborate fortifications around Portsmouth and Devonport dockyards in the 1850s and 1860s. Furthermore, the public debate regarding strategy was dominated, at least quantitatively, by army views, which naturally denigrated the navy's capacity to thwart an invasion. Yet volume of words is no indicator of their impact (often quite the opposite), and the Admiralty's *modus operandi* in this and other inter-service tussles was to act on its own strategic views without reference to the course of the public debate with the army.

Those views not only continued to countenance blockade, but broadened to encompass more aggressive operational plans. While alarmists pointed to steam's confounding impact on interdicting an invasion fleet – i.e., its liabilities from a defensive standpoint – thoughtful naval officers almost immediately appreciated its value for conducting offensive operations independent of the wind. The successful bombardments of Acre (1840), Kinburn, and Sweaborg (both 1855) suggested to many that future naval warfare would center on littoral assault rather than on fleet-to-fleet encounters. In this operational environment, steam was not a liability but a boon. This line of thinking was reinforced by the U.S. Civil War, which demonstrated not only that powerful land fortifications were unable to bar the passage even of wooden vessels (as at New Orleans and Mobile), but that warships actually had an advantage over forts, owing to their mobility.

In sum, by the late 1850s the Royal Navy had embraced coastal assault as a critical supplement to the blockade. Rather than waiting passively for enemy ships to sortie – and running the risk of failing to intercept them, owing to darkness or weather – it planned to destroy them in harbor before they could escape. This operational strategy – known as the "Cherbourg Strategy" – has long been obscured by the Admiralty's refusal to advertise its war plans, by the lack of any neatly bound volume articulating those plans, and by the officer corps' disdain for debating strategic matters publicly, but it is plain to see in the ship-procurement policy pursued by the navy from the mid-1860s onward, and particularly in the construction of small turret ironclads and, subsequently, in the authorization of far larger, seagoing "breastwork monitors," of which HMS *Devastation* (launched 1871) is rightly regarded as the first mastless capital ship, and was in many respects a precursor of the pre-Dreadnought battleships of the post-1889 era.

Many of these warships were publicly described as "coast defence" vessels, but this was a designation intended to fool the French and Russians (albeit with little success), and domestic critics of the navy like Cobden, John Bright, and William Gladstone (with considerably more). The latter regarded national and imperial defence – sometimes only the former – as the sole legitimate functions of the navy, thus the Admiralty's refusal publicly to state its intentions for their use in wartime. The internal evidence is unequivocal, however.[5]

THE ECONOMIC AND POLITICAL CONTEXT, 1870–1889

The Franco-German War provided the Royal Navy with an unexpected "peace dividend." The French navy's shipbuilding program had already slowed markedly by the mid-1860s following the realization that Britain had beaten back the technological challenge posed by ironclads. But the defeat of 1870–71, in which the navy had played no meaningful role, prompted the Third Republic to concentrate its resources on rebuilding its army.[6] Although the Royal Navy was simultaneously enduring a period of rigid economizing, the diminution of the French threat during the 1870s meant that it enjoyed a greater level of superiority over its only significant rival than at any point since the late 1840s.

Furthermore, as Britain's willingness to push the design envelope outdistanced France's in the late 1860s, that superiority was more and more a matter of quality as well as quantity, although it maintained the "two power standard" which had been the benchmark for battlefleet strength since 1817. By 1873 the First Lord of the Admiralty could boast to Parliament that the navy's frontline battlefleet consisted of twelve ironclads of such power that they had no rivals in the world.[7] On this solid foundation the Liberal Party's naval policy, which prioritized deterrence, was grounded.

Longer-term portents were less auspicious, however. Britain's share of world trade, 25.2 percent as of 1860, declined thereafter: to 24.9 percent in 1870, 23.2 percent in 1880, and barely 18 percent in 1889.[8] In 1860 Britain produced 3.9 million tons of pig iron, to Germany's 529,000 and America's 821,000 tons. By 1890 the latter had surpassed Britain's production, 9.3 to 8 million tons; Germany's output had risen to 4.1 million tons, and the latter country surpassed Britain in steel production within another decade.[9] Furthermore, the gap between imports and exports, which existed across the 19th century, grew significantly in its latter decades. The former were about 24 percent above the latter during the 1860s. By

---

[5] See BEELER, *The Birth of the Battleship*, pp. 89–91, 102–3.
[6] BEELER J., *British Naval Policy in the Gladstone-Disraeli Era, 1866–1880* (Stanford, 1997), p. 192.
[7] Ibid., p. 204.
[8] KENNEDY P., *The Rise and Fall of British Naval Mastery* (reprint edn, Malabar, FL, 1982), p. 190.
[9] MITCHELL B.R., *European Historical Statistics* (New York, 1975), p. 392; 'Statistics of iron and cotton 1830–1860', *The Quarterly Journal of Economics* 2.3 (1888), 379; KENNEDY, *Rise and Fall of the Great Powers*, p. 200.

the 1870s the percentage had risen to 33.6, and dropped only incrementally in the subsequent decade.[10] The resulting balance of payments deficit was partially offset by returns of overseas investments, which reached £80 million in 1887, and by the growth of the British merchant marine, which by 1890 amounted to more registered tonnage than the rest of the world combined.[11]

But the remarkable growth of the merchant marine was a potentially grave liability in wartime, especially since the naval strategies of both France and Russia encompassed commerce raiding, at least in theory. Of equal gravity, total overseas trade, which averaged £285 million *per annum* during the 1850s, swelled to almost £650 million in the 1870s and more than £690 million a year in the 1880s.[12] Of even greater ominousness, by the final quarter of the century Britain had become the world's greatest food importer: between 1871 and 1891 food imports increased by 88 percent. By 1886 two-thirds of Britain's grain came from overseas.[13] Britain, its Empire, its global trade, its overseas assets, even its survival, became increasingly dependent on control of oceanic trade routes, and hence on the navy, as the 19th century waned. Put another way, the sea, already essential to Britain, became still more critical during these years.

Overlaid on these economic concerns was the revived popularity of imperialism in the final quarter of the century, which, combined with Social Darwinism and other intellectual currents, generated an "us against them" mentality in which *si vis pacem, para bellum* became a widely held belief, and warfare itself was increasingly regarded not only as inevitable, but desirable: the ultimate test of fitness in the Darwinian "struggle for survival." In this climate the growth of the public's interest in the Royal Navy during the 1880s and questioning of its capacity to defend the home islands, Empire, and trade routes on which their economic prosperity (and food supply) depended, are understandable. Likewise, the expansion of the electorate and the proliferation of newspapers meant that debates about the navy's proper strength and composition were increasingly conducted in public, rather than being settled behind closed doors by the Cabinet.

Economics, Technology, and Strategy, 1870–1889

Concerns about the navy's adequacy were also fueled by a slowing rate of ironclad construction in the latter 1870s, coupled with a seemingly ambitious French armoured shipbuilding program. The reasons for this disparity were several, but three stand out. First, the Conservative government then in power placed less emphasis on deterrence than did the Liberals, preferring to devote

---

[10] MITCHELL, *British Historical Statistics*, p. 453.
[11] KENNEDY, *Rise and Fall of British Naval Mastery*, p. 151.
[12] MITCHELL, *British Historical Statistics*, p. 453.
[13] MARDER A., *The Anatomy of British Sea Power: A History of British Naval Policy in the Pre-Dreadnought Era, 1880–1905* (New York, 1940), p. 85.

more funding to unarmoured ship construction and to policing operations. Second, the French had to replace the first-generation ironclads built in the late 1850s and early 1860s, all of which were thoroughly obsolete and many of which had rotten hulls. Third, and most importantly, 1870-1889 witnessed the greatest period of confusion in naval architecture, technology, strategy, and tactics in the 19th century, and this confusion led to near-paralysis in British capital ship construction between 1876 and 1882.

The chief source of this confusion was the locomotive torpedo. Put simply, although decades away from being a practical weapon, from the start the torpedo cast into doubt the utility of building heavily armed and armoured capital ships. Indeed, by the early 1870s some authorities were advocating the abandonment of armour in order to increase firepower and speed, to enable capital ships to "outgun or outrun" torpedo vessels. Moreover, the torpedo added a confounding element to contemporary tactical debates, which revolved around close-range *mêlées* involving ramming, and threw into doubt the Royal Navy's "Cherbourg Strategy," which appeared to many to be far too dangerous to risk in the face of enemy torpedoes. The tactical and strategic confusion in turn reinforced the belief that the lumbering ironclad's day had passed. As late as 1886 former First Naval Lord Sir Astley Cooper Key stated in the *Times* "I believe the time ... is already arrived, when no more iron-clad ships will be laid down."[14]

But other navies, in particular that of France, joined in the early 1880s by Russia, *were* still building heavily armoured "battleships," as they began to be called in the late 1870s, and Britain had to follow suit or cede naval supremacy to its cross-channel rival. The latter course was not an option, so build the Royal Navy did, first HMS *Collingwood*, again imitative of a foreign (French) design, and then, when the French battleship building program seemed to reach an alarming level in the early 1880s, the subsequent "Admiral" class of battleships. As had been the case in the early 1860s, the apparent French challenge was faced down.

Several ironies attached to this episode and its aftermath. First, the French "challenge," unlike that of two decades earlier, was a chimera. The Third Republic was not attempting to contest Britain's naval supremacy; it was simply replacing Louis Napoleon's outdated and almost worthless fleet, as is evident in the overall size of the French ironclad/battleship fleet, which scarcely grew between 1880 and 1890, ambitious building program or no.[15] Second, that battlefleet was designed for defensive purposes – to protect France from a British assault – rather than *vice versa*. Third, in so far as French naval strategy posed any threat to Britain, that threat came in the form of commerce warfare, for which cruisers and overseas coaling stations, not battleships, constituted the coin of the realm. Fourth, the *guerre de course* threat was almost wholly hypothetical throughout the 1880s because the French navy lacked the vessels capable of carrying out large-scale, wide-ranging depredations against British commerce, to say nothing of the coaling stations needed to support them.

---

[14] Quoted in *Hansard's Parliamentary Debates*, 3rd ser., vol. 306 (1886), col. 1387.
[15] BEELER, *British Naval Policy in the Gladstone-Disraeli Era*, pp. 269-74.

Finally, just as the loans funding the French rebuilding program dried up, and Britain's naval supremacy was reasserted, muckraking journalist W.T. Stead managed to stoke a public and political furore with an 1884 series in the *Pall Mall Gazette* titled "The Truth about the Navy by One who knows the Facts." Stead's lurid, exaggerated, and irresponsible allegations of the navy's inadequacy, provided by disgruntled insiders including Captain John A. Fisher, gained considerable traction with the newspaper-reading public and Parliament, resulting in a supplementary Navy Estimate of £5.525 million in early 1885 to augment shipbuilding and coaling-station defence. The government and Admiralty, which had quietly taken effectual steps to counter the French battleship building program three years earlier, rightly recognized that the navy's most pressing wants were cruisers for trade protection and securing coaling stations abroad from enemy attack, and acted accordingly.

The Stead "Navy scare" of 1884 established the pattern for the course of British shipbuilding policy for the remainder of the decade and long thereafter. In the absence of public and press agitation, annual shipbuilding programs were determined by accurate reports on the states of foreign navies furnished by naval *attachés* to the Admiralty's intelligence department. During mid and late 1880s these reports consistently laid bare the glaring weaknesses of the French and Russian navies.[16] When press, public, and Parliament were sufficiently aroused by alarmist claims, however, as they were again in 1888, courtesy of a group of naval officers led by Captain Lord Charles Beresford, government and Admiralty had to give way with the 1889 Naval Defence Act, which authorized the construction of more than seventy warships, including ten battleships and forty-two cruisers, at a cost of £21 million and formally bound the government to the "two power standard."

Several aspects of the circumstances leading to, and consequences of, the Naval Defence Act (NDA) are worthy of note. To begin with, its shipbuilding program was closely modeled on an 1888 Naval Intelligence Department (NID) force-planning memorandum based on a worst-case scenario of a naval war against France and Russia in which Britain fought without allies. It also seriously exaggerated the strength of and threat posed by both "enemy" navies, especially that of France, and failed to take into consideration the qualitative advantages of British warships.[17]

Second, it also reflected a renewed commitment to blockade as the default naval strategy in a war with France or Russia. Given the threat posed by torpedoes, however, the close blockade employed by the sailing-era Royal Navy was abandoned in favor of a distant or "masking" blockade in which enemy ports were watched by an inshore force of small vessels – light or "scout" cruisers and torpedo-boat destroyers – while the main fleet was stationed out of immediate

---

[16] MULLINS R., 'Sharpening the Trident: The Decisions of 1889 and the Creation of Modern Sea Power' (PhD thesis, King's College London. 2000), pp. 43–6, 47–52.
[17] *Ibid.*, pp. 89–90.

harm's way, further out to sea.[18] Given the difficulty of intercepting a sortieing enemy force, however, coupled with the need frequently to detach vessels from the blockading fleet to coal and re-provision, the NID claimed that the latter required a large margin of superiority over the enemy force to be effectual. This ratio was based not on experience but on theoretical calculations made by the NID in December 1887, designed chiefly to extract more funding for shipbuilding.[19]

Third, while the NID and Admiralty relied on the blockade to keep most enemy commerce raiders at bay, individual cruisers would almost inevitably escape, as they had in the days of sail. To counteract the menace they would pose, the Admiralty had by the late 1880s adopted a policy of stationing British cruisers along the most heavily traveled trade routes, especially at major "choke points" such as the western entrance to the English Channel, where trade routes converged. These cruiser forces were supported by a global network of coaling stations defended by fortifications.

Fourth, and most critically, the NDA resulted not from a real foreign threat, nor even from an understandable misapprehension thereof, but from domestic panic fanned by alarmists whose largely baseless claims could be and were refuted by calmer, better-informed heads.[20] Not only was there little prospect of a Franco-Russian alliance as of 1888-89 (and no provision for naval cooperation in the one finally signed in 1892); even had there been, the French and Russian "battle-fleets," whether individually or combined, posed no threat either to Britain or to any portion of the Empire. Both forces' strategic postures were defensive, a point on which the naval *attachés'* reports were clear and convincing. Moreover, the Royal Navy *already possessed* a two-power standard of superiority in capital ships over France and Russia immediately prior to the NDA.[21]

As for the vast and largely undefended Empire, the unrivalled merchant marine, and the huge volume of commerce that the latter carried, it is true that the Royal Navy's existing cruiser force would have been inadequate to counter an enemy *guerre de course à outrance*. It is equally true, however, that there was no threat whatever of such a campaign, for the simple reason that neither the French nor the Russians had the ships with which to wage it. Russia had two fast armoured cruisers as of 1889-89, France none. Each possessed exactly one fast protected cruiser in 1889, and France five speedy unprotected cruisers.[22]

Alarmists in Britain pointed to the menace posed by Russia's plans to employ converted merchant vessels as commerce raiders, and to France's intention of using torpedo boats against British merchant shipping, to bolster their arguments, but these schemes were more indicative of Russia's pathetic steam

---

[18] GRIMES S., *Strategy and War Planning in the British Navy, 1887-1918* (Woodbridge, 2012), pp. 19-32.
[19] MULLINS, 'Sharpening the Trident', p. 85.
[20] *Ibid.*, pp. 89-90, 101-2.
[21] PARKES O., *British Battleships, 1860-1950* (London, 1957), pp. 352-3.
[22] CHESNEAU and KOLESNIK, *Conway's all the World's Fighting Ships, 1860-1905*, pp. 186-8; 192-3, 303, 308-10, 317-20.

engineering and shipbuilding sectors and France's incoherent naval strategy than of substantive threats. Moreover, few scare-mongers in Britain acknowledged that neither France nor, especially, Russia had the logistical means in terms of coaling and dry-docking facilities overseas necessary to support wide-ranging anti-commerce warfare.

That France was as of 1889 busily constructing fast protected cruisers was no cause for alarm either, because Britain, as had been the case in the 1840s, 1850s, and 1860s, still held virtually all the trump cards in any shipbuilding contest. While its overall economic and industrial lead had eroded substantially, Britain still dominated global shipbuilding, being responsible for 59 percent of tonnage built annually as late as 1914.[23] Moreover, British steam engineering firms remained at the forefront of the industry. For the whole of the pre-Dreadnought and Dreadnought eras, not only could Britain build warships faster than any rivals: it could do so in larger numbers and at lower cost. And on balance it built better ships too: the protected cruisers it built in large numbers in the late 1880s and early 1890s were superior in most respects to their French counterparts. In short, there was no need for Britain to seize the shipbuilding initiative. The superior resources at its disposal enabled it to wait securely until another power or powers did so, and then bring them to bear, just as it had through the 1870s and 1880s. Instead, it took the lead in 1889.

The NDA was intended in part as a deterrent. In that regard it was a failure; so far from cowing rivals, it led them to suspect British intentions and to respond with their own shipbuilding programs. The British, in short, initiated the pre-Dreadnought naval race. The influence of Mahan's *Sea Power* volumes would doubtless have spurred such a race sooner or later, regardless of Britain's actions, but without the NDA's passage its onset might well have been delayed for a few years.

Conclusion

At the beginning of this period Britain took a risky decision for free trade. Although the immediate advantages to the manufacturing sector were evident at the time, so was the less immediate threat to British agriculture. The alarmist warnings of the protectionist Tories in 1846 were not borne out in the 1850s or 1860s, but the onset of agricultural depression in 1873 vindicated their predictions. Although the growth of Britain's population increasingly outstripped domestic productive capacity, the flood of cheap imported food by the 1870s undercut British farmers and led to the ruination of much of the agricultural sector.

Farming aside, in purely economic terms free trade was a triumphant success,

---

[23] POLLARD S. and ROBERTSON P., *The British Shipbuilding Industry, 1870-1914* (Cambridge, MA, 1979), pp. 6-7.

at least in the short run, but from a strategic standpoint it was fraught with long-term danger. Britain bought short-term industrial supremacy at the price of import dependency. The sea and sea power therefore took on new importance. By 1890, as John Fisher melodramatically claimed, the Royal Navy was Britain's sole protection against starvation. By that time, too, free trade, as manifested by inexpensive food, had become sacrosanct, especially to working-class voters. And the growth of the electorate – after 1884 three in five adult males, the bulk of them working class, were enfranchised – and the spread of literacy and proliferation of newspapers meant that the navy, on which national survival depended, was increasingly a topic of public debate. Not only was the navy's role in national and imperial defence hugely altered: so was the discourse surrounding it.

Yet, while the harbingers of long-term relative decline were evident at the time of the NDA's passage in the form of growing economic and industrial competition from states with larger productive potential, the strategic demands of an industrialized global economy did not overtax the Royal Navy, nor the British economy and industrial base on which naval hegemony rested. In terms of fleet size, British naval supremacy was nowhere near as overwhelming in 1889 as it had been in 1815, but the fleet of 1889 was nonetheless capable of meeting any challenges that could be posed by the existing forces of rivals, and Britain's economic resources and shipbuilding capacity ensured that, as had been the case over the past three decades, it was capable of meeting any future challenge over the next three. Only after World War One would that situation change.

NAVAL ARMAMENTS RACES, 1889–1922

JON T. SUMIDA is Professor in the Department of History, University of Maryland, United States

ABSTRACT. *The rise of a world economy based on maritime trade, and specifically Britain's dependence on it, encouraged her rivals to build their own fleets. The French, Russian, German, and American navies in turn challenged British strength, creating a new arena of international competition midway between diplomacy and war.*

RÉSUMÉ. *La montée d'une économie mondiale basée sur le commerce maritime, et plus particulièrement la dépendance de la Grande-Bretagne à celui-ci, encouragèrent ses rivaux à construire leurs propres flottes. Les marines françaises, russes, allemandes et américaines défièrent tour à tour la puissance britannique, créant une nouvelle arène de la compétition internationale, à mi-chemin entre diplomatie et guerre.*

. • .

The dynamics of competitive naval expansion during the period 1889–1922 were shaped by interlocking economic, technological, financial, and political changes that had taken place over the course of the 19th century. The spread of industrialization expanded global production and consumption. Industrialization also made possible technological improvements in commercial ships and long-distance communications that reduced the costs of marine transportation. The increases in demand and supply together with decreases in the expense of commercial process accelerated the growth of trans-oceanic trade, and stimulated the acquisition of colonial territory for economic exploitation. This in turn enhanced the significance of maritime commerce and imperial extension as components of national prosperity, and thus of the strategic importance of naval power needed to protect valuable and even vital economic interests. Industrialization also created surplus wealth that could be devoted to naval purposes, brought into being powerful interest groups that favored higher outlays on navies, and generated rapid advances in naval technology. As a consequence, maritime powers were both fiscally capable and politically inclined to spend more on navies, and required to update their fleets repeatedly with warships of the latest design in order to maintain fighting efficiency. For most of the 19th century, upswings in warship construction by maritime powers were the product of temporary political conditions, and thus episodic. From 1889 to 1922, however, chronic international political antagonism – exacerbated by the widely held belief that the economic and therefore political destiny of great states depended upon maritime development – provoked widespread and nearly continuous competitive naval building.

In the mid-1880s, disagreements between Britain and France, and Britain and Russia over extra-European territory and commercial opportunity, served as the starting point for competitive imperialist adventure, for which navies, acting as agents of power projection beyond home territory, were essential. Insular Britain's dependence upon imported food and raw materials, and income generated by exported manufactured goods, was the source of British fear of the catastrophic economic consequences of naval defeat.

And the fact that Britain's army was much smaller than that of any continental great power meant that it had good reason to fear invasion in the event of its navy losing control of home waters. The validity of these two concerns encouraged Britain's two rivals to build the naval forces capable of posing dire threat. In 1889, Britain's Parliament passed the Naval Defence Act in response to public concern over naval weakness. This legislation provided for the construction of ten battleships, forty-two cruisers, and eighteen torpedo boats over a five-year period. The Naval Defence Act was accompanied by a declaration of Britain's intention to match the strength of the next two strongest naval powers measured in terms of warships of the latest type with fighting characteristics equal to or greater than those of foreign fleets. This statement of what was to become known as the "two-power standard" was interpreted to mean having as many battleships and twice the number of cruisers as the next two largest navies.

The Naval Defence Act doubled the effective strength of the navy, the objective of which was to discourage further challenges to Britain's naval position. France and Russia, however, responded with increased warship production and a formal alliance. Britain then reacted to the French and Russian actions with a second five-year scheme in 1894. This in turn provoked more French and Russian building. Between 1889 and 1896, Britain ordered twenty-five battleships as opposed to twenty-two authorized by France and Russia, sixty-two cruisers (nineteen of which were first-class cruisers) against twenty-six by the coalition, and introduced a new warship type, the torpedo-boat destroyer, which was larger, faster, and more heavily armed than a torpedo boat, in numbers that were nearly as great as those of its intended French and Russian prey (88 to 110). The financial effects of these programs were enormous. In 1896, British annual expenditure on battleships was more than triple what it had been in 1889, on cruisers some 50 per cent more, and on torpedo craft almost three times as much.[1] In 1896, the annual bill for the Royal Navy had increased by some 45 per cent over that of 1889. There are no comprehensive financial statistics available for French and

---

[1] British spending on warship categories from SUMIDA J., *In Defence of Naval Supremacy: Finance, Technology and British Naval Policy, 1889-1914* (Boston, MA, 1989).

Russian warship construction by type, but the proportional growth in annual naval budgets was nearly comparable: French naval spending in 1896 was a third greater than in 1889, Russian naval spending 42 per cent more.[2]

The French introduction in 1896 of larger and better-protected first-class cruisers, which were known as armored cruisers, forced Britain to respond with many more units of similar design from 1897 onwards. Beginning in 1901, Britain increased battleship size considerably to improve both fire-power and protection in the face of the increased potency of the armored cruiser. These qualitative changes in battleships and cruisers were not offset by any decrease in numbers. Indeed, Britain overmatched French and Russian programs by ordering more battleships and first-class cruisers in the second period than it had in the first. From 1897 to 1904, Britain authorized twenty-seven battleships as opposed to twenty-three by France and Russia, forty-seven cruisers against twenty-nine by the coalition, but of these thirty-five were armored cruisers against sixteen of this type by the two continental powers, and many destroyers. The combination of more units and higher unit costs of battleships and first-class cruisers greatly inflated naval spending. British expenditure on battleships from 1897 to 1904 was nearly twice the sum appropriated between 1889 and 1896, that on first-class cruisers more than tripled, and that on torpedo craft rose some 40 per cent. The expansion of the fleet, moreover, drove up spending on personnel, fuel, and shore installations. In 1904, Britain's overall annual naval spending was 77 per cent greater than in 1897, France's up less drastically by 12 per cent, but Russia's had risen by 90 per cent.

The naval building programs of other great powers – namely Germany, Italy, Austria-Hungary, the United States, and Japan – were relatively modest during the first phase of the naval armaments race between Britain and its two continental rivals. Between 1889 and 1896, the combined orders for new battleship and cruiser construction of these five countries (seventeen battleships and thrity-eight cruisers) remained less than those of Britain. By the mid-1890s, however, the entering into service of large numbers of powerful new British, French, and Russian warships posed potential threats to any state with maritime and imperial interests. The incentive to counter the growing naval power of others with naval expansion of one's own was magnified by the influential publications of an American naval officer, Captain Alfred Thayer Mahan, the first of which, *The Influence of Sea Power upon History 1660-1783*, appeared in 1890. Most readers of Mahan believed that the main lessons of his writing were that national prosperity depended upon maritime development, and that the possession of a powerful fleet of battleships was thus essential to any great state. Between 1897 and 1904, the five naval powers uninvolved in the contest between Britain and its rivals greatly increased their authorizations for new battleships and cruisers with an emphasis on the former type. Their combined orders for battleships came to no less than fifty-one units, which was triple the number ordered during

---

[2] Overall naval spending statistics from MODELSKI G. and THOMPSON W., *Seapower in Global Politics, 1494-1993* (London, 1988).

the preceding eight years and nearly twice the number of battleships authorized by Britain in the later period. Cruiser orders totaled ninety-four, or more than twice the number of the previous eight years and double those of Britain.

While Britain maintained its lead in naval building over France and Russia from 1898 to 1904, the need for it to keep superior forces in home waters and the Mediterranean meant that the continental coalition deployed much stronger fleets in East Asian waters. This prompted Britain to redress the imbalance in 1902 with an alliance with Japan, which made the latter's rapid naval expansion a significant factor in the on-going European naval arms race. Fiscal crisis caused by the costs of the war in South Africa and the cumulative effects of sixteen years of annual increases in naval spending, however, made it politically impossible for Britain to maintain the pace of new warship construction. In 1904, the government informed the Admiralty that naval expenditure would have to be reduced substantially from the next year onwards. In the face of the certainty of severe fiscal retrenchment and the prospect of continued French and Russian building, the leadership of the navy responded with proposals to replace the existing forms of battleship and armored cruiser with new model designs. Both novel types exploited recent technological advances to achieve much greater firepower and speed without commensurate increases in cost, and these improved operational characteristics were supposed to enable them to carry out the functions of a larger number of conventional units. The effect of these attributes, the Admiralty seems to have believed, would be a significant reduction in expenditure on large armored warships. In the event, this expedient turned out to be unnecessary. In 1904, diplomatic negotiations between Britain and France mitigated major political differences. By mid-1905, war with Japan and revolution at home had destroyed most of Russia's fleet and ruined its finances. Better relations with France and the collapse of Russia's naval power effectively eliminated the threat that had been posed by their combined fleets.

The technological and financial after-effects of the sixteen-year contest between Britain and the Franco-Russian coalition set the stage for a second naval race between Britain and Germany. The completion of the British new model battleship previously described, which was named *Dreadnought*, and the three new model armored cruisers, redefined the characteristics of a first-class battleship and armored cruiser. This disrupted planned building programs of the major European naval powers, which Britain could have exploited by establishing a wide lead over rivals in the new battleship and armored cruiser types. But fiscal exigency prevented Britain from so doing. Britain's annual naval budget in 1905 was 10 per cent lower than in 1904, and by 1908 had fallen a further 3 per cent. As a consequence, Britain's orders for battleships and armored cruisers during the period 1905–1908 were eight and four respectively, which was less than half the number authorized during the preceding four-year period from 1901 to 1904. From 1908, the new model armored cruisers were called battle cruisers and regarded as the near equals of the new model battleships, and thus like the new model battleships referred to as dreadnoughts. Between 1905 and 1908, French naval spending increased only 5 per cent, while the Russian naval budget fell 14 per cent. Russia did not order dreadnoughts until 1908, France not until 1910. Germany was a different matter.

The probability that Britain's fiscal difficulties would sharply limit its naval spending appeared to offer Germany an opportunity of equaling British strength in dreadnought battleships and battle cruisers. Achievement of this objective would have enhanced Germany's international political presence and further improved its global economic prospects. By 1908, Germany had ordered eight dreadnought battleships and two battle cruisers, which was only two short of the number authorized by Britain. German naval spending had risen by 8 per cent between 1904 and 1905, and jumped 40 per cent between 1905 and 1908, a four-year period in which, as mentioned previously, British naval expenditure declined. Britain possessed an overwhelming quantitative and qualitative superiority over Germany in conventional battleships and armored cruisers, but the near parity in dreadnought battleships and battle cruisers, and the possibility that accelerated construction might result in a German superiority in warships of this type, provoked a public outcry in Britain. The combination of fear of dire foreign threat and vociferous demand for the extension of social welfare enabled the government to pass increases in taxes in 1909 that provided it with the fiscal resources to remedy both concerns. Britain's spending on its navy in 1909 was nearly 10 per cent higher than in 1908.

Britain's building program for 1909 included no fewer than six battleships and two battle cruisers, which were augmented by two battle cruisers purchased by Australia and New Zealand. Four of the battleships and the two battle cruisers of the British program were much larger and equipped with heavier-caliber guns than previous dreadnoughts, and for this reason were called super-dreadnoughts. Britain ordered five slightly improved super-dreadnought battleships and battle cruisers in 1910, did so again in 1911, and in 1912 authorized the building of four fast battleships that were significantly larger, swifter, and better armed than their predecessors, but still referred to as super-dreadnoughts. Malaya added a fifth unit to this program. In the period 1909 to 1912, Britain and its dominions authorized the building of twenty-five dreadnought and super-dreadnought battleships and battle cruisers, or more than double the number of capital ships ordered in the previous four years. Construction of cruisers, destroyers, and submarines from 1909 to 1912 also increased dramatically as compared with the preceding four years. In 1912, British naval expenditure was 38 per cent more than it had been in 1908. Britain's formal declaration in 1912 of a one-power plus 60 per cent superiority in battleships and battle cruisers over Germany specified a greater superiority over Germany than the two-power standard (measured in terms of European powers and thus excluding the United States), given the lag in French and Russian programs.

The German government's attempt to match Britain's dramatic increases in taxation failed, which restricted its ability to keep pace with British naval building. German naval spending in 1909 was 20 per cent higher than in 1908, and from 1909 to 1912 rose an additional 10 per cent to a level one third more than that of 1908. This was not, however, enough to enable Germany to catch up with British battleship and battle cruiser construction in either numbers or nominal fire-power. In 1909, the German program consisted of five dreadnoughts (including one that had actually been ordered in 1908 and counted earlier above), in 1910 four, in 1911 four, and in 1912 two. The number of dreadnoughts authorized by Germany from 1909 to 1912 came to fifteen, ten fewer than Britain and none of which was a super-dreadnought, as compared to twenty-one units of the superior type ordered by the British. In terms of overall numbers, Britain and its dominions had ordered thirty-seven dreadnoughts and super-dreadnoughts by the end of 1912, against twenty-three for Germany. German new construction of cruisers and destroyers to support the battle fleet came much closer to British numbers of these types of warships, but this did not offset the wide margin of inferiority in large armored warships. German naval expansion during this period, moreover, depended upon resort to heavy borrowing, which generated enormous political dissatisfaction in the German imperial legislature that clouded future prospects of higher naval outlays. And the navy's fiscal position was further undermined from 1912 onwards by sharp increases in spending on the army.

The reaction of other maritime powers to British and German dreadnought programs was initially modest. From 1905 to 1908, dreadnought construction by naval powers other than Britain and Germany was limited to the United States, which ordered four, Japan, which ordered three, and Brazil, which ordered two, for a total of nine units. The proliferation of British and German dreadnoughts during this four-year period, however, established a new international standard in capital ship design that appears to have provoked a drastic increase in dreadnought and even super-dreadnought building by the other maritime powers. In the next four-year period, from 1909 to 1912, the combined total of dreadnoughts and super-dreadnoughts ordered by all maritime powers other than Britain and Germany was forty-four, which was nearly five time the number of first-class capital ships these countries had authorized between 1905 and 1908. The large armored warship programs of friendly and neutral major states such as France, Russia, the United States, and Japan, or those of weaker powers such as Spain, Argentina, Brazil, and Chile, were not a source of immediate concern to Britain. Indeed, dreadnoughts and super-dreadnoughts ordered by Japan and dreadnoughts by Brazil were constructed in British yards, to the benefit of Britain's warship-building industry. The dreadnoughts of Italy and Austria-Hungary, who were allied to Germany, did threaten Britain's position in the Mediterranean, a problem that appears to have been addressed, as will be explained, with Britain's 1913 and 1914 programs.

In 1913 and 1914, the rate of German capital ship construction decreased: the 1913 program consisted of two super-dreadnought battleships and one dreadnought battle cruiser, while the 1914 program called for only a single super-dreadnought battleship. The British programs of 1913 and 1914, in contrast, provided for no fewer than nine super-dreadnought battleships, eight of which were slower than the 1912 type of fast battleship but comparably well armed and one a repeat of the 1912 program. These units, when completed, would have given Britain the ability to counter Germany's two dreadnought battleship squadrons, under-strength half-squadron of super-dreadnought battleships, and one squadron of dreadnought battle cruisers with three squadrons of super-dreadnought battleships and one squadron composed mostly of super-dreadnought battle cruisers and fast battleships. Each British squadron, as a consequence, would have possessed an overwhelming superiority in fire-power over its German counterpart. Thus a British homogenous super-dreadnought fleet – in combination with the forward deployment of submarines – offered the credible prospect of containing the German battle fleet with a smaller margin of numerical superiority in surface capital ships, which would have enabled Britain to deploy enough dreadnoughts to the Mediterranean to deal with those of Italy and Austria-Hungary.

In mid-1914, a looming budget crisis compelled the Admiralty to accept the probability that two battleships of the 1914 program would have to be replaced by the less costly expedient of building more submarines. And shortly after the outbreak of war in August 1914, the Admiralty suspended the remaining two units in order to focus now scarce industrial resources on more immediate war requirements. In late 1914 and early 1915, pre-war proponents of an alternative naval force structure based on battle cruisers and torpedo craft rather than the conventional battle fleet were able to secure approval for the construction of five battle cruisers and a large program of destroyers and submarines. German orders for more battle cruisers in 1915 then provoked a British authorization of four additional battle cruisers. But in 1916 Germany suspended work on most heavy surface ships in order to redirect effort to increased submarine building needed to execute attacks on British trade. This action enabled Britain to cancel three of the four later battle cruisers in 1917. Over the course of the First World War, Britain's completion of all the battleships and one battle cruiser of the 1911, 1912, and 1913 programs, the five battle cruisers ordered in 1914 and 1915, and three battleships under construction in British yards that were expropriated from foreign navies, enabled it to widen its numerical lead over Germany in both dreadnought and super-dreadnought battleships and battle cruisers. This did not enable Britain to achieve a decisive victory in a general fleet action, but nonetheless constituted a quantitative and qualitative victory in the naval armaments race that had begun with the German decision to build dreadnoughts in large numbers.

During the First World War, British construction of warships and naval auxiliaries in tonnage exceeded that produced in the preceding quarter century. This massive effort far outstripped war losses, and as a consequence Britain's navy was much bigger at the end of hostilities than it had been at the beginning. The naval building by all other European powers declined during the war, and heavy warship casualties during the fighting and as a result of post-war political circumstances virtually eliminated the battle fleets of Germany, Russia, and Austria-Hungary. Treaty restrictions barred German naval recovery absolutely, the effects of revolution and civil war ruled out a Russian naval resurgence for many years, Austria was reduced to the status of a minor power, and the fiscal prostration of France and Italy meant that neither was inclined to embark upon significant naval expansion in the near term. Britain's naval position in Europe in 1919, therefore, was secure for the foreseeable future. The United States and Japan were historically friends and strategically inherently less threatening than any European rival because they were geographically much more distant. Post-war American and Japanese naval ambition, however, for a time appeared likely to bring about a three-way naval armaments race of unprecedented magnitude and expense.

In 1916, the American government had declared its intention to build a "Navy second to none," and authorized the construction of 156 warships over the next five years. The completion of this program would have added ten super-dreadnought battleships and six battle cruisers to the existing force of eleven super-dreadnought and eight dreadnought battleships as well as many cruisers, destroyers, and submarines. The American entry into the war in 1917 led to delays in the start of building on all but one of the capital ships in order to concentrate effort on producing merchant ships and convoy escorts to counter German submarine attacks on vital trans-Atlantic shipping routes. With the ending of the war, however, work on the 1916 program resumed, with the objective of attaining naval parity with Britain, which in effect would have given the United States a 100 per cent naval superiority over Japan. Japan, for its part, was determined to limit the margin of American naval advantage to no more than 30 per cent. In 1917, the Japanese national legislature thus authorized extensions to a substantial program of 1916, the total new building coming to eight battleships and eight battle cruisers in addition to the existing force of nine dreadnought and super-dreadnought battleships and battle cruisers, and substantial augmentation of the cruiser, destroyer, and submarine forces. By late 1921, one American battleship of the 1916 program had been completed, with the rest of the capital ships underway, while the Japanese had finished two battleships of their "eight-eight" program and laid down two battleships and four battle cruisers, with the remainder to follow shortly. Britain responded to these actions by ordering four battle cruisers in 1921 and making preparations to order four battleships in 1922, all of which were to be considerably larger than any of the battleships and battle cruisers being built by either the United States or Japan.

The fiscal burden of these efforts was enormous. In 1921, the naval budgets of the United States and Japan (adjusted for the rapid inflation during the war) were more than double what they had been in 1913. The British naval budget in 1921 was less (in real terms) than it had been in 1913, but the construction costs of the impending battleship and battle cruiser programs were sure to increase spending greatly. In the absence of serious political antagonism and strategic danger, the expression of national pride in the form of naval strength was not enough to overcome a deep reluctance on the part of the national legislatures of all three countries to spend heavily on armaments in the face of the difficult general fiscal circumstances that followed the ending of the First World War. In late 1921 and early 1922, the deliberations of the great powers in Washington, DC settled, among other things, outstanding conflicts of interest between Britain, the United States, and Japan over the future of Asia, which included the ending of the Anglo-Japanese alliance. This laid the foundation for a comprehensive naval armaments control agreement that called for the establishing of fixed ratios that governed the relative size of navies, the imposition of strict limits on the size and armament of battleships and battle cruisers, the scrapping of many existing battleships and battle cruisers, the cancellation of most on-going and projected new construction of such vessels and suspension of further capital ship building for a decade, and limits on the size and numbers of cruisers and aircraft carriers. These arrangements insured that Britain's vital maritime interests, as well as those of the other two powers, were secure. The several treaties of the Washington naval conference were signed in February 1922, bringing over three decades of unrestrained international competition in warship construction to a close.

The major consequences of naval armaments races in the late 19th and early 20th centuries were several. First, competitive naval building accelerated the growth in size and qualitative improvement of fleets around the world, which increased the scale and ferocity of maritime warfare. Second, dreadnought rivalry aggravated the deterioration of Anglo-German political relations and exacerbated the general atmosphere of antagonism and insecurity that shaped the response of the leadership of the European great powers to the Balkans crisis in the summer of 1914, and for these reasons must be considered a significant factor with respect to the outbreak of the First World War. Third, naval armaments races required enormous expenditure over extended periods, which generated financial difficulties that were the source of serious domestic political disagreement, and extraordinary fiscal expedients. Fourth, the competitive development of navies stimulated the growth of heavy industry, pushed the pace of mechanical invention, and prompted greater government involvement in engineering research and development. And fifth, naval building rivalry constituted grand spectacles of national prowess and progress that shaped popular opinion, taste, and imagination. Naval armaments races, in short, transformed the character of naval war, influenced international relations in critical ways, and had political, financial, economic, technological, and cultural ramifications as well. In broader historical terms, naval armaments races, together with parallel contests in land armaments, constituted a new form of international politics. Standing in between diplomacy and war, they were a protracted implied conflict whose administrative and fiscal burdens prompted a considerable extension of government direction of economic and social affairs in peace-time. Naval and land armaments races, therefore, were a precursor to what would later be called "Cold War," and a major contributor to early manifestations of the "welfare/warfare state."

Bibliography

BAER G., *One Hundred Years of Seapower: The U.S. Navy, 1890-1990* (Stanford, 1994).

BERGHAHN V., *Germany and the Approach of War in 1914* (London, 1973/1993).

BÖNKER D., *Militarism in a Global Age: Naval Ambitions in Germany and the United States Before World War I* (Ithaca, NY, 2012).

DINGMAN R., *Power in the Pacific: The Origins of Naval Arms Limitation, 1914-1922* (Chicago, 1976).

EPSTEIN K., *Torpedo: Inventing the Military-Industrial Complex in the United States and Great Britain* (Cambridge, MA, 2014).

EVANS D. and PEATTIE M., *Kaigun: Strategy, Tactics, and Technology in the Imperial Japanese Navy, 1887-1941* (Annapolis, MD, 1997).

GARDINER R., CHESNEAU R. and KOLESNIK E., eds, *Conway's All the World's Fighting Ships, 1860-1905* (London, 1979).

GARDINER R. and GRAY R., eds, *Conway's All the World's Fighting Ships, 1906-1921* (London, 1985).

HALPERN P., *The Mediterranean Naval Situation, 1908-1914* (Cambridge, MA, 1971).

HERWIG H., *'Luxury' Fleet: The Imperial German Navy, 1888-1918* (London, 1980).

JOHNSTON I. and BUXTON I., *The Battleship Builders: Constructing and Arming British Capital Ships* (Barnsley, 2013).

KENNEDY P., *The Rise and Fall of British Naval Mastery* (London, 1976).

LAMBERT N., *Sir John Fisher's Naval Revolution* (Columbia, SC, 1999).

MARDER A., *The Anatomy of British Sea Power: A History of British Naval Policy in the Pre-Dreadnought Era, 1880-1905* (New York, 1940).

MARDER A., *From the Dreadnought to Scapa Flow: The Royal Navy in the Fisher Era, 1904-1919*, 5 vols (London, 1961-75).

MODELSKI G. and THOMPSON W., *Seapower in Global Politics, 1494-1993* (London, 1988).

PAPASTRATIGAKIS N., *Russian Imperialism and Naval Power: Military Strategy and Build-Up to the Russo-Japanese War* (London, 2011).

PUGH P., *The Cost of Seapower: The Influence of Money on Naval Affairs from 1815 to the Present Day* (London, 1986).

ROPP T., *The Development of a Modern Navy: French Naval Policy, 1871-1904*, ed. S. ROBERTS (Annapolis, MD, 1987).

RÜGER J., *The Great Naval Game: Britain and Germany in the Age of Empire* (Cambridge, 2007).

SUMIDA J., *In Defence of Naval Supremacy: Finance, Technology, and British Naval Policy, 1889-1914* (Boston, MA, 1989).

SUMIDA J., *Inventing Grand Strategy and Teaching Command: The Classic Works of Alfred Thayer Mahan Reconsidered* (Washington, DC, 1997).

WALSER R., *France's Search for a Battle Fleet: Naval Policy and Naval Power, 1898-1914* (New York, 1992).

WINKLARETH R., *Naval Shipbuilders of the World: From the Age of Sail to the Present Day* (London, 2000).

The British Empire and the War at Sea, 1914–1918

DAVID STEVENS is Director of Strategic and Historical Studies at the Department of Defence, Canberra, Australia

ABSTRACT. *A seaborne empire naturally depended entirely on command of the sea, but by the 20th century the Dominions were no longer content to rely solely on British warships, stationed wherever the Admiralty chose. Who owned both warships and merchantmen, and where they served, became political as well as strategic questions.*

RÉSUMÉ. *Un empire maritime dépendait certes intégralement de la maîtrise de la mer. Mais au début du XXᵉ siècle, les dominions ne se satisfirent plus de reposer uniquement sur les flottes de guerre britanniques, lesquelles étaient stationnées selon le choix de l'Amirauté. La possession de flottes de guerre et marchandes et l'endroit où elles servaient devinrent des questions aussi bien politiques que stratégiques.*

.•.

On 16 March 1909 the First Lord of the Admiralty, Reginald McKenna, warned the British Parliament of the growing strength of foreign navies and the immediate need to order at least four new battleships, with possibly four more later in the year. Fanned by the media outcry, a sense of crisis spread rapidly across the British Empire. Within a week, New Zealand had telegraphed an offer to finance a battleship, and a second if considered necessary. Within a month, Canada, Australia and various smaller settlements had rallied to provide their own "patriotic proposals". Even the Australian states of Victoria and New South Wales offered to jointly fund a battleship, should the Commonwealth Government fail to take appropriate action.

The Empire was in a period of transition. The larger colonies had but recently become dominions, and after years of dependence were only just accepting that they must play a serious part in imperial defence. The need for intimate defence cooperation between the Empire's formal members had long been recognised, and amid the confusion of separate schemes a coordinated response was deemed essential. At the end of April the British Secretary of State invited representatives from the five self-governing dominions (Australia, Canada, New Zealand, the Cape Colony and Newfoundland) to an Imperial Conference in London. The gathering took place over July and August, and although its stated object was to discuss "the general question of Naval and Military Defence of the Empire", there could be little doubt that naval defence would take centre stage.

Needing no elaboration was the understanding that the world's greatest and most complex empire was fundamentally a maritime construct, built upon the military and social foundation of sea power. Exploration, settlement and trade had all required sustained free access to the ocean commons. For all the years of their European existence the "British dominions beyond the Seas" had trusted to the Royal Navy to preserve them from foreign aggression, secure the passage of British troops and maintain the oceanic connections that allowed them to prosper. More than this, the navy had played a key role in nation building. Naval officers had regularly assumed colonial leadership roles, while the global network of bases in ports such as Halifax, Colombo and Sydney had directly encouraged the growth of local maritime infrastructure. Protected and shaped by a largely shared sea heritage, the network of English-speaking dominions became the archetype of what Dr John Reeve has termed "the lucky league", a grouping that arguably included the United States as an informal member.[1]

By the early 20th century Britain had for decades held undisputed global leadership in finance, industry, commerce and shipping. Almost 60 per cent of the world's merchant fleet sailed under the red ensign, the services were high quality and relatively low cost and shipping routes resembled nothing so much as veins and arteries radiating to and from the pumping heart in the British Isles. The dominions may have possessed only a minor national stake in the ships themselves, but with apparently limitless natural resources they remained key beneficiaries of the exchange system that saw their agricultural produce consumed and their raw materials return as manufactured goods. Trade between Britain and its empire already approached 25 per cent of the annual value of imperial trade, while another quarter represented dominion trade with foreign countries and among themselves. By 1905, Australia alone could claim an annual overseas trade of £100 million, said to be greater than that of Spain or Japan. New Zealand, "under the beneficent influence of sea-power" possessed a revenue almost double that of Denmark.[2] Neither would have disagreed with the Canadian Government when it opined that the Royal Navy's continued supremacy was "essential to the security of commerce, the safety of the Empire and the peace of the world".[3]

Yet, at the 1909 Imperial Conference, the British freely admitted that global naval preponderance could no longer be guaranteed. At a session held with the Australian representatives on 10 August, McKenna explained that the burden of armaments was falling with increasing weight upon the imperial government,

---

[1] REEVE J., 'Maritime Nations – the Lucky League', in *The Navy and the Nation*, ed. D. STEVENS and J. REEVE (Sydney, 2005), pp. 370-83.
[2] SILBURN P., *The Evolution of Sea-Power* (London, 1912), p. 226.
[3] Telegram from SECRETARY OF STATE, 30 April 1909, The National Archives (TNA), ADM 116/1100.

and that the Admiralty could not bear indefinitely the heavy responsibilities. The risks, it seemed, lay primarily in the Pacific. By 1915, the Anglo-Japanese Alliance would have terminated, the Japanese and German fleets would be "very formidable" and, in areas remote from the main theatre of operations, British naval forces might well remain inferior to an actual or potential enemy.[4]

Until recently, the Admiralty had noted the relatively low numbers of seafarers in dominion populations and remained unconvinced that local naval forces, or "tuppenny ha'penny navies" as they were often termed, could contribute usefully to imperial defence. Its general policy had therefore been to encourage the payment of subsidies. Although these represented little more than token contributions (totalling just £328,000 in 1907), they supported the understanding that the maximum strength for a given expenditure was obtained by the maintenance of a single navy, with the concomitant unity of training and command. Now, however, came recognition that considerations of imperial strategy must necessarily include differing dominion circumstances:

> Though all have in them the seeds of a great advance in population, wealth and power, they have at present time attained to different stages in their growth. Their geographical position has subjected them to internal and external strains, varying in kind and intensity. Their history and physical environment have given rise to individual national sentiment, for the expression of which room must be found.[5]

Thus, although both Canada and Australia were comparable in geographic extent and looked generally to the land for cultural traditions, unique social, political and environmental factors had been at work, and their governments had acted upon different lines in encouraging development. In Canada a highly centralised federation had been formed in 1867, in part brought about by the need to finance an expansive rail system, built on the understanding that settlers would follow the tracks. The transcontinental railway to the Pacific, the world's longest, was completed in 1885 to great fanfare. By 1909 Canada's principal centres of wealth, population and strength, including the greatest of the eastern seaports, lay many miles inland.

The six Australian colonies, by contrast, did not federate until 1901, with each retaining far more autonomy. In the reverse of the Canadian experience, rail tended to follow settlement, a transcontinental railway was not completed until 1917 and the population remained concentrated around the many coastal settlements. Indeed, with no interstate road system and five different rail gauges, Australia was entirely reliant on coastal shipping to tame distance and the separate states might as well have been so many islands. As an English traveller wrote in 1911, the nation presented a paradox, "There is a breezy buoyant

---

[4] Admiralty Conference, 10 August 1909, TNA: CAB/18/12A.
[5] Admiralty Memorandum, 20 July 1909, TNA, CAB 37/100/98.

Imperial spirit. But the national spirit, as it is understood elsewhere, is practically non-existent."[6]

Nevertheless, no single factor had been more important in the development of Canadian and Australian interests than the Royal Navy's maritime shield. Whether directly or indirectly, both populations remained equally dependent upon shipping.

As presented to the Imperial Conference by the First Sea Lord, Admiral Sir John Fisher, the practical solution to burden sharing was to encourage the major dominions to acquire their own independent "Fleet Units"; a revolutionary tactical formation centred on an all big-gun armoured cruiser (later battlecruiser) and its high-speed scout cruisers (later light cruisers). When combined with a local defence flotilla of destroyers and submarines, and suitable auxiliaries, the package represented an ideal capability balance; small enough for a dominion to manage in peacetime, but in war able to join with other units to form a powerful imperial fleet.

Having been identified as the dominion most at risk, Australia readily accepted the need to proceed fully down the Fleet Unit path, seeing advantages beyond naval defence in developing both a domestic industrial base and a credible voice on the world stage. Buoyed by assurances that Britain would fund two further units on the China and East Indies Stations, construction progressed rapidly. On 4 October 1913 the battlecruiser *Australia*, leading three light cruisers and three destroyers, entered Sydney Harbour for the first time. On the same day the Australian Station's last British Commander-in-Chief hauled down his flag, leaving both the station and the fleet under Australian control. Importantly, though the major warships had been built in British shipyards, progress had already begun on local construction, with a further three destroyers and a light cruiser destined for completion before 1917.

For its part, New Zealand persisted with its offer to fund a capital ship, accepting promises that not only would its "gift ship" (the battlecruiser HMS *New Zealand*) become the China Station's flagship, but also parts of the China squadron would be based in New Zealand ports. Nevertheless, only the Australian unit was ever completed. Following Fisher's retirement from office in late 1910, public pronouncements concerning a Pacific naval strategy faded, disappearing entirely once the Anglo-Japanese Alliance was renewed in 1911. The next year, the Admiralty announced its decision to retain *New Zealand* in home waters, arguing the overriding need to concentrate practically the whole of its fighting strength in the main theatre. The best hope in distant seas was to hold the enemy in check until a decision had been obtained at the decisive point. As the Admiralty later admitted, in such a scenario regional defeat might have serious consequences for Australia – and presumably New Zealand – but would not "necessarily involve the Empire as a whole in irretrievable disaster".[7]

---

[6] FRASER J., *Australia: The Making of a Nation* (London, 1911), p. 11.
[7] ADMIRALTY to Naval Board, 15 May 1913, National Archives of Australia (NAA), MP1049/1, 1914/157.

Unwilling to enter into a junior partnership arrangement with Australia, New Zealand thereafter remained content to subsidise the continuing local presence of two elderly British cruisers, but retained some desire to take a more active role in maritime defence. In 1913 a new administration announced plans to build a fast, modern cruiser and secured an agreement from the Admiralty to provide on loan an additional cruiser for training.

Whereas Australia and New Zealand were true islands, at the end of the world's longest shipping routes and clearly remote from centres of friendly naval strength, other dominions could generally afford to maintain a more sanguine maritime outlook. Thus Canada, fully aware that its eastern regions remained within relatively easy reach of Britain, rejected the Fleet Unit proposal but still suffered delays in the execution of more modest plans as the nation failed to achieve an agreed naval policy. As with the Royal Australian Navy (RAN), King George V granted the Royal Canadian Navy (RCN) its "Royal" prefix in 1911 and, similarly to Australia, Canadian authorities planned to establish a viable local shipbuilding industry. Unlike Australia, by July 1914 Canada had acquired only two old cruisers, one of which was laid up in Halifax for want of money and crew, leaving only the cruiser at Esquimalt capable of going to sea.

Elsewhere within the Empire, naval interest largely resided in local reserve divisions. Since the Royal Navy had long defended the Cape sea route from its major base at Simon's Town, the new Union of South Africa saw little need to develop its own navy. As a society dependent upon some of the richest fishing grounds in the world, Newfoundland's population was more intimately connected to the sea than most, but remained simply too small to support a naval force. India at least possessed the Royal Indian Marine (RIM), but, restricted in both size and capability, its employment remained constrained to surveying, troop transport and local security. Like the others, India therefore continued to contribute a limited annual subvention towards the Royal Navy's maintenance in regional waters.

Such was the naval situation of the Empire's scattered nations in August 1914 when war finally broke out. If only subconsciously, all members at least understood their maritime dependence and most would have recognised control of their coastal waters as a basic necessity of national sovereignty. But outside the imperial fleet, only Australia possessed the practical capabilities to exercise this control beyond the range of coastal artillery. Nevertheless, the challenges facing the British Empire necessarily required a global outlook, as even the transient operations of an enemy raider had the potential to cause significant alarm and disruption.

In the Pacific, the German East Asian Squadron posed the greatest threat to the British Empire's oceanic links. Based at Tsingtao in China, its tactics had long sought to be proactive. By stalking trade routes and raiding colonial and dominion harbours to acquire supplies, the Germans aimed to take advantage of the Empire's greatest strategic vulnerability – its enormous dispersal. Indeed, the Premier of the isolated Canadian western province of British Colombia felt the threat so immediate that on the night of 4 August, on his own initiative, he acquired two small submarines from a Seattle shipyard.

By contrast, on the Pacific's opposite side the existence of the Australian fleet, and especially *Australia*, had immediately acted as an effective deterrent. Faced with overwhelming Allied naval strength and ongoing supply problems, the German squadron decided that, rather than carry out its orders for commerce warfare, it would instead proceed east towards South America. On the understanding that a single raider would not suffer the same difficulties in obtaining coal, the Germans left behind the light cruiser *Emden* to carry out a lone campaign in the Indian Ocean.

Continuing uncertainty as to the German squadron's whereabouts nonetheless caused great concern in the Australasian dominions, particularly when it came to arranging the safe passage of their expeditionary forces to Europe. With the Australian fleet engaged elsewhere, the remaining cruisers were deemed inadequate, and in early October the New Zealand Prime Minister threatened to resign if the Admiralty failed to provide an appropriate escort. The resultant need to transfer additional warships from the Indian Ocean imposed a three-week delay in the first Australasian troop convoy's departure.

Emden had meanwhile begun a highly profitable campaign against Allied shipping in the Bay of Bengal, capturing or destroying more than 80,000 tons by October. The first shock of her appearance resulted in the paralysis of all shipping movements east of Colombo. Indirect effects included port congestion, cargo spoiling and, by inducing panic among moneylenders, the derangement of commerce across southern India. Without adequate and timely intelligence, Allied hunting forces proved powerless, and *Emden* was stopped only when the raider attempted to attack the British cable and wireless station in the Cocos Islands on 9 November. By chance, the Australasian convoy was then passing within 100 miles and, alerted by the station's warning, the Australian cruiser *Sydney* was despatched and successfully engaged the raider.

Chased by Australian, British and Japanese forces, the German East Asian Squadron was eventually destroyed off the Falklands, and by the end of 1914 the Allies had cleared the enemy from the Indo-Pacific. And yet the weaknesses in imperial naval preparedness had been made very clear. The RAN received some credit for its role in improving the situation, but, as the Australian Defence Minister later remarked, the Empire had "paid the penalty for withdrawal of British fleets by loss of trade and prestige".[8] In any event, despite continued unease over the depth of Britain's regional security commitment, the way was clear for the more capable dominion warships to be deployed to areas of greater need.

Two cruisers from the New Zealand squadron went to the Middle East, while *Australia* joined the Grand Fleet in the North Sea. The RAN's two most modern light cruisers, *Sydney* and *Melbourne*, operated off North America and in the

---

[8] Cover sheet to COMMANDER AUSTRALIAN FLEET, Letter No. 37, 20 March 1915, Australian War Memorial, 3DRL53, 12/4/41.

West Indies. Initially employed in chasing the few remaining German surface raiders and watching neutral harbours, they then undertook the more general protection of British and Canadian maritime interests. As such, *Sydney*'s visits to Halifax in August and September 1915 generated more than favourable media comparisons with local naval capabilities:

> *Sydney* is now, and for some time has been, forming a part of the naval protection that the Canadian coast required during the war ... Today Canada is accepting the service of the Australian cruiser to guard our soldiers as they travel to Bermuda, and to protect our coasts and to look after shipping out and in, and guard against possible submarine attack by the enemy ... If Canada had possessed a few smart cruisers like this one from Australia, which is now making up for our deficiencies in this respect, their value would have been beyond price.[9]

During 1915–17 other Australian warships were deployed to the East Indies and China Stations, where they assisted in the suppression of German schemes to raise indigenous rebellions in Britain's Far Eastern colonies. In the Bay of Bengal, Royal Navy, RAN and RIM ships together patrolled the Nicobar Islands and Burmese coast. In addition to intercepting arms and suspicious persons, the operations demonstrated to local mariners that they were under surveillance, thereby discouraging collusion with the enemy. "Showing the flag" held a similar importance around the Dutch East Indies and Borneo. Visits by the Australian sloop, *Una*, captured from the Germans in October 1914, seemed particularly effective as she had been well known in regional ports under her former flag. Her reappearance flying the White Ensign reinforced the message that the British possessed full control at sea.

The extended absence of RAN warships overseas did, however, deepen Australian concerns when in 1917 German surface raiders again became active in the Indo-Pacific. Since the beginning of 1915, Allied shipping had been able to cross the Indian Ocean without escort, but following the discovery of minefields laid by the raider *Wolf* off the Cape and India in early 1917, escorts were once more deemed necessary for troopships in the northern Indian Ocean. Convoys for transports to and from Australia and New Zealand, or between Indian and the Cape, presented greater difficulties owing to the distances involved, and relied heavily on Japanese augmentation. Merchant ships, by contrast, were expected to sail independently, relying almost entirely upon dispersal for their safety.

Nonetheless, it was in the Tasman Sea and South Pacific that *Wolf* achieved the greatest direct effect. The raider captured or sank five Allied vessels and laid minefields off Australia and New Zealand that sank another three. In February 1917 the Australian Naval Board had reminded the Admiralty that its most powerful warships were absent on imperial tasks, and of the potential risks should a raider manage to reach Australian waters: "It is of course of great

---

[9] Cited in JOSE A., *The Royal Australian Navy* (Sydney, 1928), p. 256.

importance to the welfare of Australia to keep the communication by sea open because there is no communication between Western and Eastern Australia save by sea, [if] the carriage of coal on the East Coast were held up for any time the effect on the population would ... be disastrous."[10]

The Admiralty responded by again calling on Japanese assistance, but the threat also encouraged a strengthening of Australian local defence and, most fortunately, minesweeping arrangements. Considering that Japan remained the most likely future enemy and that the RAN never ceased planning for a Pacific war, it is not surprising that the naval relationship was sometimes strained. But the benefits of the foreign presence were made clear by the captain of *Seeadler*, a second German raider that entered the Pacific by way of Cape Horn. Captured after his ship ran aground west of Tahiti, he claimed under interrogation that it was the Japanese that had deterred his operating off Australia.

The ongoing German U-boat campaign also caused difficulties for the dominions, both in the destruction of important ships and cargo and less directly through the growing fear that the Germans might use their larger submarines to extend operations into more distant areas. Only in Canadian waters were these fears realised, the first submarine attacks taking place off Nantucket Island in October 1916 and causing the rapid expansion of coastal anti-submarine patrols. Further developments came with the introduction of trans-Atlantic convoys in the summer of 1917, the east coast ports of Halifax and Sydney thereafter becoming of great importance for convoy assembly. Nevertheless, when in late 1918 three U-boats created havoc among the east coast fishing fleet, the RCN remained incapable of an effective response. It has been remarked that the clear lesson for the Canadian Government, was that "in time of crisis, no one would look after Canadian maritime interests other than Canadians".[11] It was a message that applied equally to the other dominions.

In the meantime, U-boat attacks in the Atlantic had meant the loss of parts destined for a second cruiser building for the RAN at Sydney, and thereby added to construction delays already exacerbated by shipping shortages. The combination of raider warnings and Germany's declaration of unrestricted submarine warfare in early 1917 prompted questions to Australian Prime Minister Billy Hughes over shipping safety, and the situation continued to worsen. In July, Hughes described the economic effects as "most serious", reminding Parliament of the contract with Britain to export 60,000 tons of wheat monthly and noting that not one bushel had moved in June, while other products were heaping up.[12]

The difficulties in clearing Australian wheat harvests had already resulted in the use of troopships to assist with carriage. More significantly, following the British rejection of his request for charters, in June 1916 Hughes purchased fifteen steamers to join with twenty-seven seized enemy cargo ships to create the Commonwealth Government Line of Shipping. Hughes envisioned a more

---

[10] NAVAL BOARD to Admiralty, 21 February 1917, NAA, MP1049/1, 1920/0128.
[11] MILNER M., *Canada's Navy: The First Century* (Toronto, 1999), p. 39.
[12] *Commonwealth Parliamentary Debates*, 12 July 1917, p. 131.

general role for the national flag in overseas trade and "Being seized of the vital importance of shipping to the national, economic and financial welfare of the nation", and the urgent need to increase available tonnage, he embarked on an ambitious plan to expand construction at Australia's ports.[13] Previously, local shipbuilders had catered almost exclusively for the coastal trade, but during 1918-1923 they built nineteen ocean-going steamers for the new line.

Canada embarked on a similar shipbuilding programme early in 1918 as a war measure. Local yards had previously built steamers to assist in making up the British shortfall, but these remained unavailable for Canadian use. Already owning the railway system, the Government deemed it necessary to complete the transport chain by providing cargo ships to expand overseas trade. Despite constraints imposed by a lack of steel and engineering skills, sixty-three ships were planned to be built by 1921.

The main problem for both state-owned shipyards and merchant shipping, however, was that costs were too high to remain competitive. Although the Commonwealth Line at first made a profit, freight rates fell soon after the Armistice, a situation exacerbated by the surplus tonnage that existed in the early 1920s and the entry of many new nations into the business. Any advantages from the operation of a national line were reaped mainly by producers and, with losses falling on taxpayers as a whole, in 1928 the Australian ships were all sold to private interests.

The Armistice also brought geographical shifts in overseas trading patterns. The United States had supplanted Britain as the greatest industrial and financial power, and the dominions found trade tending to become more diverse and international. Hence, although Britain remained the largest individual destination for shipping from Australia, the previous trade imbalance was reversed and only two-thirds of arriving tonnage came from European or British ports. The remaining ships came largely from the Americas, but, even so, the most dynamic sector became trade with Asia and the Pacific. In addition to traditional commodities the latter increasingly saw the import of oil from the Dutch East Indies, a reflection on the growing importance of cheap, clean energy.

There could be no mistaking the enhanced understanding of sea power that the Great War brought to the members of the British Empire. All their campaigns had taken place at sea or overseas. Without a functioning shipping system the war economy would have come to a standstill and Britain would have been unable to draw upon its global resource base. But the arrival of peace also heralded a shift in sea power's centre of gravity from the North Sea to the Pacific. Noting the collapse of the German Navy, and that Japan and the United States had resumed their naval arms race, it appeared to more than a few commentators that the Empire's extremities were now under the greatest threat. How this issue of maritime vulnerability could best be addressed was not easily answered.

Although the varied forces that existed in 1914, and more particularly the RAN,

---

[13] Cited in JEREMY J., *The Island Shipyard: Shipbuilding at Cockatoo Island 1870-1987* (Sydney, 2013), p. 82.

had proved their worth, the Admiralty seemed unconvinced that independent dominion navies offered any great benefit. Wrangling continued after the Armistice and final vindication of Australia's arrangements did not finally come until the 1919 Imperial Conference. Here the Admiralty finally conceded that "The policy of forming Dominion Navies has the great advantage of stimulating national pride and effort in naval affairs and it is therefore recommended that Canada, New Zealand and South Africa should gradually build up navies of their own on the Australian model."[14]

Yet the dominions had also been changed by the war. In 1914 they had already been strongly organised and keenly conscious of nationhood. Their subsequent sacrifice and recognition of important aid rendered to the Empire had both increased their desire for influence in defence and foreign policy and loosened imperial ties. Indeed, their status as independent states was virtually conceded when the dominion representatives appended their signatures independently to the peace treaties. When asked in the early 1920s whether the British Empire was a single state or a group of states, the political scientist and historian Sir Alfred Zimmern replied that the entity that had entered the Great War had emerged as "something looser than a confederacy or even an alliance".[15]

Being a free association of states with no central constitutional government, by 1921 the Empire had become recognised as the British Commonwealth of Nations. The combination of a more informal structure and regular consultation proved essential in keeping the grouping together but, despite some successes in regional naval relationships, remained unable to achieve either a uniform understanding of the totality of local naval needs or a comprehensive maritime strategy for its members. At the very least, however, the Great War had demonstrated what combined naval operations could achieve and shaped expectations of collective security. Moreover, it remained the sea that made the informal empire a reality and ensured that it persisted as a global force for decades afterwards.

Sea transport continues to be the basis for economic well-being, but today it is the US Navy that largely guards the ocean commons. Like the Royal Navy before it, there exist real limits on its ability to confront existing and potential challenges at sea, and so combined naval operations have become the accepted norm when seeking to influence events. A foundation of trust is essential to these operations and, although perceived interests will never be identical, those touched by the British Empire's maritime legacy have done more than most to create an effective framework of interoperability.

---

[14] Cited in TRACY N., ed., *The Collective Naval Defence of the Empire, 1900-1940* (Aldershot, 1997), pp. xxviii-xxix.
[15] ZIMMERN A., *The Third British Empire* (London, 1926), p. 42.

Steaming worldwide waters: adaptation and transformation in the Netherlands

Anita M.C. van Dissel is a Lecturer at Leiden University, the Netherlands

Abstract. *The nineteenth-century Netherlands rebuilt its overseas trade on the basis of colonial protection. The revived empire was defended by a colonial army in the East, and a middle-sized navy divided between opposite sides of the world. By the end of the century industrialization and free trade had transformed Dutch shipping and overseas trade.*

Résumé. *Au XIXe siècle, les Pays-Bas réédifièrent leur commerce extérieur sur la base de la protection coloniale. Le nouvel empire était défendu par une armée coloniale à l'est et par une marine de moyenne taille dispersée aux quatre coins du monde. Vers la fin du siècle, l'industrialisation et le libre-échange ont transformé la navigation et le commerce extérieur néerlandais.*

. • .

The long-term decline of the Dutch Republic as a maritime power encompassed a variety of institutional, financial, geographical and socio-economic factors. In the mid-18th century, the Republic of the Seven United Provinces was no longer able to compete with Great Britain and France. During the revolutionary period from 1795 to 1813 the decline of the Netherlands accelerated as a result of the Napoleonic Wars and the Continental System. Long-term trade virtually came to a standstill and warships were locked in the roads of Holland and Zeeland by enemy-blockading squadrons. The colonies and trading posts of the former Dutch East India Company and West India Company were occupied by the British. Following the victory of the Allied armies at the Battle of Leipzig, supporters of the exiled House of Orange seized power. In his famous proclamation of 17 November 1813 Gijsbert Karel van Hogendorp, head of the provisional Dutch government in the first turbulent months, optimistically stated "The sea is open, trade revives [...] The old times are coming back again."[1] Van Hogendorp and his political friends hoped the Prince of Orange would be the instrument to restore prosperity.

---

[1] https://www.200jaarkoninkrijk.nl/content/proclamatie-17-november-1813 [Accessed 10 November 2014].

With British support, the Netherlands became a monarchy under King Willem I. The United Kingdom of the Netherlands was reinstated as a colonial power to counterbalance France on the continent. All the colonies Great Britain had seized in the Napoleonic Era were returned to the Netherlands, with the exception of Ceylon, the Cape Colony and Guyana. The Dutch field of action was actually narrowed to the Indonesian Archipelago in Southeast Asia and Surinam, six Caribbean islands and, until 1872, the Dutch Gold Coast in the Atlantic. Even the best rulers and strategists could hardly have been prepared for the unprecedented changes which transformed international relations and global trade over the next hundred years. This raises the question of the ability of the Dutch political and merchant elite to adapt to the exponential growth at the pace of change that reconfigured shipping and shaped the world.

Remembering the Past and Looking Forward

King Willem I built on reforms that were introduced during the Napoleonic period. The early modern political structure of a federation of provinces was definitively replaced by a centralized state, personified by the king with absolute power. Only in 1848, the Year of Revolutions, did the Netherlands become a constitutional monarchy. The newly formed kingdom was roughly made up of the former Dutch Republic to the north and the former Austrian Netherlands to the south. Willem I, called the "Merchant-King", dedicated himself to restoring the Golden Age's thriving economy by stimulating the production of consumer goods in the southern provinces, and shipping and transport in the northern region. However, he was unable to reconcile the northern commercial and southern industrial interests. Economic, social, religious and political differences ended in the Belgian Revolution of 1830, leading to the secession of the southern provinces from the United Kingdom of the Netherlands and the establishment of an independent Kingdom of Belgium.

The return to free access to the sea in 1814 initially resulted in a recovery of Dutch trade and shipping. The Baltic trade, in the 17th century the mainspring of the country's economic primacy and maritime strength, and Rhine transport especially, saw promising growth rates. After the post-war boom the maritime sector stagnated. The main reasons were, among other things, the loss of transport capacity during the Napoleonic Era, fierce protectionism in international trade and the dominance of Britain in industrial products. The Dutch East Indies certainly offered opportunities to expand shipping and trade, but merchants seemed to have lost interest in the colonies. In 1816, only twenty ships set sail from the Netherlands to Java, eight years later not more than fifty-three. Dutch firms in Batavia, seat of the governor-general in the Dutch East Indies, met fierce competition from British business agents, who made huge profits on the export of textiles to Southeast Asia.

To restore Dutch maritime strength and prosperity, the Netherlands had to seek new methods of profiting from trade and empire. Protectionism and state regulation proved to be the best stimulus for colonial trade. The economy was stimulated by subsidies for shipbuilding to increase the capacity of the merchant fleet, and the establishment of the Nederlandsche Handel Maatschappij (NHM; Netherlands Trading Company). The NHM was founded in 1824 on the initiative of King Willem I to stimulate all Dutch trade and maritime sectors, but colonial trade profited the most. The NHM chartered ships to transport coffee, indigo and tobacco to the Netherlands. The ship owners were guaranteed high freight rates and return cargoes.

The growth of seaborne commercial activities by the NHM went hand in hand with the introduction of the Cultivation System (*Cultuurstelsel*) in 1830. The costs of the Java War (1825-1830), the Belgian Revolution of 1830 and the king's great expenses for inland infrastructure had brought the Netherlands to the brink of bankruptcy. The Cultivation System intended to increase the exploitation of the Dutch East Indies' resources. Javanese peasants were forced to devote a proportion of agricultural production to export crops. The outcome was a tremendous expansion of state-controlled commodity exports and the growth of a highly one-sided structure of merchant shipping. In the mid-19th century the Dutch merchant marine was already fourth in world rankings, numbering more than 2,300 ships and 432,000 tons of shipping. These numbers and tonnages of ships differed sharply by trade. A large fleet of small *koffs* and *tjalks* registered in Groningen and Friesland were engaged in traditional tramp trade in northern European waters. Amsterdam, home port of barques and schooners specially designed to transport both passengers and cargo around the Cape to Java, recaptured its dominant position in the distribution of colonial products. The German states and kingdoms especially offered good prospects for the export of Javanese commodities: more than 50% of the export trade to Germany in the 1840s was comprised of these goods. At first, the NHM policy proved quite successful, but in the long run the king's protectionist policy undermined the efficiency of trade and transport. It generated more and more criticism.

From 1848 liberals dominated Dutch politics. They promoted fiscal and administrative reorganization and got rid of the remaining old institutions dominated by the Amsterdam merchant elite. The new government policy facilitated the emergence of a national and modern economy. After the international liberalization of trade and shipping in the mid-19th century freight tariffs were gradually lowered and subsidies reduced to encourage a more entrepreneurial and innovative spirit. Dutch traders explored new markets in Africa, South America, California and Australia, but faced savage international competition. Within twenty-five years, the merchant fleet fell from fourth to eighth place. The relative stagnation in ocean shipping was attributed to the policy of the NHM, which had created a guided economy that was virtually protected from international competition but was actually caused by a complex of national and international factors, such as high wages and the international shipping crisis after 1857. The introduction of innovative ships, rigging and navigation techniques contradicted the supposed backwardness of Dutch shipping and lack of entrepreneurship. Fop Smit in Kinderdijk, nowadays famous in transport, towage and salvage, for example, already built the first Dutch seagoing steamship in 1830 and, following the latest designs in British and American shipbuilding, Gips in Dordrecht launched several fast clippers in the 1850s for colonial trade and passenger service to Java.

A SMALL COUNTRY WITH A LARGE EMPIRE

The Cultivation System, although linked to colonial injustice and oppression, brought the Dutch enormous wealth. The Javanese revenues were used to reduce the public debt and made an important contribution to industrial growth after the 1860s. The costs of the construction of an extensive transport network of railroads, canals, locks and bridges were substantially covered by the proceeds from the sale of sugar and other colonial products. Inland infrastructure, which integrated remote agricultural regions with the more urbanized coastal provinces, was a precondition of the industrialization and globalization of the Netherlands. International trade became closely connected with domestic agricultural and industrial production. It was no accident that these developments coincided with growing Dutch imperial ambitions in Southeast Asia. In the age of modern imperialism that began in the 1870s, European nations pursued an aggressive expansion policy that was mainly motivated by political, economic and strategic needs. Great Britain, Germany, Belgium and Italy established colonies in Africa, the Middle East and Asia. Although the Netherlands took no part in the competitive struggle for overseas territory, it cannot be denied that the country participated in the imperialistic trend of administrative, military and economic expansion within its spheres of influence overseas. By 1914 the Netherlands controlled a large empire in Southeast Asia and a few small colonies in the Atlantic.

Driving forces of empire

Dutch empire building implied a capacity to adapt to local circumstances, to subdue threats from within and to keep out European rivals, either by negotiation and diplomacy or, more often, by force and, finally, direct rule. Surinam and the Netherlands Antilles required only a small defensive force to monitor the Caribbean Sea and to watch Venezuela, but the East Indies deserved more attention.

Dutch control in the East Indies was at first limited to Java, the centre of Dutch colonial government, and some enclaves along the coast of the Moluccas, Celebes, Sumatra and Borneo. Dutch informal empire, however, covered the whole Indonesian Archipelago. Treaties with Britain, the Netherlands' far more powerful colonial neighbour in the East, and other European competitors with territorial ambitions separated the spheres of political influence and economic activity in Southeast Asia. The new territorial borders cut arbitrarily through traditional frontiers and frequently divided peoples. Many indigenous petty states regarded themselves as sovereign and were prepared to defend their autonomy. Although abstention, a policy of non-engagement in the Outer Regions, remained official Dutch policy, the Dutch gradually exerted effective authority over the archipelago. For various reasons, Dutch expansion accelerated after 1870, resulting in a succession of military expeditions and wars and, finally, the establishment of the Dutch colonial empire in the East Indies.

Imperial physical control of the colony demanded military force. Already in 1816 the maritime defence of the colonies had been taken over by the Royal Netherlands Navy from the former trading companies. The worldwide deployment of ships and personnel changed the tasks and activities of the Dutch fleet completely. The key issue here was whether the maritime forces had to be split up into separate services for Europe, the Atlantic and Southeast Asia. For practical reasons, the colonial army was divided and not part of the regular Dutch army. The division of the naval forces was less rational, because Dutch men-of-war played an important role in maintaining relations between the mother country and the overseas settlements. Proponents of an undivided imperial navy, serving Dutch interests worldwide, finally won the argument. The minister, usually a (former) naval officer, had a budget of roughly six million guilders at his disposal, rising to over twelve million by the end of the 19th century.

As a middle-ranking colonial power the Netherlands did best by a policy of neutrality and, with the exception of the attack on Algiers (1816) and the Belgian Revolution (1830-1831), was not involved in international conflicts for more than one hundred years. With Great Britain as a "natural ally" in Europe and Asia, ostentatious displays of naval power to defend Dutch sovereignty were not often needed.[2] With an expanding number of professional European and, more particularly, indigenous personnel from five thousand men in 1816 to over ten thousand around 1900 and a well-balanced fleet of approximately fifty ships, the Royal Netherlands Navy was deployed for traditional and new tasks both at home and overseas. In the middle of the 19th century more ships and personnel served in the East Indies than in home waters. This shift in emphasis was made possible by reducing tasks in Europe to coastal defence.

Dutch men-of-war convoyed merchant vessels in the Mediterranean and the Caribbean, chased escaped slaves in Surinam until the abolition of slavery in 1863, showed the flag as far as Japan (Shimonoseki, 1863-1864) and China (Boxer Rebellion, 1900), combated piracy in Indonesian waters, participated in exploration and surveying in the colonies and, last but not least, supported the army in its expeditions against insurgent local rulers. Raiding and indigenous rebels subverted Dutch authority in the Indonesian Archipelago and threatened the Netherlands' ability to ensure peaceful commercial sea lanes. The Dutch

---

[2] VAN SAS N., *Onze natuurlijkste bondgenoot. Nederland, Engeland en Europa, 1813-1831* (Groningen, 1985).

were forced to mobilize all their naval and military resources to consolidate and finally assume power in the colony.

Superior technology, improved medication to survive in the tropics and economic exploration of the so-called Outer Regions facilitated the Dutch expansion. Machine guns and steam-powered armoured warships increased the strategic mobility and striking power of the military forces and changed the balance from defence to offence. The introduction of the telegraph improved communications between the metropolis and the colonies as well as within the archipelago. The foundation of the Koninklijke Paketvaart Maatschappij, whose interregional shipping lines developed the maritime infrastructure of the archipelago and connected the periphery to Java, undeniably contributed to the economic development of the Outer Regions and to direct rule, i.e. the subordination and incorporation of the autonomous petty states. After the defeat of the sultanate of Aceh in the first decade of the 20th century, present-day Indonesia for the first time was united with one capital, Batavia.

The revival of a maritime entrepreneurial spirit

The beginnings of the Industrial Revolution in the Netherlands in the 1860s owed much to the transfer of technology from Britain, which first occurred within the Royal Netherlands Navy in shipbuilding, cartography and nautical instruments. In 1817 the Department of the Navy had set up a "model room" for ship and technical scale models. These models were used for building and equipping new warships and instructing naval personnel. The unique collection, now exhibited in the Rijksmuseum, illustrates the rich maritime history and entrepreneurial spirit of the Netherlands in the 19th century (Figure 1).

Naval innovations slowly filtered down to other maritime sectors. Engineering and shipping pioneers like Gerhard Moritz Roentgen, a former naval officer, and Paul van Vlissingen opened shipping lines to Antwerp, Cologne, Hamburg and London. The old single-expansion marine engine was not efficient enough to allow steamers to challenge sailing ships on the route to Java, but they were most suitable for passenger, mail and high-value merchandise traffic in domestic and coastal transport. The invention of the screw propeller – another British invention first adopted by the RNN – caused steam propulsion to take off at high speed, but only the introduction of the compound engine created the technological conditions to challenge the sailing ship in international trade.

Around 1870, at the start of the colonization and annexation of overseas territories by European powers, the international shipping world changed radically. The Suez Canal route significantly reduced travel time between Europe and the Indian Ocean world. The combination of overseas connections and close ties to home ports contributed to the process of globalization. The reduced fuel consumption and greater reliability of the compound engine, together with the rise of iron construction made steamer bulk trades more and more profitable.

Fig. 1. *Model of screw-propeller lifting gear, 1857. During favorable weather conditions, early steamships switched back to sail. The problem of screw propellers acting as brakes when not in use could be solved by raising the propeller into the ship. This model of a lifting gear was constructed for the corvette Prinses Amalia. Rijksmuseum, Amsterdam (MC 563).*

A new vitality did arise in the Netherlands, almost comparable to the maritime entrepreneurial spirit of the Golden Age. Although agriculture remained an important component of the Dutch economy, the country made a strong effort to revive its stake in shipping, trade and the services sector. The number of ships and volume of shipping expanded exponentially. The turn of the century witnessed the development of modern steam shipping companies, shipyards, insurance companies and other new maritime industries, as well as the exceptional growth of Amsterdam and Rotterdam. The merchant marine capacity of steam ships rose from 21,000 Gross Register Tons in 1870 to 1,446,000 in 1910 (Table 1).[3] After 1890 the capacity of oceangoing steam ships outnumbered that of sailing ships.

The Netherlands companies entered Indian Ocean steam shipping at the same time as their most prominent foreign rivals. Only the British Peninsular and Oriental Steam Navigation Company was already firmly established in all major

---

[3] See also http://nationalaccounts.niwi.knaw.nl/table/expend1i.htm [Accessed 14 November 2014].

Table 1. *Estimated numbers of ships and size of the Dutch merchant fleet, 1832-1910*

Year	Sail	Steam	Total	Sail tonnage (x1000)	Steam tonnage (x1000)	Total
1832	1,249	3	1,252	175	1.3	176
1841	1,625	3	1,628	305	1.4	306
1850	2,300	10	2,310	429	3	432
1860	2,365	41	2,406	565	13	578
1870	2,013	46	2,059	478	21	499
1880	1,044	76	1,120	794	166	960
1890	500	110	610	388	311	699
1900	432	192	624	239	668	907
1910	426	303	729	133	1,313	1,446

Source: FILARSKI R. and MOM G., *Transport en mobiliteit*, pp. 154, 312.

ports east of Suez. In 1870 the Stoomvaart Maatschappij "Nederland" (SMN) was established on the instigation of John Elder, shipbuilder and trader from Scotland, by Amsterdam shipping brokers, merchants and other investors, including Prince Hendrik, son of King Willem II, soon to be followed by the Rotterdamsche Lloyd (RL). In 1902 they ran nineteen and fifteen ships, respectively, a small number in comparison to British and German competitors. In the Netherlands, however, their capital ships represented the new maritime entrepreneurial spirit and a growing national awareness, bearing names of members of the royal family, famous Dutch painters such as Rembrandt, or Indonesian islands such as Java and Sumatra. Steam travel made it possible for many more Dutchmen to travel and settle in the archipelago, although their numbers were minuscule compared to the indentured labours who were transported from China to Java and Sumatra, and from Java to Sumatra and Surinam after the abolition of slavery in the West Indies (1863) and the Cultivation System in the East Indies (1870). The SMN and RL received government support by guaranteeing a freight rate, cargo preferences and subsidies for the transport of passengers (civil servants, troops) and mail. This demonstrates the increasing entanglement between the national state, business and empire in those years.

Global steam shipping and passenger transport involved high risks, costs and insurance. To tame competition on routes to the East Indies, the SMN and RL apportioned traffic and schedules, set prices and sustained rates through pools and participated in international shipping conferences. In 1888 the two companies set up the above-mentioned Koninklijke Paketvaart Maatschappij to maintain the connections within the Indonesian Archipelago and supported other shipping companies with regular lines to Japan, China and Bengal as well. The shipping companies developed a transoceanic network with agents in every port of call to control and promote their interests. Although the largest share of Dutch trade was still with European countries, commerce and passenger shipping with the East Indies accounted for a very considerable share of Dutch shipping. Even more important, the success of the colonial shipping companies contributed to the exceptional growth, both in port activity and population, of Amsterdam and Rotterdam.

The winning mood of Rotterdam

Dutch international shipping was dominated by Amsterdam and Rotterdam, the main ports of the Netherlands. A variety of small harbours concentrated on specific services, goods and trade such as Scheveningen (fishery and tourism), Dordrecht (wood and ore), Groningen (inland shipping and Baltic trade) and Den Helder (naval base). In the first half of the 19th century Amsterdam recaptured its strong position as a staple market in the international distribution of sugar, coffee and other colonial products. With the advent of the Industrial Revolution and a population swelled by immigrants, Amsterdam began to expand fast. The SMN and the Koninklijke Nederlandsche Stoomboot Maatschappij, one of the first and largest steam shipping companies of the Netherlands, settled in the city. In 1876 the Noordzee Kanaal gave the port the connection with the North Sea that was essential for increasing commerce and shipbuilding. In the 1870s the old commercial system and trading network collapsed, however. Geographical position, infrastructure improvements and booming Rhine shipping favoured Rotterdam. This city was ideally situated at the Rhine-Meuse-Scheldt delta, connecting the North Sea and the vast German and central European hinterland. In addition, it had an extensive inland waterway network and, since the opening of the Nieuwe Waterweg in 1872, a short and lockless connection to the sea.

The liberalization of Rhine transport especially had started a process of rapid technological progress. After the unification of Germany a large share of its import and export products (grain, ore and coal) passed through Rotterdam, leading to "a certain Germanization of the harbour".[4] A new elite of businessmen and stevedores pushed for fundamental changes to transform Rotterdam from a staple market to transit trade. The transition from entrepôt to transit port of general cargo and bulk goods was completed in the 1880s and represented a structural shift in port-hinterland relations. The expansion of Rhine transport is best illustrated by the growth in loading capacity from 4,500,000 tons in 1880 to 45,322,000 tons in 1910.

Rotterdam was also home to the Rotterdamsche Lloyd and the Holland-America Line (HAL), a company serving the Americas. Millions of European emigrants sailed from Rotterdam to New York. RL and HAL's successes drove an increase in steamship building. Initially, steamships had been imported from Great Britain in the absence of facilities and experienced engineers.

---

[4] MILLER M., *Europe and the Maritime World. A Twentieth-Century History* (Cambridge, 2012), p. 44.

Bound by government contract, the companies switched to Dutch shipyards and engineering works. In the 20th century Fijenoord in Rotterdam and the Nederlandsche Scheepsbouw Maatschappij in Amsterdam grew into one of the world's largest shipbuilding, ship repair and marine engine building industries.

With a population growth from seventy-two thousand in 1830 to three hundred thousand in 1900 by a huge influx of worker migrants, Rotterdam was a booming town. The last quarter of the 19th century saw an explosion of activities on both banks of the river Maas. In 1909 the harbour kept 55% of the urban labour force in work. Before the outbreak of the First World War, Rotterdam had become the principal harbour on the continent, at the expense of Hamburg and Antwerp.

Concluding remarks

During the 19th century the Netherlands went through processes of industrialization, nationalization and globalization. At the turn of the century the kingdom had become a liberal and modern state. It is rather fascinating that a small country with a population of approximately six million people could built and control an empire at a distance of thousands of kilometres with a population of more than forty million people. This raises the question of to what extent the sea affected these fundamental changes in the Netherlands and its colonies. It is clear that the sea made a lot of difference. The establishment of the NHM, government support of trade and transport, the deployment of the navy to secure trade routes and to show the flag worldwide, the international maritime labour market, the construction of an inland network of canals and dikes, the growth of shipping and shipbuilding companies in Amsterdam and Rotterdam and the partial autonomy of the government institutions in the colonies were all adaptations to the changing conditions and new challenges based on seventeenth- and eighteenth-century maritime traditions and culture. The Netherlands' geographical position located on the North Sea, ideally situated between two industrial countries, Great Britain and Germany, favoured Dutch maritime enterprise too. Technological innovations opened up new opportunities and started processes which influenced, linked up and reinforced each other. Engineering pioneers like Roentgen and Van Vlissingen and many more anonymous entrepreneurs, traders, adventures, sailors, soldiers, administrators and investors at home and abroad contributed to Dutch imperial ambitions. Although the Netherlands played a marginal role on the world stage, Dutch maritime and colonial enterprise in the 19th century nevertheless affected millions of inhabitants.

BIBLIOGRAPHY

À CAMPO J., *Engines of Empire: Steamshipping and State Formation in Colonial Indonesia* (Hilversum, 2002).

AERTS R. and ROOIJ P. DE, *Geschiedenis van Amsterdam*. vol 3. *Hoofdstad in aanbouw 1813-1900* (Amsterdam, 2006).

ANTUNES C. and GOMMANS J., eds, *Exploring the Dutch Empire. Agents, Networks and Institutions, 1600-2000* (London and New York, 2015).

BAETENS R., BOSSCHER P.M. and REUCHLIN H., eds, *Maritieme geschiedenis der Nederlanden*. vol 4. *Tweede helft negentien de eeuw en twintigste eeuw, van 1850-1870 tot ca 1970* (Bussum, 1978).

BOER M. DE, *100 jaar Nederlandsche scheepvaart* (Den Helder, 1939).

BROEZE F., 'The international diffusion of ocean steam navigation. The myth of the retardation of Netherlands steam navigation to the East Indies', *Economisch- en sociaal historisch jaarboek* 45 (1982), 77-96.

BROEZE F.J.A., BRUIJN J.R. and GAASTRA F.S., eds, *Maritieme geschiedenis der Nederlanden*. vol. 3. *Achttiende eeuw en eerste helft negentiende eeuw, van ca. 1680 tot 1850-1870* (Bussum, 1977).

DAVIDS C., 'The Transfer of Technology between Britain and the Netherlands, 1700-1850', in *Anglo-Dutch Mercantile Marine Relations 1700-1850*, ed. J. BRUIJN (Amsterdam and Leiden, 1991), pp. 13-17.

DIRKZWAGER J., 'Scheepsbouw', in *Geschiedenis van de techniek in Nederland. De wording van een moderne samenleving 1800-1890*, vol. IV, ed. H. LINTSEN (Zutphen, 1993), pp. 66-103.

DISSEL A. VAN, 'Embarking on a New Course: Personnel, Ships and Administrative Reforms in the Royal Netherlands Navy, 1814-1914', in *Frutta di Mare. Evolution and revolution in the Maritime world in the 19th and 20th Centuries*, ed. P. VAN ROYEN (Amsterdam, 1998), pp. 101-15.

DISSEL A. VAN and GROEN P., *In de West. De Nederlandse krijgsmacht in het Caribisch gebied* (Franeker, 2010).

DOEL W. VAN DEN, *Zo wijd de wereld strekt. De geschiedenis van Nederland overzee* (Amsterdam, 2011).

FILARSKI R. and MOM G., *Van transport naar mobiliteit. De transportrevolutie, 1800-1900* (Zutphen, 2008).

GAASTRA F., *Vragen over de koopvaardij. De 'Enquête omtrent den toestand van de Nederlandsche koopvaardijvloot' uit 1874 en de achteruitgang van de handelsvloot. Rede uitgesproken door Prof. dr. Femme S. Gaastra Bij de aanvaarding van het ambt van hoogleraar in de Zeegeschiedenis* (Leiden, 2004).

GRAAF T. DE, *Voor handel en maatschappij. Geschiedenis van de Nederlandse Handel-Maatschappij, 1824-1964* (Amsterdam, 2012).

HEADRICK D., *The Tools of Empire: Technology and European Imperialism in the Nineteenth Century* (Oxford, 1981).

HORLINGS E., *The Economic Development of the Dutch Service Sector, 1800-1850: Trade and Transport in a Premodern Economy* (Amsterdam, 1995).

HOUBEN V., 'Java in the 19th Century: Consolidation of a Territorial State', in *The*

Emergence of a National Economy: An Economic History of Indonesia, 1800-2000, ed. H. DICK (Leiden, 2002).

LAAR P. VAN DE, *Stad van formaat. Geschiedenis van Rotterdam in de negentiende en twintigste eeuw* (Zwolle, 2000).

LEMMERS A., *Techniek op schaal: modellen en het technologiebeleid van de Marine 1725-1885* (Amsterdam, 1996).

LUITEN VAN ZANDEN J. and RIEL A. VAN, *The Strictures of Inheritance: The Dutch Economy in the Nineteenth Century* (Princeton, NJ, 2004).

MILLER M.B., *Europe and the Maritime World. A Twentieth-Century History* (Cambridge, 2012).

MULLER A.J.J., ed, *De eeuw van de 'Nederland'. Geschiedenis en vloot van de Stoomvaart Maatschappij 'Nederland' 1870-1970* (Zierikzee, 2003).

SAS N. VAN, *Onze natuurlijkste bondgenoot. Nederland, Engeland en Europa, 1813-1831* (Groningen, 1985).

SMITS J., *Economische groei en structuurveranderingen in de Nederlandse dienstensector, 1850-1913* (Amsterdam, 1995).

AUSTRIA-HUNGARY: AN INLAND EMPIRE LOOKS TO THE SEA

LAWRENCE SONDHAUS is Professor in History and Director of the Graduate Program in History at the University of Indianapolis, United States

ABSTRACT. *During the 19th century Trieste grew to be a major seaport and outlet for much of the trade of central Europe. The Dual Monarchy's brief period as a serious naval power commenced in the 1890s with the building of a battleship fleet meant to fight in the Mediterranean with the Triple Alliance against a Franco-Russian alliance. The defection of Italy from the Triple Alliance in 1915 condemned the fleet to a defensive role, but it still commanded the Adriatic and tied down a greatly superior enemy fleet.*

RÉSUMÉ. *Durant le XIXe siècle, Trieste se développa pour devenir l'un des ports et points de vente principaux du commerce d'Europe central. La brève période pendant laquelle la double monarchie se constitua en puissance maritime majeure commença dans les années 1890, lors de la construction d'une flotte de guerre, destinée à combattre avec la Triplice en Méditerranée, l'alliance franco-russe. Le désengagement de l'Italie en 1915 condamna la flotte à un rôle de défense mais celle-ci garda la maîtrise de l'Adriatique et bloqua l'avancée d'une flotte ennemie largement supérieure.*

. • .

In March 1918, a United States navy memorandum characterized the Adriatic Sea as "practically an Austrian lake, in which no Allied naval operations of importance are undertaken."[1] The assessment came just four weeks after the Austro-Hungarian navy suffered its worst mutiny of the First World War, foreshadowing the complete collapse of the Dual Monarchy's armed forces, and the empire itself, a mere eight months later. The domination of the Adriatic by Austria-Hungary, right up to the eve of the Armistice, remains one of the more remarkable, and overlooked, dimensions of the conflict of 1914-1918. Indeed, the Dual Monarchy hardly rated as a strong candidate to assert local naval power effectively, even during the long prewar period of peace. Compared to Europe's other five great powers at the turn of the century, only Russia was less urbanized, only Russia and Italy less industrialized, and none had a less extensive coastline. None, too, was so dominated by another great power, as Austria-Hungary

---

[1] Quoted in HALPERN P., *The Naval War in the Mediterranean, 1914-1918* (Annapolis, 1987), p. 439.

depended on its German ally not just for support and protection in the military and diplomatic sense, but also for nearly half of its foreign trade. Worst of all, Austria-Hungary was a multinational anomaly in a Europe dominated by great-power nation states, and its own leaders – the House of Habsburg and the ministers serving it – had a long history of lacking either the imagination or the resolve to make the changes needed to ensure the long-term viability of the empire. In the one great attempt at political reform, the Compromise of 1867, the traditionally dominant German Austrian minority agreed to share power with the most recalcitrant of the host of nationalities they ruled, the Hungarians, but at the expense of all the others, thus saddling the empire with a constitutional structure that doomed it to failure. In the face of such obstacles, it appears all the more remarkable that Austria-Hungary was able to articulate maritime interests, develop overseas trade with partners as distant as China and Japan, and build a navy strong enough to safeguard the empire's Adriatic littoral as well as show the flag overseas. Indeed, the unique coalition of special interests that supported Austro-Hungarian sea power – interests that reached far inland, and united a number of otherwise-hostile national groups – serves as an intriguing example of the sort of cooperation the multinational empire needed to counter the centrifugal forces of nationalism, the forces that ultimately caused its demise.

BACKGROUND, TO 1866

Austria acquired its first seaport, Trieste, in 1382, but its foothold on the Adriatic remained insignificant until the Napoleonic wars. In 1797 the demise of the Venetian Republic added Venetia, Istria, and Dalmatia to the Habsburg empire, an inheritance confirmed after the defeat of Napoleon in 1814. From then until 1848, Venice served as base for the imperial navy, a modest force dominated by Venetians, with Italian as its language of command. While its focus remained on the Adriatic, the navy's frigates and smaller sailing warships defended Austrian interests throughout the Mediterranean, bombarding a Moroccan pirate port in 1829 and supporting the British navy in the Near Eastern Crisis of 1840. Widespread desertions during the Venetian revolution of 1848–49 facilitated the navy's rebirth as a multinational force based at Pola (Pula) on the Istrian peninsula, with German Austrians providing most of the officers and Croatians a plurality of the manpower. Venice remained Austrian until 1866 but its eclipse was well underway long before then. Trieste's status as a free port (1719–1891) attracted Greek, Armenian, and Jewish merchants whose Eastern Mediterranean connections brought lasting benefits to the city. In 1836 Trieste became home to the empire's first steamship company, the Austrian Lloyd, and in 1857 the completion of a railway across the Alps linked Trieste with Vienna and the nascent rail network of central Europe.

While Emperor Franz Joseph (reigned 1830–1916) had little appreciation for sea power, the empire's maritime interests benefited from the patronage of his younger brother, Archduke Ferdinand Max, and later of his nephew, Archduke Franz Ferdinand. Ferdinand Max, better known to history as Emperor Maximilian of Mexico, entered naval service in 1851 and became commanding admiral just three years later. The archduke accelerated the navy's transition from sail to steam power but kept Austria out of the European naval race of the 1850s, in which Britain and France built dozens of steam-powered wooden ships of the line. His wisdom paid dividends at the end of the decade, when the leading navies started to build armor-plated steam frigates as their capital ships, rendering all wooden battleships obsolete. Austria built just one steam ship of the line, the *Kaiser* (1858), which was eventually converted to an ironclad.

France's victory over Austria in the War of 1859 opened the way for Sardinia-Piedmont to become the catalyst for a united Italy, proclaimed two years later. The Austrian navy spent the brief war blockaded by a superior French force, a humiliation that gave Ferdinand Max the justification he needed to add armored warships to the fleet. After the Sardinians ordered two ironclads from a French shipyard late in 1860, the archduke placed orders for the first pair of Austrian ironclads. Over the next six years Italy commissioned twelve ironclads, eleven of them built in foreign shipyards, while Austria struggled to respond with seven, all built in Trieste. But before the two rivals met in battle in the Adriatic, the Austrian navy received a call to action from an unexpected quarter. In 1864, when Austria joined Prussia and the smaller German states in a war against Denmark over the Schleswig-Holstein question, the Danes blockaded the north German ports. Denmark's overwhelming naval superiority over Prussia left Austria holding the key to victory at sea for the German allies. The war's decisive naval battle occurred on 9 May, when a small unarmored squadron under Captain Wilhelm von Tegetthoff, in the steam frigate *Schwarzenberg*, engaged Danish forces off Helgoland. The Danes subsequently withdrew to the Skagerrak, ending their blockade. The Austrian ironclads saw no action, but two of them were included in a larger force that followed Tegetthoff's squadron to the North Sea, ensuring the Danes would not reimpose the blockade. The navy's baptism of fire in 1864 also marked the emergence of Tegetthoff, elevated to rear admiral, as the leading figure within the Austrian navy, filling the void left when Ferdinand Max had departed for Mexico earlier that year.

THE WAR OF 1866 AND ITS AFTERMATH

After the War of 1864, the Austro-Prussian relationship deteriorated over a proposed reform of the German Confederation, and the two countries began to prepare for war. Prussia concluded an alliance with Italy and, as the price of securing French neutrality, Austria accepted Emperor Napoleon III's demand that it cede Venetia to Italy after the war. The Austrians believed the cession would ensure Italian neutrality too, but Italy declared war anyway, hoping to acquire more than just Venetia. In the ensuing War of 1866, the Austrian army thus had to fight separate campaigns in the north (which it lost) and the south (which it won), while the naval action was limited to the Adriatic. The Italian ironclad fleet included just three armor-plated wooden ships along with nine ships of iron construction, and carried the latest imported ordnance; in contrast, Tegetthoff's flagship, the 5,100-ton *Erzherzog Ferdinand Max*, and the six other Austrian ironclads were armor-plated wooden ships armed with guns from the Imperial-Royal Foundry at Mariazell. After the Prussians crushed the Austrian northern army at Königgrätz (3 July 1866), then marched to the outskirts of Vienna, the Austrians had to redeploy their victorious southern army to defend the imperial capital. The Italian army then occupied Venetia unopposed, and Italian leaders planned landings in Istria and Dalmatia, now claimed for Italy because they had once been part of the Venetian Republic. To clear the way for the landings, the Italians first planned to "take possession of an important station in the Adriatic," the island of Lissa.[2] They were on the verge of putting troops ashore when Tegetthoff arrived off the island with the Austrian fleet on 20 July. In the melee that followed, inferior Austrian guns and incompetent Italian gunners ensured that neither side would inflict serious damage on the other. Tegetthoff used ramming tactics to compensate for his weaker artillery, and at the climax of the four-hour engagement, his *Erzherzog Ferdinand Max* rammed and sank the Italian flagship *Re d'Italia*. A second Italian ironclad, the *Palestro*, caught fire and exploded as the Italian fleet withdrew. "The whole thing was chaos," Tegetthoff confided afterward to a friend. "It is a miracle that we did not lose a ship."[3] The peace settlement that autumn awarded the Italians only Venetia, which they would have received without going to war at all.

The stunning victory earned Tegetthoff a promotion to vice admiral, but it was his role leading the mission to bring Maximilian's body back from Mexico the following year that earned him the undying gratitude of Franz Joseph. In 1868 the emperor confirmed Tegetthoff as commander of the navy and lent his support to a fleet plan including fifteen ironclads. Tegetthoff's premature death in 1871 left it unrealized, and also ushered in a long period of less effective naval leadership. His legacy included the widespread emulation of his ramming tactics, reflected in warship designs that continued to include exaggerated ram bows long after the increasing range of naval artillery rendered fanciful any notion of one warship ramming another in battle. More important for Austria-Hungary, the memory of Tegetthoff's decisive victory against a superior Italian foe heartened the Habsburg fleet, and haunted the Italian navy, right down to 1918.

Meanwhile, amid the post-Tegetthoff malaise, the navy grew weaker than its Italian rival. It registered few accomplishments aside from being the first

---

[2] Instructions to Admiral Count Carlo Pellion de Persano summarized in Agostino Depretis to Bettino Ricasoli, Florence, 17 July 1866, in *Carteggi di Bettino Ricasoli*, vol. 22: *20 giungno–31 luglio 1866*, ed. S. CAMERANI and G. ARFE (Rome, 1967), p. 298, no. 421.

[3] TEGETTHOFF to Baroness Emma Lutteroth, 22 July 1866, text in *Admiral Max Freiherr von Sterneck: Erinnerungen aus den Jahren 1847 bis 1897*, ed. J. BENKO VON BOINIK (Vienna, 1901), pp. 149–50.

to adopt the self-propelled torpedo, invented by Johann Luppis, an Austrian captain, and developed by British expatriate Robert Whitehead at a factory at Fiume (Rijeka), Hungary's leading port after the subdivision of the empire in 1867. The new torpedo technology laid the foundation for the Jeune École, the French navy's "Young School," which by the 1880s promoted a strategy of cruiser and torpedo warfare as the key to challenging British naval power worldwide. During that decade the Jeune École had a near-universal impact, as most of the great powers built many more cruisers and torpedo boats, and fewer battleships. Austria-Hungary embraced the new strategy after the conclusion of the Triple Alliance (1882), which united the Dual Monarchy with Germany and Italy, eliminating the navy's anti-Italian *raison d'être*. While Italy, thereafter, dreamed of becoming a Mediterranean power on a par with France, Austria-Hungary hedged its bets by developing a torpedo deterrent in the Adriatic to defend itself in case Italy changed its foreign policy. Between 1876 and 1893, the navy commissioned just two battleships. Otherwise, its largest new units were the 4,000-ton "ram cruisers" *Kaiser Franz Joseph I* (1890) and *Kaiserin Elisabeth* (1892), protected cruisers intended for service as flotilla leaders for torpedo boats. By the early 1890s Austria-Hungary had the weakest navy, by far, of any of the six great powers of Europe.

NAVAL REVIVAL

In the first years after Austria-Hungary resumed its battleship program in 1893, the buildup was justified not by a deterioration of relations with Italy but by the goal of putting the Triple Alliance in a better position to counter the new Franco-Russian alliance in the Mediterranean. Over the next thirteen years Austria-Hungary ordered twelve battleships: three each of the 5,600-ton *Monarch* class, the 8,300-ton *Habsburg* class, the 10,600-ton *Erzherzog* class, and the 14,500-ton *Radetzky* class. The navy also commissioned three armored cruisers. Aside from one battleship and one armored cruiser laid down in the Pola arsenal, all were built in Trieste by the Stabilimento Tecnico Triestino. Starting with the armored cruiser *Maria Theresia* (1895), the navy ordered all of its armor plate from Witkowitz of Moravia, and from 1901 it ordered its guns from Bohemia's Skoda works rather than Germany's Krupp. In 1901 the navy leadership won over traditionally anti-navy Hungarian leaders by promising Hungarian firms a share of naval spending equal to the Hungarian contribution to the joint budget of the Dual Monarchy. Thus, in a divided domestic political landscape a broad pro-navy coalition evolved which represented the interests of nationalities far from the Adriatic.

During the same years, Archduke Franz Ferdinand, heir to the Habsburg throne, became the empire's leading naval enthusiast after travelling to Japan in 1892–93 aboard the cruiser *Kaiserin Elisabeth*. The archduke's patronage of the navy became more significant as Franz Joseph grew older and allowed his heir to assert more influence, especially over the armed forces. While Franz Ferdinand never openly opposed Austria-Hungary's alignment with Germany, the degree of dependence troubled him more than it did most of the empire's leaders. As a result, he viewed the development of overseas trade, and of the naval forces to support it, as crucial to the Dual Monarchy's future as an autonomous great power. In the years after the completion of the Suez Canal (1869), the Austrian Lloyd had extended its service to the Far East, enabling Trieste to establish itself as a leading point of entry for European imports from Asia. Amid the ensuing prosperity, Trieste grew to become continental Europe's fifth-busiest port (after Hamburg, Rotterdam, Marseilles, and Genoa). By 1913, the overall value of the city's trade with Asia far surpassed the figure for the Asian trade of all ports of the kingdom of Italy combined. While the Lloyd eventually opened a line to Brazil it did not add service to North America, leaving a void that was filled after 1895 by the Austro-Americana, which ultimately handled over half of Trieste's emigrant traffic with the United States. The Lloyd also never served the Western Mediterranean and Western European ports, leaving that trade to a Hungarian company, the Adria Line, established in 1882 at Fiume. The growth of Fiume, modest compared to Trieste, nevertheless sufficed to make it continental Europe's seventh-busiest port by 1913.

At the turn of the century, Germany's decision to challenge Britain's hegemony at sea transformed the Triple Alliance into an anti-British bloc no longer attractive to Italy. The program outlined in Admiral Alfred von Tirpitz's navy laws of 1898 and 1900 made the German fleet the world's second-strongest as of 1905; by then, Britain had resolved its differences with France (1904) and would soon achieve a rapprochement with Russia (1907), creating the Triple Entente. A visit to Toulon by the Italian fleet in 1901 provided the first sign of a warming of Franco-Italian relations; Italian navy leaders soon considered Austria-Hungary, not France, to be their most likely future rival. Thus, for more than a decade before the outbreak of the First World War, Europe's greatest naval race outside of the North Sea occurred in the Adriatic, where the nominal allies renewed their old rivalry. Counting all battleships laid down in the past twenty-five years, by 1905 Austria-Hungary had just twelve to Italy's eighteen. As the navy scrambled to catch up, it continued to benefit from the patronage of Franz Ferdinand and the support of a broad domestic political coalition. The web of connections linking Skoda, Witkowitz, and the Stabilimento Tecnico Triestino coalesced into a first-rate naval-industrial complex, enabling Austria-Hungary to build larger warships much faster than Italy, indeed, faster than any country other than Britain and Germany.

In December 1906, the commissioning of Britain's 18,110-ton *Dreadnought* – the largest, fastest, and most heavily armed warship yet built – rendered all existing battleships obsolete. The resulting clean slate gave fresh hope to inferior naval powers willing to pay the price to catch up with superior rivals, but Austria-Hungary decided to proceed with the construction of the three 14,500-ton *Radetzky* class pre-dreadnoughts, just funded in the autumn of 1906, before considering dreadnoughts of its own. Italy laid down its first dreadnought in June 1909, after learning that the Dual Monarchy was considering a fleet plan including four 20,000-ton dreadnoughts. A constitutional crisis in Hungary delayed the implementation of this plan, and Austria-Hungary finally laid down its first dreadnought, the *Viribus Unitis*, in July 1910, followed two months later by the *Tegetthoff*, for which the class of warships was named. Meanwhile, in the summer of 1910, the Italians laid down three more dreadnoughts, prompting Austro-Hungarian legislators to approve a second pair in March 1911, to give both navies four. Like the older battleships of the fleet, the Austro-Hungarian dreadnoughts were built entirely from domestic resources, at an exorbitant cost ultimately covered only by giving the navy one quarter of the entire defense outlay in the last fiscal year before the First World War. Work began on the third and fourth dreadnoughts in January 1912, the *Prinz Eugen* at Trieste and the *Szent István* at Fiume's Danubius shipyard, the first firm in the empire's Hungarian half to receive a major warship contract. Italy responded later that winter with its fifth and sixth dreadnoughts. Thanks to its more efficient shipyards, in October 1912 the Dual Monarchy became the third European power to have a dreadnought in commission, when the *Viribus Unitis* entered service after a building time of just twenty-seven months. Italy's first dreadnought, completed in forty-three months, finally entered service in January 1913.

Each navy would have three dreadnoughts in service by the time the war began in July 1914, but before then their rivalry took an unexpected turn. After the Italo-Turkish War (1911–12) temporarily strained Italy's relations with the Triple Entente, the Italians, in December 1912, agreed to an extension of the Triple Alliance, then, in June 1913, to a Triple Alliance naval convention. War plans called for Admiral Anton Haus, the Austro-Hungarian naval commander, to head a battle fleet including the newest units of the Austro-Hungarian and Italian navies, joined by any German warships that happened to be in the Mediterranean, with the mission of engaging the French fleet and blocking the transport of colonial troops from North Africa to France. The convention became moot on 31 July 1914, when Italy condemned Austria-Hungary's declaration of war against Serbia as an act of aggression. Over the months that followed, Italy pursued a policy of neutrality that was increasingly hostile to the Dual Monarchy, before finally joining the Entente under the terms of the Treaty of London (26 April 1915).

THE FIRST WORLD WAR

A week after the assassination of Franz Ferdinand at Sarajevo, Austria-Hungary secured the support of Germany for a war against Serbia, assuming that the threat of German intervention would suffice to keep Russia out of the conflict. Russia's decision to stand behind the Serbs gave Germany the continental war it wanted and left Austria-Hungary fighting for German war aims under German direction. While the British navy, concentrated in the North Sea, imposed a blockade on Germany, the French blockaded the mouth of the Adriatic. The access to overseas trade that had been such an important corrective to the empire's economic dependence on Germany thus ended, leaving Austria-Hungary even more at the mercy of its ally. Haus kept the fleet at Pola throughout the initial phase of the war, explaining to a subordinate that "so long as the possibility exists that Italy will declare war against us, I consider it my first duty to keep the fleet intact."[4] The French initially deployed dreadnoughts and pre-dreadnoughts in the lower Adriatic but grew less aggressive after Haus transferred his small submarine force from Pola to Cattaro (Kotor), the Austro-Hungarian base at the southern tip of Dalmatia. Following the torpedoing and near loss of the dreadnought *Jean Bart* in December 1914, the French navy sent no capital ships into the Adriatic. After a U-boat torpedoed and sank the armored cruiser *Léon Gambetta* off the southeastern tip of Italy on 27 April 1915, the French no longer deployed any warship larger than a destroyer north of a line approximately three hundred miles (480km) south of Cattaro.

The prudence of Haus in the face of a vastly superior foe left his fleet intact to take on the Italian navy. On the evening of 23 May 1915, within hours of Italy's declaration of war against Austria-Hungary, he steamed out of Pola with the three dreadnoughts then in commission, backed by nine pre-dreadnoughts and a host of smaller warships, for a punitive bombardment of the Italian coastline. The Italians entered the war supremely confident but within two months assumed the same cautious posture as the French, after they lost the armored cruisers *Amalfi* and *Garibaldi* to submarine attacks within a span of eleven days in July. That autumn the Italians learned that their warships were not necessarily safe even in port, when Austrian saboteurs, on the night of 27 September, blew up the pre-dreadnought *Benedetto Brin* at Brindisi. During 1916 the Italians moved their dreadnoughts to Taranto, well out of harm's way, and repeatedly pleaded for more help to contain the Austro-Hungarian threat. The French and British appeased them by sending more warships to the mouth of the Adriatic, enabling the Dual Monarchy's "fleet in being" to tie down an ever-greater number of Allied warships that could have been put to better use elsewhere. Further Italian losses during 1916 only reinforced their timidity, most notably the dreadnought *Leonardo da Vinci*, sunk on 2 August at Taranto by Austrian saboteurs, and the pre-dreadnought *Regina Margherita*, which on 11 December fell victim to a minefield off Valona, Albania. By then, confirming that they had conceded the Adriatic to the Austrians, the Allies attempted to close the mouth of the sea by deploying the Otranto Barrage, anti-submarine nets dragged by trawlers and drifters commandeered from fishing fleets, backed by minefields, on the model of the Dover Barrage, deployed by the British to block German access to the English Channel from the North Sea.

After making Pola and Cattaro available to German U-boats during the first round of unrestricted submarine warfare in 1915, Austria-Hungary again

---

[4] HAUS to Rear Admiral Karl Kailer, Pola, 6 September 1914, quoted in HALPERN, *The Naval War in the Mediterranean*, p. 30.

supported the Germans after their fateful decision to resume the campaign early in 1917, despite the American intervention it was likely to provoke. The Austro-Hungarian navy agreed to send its own submarines out of the Adriatic to attack Allied convoys in the central Mediterranean, and to assign more personnel to support the German U-boats operating out of Cattaro. To weaken the anti-submarine barrage at the mouth of the Adriatic, the navy launched a series of ever-larger and more aggressive attacks, culminating in the Battle of the Otranto Straits (15 May 1917), a successful cruiser raid led by Captain Miklós Horthy that opened the straits to German and Austro-Hungarian submarines for the following six weeks. But for the Central Powers, the shift away from large-unit surface operations idled most of the sailors of their fleets and increased the likelihood of unrest aboard those ships. In July 1917 the first demonstrations swept the Austro-Hungarian fleet at Pola. Then, during January 1918, sailors of the fleet joined in a strike by workers in the Pola arsenal. Finally, on 1–3 February 1918, a serious mutiny temporarily paralyzed the naval forces at Cattaro. The uprising included sailors of all nationalities of the empire, reflecting the predominant influence of war weariness encouraged by socialist politics, which gave it more in common with the mutinies that swept the Russian and German navies in 1917 and 1918 than with the concurrent unrest in the Austro-Hungarian army and home front. Following the suppression of the Cattaro mutiny, four of its leaders were executed and almost four hundred others imprisoned. Afterward, a radical reorganization of the naval hierarchy left Horthy as fleet commander in place of the ineffective Admiral Maximilian Njegovan, who had succeeded Haus upon his death twelve months earlier. The Hungarian captain's extraordinary promotion to rear admiral forced the twenty-eight senior officers who outranked him either to retire or to accept posts on land.

In the war's last year, Horthy's one bold stroke met with disaster on 10 June 1918, when the dreadnought *Szent István* was torpedoed and sunk by an Italian torpedo boat while making its way down the Dalmatian coast from Pola, along with the other three dreadnoughts of the *Tegetthoff* class, for an attack on the Otranto Barrage. Horthy hoped the attack would force Italian and French dreadnoughts out of Taranto for a battle at the mouth of the Adriatic, but the sinking of the *Szent István* – the only major warship lost by Austria-Hungary in the entire war – forced the cancellation of the operation. Afterward Austro-Hungarian morale plummeted, dashing Horthy's hopes for a revitalizing victory. He continued to vouch for the battle-readiness of the fleet, at least through the summer months, but it never sortied again. In the autumn of 1918, while Germany made peace overtures to the Allies, the Dual Monarchy began to disintegrate internally as Emperor Charles (who had succeeded Franz Joseph in 1916) tried in vain to salvage the situation. On 30 October, one week after the Austro-Hungarian army crumbled in the face of the final Allied offensive on the Italian front, Charles ordered Horthy to turn over the navy to the Yugoslav national council, whose members by that time included some of the leading Slovenian and Croatian officers serving under him. The transfer ceremonies occurred at Pola the following day. The Allies ultimately did not allow postwar Yugoslavia, an amalgamation of Serbia with the former South Slav lands of Austria-Hungary, to keep the ships, which first were distributed among the victorious Allies as reparations, then, in most cases, scrapped. During the interwar years, Italy, in possession of Trieste, Fiume, and Pola, finally enjoyed the hegemony over the Adriatic that had been denied to it by the Habsburg empire's effective development of local naval power.

Conclusion

While the demise of Austria-Hungary brought the dismantling of the naval-industrial complex that had enabled it to build a great-power navy on domestic resources, the introduction of new international borders, tariffs, and currencies disrupted the trade networks that had linked the central European interior to Trieste and Fiume. Fatefully, a region already economically dependent on Germany in the days of the Dual Monarchy became even more so after being subdivided into a collection of smaller, weaker states. Most historians consider the demise of Austria-Hungary to have been inevitable; indeed, a number of contemporary observers felt the same way. But lost in the debate over the measures that could have been taken to prolong its history or remedy its problems is the question of whether measures that were taken, such as the development of maritime interests and naval power, actually enabled Austria-Hungary to last longer than it otherwise would have. It would not be unreasonable to conclude that if the Habsburg empire had not turned to the sea in the 19th century, it would not have survived into the 20th.

Bibliography

BABUDIERI F., *Industrie, commerci e navigazione a Trieste e nella regione Giulia* (Milan, 1982).

CASALI A. and CATTARUZZA M., *Sotto i mari del mondo: La Whitehead, 1875-1990* (Rome, 1990).

CATTARUZZA M., 'Population Dynamics and Economic Change in Trieste and its Hinterland, 1850-1914', in *Population and Society in Western European Port-Cities, c. 1650-1939*, ed. R. LAWTON and R. LEE (Liverpool, 2002), pp. 176-211.

GARDINER R., ed., *Steam, Steel, and Shellfire: The Steam Warship, 1815-1905* (London, 1992).

HALPERN P., *The Naval War in the Mediterranean, 1914-1918* (Annapolis, MD, 1987).

HALPERN P., *The Battle of the Otranto Straits* (Bloomington, IN, 2004).

LAMBERT A., *Battleships in Transition* (Annapolis, MD, 1984).

MAYER H. and WINKLER D., *In allen Häfen war Österreich: Die österreichisch-ungarische Handelsmarine* (Vienna, 1987).

SONDHAUS L., *The Habsburg Empire and the Sea: Austrian Naval Policy, 1797-1866* (West Lafayette, IN, 1989).
SONDHAUS L., 'Strategy, tactics, and the politics of penury: Austria-Hungary and the Jeune École', *Journal of Military History* 56 (1992), 587-602.
SONDHAUS L., *The Naval Policy of Austria-Hungary: Navalism, Industrial Development, and the Politics of Dualism, 1867-1918* (West Lafayette, IN, 1994).
SONDHAUS L., *The Great War at Sea: A Naval History of the First World War* (Cambridge, 2014).

The Ottoman Empire and the Sea, 1789–1922

Colin Heywood is Honorary Research Fellow at the Maritime Historical Studies Centre, University of Hull, United Kingdom

Abstract. *Even at its height around 1800, the Ottoman navy could not project its power far beyond the Eastern Mediterranean and Black Sea. The loss of Greece and Egypt cost the empire most of its ships and seamen, and neither the efficiency of its government nor the strength of its industrial base were enough to bring it effectively into the industrial era. In the Balkan wars of 1911–1913 Italy and Greece made extensive conquests of Ottoman territory which the navy could not protect.*

Résumé. *Même au sommet de sa puissance, autour de 1800, la marine ottomane ne parvint pas à étendre son pouvoir au-delà de la Méditerranée orientale et de la mer Morte. La perte de la Grèce et de l'Égypte coûta à l'empire la plupart de ses vaisseaux et marins, et ni l'efficience de son gouvernement ni sa forte assise industrielle ne suffirent à le conduire efficacement dans l'ère industrielle. Lors des guerres balkaniques de 1911–1913, l'Italie et la Grèce firent d'importantes conquêtes sur les territoires ottomans que la marine ne pouvait protéger.*

.•.

The first among the problems which the Ottoman Empire faced as a naval power were the constraints of geography. Territorially, as a land empire stretching across large parts of three continents, the Ottoman state at its apogee in the 16th century had controlled (at least in theory) some of the major maritime "pinch points" of the Old World: the Black Sea Straits (the Bosphorus and the Dardanelles); the exits into the Black Sea of the Don and Dnestr rivers; the Bâb al-Mandab; the Straits of Hormuz. But the whole was a sum much less than that which its disparate parts might suggest: the Ottomans, even at their height, were a naval power predominating mainly in the Black Sea and the eastern half of the Mediterranean basin which, until the construction of the Suez Canal, was a maritime cul-de-sac. The Ottoman galley fleet of the 16th/early 17th centuries had never been able to get beyond the Straits of Gibraltar, and was rarely strong enough to penetrate even beyond the Tunis-Sicily narrows. Nor did matters change very much after the Ottomans' tardy adoption (tardy, that is, in contrast with their North African corsair allies and confrères) of the three-masted, sail-driven man-of-war. In the 18th century the post-Petrine Russian navy could get its Baltic fleet out into the North Sea and through the Straits into the Mediterranean; but there was never the remotest possibility that the Ottomans could get *their* sail-driven fleet through the Straits, let alone (to venture into the realm of speculative history) to confront the Russians in the Baltic.

Why was this? Ottoman political and social culture, which was strongly conservative, together with a lack of know-how of how to go about it, had all played a part. Russia, after 1700, could purchase technical knowledge from England and Holland, and hire British and Dutch (and German) officers, who could be more or less effortlessly incorporated into the Russian naval establishment. For more than a century after the Petrine reforms in Russia, the Ottomans could not replicate the Russian example and bring in foreign (Christian) experts in any large numbers, nor could the indigenous Greek maritime *reâyâ*, who in part manned and in large part constructed the Ottoman war fleet, ascend the maritime chain of command, access to which was virtually limited to Muslims until the 19th century. Nor, later in the 19th century, was the opening of the Suez Canal anything other than a two-edged sword for the Ottomans: potentially it opened up their Gulf and Red Sea provinces to direct naval access from the Mediterranean, and in theory rendered the oceans of Asia open to the Ottoman navy, but at same time it reinforced the British need to dominate the Mediterranean and Ottoman seaways as a vital part of the direct route to and from India: the British occupation of a nominally Ottoman Egypt – and of the Suez Canal – would occur a bare decade after its opening.

The question may therefore be asked, could the Ottoman Empire have used the sea to regain, in the 19th century, the status of a maritime great power which once, two and a half centuries previously, it had appeared to possess? There were two significant obstacles to achieving this, and one fundamental reason why it was impossible. In the first place there was the overwhelming maritime preponderance of Britain, not just worldwide post-1815, but especially in the Mediterranean, which was seen, not only as the major artery of Britain's South European and Levantine trade, but as the vital corridor between Britain and its growing preponderance in India, even before the opening of the Suez Canal. Second, there were the capital and revenue, as well as manpower and material, costs of building and maintaining a great navy. It would not be entirely correct to say that, like Spain, like China, the Ottoman Empire lacked an indigenous industrial base: in the early modern period it was rich in resources such as timber, coal and iron, and with an equally solid demographic base for building and crewing its navy, but its growing structural and demographic deficiencies, particularly post-1821, which the reforms of the nineteenth century were ultimately unable to solve, coupled with a lack of capital or of an indigenous entrepreneurial class, meant that the empire's quasi-great-power status via its post-1856 membership of the Concert of Europe was never to be other than an illusion. Furthermore, the rise of nationalism, either internal or external, exacerbated Ottoman vulnerability and promoted Mediterranean rivals or potential rivals: first and foremost Greece; then Italy after 1860; and even Austria-Hungary, the Ottomans' European *doppelgänger* as a multi-ethnic would-be great power, with its naval bases at Trieste and Fiume (Rijeka) on the Dalmatian littoral of the Adriatic.

What, then, given these constraints, was the function of the Ottoman navy in the "long" 19th century, from the accession of Selim III in 1789 to the final disappearance of the Ottoman Empire as a state entity in 1922? The year 1800 may be seen to mark the apogee of the rebuilt and reformed Ottoman navy of the "New Order" (*Nizâm-i Cedîd*) era, the creation of which was one of the most impressive achievements of the reforming sultan Selim III. In the years between 1791 and 1800, sixteen navy yards – Istanbul, Rhodes, Mytilene, Sinop, Bodrum, Gemlik, and ten other new, smaller ones – constructed between them sixty-nine of the seventy ships which comprised the programme. The construction of more than a half of these vessels was supervised by foreign builders, Swedish or French; of the Ottoman builders, six were Muslim and eight were Greek. In terms of numbers, the Ottoman fleet of this era, while less than a fifth of the size of Britain's and roughly half that of France or of Russia's combined Baltic and Black Sea fleets, was smaller also than Spain's but larger than that of Portugal: an indication of the Ottoman Empire's somewhat indeterminate status as a major or less-than-major power. After 1800 naval construction marked time, as the empire was confronted both by internal crises (Wahhabi revolts in Arabia, the Serbian revolt on the Danube and the revolts of provincial governors in the Balkans and the Levant, often allied with conservative, anti-reform elements at the centre) and by an escalating financial crisis.

None of the above-mentioned internal crises in the Ottoman state in the first quarter of the 19th century impacted to any great degree on the Ottoman state as a naval power. Conversely, the outbreak in 1821 of the Greek revolt may be seen to have produced the most serious and long-reaching effects on the entire Ottoman maritime establishment, effects which were both demographic, in terms of the manning of the Ottoman war fleet, and territorial, in terms of the loss to the Ottomans of naval bases and strategic harbours in the islands and on the coasts of the Aegean, as well as on the west coast of the Peloponnesus.

In the first place, what may be termed the "Greeks", i.e., the Greek Orthodox subjects of the sultan, had come, in the course of the previous century and a half, to play a preponderant role in the merchant shipping of the empire, both as entrepreneurs and as seamen on board "Greek" – i.e. Greek-manned but Ottoman-flagged – merchant ships. This process of (for want of a better term) the "Hellenization" of Ottoman maritime trade had begun with the exclusion of Venetian shipping from Ottoman waters from the mid-17th century, but had been strengthened by growing Russian preponderance in the Black Sea post-1774 and the rise of grain-exporting "new ports" such as Odessa, which also allowed enterprising Greek shippers to operate under Russian flags of convenience. Finally, in the period of the Napoleonic wars, the Greek-Ottoman merchant marine reached the height of its pre-1821 prosperity as the only neutral merchant fleet able to assure the essential commercial exchanges in the Mediterranean and the Black Sea, and even beyond, as far as the Spanish colonies in the New World.

The Greek-Ottoman maritime trade, in a period of general warfare, was a dangerous one, and the ships, with Greek shipowners and entrepreneurs, the majority of whom (as well as the crews) came from a handful of the major islands of the Aegean – Hydra, Spetses, Psaras, Andros, Skopelos and Santorin – were stoutly built, many with a tonnage of at least 200 to 400 tons, heavily crewed and strongly armed, and thus transformable into the fighting ships of the nascent post-Revolt Greek navy.

From the outset of the Greek revolt the Ottoman navy was faced with a well-nigh impossible task, and one to which its fleet and its monolithic command structure were ill-suited. In the initial stages of the war, the Ottoman admirals and their subordinates proved to be no match for a multiplicity of independent, anarchic Greek commanders from the various Aegean islands, often at odds with each other, and able by their hit-and-run tactics in command of smaller, more nimble vessels, to dominate the larger and better-equipped warships of the Ottoman fleet, and to mount an effective blockade of Ottoman ports. The cards were stacked against the Ottomans: Great Power recognition of the Greeks as belligerents, and a rising tide of Graecophilia in Europe, and the unwelcome but necessary intervention on the Ottoman side of their nominal vassal Mehmed Ali Pasha of Egypt, led not to Ottoman but to Egyptian naval and military intervention, and the effective Egyptian occupation of the Morea.

Ottoman naval strategy in fact lacked all autonomy of action. Attempts to capitalise on a more favourable situation through cooperation with Mehmed Ali and the assembling of a large Ottoman-Egyptian naval expeditionary force at Alexandria in the summer of 1827 were opposed by the Powers. British, French and Russian squadrons were sent to prevent Ottoman-Egyptian action against the Greeks and to bring about the return of the joint fleet to its bases. The destruction of the Ottoman-Egyptian fleet at Navarino was little more than an inevitable outcome of Ottoman intransigence.

In the Ottoman navy the age of sail, characterised by the hesitant and tardy adoption but rapid pre-eminence of the three-masted warship, lasted barely two centuries, from the Ottoman–Venetian war for Crete to the Crimean war with Russia. For the Ottomans, it ended violently, wooden sailing ships against wooden sailing ships, with the Russian destruction of a Turkish squadron at Sinop in November 1853. In little more than an hour eight Russian battleships, including three 120s, defeated ten relatively underarmed Turkish vessels; but it was a pyrrhic victory in that by the end of the war the Russian Black Sea fleet of sailing warships had all either been sunk or destroyed by their own crews.

Thereafter, for almost a quarter of a century, the Ottoman and Russian empires remained at peace with each other. The two decades from the mid-1850s to the mid-1870s witnessed the Ottoman navy's rapid transition from wooden sailing ships to ironclad steamers. This gave the Ottomans a considerable superiority, at least on paper, with Russia forbidden (until 1871) to maintain a war fleet in the Black Sea. In 1875 the Ottomans possessed the third-largest navy in the world after Britain and France – 21 battleships and 173 other types of warship. It was a superiority which failed to have any noticeable positive effect on the course of the Russo-Turkish war of 1877–78, and which was rapidly eroded thereafter by a combination of Russian naval expansionism, the post-war Ottoman financial crisis and meltdown, and the still not fully understood naval policies of Abdülhamid II.

The Hamidian era has traditionally been seen as one of decline in the fortunes of the Ottoman navy in the face of the sultan's deep suspicion of its political loyalty, coupled with official neglect and underfunding. The increasingly outdated fleet was largely left to rot at anchor in the Golden Horn for thirty years (1878–1908). Recent research has questioned whether the neglect of the navy sprang more from the parlous state of the empire's finances than the sultan's suspicions. In reality, both views can be backed by evidence. Abdülhamid was preternaturally suspicious, and the navy was starved of funds: its allocated budget could barely cover the pay, food and clothing of the sailors and minor maintenance and repair to the fleet. The inability of the state to take out foreign loans for major capital expenditure such as the purchase abroad of new ships was compounded by the empire's relative technological and industrial backwardness, and the lack of an entrepreneurial arms and shipbuilding industry. The inward-looking policies of Abdülhamid II foundered on the state's inability to provide what was needed, either in men or matériel, to keep pace with the late-nineteenth-century advances in naval technology.

Under the circumstances in which the empire found itself the preference of Abdülhamid II for using what funds were available to build up the army at the expense of the navy, and the "turn" away from Britain and towards a growing reliance on Germany, becomes understandable.

By the last years of Abdülhamid's reign the weakness, both comparative and absolute, of the Ottoman navy becomes apparent from the figures. The year 1904 is an instructive one: it was the last year of the corrupt regime of the minister of marine Hasan Pasha who, over the previous seven years, had stolen most of the credits advanced for modernising the fleet, and issued false and misleading progress reports to the sultan. In 1904 the Ottoman navy budget was equivalent to twelve million gold francs; that of Great Britain was 940 million. With closer control and American technical assistance, improvements were put in hand: warships were purchased from Italy, France and Germany, but in that year, of fifty-four vessels in the Ottoman fleet, twenty-four (including two submarines) were unseaworthy, and most of the remainder were unusable due to chronic or acute shortages of parts and a lack of experienced sea officers. (To look ahead, in 1913, the last year of relative peace, the Ottoman navy budget amounted to twenty-nine million gold francs; that of Britain to 1,181 million. The British naval budget was almost half as much again as the army's; in the Ottoman Empire the naval budget amounted to one-seventh of that of the army.)

The increasing subordination of naval strategy and planning to chimerical politico-religious obsessions during the reign of Abdülhamid II is best seen in the tragi-comic episode of the Far Eastern cruise in 1889–90 of the cruiser *Ertoghrul*. The voyage of the *Ertoghrul* to the Far East, decided on by Abdülhamid early in 1889, was intended to be both a symbol of the rejuvenated Ottoman navy and a demonstration of the pan-Asian reach of the sultan's claimed role as Caliph.

The *Ertoghrul* was an old wooden frigate of two thousand tons, dating back to the last years of sail, and originally constructed in Istanbul during and just after the Crimean War. It was later converted – in a British yard – to steam power, and fitted out by the Ottomans with a modern armament, all of which failed in the main to compensate for its antiquated construction and lack of seaworthiness. In the summer of 1889, with its normal complement of 400 increased to over 650, including two rear-admirals, it was despatched on a propaganda tour to the Far East. After visiting various ports in British India and the Dutch East Indies where, to the intense irritation of the British and Dutch colonial authorities, it was enthusiastically received by the local Muslim population, the *Ertoghrul* made its way to the Japanese port and naval base of Yokohama. There, in September 1890, the *Ertoghrul*'s orders were suddenly countermanded by the sultan, and the vessel was ordered to return home. To disobey the sultan's capricious will was impossible; to embark at the height of the typhoon season was to court disaster. On 18 September 1890, the *Ertoghrul* was caught in a violent storm off the coast of Japan and foundered, with the loss of all but sixty-nine of its crew.

The disaster, both avoidable and predictable, which befell the *Ertoghrul*, and the official reaction to the tragedy, neatly epitomise the weakness of the Hamidian autocracy. The true, immediate cause of the disaster, suppressed, and attributed to unavoidable natural causes, was kept secret. The wider causes: an improvised and personalised naval policy; a reliance on antiquated equipment and mediocre personnel; and above all, the paralysing effect of a sultanic autocracy which stifled and proscribed all initiative, were all too self-evident.

The low point of the Ottoman navy in the reign of Abdülhamid II was reached in the short and inglorious Greco-Ottoman war which followed a Greek-inspired insurrection on the island of Crete in 1896, and the sending of Greek ships and troops to Crete early in the following year. By this time, the Ottoman war fleet had been laid up in the Golden Horn for over nineteen years; ships had rotted at their moorings; their crews and officers were untrained; and all attempts to put elements of the fleet to sea proved abortive. The ambitious plans to activate the fleet to transport troops from Izmir to Thessaloniki and Crete were abandoned; the few fighting ships that ventured beyond the Dardanelles were found to be not battle worthy in almost every particular; and the Cretan rebellion was eventually crushed by troops transported by commandeered merchant vessels from Anatolia. Conversely, on land, the Ottoman forces, after fifteen years of reform spearheaded by the German General Colmar von der Goltz Pasha, were able to inflict a severe defeat on Greece, a defeat in which the navy played no part.

Abdülhamid II appeared, for the moment, to have learned the lessons of the Greco-Ottoman war. A naval reorganisation plan, proposing the modernisation of the existing fleet and the purchase abroad of new warships, was set in train. A grandiose scheme for the construction of two battleships and six cruisers was deemed by foreign experts to be unrealisable, while the existing fleet was found to be incapable of modernisation. The Ottoman government, meanwhile, found itself the object of unremitting attention from German and British and, to a lesser extent, from French and Italian constructors, in which the German builders Krupp and the British firm of Armstrong, in cooperation with the Italian firm of Ansaldo, played preponderating and rival roles. The results were patchy: the *Mecidiye* (1903), a new cruiser built in the United States as part of compensation for US losses in the course of the Armenian uprisings a decade earlier, was found to be a failure, unseaworthy and unstable; the *Hamidiye*, built by Armstrong, and also completed in 1903, proved a success, remaining in service until long after the disappearance of the Ottoman Empire. Further rebuilding and reconstruction, together with the construction of new vessels, although a process bedevilled by financial and contractual disputes and scandals, proceeded at a fast pace in the yards of the major European naval powers.

All these developments took place against a background of rising opposition to the rule of Abdülhamid. This was led mainly from the Macedonian corps of the army, and culminated in 1908 with the so-called Young Turk revolution and the deposition of Abdulhamid II in the following year, events in which the navy played no significant part.

The new Young Turk regime inherited from its predecessor a navy that appeared to be in better shape than for many decades previously. The revival at this time of the fortunes of the British naval mission under Rear-Admiral Sir Douglas Gamble (1908–10) also appeared to promise much, but it rapidly fell foul of vested interests in an over-age, over-manned officer corps, and of interministerial rivalries at the Porte, as well as a dearth of money to implement Gamble's far-reaching proposals for reform. His unimpressive successor, Rear-Admiral Hugh Williams (1910–12), did no better, and even the efficient Arthur Limpus (1912–14) never fully overcame the implacable xenophobia and bureaucratic obstructionism in the Ottoman Admiralty. The débacle of their project for a vast floating dock at Izmid on the eastern shore of the Sea of Marmara forms a classic example of the gap between appearance and reality.

War with Italy, which broke out in the autumn of 1911, demonstrated the inability of the Ottoman navy to protect the extended coastlines of the empire or to defend itself against a superior force. The conquest and occupation of Tripoli was rapidly followed by the retreat of the Ottoman fleet into the shelter of the Dardanelles, and unopposed Italian naval operations against the Ottomans in the Red Sea, the eastern Mediterranean, the Aegean and the Adriatic, aimed at eliminating the last vestiges of Ottoman naval power and securing by conquest an Italian presence in the major Aegean islands off the west coast of Anatolia (the so-called Dodecanese). Further disasters accompanied the First and Second Balkan wars in the shape of Greek occupation of the remaining Ottoman islands in the Aegean and the loss of Thessaloniki, the last Ottoman port of significance in its now largely lost European provinces, which the Ottoman navy had been powerless to protect.

The disastrous outcome of the Libyan Balkan wars demonstrated the sclerotic and incompetent top-loading of the Ottoman navy with officers of twenty, thirty and forty years' service, and for a short period, from the appointment of the Young Turk leader Cemal Pasha as Navy Minister in March 1914, matters improved. Hundreds of elderly and incompetent officers were forced into retirement; far-reaching and logical administrative reforms were put in place; new departments for torpedos, mines and naval aviation were set up; and Admiral Limpus was persuaded to prolong his secondment to the Porte for a further year.

All these domestic developments were now rapidly overtaken by a major European crisis. In the weeks following the assassination of the Austrian archduke Franz Ferdinand at Sarajevo in June 1914, considerations of naval strategy appear to have played some part in the secret negotiations between elements of the Young Turk régime and Germany which led to the momentous and fatal Ottoman–German secret agreement of 2 August 1914, committing the Ottoman Empire to join the Central Powers if Russia were to enter the escalating conflict and thereby force Germany into the war. The decision was made on the basis of false perceptions on both sides. The Ottomans looked forward to a war with Russia only, which they expected Germany and Austria would win, yielding concrete results in the Balkans and the Caucasus. Germany anticipated the positive effect of an Ottoman alliance on the Muslim populations of the British and French empires in Africa and Asia, plus the effective neutralization of Russian naval forces in the Black Sea by the closing of the Straits.

Events thereafter took an unexpected turn. In the first days of August 1914 the links between Britain and the Young Turk régime in naval matters still appeared to be firmly established. Three years previously, in 1911, the Ottomans, alarmed by the growing strength of the Greek navy, and in particular by Greece's purchase from an Italian yard of the armoured cruiser *Georgios Averoff*, had ordered two modern battleships from Britain, the purchase of which had been financed in part by fund-raising activities throughout the empire. This development formed part of a general naval arms race amongst the Mediterranean and Black Sea states which had begun at the time of the Libyan crisis and accelerated in the years immediately preceding the outbreak of the First World War. When the 1914 crisis broke, the two battleships under construction in Britain were complete but not yet handed over, while awaiting further tests and the remaining tranches of payment. By the end of July, the tests had been completed; the final payments had been made, and a party of Ottoman officers and crew members were already in England to take delivery, when, on 1 August, the British Admiralty requisitioned both the *Reşadiye* and the *Sultan Osman*. This enraged Turkish opinion, and handed a major propaganda victory to both the Ottoman government and Germany. The German naval high command ordered its Mediterranean squadron, which consisted of the battle-cruiser *Goeben* and the light cruiser *Breslau*, under the command of Admiral Souchon, to proceed to the Dardanelles. The two German vessels managed to avoid British and French attempts to intercept them; on 10 August, by which time Britain and Germany were at war (though the Ottomans were not), they entered the Dardanelles and, in response to British demands for their extradition, were bought by the Ottomans in a fictitious sale as the *Yavuz Sultan Selim* and the *Midilli*.

Debate has raged over whether or not the Ottomans were only pawns in a deep German game, spearheaded by Souchon, to bring the Ottoman Empire into the war on the side of the Central Powers. It would seem now that the innermost circles of the "Committee of Union and Progress" were well aware of Souchon's plans, and that increased German interest in promoting Ottoman belligerency after mid-September, when the German land offensive in the west stalled on the Marne, was matched by the active involvement of Enver Pasha and the increasingly desperate Ottoman need for loans in the shape of German gold. Souchon was now commander-in-chief of the Ottoman fleet. On 27 October the fleet entered the Black Sea to attack Russian ports and shipping. This cannot be regarded as an independent coup by a headstrong German commander, but was an act planned in close collaboration with the Porte, and executed on the explicit orders of the Ottoman war ministry.

Following on the exploits of the *Goeben* and *Breslau*, which had spectacularly precipitated the outbreak of war with Russia, the Ottomans retreated to a mainly defensive stance in the face of Russian naval superiority in the Black Sea. In the Mediterranean, the Ottomans were unable to operate beyond the Straits in the face of overwhelming British and allied superiority at sea and a blockade, sustained by a strong British fleet presence at Lemnos, which was even more effective than that which Venice had imposed on the Straits two and half centuries previously. In the Black Sea, the Ottoman navy was constrained to perform humdrum but vital duties. Chief of these was to protect the coal traffic from Zonguldak to Istanbul, on which both the fleet and the capital relied. The mines at Ereğli were able to supply less than half the state's needs: down to the outbreak of war the Ottoman navy had been in large part dependent on Welsh steam coal, a source which was now closed to them. Also vital, in view of the weakness of the Anatolian railway network, was the maintenance of the fleet's ability to ferry large bodies of troops from Istanbul to Trabzon for service on the eastern Anatolian and Caucasian fronts.

In the course of 1915 the inadequacy of the Ottoman navy to sustain these two roles became ever more obvious: by the end of 1915 it had lost most of its colliers. Equally, the dependence of the German-built ships in the fleet on spare parts and technical expertise, the procurement of which had become ever more difficult, limited the amount of time for which they could be at sea. By November 1917, when the new revolutionary regime in Russia withdrew from the war, the Ottoman navy in the Black Sea was no longer a fighting force, but the signing of an armistice (December 1917) between Russia and its former enemies brought some respite to the remaining active ships.

By the end of the war, the Ottomans had been forced almost entirely onto the defensive. The defences of the Dardanelles and the Bosphorus, through the expenditure of men, munitions and treasure, and through systematic use of mines and anti-submarine nets, remained for the most part unbreached: the abortive allied attempt in 1915 to force the Dardanelles foundered as a result of indecisive allied leadership and determined Ottoman resistance in which large-scale mining and the use of torpedo boats, as well as resolute defence on land, played a part. Thus, while the Ottomans were largely bottled up in the

Dardanelles, the allied forces were unable to breach the Turkish land and sea defences except by submarine warfare, which, in 1915, was surprisingly effective, penetrating into the Sea of Marmara as far as Istanbul. In the Black Sea, likewise, the Bosphorus defences had remained unbreached.

After the cessation of hostilities, the Ottoman navy was dissolved by the allies and the larger ships of the fleet were interned in the Golden Horn or at the islands in the Sea of Marmara. Eventually, under the newly constituted and recognised Republic of Turkey, the surviving major warships, including the *Goeben/Yavuz* and the *Hamidiye*, were repaired and modernised to form the nucleus of the new republic's navy.

In retrospect, the history of the Ottoman navy in the "long" 19th century cannot be seen as much more than a footnote to the history of the empire itself in this period. The paradigm of decline and fall has now become distinctly unfashionable – but in this period the empire did decline, and it did, eventually, fall. The forces which contributed to that fall – national feeling among the subject population of the empire; the Ottoman state as a perceived "other" amongst the powers of the time and the xenophobia which this view both precipitated and reflected; the empire's technological and demographic backwardness – had for the most part little to do with naval and maritime matters, and the relegation of the navy to a junior role vis-à-vis the army, in funding terms, throughout this period reflected little more than reality for an institution which was incapable either of adequately defending the maritime frontiers of the empire or of acting decisively in the face of great-power pressure to suppress rebellion within it.

SUGGESTED READING

For a general introduction to the period: ZÜRCHER E.J., *Turkey: A Modern History* (2nd edn, London, 1997), Chs 1-9. For Ottoman naval history see PANZAC D., *La marine ottomane: de l'apogée à la chute de l'Empire (1572-1923)* (Paris, 2009); SOUCEK S., *Ottoman maritime wars, 1700-1914* (Istanbul, 2013); ÖZVEREN E. and YILDIRIM O., 'An Outline of Ottoman maritime history', in *New Directions in Mediterranean Maritime History*, ed. G. HARLAFTIS and C. VASSALLO, Research in Maritime History, no. 28 (St John's, Newfoundland, 2004); ANDERSON R.C., *Naval Wars in the Levant, 1559-1853* (Liverpool, 1952); PANZAC P., 'The Manning of the Ottoman Navy in the Heyday of Sail (1660-1850)', in *Arming the State: Military Conscription in the Middle East and Central Asia, 1775-1925*, ed. E.J. ZÜRCHER (London, 1999); LEON G.B., 'The Greek Merchant Marine (1453-1850)', in *The Greek Merchant Marine (1453-1850)*, ed. S.A. PAPADOPOULOS ([Athens], 1972).

On the technical details of the Ottoman navy in the post-sail era, see LANGENSIEPEN B. and GÜLERYÜZ A., *The Ottoman Steam Navy 1828-1923* (Annapolis, MD, 1995), with useful chronology; GÜLERYÜZ A., *Ottoman Navy's Cruisers* (Istanbul, 2011).

On specific episodes: KOMATSU K., 'Financial Problems of the Navy during the

Reign of Abdülhamid II'; and ZHUKOV, K. 'The Origins of the Ottoman Submarine Fleet', both in *The Ottomans and the Sea*, ed. K. FLEET (Naples, 2001); ROONEY C.B., 'The international significance of British naval missions to the Ottoman Empire, 1908-14', *Middle Eastern Studies* 34 (1998), 1-29. On the *Goeben* and *Breslau*: TRUMPENER U., 'Turkey's entry into World War I: an assessment of responsibilities', *Journal of Modern History* 34 (1962), 369-80; LANGENSIEPEN B., NOTTELMANN D. and KRÜSMANN J., *Halbmond und Kaiseradler: Goeben und Breslau am Bosporus, 1914-1918* (Hamburg, 1999).

Empire and trade without a major navy: Portugal[1]

Francisco Contente Domingues is Professor of History in the Faculty of Humanities of the University of Lisbon and Rear-Admiral Fernando David e Silva, Portuguese Navy, is attached to the Centre for Naval Research

ABSTRACT. *First and last of all the European seaborne empires, the Portuguese was distinguished throughout by its flexibility and adaptability. Initially an Eastern empire, later centred on the South Atlantic and finally on southern Africa, it followed different models in different areas. Never backed by a powerful navy or even an adequate merchant fleet, it survived and at some periods flourished thanks to its capacity to adjust to circumstances.*

RÉSUMÉ. *Premier et dernier empire maritime européen, le Portugal s'est distingué par sa flexibilité et sa capacité d'adaptation. Au départ, l'empire s'étendait plutôt en Orient, avant de concentrer sa présence sur l'Atlantique sud puis au final sur l'Afrique du sud. Il suivit par conséquent différents modèles dans différentes régions. Bien qu'il n'ait jamais été doté d'une marine puissante ou même d'une flotte marchande adéquate, il réussit à subsister et, à certaines périodes, parvint à grandement prospérer grâce à son aptitude à s'adapter aux circonstances.*

.•.

Between Ceuta in 1415 and Macao in 1999, the beginning and end of the empire, stretch six centuries, fifteen thousand nautical miles and two different models of colonisation. The last act of the Portuguese empire was in 1999 to hand over Macao to Chinese rule, after 450 years of a Portuguese presence marked by a way of life of mutual tolerance. Its rules changed over time, and many of them were scarcely written down; sometimes they were remote from official regulations, often they were shaped by local interests.

Ceuta was captured by King John I with an army of twenty thousand men carried in over two hundred ships. It was an enormous and formidable force for a country with a population of no more than a million: 2% of the population sailed to Ceuta. The expedition was for a long time explained as a crusade, or a means of glory for the princes Duarte and Pedro, and Henrique, Duke of Viseu (known to

---

[1] Translated by Gonçalo Couceiro Feio. This work is state-funded by FCT (Foundation for Science and Technology) under project UID/HIS/04311/2013.

history as Henry the Navigator). The truth is that Ceuta was a trading centre in a strategic position to control the Strait of Gibraltar and communication between the Mediterranean and Atlantic. Its capture served the political interests of a new dynasty in need of international recognition, and opened opportunities of expansion for a small kingdom trapped between Castile and the sea. Much later, in 1580, Portugal fell into Spanish hands with the failure of the dynasty and, when Portugal regained her independence in 1640, Ceuta alone of her former possessions never returned.

In some quarters it is still fashionable to argue that the capture of Ceuta, the first milestone of Portuguese expansion, was the fruit of naval superiority, excellent weapons and flourishing trade. Others ask how a small population inhabiting a poor country could succeed in an enterprise scarcely within the reach of much richer and more powerful states. Others attribute the expansion to the crusading spirit, or the drive to escape a life of poverty and isolation on the western margin of Europe. All these explanations are worth attention, and together they led to the creation of a Portuguese seaborne empire which outlasted all the other European colonial empires.

Although fifteenth- and sixteenth-century land expeditions gathered much useful information, all the bases of the Portuguese empire were reached by sea. Ships sent by the Portuguese crown reached – and returned – from Madeira (c. 1419), India (1498), Brazil (1500), Malacca (1511) and the Moluccas (1512). The Portuguese were also the first European to reach Vietnam by sea (1507), the kingdom of Siam (Thailand) (1511), China (1513), Japan (1542) and Korea (1578).

The credit for these voyages belongs not only to the captains and pilots, but to the mathematicians, astronomers and cartographers who laid the foundations of a new art of navigation. Crossing first the Atlantic and then other oceans forced the pilots to navigate by the stars, from which they determined their latitude, relying on dead reckoning for longitude to make long open ocean passages. On their charts they laid down many countries hitherto unknown to Europeans, and with them a huge quantity of hydrographic information about oceans, seas, rivers, coastlines, shoals, winds and currents: a great database of information stretching from the Atlantic to the seas of China and Japan which was to be of great benefit to navigators from other parts of Western Europe. At the same time, the first written texts on the construction of ocean sailing ships began to appear in Portuguese and other languages from the last quarter of the 16th century. All this was the fruit of a great effort; navigating unknown or uncharted waters required an intellectual drive to organise information drawn from different branches of knowledge, and a critical attitude towards the classics: the world turned out not to be as Pliny and Ptolemy had described. The paradox of the Portuguese empire rests partly on the interaction of experience with organised and formalised learning.

The question has to be asked, whether the growth of the Portuguese empire was the result of Portugal gaining command of the sea and sweeping aside opposition to its trade and conquests. The answer is no: the Portuguese navy was never large enough to gain supremacy over the naval powers of Europe. However, the crown monopoly of overseas trade meant that the success of the first voyages depended on the projection of state power, and on the building of more than three hundred forts in the Americas and Asia. This heroic effort exceeded the country's capital resources, as witnessed by the funding of Portuguese trading fleets by German and Italian bankers, and the Portuguese model showed itself to be less efficient in direct competition with Dutch and English public companies, underwritten by merchants with deeper financial resources than Portuguese bankers or even the Portuguese state.

Thus the Portuguese case differed from that of the Dutch who were the first to defy Portuguese power. Luís Filipe Thomaz wrote that capitalism "was a graft on the trunk of Portuguese maritime expansion ... Therefore we find outmoded institutions and ways of thinking which become conspicuous ... when we compare the Portuguese expansion in the Indian Ocean with the authentically bourgeois and commercial Dutch expansion."[2] He stresses that the Portuguese model based on state power offered weak resistance to a strategy planned, financed and managed by a trading organisation such as the Dutch East India Company, especially in the context of the war generated by the union of the crowns of Portugal and Spain between 1580 and 1640.

Next we must consider the ships required by the empire, especially the eastern empire which had the most pressing need due to the sheer distance from the Persian Gulf to the Malay Peninsula, the Moluccas, the China Seas and Japan. In 1525, for example, Portuguese Asia from Hormuz to Calicut possessed no more than six carracks, of which three were under repair, eleven galleons (five of them under repair), about twenty galleys and smaller craft, and eleven privately owned ships.[3] This shortage of shipping remained standard for centuries, and Portugal could never match the naval strength of England or the Netherlands.

Despite losing some Asian forts (and a few in Brazil and Africa) in the first decades of the 17th century, the Portuguese continued to operate their trading network in the eastern seas, but with a growing number of private entrepreneurs. The Dutch and English made no systematic attempt to eliminate Portuguese power in Asia, which would have been very costly and would have aroused the resistance of local powers which did not welcome outside competition.

A peace with the Dutch was reached in 1661, at the cost of paying compensation and abandoning claims to forts in the East. By the end of this century a new phase of empire was about to begin. From the 16th century sugar, gold and diamonds drew Portuguese interest towards Brazil, and generated a trade in slaves from Angola, Mina and São Tomé on the eastern shores of the South Atlantic. As the eastern empire weakened, the Atlantic empire grew. Brazil was linked to Africa, the source of the slave workforce essential to the plantation economy in both North and South America. Brazilian gold (of which the crown took a fifth) and wine exports paid for the trade deficit with Britain. This legally

---

[2] THOMAZ L.F., *De Ceuta a Timor* (Lisbon, 1994), p. 35.
[3] SUBRAHMANYAM S., *The Portuguese Empire in Asia, 1500-1700: A Political and Economic History* (London and New York, 1993), p. 75.

exported gold, together with gold smuggled out of Brazil by British ships, contributed to the Industrial Revolution, but excluded Portugal and Brazil from it.[4] Moreover, from the mid 18th century up to the First World War, Britain was increasingly important in indirectly protecting Portuguese transatlantic trade.

Around 1750 the Portuguese navy had only five ships of the line and seven frigates, none in good condition. Thanks to the work of two energetic ministers the number of ships of the line and the navy's infrastructure were increased, but by the end of the century the total was only twenty ships of the line (of which four were in Brazil and three in India), and the same number of frigates. This weakness reflects the real condition of the empire, essentially concentrated on Brazil, with too few ships to protect the trade to the East.

When France invaded Portugal in November 1807 to force her to participate in the "Continental System" and close her ports to Britain, John VI (then Prince Regent) decided to transfer the crown to Brazil. Though executed in haste as Junot's troops entered Lisbon, this move to what was arguably the richest part of the empire had been contemplated since the 16th century. It was a major maritime operation to move the court, involving twenty thousand people on board thirty merchantmen escorted by all the Portuguese warships fit to sail (twenty-three ships with a total of a thousand guns, including eight ships of the line, the jewels in the navy's crown), plus some British ships of which four went all the way to Brazil.

The decision in 1808 to open Brazil to foreign trade (essentially meaning British trade) tended to make Brazil the real centre of the new empire. Lisbon gradually lost importance as a centre of trade, though transatlantic links never disappeared, showing the continued flexibility which the empire had shown in the past.

In 1820, a Liberal revolution in Portugal overthrew the *ancien régime* and rejected the British protectorate which had lasted since the expulsion of the French. In 1821 this new government called back King John VI from Brazil, leaving his eldest son Dom Pedro in Rio de Janeiro as Regent of Brazil. The following year Dom Pedro refused to return to Portugal and was proclaimed Emperor of Brazil; a paradox of the colonial empire in which a colony had to become independent to create a Portuguese emperor.

After the declaration of Brazilian independence in 1822, the Lisbon government tried to reduce it once more to a colony (although it had officially been a separate kingdom since 1815). For want of good ships and good troops the expeditions failed, and the effort to recreate the empire by force exacerbated the economic difficulties of Portugal, as exports to Brazil and re-exports from Brazil collapsed, and customs revenues with them.

When the king returned to Lisbon in 1822 he brought back only two ships of the line and seven frigates, a mere shadow of the navy which had been relatively

---

[4] MARTINIÈRE, G., 'A Implantação das Estruturas de Portugal na América', in *O Império Luso-Brasileiro 1620-1750* (*Nova História da Expansão Portuguesa*, vol. 7), ed. F. MAURO (Lisbon, 1991), pp. 90–261 (p. 251).

flourishing thirty years before. The years 1820 to 1851 were a turbulent time in Portugal, with a succession of civil wars, internal struggles and foreign interventions. The period of war between the Liberals and Absolutists, from 1828 to 1834, was especially violent. After their victory in 1834 the Liberals aimed to revive the decaying African empire in order to restore the fortunes of the country. Speaking in the Chamber of Deputies in 1840, the writer and historian Alexandre Herculano urged the government to defend the colonies in the name of "the ashes of our ancient knights", and "the legacy of glory we have inherited". This was the beginning of the myth of the "sacred inheritance", the basis of Portuguese colonial claims which were maintained with little variation throughout the Constitutional Monarchy (1834-1910), the First Republic (1910-26), the Dictatorship (1926-33) and the "New State" (1933-74). Initially directed towards the élites, the myth filtered down through society and became an instrument of mass propaganda, much as happened until the 1960s in Britain, France, Belgium, the Netherlands, Italy and Germany.

The impulses behind the imperial project in the 19th century have been variously identified as historical national prestige, foreign interests (British in particular) or mercantilist ambitions.[5] Such a range of explanations suggests that there was no true colonial strategy, although all these elements were present to varying degrees.

On a practical level, Portugal still lacked resources. She controlled vast and distant territories, but lacked a navy or merchant fleet capable of defending the empire or assuring its links with the mother country. Poor communications helped to preserve something of the *ancien régime* in the colonies, where traditional powers and forms of government still survived.

In the first half of the 19th century, abolitionism and the slave trade were important questions. Under British pressure, internal debates grew while governors and slavers more or less openly continued the trade. In this context again an inadequate navy revealed the weakness of the state.

The Industrial Revolution arrived late (some would say, never); the first steamer reached Portugal in 1820 in an unsuccessful attempt to enter the coasting trade. Not until the late 1850s did the navy acquire its first two steam corvettes. These small warships, and the even smaller gunboats, became the backbone of the Portuguese Navy, now truly a colonial navy, which used them for long voyages and as station ships from Angola to Macao.

In 1875 the Portuguese Navy was a small and weak force of ten corvettes, seven gunboats and two steam transports. It evolved into two groups; the colonial force and the ships intended for home defence, especially of Lisbon. The core of the colonial navy was the gunboats; at its greatest strength in 1890 there were twenty-three ships including eight steam-and-sail corvettes. The empire still depended on small ships and a small fleet, which was all that national resources and policy priorities could support.

---

[5] ALEXANDRE V., 'A questão colonial no Portugal oitocentista', V. ALEXANDRE and J. DIAS, *O Império Africano (1825-1890)* (Lisbon, 1998), pp. 21-132 (pp. 120-6).

In the 1890s, military campaigns in inland Africa reduced the importance of the colonial navy. Between 1896 and 1901 five small cruisers were built, which varied their employment between defence of the capital and periods on station at Angola or Mozambique, with visits to Macao. Such was the poor state of the Portuguese economy, business and finance that there were then no regular shipping lines from Portugal to Angola, Mozambique or Brazil, still an important part of Portuguese foreign trade since its independence.

At the time of the partition of Africa in the 1890s, Portugal tried to strengthen its empire by claiming the lands lying between Angola and Mozambique, alleging historical rights and effective occupation. In the spirit of the Berlin Conference, Portugal mounted transcontinental expeditions linking the Atlantic and Indian oceans, but these were opposed by Britain because they cut across Cecil Rhodes' projects. The colonial question thus became central to both internal and foreign policies.

When the monarchy ended in 1910, Angola and Mozambique were far from the hoped-for "new Brazils", and the First Republic was no more successful. One of its first decisions was to divide the Ministries of Colonies and the Navy, which had been united since 1736. The intention was to strengthen the autonomy of the colonies, as France (1894) and Germany (1907) had done, but lack of money, the First World War and a failure to decentralise colonial administration all undermined the project.

In 1912, the parliament approved an ambitious plan to strengthen the navy, based on ideas in circulation for a decade. The plan to build three dreadnought battleships, three cruisers, fifteen destroyers and six submarines represented a technological and strategic leap. These ships were not meant to serve in Africa; they expressed an understanding that the defence of the colonies in the approaching war would start in European waters. The war came too soon, however, and none of the ships was built. There are hints that the underlying motive of the scheme was to buy the navy's loyalty to the young republic.

When the war broke out, the Portuguese government's first concern was to obtain assurances from Britain that the frontiers of the colonies would be respected, since Angola bordered on German West Africa and Mozambique on German East Africa. Britain did not seek Portuguese participation in the war, for in her state of unpreparedness she would be more of an embarrassment than a help; but neither did Britain want Portugal neutral, which would restrict Britain's freedom to use Portuguese ports. Portugal was thus a non-belligerent state until March 1916, when Germany declared war after the Portuguese government seized seventy German merchant ships interned in Portuguese ports since 1914. The *casus belli* here was the fact that some of these ships were to be chartered by the British government in compensation for losses inflicted by German U-boats and auxiliary cruisers.

The European war had an immediate impact in Africa. There were incidents with German troops on the northern frontier of Mozambique in August 1914, and on the southern frontier of Angola in October. Troops and ships were deployed, but most of the fighting was against local powers rather than the Germans.

Although none of the planned additions to the navy had been realised, the navy had to transport troops from Portugal to Africa (mostly in chartered steamers) and supply naval support, especially in northern Mozambique.

The fighting in the two colonies cost 5,600 dead and the same number missing, mostly from disease since the health of the forces was poor; this was a heavier toll than in the operations of the Great War. No fewer than 13,500 Portuguese were lost in Africa, a crushing toll of victims of the empire.

The First Republic was overthrown by a military coup in 1926 and Portugal was governed by a dictatorship until 1933, followed by an authoritarian constitutional government. The Colonial Act of 1930 established the "Portuguese Colonial Empire" and defined its mission to "colonise overseas territories and civilise the inhabitants, exercising the moral influence belonging to the Patron of the East". Here we see the essential elements of the three phases of the empire: to dominate, to convert and to civilise.

A revised constitution in 1951, under the "New State", stressed the integration of the "overseas provinces". But this strategy failed where it was most likely to, in Goa, the first part of the empire to be touched by the "winds of change" which had been blowing since the end of the Second World War, and especially since the Bandung Conference of 1955.

Portuguese India fell in December 1961, to a brief but overwhelming invasion by India's armed forces. In February of that year violent uprisings erupted in Angola, rapidly spreading to Guinea-Bissau and Mozambique. The Portuguese authoritarian regime, led by Oliveira Salazar until 1968 and Marcelo Caetano until 1974, shifted its policy towards increased public investment and new white migration to the colonies, which also supported its legal and diplomatic arguments.

There followed a thirteen-year guerrilla war against the liberation movements, during which the navy was heavily involved in coastal, riverine and inland operations. In its dying days the empire really depended on the sea, but the nation was socially and economically exhausted by the war and diplomatically defeated. Between 1974 and 1975, Guinea-Bissau, Angola and Mozambique became independent, followed by Cape Verde and São Tomé e Príncipe, where there had been no fighting. Timor was invaded by Indonesia after some resistance by the small Portuguese garrison; it was returned in 2002 on condition of becoming independent. Macao, which to satisfy the Chinese had never been declared a colony, was handed over to China by mutual agreement in 1999.

The Portuguese empire was the longest-lasting maritime empire in history. It was an empire which never had an emperor, though it produced the first Emperor of Brazil. It survived thanks to its talent for metamorphosis into new forms of sovereignty adapted to changing circumstances. At some periods the empire enriched its elites and clients, but it was unable to do so consistently. It was a maritime empire belonging to a small country, poor in natural resources, and never able to command the sea outside certain regions and periods.

What was distinctive about the Portuguese empire was its flexibility and resilience. It continually sought to adapt its form and methods to changing circumstances, with varying success. In all its successive forms up to 1974, the empire was central to Portuguese strategy. In the judgement of a political scientist like Adriano Moreira, Portugal is still redefining a new concept, based now on a European rather than a Portuguese sea.

Ultimately, the key question is to understand whether the Portuguese empire existed because of the sea, or in spite of it.

BIBLIOGRAPHY

ALEXANDRE V., 'A questão colonial no Portugal oitocentista', V. ALEXANDRE and J. DIAS, *O Império Africano (1825-1890)* (Lisbon, 1998), pp. 21-132.

BETHENCOURT F. and CURTO D.R., eds., *Portuguese Oceanic Expansion, 1400-1800* (Cambridge, 2007).

BOXER C., *The Portuguese Seaborne Empire 1415-1825* (London, 1969).

MARTINIÈRE, G., 'A Implantação das Estruturas de Portugal na América', in *O Império Luso-Brasileiro 1620-1750* (*Nova História da Expansão Portuguesa*, vol. 7), ed. F. MAURO (Lisbon, 1991), pp. 90-261.

OLIVEIRA E COSTA J.P., RODRIGUES J.D. and OLIVEIRA P.A., *História da Expansão e do Império Português* (Lisbon, 2014).

SUBRAHMANYAM S., *The Portuguese Empire in Asia, 1500-1700: A Political and Economic History* (London and New York, 1993).

THOMAZ L.F., *De Ceuta a Timor* (Lisbon, 1994).

Italy, 1861–1914: did the sea build a state and an empire?

Francesco Zampieri is a lecturer at the Naval Staff College, Italy

Abstract. *Italy's geographical situation as a peninsula in the central Mediterranean seems to offer large opportunities for seaborne trade linked to overland routes, but in practice Italy's underdeveloped industries, ports and railways left it behind its neighbours until well into the 20th century. The navy was intended to defend the vulnerable coastline and to seek an empire overseas, which was found in parts of East Africa and, in the Turkish War of 1911, in Libya. In a state marked by poverty and structural weakness, the navy was one the more efficient agencies.*

Résumé. *En tant que péninsule au centre de la Méditerranée, la situation géographique de l'Italie semble lui offrir de nombreuses opportunités de commerce maritime associé à des itinéraires terrestres. En réalité, le sous-développement des industries, ports et chemins de fer italiens la laissèrent loin derrière ses voisins jusqu'au milieu du XXe siècle. La marine avait pour rôle la défense des côtes littorales vulnérables et la formation d'un empire colonial, qui se constitua de certaines régions d'Afrique de l'est, puis de la Libye pendant la guerre italo-turque de 1911. Dans un état marqué par la pauvreté et la faiblesse structurelle, la marine fut l'une des organisations les plus efficaces.*

.•.

Introduction

This study examines the influence of the sea on the Italian Kingdom from 1861 to 1914. The aim is to understand if Italy was a sea power and if the naval and maritime components of the state were important. Writing in 1893, Major Cristoforo Manfredi argued that Italy had never understood whether she was a continental or a maritime power. He argued that she was both, and that the sea was the key to her future development.

> We fought for unity and independence and we have won. Now we have to fight for prosperity. ... We must give the Italian State what it needs to be respected, feared and, as a result, prosperous. A great nation that is not respected and feared cannot be prosperous. Our field of expansion is the sea, and beyond the sea.[1]

---

[1] Manfredi C., *L'Italia deve essere potenza terrestre o marittima?* (Roma, 1893), p. 36.

This was the roadmap for some opinion makers and some politicians. In fact, a lot of backwardness blocked Italian sea power: natural gaps, economic poverty, lack of commercial mindset, a difficult geopolitical situation and national traditions, according to which Italians were farmers more than they were seamen.

In the following pages I will analyze the history of the relationship between Italians and the sea during the period 1861-1914. My roadmap will be Admiral Mahan's definition of sea power: a complex combination of naval power, maritime power, geographical, and human characteristics.

LAND AND SEA

The Italian Kingdom was a peninsula at the crossroads of the most important sea lines of communication in the Mediterranean Sea, but in the years after national unification access to the sea was practically non-existent. The Tyrrhenian coast, from the Gulf of La Spezia to Naples, excepting the populous coastal centers, was dominated by a succession of coastal plains covered by malarial swamps. This kind of landscape is the same as the Pontine and Calabrian coasts and, on the Ionian Sea, as the Lucanian and Calabrian coasts. Here the local population withdrew to the hills. The same conditions pertained in Apulia, down to Santa Maria di Leuca. Everywhere there was malaria, a tangible sign of the degradation of coastal areas, as reported in the medical records. Even in the early 20th century, in 1910, the situation was unchanged: the Venetian and Emilian coasts were described as an uninhabited strip of lagoons and marshes, impoverished by malaria, and it was the same in Gargano and Salento. In the early years of the 20th century something changed: in 1911 the population along the coastal areas, outside of the major port cities, had increased.[2] Changes in agricultural practice, a new geographical distribution of the rural population, and national health and economic policies led to the repopulation of the coastal areas. The development of the railways was the greatest factor in the transformation of Italy in the second half of the 19th century and the first decades of the following century.[3]

---

[2] Between 1871 and 1911, the coastal population from the Venetian lagoon to Salento increased from 352,000 to 513,000 (46%). In Apulia, the population of the maritime centres, between 1828 and 1911, had trebled. The increase in the population density, within a radius of 15 km from the sea, was evident also in Tuscany, Lazio, Sardinia, Basilicata and Calabria.

[3] In 1861, the Italian railway network was undeveloped: in Italy, there were only 1,829km of track, in France 9,300km and in Great Britain 17,000km. The Italian railway network was designed for the needs of the pre-unification states and not the new national kingdom. The new national state committed itself heavily to the construction of railways: in 1865, 4,500km of railway were in operation; by 1876, the railway system had quadrupled; at the end of the century, Italy could count almost 15,000km of railways. Along the peninsula two major lines were built: the Adriatic, from Bologna to Brindisi (760km) and the Tyrrhenian, from Ventimiglia to Rome (653km), which would be completed only at the beginning of the 20th century with the stub from Naples to Reggio Calabria. The Milan–Bologna–Florence–Rome railway became very important to assure communications between the north and the south.

The railways along the Adriatic and Tyrrhenian coasts were close to the sea and this encouraged the gradual transfer of population to the coastal areas. The railways boosted the reclamation of the marshes, the birth of factories, the depopulation of the mountains, and the development of tourism. Furthermore, the industrial settlements were situated along the railways and near ti the stations, in the North (Milano-Bergamo-Brescia), in the center (Pontedera, Figline-San Giovanni-Montevarchi, Narni), and in the South (Bussi-Scafa, Augusta-Priolo, Gargallo). The railways encouraged the migration of the population; many villages in Romagna and Versilia shifted to the shoreline and from there expanded inland. The impact of the railways on the transfer of population to the coast was enormous: in the period 1861-1911 the population of coastal towns served by railway grew by 131%, compared to 28% in the cities that were not touched by the railway.[4]

These developments were very important in defining the relationship between the young, post-unification Italian State and the sea. The coastal area changed from "no man's land" to public land. In the Civil Code of 1865 and in further laws, the coastal and maritime areas were transferred increasingly into public ownership. State property was identified with maritime military assets (navy yards, naval bases, etc.), but also with the coasts, because they represented a public interest in the communication between land and sea.

The role of the Italian merchant navy

The Italian merchant navy was a fundamental component of national sea power, but in the second half of the 19th century it was affected by an evident technological backwardness: it was one of the last fleets to complete the transition from sail to steam. Even in the coasting trades, Italian shipping suffered from the competition of foreign fleets that had adopted steam propulsion and iron hulls. Consequently, the Italian merchant navy concentrated on the ports of the Black Sea and the Danube, as well as the coasts of Dalmatia, Croatia-Istria, and the French coast of the Mediterranean and Tunisia, where the technological gap could somehow be compensated. The situation became untenable after 1870. The opening of the Suez Canal (1869) was a disaster for the Italian merchant fleet; the winds of the Red Sea prevented Italian sailing ships from taking that route and forced them to take the longer and more expensive route round the Cape. In this way, the Italian merchant navy began to decline. The opening of the Alpine passes – which could have transformed the Italian peninsula into a hub for goods coming from the rest of Europe – did not help the Italian merchant navy, either. The real winners in the Mediterranean routes were the French port of Marseille and the Austrian port of Trieste, while the Italian ports played only secondary roles. The Law of 14 July 1907, n. 542 – which financed works for the

---

[4] Frascani P., *Il mare* (Bologna, 2008).

improvement of the national ports – was the first attempt to create an integrated system, including inland waterways and the link between railways and ports, in order to stimulate and support navigation coast to coast. In fact, only a few ports in the north and center of the peninsula could benefit from these important investments, because public funding was feasible only in partnership with municipalities and provinces, which did nothing to correct the economic imbalance in favour of the north.

Despite the deficiencies of the port system, the lack of iron and steam ships was largely due to the high cost of raw materials (primarily iron and coal). To overcome these obstacles, a large supply of money for investment in the maritime industries was needed: this was very difficult for the small Italian shipping companies. Larger shipping companies were needed. The law of 23 July 1881, n. 339, created the Navigazione Generale Italiana (NGI) from the merger of the two most important existing shipping companies (Raffaele Rubattino e C. and Ignazio e Vincenzo Florio e C.). The modernization of the Italian merchant fleet was also affected by the burden of maritime taxes (port duties, health duties, consular registration and stamp duties, insurances, etc.), which was significantly higher than abroad. Only the laws of 1885 and of 13 June 1910, n. 306 introduced measures in favor of maritime industries and reduced taxes and duties.[5]

However, the biggest problem remained the lack of funds to modernize the merchant fleet. To correct this, Italy began a strong policy of protectionism in favor of Italian shipping companies and shipyards, but its effects on the modernization of the fleet were negative. We can estimate that the total funds paid by the Italian state to the shipping companies would have sufficed to buy modern ships from Britain. However, just to make money, the Italian shipping companies preferred to buy obsolete but very cheap British ships, rather than more modern and more expensive Italian ships.

Another vulnerability of the merchant navy was represented by a big gap between imports and exports. Heavy goods (coal, metals, cotton, and corn) came to the Italian ports, while exports were equivalent to only a quarter of what was imported. This meant that Italian ports were full of foreign ships unloading foreign products, while Italian ships could be loaded only with the few products that the limited agricultural and industrial hinterland of the country could offer. An active maritime trade policy would have allowed greater development for an economy such as the Italian one, which was primarily agricultural. It would have been better to use Italian ships for imports in order to reduce costs, and Italy would have increased the value of its exports if it had adopted the same solution.

The merchant fleet specialized in the transport of migrants. Shipping emigrants contributed much more to the development of the Italian merchant navy than the law of 1885; but despite the growth in their earnings, the shipping companies still required public subsidy. The Italian shipping companies transported emigrants in old ships: about half of the ships used for this purpose were

---

[5] DE COURTEN L., *La marina mercantile italiana nella politica di espansione (1860-1914). Industria, finanza e trasporti marittimi* (Rome, 1989), pp. 84–5.

between twenty and twenty-five years old, and 30% of them did not exceed three thousand tons. Migrants were embarked as third-class passengers; their sanitary conditions were intolerable: epidemics that forced foreign authorities to reject Italian merchant ships. The profits of emigration encouraged the birth of new shipping companies. Lloyd Italiano – founded in Genoa by Erasmo Piaggio in 1904 – served the Americas; Lloyd Sabaudo, which was founded in Turin in 1906; Sicula-Americana which was founded in Messina in 1906 by the Peirce Brothers (two English merchants of Sicilian wines) and which specialized in the transport of emigrants from the island.

The Royal Decree of 10 July 1901, n. 375 on Emigration excluded from the transport of migrants companies that did not respect the rules on hygiene and safety. These laws opened a lucrative market to foreign competitors, who were bound to the same conditions as the national shipping companies. The high profits in this market encouraged the renewal of the Italian merchant fleet: between 1904 and 1909 the Italian shipping companies modernized their fleets through orders from Italian and English shipyards.

Steel industry and shipbuilding industry

The steel industry and the shipbuilding industry had an important effect in transforming Italy from an agricultural to an industrial economy. In order to promote the growth of the shipbuilding industry, the Italian state supported numerous investments. First, it was important to ensure autonomous capacity in military shipbuilding. The Società degli Altiforni, Acciaierie e Fonderie di Terni, for example, was founded on 10 March 1884, thanks to the great efforts of naval architect Vice Admiral Benedetto Brin, later Minister of the Navy.[6] The Minister wanted to create an armour manufacturing industry for the battleships of the navy. The companies Franco Tosi (1882) and Breda (1886) both benefited from public funding granted either directly by the state or by the banks. This public funding attracted numerous national and international investors, especially banks, to the steel industry and shipbuilding.

Economic historians agree that the creation of consortia among steel firms, shipyards, and shipping companies started with the great banking revolution of 1893-94, after the crisis of the Italian banking system. After this crisis new banks were born, designed to finance all the industrial activities of the kingdom. The new banks received a massive injection of foreign – in particular, German – capital, because from 1882 the Italian state was in alliance with the German and Austro-Hungarian empires. Italian banking was now monopolized by two new major banks, the Banca Commerciale and the Credito Italiano, which were a formidable coalition of interests drawn from the steel industry, shipbuilding,

---

[6] BONELLI F., *Lo sviluppo di una grande impresa in Italia. La Terni dal 1884 al 1962* (Turin, 1975), pp. 16–20.

shipping companies, cotton and wool producers, and southern agricultural landowners.[7] Their links with the merchant navy were considerable: for example, the NGI fell under the control of the Comit Bank, dominated by German interests.[8] Due to the technological backwardness of the Italian merchant navy, the financial investments of the banks were of primary importance. However, in addition to the lack of raw materials (iron and coal) and the inadequate infrastructure of the Italian ports, there was another problem for the Italian shipbuilding industry. Many steel plants and shipbuilding companies were built to meet the aspirations of the regional governments rather than to provide the country with an efficient shipbuilding industry. The correct solution to this problem should have been the concentration of production in a few big sites. This policy should have been used also for the naval dockyards (Spezia, Naples, Taranto, and Venice) and for the private shipyards (Ansaldo and Odero in Sestri Ponente, Odero della Foce, Orlando in Livorno, Pattison and Armstrong in Naples and Pozzuoli), most of them concentrated in the North. This occurred only in 1898, when Terni joined Odero and Orlando, and became a monopolistic supplier of naval vessels for the Italian state.[9]

In the early years of the 20th century there were similar cases of joint venture between steel companies and shipbuilders: in 1903 the merger between Gio. Ansaldo e Co. of Genoa and Armstrong-Whitworth Limited of Newcastle on Tyne (with a branch in Pozzuoli since 1885) gave birth to the Società anonima italiana Gio. Ansaldo Armstrong e Co.; in 1907 the Cantieri navali riuniti (Ancona, Messina, Palermo, and Spezia) were founded. These industrial trusts were extremely stratified and were based on interests that linked banks, steel and metallurgical industries, shipyards, and shipowners. For example, Federico Weil, managing director of Comit, was also the managing director of the NGI; on the Comit board there were also Ignazio Florio and Carlo Raggio. Erasmo Piaggio, the former manager of NGI and founder of the Lloyd Italiano, was president both of the Banca di Genova and of the Credito Italiano.

These companies were able to finance newspapers and magazines: we refer to *La Rassegna Nazionale*, *la Rivista Coloniale*, *la Rivista nautica*, *La Marina mercantile italiana*, *La Lega Navale* or newspapers – mainly edited in Rome and Genoa – such as *La Tribuna*, *Il Messaggero*, *La Vita*, *Il Giornale d'Italia*, *Corriere mercantile*. As a further example, we can quote the case of the leading shipbuilder Ansaldo which bought some major newspapers, such as *Il Secolo XIX* of Genoa in 1897 and *Il Messaggero* of Rome in May 1915; also the magazine *La marina mercantile italiana*, edited by Oreste Calamai, was a voice of the Ansaldo company.

---

[7] BORELLI G., *La forma e l'organizzazione. Aspetti del capitalismo industriale tra '800 e '900* (Padua, 1997), pp. 90 ff.; Idem., *Temi e problemi di storia economica europea* (Verona, 1994), pp. 507–8.
[8] Italian shipping companies under foreign control were La Veloce of Genoa (by two major German banks, the Berliner HandelsGesellschaft and the Bank für Handel und Industrie); the Ligure-Brasiliana, a subsidiary of the Hamburg-Amerika Line; the Lloyd Sabaudo and Sicula Americana, which were under the control of English capital; and the Transatlantica-Italiana, under the complete control of the Hamburg-Amerika Line (in 1913).
[9] AA.VV., *Storia dell'Ansaldo*, vol. III *Dai Bombrini ai Perrone (1903-1914)* (Rome, 1996), pp. 81–3.

The naval component of sea power

After national unification, the potential enemies of the new Italian kingdom were France and the Habsburg Empire: two giants compared to the new state. The Habsburg Empire was a continental power and France would have been able to attack Italy both from the land and from the sea. The Alps protected Italy from a possible ground invasion, while the long and undefended coastline was exposed to threats from the West, from the East and from the South. If the Italian Army had remained in being in the Po Valley, it could have defeated any enemy that attacked Italy through the Alps, but the long, low, and sandy coasts of the Italian peninsula were suitable for amphibious landings. To avoid this danger, Italy needed a powerful navy, sufficient to acquire command of the sea and destroy enemy transports and their troops on board. Moreover, the national government feared possible riots or even secessionist movements in the less developed regions of the kingdom, and kept many troops in the islands and near the vulnerable coasts. In addition to that, it was necessary to have an adequate military reserve; the railways could ensure easy mobility for this reserve. However, the railways were near enough to the coasts to be exposed to enemy naval gunfire.

The rivalry with France increased in the years following national unification, especially after the Congress of Berlin (1878) and the occupation of Tunisia by France (1881): for this reason, France was identified as the main enemy of the new Italian state. Against so formidable an opponent, it was necessary to improve the fleet, and this was the goal of Italian naval policy until the First World War. Since Italy relied on the alliance with the German Empire – and the more unnatural alliance with the Austro-Hungarian Empire (1882) – the primary political and military objective of the Italian government was the defense of the western frontiers, both terrestrial and maritime. The task of countering the French fleet in the Tyrrhenian Sea and in the western Mediterranean appeared extremely problematic for the navy. In Italy there was a perception that the Italian Navy was inferior to the French Navy. As a result, Italian maritime strategy from 1882 to 1914 was designed to ensure some naval support in the Mediterranean from allies of the Triple Alliance as well as from Britain, whose clash with France was used by Italy to its advantage. Therefore, Italy was able to obtain from the German and the Austro-Hungarian empires a real commitment to joint military intervention in the Mediterranean Sea (first and second Naval Conventions of the Triple Alliance, 1900 and 1913). The Italian Royal Navy was continually reinforced against the threat of France and, to discharge military duties, included in the alliance signed with Germany. According to the Treaty, Italy had to prevent the French Army from being transported from the African colonies to the Rhine frontier. Furthermore, the Italian Navy was to fight against the French Navy for the command of the Tyrrhenian Sea and the Mediterranean. To improve Italian naval capabilities the government provided increasing funds. From 1881 – the year when France occupied Tunisia, ending the "peaceful coexistence" with Italy – the budget of the navy was progressively increased, reaching an average of about 118 million lire between the financial years 1887-88 and 1905-6. Furthermore, from 1896-97 onwards, the increase was constant (excepting one brief decline) and accelerated sharply in the financial year 1906-7, when there was a significant increase of 25.5 million lire over the previous year. However, the great leap occurred in the first two decades of the 20th century, when the naval budget increased in the financial year 1910-11 by 81.2 million lire. This was not an isolated case: the subsequent growth of the navy's budget was equally impressive (Figure 1).

The Navy was seen by the national leadership as an essential means to achieve Italy's geopolitical and diplomatic aspirations in the Mediterranean. In 1864 the Squadra d'Evoluzione – basically, the core of the fleet – was engaged in the crisis of Tunis, in an international peacekeeping operation, which also involved British and French warships. The Italian Kingdom – just a few years after unification – had become a power with capabilities of power projection from the sea.

The government identified in the navy a tool to build an empire and to realize national political ambitions. The mission of the corvette *Magenta* (January 1866–March 1868) – which made the first circumnavigation of the globe by an Italian warship – was the first demonstration of the geopolitical ambitions of the kingdom. The Italian government intended to establish official relations and conclude treaties of friendship and trade with Japan and China, to the advantage of the domestic textile industry and the silk trade. In Tokyo, Commander Vittorio Arminjon signed the first treaty of friendship, trade, and navigation between Japan and Italy, which was recognized as the "most favored nation" in trade; with China too, the *Magenta*'s captain concluded and signed a similar treaty. This opened trade between Italy and sixteen Chinese ports and allowed Italy the privilege (already granted to Britain and France) to establish diplomats in Beijing rather than in Tianjin.

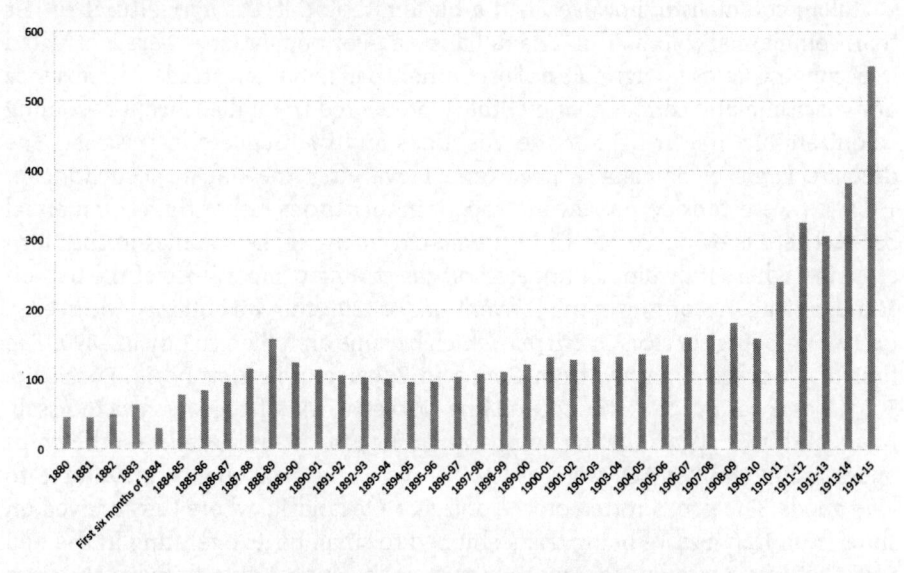

Fig. 1. *The Italian Royal Navy's budget from 1880 to 1914 (million lire)* (FIORAVANZO G., La Marina militare nel suo primo secolo di vita, 1861-1961 (Rome, 1961), pp. 53-4)

From July 1868 to July 1871 the corvette *Principessa Clotilde* undertook a three-year mission under the command of Commander Carlo Alberto Racchia, who had been sent to seek for an area of the archipelago of Borneo to set up a penal colony. Commander Racchia suggested the island of Giada and, in February 1870, began negotiations with the Sultan of Brunei. On 1 January 1871, in Bangkok, he signed a treaty of friendship and trade with Siam (Thailand) and on 3 March of that year he signed another treaty with Burma. Such naval diplomacy was very important in the years which immediately followed complete national unification and the real "civil war" between the North and the South of the kingdom: the fight against bandits and the former governments in the southern regions.

It is important to remember that the Italian Navy performed numerous missions of naval diplomacy and opened markets to products both civil and military. These events are even more emblematic, considering that from 1866 to 1882 Italy experienced a long diplomatic isolation. In this period, only the ships of the navy guaranteed some visibility to the national flag, aided emigrants, promoted Italian business, and re-established national prestige.

The Italian Navy was very important for the foundation of the Italian colonial empire. From the 1860s, the navy acquired bases along the African coast of the Red Sea. The private Rubattino shipping company launched the first phase of Italian colonial expansionism by purchasing the Bay of Assab in 1869. However, the navy was used to improve the local port facilities. In the 1870s and in the early 1880s, the crews of warships built the first port installations in the Italian colonies: the navy was the main instrument of Italian colonialism in the Red Sea. In 1885, a Naval Division of the Red Sea was founded; its tasks were to show the flag, control colonial waters, suppress piracy and arms smuggling (1885–1896), and maintain undersea telegraph cables.

Italian colonialism, however, had a big limitation: it was agricultural rather than commercial colonialism. The Italians – a poor population – were interested in occupying lands for agricultural use rather than in building trade. The absence of a maritime and commercial mentality prevented the Italians from becoming colonizers like the British, or the Venetians and the Genoese in the past. The desolate lands of Somalia, Eritrea (and Libya after the Italian occupation of 1911–12) were considered new metropolitan territories rather than commercial bases. There is evidence of this in the management of the colonies in the Horn of Africa, where Italy did not understand the strategic importance of the Bab-el-Mandeb strait. According to the conventions of 1893, the NGI obtained the license for two shipping services in Eritrea, which became an Italian colony in 1890. The first line worked monthly, from Genoa to Zanzibar, via Alexandria, Port Said, Suez, Massawa, and back; the second line worked weekly, from Massawa to Assab, Aden, and back. The shipping company did not invest in these lines: the ships operating in the Red Sea were of low tonnage and poor quality, unsuitable to load goods. The goods rotted on the docks of Alexandria, where they arrived on ships from Italy before being trans-shipped to small boats operating in the Red Sea. That was a wrong decision: Italy missed the opportunity to make Massawa a transit point as well as a concentration and distribution point for cargo for the

Far East and Bombay, and left to the British the commercial monopoly of the Red Sea. The Bab-el-Mandeb could have rivalled Suez, if the Italians had been clever colonizers! The national service was so poor that the Italian colonial administration in Eritrea, and then in Somalia, preferred to rely on local companies (British or British-subsidized) because of the high prices of the NGI.

The Italian Navy was an instrument of national policy and diplomacy in the eastern Mediterranean too. Very important in this regard was the peace-keeping mission in Crete (1896–1899), when the command of the multinational naval force was assigned to an Italian Admiral, Napoleone Canevaro. The Italian command of the military operation in Crete and the collaboration with France and Britain also had political and diplomatic effects: cooling Italian relations with the Triple Alliance powers (Germany and Austria-Hungary) and directing Italian friendship to the West.

The role of the Italian Navy in the defense of national interests in Latin America was irreplaceable. In 1893, for example, it was engaged in a mission to protect Italian immigrants in Brazil who were endangered by riots. In 1895 Italian–Brazilian relations were again so strained that the navy planned an operation of power projection and gunboat diplomacy off Brazil. The crisis cooled without the need of naval action, but the Italian Naval Division in South America, established in early 1898, remained operational until 1906. After that date the Italian naval presence in Latin America became occasional.

In the early 1880s, the navy began to operate in the Far East and, at the beginning of the 1890s, a naval base was established there. Here the Italian presence lasted, except for a few interruptions, until the beginning of the Second World War. At beginning of the 20th century the navy was involved in the suppression of nationalist rebellion in China (the Boxer rebellion), when the gunboats and the Italian marines were combined with the military assets of the Great Powers. The Italian marines were in Admiral Seymour's relief expedition and were very strong combatants in the fight against the Boxers.

Conclusion

The role of the sea in the building of the Italian state and empire was ambiguous. Italian industrialization started with the creation of a modern military navy, and was strongly influenced by the merchant navy. The economic policy of the Italian Kingdom during the period 1861–1914 was inspired by protectionism, as was the same in other European countries. The failure of Italian colonialism was the consequence not of an inadequate maritime instrument, but of the poverty and structural weakness of the Italian state. The main weakness of the state was its incapacity to organize the peripheral individualism and coordinate the political, military, economic, cultural, and scientific assets of the nation. As a result, the existence of the Italian state was a miracle! In this state, the Royal Italian Navy was one of the most serious and efficient agencies.

IMPERIAL FAILURE OF THE INDUSTRIAL AGE: SPAIN, 1805–1898

JESÚS M. VALDALISO is Professor of Economic History and Institutions at the University of the Basque Country, Spain

ABSTRACT. *This period began and ended with disastrous naval defeats which lost Spain all her overseas empire. In merchant shipping and fishing, however, the second half of the century was a period of remarkable growth which helped to lift Spain into the industrial era and integrate it into the world economy.*

RÉSUMÉ. *Cette période s'ouvrit et se ferma par de désastreuses défaites navales qui firent perdre à l'Espagne tout son empire colonial. Dans le domaine de la navigation marchande et de la pêche, la seconde moitié du siècle fut toutefois une période de croissance remarquable, permettant au pays de se hisser vers l'ère industrielle et de rejoindre l'économie mondiale.*

.•.

INTRODUCTION

The 19th century in Spain opened and closed with two calamitous naval defeats: at Trafalgar in 1805, at the hands of Great Britain, and at Santiago de Cuba and Cavite (Philippines), in 1898, against the United States. The latter naval debacles, widely labelled by the media as the "Disaster of 1898", lost Spain her last colonies of Cuba, Porto Rico and Philippines, reducing her definitively to a second-rank maritime and global power. Spanish Prime Minister Francisco Silvela made it very clear in the autumn of 1898: "the first lesson to be learned from the 'disaster', although not the most popular, is that ... to give up a navy is to abandon independence and a future in the world".[1]

Silvela's statement appeared in the prologue of a book by Joaquín Sánchez de Toca, which appeared a few months after the disaster, attempting to explain the influence of sea power upon Spanish history in accordance with Mahan's theory. According to Mahan, Spain had never been a significant sea power, ultimately because of her people's lack of maritime interest and expertise.

---

[1] SÁNCHEZ DE TOCA J., *Del poder naval en España y su política económica para la nacionalidad iberoamericana* (Madrid, 1898), Prologue.

This negative assessment of the relationship between the country and the sea became widespread among the media, the politicians and even the intellectuals of the time. Along with Sánchez de Toca, who became Navy Minister in 1902, his comrade in the Conservative Party, Antonio Maura, stated in 1899 that "for centuries Spain has launched fleet after fleet, and won with them nothing but defeat and disgrace". Joaquín Costa, another politician leader of the "regenerative" movement, claimed in 1907 that "Spain has never exhibited the attitudes of a naval power", and that this was one of the causes of Spanish decline.[2] José Ricart, merchant captain and influential voice in maritime circles, had the same opinion.[3]

The naval defeats and their consequences, therefore, generated a pessimistic feeling, a sort of inferiority complex, that became widespread in the country, affected other sectors such as the economy and commerce, and even became entrenched in the historiography of the Spanish economy in the 19th century. Although the disaster of 1898 had hardly any negative effect on the Spanish economy (rather the reverse), it exerted a strong impact on the Spanish media and public opinion, and became the catalyst for a great debate about the national identity and the ways to regenerate the country and to recover her lost place among the most important international powers. For J. Costa, leader of the "regenerative" movement and founder of the Liga Nacional de Productores in 1899, Spain should no longer waste her revenue on the army and navy, but allocate it to education and agriculture instead. In reaction to this, another interest-group, led by A. Maura and J. Sánchez de Toca, more influential in the dominant parties, attempted to bring the maritime interests of the country together in the Spanish Maritime League in 1900. It lobbied the government for a new policy to restore sea power, based not only on new building programmes for the navy but on the support of shipping and trade as well. The Liga Marítima Española, with more than sixteen thousand members and affiliates in the navy, the merchant shipping, shipbuilding and other auxiliary industries, eventually succeeded and the government headed by A. Maura passed laws in 1908 and 1909, aimed at encouraging the development of the navy and merchant shipping respectively.[4]

The sea, or more precisely, the diverse interest groups created around the sea, was at the forefront of the political debate in Spain at the beginning of the 20th century. The sense of pessimism dominant at that time impregnated the analysis of the different maritime sectors, from the navy to shipping and the fisheries,

---

[2] COSTA J., *Marina española o la cuestión de la escuadra* (Huesca, 1912), pp. 120-1; and M. FERNÁNDEZ ALMAGRO, *Política Naval de la España Moderna y Contemporánea* (Madrid, 1946), p. 228.

[3] RICART J., *Potencialidad naval de España. Lo que ha sido, lo que es y lo que puede ser* (Barcelona, 1899), pp. 33 and 36.

[4] VIAÑA E., '¿Pantanos o acorazados? Economía y defensa en la España del novecientos', in *Economía española, cultura y sociedad. Homenaje a Juan Velarde fuertes* ed. J.L. GARCÍA DELGADO (Madrid, 1992), pp. 299-316; and RODRIGO M., 'Los dividendos de la presión política: La Liga Marítima Española (1899-1910)', *Revista de Historia Económica* 22 (2004), 707-34.

and continued to affect Spanish historiography at least until the 1980s. The sea was seen as a key factor in Spain's imperial failure and economic backwardness in the 19th century. The loss of the Spanish colonies, the disappearance of the sailing fleet and of the wooden shipbuilding industry were all seen as examples of Spaniards' the lack of aptitude for and interest in the sea.

In recent decades, however, new studies on the maritime industries have modified the negative assessment of Spanish historiography on the role of the sea in Spain's nineteenth-century history. Building on a former essay that labelled the shipping and fishing industries of Spain as the Cinderella of Spanish historiography,[5] I argue here that, in spite of the naval defeats, the loss of the colonies and the significant changes undergone in most of the maritime sectors, the sea continued to play a key role in Spain's development in the 19th century as a source of food (fisheries), as a means of transport of goods and people (trade and shipping), as a means of colonial control, as a source of employment and as market for different industries and services. In these ways, the sea was a key asset for different communities and interest groups such as the navy, politics, fishermen, merchants, shippers, shipowners, shipbuilders and other auxiliary and related industries, colonial elites and even the thousands of Spanish emigrants to the Americas.

THE SEA AS A SOURCE OF FOOD: FISHERMEN AND FISHING RESOURCES

At the middle of the 19th century fishing was still a pre-industrial activity, heavily regulated by the state and subordinated to the navy. The *Matrícula de Mar*, whose origins went back to the early 17th century, established compulsory naval service for all those between the ages of fourteen and sixty who were engaged in fishing, shipping and shipbuilding, giving them, in compensation, the monopoly of these activities. In addition, the state regulated access to the fisheries, the type of vessels and the fishing methods. In Cantabrian ports, fishing was managed by maritime guilds that controlled fish landings and distribution and excluded non-members. Scattered estimates of both employment and fish landings point to a significant growth between c. 1830 and c. 1860. The number of people registered in the *Matrícula de Mar* (including those in shipping and shipbuilding) increased from under 20,000 in 1815 to 64,094 in 1860. Fish landings also grew, from 55,481 metric tons in 1831 to a figure close to 70,000 tons in the 1860s. Fish consumption in Spain in that decade amounted to c. 6 kilograms per capita, of

---

[5] VALDALISO J.M. and LÓPEZ E., 'Las "Cenicientas" de la historia económica española: la historiografía económica sobre las industrias marítimas desde finales del siglo XIX hasta la actualidad', in *La Storiografia marittima in Italia e in Spagna in età moderna e contemporánea*, ed. A. DI VITTORIO and C. BARCIELA (Bari, 2001), pp. 427-50.

which about 60% was preserved, either salted or pickled, because of the lack of a modern transport system (i.e. railways) at that time.[6]

The abolition of both the *Matrícula* and the maritime guilds in 1873 liberalized fishing and attracted new capital and entrepreneurs. Besides, by the early 1880s railways had connected the most important fishing ports with inland Spain, and made it possible to distribute fresh fish to a broader domestic market. In the 1880s the combination of new canning technologies and better, faster transport resulted in new products such as tinned sardines, anchovies and tuna, increasingly sold on international markets. At the same time new and more intensive fishing techniques, and steam-powered vessels like the steam trawler, were adopted, particularly in Galicia, the Basque Country and the south of Spain's Atlantic coast, making possible a sustained high growth in fish landings, employment and productivity. Between 1883 and 1908 fish landings grew by 54%, employment by 41% and landings per vessel by 70%.[7] The modern fishing industry became increasingly concentrated in a few large ports, particularly in Vigo and Corunna in Galicia, Bermeo in Biscay and Ayamonte in Huelva, whereas in the small fishing communities it continued as a more traditional activity, conducted in small sailing boats.

At the beginning of the 20th century both the fishing and the fish canning industries, although small in terms of employment and valued added in comparison to agriculture, stood out as two of the most dynamic sectors of the Spanish economy. By volume of catch, Spain ranked in a second group of European fishing powers with Germany and France, and far below Britain and Norway. However, it became the most important European exporter of canned fish, surpassing France.[8] Arguably the foundations of the Spanish fishing fleet's later expansion into international waters lay in this modernization period that started in the 1880s.

THE SEA AS A MEANS OF TRADE AND TRANSPORT OF GOODS AND PEOPLE: MERCHANT SHIPPING AND PORTS

However, for most Spaniards in the 19th century the sea meant first and foremost trade and colonies. The overwhelming bulk of Spanish foreign trade was conducted by sea, and the sea integrated Spain into the international economy.

---

[6] CARMONA J. and LÓPEZ E., 'Spain's Atlantic Coast Fisheries, c. 1100–1880', in *A History of the North Atlantic Fisheries. Volume 1: From Early Times to the Mid-Nineteenth Century*, ed. D.J. STARKEY et al. (Bremen, 2009); and GARCÍA E., 'El trabajo en la marina mercante española en la transición de la vela al vapor (1834–1914)' (PhD thesis, Barcelona University, 2013).

[7] CARMONA and LÓPEZ, 'Spain's Atlantic Coast Fisheries,' pp. 259–60 and 274.

[8] GIRÁLDEZ J., 'Fuentes estadísticas y producción pesquera en España (1880–1936): una primera aproximación', *Revista de Historia Económica* 9 (1991), 526–9; and CARMONA J., 'Recursos, organización y tecnología en el crecimiento de la industria española de conservas de pescado, 1900–1936', in *La cara oculta de la industrialización española*, ed. J. NADAL and J. CATALÁN (Madrid, 1994), pp. 134–5.

Maritime trade, measured both by value and by volume, experienced a very high growth, higher than the country's GDP, thanks to the export boom in foodstuffs and, above all, ores like iron, lead or copper, of which Spain became one of the largest exporters in that century. Imports and coastal trade also grew, although not so rapidly.[9] Whereas railways integrated the domestic market and connected ports and inland, shipping was responsible for the international integration of the Spanish economy. Even after the loss of the American mainland colonies and until 1850, the Americas still absorbed between one fourth and one third of all Spanish foreign trade.[10] By then, Europe, in particular Britain and France, accounted for most of Spanish exports and imports, followed by the remaining Spanish colonies of Cuba and Porto Rico and by the United States.[11]

To a great extent, the remarkable growth of sea trade in Spain was due to the export boom in bulk cargoes such as ores and foodstuffs that accounted for the largest share of Spanish exports. However, general cargo carried by shipping lines, mostly in import and coastal trade, also grew substantially. Changes in the distribution of cargoes and in the geography of the maritime trade altered the ranking of top Spanish ports. Until mid-19th century Barcelona and Cadiz were the most important Spanish trading ports (foreign and coastal), followed by Bilbao, Santander and Malaga, and general cargo predominated. The high growth of ore exports in the last third of the 19th century changed that. Bilbao, driven by its iron exports, became the most important port by trade volume, followed by other similar ports like Huelva or Cartagena that surpassed Barcelona.

Overseas trade became one of the most dynamic sectors of the Spanish economy, but only part of it was carried in Spanish bottoms. The Spanish flag's share in foreign trade, which amounted to 50% around 1850, began to experience a sustained decline that lasted until the end of the century. In 1898 Spanish-flagged merchant ships carried less than 20% of Spanish exports and 30% of imports. This decline, which also happened to the rest of European nations with the exception of Britain and Norway, was not due to a crisis in the Spanish merchant fleet, which experienced a process of growth and modernization during the last quarter of the 19th century, but to the early and unstoppable internationalization of world shipping.[12]

The sea also became the means of transport for increasing numbers of people who left Spain in search of a better life in the "new world", following a tradition that had started in the 16th century. Although absolute numbers of

---

[9] VALDALISO J.M., 'El transporte marítimo en España, 1850–1936', in *Vie e mezzi di comunicazione in Italia e Spagna in età contemporánea*, ed. C. BARCIELA et al. (Soveria Mannelli, 2013).

[10] FERNÁNDEZ DE PINEDO E., 'La recuperación del comercio español con América a mediados del siglo XIX', in *Antiguo Régimen y liberalismo. Homenaje a Miguel Artola. 1. Visiones generales* (Madrid, 1994), pp. 51-66.

[11] VALDALISO J.M., *Los navieros vascos y la marina mercante en España, 1860-1935. Una historia económica* (Bilbao, 1991), pp. 54 and 57.

[12] VALDALISO J.M., 'Trade, colonies and navigation laws: the Flag Differential Duty and the international competitiveness of Spanish shipping in the 19th century', *International Journal of Maritime History* 17.2 (2005), 43.

Spanish emigrants are lower than those of other European nations, they were significant for the national economy and labour market, particularly in the last quarter of the 19th century. More than 1.4 million people left Spain and went to the Americas between 1830 and 1900, and this figure was even higher for the first thirteen years of the new century.[13] With the exception of two Spanish companies, this traffic was controlled by foreign shipping lines that departed from Britain, Germany, France or Italy and called at Barcelona, Cadiz, Corunna or the ports of the Canary Islands, the most important ports for the emigrant trade.

The increasing demand for sea transport of both goods and people drove the growth of the Spanish merchant marine. After a severe crisis during the first three decades of the century, the merchant fleet began to recover from 1830 onwards, thanks to the recovery of the trade between Spain and the Americas, and to state support with a differential duty on foreign shipping (a surcharge of between 50 and 300%, reduced to 20% in 1849, on the import duties payable on the cargoes of foreign vessels). The Spanish sailing fleet experienced a last golden age between the 1830s and the 1850s, increasing its share of most of the import and export trades, particularly with the Americas.[14] However, the Spanish merchant fleet overall consisted of smaller and more expensive vessels, with more seamen per ton and paid higher wages than those of other fleets. Besides, the state regulated the labour market (by the *Matrícula de Mar*), severely restricted the import of foreign ships and the methods of finance, and laid a vast array of different levies and burdens on vessels in Spanish ports. By the early 1860s the Spanish sailing fleet faced increasing competition both from other sailing vessels and from the new steamers that were appearing in European waters, which they were unable to meet even with the help of differential duties.[15]

As in Britain with the repeal of the Navigation Acts, shipping was at the forefront of the political debate in Spain between free traders and protectionists in the late 1860s. The shipowners of Barcelona and Bilbao, the most important Spanish ports of registry, along with those of Santander and Corunna, demanded more freedom and less state intervention in order to compete internationally. The new liberal government that took office in 1869 liberalized the market for labour, ships and capital, abolished the flag differential duty (except for the colonial trade), reduced navigation taxes and simplified the administrative regime. In the words of a Parliamentary Commission which analysed the state of the shipping industry in 1879,

> What the merchant marine needs to thrive is to have many cargoes to carry, and this cannot be achieved by bounties or privileges, but only by free trade, free industry and free navigation; with very low tariffs, cheap raw materials and diligent and intelligent shipowners.[16]

---

[13] YÁÑEZ C., *La emigración española a América (siglos XIX y XX)* (Gijón, 1994).
[14] VALDALISO, 'Trade, colonies and navigation laws', 35–42.
[15] *Ibid.*, 43–6; and VALDALISO, *Los navieros vascos*, pp. 91–8.
[16] VALDALISO, *Los navieros vascos*, p. 110.

Institutional change, growth in demand, intelligent and diligent shipowners help to explain the fast pace of technological change in Spanish merchant shipping in the last three decades of the 19th century, when wooden sailing vessels were replaced by iron and steel steamers in one of the fastest transitions from sail to steam in Europe, only comparable to that of the world carrier, Britain. By 1900, steamships accounted for 83% of Spanish tonnage, whereas in Britain this percentage was only 79%, and France and Italy it barely reached 60%. In absolute figures, the Spanish steam fleet ranked fifth between the mid-1880s and 1896, below Britain, France, Germany and the United States; and sixth, after Norway, in the closing years of the century.[17]

The new steam vessels, mostly imported from Britain, were acquired by shipowners of Barcelona and Bilbao, ports which accounted for 32% and 34% of Spanish steam tonnage in 1885, followed, but at a great distance, by Cadiz, Santander and Seville. In the 1870s and 1880s, Spanish shipowners deployed their steam vessels in the transport of general cargo in regular lines in the Spanish coastal trade and in the colonial trade with Cuba and Porto Rico. From the 1890s onwards, the Spanish fleet, led by Bilbao shipowners, moved *en masse* into bulk cargoes (ores, coal, grain and timber, among others) chartered in the tramp market. In 1900 Bilbao concentrated 46% of the Spanish merchant fleet and hosted the headquarters of more than 50% of the Spanish shipping companies.[18]

Steam changed the business of shipping in Spain. The striking growth of capital requirements, along with the increasing speed of trading operations, resulted in the appearance of new specialist shipping firms, mostly joint-stock limited companies with professional managers who were also shareholders. The patterns of ownership and finance were imported from Britain, and some trading houses and shipping companies from London and Liverpool even directly financed Spanish shipping. Nine out of the twenty largest shipping companies in Spain in 1885 had a strong relationship with British companies, which not only participated as shareholders, but also took responsibility for ship management, agency and cargo chartering. Another two, although Spanish-owned and managed, operated from London and Liverpool. In Bilbao, which had a very close commercial relationship with Britain from early modern times, those companies were widely known as "Anglo-Biscayan".[19]

Last, but not least, the remarkable growth of trade and navigation in nineteenth-century Spain stimulated substantial investments in port infrastructure, although these were located in only a few ports (Pasajes, Bilbao, Santander and Gijon on the Cantabrian coast; Huelva on the Atlantic coast; Cartagena, Valencia and Barcelona in the Mediterranean; and Las Palmas and Santa Cruz de Tenerife in the Canary Islands) and took place, mostly, in the last

---

[17] VALDALISO J.M., 'Growth and modernization of the Spanish merchant marine, 1860–1935', *International Journal of Maritime History* 3.1 (1991), 33–58.

[18] VALDALISO J.M., 'The rise of specialist firms in Spanish shipping, 1860 to 1930', *Business History Review* 74 (2000), 267–300.

[19] *Ibid.*, p. 276–77; and VALDALISO, 'Trade, colonies and navigation laws', pp. 51–3.

three decades of the century. Overall, gross capital investment in port infrastructure in Spain was substantially smaller than that allocated to railways and roads, and it was not financed by the state budget, but by dues levied by the port authorities.[20] Shipping and trade, through employment growth in stevedoring and other shipping-related jobs such as shipbuilding, ship-repairing and auxiliary industries, ship agency, ship handling, coaling and water stations, and through other external economies, helped to transform substantially the geography of port cities, as had been the case with the fishing ports.

To sum up, the growth of maritime transport drove the development of both merchant shipping and port infrastructure in Spain, mostly concentrated in the last third of the 19th century. Equally, the improvement in ships' and ports' productivity increased the speed, quality and reliability of the service and reduced costs and prices, facilitating the integration of the Spanish economy into the international market.

THE SEA AS A SOURCE OF JOBS AND AS A MARKET

Rough and scattered estimates of employment in sea-related activities point to a significant increase in the absolute number of jobs during the 19th century, mostly as a result of the remarkable development of fishing, trade and shipping. By the beginning of the 20th century, the overall number of people employed in Spanish shipping both afloat and in ports must have been close to fifty thousand, and the number of fishermen close to ninety thousand, to which should be added people employed in related industrial activities and naval personnel (between ten thousand and fifteen thousand people). Whereas this overall figure was not very large (around 2.5%) in relation to the working population of a mostly inland and agriculture-based economy, its significance was much greater in large port cities and small fishing towns and villages.[21]

At the beginning of the 19th century the fishing and shipping fleets and the navy drew on a shipbuilding industry that was concentrated mainly in the Basque Country and Catalonia, and in the naval yards of Ferrol, Cadiz and Cartagena. These last almost collapsed during the first third of the 19th century – the 3,500 workers of the Ferrol shipyard in 1790 had been reduced to thirty-seven in 1833 – but recovered from the 1850s, thanks to the new building plans of the navy.[22] The merchant shipbuilding industry experienced a last golden age between 1830 and 1860, thanks to the growth of the merchant and fishing fleets and to state

---

[20] VALDALISO, 'El transporte marítimo', pp. 369–70.
[21] GARCÍA, *El trabajo*; CARMONA and LÓPEZ, 'Spain's Atlantic Coast Fisheries'; SUAREZ M. and IBARZ J., 'La organización del trabajo portuario: los casos de Barcelona y de la Luz en Las Palmas de Gran Canaria (1890–1936)', *Parabiblos* 11 (1998), 10–11; and JORDANA J. and RAMIO C., 'Gobierno y Administración', in *Estadísticas Históricas de España. Siglos XIX-XX*, vol. III, ed. A. CARRERAS and X. TAFUNELL (Barcelona, 2005), pp. 1004, 1016–17.
[22] RODRÍGUEZ A.R., *Política naval de la Restauración (1875-1898)* (Madrid, 1988), pp. 91 and 179–96.

protection, but collapsed in the 1870s due to technical change and import liberalization. Only a few traditional shipyards survived, focused on supplying the needs of small fishing communities.[23]

The modernization of Spanish merchant shipping demanded a great volume of modern tonnage, overwhelmingly supplied by British shipyards, which found in Spain one of their largest markets. Maritime demand between 1870 and 1900, crudely measured by imports of ships, constituted a market about 40% larger than the total industrial production of transport equipment in Spain in those years, and accounted for 31% of the gross fixed capital investment of the country.[24] Naval demand, although much less important in volume than that of merchant shipping, continued to be supplied mostly by Spanish industry, either the naval yards or, increasingly from the 1890s, private shipyards. Public expenditure on naval shipbuilding accounted for about 4% of the industrial production of equipment goods in Spain between 1888 and 1899.[25] Besides this, shipyards demanded steel, marine equipment and other goods that became a source of growth for the steel, machinery and auxiliary industries.

The first modern shipyards with the facilities and technical capabilities to build steamships appeared in Bilbao and Cadiz in the late 1880s in response to the demands either of the navy or of Spanish shipping companies. However, most of the needs of Spanish shipowners and fishermen continued to be met by British shipyards: at the beginning of the 20th century, less than 5% of Spanish merchant tonnage had been built in Spain.[26]

THE SEA AS A VEHICLE OF IMPERIALISM: THE NAVY AND THE COLONIES

In spite of all the achievements of the economic sectors related to the sea in Spain in the 19th century, the great naval defeats of the beginning and end of that century and the loss of the colonies were responsible for that feeling of imperial failure that marked the maritime vision of the Spaniards and left a long-lasting imprint on public opinion, political circles and foreign policy.

From 1801, when Spain was still the third-largest sea power in the world, to 1808, Trafalgar and other naval defeats had reduced the Spanish navy by close to 40%, and things got worse thereafter. The war against the American colonies, and particularly the increasing economic and financial problems of Spain in the 1810s and 1820s, made it impossible to build new vessels and wrecked the navy. In 1833 it consisted of barely twelve very old ships plus another twenty-three

---

[23] VALDALISO, *Los navieros vascos*, pp. 273-6.
[24] *Estadísticas Históricas de España. Siglos XIX-XX*, ed. A. CARRERAS and X. TAFUNELL (Barcelona, 2005).
[25] CUBEL A., 'Los efectos del gasto del Estado en la industria de construcción naval militar en España, 1887-1936', *Revista de Historia Industrial* 5 (1994), 93-119.
[26] VALDALISO, *Los navieros vascos*, pp. 277-96.

smaller vessels, far from the 115 ships and 108 vessels of 1801. The Navy, which absorbed 27% of the expenditure of the Bourbon monarchy in 1788-1792, accounted for only 9% of expenditure in 1829-1833.[27]

However, Spain was able to retain part of her former empire, after 1824 reduced to four island groups (the Spanish Antilles, the Philippines and the Carolinas), and still needed a navy to manage and to defend it. Moreover, this relatively small colonial empire, Cuba in particular, was very important for the Spanish economy, providing a substantial reserved market for her exports, a privileged trade for her shipping and a source of new business opportunities for Spaniards linked to the booming sugar economy.[28] In the first half of the 1890s, 24% of Spain's exports went to her colonies, a figure surpassed only by that of Britain among the main imperial nations.[29] The positive surplus of the commodity balance with Cuba and Porto Rico helped Spain to finance her imports from other countries. In the words of a Spanish MP in 1872, "the Antilles ... are the market for our grains, our flour, our wines ..., they feed our merchant marine and our Navy".[30] Colonial interests shaped the political course of Spain throughout the 19th century.

The benefits of maintaining that colonial empire were clear for the metropolis, but it also involved some costs that were increasing in the context of the global colonial and military race of the last third of the 19th century. Between 1868 and 1898 Spain waged two Cuban wars (1868-1878 and 1895-1898), financed by the issuing of public debt which aggravated the state's indebtedness and eventually forced the country to default in 1881 and 1899. Between 1848 and 1887 Spain launched several building plans to renovate and enlarge a long-needed navy, but with few funds and little success.[31] The navy's share of Spain's public expenditure steadily declined in the second half of the 19th century, from 5% to 6% in the 1850s, and even more in the 1860s, to below 3% in the late 1890s, this latter being much lower than that of other imperial powers such as Britain (22%), Japan

---

[27] CASTILLO P., *La marina de guerra española en el primer tercio del siglo XX* (Madrid, 1992); and FERNÁNDEZ DE PINEDO E., 'Coyuntura y Políticas Económicas', in *Historia de España vol. VII. Centralismo, Ilustración y Crisis del Antiguo Régimen* ed. M. TUÑÓN DE LARA (Barcelona, 1980), p. 86.

[28] RODRIGO M., '¿Más costes que beneficios? La España liberal y la perla de las Antillas', in *De Tartessos a Manila. Siete estudios coloniales y poscoloniales*, ed. G. CANO and A. DELGADO (Valencia, 2008), pp. 119-51; and VALDALISO, 'Trade, colonies and navigation laws.

[29] FLUX A.W., 'The flag and trade: a summary review of the trade of the chief colonial empires', *Journal of the Royal Statistical Society* 62 (1899), 491.

[30] MALUQUER DE MOTES J., 'El mercado colonial antillano en el siglo XIX', in *Agricultura, comercio colonial y crecimiento económico en la España Contemporánea*, ed. J. NADAL and G. TORTELLA (Barcelona, 1974), p. 325.

[31] COMÍN F., 'Los gastos militares en España durante los siglos XIX y XX', in *El alimento del Estado y la salud de la res publica: orígenes, estructura y desarrollo del gasto público en Europa*, ed. A. GALÁN and J.M. CARRETERO (Madrid, 2013); and RODRÍGUEZ, *Política naval de la Restauración*.

(15%), Germany or France (9% each) at that time.[32] Accordingly, the Spanish navy lagged behind those of other countries by size, ship types and naval armaments.

The ultimate lesson from this was clear: in the words of the Spanish Prime Minister after the 1898 disaster, quoted at the beginning of this essay, "to give up a Navy is to abandon independence and a future in the world". At the beginning of the 20th century maritime interests, for better or for worse, still stood at the centre of political debate in Spain.

---

[32] COMIN F. and DIAZ-FUENTES D., 'Sector público administrativo y estado del bienestar', in *Estadísticas Históricas de España. Siglos XIX-XX. Vol. II*, ed. A. CARRERAS and X. TAFUNELL (Barcelona, 2005); and VIAÑA, '¿Pantanos o acorazados?', p. 303.

Denmark: a small power with a growing shipping industry

Anders Monrad Møller is a former lecturer at the University of Copenhagen, Denmark

ABSTRACT. *Denmark with its possessions of Norway (to 1814), Iceland and Greenland was formed of numerous islands and depended on seaborne trade. So did the capital, Copenhagen, which drew food and commodities from all over the kingdom. Danish shipowners exploited their position to trade between the Baltic and North Sea, while others captured cargoes throughout the world, trading between hundreds of ports remote from Denmark or Danish products.*

RÉSUMÉ. *Le Danemark, auquel appartenaient la Norvège (jusqu'en 1814), l'Islande et le Groenland, était formé de nombreuses îles et dépendait du commerce maritime, tout comme Copenhague, sa capitale, qui faisait venir denrées alimentaires et produits de base de tout le royaume. Les armateurs danois profitèrent de leur situation géographique pour installer leur marché entre la mer Baltique et la mer du Nord. D'autres s'emparèrent de cargos partout dans le monde, ce qui leur permit d'établir des échanges commerciaux avec des centaines de ports éloignés du Danemark ou de ses produits.*

.•.

The Royal Danish navy

Nearly all the ships of the Danish navy were taken by the British in 1807 and after the Napoleonic Wars the economy was so bad that in 1820 the navy consisted of only two ships of the line, five frigates, one corvette and two brigs. More men-of-war were built in the following years; in 1850 four ships of the line, eight frigates, five corvettes and four brigs were available, as well as a handful of paddle steamers.

In the years 1848–1850 Denmark was at war against insurgents in the duchies of Schleswig and Holstein who were for a time supported by Prussia. At that time no German state possessed a navy, so Denmark was superior at sea and could blockade Hamburg as well as the Prussian harbours in the Baltic. The Danish navy still held its own in the second war in 1864, although as a result of that war the duchies were lost to Prussia and Austria. At that time several of the wooden frigates were provided with steam boilers and auxiliary propellers. On the eve of the First World War the Danish navy had four cruisers, five smaller armour-plated warships, thirty torpedo boats, four submarines and a lot of smaller vessels.

In most years during the 19th century a brig was sent to the Danish Caribbean islands of St Thomas, St Jan and St Croix. Its task was to maintain Danish supremacy and to protect trade – the port of St Thomas, Charlotte Amalia, was known as one of the best in the Caribbean Sea and this entrepôt was visited by numerous foreign ships.

Danish colonial trade

After the Napoleonic Wars the interrupted trade of the Danish Caribbean Islands was taken up again. In 1816 no fewer than seventy big ships left Copenhagen for the islands and returned laden with sugar and rum. But since many seafaring nations did the same, the market was flooded, prices went down and in the early 1820s many merchants in Copenhagen went bankrupt.

The trade soon found a more realistic level. By 1828 the number of ships had fallen to twenty-eight, which was enough to supply unrefined sugar to the refineries. In 1844 the number of ships in this trade was twenty-two from Copenhagen and twenty-one from Flensburg, the biggest town in the duchy of Schleswig. In 1854 the numbers were twenty-two and eight, respectively; six years later they had reduced to twelve and eight. The trade diminished further in the later part of the century as beet sugar competed with cane. The economy of the islands deteriorated, the population was interested in joining the United States of America, and in 1917 the islands were sold.

The oldest of the Danish colonies were in India: Tranquebar on the Coromandel coast, acquired in 1620, and the town of Serampore in Bengal from 1755. In the last decade of the 18th century the East India trade had flourished, handled by the Danish Asiatic Company and some private shipowners. But after the Napoleonic Wars the traffic diminished. About a dozen ships visited the colonies in 1818, but ten years later only three did so. The local administration needed annual subsidies from Denmark and this deficit was felt to be untenable, so in 1845 the colonies were sold to the British East India Company.

Before the Napoleonic Wars the Danish Asiatic Company's most important trade had been in tea and porcelain from China. The revival of this trade was organized in 1815 by private shipowners who sent a big ship to Canton, and this was repeated the following year. In 1819 the Company equipped the biggest ship in Copenhagen for the first of its five expeditions, the last of which was in the 1833–34. This was the end of the trade in tea and in 1846 the Danish Asiatic Company was finally dissolved.

From the middle of the 17th century Denmark had some forts on the coast of Guinea which supplied slaves to the Caribbean. After 1814 communication with Copenhagen was infrequent, less than one ship a year. To maintain the forts seemed hopeless and in 1850 they were sold to Great Britain.

The North Atlantic colonies were Greenland, Iceland and the Faroe Islands, and they were traditionally of great importance to the shipping of Copenhagen. Greenland was supplied with guns, ammunition, coffee, tobacco and the like, and the return freight was blubber, sealskins, bearskins, fish and feathers. The Greenland trade was a monopoly, and every year the Greenland Company sent five or six of its ships north. In 1887 the first bark with an auxiliary steam engine was sent to Greenland, but barks without engines were in use until after the First World War.

Iceland was supplied with grain and other provisions, and from Iceland stockfish was exported by Danish ships mostly coming from Copenhagen. They did not always return directly to the home port. Some went to Great Britain with the Icelandic fish, which were in great demand, and in some instances the ships even proceeded to the Mediterranean.

In comparison with Iceland the population of the Faroe Islands was much smaller, so only a handful of ships each year provided the islands with grain and other provisions and returned with woollen goods, especially stockings, and in the second half of the century with fish as well.

THE INLAND TRADE

For historical reasons the Danish capital, Copenhagen, is relatively big in comparison with the rest of the country. The population of Copenhagen was supplied by many small vessels laden with firewood, rye, barley, wheat, oats, eggs, cheese, butter, pork, beef, chickens, turkeys, apples and pears, pottery, linen etc. These ships came from all the provincial ports east of the Skaw. For example, in the year 1834 there were 3,632 arrivals in Copenhagen of ships with an average size of 14 tons. This was a growing trade: in 1857 the number was 6,551 with an average size of 11½ tons. The return freights were smaller, consisting of colonial goods such as coffee, tea, tobacco, spices, rice and sugar, also wine, spirits, paper and other industrial products. In both directions the ships carried passengers and parcels. When in Copenhagen the skippers often advertised in the newspapers, telling where they lay in the harbour and when they intended to return to their home port, offering cheap voyages for people of limited means. A vessel could normally make four to six voyages in the season from March/April to the end of the year. In reality it was a system of packet boats, as reflected in the names of ships like the *Paketten* of Fåborg, a town on the island of Funen.

The first Danish paddle steamer was imported from Glasgow in 1819 and was used to connect Copenhagen with Kiel in Holstein. The early steamers transported only post and passengers because they consumed so much coal that there was no room for cargo in bulk. After the middle of the century steamers transported horses and cattle, and soon in the case of a new steamer, both its modern conveniences for the passengers and the capacity of the hold were announced.

In the second half of the century, the skippers of the sailing packets gradually stopped advertising for passengers.

Many of the early steamers were owned by the government, but from the 1840s expensive purchases were made by limited companies all over the country. For a couple of decades local initiative and local capital marked the Danish steamship companies, but in 1866 the two biggest shipowners joined in a new limited company founded by twenty-two prominent businessmen mostly from Copenhagen. Its name was DFDS (The United Steamship Company), and in a very short time nearly all the other firms followed, so that in 1867 the fleet numbered twenty steamers all in regular service. Sailing plans were announced, local facilities in the form of storehouses were established, etc. The steamers took over the transport of more and more of the general cargo and gradually the sailing packets were ousted.

The Danish routes in 1867 included most ports in southern Zealand and the isles of Lolland, Falster, Funen and eastern Jutland. The first routes in the Baltic were to Königsberg, Danzig and Stettin. There was a route to Oslo and another to the Norwegian ports of Kristiansand, Stavanger, Bergen, Ålesund, Kristiansund and Trondheim. A route west and north via Granton near Edinburgh continued to the Faroe Islands and ended in Iceland. Three routes connected Copenhagen with, respectively, Hull, London and Antwerp.

The ambition behind the foundation of DFDS lay in the possibility of using the safe income from the inland routes to invest in the new, more risky routes to foreign countries. And DFDS certainly succeeded in this, as will be seen.

Trade to Norway and Western Europe

Until 1814 Denmark and Norway were governed by the same king, and the provision of Norway with grain was reserved to Denmark. This monopoly was ended after the war; but the Norwegians still needed grain, old business connections were still in existence and the trade was taken up again.

The ships in this trade were of very different size. In 1843 a cutter of eighty tons took a cargo of grain to Trondheim and returned in ballast. The same year a small vessel of 3½ tons made six trips to the southern Norwegian ports of Porsgrunn, Arendal and Grimstad.

The ships were loaded primarily with grain, and in some instances with pork, beef, butter and other provisions. The return freight was timber, and in the first part of the century iron products as well, in the form of stoves and bar iron – later Danish iron foundries were founded and took over. The return cargoes from Bergen and destinations more to the north were fish.

At the beginning of the period the trade was nearly always a voyage to a harbour in Norway followed by an immediately return to the home port. Later the pattern of the voyages became more complex. For example, a voyage could be a Danish ship loaded with bones going to Hull and then proceeding in ballast to a port in southern Norway to fetch timber to be delivered in a Danish port. In 1828 a cutter began the sailing season with a passage to Bergen loaded with grain, then herrings were shipped to Königsberg in the Baltic and from here the cutter took a load of grain to Amsterdam. Later in the year she returned in ballast to Königsberg to fetch grain, linseed and hemp to be transported to Bergen.

In 1857 a Danish ship began the year by going to the northern part of Norway and unloading grain in Ålesund and Kristiansund and then continued in ballast to Archangel, where she loaded rye which was brought back to Kristiansund in exchange for herring to be delivered in Stettin, whence she carried timber to a Danish port. Many more examples could be given of the more complex patterns of sailing.

Some years after the middle of the century steamers began to share in the trade to Norway. In 1870 Bergen was visited by nineteen steamers; ten years later the number had risen to thirty-five and by 1890 it had risen again, to thirty-nine. In the years before the First World War the steamers had ousted most of the sailing ships from this trade.

Denmark had more grain than could be consumed in Norway, so the merchants found new markets in England and, to a certain degree, in the Netherlands. In 1828 most Danish ships after having delivered their grain to Hull, Leith, London and Amsterdam returned in ballast. Later coal became of great interest for the Danish shipowners. Coal had been delivered by British ships for use in breweries and distilleries in Copenhagen; the British ships then proceeded into the Baltic to get their cargoes for the return voyage.

From about 1830 iron foundries were established in most provincial towns in Denmark, which naturally generated a growing need for coal all over the country. What could be more obvious than that the ships transporting grain should return with coal? To have a cargo both ways was certainly the ideal situation for the shipowners. Table 1 shows the tonnage going from Danish provincial towns to harbours in Great Britain and back. The percentage of the ship's carrying capacity used has been calculated. It should be noted that the grain often was unloaded in one port and the coal taken on in another. For example, if grain was delivered to Leith, the return freight might be found in Alloa, Dysart, Bo'ness, Clackmannan or Inverkeithing. In 1863 the returning tonnage was much bigger than the outgoing.

Table 1. *Danish sailing ships going to and returning from Great Britain*

	Going to Great Britain		Returning to Danish provincial ports	
	Tonnage	%	Tonnage	%
1826	16,779	92.6	16,880	31.9
1834	21,584	91.5	22,102	59.2
1843	36,036	84.1	35,190	83.0
1855	112,638	91.7	103,576	94.3
1863	129,320	87.6	138,696	97.6

The explanation is that ships which had been elsewhere, instead of returning to Denmark in ballast, would call at a British port for a load of coal.

The growing export of grain to Great Britain was of course of great importance for the Danish economy, and the growth in the import of coal was crucial for the early industrialization of Denmark.

The Danish export of grain to Great Britain was in competition with grain from the United States from the 1880s; prices were falling and the situation was precarious for Danish farmers, so they increasingly used the grain to feed cattle and pigs which were exported to Germany by rail or shipped to Britain from Esbjerg, a North Sea port founded in 1868. To begin with, the export of cattle was predominant; from about 1880 butter became more and more important; and just before 1890 bacon replaced the cattle and pigs.

Table 2. *The ports in Great Britain most commonly visited by Danish steamers*

	1870 Number	1870 Tonnage	1880 Number	1880 Tonnage	1890 Number	1890 Tonnage
London	50	21,687½	73	45,107	131	105,123
Hull	36	14,639	67	40,014	132	60,918
Newcastle	25	11,511	363	182,693	488	204,716
Leith	22	7,775½	44	10,596	60	20,179
Harwich			37	12,106	154	72,557
Grimsby					73	47,536
Sunderland					40	32,696
Grangemouth					82	61,286
Bo'ness					68	35,357
Burntisland					99	56,088

Table 3. *The ports in the Netherlands, France, Portugal and Spain most commonly visited by Danish steamers*

	1870 Number	1870 Tonnage	1880 Number	1880 Tonnage	1890 Number	1890 Tonnage
Rotterdam	8	3,862½	13	10,329	71	63,933
Antwerp	18	8,358	91	65,760	139	122,727
Ghent					24	16,263
Dunkirk	6	3,010½	22	15,677	76	61,315
Le Havre					32	23,071
Rouen					30	26,233
Bordeaux	6	2,043	14	10,662	40	28,157
Lisbon					28	18,724
Cadiz					26	20,424

The steamers of DFDS very soon took part in exports to British ports – some of them in scheduled services. The number and tonnage of incoming Danish steamers to the most important British ports in the years 1870, 1880 and 1890 can be seen in Table 2. The rising figures for Newcastle show that steamers were increasingly involved in the transport of coal to Danish ports, thereby partly taking over from the sailing ships.

Danish grain was also exported to Amsterdam and elsewhere in Western Europe. The development in this field is seen in Table 3. In comparison with the steamer trade between ports in Denmark and Great Britain, the connections with other harbours are a lot more complex. In some cases the steamers were owned by DFDS in regular service, in other cases the traffic was more casual. But part of it had to do with goods from the Baltic.

The role of the Baltic

Every year thousands of ships passed the Sound at the beginning of the year, going east to fetch Baltic products for Western Europe. Danish shipowners had the advantage of being located nearest the Baltic and at the beginning of the season could be the first to go east and, later, west. This advantage was of course made use of.

The Baltic ports were Rostock, Wismar, Stralsund, Greifswald, Wolgast, Stettin, Colberg, Danzig, Pillau, Königsberg, Memel, Libau, Riga and St Petersburg. The goods exported could be grain, peas, beans, hemp, linseed, oilcake and timber. Many ships entered the Baltic in ballast; fewer were loaded with colonial products and general merchandise.

The steamers of course soon entered the Baltic trade, as can be seen in Table 4. In 1870 the Danish steamer *Valdemar* entered Pillau and Königsberg eight times, and St Petersburg twice, and each time called at Copenhagen on its way to London. In the same year the *Arcturus* sailed north and called at the Norwegian

Table 4. *The ports in the Baltic most commonly visited by Danish steamers*

	1870		1880		1890	
	Number	Tonnage	Number	Tonnage	Number	Tonnage
St Petersburg	11	5,007	37	25,290	104	103,684
Reval			19	10,301	39	31,184
Riga			64	39,755	173	140,979
Libau			102	47,691	220	107,421
Memel					27	14,123
Pillau and Königsb.	75	30,608½	77	53,997	139	77,773
Danzig	20	6,516	16	5,698	137	56,146
Stettin	37	7,168½	150	40,744	325	175,087

ports of Bergen and Trondheim four times, and from there sailed south though the Sound to the Baltic and called at Stettin or Königsberg.

In the year 1880 the *Anglo-Dane* was seen ten times in Libau, and then times in Antwerp as well. In addition, it called three times at British ports. Now, Danish steamers also sailed between the Baltic and ports in the Mediterranean.

Mediterranean trade

There were few ships under the Danish flag in the Mediterranean in the first decades of the 19th century. Reports from Danish consuls show the number of arrivals and departures and give information on the cargoes. Malaga was often visited in the beginning, mostly in ballast, later on often with coal from English or Scottish harbours. The goods returned to Denmark were wine, olive oil and fruit.

Spanish harbours such as Cartagena, Torrevieja, Alicante, Denia, Valencia, Benicarlo, Vinaros and Tarragona were seldom called at, but Barcelona was visited more often. In this case some ships were laden with coal from Great Britain. The French harbours of Cette and Marseilles received grain or timber; and salt and wine were fetched from Cette, and general cargo from Marseilles.

The Italian ports of Genoa and Leghorn were visited by a small number of Danish ships bringing grain, fish or coal, but most sailed out again in ballast. Messina was a "fruit port", where a rising number of Danish ships, after delivering a cargo of coal, loaded lemons, oranges, almonds and nuts. Trieste was a free harbour and Danish ships arrived here from America laden with coffee, sugar and general cargo and sailed with general cargo or in ballast.

In the Black Sea, from 1840 onwards a rising number Danish ships arrived in Odessa, Galatz or Taganrog with coal and returned west with corn and wheat.

The ships in the Mediterranean were on average more than a hundred tons, although in 1857 there was still a small schooner of sixty-nine tons. The schooner was in the fruit trade going to Malaga, in which speed was of greater importance than carrying capacity.

Between 1880 and 1890 rising numbers of Danish steamers called at ports in the Mediterranean as can be seen in Table 5. The goods transported could be grain from Kronstadt to Amsterdam, coal from Newcastle to Malaga, and from there wine to Copenhagen. The *H.J. Pallisen* brought oranges and lemons from Catania to Reval. This was certainly a steamer not in regular service but in the tramping trade, which become more common between 1870 and 1890.

The leading Danish shipping firm, DFDS, extended its scheduled service to ports in the Mediterranean in 1883. Eight years later, in 1891, the voyage might start in one of the most important ports of the Baltic, and after passing Copenhagen and the Sound the ship might call at one or more ports in Western Europe before passing the Straits of Gibraltar. In the Mediterranean there were regular calls at Malaga, Valencia, Tarragona, Barcelona, Marseille, Genoa, Leghorn, Naples,

Table 5. *The ports in the Mediterranean and the Black Sea most commonly visited by Danish steamers*

	1880		1890	
	Number	Tonnage	Number	Tonnage
Messina	9	8,184	20	14,467
Palermo	6	4,942		
Malaga			24	19,404
Valencia			35	28,501
Genoa			19	16,068
Salonica			16	19,283
Piræus			31	36,252
Smyrna			19	22,211
Constantinople			60	69,720
Odessa	5	4,929	25	29,273
Batum			21	15,236
Alexandria	5	3,833		

Messina, Catania, Licata, Palermo, Piræus, Smyrna, Salonica, Istanbul, and in the Black Sea, Odessa, Sevastopol, Novorossiisk, Batumi, Trebizond and Samsun. The steamers in scheduled service primarily carried general cargo but had accommodation for passengers as well.

Irregularly the ships would call at the Spanish ports of Almeria, Cartagena, Alicante, Denia and Benicarlo, and Cette; and also at the Italian ports of Bari, Barletta and Trieste. In North Africa they might visit Oran, Algier, Tunis, Sfax, Alexandria, Port Said and, in the easternmost part of the Mediterranean Akka, Tripoli, Alexandretta and Alanya. This category of ports occasionally would be called at after a telegram received earlier.

Overseas

The trade to the Danish Caribbean Islands has been mentioned, but there were other destinations far west. In 1828 the ship *Caravane* of Åbenrå in Southern Jutland was first seen in the month of May calling at Pernau in the Baltic, where she loaded for Porto. From there the ship proceeded with wine to Bahia in Brazil, arriving in October. On Christmas Day *Caravane* again put to sea, with sugar which was unloaded in Trieste the following year.

Ports in Uruguay and Argentina were also visited. In 1843 *Creole* of Åbenrå transported salt from Cadiz to Buenos Aires. The bark *Sara & Johanne* of Aarhus transported general cargo from Hamburg to Montevideo, where it was partly unloaded, and then proceeded with the rest to Buenos Aires. She returned to Altona in Holstein with a cargo of hides.

Danish ships also rounded the Horn. In October 1842 the bark *Waldemar* of Korsør departed from Valparaiso laden with cocoa, coffee, copper and hides and unloaded in Hamburg, returning to Chile with general cargo. In all, twenty-seven Danish ships called at Valparaiso in the year 1843.

So, Danish ships were sailing in increasing numbers to South America. In 1843 the following home ports are mentioned: the island of Fanø, and the ports of Åbenrå, Elsinore, Korsør, Nakskov, Nyborg, Randers, Rønne, Aalborg and Aarhus.

In 1857 a lot of guano was shipped from Peru to fertilize European farms. Here the biggest Danish ships were used, such as the *Cimber* of Åbenrå, of 1,640 tons. She sailed in ballast north from Valparaiso to Las Chinchas (the Bird Islands) to fetch guano and returned to Europe to unload at Antwerp.

At this time Danish ships were also sailing to the Far East. In February 1857 the *Calløe* of Åbenrå left Liverpool with general cargo and called at Batavia in May, from whence she seemingly intended to proceed to China. In Batavia the same year the *Hindoo* of Åbenrå sailed rice to China. Later that year she called at Singapore, coming from Macao in ballast. In the year 1857, in all, thirteen Danish ships visited Batavia and thirty arrived at Hong Kong.

A last example from the Far East is the *Adele* of Ribe, which in January 1857 arrived at Hong Kong from Melbourne in Australia. In March she arrived in Akyab in Burma in ballast from Singapore, thence shipped rice to Macao and arrived at Hong Kong in June in ballast. On the next voyage the *Adele* went to the Sunda Islands, Lombok, to fetch rice and coffee, which were unloaded in Hong Kong, and in October she sailed for Bangkok.

On 25 October 1879 the biggest Danish steamer, the *Thingvalla* of Copenhagen, left for New York for the first time as an emigrant ship. In 1890 the Thingvalla Company owned four steamers which crossed the Atlantic twenty-four times between them and brought 6,362 passengers to New York. General cargo was carried both ways. The economy of the company, however, was not too good, and in 1898 DFDS took over and the name was changed to Skandinavien-Amerika Linien (Scandinavian-America Line).

At that time another line was established and in 1895 DFDS began a regular service to New Orleans to load corn, wheat, flour, oilcake, resin, cotton, machinery and general cargo. After the turn of the century a line to Boston, Massachusetts was opened, and a little later Baltimore and Philadelphia were added. Further, in 1907 DFDS established a line to Buenos Aires in South America.

DFDS did not remain alone in the overseas steamer trades. In 1897 Det Østasiatiske Kompagni (The East Asiatic Company) was founded. The following year its steamer *Siam* left Copenhagen for Colombo (Sri Lanka) and proceeded to Singapore, Bangkok and Hong Kong. Later the line was extended to Vladivostok and ports in Japan. In 1900 the Company established a line to South Africa and in 1905 to the Danish Caribbean Islands. In anticipation of the opening of the Panama Canal in 1914 the Company founded lines in the Pacific, one going north to San Francisco and Canada, another going south and calling at ports in Peru and Chile. And finally, in the year 1914 a line was established round Australia and home via Java.

Conclusion

Overseas colonial trade decreased during the period and the colonies were sold – the last, the Danish Caribbean Islands, in 1917. The trade of the North Atlantic colonies was steady but became relatively less important during the 19th century.

The Danish shipping industry, however, was indispensable for the provisioning of Copenhagen and for the growing export of grain and, later, animal products to Norway and Great Britain. Danish exports in the 19th century consisted almost exclusively of agricultural products.

Danish industrial products were mostly for the home market. Coal was of vital importance for the growing Danish industry and was transported from British ports by Danish ships.

In the second part of the century shipping under the Danish flag was extended worldwide and became an industry of its own, first using sailing ships and later steamers as well. The first paddle steamer was built in Glasgow, but about the middle of the period Denmark was beginning to be self-sufficient in this field. Technically, Danish shipbuilding on the eve of the First World War was advanced. In 1912 the leading Danish shipyard launched the *Selandia*, the first ocean-going ship in the world with a diesel engine.[1]

---

[1] MØLLER A.M., *Med korn og kul*, Dansk Søfarts Historie vol. 4 (Copenhagen 1998); and MØLLER A.M., DETHLEFSEN H. and JOHANSEN H.C., *Sejl og damp*, Dansk Søfarts Historie vol. 5 (Copenhagen 1998).

Sweden and the Sea in the 19th Century

Leos Müller is Professor of History at Stockholm University, Sweden

ABSTRACT. *In the war of 1808-9 Sweden lost Finland to Russia and ceased to be a Baltic imperial power. Swedish foreign policy came to be based on neutrality, but Russia, and later Germany, remained real threats across the Baltic. Swedish shipping grew slowly, mainly carrying Swedish imports and exports. As Sweden industrialised, shipowning concentrated in the ports of Gothenburg and Stockholm.*

RÉSUMÉ. *Lors de la guerre de 1808-1809, la Suède perdit la Finlande au profit de la Russie et cessa d'être une puissance impériale balte. La politique étrangère suédoise se fonda par la suite sur la neutralité mais la Russie, et plus tard l'Allemagne, demeurèrent de véritables menaces de l'autre côté de la mer Baltique. La navigation suédoise se développa lentement et eut principalement pour rôle l'importation et l'exportation. Avec l'industrialisation de la Suède, l'activité maritime se concentra dans les ports de Göteborg et de Stockholm.*

.•.

The two hundred years of peace that characterise Sweden's modern history began with a disastrous war against Russia, 1808–1809. Part of the French Revolutionary and Napoleonic Wars, it is probably little known on the Continent, yet it had lasting consequences. Sweden lost Finland, accounting for a third of Sweden's territory and a quarter of her population. From being a maritime empire in the Baltic Sea, Sweden contracted into the territorial state of its present shape. Stockholm, the capital at the heart of the old Swedish Baltic Sea empire ended up on the easternmost corner of the new territory that took shape in 1809, just hours in distance from the Russian-controlled Åland islands – a part of then Russian Finland. This was perhaps the biggest geopolitical shift in Sweden's history.

The disastrous war entailed a political revolution that removed King Gustaf IV Adolph; within a year he was replaced by the French General Jean Bernadotte, the future King Karl XIV Johan. Sweden became a constitutional monarchy. In the final years of the French Revolutionary and Napoleonic Wars Sweden also accepted Prussia's incorporation of Swedish Pomerania, a remnant of the seventeenth-century great-power period. In exchange, in the European settlement of states 1814–15, Norway was transferred to Sweden from Denmark.

While Sweden under Bernadotte took an active part in the campaign against Napoleon, Denmark stayed a loyal ally to France until the end. The union of Sweden–Norway was forged by force, against Norwegian will, in 1814. The union was a very loose one. It rested on the person of the king, and a common foreign policy only. In all other respects the states of Sweden and Norway were governed separately for the rest of the century, not least economically – which later on caused political troubles and eventually led to the dissolution of the loose union in 1905.

NEW DEFENCE STRATEGY

The transformation of Sweden from a middle-ranking maritime power to a "small" territorial state entailed serious changes in the state's defence strategy and its foreign policy. For almost three centuries, since the early 16th century, Sweden's defence strategy had been built on its ability to prevent the enemy from landing on Swedish territory and, more specifically, attacking Stockholm. The strategy required a navy strong enough to meet any enemy fleet in the Baltic Sea: in the 16th and 17th centuries the Danes, in the 18th century the Danes and the Russians. Another part of the strategy was to meet the enemy on the enemy's territory, which until 1721 meant on the southern and eastern coasts of the Baltic. This required the navy to be able to transport the Swedish armies across the Baltic Sea. These two tasks promoted Sweden to one of the biggest naval powers in the early modern era.[1]

With the occupation of Finland and with Russian troops stationed in the Åland islands, Sweden's war planners began to prepare for a different kind of defence. The Swedish army could not halt an enemy landing in central Sweden; instead they had to concentrate on territorial defence inland. This new strategy, the so-called central defence doctrine, called for a number of inland fortresses. The best-known is Karlsborg, begun in 1819 on Lake Vättern, some 300km southwest of Stockholm. It was planned to protect the Swedish central administration in the case of Stockholm's being attacked.

The new defence doctrine also produced a strategic reconsideration of the navy's role in Sweden's defence, and especially that of the naval base of Karlskrona, built in southern Sweden to fend off the Danish fleet. The new situation made Karlskrona redundant. However, due to limited resources the new defence doctrine was put in place only gradually, the inland fortress building proceeded slowly and Karlskrona continued to consume large resources. In a

---

[1] GLETE J., 'Bridge and Bulwark. the Swedish Navy and the Baltic, 1500–1809', in *In Quest of Trade and Security. The Baltic in Power Politics, 1500–1990*, Vol. 1, ed. G. RYSTAD, K-R. BÖHME and W.M. CARLGREN (Lund 1994), pp. 9–59. For a useful recent summary of Sweden's naval history see WOLKE L.E. and HÅRDSTEDT M., *Svenska sjöslag* (Stockholm, 2009). For a comparison of navies in early modern times see GLETE J., *Navies and Nations. Warships, Navies and State Building in Europe and America, 1500–1860*, 2 vols (Stockholm, 1993).

way it is surprising that the changed strategic situation and the adaptation of new central defence doctrine did not have a more profound impact on the navy. One explanation is the policy of neutrality and the friendly relations between Sweden and Russia during the reign of Karl XIV Johan (1818–1844).

NEUTRALITY – OLD OR NEW FOREIGN POLICY?

Sweden was a neutral state during the 18th century and adopted neutrality in the many great-power conflicts taking place outside the Baltic Sea (1756, 1778–1783 and 1793–1805).[2] But this eighteenth-century neutrality was inconsistent and unpredictable, and very different to the neutrality of the 19th century. Economic opportunities were paramount to the neutrality of the 18th century, which provides an important explanation for the growth in Swedish exports and tramp shipping, in particular in Southern Europe. Yet, in the Baltic Sea Sweden continued to play an active and often aggressive role towards Russia and Denmark.

The British domination of the seas in the 19th century changed the situation. On the one hand, neutrality at sea was no longer a competitive advantage as the seas in general saw fewer conflicts (*Pax Britannica*). On the other hand, after 1815 neutrality became the preferred foreign policy of small European states more generally. The reason for this was not the benefit of trading under a neutral flag, but the greater security of the state. One of the evident outcomes of the French Revolutionary and Napoleonic Wars was the increasing gap between the great powers – the pentagon of Britain, Russia, France, Prussia and Austria – and the large number of small states – like Sweden or Portugal in Europe, but also the many new republics in the Americas. While the great powers continued to expand their armed forces, as they could put more and more resources into them, for small states the arms race was no viable way to guarantee security, territorial integrity or even the survival of the state. They simply could not match the economic and military resources of the great powers.

Instead, the small states increasingly relied on non-military solutions to security problems; they took part in international settlements and they declared their neutrality. The Congress of Vienna in 1815 and the following settlements: the Congresses of Aachen in 1818 and Paris in 1856 and the Berlin Conference of 1884–85 made the nineteenth-century international environment more predictable and safer for small states. The big settlements included guarantees for the small states' integrity. The policy of neutrality meant primarily that small states did not engage in great-power politics. However they could not avoid the reverse, i.e. the great powers drawing small states into their conflicts. Denmark's neutrality, for example, did not stop the war of 1864 when Prussia and Austria occupied the Duchies of Slesvig and Holstein, part of the Danish conglomerate state.

---

[2] AF MALMBORG M., *Neutrality and State-Building in Sweden* (Basingstoke, 2001).

The neutrality of the 19th century was in a way contrary to the idea of collective security that has dominated twentieth-century security solutions. Nineteenth-century neutrality presupposed two separate kinds of international relations and regimes: on the one hand, a regime where the relations between the great powers were based on real power – *realpolitik*, and on the other hand, one where relations between states were based on the concept of international law – a law of nations, incorporating neutrality as a key principle. The second regime was not so weak (and naïve) as we might think in the light of our twentieth-century experience. It was viable and for a time a functional system. In addition to the many European states that adopted it, neutrality was the leading principle for the nineteenth-century foreign policy of the United States and the Latin American republics. The heyday of neutrality appeared to be the Hague Conference in 1907. The First World War, however, discredited neutrality as a viable concept of foreign policy, and in 1917 even the biggest and internationally most important neutral state, the US, entered the war.

For Sweden, neutral foreign policy was one of the consequences of her weakened strategic situation in the Baltic Sea. Yet Sweden's foreign policy was shaped not only by the Russian threat. Cultural nationalism, unlike the older civic nationalism, gave rise to the movement of *Skandinavism* that influenced Swedish and Danish politics in the mid-century. *Skandinavism* propagated the cultural and political brotherhood of the three Scandinavian nations; in foreign policy it was mainly expressed by Swedish support for Denmark in the case of Slesvig and Holstein. In 1864 the joint Swedish–Norwegian fleet patrolled the Kattegat, deterring Prussian ships from attacking Copenhagen. But the union of Sweden and Norway declined to send troops to Denmark, and Denmark's defeat and the loss of the Duchies marked the end of *Skandinavism* as an effective political ideology. Instead, the late 19th century was marked by increasing differences and political disagreements between the Scandinavian nations.

Sweden and Norway's economic interests also shaped the union's foreign policy. Before 1800 the two countries were among the leading European carriers, with extensive tramp shipping in Southern Europe and the North Sea. After 1815 Sweden's tramp shipping shrank, but some new markets appeared. The independence movement in Latin America opened new shipping routes for the Swedes, as we will show below.

One of the diplomatic incidents of the early 1820s that attracted much attention in Sweden was linked to developments in Latin America. In 1825 and 1826 Sweden attempted to sell five second-hand warships to the young American republics of Mexico and Colombia. The affair was carried out via British intermediaries but became public and naturally raised intense resistance in Spain, and in Russia, which perceived the independence movements in Latin America as illegal rebellions which Russia had to oppose. In the face of Russian threat, the sale was cancelled and three Swedish ships returned home. The remaining two, *Tapperheten* and *Af Chapman*, which had already reached Cartagena in Colombia, were sent back to New York and sold at public auction.

Another maritime expression of the union's foreign policy was the expansion of consular services across the globe. In a first wave, in the 1820s and 1830s, new Swedish-Norwegian consuls were appointed in the newly independent American republics; in a second wave, in the mid-century, consuls were sent to Asia, Africa and Australia. As the majority of appointments were for port cities it is apparent that the purpose was to serve Swedish and Norwegian maritime and commercial interests.

THE CRIMEAN WAR AND SWEDEN'S SITUATION IN THE SECOND HALF OF THE CENTURY

The Baltic Sea might appear as an unexpected war theatre in the Crimean War (1853–1856), but was important in the plans of the Franco-British coalition, which sent a joint fleet to the area, under the command of Sir Charles Napier. The ultimate aim of the Baltic campaigns was St Petersburg, but the allies were not able to pass the naval base of Kronstadt in front of the Russian capital. From the Swedish point of view the most important part of the campaigns was the initial allied attack on the Russian fortress of Bomarsund in the Åland islands, a dangerous threat to Stockholm. After an intensive Franco-British bombardment the Russian fortress surrendered in August 1854 and was destroyed.

The Scandinavian states, Denmark and Sweden-Norway, declared their neutrality at the beginning of the conflict, in December 1853, but already in 1854 the allies tried to draw Sweden-Norway into the war with promises of territorial gain. The stake was the Russian-controlled Åland islands with their Swedish-speaking population. The invitation caused a conflict between King Oscar I, who wanted a more bellicose policy, and the cautious *Riksdag*, which stressed the need to follow strict neutrality in the conflict. In November 1855 the western allies signed a treaty with Sweden-Norway in which they guaranteed the integrity of the Scandinavian state. The treaty did not oblige Sweden to support the allies, but it marked a shift in foreign policy orientation in comparison with Karl XIV Johan's pro-Russian strategy.

The peace was signed in Paris in 1856 and had one lasting outcome for Sweden: it guaranteed a demilitarised and neutral status for the Åland islands, which reduced the threat of a Russian attack on Stockholm. The so-called Åland Convention is still an important component of Åland's special status in Finland and the Baltic Sea.

In 1861 Sweden adopted a new naval doctrine which marked a shift from the central defence doctrine.[3] The navy's task was now to meet the enemy on the coast and hinder it from landing. For the new defence task special coastal artillery was created, which at some periods was directly integrated within the navy. In the 1850s and 1860s Sweden's sailing warships were equipped with

---

[3] GLETE J., *Kustförsvar och teknisk omvandling. Teknik, doktriner och organisation inom svenskt kustförsvar 1850-1880* (Stockholm, 1985).

steam power, yet the modernization progressed slowly. Technically interesting is Sweden's introduction of small but heavily armoured naval ships from the US in the 1860s, the so-called "Monitors", designed by the Swedish engineer John Ericsson.

In general the situation in last three decades of the century was characterised by an increased interest in the navy. Swedish officers went abroad to Britain and the US to learn more. Alfred T. Mahan's ideas were introduced and discussed in the Swedish naval context. The rise of German power and the weakening of Russia did not make much difference to Sweden's neutrality policy, but they made the navy once again relevant to Sweden's defence strategy. In a limited sense Sweden took part in the global build-up of ironclad ships. In 1907 Sweden had twelve ironclad warships (c. 3,000–7,500 tons). This reflected more on Sweden's new confidence as a modern industrial nation than on any ambition to be a naval power.

SWEDISH SHIPPING, 1815–1914

The decades following the end of the French Revolutionary and Napoleonic Wars were characterised by problems in Sweden's shipping sector. The end of the wars brought a deep economic crisis in Gothenburg, which had profited enormously by the wartime boom and the Continental system. In a couple of years (1808–1814) a large share of British and US exports and colonial re-exports were channelled through Gothenburg. After 1814 all this traffic returned to the normal routes, with predictable consequences for Gothenburg. Moreover, the introduction of coke-produced iron in Britain wiped out a major market for Sweden's main export commodity – charcoal-produced bar iron. However, in two critical decades, the 1820s and 1830s, the US replaced Britain as *the* market for Swedish bar iron.[4]

The connection between Sweden and the US was established in the war years, when American ships came with colonial produce to Sweden's western coast. Swedish bar iron made a suitable return cargo, and so a new trade route between Sweden and the US was born that survived the peacetime decline in trade. In the 1820s the American ships found more profitable cargoes on other routes and were replaced by Swedish vessels carrying bar iron to the US. These Swedish ships were looking for return cargoes not only in the US but also in Latin America. This shaped a new pattern for Sweden's Atlantic trade in the early decades of 19th century, based on exports of bar iron and imports of colonial goods, for example coffee and sugar from Brazil. Already around 1820 we find many Swedish ships in Rio de Janeiro and Buenos Aires loading sugar, coffee, hides etc. for Europe. This became typical of the trade of the iron-exporting port of Gävle, after Stockholm

---

[4] MÜLLER L., *Consuls, Corsairs, and Commerce. The Swedish Consular Service and Long-Distance Shipping, 1720–1815* (Uppsala, 2004), pp. 199-223.

and Gothenburg the third most important shipping town in Sweden. In the 1840s the Gävle firm of Eckhoff & Co. exported bar iron to the US and brought home coffee and sugar.

Nevertheless, the numbers of ships engaged in this new Atlantic trade were limited. The number of registered Swedish ships engaged in international trade between 1820 and 1850 stagnated at between eight hundred and nine hundred (in tonnage, c. 125,000 tons), roughly the same figure as the Swedish merchant fleet of the late 18th century.[5] But the pattern of shipping changed. As mentioned above, the tramp shipping to Southern Europe disappeared, and the new Atlantic routes required a quite limited number of vessels. The only shipping that rapidly expanded in tonnage was transport of sawn timber from northern Sweden.

Looking at the history of commercial shipping in the 19th century, historians point to two factors that at different stages and at different speeds influenced the transformation of the maritime sector. The growing liberalism of the first half of the century was one factor. The Swedish Navigation Act (*produktplakatet*) was abandoned in stages as bilateral trade treaties between Sweden and other countries gave Sweden and her treaty partners the status of most favoured nation. This opened up the shipping of Swedish sawn timber to other fleets. Britain was the major market for Swedish timber and consequently many British vessels entered this trade. Norwegian ships likewise entered the carrying business from northern Sweden in large numbers. Moreover, trades in other key export goods were liberated, which opened up an export trade boom in Sweden after 1850.

The second factor was technological change – the transition from sail to steam and from wooden ships to iron and steel. Especially in relation to Atlantic and global trade, this transition has been perceived as the cause of globalization in the mid-19th century.[6] The argument is that the technological shift dramatically reduced freight costs and hence stimulated growth in the trade in bulky export goods: grain, iron, sawn goods, coal, ores and so on. These were typical Swedish exports. In Sweden, however, the transition from sail to steam was a long drawn-out history, and indeed no transport revolution. Steamboats appeared in Sweden early; already in 1824 there was a postal steamboat going between Ystad in southern Sweden and Germany. In the 1830s and 1840s steamboats entered the traffic on inland lakes, preceding railways in waterway-abundant Sweden. But the penetration of steam into long-distance shipping was a much slower process. As late as 1892 70% of Swedish-registered tonnage consisted of sailing ships.[7] This was not in any way exceptional, in comparison with, for example, Norwegian and Finnish fleets. There was simply too little incentive to invest in

---

[5] KILBORN J., *Fartyg i Europas periferi under den industriella revolutionen. Den svenska utrikeshandelsflottan 1795-1845* (Göteborg, 2010).
[6] O'ROURKE K.H. and WILLIAMSON J., *Globalization and History. The Evolution of a Nineteenth-Century Atlantic Economy* (Cambridge, MA, 1999).
[7] For an overview of the transition of the Swedish fleet from sail to steam see LARSSON B., *Svenska varor på svenska kölar. Staten, industrialiseringen och linjesjöfartens framväxt i Sverige 1890-1925* (Göteborg 2000).

new steam tonnage when sailing tonnage could be acquired cheaply abroad (in Britain) and when foreign ships were carrying Swedish exports. Steam vessels also required different forms of organization and financing of both shipyards and shipping companies. For most of the 19th century Sweden's shipping industry was still dominated by small family firms dispersed all around its long coast. At the same time Sweden's export trade went though a rapid expansion. In addition to sawn goods, Sweden became one of the biggest exporters of paper and pulp. All these were forest products, but oats for the British market also become an important export item in the mid-century.

The boom in global trade after 1850 had different outcomes in different parts of the union. Norway's shipping industry expanded rapidly. Between 1854 and 1874 the Norwegian fleet expanded four-fold and Norway became the world's fifth shipping nation. Sweden's fleet expanded too, but at a much slower pace. In 1870 Norway's merchant tonnage accounted for 974,000 net tons, while Sweden's was just 347,000 net tons. In 1888 Norway's fleet had expanded to 1.4 million tons, as compared to Sweden's 374,000 tons.[8] If we look at the export trade values, the relationship was reversed; Sweden's foreign trade was much bigger than that of Norway and it expanded fast. Between 1854 and 1874 Sweden's foreign trade expanded from 160 million Swedish crowns to 540 million crowns. In the same years Norway's foreign trade rose from 98 million to 310 million crowns.[9]

Thus, the two economies followed very different paths of development. In Sweden, industrialization and exports were the priority, while the merchant fleet was perceived primarily as the carrier of Swedish products. Germany and Britain were the major markets, and so the carrying trade in the North Sea and Baltic Sea completely dominated Swedish shipping demand. As mentioned, there was a Swedish oceanic shipping fleet (for example to the US), but it was not very significant. The Norwegian merchant fleet, in contrast, grew into a global carrier, for which the exports of domestic products played a much more limited role than in Sweden. Comparatively, the shipping sector of the economy was more important than the export sector.

The different development paths also generated different foreign policy interests. While the Norwegians argued for the needs of their maritime sector, asking for an extended consular representation in the world and eventually their own department of foreign affairs, the Swedes had only a limited interest in the global maritime sector, arguing for representation that would promote their foreign trade. In the 1890s the different interests in consular issues resulted in the crisis of the union and the final dissolution of 1905.

The modernization of the Swedish merchant fleet began only around 1900, but then it proceeded fast. A modern fleet required a lot of capital and, consequently, new organizational forms. The shipping companies became concentrated in two maritime centres, Stockholm and Gothenburg, while smaller shipping ports

---

[8] KAUKIAINEN Y., *History of Finnish Shipping* (London, 1993), p. 100.
[9] *Underdånigt betänkande angående svenska och norska konsulväsendet ... avgifvet den 4 November 1876 ...* (Stockholm, 1876), p. 4.

declined in significance. At the same time modern shipyards grew in western and southern Sweden (Malmö and Gothenburg); the traditional wooden shipbuilding, dispersed along the coast of northern Sweden, had disappeared already by the late 19th century. The modernization of the shipping sector was directly related to the interests of banks and industries, and there were ownership links between the different sectors of the economy. The shift of the Swedish economy towards managerial capitalism entailed a participation in global trade which required a different kind of shipping. Swedish industrial products as well as paper and pulp were now carried to distant markets in Africa, Latin America, Asia and Australia.

The transformation of the Swedish shipping industry about 1900 was also related to increasing economic protectionism. In shipping, an expression of this trend was the growth of big shipping lines and the liner conference system that regulated markets for liner shipping. Swedish shipping lines became included in the liner conference system and thrived until the outbreak of First World War. In a way, the situation with protectionism in shipping resembled the eighteenth-century situation when Swedish shipping prospered under the protection of the *produktplakatet*. But while in the eighteenth-century tramp shipping was of key importance for Swedish ships, in 1900 there was only a limited market for Swedish tramp shipping. The modern Swedish shipping industry was built to transport Swedish export goods.

About 1900 three types of export goods required three different kinds of tonnage, something that shaped the establishment of shipping companies. Iron ore exports from northern Sweden (Kiruna area) required a big carrying capacity designed for ore. The ore-exporting ports were Narvik in Norway and Luleå in Sweden, and the major company was Nordstjernan (founded 1890). The markets for ore were located in Europe and ore-carrying ships took home coal and coke, used in the Swedish iron and steel industries. The forest products, sawn goods, paper and pulp, were traded globally with markets in the Americas, Asia, South Africa and Australia, as well as in the Baltic and North Seas. Forest products required relatively large carrying capacity and more diversified ships. The third group of exports were products of the new engineering industries (AGA, L.M. Ericsson, Separator, SKF) such as telephones, creamers, gas burners, ball bearings and similar goods. These engineering products were traded globally and made Sweden's name as an industrial nation, but they did not require so much tonnage as iron ore or forest products.

As mentioned above, the new shipping companies grew up in two maritime centres, Gothenburg and Stockholm. In Gothenburg the shipping industry cluster was connected to Dan Broström (1870–1925), who founded a number of liner companies. The Broström family also played a key role in development of the shipbuilding industry in Gothenburg. In Stockholm the dominant figure was Axel Johnson (1844–1910), the founder of the Nordstjernan company. The Johnson and Broström families continued to play important roles in Sweden's economy in the 20th century. For example, Axel Johnson AB is today one of the biggest Swedish holding companies in trade and trade-related sectors.

Concluding remarks

Sweden's relationship with the sea in the 19th century might be defined by two turning points, very different in their nature but significant for an understanding of Sweden's modern history. The disastrous outcome of the war 1808-9 marked the end of Sweden as a Baltic Sea empire. From being an important naval power in the North, and a middle-range state in the 18th century, Sweden became one of many small European states, in spite of its large territory. The Russian annexation of Finland dramatically worsened Sweden's strategic situation and required a new defence doctrine in which the role of a navy was limited. In the new situation Sweden' security was guaranteed by a cautious foreign policy towards the great powers, and a consistent neutrality – a favourite standpoint of many small states in the 19th century. In the second half of the century Russia's relative strength in the Baltic declined, partly as a consequence of the Crimean War, and partly due Germany's rise as a new economic and military power in northern Europe. Yet neutrality continues to be a central part of Sweden's security policy today.

The decades 1890-1910 might be seen as another turning point in Sweden's relation to the sea, this time determined by the new golden age of the Swedish shipping industry. Economic success compensated for the loss of political and military status in 1809. In the second half of the century Sweden's economy and foreign trade developed very quickly; in fact, Sweden had the fastest-growing economy in Europe between 1870 and 1910. About 1900 the modernization of the Swedish shipping industry and the rise of Gothenburg and Stockholm as important maritime centres with global shipping companies marked a new kind of economic power. The early modern territorial expansion on the other side of the Baltic Sea was replaced by expansion in global markets for Swedish products. New and modern liner companies were carrying Swedish products to all corners of the world.

Navies, internal order and trade in South America, 1830–1914

BRIAN VALE is an independent researcher, United Kingdom

ABSTRACT. *The South American states are linked by the sea and the great rivers, which have always been their means of access to the outside world and to each other. The trade of the nineteenth-century South American states was seaborne, and their rivalries were expressed by naval wars at sea and on the great rivers.*

RÉSUMÉ. *Les États d'Amérique du Sud sont reliés par la mer et les grands fleuves. Cela a toujours été leurs moyens d'accès au monde extérieur et à leurs voisins. Le commerce des États sud-américains du XIXe siècle était maritime, et leurs rivalités s'exprimèrent par des guerres navales sur la mer et les grands fleuves.*

. • .

Bordered by the Pacific and Atlantic oceans, South America comprises a conical-shaped landmass stretching from the equator in the north to the icy wastes of Tierra del Fuego in the south. Topographically, it comprises three zones – the peaks of the Andes which run down the western side; the highlands of Brazil which, with their associated plateau, occupy the eastern corner; and, in the centre, two huge river systems – the Amazon, which flows east through tropical rainforests from Peru to the sea, and the Paraná, which, with its tributaries, flows south from the Brazil–Bolivia border, through Paraguay, to the temperate grasslands of the River Plate.

In the 1820s, South America was emerging after centuries of Spanish and Portuguese rule and was partially explored, imperfectly exploited and thinly populated. Its topography was reflected in three major socio-economic zones – the Peruvian highlands, which silver made the engine of the Spanish Empire; North East Brazil, the source of labour-intensive tropical crops worked by African slaves; and the lowlands of Southern Brazil and the River Plate, then thinly populated and the source of hides and beef. All these commodities were produced in large economic units owned – whether mines, plantations or ranches – by a creole elite and worked by an indigenous or imported labour force held in various degrees of subjugation.

The bulk of the population lived within two hundred miles of the sea – on coastal lowlands or the lower reaches of the rivers which penetrated the interior. The only exception was Upper Peru. The coastal settlements did not, however, comprise a continuous strip but a series of independent entities based on the ports through which their products were sent to the outside world via the open sea. They had little contact with their neighbours, and distance and physical barriers made overland connections tortuous. The only reliable links were by sea.

The importance of the sea to internal communications and external trade did not, however, result in the development of maritime skills nor, indeed, interest. In spite of its huge coastline, South America was a continent of miners, cattle herders and plantation workers who looked to a vast interior as the place of opportunity, and not to the sea. Fishing methods were primitive; coastal shipping was in the hands of resident Spanish or Portuguese; and the whalers which hunted the seas were British or North American. During the wars of independence, in which command of the seas was vital, the revolutionary leaders had had to recruit foreign officers and sailors to man their navies, most of them British, and many the veterans of the Napoleonic Wars.

The primary reason for this lack of interest in the sea lay in the specialized role that South America performed in the Iberian colonial systems. This was to supply Spain and Portugal with the products of mine and plantation – significantly, silver from Upper Peru and sugar from Brazil. Cotton, tobacco and cocoa were also grown, but they were economically insignificant: indeed, activity other than on the major export crops was discouraged by the authorities and of no interest to investors. Within this global system, it was the role of Spain and Portugal to provide naval protection and the ships needed both to export South American products and to supply manufactured goods and the millions of slaves needed by the plantations of Brazil. Trade was a Portuguese or Spanish monopoly; and local manufacturing was prohibited.

The Napoleonic Wars shattered the Spanish colonial system and, from Peru to the Plate, local politicians and military strong men led successful wars of independence which resulted in republican regimes of one hue or another. Brazil was different. There, the Portuguese government had moved to Rio de Janeiro during the Napoleonic Wars and when, on its return, it tried to restore Brazil to colonial status there had been widespread resistance. To save the Braganza dynasty, the Prince Regent Pedro seized the initiative and took the lead in a war which secured Brazilian independence, with himself as emperor. Thus, whereas in Spanish America the independence movement which swept away the old institutions was republican, in Brazil it was monarchical and left the machinery of government intact.

Conflict and consolidation

By 1830, independence had been won and the local elites had achieved their main objectives, which were to take political control and gain direct access to foreign markets. There were changes, but the fundamentals remained the same. British merchants and ships supplanted those of Spain and Portugal, but external trade remained in foreign hands; and although guano, nitrates, coffee and meat replaced silver and sugar, South America was still dedicated to the production of raw materials.

Alas, the economic benefits of independence were delayed for thirty years by a series of internal rebellions and external wars. The problem was that the local elites could not agree on how to convert the vague liberal ideas on which independence had been fought into concrete programmes. Urban liberals wanted a centralized state, representative government, free trade, European immigration and foreign investment. In the rural areas, however, liberalism was only skin deep: most of the population yearned for the stability of Catholic monarchy and wished to maintain traditional social and political relationships. Added to this mix was the phenomenon of the provincial strong man – the "caudillo" in Spanish America or "coronel" in Brazil – who wanted a federal system of government with a conservative and protectionist agenda and was often able, with the aid of a private army and support from Indians, peasants and the poor, to gain power.

At first the liberals were in the ascendant, but continuing instability led to more authoritarian regimes. In 1831, the caudillo Juan Manuel Rosas took power in the United Provinces (as Argentina was called) and kept it until 1852, ruling as a despot until he was overthrown by rivals backed by Brazil. In Brazil, a relaxation of central control after the abdication of Pedro I in 1831 led to a succession of regional rebellions which went on for fifteen years. Stability only returned when fourteen-year-old Pedro II was crowned emperor in 1840 and centralized power was restored. In Chile, the pattern was similar. A decade of turmoil was followed in the 1830s by an "autocratic republic" which centralized authority and brought political stability and increased trade.

There was also unfinished business from the Spanish Empire. The United Provinces was unable to control the huge area inherited from the Viceroyalty of the River Plate, and Paraguay and Upper Peru declared their independence, the former becoming the personal fiefdom of the Lopez family, the latter – which in 1774 had been detached from its natural partner, Peru – becoming Bolivia. Then there were border disputes – in 1826 between Brazil and the United Provinces, and in 1828 between Peru and Columbia. The first led to the creation of Uruguay, where political instability – combined with aggressive policies from Rosas and then from Paraguay – triggered British and French intervention in 1838 and 1845, regional conflicts in 1839, 1851 and 1863, and the disastrous War of the Triple Alliance in 1864–1870 when Brazil, Argentina and Uruguay devastated Paraguay. Meanwhile, Chile, a small, manageable country with an elongated coastline and a balanced economy based on wheat and minerals, had become a regional power. In 1836-1839, it intervened to prevent Peru from reuniting with Bolivia in a confederation; and in 1879-1883 it crushed the same foes in the War of the Pacific and annexed the provinces that contained the nitrate deposits of the Atacama Desert.

Fighting at sea or on South America's internal rivers played a major part in all of these conflicts. The importance of maritime power was clear to all, but the attitude of governments towards national navies varied. In imperial Brazil, the existence of a permanent and prestigious naval force was accepted as a necessary feature of any monarchy. Every ministry maintained it and ensured that it had the latest ships and equipment from Europe, successively introducing steam, Paixhans guns, screw propulsion and armour plate. Improved education of officers and schemes for the recruitment and training of seamen were introduced.[1] Nor was there any problem of leadership. As in other South American navies, many British officers stayed on to provide skills and experience while a new generation of nationals grew up. In Brazil, they were joined by Portuguese-born officers who had thrown in their lot with the country at the time of independence.

In republican Spanish America, the attitude to navies was different. A sense of nationhood in the new states was weak and, although the sea was important, the landowners and army officers who dominated the various governments did not give navies any priority, and were reluctant to spend scarce resources on them. At the end of a war, they were just disbanded – except for a few vessels needed for communications and surveying. Chile did this after independence in 1822 and the Confederation War in 1839. Peru did the same; as did Argentina in 1828, 1862 and even as late as 1870, after the Paraguayan War.

There was also little interest in merchant shipping. South Americans were used to the old colonial system and had no difficulty with the fact that the exports which were crucial to their prosperity were transported in foreign ships. This trade was originally carried by sail, but in the 1830s steam made its appearance. Inevitably, in view of its advanced technology and local interests, Britain took the lead. In 1839, the Pacific Steam Navigation Co. began operations in the Pacific; and in 1841, the Royal Mail Steam Packet Co. opened a service to the Caribbean. In 1846, Pacific Steam extended its routes to Panama so as to link with Royal Mail across the isthmus; and five years later, Royal Mail began operating to Rio and the River Plate.

Steamship lines were costly to operate and viable only because of government mail contracts. Carrying passengers, mail and luxuries, they made little impact on oceanic trade, which continued to be carried in sailing ships – indeed, high-bulk, low-value cargoes like copper and nitrates were transported by sail up to the First World War. But steamers showed the value of speed, fixed timetables and independence of the wind.[2] They also allowed the penetration of the great inland

---

[1] BARMAN R., *Brazil: The Forging of a Nation, 1798-1852* (Stanford, 1988), p. 131.
[2] VON SCHIRACH-SZMIGIEL C., 'Liner Shipping and General Cargo Transport' (Dissertation, Economic Research Institute, Stockholm, 1979), pp. 11-12.

rivers. Between 1845 and 1856, Paraguay, Uruguay and Argentina all confirmed free navigation on the Paraná, while Brazil did the same for the Amazon in 1867.

Intermittently, South American countries reserved the coastal trade for their own ships and offered inducements to encourage nationals to form shipping lines to replace those of locally resident foreigners. In 1835, most Chilean coasting vessels were owned by the British.[3] The policy did not work, and the number and quality of national vessels was poor. They were also unreliable, as when, in the 1849 Gold Rush, most of the Chilean merchant marine went off with lucrative cargoes to California, to be abandoned by their crews. Chile had to reopen its coastal trade to foreign shipping but continued to offer incentives to encourage a revival of local shipping. Meanwhile, Brazil's ocean-going marine shrank, since it consisted largely of slavers which were laid up when British pressure caused the trade to be suppressed in 1850.

National unity made the coasting trade a priority for Brazil, and there were enough Portuguese shipowners settled in the country to provide it. Brazilians had been using steamers since 1819, but the first serious initiative came in 1838 with the creation of a company to ply between Rio and Belem. Three years later, it extended its routes to Rio Grande do Sul. Services were not, however, regular enough and shippers applied pressure to allow them to use empty cargo space in foreign ocean-going ships traversing the east coast, instead of local carriers. In 1861, the ban on foreign vessels was accordingly lifted and Lamport and Holt eventually took over the lucrative parts of the coastal trade, leaving subsidized Brazilian firms to provide unprofitable steamer services to the north coast and up the Amazon and the Paraguay.

EXPORTS, ORDER AND PROGRESS

After 1860, the fortunes of South America were transformed. The return of stability enabled it to satisfy an apparently insatiable demand for its products. Exports boomed and the continent dedicated itself to producing valuable primary commodities. Some enjoyed a monopoly – guano in Peru, nitrates in Chile, coffee and rubber in Brazil. Coffee in particular flourished. With cheap labour and ample land for expansion, coffee exports increased six-fold, and by 1906 Brazil was producing five times as much as the rest of the world put together.[4] Profits were immense. With the taming of the pampas, beef production also soared, and the arrival of refrigeration led to the export of tons of frozen meat and helped Argentina become the world's tenth-largest economy.[5] South America benefited further when improved efficiency and industrial competition from Germany and the United States caused a fall in the price of the goods it purchased with its

---

[3] VELIZ C., História de la Marina Mercante Chilena (Santiago, 1961), pp. 55–6.
[4] TOPIK S., The World Coffee Market in the Eighteenth And Nineteenth Centuries, from Colonial to National Regimes (Working Paper no. 4, University of California, Irvine, 2004), pp. 20, 22.
[5] LEWIS C., A Short History of Argentina (Oxford, 2002), p. 1.

export earnings. Meanwhile, Brazil, Argentina and Chile were producing even more by opening new territories for exploitation and settlement, crushing any resistance from indigenous peoples.

Developments in transport improved the position further. In the 1850s, railway lines proliferated, extending the coffee-growing and cattle-raising areas, linking them to ports and meat-packing plants and lowering costs. Advances in maritime engineering led to a steady fall in tariffs.[6] Screw propellers and compound engines made ships faster and more economical, while steel construction enabled size and cargo capacity to increase. By 1870 freight rates from Europe were 40% of their 1820 figure.[7] Britain dominated: by the 1850s it owned half of the world's shipping, and by the 1880s its steam tonnage exceeded that of sail.[8] In 1864, Pacific Steam opened a route to Europe around Cape Horn; while the Liverpool, Brazil and River Plate Steamship Co. (better known as Lamport and Holt) extended its operations to Rio, Montevideo and Buenos Aires. The two firms achieved a dominant position in both the oceanic and coastal trades and ruthlessly drove competition to the wall.

As its economy boomed, so South America was transformed. Roads, railways, telegraph lines and steamships linked distant provinces. Cities like Buenos Aires and Rio were redeveloped with boulevards and public buildings; cultural and scientific institutions; and gas, sanitation and electricity. Trade brought huge increases in government revenues, largely due to rising customs duties, which provided an average of 70% of the total revenues between 1850 and 1872.[9] Governments grew richer and stronger, using the money to develop public works, education and the apparatus of the state. A side-effect of raising import duties to increase revenues was that it gave protection to local industries and enabled them to grow. This was, however, an accident: South American governments were not pro-business and were principally concerned with expanding the production of the export commodities which generated so much prosperity.

Development in South American countries was, however, uneven, and economic rankings reflected distance from the sea. Those bordering the Atlantic like Argentina and Uruguay, with navigable rivers and good harbours, formed the top group; southeast Brazil the second; Chile and Peru, round Cape Horn, came next; while landlocked Bolivia and Paraguay came last.[10] In thinly populated Argentina and in Brazil, where slavery was declining as an economic and politically acceptable source of labour and was abolished in 1888, the problem was

---

[6] HARLEY C., 'Ocean freight rates and productivity, 1740-1913,' *Journal of Economic History* 48 (1988), 851-76.
[7] DE LA ESCOSURA L., 'The Economic Consequences of Independence in Latin America', *Cambridge Economic History of Latin America*, ed. V. BULMER-THOMAS, J. COATSWORTH and R. CORTES-CONDE, vol. I, p. 488.
[8] VON SCHIRACH-SZMIGIEL, 'Liner Shipping and General Cargo Transport', p. 13.
[9] CENTENO M., 'Blood and debt: war and taxation in 19th century Latin America', *American Journal of Sociology* 102 (1997), 1579.
[10] BÉRTOLA L. and WILLIAMSON J., 'Globalization in Latin America before 1940', in *Cambridge Economic History of Latin America*, vol. II, p. 15.

not access but a manpower shortage. The answer lay in immigration. Between 1881 and 1930, immigrant ships carried over eight million Italian, Spanish, German and French migrants to Brazil, Uruguay and Argentina, changing the racial balance of the first and the urban and social landscape of the last. Unable to settle on the land, most went to the cities to man the new factories. Meanwhile, a discontented industrial and commercial elite and an urban middle class had developed. While the old system continued to produce wealth, the landowners and rural political bosses who ran it were able to maintain their positions; but as commodity prices fell and industrialization increased, the strains on the social fabric mounted. By 1914, they had become intolerable.

Dependence on a narrow range of exports made South America vulnerable to falls in world prices and to cycles of boom and bust; while reliance on imported manufactures led to crippling foreign loans when income fell. Likewise, although the flood of investment was beneficial, it put the ownership of large parts of the economy – like mines, nitrates, railways and meat packing – in foreign hands. Little investment in manufacturing or shipping came from local sources. South Americans preferred to spend their profits on expanding existing commodity production, and not on diversification.

Merchant Shipping and the Naval Race

The post-1860 period saw a growing interest in shipping, largely in Brazil and Chile. Bolivia was landlocked and crippled by the war in the Pacific. Peru was in decline following the end of the guano boom and the loss of its nitrates. Argentina, which was busy extending its frontiers, left oceanic trade to foreigners and neglected coastal shipping. Its push to Patagonia was done by land and supported by railways, not by ships. Only river transport up the Paraná was developed to provide access to territories ceded after the Paraguayan War.

Various governments tried unsuccessfully to challenge Britain's grip on oceanic shipping. Even in Brazil, where, by 1889, local steamship lines were running services to all major ports and riverine cities, the export trade was still dominated by British carriers. By then, however, the United States had become the main market for coffee, and an American shipping line was formed to exploit the situation. The Brazilian government, increasingly resentful of the British position, awarded a subsidy, but the new line could not compete with Lamport and Holt's interlocking interests and went out of business in 1893.

Republican Brazil restored the national monopoly of the coastal trade and backed the ambitions of a new company called Lloyd Brasileiro. Unfortunately, the government saw it as a prestige symbol and a source of political patronage and constantly interfered in its management. It frustrated plans for a profitable direct service to New York by insisting on calls at all major Brazilian ports *en route*, and forced the company to keep cargo rates unprofitably low. With income cut further by a price war between Hamburg-America and Lamport and Holt, by 1914 Lloyd Brasileiro was bankrupt.

In Chile, a silver boom funded a rash of local companies, the most significant of which was the Compañia Sud Americana de Vapores. It incurred the wrath of Pacific Steam, then the largest shipping company in the world,[11] but survived by signing a one-sided agreement with that company, which was increasingly worried by international competition. This was growing, and by 1872 six companies were operating on the Pacific coast, although none could rival Pacific Steam's fifty-six steamers – or even Sud Americana's ten.

After 1882, relations were still bad, but Sud Americana was given a lifeline in the form of a subsidy from the Chilean government, which suspected Pacific Steam of Peruvian sympathies in the Pacific War and wanted to reward Sud Americana for its help. But there were commercial set-backs, earthquakes in Chile and competition from Kosmos and a newly created Peruvian line. In 1910, Sud Americana almost went into liquidation, but was saved again when investments rose as the benefits of the imminent opening of the Panama Canal began to be appreciated.

Growing national consciousness after 1860 was accompanied by a conviction that navies were necessary for defence and security. Brazil had already learnt that only a navy could ensure national unity; and Chile was stirred into action when a Spanish clash with Peru in 1863–1865 led to the bombardment of Valparaiso. It was also clear that the sophistication of ships and tactics meant that navies had to be modern and professional. In Chile, Peru and Argentina institutions to train officers and seamen were created or overhauled. Dockyards were expanded – Brazil even developed a shipbuilding capability in iron and steel. In the 1870s, Argentina's still riverine navy was modernized with monitors and gunboats; and Chile and Peru, with revenues from minerals and guano, bought British-built ironclads – although after the war in the Pacific, Peru could afford only gunboats. Chile, however, expanded further, buying cruisers, torpedo gunboats and, in 1890, a battleship.

As Britain was the major source of warships and the leading naval power, South American navies emulated the practices of the Royal Navy and adopted British-style naval uniforms – just as their armies wore French uniforms until 1870 and German thereafter. They did not, however, follow Britain in terms of political neutrality. Navies in South America were more aristocratic than the predominantly middle-class armies and began to intervene on the conservative side. The Brazilian navy had been loyal during the Empire, but mounted two pro-monarchical revolts after the creation of the Republic in 1889; and the Chilean navy overthrew a radical president in 1891. After 1918, when society started to fragment, the armed forces began to intervene more regularly in their supposed role as guardians of the *patria*.

There were no South American wars after 1883, but there were clashes

[11] DE LA PEDRAJA R., *Oil and Coffee: Latin American Merchant shipping from the Imperial Era to the 1950s* (Westport, 1998), p. 18.

between Argentina and Chile in the 1870s as they pushed south into Patagonia. Argentina now had a sea-going navy and the two countries became locked in an arms race. Backed by ample revenues, they leap-frogged each other as they acquired progressively bigger warships until 1901, when Argentina ordered heavy cruisers from Italy and the Chileans battleships from Britain. International pressure then called a halt.

During the last years of the empire, the Brazilian navy continued to grow until it became the fifth-largest in the world and had the most powerful battleships in South America.[12] After the naval revolts of the 1890s, however, the republican government halted any expansion. But by 1900, politicians were alarmed by the growing strength of Argentina and were anxious to establish their country as a world power. In 1905, therefore, with coffee and rubber exports booming, Brazil ordered two dreadnoughts from Britain – with the possibility of a third – and triggered another naval race.[13] Argentina responded by ordering two dreadnoughts from the United States, and Chile followed with an order of two from Britain. Even Peru joined in, with two British-built cruisers and two French submarines. The cost of these ships, and of their accompanying destroyers, was colossal. Eventually, a fall in commodity prices and the realization that the race was taking a quarter of each country's national income[14] brought it to an end. In 1914, the battleships nearing completion in Britain were acquired by the Royal Navy.

Epilogue

The export orientation which dominated South America in the 19th century was little different to the system which had operated under Portuguese and Spanish colonial rule. Yet no one complained: indeed, the material progress it generated seemed to justify it. The landowners and merchants grew richer, government revenue and expenditure expanded and overseas investment soared, enabling the taming of the pampas, the development of mining and food processing and the creation of public utilities and the railways.

The sea and maritime affairs played a crucial role in this scenario, yet South Americans did not share the usual ideas on the subject – namely, that the sea was the route to national prosperity through commerce; that the resulting trade should be carried in national ships; and that a major job of navies was to protect it. They were content that their trade was carried in foreign vessels, and that the role of their navies was not commerce protection but the achievement of occasional military objectives. It was the development of a sense of nationhood

---

[12] PARKINSON R., *The Late Victorian Navy: The Pre-Dreadnought Era and the Origins of the First World War* (Woodbridge, 2008), p. 128.
[13] SONDHAUS L., *Naval Warfare 1815–1914* (London, 2001), p. 216.
[14] MASSIE R., *Castles of Steel; Britain, Germany and the Winning of the First World War* (London, 2003), p. 22.

after 1860 that caused navies to be seen as necessary attributes of the state, and burgeoning exports enabled them to be paid for.

Government attempts to stimulate local shipping by excluding foreign vessels from the coastal trade met with little success. Competition was intense, local elites preferred to invest in more lucrative fields than ships and those that did could be deflected by any chance to make more money – as in the California Gold Rush. Attempts were also frustrated by foreign residents who re-registered their ships in the names of local relatives or employees, and by shippers who believed that only foreign firms had the competence to handle profitable cargoes and that national firms with exclusive rights would become expensive monopolies.[15] With the arrival of steam the problem became worse. In Chile, foreign ownership was greater in 1875 than in 1835.[16] The shortage of maritime skills also continued to be a handicap. In 1835 and 1854, 90% of Chilean ships had foreign officers and crews – mostly British. And in the 1880s all the officers even of Sud Americana ships were British. When the company felt obliged to replace them, it had to recruit US citizens, as few Chileans were available. The extent of the problem can be seen in the percentages of officers and men on national ships which local law required to be citizens. In Chile in 1837, it was 25%. By 1892, it had risen only to one officer and 75% of the crew. An Argentine law of 1910 showed a worse situation, with a requirement of 33%. And only in 1930 was Brazil able to restrict command of its ships to nationals.

Lack of investment also hampered the growth of local oceanic shipping, but the major obstacle was the stranglehold of existing British and American lines. Competition was fierce, especially after falling freight rates and reduced profits led to global price wars. The extension of the "Conference System" – a cartel of established shipowners designed to fix prices and exclude outsiders – to South America in the 1890s added to the problem.

South America had little military involvement in the 1914-1918 war, but the conflict shattered the economic system on which its prosperity depended. Exports collapsed as European ships were redeployed to war duties and disappeared, and although Lloyd Brasileiro, Sud Americana and the Peruvian line revived, they were unable to fill the gap. Their recovery was only temporary: they remained inefficient and subject to political interference. The renewal of coastal trade restrictions after the war helped, but low rates and a decline in cargoes after the 1929 economic crash prevented any serious recovery.

The war saw the end of British supremacy in the South Atlantic – and competition ensured that it was never regained. The opening of the Panama Canal in 1914 had a similar effect in the Pacific. The United States now became the principal – and nearest – trading partner of Chile and Peru, and it was the American Grace Line which dominated the seas, and not Pacific Steam.

The First World War also initiated wider economic changes. Foreign

---

[15] McGARRY J., *Ploughing the South Seas A History of Merchant Shipping on the West Coast of South America* (Milton Keynes, 2006), pp. 217-20.
[16] *Ibid.*, p. 155.

investment came to a standstill and manufactured goods became unavailable, thus stimulating local production. More significantly, the conflict, and the depression which followed, initiated a steep decline in world demand for primary commodities and in the profits which had previously funded the continent's prosperity. Within a decade, the export orientation which had been the defining feature of South America in the 19th century had disappeared forever.

The Sea and the American Civil War

CRAIG L. SYMONDS is Professor Emeritus, US Naval Academy, United States

ABSTRACT. *The U.S. Civil War was a land war, but the Confederate States depended on overseas trade for their livelihood and military supplies, so that the Federal blockade became an essential instrument of victory. So did inland fighting along the great rivers which opened the interior of the Continent.*

RÉSUMÉ. *La guerre de sécession fut une guerre au sol mais les États confédérés dépendaient du commerce extérieur pour leur subsistance et leur approvisionnement militaire. Ainsi, le blocus fédéral devint un instrument essentiel à la victoire, tout comme les combats intérieurs le long des fleuves qui ouvrirent l'accès à l'intérieur du continent.*

⋅•⋅

At its core, the American Civil War was a land conflict. More than three million men (and a handful of women) fought for four years along a thousand-mile front, and more than seven hundred thousand of them died either of battlefield wounds or (more often) of disease. The national government won the war and preserved the union because the northern public proved willing to sustain the Lincoln administration through four long years of bloodshed and sacrifice, and the South lost it because it could not match northern superiority in either manpower or industrial production. Nevertheless, sea forces played an important role in the conflict, and helped to determine both the trajectory and, very likely, the length of the war. Moreover, the two sides embraced dramatically different conceptions of the role that sea forces could or should play in the war, conceptions that were the product of divergent cultures and economies.

From the beginning, a significant part of the economy of the British colonies in New England and New York had derived from maritime activities – fishing, whaling, and of course trade – and this sea-based economy continued after independence was secured in 1783. For a time, the southern states, too, maintained a symbiotic relationship with the sea. From the Potomac River in Virginia to the Rio Grande in Texas, the southern coastline was more than 3,500 miles long, and included both the commodious sounds of the Carolinas as well as scores of natural harbors. Along the Atlantic seaboard, the rivers that flowed across the Piedmont and Tidewater from the Appalachian Mountains to the Atlantic, combined with the natural waterway along the coast created by the offshore islands, meant that most of the commerce in the southern states moved by water. The navigable Mississippi River drained a continent and debouched into the Gulf of Mexico below the thriving port of New Orleans. Nor was the South poor in the raw materials essential to maritime enterprise. The wood of Georgia live oak trees was greatly prized both for its density and for its irregular shape that made it particularly useful for the knees of sailing ships. The tall pines and firs of the Carolinas made excellent masts, and the southern states also produced the tar, pitch, turpentine, and hemp essential to a thriving maritime industry. Indeed, given its geography and resources, the South might have been expected to continue to develop as a maritime power. Instead, after 1830 southerners effectively turned their backs on the sea in order to pursue the far greater profits to be found in the cultivation of cotton.

When the United States secured its independence, chattel slavery existed in all thirteen states, though it had never been as profitable or as widespread in the North as in the South. Because the North's dependence on slavery was far weaker, the impact of Enlightenment thinking about human rights was more compelling there, and one by one the northern states abolished slavery, until it existed only in the South. Slavery might have died out there, too, but for the cotton gin. That invention made it possible for southerners to grow and market not only the long-staple cotton that grew on the offshore islands of Georgia and South Carolina, but also the short-staple boll cotton that grew inland. This created a virtual economic revolution in the South. The potential profit from this cash crop was so great that the southern economy became unidimensional, as banking, commerce, and trade were all subordinated to a cotton-centric economy. In this case, at least, culture and economics trumped geography and resources. It also breathed new life into the slave-labor system.

Southerners who profited from the system convinced themselves that it was not only more efficient than what they derisively called "wage slavery" in the North and in Europe, but also that it was more humane – that they were doing their chattels a service by ensuring lifetime employment with guaranteed shelter and sustenance, even free medical care. This self-justifying philosophy, combined with the lure of unprecedented profits, directed the attention of most southerners inland: westward toward the fecund lands of Mississippi, Alabama, and east Texas, rather than outward, toward the sea.

Even as the South wed itself to chattel slavery, a movement to abolish or at least to limit the expansion of this labor system took root in the North. In the midst of the ensuing sectional dispute, southern champions of slavery became defensive and distrustful, convinced that any restriction of slavery would put it on a course of ultimate extinction. When in 1860 Abraham Lincoln was elected president on a platform of stopping the expansion of slavery entirely, seven southern states declared their separation from the union and formed their own pro-slavery government. Once it became clear that Lincoln intended to use force to compel their continued adherence to the union, four more southern states joined the separatist Confederacy.

In the conflict thus begun, the maritime tradition of the northern states, in combination with the absence of any serious commitment to the sea by the southern states, gave the North overwhelming naval superiority. Only one U.S. Navy warship – the steam frigate USS *Merrimack* – ended up in southern hands, and that was because it was undergoing repair in a southern port when the war started. The South acquired a few revenue cutters (part of the Treasury Department), but for all practical purposes it began the war with no navy at all. This caused southern leaders few qualms, however, for they did not believe that naval forces would be decisive or even particularly important in the war. Just as southerners had looked inland for economic success before the war, so, too, did they plan to defend their proclaimed independence with land armies, relying on shore fortifications to protect their rivers and sea coast.

Though southerners asserted that they could win their independence unaided, they looked to Europe – and especially to Britain and France – both for material assistance and for the kind of diplomatic recognition that would validate their claim to sovereignty. In conformance with this ambition, Confederate leaders sought to convince the British, who had abolished slavery in their empire three decades earlier, that the objective of the war was southern self-government, and not the defense of slavery. To emphasize the trade advantages that would redound to Britain from a divided America, the Confederacy decided early on to embargo its own cotton, convinced that the resulting shortage would compel the British to intervene in the war to get it. Instead, Britain found other sources for cotton in India and Egypt.

Though British leaders recognized potential diplomatic and economic opportunity in the American schism, the only moment when British intervention became a serious possibility was in the late fall of 1862, during the so-called *Trent* Affair. On 8 November of that year, a mercurial U.S. Navy captain named Charles Wilkes stopped the British mail packet *Trent* off the north coast of Cuba and forcibly removed four men: the Confederate ministers to Britain and France and their two secretaries. Wilkes' patently illegal act was hugely popular in America, but Lincoln recognized at once that it seriously endangered Anglo-American relations. In the event, war was avoided when Lincoln agreed to release the four men, though he did so in such a way as to make it appear that Britain had accepted an American interpretation of neutral rights.

The very first strategic decision Lincoln made once the war began was to declare a naval blockade of the southern coast. Historians have often presented this decision as part of a grand scheme devised by Lieutenant General Winfield Scott for the suppression of the rebellion. Besides a blockade, the other key elements of this strategic blueprint were a holding action in Virginia to prevent southern armies from taking the initiative, and a combined army–navy campaign to secure the Mississippi River Valley, thus sundering the Confederacy not quite in half. Critics who believed this too passive derisively likened it to an Anaconda, the South American reptile that slowly strangled its prey, and the "Anaconda Plan" it has been labeled ever since.

Measured either by the number of ships involved or the amount of money spent, the blockade of the South was the single largest undertaking of the U.S. Navy during the Civil War. A blockade was (and is) an act of war, and some of Lincoln's advisors feared that his proclamation effectively conceded belligerent status to the Confederacy. That ran up against Lincoln's official insistence that the Confederacy was not a nation, or even a belligerent power, but simply a group of rebels in arms. Secretary of State William H. Seward was especially concerned that Britain, France, and the other major powers of Europe would seize upon Lincoln's blockade proclamation to confer recognition on the Confederate government.

Seward's fears were partially justified. Britain did recognize the Confederacy as a belligerent, but did so in the context of acknowledging the Union blockade, and that proved to be a victory for Lincoln's policy. Determined to do nothing that would weaken the laws of blockade on which Britain had relied for more than two centuries, the British government accepted Lincoln's blockade proclamation at face value, even though the U.S. Navy warships necessary to enforce it did not yet exist. Moreover, by accepting the obligations of a neutral, Britain closed its ports to the warships of both sides. Most European powers followed suit, and the practical result was that the Confederacy was denied access to important ports in the Caribbean and elsewhere. Despite Seward's blustering, Britain's neutrality announcement hurt the Confederacy far more than it did the Union.

To make the blockade effective, the national government sought to expand the U.S. Navy to unprecedented size. International law held that for a blockade to be binding on neutrals, the declaring power had to maintain a naval force offshore sufficient to deter trade, and it was self-evident that the U.S. Navy, which consisted of some forty-two active service warships, could not blockade a coastline of 3,500 miles. To fulfill the president's declared intent, therefore, the U.S. Navy had to expand exponentially to five, ten, even fifteen times its pre-war strength.

It did so largely by converting existing merchant ships into ersatz warships. The middle of the 19th century was very nearly the last moment in history when such a transformation was possible, since it involved little more than strengthening the decks of steam-powered merchantmen to allow them to bear the weight of naval ordnance, and constructing a magazine below the waterline. Before the end of the war, the northern states converted no fewer than 418 vessels into warships. In one exceptional case, the merchant steamer *Monticello* was transformed in less than twenty-four hours. The United States also built entirely new warships, and its mature maritime infrastructure allowed it to construct hundreds of them relatively quickly, completing twenty-three new ocean-going, steam-powered gunboats in the first ninety days after the first shot of the war was fired in Charleston Harbor.

Of course, the government also had to supply and sustain these ships off a hostile coast for an extended period. Horatio Nelson had famously maintained a blockade of Toulon for nearly two years during the Napoleonic Wars, but the technology of naval warfare had changed since then. The steam-powered warships of the Union's blockading squadrons needed to re-coal frequently, and to do that the U.S. government sought to seize and hold a number of supply bases along the enemy coast. The first, and in many ways the most important, of these was Port Royal, South Carolina.

On 7 November 1861, a squadron of eight U.S. Navy steam warships (and one sailing ship under tow) entered Port Royal Sound and battered the Confederate forts there into submission. This not only provided the South Atlantic Blockading Squadron with an important supply base, it demonstrated in a dramatic way the new relationship between guns afloat and guns ashore. Until the American Civil War, conventional wisdom was that forts were innately superior to ships; only a foolish or a desperate captain would pit his wooden-hulled vessel against a shore fortification. The Union seizure of Port Royal demonstrated that assumptions about the superiority of shore fortifications were, at best, uncertain.

An appreciation of this led the separatist Confederates to pull back even more from the sea. Confederate Major General Robert E. Lee, who was present in South Carolina to witness the fall of Port Royal, recommended to Confederate President Jefferson Davis that the South should no longer even attempt to defend its coastline. Except for a handful of seaports needed for the blockade-running trade, where geography made them defensible, the Confederacy effectively abandoned its coastline. For the rest of the war, the Confederacy energetically defended only a half-dozen places: Galveston, Texas; New Orleans, Louisiana; Mobile, Alabama; Savannah, Georgia; Charleston, South Carolina; and Wilmington, North Carolina. Over the ensuing months and years, the Union Navy gradually occupied most of the rest of the southern coastline, which not only crippled the coastwise trade, it also undercut southern claims of sovereignty. In the end, Union forces also seized most of the well-defended sites as well, including New Orleans, which fell in April of 1862, effectively closing the Mississippi River.

Both at the time and later, critics pointed out that the Union blockade of the Confederacy was never fully effective; until the very last days of the war, blockade-running vessels managed to slip in and out of southern ports. Yet the blockade did have a significant impact on the course of the war, including a long-term crippling effect on the southern economy. While many of the ships that sought to run through the blockade did so successfully, the total number of vessels entering or departing southern ports declined by as much as 90 percent. It is difficult to ascertain the precise impact of such a reduction, but anecdotal evidence suggests that the blockade weakened the southern economy, contributed to inflation, depressed civilian morale, and encouraged desertion among southern soldiers who abandoned the army to go home and care for their suffering families. Then, too, the blockade effectively isolated the Confederacy not only physically and economically, but also diplomatically. In effect, the northern blockade of the South served to contain the war to the North American continent and helped to ensure that it remained a civil war rather than an international one.

One particularly noteworthy aspect of the American Civil War was that it took place in the immediate wake of a virtual technological revolution. Steam-powered warships had been common in the navies of the European powers for several decades, but the U.S. Navy had clung to sail power well into the 1850s, partly because the United States lacked any overseas bases where coal-burning warships could re-fuel. (America's first overseas possession was the tiny Pacific atoll of Midway, acquired in 1867.) Nevertheless, in the half-decade before the Civil War, the United States embarked on a program to build several new classes of steam-powered warships. This was not done in anticipation of looming war, but simply because the older sailing ships had become notoriously obsolete. As a result, while the U.S. Navy in 1861 remained relatively small by European standards, it boasted two dozen modern steam warships, which made it quite robust by American standards.

Besides steam, another aspect of the technological revolution was the increased size and accuracy of naval guns, evidenced by the easy victory of the Union squadron at Port Royal. For centuries, western navies had relied on cast-iron smoothbore gun tubes that fired solid shot ranging in size from three to sixty-four pounds. In the 19th century, improvements in metallurgy allowed naval guns to become much larger so that they were often categorized by the diameter of their muzzles (e.g. eight inches) rather than by the weight of the shot (e.g. twenty-four-pounders). Then, too, many of the new heavy guns were rifled, which dramatically increased both their range and their accuracy, and they were capable of firing explosive shells as well as solid shot. All of these changes preceded the American Civil War, but the Civil War provided a kind of testing ground for the new generation of naval weaponry.

A third innovation that met its trial by fire during the Civil War was iron armor. Here, too, European navies had led the way. The French had commissioned the *Gloire* in 1859, and the British commissioned the *Warrior* a year later. Still, it was in the Civil War that iron-armored ships first fought one another in battle.

It is often the weaker naval power that proves most willing to experiment with cutting-edge weaponry, and from the first days of the war, the Confederate Secretary of the Navy, Stephen Mallory, had sought to acquire an armored warship. He even proposed buying the *Gloire* from the French, though the French turned him down. In the end, Mallory embraced the proposal of William P. Williamson to convert the wooden steam frigate USS *Merrimack*, abandoned in Portsmouth Navy Yard when Virginia seceded, into an ironclad. This vessel, christened the CSS *Virginia* (though often still referred to as the *Merrimack* in modern histories), was essentially an iron-sheathed wooden casemate built atop a wooden hull. Far more creative was the Union response to this threat: a much smaller iron vessel designed by the Swedish immigrant John Ericsson. The hull of this ship, subsequently christened the *Monitor*, was mostly below the waterline, with only a few inches of exposed freeboard. In the middle of its flat deck was a twenty-one-foot rotating iron cylinder made of nine layers of one-inch curved iron plate, and inside this turret were two 11-inch guns.

These two armored vessels met one another in Hampton Roads, Virginia, on 9 March 1862, and fought to a tactical draw in the most famous naval engagement of the war. The real watershed, however, was the confrontation that took place the day before, when the *Virginia* sank two wooden sailing warships, the *Cumberland* and the *Congress*, thus inflicting on the U.S. Navy the worst defeat in its history until the Japanese attack on Pearl Harbor in 1941.

Other nations took note. The British, who had launched the partially-armored *Warrior* two years before, remained publicly skeptical that the revolutionary design of the *Monitor* posed a significant threat. The British First Lord of the Admiralty famously mocked the *Monitor* in the House of Lords as "something between a raft and a diving bell." At least some of this professed unconcern was whistling in the dark, for as the London *Times* noted, the Royal Navy possessed "but two vessels that could be relied upon to meet such a ship." If nothing else, this first clash of ironclads cast doubt on the ability of the Royal Navy's fleet of conventional ships-of-the-line to establish and maintain a blockade of a coastline defended by ironclads. Though Royal Navy experts did not believe that the North's monitors could challenge Britain for command of the sea, the London *Times* acknowledged that their prowess as coastal and harbor defense vessels rendered "the Americans practically unassailable in their own waters."

Encouraged by the initial success of the *Merrimack/Virginia*, the Confederacy began work on more than fifty ironclads, though only about a third of them were ever completed. All of them were of the casemate design, conscious clones of the original. This was due less to a faith in the superiority of that design than to the South's inability to produce curved iron plate. Indeed, a shortage of iron plate of any kind, plus the inability to fabricate marine engines, created significant construction bottlenecks for the Confederacy. Marine engines had to be brought in from Europe through the increasingly effective blockade or, more often, cannibalized from existing ships, which meant that even when the Confederacy completed an ironclad warship it was almost certainly severely underpowered.

The Confederates embraced other maritime innovations, including mines (called torpedoes), David boats (essentially early PT boats), and even an operational submarine, the *H.L. Hunley*, which sank the USS *Housatonic* off Charleston on 17 February 1864, though the *Hunley* did not survive the sortie. Like the *Virginia*, each of these innovations proved dramatically successful when first introduced, yet none of them changed the existing maritime balance of power because the South could not produce them in numbers. The North could – and did, building more than sixty ironclad warships, most of them of the monitor type, with each successive class larger than the one before.

The guns, too, became larger and much more powerful during the war. The original *Monitor* carried two 11-inch guns. Succeeding classes carried 12-inch, and then 15-inch guns. The *Miantonomah*-class monitors, built toward the end of the war, were 260 feet long, displaced 3,400 tons, and had two rotating turrets, each of which housed two 15-inch guns. The United States even manufactured a 20-inch naval gun, though it was never deployed. The South struggled to keep up and continued to innovate. John Mercer Brooke produced effective 6.4-inch and 7-inch rifled artillery pieces that proved especially effective, but even when the

South successfully innovated, it was the North that most effectively exploited and expanded on the innovation.

The Union Navy also played a critical role in the campaigns on America's western rivers. Whereas the rivers in the Eastern Theater of war all ran west to east (horizontally as viewed on a map) and thus acted as barriers to any military advance, rivers in the West mostly flowed vertically – either north to south like the Mississippi, or south to north like the Tennessee and the Cumberland. As a result, these rivers served not as barriers to be defended, but as potential avenues for a military advance. Both sides knew that whoever commanded the rivers had a tremendous strategic advantage in this vital theater.

As in the salt-water war, the Union had the benefit of possessing an industrial base that allowed it to produce more and better warships for use in the river war. Months before the transformation of the USS *Merrimack* into the CSS *Virginia* or the construction of the USS *Monitor*, the Union salvage expert James Buchanan Eads of St. Louis began to build a flotilla of armor-plated and powerfully armed river gunboats. Though their armor was thinner than the heavy shields on either the *Monitor* or *Virginia*, their broad beam and flat bottom enabled them to maneuver in remarkably shallow water. Union Major General William T. Sherman is said to have remarked admiringly that they could navigate in a heavy dew.

The South, too, initiated an ironclad building program for the western rivers, laying down two big ironclads at New Orleans at the southern end of the Mississippi, and two more 360 miles to the north at Memphis. Once again, however, the South's inferior industrial base, and the early Union conquest of both Memphis and New Orleans, derailed this effort. Only one of the four ironclads was ever completed (the CSS *Arkansas*), and for the most part, the South had to depend on shore fortifications in a vain effort to prevent Union armies from using the rivers as avenues of advance.

One milestone event in the river war took place in April of 1862, when U.S. Navy Flag Officer David Glasgow Farragut, who was destined to become America's first admiral, ran his ocean-going wooden-hulled warships up from the mouth of the Mississippi past the Confederate forts that had been built to protect the city of New Orleans from a naval assault. Easily dispatching the small squadron of Confederate gunboats that came out to contest their passage, Farragut's ships steamed up to New Orleans, anchored off the city, and demanded its surrender. Having counted on the forts to thwart the Union Navy, Confederate authorities had little option but to capitulate. New Orleans was the largest city in the Confederacy and its most important seaport, and its fall so early in the war was a tremendous blow to southern hopes.

After that, the Confederate citadel of Vicksburg, Mississippi, located on a high bluff on the eastern bank of the river, became the buckle on the strap that held the two halves of the Confederacy together. The key to the eventual Union capture of this strong point was the cooperation of Union Army and Navy commanders. In April of 1863, a full year after Farragut ran past the forts below New Orleans, Rear Admiral David Dixon Porter ran his river squadron past the

Vicksburg Batteries. That enabled him to escort the army of Major General Ulysses S. Grant across the river so that it could assail Vicksburg from the east. After several fierce battles, and a forty-seven-day siege, Vicksburg fell to Grant's army on 4 July 1863. Neither the Union Army nor Navy could have achieved this victory by itself, but working together they proved irresistible. It was a case of the whole being greater than the sum of the parts.

Cooperation proved essential, too, in the Union effort to close down the last of the Confederate ports along the Atlantic coast: Charleston, Mobile, and Wilmington. At each of these places, effective cooperation proved both essential and occasionally elusive. Where the army and navy commanders sought to compete with one another, as they did at Charleston, South Carolina and Wilmington, North Carolina, it caused delays and frustration. When they were able to work together, success came more quickly.

The Union assault on Mobile was also a joint operation, though the city was effectively neutralized as a haven for blockade runners when Farragut ran his squadron past the defending forts and into the bay in August of 1864. In the midst of that maneuver, Farragut's lead ironclad, the *Tecumseh*, hit a mine and went down in just a few seconds with ninety-three crewmen still on board, thus proving that the big ironclads were not invulnerable after all. The captain of the USS *Brooklyn*, just ahead of Farragut's flagship, called out to the admiral that the Confederates had sown mines, or torpedoes, in the channel. Unwilling to stop in the midst of his assault, Farragut supposedly exclaimed "Damn the torpedoes," and continued successfully into the bay.

As weaker naval powers had done since the 16th century, the Confederacy turned to commerce raiding as a cheap and effective way of assailing the maritime economy of the Union. *Guerre de course* had been a principal strategy of the United States in both of its wars with Britain, and Confederates believed it would hurt the Yankees where they were most sensitive – in their pocketbooks. Initially, Confederate President Jefferson Davis hoped to accomplish this by issuing letters of marque to southern privateers. But the Confederate experiment with privateering was short lived, largely because the combination of the Union blockade and the British declaration of neutrality closed off most of the ports where prizes might be sent for adjudication and condemnation. Without the opportunity to make a profit, the whole *raison d'être* for privateering disappeared. Would-be privateers turned instead to blockade running, which was both more profitable and less dangerous.

Unable to rely on privateers, the Confederacy assigned the *guerre de course* mission to a handful of Confederate Navy warships, most of them built in England and manned by international crews. There was more than a bit of subterfuge involved in this enterprise. Though it was an open secret that several of the ships being constructed in the Birkenhead shipyard on the Mersey River opposite Liverpool were intended for the Confederacy, the builders professed a guileless innocence. After the war, the British agreed to accept arbitration to assess their culpability for the damage wrought by these raiders, and in 1872 Britain paid the United States $15.5 million in damages.

Confederates were less successful in their effort to obtain French-built warships. They had failed to convince the French to sell the *Gloire* in 1861, though two years later a French company in Bordeaux laid down two powerful ironclad rams that were intended for the Confederacy. As in Britain, the builders invented a cover story that the ships were being built for a different power, in this case Egypt. In February of 1864, however, the French government stopped delivery of the ships, though one of them, subsequently named the CSS *Stonewall*, was surreptitiously sold to the Confederates anyway and got as far as Cuba before the war ended.

The best-known and most successful of all the European-built Confederate warships ships was the CSS *Alabama*, commanded by Captain Raphael Semmes. Over the course of two years (July 1862–June 1864) Semmes and the *Alabama* captured and burned no fewer than sixty-four Union merchant ships, and sunk one Union warship, the USS *Hatteras*. Altogether, Confederate commerce raiders destroyed 284 Union merchant ships. Such losses created a near panic among the merchants of northern cities, especially New York. Maritime insurance rates skyrocketed, and many ship owners re-registered their vessels under foreign flags. In the fall of 1863, an observer in New York noted that of 176 merchant ships then in the harbor, only nineteen flew the U.S. flag. Whereas in 1860 U.S. merchant ships had carried 2.2 million tons of cargo in and out of American ports, by 1865 that number had shrunk to under half a million. Some scholars have cited this as the origin of a century-long contraction of the American merchant marine, yet the re-flagging of U.S. ships during the war was more a gambit of convenience, and the gradual reduction of the American carrying trade in the late 19th and early 20th centuries was the result of a variety of factors.

Northern merchants pressed the administration to do something about these "Anglo-Rebel pirates," as they were labeled in northern newspapers. The New York Chamber of Commerce wanted Union Navy Secretary Gideon Welles to establish convoys to protect American shipping. Convoys might well have worked, but the concept was unpopular with professional navy men (as it was when the Germans employed *guerre de course* against the British in both world wars), and Welles rejected the idea. He could not inaugurate a convoy system without weakening the blockade, which he considered more important. Instead, he sent out fast, heavily armed ships to try to hunt down the raiders. Mostly this proved frustrating and ineffectual, for by the time a cruiser responded to a reported sighting, the commerce raider had moved on.

These circumstances contributed to the authorization of a new, experimental class of United States warship in 1863, the lead vessel of which was the USS *Wampanoag*. Launched in December of 1864, the *Wampanoag* was nearly as revolutionary as the *Monitor*. Designed for speed, she set a world record of 17.4 knots on her trials (though the numbers may have been fudged). She was also heavily armed with ten 8-inch guns, plus a mixed battery of smaller guns. She was designed to catch and destroy rebel raiders like the *Alabama*, and some

U.S. Navy men also conceived of her as the kind of vessel that could savage British commerce, or even assail the British coast, in the event of a third Anglo-American naval conflict. Before the *Wampanoag* and her planned sister ships were commissioned, however, the war ended, and with it the need to pursue commerce raiders – or to confront the British – and, advanced as she was, the *Wampanoag* was decommissioned in 1868.

Even without the *Wampanoag*, U.S. Navy warships managed to find and destroy two of the most notorious rebel raiders in 1864. The USS *Kearsarge* sunk the *Alabama* in a classic ship-to-ship duel off Cherbourg in July, and three months later Captain Napoleon Collins in the USS *Wachusett* cut out the Confederate raider *Florida* in the neutral port of Bahia, Brazil. The sinking of the *Alabama* triggered wild celebrations in the United States, but the seizure of the *Florida* in a neutral port caused more controversy. Collins was subsequently found guilty by a court martial of exceeding his orders, though later, after the war ended and tempers cooled, he was quietly restored to duty.

The last of the rebel raiders was the CSS *Shenandoah*, commanded by James I. Waddell. After savaging the Pacific whaling fleet in the spring and summer of 1865, Waddell learned that the war had ended in May, and fearing reprisal for the many captures he had made after that, he directed the *Shenandoah* back to Liverpool, where it hauled down its flag in November of 1865, the last Confederate surrender of the war.

The Union did not win the Civil War because of its naval superiority, but its navy was an important element in that victory. The blockade created shortages and hardship within the Confederacy, and the Union Navy was a full partner in the strategically important victories in the Western Theater that effectively split the Confederacy in half. Annoying and costly as the rebel commerce raiders were, they could not threaten Union naval superiority or change the outcome of the war. In the end, despite exploiting new technology, the South simply found itself overmatched at sea.

The U.S. Navy emerged from the war with a remarkable 671 warships on active service. Its astonishing growth had caused ripples of concern in London and elsewhere, but most of that concern was premature. Among the 671 ships on the U.S. Navy register were 418 converted merchantmen, a hundred or so river gunboats, and fifty-two coastal monitors. None of these was capable of serving effectively as part of a standing peacetime navy, and within five years they were sold off, mothballed, or simply scrapped. By 1870, the U.S. Navy had only fifty-two active warships, just ten more than it had had in 1861. It would be another generation before the United States emerged from its chrysalis as a legitimate global naval power during the 1890s.

THE WIDER CARIBBEAN DURING THE 19TH AND 20TH CENTURIES

JOHANNA VON GRAFENSTEIN is Professor in Latin American Studies at the Instituto Mora, Mexico

ABSTRACT. *The Caribbean basin and the Gulf of Mexico together occupy a central position commanding communications between North and South America, the Atlantic and the Pacific. Goods, people and ideas circulated within and through these waters. The original core of the Spanish American empire, they became dominated (though by no means controlled) in the 20th century by the United States.*

RÉSUMÉ. *Le bassin caribéen et le golfe du Mexique occupent ensemble une position centrale, gouvernant les communications entre l'Amérique du Nord et du Sud, l'Atlantique et le Pacifique. Les biens, personnes et idées circulèrent au sein et par ces eaux. Initialement au cœur de l'empire américain d'Espagne, ils furent au XXe siècle dominés (bien qu'en aucun cas contrôlés) par les États-Unis.*

.•.

In this contribution the "Wider Caribbean" is understood as the union of two seas or basins: the Gulf of Mexico and the Caribbean Sea, with their islands and continental coasts that extend from the Floridian peninsula to the east of Venezuela, and even beyond, including the Guayanas, historically related to the Caribbean because of their similarity in development and island character. How do the two seas influence the history and development of the countries located around them? What significance do they have for their inhabitants, of different social conditions and geographic origins? What has been their importance in global historical terms, from the end of the 18th century to the beginnings of the 21st?

Important geographic resources determined the role of the two basins in the history of colonial and post-colonial America. The islands of the Caribbean Sea were the first strongholds of European colonial expansionism, where the Spanish monarchy rehearsed schemes of political and social organization as well as economic exploitation. With the conquest of the continental territories the two seas began to host important maritime routes as well as the principal entrances to the viceroyalties of New Spain and Peru. Magnificent bays served as harbours for the fleets that transported American treasures to Spain and European merchandise in return. The wide and protected bays of San Juan of Puerto Rico, Cartagena de Indias and Havana could give shelter to hundreds of merchant and war ships. "These two cords" (*cordones*), wrote Bernardo de Ulloa in 1740 – referring to the Antillean archipelago and the continental coasts that limit the Gulf of Mexico and Caribbean Sea – "enclose a space where are located the most precious harbours, bays and shelters which are the envy of the nations."[1] While the Gulf coast is without good harbours on its southern and eastern side, except some protected up-river ports, the north-west coast possesses the excellent ports of Pensacola and Mobile. Up to 1740, the port complex of Cartagena de Indias, Portobelo and Panama was crucial for the commerce with Peru, while Veracruz was the only Atlantic harbour authorized for the commerce between the Spanish metropolis and New Spain. Count Floridablanca considered San Juan, Puerto Rico strategically so important that it never should be a subject of negotiation with Great Britain about the return of Gibraltar; nor should Samaná Bay in the eastern part of Santo Domingo. In case of negotiations about the latter, Floridablanca suggested ceding the whole colony rather than just Samaná Bay, which he considered its most important resource. The minister of state also attributed a high strategic value to the Bay of Port-of-Spain on Trinidad Island. Its closeness to the continent and its protected harbour were elements which could transform it into an important basis of communications between the Spanish ports of the Wider Caribbean.[2]

In the second half of the 19th century the deep-water bay and harbour of Môle Saint-Nicolas at the extreme west of the northern peninsula of Haiti, and Samaná Bay on the east side of the Dominican Republic, the first strategically located on the Windward Passage and the second on the Mona Channel, became matters of negotiations between local governments and external powers. Both bays offered possibilities as naval bases and coaling stations. The Haitian presidents Sylvain Salnave and Lysius F. Salomon offered Môle Saint-Nicolas to the United States in exchange for support during civil wars. The US government refused the propositions, but in 1891 demanded the cession of the port because of the support sent to the Revolution in the North. Also the lease of Samaná Bay was an issue of negotiations between the Dominican government of Buenaventura Báez and private US companies in order to increase public revenue during the 1870s. In the Spanish-American War of 1898 the battles for the control of the bays of Guantánamo and Santiago de Cuba were decisive, and in the 20th century Guantánamo became a symbol of US–Cuban conflict. The Cuban–American Treaty of 1934 confirmed the lease of the bay guaranteed in 1903, and the military base installed there played an important role in ensuring American strategic interests in the region until 1991. After 1959 the treaty and occupation of Guantánamo were declared illegal by Fidel Castro.

---

[1] DE ULLOA B., *Restablecimiento de las fábricas, tráfico y comercio español* (Madrid, 1740), Segunda Parte, pp. 26–7.
[2] FERRER DEL RÍO A., ed., *Obras originales del conde de Floridablanca* (Madrid, 1899), pp. 229 ff.

Another important resource of both seas is their location between two oceans separated only by narrow portions of land at some spots of Mexico, Central America and Colombia. Since the 16th century this has inspired plans to connect the Atlantic and Pacific Oceans by different land and waterways. The early nineteenth-century US writer William D. Robinson outlined five possible routes. Two were in the New Kingdom of Granada, the first in the province of Chocó, where around 1700 a monk actually summoned up the Indians of his parish to dig a channel between the rivers Atrata and San Juan, named the Canal de Raspadura, which was navigable by small boats and was used to transport cocoa from one ocean coast to the other until its transit was prohibited by the Spanish crown. The second Granadian connection mentioned by Robinson was via the river Naipí. Robinson added two more possible interoceanic links in Central America (the Isthmus of Darién, i.e. Panama, and Nicaragua) and another one through the Isthmus of Tehuantepec in Oaxaca, Mexico.[3] Alexander von Humboldt also considered an interoceanic link in the Isthmus of Tehuantepec, remembering the expedition of Hernán Cortés in the region, as well as the project of viceroy Antonio Bucareli and the engineer Agustín Kramer to connect the rivers Coatzacoalcos and Chimalapa, around 1775.[4] From 1820 the United States became interested in an interoceanic connection in Panama or Nicaragua in order to increase communication with Asia. The Treaty of 1846 which settled the boundaries of Oregon, and the incorporation of California and other territories after the war with Mexico, gave the country a transcontinental character and increased interest in linking the Atlantic with the Pacific. The rival projects, with their supporters located in New York or New Orleans, included also the plan to construct a railroad through the Isthmus of Tehuantepec in southern Mexico. British and French interests complicated yet more the struggle for a successful interoceanic communication. After the failure of Ferdinand de Lesseps to connect the Pacific and Atlantic in Panama, the US Project started in 1904 and concluded successfully a decade later. The concession of ninety-nine years to the United States ended in 1999, in consequence of the signature of the Torrijos-Carter Treaty in 1977. The importance of the canal to the economy of Panama is huge; in 2006, services (transport, business, finance, real estate) counted for 41% of GDP and employment. These activities are concentrated in the Canal Zone. In 2014, 5% of international seaborne trade passed through the canal and almost 22% (by tonnage) of all US imports and exports went the same way. The enlargement of the canal, initiated in 2007, will permit the passage of ships "Post-Panamax" of forty metres beam. In December 2014 the Nicaraguan and Chinese governments

---

[3] ROBINSON W.D., *Memoirs of the Mexican Revolution: including a Narrative of the Expedition of General Xavier Mina. With some Observations on the Practicability of Opening a Commerce between the Pacific and Atlantic Oceans through the Mexican Isthmus in the Province of Oaxaca, and the Lake of Nicaragua; and the Future Importance of such a Commerce to the Civilized World, and more especially to the United States* (Philadelphia, 1820), pp. 340-55.

[4] VON HUMBOLDT A.F., *Ensayo político sobre el reino de la Nueva España*, ed. J.A. ORTEGA Y MEDINA (Porrúa, México, 7th edn, 2006), pp. 469-71.

signed a treaty for the construction of an interoceanic connection on Nicaraguan territory.

Of great interest also were the different entrances and exits of the two seas. During the age of navigation under sail the trade winds and sea currents from south-east to north-west determined the use of various entrances to the Caribbean Sea through the Lesser Antilles, the principal ones being in the north in the latitude of the Virgin Islands (Anegada Channel), another between Guadaloupe and St Lucia and the third near Trinidad. The principal exit of the two seas was the Florida Straits, with its strong currents that turn into the Gulf Stream, determining thus the paths of return to Europe. On this exit route Havana and St Augustine in Florida were strategically located to guarantee a secure passage for the Spanish fleets. This pattern of protection was successful for most of the three hundred years of navigation from Spanish America to the Iberian peninsula, and only once did a whole treasure fleet fall into the hands of the enemy, when in 1628 the fleet commanded by Juan de Benavides was chased by the Dutch Piet Heyn into the bay of Matanzas on the northern coast of Cuba, where it ran aground, possibly because of the pilots' lack of experience. Other important exit and entrance routes to the Caribbean Sea are the Windward Passage, located between Cuba and Haiti, and the Mona Channel, between the Dominican Republic and Puerto Rico.

The importance of the Gulf–Caribbean basins for the maritime interests of the United States was the subject of an influential analysis by Alfred Thayer Mahan in 1897. He saw the Caribbean "pre-eminently [as] the domain of sea-power", and distinguished in each of its two "sheets of water" one pre-eminent commercial position: in the Gulf of Mexico, the mouth of the Mississippi, and in the Caribbean Sea, the Isthmus of Panama. In the former meet all the exports and imports, by water, of the Mississippi valley, interior "to a great state whose resources they bear", whereas in the latter converge the roads of the ocean, "the common possession of all nations". To control the isthmus, it was necessary to control the isthmus itself, to control the approaches, or to possess a "preponderant navy" as a mobile force.[5] In a famous map, Mahan marks the locations that are essential to guarantee the free movement from and to the two central positions mentioned before. The principal of them are Cuba and Jamaica, seen by Mahan as rivals for control of the navigation routes in the Gulf of Mexico and Caribbean Sea.

In terms of communication, what does the sea mean to the inhabitants of these islands and continental shores? In many circumstances, the sea meant liberty, security from persecution, news about foreign libertarian projects, and support for their own. Slaves from Curaçao often gained liberty *de facto*, working as seamen for Dutch ship owners, who practised commerce with Venezuelan and other ports, easily passing as free coloured on the ships they served and at the ports where they landed. The conspiracy of Coro (1795) in the Captaincy of Venezuela was greatly inspired by revolutionary movements in French

---

[5] MAHAN A.T., *The Interest of America in Sea Power, Present and Future* (Boston, MA, 1918), pp. 277–81.

Saint-Domingue and the ideas of the French revolution. José Leonardo Chirinos often accompanied his wife's master to Saint Domingue on business and knew the new political and social ideas which he spread through the popular sectors of Coro. The conspirators proclaimed their intention to introduce the laws of the French into the colony, that, is liberty, equality and fraternity. For the white planters, the vicinity of Cuba, with the Punta Maisí only 90km from Cape Saint Nicolas, meant refuge in the turmoil of the slave revolt in the north of the French colony, but they also chose other destinations such as New Orleans and Mayagüez in Puerto Rico or the island of Trinidad, and after their expulsion from Cuba in 1809 moved especially to eastern US ports, and again to New Orleans. A few of them came also to New Spain, as primary sources reveal. In the Lesser Antilles, movement during the revolutionary years from one island to the other was even easier and more frequent. During the wars of Independence of the Spanish continental possessions, the Gulf of Mexico and the Caribbean Sea served as areas of operations for the insurgents and their international allies, who shipped arms, provisions and even slaves, attacked Spanish merchant ships and besieged ports in order to interrupt and damage Spanish commerce. Islands such as Amelia on the east coast of Florida, Barataria in the Mississippi delta, Galveston, Matagorda, Mujeres Island, Old Providence and Margarita Island near the Venezuelan coast served as retreats for the international revolutionary community. Here smugglers also established admiralty courts to condemn prize goods which later could be sold as legal merchandize in ports such as New Orleans, Jacmel and Les Cayes in independent Haiti, in the neutral ports of Charlotte Amelie in Danish Saint-Thomas or Gustavia in Swedish Saint-Barthélémy.

During the frequent civil wars in independent Mexico, Colombia and Central American countries, political opponents often escaped through Caribbean sea ports like Veracruz, Tampico, Barranquilla or Cartagena. Important port-cities and islands which offered refuge were New Orleans, Havana or St Thomas. Another aspect of connections across the Wider Caribbean are the attempts to support internal social and political movements by landing troops and arms. During the wars of Independence of the Spanish continental colonies the Spanish liberal Xavier Mina passed through Port-au-Prince in Haiti and then Galveston and New Orleans before landing troops and military equipment in Soto la Marina in Nuevo Santander (southwards of Texas) in order to join local insurgent groups and "liberate New Spain from the tyranny of Fernand VII".[6] Simón Bolivar sought refuge in Jamaica, and then twice in Haiti, preparing his two expeditions to Venezuela. Other expeditions were fitted out in Haitian ports, like the ones of Gregor Mc Gregor, the brothers Carabaño or Pierre Labatut, organized to invade New Granada or other Spanish strongholds. Troops, arms and important leaders arriving by sea also played a major role during the war of Cuban independence when exiled combatants like José Martí, Antonio Maceo or Máximo Gómez arrived on the coast. Also during the 20th century opponents of

---

[6] See ROBINSON, *Memoirs*, p. 51.

François Duvalier and Rafael Leónidas Trujillo several times tried invasions by sea to overthrow these dictators. All these examples show that in war situations, revolts and opposition movements the sea offered the possibility of bringing in support from outside. But also the contrary was the case. From the sea could appear important threats to national sovereignty such as the bombardment of the port of Veracruz by the French in 1839, the invasion by French and Spanish troops in 1863 and the occupation by US forces in 1914. The military occupations of Haiti and the Dominican Republic, which began in the respective capitals and sea ports of Port-au-Prince and Santo Domingo in 1915 and 1916, are also examples of such invasions, as well as the failed military invasion of Playa Girón in Cuba in 1962.

Sea communications served not only political movements and invasion projects, but also unemployed or badly paid working people during periods of economic crisis, or during moments of high labour demand in other countries of the region. An important example is the exodus by sea in flimsy boats from Cuba to Miami during the last decade of the 20th century, when the interruption of and support from the former socialist bloc caused shortages of all kinds. Haitian "boat people" tried to reach the Florida coast to escape political oppression and lack of economic opportunities for at least two decades after the fall of the dictator "Baby Doc" Duvalier in 1986. In some economic situations communications by sea also allowed significant labour mobility, for example, during the two periods of the construction of the Panama Canal, or during the second half of the 19th and the first half of the 20th centuries, when workers from Jamaica and other Caribbean islands moved to Port Limon in Costa Rica in order to find employment in the construction of the railroad, in the enlargement of the port and on banana plantations. This was also the case for the extension and modernization of the ports of Veracruz and Tampico in the same period. On the other side, Haitian and Jamaican workers found employment in the Cuban sugar mills, Dominicans worked in Puerto Rico, or moved to St Maarten and other islands with a strong tourist trade.

An important issue to discuss is that of the sea and its importance in war. While the sovereignty of the Caribbean islands changed often during the international conflicts of the 18th century, depending on the maritime superiority of the different European powers, after 1815 control of the islands and certain coastal territories did not change until the Spanish–American War of 1898. Only St Barthélémy returned to France in 1878 and the Dominican Republic gained its independence from Haiti in 1844. After 1815, Great Britain held the major part of the islands, while France, the Netherlands and Denmark maintained small island territories, and the first two also part of the Guayanas. The Caribbean Sea ceased to represent an important theatre of war for the European navies and small fleets of corsairs which during previous centuries had assaulted the possessions and shipping of their enemies. During World War II German U-boats and Italian submarines attacked targets in the region. Oil tankers and transporters of bauxite were sunk, and refineries were attacked at Trinidad Island, Aruba and Curaçao. The oil production of Venezuela was of great importance for the British

Empire during the war, while the vital Panama Canal was heavily protected by US forces.

There is, finally, the important subject of the sea as a vehicle for trade relations, for the operations of shipping lines and cruise ships. The region has been an important commercial zone since the Europeans first appeared. Trade between the islands and Europe, as well as regional trade, illicit and legal, were important sources of wealth for merchant families with Atlantic connections. Exports of tropical agricultural and forest products, and imports of manufactured goods from Europe, together with the African slave trade, were responsible for a huge maritime movement in the Gulf–Caribbean region and the Atlantic during the 18th and part of the 19th centuries. The appearance of steamers in the 19th century changed the connections between islands, mainland countries and Atlantic destinations and shortened the distances. Until the introduction of the charter flights in the 1960s, the expansion and improvement of international shipping lines permitted an increasing transport of passengers. The transport of goods through the Caribbean Sea is still of enormous proportions.

What other resources and ways of development do the Gulf of Mexico and Caribbean Sea offer for the countries located around them? The sea as a source of food – fish, crustaceans, for a long time also turtles – always has been important for the peoples living along the coasts. During the 16th and 17th centuries European explorers, conquerors and pirates provided themselves with food by trading with or attacking the small fishing communities along the shores. Through centuries these communities survived without great changes in their way of life, sustained by artisanal fishing. One of the threats to these communities is industrial fishing, which has diminished the stocks of fish and crustaceans, mainly of the most commercial species, and also has affected the biodiversity of sea life. Many modern tourist centres displaced old fishing communities like Playa del Carmen. The Mujeres and Cozumel islands had a longer tradition as international vacation destinations, since the 1920s or 1940s. The mass tourist centre of Cancún was developed in the 1970s in a place considered an "abandoned space" on the frontier, which needed to be "settled, employed and occupied".[7]

The biodiversity of mangrove forests and lagoons, characteristic of many of the coastlines around the Gulf of Mexico and Caribbean Sea, is immense. Hundreds of bird species have their breeding grounds there; these vital zones are also the habitat for fish, shrimps, crabs, shellfish and other species. Another source of biodiversity are the seagrass meadows and the coral reefs that extend around the islands and at a certain distance along the continental shores. The latter serve also as protective walls against high waves, especially during storms, which on the other hand can damage the fragile reef ecosystems, especially when they reach the velocity of hurricanes. The most important of them is the Mesoamerican Barrier Reef System, the second-largest in the world with its

---

[7] REDCLIFT M., '"A convulsed and magic country": tourism and resource histories in the Mexican Caribbean', *Environment and History* 11.1 (2005), 89, note 8; DACHARY A.C. and BURNE S.M.A., *El Caribe mexicano, una frontera olvidada* (Chetumal, 1998), pp. 398–405.

almost 1,000km of length. It extends from Cotoy Island at the north-eastern end of Yucatán to the Bay Islands in the Gulf of Honduras. In the Gulf of Mexico the Florida reef is also of importance, stretching around the south coast of the peninsula near the Florida Keys. Around Cuba are located some of the richest and most unspoiled coral reefs in the region; especially famous are the Jardines de la Reina along the southern coast.

Another resource provided by the Gulf of Mexico and the Caribbean Sea was salt, exploited since the 17th century on the west coast of Yucatán, on the islands of San Maarten and Curaçao and on the coast of eastern Venezuela, in the province of Cumaná. Since the first decades of the 20th century, oil fields in the Gulf of Mexico and off Venezuela have been exploited commercially. The offshore exploitation of oil and natural gas is greatly developed in the waters of Louisiana, Mississippi and Alabama, as well as in the "Sonda de Campeche", Mexico, and east of Trinidad Island.

The beauty of the coastal zones of the Caribbean Sea determines increasingly the development of the countries located around it, making the tourist sector one of the most important source of incomes. Seaside tourism in tropical climates began to appear during the last decades of the 19th century. Before 1959 Cuba was the most visited, especially by citizens from the United States, followed by Puerto Rico, the Bahamas and Bermuda. Jamaica also received tourists from the 1940s, as well as Haiti. Around the Gulf of Mexico, important tourist zones grew up in the southern part of Florida and at the beaches southwards of Veracruz. This was almost exclusively oriented to national tourism, although it was always behind Acapulco, the most important Pacific tourist centre. With the rise of charter flights in the 1960s and 1970s, the Caribbean began to be accessible to European and US tourists on a large scale. Cancún on the east coast of the Yucatán peninsula emerged as the most successful destination for mass tourism. The Caribbean offered the most attractive tropical sun, sea and sand holidays, before other regions in the world with similar characteristics began to develop their coastal zones.

Most of the publicity photos which announce the beauties of the region could have been taken at any island or continental coast of the Caribbean: beaches of white fine sand, tropical vegetation with picturesque palm trees, crystal-blue water and eternal sunshine are invariably represented. With the development of different water sports, other beauties of the sea were accessible by snorkelling and scuba diving in rocky coastal zones and coral reefs offshore. Some places are known for their deep-water fishing, like the north coast of the Dominican Republic near Monte Cristi; the Florida reef and the Banco Chinchorro of the Mesoamerican Barrier Reef offer rich grounds for wreck diving; the north coast of Yucatán is another place for "special interest tourism" in summer, when swimming with whale sharks has become an attraction. Finally, the infrastructure of marinas for sailing and motor yachts is well developed and the Caribbean islands are highly appreciated destinations for these sports.

Since the decay of the traditional agricultural production (coffee, sugar and bananas), mining (bauxite) and assembly industries in the region, tourism dominates the development of many of the countries around the Caribbean basin. According to the Caribbean Tourist Organization (CTO), which counts thirty-four members, including the Antilles, Bahamas, Bermuda, Cozumel-Cancun, Belize, Surinam and Venezuela, in 2014 the region attracted 26.3 million stop-over tourists and 24 million cruise-passenger arrivals. They spent 29.2 billion US dollars, contributing 14% to the Gross Domestic Product (GDP) of the CTO members.[8] Nearly 50% of the stop-over tourists in 2014 were from the USA, followed by Canadians and Europeans. In 2013, 11.3% of total employment in the region depended on tourism: the direct contribution of this sector to employment was 3.6%; the induced one 1.9% and the indirect 5.8 %. Cruise-ship tourism contributes little to the local economy of islands and continental tourist zones.[9] A few hours of local shopping is the most a cruise-ship passenger will spend onshore. "The bulk of the tourist expenditure is retained by transnational companies", observed Amalia L. Cabezas in 2008, "and only 22–25% of the retail price remains in the host country."[10]

Politicians, private investors and developers consider the recreative use of the sea and its shores by international tourism as the most important source of prosperity for the Caribbean countries, but there are also many critics who underline the limited impact of this industry on employment, especially on the creation of skilled jobs. Tourism offers only menial tasks and seasonal work for local people, they point out, while the well-paid and specialized jobs are reserved for foreign employees of the transnational corporations that control up to 89% of the sales of all-inclusive package holidays. There is also claimed to be a negative sociocultural impact by "the suggestion of permanent luxury and idleness" projected by guests of the high-category hotels and resorts.[11] The critics of tourism in its massive and invasive patterns warn against the impact on local ecosystems by pollution of ground water and lagoons, devastation of mangrove forests and coral reefs and, as a final result, deterioration and destruction of biodiversity and ecological equilibrium. However, there are nature-friendly tourist projects with low environmental impacts. Especially, the small Caribbean islands are developing schemes of ecotourism and small resorts encouraging the use of local resources for construction and food and offering opportunities to small investors and local employees. The foundation of national parks and biosphere reserves are also important measures to protect natural resources on the islands and mainland coasts.

Finally, it is important to consider the jurisdictional development of maritime

---

[8] World Travel and Tourism Council, *The Economic Impact of Travel and Tourism*, 2014, p. 3, http://www.wttc.org/~/media/files/reports/economic%20impact%20research/regional%20reports/world2014.ashx.

[9] BULMER-THOMAS V., *The Economic History of the Caribbean since the Napoleonic Wars* (Cambridge, 2012), p. 363.

[10] CABEZAS A.L., 'Tropical blues: tourism and social exclusion in the Dominican Republic', *Latin American Perspectives* 35.3, 'The Impact of Tourism in Latin America' (May 2008), 27.

[11] GORMSEN E., 'The impact of tourism on coastal areas', *GeoJournal* 42.1, 'Land, Sea and Human Effort' (May 1997), 47–8.

frontier zones in the second half of the 20th century. In historical terms we can say that the status of an exclusive Spanish *mare clausum* did not last long; in the 1530s a dozen French, English and Dutch privateers and pirates penetrated into the Caribbean Sea, only one into the Gulf of Mexico. From the 1620s onwards, Spain's rivals formed their first settlements on the small Antillian islands and on the northern and western coasts of Hispaniola. Spain held only the Islands of Cuba, Puerto Rico, Trinidad, Margarita and the eastern part of Hispaniola. The purchase of Louisiana by the United States of America in 1803, its acquisition of Florida in 1819, the formation of the first national state in the area in 1804 when Haiti proclaimed its independence, the appearance of independent states on the continent during the second and third decades of the 19th century, followed by the Dominican Republic and Cuba, and finally by thirteen new independent states during the second half of the 20th century, were all elements that created an extremely complicated maritime frontier situation. At present the rights of the coastal states of the Caribbean Sea relative to Territorial Waters, Contiguous Zone, Economic Exclusive Zone and Continental Shelfs are not clearly defined in many cases. In the whole area, affirms Chris Carleton, "there are some 78 maritime boundaries of which only 23 are fully delimited with a further 4 that have been agreed but are not in force for one reason or another".[12] In some of the cases, the International Court of Justice (ICJ) and the Organization of American States are intervening to settle disputes or facilitate agreements. The definition of maritime boundaries between Nicaragua and Colombia and between Nicaragua and Honduras is before the ICJ and the arrangement of the Belize and Guatemala *differendum* has been the matter of negotiations in the OEA.

The preceding study has shown that the sea has defined decisively the economic, political and cultural development of the islands and coasts located around the two Wider Caribbean basins. The frequent and rapid communications by water between the multiple island and continental port cities favoured an easy flow of material and immaterial goods and forged the cosmopolitan character of their inhabitants.[13] Between the many consequences of this steady exchange was the flourishing of the port societies and the accumulation of wealth in them. Not only the elites profited from the advantages of easy external communications, but also members of the lower classes who moved around the region to benefit from work and trade opportunities. As we have shown in this contribution, some of the bays and ports of the two sheets of water have occupied strategic positions

---

[12] CARLETON C., 'Maritime Delimitation in Complex Island Situations: A Case Study on the Caribbean Sea' (unpublished lecture, Harte Research Institute for Gulf of Mexico Studies, Texas A&M University, 2007), p. 11.

[13] Alexander von Humboldt attributed certain capacities to the inhabitants and societies of La Havana and Caracas: 'more progress' and a 'European aspect of their civilization', 'more knowledge about political relations, ... about the situation of colonies and metropolis', capacities that were seen by the author as a direct consequence of communications and trade. VON HUMBOLDT A.F., *Viaje a las regiones equinocciales del nuevo continente hecho en 1799, 1800, 1801, 1802, 1803 y 1804* (Ministerio de Educación Nacional, Caracas, 1941-1942), Vol. II, p. 302.

in the international communication systems and therefore enjoy special advantages. On the other hand, the Gulf of Mexico and Caribbean Sea provided their residents with a variety of food throughout the history of settlement on their coasts, and were also the source of raw materials, especially oil. Its extraction has benefited local economies as well as international investors. In recent decades the recreative exploitation of the beauties of the sea and its shores has become the most important factor of economic growth, especially of the small islands and some continental areas. But the benefits of this recent development accrue largely to great investors, especially transnational ones. As we have argued in this contribution, it will be necessary to implement new forms of tourism more vigorously in order to preserve the rich biodiversity of sea and shores and to allow the local population to benefit on a larger scale from the millions of visitors who each year come to enjoy the attractions of tropical water life and the cultural riches of the local human communities living by the sea.

Ship Canals

GRAEME J. MILNE is Senior Lecturer in Modern History at the University of Liverpool, United Kingdom

ABSTRACT. *Ship canals bring the advantages of the sea inland and overland, giving physical expression to the high economic and political value of sea transport. The Suez and Panama Canals linked empires as well as shortening trade routes and favouring steam over sail. They have often taken on a powerful symbolic value, embodying the power of empire and even of mankind over nature.*

RÉSUMÉ. *Les canaux de navigation offrent les avantages de la mer au transport intérieur terrestre. Ils sont la manifestation physique de l'importance économique et politique du transport maritime. Le canal de Suez et le canal de Panama permirent de relier des empires tout en raccourcissant les itinéraires commerciaux et favorisèrent l'utilisation de la vapeur sur la voile. Ils ont souvent pris une puissante valeur symbolique en incarnant le pouvoir d'un empire voire même du genre humain sur la nature.*

.•.

Ship canals distort space and time. Some of them create routes across landmasses that would otherwise have to be circumnavigated, dramatically shortening the maritime distance between two points. Others turn landlocked towns into seaports, bringing ocean-going vessels far inland and challenging the interests of older ports. Ship canals are therefore a disruptive force in their own right, and they have historically served as enablers of others, not least the steamship. Canals offer important lessons in how states, navies, entrepreneurs, port authorities and engineers have visualised and manipulated the relationship between land and sea, often on a monumental scale, and also in how those institutions and individuals have adapted to the consequences of such actions. Most major ship canals were a product of a particular time, and need to be interpreted as part of European and American economic and imperial expansion from the second half of the 19th century. Their role changed, but was still important, in the 20th century. Even with the development of aviation, the sea remained fundamental to the security and prosperity of states. Warships did not lose their strategic importance in projecting state influence overseas, while cargo shipping has always been the cheapest means of carrying most goods. Today, the shipping industry defines classes of vessels according to whether they can navigate the world's major canals, and the demands of ever-larger ships drive periodic reassessments of the operation and capacity of the canals themselves. For all these reasons the larger ship canals continue to be notable pressure points in the political economy of the 21st century.

The building, ownership and operation of ship canals require many levels of interpretation and understanding. They have repeatedly tested the abilities of naval planners and shipping managers. Statesmen find themselves judged on their ability to comprehend a geopolitical map suddenly altered for the first time in generations. The scale and symbolism of the great ship canals has often taken them to an imaginary level, inspiring still wilder schemes, fictions and imperial visions, and in turn making them targets for anti-colonial and national independence movements. They have been a formidable challenge to the skills of civil engineers and construction workers, and a driver of new processes in project management. This essay therefore takes advantage of the amphibious status of ship canals to address questions about the impact of the maritime world on the land, and vice versa. It begins by considering antecedents, briefly surveying a long history of canal visions that were mostly brought to fruition only in the steam age of the 19th century. The technological, economic and strategic challenges posed by the construction and operation of ship canals are then examined in light of what they reveal about attitudes toward the sea, its opportunities and its threats.[1]

ROUTES, ANTECEDENTS AND VISIONS

The major ship canals built in the second half of the 19th century almost all had antecedents going back centuries. They had been envisaged long before economics, finance, state power and engineering developed the capacities to construct them. The ancient Egyptians built a succession of canals in the desert, and while none was a direct precursor of the Suez Canal (1869), they inspired the French intelligentsia of the 19th century in their visions of uniting East and West more directly by sea.[2] In the Americas, sixteenth-century explorers already knew the general area that would provide the shortest way from the Caribbean to the Pacific, and searched in vain for a natural channel; their paths eventually evolved into the route chosen by the builders of the Panama Canal (1914).[3]

Indeed, generations of mariners did not wait for canals. They strung together routes using rivers, lakes and transhipment points, even dragging their vessels

---

[1] For key facts, maps and bibliography, see entries for individual canals in *The Oxford Encyclopaedia of Maritime History*, 4 vols, ed. J.B. HATTENDORF (Oxford, 2007).
[2] ABI-MERSHED O., *Apostles of Modernity: Saint-Simonians and the Civilizing Mission in Algeria* (Stanford, 2010).
[3] TAYLOR H.C., 'The Nicaragua canal', *Journal of the American Geographical Society of New York* 18 (1886), 95–126; AGUIRRE R., *The Panama Canal* (Leiden, 2010).

overland where necessary. This pragmatic and flexible approach is a reminder that the separation between land and sea was not as rigid historically as it has since become. The scale of shipping and port construction since the mid-19th century has delineated the boundary between land and sea to the point that it is inconceivable for a ship to be pulled across an isthmus, or to have its cargo repeatedly man-handled to other forms of transport across a chain of short stages. In the long centuries of small, shallow vessels powered by sails and oars, however, it was common to visualise water transport as part of a landscape, not as separate from it. Viking seafarers used a mix of river and land routes to cross the north of Germany, bypassing the dangerous and long-feared route from the Baltic to the North Sea round Denmark. This signalled the benefits, far in the future, of the Kiel Canal (1895). A succession of ancient Greek and Roman rulers planned a canal across the Corinthian isthmus, settling for track-ways instead, and the eventual builders of the Corinth Canal (1893) followed the same route. Caravans and railways, run by the "Industrial Pasha" Muhammad Ali and the Peninsular & Oriental Steam Navigation Company, bridged the Arabian isthmus before the Suez Canal. Stagecoaches, then a railway, crossed Panama before a canal could be built there.

The openings of the Suez and Panama Canals can be seen as bookends to half a century of canal-building that reconfigured world shipping patterns. Both canals enabled many long-distance shipping routes to concentrate in equatorial waters, rather than having to make dangerous and time-consuming arcs around the southern capes of Africa and South America. They remain in a class of their own, serving a genuinely global purpose, and able to accommodate much larger shipping than any of the other ship canals. Indeed, it is important to remember that even in that defining era, most canal schemes did not have such world-shaping aspirations but were, rather, focused on the particular ambitions of individual towns. Although less dramatic and romantic than the major projects, these efforts to build smaller canals offer a significant insight into the place of the sea in the world-view of civic leaders in the 19th century. As well as revealing economic priorities, canals were clearly symbolic, being at least on a par with the later determination to have a major airport, or to host prestigious international events. The city of Manchester, increasingly confident in its ambitions as the industrial and commercial capital of the north of England, saw its Ship Canal (1894) as a logical consolidation of that power, literally bypassing its dependence on the port of Liverpool and creating its own gateway to the oceans.[4] In Texas, Houston's desire to be a major seaport, and not to concede larger shipping to coastal towns like Galveston, required large investment in dredging its Ship Channel (1914) throughout the 20th century.

In the mid-20th century, new canal projects took another turn, focusing on developing regional transport capacities, connecting existing waterways and often making no attempt to accommodate the very largest shipping. As such,

---

[4] FARNIE D., *The Manchester Ship Canal and the Rise of the Port of Manchester, 1894-1975* (Manchester, 1980).

their planners had to be more collaborative than competitive, although conflicts over funding, management and ownership remained common. The St Lawrence Seaway (1959) was eventually heralded as a flagship venture between Canada and the United States, but only after Canada started building on its own in the face of a reluctant US Congress. In Europe, even projects in a single national territory, such as Germany's Rhine-Main-Danube Canal (1992), have far-reaching implications for the economies of neighbouring countries and indeed the entire continent. Both these schemes, like those of the late 19th century, had been long envisaged, but it required a particular conjunction of political, economic and technological forces to bring them to eventual fruition.

Technologies of Land and Sea

Ship canals represent an important case study in technological development, both in their own terms and in their interaction with the shipping, port and logistics industries. They are a reminder to maritime scholars that the technological aspects of our discipline cannot be understood exclusively through the building and operation of ships, and that the broader infrastructural context often has sufficient inertia to constrain the choices of shipbuilders and operators. That relationship is a mix of contest and cooperation as the relative power of users and providers of strategic facilities changes over time. It also encompasses various levels of engagement, from the day-by-day physical realities of fitting a ship through a set of locks to more abstract negotiations of future needs and possibilities for a cluster of related technologies.

Sometimes, new technology worked to the canal-builders' advantage. The Panama Canal, for example, was finally dug with steam-powered excavators that had not been available when the project started. Canal projects were drivers of new techniques as well as technologies. They demanded innovation in project management and the emerging concerns of health, safety and welfare at work, especially in tropical disease-environments. Canals also offer lessons about the political and economic constraints on technological application, and the extent to which successive projects follow the lead of their predecessors, accepting norms and models that become standards for the industry. Such path dependency is then challenged by the next generation of larger ships, or by a new economic or military demand for security or predictability of passage.

The Suez Canal was the defining achievement of the ship canal age, because for good and ill it became a key reference point for subsequent developments. Ports around the Indian Ocean used its depth as a benchmark for their harbour improvements. Manchester built its own canal to the same depth, a practical scheme but also one that signalled the new port's interest in raw cotton from production regions in the East. In other ways, however, Suez was not a useful model. The Mediterranean and the Red Sea being at the same level, and the terrain being reasonably flat, it was possible to build a sea-level canal without locks. There were great financial and logistical advantages to this, but it turned out that such conditions were relatively unusual, and trying to apply the same approach to other projects proved disastrous.

In particular, what worked in Egypt did not work in Central America, and the path-dependence of the canal-building profession resulted in a false start on the Panama Canal that cost lives and capital on a huge scale. Ferdinand de Lesseps, builder of the Suez Canal, tried to repeat his approach in Panama's mountainous jungle terrain. His venture collapsed in 1893 after twelve years of digging and the deaths of some twenty thousand workers, mostly from the Caribbean, China and Ireland. Even after the United States government took over the project in 1904, a sea-level canal remained the favoured option, until a major engineering survey opted for the lock system that was finally completed in 1914. Although the Panama project stuck with its original plan for too long, there was good reason to avoid lock-based canals if at all possible. Canal-builders knew that enlarging locks and gates to accommodate bigger shipping was always many times more expensive than deepening or widening a canal itself.

That technological entanglement between the builders of canals and the builders of ships has never ceased. The most immediate impact of the Suez Canal on the maritime world was to accelerate the transition from sail to steam. Early steamships were economical only over short distances, not carrying so much fuel that it compromised their cargo capacity. Because the feasible distance between any two ports remained the same, the only way to bring a given port into range was to design, build and fit more efficient engines, a process that took years. A ship canal could change the fixed element in that equation. Suddenly, the 17,000km voyage from London to Bombay became a 9,900km journey. Existing steamships with the latest compound engines could economically reach India, and shipping firms in Liverpool and Glasgow were among the earliest to take advantage of the new Suez route after 1869. As well as that broad economic blow, the canal had a more direct impact on sailing vessels, which had to be towed through for their own safety and for that of other shipping. In any case, the Red Sea was a dangerous place for sailing ships. More than five thousand vessels used the Suez Canal in its first five years of operation, but fewer than three hundred were sailing ships.

By the 1870s, therefore, it was clear that ever-larger steamships would dominate global trade routes, and that this process would demand both new canal projects and the regular updating of existing crossings. Shipowners came to view the dimensions of ship canals as targets, satisfying them only until the next set of economic changes in the industry made them revisit the calculations. In the 20th century, the major ship canals, and in particular Suez and Panama, became reference points for successive generations of ship design, and vice versa, with a new jargon of "Panamax" and "Suezmax" invented to classify shipping. Even building close to that "target" causes problems for the canal operators, because vessels that only just fit have to be handled with extra care, and take more time to safely navigate through the Panama Canal locks, especially.

Nor can canal operators assume that once their canal is established as a key route it will always be used as such. Trade routes have considerable inertia, but it is far from overwhelming. Closures of the Suez Canal during periods of armed conflict in the 1950s and 1970s encouraged the building of very large oil tankers, which offered such economies of scale that they made it less important to take the most direct route. This pattern has continued with the construction of the very largest container ships, which are unable to pass through the Panama Canal's locks but which are nonetheless economic on other routes. Technological considerations therefore need to be studied as a crucial element in the operation and evolution, as well as the construction, of ship canals. They are, however, only part of a broader set of forces and drivers in the interaction between land and sea routes, shipping firms, ports and canal operators.

Strategies, winners and losers

Ship canals had a powerful disruptive effect on incumbents of all kinds in the 19th century. Canals became an element in the broader liberalisation of the maritime world, offering entrepreneurial shipping firms an entry into trades that had previously been monopolised by state-chartered or subsidised companies. In addition, by distorting long-established sea routes, canals presented some seaports with unexpected windfalls, while relegating others to backwaters. Pireaus and Trieste, for example, grew as entrepôts for the Far East trades via the Suez Canal, benefiting from their locations in the eastern Mediterranean. The Chilean port of Valparaiso, however, lost much of its old passing trade when the Panama Canal opened. The Suez Canal turned many sections of the voyage from Europe to East Asia into a chain of short sea routes. Whereas the old sailing tracks had taken vessels into deep water for weeks at a time, canals encouraged shipowners and port authorities to create coaling stations and other port-of-call facilities along the way. The availability of coal at intermediate stops further altered the fuel-efficiency equation, encouraging regular liner services that in turn generated hinterland trades for previously minor ports. None of those ports had been involved in the decisions to build the canals, of course. Canal-builders and the great powers that sat behind them had far-reaching and largely unaccountable power to disrupt long-established maritime relationships for good or ill.

It is important to stress, however, that the impact of ship canals cannot be assessed through any crude geographical determinism, and that many initial assumptions were not borne out by events. A canal's distortion of distance was a necessary, but far from sufficient, condition of its realignment of trading patterns and relationships. This is demonstrated most clearly in the number of predictions about the Suez Canal that turned out to be wrong. In particular, French investors in the canal believed that their national shipping lines would have substantial advantages in the new route to the East, turning ports like Marseilles into new hubs of global commerce. This proved over-optimistic. Britain, while much further from the canal, produced coal, iron and manufactures on such a scale that British ports remained the default beginning and end for a very large proportion of the world's trade routes. An increasing share of India's exports to Europe did go directly to Continental ports rather than their old entrepôt in London, but they were still carried in large part on British vessels. Ownership of the focal points of the industrial economy outweighed even the dramatic realignment of geography promised by canals. Not until the very end of the 19th century, when Germany's industrial and maritime strength was increasing rapidly, did the Suez Canal see any noticeable fall in the proportion of British shipping passing through.

As those patterns suggest, the building, ownership and operation of ship canals have always raised questions of international rivalry, and the political and diplomatic aspects of the history of canals raise some ironies. Advocates of commercial shipping and naval power alike have long complained that politicians and policy-makers are ignorant of maritime affairs, but ship canals and their immediate zones may be an exception, offering solid locations that can be visualised and comprehended amid the more abstract concepts of seaborne trade and strategy. The Panama and Suez Canals especially took on high levels of symbolism for US and British statesmen, and for wider public opinion, at several points in the 19th and 20th centuries. They also became a focus of anti-colonial movements in Egypt, in Panama, and in the Middle East and Central America more generally. The physical territoriality of a canal can make it seem more important than the navies and merchant fleets that use it, which can lead to distortions in priorities.

The ability of ship canal projects to capture national and imperial imaginations has posed significant dilemmas to states with an existing stake in the regions concerned. Despite the enthusiasm of many of its shipowners and merchants, the British state resisted the idea of a Suez Canal for decades, believing that it would distort balances of power that had hitherto worked largely in Britain's favour. Better, the argument went, to have substantial control over inefficient overland routes than to give competing powers access to a new shipping channel. The Suez and Panama Canals forced strategists and politicians to envisage new implications for maintaining naval power, and the security of commercial shipping. This was an extension of existing thinking about having naval bases abroad. It had long been the case that global naval reach required some presence on land, and often in circumstances that might prove vulnerable to changing attitudes in host countries. The major canals shifted that commitment to an appreciably higher level, however. As soon as the implications of gaining a canal route had begun to be absorbed, planners had to contemplate the possibility of losing it again, and develop strategies for avoiding such an event. An entire zone had to be defined and, potentially, defended with sufficient force to keep the navigation open.

Canals therefore blurred the line between naval and territorial power. The Suez and Panama Canals made Britain and the United States responsible for territory, when they might have preferred to maintain their influence from the sea. Worse, the symbolism of the canals in public opinion meant that any pragmatic step back from a canal would be seen as a national humiliation. When Britain bought out the Khedive's shares in the Suez Canal Company in 1875, the British public interpreted this as a boost to national prestige, and also to British influence in the eastern Mediterranean. British imperial occupation of Egypt from the 1880s was sometimes explained as defence of the canal, but that rhetoric became a hostage to fortune in later decades when the canal was actually threatened. The obvious inconsistency between Britain's imperial actions and its free trade internationalist rhetoric gave increasing ammunition to Egypt's national resistance movement. This set up a long chain of events that would ultimately see Egypt's nationalisation of the canal in the 1950s, and the subsequent failure of the British and French to take it back, being widely interpreted as the end of the British Empire.[5]

Canals forced planners to rethink issues of internationalisation, neutrality, extra-territoriality and free transit. Historians have tended to study these questions in relation to informal empire, most obviously in the treaty ports of China and Japan, but the major ship canals also offer an important set of lessons. Each canal had a dominant power with an interest in favouring free transit rather than strict neutrality, because the latter practice would question its own right to send warships through during times of international conflict. International conferences agreed a series of conventions in the 19th century, but these were exposed to new stresses in the 20th, and the result was generally a more explicit annexation of authority by the great powers. During the First World War, Britain steadily increased its control of the Suez Canal to the point where it could be used only by British and allied shipping. Although free navigation resumed after the war, there was never any doubt that it would be suspended again in the event of future conflict. The international laws and strategic realities surrounding ship canals were repeatedly tested in the series of crises of the middle decades of the century, and became much debated by military, legal and diplomatic thinkers.[6] The Second World War revealed another, different strategic reality, when Axis air power made the Mediterranean too dangerous for Allied shipping. Normal use of the Suez Canal would have required not only control of the canal-side zone, but the extension of that secure zone all the way to Gibraltar. British forces in Egypt, deprived of their route through the Mediterranean, had to return to the pre-1869 world of circumnavigation of the Cape of Good Hope. The Mediterranean route regained its traffic only after the Allied invasions of North Africa and Sicily made the sea safer again. In the meantime, however, the canal zone had been transformed into a series of major military bases, reflecting the importance of the Middle East theatre in the wider conflict.

The United States' vision of a crossing in Central America also became more interventionist over time, reflecting broader strategic priorities. Although the US was willing to develop a series of treaties with Britain and the Latin American

---

[5] FARNIE D., *East and West of Suez: The Suez Canal in History, 1854-1956* (Oxford, 1969).
[6] HOSKINS H., 'The Suez Canal in time of war', *Foreign Affairs* 14.1 (1935), pp. 93–101.

states in the decades prior to the construction of the canal, by the time it became a reality Theodore Roosevelt's pursuit of expansionist American power had changed the hemispheric landscape dramatically. From accepting a world in which no European power would dominate a prospective canal, the US moved to the position that it alone should control the real one, even if it never actually owned the canal or the territory. Having built the canal, the United States expanded its naval and military capacity not only in the heavily militarised Canal Zone, but also in the Caribbean to defend the approaches. The Canal became part of a chain of US imperial outposts that included Hawaii and the Philippines. It was justified on commercial grounds as a means of linking the east coast cotton and industrial economy with markets in the Far East, and also as a route for moving warships quickly from one coast of the US to the other.[7]

In the 20th century, the United States was well aware of uncomfortable parallels between its own situation in relation to Panama and that of the British in Egypt, but ultimately refused to accept any moral equivalence. Such assumptions go some way to explaining British Prime Minister Anthony Eden's shock when the United States refused to support him during the Suez Crisis in 1956.[8] By then, the strategic importance of the Panama Canal to the United States had lessened because the US Navy had the capacity to operate fleets in more than one ocean, and no longer needed to move warships quickly from coast to coast. Still, Soviet warships never used the canal during the Cold War, pointing to the political realities underpinning the theory of free transit. In 1979, the United States agreed to cede the canal to Panama in 1999. Panama remained important to the US world-view, but more for its role in the "war on drugs" than for its canal, adding another twist to the multiplicity of factors surrounding superpower attitudes toward global pressure points.

CONCLUSIONS

Alongside the world's real ship canals sit a plethora of schemes that were planned and sometimes even started, but never built. Like railways but on a grander scale, canals became a speculative mania at times, with many competing proposals and visions. There were a number of alternative routes across Central America, for example, and a canal using Lake Nicaragua for part of its length has been proposed several times over the centuries.[9] There is evidently something very attractive and inspiring in projects that promise to alter the relationship between land and sea and suddenly change realities that have for millennia been literally set in stone. Such huge undertakings have also appealed to the military-industrial complex. A clear institutional thread runs from the joint US military

---

[7] LAFEBER W., *The Panama Canal: The Crisis in Historical Perspective* (New York, 1978).
[8] MAJOR J., *Prize Possession: The United States and the Panama Canal, 1903-1979* (Cambridge, 1993).
[9] BRANNSTROM C., 'Almost a canal: visions of interoceanic communication across southern Nicaragua', *Cultural Geographies* 2 (1995), 65-87.

and civilian builders of the Panama Canal to later ventures like the Manhattan Project, and – almost – back again, in plans to "dig" a new sea-level canal across Central America in the 1950s using atomic explosives.[10]

Ship canals have also taken on a symbolic role in successive issues of public and official concern, whether focused on freedom of the seas, naval strategy or the independence of small states. Most recently, they have been part of debates about environmental change and globalisation. Activists criticise new projects in Central America for the damage they would do to rainforests and watersheds, while anti-capitalist voices question the need for ever-larger canals and ships just to satisfy increasing world consumerism. Pollution caused by ships themselves is a growing issue, and ports and canals naturally serve as focal points for such concerns, which are otherwise out at sea and out of sight. On another environmental level, there is an expanding branch of ocean science studying ship canals as "bio-invasion corridors", plotting the ability of marine organisms to use canals to pass from one previously separate ocean to another, in a process named Lessepsian migration after the builder of the Suez Canal.[11]

The major ship canals no longer seem as important to the world's great powers as they were in the first half of the 20th century. It is possible that this might change once again, if, for example, Chinese companies succeed in building their proposed Nicaragua Canal, altering the geopolitical map in an area of sensitive US interest. For now, though, naval strategists and commercial operators value the canals, but are always aware of alternative routes, and of the ongoing contest of technologies and techniques. The smaller regional canals retain their importance for trade, but are conceptualised more on the level of rail or road corridors, crucial in their way, while hardly romantic objects of national prestige. This seems to be a healthy maturity of perspective in this aspect of the relationship between the land and sea.

---

[10] FRENKEL S., 'A hot idea? Planning a nuclear canal in Panama', *Cultural Geographies* 5 (1998), 303–9.
[11] GOLLASCH S., GALIL B. and COHEN A., eds, *Bridging Divides: Maritime Canals as Invasion Corridors* (Dordrecht, 2006).

Oil and water

Patrick Alderton is a researcher in Maritime Economy, United Kingdom.

ABSTRACT. *The exploitation of mineral oil on a world scale has been made possible by the development of tanker shipping, without which the international oil trade would scarcely exist. This sea-borne oil trade has radically transformed the shape of the world economy, and the wealth of particular countries.*

RÉSUMÉ. *C'est l'essor du navire-citerne comme moyen de transport maritime qui a rendu possible l'exploitation de l'huile minérale à l'échelle mondiale. Sans ces navires, le commerce international du pétrole existerait à peine. Ce commerce pétrolier par voie maritime a changé radicalement l'état de l'économie mondiale, et le niveau de richesse de certains pays.*

.•.

Brief introduction

For thousands of years oil has been found in various parts of the world in the form of natural seepage through the earth's crust, and those near its sources found uses for it. The Greek historian Herodotus wrote that it had been used in building the walls of Babylon. Oil was used as a fuel in Persia and the surrounding area in the 8th century. It is also possible that around the same time Chinese junks carried oil in the expansion trunks designed for water. In 1725 Peter the Great issued instructions regulating the carriage of oil in bulk on the Volga.

The growing geographical distribution of oilfields with the ability to utilise liquefied natural gases (LNG)

However, the real commercial potential of oil emerged only in the middle of the 19th century. There are indications that natural sources were being commercially exploited in Russia in 1856 and in Romania in 1857, but the best-documented early oil production is in the United States, when in 1859 crude oil was produced by drilling in Pennsylvania where Colonel Edwin Drake struck oil at Titusville. Originally it was moved in barrels, and then in tin cases. The development of

Table 1. *Percentage share of world oil production, 1890-2000*

Region	1890	1910	1930	1950	1970	1990–2000
Middle East	0.0	0.0	1.8	3.3	30.9	31.0
North America	64.6	65.6	86.5	66.7	24.6	18.2
Russia/USSR	35.4	27.2	6.4	12.2	16.3	11.0
Asia Pacific	0.0	6.3	4.3	4.0	3.9	10.6
Africa	0.0	0.0	0.1	0.2	13.2	10.4
South America	0.0	0.4	1.1	13.5	10.4	9.7
West Europe	0.0	0.4	0.1	0.1	0.7	9.2
World total in mn metric tons	9.9	44.5	95	192.9	2288.4	3589.6

Source: BP *Statistical Annual Review of Oil Industry et al.*

Table 2. *World tanker cargo, 1929-2000*

Year	Tanker cargo mn.tons	Total cargo mn.tons	% tanker cargo
1929	65	455	14.3
1950	225	524	42.9
1960	540	1080	50.0
1970	1241	2482	50.0
1980	1432	3387	42.3
1990	1526	3977	38.4
2000	2024	5374	37.7

Table 3. *Oil consumption per head, 2000*

Country	Oil consumption in US barrels per head, per year
India	0.8
China	1.3
Korea	17.2
Japan	16.4
UK	10.7
Germany	12.6
USA	24.6

Source: Poten & Partners.

drilling techniques enabled the oil industry to expand. By the end of the 19th century the United States and Russia were the major producers of petroleum products. By 1902 Mexico and Venezuela had become major producers, and in 1909 the Anglo-Persian Oil Company was formed. By 1970 Nigeria was an important producer but it was not until the oil price rise of 1973 that many relatively small and expensive oil fields were developed around the world (Table 1). As prices became competitive, so did the transportation pattern of crude oil change. It is important to note how slow the Middle East was to join the major players. Was it the Second World War that made the rest of the world realise the importance of oil?

USES OF OIL

It did not take long for industrial nations to grasp the possibilities of this new major source of energy for heating, lighting, transport and lubrication. Table 2 indicates the growth of tanker cargo during the 20th century, showing how, in the latter years, oil cargoes were the largest single commodity traded by far. It is not surprising that politicians and powerful industries sought to control it.

Assuming that India and China will increase their oil consumption per head of population to, say, only half that of Europe or Japan, the demand in this sector will be tremendous (Table 3).

METHODS OF TRANSPORTING OIL

Oil traded on the competitive oil market is mainly transported by tanker. There have been many discussions concerning the transport of oil by pipelines on the competitive trading markets. There was some enthusiasm for this in the early 1950s when some producers built pipelines to facilitate a better connection to maritime trade routes, such as the 1,068-mile pipeline from Saudi Arabia to Sidon in Lebanon in 1951, and the 558-mile pipeline from Iraq to Banias in Syria in 1952, but there have been few such projects since. For such a competitive market as the international maritime oil market, pipelines lack the flexibility and choice required by any potential buyer. They have also presented attractive targets for various revolutionary groups. As Table 4 indicates, sea transport dominates the world oil trade.

At the moment, some 32,000km of new pipelines are constructed each year, and 50% of these developments are expected in North and South America. Additionally, 8,000km of offshore pipelines are being built per year, with 60% in North West Europe, Asia-Pacific and the Gulf of Mexico. Sixty-four per cent carry natural gas, 19% carry petroleum products and 17% carry crude oil. Further, most of the pipelines are used by the owners of the oil products to distribute their own commodities to link with the commercial oil trading markets where

Table 4. *International oil trade by mode in 2006*

	By volume	By value
Sea	75%	59%
Land	16%	28%
Pipeline	9%	2%
Air	0.3%	1%
Other	0.4%	10%

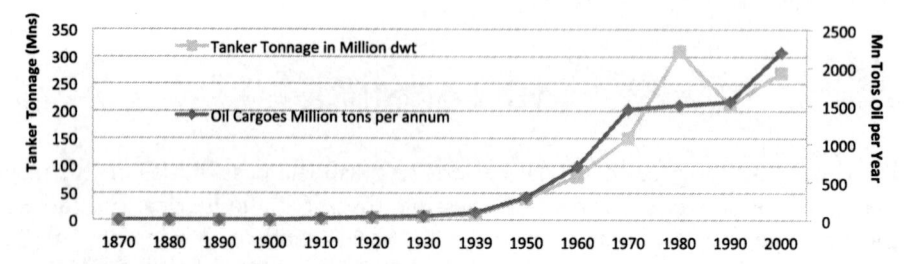

Fig. 1. *Tanker tonnage vs oil transported, 1870–2000*
Source: BP *Statistical Annual Review of Oil Industry et al.*

oil products are bought and sold. Individual organisations such as oil companies will use pipelines, road or rail tankers as required to move their own oil, but the economics and logistics of buying and selling oil on international markets have to be more sophisticated.

As can be seen from the graph in Figure 1, tanker supply and demand have generally been in step, although after the oil price rise in 1973 there was, in the short term, a reduction in demand and an excess of supply. This was mainly the result of the growth of shorter regional supply routes, reducing the distances oil had to be carried.

NEW TANKER TYPES

Experiments had been tried in the 1920s with "combos", meaning ships that could carry bulk oil in one direction and dry bulk in the inevitable ballast voyage, but it was not until the 1950s that the combination types were built in any numbers and Universal Bulk Carriers (UBCs) were developed. For various reasons, by the 1980s this type had largely disappeared. From the early 1950s "oil or ore" carriers (O/Os) appeared, and around 1965 oil and bulk ore carriers (OBOs) superseded them. By the mid-1980s "combos" had largely disappeared and the popularity of OBOs seemed to have peaked, though in 2010 one or two owners were again building, tempted by improved cleaning techniques and the added possibilities of switching vessels between the dry cargo and oil markets.

Table 5. *Tanker development*

1861	The first long-distance trade in oil (lubricating and illuminating oils) was carried by the brig *Elizabeth Watts* of 224 tons, which sailed from the USA to London with 201 barrels of oil in December 1861. She had difficulty in getting a crew, as the cargo was considered dangerous. It was not until 1900 that the term "tanker" came into use.
1865	The first successful movement of oil by pipeline.
1869	Sailing vessels with iron tanks used for the carriage of oil.
1872	The *Vaderland* was the first purpose-built tanker but never carried any oil, as she was also designed to carry passengers and new regulations did not allow both.
1876	The *Andromeda* had square iron tanks on three decks with pipes and pumps
1878	Tank steamers were employed by Nobel Brothers on the Caspian Sea. In 1878 the *Zoroaster* was the first ship converted to a tanker.
1883	There were about thirty tankers in service and a much larger number of vessels carrying oil in barrels and cases.
1885	The first purpose-built tanker to carry oil, the *Glückauf* of 2,300 dwt, was launched.
1887	*Charles Howard*, the first oil burning tanker
1892	Two serious tanker explosions. The British Board of Trade imposed increased safety measures and the first Shell tanker was built, which was also the first tanker to sail through the Suez Canal.
1901	The birth of the oil industry in Texas, when oil was found at Spindletop Hill.
1902	Loaded tankers allowed through the Suez Canal.
1903	The *Vandal* and *Sarmat* were the first diesel-powered tankers. Largest tanker 12,850 dwt.
1906	Longitudinal framing patented and soon became standard in tanker construction.
1911	Forty-eight sailing vessels and 234 steamers carrying oil in bulk. One sailing vessel, the *Navahoe*, was a six-masted schooner that could carry 12,000 tons of oil in bulk (sometimes towed).
1914	Tanker tonnage around 1.25mn dwt, which increased in 1931 to 9mn dwt.
1923	9.1mn tons of coal bunkers and 10.5 mn tons of bunker oil carried by sea.
1952	28,000 dwt largest tanker of the period – known as a "super tanker".
1960	9 September, OPEC formed by Iran, Iraq, Saudi Arabia and Venezuela, in response to the US cutting the posted price of Middle East Oil.
1964	LNG trade between Algeria and Canvey Island, carried by the *Methane Princess* and *Methane Progress*.
1967	Closure of the Suez canal, causing a surge in the demand for tankers.
1973	Oil price rise, transferring power to OPEC and leading to the growth of oil traders as charterers.
2007	Kogas. S. Korea introduces a new liquefied natural gas type of vessels.

Liquefied Gas Carriers

The seaborne transport of liquefied gases began in the late 1920s and early 1930s when a major international company put two combined oil/LPG (liquefied petroleum gas) vessels into operation, but it was not until 1959 that the *Methane Pioneer*, a converted American C1 freighter, became the first ship to carry LNG (liquefied natural gas). By 1993 there were about 946 such tankers, divided into two basic types to suit the two main cargoes concerned, i.e. natural gas (methane) and various petroleum gases such as butane. They are carried in liquefied form as this reduces the volume about six hundred times. LNG is carried either by reducing the temperature to minus 160°C and shipping it in fast, well-insulated and expensive ships or by converting it (an expensive process) into methyl alcohol and carrying it in conventional tankers. The economic advantages of each method depend fundamentally on the distance the gas has to be carried. The methyl alcohol method is better for longer distances and inherently safer. The first LPG to be shipped internationally was transported in the deck tanks of cargo liners. Dry cargo ships were then converted and refitted with cylindrical pressure tanks for LPG. It was not until 1953 that the first purpose-built LPG tanker, the *Rasmus Tholstrup*, was constructed in Sweden. Later on in the decade, these pressure ships became commonplace in Europe. But the thickness of the tanks usually limited an efficient design to a carrying capacity of around 2,500 cubic metres. LPG can be liquefied at higher temperatures than LNG, by pressure or a combination of pressure and refrigeration. LPG carriers tend to be smaller than LNG carriers.

The International Gas Carrier Code (IGC Code) governs the construction of all gas tankers constructed after 1 July 1986. It requires the following.

- All LNG carriers must have double skins and tanks must be constructed of material such as aluminium or nickel that will not become brittle at very low temperatures.
- Tanks must be insulated both to protect the mild steel outer hull and to reduce the cargo loss due to boil-off. These tankers are possibly the only steam turbine ships still being built, as the "boil off" can be used in the boilers to power the ship.
- Two main types of tank construction: independent or free-standing tanks, and "membrane "tanks. The tanks which carry the liquefied gas within the outer hull must be adequately supported. Very strict safety precautions are needed for both the construction and the operation of such ships.

In 2004 new gas-carrying ships were being developed as Compressed Natural Gas (CNG) carriers. It was hoped that CNG carriers would load directly from the supply source and discharge directly to the power point, likewise Pressurised Natural Gas (PNG) carriers. CNG and PNG vessels would be designed for relatively short routes. For longer routes Natural Gas Hydrate (NGH) carriers would carry frozen hydrate pellets.

The strategies involved in the trading market

Before the Second World War the Dutch through Shell, the British through BP and the five major US oil companies enjoyed good concessions of oil in various parts of the world. In the post-war years many oilfields fell under the control of local governments, as in 1951 when the oil refineries of the Anglo-Iranian Oil Co. were nationalised. This led many oil-importing countries to refine the oil under their own control at home rather than at the oilfields. Others argue that the main reason for the change in refining practice was the rapid development of the chemical industry at this time. Whatever the reason, there were significant changes in the tanker industry in the 1950s. There was a large growth in tanker cargoes in the 1950s and 1960s as the oil was now carried twice, first as crude oil from source to refinery, and then as refined oil distributed to markets.

   1950: tankers carried 225 million tons of oil.
   1960: tankers carried 540 million tons of oil.
   1970: tankers carried 1,440 million tons of oil.

This development also drove an increase in tanker size. At the end of the Second World War the largest tankers were of 16,000dwt, whereas by the end of the 1950s there were 100,000dwt tankers, and by the end of the 1960s the VLCC (Very Large Crude Oil Carrier) of around 250,000dwt was developed. When the Suez Canal was closed in 1967 and shipping was diverted around the African Cape, the VLCC of 250,000 dwt became a standard size.

The US standard "T2" 16,000-dwt tanker, built in the hundreds during the Second World War, was so commonplace that it became the unit of measure for refineries, which would measure their requirements in the number of T2s per month. Another, different unit of measure in the oil industry is the barrel. Because of the American dominance in the market, crude oil price and quantity are often quoted in US barrels. As it is a measure of volume, its conversion to tons depends on the density of the oil. There are approximately seven barrels to the ton; Valdez crude is 7.054, Kuwait crude is 7.253, Bonny crude is 7.410.

The growth in the global tanker fleet also involved growing numbers of tanker owners independent of the major oil companies. Before the Second World War the oil companies owned 70% of the tanker fleet and the independents 30%. By the mid-1970s the situation had reversed, with the oil companies owning only 30% of the tonnage, and since then this percentage has been steadily decreasing. In 1984 oil companies owned 24%, independent owners 67% and governments 9%. This growth of independents has meant a growth in tanker chartering. In the late 1970s Saudi Arabia built two 25-million-ton oil refineries which started to reverse the trend of the 1950s and see a return to refining more oil at source.

The growth of the large crude carriers allowed the oil industry to enjoy the economies of scale, but the large ships drew so much water that when they were first introduced there were few ports, especially in the USA and USSR, that could accept a loaded VLCC (Figure 2).

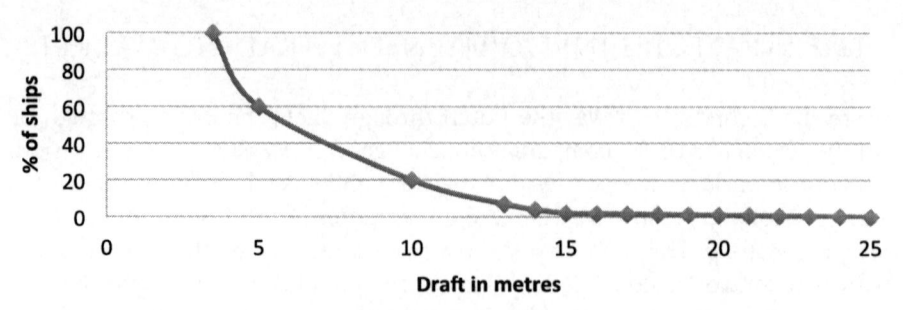

Fig. 2. *Percentage of ships versus draught (vessels over 500 GT)*

OPEC

The Organization of the Petroleum Exporting Countries (OPEC) was formed in 1960 as an intergovernmental organization of many oil-producing countries. The rise of oil prices in 1973 increased the power of OPEC, reduced the power of the large oil companies and encouraged the growth of oil traders speculating in the market. These oil traders then formed a large proportion of the tanker charterers and affected tanker chartering in several ways.

- They bought the oil, chartered and loaded a tanker and then tried to sell the cargo at a profit during the voyage. This explains why much tanker chartering during this period became "open ended", i.e. the precise destination of the ship is not stated when the fixture is made.
- As the shipload of cargo with its unknown port of delivery may be sold several times during a voyage, care must be taken to deliver the cargo to the right owner. In this context masters are well advised not to discharge without sight of the Bill of Lading. This can create problems if the ship and cargo arrive before the documents. Further, although oil companies can be considered reliable charterers, the same may not be said of all oil traders. So it may be worth checking the financial credibility of unknown charterers. For this sort of service the IMB (International Maritime Bureau) can be very helpful.

Table 6. *World crude oil production in million barrels (approx.), 1970–1995*

	Total	Non OPEC	OPEC
1970	48		24
1975	56		26
1980	63	35	28
1985	57	40	17
1990	64	41	23
1995	69	46	23

The rise in oil prices encouraged the development of new oil fields all around the world, for example in the North Sea. This in its turn had a great impact on oil trading patterns, tanker requirements and the power of OPEC. In tanker chartering, instead of quoting the freight in actual cash terms for a given voyage, it is quoted in "scale values", a price per ton-mile of the charter. The Tanker Freight Scale was introduced by the British and American authorities in the Second World War. As the scales became popular the system was privatised, and in 1962 the International Tanker Nominal Freight Scale Association Ltd published INTASCALE. In 1969 the Association revised the scale and called it World Scale, again updated in 1989 as New World Scale.

Under the World Scale, 72 hours are allowed to discharge and reload the ship. As tankers are handling liquids, which can be easily pumped, very fast handling speeds are possible. This is one of the reasons why tankers were the first ship type to grow in size after the Second World War. Virtually all tankers are allowed the same port time because larger tankers have larger pipelines and larger pumps and so can handle the cargo proportionally faster. As a simple rule of thumb, a tanker can be estimated to have a maximum pumping speed per hour of 10% of her deadweight tonnage. This does not mean that a tanker can discharge in ten hours, since time has to be allowed for the more viscous oils to drain, hence the discharge time is usually slightly longer than loading time. However, prior to 1950, when 10,000dwt could be considered to be the typical tanker, two hundred tons an hour could be considered a typical cargo-handling figure.

THE INITIAL COST OF PURCHASING A NEW TANKER

This is invariably one of the largest single costs in tanker operation, but it is also one of the most difficult to quantify with any precision. There are large variations in the price of similar ships built at the same time, depending on quality, speed of delivery and the fluctuations in the supply and demand for ships that can cause new prices to go up or down by 20% in one year. Second-hand prices can be even more unstable. For example, as the oil freight rates fell in 1974 the second-hand price of one particular VLCC dropped from over £30 million to £12 million in just a few months. This is why ship owners (many Greek owners, for example) with a simple management structure that allows them to react quickly in periods of rapidly changing prices can prosper, while nationalised fleets are usually too slow to grasp these market opportunities.

Following the end of the Second World War there were geographical variations in price, with the Japanese yards, for example, offering lower prices for certain types of ship. For new buildings, most countries provide official shipbuilding credit schemes to support their shipyards. In order to regulate competition on this front most shipbuilding countries would attempt to be seen to follow the financing regulations laid down by the OECD, but during the years when shipyards were desperate for work some ship owners, one suspects, have had some very good deals. Second-hand ships, on the other hand, have nearly always to be purchased with a bank loan paid back over a period of five years and with higher rates of interest than most credit packages for new ships. The irony of this is that some ship owners or potential ship owners with cash-flow problems may find it more advantageous to obtain financing for a new ship rather than a second-hand ship, as some "imaginative" credit schemes for new vessels allow the "pay back" to be over a much longer period.

It is interesting to note that in 1956 the UK shipyards still had 35% of the market, but this had dropped to 3.5% by 1976.

Environmental and Political Effects of Development in Mineral Oil

Joint Forces Quarterly 2001 gives an example of the environmental and political effects of using oil as a major oil source and I have taken a few of the following indications from that longer analysis of power for naval vessels.

Coal was widely available in Britain, and Britain had a global network of coaling stations. In addition, coal was inert and thus supplemented armour by reducing damage from shells exploding in coal storage bins. But coal also had disadvantages. Moving it from shore to ship, and aboard ship, was dirty and strenuous work that required extensive manpower. Oil had greater thermal content than coal, so that boilers could be smaller and ships had a longer range. As Churchill also noted, oil offered many other benefits. Greater speed was possible, and oil burned with less smoke, so the fleet would not reveal its presence as quickly. Oil could be stored in tanks anywhere, allowing more efficient design of ships, and it could be transferred through pipes without reliance on stokers, reducing manning. Refuelling at sea was feasible, which provided greater flexibility.

Finding and securing sources of oil seemed to be the most difficult part of the venture. The world's oil supplies were in the hands of vast oil trusts under foreign control. If the Royal Navy overcame the difficulties and surmounted the risks, it should be able to raise the whole power and efficiency of the navy to a definitely higher level; better ships, better crews, higher economies. Supporting change was Admiral Sir John Fisher, the First Sea Lord from 1904 to 1910 and friend and advisor to Churchill during his tenure as First Lord of the Admiralty. Fisher, who dominated the Royal Navy in his day, was renowned for many innovations in administration and engineering.

The final step was finding a source, and toward that end a delegation went to the Persian Gulf to examine oil fields. Two companies were the likely choice of supply: the powerful Royal Dutch Shell Group and the smaller Anglo-Persian Oil Company. After considerable manoeuvring, and largely through Churchill's encouragement, the government decided to maintain competition in the oil industry and ensure supplies by investing directly in Anglo-Persian. The government acquired 51% of company stock, placed two directors on the board and negotiated a secret contract to provide the Admiralty with a 20-year supply of oil under attractive terms.

SAFETY AND OIL POLLUTION OF THE SEAS

The IMO (International Maritime Organisation) was conceived at a UN conference in 1948 but it did not come into being until 1958. Its achievements mainly concern safety and anti-pollution and these functions have become paramount issues in the economics and operation of oil and the sea.

Governments will seldom act on environmental issues unless spurred on by public outrage following a tanker catastrophe. Few news items generate such public outrage as oil pollution of the sea. When such an environmental disaster is announced, the media coverage talks of sterile coastlines for many years to come. However in most cases, after a couple of years the environment seems to have quite recovered and much of the damage that was caused seems to have been due to the unnecessary use of powerful detergents. Many serious researchers have also produced data to indicate that nowadays most oil pollution of the seas comes either from natural causes or from discharges ashore.

Ship owners through their Protection and Indemnity Clubs,[1] realising that there would be public demand for punitive legislation to prevent oil pollution, tried to remove the necessity for it by instigating a scheme known as TOVALOP (Tanker Owners' Voluntary Association for the Liability for Oil Pollution). Under this scheme tanker owners voluntarily cleaned up any pollution they caused. The oil industry also increased the money available for this procedure through a scheme known as CRISTAL. These offers however, were made too late, in that the mechanism for severe anti-pollution laws had already been set in motion. TOVALOP and CRISTAL ended on 20 February 1997.

The stranding of the *Torrey Canyon* near the Scilly Isles in 1967 brought international support for the compulsory routing of ships, which had been under discussion for several years. It also inspired the 1969 Brussels Convention on Oil Pollution. This was the first of a series of international conventions propelled by public anger at oil pollution, each of which laid heavier obligations on tanker owners to ship oil in safe conditions, and heavier liabilities to pay compensation for oil spills. In response to the *Exxon Valdez* oil spill, which occurred in Prince

---

[1] Protection and Indemnity (P&I) Clubs are mutual insurance clubs which shipowners have formed (the first was started in 1855) to meet financial liabilities that they could not insure with Lloyd's or with any of the large insurance companies. P&I insurance also covers claims for oil pollution and personal injury. It covers the shipowner for damage done by his ship to docks, piers and other fixed objects. If the owner's ship sinks, the insurance will pay up on the value of the ship, but the shipowner is left with the responsibility of perhaps having to remove the wreck. This will be paid for by the club. Many of the fines that might be imposed by governments can be covered, as also are claims for loss, short delivery, pilferage or damage to cargo. In other words, P&I insurance covers claims and losses incident to the business of ship owning which the committee considers come within the scope of the club.

William Sound, Alaska on 24 March 1989, the United States Congress passed the Oil Pollution Act of 1990 (OPA), which greatly increased ship owners' liability concerning oil spills when trading to the USA. This Act also rules that all tankers trading with the USA must be double hulled and the effect of this has been that virtually all new tankers constructed since the Act came into force are double hulled.

The growth of legislation on oil pollution has been complex and changing. However, the international regime of compensation for damage caused by oil pollution is currently based on the two updated international conventions: the 1992 Civil Liability Convention (1992 CLC) and the 1992 Fund Convention. The 1992 CLC provides a first tier of compensation which is paid by the owner of a ship which causes pollution damage. Under the 1992 CLC, the ship owner has strict liability for any pollution damage caused by the oil, i.e. the owner is liable even if there was no fault on the part of the ship or its crew. However, the ship owner can normally limit his financial liability to an amount that is determined by the tonnage of the ship. This brief précis of some of the highlights of the pollution legislation shows that it can be a serious headache for ship owners.

In 1998 the IMO introduced the International Safety Management (ISM) Code, which became mandatory for passenger ships, tankers and bulk carriers over 500gt on 1 July 1998.

In November 2002, the 70,000dwt tanker *Prestige* sank in the Atlantic off the Spanish coast. It was built in Japan in 1975, owned by Greeks, chartered by Russians, registered in Bermuda, with crew from the Philippines and a Greek master, bound for Singapore. Note in addition that the ship's classification society was American, thus showing how international one ship can be. As a result of this accident, in December 2002 France, Spain and Portugal ordered single-hull tankers loaded with crude and fuel oil to stay more than two hundred miles from their coasts.

Although there have often been bursts of media anger against the safety of tankers, Table 7 shows in fact that tankers have a very good safety record. The number of oil spills over seven hundred tons is reducing. From 1970 to 1979 there

Table 7. *Merchant shipping losses, 1987–1992*

Ship type	Annual average % of ships lost (1987–92)	Average loss ratio (% of type of ship lost)	Average age of type (years)
Tanker	7.3	0.16	16
Dry bulker	10.1	0.24	14
General cargo ships	69.7	0.58	20
Ro/Ro cargo	5.2	0.48	14
Containership	1.8	0.17	11
Ferry/passenger	0.9	0.18	18

Source: Lloyds Register of Shipping, the usual accepted major source of ship-type statistics.

Table 8. *Environmental pollution by ships, 1993*

Pollution claims	Percentage 1993	Average value ($ mn)
Grounding	23	1.6
Bunkering	12	1.5
Collision	12	0.9
Valve failure	12	0.3
Shell plate failure	11	1.1
Wrong valve	8	0.6
Pipe failure	5	0.2
Fire/sinking	4	5.0
Other	13	1.3

Source: UK P&I Club – Analysis of Major Claims 1993.

were on average 24.2 spills a year, while in 1980–1989 there were 8.9 spills per year, and in 1990–1999 only 7.3 per year.

The pollution analysis in Table 8 is for all ships and it is interesting to note that in 1993 tanker groundings accounted for only 5% of the UK P&I Club pollution claims. For tankers, the most common causes of pollution were valve and shell plate failure, although the greatest expense was caused by grounding, fire and sinking. Between 1974 and 2004 there were 3,174 spills from tankers during loading and discharging, 545 spills due to collision, 563 spills due to groundings and 704 due to hull failure. However, since 2002 the tonnage spilt has been reducing significantly and 91% of the spills have been less than seven tons. In 1977 1.3 million tons of oil were estimated to be discharged annually into the sea. Of this only a small percentage was caused by tanker accidents.

In the early 1950s a BP house magazine speculated that the commercial availability of mineral oil would come to an end in the early1990s. As can be seen, the speculation was wrong as regards its timing but not as regards its inevitability. However, the loss of such a vital commodity does not necessarily mean a catastrophic economic situation. When the UK ran out of wood for shipbuilding it moved to iron, which turned out to be a blessing in disguise.

IMPERIAL FAILURE IN THE INDUSTRIAL AGE: CHINA, 1842–1911

S.C.M. PAINE is William S. Sims Professor of History and Grand Strategy at the US Naval War College, United States

ABSTRACT. *Never having met the industrial world or any serious threat by sea, China was slow to understand the challenge of the West, and of the westernizing Japanese. Preoccupied by major civil wars, the Qing empire was willing to buy foreign naval technology, but (unlike Japan) had no idea of changing its traditional policies. When it did attempt fundamental reform in the early 20th century, it unleashed half a century of civil war.*

RÉSUMÉ. *N'ayant jamais rencontré de sérieuse menace par la mer ou fréquenté le monde industriel, la Chine mit du temps à comprendre le défi que représentaient l'Occident et l'occidentalisation du Japon. Pour faire face aux importants conflits civils qu'il subissait, l'empire Quing désira acquérir la technologie navale étrangère sans pour autant, contrairement au Japon, se soucier de changer sa politique traditionnelle. Au début du XXe siècle, le pays entreprit finalement une réforme fondamentale de son système, déchaînant une guerre civile qui dura un demi-siècle.*

. • .

During the Qing dynasty, the Chinese did not understand the developing maritime dimension of their national security and prosperity. Prior to the Industrial Revolution, there was no significant maritime dimension to either, beyond pirates who sometimes harassed the coast, and the domestic coastal junk trade, which was secondary to the internal overland, riverine, and canal trade and tax-collection system. So the Qing dynasty, beyond buying an assortment of incompatible naval ships late in the dynasty, never turned to the sea and suffered dire foreign policy consequences as a result. China illustrates the problem of not understanding the problem.

China became the victim of its highly successful traditional national security paradigm that focused on landward threats. The Industrial Revolution, however, brought a seaward threat that the Chinese government failed to understand until the last decade of the Qing dynasty. Initially, China's leaders construed the emerging maritime problem narrowly in terms of military technology and imported a great deal during the Self-strengthening Movement (1861–1895). But they failed to understand the civil as opposed to military origins of Western power, let alone the organizational and institutional origins. The Industrial Revolution ushered in a global maritime order based initially on overseas trade, freedom of navigation, and international law to facilitate trade and diplomacy. Ultimately, the Industrial Revolution would spell the end for the traditional world of continental empires that had spawned so many great civilizations, China's included.

CHINA THE GREAT CONTINENTAL EMPIRE

Kenneth Boulding, the eminent twentieth-century social scientist, observed, "There is no failure like success and no success like failure."[1] China became the victim of its own success. For thousands of years it had militarily, politically, economically, and culturally dominated the known world (meaning the world known to China). Its neighbors emulated its institutions and coveted its manufactures. Its settled agriculture, handicrafts, and domestic commerce funded an empire protected by huge armies and governed by a literati elite. For millennia, the Chinese empire produced wealth on a scale that no neighbor could match.

The Han, the dominant ethnic group of China, considered their civilization to be the acme of human achievement and did not recognize the existence of other civilizations. China's destiny was to spread its civilization across the known world to unite "all under heaven" (*tianxia*, 天下), one of the names that the Han used to designate China. Each emperor sought to maintain and, if possible, to expand his territorial inheritance. In times of population growth, the Han migrated outward in search of arable lands. They encouraged or coerced minority peoples to adopt Han cultural norms and, over time, many minorities lost their original ethnic identities to become Han. Those who refused to assimilate were driven first into the hills – areas not suitable for the settled agriculture of the Han – and eventually to the frontier. Many of China's minority peoples, such as the Hakka, the Zhuang, and the Miao, who by the time of the Qing dynasty inhabited the periphery of the empire, had originated in the Yellow River or Yangzi River valleys but had been chased southward over the centuries. The Han strategy for empire produced ethnic homogeneity in the core territories and gradual assimilation on the periphery.

Many of China's immediate neighbors emulated its governmental institutions, educational system, and social practices. Burma, Thailand, Indochina, Korea, and Japan belonged to China's Sinicized world order. Their governments followed the norms of the Chinese global order, the *Pax Sinica*, in which China was the suzerain over all, mediating their disputes with each other and setting the outlines of their foreign but not domestic policies. China's name for itself

---

[1] Cited in HANDEL M.I., *Masters of War: Classical Strategic Thought* (3rd rev. edn, London, 2001), p. 97.

was apt: "the Central Kingdom" (中國, *zhongguo*), with an emphasis on China's central position in the human universe.

The Han considered those who did not follow their practices to be barbarians, ignorant people living on the periphery, whom the Han would either placate with trade or crush militarily when necessary. Historically, dire security threats came not from the Sinicized world but overland from the nomadic peoples living in the northwest and north, the Muslims, the Mongols, and the Manchus. Two had overthrown Han dynasties to form conquest dynasties, the Mongol Yuan dynasty (1271-1368) and the Manchu Qing dynasty (1644-1911), the two territorially largest dynasties in Han history. Mountains or seas protected China's other borders.

China administered this global order through the tributary system, under which China maintained bilateral relations with its neighbors, who over time became increasingly Sinicized. The neighbors made occasional and eventually annual tribute missions to Beijing bearing gifts of local manufactures. In return, they received far more valuable Chinese manufactures intended to buy peace on the frontier and compliance with Han norms for foreign policy. China dealt separately with its neighbors in order to prevent them from coordinating. If facing multiple adversaries, China would appease the least-menacing – often through preferential trade arrangements – while it annihilated the most dangerous threat. During the Opium Wars, China's rulers eventually decided to appease the West through trade while they annihilated the far more dangerous threat, a succession of internal rebellions. As long as China remained technologically and organizationally superior to its neighbors, and as long as the neighbors could not coordinate, the traditional security paradigm, known as the tributary system, worked.

In the 19th century, the very success of Chinese civilization blinded both the Manchu dynasty and the Han literati to the unprecedented nature of the changes taking place in Europe, a region that barely figured in their consciousness. In the 18th century, China was probably the richest empire in human history. It produced the most technologically sophisticated luxury goods. It could organize armies on a scale unimaginable to its enemies – only during the Napoleonic Wars did Europeans field forces measured in the hundreds of thousands, whereas China had been doing so for over two thousand years. A very small bureaucracy in Beijing ruled the empire. Beyond the royal house, the elite were those who scored highest on government examinations that tested the humanities. This elite scorned commercial achievements. Merchants were the lowest social class in the traditional hierarchy of scholars at the top, followed by farmers, laborers, and merchants at the bottom. The Industrial Revolution would upend the world as the Chinese knew it. In the West, merchants eventually held high social status; profits from trade increasingly animated Western foreign policy; and the Industrial Revolution would transform the proficiency and reach of Western militaries.

Prior to these changes, although from time to time pirates marauded along Chinese shores, they threatened primarily local economic and commercial interests and never the survival of the provincial government, let alone the central government. Although the junk trade linked coastal communities, prior to the Industrial Revolution China's main cities were located inland and connected primarily by rivers, roads, and canals. While fish formed a important part of the diet, control of fisheries was not a source of international conflict.

The emerging global maritime order

In the late 18th century, a new era dawned in Britain that after the Napoleonic Wars spread to continental Europe, and by the mid-19th century it began to make itself felt in Asia. It became known as the Industrial Revolution: a revolution because it irrevocably overturned the way the world was. A combination of steam power, the iron industry, textiles, the insurance industry, banking, and, in its later stages, railways, telegraphs, and steamships, among other technological and institutional innovations, together transformed once-static societies into the rapidly changing world that is today taken for granted. These domestic innovations produced economic growth, initially at the modest rate of 3 percent per annum. Compounded growth then doubled per capita standards of living each generation. Over time, those whose economies grew became dramatically richer and more powerful than those whose economies did not. The Industrial Revolution overturned the traditional hierarchy among nations. Those who adopted and adapted to the emerging industrial economic order most rapidly and most completely remain the world's most wealthy and most powerful nations.

The Industrial Revolution gave rise to an emerging westernized global order conducive to the promotion of trade and the creation of wealth. It was based on freedom of navigation, freedom of trade, international law, and eventually on an expanding set of international institutions to facilitate trade and communication. At its root, it was a maritime global order because its members were bound together by maritime shipping, which was far cheaper than the overland trade, which it soon eclipsed. In the traditional world of continental empires, wealth was based on agriculture and therefore on land. Land produced the agricultural surplus to fund armies and peasant families produced the children to man armies. The land power with the most proficient army best defended the homeland and most rapidly expanded the empire at the expense of its less proficient neighbors. The more land, the greater the wealth and armies to keep expanding.

In the emerging maritime world of the Industrial Revolution, wealth became based on the comparative advantages derived from trade, the mass production of industry, and economies of scale. People could consume on an unprecedented scale. Land was no longer key. In this new maritime world, the highly successful national security paradigms of traditional societies suddenly no longer worked. Societies that had once been comparatively rich became comparatively poor not because they had become less capable but because exogenous changes taking place in Europe had made Europe so much more economically efficient. These economic efficiencies then had a cascade effect throughout society, most blatantly on relative military power. The Industrial Revolution was unprecedented in human history both in scale and in effects.

China, whose educational system emphasized the study of precedents, was singularly ill-prepared to meet the challenge presented by these unprecedented changes. The timing could not have been worse. The first impact of these changes coincided with a wave of huge internal rebellions. The largest were the Nian (1851–1868), the Taiping (1851–1864), the Donggan (1862–1873), and the Xinjiang (1862–1878) rebellions that nearly toppled the dynasty. But there were many other rebellions throughout the 19th century. In reality they were full-fledged civil wars; not just one, but many. Together they killed tens of millions of people and caused long-term devastation throughout China that crippled local economies for decades.

Westerners, like so many barbarians before them, came to China in pursuit of high-quality manufactures and commodities, most particularly tea. But, unlike past barbarians, they possessed superior military technology. They also arrived at a time when the Qing dynasty had to deploy its main armies against the internal foes seeking regime change, not the external foes greedy for better terms of trade. The real beneficiary of China's perfect storm of threats was Russia, which moved in to formalize the Russo-Chinese border and walked away with sovereignty over new territories exceeding US territory east of the Mississippi River.

Resistance and appeasement

The Industrial Revolution brought a maritime dimension to Chinese security that successive governments found hard to understand. A highly lucrative triangular trade developed among Britain, India, and China. Britain traded its manufactures for Indian opium, which it exchanged for Chinese tea. Britain wished to regularize this trade, while the Manchu government (but not the Han merchants) wanted to eliminate it. The government blamed the trade for an outflow of silver that inflated domestic land taxes – paid in copper but assessed in silver. The silver outflow caused acute rural distress because silver prices rose relative to copper prices, creating a de facto tax increase on a peasantry already suffering from overpopulation, land degradation, and economic dislocations from the many internal rebellions. These tax problems, not opium consumption per se, made the Qing dynasty determined to stop the trade. Opium in the 19th century was not the bugaboo that it became in the 20th century; indeed, its sale was legal in Britain until World War I. The solution to the silver outflow would have been an adjustment of land tax rates and the taxation of commerce. Instead, China went to war to expel Westerners and close down the trade.

Britain won the ensuing Opium War (1839–1842) by deploying naval forces to take the intersection of the Grand Canal and the Yangzi River, and thus cutting the delivery of the vital rice tribute to Beijing. China capitulated without intending to honor the provisions of the 1842 Treaty of Nanjing, which opened five ports to international trade, demanded an indemnity, and envisioned the Western payment to the Chinese government of customs on the trade. A Second Opium War (1856–1860) erupted when France joined forces with Britain to enforce the treaty terms. This time Anglo-French expeditionary forces threatened Beijing. Mid-war in 1858, Qing representatives signed four treaties of Tianjin with Britain, France, the United States, and Russia, respectively, opening an additional eleven treaty ports, allowing the stationing of foreign representatives in the capital, permitting foreigners to travel within China, detailing trade regulations, and demanding another indemnity. Russia's treaty promised prompt demarcation of their mutual frontier. When the emperor learned of the treaty terms, he had the negotiator commit suicide and refused to enforce the terms.

In the summer of 1860, the Second Opium War and the Taiping Rebellion reached critical stages. Anglo-French naval forces had blockaded the Gulf of Bohai, again preventing rice shipments from reaching Beijing, and a large Taiping force was heading toward the capital. In August, Anglo-French forces took the fortifications at Dagu on the Gulf of Bohai and protecting Beijing's port city of Tianjin. They then took Tianjin and in September began marching on Beijing, whereupon the emperor fled the capital. In October, British forces burned his summer palace on the city outskirts in order to put direct pressure on the royal house. The strategy succeeded. Four days later the emperor sued for peace and his half-brother signed the Treaty of Beijing, which guaranteed the enforcement of the previous treaties, increased the indemnity, and ceded Kowloon to Britain.

The Western treaties focused on trade and on diplomatic representation to facilitate trade. Rather than fight, the Qing dynasty would have been far wiser to tax the trade and use commerce to promote economic growth at home. Economic growth, however, did not exist as an intellectual concept in China at that time.

Russia's treaties focused on territory. Simultaneously with the Second Opium War, Russia sent several flotillas down the Amur River (which today forms the border between Russia and China) and, like the British, signed a set of treaties, two of which (the 1858 treaties of Aigun and Tianjin) the Chinese tried to ignore, but the third of which (the 1860 Treaty of Beijing) they followed. Russia gained sovereignty over much of Central Asia, the northern bank of the Amur River, and the Pacific coast between the Ussuri River and the sea without firing a shot but by piggybacking on the British and French victories and posing as China's mediator with the West. Russia played on Chinese fears that the Western powers intended regime change, when they wanted only commerce. Meanwhile, prior to the development of the railways, Russia had no ability to hold the territory that China ceded and so China had no need to cede the territory, particularly since Russia rendered no services as a mediator.

China appeased the European barbarians with trade privileges for the Western Europeans and land for the Russians so that it could focus on putting down the far more important internal rebellions. The Chinese government did not see the peace treaties as permanent documents but intended to overturn them later when it recovered its strength. But China never recovered its technological or military superiority, so the treaty terms endured.

Although Western naval forces defeated China in both Opium Wars, not until 1874 was there a major foreign policy debate over the prioritization of land versus naval defense. Those favoring the traditional preeminence of land forces won the day, although China went on to acquire a variety of capital ships, which, by the last decade of the 19th century, still put its navy among the world's top ten.

Defeats in the Opium Wars did make clear to China's leaders the superiority of Western military technologies. As the Chinese had done in the past when they had encountered superior military technology, such as cannon introduced by the Portuguese during the Ming dynasty, they set about reverse-engineering the armaments in order to manufacture their own. Those who organized these efforts from the 1860s through the 1890s became known as the self-strengtheners. They often were Han officials serving as provincial governors, and they were concerned with defense issues because China had no national defense; governors were responsible for the defense of their provinces.

These governors established provincial arsenals, built factories to produce modern armaments, sent students abroad to study foreign technology and militaries, and hired foreign mercenaries to form Western-drilled armies. Given the nature of their administrative positions, they could not easily coordinate with each other, so they introduced a hodgepodge of foreign technology.

The self-strengtheners understood Western power strictly in military terms. In 1881, after the Xinjiang Rebellion, when China had a large standing army in place, it forced Russia, a continental foe, which lacked the transportation system to deploy troops in sufficient numbers, to withdraw from and rescind its 1873 declaration of Russia's newest region of Kuldja (the Ili Valley of modern-day northwestern Xinjiang). With this success, Chinese authorities incorrectly believed that they could resume foreign policy as usual. They did not differentiate the traditional continental problem that they had just solved with Russia from the maritime problem posed by naval powers. They failed to see the harbinger of enduring and even growing vulnerabilities in Japan's annexation, with a naval expeditionary force, of the Ryukyu Kingdom in 1879, formerly a Chinese tributary.

Defeat in the Sino-French War (1883–1885) soon followed. The French had been gradually extending their control over Annam (northern and central Vietnam), another tributary of China. The government of Annam called on China, as its suzerain, to protect it from the predations of France. China sent ground troops, which fought well. Its naval forces, however, did not. Its Nanyang and Fuzhou fleets were poorly equipped and the state-of-the-art Beiyang Fleet, based in North China, refused to assist. France responded by attacking Taiwan, an island vulnerable to French sea power. France sank the Fuzhou Fleet in port, as Japan would later do to the Beiyang Fleet in the First Sino-Japanese War. Just as the British had done in the First Opium War, the French cut Qing tax revenues via the Grand Canal, this time by blockading the Nanyang Fleet on the Yangzi River. Again the Qing settled on enemy terms. Vietnam became a French protectorate.

FAILURE TO UNDERSTAND THE THREAT

In 1894, Sir Thomas Francis Wade, the British minister to Beijing from 1871 to 1882, the co-developer of the Wade-Giles Romanization system for Chinese, and resident of China for over forty years, told an interviewer: "The sentiment of China was very well represented by a Chinese statesman who said to me, 'We intend to adopt Western machinery, but we shall keep our old customs and our old morality.' The more astute Japanese, on the other hand, clearly perceives that you cannot have one without the other: and that the machinery of Western life is merely the fruit, so to speak, of the ideas that underlie it. The consequence with China is that her attempts to adopt Western ideas have been continually defeated by her adherence to ancient and invincible custom."[2]

The Chinese perceived the security threat posed by the West in terms of military technology and set about buying and manufacturing state-of-the-art armaments. But they could not match the West. The Japanese, who carefully observed events in China and sent year-long fact-finding missions to the West to study the underpinnings of Western military power, concluded that the problem was not simply modernization, meaning the acquisition, use, and manufacture of state-of-the-art technology, let alone simply military technology, but more fundamentally a problem of westernization, meaning the adaptation of the institutional innovations of the West, not only those concerning military institutions but also those concerning a whole array of civil institutions. The Japanese concluded that they must westernize their political, military, economic, educational, and social institutions, not out of any affinity for Western culture, but from a cold-headed calculation that only by westernizing could Japan defend itself against the West. In short, they believed that the technological fruits could not be had without the garden in which they grew.

Japan brought home this conclusion to China with its victory in the First Sino-Japanese War (1894–95), fought over the domination of Korea. In 1894 Korea called on China, its suzerain, to protect it from Japan. Again China succumbed to expeditionary forces totally dependent on naval supply lines. China, to its shock and dismay, lost every battle in the ensuing war that rapidly eliminated the Chinese presence in Korea, destroyed China's two naval bases at Port Arthur (Lüshun) and Weihaiwei on facing shores of the entrance to the Gulf of Bohai, and threatened a march on Beijing via Manchuria. The Nanyang Fleet paid back the Beiyang Fleet by refusing to come to its aid. In the end, China sued for peace, ceded Taiwan and the Pescadores, and paid an indemnity that funded the

---

[2] 'Some English Views on the War', in *The Japan Weekly Mail* (Yokohama), 29 December 1894, p. 732.

Japanese side of a post-war Russo-Japanese arms race. The combination of the destruction of the Beiyang Fleet and a heavy indemnity ended Chinese naval power for the next century. Only in the 1990s did China begin to reconstitute itself as a naval power.

The war fully discredited both the tributary system (China's global order) and Confucianism at home in the way that the defeats against the European powers could not. Japan, a member of China's Sinified world, had proven that Sinification was not a one-way process after all, the world had other civilizations, and a subject nation could emulate another civilization (by westernizing) and use the technological and organizational accomplishments of that alien civilization to trounce China in war. Japan detonated the foundations of China's traditional order at home and abroad. To the present day, China has yet to find a satisfactory replacement for either.

SINS OF OMISSION

The Chinese still failed to understand why they had lost the First Sino-Japanese War. They had grasped defeat from the jaws of victory. Both countries had comparable fleets at the start of hostilities. Japan required its navy to reach the theater, whereas China did not. So China could afford to risk its fleet in a way that Japan could not. Yet China failed to use its ships but allowed the Japanese to blockade and sink them in port, getting little military advantage from its considerable naval investments. If China had used its fleet offensively, particularly its two armored battleships for which Japan had no counterpart, at a minimum China could have disrupted if not prevented Japanese troop landings and possibly could have sunk a good part of the Japanese fleet and merchant marine. In addition, Chinese forces could have attacked Japanese troops during river crossings and at mountain passes, instead of waiting in static positions behind city walls that Japan's modern artillery rapidly destroyed. China could have drawn the Japanese as far inland as possible so they would fight on extended logistical lines. China was organizationally inept. Because China had dominated others for the duration of known history, the Chinese saw no need to undertake the sort of radical reforms that allowed Japan to defeat them. China's loss of the First-Sino Japanese War marked the end of the Self-strengthening Movement, which the war had proved to be inadequate.

Belatedly, the Qing dynasty became interested in the Meiji Restoration and introduced its own version of Japan's westernizing reforms. In 1901 the Qing dynasty created a Ministry of Foreign Affairs, westernized its civil service and military exams, promoted railway construction, and ordered the drafting of a westernized commercial code; in 1902 it promoted study abroad, condemned footbinding, and created a national curriculum; in 1903 it established ministries of Trade and Commerce, and westernized its military training; in 1904 it authorized the creation of a thirty-six-division national army and opened the higher military ranks to Han officers, and drafted a commercial code; in 1905 it created ministries of Police and Education, a central mint, and a central bank; in 1906 it authorized the drafting of a constitution, replaced earlier administrative structures with eleven ministries, and banned opium; in 1907 it created a national system of education for girls and curtailed Manchu privileges; in 1908 it completed a draft criminal code and established nationwide committees to reorganize financial affairs; in 1909 it held elections for provincial assemblies and centralized financial authority under the Ministry of Finance; in 1910 it convened the National Assembly, which passed the first budget, reorganized the navy, and authorized only the central bank to issue paper notes; and in 1911 it created a General Staff, completed the draft civil code, and nationalized the railway system.

There was only one fly in the ointment. The creation of a unified Han military led to the overthrow of Manchu minority rule, eliminating the Manchus from the political map of China and also virtually from the ethnic map as well. The late-Qing reforms were all for naught when China devolved into a nationwide civil war that continued until the Communist victory in 1949. As Alexis de Tocqueville correctly observed, "[T]he most dangerous moment for a bad government is when it begins to reform itself."[3]

The sea was a critical factor in the destruction of imperial China. The oceanic agents of change came in the form of international commerce by sea and naval fleets to impose commerce on foreign terms. Thus there were both military and civil dimensions to the sea. Japan understood this, whereas China perceived only Western military superiority. While China went to war against the West, Japan westernized in order to defend against the West and, more importantly, to supplant China as the dominant regional power of Asia. Japan toppled China from its historical preeminence by means of war, which required expeditionary forces supported by the navy. China's leaders did not perceive that its maritime enemies could lose by either land or sea, whereas China could lose only by land. They failed to develop a strategy that leveraged this great strength along with the sheer size of the theater, its huge manpower reserves, and its interior lines. Degrade Japan's naval strength and then draw its forces inland, extend its logistical links to the sea, and the Chinese would have won.

BIBLIOGRAPHY

ELLEMAN B.A. *Modern Chinese Warfare, 1795-1989* (London, 2001).
ELLEMAN B.A. and PAINE S.C.M., *Modern China: Continuity and Change 1644 to the Present* (Boston, MA, 2010).

---

[3] DE TOCQUEVILLE A., *The Old Regime and the Revolution*, ed. F. FURET and F. MÉLONIO, trans. A.S. KAHAN, 2 vols (Chicago, 1998-2001) vol. 1, p. 222.

FAIRBANK J.K., *Trade and Diplomacy on the China Coast: The Opening of the Treaty Ports, 1842-1854* (Cambridge, MA, 1953).

HSU I.C.Y., *China's Entrance into the Family of Nations: The Diplomatic Phase 1858-1880* (Cambridge, MA, 1968).

HSU I.C.Y., 'The great policy debate in China, 1874: maritime defense vs. frontier defense', *Harvard Journal of Asiatic Studies* 24 (1964-1965), 212-28.

MANCALL M., *China at the Center: Three Hundred Years of Foreign Policy* (New York, 1984).

PAINE S.C.M., *Imperial Rivals: China, Russia, and Their Disputed Frontier* (Armonk, NY, 1996).

PAINE S.C.M., *The Sino-Japanese War: Perceptions, Power, and Primacy* (Cambridge, 2003).

RAWLINSON J.L., *China's Struggle for Naval Development 1839-1895* (Cambridge, 1967).

CHINA TURNS TO THE SEA, 1912-1990

BRUCE A. ELLEMAN is Professor of Maritime History, William V. Pratt Professor of International History at the US Naval War College, Newport, United States

ABSTRACT. *The modern Chinese navy, established by the Nationalist government in 1928, was ruined by the Japanese invasion. Reconstructed after the war with transferred U.S., British and Canadian ships, it disintegrated during the civil war when key units defected, opening the way to the Communist victory. Only after the retreat to Taiwan did the Nationalist government build up an effective modern navy. The communists, meanwhile, kept their own warships divided between different fleets to minimize the danger of mutiny. Not till the 1990s were they fully liberated from Russian technology. Now backed by a wealthy economy, the Chinese navy is able to support an expansionist policy at sea, but it is still not fully trusted by the régime.*

RÉSUMÉ. *La marine chinoise moderne, établie par le gouvernement nationaliste en 1928, fut complètement détruite par l'invasion japonaise puis reformée après la guerre grâce au transfert de navires américains, britanniques et canadiens. Pendant la guerre civile, elle se désintégra à nouveau par la désertion des unités principales, ouvrant la voie à la victoire communiste. Ce ne fut qu'après sa retraite vers Taiwan que le gouvernement nationaliste parvint à construire une marine moderne et efficace. Dans le même temps, les communistes gardèrent leurs propres navires de guerre séparés entre différentes flottes pour minimiser le danger lié à la mutinerie. Ils ne furent entièrement libérés de la technologie russe que dans les années 1990. Soutenue par une économie solide, la marine chinoise peut désormais défendre une politique expansionniste en mer mais n'est toujours pas complètement acceptée par le régime.*

. • .

During the 19th century, China endured many maritime defeats, including the first and second Opium Wars (1839-1841, 1856-1860), the Sino-French conflict (1884-1885), and the first Sino-Japanese War (1894-1895). As a result, China lost its formerly unchallenged position as Asia's hegemon. During much of the 20th century, China's almost constant civil wars meant that its naval forces were often divided, sometimes into as many as half a dozen competing fleets. Fear of naval mutiny, the opposing demands of a land power versus an emerging sea power, and great power competition with Russia on its land border, and with the United States and its allies on the sea, have challenged the naval development of warlord, Nationalist, and Communist governments alike. Only with the end of the Cold War in 1990 have economic relations between China and Taiwan started to heal the post-World War II division of China.

THE REPUBLIC OF CHINA AND WARLORD NAVIES

In the early years of the 20th century, reform-minded Chinese officials began to consider how to create a modern government, including adopting new educational, social, and military programs. Copying Japan's success in the Meiji Restoration, these reforms were based on the study of Western history and politics, the adoption of science and technology, and the encouragement of travel and study abroad by Chinese officials, merchants, and intellectuals. Rather than catching up with the West, however, the "New Army" military and naval reforms weakened the Manchus' authority. On 10 October 1911, military units in Hankou rebelled, sparking a nation-wide revolution. Beijing ordered Admiral Sa Zhenbing to lead one cruiser and seven gunboats up the Yangzi River to put down the rebellion. During 18–19 October, Sa's task force bombarded the city, but on 12 November the Han Chinese sailors mutinied and joined the revolutionaries, forcing Sa to flee.

Without a loyal navy to stop the rebellion it quickly spread, and eventually fifteen provinces announced their secession from the Qing dynasty. On 1 January 1912, the Republic of China (ROC) was formed, with Sun Yat-sen as its first president. But true power still resided in the army and the navy under the leadership of Yuan Shikai, a Qing dynasty general who negotiated the Manchu dynasty's abdication on the condition that he should become president. Puyi, the last Qing Emperor, abdicated on 12 February 1912, Sun resigned, and Yuan became the new president of the ROC on 14 February 1912.

The years from 1912 to 1928 were characterized by almost constant civil war, both among the northern warlords and between the warlords and the independent Nationalist movement in the south. Following Yuan's death in 1916, warlords fought for power. From its base in South China, the Nationalist – Guomindang – party reunified China in 1928 and established a single Chinese navy that combined six separate regional fleets previously under the control of various warlords. Admiral Chen Shaokuan (1889–1969), the Minister of the Navy, adopted comprehensive naval reforms. He envisioned seventy-one first-line ships, including battleships, cruisers, and destroyers, plus thirty-four support ships, including submarines, depot ships, mine sweepers, torpedo boats, and a hospital ship. The formation of this new naval force was to be divided into a Central, Northeast, and Guangdong fleet, with the Central fleet being the largest and composed of two regular squadrons and a training squadron. The presence of three fleets mirrored the Qing navy, but establishing squadrons based on function was a more Western concept.

Admiral Chen requested that Britain send a naval mission to help organize and train the Nationalist navy. The head of this mission, Captain Baillie-Grohman, reported back to London during 1932 that while it was large, consisting of fifty-six ships and nearly 8,017 sailors, the Nationalist navy was "purely a paper one, and ships are moved round at a moment's notice without any reference to the Flag Officer under whom they are supposed to be." The biggest handicap was lack of a coherent policy. The equipment and armament were not standard, the ships were a "compromise between river and seagoing craft," and the lack of "*regular* funds" made the navy's existence precarious.[1]

When the second Sino-Japanese War escalated in July 1937, the Nationalist navy was insufficiently prepared to face this new threat. Beginning in August 1937, it held off the Japanese advance up the Yangzi River for almost fifty days. On 23 September 1937, however, Japanese bombers sank the Nationalists' most important warships, *Pinghai* and *Ninghai*. China's naval defenses were broken by early December. Most of the Nationalist navy's 120 vessels, totaling more than 68,000 tons, were used as blockships in a vain attempt to stop Japanese forces. The few surviving Nationalist ships continued to conduct a naval blockade at Matang, in Anhui province. By 1940, however, the "remaining ships were scuttled near the Yangzi Gorges at Yizhang in Hubei Province ... [and] Chiang K'ai-shek ordered the Navy Ministry dissolved."[2] The last remnants of the Nationalist navy were disbanded in 1940 and the crews dispersed until after World War II.

THE CHINESE CIVIL WAR

After World War II, the Nationalist navy was reconstituted from a wide range of confiscated ships from Japan and the Chinese puppet government under Wang Jingwei, plus surplus vessels from the United States, Britain, and Canada. The U.S. would eventually transfer to China a total of 271 surplus ships, while Britain and Canada provided 15 ships, and another 33 were transferred from Japan as war reparations. China's most advanced ship was a British cruiser, *Aurora*, renamed *Chongqing* in honor of the Nationalists' wartime capital. By 1947, the navy controlled a total of 824 vessels of various types, including many modern ships. As of 31 October 1948, the navy had 40,859 personnel, including a total of 8,062 officers.

The Chinese civil war undermined morale in the Nationalist navy. Beginning in 1947 there were several important cases of sabotage and defections. On 25 February 1949 the Nationalist flagship, *Chongqing*, mutinied and defected. This was considered an enormous "loss of face" to Chiang Kai-shek personally, who ordered the ship destroyed. While dockside in the Communist-held port of Huludao, *Chongqing* was attacked by B-24s and B-25s sent by the Chinese National Air Force and was severely damaged. Fearful that the Nationalist navy might

---

[1] 'Naval Mission in China, 1931–1932, Report by Captain Baillie-Grohman', with index, British National Archives, ADM 1/8756/133, pp. 4, 65; underlining in the original.

[2] SWANSON B., *Eighth Voyage of the Dragon: A History of China's Quest for Seapower* (Annapolis, MD, 1982), p. 166.

send in ships to reclaim it, the Communists scuttled *Chongqing*; during the early 1950s they refloated it and renamed it *Beijing*.

Because the USSR retained sea control in Manchuria, and refused to let Nationalist ships dock in Lüshun (Port Arthur) and Dalian (Dairen), the Nationalist navy could play only a minor role during the final stage of the civil war. By spring 1949, about a quarter of the Nationalist navy's total tonnage, and many of its best ships, had defected to the Communists. If the Nationalists had retained their navy intact, the Yangzi River might have become the dividing line between North and South China. But with naval vessels of their own, Communist forces could now cross into South China and directly threaten Nanjing and Shanghai. This forced Chiang Kai-shek and his followers to retreat to Taiwan. During this seaborne retreat, the Nationalist navy helped transport more than six hundred thousand military personnel and two million civilians.

During the early-to-mid 1950s the Communist and Nationalist forces fought over numerous off-shore islands in the Taiwan Strait. The Nationalists' successful hold over twenty-five islands was an important deterrent to a cross-strait invasion. The Nationalists also adopted a naval blockade against the mainland beginning in July 1949. By early 1954, patrolling the naval blockade shifted from warships to a more intensive use of air power with the addition of American-made jet bombers. In December 1954, Taipei and Washington signed a mutual-security pact reaffirming that the U.S. government would defend Taiwan and the Penghus, but it was left deliberately vague how the U.S. might react to an attack on the off-shore islands. In early 1955, the People's Liberation Army (PLA) attacked the Dachen Islands, the northernmost off-shore islands used in the blockade, which forced the Nationalists to evacuate. Backing Taiwan, on 29 January 1955 Congress passed the "Formosa Resolution," stating that the U.S. President could judge whether a Communist attack on the off-shore islands constituted part of an invasion of Taiwan.

The Communist strategy of breaking up the U.S.-Taiwan alliance backfired. With active American assistance, the Nationalist navy developed rapidly. By early 1955, the Nationalists had 228 vessels listed as active, 85 of which were considered sea-going vessels, and the ships were reorganized into squadrons determined by function. Training was also improved, with the Chinese Naval Academy adopting a curriculum similar to that of the U.S. Naval Academy. During July 1956 the Naval College of Technology was changed into a Naval Postgraduate School, and in 1957 a special course for advanced junior officers was offered by the Naval Command and Staff College.

A second cross-strait crisis broke out in August 1958, focusing on the Nationalist-controlled island of Jinmen (Quemoy). Communist leaders explained that they were most "concerned by the fact that the off-shore islands are being used to mount Commando attacks on the mainland and to impose a blockade."[3] In October 1958 Secretary-of-State John Foster Dulles flew to Taiwan to persuade

---

[3] Memorandum of conversation between Prince Norodom Sihanouk, the president of the Council of Ministers of Cambodia, and Walter S. Robertson, assistant secretary to the U.S.

Chiang Kai-shek to reduce the size of Nationalist forces on the islands. This decision effectively ended the Nationalists' naval blockade, which had already lasted over ten years. An American-backed embargo on strategic goods continued, however, until 1971.

The Nationalist goal of retaking mainland China by force remained out of reach. Taking full advantage of its geographic position straddling East Asia's most important sea lanes, Taiwan focused instead on economic growth. A unique combination of Han Chinese culture, Japanese agricultural and business models, technical and financial assistance from the United States, and Nationalist Party leadership thrust Taiwan from third world to first world status in only two generations. During the 1980s, Taiwan's foreign exchange reserve of $70 billion was almost half of the mainland's entire GNP, sparking jokes that perhaps Taiwan could buy back mainland China a piece at a time. This incredible economic turnaround was called the Taiwan miracle.

SOVIET SUPPORT FOR THE PLA NAVY

On 23 March 1949, Mao Zedong and Zhu De formed a PLA Navy (PLAN), with the *Chongqing* as the Communists' first warship. Other Nationalist ships soon defected and joined the PLAN, including most of the Yangzi fleet under Admiral Lin Zun. By the end of April 1949, the Communists successfully crossed the Yangzi River and advanced on Shanghai, which fell during the following month. With the founding of the People's Republic of China (PRC) on 1 October 1949, the so-called Two Chinas standoff between the PRC on the mainland and the ROC on Taiwan was created and has continued to the present day.

The PLAN received the bulk of its naval equipment, plus many of its earliest sailors, from the Nationalists. During spring 1950, Chinese military and naval forces retook the Miao Islands, north of Shandong Peninsula, as well as attacking Hainan Island, ten miles from China's southern coast, in the process pushing Nationalist troops off many other off-shore islands. Once Communist forces had retaken the northernmost and southernmost islands, however, they halted their offensive. To invade the remaining Nationalist-controlled off-shore islands required more advanced naval technology, such as amphibious landing craft, which the PLAN could get only from the USSR.

It appeared to many outside observers that it was simply a matter of time before the PRC reunified with Taiwan. During spring 1950 there were rumors that the PLAN might try to replicate its success in storming Hainan by attacking Taiwan. The PRC began collecting 4,000 motorized junks in port cities along the Taiwan Strait in preparation for an amphibious invasion. Following the beginning of the Korean War during late June 1950, however, President Harry S.

Mission to the UN, 16 September 1958, 'China; 1958–1960', *Foreign Relations of the United States*, vol. XIX, pp. 201–3.

Truman ordered the U.S. Seventh Fleet to intervene and "neutralize" the Taiwan Strait so as to insure that the Korean war did not escalate into World War III. The Communist invasion of Taiwan was delayed, and then canceled altogether. The U.S. Navy's Taiwan Patrol Force conducted both constant and intermittent patrols in the Taiwan Strait for the next twenty-nine years.[4]

PRC leaders did not fully trust the PLAN. Unlike the Nationalist navy, which was divided into squadrons organized by function, the PLAN was divided into three regional fleets. The Guangdong Riverine Defense Command was changed into the South Sea Fleet (*Nanhai jiandui*). Near Shanghai, the Huadong Military Region naval forces became the East Sea Fleet (*Donghai jiandui*). Finally, following the Soviet departure from Lüshun and Dalian in 1955, the Northeast Navy and the North China Navy merged into the North Sea Fleet (*Beihai jiandui*), which included China's first submarine corps, founded on 19 June 1954, and the first destroyer unit, created on 22 July 1954. By the mid-1950s, the PLAN's structure exactly replicated the Qing-era division into separate fleets, a balance-of-power structure designed to mitigate the chance of naval mutiny.

Soon after signing a thirty-year friendship treaty with China in February 1950, the USSR began to assist the PRC with ships and naval advisers. During its first six years, the PLAN grew from being little more than a motley collection of used warships to the largest and most powerful indigenous East Asian navy south of the USSR. Between 1953 and 1955, Moscow transferred to Beijing four destroyers, twelve large submarine chasers, two fleet minesweepers, and over fifty motor torpedo boats. Soviet assistance for China's submarine program was particularly important. Four World War II-era S-type submarines were transferred to China in 1954. Beginning in 1956, Soviet advisers helped the PRC to establish a diversified shipbuilding program. Based mainly at the Jiangnan dockyard and the Huadong shipyard in Shanghai, the PLAN completed as many as four submarines in 1956, with at least four more being built. The Chinese eventually produced over a hundred of the *Whiskey*-class diesel submarines, and later built sixty-four *Romeo*-class diesel submarines.

After years of tense negotiations, the Soviet naval base at Lüshun and the nearby civilian port at Dalian were finally returned to China in 1955. The Sino-Soviet alliance was under increasing strain. Beginning in 1958, tensions soared when Moscow and Beijing began to discuss developing a joint naval force, including basing Soviet nuclear submarines in Chinese ports. What Mao wanted was to use the joint submarine program to transfer Soviet nuclear technology to China. But the Soviet leadership refused to do this, insisting instead on retaining full administrative control over the submarine fleet, even though it would be based on Chinese sovereign territory. Mao balked at accepting these unequal terms.

There were equally important economic factors at work. The combination of Nationalist blockade and U.S. strategic embargo forced China to rely on the USSR

---

[4] ELLEMAN B.A., *High Seas Buffer: The Taiwan Patrol Force, 1950-1979* (Newport, RI, 2012).

for most of its foreign trade. During the 1950s, most of the PRC's domestic North–South trade was diverted inland, while sea-going trade was largely conducted by either foreign-registered or Hong Kong ships, which were neutral vessels. As a result of the blockade, 75% of China's foreign trade was transported overland, in particular that with the USSR and a number of Eastern European countries, via the Trans-Siberian Railway. Before World War II, only 1% of China's foreign trade was with Russia, while by 1957 this figure had increased to well over 50%.[5] The Nationalist naval blockade, which finally ended during 1958, was instrumental in increasing Sino-Soviet trade tensions, leading to a rift. The economic friction resulting from this dispute also contributed to an ever-widening political split between China and the USSR.

THE SINO-SOVIET SPLIT

The rapid expansion of the PLAN during 1955–1959 tapered off in 1960, due to the impact of the Sino-Soviet split. The transfer of naval technology from the USSR soon slowed to a trickle. Throughout much of the early 1960s, the PLAN's total force remained static, including about two dozen submarines, four destroyers, four destroyer escorts, and about 250 patrol craft. Arguably, the PLAN remained a coastal defense force with only limited capability to conduct offensive operations. The one success was China's detonation of its own indigenously produced atomic bomb during October 1964. This elevated the PRC to the position of a nuclear power, and reemphasized that Beijing no longer had to follow Moscow's orders.

By the mid-1960s, the PRC began to produce a whole new generation of indigenous Chinese-made naval equipment. In 1965, China improved on the *Riga*-class ship design obtained from the USSR and produced five Type 065 *Jiangnan*-class frigates. The Soviet-style steam boilers were replaced with French-licensed twin-mounted SEMT-Pielstick 12 PA6 diesels. Much of the on-board equipment, including sensors, fire control, and many of the weapons systems, either remained the same equipment as provided by the Soviet Union or was reverse-engineered copies of earlier Soviet models.

In 1967, China began to produce its own indigenous *Luda*-class guided missile destroyer. Eight vessels were completed during the 1970s, while another ten were built after 1980. These early *Luda*s were quite simple, and they were not equipped with advanced combat direction systems, firing displays, variable depth sonar, or anti-submarine defenses. For naval air support, China depended on MiG-15s, MiG-19s, Tu-2 bombers, and a dozen Be-6 seaplanes transferred from the USSR during the 1950s. Beginning in 1966, China also began building its own H-5 naval bombers, which were reverse-engineered from the Soviet twin-jet IL-28. By 1969,

---

[5] ELLEMAN B.A. and KOTKIN S., *Manchurian Railways and the Opening of China: An International History* (Armonk, NY, 2012).

at the time of the Sino-Soviet border clashes, the PLA Air Force reportedly had about four hundred aircraft.

Increasingly tense Sino-Soviet border relations resulted in the 1969 conflict, which almost escalated into a nuclear confrontation. Mao Zedong reacted by opening secret talks with the United States. Following President Richard Nixon's visit to China in 1972, the PRC began to obtain Western naval equipment, in particular from the United States and Europe, in order to strengthen the PLAN. From the early 1970s through until the USSR's collapse in 1991, the Chinese goal of reunification with Taiwan became secondary to that of countering Soviet attempts to encircle China.

During the mid-1970s the PLAN started to play a larger international role by undertaking expeditionary warfare for the first time. In January 1974 the PLAN used naval forces to seize the Paracel (Xisha) Islands from South Vietnam, a group of islands in the South China Sea that were also claimed by North Vietnam. Deng Xiaoping was chief of the PLA general staff and oversaw the operation, which included a successful PLAN amphibious operation. This maritime action was accomplished in the face of Soviet protests on behalf of Hanoi. Arguably for the first time since the collapse of the Qing in 1911, a Chinese naval force successfully defeated a foreign opponent.

One Soviet goal was to surround China to the north and south. In 1979, the PLA fought a short but intense war against Vietnam in reaction to a recently signed Soviet–Vietnamese treaty of alliance. The USSR did not actively intervene to assist North Vietnam, in part because of the presence of naval ships stationed in the Paracels. Moscow's reluctance to intervene undermined the ever-present threat to China of a two-front war. In the aftermath of this conflict, Beijing indicated that it would not renew its 1950 treaty with the USSR.

On 1 January 1979 President Jimmy Carter and Deng Xiaoping opened diplomatic relations. At the same time, Deng opened up China economically to the West in his so-called "Open Door" reforms. The peasant commune system was dismantled, resulting in a huge increase in agricultural productivity. Companies were no longer required to give up all profits to the government, but could reinvest them, creating market-driven incentives. Special Economic Zones were also opened to attract foreign investment, and by the early 1990s there were almost nine thousand of them. As a result of these economic reforms, the PRC was able to replicate Taiwan's economic miracle of 10 percent annual growth rates.

The PLAN began to purchase more advanced naval weaponry from abroad. The Navy's commander, Liu Huaqing, shifted China away from a purely coastal defense strategy (*Jinan Fangyu*) to a strategy relying on high-tech naval equipment. During most of the 1980s, China's total defense budget dropped, but the PLAN avoided these cuts. The size of the PLAN's manpower rose from 8 percent to 10 percent of the PLA's total force, and its share of China's defense budget grew to almost one-third of the total. By the late 1980s, China was well on its way to achieving its goal of asserting naval power not just defensively along its coastline, but also offensively in the Yellow Sea, East China Sea, and the South China Sea.

The PRC's goal of building a blue-water navy was greatly simplified by the end of the Cold War in 1990, which resulted in the collapse of the USSR the following year. Almost overnight, the balance of power throughout Asia shifted, granting the PRC status as a "great power." The PLAN had approximately 270,000 personnel, including 28,000 coastal-defense forces and 25,000 naval air forces. It had over four hundred fast attack boats, sixty submarines, and over seven hundred aircraft. Its "active defense" policy called for extending China's reach beyond the first island chain, composed of the Kurils, Japan, Okinawa, Taiwan, and the Philippines. The PLAN's immediate goals included reclaiming Taiwan, preparing for a possible conflict with the Philippines or Vietnam over the Spratlys, or naval encounter with the Japanese Maritime Self-Defence Force, most likely backed by the U.S. Navy, over the Senkaku (Diaoyu) islands. Long-term goals included expanding the PLAN from a one-ocean to a two-ocean – Pacific and Indian – navy by the year 2035.

Without a doubt, it is in the field of economics that China's turn to the sea has been most pronounced. During the early 19th century, it was estimated that Qing China accounted for almost a third of the world's wealth. By 1900 this had fallen to 10 percent, and by the 1930s to under 5 percent. China's economy remained stagnant for many decades because of the Great Leap Forward and the Cultural Revolution. Due mainly to Deng Xiaoping's 1978 economic reforms, but also greatly assisted by geopolitical events such as the end of the Cold War and the collapse of the Soviet Union, China's total merchandise trade had grown 143 times by 2010, from $20 billion in 1978 to over $3 trillion in 2010. China now accounts for over 10 percent of global exports and 9 percent of imports. By some measures, China may soon reclaim its former standing as the wealthiest country in the world. Most of this enormous growth rate is due to the opening of China's markets to maritime trade.

Conclusions

As China has turned to the sea it has focused more resources on developing its navy. There are many historical parallels between earlier periods of Chinese naval development and the post-1949 PLAN. Once Communist power over the mainland was consolidated, the PLAN's primary task was to defend the coastline, regain control over as many of the off-shore islands as possible, and prepare to retake Taiwan, so as to end the civil war once and for all. If successful, this would allow the Communist Party to reunify all of the lands formerly under the Chinese empire. To date, the PLAN has failed to adopt a strategy that is capable of achieving these goals. The sixty-five-year separation between the PRC and Taiwan is perhaps the most remarkable impact of its ocean geography.

China's Communist leaders do not trust their own navy. With Nationalist defections clearly in mind, the PLAN's organization into three fleets proved remarkably similar to the mid-nineteenth-century Qing navy. While dividing power helped to protect the Communists from the possibility of naval mutinies, it has hampered China's joint operations among the various regional fleets. The PLAN enjoyed some early success in taking off-shore islands controlled by the Nationalists, but it failed to gain control of Jinmen (Quemoy) Island, Mazu (Matsu) Island, the Penghu (Pescadores) Islands, or Taiwan.

Throughout the Cold War, the United States and China worked hand in hand to counter the USSR. With the 1989 fall of the Berlin Wall, the 1990 end of the Cold War, and the 1991 collapse of the Soviet Union, however, the U.S. government no longer needed China to act as the Eastern "pincer" in this two-front strategy. The PRC's strategic objectives switched from continental to maritime concerns, including, most importantly, settling the Taiwan question and asserting control over its near seas, particularly the East and South China Seas. Ever since 1991, even as China has experienced 8 percent growth rates due to maritime trade, the PRC government's determination to solve these strategic challenges has continued to dominate the structure, organization, and training of the PLAN.

BIBLIOGRAPHY

DREYER E.L., *China at War, 1901-1949* (London, 1995).

ELLEMAN B.A., *High Seas Buffer: The Taiwan Patrol Force, 1950-1979* (Newport, RI, 2012).

ELLEMAN B.A. and KOTKIN S., *Manchurian Railways and the Opening of China: An International History* (Armonk, NY, 2012).

ESHERICK J.W., *Reform and Revolution in China: The 1911 Revolution in Hunan and Hubeh* (Berkeley, CA, 1976).

HSÜ I.C.Y., *The Rise of Modern China* (New York, 1990).

KONDAPALLI S., *China's Naval Power* (New Delhi, 2001).

MCDEVITT M., *The PLA Navy: Past, Present, and Future Prospects* (Alexandria, VA, 2000).

MULLER D.G., JR, *China as a Maritime Power* (Boulder, CO, 1983).

PAINE S.C.M., *The Sino-Japanese War of 1894-1895: Perceptions, Power, and Primacy* (New York, 2005).

SWANSON B., *Eighth Voyage of the Dragon: A History of China's Quest for Seapower* (Annapolis, MD, 1982).

INDIA AND THE SEA

JAMES GOLDRICK is Rear Admiral, RAN(Ret), Adjunct Professor at the University of New South Wales at Canberra (ADFA), Australia

ABSTRACT. *Although unified modern India was a product of British sea power, it inherited a weak awareness of the sea and gained independence with few warships or merchant ships of its own. Growth was initially modest, but by the 1970s Indian governments were becoming aware of the risks of not controlling the Indian Ocean. Only the economic liberalization of 1991 revealed India's potential gains from world trade, and much of that still remains unrealised.*

RÉSUMÉ. *Bien que son unification fût le produit du pouvoir maritime britannique, l'Inde moderne n'hérita que d'une faible connaissance de la mer et gagna son indépendance avec peu de navires de guerres ou vaisseaux marchands lui appartenant. Sa croissance fut au départ modeste mais dans les années 1970, les gouvernements indiens commencèrent à prendre conscience des risques générés par le non-contrôle de l'océan indien. Seule la libéralisation économique de 1991 révéla les bénéfices potentiels que l'Inde pouvait tirer du commerce international, lesquels restent pour la plupart encore aujourd'hui irréalisés.*

.•.

India has strong maritime traditions, but it is not a nation with a maritime outlook. This is the result in part of geography and in part of its history. It is a simple strategic reality that India, although a peninsula, has land borders that are twice the length of its coast. Equally significant is that relations with Pakistan have been tense, when not overtly hostile, over the entire period since partition and independence in 1947, while an undeclared war was fought with China on the disputed northern border in 1962, over a boundary that has yet to be agreed in 2015. Relations with other neighbours on land, such as Nepal and Bangladesh, have been somewhat less fractious, but never entirely comfortable.

And it is a simple historical fact that "India" as an entity is the result much more of its domination by the British than of its pre-colonial past, and that diversity marked – and continues to mark – the Indian maritime domain as much as that of the land. The sub-continent, made up of a patchwork of competing states, fell to the British as much through the latter's successful division of local rivals as through outright conquest. This was just as true at sea. Later proponents of Indian sea power were quick to point out that such a lack of Indian unity benefited the intruders much more than their undoubted technological superiority. Underlining the lesson was the fact that the last real seaborne resistance to the British, on the part of the Marathas, had ended in 1756 with the fall of the naval base and fortress at Vijaydurg, a year *before* the battle of Plassey.

Once India was incorporated within the British Empire, its relationship with its new rulers limited its maritime development. If India was required to fund much of its own defence on land, the bargain at sea did not extend to more than limited support for coastal defences and small subsidies for the British Royal Navy. The East India Company had its own navy, but this did not survive as a significant combatant force past the assumption of direct British government control of the sub-continent in 1858. From 1863, the Royal Indian Marine functioned as a subsidiary transport, maritime security and hydrographic service, while India's naval defence and the protection of its sea communications were effectively left to the British Admiralty. This situation began to change only as the Royal Navy came under increasing pressure from would-be rivals in the first decade of the 20th century but, significantly, there was much less interest in India than in other parts of the Empire, such as Australia and New Zealand, in developing national naval capabilities to compensate. A limited subsidy to the Admiralty not only seemed to provide best value for money, but also did not threaten the Indian Army's domination of strategic planning, or its overwhelming claim on the available budget. Furthermore, if even India were to create a capable naval service, constructing a fleet would require the expenditure of funds in the United Kingdom, not in the sub-continent.

This was a key reason why there was relatively little in the way of either an official or a domestic constituency for naval development. Furthermore, India was not a country of immigrants who had travelled by sea, and awareness of maritime issues was not great in the educated classes, despite the combination of an increasingly nationalist outlook and an ever-larger cadre of the elite who had been educated overseas (largely in the United Kingdom) and thus had some first-hand experience of the maritime world. Matters were not helped by the preoccupation of the British Admiralty with racial purity. The white colonies could provide cadets for the Royal Navy, but it would be 1928 before an Indian officer was commissioned even within the Indian naval service.

There were other good reasons why Indian industry was unready to support a navy, although a small naval dockyard was maintained in Bombay. Indian shipbuilding had flourished as late as the early 19th century. Local expertise rivalled the shipyards of the United Kingdom, while Indian wood, particularly teak, allowed for high-quality, long-lasting ships to be built at competitive prices, but this situation did not continue into the era of iron hulls and mechanical propulsion. Thereafter, domestic shipbuilding steadily regressed to the construction of "country" vessels for the coastal trade, still largely of wood and propelled by sail.

Existing indigenous commercial activity was also profoundly affected by the increasing European domination of the maritime sector in the Indian Ocean. There were few commercial elements in India with both the inclination and the money necessary to create a modern shipbuilding industry or modern shipping lines, and it is arguable in any case whether the natural advantages enjoyed by the British in producing cheap and efficient ships could have been overcome, particularly in view of Britain's domination of the world's supplies of steaming coal. The Indian government itself had little motivation to support such efforts. Apart from the political influence in Whitehall wielded by British shipping interests, successive viceroys were much more focused on the development of India-wide railway networks to invest India's limited capital in transportation.

As the 19th century wore on, Indian trade to the east and west was increasingly carried in British-built and British-owned ships. National maritime activity became largely confined to semi-subsistence fishing, together with what was effectively internal coastal traffic around the Indian Empire termed the "adjacent trade", albeit with a reach that encompassed Burma in the west and went offshore as far as the Arabian peninsula in the east, as it had done for hundreds of years. Thus, to a limited extent, historical patterns of commerce continued, but the growth of local shipping to meet new requirements was much slower than it might have been because of the availability of British hulls.

Only in the last years of the century did significant Indian efforts begin to operate more capable merchant vessels over longer distances. These met with ferocious resistance from British shippers, who did not hesitate to use their greater resources to undercut any would-be competition (as they did elsewhere in the British Empire). The battle continued at intervals from 1890 until the start of the First World War and it was only in 1919 that the Scindia Steam Navigation Company, the first modern national shipping firm, was established. Its ambitions to engage in the tramping and liner trades immediately faced British commercial efforts to drive it out of the market. In 1923 a barely acceptable ten-year agreement was reached between Scindia and the established international shipping lines such as the P&O. This effectively restricted Scindia to the coastal trade but at least allowed the young company some space to expand.

Scindia's travails did not pass unnoticed and interest in maritime affairs began to grow amongst the nationalist politicians in the new Indian Central Legislative Assembly, taking the form of efforts to promote Indian international and coastal shipping in the 1920s. These were largely unsuccessful, but a small seed was sown in the form of the training ship *Dufferin*, commissioned in 1927 to prepare Indian cadets for the merchant service. *Dufferin* would also form something of a nursery for a revived Indian Navy, but above all marked the start of an Indian contribution to the global shipping industry in the form of trained personnel that would increase steadily in the decades ahead.

An Indian National Steamship Owners Association was formed in 1930. Scindia managed to survive a renewed "rate war" on the lapse of the existing agreement in 1933, at a time when global shipping was suffering from the Great Depression and shipping lines were out for any work that they could get. Although Britain had embarked on a policy of "imperial preference", the protection that this gave was to India's emerging steel industry and the textile trade against foreign competition, not to Indian shipping companies against British interests. Nevertheless, Scindia had the foresight to start the development of a shipyard at

Vishakhapatnam on India's east coast in 1941. Some small ships were produced, but the onset of the Japanese war meant that progress was slow and it was not until 1946 that the yard was ready to build large merchant ships. The first of these was completed in 1948 and nine more vessels had been put into service by 1952. New Delhi was eventually forced to take the shipyard over from Scindia in 1952 and it was reorganised as the state-owned and controlled "Hindustan Shipyard". From this point, production continued steadily. Although Indian-built ships did not necessarily represent the latest technology, they were workmanlike units which were to give good service.

The travails of the new shipyard represented in microcosm many of the tensions inherent in achieving the systematic development of India's maritime industries. Productivity and finance both proved difficult to manage. The commercial interests sought subsidy and protection, particularly against overseas companies, while the government, wedded to central planning, wanted greater control than business was ready to accept.

There were other reasons why India did not turn to the sea on independence in 1947. The government's overall approach, derived in part from the Mahatma's ideas of national self-reliance as well as from Nehru's socialism, concentrated upon economic development within India much more than initiatives to develop the country as an international trading nation. Plans were soon in hand to increase Indian-flagged merchant tonnage to two million gross, but this was very much a long-term target and the fleet did not reach a million tons for more than a decade. There were other constraints. The partition of India and Pakistan and the independence of Burma and Ceylon had their effects on coastal shipping. The old adjacent trade suffered increasing interference from national customs and other authorities, while the motivation to trade at all, particularly between India and Pakistan, was steadily eroded by repeated armed confrontations. Matters were not helped by domestic over-regulation of the coastal industry, which drove up costs. Furthermore, in a repetition of the 19th century, the national government's priority (such as it was) for funding transportation went principally to India's railways or to roads.

More successful were efforts to increase the training effort for deck officers and engineers. A Marine Engineering College began operations at Calcutta in 1948 and a Nautical and Engineering College was established at Bombay shortly afterwards. Training for merchant seamen began in Calcutta in 1950, with similar arrangements being made in Visakhapatnam and Saurashtra in later years.

In military terms, there was an unspoken dependence upon the remnants of the *Pax Britannica* in India being free to adopt its global policy of non-alignment and focus locally on its land borders. For some twenty years, the Royal Navy remained the major force in the Indian Ocean, initially with the East Indies Station based in Ceylon and then from the Eastern Fleet's base at Singapore. Pakistan's small fleet, a third of the old Royal Indian Navy, did not at first constitute any significant threat. On the other hand, the Pakistan Army and later Pakistan's Air Force represented much more substantial and immediate problems over land and from both east and west. This meant that the threat axis hitherto focused on the north-west and Afghanistan was greatly widened, particularly as it came to include the northern borders with China. The Army's problems were thus much greater in magnitude but, after the initial turmoil of partition, not greatly different in nature than its experience under the British Raj. It would continue to be by far the largest of the military services, a domination confirmed by its assumption from the Navy of the formal status of "Senior Service" after India became a republic in 1950. That the Navy was never completely overwhelmed by the Army was probably the result of the determination by politicians and the public service to keep control of the armed forces out of the hands of a single military officer. While this would hinder the development of Joint doctrine for many decades, it did at least allow the smaller services to have their voices heard.

The problem was that the Navy's doctrine, training and force structure were based much more on contributing to the maintenance of the western maritime system than on national territorial defence, even if the naval staff (including its British members on loan) recognised Pakistan as "the enemy".[1] That India was a part of this system was understood within the service, if more instinctively than consciously, but it was not a point of much relevance to the Indian elites after independence. The Indian Navy thus entered something of a twilight world, being regarded by many as British not only in style, but in strategic outlook. It is arguable that even the very moderate development of the Navy in the late 1940s and into the 1950s would not have occurred without the personal influence of Lord Louis Mountbatten, particularly with Prime Minister Nehru. The Navy was, however, also helped by the fact that it constituted both an external symbol and internally something of a model for the new India. Both aspects were demonstrated when the cruiser *Delhi* conveyed Nehru and his family on a state visit to Indonesia in 1950. Their hosts were deeply impressed by the military capability demonstrated, while Nehru himself was pleased by the wide diversity of the crews and their working and living together at such close quarters, despite the constraints of race, caste and language.

Through the 1950s the maritime development of India was steady, but, as with so many other national efforts, slow. Successive five-year plans allocated relatively small amounts to port development. An Eastern Shipping Corporation was formed in 1950, followed by a Western Shipping Corporation in 1956 (the groups were combined in 1961) and the tonnage of the Indian fleet began to grow. The availability of capital remained a problem but the Indian government's tentative attempts to set up cooperative arrangements with overseas shipping companies encountered strong resistance from Indian industry, even when a 25% limit was set on foreign ownership. In these circumstances there was little international interest and the single cooperative venture in the 1950s was with a Greek company. Only in 1963 was the limit raised to 40%, but this was not enough to overcome the concerns which foreign business had with Indian bureaucracy, as well as capacity and workforce problems in India's ports.

---

[1] Admiralty M Branch Minute M 01679/49 of 19 November 1949, The National Archives (UK), ADM 116/5852.

At least Indian science began to move seaward. The Indian Navy slowly expanded the small hydrographic force which had been in being at independence, while other departments and academic institutions embarked on research programmes. From 1962 to 1964, India played a key part in the work of the International Oceanographic Expedition in the Indian Ocean, contributing three ships from different authorities as well as one from the Navy itself. Discoveries from these and subsequent research expeditions were to allow India to become a relatively early player in exploiting offshore oil fields.

India's close interest in the development of the law of the sea had more than economic dimensions. There was considerable resentment over the way in which Indian attempts to restrict the movement of foreign warships in the territorial sea were rebuffed by the western powers. Such restrictions were not included in the 1958 Convention on the Territorial Sea and Contiguous Zone, which India initially refused to ratify. From 1973, when formal negotiations began for a new convention, India continued to press for such restrictions. It moderated its requirements to approve foreign warship movements, but continued to insist on prior notification, something still rejected by the West. India also took the view that military activities, particularly intelligence gathering, should not be conducted in other nations' economic zones. This was to be the source of some friction between the Indian Navy and the western powers, although the implications for restricting the exercise of India's increasing naval capabilities in other nations' zones were eventually to create increasing ambivalence in some elements of the Navy.

Despite the considerable development of Pakistan's fleet in the late 1950s and the threat that it posed to shipping and coasts, the Indian Navy remained at the margins of strategic policy. It received a fillip through its part in the capture of the Portugese enclave of Goa, although the operations revealed many problems, but could obviously contribute little to the "frontier war" with China in 1962, and its lack of wider relevance in New Delhi was sharply demonstrated by reductions in spending to find more money for the Army and Air Force. The situation did not improve during the short conflict with Pakistan in 1965. The majority of the Indian fleet was caught on the wrong side of the sub-continent and was late in beginning operations in the main naval theatre of the Arabian Sea, on which the government in any case placed significant restrictions. Matters were made worse by the very poor material state of many ships. Many had significant speed restrictions, while some were unable to sail at all. The Pakistan Navy was not notably aggressive, but conducted a token bombardment of the Indian coast, to the Indian Navy's mortification. An even more pointed demonstration of India's vulnerability came with the despatch by Indonesia of submarines and missile craft as a gesture of support to Pakistan. These arrived in the latter's waters only after the conclusion of hostilities. Although their intended role remains unclear, it was an indication of the increasing complexities of the region. The Indian Navy had already made this point within government as a result of earlier Indonesian submarine operations in the vicinity of the Nicobars.

The Indian Navy initially approached the acquisition of Soviet ships and technology with reservations. Given, however, that the lack of an alliance relationship and the unavailability of hard currency combined to make the latest western technology inaccessible, the Navy had few alternatives if it were to avoid becoming completely moribund. Submarines and missile craft were the key attraction, although the Navy soon extended its purchases to include larger surface ships and aircraft. Nevertheless, the relationship was conducted at something of an arm's length, particularly as the Soviets initially gave little information on their operating procedures and tactics. Such reticence accelerated the Indian Navy's efforts to develop its own doctrine, since access to Royal Navy sources was becoming more tenuous as the British became more closely integrated with the United States Navy and NATO.

With the Navy determined to settle scores with Pakistan, work to exploit the newly available Soviet technology accelerated after 1968. This bore fruit in the 1971 Indo-Pakistan War, which resulted in the break-up of Pakistan and the formation of Bangladesh from the country's eastern wing. While the Indian government placed too many restrictions on the rules of engagement of the new submarine force for it to prove effective, the reins lay much more loosely on the new missile boats, which scored some spectacular successes. The aircraft carrier *Vikrant*, despite mechanical restrictions, also proved extremely useful in providing close air support and strike for the Indian Army units operating in East Pakistan. Only just capable of launching her aircraft, the *Vikrant* demonstrated to the Indian Navy that capability has to be considered in relative as well as absolute terms. Just enough, in this case, was certainly good enough.

These successes came at a time when the maritime balance of power was shifting. The Indians did not object to a Soviet naval presence in the Indian Ocean, particularly as India's relationship with the United States was becoming increasingly fraught and that with the USSR much closer, but the Russians' activities drew attention to the maritime security of the region and India's vulnerabilities at sea in a way that was wholly new to many in the Indian government, despite the warning of the 1965 experience with Indonesia. That a new order was emerging was starkly confirmed by Britain's decision in 1968 to withdraw from east of Suez. India was faced by the termination of its unacknowledged maritime protector's efforts and their substitution by much less comfortable – and, arguably, much less sympathetic actors. The watershed came in 1971, during the war over East Pakistan. Initially supporters of Pakistan, the Americans demonstrated their concern somewhat ham-fistedly with the deployment of the aircraft carrier *Enterprise* into the Bay of Bengal. Embroiled as the United States was in Vietnam, this sortie could only be a token gesture, but it was deeply resented in India. The desire to keep the Americans out of the Indian Ocean created support for the concept of a "Zone of Peace", with a ban on military activities by non-littoral states, but the implicit restrictions on India's ability to deploy force within the region meant that it was an idea viewed with little enthusiasm by many areas of government. Much more to Indian tastes was an emerging consciousness that India had the potential to be the leading actor in the maritime domain, provided that its capabilities evolved to match its geographic advantages.

The Indian Navy thus emerged from the 1971 conflict in a somewhat better position to argue for resources, but it remained very much the third service, in spite of the government's new interest. Problems on land, both domestic and external, continued to beset successive administrations. Over the next two decades the Navy's budget increased much more from the general, albeit slow and sometimes fitful growth of the Indian economy and the trickle through to government spending than it did from any reallocation of funding within the defence portfolio. The flow of Soviet ships and equipment depended largely upon "soft" currency arrangements, although these were to come under increasing strain in the 1980s, while the Indian government's approval of domestic ship-construction programmes resulted as much from the desire for technology transfer and local employment as actual naval capability. The result was a combination of frustrating delays and ingenious adaptation to the situation, including the production of modern surface combatants which successfully integrated western and Soviet technology.

From the early 1970s, a more confident Indian Navy nevertheless proved a useful instrument for a government at least more aware of the maritime domain and eager to engage with the newly independent littoral states, including Mauritius, the Seychelles, the Maldives and the Comoros. The Indian Navy not only provided equipment and training to a number of navies and coast guards but also initiated a comprehensive programme of hydrographic surveying. Indian naval schools began to be used by an increasing number of other countries as the value of such soft power was recognised. From the first international training for Malaysia and Sri Lanka in 1965, a total of twenty-two nations had used Indian facilities by 1980, and the number would increase further.

As the decade wore on, India was also quick to identify the benefits emerging from the new consensus of the law of the sea. As early as 1976 the government passed its Maritime Zones Act, establishing a twelve-nautical-mile territorial sea, as well as a twenty-mile contiguous zone and a two-hundred-mile exclusive economic zone. The clearest incentive lay in the development of the Bombay High oil field, discovered by an Indo-Soviet scientific team in the 1960s and first drilled in 1974. By 1980, five million metric tons were being pumped a year and output would increase steadily over the next decade. Bombay High could not provide all of India's petroleum requirements, but became a key source of supply, accounting for more than a third of domestic production. It was also a source of concern for the Indian Navy, offering as it did so many potential targets to the Pakistani fleet.

Set up in interim form in 1977, a Coast Guard was formally established the following year, based on a handful of old frigates and patrol vessels. This was a logical step and the new organisation had the necessary legal remit, but its relationship with the Indian Navy was uneasy, even when the latter was providing the lion's share of qualified personnel. The new service was often seen as a competitor for the limited funds available, rather than a welcome relief for an over-extended Navy.

The expansion of India's merchant fleet continued, as did the growth of India's international trade, but they were slower than they should have been. Both remained hamstrung by the combination of the government's economic policies, inadequate infrastructure and the mass of regulation, seasoned with a good measure of local corruption. Fishing and coastal trading continued largely independent of all this as part of India's "grey economy", the unregulated trade often being little less (and sometimes more) than outright smuggling, but they inevitably remained somewhat primitive and makeshift. Over-fishing, driven domestically by the demands of India's growing population for protein and externally from the pressure of foreign fishing, as well as environmental degradation, also began to create concern within coastal communities. This problem would defy solution.

India's ports, particularly Bombay, had become a global byword for inefficiency. The potential international advantages of a large, low-wage and relatively well-educated workforce were being dissipated, even as they were being demonstrated by the diaspora of Indian officers and seamen in the global merchant fleet. The fact that no Indian port could take a vessel larger than 50,000 tons deadweight until well into the 1970s was another symptom of the accumulating lag in capacity, one soon exacerbated by the container trade, which promised enormous efficiencies but depended upon facilities which India had yet to create. Makeshift arrangements, such as transhipment from bulk tankers to smaller ships, helped a little, but not enough. Yet the national government was still obsessed with internal development. Even in the 1980s, the annual *Budget and Economic Survey* enlarged extensively on the achievements in manufacturing land vehicles, as well as the activities of the railways, while shipbuilding and shipping received little or no attention.[2] The Sixth Five Year Plan attempted to improve the situation and, perhaps just in time for the economic reforms after 1991, new ports and loading systems began to come on line in the later 1980s, even if many problems of organisation had yet to be solved. By 1989, India had nearly six million tonnes of shipping on the national register, but this continued to carry a frustratingly low proportion of the country's international trade.

The Navy demonstrated a similar range of achievement and at least partial failure. It strove to create a fully balanced fleet, inducting a nuclear submarine on loan from the Soviets at the same time as it tried to keep two aircraft carriers in commission. Yet there was not enough money and arguably too little technical expertise to maintain the whole force in an operational state, a situation complicated by the progressive breakdown of the logistics chain from the Soviet Union as the latter moved towards collapse. Matters came to a head with the sinking of

---

[2] MINISTRY OF FINANCE, Government of India, *Economic Survey 1980-81*. See Table 1.16 'Production of selected industries' and Table 1.20 'Operations of Indian Government Railways'.

the ill-maintained corvette *Andaman*, which demonstrated not only the parlous material state of the fleet but equally serious problems of training and command.

The 1980s nevertheless saw India assume in some ways the regional maritime pre-eminence which had long been the goal of the maritime lobby, even if the limits on the nation's ability to act were soon made clear. Indian units suppressed a coup in the Maldives in 1988 and arrested the mercenaries involved in a well-conducted operation at sea. Operations in Sri Lanka, however, were by no means so neatly confined. A long-running Tamil insurgency had gone beyond the resources of the Sri Lankan government to control. Indian forces had been involved since the early 1970s in efforts to patrol the Palk Strait between the two nations to prevent the smuggling of arms and war materials but, in 1987, a formal intervention was attempted at Sri Lankan request. It rapidly proved a quagmire for the Indian armed forces, soon regarded not as peacekeepers but as an occupying power. By late 1989 the bulk of the force had been withdrawn, and the commitment was formally concluded in March 1990.

In 1990 the reforms that would set India on a very different path had yet to come. Liberalisation of the national economy would not begin until the election of the government of P.V. Narasimha Rao in 1991. The success of this effort, however incomplete, would have important benefits for India's maritime interests. Port facilities received renewed priority, as did expansion of the merchant navy, whose tonnage doubled by 2000. India's international trade grew at a much faster rate than ever before. These developments both depended upon and were funded by the boom which followed the reforms. The Indian Navy and Coast Guard benefited in similar ways. The 1990s gave both a breathing space and some improvement in their budgets. While logistical problems continued and indigenous shipbuilding was bedevilled by delays and cost over-runs, the decade allowed both services to consolidate and prepare for the future. This was no bad thing, for the conflicts in the Middle East, India's rivalry with Pakistan, a fractious relationship with a rising China and a multitude of other political, economic and environmental problems would provide a host of challenges in the years ahead, as they would for India's other actors in the maritime domain.

Even the semi-subsistence existence of India's coastal fishermen was about to change profoundly. They, as much as any other group, were to benefit from the explosion of mobile communications which accompanied the economic reforms of the 1990s. Before the end of the century it would be commonplace for a captain to interrogate contacts ashore to establish in which port the highest prices were to be found for his catch.

It may be an exaggeration to assert that the first half-century after independence was marked by India's failure to exploit the sea, but there can be no doubt that there were many missed opportunities. Arguably, India's inability to make use of all its chances in the maritime domain was caused by the same factors which hindered development in so many areas on land. Perhaps most important was the national government's attempt to evolve India into a self-sustaining entity, largely divorced from the global economy. While this remained the intent, India could never properly fulfil its maritime potential. It took the reforms of 1991 to break the dam and show what could be achieved and what might yet come. Perhaps the cameo of the fisherman and his mobile phone encapsulates the likely future of India's relationship with the sea, one that will continue to reflect the extraordinary diversity, complexity and contradictions of a huge, dynamic and dysfunctional nation.

Bibliography

ARASARATNAM S., *Maritime India in the Seventeenth Century* (New Delhi, 2004).
BULLION A.J., *India, Sri Lanka and the Tamil Crisis 1976-1994* (London, 1995).
GOLDRICK J., *No Easy Answers: The Development of the Navies of India, Pakistan, Bangladesh and Sri Lanka* (New Delhi, 1997).
HASTINGS D.J., *The Royal Indian Navy, 1612-1950* (Jefferson, NC, 1988).
HEADLAM E.J., 'History of the Royal Indian Marine', *Journal of the Royal Society of Arts* 77. 3985 (1929), 519-40.
HIRANANDANI G.M., *Transition to Eminence: The Indian Navy 1976-1990* (New Delhi, 2005).
HIRANANDANI G.M., *Transition to Triumph: History of the Indian Navy 1965-1975* (New Delhi, 2000).
KOHLI S.N., *We Dared* (New Delhi, 1979).
MCPHERSON K., *The Indian Ocean: A History of People and the Sea* in *Maritime India* (New Delhi, 2004).
MISHRA S.R., *Fisheries in India* (New Delhi, 1987).
NATIONAL COUNCIL OF APPLIED ECONOMIC RESEARCH, *Indian Shipping Industry: Retrospect and Prospect* (New Delhi, 1993).
RAO T.S.S., *A Short History of Modern Indian Shipping* (Bombay, 1965).
ROTHERMUND D., *India: The Rise of an Asian Giant* (New Haven, 2008).
SINGH S., *Under Two Ensigns: The Indian Navy 1945-1950* (New Delhi, 1986).
SRIDHARAN K., *A Maritime History of India* (New Delhi, 1981).

Les îles d'Océanie et l'ouverture sur la mer à l'heure de la première mondialisation contemporaine

CLAIRE LAUX is professor in contemporary history at Sciences Po Bordeaux, France.

RÉSUMÉ. *Les voyageurs européens se passionnèrent pour la question de la colonisation des îles du Pacifique. Cook proposa en premier la thèse de migrations successives venant de l'Ouest par voie de mer. Mais un tel accomplissement semblait impossible pour ceux qui ne comprenaient pas le système de navigation polynésien et qui considéraient ses habitants comme des analphabètes à la culture digne de l'Âge de pierre. En les fréquentant davantage, les Européens préférèrent les Polynésiens aux autres natifs des îles. Leurs sociétés hiérarchisées et leurs savoir-faire en matière de navigation et de commerce leur valurent d'être admis à un rang relativement élevé dans le nouvel ordre impérial.*

ABSTRACT. *European voyagers were fascinated by the question of how Pacific islands had been settled. Cook was the first to propose successive seaborne migrations spreading from the West, but to those who did not understand Polynesian navigation such an achievement seemed impossible for illiterate people with a Stone Age culture. On further acquaintance the Europeans preferred the Polynesians to the other islanders. Their hierarchical societies and their skills in navigation and commerce admitted them to a relatively high status in the new imperial order.*

. • .

Dans le vaste ensemble que constitue l'Océanie, les différents groupes insulaires définissent leur identité par rapport à la mer, mais de manière très différente selon les archipels. Les premiers Européens qui rencontrent ces îles sont frappés par ces contrastes, même s'ils attendent le XIXe siècle pour en proposer une approche prétendument scientifique. C'est en effet Dumont d'Urville qui est à l'origine, dès 1834, de la partition de l'Océanie, aujourd'hui contestée par les Océaniens eux-mêmes, en trois grands ensembles: Micronésie (« petites îles » disséminées au nord de l'équateur), Polynésie (îles nombreuses) et Mélanésie (îles noires). Ces divisions se fondent sur des appréciations physiologiques des populations, jugements très à la mode à l'époque, comme les caractères plus « négroïdes » des Mélanésiens que des Polynésiens, mais aussi sur les relations qu'entretiennent les populations avec la mer qui les entoure. Contrairement aux navigateurs du XVIIIe siècle, c'est sur fond de darwinisme et d'affrontement entre polygénistes et monogénistes que les voyageurs tirent de leurs observations les théories les plus variées: ainsi Pierre-Adolphe Lesson avance, certes avec prudence, l'hypothèse selon laquelle les Maoris descendraient des phoques[1] ! La relation avec la mer est en effet aussi déterminante que l'aspect physique des populations rencontrées. Les sociétés maritimes de Polynésie apparaissent comme des sociétés dynamiques et hiérarchisées alors que les sociétés terriennes mélanésiennes demeurent bien plus émiettées, comme incapables de produire des structures organisées et hiérarchisées.

Lors de la rencontre avec l'Occident, cette dimension d'ouverture par la mer devient alors déterminante, le paysage des îles étant désormais façonné par leur insertion dans des réseaux transnationaux. Nous montrerons donc ici comment la relation avec la mer devient l'élément le plus important à la fois de la personnalité et de l'histoire économique, culturelle et politique de ces îles, d'abord à l'époque des premiers contacts, puis de leur place dans les grandes routes maritimes qui s'établissent au XIXe siècle, enfin lorsque l'Océanie devient l'enjeu d'un partage colonial entre les grandes puissances.

Un 'peuple de la mer dont l'aventure est unique dans l'histoire de l'humanité' (José Garanger)

Les premiers voyageurs européens, dans le dernier tiers du XVIIIe siècle, déjà, sont saisis à la fois par les qualités de navigateurs des Polynésiens et par le mystère du peuplement d'îles aussi dispersées: la tentation est alors grande de lier les deux. Le premier signe pour les navigateurs occidentaux de cette ouverture des Polynésiens sur la mer et sur l'Autre est évidemment l'accueil fait par les femmes, qui montent sans hésiter leur souhaiter la bienvenue à bord de leurs navires, alors qu'ils n'aperçoivent pas les Mélanésiennes ce qui ne va pas sans générer une certaine frustration. Dès lors, le 'bon sauvage' est le Polynésien, le Mélanésien, lui, incarne la face sombre, terrienne, de l'état de nature.

Des îles dispersées et ... peuplées !

De fait, si l'insularité accentuée de l'espace polynésien a longtemps et lourdement pesé sur les formes et l'histoire de l'occupation humaine, elle n'a paradoxalement pas empêché l'essaimage dans tous les archipels du grand Océan, si isolés fussent-ils, d'un peuplement polynésien témoignant par-là des étonnantes capacités nautiques de ces populations. Compte-tenu des distances, l'odyssée des Polynésiens à travers le Pacifique – et jusqu'à la côte de l'Amérique du Sud – constitue la plus impressionnante saga maritime de l'histoire de l'humanité.

---

[1] LESSON P.A., *La légende des îles Hawaii, tirées de Fornander et commentées avec une réponse à M. de Quatrefages, par le Dr A. Lesson*, Niort: M. Clouzot (1884).

Elle a été rendue possible par des moyens et des techniques de navigation remarquables (catamarans et pirogues à balanciers, observation de la voûte céleste,[2] etc.).

La question de l'origine des Polynésiens fascine les Européens dès les premiers contacts. A partir de cette époque et durant tout le siècle, nombreux sont les écrivains, marins, savants ou missionnaires qui avancent leur hypothèse, dont certaines surprenantes. Une myriade d'îles de tailles variées, toutes peuplées,[3] remplace le continent austral, et forme l'étonnant « triangle maori ». Dans la plupart des mythologies locales, ces îles océaniennes ont été remontées du fond de l'océan par un dieu, le dieu Mani par exemple pour les îles de la Société. Les voyageurs rapportent cette tradition orale en soulignant toujours cette osmose entre les Polynésiens et la mer. Trois grands types d'explications à ce « peuplement polynésien » se côtoient plus qu'ils ne se succèdent chez les observateurs:

- L'hypothèse des restes du grand continent englouti: les îles en seraient les ultimes vestiges émergés et les Polynésiens des survivants d'une seule et unique civilisation. À la fin des années 1840 encore, le Belge Jacques-Antoine de Moerenhout, consul des États-Unis aux Hawaii puis de France à Tahiti, continue à défendre ce vieux rêve, réminiscence du mythe du continent austral, bientôt infirmé par l'étude de la formation géologique des archipels.
- L'hypothèse de l'origine américaine des Polynésiens, aujourd'hui réfutée par les anthropologues, part de la découverte de traces de contacts entre les civilisations comme une épidémie de syphilis aux îles de la Société avant même le passage de Cook ou la présence de patate douce dans certains archipels comme la Nouvelle-Zélande ou les Hawaii. En fait, ces apports témoignent vraisemblablement de visites des Polynésiens dans le sud du continent américain d'où, mangeurs de tubercules, mais guère cultivateurs de céréales, ils rapportent des racines en délaissant le maïs.
- Déjà en 1784 Cook formule la théorie d'un peuplement de la Polynésie par l'ouest du Pacifique, par étapes successives, entre 2000 et 1000 avant notre ère, à partir de l'Indonésie ou des Philippines à travers la Micronésie ou la Mélanésie, théorie que complète le linguiste Horatio Hale en 1848.[4] Cette hypothèse est aujourd'hui confirmée en particulier par les études de la linguistique comparée.

---

[2] BOULINIER G. et BOULINIER G., 'Les Polynésiens et la navigation astronomique', *Journal de la Société des Océanistes* 36 (septembre 1972), 275–284.
[3] Tant dans l'Atlantique – Açores, Madère – que dans l'océan Indien – Mascareignes – malgré des distances beaucoup plus faibles, bon nombre d'îles étaient demeurées vides d'hommes jusqu'à l'arrivée des Européens.
[4] Cité par BENOIT C., dans 'Le Grand Océan, les Polynésiens, le triangle maori', dans *Sillages polynésiens* Paris: L'Harmattan (1985), p. 16.

Cook a beau penser que l'idée d'une 'navigation accidentelle', c'est-à-dire d'un peuplement de certaines îles par des voyageurs perdus en mer pouvait 'mieux que mille hypothèses conjoncturales ... expliquer le peuplement des Mers du Sud,[5] d'autres auteurs envisagent des migrations sur une longue distance délibérées et organisées, ce qui suppose à la fois des embarcations fiables et une très bonne maîtrise des arts nautiques,[6] ce que souligne par exemple Armand de Quatrefages: 'Les Polynésiens savaient fort bien se diriger en mer en se guidant sur les étoiles'.[7]

Il y a certes quelques observateurs, souvent de seconde main, qui ne partagent pas cette admiration pour la 'maritimité' polynésienne. Malthus par exemple penche pour des sociétés océaniennes en 'systèmes clos,' ce qui apparaît comme le premier défaut de sa théorie sur la régulation démographique des sociétés du Pacifique: pour lui, les Tahitiens auraient été enfermés sur leurs îles, leurs techniques de navigation ne leur permettant pas d'émigrer quand le besoin s'en fait sentir.[8] L'hypothèse semble étonnante pour un lecteur de Cook et ses successeurs – tous admiratifs de l'art nautique des Polynésiens – et de textes sur les mutins de la *Bounty*, lesquels peuvent rejoindre Pitcairn avec les moyens offerts par leurs amis insulaires. Tout semble prouver que les migrations polynésiennes furent intentionnelles, conçues comme une véritable entreprise de colonisation – les pirogues doubles contenant jusqu'à soixante personnes, des familles entières donc avec animaux et plantes – avec des contacts réguliers entre les îles et non ces 'voyages sans retour' auxquels pensent les premiers voyageurs. Si les études plus récentes – réalisées en particulier avec ordinateurs – montrent que les techniques de navigation des Polynésiens les rendaient bien capables de tels voyages, pour les Européens une telle maîtrise de la mer avec de simples navires plats et posés sur l'océan est proprement impensable. La manière des Océaniens de se repérer dans le ciel, la nuit, en se dirigeant à la fois à la proue et à la poupe et de se transmettre oralement la localisation des îles –, mais sans aucun terme pour désigner les distances, ces dernières étant remplacées par le temps mis à les parcourir –, récitant par cœur les plans de navigation, tout comme la litanie de leurs généalogies sur trente générations, ne leur paraît guère plus concevable. Les Européens qui ont mis des siècles et toutes leurs sciences à améliorer les coques de leurs navires afin de pouvoir affronter des mers lointaines et chaudes et à élaborer des cartes marines avec la grille abstraite des longitudes et des latitudes, ont grand mal à comprendre ces civilisations cosmiques et ces hommes pour lesquels le ciel est 'horloge, calendrier, boussole.'[9] Devant ces navigateurs qui voyagent essentiellement la nuit pour se diriger avec les étoiles, les Européens ont vraiment le sentiment de

---

[5] COOK J., *A voyage to the Pacific ocean ... in the years 1776-1780*, Londres (1984), t. I, p. 367.
[6] SUGGS R.C., 'Methodological problems for "accidental voyagers",' dans *Journal of Polynesian Society*, 70 (1961), 474–476.
[7] DE QUATREFAGES A., *L'espèce humaine*, Paris, 3e édition (1977), p. 143.
[8] MALTHUS T.R., *Essai sur le principe de population*, Paris et Genève, t. I (1823), p. 103.
[9] Cité par C. BENOIT, dans 'Le Grand Océan, les Polynésiens, le triangle maori', *op. cit.*, p. 21.

se trouver face à des antipodes où tout est inversé. Ils constatent une intégration profonde de la maritimité à des cultures orales tout en s'interrogeant sur la cartographie 'pour se souvenir' des Océaniens, avec par exemple les cartes de baguettes de bois et de coquillages en Mélanésie, qui rappellent dans une certaine mesure les portulans.

Cette admiration matinée d'incompréhension pour ces peuples de la mer, est renforcée quand les Occidentaux ont eux-mêmes à utiliser les talents de navigateurs des Polynésiens.

L'expérimentation par les Européens des qualités de navigateurs des Polynésiens

Les désertions touchent en effet fréquemment les flottes de passage dans le Pacifique. Elles sont le produit de la conjonction de voyages particulièrement longs et souvent pénibles – surtout à bord des baleiniers – et des attraits réels ou supposés des îles d'Océanie. Pour compenser une grande versatilité des équipages,[10] de baleiniers en particulier, les marins polynésiens, souvent excellents, sont très appréciés, comme le remarque *L'Indicateur* de Bordeaux:

> Nous avons vu à bord du *Comte-de-Paris* deux jeunes Zélandais, habillés « à la française », et qui sont employés comme marins: l'un de ces jeunes gens est surtout remarquable par la vigueur de ses membres, bien qu'il ait une figure efféminée comme tous les naturels du pays. Ils sont tous deux agiles, courageux, d'une douceur et d'une docilité admirable: le capitaine n'a eu qu'à se louer de leurs services.[11]

Les Polynésiens apparaissent donc comme un peuple 'naturellement maritime' et leurs îles comme idéales pour la relâche. La relâche a elle-même un certain nombre de fonctions qu'Annick Foucrier regroupe sous le nom des 'trois R': renseignement, repos, ravitaillement,[12] auquel, après de longs périples dans le Grand Océan il faut souvent ajouter un quatrième 'R', celui de la réparation des navires[13] et un cinquième, celui de 'recrutement' ... Au ravitaillement en vivres

---

[10] Étudiée par exemple par Paul Huetz de Lemps à propos de l'échouage du *Napoléon III*, navire de 704 tonneaux en 1858, au cours duquel les marins se dépêchent de contracter de nouveaux engagements à bord du navire qui les a recueillis, l'affaire étant compliquée par les fraudes du capitaine Morel. *Cf.* HUETZ DE LEMPS P., *Les Français acteurs et spectateurs de l'histoire de Hawaii (1837-1898)*, thèse dactylographiée. pour le diplôme d'archiviste paléographe, École nationale des chartes, Paris (2001), pp. 262 et 447-448.

[11] TREMEWAN P., 'French Whalers and the Maori', in *Pacific Journeys, Essays in Honour of Dunmore*, Wellington: Victoria University Press (2005), pp. 141-143.

[12] FOUCRIER A., 'La Californie, nœud gordien du Pacifique Nord (1769-1848)', in *Marins et Océans*, t. III (Paris, 1992), pp. 123-149 et *La France et la Californie avant la ruée vers l'or (1788-1848)*, thèse EHESS, 2 vols (1991).

[13] Voir aussi LAUX C., 'Des Français dans le commerce maritime des îles du Pacifique au XIXe siècle: des trafiquants aux négociants', *Revue d'histoire maritime*, octobre (2006), 29-48.

et en eau potable, il faut ajouter le recrutement de marins océaniens afin de remplacer les pertes et les désertions.

Ces qualités de marins des Polynésiens sont déterminantes quant à l'opinion qu'en ont les Occidentaux dans leur ensemble et, par voie de conséquence, sur la manière dont ils sont traités. Aux Hawaii, les navires trouvent un havre, de quoi se ravitailler mais aussi un vivier d'excellents matelots. Dès 1812, un agent commercial d'une maison de Boston est établi à demeure à Honolulu afin de superviser le commerce des îles et de coordonner les opérations de plusieurs navires. Les cargaisons de ces navires sont vite complétées sur place par du bois de santal.[14] C'est par la mer et par ces dispositions pour l'ouverture que passent toutes les ouvertures, commerciales mais aussi religieuses. Si l'*American Board of Commissioners for Foreign Missions* de Boston, fondé en 1810 par des presbytériens et congrégationalistes très actifs sur le territoire nord-américain, se tourne dès 1819 vers les Hawaii, c'est avant tout en raison des rapports des marchands ainsi que de la présence à Boston de jeunes indigènes engagés comme complément d'équipage sur les navires faisant la traite des fourrures et du santal et plus tard sur les baleiniers. Ce sont les dispositions manifestes de ces Polynésiens pour le commerce qui conduisirent les missionnaires puritains à les considérer comme une population digne d'être évangélisée. Un dénommé Obookiah en particulier demeure en Nouvelle Angleterre jusqu'à sa mort en 1818 et est le premier à transcrire en hawaiien quelques textes bibliques. Ce sont alors les marchands de Boston et les baleiniers de Nantucket qui assuraient le transport des missionnaires vers ces régions encore païennes.

L'ouverture sur la mer produit donc, selon les Occidentaux, des sociétés capables de s'ouvrir au commerce et donc d'entrer dans un processus de mondialisation qui touche le Pacifique avant même que celui-ci ne soit absorbé par la colonisation. Mais le rapport à la mer détermine aussi les structures sociales et politiques des îles: la Polynésie offre, en dépit de conflits intestins, un paysage de monarchies centralisées, en grande partie grâce aux influences extérieures, en particulier celles des missionnaires: on pense à George Tupou Premier des Tonga sur lequel nous reviendrons, mais aussi à Kamehameha aux Hawaii, à Pomare à Tahiti ... Ces systèmes politiques engendrent des sociétés fortement hiérarchisées, alors que les sociétés terriennes mélanésiennes apparaissent comme morcelées en chefferies et clans rivaux.

Dans ce contexte, alors que se met en place au XIXe siècle une mondialisation essentiellement maritime, la capacité d'ouverture des îles océaniennes détermine leur place dans cette mondialisation.

---

[14] Pour tout ce qui concerne l'histoire des Hawaii, voir essentiellement: HUETZ DE LEMPS C., *Les Iles Hawaii: étude de géographie humaine*, 5 vols, Bordeaux: Université Michel de Montaigne (1977) dont deux volumes consacrés à l'histoire de l'archipel, et KUYKENDALL R.S., *The Hawaiian Kingdom*, 3 vols, Honolulu: University of Hawaii Press (1938–1967).

L'OUVERTURE MARITIME COMME ÉLÉMENT ESSENTIEL DE L'INSERTION DES PEUPLES D'OCÉANIE DANS LA MONDIALISATION ORCHESTRÉE PAR LES OCCIDENTAUX AU XIXE SIÈCLE

L'Océan, facteur d'isolement géographique ?

Les échanges qu'ils soient d'ailleurs économiques, religieux ou culturels sont tout d'abord déterminés par le degré d'isolement des îles concernées. L'isolement dépend d'abord de paramètres géographiques. L'indice d'isolement proposé par François Doumenge est calculé à partir du rapport entre la surface émergée de l'ensemble insulaire et une surface marine adjacente libre de toute terre assimilée à la zone économique exclusive dite des 'deux cents milles' – convention récente, puisqu'établie par l'accord international de Montego Bay en 1984, mais qui peut être néanmoins opérante pour se faire une idée du degré d'isolement de certaines îles. S'il n'existe d'autre terre émergée à cette distance, une île de 1km^2, peut être associée à une surface maritime de 380 000km^2, ce que l'on définit comme l'isolement absolu – l'île inhabitée de Clipperton n'en est pas loin. Dans le cas de certaines petites îles particulièrement isolées, le degré d'isolement est tel que certains historiens, anthropologues et géographes ont inventé la notion d'"insularisme', mais celle de 'surinsularité' nous parait plus adaptée dans la mesure où il s'agit surtout d'une accentuation des traits de l'insularité pour des raisons physiques. À Pitcairn, où se réfugièrent les mutins de la *Bounty*, l'indice tombe à 1/160.000. Il est de 1/800 seulement pour l'île Maurice ! Les Hawaii, quant à eux, constituent l'un des grands archipels les plus isolés du monde. Si le Pacifique Sud Ouest donne une impression de bien plus grande proximité entre les îles, les distances n'en demeurent pas moins considérables: ainsi la Nouvelle-Calédonie est-elle à 1600km de l'Australie, 1400 des Fidji et 700 du Vanuatu dont elle semble 'voisine'.

Il est également nécessaire d'opérer un *distinguo* entre 'petites îles' (avec de véritables microcosmes qui peuvent faire office de laboratoires pour les contacts avec l'Occident, en particulier pour l'évangélisation, comme les îles Gambier ou Futuna)[15] et 'îles-continents', comme la Nouvelle-Zélande, dernier grand pays peuplé par l'homme, ou *a fortiori* l'Australie. Plus largement, il faut souligner que la faible superficie des îles renforce l'effet d'isolement. Cela conduit à d'importantes nuances géographiques entre les grands archipels du sud-ouest du Pacifique et les nettement plus petites îles du Pacifique austral et oriental: 28 796km^2 pour les Salomon, 18 272km^2 des Fidji, pour seulement 3000km^2 de l'ensemble de l'archipel des Samoa et 4000km^2 pour la totalité des îles de la Polynésie Française. Seule Hawaii (16 638km^2) est de taille comparable dans le Nord Est Pacifique. De nombreuses îles ou archipels de Polynésie ou de

---

[15] Avec des cas extrêmes comme par exemple Futuna. Voir à ce sujet ANGLEVIEL F., 'Uvéa et Futuna, 1616–1767–1887. D'une découverte tardive à la non-colonisation', *Actes du Ve colloque CORAIL*, Nouméa (1993), pp. 41–45, ou encore les travaux de Marc Soule.

Micronésie ne dépassent pas quelques centaines de kilomètres carrés et parfois moins: 26km² pour Tuvalu, 21km² pour Nauru.

Ouverture maritime et intégration dans les courants d'échanges à la fin du XVIIIe et au début du XIXe siècle

Jusqu'au percement du canal de Panama, l'accès au Pacifique Nord est difficile pour les Européens, davantage bien entendu que pour les Américains. Avec leur implantation en Californie en 1848, ces derniers se considèrent comme une puissance du Pacifique. Malgré tout, paradoxalement, le plus isolé des archipels océaniens et le dernier découvert par les Occidentaux, les îles Hawaii, est celui qui s'intégra le mieux et le plus vite aux grands courants d'échanges internationaux. Pour certains archipels, en effet, l'isolement peut devenir un atout dans la mesure où ils deviennent des escales quasi-obligées sur de grandes routes maritimes. Ainsi donc des Hawaii dont le futur consul de France à Manille Albert Barrot écrit lorsqu'il les visite avec la *Bonite* en 1836:

> Placées au centre du grand Océan Pacifique septentrional, elles sont là comme un relais au milieu de cette immense mer qui sépare l'Inde et la Chine de l'Amérique méridionale; elles acquerront de l'importance à mesure que les relations des deux continent se développeront.

et il évoque la possibilité du canal de Panama, déjà pensé par Nuñez de Balboa, rejeté car jugé trop coûteux par Charles Quint mais auquel les saint-simoniens accordent un grand intérêt: 'Si l'isthme de Panama s'ouvre, les îles Sandwich deviendront nécessairement l'un des points les plus intéressants du globe ...'[16]

Dans le dernier tiers du Siècle des Lumières, en parallèle avec les efforts mis en œuvre pour découvrir le continent austral puis le passage du nord-ouest, les Européens mettent certains espoirs dans le développement de flux marchands trans-Pacifique (entre les côtes nord-américaines et la Chine pour le commerce des fourrures par exemple), et l'exploitation de ressources propres au grand océan (troupeaux de baleines), voire à ses îles (bois de santal ...). Les îles du Pacifique en elles-mêmes ont déçu économiquement même si leurs milieux naturels et leurs populations continuent d'être l'objet d'un grand intérêt. Après avoir suscité d'immenses espérances, fasciné par l'"abondance primitive"[17] dans laquelle vivaient ses populations, il est loin de procurer à l'Europe des trésors comparables à ceux des Amériques. Point non plus, du moins dans les premiers temps, de produits tropicaux comparables à ceux offerts par les Antilles ou les îles de l'océan Indien. A la fin du XVIIIe siècle, une seule tentative d'exploitation des ressources propres au Pacifique suffit aux Européens: un navire britannique est envoyé, à l'initiative de Joseph Banks, à Tahiti pour ramener des plants du

---

[16] BARROT A., 'Les îles Sandwich', *Revue des Deux Mondes*, 1er et 15 août (1839), 539.
[17] FISK E.K., 'Planning in a primitive economy; from a pure subsistence to the production of a market surplus', *Economic Record* 40.90 (1964), 156–174.

fameux 'arbre à pain' que l'on pense pouvoir planter dans la Caraïbe afin d'obtenir un aliment roboratif et bon marché pour la main d'œuvre servile. Son capitaine est William Bligh et le navire, la *Bounty*, se mutine comme on le sait. Après les voyages de Bligh le Pacifique est largement laissé aux trafiquants et aventuriers.[18] Les Français connaissent une déception par certains aspects comparable à celle qu'ils avaient connue en Nouvelle-France au XVIIe siècle. Point d'or ni d'argent donc sur cette poussière d'îles si difficilement accessibles: pour toute richesse, le Grand Océan n'offre aux Européens qu'une immense aire de chasse à la baleine, cétacé dont l'huile, entre autres, est recherchée pour l'éclairage.

Les déceptions économiques précédemment évoquées n'empêchent pas des armateurs privés de donner l'impulsion à de grands voyages de découverte à visées économiques: santal, fourrures puis baleines. Ainsi que le souligne John Dunmore, ce n'est pas un hasard si la reprise des expéditions françaises vers le Pacifique se fait sur des objectifs commerciaux.[19] Dans le même temps, à côté de ces marchands 'officiels', un grand nombre de petits trafiquants, d'aventuriers, viennent tenter leur chance dans les Mers du Sud.

Durant les premières décennies du siècle, les Français et les Britanniques, mais aussi les Américains dans le Pacifique Nord, expérimentent différentes options économiques, plus ou moins durables, dans les îles océaniennes. Toutes sont liées, à divers degrés, à leur intégration dans les flux d'échanges trans-Pacifiques: fourrures, baleines, bois de santal et diverses productions insulaires qui au départ servent à compléter les cargaisons ou à satisfaire les besoins de ceux qui pratiquent ces échanges.

En Polynésie, les chefs locaux cherchent à tirer le meilleur parti possible de ces courants d'échanges, confirmant leur aptitude à faire de la mer leur alliée. Aux Hawaii, le roi Kamehameha Ier garde le monopole du commerce du santal et tente même en 1818 d'envoyer un santalier sous son propre pavillon vers la Chine, sans grand succès d'ailleurs. Son successeur, Kamehameha II libéralise le commerce du santal, permettant ainsi aux chefs de participer aux profits. Ces derniers se lancent alors dans une course effrénée à la coupe de la précieuse essence. Cette libéralisation sans la moindre retenue n'a pas que des effets positifs, elle a en effet des conséquences dramatiques tant au plan écologique que sur celui des sociétés océaniennes: la surexploitation des ressources en bois entraîne leur épuisement. Malgré cela, cette capacité à se tourner vers la mer, permet aux chefs polynésiens de jouer longtemps un rôle actif dans leur propre histoire et ne pas s'en laisser déposséder, en dépit d'un certain nombre d'erreurs de jugement, contrairement aux Mélanésiens. Leur ouverture par la mer se caractérise par la capacité des chefs à quitter leur archipel pour voyager. Le voyage officiel de Kamehameha II et de son épouse, rebaptisée Victoria à Londres, par exemple en 1824, fait grande impression. Chateaubriand voit bien dans cette visite du roi des Hawaii dans la capitale britannique le symbole des

---

[18] HAUDRÈRE P., *Le grand commerce maritime au xviiie siècle*, Paris: SEDES (1997).
[19] DUNMORE J., *Visions and Realities, France in Pacific, 1695-1995*, Waikanae, N.Z.: Heritage Press (1997) p. 155.

transformations vertigineuses qu'a connues l'archipel: 'On a vu dernièrement, à l'opéra de Londres, un roi et une reine de ces insulaires qui avaient mangé le capitaine Cook, tout en adorant ses os dans le temple au roi Rono [Lono].[20] Les monarques hawaiiens meurent d'ailleurs de la rougeole en Angleterre, comme tant de leurs sujets dans l'archipel. Le capitaine britannique Byron ramène la triste nouvelle aux Hawaii en même temps que les dépouilles royales. Les deux monarques sont inhumés 'à l'anglaise', dans la retenue et sans débordement. Le roi Kamehameha IV, quant à lui, petit-fils du grand Kamehameha et qui monte sur le trône des Hawaii en 1854, s'est aussi rendu en visite en Angleterre, en 1849–1850, d'autant qu'il est marié à Emma Rooke, fille métisse d'un marin.

Ouverture sur la mer et destinée des îles en situation coloniale

Si dès les années 1870, on assiste à ce que les historiens appellent le 'scramble for Africa', le Pacifique des années 1880 subit un 'scramble for Oceania' qui conduit à un partage rapide des archipels du Grand Océan entre les grandes puissances. La plus petite île, même sans intérêt géopolitique ou économique se retrouve âprement disputée. Là aussi, la place que prennent les îles dans le système colonial est très largement fonction de leur capacité à s'ouvrir ou non sur la mer. Des archipels comme les Hawaii ou les Tonga semblent contrôler relativement longtemps leur insertion dans le processus de mondialisation. En dépit de la réelle influence des premiers missionnaires, Turner mais surtout Thomas, la fascination pour le modèle britannique apparait au départ comme relativement spontanée dans l'archipel des Tonga, en tous cas chez cette personnalité extraordinaire que fut le chef Taufa'ahau, futur roi George Ier. Les missionnaires sont les vecteurs de cette influence, en tant que représentants de la civilisation britannique, ils ne l'imposent pas.

Les Tongiens avaient, avant même l'arrivée des premiers missionnaires, connu un contact prolongé avec un représentant de la civilisation britannique, un aventurier, William Mariner, qui y séjourna plusieurs années au début du XIXe siècle.

Taufa'ahau, qui n'est encore qu'un chef parmi d'autres dans l'archipel, sans légitimité particulière pour capter la souveraineté, se fait dès 1833 appeler Georges Ier en raison de son admiration pour Georges III d'Angleterre. Le seul soutien britannique qu'il reçoit est alors celui des missionnaires, les pasteurs de la *Wesleyan Methodist Missionary Society* faisant office de conseillers militaires auprès de ce chef sur lequel ils ont tout misé. Cet appui missionnaire permet à Taufa'ahau de mettre fin à la situation de guerre civile qui déchire l'archipel et d'évincer les prétendants de l'étrange monarchie tricéphale tongienne, où la souveraineté est partagée entre le Tui Tonga, le Ha'atakalau, et le Tui Kanakupolu.[21] Il fonde

---

[20] DE CHATEAUBRIAND F.-R., *Voyage en Amérique*, in *Œuvres romanesques et voyages*, 2 vols, Paris: Gallimard (1986), II, 647.

[21] La dynastie des Tui Tonga remonte probablement au Xe siècle et peut être comparée à celle du Dalaï Lama au Tibet ou à celle de l'empereur du Japon. La crainte de l'assassinat

alors la dynastie qui règne aujourd'hui encore sur les Tonga. Son admiration pour la Grande-Bretagne se traduit par un désir d'imitation dans de nombreux domaines: ainsi, il se plaît à inviter ses amis missionnaires à prendre le thé tout en parlant des affaires du royaume. L'un des missionnaires, Tucker, raconte par exemple comment, par l'évocation du modèle de civilisation anglais, les missionnaires parviennent à convaincre le monarque de faire preuve de magnanimité sur la question problématique de l'esclavage:

> J'ai eu ce matin une longue et très intéressante conversation avec le roi durant laquelle, entre autre sujets, fut abordée la question de l'esclavage. Je lui donnai mon point de vue sur le sujet et lui mentionnai ce qui avait été fait récemment en Angleterre et dans d'autres pays pour abolir ce système et libérer les opprimés ... Dans la soirée nous entendîmes plusieurs personnes criant très fort et l'on découvrit que cela se passait à la maison du roi; il a commandé à tous les servants de venir et là ensuite, il leur rendit la liberté. La scène était des plus émouvantes ...[22]

L'alliance entre le roi George et les missionnaires ne doit pas être interprété comme un simple 'malentendu productif'[23] car, contrairement probablement à Pomaré II de Tahiti, sa conversion fut sincère et il demeura toute sa vie un homme de foi. Son admiration pour l'Angleterre ne fut pas non plus simplement le fruit d'une grande habileté politique; même si cette dimension est indéniable, il ne faudrait pas en sous-estimer l'authenticité. Contrairement à Pomaré ou à Kamehameha, il choisit d'ailleurs d'abandonner son nom polynésien pour prendre un patronyme britannique. Ce sont néanmoins indubitablement la nouvelle religion et l'adoption du modèle anglais qui permettent au nouveau roi de fonder sa légitimité après une phase d'hénothéisme durant laquelle le Dieu chrétien s'impose comme *primus inter pares* au sein du panthéon tongien. A son image, George Ier s'impose d'abord comme un chef parmi d'autres avant de devenir véritablement roi, en investissant son titre d'une sacralité particulière, sacralité protestante et ... britannique.[24]

George Ier a certes sa propre conception du modèle britannique: c'est davantage en monarque éclairé qu'en monarque parlementaire qu'il modernise son pays et il n'hésite pas à imposer à ses sujets le protestantisme comme religion d'État, ce qui n'est pas pour déplaire à ses alliés missionnaires wesleyens. Il devient chef de la nouvelle Église tongienne et ses amis pasteurs évoquent fréquemment et avec

---

politique ou simplement la nécessité des rapports de force imposèrent une division de la souveraineté en deux puis en trois. Sur l'interprétation de ce phénomène voir par exemple CAMPBELL I.C., *Classical Tongan Kingship*, Nuku'alofa, Tonga: 'Atenisi University (1989).

[22] SOAS, Londres, Methodist Missionary Society Archives, box 540, file 1834, Tucker, Journal, 1834, 21 août.

[23] Pour reprendre l'expression de Jean-François Baré: J.-F. BARÉ, *Le malentendu Pacifique*, Paris: Hachette (1985).

[24] Voir LAUX C., 'L'hénothéisme, transition essentielle dans l'évolution religieuse et politique des îles de Polynésie', *Bulletin de la Société d'histoire du protestantisme français* CXLVII, avril-mai-juin (2001), pp. 251–281.

admiration ses prêches.[25] Ils entraînent dès leur arrivée les Tonga dans la voie de l'ouverture économique et du libéralisme, si essentiels soubassements de l'idéologie impérialiste britannique de l'époque, ce que ne manquaient pas d'ailleurs de dénoncer leurs rivaux maristes.[26] Àl'intérieur, son code de loi de 1850, qui fait l'admiration des autres monarques polynésiens, cherche certes à imiter là encore les souverains britanniques dont il entend louer le juste et équitable gouvernement, mais il est surtout calqué sur le Décalogue et le respect des principes bibliques.

Sa longévité remarquable lui permet jusqu'à la fin du siècle de préserver l'essentiel de sa souveraineté sur les Tonga et de les protéger de toute domination étrangère, y compris celle des Anglais.

Il peut compter pour cela dans les années 1870 sur un Premier ministre particulièrement avisé: un missionnaire et aventurier, le très célèbre Shirley Baker, fort peu prisé par ses compatriotes britanniques. Pendant longtemps, il fut même l'objet d'une sorte de 'mythe noir' parti de l'ouvrage de Basil Thomson, *Diversions of a Prime Minister*, publié à Londres en 1894, mais ce témoignage est trop favorable aux Anglais pour ne pas être sujet à caution. Il n'a de cesse en effet que d'abaisser celui qui a fait tant d'effort pour éviter aux Tonga de tomber sous le joug britannique.[27]

Sur le plan religieux, logiquement, les velléités de Baker et du roi George de maintenir l'indépendance des Tonga le conduisent à rompre avec sa mission d'origine, la *Wesleyan Missionary Society*, et à se créer une Église tongienne indépendante, la *Free Church of Tonga*, schisme qui n'est évidemment pas fait pour rehausser son image auprès de ses compatriotes.[28]

CONCLUSION

La relation à l'histoire des îles d'Océanie, prise dans le temps long, montre parfaitement la pertinence des concepts « d'îléité » et d'insularité tels que les définit Joel Bonnemaison, qui différencie les îles polynésiennes et micronésiennes, îles du rivage tournées vers la mer, des îles mélanésiennes, îles continentales, indépendamment même de la taille, même si celle-ci a évidemment une importance capitale. Cette différence culturelle dans la perception et l'usage fait des immensités océaniques dans lesquelles sont perdues les îles est évidemment fondamentale dans leur histoire ancienne, celle d'avant les contacts avec les Occidentaux, et elle façonne leur personnalité. Mais il nous a paru intéressant

---

[25] SOAS, Londres, Methodist Missionary Society 9, box 541, Tucker, journal, 1835, 24 mars et 8 juillet.
[26] DURIEZ C., *Contribution mariste à l'histoire de Tonga*, thèse: Université de Paris VII, (1994), p. 102.
[27] Le témoignage de Thomson est critiqué de manière fort pertinente par Noel RUTHERFORD dans son *Shirley Baker and the King of Tonga*, Melbourne: Oxford University Press (1971).
[28] FINDLAY G.G. et HOLDSWORTH W.W., *The History of the Wesleyan Methodist Missionary Society*, 5 vols, Londres: Epworth (1921), III, 337.

de montrer ici comment la plus ou moins grande 'maritimité' des îles continue à jouer un rôle non négligeable dans la période contemporaine. Être tournés vers la mer pour les habitants des îles confère des facultés d'adaptation, et parfois de résistance, à l'intensification des échanges, à la participation à un processus de globalisation, et même à l'entreprise coloniale. Dans ces îles comme ailleurs, les individus les plus dynamiques, les plus parties prenantes dans cette ouverture, sont alors les 'gens du contact', en particulier les métis dont l'existence même est fruit de la rencontre maritime ...

Maritime labour

ALASTAIR COUPER is Professor Emeritus in Maritime Studies at Cardiff University, United Kingdom

ABSTRACT. *Seafaring has always been a dangerous and isolated livelihood. Shipowners nowadays can recruit from low-wage countries far from the ships' home ports, and sometimes far from the sea; deep-sea fishing boats are sometimes manned by semi-slave labour. Owners use flags of convenience to avoid safety regulations and to undermine the International Labour Organisation, but port states may enforce regulations adopted by international agreement on shipping frequenting their ports.*

RÉSUMÉ. *La navigation a toujours été un gagne-pain isolé et dangereux. Les propriétaires de navires peuvent aujourd'hui recruter dans des pays aux bas salaires, éloignés des ports d'attache des navires et parfois même de la mer. L'équipage des bateaux de pêche en haute mer travaille souvent dans des conditions proches de l'esclavage. Les armateurs utilisent des pavillons de complaisance pour passer outre les règlementations de sécurité et nuire à l'Organisation internationale du travail (OIT) mais les États portuaires peuvent renforcer la législation adoptée par accord international sur les bateaux qui fréquentent leurs ports.*

. • .

The sea has seldom been a barrier to the movement of people or trade. It has served as a means of long-distance communication and a source of food whenever reliable vessels could be constructed and crewed by competent seafarers. When Captain Cook met with the Polynesian priest navigator Tupaia in Tahiti during 1769 he was told of 130 distant Pacific islands which Tupaia knew from his voyaging and ancient oral history. Tupaia drew a chart showing seventy-five of these that would be of interest to Cook. They were distributed 2,500 miles east and west from the position of Tahiti, and he described some of their products and people. Tupaia knew the relationship between sea, ship and crew in traversing such distances with accuracy and safety.[1]

This chapter focuses on these three components with emphasis on the crew in the period from the mid-19th century to the present. It considers seafarers on merchant vessels, and then, because of their different functions, the crews of fishing craft. The period includes the great changes in technology and organisational

---

[1] COUPER A.D., *Sailors and Traders: A Maritime History of the Pacific Peoples* (Hawaii, 2000), p. 68.

structures that came about in the transition from sail to steam, and the intervention by nation-states and international bodies in the regime of labour at sea.

As a means of earning a living, and way of life, going to sea has always had its dangers. It was, and still is, the most hazardous of all occupations. Precise figures are still not widely available even in modern times. Historically in Britain between 1872 and 1884 on average three thousand seafarers were lost at sea each year and 2,300 died from other causes.[2] This in many ways reflected insufficient responses to the vagaries of the sea, inadequate vessels and poor life-saving equipment. Seafarers were well aware of the risks and regarded the sea with respect. It could overwhelm a ship, or snatch an unwary sailor from the deck. Joseph Conrad consistently depicts the sea and ship in such anthropomorphic terms. He gives a graphic account of the struggle between his ship the *Narcissus* and the sea as she fought for survival.

> A great sea came running up aft and hung for a moment over us with a curling top; then crashed down under the counter and spread out on both sides into a great sheet of bursting froth ... the ship trembled, trying to lift her side, lurched back, seemed to give up with a nervous dip, and suddenly with an unexpected jerk swung violently to windward, as though she had torn herself from a deadly grasp.[3]

Conrad cautions his fellow mariners that they must always treat the ship with "an understanding of the mysteries of her feminine nature, then she will stand by you faithfully",[4] and when it comes to seamanship he reminds them that "the sea will not put up with a mere pretender". These are not simply literary romanticisms, they resonate over time and space in ancient myths and traditions of peoples of the sea.

While the ship may be referred to as feminine the crew has always primarily been masculine, there have been only a few women employed at sea and these days they are mainly in domestic service on cruise ships and passenger vessels. Sailors have generally looked after themselves and conformed to customary laws on board. They had to make and mend and improvise, independent of the shore. Foreign seamen could take their place on most sailing ships and, independent of language, carry out skilled tasks aloft and on deck at a command, and could always depend on one another for safety:

> You'd be slithering about a deck you know, and a hand'll catch you and pull you up, and something like by Christ you were bloody near for it then weren't you.[5]

For most people ashore the ways of the sea and lifestyles of seafarers were

---

[2] HOPE R., *A New History of British Shipping* (London, 1990), p. 281.
[3] AYMAR B., *Men at Sea: The Best Sea Stories of All Time* (New York, 1988), p. 473.
[4] MASON M., GREENHILL B. and CRAIG R., *The British Seafarer* (London, 1975).
[5] SAGER, E.W.S., *Seafaring Labour: The Merchant Marine of Atlantic Canada, 1820-1914* (Kingston and London, 1989), p. 130.

generally out of sight and out of mind. Sailors were usually only encountered by land people in the disreputable districts of port towns. These "sailor towns" included parts of Limehouse in London, Paradise Street Liverpool, Tiger Bay Cardiff, St Pauli Hamburg and the Barbary Coast San Francisco.[6] It was there that seafarers paid off and said goodbyes to shipmates or signed on and bonded with new crews before sailing. There were informal networks of information in the various port establishments where views were exchanged on ships and captains. For the local citizens these districts were regarded as necessary evils in the vital commerce of a port.

The images of the sailor ashore belied his hard, responsible and sober ways of life at sea. They made it difficult for sailors to be heard in protest over unsafe ships and conditions. The American Supreme Court Judge Joseph Storey in 1823 described them patronisingly as "thoughtless and required indulgence", and the British Judge Lord Stowell in 1825 saw sailors as "a set of men generally ignorant and illiterate, requiring protection even against themselves".[7]

The sea-going conditions of seafarers were given some publicity by evangelical groups who established missions, sailors' homes and orphanages.[8] Awareness and some outrage became apparent in America with the book by Richard Henry Dana *Two Years Before the Mast*. He described the power of a captain over legally isolated seafarers from his experience on the American ship *Pilgrim* in 1834. The sailor John the Swede asked Captain Thompson why his shipmate Sam was being flogged. Captain Thompson told him to shut up "nobody shall open his mouth aboard this vessel but myself", he then personally flogged the Swede. The sailor cried out in pain "Oh Jesus Christ", to which Captain Thompson retorted "don't call on Jesus Christ, he can't help you".[9] He was making it plain to the crew that there was nobody above him, the Master.

In 1836 the British Parliamentary Select Committee on Shipwrecks finally gathered evidence from seafarers, owners and ship insurers (Lloyd's of London) on the situation in merchant shipping. They reported defective construction, inadequate equipment, improper loading, incompetent masters and officers and drunkenness of masters and officers.[10] But little changed. In three days in January 1843 some 240 vessels sank in bad weather.[11]

Between 1850 and 1880 the nation-states moved towards the protection of labour at sea and there were a series of reforms, including the British Merchant Shipping Acts (MSA), which were replicated elsewhere. These included compulsory Articles of Agreement when joining a ship, improvements in provisions, accommodation and certificates of competency.[12]

---

[6] HUGILL S., *Sailortown* (London, 1967).
[7] FITZPATRICK D. and ANDERSON M., *Seafarers' Rights* (Oxford, 2004).
[8] KVERNDAL R., *Seamen's Missions: Their Origin and Early Growth* (Pasadena, CA, 1986), p. 18.
[9] DANA R.H., *Two Years before the Mast* (New York, 2001), p. 14.
[10] *British House of Commons Select Committee Appointed to Inquire into the Cause of Shipwrecks.* HC 1836 XVIII, p. 373.
[11] HOPE, *A New History of British Shipping*, p. 281.
[12] COUPER A.D., 'Perceptions and Attitudes of Seafarers Towards Maritime Regulations: An Historical Perspective', in *The Regulation of International Shipping: International and Comparative*

In 1870 a major cause of ship loss was further revealed by the Tyne shipowner James Hall as overloading. This was ameliorated eventually after the publication of the book *Our Seamen* by Samuel Plimsoll in 1876. On the navigational side, the Comité Maritime International was discussing safety, but it was not until 1910 that the Rule of the Road[13] was set out through the efforts of France and Britain. The major convention on Safety of Life at Sea (SOLAS) was drafted only after the loss of the *Titanic* in 1912, and not ratified until 1929.[14] The health of seafarers had, on the other hand, quickly benefited from the publication of the book *A Ship Captain's Medical Guide* by the medical reformer Dr Harry Leach in 1868,[15] although as late as 1924 Dr W.E. Home complained about unreliable figures on the health of seafarers:

> If the figures referred to bags of coffee or tons of coal, that would be alright, it would be in the financial interests of certain people to keep a watchful eye on the returns. But the deaths of seamen are nobody's concern.[16]

A CHANGE FROM SAIL TO STEAM

On the nineteenth-century sailing ship the division of labour and the hierarchy of the crew were clear. There were a captain, three mates, four apprentices (officer cadets), a bosun, carpenter, sail maker (non-commissioned officers), about ten able-bodied seamen (AB), skilled in the high-top duties, and ten or so ordinary seamen, plus a cook, two stewards and several boys working on deck, galley and pantry. The segregated social order was also clear. The captain had a bedroom, day room and bath aft, and the three mates lived aft in small cabins. The non-commissioned group were in a structure amidships along with the galley. The rest of the crew were in the crowded, wedge-shaped forecastle at the bow. They had tiered bunks with straw-filled mattresses all laid out according to seniority. It was also a class system, since with a few exceptions there was little mobility from ratings to officer rank, due to the poor educational origins of young boys recruited for seagoing. The crew generally signed on for a voyage after some bargaining with the captain over wages. The levels of these depended on supply and demand.

Sail and steam coexisted until the end of the century, and longer in the carriage of grain and coal on long hauls. For the seamen who moved from sail

---

Perspectives: Essays in Honor of Edgar Gold, ed. A. CHIRCOP, N. LETALIK, T.L. McDORMAN and S. ROLSTON (Leiden, 2012), p. 429.

[13] CHIRCOP A., 'Introduction to the Regulation of International Shipping', in *The Regulation of International Shipping*, ed. CHIRCOP et al., p. 1.

[14] CHIRCOP A., 'Seafaring and Maritime Labour Law', in *The Regulation of International Shipping*, ed. CHIRCOP et al., p. 434.

[15] COUPER A.D., 'A Historical Perspective on Seafarers and the Law,' in *Seafarers' Rights*, ed. D. FITZPATRICK and M. ANDERSON (Oxford, 2005), p. 16.

[16] HOME W.E., 'The health of merchant seamen,' *The Lancet* 204.5280 (1924), 981–2.

to steamships there were considerable deskilling and new divisions of labour on board. These included the additions of chief engineer and engineering officers, and greasers, firemen and trimmers. The designs of ships changed radically, as did the allocation of space for officers and crew. Cargo vessels had mid-ship structures for the navigation bridge, engine room and accommodation for the captain and officers. Deck officers lived in the starboard side and engineer officers on the port side. The crew remained in the forecastle but were later housed aft on newer vessels, although there were separate mess rooms for sailors and for firemen and trimmers. The crews on steamships became more multi-racial, although European ratings generally carried out deck work while Asiatic and Arab ratings worked in the dark, dirty, airless conditions of the engine room. The mixed crews were increasingly drawn from countries with colonial possessions, and more women became employed at sea with the passenger and cargo liner services as stewardesses and nurses. There were generally amalgamations of companies, particularly in the liner services, and as they concentrated on more specific large ports there was more contact between seafarers and port workers in attempts to organise concerted industrial action.

MARITIME TRADE UNIONS AND INTERNATIONAL NEGOTIATIONS

Trade unions were already established for skilled crafts ashore and extended to general workers. One of the first maritime unions in seagoing was the Federated Seamen's Union of Australia in 1878. In Britain the National Amalgamated Sailors and Firemen's Union was formed in 1880, along with the beginning of seamen's and dockers' unions in France, Holland, Belgium and Germany. In America the Coast Seamen's Union started in 1885, the American Longshoremen's Union in 1890 and the International Seamen's Union of the United States soon afterwards. A number of strikes in the late 19th century showed the power of the unions if they acted together. The port strike in Rotterdam in 1896 was supported by the crews of British ships in the port who refused to work cargo. The new unions met in London in 1897 and in 1898 they formed the International Transport Workers' Federation (ITF), comprising a strong seagoing section along with port workers. This was eventually followed by the Shipowners International Shipping Federation (ISF), formed in 1908.[17]

The turn of the century was also a period of more mobility of indentured labour internationally, moving to plantations, goldfields, mines and railway building. They came largely from colonial possessions and were also recruited into seagoing. The Australian Steam Navigation Company in 1887 started to employ low-waged Chinese seafarers on their ships. The unions called a strike.[18]

---

[17] ITF. *Solidarity: ITF Centenary Book* (London, 1996).
[18] Ibid., p. 40.

They were successful in stopping this and their action also resulted in the introduction of the so called "White Australia Policy" from 1891 to 1901. In the US the "yellow peril" was identified partly because large numbers of Chinese who had been working on the transcontinental railways were looking for positions at sea in San Francisco. The trade unions denied racial discrimination, arguing that they would tolerate any foreign labour provided it was on the correct rates of pay. The American government ultimately introduced the 1882 China Exclusion Act. Chinese seamen were still signed on in Hong Kong and elsewhere but were not allowed to go ashore in the United States when on American vessels. This resulted in a reduction in the employment of Chinese crews on American ships.[19]

In Britain there were special Lascar Agreements on British ships, allowing Indian crewing in certain routes. In 1913 British ships employed 212,570 British seafarers, 46,848 Lascars (Indians) and 32,639 non-British Europeans.[20] Efforts were made to spread union membership amongst these groups and through the ITF there was an anti-racist stance, but riots and strikes still occurred over cheap labour at sea. The need for an international approach to labour issues resulted in the establishment in 1919 of the International Labour Organisation (ILO) in Geneva. The ILO had a commitment to the provision of conventions and recommendations for the improvement of life and labour relations at sea. Negotiations on proposed regulations were conducted by the ITF and ISF at the ILO. One of the first conventions to be promulgated was the 1920 Placing of Seamen Convention to eliminate the charging fees paid by seafarers and not by the shipowners to agencies that were recruiting labour for shipping. Subsequently there were forty maritime ILO Conventions and thirty Recommendations. Many remained unratified and others were not implemented primarily because of the flag of convenience system. Through this the registration of a ship could be moved to states which had neither the willingness nor the capacity to enforce the measures being agreed as conventions at the ILO.

An important addition in the ILO system was the facility under the Joint Maritime Commission within which the ITF and the ISF could contribute to the establishment of a minimum wage internationally for an AB as the basis around which other rates would be geared. To the basic wage would be added overtime and leave payments to reach a final sum by any company. The ITF interpreted its own final sum and sought separate agreements with shipping companies.

Modern labour relations

Not all the ILO Conventions were ratified by member states; to those that were, there was scant attention paid by some sectors of the industry. Their avoidance of these measures was through the adoption of flags of convenience (FOC). This

---

[19] GIBSON A. and ARTHUR D., *Abandoned Ocean: A History of United States Maritime Policy* (Columbia, SC, 2000), p. 117.
[20] HOPE, *British Shipping*, p. 342.

became most prevalent after the 1973 rise in the price of fuel and, with that, the search for economies in production and transport. The modern period also saw shifts of manufacturing to low-cost areas and increases in the volume of carriage of goods by sea. Economies of scale were likewise obtained by the introduction of giant ships in oil and dry-bulk transport, and the containerisation of general cargos. Crew sizes were reduced and there was systematic recruitment of crews from lower-paid economies. This was facilitated by the simple device of shift of flags to FOC.

The FOC system was opposed by the ITF. It ran a campaign and introduced methods to retain a "genuine link" between the flag of the ship and the country of ownership of the vessel. However, in the modern world, control of the ship would not necessarily be in the country of ownership. It could be elsewhere through a management company, or by charterers of the ship. Wage differentials between FOC and national-flag vessels were not the only difficulties. There were national-flag ships with worse conditions and pay than on some of the FOC vessels. Several unions that were affiliated to ITF were not dismayed by the lower wages on FOC, since these could be twice the amount their members would obtain under their own flags, and in any case they would probably not find work whatsoever. The ITF came to agreements with FOC companies that were prepared to raise their standards in rates and conditions and issued them with a Blue Certificate of Approval, thereby avoiding problems of boycotts in several ports.[21]

In 1948, after the vast losses at sea during the Second World War, the concern over safety of ships internationally came into the province of what became the International Maritime Organisation (IMO), a UN agency related to the ILO. The IMO developed further the SOLAS Convention. It also had responsibility for a new Convention on the Standards of Training, Certification and Watchkeeping (STCW) and a third major Convention related to the protection of the marine environment against pollution from ships – MARPOL.

These various legal instruments required implementation by flag states, additional skills of seafarers and responsibilities from the masters of ships. Port states were also given authority to monitor and take actions in cases of violations of the Conventions. The ILO in conjunction with the IMO, the ITF and the ISF went on to clarify the rights and obligations of seafarers by combining thirty-seven existing ILO Conventions into the Maritime Labour Convention (MLC 2006).[22] This thereby established the four pillars of a legislative structure which would support work, health and safety on merchant ships, provided it was implemented by flag states and merchant seafarers of the world.

---

[21] ITF, *Solidarity*.
[22] International Labour Organisation, 'Maritime Labour Convention, 2006', http://www.ilo.org/global/standards/maritime-labour-convention/lang--en/index.htm [Accessed 3 February 2014].

The Numbers of World Merchant Seafarers

A brief analysis of labour shows that in 2010 there were 1.4 million seafarers supplied to merchant ships worldwide. Of these 445,000 were officers and 648,914 were ratings.[23] Table 1 shows the most significant places of origin of these seafarers, although not the flags they served under nor the shipowners they worked for.

It is clear from Table 1 that most ratings and increasing numbers of officers are now drawn from the developing countries and Russia, along with other countries of the former communist bloc. The shipping companies owning ships are in the richer countries, consequently there are now fewer ratings from the once-traditional maritime states that still control shipping companies. The US seems anomalous in its position of employment. This is due partly to the Jones Act, which requires American coastal vessels, and some of those on other routes to be crewed by US seafarers.[24] China shows dominance in supply, but most Chinese seafarers are on Chinese ships, with large numbers in the coastal trade of China. The Philippines leads in the people export states to the sea. In particular, Philippine ratings occupy over 30% of ratings on cruise ships. They are selected by the criteria of English language, hardworking, friendly and with musical talent. The cruise industry is also the main employer of women at sea. According to the Philippines Overseas Employment Administration (POEA), in 2010 the Philippines provided 339,608 seafarers to world shipping, which included 81,761 officers and 124,765 ratings. On the demand side of maritime labour, according to BIMCO/ISF there was a ten thousand deficit of officers in 2010, often for very specialised vessels, and a surplus of 135,000 ratings.[25] This indicates some difficulties in determining the numbers of ratings as compared with the BIMCO/ISF figures in Table 1.

Work in Fishing

There are several labour issues over wage differentials in fishing, similar to those in the merchant shipping sector, but even higher mortality rates and more fundamental differences over recruitment and the work at sea. About sixteen million fishermen catch fish at sea from some four million craft, and women are engaged in lagoon and estuary netting, but much more in the processing of landings. Most fishing is from small boats of less than ten metres working out of villages in local waters. Bigger ships employ nearly two million fishers out of national

---

[23] BIMCO/ISF. *BIMCO/ISF Manpower 2010 Update: The Worldwide Demand for and Supply of Seafarers, Main Report* (London, 2010).

[24] 'Merchant Marine Act, 1920', https://www.law.cornell.edu/uscode/html/uscode46a/usc_sup_05_46_10_24.html [Accessed 23 February 2015].

[25] BIMCO/ISF, *BIMCO/ISF Manpower 2010 Update: The Worldwide Demand for and Supply of Seafarers, Main Report*.

Table 1. *Numbers of world merchant seafarers, 2010*

Flag	Officers	Ratings	Total
China, People's Republic	51,511	90,296	141,807
Turkey	36,734	51,009	87,743
Philippines	57,688	23,492	81,180
Indonesia	15,906	61,821	77,727
Russia	25,000	40,000	65,000
India	46,497	16,176	62,673
United States of America	21,810	16,644	38,454
Ukraine	27,172	11,000	38,172
Malaysia	6,313	28,687	35,000
Bulgaria	10,890	22,379	33,269
Myanmar	10,950	20,145	31,095
Japan	21,297	7,308	28,605
Romania	18,575	5,768	24,343
Norway	16,082	7,300	23,382
United Kingdom	14,657	8,536	23,193
Poland	17,923	4,746	22,669
Vietnam	10,738	11,438	22,176
Sri Lanka	2,282	19,511	21,793
Italy	9,560	11,390	20,950
Cambodia	8,053	12,004	20,057
Honduras	4,239	15,341	19,580
Croatia	11,704	6,954	18,658
Canada	13,994	3,109	17,103
Chile	7,348	7,759	15,107
France	4,568	9,128	13,696

Source: BIMCO/ISF. *BIMCO/ISF Manpower 2010 Update: The Worldwide Demand for and Supply of Seafarers, Main Report*. London BIMCO/ISF, 2010.

ports; big ships also fish internationally in distant waters from many countries. The small craft are often run on a family basis, with payments including shares in the catch. Distant-water vessels are frequently owned by national or transnational companies and are crewed by migrant workers recruited from elsewhere in the developing world.

All fishers have multiple problems and conflicts. These include depletion of stocks due to overfishing and the excess capacity of modern boats and gear, along with the destruction of the marine environment. The small-scale fishers are also denied opportunities to earn a decent living, due to fishing by large-scale vessels from urban and foreign countries fishing over their zones. In the race for fish the distant-water vessels make economies by trafficking young men and boys from the poorest countries through deception and subjecting them to forced labour at sea. This supply of crews for distant-water fishing fleets is through networks of company agents that recruit workers in remote areas and deliver them to the ships. The fishers pay to obtain the work and other expenses are deducted from their earnings, so that they are debt bound for months and sometimes years at sea.

There are regional patterns of obtaining labour for foreign fishing vessels. Thailand is a focus for recruitment of many young men and boys from Cambodia, Myanmar and Laos.[26] Ships with virtual slave labour from these sources are owned by Japan, Taiwan, South Korea, Turkey and Russia. Both the Philippines and the People's Republic of China are also people-exporting countries for fishing. They are very competitive in cost cutting, mainly on wages and conditions. Many countries in Europe likewise engage low-cost fishers from Asia, India and Africa to supplement their crew, due, they claim, to the difficulties of getting people in the traditional home areas to take up a fishing career.

Another problem for the modern-day fishers, especially in Asia, is the possibility of being arrested and spending time in jail, resulting in the destitution of families. There are many disputes over divisions of the sea throughout Asia, and also conflicting national claims over small islands, rocks and reefs. Ordinary fishers are unaware of these political issues but are arrested by a series of countries for territorial and resource violations. Regular sinking of boats, killings and imprisonment are involved. Some countries subsidise and encourage their boats to fish in these disputed zones, as not to do so would indicate abandonment of claims; in turn, all other countries with claims arrest all other boats, as not to do so would be to concede their right to fish. Thousands of fishers are used as political pawns in these circumstances.[27]

CONCLUSIONS

This brief review of maritime labour at sea shows several of the major changes that have occurred over time in the context of concepts, technology and legal developments. Over the period reviewed the sea has continued to exert a dominance as a result of its vast space and unpredictable and frequently hazardous nature. Mariners have always respected the power of the sea and been well aware of the risks of working at sea. Even in the modern age, deaths at sea are high, varying between ten and thirty times above the levels of occupational mortality in other occupations in the countries from which they are drawn.[28]

---

[26] International Organization for Migration, *Trafficking of Fishermen in Thailand* (Bangkok, 2011).
[27] COUPER A.D., SMITH H.D. and CICERI B., *Fishers and Plunderers: Theft, Slavery and Violence at Sea* (London, 2015).
[28] WINDLE M.J.S., NEIS B., BORNSTEIN S. and NAVARRO P., *Fishing Occupational Health and Safety: A Comparative Analysis of Regulatory Regimes* (Memorial University of Newfoundland).

Attitudes to the hazards of sea employment as perceived by the public and authorities have usually been influenced by catastrophic events. The view that technological advances could master the sea was shattered with the loss of the RMS *Titanic*. This advanced and magnificent vessel simply slid beneath the sea four hours after colliding at full speed with a predictable iceberg on the clear night of 12 April 1912, taking 1,490 people to their deaths. Two of the many questions raised were, why out of a crew of four hundred, were there only eighty-five experienced seafarers, and why was there only sufficient life-saving equipment for less than half the people on board?[29] Perceptions of the perils of the sea were altered, and with this came the important SOLAS Convention, but not until after the First World War. Despite subsequent improvements to navigational aids, communications, life-saving facilities and Rules into recent times, the major cause of loss of ships and life remain storms at sea, as well as accidents attributable to the human errors of seafarers. The term "human error", so consistently used in the past, is now recognised as a symptom, not a cause of accidents. Causes lie in factors such as under-manning of ships, minimum time in port and fatigue. There are also delays in responses to accidents to ships, due to the undermining of masters by decisions from the shore side. The master still has absolute responsibility and liability, but a much-eroded authority, at sea.[30]

Attitudes to the sea have changed in other ways with the realisation that maintaining the health of the ocean is also a requirement of mariners and managers. The implementation of the MARPOL Convention of the IMO has become part of the daily routines in good seamanship on all well-run merchant vessels from tankers to cruise ships.

The crews of fishing craft have primary contact and close working relationships with the sea. Fishers are required in all weathers to find, catch and preserve the seafood they are expected to deliver to markets. The greatly depleted fish stocks, arising from intense competition, subsidies, illegal fishing, destructive gear and rapacious methods of fishing can result in economic and social decline in fishing communities, and irreversible ecological consequences for the sea.

The actions of the United Nations Food and Agricultural Organisation (FAO) and of some governments and NGOs are attempting to control the excessive effort and greed in commercial fishing. The ILO, supported by the IMO, is in turn attempting to obtain ratification for a new instrument, "Work in Fishing Convention (188)".[31] This will help to solve many of the labour issues that beset the industry and will help crews on board and the poorest fishing communities on shore who depend for their living on a healthy sea. As always, success will depend on implementation.

---

[29] National Maritime Museum Records and Exhibitions, Greenwich, London, 1987.
[30] GOLD E., 'Empowering the Shipmaster', *Seaways* (2008), p. 9.
[31] ILO, 'C188 – Work in Fishing Convention, 2007 (No. 188)', International Labour Organisation http://www.ilo.org/dyn/normlex/en/f?p=NORMLEXPUB:12100:0::NO::P12100_ILO_CODE:C188 [Accessed 25 January 2015].

Fisheries

INGO HEIDBRINK is Professor in History at the Old Dominion University, Norfolk, United States and Honorary Research Fellow at the Maritime Historical Studies Centre, University of Hull, United Kingdom

ABSTRACT. *Sea fishing provides a rich source of protein, but requires access to suitable sea areas and mastery of appropriate technology. Societies with sufficient protein sources on land have not needed to develop fisheries. Commercial fishing requires means of preservation; initially salt. Later, railways allowed fresh fish to be sold to large inland markets, while canning and freezing extended the technologies of preservation.*

RÉSUMÉ. *Les poissons d'eau de mer sont une excellente source de protéines, mais leur pêche nécessite l'accès à des zones maritimes particulières et la maîtrise d'une technologie adaptée. Les sociétés qui possèdent suffisamment de sources terrestres en protéines n'ont pas eu besoin de développer la pêche. À des fins commerciales, celle-ci exige des moyens de conservation, dont le premier exemple fut le sel. Par la suite, le transport ferroviaire rendit possible la vente de poissons frais dans les grands marchés de l'intérieur des terres tandis que la mise en boîte et la congélation élargirent les techniques de conservation.*

.•.

With an annual global fish consumption of 17.0kg per capita, fisheries and aquaculture today provide about 20% of protein consumed, but fish consumption is not evenly distributed around the globe, with some regions consuming as much as 90kg a year per capita, and others close to nil. While it is obvious why coastal nations eat more sea fish than landlocked countries do, it is less obvious why certain nations more or less without a coast developed intensive fisheries too. This raises the question of whether geography alone was the main factor in the development of fisheries. It also needs to be asked why nations with short coastlines but large agricultural areas built up fisheries. The pattern of fish consumption is a matter of scientific analysis, since fish are by no means evenly distributed throughout the oceans, and certain species are better suited for the development of large-scale fisheries than others. To answer the second question we have to assess what difference fishing made and what benefits it offered – which is more challenging. The main reason why certain societies opted to use maritime protein might simply be that the ocean provided a more or less endless supply, while land-based protein sources were more limited.

Before we look into some examples of nations that have opted for fisheries as part of their protein supply, some basic facts about men and the oceans need to be discussed. First and most important, it needs to be understood that every fishery has required a certain amount of technology. As humans are land-based animals that cannot survive unaided on the water, the availability of some technology was always a prerequisite for any fishing, and more sophisticated maritime technology nearly always resulted in more efficient fisheries. Second, and maybe of equal relevance, it needs to be understood that only certain areas of the world's oceans provide the natural conditions for the development of efficient fisheries.

Maybe the easiest situation to understand is an isolated island. Living on an island means that the coast and the oceans are always available, but also that land available for food production is limited. Island nations like Iceland or Greenland are prime examples of this situation, the more so as the climates of these islands have always limited traditional agriculture. Moreover, land-based resources are a prerequisite for developing a fishery, most notably for the construction of fishing vessels. While medieval Norse populations on Iceland had access to such resources, the Inuit population of Greenland had little or none. Their driftwood boats like the kayak or umiak remained small in size and better suited for hunting marine mammals than for fisheries. Hunting marine mammals provided not only protein, but a wide variety of raw materials such as sealskin, furs, ivory, bones, and blubber for heating purposes, and thus hunting was much more attractive to some societies than fishing. There was no need to develop sizeable fisheries, and thus some societies refrained from fishing in spite of living in proximity to an abundance of fish. While the situation of the medieval Norse population of Iceland was different, it too had enough protein to feed the population available from another source than fish – sheep – and thus no need to develop sea fisheries. Of course, Inuit and Norse societies developed some fisheries to supplement other protein sources, but they remained extremely limited in size, effort and result. A very different situation can be observed in isolated Pacific island societies, few of which had the opportunity either to hunt marine mammals or to breed sufficient numbers of land-based animals. Consequently nearly all of them developed fisheries as one of their main protein supplies, even though the natural conditions of the Pacific were not as favourable for fishing as those of the North Atlantic. In summary and oversimplification, it can be stated that societies opted for fishing only when other protein sources were not easily available.

While this pattern has continued throughout history, there is another factor that became particularly important in the development of fisheries in densely populated areas like Europe: the market. While the growing population might by itself have generated greater demand for protein and thus for fish, population increases were also accompanied by major advances in agriculture and animal breeding, which might have cancelled the effect. However, the main period of medieval population growth in Europe was also the period in which Christianity finally reached even the most remote areas. The market for food was therefore determined not only by natural demand but also by religious regulations, most notably fasting rules.

The merchants of the medieval Hanseatic League profited most from this demand. The main reason for their success was their access to salt. Salt allowed the merchants to solve the main problem of any fish trade, the natural decay of fish. While hard-salted fish might not be to everybody's taste, and is of less nutritional value than fresh fish, salted fish satisfied the fasting rules and could be traded over long distances. As the Hanseatic merchants were not fishermen but traders, the fisheries in Scandinavia which supplied them flourished in spite of the small local population and the lack of local salt supplies. When the Hanseatic trade finally collapsed during the Early Modern period, owing to a variety of factors not related to the fish trade, other European nations had a chance to step in as the main suppliers of fish, and thus of protein acceptable on fast days. Even though the claim that Basque fishermen crossed the Atlantic before Columbus is disputed, it is interesting to look at developments in the Iberian Peninsula during the age of exploration. Improvements in shipbuilding and navigation not only enabled explorers to reach unknown coasts but also allowed fishermen to work far from their home ports, and to supply a market with a high demand for marine protein. The fishing grounds of the Northwest Atlantic became more and more important for fishermen from the Iberian Peninsula, Basques in particular – another group with limited opportunities for the development of large-scale protein production on land.

Another interesting case of a society which opted for the development of sea fisheries instead of land-based protein production is the Dutch and their herring fisheries. While earlier herring trades required much salt to preserve the fish, the Dutch herring fisheries were stimulated by an important innovation. Instead of gutting and salting the herring, the Dutch realized that gibbing (gutting the herring, leaving the liver and the pancreas in the fish), allowed preservation with much less salt. This technique freed Dutch fishermen from dependence on huge quantities of salt and enabled them to produce in unprecedented quantities. Their dominance, indeed *de facto* monopoly, of the European trade was reinforced by a strict organization which regulated participation in the herring fisheries and imposed measures which can be understood as early fisheries management. Again, a nation with limited means for land-based protein production had opted for sea fisheries and made them into a most successful business.

In the pre-industrial era the main structure of fisheries all over the world remained unchanged. In the North Sea and the Atlantic as well as the Indian Ocean and the Pacific, coastal and island nations with limited land-based protein production supplemented their diet with fish. The total catch capacity of fishing fleets was still well below the maximum sustainable yield or the natural reproduction capacity of the fish stocks, and Grotius' description of the fisheries as "an endless resource" may have been literally true. This situation changed in the second half of the 19th century, when steam engines became available. Steam engines affected fishing directly, but railways were of equal relevance. Once the railways reached the fishing ports, their market area expanded hugely. Hitherto the hinterland had provided no real market for fish unless dried or salted; now the railways allowed fresh fish to be transported deep into the hinterlands. Thus it was no longer only in coastal regions or islands where fisheries competed with other means of protein production.

Moreover, industrialization created densely populated large cities which depended on food produced elsewhere. These new industrial centres became major markets for cheap protein, including fish. Similar things happened in all industrialized nations, but the German steam fishing industry is an example. Traditionally, consumption of sea fish was limited to coastal areas of Germany and their immediate hinterland. The railways changed this, and made it possible to transport fish inland in less than two or three days. The growing populations of industrial areas like Berlin, Munich or the Ruhr demanded cheap protein, and the railways allowed the fisheries to compete with agriculture. Fish merchants in the port cities realized the opportunity for expanding their business and started inland trade. They soon realized that the traditional fisheries could not satisfy the new urban demand, and so they built the first steam trawlers to increase fish landings. For the first time in Germany sea fish had become a cheaper alternative to land-based protein sources, and fishing supplied a national market. Fishermen no longer worked in local or family networks, with the crew of a boat often belonging to the same family; the crews of the steam trawlers were industrial employees. Soon companies became involved. As early as 1896 a group of shipowners and merchants from Bremen founded the Deutsche Dampffischerei-Gesellschaft Nordsee. Unlike earlier fisheries and the first steam trawling companies, the Nordsee operated a whole fleet. Consequently the company needed a large number of crewmen, who had to be hired on the labour market. Living conditions on board the trawlers were poor and the work was hard, but fishermen were attracted by the high wages. In the same way, capitalists invested in steam-trawling companies to make profits. While it would be naïve to state that earlier fishermen were not interested in earning money, the difference was that traditional fishing was also a way of life, carried on in the same families over generations, comparable to farming on an inherited farm. Steam fishing, on the other hand, was from the very beginning just a money-earning employment.

Though steam trawlers from North Sea ports started operations on the traditional fishing grounds of the North Sea, their operational area expanded quickly, and as early as the 1890s the waters off Iceland and Northern Norway had become regular fishing grounds. This generated competition between distant-water and local fisheries. This competition was asymmetrical, as the distant-water fisheries utilized sophisticated vessels and gear while the local fisheries continued using small vessels and somewhat primitive gear. The only reason why this situation did not immediately result in conflicts was the fact that the distant-water fishing grounds were normally not accessible to fishermen using small, unmotorized vessels.

Any analysis of the development of ocean fisheries would be incomplete without some brief remarks on the Law of the Sea. Probably the most influential book on the Law of the Sea is Hugo Grotius' *De Mare Liberum* of 1609, which argued that the oceans did not belong to any particular nation and might be used by all. While *De Mare Liberum* dealt mainly with oceanic trade, Grotius argued also that fish were available to all nations, because fish were a limitless resource, which could be exploited without causing any damage. While such an argument sounds naïve today, it was true at the beginning of the 17th century. Nevertheless, Grotius' concept of the "Freedom of the Seas" became one of the main issues of international fisheries in the next centuries. As soon as fishing technology reached such a level that fish could no longer be understood as an endless resource, the question of ownership of the fish stocks arose. Icelandic fisheries around 1900 were small-scale fisheries operating on inshore grounds with small, unmotorized vessels. Icelandic fishermen were often part-time subsistence farmers. Their market was small and mainly domestic. By contrast, distant-water fishing fleets from England and other European nations used highly sophisticated vessels and full-time professional crews and had a nearly endless market for their catch. Even their understanding of the Law of the Sea was completely opposite. For Icelanders, the fishing grounds off the coast were an extension of the land, over which they had an exclusive right of ownership, while for distant-water fishermen the same fishing grounds were part of the free seas, which could be utilized by anybody. With no ultimate authority to rule between them, conflicts were inevitable, and the only reason why conflict did not occur at this time was that the fish stocks still provided enough for all.

The rise of distant-water fisheries in many European nations during the first decades of the 20th century depended on markets, mainly the population of big cities and industrial areas. They chose fish simply because it was a cheaper source of protein than the alternatives. In addition, national governments encouraged the consumption of sea fish and the building up of the trawler fleets for a number of reasons. While the concept of economic autarky was not yet developed, national governments already understood that increasing trawl fishing was an easy way to provide sufficient protein supplies to the masses. At least theoretically, the development of distant-water trawling industries also fitted the ambitions of nations like Germany, which were not traditional colonial powers, by providing a potential source of raw materials. As early as 1904 the Nordsee company sent trawlers to fish off the coast of Morocco, and German colonial activities even in China included attempts to build up trawl fisheries. Both enterprises ultimately failed, but they were characteristic of the development of fisheries in a nation like Germany.

World War I affected all kind of fisheries, as fishing grounds became theatres of war and trawlers and crews were recruited by the navies. Many trawlers were lost, and the few still fishing during the war were confined to limited areas. But the war also resulted in a modernization of the trawling fleets, as the navies of the belligerent nations constructed auxiliary warships based on the most advanced trawler designs, which were converted to fishing as soon as the war was over. As the war also blocked the international trade in foodstuffs it caused an increase in demand for fish in nearly all nations. Coastal nations like Iceland were cut off from food imports and thus needed to focus on domestic protein supplies like fish, and distant-water fishing nations returned to the fisheries immediately after the war, as it was easier to increase fish landings than to restore agricultural production. Starving people were willing to accept any source of food after the war, whether or not they had eaten fish before. While this caused a short-lived increase in fish consumption during the immediate post-war years, as soon as agricultural production returned to normal levels the demand for fish declined again. But, as the fishing industry had tasted periods of high demand for its catch, and as governments had invested in the rebuilding of the fishing fleets, a new phenomenon occurred in a number of distant-water fishing nations: the centralized promotion and marketing of fish. Hitherto fish had been seen in most inland areas mainly as a substitute protein source, with demand high only when land-based protein was scarce. Now fish was marketed as a protein supply in its own right. In addition, it became a well-known "fast food", with the typical British fish and chips only the most prominent example.

The general pattern, however, remained the same. Outside those countries with domestic fisheries and a tradition of eating fish, it was mainly an alternative protein source most often consumed by those who could not afford anything better. The Great Depression reinforced this pattern. The effects were by no means the same in all countries, and outside the United States the countries most affected were those which relied on imported food. Thus, countries like Germany were hit extremely hard, but countries like France less so. Nations like Spain or Portugal promoted self-sufficiency, so fisheries gained importance as kind of a hybrid between domestic and imported protein production. The effect of the Great Depression on fisheries was paradoxical, as the decline of international trade promoted fishing. Again, fish became popular because of a lack of alternative protein supplies, and working on board a trawler was at least better than being unemployed.

Besides the Great Depression, there were two other factors that affected the fisheries in the inter-war period. New preservation technologies gave processed fish a longer shelf-life, and a modest modernization of small-scale fisheries all around the globe began with the motorization of many fishing boats. Unlike steam engines, internal combustion engines could easily be integrated into existing small fishing boats, and, more important, the required investment was much less than for a steam engine. As a number of governments subsidized this motorization of local fishing fleets, the inter-war period saw a rapid modernization of the fishing fleets which mainly supplied their own domestic markets. Many fishermen now became full-time professionals. While there were still substantial structural differences between the now motorized local fisheries of coastal nations and the steam-trawler fleets of distant-water fishing nations, the two fleets were now capable of operating on the same fishing grounds. Immediate conflicts were avoided in the short period up to the outbreak of another world war, perhaps partly because most coastal nations with fishing grounds had not yet gained complete sovereignty.

The other factor affecting the inter-war period was the development of new preservation technologies. Deep-freezing was still only experimental and not very successful, but canning became more important than before. The consequences were only indirectly felt by the fisheries themselves, but affected the market and distribution side of the industry. Unlike fresh fish, canned fish products required no specialized handling, but could be traded like any other non-perishable products. Fish could be sold everywhere, regardless of available infrastructure. But not all fishermen could benefit from this market expansion, as participation in the new markets required investment in canneries, an insuperable obstacle for small-scale fishermen, but easily surmountable by the already highly capitalized trawling industry. In practice the outbreak of World War II concealed the consequences of these developments as trawlers and fishermen were recruited again for a war. While the basic pattern was similar to World War I, many of the belligerent nations were more aware than before that war was not only a military affair, and that food supplies were crucial too.

Again it was Germany that was not only responsible for the war, but that demonstrated how the fishing industry could be integrated into the war effort. Besides expanding catch capacity to the maximum and subsidizing additional trawler construction, Germany's autarkic policy extended to more complex concepts. Under the slogans *Ernten ohne zu säen*, "Harvesting without Sowing", and *Deutschlands einzige Kolonie ist das Meer*, "Germany's only Colony is the Sea", a programme was developed to utilize the oceans as much as possible as a source of supply of all kind of industrial raw materials. One of the cornerstones of this programme was whaling in the Southern Ocean, with the object of providing fats, detergents and other products to replace imports. Other less well-known activities included an expedition sent out to catch sharks and sea turtles to provide supplies of industrial leather for drive belts, abrasives and tortoise shell for products like spectacle frames. The fish caught by the trawling fleets was no longer used only as a food supply, but became a universal raw material, with nearly 100% of the fish used for a wide variety of products.

Nazi Germany turned towards an increased use of marine resources as a command economy, not through the free choice of consumers to eat more fish or the decision of the industry to increase production. Though the sea was not Germany's only colony, it was the easiest accessible reservoir of raw materials. Wartime efforts also resulted in a breakthrough in deep-freezing technology, and in particular the technological concept of the factory-freezer trawler. Though the factory-freezer trawlers built during the Nazi period were not practically important during the war, the technology was developed to an operational level. For other nations the effects of World War II on the fisheries were more or less similar to those of World War I. Substantial numbers of trawlers and fishermen were recruited for naval service, but at the end of the war many auxiliary warships were converted to civilian trawlers and thousands of wartime seamen were looking for employment. Wartime losses reduced the fishing fleets, but when the war was over the remaining vessels could restart fishing more or less immediately, while agricultural production needed much longer for the transition from war to peace. Thus the fisheries of all the belligerent nations played an important role in rebuilding food production, and since fishermen could harvest without seeding, they could deliver protein to the starving populations when agriculture was still far away from bringing in the first post-war harvests.

Finally, it needs to be mentioned that World War II also resulted in changes to the political map of the world. In the North Atlantic, Iceland became a fully sovereign nation, and Newfoundland joined the Canadian Federation. In the new world order the western-style democracies gathered on one side and the socialist nations under the leadership of the Soviet Union on the other. Many former colonies, now becoming independent nations, were already active in deep-sea fisheries. For nations like Iceland without major mineral deposits, fishing was now the most important export industry, and it was no longer acceptable that distant-water fishing nations exploited the fishing grounds off their coasts. Coastal nations no longer confined themselves to small-scale local fishing, but became substantially engaged in the international fish trade. Thus the economic structures of fisheries in the coastal nations and the distant-water fishing nations began to resemble each other. Local fisheries were no longer oriented towards subsistence, but towards maximizing catch and profit. Nations like Iceland and Norway therefore started using fishing vessels comparable to those of traditional distant-water fishing nations. Naturally they worked the same fishing grounds, and international fishing conflicts became unavoidable. While the distant-water fishing nations favoured the concept of Freedom of the Seas, the coastal nations now fishing for global markets claimed the fishing grounds and the fish stocks off their respective coasts as national property. Nations like Iceland or the United Kingdom were willing to fight these conflicts not only on a diplomatic level, but on the fishing grounds themselves in the Cod Wars of 1958 to 1976.

Another factor contributing to conflicts was that distant-water fishing nations, now including a number of socialist nations, continued the development of factory-freezer trawlers and started successfully operating these vessels as early as the late 1950s. As these ships now had an almost unlimited operational range and endurance, they caused substantial concern to the coastal nations. Factory trawlers became one of the main causes of dispute about the fishing limits of the coastal nations, and probably the main reason why such negotiations regularly failed. The introduction of factory trawlers was linked to changes within the market, particularly the new, pre-prepared convenience foods like fish fingers. Originally developed in the late 1950s, fish fingers became the real game-changer for the global fish markets. While they were basically nothing more than a frozen and battered portion of fish fillet, fish fingers managed to achieve what no other fish product had achieved before: they were no longer regarded as a substitute for other sources of protein, but as a cheap and convenient product in their own right. Thanks to their ease of preparation, the small portions and the conviction that fish was healthy, fish fingers became particularly popular among families with young children. Fish fingers were also the first fish product suitable for the development of brands. It was no longer fish as such that was advertised, but Birdseye or Käpt'n Iglo fish fingers. Interestingly enough, what fish was processed into fish fingers did not really matter, as long as it was white fish, so processing companies used whatever species was available on the market. To a degree, fish fingers had reached the ultimate goal of the fish-processing industry: the squaring of the circle. With round white fish now marketed as a rectangular, pre-processed product, and the fish itself camouflaged behind a thick crust of batter, fish now attained unprecedented popularity in countries which had not traditionally eaten it.

For the fisheries themselves the introduction of fish fingers meant that the most important product landed by the trawlers was no longer fresh or frozen fish, but standardized frozen blocks of fish fillet which could be traded on a global market. In economic terms this implied a complete separation of catch and processing, as there was no longer any need for a processing company to maintain its own fishing fleet. Standard frozen fillet blocks could be traded all over the globe, and as long as quality standards were met, the raw material for fish finger production could be bought wherever it was cheapest. Although some distant-water fishing nations had developed highly sophisticated factory-freezer trawlers and built up fishing fleets capable of operating on all fishing grounds of the globe, the separation of catch and processing meant that it no longer made sense for the fish-processing companies to maintain these fleets. Moreover, the three United Nations Conferences on the Law of the Sea, and claims by coastal nations for substantial extensions of their national fishing limits, left the distant-water fishing nations without fishing grounds.

These developments raised the global catch to levels unknown before, and far beyond the maximum sustainable yield for many species. A new era had begun in which fisheries were mainly characterized by management schemes and extended fishing limits or exclusive economic zones. Distant-water fishing nations like Germany gave up the idea of national fishing fleets and focused on fish processing, while coastal nations developed highly sophisticated fishing fleets to supply these industries with raw material. Most importantly, fish was no longer a cheap substitute protein source, but had become a high-priced commodity with global supply often below demand. Fishing fleets all around the world were scrapped to adjust catch capacity to levels that could be considered as sustainable, and maybe fish has finally become a highly valued protein supply in its own right. Of course, scrapping the fleets resulted in a reduction of active fishermen too. Now the fisherman is no longer somebody who has gone to sea to make quick money, but a well-educated professional who has chosen to work afloat in spite of the alternatives available on land.

Select bibliography

Ashcroft N., Starkey D.J. and Reid C., *England's Sea Fisheries: The Commercial Sea Fisheries of England and Wales since 1300* (London, 2000).

Candow J.E., *How Deep Is the Ocean?* (Sydney, 1996).

Fagan B.M., *Fish on Friday: Feasting, Fasting, and the Discovery of the New World* (New York, 2006).

FINLEY C., *All the Fish in the Sea: Maximum Sustainable Yield and the Failure of Fisheries Management* (Chicago, 2011).
GARCIA-ORELLAN R., *Terranova: The Spanish Cod Fishery on the Grand Banks of Newfoundland in the Twentieth Century* (Boca Raton, FL, 2010).
GERHARDSEN G.M., *Fifty Years of Norwegian Fisheries, 1905-1955* (Bergen, 1955).
HEIDBRINK I., *'Deutschlands Einzige Kolonie ist Das Meer!' Die Deutsche Hochseefischerei und die Fischereikonflikte des 20. Jahrhunderts* (Hamburg, 2004).
HEIDBRINK I. and STARKEY D.J., eds, *A History of the North Atlantic Fisheries - from the Mid 19th Century to Today* (Bremen, 2012).
HEIDBRINK I., STARKEY D.J. and THÓR J.T., *A History of the North Atlantic Fisheries - from Early Times to the Mid-Nineteenth Century* (Bremen, 2009).
HOLM P., SMITH T.D. and STARKEY D.J., *The Exploited Seas: New Directions for Marine Environmental History* (St John's, Newfoundland, 2001).
HORSTED S.A., *A Review of the Cod Fisheries at Greenland, 1910-1995* (Nova Scotia, 2000).
INNIS H.A., *The Cod Fisheries; the History of an International Economy* (New Haven, 1940).
JACOBSEN A.L.L., 'Steam Trawling on the South-East Continental Shelf of Australia: An Environmental History of Fishing, Management and Science in NSW, 1865-1961' (2010).
JANTZEN K., *Cod in Crisis? Quota Management and the Sustainability of the North Atlantic Fisheries, 1977-2007* (Bremen, 2010).
JÓHANNESSON G.T., *Troubled Waters: Cod War, Fishing Disputes, and Britain's Fight for the Freedom of the High Seas, 1948-1964* (Reykjavík, 2007).
JÓNSSON H., *Friends in Conflict: The Anglo-Icelandic Cod Wars and the Law of the Sea* (London, 1982).
LOOMEIJER F.R., *De Nederlandse Visserij 1900-1935 = Dutch Fishing Industry 1900-1935* (Alkmaar, 1995).
MATHISEN O.A. and BEVAN D.E., *Some International Aspects of Soviet Fisheries* (Columbus, 1968).
ORREGO VICUÑA F., *The Changing International Law of High Seas Fisheries* (Cambridge, 1999).
PAYNE B.J., *Fishing a Borderless Sea: Environmental Territorialism in the North Atlantic, 1818-1910* (East Lansing, MI, 2010).
POULSEN R.T., *An Environmental History of North Sea Ling and Cod Fisheries, 1840-1914* (Esbjerg, 2007).
ROBINSON R., *Trawling: The Rise and Fall of the British Trawl Fishery* (Exeter, 1996).
SMYLIE M., *Herring: A History of the Silver Darlings* (Stroud, 2004).
TULL M., 'The development of the Australian fishing industry: a preliminary survey', *International Journal of Maritime History* 5.1 (1993), 95-126.
WALTER W., *Deutsche Fischdampfer: Technik, Entwicklung, Einsatz, Schiffsregister* (Hamburg, 1999).
WRIGHT M.C., *A Fishery for Modern Times: The State and the Industrialization of the Newfoundland Fishery, 1934-1968* (Dons Mills, ONT, 2001).
ÞÓR J.Þ., *British Trawlers and Iceland, 1919-1976* (Göteborg, 1995).

Geographical determinism and the growth of the American whaling and sealing industries

MICHAEL P. DYER is a Senior Maritime Historian at the New Bedford Whaling Museum, United States

ABSTRACT. *From the 18th century New England ports dominated deep-sea whaling, above all for sperm whales. After the American Revolution loyalist Quakers took the techniques to British and French ports, and Pacific waters. The hunt for whales and seals in waters remote from Europe and America played a major role in rapid social, political and ecological change.*

RÉSUMÉ. *Les ports de Nouvelle Angleterre dominaient la pêche à la baleine en haute mer, et en particulier celle du cachalot, depuis le XVIIIe siècle. Après la révolution américaine, les Quakers loyalistes transmirent leurs techniques aux ports français et britanniques et jusqu'aux eaux du Pacifique. La chasse à la baleine et au phoque dans des eaux éloignées de l'Europe ou de l'Amérique joua un rôle prépondérant dans le rapide changement social, politique et écologique.*

．•．

From the moment in June of 1602 that Gabriel Archer set eyes on the Acushnet River on the south coast of Massachusetts his commentary was aimed purely at its advantages to commercial navigation. Companion to English explorer Bartholomew Gosnold (1571-1607), he observed with a seaman's eye that the place "may happily become good harbors, and conduct us to the hopes men so greedily do thirst after." His was an immediate recognition that here, along the complicated west side of Buzzards Bay, was a broad, deep, and protected haven with unlimited potential for development. Facing southeast, the mouth of the Acushnet River is protected from the prevailing southwest wind by a peninsula at its mouth, allowing safe passage for vessels bound in. Periodic northerly breezes allow any outbound vessels safe passage to the broad Atlantic. Archer's prophetic observation truly resonated down the ages, as by 1765 Bedford Village had been built on the west bank of the river and by the 1850s the harbor of the Acushnet had become home to one of the greatest whaling fleets in history. By the 1890s the harbor was a rail head and a center for sea-borne coal distribution and one of the largest textile manufacturing cities in the U.S.A. Today the port

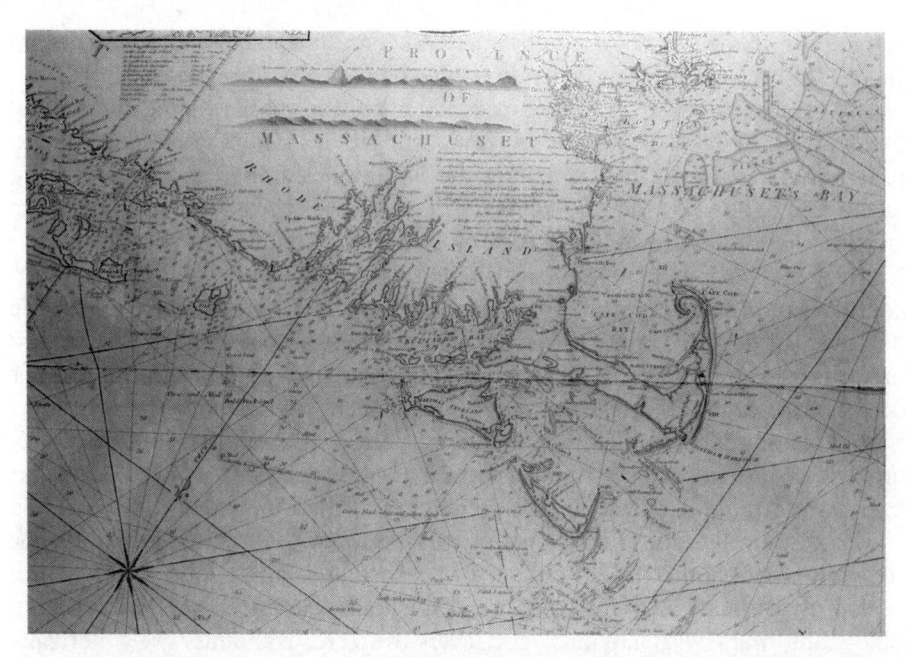

Fig. 1. *This chart shows the entire coast of New England, including the eastern tip of Long Island, New York, from which the American whaling and sealing industries arose. A New Chart of the Coast of America from Philadelphia to Halifax shewing [sic] the tracks of the American Surveying Vessels Science and Orbit, 1825. A new edition improved by J.W. Norie. London: William Heather, 1812 (Courtesy of the New Bedford Whaling Museum, New Bedford, MA, U.S.A.).*

of New Bedford on the banks of the Acushnet River is home to the largest profit-grossing fishing fleet in the United States.

As astonishing as it seems, Archer predicted this. After all, in 1602 the great ocean highway of the Atlantic was fast becoming the pathway to wealth, economic stability, and advances in hydrography, marine technology, shipbuilding, cartography, and a sense of the world growing smaller, or, if not smaller, at least, better defined. Indeed, it was the fundamental ability of colonial and, later, free Americans to maintain their trans-Atlantic trade that allowed a crooked but unbroken line to be drawn from the Gosnold voyage of 1602 to the nineteenth-century annexations of Hawaii and Alaska. These events seem universes apart, yet to a nation that built its commerce first on the sea, the gaps shrink, and, in combination with fleets of vessels exploring every square mile of the watery world in pursuit of unknown populations of animals for economic gain, the gaps shrink even further. If the United States had later come to be seen as a land of wide-open spaces synonymous with buffalo herds, the Great Plains and the Westward Movement, the California Gold Rush, Yosemite Falls, and the magnificent vistas of the Grand Canyon, navigating the Atlantic Ocean in ships built of native timber was its first great national profile. Once the frigate U.S.S. *Constitution*, "Old Ironsides," built of native North American white oak, live oak, white pine, yellow pine and locust, together with the many other famous warships of the U.S. Navy, secured American "Free Trade and Sailor's Rights" in the War of 1812, the U.S.A. had firmly established itself as a sea power. With sovereignty gained, commerce could proceed, and thus the great whaling and sealing fleets of the 19th century began to grow. That growth had taken a long time to fully mature, however. It was among the high dunes along the coasts of Long Island and Cape Cod over 130 years earlier that a distinct American maritime culture was born, with whaling as one of its defining commercial successes.

Northern European commercial whaling was in its infancy in the early 17th century, from around the time that Gosnold and Archer were exploring Buzzards Bay. Over the next two hundred years it would develop into a significant economic driver for several European nations, providing the raw materials in the form of oil for soap, lamps, and leather tanning, and springy whalebone (baleen) for a host of commercial applications including parasols, umbrellas, knife handles, utensils, boxes, musical instrument parts, and corset stays. It rapidly became an important economic driver for the colonies, and then for young United States as well, especially along the banks of the Acushnet River, an eventuality not remotely accidental. While the story of the rise and fall of American whaling is tied up with questions of theocracy, religious tolerance, wars with Native Americans, wars with England, and even the Civil War amongst Americans themselves, at bottom, Yankee whaling, and seal hunting as well, were enmeshed with geography. New England's limited capability for large-scale agricultural production, due to poor soil and lots of rocks, drove her people to the commerce of the seas. If the Puritan colonists of the Massachusetts Bay Colony couldn't abide Quakers, Baptists, Jews, blacks, and Native Americans, it was these very marginalized populations who would settle seaside Massachusetts; Dartmouth (1670s), Bedford Village (1765), Nantucket Island (1690s), Cape Cod, and the ports of Providence and Newport in Rhode Island (1640s), and develop American maritime trades in these places. It was also these very people who transformed American shore-side whaling into a sophisticated pelagic endeavor targeting a species, the sperm whale (*Physeter macrocephalus*), hitherto only available to Europeans by stranded animals. Sperm whales provided unique raw materials, namely refined sperm whale-body oil and spermaceti "head matter." The latter could be molded into candles, and the former burned beautifully and was a fine lubricant for machinery.

By 1750 Americans were systematically hunting sperm whales on the high seas. Nantucket whalers took them at every opportunity and had developed the means of boiling blubber into oil on shipboard using a try-works, a brick furnace holding two iron pots. Before try-works were employed, whale blubber would be "cut into cask," meaning that the blubber would be chopped up small enough to fit into wooden storage casks and stored raw to be processed ashore when the vessel returned to port. This process worked well in the frigid Arctic, but the blubber quickly deteriorated in the more temperate climes where sperm whales were hunted. By combining heavy blocks and tackles and iron hooks with the mechanical advantage of the ship's windlass or capstan, larger sheets of blubber, called "blankets," could be flensed from the whale floating alongside the vessel.

That blubber could then be cut into smaller pieces and minced into thin slices before being put in the try-pots and boiled into oil that could be stored in casks indefinitely. This practice eventually resulted in an increase in the size of the vessels employed, from sloops and schooners of forty to ninety tons before the American Revolution to full-rigged ships of close to two hundred tons by the 1790s. By the 1830s and 1840s, the industry had become so sophisticated that whaling vessels of several sizes and types were in general use, sailing to waters all around the world. Agents commonly outfitted sperm and right whalers of between three hundred and four hundred tons for voyages lasting between two and four years. They would also outfit smaller vessels for voyages closer to home. Provincetown, Massachusetts, for instance, specialized in using schooners, brigs, and small barks to hunt sperm whales in the North Atlantic, South Atlantic, and the Caribbean. Fairhaven, Mattapoisett, Dartmouth, Westport, and New Bedford, the very regions included in the original 1653 Old Dartmouth Purchase that the Plymouth Colony bought from the Wampanoags, all became shipbuilding centers with expertise in whaling. The vessels were built to exact specifications, determined over decades of experience, and were designed for heavy-duty work in the ice of the Western Arctic, the treacherous waters of the Sea of Okhotsk, and the uncharted islands of the Pacific, the East Indies, and in the Southern Ocean.

As it grew, American whaling saw several important moments of innovation and these included both technology and management. From a management perspective, as far as records indicate, from at least as early as the 1790s each voyage was a unique corporate entity. While a vessel may have had one or two primary owners, the investors in each voyage would often change from voyage to voyage. Diverse investment helped to spread risk and brought considerable returns, potentially throughout the whole community. Likewise, many of the same individuals who were investing in voyages also owned or managed other important components of the industry like wharves, ropewalks, iron foundries, nail factories, flour mills, oil refineries, and candleworks. As fresh innovations developed, like the railroad in the 1830s, for instance, they were seamlessly incorporated into the whole.

Technologically, the shipboard try-works transformed the industry completely. Where colonial Americans had first pursued black whales (*Eubalaena glacialis*, commonly called the North Atlantic right whale) in a seasonal, opportunistic fashion from shore, once shipboard try-works were adopted voyages could be extended further and a higher-quality product could be made without the need of returning to a try-house on shore. Colonial whalers pursued their craft steadily, hunting sperm whales and black whales too, in warmer climates and in a different way from the main target of European commercial whaling, the polar right whales (*Balaena mysticetus* or bowhead whale) of the Davis Strait and Labrador. After heavy hunting pressure, the small population of migratory black whales that had so frequently passed Long Island and Nantucket on the way to their spring and summer feeding grounds in Cape Cod Bay, the Bay of Fundy, and the Gulf of Maine between 1650 and 1790 had disappeared from

Fig. 2. *In his 1854 oil painting View of New Bedford Harbor from Crow Island, William Bradford (1823-1892) captures the essential elements of this active whaling port, including fully laden whalers bound in to the wharves, outbound cargo vessels, small craft, shipbuilding, and ship repair on the Fairhaven side of the river at the height of the industry (Courtesy of the New Bedford Whaling Museum, New Bedford, MA, U.S.A., 1975.18)*

their range in the western North Atlantic. In 1792, Secretary of State Thomas Jefferson phrased the situation curiously in his "Report on the subject of the Cod and Whale Fisheries," that the whales, "being infested, retired from the coast." This was simply another way of saying that the whales had been either killed or completely driven off. The phrasing begs the question as to whether or not Jefferson believed that the animals had been killed off, chased off, or *chose* to move someplace safer. In any event, off-shore sperm whaling was a far more lucrative adventure and had been developed into a real American specialty. By the 1800s, fortunes would be made from sperm whaling, but the groundwork built during the colonial era is important to understand.

Refining spermaceti into candles provided a much-needed influx of cash into the economy of New England, especially in the post-war years at the turn of the 19th century. But more than that, the processes and equipment involved in hunting sperm whales and processing the oil and spermaceti were jealously guarded and known only to a few, thus insuring the stability of the enterprise until those processes were discovered and developed elsewhere. In Newport, Rhode Island, in the mid-18th century, a few merchants, namely the Sephardic Jews Aaron Lopez and Jacob Riviera, another man named Benjamin Crabbe from nearby Rehoboth, Massachusetts, and a few others, had developed a process for "pressing, fluxing and chrystalizing" spermaceti and molding it into high-quality candles. As a commercial enterprise it was ideal for New Englanders. Strong populations of animals roamed within easy sail of harbors all around Massachusetts, Connecticut and Rhode Island and, in combination with a strengthening tradition of shipbuilding that utilized the combined resources of extensive timber and plentiful bog iron, New England's maritime culture easily adopted whaling as a viable commercial endeavor.

Shipbuilding was not the only specialty being applied to this industry. American whaleboats had developed from shore-whaling craft needing to be launched into the surf and rowed rapidly across open, ice-free waters, often in strong currents, into fast, lightweight craft built of native Atlantic white cedar, a tough, light, durable wood. Their utility was easily adapted to pelagic whaling. Likewise, Yankee harpoons and other whalecraft such as lances, spades, mincing knives, and boarding knives were equally light and tough compared with their European counterparts, which had been intended for heavy use in the Arctic ice. The head of a British Arctic harpoon, for instance, was three times as large as an American one and very heavy. By the 1820s, American whaling tools were being made from the finest materials; steel in the case of mincing knives, boarding knives, and spades, and in the case of harpoons and lances, wrought iron, designed to bend but not break under the incredible strains generated between the whales, the line, and the boat.

The manufacture of whalecraft, like many crafts associated with the industry, was a specialized business in American whaling ports, and while the design of a harpoon had not changed appreciably from those used by the Basques three centuries earlier, by the 1840s even this ancient design came to be improved. At 1850 over a dozen specialized shipsmiths were making whalecraft in New Bedford alone, not counting those working on Nantucket and in Norwich, Connecticut and other whaling ports. One such man, Lewis Temple, the much-acclaimed African-American shipsmith whose shop was located near Merrill's wharf at the foot of Walnut Street in New Bedford, is credited with having invented a harpoon in 1845 that had a barbed head that would "toggle" open when struck into a whale's blubber, dramatically increasing the likelihood that a whale struck could be captured. Like the try-works and the Yankee whaleboat, and the innovative management techniques, the Temple toggle iron was another technological innovation that was the direct result of a concentration of skilled craftsmen working closely together in an entire community devoted to one industry. It came about in this way.

Joseph Russell (1719–1804), a Quaker from Dartmouth on the south coast of Massachusetts who owned considerable land along the banks of the Acushnet River, laid out a plan in 1765 to build a whaling port. His aim was to gather, to "muster in a gleaming row" as one historian described it, as many craftsmen, artisans, shipbuilders, and other specialized mechanics as he could with the express purpose of pursuing the whale fishery completely, from the outfitting of the vessels to processing the cargo. Originally named "Bedford" for the part of southeast England where Russell family members held title as the Duke of Bedford, the name was changed later in the 18th century to "New Bedford," as there was already a town in Massachusetts called "Bedford." Russell's plan attracted Joseph Rotch (1704–1784), a Quaker whaling merchant of Nantucket, and his sons including William Rotch, Sr. William Rotch, Sr. (1734–1828) is a figure who, for his exact knowledge, business acumen, and sober diplomatic perspicacity in the face of potentially disastrous wartime depredations by the British navy, has been described as the father of the American whale fishery. The Quaker Rotches, including William Rotch, Jr. (1759–1850) and Samuel Rodman (1753–1835), a Newport Quaker who learned the candle trade from Jacob Riviera and married William Rotch, Sr.'s daughter Elizabeth, created a dynasty between Nantucket and Bedford Village. Rodman's daughter, Sarah, would go on to marry the Philadelphia Quaker merchant Charles W. Morgan (1796–1861), and his son Samuel, Jr. would himself become a whaling merchant. The potential of this port with its excellent harbor, deep, wooded hinterland, and ample land attracted young candle makers trained in the factories of Newport to build their own refineries and candle houses in the new whaling port.

Shipbuilding, too, was an important part of the plan and the first large vessel built in Bedford Village was the ship *Dartmouth*, built in 1767 to the order of Joseph Rotch. Not a whaler, the *Dartmouth* was a merchant ship designed to carry whale oil to England and return with manufactured and other taxable goods to the colonies. It was famously involved in one of the defining events leading up to the American Revolution, the Destruction of the Tea in Boston in 1773. The "Boston Tea Party," as it came to be known, prominently brought to the fore the aggravated state of the maritime, mercantile interests of the colonies with Great Britain. That a ship built on the Acushnet River should be the focal point of this antagonism seems a poetic justification tying Archer's ancient prophesy directly to colonial ambitions.

By the late 1820s, the town was the center of the Federal Port District that included Wareham, Marion, Mattapoisett, Fairhaven, Dartmouth, and Westport. The Custom House, built between 1833 and 1835, remains standing today as the oldest continuously operating Custom House in the nation. The dynamic seaport had its own shipyards, including the yard of Jethro and Zachariah Hillman where the famous whaler the *Charles W. Morgan* was built in 1841. It had ropewalks, twelve candle houses and oil refineries, stores for navigating instruments and stationery, pump and block makers, spar yards, tool manufactures, sail lofts, cooperage shops, salt works, five banks, and three insurance companies. It had fifteen wharves and these carried the commerce of the world, but primarily the products of the whale fishery, which by the mid-1830s numbered between seventy thousand and a hundred thousand barrels of sperm and whale oil and between thirty thousand and two hundred thousand pounds of whalebone with an annual value of approximately $200,000.00.

The successful and lucrative voyages over the decades of the 18th century had additionally created a body of knowledge useful to sea hunters that was so extensive that by the 1800s voyages were becoming carefully planned. For instance, by the 1830s new black whaling grounds had been discovered on the northwestern coast of North America. In combination with the sperm whaling grounds discovered in the Northwest Pacific in the 1820s, the stage was set for a rapid and lucrative expansion of the industry. By the 1840s there was nothing random about the American whale fishery. Masters and agents relied upon the increasingly accurate qualities of sea charts and navigating instruments to chart their whaling grounds. These in turn created the conditions under which the whalers themselves could begin contributing new knowledge about the whereabouts of islands, currents, shoals, shores, and the deep ocean. Collecting information about the habits of sperm whales and naming various regional whaling grounds helped the whalers to predict where whales might be found. Among the earliest regions where sperm whaling took place was the "Hatteras Grounds." This body of water of about 46,000 square miles is located four hundred miles due south of Martha's Vineyard along the 36th parallel, east of the coast of Virginia, along the edge of the continental shelf. Not surprisingly, these waters were on the direct trade route from New England to the Caribbean, a primary trading destination for colonial merchants. Sperm whales were hunted in these waters throughout the entire history of Yankee whaling and the hunt extended into the Caribbean, the Gulf of Mexico, and the Bahama Banks from a very early date. Among the earliest voyages and the very last American sperm whaling voyages under sail were made to the Hatteras Grounds. Likewise, mid-Atlantic voyages due east from Nantucket became increasingly common. As early as the 1760s, Nantucket whalers were hunting as far eastward as the Azores. This region, just along the southern margin of the Gulf Stream, came to be called the "Western Grounds" named for the waters westward of the Western Islands, as the Azores were commonly known. It is easy to forget that on the eve of the American Revolution, Nantucket's whaling fleet numbered 150 vessels with an aggregate tonnage of fifteen thousand tons. This fleet had grown very rapidly from about 1720, thus, by the 19th century, the accrued knowledge of whale habitats, seasons, and whaling grounds was solidly in the possession of Nantucket masters and merchants. William Rotch, Sr., his son, and son-in law were not the least among these, and as they shifted their operations from Nantucket to New Bedford all of that knowledge came with them.

For all of its obvious success, the details and full extent of the activities of the colonial whaling fleet remain relatively sparsely documented. Few logbooks have survived, but those that have point to voyages manned by family, friends, close associates, and members of a tight-knit community. Voyages commonly sailed in close company with other vessels and took relatively few animals per voyage, compared to later in the 19th century. In the 1760s a single vessel returning three hundred barrels of oil was notable, and in 1763 eighty vessels sailed from Massachusetts ports to the Gulf of St Lawrence. On average, these vessels returned about 170 barrels each or the quantity (on average) of two or three adult sperm whales or black whales. By the 1840s the industry was very well documented. There was a trade newspaper published in New Bedford, *The Whaleman's Shipping List and Merchants' Transcript*. This paper kept track of prices current, new navigation knowledge, crew lists, and a running list of all whaling voyages sailing from American ports.

At this time it was common for a two- to four-year voyage to take between twenty-five and sixty-five animals and to return thousands of barrels of oil. Nineteenth-century voyages to the Pacific, Western Arctic, and Indian Oceans

Fig. 3. *Whaleman James Carter captures the action while sperm whaling in the Indian Ocean, in this watercolor view from his journal kept onboard the ship St. Peter of New Bedford in 1850 (Courtesy of the New Bedford Whaling Museum, New Bedford, MA, U.S.A., KWM #1047).*

commonly lasted years and the crews were no longer made up of close associates from the community but were compiled from a global pool of men, some experienced sailors, some "greenhands" who either from economic necessity or from a spirit of adventure chose whaling for their livelihood. Unlike these later voyages, the earlier voyages lasted anywhere from a few days, as in the case of a cruise to the waters "offshore" of Nantucket, up to three months when sailing to Davis Strait, the Grand Banks, Newfoundland, or the Bahama Banks, and up to a year if going so far as the coast of Brazil, the coast of Africa, or even further south where other valuable marine mammals like elephant seals could be found. By the 1780s and 1790s, whalers and sealers had begun extensive voyages around the southern capes.

The first American whaler to round Cape Horn was the ship *Beaver* of Nantucket in 1789, closely followed by the ship *Rebecca* of New Bedford. These were, in turn, close behind the first recorded seal-hunting voyage to the Falkland Islands by the brig *States* of Boston in 1783. By the first decades of the 19th century it was not uncommon for Nantucket, occasionally New Bedford, and more frequently Stonington, New London, and ports in New York to outfit voyages combining whaling and elephant seal hunting. New London, itself a major whaling and seal-hunting port located along the banks of the Thames River in Connecticut, was the largest sealing port in the U.S.A., sending from four to twelve voyages annually between 1841 and 1881. Southern elephant seals (*Mirounga leonina*) were a prime target and, as voyages extended further into the Pacific, the northern elephant seal (*Mirounga angustirostris*) was also extensively hunted. These species were found congregating on the Antarctic islands of the Southern Ocean in certain seasons, and likewise on the coast of California. Unlike fur seals, hair seals, and sea lions, elephant seals were not hunted for their skins or other body parts, but for oil. Elephant seal oil was classed in almost the same category as sperm oil for lubrication, and many hundreds were often to be found on isolated beaches at one time. As the movements of the seals were somewhat predictable, once the rookeries had been found, a sea elephant voyage was deemed less financially risky than a whaling voyage, although combined whaling and sea elephant voyages were common, as the oil was the prime target of each. If the animals were relatively easy to find, the voyages themselves could be hazardous, as men and supplies needed to be ferried back and forth through the surf to remote locations and dangerous seacoasts. Once on land, however, the men would build a camp and proceed with their hunting from a base of operations.

Other kinds of sea hunting voyages, however, were conducted with very different ends in mind, and they were conducted from many ports other than the great whaling ports. Seal hunting is a good example. Seals of the hair and fur variety were to be found in both hemispheres, and in the process of searching out new rookeries sea hunters explored the islands around Antarctica, the Indian Ocean, the coasts of South America, including Tierra del Fuego, the Jasons, the Falklands, the coast of California, and the Aleutian Islands. Masafuera, Juan Fernandez, and Mocha off the coast of Chile were particularly productive places to obtain fur seal skins. These furs had value in several markets including in London, where the furriers were highly skilled at preparing and dying the furs for fine apparel. They were also of value in the China trade. Vessels engaged in sealing for the China trade were often gone for years, as the skins needed to be collected before proceeding to Canton to negotiate trade for valuable goods including tea, silks, satins, nankeen printed cloth, and crockery.

To imagine the importance of the sea hunting trades to the American national experience is to look beyond their economic impact. There were social and political ramifications to the constant influx of American vessels and crews to ports from Pernambuco to Cape Town and from Sydney to Paita, Peru. As whaling crews were made up of men hired from potentially every port of call the world round, as they either were discharged or deserted they could find themselves just about anywhere. This was an issue in ports throughout the Pacific and in Alaska. Shipwrecked mariners on the North Slope of Alaska had become so frequent that the American Revenue Service installed the Point Barrow Refuge Station in 1889, where men could spend the winter if need be. By mid-century the installation of American consuls in many seaports solidified American influence and growing hegemony, especially in the eastern and central Pacific. It all happened in a relatively short time. San Francisco was merely a Spanish mission and hide-trading port in the 1820s and by the end of the 1860s was a major American seaport. Granted, the Gold Rush pushed San Francisco's growth, but a deep-water port on the California coast was a boon to whalers, sealers, and other merchantmen and, as the waters of the Western Arctic became the source for quality bowhead whalebone, San Francisco itself became the largest whaling port in the U.S.A.

The expansion of American marine commerce, especially after the War of 1812, was dizzying. What the American Revolution had won encouraged maritime trade without absolutely securing it. In 1804, for example, the Lewis and Clark expedition set out to explore the full extent of the land acquisition of the Louisiana Purchase. While the North American Native Americans who lived on the continent had good knowledge of its full scale, few others did, but when the expedition finally reached the Pacific Ocean its leaders actually anticipated and expected to meet Boston fur-traders on the Northwest Coast. This fact alone speaks to the incredible reach of American mariners. As they sought commodities for trade with China, and in doing so built up the national coffers through the importation of dutiable goods, they also built up networks of relationships all around the world. Ultimately these actions led to much larger settlements on the west coast and increasing populations of discharged sailors, immigrants from the Portuguese islands of the Atlantic, and settlers from all across the continental United States. With the construction of the trans-continental railroad in 1869 an astonishing transformation had taken place. The pioneering voyages that had rounded Cape Horn only eighty-six years earlier had effectively served to create a web of commerce and political influence so extensive that it now extended across the continent.

At the turn of the 19th century and for the next fifty years, American whalers, sealers, and traders in sea-otter pelts were regularly rounding Cape Horn. In the process of their hunts, mariners found themselves negotiating with the Spanish authorities of South American ports for port access for refreshments or in emergencies, making contact with many different groups of native peoples around the Pacific, even to the newly settled penal colonies of Australia. During the War of 1812, Captain David Porter of the U.S. frigate *Essex* especially targeted British whalers on the coast of Chile, and while the British Navy eventually caught up with him and captured the *Essex*, he had nonetheless helped to define the reach of American sea power into these important waters. Porter sailed as far as the Marquesas Islands and wrote about it in his narrative *Journal of a Cruise* (New York, 1822), a valuable guidebook for mariners who came after him – one more stepping-stone in the rapid expansion of American influence. While he did not make it as far as Hawaii, his published descriptions of the islands helped to enable American whalers and traders to use the safe harbors in their explorations of the vast ocean.

Just as the Azores were of central importance (indeed one of the first U.S. consuls, John Street, was appointed to Horta, Fayal in 1795), Hawaii's central location in the North Pacific enabled a great deal of American commerce. The first American whaler to visit Honolulu was the ship *Balaena* of New Bedford in

Fig. 4. *A Shoal of Sperm Whale. Off the Island of Hawaii. In which the Ships Enterprise, Wm. Roach, Pocahontas & Houqua were engaged 16th Decr. 1833. To the Merchants, Capts., Officers & Crews engaged in the Whale fishing. This print is respectfully inscribed by Corns. B. Hulsart who lost an arm on board the whale ship Superior of New London and was on board of the Enterprise at the time.* Colored aquatint. Painted by Thomas Birch from a sketch by C.B. Hulsart, engraved printed and colored by J. Hill. Published by Cornelius B. Hulsart and for sale at the Office of the Seamans Friend Society, 82 Nassau St., N. York, 1838. Courtesy of the New Bedford Whaling Museum, New Bedford, MA, U.S.A., 2001.100.7581.

1819 under the command of Edmund Gardner; the ship *Equator* of Nantucket, Elisha Folger, master sailed in just behind. In the wake of Gardner and Folger's visit to Hawaii, came hundreds and then thousands of visits by American whalers. Hawaii became the hub of American Pacific whaling as a system of seasonal cruises came into regular practice. By the 1850s whalers would use Hawaii as a port to refresh and transship their oil home before making another four-to-six months' cruise to the Sea of Okhotsk, the Sea of Japan, the Bering Sea, south into Polynesian islands "on the line," or southwest to Fiji, Samoa, or New Zealand. Much of the oil and bone captured on the thousands of whaling voyages to the Pacific Ocean passed through the Hawaiian Islands on its way to the markets of the old east coast. In 1855, a railroad opened across the Isthmus of Darien, making Hawaii even more important as goods, people, and services could more easily access the important port in the central Pacific. It was now easier to transship oil back to the east coast ports, mail was more efficient and crew members, particularly officers, were more easily replaced or added in case of death, injury, illness, or other discharge.

New England's maritime trades, especially whaling and sealing, grew out of necessity supported by geography. From Nantucket's isolated locale to the broken coastline of Buzzards Bay, the Narragansett River in Rhode Island, and the Thames River estuary on the coast of Connecticut, Yankee mariners left the scoria of their landscape behind and sought the riches of the seas. So successful were these voyages, and they amounted to many thousands involving hundreds of thousands of people all around the globe, that their influence transcended their intent. Yes, many people made a lot of money, and in New Bedford many made millions. But apart from that, whaling voyages dispersed people everywhere, demanded government support in the form of consuls and strong diplomatic relations with foreign governments, and heavily impacted on the populations of sea mammals the world round. Yankee whaling deteriorated to nothing as the fortunes of whaling were invested in other industries, but its legacy was permanent.

La France et la mer, 1815–1914

Michèle Battesti is a researcher, director of the department of 'Defense and Society' at the Institut de recherche stratégique de l'École militaire, Paris, France

Résumé. *La reconstitution de la puissance française pendant la Restauration nécessita la reconstruction de sa marine, sans qu'il fût question de raviver l'ancienne rivalité maritime avec la Grande-Bretagne. L'introduction de la propulsion à vapeur, l'emploi de l'obus explosif et l'apparition du blindage, des innovations qui furent mises à l'épreuve pendant la guerre de Crimée (1854–56), poussèrent Napoléon III à recourir à la stratégie des moyens pour compenser la supériorité navale de la Grande-Bretagne. La France impériale prit ainsi la tête du progrès technique et se dota d'une flotte cuirassée, ce qui provoqua l'inquiétude des Britanniques, hostiles à l'essor d'une marine sur le continent. Durant la guerre de 1870, la marine impériale surclassait l'embryon de marine allemande, mais dans ce conflit de dimension continentale elle fut employée à contre-emploi et impuissante à sauver le régime impérial. Elle n'en fut pas moins jugée responsable de la défaite eu égard aux trois milliards de francs dépensés pour sa modernisation et connut une décennie de « recueillement ». Dans les années 1880, l'engouement de la Jeune École et de l'opinion publique pour les torpilleurs acheva d'oblitérer la puissance navale de la France qui rétrograda au quatrième rang des puissances maritimes et fut désarmée dans la compétition coloniale avec les Britanniques. Cette situation mena à la conclusion de l'Entente cordiale en 1904 à la faveur de laquelle la Grande-Bretagne et la France unirent leurs puissances impériales pour affronter l'émergence de l'Allemagne.*

Abstract. *The restored Bourbon regime required a rebuilt navy, but there was no question of reviving naval rivalry with Britain. The development of steamers in the 1840s, followed by the first ironclads (both of which were used during the Russian War of 1854–56), encouraged hope that French genius might make up for British superiority in numbers. Napoleon III favoured his navy, which (the British feared) was intended to favour his ambitions, but in spite of building the first ironclad it was unable to compete with British industrial superiority, and did not save him in 1870. In the 1880s a radical (and Radical) experiment with torpedo-craft failed to overturn the ironclad's command of the sea, and naval weakness betrayed France in colonial disputes with Britain. All this led to the 1904 reversal of alliances after which Britain and France confronted the rise of Germany as successful imperial powers together.*

. • .

1ʳᵉ PARTIE: 1815-1850

En 1815, la France est une puissance maritime déchue qui s'est 'détournée du grand large'. Ses ports et arsenaux sont ruinés. Sa flotte de commerce est anéantie – à l'exception de la flotte de cabotage. Sa flotte de guerre aligne 71 vaisseaux et 41 frégates, mais elle accuse un retard technique rédhibitoire et souffre du manque d'entraînement des équipages. La marine pâtit d'un '*discrédit inconcevable*' (baron Portal) auprès de l'opinion, traumatisée par les 'insultes' de la Royal Navy contre les côtes françaises, d'autant qu'elle n'a pas, à la différence de l'armée, participé à la gloire napoléonienne. Une seule bataille navale – celle de Grand-Port du 23 août 1810 à l'Île de France – est appelée à être célébrée sur l'Arc de triomphe. La perte d'influence de la France est sensible dans le monde extraeuropéen. Les traités de 1815 lui ont restitué '*ses colonies, pêcheries, comptoirs et établissements en tous genres*' dans leur état de 1792, mais amputés de Tabago, Sainte-Lucie et l'île de triomphe (rebaptisée Maurice). Certains '*ne croyant plus à son avenir*' préconisent la disparition d'un instrument si décevant.

Face à ce constat de faillite, Louis XVIII oppose une réponse sommaire, la 'restauration de l'ordre ancien' qui accélère la dégradation de l'instrument naval. Le ministre de la Marine Du Bouchage s'escrime à gommer toute trace de la période napoléonienne: mise en disponibilité de 400 officiers; reconstitution de carrière d'officiers émigrés qui ont eu le temps d'oublier leur métier; élimination des institutions impériales. Le budget plafonne à 40 millions de francs. Le 'Collège royal de la Marine', ancêtre de l'École navale, est créé au milieu du terroir français, à Angoulême !

Mais Louis XVIII, qui a un besoin impérieux d'une politique de prestige pour effacer la tare 'd'être revenu dans les fourgons de l'étranger', ne peut renoncer à un rôle international. Un de ses premiers actes internationaux est de reconstituer la station du Levant (28 septembre 1815) afin de ranimer la séculaire implantation diplomatique et commerciale de la France en Méditerranée orientale. La marine royale récupère les territoires coloniaux dès 1817, à l'exception de Saint-Domingue dont l'indépendance sera reconnue en 1825. Le domaine colonial n'atteint que le cinquième rang mondial avec moins de 7 000km² de territoires épars, morcelés et sans réelle valeur stratégique et économique. Sa récupération est entachée par le tragique naufrage de la *Méduse* (2 juillet 1816) au large de la Mauritanie. Le drame immortalisé par Géricault porte un coup sévère au prestige de la marine. Il est à son étiage. Conséquence bénéfique, le programme de 'restauration' est arrêté et les officiers 'rentrés' sont renvoyés dans leurs foyers. Reste à procéder à la reconstitution morale et matérielle de la France maritime. Comme c'est souvent le cas en France, celle-ci est l'œuvre d'un homme providentiel, le baron Portal, un ancien armateur bordelais, ministre de la Marine et des Colonies du 29 décembre 1818 au 14 décembre 1821.

Tirant les leçons des guerres de la Révolution et de l'Empire, Portal est convaincu, à l'instar des milieux maritimes et politiques, que la France n'est plus en mesure, avec ses seules ressources humaines et matérielles, de prétendre à la parité avec l'Angleterre qui caracole en tête de la hiérarchie navale, mais qu'elle peut prétendre au second rang des puissances navales dans le cadre d'une stratégie générale à dominante continentale et d'une alliance avec les autres puissances. Il préconise une vaste politique nationale basée sur la mise en valeur des colonies, le grand commerce et la marine marchande, qui exige l'existence d'une flotte *'suffisante pour protéger les principaux intérêts'*. Il pose en principe qu'un budget de 65 millions de francs permettrait d'entretenir des forces navales composées de 40 vaisseaux et 50 frégates, *'suffisantes'* pour défendre le littoral de la France, protéger ses établissements d'outre-mer, attaquer les possessions de l'ennemi et ses convois, *'fusionner'* avec les flottes des puissances maritimes secondaires (États-Unis, Russie, etc.). En cas d'échec de la dissuasion et d'une guerre directe avec l'Angleterre, il préconise de *'renoncer à la vanité des batailles navales'* et de recourir à la guerre de course contre le commerce britannique. Il compte en appeler à l'initiative privée – armateurs, corsaires occasionnels – et 'nationaliser' la guerre maritime. Sa 'doctrine' influe la politique navale pour plusieurs décennies. Le cadre administratif est réédifié grâce au rétablissement des institutions supprimées durant la première Restauration: équipages de ligne (1825), préfecture maritime (1826), école flottante sur le vaisseau *Orion* à Brest (1827), etc.

De 1815 jusqu'au mitan du siècle, la monarchie constitutionnelle s'attache à relever et maintenir le rang de la France au sein du concert européen tout en rassurant les puissances européennes, d'où une politique étrangère axée sur la recherche de la paix et de l'alliance anglaise. Toutefois la marine marchande, protégée par des surtaxes, mais entravée dans son développement par le manque de capitaux, progresse lentement, atteignant presque en 1848 le chiffre de 1789 (700 000 tonneaux contre 4 millions pour la Grande-Bretagne). La marine de guerre exécute des opérations de détail en Europe: Espagne (1823), Portugal (1831), Anvers (1831), Ancône (1832). Elle conduit plusieurs opérations de défense des intérêts français aux Antilles, en Colombie, en Argentine et au Mexique où la flotte procède au bombardement du fort de Saint-Jean d'Ulloa qui commande l'accès de Veracruz (1838): *'Le seul exemple d'une place régulièrement fortifiée réduite par une force purement navale'* (Wellington). La marine participe à la constitution du 'second' empire colonial grâce à la politique dite des 'points d'appui': Grand-Bassam (1838), Nossi-Bé et Mayotte (1843), Tahiti, les Marquises et les Wallis (1842–1844). Le domaine colonial passe à 300 000 km² (200 millions de chiffre d'affaires). En 1827, la marine participe à une opération de sécurité collective au profit des Grecs, qui secouent le joug ottoman. Mais l'événement majeur est la prise d'Alger (1830), à la faveur de la plus grande opération de débarquement en pleine côte qui ait été effectuée au temps de la marine à voile. La flotte met pour la première fois en œuvre avec succès des navires auxiliaires à vapeur et des chalands de débarquement à fond plat. La prise d'Alger consacre la Méditerranée comme centre de gravité de la politique française.

L'escadre d'évolutions est recréée sous la férule du contre-amiral Lalande pour entraîner les équipages et les états-majors. L'hydrographie des côtes est refaite par Beautemps-Beaupré. La marine renoue aussi avec la tradition des voyages d'exploration dans le Pacifique et vers l'Antarctique où s'illustrent Freycinet, Duperrey, Dumont d'Urville, et participe à des opérations de prestige comme le transport de l'obélisque ou le retour des cendres de Napoléon sur la *Belle Poule*.

La France de Louis-Philippe a beau ménager l'Angleterre et célébrer la première 'entente cordiale', la compétition reste 'active' entre les deux pays et génère des crises. L'une d'elles manque dégénérer en 1840 lorsque la France se pose en alliée inconditionnelle de l'Égyptien Méhémet Ali. Devant le danger d'une coalition européenne anti-française, Louis-Philippe abandonne le pacha égyptien à son sort, au grand dam des boutefeux arguant que l'escadre de Méditerranée était en mesure de tenir la dragée haute à la Royal Navy. En fait la France navale est '*désarmée*' de l'aveu même du ministre de la Marine.

La prise de conscience est brutale. Les Français piqués au vif réclament une flotte susceptible '*non de dominer, mais d'empêcher toute domination sur les mers*' (Thiers). Or dans ce premier XIXe siècle, le voilier est parvenu à l'ère des investissements prohibitifs. Sous l'impulsion de la révolution industrielle, trois filières de l'innovation – la propulsion à vapeur, l'artillerie et la construction métallique – bouleversent l'art naval et rebattent les cartes stratégiques. L'idée s'impose qu'une percée technologique pourrait niveler par le 'qualitatif' l'écart 'quantitatif' entre la marine française et la Royal Navy. La généralisation des canons obusiers et de l'obus explosif voue les coques en bois à l'obsolescence. Le fer est envisagé comme matériau de substitution, mais il est réputé non militaire. La propulsion à vapeur confirme sa supériorité sur la voile. Mais en attendant la mise au point de l'hélice, les machines sont fragiles, les roues à aubes vulnérables et diminuent la place de l'artillerie. Toutes les incertitudes techniques sont loin d'être levées. Cela n'empêche pas en mai 1844, le prince de Joinville dans un article 'anonyme' de la *Revue des deux mondes* de préconiser, pour compenser l'infériorité française, de construire une flotte à vapeur capable d'opérer des 'descentes' en Angleterre et courir sus à son commerce. En 1846, l'amiral de Mackau obtient du Parlement à l'unanimité le vote d'un crédit extraordinaire de 93 millions de francs, échelonné sur sept ans, pour construire une flotte comprenant 44 vaisseaux et 66 frégates à voile, 100 bâtiments à vapeur, mais les 'modernes' n'ont pu imposer la propulsion à hélice.

Pendant le court intermède de la IIe République, qu'il est de bon ton de dénigrer à cause de ses 'réformes' démagogiques comme l'abolition des peines corporelles, la substitution du titre d'élève par le grade d'aspirant, le budget de la marine retombe au niveau de 1839 et le programme de Mackau est arrêté. La marine est de nouveau sur la sellette. Elle ne se laisse pas distraire et procède au lancement de la frégate le *24 février* (futur *Napoléon*), parrainée par le prince de Joinville. Cette frégate révolutionnaire, œuvre de l'ingénieur Dupuy de Lôme, est spécialement conçue pour la propulsion à hélice. Avec ses 13 nœuds aux essais, elle va surclasser tous les bâtiments existants. En octobre 1849, l'Assemblée législative décide la création d'une commission d'enquête parlementaire sur la situation et l'organisation des services de la marine. Celle-ci auditionne toutes les personnalités qui comptent dans le milieu maritime et constitue une formidable base de données sur le département. Ses 203 propositions sont perçues comme un programme. La preuve, le 18 février 1873 le ministre de la Marine demandera si leur exécution a été effective, comme si l'Empire n'avait été qu'un intermède !

2ᵉ PARTIE: L'« EMBELLIE » DU SECOND EMPIRE

Porté au pouvoir par l'opinion publique et la légende napoléonienne, Napoléon III rétablit l'Empire le 2 décembre 1852 contre l'avis des puissances européennes. Il hérite de la problématique stratégique de ses prédécesseurs, aggravée par la crainte que son seul nom suscite. Or il lui faut réussir son pari dynastique et rehausser la France dans le peloton de tête des pays européens. Plusieurs séjours en Grande-Bretagne lui ont fait comprendre les arcanes de la puissance britannique. Il est programmé pour imiter les recettes de la première puissance maritime du XIXᵉ siècle. Mais s'il souhaite disposer d'une grande marine, c'est dans les limites imparties par la politique générale. Napoléon III est persuadé que l'échec de Napoléon Iᵉʳ de recomposer la carte européenne – son propre dessein en fonction du principe des nationalités – est dû au fait qu'il n'a pas su ou pu éviter l'affrontement avec l'Angleterre. Comme pour ses prédécesseurs, la pierre angulaire de sa politique extérieure est l'alliance anglaise. Il n'a pas l'intention d'effrayer la Grande-Bretagne, jalouse de sa suprématie sur mer et prompte à s'émouvoir lorsqu'une puissance continentale prétend développer sa marine. Au contraire, il tient absolument à la ménager. Pour Napoléon III, il est donc exclu que la marine impériale atteigne la parité avec la Royal Navy. Par contre, elle doit tenir le second rang des puissances maritimes et détenir une flotte à la composition identique et même supérieure en qualité à celle de la Royal Navy, mais en quantité inférieure. Sa stratégie navale s'inscrit dans le droit fil de la doctrine Portal. La France doit disposer d'une flotte *'d'élite, très-effective, très menaçante'*, capable d'exercer de *'terribles représailles sur les côtes'* d'un quelconque agresseur, pour défendre le littoral français, l'Algérie et ses intérêts outre-mer.

La question d'Orient lui fournit très vite l'opportunité de sortir de son isolement et de rompre le front des puissances européennes. Elle est ouverte par les prétentions du tsar Nicolas Iᵉʳ de dépecer *'l'homme malade de l'Europe'* pour accéder à la Méditerranée ce qu'exclut la Grande-Bretagne. Dès le début de la crise, Napoléon III se déclare aux côtés de Londres et de la Sublime Porte sous prétexte de protéger les Lieux saints. La guerre contre la Russie est une gageure pour les deux puissances maritimes face à la masse continentale de leur adversaire, alors que les pays limitrophes (Autriche, Prusse, Suède) se déclarent neutres. Ils usent de leur écrasante supériorité navale pour bloquer ou attaquer les 'fenêtres maritimes' de leur adversaire (mer Noire, Baltique, mer Blanche, Pacifique) sans pouvoir attenter à ses intérêts vitaux. La guerre s'en trouve circonscrite à des descentes et bombardements en Baltique, et à un point de fixation à Sébastopol en Crimée. 'Première guerre moderne pour les marines', elle met à l'épreuve les matériels existants et lève des incertitudes techniques. Elle révèle aussi les déficiences françaises en navires de transport faute de flotte de commerce, en bâtiments à vapeur et en équipages, traditionnel goulot d'étranglement. Voulant obtenir la décision en attaquant Saint-Pétersbourg protégé par les 3 000 bouches à feu de l'île-forteresse de Cronstadt, Napoléon III met en place une commission *ad hoc* pour construire des bâtiments cuirassés. Quelques semaines suffisent à trouver un système de blindage – un matelas de bois de

44 cm recouvert de 11 cm de fer forgé – sur lequel les ingénieurs achoppaient depuis plusieurs décennies. Cinq batteries flottantes sont aussitôt mises en construction et les plans de cette innovation de matériel sensible sont communiqués aux Britanniques. Les batteries françaises interviennent à Kinburn, le 17 octobre 1855, ouvrant l'ère des cuirassés. Entre-temps Sébastopol est tombé. En 1856, le tsar se résout à conclure la paix. Avec cette victoire militaire, la France retrouve l'héritage napoléonien et son prestige est fortifié par la tenue de la conférence internationale de la paix à Paris. La France est au centre de la scène européenne, rien ne se fera sans elle.

La guerre de Crimée assoit la légitimité de la marine, force de projection à l'échelle planétaire. Les leçons en sont rapidement tirées. Dès 1855, une commission composée d'amiraux a déclaré qu'un bâtiment de guerre doit être à vapeur. La loi de programmation navale du 23 novembre 1857 prévoit de consacrer 65 millions de francs sur 13 annuités pour la transformation de la flotte et la modernisation des infrastructures (flotte de combat à grande vitesse de 150 bâtiments; une flotte de transports de 74 bâtiments à hélice pour enlever 40 000 hommes et 12 000 chevaux). En 1860 et 1865, la loi est infléchie pour tenir compte du progrès technique. La flotte de combat ne doit être composée que de bâtiments cuirassés: 40 frégates cuirassées pour l'Europe; 20 corvettes cuirassées pour l'outre-mer pour parer la menace de puissances maritimes émergentes en Amérique latine et en Asie; 30 batteries flottantes et béliers garde-côtes.

Dans un contexte de forte croissance économique propice aux grands travaux, Napoléon III consacre 3,7 milliards de francs à la marine et aux colonies, soit 9,2% des dépenses de l'État contre 6% durant les 35 années précédentes. Il privilégie la stratégie des moyens. Un choix de challenger. Dupuy de Lôme, l'inventeur du *Napoléon*, réédite son exploit de devancer la Royal Navy en créant la frégate cuirassée *Gloire*. Sa nouveauté est de disposer d'une ceinture en fer forgé de 12 cm d'épaisseur descendant à 2 mètres en dessous de la ligne de flottaison. Pour intégrer les 820 tonnes du blindage, Dupuy de Lôme a rasé une batterie, d'où l'appellation de frégate, et l'artillerie se limite à 34 canons de 160 mm. Même avec cette artillerie réduite la *Gloire*, mise en service en 1860, surclasse tous les bâtiments existants, ce qui provoque une panique à Londres. Après la construction de *sister-ships*, d'autres séries homogènes sont mises en chantier pour intégrer l'éperon pour le combat par le choc, l'augmentation de l'épaisseur du blindage portée à 20–22 cm et la modification de la disposition de l'artillerie. En septembre 1863, la première escadre cuirassée de l'histoire appareille de Brest. C'est l'apogée de la marine impériale. L'artillerie fait des progrès spectaculaires grâce à la collaboration avec l'armée et Treüille de Beaulieu. Les canons sont frettés en acier, rayés, chargés par la culasse, et montent dans l'échelle des calibres. Toutefois, la France rate la révolution de la tourelle impulsée par le *monitor*. Toutes les filières de l'innovation sont explorées: le sous-marin et la torpille.

Pour optimiser un matériel à la pointe du progrès, l'accent est mis sur le personnel et sa formation dans le but d'obtenir un corps permanent, homogène et militaire. Le décret du 5 juin 1856 – un décret jugé le plus important depuis

Colbert – crée les *équipages de la flotte* (et non plus les équipages de ligne). L'unité est l'*individu* (et non plus la compagnie), incorporé dans des *compagnies de dépôt* organisées par *spécialité professionnelle*. Des spécialités associées à des écoles se multiplient – canonnage (1837), fusiliers (1856), timonerie (1860), gabier (1866), mécaniciens et chauffeurs. L'inscription maritime est réformée.

Les infrastructures portuaires et les arsenaux, négligés depuis 1815, sont modernisés pour garantir l'efficacité opérationnelle de la flotte en toute indépendance vis-à-vis du privé. Tous les ports sont désenclavés par l'extension du réseau ferroviaire. La mécanisation se généralise. Le grand événement du règne est l'achèvement de la digue (1853) et des bassins (1858) de Cherbourg, offrant la base sur la Manche qui a manqué à la France depuis Louis XIV. Les souverains britanniques ne s'y trompent pas et l'inauguration en 1858 provoque un fort rafraîchissement des relations franco-britanniques, signe de l'étroite marge de manœuvre de l'empereur.

Napoléon III ambitionne de faire de la France une grande puissance commerciale. Grâce à une politique dirigiste de subventions et de primes, au dynamisme de quelques armateurs et banquiers comme les frères Pereire, Armand Béhic, la flotte de commerce passe de 600 000 à 1 million de tonneaux et les vapeurs de 11 000 à 200 000 tonneaux. De multiples compagnies sont créées: Messageries Impériales (1851), Compagnie de Navigation Mixte, Compagnie Générale Maritime (1855) – future Compagnie Générale Transatlantique. Les paquebots français sillonnent tous les océans. Autre réalisation française aux retombées commerciales et stratégiques: le canal de Suez réalisé grâce à la ténacité de Ferdinand de Lesseps, aux capitaux des petits porteurs français et à l'arbitrage de Napoléon III.

La marine impériale est constamment sur la brèche avec en moyenne plus de 300 bâtiments armés en permanence. Le cumul des campagnes de guerre donne le total aberrant de 32 ans de guerre (hors Algérie) sur 18 ans de règne. La flotte participe à de multiples opérations de 'maintien de la paix' dans le monde extraeuropéen pour faire respecter le droit des gens et se pose en 'gendarme de l'Occident chrétien'. Mais elle n'intervient pas seule: en Chine (1857-1859 et 1860) avec la Grande-Bretagne; en Cochinchine (1858-1859 et 1860-1862) avec l'Espagne; au Mexique (1861-1862) dans la première phase avec l'Espagne et la Grande-Bretagne; en Chine contre les Taiping (1861-1864) avec la Grande-Bretagne et les États-Unis. Une fausse exception au Liban (1860) où elle s'interpose en faveur des chrétiens sous mandat international délivré par les quatre puissances européennes (Grande-Bretagne, Autriche, Prusse, Russie) pour une opération de police limitée à six mois. La marine impériale participe également à l'acquisition et à l'extension des colonies dans des régions préemptées par la France (Sénégal, Gabon, Cochinchine, Cambodge, Nouvelle-Calédonie, Obock). Le domaine colonial passe à un million de km^2, peuplé de 7 millions d'habitants. Un réseau de base est esquissé avec l'essor de Dakar et de Saigon.

Napoléon III a mené une politique maritime, globale, volontariste, cohérente tant navale que maritime et doté la France d'une des plus belles flottes qu'elle n'ait eues, forte de 321 bâtiments à vapeur à l'avant-garde de la révolution technique dont 55 bâtiments cuirassés, 115 croiseurs et avisos, 52 transports. Mais l'empereur a commis la faute de ne pas endiguer la puissance de la Prusse. La guerre est inévitable en 1870 et le rôle de la marine mal compris. Pourtant grâce à son écrasante supériorité elle dispose de la maîtrise de la mer et assure le blocus des fenêtres maritimes de l'Allemagne, la capture de 90 navires ennemis, la liaison avec l'Algérie, les livraisons d'armes et de matériels fournis par ses arsenaux, la libre circulation des navires de commerce ce qui permet l'approvisionnement en armes provenant des États-Unis. Elle est aussi utilisée à contre-emploi: plus de 57 000 hommes sont déployés à terre pour la défense de Paris et dans les armées. Ses pertes sont lourdes. Paradoxalement, les marins n'ont jamais été aussi populaires et la marine aussi décriée. Accusée d'avoir dilapidé plus de 3 milliards de francs au détriment de l'armée, elle est jugée responsable de la défaite de 1871. Thiers scelle son destin en la qualifiant d' 'instrument de luxe'.

3ᴱ PARTIE: 'RECUEILLEMENT', CONQUÊTE COLONIALE, RÉTROGRESSION

Pour la seconde fois du siècle, la France se détourne du 'grand large'. Le syndrome de l'invasion et l'obsession de la reconquête de l'Alsace-Lorraine axent les efforts en matière de défense sur la reconstruction d'une armée de terre moderne et la défense des frontières de l'Est. La stratégie française est plus continentale que jamais. La France maritime entre dans une phase de 'recueillement' selon l'expression consacrée. Celle-ci se traduit par une baisse significative du budget et le ralentissement, voire l'arrêt des constructions neuves. Mais la tradition française de l'expansion d'outre-mer est réactualisée et présentée comme le seul moyen d'éviter l'irrémédiable déchéance qui menace la France au lendemain de la perte de l'Alsace-Lorraine, une réponse à la récession économique des années 1873–1874, ainsi qu'une quête stratégique de matières premières et de débouchés pour les produits manufacturés français.

Cette aspiration coïncide avec la course aux armements navals et la poussée impérialiste qui touchent l'Europe et même les États-Unis dans les années 1880. Elle ne fait pas l'unanimité en France. Les gouvernements successifs doivent ruser avec l'opinion et le Parlement. Ils agissent en catimini pratiquant une politique des 'petits paquets' pour masquer l'ampleur de leurs ambitions. Puis, les 'difficultés' s'accumulant, ils obtiennent insensiblement un accroissement des crédits, l'envoi de renforts de plus en plus conséquents et entraîne irrésistiblement la représentation nationale dans l'engrenage de la conquête.

En 1881, la France donne le coup d'envoi de la 'curée' impérialiste avec la conquête de la Tunisie. Cette première entreprise reçoit l'aval des grandes puissances non sans arrière-pensées. L'incursion des tribus Kroumirs sur les confins algéro-tunisiens fournit opportunément le prétexte d'intervenir. Les forces navales contribuent à la conquête grâce au contrôle de la façade maritime. Mais le principal succès de la marine a lieu en Extrême-Orient pour préserver sa 'chasse gardée'. La question du Tonkin se pose dès 1873. Elle n'est résolue que dix ans plus tard grâce à la campagne foudroyante menée par le contre-amiral Courbet, avec deux petits cuirassés, un croiseur, 3 canonnières, qui se conclut par la prise de la capitale de l'Annam. Le traité de Hué (6 juin 1884) reconnaît le protectorat sur l'empire d'Annam contre l'avis de la Chine, son suzerain théorique, dont les troupes continuent d'occuper le Tonkin. Les Chinois finissent par signer les préliminaires du traité de Tientsin, mais tergiversent. Pour les amener à résipiscence, Courbet leur livre une guerre, non déclarée officiellement, où sa marge de manœuvre est faible pour trouver la faille stratégique de l'empire du Milieu d'autant qu'il lui est interdit – en raison de la modicité de ses moyens navals et de la nécessité de ne pas indisposer les puissances européennes, d'intervenir au nord du Yang Tsé Kiang où se trouvent les points sensibles de la Chine maritime. Les actions navales sont circonscrites à 'des prises de gage'. Lors de l'attaque contre Fuzhou, arsenal et mouillage de la flotte chinoise du Sud sur la rivière Min, il utilise avec succès des torpilles portées sur une hampe rétractable pour couler ou endommager deux croiseurs chinois. L'exploit n'influe pas sur le cours des événements. Courbet tente alors d'instaurer le blocus de Formose. Il torpille deux autres bâtiments chinois réfugiés à Shipu. Dans une interprétation très contestable du droit de la guerre, il déclare le riz « contrebande de guerre » pour affamer la Chine du Nord. La Grande-Bretagne proteste et ferme ses ports aux bâtiments de guerre français. Courbet occupe l'archipel des Pescadores, persuadé avoir trouvé en Makung la 'réplique de Hong Kong', recherchée depuis quatre décennies. Les préliminaires de paix sont signés, le 4 avril 1885, à Pékin. La Chine renonce à sa suzeraineté sur l'Annam et le Tonkin et ouvre en deux points sa frontière méridionale, donnant accès au Yunnan et Kangxi, par où les marchandises acquittent des droits de douane inférieurs au tarif maritime. La conquête des Pescadores, intervenue trop tardivement, n'est pas prise en compte éloignant définitivement la possibilité de créer une base navale en mer de Chine. Deux jours plus tard, Courbet, exténué par sa longue campagne, meurt à 58 ans à bord du *Bayard*, en rade de Makung, après avoir joué un rôle décisif dans l'acquisition et la formation de l'Indochine française. La pacification du Tonkin se prolonge jusqu'en 1896.

Une sorte de guerre froide s'instaure entre la France et la Grande-Bretagne au gré des incidents coloniaux: Égypte (1882–1883), Congo (1884–1885), Afrique occidentale (1880–1890), Siam (1893), Madagascar (1884–1895). Paris décide de mettre en valeur les acquisitions du Second Empire. Obock est l'objet de toutes les attentions. Un dépôt de charbon y est installé lequel est transféré en 1888 à Djibouti qui s'érige en débouché commercial de l'Abyssinie. L'Afrique noire est un des théâtres sur lequel s'exaspère la compétition franco-britannique, elle est la 'chasse gardée' de l'armée d'Afrique, avide de gloire et de promotions. Mais les marins, fidèles à leur tradition d'explorateurs, y prennent une part active même si elle est localisée, épisodique, voire même individuelle. En Afrique occidentale, les flottilles de canonnières continuent à contribuer à la conquête de Tombouctou

(1894) et à l'exploration du Niger (lieutenant de vaisseau Hourst, 1896), de la Bénaoué (enseigne de vaisseau Mizon, 1894). Ces expéditions pacifiques ne sont pas toujours prises en compte pour la définition des zones d'influence de la France, mais elles ont collationné des renseignements politiques, ethnographiques, économiques, hydrographiques qui ont fait régresser les *terrae incognitae*. En Afrique équatoriale, la marine est avantageusement représentée par Pierre Savorgnan de Brazza qui explore à partir de 1875 la voie de l'Ogooué et jette les bases d'une nouvelle colonie dans le bassin du Congo. Mais le duel à fleuret moucheté avec l'Angleterre manque de dégénérer dans la vallée du Nil. La mission Marchand établit le protectorat nominal de la France sur la région du haut-Nil considérée *res nullius* depuis 1885, quand survient Kitchener qui exige son évacuation au nom du Khédive d'Égypte. La crise est son paroxysme, quand le 3 novembre Marchand est rappelé. La France s'est inclinée. La prise de gage a tourné à l'affront. La partie a été perdue sur mer.

Le président Félix Faure avoue que '*notre action dépassait tout à fait notre force maritime*'. La marine sans le vouloir se retrouve sur la sellette et confrontée à une nouvelle épreuve de vérité. La flotte de 1898 dispose d'une 'poussière navale' composée de 180 torpilleurs de défense mobile et de 71 torpilleurs de haute mer dont le rayon d'action est insuffisant et qui tiennent mal à la mer; ses croiseurs deux fois moins nombreux sont surclassés en vitesse, en puissance de feu et en protection rapport à leurs homologues britanniques; ses bases sont mal équipées, mal approvisionnées, excentrées par rapport aux routes empruntées par les Britanniques lesquels disposent de 25 bases réparties dans tous les océans. La marine doit admettre qu'elle est incapable de protéger les côtes françaises contre les bombardements et le blocus, de mener une guerre de course contre le commerce anglais et même d'affronter la Triplice. L'alliance russe de 1891 et les gesticulations navales se sont révélées inopérantes face à la Royal Navy, plus que jamais maîtresse des mers. Ce constat amer résulte de trois décennies d'errements.

De 1870 à 1914, la marine est un champ d'expérimentation pour les ingénieurs débordés par les innovations techniques portant sur la vitesse, l'armement, la protection. Les esprits sont brouillés par la torpille. Le torpilleur, bâtiment léger et peu coûteux, est, en effet, censé pouvoir détruire les puissants cuirassés. Une aubaine en période de disette budgétaire étayée par la croyance que la marine française pourrait pallier son infériorité structurelle. L'arme 'panacée' tombe dans le domaine public et politique. Elle suscite un courant de pensée, la *Jeune École*, pour qui la guerre d'escadre est dépassée et seule la guerre de course est envisagée, d'où la construction boulimique de torpilleurs et de croiseurs. L'accent est également mis sur le sous-marin. Mais les crédits sont mal employés, les bâtiments trop petits, expérimentaux et manquants de robustesse. Durant cette même période, la flotte marchande stagne. En 1900, son tonnage est inférieur à celui de 1870 alors que la flotte mondiale a doublé. Elle couvre 27% du trafic national. À la veille de 1914, elle connaît toutefois un certain redressement et atteint 2 500 000 tonnes grâce aux primes à la construction (création des Chantiers de la Loire, des Chantiers et Ateliers de la Gironde, des Chantiers de

Saint-Nazaire-Penhoët, des Forges et Chantiers de la Méditerranée, des chantiers Augustin-Normand au Havre) et à la navigation.

La crise de Fachoda a pour conséquence indirecte de démontrer la complémentarité des forces de la France et de la Grande-Bretagne. Elle contribue au retournement d'alliance de 1904 et à la conclusion de l'Entente cordiale. Par ailleurs, la guerre russo-japonaise démontre l'importance de l'artillerie. Les Britanniques innovent avec le *Dreadnought* caractérisé par l'unification des grosses pièces (8 ou 10 canons de calibre 381mm) et l'imposent comme le *capital ship* des flottes. Taraudée par la montée de la menace des puissances centrales, la France se résout à édicter la loi du 30 mars 1912, un vrai programme naval, qui prévoit la construction de 194 bâtiments, dont 28 cuirassés et 94 sous-marins à l'échéance de 1920. Le rythme des constructions est accéléré. Les deux premiers dreadnoughts ont été mis en chantier, les *Courbet*, en 1910; 12 autres suivent de 1911 à 1914. Pour pallier les faiblesses françaises, les conventions franco-anglaises de 1913 renforcent l'Entente cordiale et aboutissent à une répartition des tâches: à la Royal Navy la responsabilité de la mer du Nord à l'Atlantique; à la marine française, celle de la Méditerranée. La guerre en 1914 surprend la marine française en plein redressement moral et matériel entrepris trop tardivement. *In fine*, en ce XIXe siècle de détente internationale, et compte tenu de ses contingences géostratégiques, la France a tiré son épingle du jeu. Elle est présente sur tous les océans. Elle a tenu son rang aussi bien en Europe que dans le monde. Puissance à dominante continentale meurtrie par les invasions, la France a réussi en partie grâce à la marine à transformer ses 'confettis' coloniaux, hérités en 1815, en un empire de quelque 14 millions de km², peuplé par près de 48 millions d'habitants. Il n'en reste pas moins qu'à cause des errements de la Jeune École elle a rétrogradé depuis 1870 au quatrième rang des puissances navales.

RUSSIA TRIES THE NEW NAVAL TECHNOLOGIES, 1815-1914

NORMAN SAUL is Professor Emeritus of History at the University of Kansas, United States

ABSTRACT. *From its notional foundation by Peter the Great in the 17th century, and its real origin under Catherine the Great in the 18th century, the Russian navy had many achievements, but it never succeeded in escaping the destructive effects of geography, which separated the fleets of the Baltic, Black Sea, Arctic, and Pacific. Moreover the high-technology enterprise of a navy was built on a society weakly connected to modern industry and technology, and heavily dependent on foreign equipment and foreign experts. The result was a series of wartime failures, the last and worst during the war with Japan in 1904-5.*

RÉSUMÉ. *Depuis sa fondation théorique par Pierre le Grand au XVIIe siècle, et ses véritables débuts sous Catherine II au XVIIIe, la marine russe connut de nombreux succès, mais ne parvint jamais à échapper aux effets nuisibles de la géographie, qui séparait les flottes situées sur la mer Baltique, sur la mer Noir, dans l'océan Arctique et dans le Pacifique. En outre, entreprendre la construction d'une marine de pointe, dans une société avec peu de contact avec la technologie et l'industrie moderne, et fortement dépendante des équipements et experts étrangers, résulta en une série de défaites militaires, la dernière et la plus terrible pendant la guerre avec le Japon en 1904-1905.*

. • .

The rise of Russia as a naval power in the 19th century was a major factor in international, military, and economic relations. It commanded the attention of other countries in forging political alliances and business connections, though Russia's naval history has not been given the attention in historical literature as a recognized naval power of the period, such as Great Britain, France, the United States, Germany, and, by the end of the century, Japan. There is no comparison, for example, between Russia and Great Britain in the amount of material produced by historians in regard to naval developments. Russian naval history has also witnessed a considerable impetus in recent years, due to the celebration of the 300th anniversary of the birth of the fleet and of the founding of St. Petersburg, with which it was closely connected.[1]

---

[1] See especially, KELLER E. and KELLER A., *Peterburg: morskoi stolitsa Rossii* [Petersburg: Naval Capital of Russia] (St Petersburg, 2003); and *Tri veka Rossiiskogo flota, 1696-1996* [Three

THE BIRTH OF THE RUSSIAN NAVY

In one sense Peter the Great did not found the navy, it discovered him, or at least, the technology to build it. The state of Muscovy that he inherited at age ten in 1682 was virtually land locked and sealed off from the West by superior powers, Poland-Lithuania, Sweden, and the Ottoman Empire. In the middle of the 16th century, during the reign of Ivan IV (the Terrible), an English adventurer, Richard Chancellor, forged a sea path to Russia through the Arctic Ocean and the White Sea to the fishing port of Arkhangelsk. Merchants of the London Muscovy Company were soon plying this route, closed by ice half the year, and soon were followed by Dutch traders, to seek profits from exploiting the resources of Russia, mainly furs and linens, and introducing Western products. This led to the establishment of a foreign community in Moscow that dealt with this commerce.

The young Romanov heir was drawn to the strange objects and people of that community and found friends there who became allies and supporters of Russia's westernization. Foremost and early among them were the Swiss (Genevan) Francis Lefort, a Scottish mercenary-adventurer Patrick Gordon, and the Dutch ship builder Franz Timmerman. As a teenager, Peter relished learning of new things from the West, including sailing ships, which he could also see for himself on the White Sea. With his friends' help he discovered a small English sail boat, had it restored, and learned to sail. Dubbed in legend as the "grandfather of the Russian navy," he soon had a "toy" fleet on Lake Periaslavl to wage play sea battles.

The creation of a real Russian navy is thus attributed in legend and myth, and in some reality, to one person, Peter the Great, and to a war with the Ottoman Empire.[2] Muscovy/Russia would fight many wars against the Turks, who at this time controlled the northern shores of the Black Sea. After the death of his mother in 1694 and his real ascendancy to rule, Peter mapped out a campaign to capture the fortress-port of Azov at the mouth of the Don River. The first, in 1695, mainly by land, was unsuccessful. After hurried construction of river galleys, managed by Lefort, a second venture succeeded the following year, resulting in the first naval victory in Russian history, and in a "beachhead" in the south on the Sea of Azov.[3]

To further his aim to gather a coalition in pursuit of more gains in that sphere, Peter went on a "grand embassy" to Europe (1697-98) to gather information and allies. Focusing on the Netherlands and England and on shipyards, and

---

Centuries of the Russian Navy, 1696-1996] ed. F. GROMOV (3 vols., St Petersburg, 1996), vol. 1. Interest in Russian naval history revived after the collapse of the Soviet Union, with a new naval journal, *Gangut*, supplementing the long-existing (since 1848) *Morskoi Sbornik*.

[2] A fresh approach to legend and history is DOTSENKO V., *Mify i legendy rossiiskogo flota* [Myths and Legends of the Russian Navy] (St Petersburg, 2004).

[3] A good account is PHILLIPS E., *The Founding of Russia's Navy: Peter the Great and the Azov Fleet, 1688-1714* (Westport, CT, 1995). See also the pioneering works of ANDERSON R., *Naval Wars in the Levant, 1559-1853* (Liverpool, 1952) and *Naval Wars in the Baltic, 1522-1850* (2nd edn, London, 1969).

encouraged by Lefort and Peter's advocate, Alexander Menshikov, he brought a retinue of Russians to follow his example of learning on the spot, and he brought back skilled Dutch and British craftsman to improve and enlarge his naval ambitions as an example for the future. Rather than continuing his preference for advances in the south, he agreed to join a coalition against Sweden and Poland in the Great Northern War.[4] After initial setbacks, the contest resulted in Peter's being crowned emperor of Russia, the establishment of a new capital in St. Petersburg, and the advent of a Russian Baltic fleet, mainly a hundred coastal galleys, by 1709 including nine frigates, and the establishment of a naval base at Kronstadt on an island about fifteen miles from St. Petersburg. A feature of both Kronstadt and St. Petersburg was shipyards, hampered initially by contrasting rival British and Dutch techniques of construction.

An important aspect of Peter the Great's naval ambitions was the sending of a voyage of exploration under Vitus Bering, a Dane in Russian service, to the North Pacific, where he left his name on world maps in discovering the separation of North America from Asia and in exploration of the northwest American coast, achieved mostly by Russian subordinates. This would set the stage for future Russian activities in the Pacific Ocean, the Far East, and expansion into Alaska. With the assistance of Western experts, a practice to be followed in the future, Peter had brought the Russian Empire into the sailing age.

But was the tsar the real founder of the Russian navy? His several successors in the 18th century left the Baltic fleet to fall into decay and virtually disappear. By the 1760s, however, currents of change appeared, coinciding with the beginning of the reign of Catherine the Great, who could lay claim to being the real founder of a permanent Russian naval power. She, like Peter, was the subject of many biographies, though few of them view the Russian navy as a major achievement of her rule. Following her famous predecessor, Catherine, a German, was even more systematic in borrowing Western expertise from British, Swedish, Italian, Greek, and other advisors and officers.

New factors effected the development of naval rise under Catherine the Great: lessons learned from the naval engagements of the Seven Years' War, a major increase in the size and number of both commercial and military vessels after that war (the commercial revolution), and Russia becoming the most important supplier of vital resources for ship construction: iron for anchors, nails, and chains; rough linen for sail cloth; hemp for rope; and to some extent masts and wood. Most of the navies of the world were at least partially dependent on sources from Russia, resulting in a considerable increase in shipping in the Baltic ports of St. Petersburg, Revel, and Riga. Russia in the last half of the 18th century

---

[4] For brief entries on Lefort, Gordon, Northern Sea Route, Azov campaigns, the grand embassy, and others, consult SAUL N., *Historical Dictionary of Russian and Soviet Foreign Policy* (Lanham, MD, 2015). For Russian readers there is a similar, more specifically naval 'directory', *Rossiiskii imperatorskii flot, 1696-1917: voenno-istoricheskuu spravochnik* [The Russian Imperial Navy, 1696–1917: A Military-Historical Directory] ed. N. BEREZOVSKII et al. (Moscow, 1993).

had joined the international economic world.⁵ It brought prosperity to Russia in a favorable balance of trade that facilitated domestic and foreign development, including naval expansion.

A result was the overwhelming Russian success in the Russo-Turkish War of 1768-1774. In this conflict the revitalized Baltic fleet, a virtual armada of thirteen line-of-battle ships, sixteen frigates, and eleven support vessels, sailed around Europe (finding repairs in British ports) to the Eastern Mediterranean, where the main Ottoman fleet was surprised and destroyed at Chesma on the southwest Anatolian coast in July 1770, a battle that rivaled Trafalgar in terms of changing the balance of power in the area. Though the fleet was formally under the command of Aleksei Orlov, a lover of Catherine the Great, real credit is due to Admiral Grigory Spiridov and the British officers, John Elphinston and Samuel Greig, who were recruited for Russian service. Grigory Potemkin, another lover, deserves much of the credit for the grand design of the expedition, which also included the replacement of the Ottoman Empire by a revived Byzantine Empire with Catherine's grandson Constantin as emperor, the so-called "Greek Plan."⁶

The broader significance of the Russian success was the acquisition of the northern shore of the Black Sea, the annexation of the Crimea in 1783 that followed with bases and shipyards for a new Black Sea fleet, and the subsequent establishment of a new commercial port and naval base at Odessa in 1792. Other European powers now recognized Russia as the dominant naval power in the Baltic and Black Seas. This would be extended with the beginning of the Napoleonic Wars at the end of the century. But the sudden French penetration into the Eastern Mediterranean in 1797-98 with the Treaty of Campformio, and Napoleon Bonaparte's expedition to Egypt, threatened the interests of both Russia and the Ottoman Empire. The result was that both joined the Second Coalition against France. A Black Sea fleet under the command of Admiral Fedor Ushakov passed through the Straits to join the Turks in an expedition that targeted the Ionian Islands which had been ceded to France at Campoformio. Seized with little opposition, a Republic of the Seven Islands was created, centered on Corfu; a complicating factor was that Emperor Paul I had become Grand Master of the religious Order of Malta in 1798, that island having also been occupied by the French. A second squadron was sent from the Baltic under Admiral Dmitri Seniavin in 1804 to augment the Russian force, which now challenged both French and British interests in the Mediterranean.⁷

---

⁵ See KAHAN A., *The Plow, the Hammer, and the Knout: An Economic History of Eighteenth-Century Russia* (Chicago, 1985), especially ch. 6, pp. 283-310.
⁶ Details are in the work of BESKROVNYI L., *Russkaia armiia i flot v XVIII veka* [The Russian Army and Fleet in the XVIII Century] (Moscow, 1958), pp. 484-94; and in ANDERSON, *Naval Wars in the Levant*, pp. 299-304.
⁷ For a full account, SAUL N., *Russia and the Mediterranean, 1797-1807* (Chicago, 1970); and STANISLAVSKAIA A., *Russko-angliskie otnosheniia i problemy sredizemnomor'ia 1798-1807* [Russo-English Relations and the Problems of the Mediterranean Sea, 1798-1807] (Moscow, 1962); TARLE E., *Tri ekspeditii russkogo flota* [Three Expeditions of the Russian Navy] (Moscow, 1956); SHAPIRO A., *Admiral D.N. Seniavin* (Moscow, 1958).

At the same time a Russian round-the-world voyage, under the direction of Captains Adam Johann von Kruzenstern, a Baltic German, and Yury Lisiansky, attracted world-wide attention. Promoted by the Russian America Company and the wealthy aristocrat, Nikolai Rumiantsev, the expedition of two naval ships, *Nadezhna* (Kruzenstern) and *Neva* (Lisiansky), left Kronstadt in 1803 for the Pacific Ocean. Their accounts of the voyage, published in German, Russian, and English, were widely read and brought Russia acclaim as a world power on distant seas and as instruments of technological prowess.[8] The scientific and technological importance of these voyages have been analyzed in a number of subsequent studies.[9]

Having established a strong position in the Mediterranean, but suffering defeats on land in central Europe, Alexander I abruptly withdrew from it in signing the Treaty of Tilsit in 1807, with most of the remaining ships and crews becoming interned in British ports until 1812. The new situation allowed Russia to pursue additional gains in the Baltic in a brief war against Sweden in 1808 that resulted in the annexation of Finland as an autonomous grand duchy, and a considerable gain of Baltic coastline, harbors and ports such as Helsingfors (Helsinki) and Åbo (Turku), and an economically advanced population of Finns and Swedes.[10]

Other events impacted on Russian domination of Baltic waters. The arrival of John Quincy Adams in St. Petersburg in 1809 heralded the establishment of diplomatic relations with the United States, which took advantage of its neutral status to expand significantly its commerce with Russia in 1809–1811. Many of the departing cargoes of naval stores ended up in Great Britain. This infuriated Napoleon for being an obvious Russian violation of the strictures of the "Continental System" that banned British trade with the Continent, and this was a major cause of his rash decision to invade Russia in 1812.[11]

---

[8] LISIANSKY U., *A Voyage Around the World in the Years 1803, 4, 5 and 6; performed by Order of His Imperial Majesty Alexander the First, Emperor of Russia in the Ship Neva* (London, 1814); KRUZENSTERN I., *Puteshestviiu vokrug sveta v 1803 ...* [A Journey Around the World in 1803 ...], 3 vols (St Petersburg, 1809-13).

[9] LOWENSTEIN H., *The First Voyage around the World: The Journal of Herman Ludwig von Lowenstein, 1803-1806*, trans. V.J. MOESSNER (Fairbanks, AK, 2003); VINKOVETSKY I., 'Circumnavigation, empire, modernity, race: the impact of round-the-world voyages on Russia's imperial consciousness', *Ab Imperio* 1-2 (2001), 191-210; WERRETT S., 'Technology on display: instruments and identities on Russian voyages of exploration', *Russian Review* 70.3 (2011), 380-96.

[10] For long-term implications of Helsinki's being the main base of the Russian Baltic fleet, LUNTINEN P., *The Imperial Russian Army and Navy in Finland, 1808-1918* (Helsinki, 1997).

[11] For details, see CROSBY A., *America, Russia, Hemp and Napoleon: American Trade with Russia and the Baltic, 1783-1812* (Columbus, OH, 1965) and SAUL N., *Distant Friends: The United States and Russia, 1763-1867* (Lawrence, KS, 1996).

Russia enters the steam age

Pavel Svin'in, who had served in a diplomatic capacity with Seniavin's squadron in the Mediterranean, subsequently was appointed secretary to the Russian legation in the United States.[12] He traveled extensively throughout eastern America, artistically recording what he saw, especially becoming intrigued by the steam boat *Clermont* launched by Robert Fulton on the Hudson River and its potential use in Russian waters. His book featuring this circulated widely in Russia, though he was unsuccessful in his attempt to enlist Fulton into Russian service.[13]

A steam ship modeled on Fulton's was built at the Berg shipyard in St. Petersburg in 1815, followed quickly by others there and on the Volga River and at Arkhangelsk for commercial transportation. In 1817 the first Russian naval steam ship, the *Skory*, was built for the Baltic fleet, followed by others such as the *Vesuvius* built at Nikolaev for service on the Black Sea.[14] Several more followed with increasing size and horsepower. These paddle-wheel steam boats were unwieldy in open waters and quite vulnerable to battle damage, and were employed mainly on rivers and in coastal areas, for example, as ferries between Kronstadt and St. Petersburg. Ships with screw propulsion were not introduced until the 1840s.

By 1825 the Russian Baltic fleet had 217 commissioned ships of all sizes, including twenty-six ships of the line and twenty-one smaller steam powered vessels; the Black Sea fleet possessed around 180 (fourteen of them ships of the line) but not all of these were in service. Nevertheless, at the end of that year the new emperor, Nicholas I, declared, "Russia must become the third naval power after England and France and must be more powerful than any coalition of secondary naval powers." He also authorized an "1826 Table of Organization" for future planning, thus initiating the major role that the Romanovs would play in naval expansion throughout their rule.[15] In addition, ship construction and repair facilities were a major factor in St. Petersburg's transformation from Peter the Great's model eighteenth-century city into the largest industrial center in Russia, though the shipyards were concentrated at the mouth of the Neva (New Admiralty, New Holland, and Putilov yards) and up the river at the Alexandrovsk iron works, and at Kronstadt, leaving the heart of the city around the Winter Palace and Nevsky Prospect "unspoiled."

---

[12] Coincidentally, Seniavin had also visited America in the 1760s while serving as a trainee officer on a British frigate, *Coventry*. SAUL, *Distant Friends*, p. 4.
[13] SVIN'IN P., *Opyt'zhivopishago puteshestviia po Severnoi Amerike* [An Illustrated Journey through North America] (St Petersburg, 1815). This is available in an excellent annotated translation: WHISTENHUNT W. and SWOBODA M., *A Russian Paints America: The Travels of Pavel P. Svin'in, 1811-1813* (Montreal and Kingston, 2008). For a brief review, SAUL, *Distant Friends*, pp. 64–70, 151.
[14] BESKROVNY L., *The Russian Army and Navy in the Nineteenth Century: Handbook of Armaments, Personnel and Policy*, ed. and trans. G.E. SMITH from the original Russian edition of 1973 (Gulf Breeze, FL, 1996), pp. 295–96.
[15] *Ibid.*, pp. 296–7.

Navarino

By the early 19th century the Eastern Question was complicated by the Napoleonic wars and the emphasis on national liberation and the support of the Greek revolt that began in 1821. The result was the Treaty of London (1827), in which Great Britain, France, and Russia agreed to support Greek independence. A Russian Baltic squadron of four ships of the line and four frigates under Rear Admiral Logan Geiden (or Heyden of Dutch origin) was sent to the Eastern Mediterranean, where it joined similar squadrons of Great Britain and France under the overall command of Vice Admiral Edward Codrington. This allied fleet met an Ottoman–Egyptian "armada" of over sixty ships along the Peloponnesian coast on 20 October 1827 and thoroughly destroyed it through superior gunnery and deployment with a loss over four thousand killed or wounded, and few of the allied force. This was followed by additional Russian success in the Black Sea during the Russo-Turkish War of 1828–29, and a French expedition to Greece that precipitated Ottoman withdrawal from Greek territory by 1830, and the permanent establishment of Greek independence. This, however, did not solve the Eastern Question, as most of the Balkans remained under Ottoman control, but it certainly promoted their eventual liberation into several rival states such as Bulgaria and Serbia and provoked a continuing interest in the expansion of Russian naval power in the region.

The American connection

Another country was also rising on the seas, the United States, and it would many times act in harmony with Russia in the 19th century. A new US minister to Russia, George Mifflin Dallas, arrived in July 1837 on board the USS *Independence*, a ninety-gun, 2,250-ton ship of the line built in Boston in 1814 to defend New England from the British in the War of 1812. It subsequently served in the Mediterranean and was refitted as a fast frigate of fifty-four guns in 1836 with auxiliary steam power. Crossing the Atlantic in record speed in 1837, it called at Portsmouth and Copenhagen before dropping anchor at Kronstadt, where it was unofficially inspected in detail by Nicholas I himself, who was quite impressed. A special naval mission, headed by Captain Johann von Schantz of Finno-Swedish background, was promptly dispatched to America. This resulted in a contract in 1839 with the John H. Brown shipyard of New York for the construction of the *Kamchatka*.[16]

The largest ship yet built in America, according to newspaper reports it registered fully loaded at 2,468 tons with a six-hundred horsepower engine at a cost of over $450,000. The *Kamchatka* attracted much publicity and a crowd of

---

[16] Saul, *Distant Friends*, pp. 131–3.

over ten thousand when it was launched into the East River in November 1840.[17] After its delivery to Kronstadt by an American crew, it was mainly a show piece for the Baltic fleet. With the introduction of screw propulsion, it soon became obsolete. One could argue that such extravagance, especially in regard to the social and economic condition of most of the Russian population, was unwise, but the Russian trait of "gigantomania" would continue through the Soviet era.

Meanwhile, American shipping continued to prevail in the Baltic for decades after the Napoleonic Wars, with New England-based brigs of around five hundred tons plying a triangular route from such ports as Boston, south to the Carolinas and Georgia or Havana to load with rice, cotton, sugar, and coffee, and bringing back iron, rope, and linen sailcloth. The *Czarina*, appropriately named, made more than thirty such voyages from Boston, often twice in a year. By the 1850s "Yankee Clippers" of over a thousand tons were delivering cotton directly from Mobile and New Orleans, promoting a boom in the Russian textile industry. Since such ships were too large to enter the Neva, Kronstadt became the main commercial port, as well as naval base, with commodities shuttled back and forth on lighters or flatboats into and out of St. Petersburg.

This commerce was a factor in Russia's seeking American assistance in the construction of railroads, owing to US experience in building long-distance railways. Another special Russian mission was sent in the 1840s that led to the hiring of George Washington Whistler of Connecticut to survey and supervise the building of a railroad between Moscow and St. Petersburg, and a contract was signed with Ross Winans and his sons of Baltimore for the manufacture of locomotives and cars for that road at the Petersburg suburb of Aleksandrovsk.[18] Thus Russia entered the railroad age, American-style, that would culminate with the construction of the Trans-Siberian at the end of the century.

While all of this was taking place, Russian–American naval cooperation was rising in Pacific waters. Enterprising Bostonian sea captains entered that arena to find the Russians already there, in need of ships to carry furs (mainly sea otter) to China, where they were much in demand. One of the early Bostonians, John D'Wolfe, sold his ship, the *Juno*, to the Russian America Company to facilitate a Russian mission, led by Nikolai Rezanov, to Monterey in Spanish California in 1807. After the Mexican War and the US annexation of California, a lively trade developed between Russian Alaska and California in the 1840s and 1850s, with America providing foodstuffs and building materials, while the main product from Alaska became ice. In 1858 the Russian company acquired in Hamburg a "Yankee Clipper" of 1,200 tons for hauling ice, a major investment. Built in Portsmouth, New Hampshire, and renamed the *Tsaritsa*, it would supply booming San Francisco (before artificial refrigeration) with that commodity until the sale of Alaska.[19]

---

[17] *Ibid.*, pp. 132–4.
[18] *Ibid.*, pp. 139–41 and *passim*.
[19] *Ibid.*, pp. 44–5 and *passim*. For more far-reaching Russian naval activities in the Pacific, see BARRATT G., *Russia in Pacific Waters, 1715–1825: A Survey of Russia's Naval Presence in the*

The Crimean War

A number of factors led to an allied (Great Britain, France, and Sardinia) invasion of Russia in the Black Sea in the 1850s: the rise of liberation movements in the Balkans coupled with the advent of pan-Slavism in Russia (Russia as the big brother of Slavic peoples), minor controversies in Palestine, British and French loans to the Ottoman Empire that encouraged the Turks to take the initiative in the Balkans and the Caucasus in October 1853, what historian A.J.P. Taylor termed "the struggle for mastery in Europe", and the destruction at the end of November of the Ottoman Black Sea squadron by Admiral Pavel Nakhimov's Russian Black Sea squadron at Sinope, where it had just anchored for the winter.[20] Some in the West considered attacking ships at anchor was unfair, but they were defended by coastal batteries.

Nakhimov had new and revamped ships in the attack: six ships of the line (four of 120 guns), two frigates, and three steam ships against the Ottoman force of seven frigates (44–62 guns), three corvettes, and two steamers, with only one small steamer managing to escape. The others were destroyed by shelling or deliberately grounded to avoid capture or sinking. The main Russian advantage was that the ships were equipped with new rifled guns firing exploding shells, a major change over smooth-bore cannon firing balls or grapeshot.[21] In fear that the Ottoman Empire was about to collapse to Russia's profit, Great Britain and France quickly reacted in a joint attack on Sevastopol, the main Russian naval base, where Nakhimov's victorious squadron was sacrificed to block the entrance.[22]

A prolonged land war in Crimea produced several defeats of the Russian army but accomplished little definitive, except for legends created by some of its participants, such as Leo Tolstoy, Florence Nightingale, and around forty American surgeons, half of whom succumbed to disease in treating the Russian wounded. In the meantime, the Baltic fleet was enlarged and improved to ward off the possibility of a serious British attack on St. Petersburg, where the Winans' factory produced a number of modern torpedo boats and other smaller craft. The Crimean War experience produced another search by Russia for improvement and modernization.[23]

At least partly due to American benevolent neutrality during the war, which even included smuggling in Colt revolvers in bales of cotton, Russia turned again

---

North and South Pacific (Vancouver, 1981), and *Russian Shadows on the Northwest Coast of North America, 1810–1890* (Vancouver, 1983).

[20] The Crimean War has been a focus of recent historical literature: especially recommended is FIGES O., *The Crimea War: A History* (London, 2012).

[21] For a discussion of these innovations: SONDHAUS L., *Naval Warfare, 1815–1914* (London, 2001).

[22] BEREZOVSKII, *Russkii imperatorskii flot*, pp. 214–15.

[23] See especially, KIPP J., 'Consequences of defeat: modernizing the Russian navy, 1856–1863', in *Jahrbücher fur Geschichte Osteuropas* 20.2 (1972), 210–25, and VIOLETTE A., 'The Grand Duke Konstantin Nikolayevich and the reform of naval administration, 1855–1870', *Slavonic and East European Review* 52.129 (1974).

to that "far shore" for more naval expansion under the leadership of Grand Duke Constantine Nikolaevich, younger brother of Alexander II, as minister of navy, who began his role by a tour of inspection of Great Britain and France. In 1857 Russia contracted with the William H. Webb shipyard in lower Manhattan for the construction of a steam corvette, *Iaponetz*, of 1,400 tons, designed for the Russian Pacific fleet with ability to navigate the Amur River – with six hundred horsepower and at a cost of $250,000. Another smaller corvette, *Manzhur*, was assembled in Boston to accompany the *Iaponetz* to the Pacific, once more with much local and Russian publicity.[24]

These were dwarfed by another project, the construction of the *General-Admiral* at the Webb yards. The keel was laid on 27 September 1857, on the grand duke's thirtieth birthday, with much ceremony. Its construction was covered in detail in the news media at its various stages, for example, "The entire frame of the Russian frigate ... is now raised showing the immense vessel in all her proportions. The iron diagonal truss framing, composed of the longest iron bars ever rolled, is also in place. ... The frigate is pierced for 72 guns and is intended to mount an unusual heavy battery of eight and nine inch shell guns."[25] At a displacement of seven thousand tons it was arguably the largest wooden warship ever built. It was delivered to Kronstadt on 14 July 1859 with much fanfare. Grand Duke Constantine formally received the ship and expressed his pleasure at the *"tout ensemble"* of the vessel.[26] At a cost of over a million dollars, not counting extravagant celebrations on both sides of the Atlantic, one must wonder if it was worth it, especially since it was soon outmoded by the advent of ironclads. The addition of four-inch armor in Kronstadt added to the expense, and the ship was never employed in combat.

THE RUSSIAN NAVY AS AN INSTRUMENT OF FOREIGN POLICY

The major European powers were in a quandary over a conflict that erupted in the United States that resulted in a long and costly civil war in the 1860s. Great Britain and France, while having no desire to support slavery in the South, were unhappy about the Union blockade of ports of the Confederacy and, especially Britain, favored the weakening and division of the growing American economic and naval power that would result from a Confederate victory that seemed quite possible in 1863, after the Battle of Gettysburg. Russia, on the other hand, having just emancipated the serfs, felt a common interest with the North, and above all to maintain a strong United States as a counterweight to Great Britain. It feared that Britain and France might intervene in the war by granting diplomatic

---

[24] 'The Russian Corvette *Japanese*', *Frank Leslie's Illustrated Newspaper*, 1 May 1858, p. 345; SAUL, *Distant Friends*, pp. 256–7.
[25] 'The New Russian Frigate', *New York Herald*, 21 March 1858.
[26] SAUL, *Distant Friends*, pp. 258–9.

recognition to the Confederacy or even going farther by initiating a blockade of northern ports in retaliation of the Union's blockade of the South, which could be considered an act of war and widen the American conflict into a world war. Russians remembered American friendship and support during the Crimean War, and the recent construction of Russian warships.

In any event, Grand Duke Constantine, one of the leaders of the emancipation/reform movement, sent a squadron of the Baltic fleet to visit New York in September 1863, commanded by Admiral Stepan Lesovsky on board the flagship *Alexander Nevsky*, a 4,500-ton, eight-hundred-horsepower steam frigate, modeled on the *General-Admiral*, and six smaller frigates. They carried double crews to add to the squadron in case of need. This was obviously not a random port call, since the squadron remained in Union ports for four months, and it was augmented by a Pacific squadron simultaneously docking in San Francisco. Attended by parades, receptions, balls, and banquets, the Russian visit certainly lifted the morale of the Union. And it could be credited with warding off any precipitous action by Great Britain and France in favor of the Confederacy and "saving the Union."[27]

Two other minor technological developments were related to Russia and the American Civil War. The Winans' company (Alexandrovsky) in St. Petersburg had been building various small craft for the Baltic fleet for a number of years and began to experiment with a "cigar ship." This was essentially a monitor-type vessel with sharply pointed ends, designed for ramming, with guns on top but the ship was mostly submerged – a floating submarine. A Russian prototype was launched in St. Petersburg in 1865, with more trials and construction in England, but no buyers could be found.[28] Related to this was the sending of a true monitor, the *Miantonomoh*, to Russia in 1866 on an official mission of thanks for support during the war. Displacing 2,400 tons and mounting a 450-pound cannon, it lay low in the water, the first and last such vessel to cross the Atlantic. The object was to sell it. Russia, wisely this time, was not interested, nor were other buyers to be found.

Meanwhile, Grand Duke Constantine had his eyes on the Pacific. The acquisition of the Amur Provinces in 1860 made possible the foundation of a naval base at Vladivostok. The Russian America Company, previously the main Russian naval presence in the Pacific, was soon sacrificed by the sale of Alaska to the United States. For many years the company had relied on the navy to provide transportation and administration. With the depletion of sea otters, its revenues were declining; a major reason for the sale was the grand duke's strategy of concentrating naval resources in the Far East at Vladivostok.

Other seas were not neglected as major building programs promoted by Constantine were emphasized. By 1870, however, Russia had clearly fallen behind, especially in new iron-clad ships, having less than half the number of the British and French fleets, as private shipyards were slow in adapting to new technologies.[29] The answer would be a shift to government-operated shipyards.

---

[27] *Ibid.*, pp. 337–54.
[28] 'The Winans Cigar Ships', http://www.vernianera.com/CigarBoats.html.
[29] BESKROVNY, *The Russian Army and Navy*, pp. 308–9.

The grand duke was handicapped by other responsibilities: serving as viceroy in Poland, chairman of the State Council, and family issues (an estranged wife with six children and a mistress with five). He still managed to steer the navy through the important military reforms of 1874, which abandoned the Russian practice of permanent service (twenty-five years) in favor of limited terms, more selective recruitment, and the creation of reserves. The navy was assigned districts that were mainly industrial and coastal areas. Recruits then had more factory, shipping or port experience before entering naval service than did those drafted for the army. Naval training schools would accompany and enhance these new directions.[30]

As usual in Russia, all of this took time, was expensive, and was disrupted by both foreign and domestic events. Though personnel were paid less, more were recruited per gun in the Russian navy than in other states, and ship building was more costly because of outdated machinery and an inflated labor force. It is calculated by one source that each ton of ship construction was more than double the expense in Russia than in Germany or Great Britain in the 1870s, and bureaucratic logjams were excessive.[31] After the assassination of Alexander II in 1881, his more conservative successor, Alexander III, abruptly dismissed Constantine from all offices and installed his own brother, Alexis Alexandrovich, as "grand admiral". Alexis had been groomed for the navy from an early age, including a celebrated round the world voyage in 1871-72 at age 20-21 that included several months in the United States.[32]

Though lacking the vision of his predecessor, Alexis pursued the same naval expansion goals in the 1890s, supported by Nicholas II, in an arms race with Great Britain and Germany. This was financed mainly by loans from France, which Russia could ill afford. By this means Russia succeeded in maintaining a solid third-place position as a naval power in number and quality of warships by 1898: Great Britain 355, France 205, Russia 107, Germany 77, with about the same proportion under construction. The emphasis in Russia, however, was more on shore defense than it was in the other countries.[33] The imperial family's favoritism toward the navy is vividly portrayed in a recent illustrated album assembled from archives.[34] Clearly, Nicholas II's happiest days were spent in naval uniform aboard his large yacht, the *Standart*, on the Gulf of Finland.[35]

The Russian government shipyards could not keep up with orders in the naval

---

[30] For details, see GROMOV, *Tri veka*, pp. 232-48 and *passim*.
[31] SHEVYREV A., *Russkii flot posle Krymskoi voiny: liberal'naia biurokratiia i morskoi reformy* [The Russian Navy after the Crimean War: Liberal Bureaucracy and Naval Reforms] (Moscow, 1990), pp. 156-7.
[32] SAUL N., *Concord and Conflict: The United States and Russia, 1867-1914* (Lawrence, KS, 1996), pp. 64-8.
[33] BESKROVNY, *The Russian Army and Navy*, pp. 316-17.
[34] KRESTIANINOV V., *Imperial Russian Navy in Photographs from the Late 19th and Early 20th Centuries* (St Petersburg and London, 2013).
[35] *Ibid.*, pp. 52-3. By the 20th century a battleship of 15,000 tons would typically carry six 12-inch guns and twelve 6-inch guns and many appropriate shells.

arms race. Since they usually fell behind schedule, some of the demand for new ships was contracted out to private concerns and to foreign countries, especially Germany, Great Britain, and the United States, and older vessels in the meantime remained in service. Recruitment for the navy in the 1890s had to be extended to inland provinces, usually along rivers, to avoid over-depletion of shipyard workers. The navy received preference in these areas, the result being that naval recruits had more water and factory experience and a much higher literacy rate than those for the army – but exposed the navy to the labor disputes and strife they brought into naval service. As the navy entered the 20th century, ship crews in the Baltic were normally contained in cold, ice-bound ships in frozen harbors, such as Kronstadt, Helsinki, and Revel (Tallinn) during the winter, while most of the officers lived in comfortable housing on shore with their families. This apartheid reinforced the gap between the aristocratic, often non-Russian (Finnish and Baltic German) officer caste and the Russian, Estonian, and Latvian sailors (conscription did not apply to Finland), which fostered resentment. The Russian navy would soon be tested.

THE RUSSO-JAPANESE WAR

Japan was also involved in naval expansion and was particularly concerned about Russian advances in its direction, notably the building of the Trans-Siberian Railroad, the short-cut across "Chinese" Manchuria, the acquisition in 1898 of a new warm-water naval base at Port Arthur in 1898 (which Japan had just relinquished under pressure after the Sino-Japanese War), and attendant Russian economic advances in Korea and Northern China. The establishment of a new naval base in the Far East divided the Russian Pacific fleet between it and Vladivostok far to the north – with the expanding Japanese navy concentrated in between.

These developments magnified problems for government and military leaders who were already confronting budget and shipyard limitations, none of the latter in the Pacific bases. There were divisions among them regarding concentration of resources, with the General Admiral (Grand Duke Alexis) and Nicholas II favoring the Baltic arena, while a number of ranking naval officers leaned toward the south, to the Black Sea and the Mediterranean, where a Russian squadron was based in Greece at Pireaus. Grand Duke Alexander Mikhailovich, director of navy, and Minister of Finance Sergei Witte and others wanted to concentrate resources in the Far East to challenge the rise of Japan and promote Russian economic interests in Korea and China. Witte, however, preferred funding the completion of the Trans-Siberian Railroad, with its extension to Port Arthur, over fleet expansion.[36]

---

[36] See the excellent discussion in PAPASTRATIGAKIS N., *Russian Imperialism and Naval Power: Military Strategy and the Build-Up to the Russo-Japanese War* (London, 2011), pp. 125–53.

Diplomatic measures having failed, Japan launched a surprise attack on the Russian bases at Port Arthur and Vladivostok in February 1904, blockading the Russian warships in their harbors. After evidence of a subsequent Japanese land offensive in Manchuria, especially to accomplish the capture of Port Arthur, the Russian government decided to send a "Second Pacific Squadron" to the rescue.

A hastily assembled armada from the Baltic Fleet was sent under Rear Admiral Zinovy Rozhdestvensky all of the way around Africa to the Pacific. It was a motley, ill-prepared fleet of new and old, large and small craft, dependent on frequent coaling en route, destined to meet its doom in the Battle of Tsushima in May 1905.[37] The consequence of defeat attributed to growing unrest at home, the mutiny on the battleship *Potemkin* in the Black Sea in June, and the Russian Revolution of 1905 that reached its zenith later that year, and a lasting demoralization of the Russian navy. The response was more of the same: concentration on expending resources on rebuilding, now advancing into the dreadnought era, further burdening ship-building capacity, renewal of disciplinary measures, and a worsening of tensions between officers and crews, setting the stage for a real revolution in the navy in 1917.[38]

In retrospect, considering its uselessness in World War I, the Russian navy was a luxury extension of a land-based empire, an effort to demonstrate a mastery of a technology it had little real need for. Money and personnel might have been better spent on modernizing the army, which by 1914 was badly deficient in basic equipment (small arms and artillery), transport, management, and vision. Russia succeeded in meeting the demand for new naval technology and innovation, but, in Loren Graham's phrase, it lacked the will, determination, and especially administrative capability to "make it work."[39] One aspect of confronting the demands of naval power for a century was to turn Russia more to the West and away from the alternative of a Eurasian direction.

---

[37] The story is well told in GROMOV, *Tri veka*, pp. 317–50. See also PIOUFFRE G., *La guerre russo-japonaise sur mer* (Nantes, 1999); CORBETT J., *Maritime Operations in the Russo-Japanese War*, 2 vols (Annapolis, 1994); PLESHAKOV C., *The Tsar's Last Armada: The Epic Journey to the Battle of Tsushima* (New York, 2002); and an able summary by LUNTINEN P. and MENNING B., 'The Russian Navy at War, 1904–05', in *The Russo-Japanese War in Global Perspective: World War Zero*, ed. J. STEINBERG et al. (Leiden, 2005), pp. 229–59.

[38] For more analysis, SAUL N., *Sailors in Revolt: The Russian Baltic Fleet in 1917* (Lawrence, KS, 1978).

[39] GRAHAM L., *Lonely Ideas: Can Russia Compete?* (Cambridge, MA, 2013).

The First World War and Japan: from the Anglo-Japanese Alliance to the Washington Treaty

Yoichi Hirama is Rear Admiral, Ret. in the Japanese Maritime Self-Defense Force

Abstract. *The Anglo-Japanese alliance served both parties well in the original context of the Russo-Japanese War, but came under strain during the First World War, and even more at the Versailles Conference, before being cancelled under U.S. pressure in 1923. Japanese strategy in the Meiji Era was divided, the army standing for the "northward advance" on land against Russia, the navy for a "southward advance" by sea against western powers. Both were intended to control Chinese resources to sustain a major war.*

Résumé. *L'alliance anglo-japonaise fut profitable aux deux pays dans le contexte originel de la guerre russo-japonaise, mais subit des tensions pendant la première guerre mondiale et même davantage lors du Traité de Versailles. Elle fut par la suite annulée, sous la pression des États-Unis, en 1923. La stratégie militaire japonaise pendant l'ère Meiji était divisée, l'armée se portant en faveur d'une « avancée vers le nord » par les terres contre la Russie, tandis que la marine promouvait une « avancée vers le sud » par la mer contre les puissances occidentales. Les deux avaient pour but de contrôler les ressources chinoises en cas de guerre grave.*

.•.

Russia's southward advance and the Anglo-Japanese Alliance

From a historical and geopolitical view, the Korean Peninsula has always been surrounded by powerful land powers – Mongolia, the Chinese Empire, and Russia or the Soviet Union. For a long time, this peninsula was a bridge connecting Japan and the Eurasian continent. It helped bring culture to Japan, but the Mongols and the Goryeo dynasty also threatened Japan across this bridge. On entering the modern period, Japan maintained its security by allying with sea powers against the land powers.

Seeking ice-free ports, Russia built a coaling station in Jeoryeongdo, Korea, in 1888. Following the Triple Intervention, concluded in 1895, Russia leased the territory of Dalian and then began to show interest in the Korean Peninsula. As Russia increased its interference in Northeast Asia, Korea's King Ko Jong leaned toward Russia. Japan negotiated with Russia and offered to recognize Russian dominance in Manchuria in exchange for Russia's recognition of Japan's sphere of influence in Korea. This resulted in the Yamagata-Lobanov Agreement in 1896 and the Nishi-Rosen Agreement of 1898. However, Russia ignored these conventions by deploying its military forces and financial advisors to Korea.

In 1896, the Russian cruiser *Admiral Nakhimov* entered the port of Inchon and invited King Ko Jong to stay in the Russian legation. King Ko Jong ordered the cabinet of the reform faction to dissolve, and he gave orders to kill reform and purge members of the pro-Japanese faction. Afterward, Russia sent three warships to the port of Masanpo, where they built another coal-storage facility and leased Yongampo to establish a military base.

In response to Russia's advance to Korea, the Anglo-Japanese Alliance was concluded in 1902. It enabled Japan to challenge Russian expansion without fear of French and German intervention. It won great prestige for Japan, as it was the first alliance between an Asian nation and an advanced Western nation, even though it was not so much an equal treaty as a pact between a junior and a senior partner. The Japanese were very much delighted, as the treaty fulfilled their dream of "prosperity and strong defense" which they had been working hard to achieve since the Meiji Restoration. There were, however, reasons for Britain to have abandoned her "Splendid Isolation" and step into an alliance with a small country in the Far East – her confrontation with Russia and Russia's advance into China. Deeply involved in the Boer War, Britain was not in a position, even if she wanted, to increase her army in China to maintain her influence. Meanwhile, Britain could not depend on the United States, which did not have many concessions in China or the capacity to send an army while she was putting eighty thousand soldiers into the Philippines to suppress independence movements.

In the meantime, Japan had no clear idea whether she would choose Britain or Russia. Britain took the plunge to conclude the alliance with Japan after Ito Hirobumi's visit to Russia. Britain had calculated Japan's military power, especially her naval strength and logistical capabilities. Table 1 shows the naval vessels of the major powers in the Far East at that time.

In Japan, logistical facilities such as the dry docks at Kure and the Yokosuka

Table 1. *Major warships in the Far East, 1904*

	Japan	Britain	Russia	France
Battleships	6 (1st–2nd class)	4	5 (1st–2nd class)	1 (2nd class)
1st class cruiser (armored)	7 (6 new type)	3 (2 old type)	6	2 (old type)
1st class cruiser (protected)		4		2
2nd class cruiser (protected)	10	8	1	5
3rd class cruiser (protected)	14	1		

Naval Arsenals, as well as the collieries at Miike and Karatsu, were the only such facilities available in Northeast Asia. One clause of the Anglo-Japanese Alliance, stipulating that "Mutual facilities shall be given for the docking and coaling of vessels of war of one country in the ports of other", was added at Britain's request.[1]

THE RUSSO-JAPANESE WAR AND U.S.–JAPANESE RELATIONS

On the night of 8 February 1904, the Japanese fleet under Admiral Togo Heihachiro opened fire on the Russian ships off Port Arthur. A series of indecisive naval engagements followed until August, when the Russian Pacific (Far Eastern) fleet, hoping to deploy to Vladivostok, was defeated in the Battle of the Yellow Sea. Meanwhile, to weaken the Russian defense of the Lushun fortress, the Japanese Army under General Kuroki Tamemoto crossed the Yalu River into Russian-occupied Manchuria by the end of April, and the Japanese 3rd Army under General Nogi Maresuke captured the key bastion, Hill 203, in December. From this vantage point, long-range artillery was able to shell the remaining Russian vessels to destroy them in the port. After the Battle of Liaoyang in late August, the northern Russian force that might have been able to relieve Port Arthur had already retreated to Mukden. Major General Anatoly Stessel, commander of the Port Arthur garrison, surrendered on 2 January 1905.

With the fall of Port Arthur, the Japanese 3rd Army continued northward to reinforce the Japanese forces under General Oyama Iwao. The Battle of Mukden commenced on 20 February 1905. After three weeks of harsh fighting, on 10 March 1905 General Aleksei Kuropatkin decided to withdraw to the north. Having sustained heavy casualties, the Japanese lacked ammunition and reserve forces to destroy the retreating Russian army, so the final victory depended on the navy.

The Russian navy was preparing to reinforce the Pacific Fleet by sending the Baltic Fleet, under the command of Admiral Zinovy Rozhestvensky. The main squadron, renamed the Second Pacific Squadron, departed Libau on 15 October 1904 for a seven-month voyage to the Pacific via the Cape of Good Hope. It contained eight battleships, including four new battleships of the *Borodino*-class, as well as thirty cruisers, destroyers and other auxiliaries. During a stop-over of several weeks at Nossi-Bé, Madagascar, which had been reluctantly allowed by neutral France, the demoralizing news that Port Arthur had fallen reached the fleet.

The Japanese Combined Fleet had lost two of its original six battleships to mines, but still retained its cruisers, destroyers, and torpedo boats. By the end of May, the 2nd Pacific Squadron was on the last leg of its journey to Vladivostok,

---

[1] GAIMUSHO [Ministry of Foreign Affairs] ed., *Nippon Gaiko Bunsho* [Japanese Diplomatic Documents], vol. 35 (Nihon Kokusairengo Koyokai, 1957), p. 86.

taking the shorter, riskier route between Korea and Japan. The Japanese engaged the Russians in the Tsushima Straits on 27–28 May 1905. The Russian fleet was virtually annihilated, losing twenty-seven ships, including eight battleships, numerous cruisers and destroyers as well as over five thousand men, while the Japanese lost three torpedo boats and 116 men. Only three Russian ships escaped to Vladivostok.

The defeats of the Russian army and navy shocked Tsar Nicholas II, and he elected to negotiate peace. The negotiations took place in August in Portsmouth, New Hampshire and were brokered by U.S. President Theodore Roosevelt. The final agreement was signed on 5 September 1905. As a result, Russia lost the southern half of Sakhalin Island and many mineral rights in Manchuria. In addition, Russia's defeat cleared the way for Japan to annex Korea outright in 1910. The victory greatly raised Japan's international stature, but the Treaty of Portsmouth marked the last real event in the era of U.S.–Japanese cooperation that had begun with the Meiji Restoration in 1868. In the Russo-Japanese War, the United States supported Japan to check the Russian southward advance to China. Once the war was over, however, the military, racist groups, and yellow journalism in the United States started to voice the threat of the Japanese "Menace".

World War I and the Anglo-Japanese Alliance

Japan entered World War I by declaring war on Germany on 23 August 1914. The Japanese navy and army soon moved to occupy the German East Asia Squadron base of Qingdao, German-leased territories in China's Shandong Province, as well as the Marianas, Caroline, and Marshall Islands in the Pacific. During the war, the Japanese navy completely established sea control of the Pacific and the Indian Ocean for the Allied Powers. With Japan's assistance, Great Britain was able to maintain its control of the sea-line communication in the Pacific and the Indian Ocean without any interruption.

To borrow the words of the Genro, or elder statesman, Inoue Kaoru, "the First World War was a miracle and a boon for expanding Japan's exports and realizing its industrial modernization." However, in Britain there was great distrust and dissatisfaction over Japan's role in the war. The British perceived Japan negatively for having hesitated to co-operate and for demanding rewards despite being an ally. Britain's naval attaché, Captain Edward H. Rymer, reported this dissatisfaction in his report on "The present situation of Japan":

> Every Japanese is an absolute Japanophile – an egoist who thinks about only himself and has no feeling of sacrificing himself for other countries. ... The Japanese are not interested in War and Alliance. If we strongly suggest how Britain supported Japan in the past, what Japan should do as an ally, and Japan should have an obligation as an ally, Japan would desert us. If Britain conceded and begs for their support, the wise Japanese simply increases his complacency

inwardly with doing well or the ignorant Japanese would simply increase his confidence and escalate his demands. ... Japan was spellbound by money and blinded by the dream of being the leader in the Pacific.[2]

Britain's formal criticism of the Japanese might best be shown by the "Memorandum on Anglo-Japanese Relations." This report was distributed at the Imperial Conference held in March 1917, one year before the end of the war, and concluded as follows:

> Every Japanese is born and bred with ideas of aggressive patriotism, of his superiority to foreigners, of his national call to head a revival of the neighboring brown and yellow races. His success in the Russo-Japanese war had made these ideas a practical and living force in the national life. His training, military and commercial, is on German lines, and his character appears naturally to assimilate German methods of organization and discipline. It is no exaggeration to say that he has become the Prussian of the Far East – fanatically patriotic, nationally aggressive, individually truculent, fundamentally deceitful, imbued with the idea that he is under a moral obligation to impose his own particular form of *Kultur* on his neighbors ... It is, and must remain, impossible to give gratuitously to Japan enough to satisfy her ambition. Should we not make up our mind that the moment will come when that ambition must be curbed by force?[3]

This report also shows British criticisms and complaints.

> Japan has proved lukewarm or actively disloyal to the Allied cause in the following ways:-
> 1. She has permitted and even encouraged the use of her territory as a focus of intrigue on the part of the most active and dangerous Indian seditionists, and has placed every obstacle in the way of British authorities investigating the activities and preventing the passage by sea and subsequent arrest of such seditionists.
> 2. Up to the end of 1916 she had refused to adopt any adequate measures for suppressing the commercial activities of enemy subjects in Japan.
> 3. She has refused to curtail the profits of her own traders and industrialists by controlling the export of contraband articles which might reach the enemy, e.g., minerals to America, soya beans to Sweden.
> 4. She has permitted, if not encouraged, a series of violent press campaigns in opposition to the Anglo-Japanese Alliance, and to the adherence of Japan

---

[2] Doc. (XC3347), Japan at War 1914-1918 (British Embassy in Tokyo, 21 February 1918), FO.371/3233. Public Record Office, London.
[3] Memorandum on Anglo-Japanese Relations (Written for the Imperial Conference in March 1917), in *British Documents on Foreign Affairs ... Part II, From the First to the Second World War. Series E, Asia, 1914-1939*, ed. K. BOURNE, A. TROTTER and D.C. WATT, 50 vols (Frederick, MD, 1990-97), vol. II, Doc. 242, pp. 218-227, at p. 226.

to the Allied cause, thereby casting doubt among neutrals as to the real solidarity of the Allies.
5. She has completely ignored the needs of this country for the raw material and manufactured products which [are] essential for carrying on the war ...
6. She has equally ignored our need to husband tonnage, and has protested continuously and violently against every attempt on the part of His Majesty's Government to restrict unnecessary imports.
7. She has done her best – and with a large measure of success – to undermine our political position in China.[4]

This report also lists Japan's contributions as an ally:

1. By Capturing Tsing-tao and destroying the principal German base in the Far East.
2. By seizing the German islands north of the Equator, and destroying the subsidiary bases there established.
3. By providing a naval force which co-operated in hunting down the German Far Eastern Squadron (*Gneisenau, Scharnhorst*, &c.), and providing escorts for Australian transports.
4. Subsequently, by providing two cruisers for the Indian Ocean, a destroyer flotilla for the Malacca patrol, and two cruisers to watch the German merchantmen sheltering in Chinese harbours.
5. Recently, by agreeing to allocate eight destroyers for patrol duties in the Mediterranean [finally two cruisers and twelve destroyers were sent], and two cruisers for the Cape Station.
6. By supplying munitions of all kinds to the Allies, and especially to Russia.
7. By taking up British and Russian Exchequer Bonds.
8. By redeeming some considerable proportion of her external debt outstanding in France and England.
9. By providing, on two occasions, cruisers to convoy bullion from Vladivostok to Esquimalt. [Two escorts followed].[5]

Foreign Secretary Edward Grey, however, evaluated Japan's support during the war more favorably:

During the last year that I served as Foreign Secretary Japan was always fair in her obligations as an ally and in sharing the benefits. The Japanese government and ambassadors stationed in UK were honorable and faithful allies. ... The First World War was a great opportunity for Japan to expand its territories. If there were any European country like Japan which had surplus population and if they needed territories, it is doubtful that they (the European countries) would have managed to control themselves in the face of such an immediate opportunity as Japan did.[6]

---

[4] *Ibid.*, p. 222.
[5] *Ibid.*
[6] GREY E., VISCOUNT, *Twenty-five Years, 1892–1916* (London, 1925), vol. 3, pp. 33–4.

The Japanese responses and the background

When World War I ended, Japan was internationally isolated. Anti-British feelings, touched off by Britain's high-handed Indian policy, intensified the Indian refugee extradition issue. In July 1915 Indian independence hard-liners Bhagawan Sing and Raj Bibari Bose had defected to Japan as Britain tightened its control in India.

The Indian Tarakanath Das and the Chinese professor at Shanghai University Dr. Fan Chun Zong asserted that because Japan could neither confront the great European powers alone nor acquire real allies in Europe, it would therefore be natural for Japan to seek allies in Asia.[7] This idea of "Along with Asia" became influential in Japan. Dr. Okawa Shumei wrote *The Present State and the Future of National Movements in India*, in which he contended that the Indian people detested British tyranny, desired independence and expected Japanese help. The Japanese, Dr. Okawa wrote, had to bravely take on this holy task – Japan as an Asian leader had to acquire real power in order to spread justice throughout the world.[8]

During the Paris Peace Conference of 1919 Japan proposed a clause on racial equality to be included in the League of Nations Covenant. The clause was rejected, due to opposition from the British dominions of Canada and Australia. This rejection helped to turn Japan away from cooperation with the West and toward nationalistic policies.

German propaganda efforts to spread anti-Japanese racial animosity among the Western countries were effective during the war and did not diminish after the war, in spite of Japan's contribution to the Allied victory. While the Japanese navy was escorting British troops in the Mediterranean, London refused to loan submarine detection devices to the Japanese destroyers and did not allow Japan's liaison officers to handle cryptological intelligence. After the war, the Anglo-Japanese Alliance was increasingly viewed as of small benefit for Japan but of great benefit for the UK. Arguments concerning revision or abrogation of the alliance increasingly appeared in public in Japan.

After the war, why did the British and the Allied countries so quickly forget Japan's assistance, and why have Western naval histories neglected Japanese contributions to the Allies? In Australia, Japanese loyalty and service were discredited by the First Naval Member, and a report titled the "Misleading Reference to Japanese Naval Action in the Pacific Ocean during the War" was submitted to Prime Minister William M. Hughes. Thus Japanese help quickly and completely disappeared from Western naval history.

---

[7] *Kaigun Senshi* [Naval War History] 3-4 Nen, vol. 2, pp. 56-57, 'Yahagi Senji Nitsushi [Yahagi War Dairy]', National Ministry of Defense War History Center, 'Indo-Jin Dasu ni Kansuru Ken [Issue on Indian Das]', 'Shinbun, Zatsushi, Torisimari Zatsuken Indo-Jin Torisimari no Ken [Control of Newspapers and Magazines: The Indian Activities], Japanese Diplomatic Achieves.

[8] SHUMEI O., *The Present State and the Future of National Movements in India Okawa Shumei Shu* [Collection of the Writings of Okawa Shumei] (Chikuma-Shob 1975), p. 13.

After the Germans were eliminated in Northeast Asia, the Pacific was considered secured. However, for Australia and New Zealand this simply meant that the German threat was replaced by a Japanese threat. Australia began prohibiting colored immigration, even though many nations in Asia were suffering from poverty due to overpopulation. Paradoxically, Australians feared that their policy of a "White Australia" might offer the newly powerful Japan an excuse for invasion. Japan's occupation of the former German Pacific territories, despite the Versailles Treaty's requirement that they not be fortified, had given rise to suspicions that these islands were being developed as bases to protect against America's westward advance and to use for Japan's southward advance toward Australia.

Meanwhile, British industrialists urged the annulment of the Anglo-Japanese Alliance. Soldiers and diplomats, dissatisfied with the amount of Japan's wartime cooperation, also pushed for annulment. In the British Parliament arguments intensified over ending the alliance, with many believing that Japan was planning to invade China by abusing the alliance.

The Anglo-Japanese Alliance was diluted in its significance because the two countries' common enemies, Russia and Germany, were weakened and because Britain had made it clear to the United States that it had no intention of carrying out its obligations under the alliance. The alliance had become ineffective. But to avoid international isolation Japan wanted to continue with it, and planned a cooperative arrangement with Britain. Britain also wanted to continue the alliance, fearing that if it were abolished, Japan would become a threat to its dominions such as Australia and New Zealand. Britain also hoped to use it as a diplomatic channel to settle conflicts of interest in China.

European naval power had been shattered in Asian waters, leaving Japan and the United States as the foremost powers. Japan and the United States, however, soon clashed on the Shandong issue at the Peace Conference in Paris, and tensions intensified with Japan's continued dispatch of troops against the Red Army in Siberia and with the United States' restrictions on Japanese immigration. Under the slogan of "Open Door" in China, U.S. diplomatic policy toward Japan during the interwar period sought to change Japan's policies on the continent by directing international criticism toward Japan and by denying the reality of Japanese successes in China during the war.

Fearing that Britain would take the initiative, on 11 July 1921 President Warren G. Harding called for a conference to be held in Washington, DC. France was added to the attending powers to prevent rapprochement between Britain and Japan. The resulting Four-Power Pacific Treaty was signed and simultaneously brought the Anglo-Japanese Alliance to an end. The Four-Power Treaty was a general agreement recognizing and mutually respecting the rights of the four signatories toward the islands and territories in the Pacific.

Furthermore, the Nine-Power Treaty, which protected Chinese interests and defined the principles of the "open door" and equal opportunity in the Chinese market, was concluded. The United States annulled the Ishii-Lansing Agreement, which had allowed Japan to hold special privileges in China. Thus, by the events of the Washington Conference, the United States had succeeded not only in annulling the Anglo-Japanese Alliance but also in securing the safety of the Philippines. The United States had also obtained international recognition of the "open door" and equal opportunity policies, which had been an objective since the days of John Hay. At the Washington Naval Conference, Japan also signed the Five-Power Naval Disarmament Treaty. By this treaty, Japan conceded a 40 percent disadvantage in tonnage of capital ships compared to the United States and Britain. These three treaties established the so-called Washington Treaty System as a comprehensive, international, cooperative peace organization.

The Imperial defense policy and Japanese tendencies

In the early Meiji era, Japan's navy took a secondary position to the army, both functionally and organizationally. In 1892, Lt. Commander Sato Tetsutaro (later Vice Admiral) wrote *Teikoku Kokuboron* [Theory on Imperial National Defense]. In this book, he insisted that the best defense was never to let a foe reach the homeland. He emphasized naval defense and foresaw Japan as a maritime nation. He argued that Japan should not involve itself in continental matters. *Teikoku-kokuboron* became the fundamental text for naval officers and influenced Japan's population. The Japanese navy, however, could not change Japan's national strategy, preferred by many Japanese leaders, who envisioned their nation as the dominant continental power of Northeast Asia rather than as a leading maritime state. To gain standing, the navy utilized the doctrine of navalism – the idea of sea power, based on great battle fleets, was the key to national greatness propounded by the "Blue Water" school. Alfred Thayer Mahan gained the attention of Japanese naval circles. His *The Influence of Sea Power upon History* was translated and published by Suikosha, the naval officers' professional association, in 1896.

Japan's highest and most authorized formulation of military policy, approved by the emperor, was the Imperial Defense Policy and its allied documents, the Forces Necessary for Defense and Imperial Defense Methods. These documents were first formulated in 1907, immediately after the Russo-Japanese War.[9]

In this policy, however, the strategies of the army and of the navy were split. The army insisted that Russia was preparing for revenge against Japan and was readying the Siberian Railway to return Manchuria. Considering the heavy casualties and high cost of the Russo-Japanese War, the army quoted public opinion that favored Japan's maintaining her hold over Manchuria and Korea. Meanwhile, the navy upheld Mahan's maxim, "Sea power brings greatness for countries and prosperity for peoples." Specifically, the navy's slogan was

---

[9] Ref. Kurono Taeru, *Teikoku Kokubou Houshin no Kenkyu* [A Study on the Defense Policies of Imperial Japan] (Sowa-sha 2000).

to prepare "sufficiently for defense but not enough to attack." In the simultaneous adoption of the policies of Nanshin (southward advance) and Hokushin (northward advance), the army foresaw Russia, while the navy viewed the United States, as potential enemies.

Lessons having been from World War I, the policy of 1918 stressed an initial offensive operation to achieve a quick victory. The new thinking also recognized the need to move to a long-range, total war strategy if the initial campaign failed to end hostilities. While Japanese strategists recognized the possibilities of a total war, they formed no concrete plan to prepare for one. With increasing demands for disarmament within Japan and throughout the world, the army and the navy parochially concentrated on building up their own separate forces.

The Defense Policy was revised again in 1923. The navy disagreed with the army's strategy of northward advance because of U.S. advances in China and friction with Great Britain, while the army declined to stand on the defensive in the North and strongly insisted on facing the USSR and China. But both understood that Japan could not fight a total war without having significant control over Chinese resources. Thus the army and the navy were condemned to advance into Northeast Asia. The navy adapted a strategy of defense of the mainland and added the maintenance of sea communications between Japan and the Chinese mainland. However, no plan was offered for the possibility of the U.S.,USSR, Britain, and China being united: it was noted to be "decided at that time."

The Defense Policy of 1936 showed an even wider divergence of strategies between the army and the navy – the army saw the Soviet Union as a potential rival for control of the Asian continent, while the navy saw the United States as a potential rival for control of the western Pacific. Furthermore, Japan needed to prepare for possible conflicts against China and Britain, and the army and the navy both insisted on "the enclosed military power – The Force Necessary for Defense" for this purpose.

After being subjected to inferior ratios for capital ships at the Washington Conference and for auxiliary ships at the London Naval Conference, the Imperial Japanese Navy's strategic thinking was preoccupied by the question of "how to contend successfully against heavy odds." The navy formulated an "interception-attrition-strategy" to deal with American naval power by efficient utilization of airplanes, submarines, and torpedo squadrons (cruisers and destroyers). The navy began to manage naval education and training, fleet formations, and armaments, all with an American enemy – an overwhelmingly powerful one – in mind. This became its dogma by the late 1930s.[10]

In evaluating Japan's path to World War II, some suggest that Japan should have gradually developed its economic and industrial power and should have chosen Communist Russia as its main enemy. This would have kept Japan within the Washington Treaty System and would have avoided friction with Britain and

---

[10] YOICHI H., 'Japanese Preparations for World War II: Strategy and Weapons Systems', *U.S. Naval War College Review* 54, No. 2 (Spring 1991) pp. 63–81.

the United States. But China at the time was in chaos and was ignoring international laws. Its central government had broken down, and multiple governments were competing for power. This produced constant civil war among war lords, between the Communists and the Nationalists as well as within the Nationalist Party itself. None was able to assume their responsibilities abroad. In Japan, anti-Chinese feeling was aroused, and state leaders agitated the population through journalism. The army and the navy also used this populism to build up their strength.

Japanese tendencies after the Washington Conference

What could Japan have done when she lost her strong partner? After the annulment of the Anglo-Japanese Alliance, which path could Japan have taken? Japan was isolated and had to take the option of independent armament. Vice Admiral Sato Tetsutaro wrote in 1933, that "Diplomatically, Japan must pursue peace in the Pacific area. Because this peace falls on the shoulders of Japan and the United States, which are both located on the North Pacific, whatever happens, Japan and the United States should not be hostile but must maintain peace by mutual cooperation so long as they exist. For this, mutual respect is important."

After the annulment of the Anglo-Japanese Alliance, the Japanese navy still had a stronger affinity with Britain. This was indicated by the message sent from Naval Minister Admiral Kato Tomosaburo while staying in Washington as the plenipotentiary for the conference, to the Naval Deputy Minister: "Henceforth a system of civilian ministers will appear, therefore we must prepare for it. It should be similar to the British system."[11]

But, at the Peace Conference in Paris, the clause abolishing racial discrimination was rejected because of opposition from Australia, a dominion of Japan's ally. Then the fortification of Singapore began immediately after the Anglo-Japanese Alliance was brought to an end. These developments portrayed an image of "ungrateful Britain" to the Japanese people. Humiliating memories and dissatisfaction among those who participated in joint maneuvers became an issue, thus anti-British sentiment increased even in the navy, which previously had been strongly pro-British. The reason for these aggravated anti-British feelings is explained by the Japanese navy's confidential document, as follows:

> Until World War I, Britain took full advantage of its relationship with Japan; fully employing Japan's military strength and goodwill at all times, including the period of Imperial Russia's aggression against China, the restraining of the Indian independence movement, the blocking of China's anti-foreign activities,

---

[11] JYUN I.M.K., ed., *Taiheiyo Senso Heno Michi* [The Road to the Pacific War] *Kaisen Gaiko* [Diplomacy to War] *Shiryo-He* [Historical Docummments] (Asahi-Shinbun, 1963), p. 7.

and the protection of its dominions after it concentrated its fleets in the North Sea. Once peace resumed, however, its attitude suddenly changed and Britain refused to give Japan even the slightest concessions. This led to the Japanese isolation at the Paris Conference and the demand for the ratios of 5–5–3 for battleships at the Washington Conference, the return of Shandong, the annulment of the Anglo-Japanese Alliance, the conclusion of the Nine Power Treaty, and eventually to all-out oppression of Japanese trade.[12]

The British door was closed to Japanese officers following the annulment of the alliance, so the Japanese navy gradually changed its destination for study abroad and technical transfers to Germany. As a result, the numbers of those returning from Germany gradually increased in the navy. Admiral Sato's assertions changed. In his book, *On Defense*, published in 1934, he wrote, "Every alliance or agreement is based on one's own interests and never a pure spiritual combination. Therefore, whenever any difference arises in interests, a friend yesterday will be discarded almost without hesitation." He also asserted the necessity of self-armament, stating, "Those who have no real power on their own cannot remain independent."

One year before, for the Naval Limitation Conference, Captain Yamashita Tomohiko and Lt. Commander Waraya Hidehiko, who had studied in Germany, presented a "Proposal to cooperate with Germany" to the Naval Counselor Admiral Kato Kanji.[13]

> Promote an alliance with Germany, whose armaments are restricted and would be the only country to support Japan's claim for equal armaments at the disarmament conference. Japan should renounce reparations from Germany, promote pro-Japanese feelings in Germany, and turn the disarmament conference to its advantage by collaborating with Germany to break the unequal armament of nations.

The unfavorable Japanese naval ratios, driven by an apparent conspiracy by the United States and Britain at the Washington and London Conferences, brought the Japanese navy, which was increasingly dissatisfied with the Washington Treaty System, closer to Germany. During 1939 and 1940, a period in which crucial events (the 1st Nankin Incident, Jinsn Incident, Marco Polo-Bridge Incident, 2nd Shanghai Incident, etc.) altered Japan's destiny, the pro-German faction, represented by those who had studied in Germany, became the driving force in the navy and had a large hand in Japan's decision to join with Germany in World War II.

---

[12] IMPERIAL NAVY INTELLIGENCE DIVISION, 'Why Anti-British Feeling Became Strong in Japan', in *Showa Shakai Keizaishi* [History of Social and Economic History of the Showa-Period], ed. O. TATUMASA (Daito Bunka Kenkyusho, 1989), vol. 6, pp. 133–4.

[13] 'Proposal to cooperate with Germany', in *Zoku Gendaishi Siryo (5) Kato Kanji Nitsuki* [Modern Historical Documents (5) Diary of Kato Kanji], ed. I. TAKASHI (Misuzu-Shobo, 1994), pp. 557–63.

The Miscalculations of Annulling the Anglo-Japanese Alliance

The termination of the Anglo-Japanese Alliance in August 1923 was a psychological blow to the Japanese. Japan was to remain without allies until the conclusion of the Tripartite Pact with Germany and Italy in 1940. Thus, independent armament increased the military, strengthened the voice of the military, and led Japan to become a country led by the military.

In concluding this paper, I would like to quote from two books, first Winston Churchill's *The Second World War: The Gathering Storm*.

> The United States made it clear to Britain that the continuance of her alliance with Japan, to which the Japanese had unctuously conformed, would constitute a barrier in Anglo-Japanese relations. Accordingly this alliance was brought to an end. The annulment caused a profound impression in Japan, and was viewed as the spurning of an Asiatic Power by the Western world. Many links were sundered which might afterwards have proved of decisive value to peace. At the same time, Japan could console herself with the fact that the downfall of Germany and Russia had, for a time, raised her to the third place among the world's naval Powers, and certainly to the highest rank. Although the Washington Naval Agreement prescribed a lower ratio of strength in capital ships for Japan than for Britain and the United States (five: five: three), the quota assigned to her was well up to her building and financial capacity for a good many years, and she watched with an attentive eye the two leading naval Powers cutting each other down far below what their resources would have permitted and what their responsibilities enjoined. Thus, both in Europe and in Asia, conditions were swiftly created by the victorious Allies which, in the name of peace, cleared the way for the renewal of war.[14]

Fredrick Moore, an American who served as adviser at the Japanese embassy in Washington, DC for fourteen years, attributed the outbreak of the Pacific War to the annulment of the Anglo-Japanese Alliance eighteen years before.

> I felt strongly that it was a mistake in foreign policy for the United States to press the British for a termination of their Alliance with Japan. The Alliance could not menace us. The charge that it could was, I thought, false ... The Japanese were shocked by its termination ... This was the beginning of the nation's turn toward independent action. ... It opened the way psychologically for cooperation with Germany. It is, I think, even probable that had the Alliance between permitted to continue there would have been enough restraint kept upon the Army by civilian and naval influence in Japan to prevent the alignment of Japan with the Axis Powers. Because of the Alliance with Britain, Japan took

---

[14] CHURCHILL W.S., *The Second World War: The Gathering Storm* (London, 1948), vol. 1, p. 13.

part in the First World War on the side of the Allies. I am sure the termination of it was a blunder on the part of our people and Government.[15]

The Japanese navy rose to be the third-largest navy by learning the idea of sea power from the "Blue Water" school, especially from the Royal Navy. But, under the influence of a strong continental political system and thinking from ancient China and Germany, co-prosperity with maritime countries was dropped in favour of a dream of "Great East Asian Co-Prosperity." Thus Japan fought against the maritime powers, the U.S.A. and U.K., and invited the tragedies of the Pacific War.

---

[15] PIGGOTT F.S.G., *Broken Thread – An autobiography* (Aldershot, 1950), p. 148.

The Sea in the Great War

AVNER OFFER is Chichele Professor Emeritus of Economic History at the University of Oxford, and a Fellow of All Souls College, Oxford, United Kingdom

ABSTRACT. *The role of the sea in the war is best understood in facilitating or denying food supplies to the combatants. The balance of power is presented here as a balance of energy. Coal, in which the allies were rich, multiplied human effort about forty times. Grain only multiplied human effort by 1.5. The allies were able to import food, and to send their men to war. The central powers (and Russia) did not realize that mobilizing their manpower threatened them with starvation. Submarine warfare was dangerous, but failed to reduce British food consumption.*

RÉSUMÉ. *Le rôle de la mer dans la guerre est mieux compris lorsqu'il est envisagé comme un moyen de faciliter ou d'empêcher l'approvisionnement des combattants. L'équilibre des puissances est ici présenté comme un équilibre des moyens énergétiques. Le charbon, dont les Alliés étaient riches, multipliait les efforts humains par environ 40. Le grain, quant à lui, ne le multipliait que par 1,5. Les Alliés étaient en mesure d'importer de la nourriture et d'envoyer leurs hommes au combat. Les puissances centrales - et la Russie - ne réalisèrent pas que la mobilisation de leur main d'oeuvre les menaçait de famine. La guerre sous-marine était dangereuse mais échoua à faire diminuer la consommation alimentaire britannique.*

.•.

Viewed from space in August 1914, the earth was a shimmering blue globe, clad in a mantle of saltwater. From that height, the war that had just broken out was contained in two slender bands, neither of them visible, the one running through Belgium and France, the other through the Eastern boundaries of Germany and Austro-Hungary. On the ground, for the combatants, the grey sea was a lifeline, either for their side or for the other. The problem was how to keep it open, or how to shut it down. Historians are divided about the role of the sea. Paul Kennedy regards it as a sideshow.[1] For Norman Friedman, however, "The First World War was above all a maritime war, not in the sense that most of the action was at sea, but rather in the sense that maritime realities shaped it."[2] We

---

[1] KENNEDY P., 'The War at Sea', in *The Cambridge History of the First World War*, ed. J.M. Winter, vol. 1 (Cambridge, 2014), pp. 321-48, 321.

[2] FRIEDMAN N., *Fighting the Great War at Sea: Strategy, Tactics and Technology* (Barnsley, UK, 2014), p. 12; also SONDHAUS L., *The Great War at Sea: A Naval History of the First World War* (Cambridge, 2014), p. 2.

concur. Once a quick decision on land eluded the combatants, the sea loomed increasingly larger, until, in the final two years, its massive, inert presence determined the outcome.

I

The international division of labour is where the sea becomes a factor in the war. Interdependencies reached like gossamer threads over the shipping routes, controlled by Morse-code signals over copper cables on the ocean floor. Britain's position as the leading economic power was underpinned by the energy windfall of rich deposits of coal opened up more than a century before. Its economy responded by reaching out beyond the seas for cotton to feed its factories, and for sugar, tea, wheat, butter and meat to feed to its workers. In return, British factories and shipyards exported manufactures and constructed the bottoms to carry the goods. For Britain in 1914 the existence of this trans-oceanic economy was at risk.

War is trying to get your way by force. Force is the application of energy. Hence war is an exchange of energy. This provides a novel framing for the conflict. Energy endowment may be classified into three categories: chemical high explosive energy, underground deposits of high-density fossil fuel and low-density renewable energy in the form of vegetable and animal products. Alfred Nobel was the foremost innovator and manufacturer of explosives in the world, and, in expiation, also the founder of a Nobel Peace Prize. In 1892 he said to his friend the peace activist Bertha von Stuttner, "My factories may put an end to war sooner than your congresses. The very day when two army corps can annihilate each other within one second, would not all civilised nations shrink back from a war and dismiss their troops?"[3] But high explosive was not explosive enough: the environment was vast enough to absorb it. It had two different uses, destruction and propellant. Due to instability, it had no other uses. In the larger scheme of things, and despite recurrent anxieties about shortages on both sides, high explosive was available to both of them, and thus was effectively cancelled out as a decisive factor, apart from its role in delivering a *coup de grâce* first to the weakened armies of Russia and then to the Central Powers.

Fossil fuels and renewables have different attributes, and cannot be substituted for each other. For simplicity, call them coal and grain, respectively. Both derive from the sun. Coal is the fossilized sunshine energy accumulated in carbon deposits over hundreds of millions of years, which (together with oil) represents most of the globe's energy savings. In contrast, grain energy has to be reproduced every year by tillage of vast tracts of land, applying sunshine to photosynthesis during several months of growth. The annual carry-over of

---

[3] NOBEL P., 'Alfred Bernhard Nobel and the Peace Prize', *International Review of the Red Cross* 83.842 (2001), 259–74, p. 266.

grain is small, and you cannot eat coal. But coal and grain enter into each other's production. Miners eat, and coal is fired to fabricate tools and machinery, to make fertilizer and to drive ships and locomotives. Oil had only just emerged as motive power, but at sea it already drove the most important fighting units: British battleships and German submarines.

Beyond the railheads, energy in wartime was muscle power, which converted grain, meat and potatoes into heat and motion, in horses, mules and men. On land, the critical military factor was still the number of bayonets. Power was counted in divisions of infantry. Numbers were decisive, and they had to be fed. Muscular effort was dissipated by the frictions of surface: terrain required energy to overcome it, especially when trussed with fortifications, flooding, trenches, barbed wire and contours.

Coal has a high energy density, i.e. it contains a great deal of energy per units of volume and weight; in fact, more than three times as much as dynamite.[4] In comparison, vegetable and animal renewables have very low energy content. A recent unit of measurement for energy density is the Energy Return on Investment (EROI). It is the number energy units obtained by sacrificing a single unit: e.g. how many barrels of oil can you extract by burning just one? For coal, under the very best conditions, the EROI in 2005 was as high as 80, while the EROI of Saudi Arabian oil was around 100 in 1930.[5] These are extreme figures, and about half those levels is more typical. EROI varies depending on the technology used, the quality of the source and its location. A simple proxy which captures similar ratios is how many people can be supported by those working to extract energy. For a self-sufficient energy economy like Britain's (which exported a surplus), a measure of this windfall was the proportion of the adult population working in coal mining. In 1911, this was about 4 per cent.[6] Each miner provided fossil energy for twenty-seven adults in the UK, and for about ten more overseas. The Allies were better endowed with coal than the Central Powers: in the course of the war, Britain alone used a little more coal than Germany and Austro-Hungary together, with France and Italy adding almost a third more and Russia another 20 per cent. United States' consumption during its two war years raised the Allied margin of superiority to nearly three to one, and this still leaves out Australia and Canada.[7] Other things being equal, then, the Central Powers were handicapped from the outset by an inferior fossil-fuel energy endowment.

In contrast to coal, the stock of grain has to be replenished every year. It has an EROI in low single figures. Even today, with inputs of oil energy for tillage,

---

[4] Wikipedia entries on gasoline and dynamite; Electropaedia, 'Energy Resources', in http://www.mpoweruk.com/energy_resources.htm [Accessed 14 February, 2015].

[5] HALL C.A.S. and DAY J.W., 'Revisiting the limits to growth after peak oil', *American Scientist* 97 (2009), 230-37; HALL C.A.S., LAMBERT J.G. and BALOGH S.B., 'EROI of different fuels and the implications for society', *Energy Policy* 64 (2014), 141-52.

[6] MITCHELL B.R., *British Historical Statistics* (Cambridge, 1988), p. 104.

[7] Correlates of War Project, *Material Capabilities Dataset: National Material Capabilities* (2005), in http://www.correlatesofwar.org/COW%20Data/Capabilities/nmc3-02.htm#data [Accessed 4 September 2014].

fertilizer, irrigation and haulage, the EROI of wheat in Pakistan is about three, and typical early modern yields may have been only slightly above one.[8] What this means is that in self-sufficient societies most of the labour effort is absorbed in growing food. It required a great deal of muscle power to produce muscle power. In Russia in 1910, more than 85 per cent of the population lived in settlements of fewer than five thousand.[9] They fed the country and left a good deal for export. If small towns are taken to be part of the rural infrastructure, that gives a rough EROI of 1.5, taking wheat exports into account.[10] Each country-dweller could feed only himself and another one-half of a person. On this measure, even the United States still had almost 60 per cent on the farm and in small towns. But the residue, the 40 per cent resident in towns, provided some 23.5 million adults free to do other things.

In agrarian societies, workers on the land could not be mobilised for war without reducing food supplies. So Russia (and Austro-Hungary, another agrarian empire with a rural and small-town proportion of 81.5 per cent) were destined to suffer severe and eventually disabling shortages in World War One. The EROI of grain could be enhanced with fossil energy inputs, and this was achieved further west, in Germany, France and Britain, with fertilizers, oilmeal cake and farm machinery, either produced at home or transported using coal. Hence the proportion of the rural population could be smaller than in the less-developed countries further east; it was about one-half in Germany in 1914. That was still a sufficiently large proportion for its partial withdrawal for military service to diminish food production at a time when fertilizer production was competing with high explosive and imports of food, feed and manures had largely stopped. In terms of calories consumed per head, Germany lost a pre-war nutritional surplus of about 20 per cent, pushing the ration down to the margin of physical efficiency, and below it in many cases.[11] Rye and wheat production both fell by some 50 per cent till 1917, and the harvest per hectare fell by about 35 per cent, suggesting a substantial contraction of the area under cultivation.[12] Even in Britain more than 30 per cent of the population lived in the countryside or in small towns, although the proportion of farmworkers in the adult population was only 4.5 per cent, i.e. about the same as coal-miners. The male population was not tied down by food production, and was able to deploy high-density energy at work and at home, or to go off and fight.

[8] PRACHA A.S. and VOLK T.A., 'An edible energy return on investment (EEROI) analysis of wheat and rice in Pakistan', *Sustainability* 3 (2011), 2358–2391; STANIFORD S., 'The Net Energy of Pre-Industrial Agriculture' (2010), in http://earlywarn.blogspot.co.uk/2010/03/net-energy-of-pre-industrial.html [Accessed 6 September 2014].
[9] BAIROCH P. and GOERTZ G., 'Factors of urbanization in the 19th-century developed-countries – a descriptive and econometric-analysis', *Urban Studies* 23 (1986), 285–305 (p. 288, table 3).
[10] O'CONNOR M.O., 'World Wheat Supplies 1865–1913', Woodrow Wilson School, Discussion Paper 12 (Princeton University, July 1970); OFFER A., *The First World War: An Agrarian Interpretation* (Oxford, 1989), p. 86.
[11] OFFER, *Agrarian Interpretation*, ch. 3.
[12] DAVIS L.E. and ENGERMAN S.L., *Naval Blockades in Peace and War: An Economic History since 1750* (Cambridge, 2006), p. 199, table 5.23.

For the Central Powers, self-sufficiency provided internal lines of communication and some operational flexibility, but it also carried a cost: a high proportion of men had to be left on the land, in a difficult trade-off between the short-term and the long-term. In initial battles, numbers counted, and farmworkers could be called up. But the longer the war lasted, and especially as it froze into stasis (at least on the Western front), ploughmen in uniform produced no food. Eventually the war was decided on the wheat fields as much as on the battlefields. All three of the main landlocked powers, Germany, Austria and Russia, suffered severe domestic shortages, which led directly to their collapse. The sea acted as a barrier, denying them access to imports.

For the Allies, the situation was the opposite. Despite Britain's commitment to the land war, it had the luxury of delaying conscription for more than a year. Even if it agonised over the deployment of men, it only required a small fraction for low-productivity farmwork, because production of low-energy-density food had long been outsourced overseas. Due to this international division of labour, Britain's "military participation ratio" was considerably lower. It mobilised proportionately fewer men than Germany in the fifteen to forty-nine age group (53 per cent vs 81 per cent, respectively). At 12.5 per cent, the proportion killed among men of that age in Germany was twice as high as in the UK.[13] The prairie farmers of the USA, Canada, Australasia and Argentina were not called up at the outset, and most of them never were; they continued to ship grain to Britain as before. Germany's pre-war share of transatlantic food imports could now go to France and Italy.

In a balance of energy, calories are the appropriate measure for the low-density kind. Before the war, Britain imported some 60 per cent of its food calories, and it continued to do so throughout the war, with a small increase in home supply during the last two years. Imported cereals made up some 30 per cent of total UK calorie supply during the war, which required high tonnages for transport: about five million tons a year of grain had to be carried to Britain. A loss of this magnitude could not be sustained for long. In the year of peak shipping destruction, some 3.8 million gross tons of shipping were lost. Now a million gross tons of shipping can carry much less than a million tons of grain. On the other hand, a ton of shipping can make several journeys. What this tells us is that the tonnage destroyed was of a similar order of magnitude to grain-carrying capacity; but that new construction and the reallocation of cargoes ensured that the actual amounts of grain carried were not greatly affected (Table 1).[14]

To import the low-density renewable energy required for a major industrial country required access to large endowments of land, and to workers willing to till it. The United Kingdom had built up a grain-supply chain in the decades before the war and was able to keep it going at the same pace throughout. France, although largely self-sufficient before the war, was able to access overseas supplies as well. Germany was importing about 15 per cent of its calories before

---

[13] WINTER J.M., *The Great War and the British People* (London, 1986), p. 75, table 3.4.
[14] DAVIS and ENGERMAN, *Naval Blockades*, p. 178, table 5.7 and p. 189, table 5.14.

Table 1. *UK food supply, 1909-1918, in billions of calories*

	1909–1913	1914	1915	1916	1917	1918
Imports	29.6	34.2	31.8	31.1	29.2	27.9
Of which cereals	14.0	16.3	15.0	16.5	16.6	15.2
Home supply	21.1	21.4	21.9	19.4	20.6	21.2
Total supply	50.7	55.6	53.7	50.5	49.8	49.1

Source: DEWEY P.E., 'Food production and policy in the United Kingdom, 1914–1918', *Transactions of the Royal Historical Society* 30 (1980), 71–89 (pp. 81, 88).

the war, but had only limited access to imports from contiguous neighbours to compensate for the decline of its own productive capacity.

These issues were contemplated before the war both in Britain and in Germany, by naval and military planners, and also in public debate. Provided that its own supply chains were not challenged, Britain had access to the requisite low-density energy and could prevent the sea-borne fraction of Germany's usual supply from reaching that country. Admiralty planners did not examine domestic production in Germany very closely: they were sure that the denial of imports would be decisive in itself, if the war lasted for long enough: a committee on "the Military Needs of the Empire" chaired by the Prime Minister, concluded its report in July 1909 with the words "a serious situation would be created in Germany owing to the blockade of its ports, and [...] the longer the duration of the war the more serious the situation would become".[15] The Director of Naval Intelligence had written a few months before that, "grass would sooner or later grow in the streets of Hamburg and wide-spread dearth and ruin would be inflicted".[16] Maurice Hankey, the staff officer at the centre of British war preparations, later recalled his thoughts at the outbreak of war: "The Germans, like Napoleon, might overrun the Continent; this might prolong the war, but could not affect the final issue, which would be determined by economic pressure. Hence, on that eventful night, I went to bed excited but confident."[17]

For Germany it was imperative to conclude the war quickly. British officers and officials also considered the mechanism of financial collapse, but there were no grounds to regard it even as potentially decisive – a country may not be able to feed its people, but it can always suspend contracts and print paper money, especially if it is not trading overseas. Nicholas Lambert's speculations to the contrary find little support in the sources, and make little sense.[18] In wartime, Germany was not short of money but often short of food. Germany was able to use its own currency to pay for imports, and built up a trade deficit of about

---

[15] OFFER, *Agrarian Interpretation*, p. 243.
[16] Ibid., p. 232.
[17] Ibid., p. 317.
[18] LAMBERT, N.A., *Planning Armageddon: British Economic Warfare and the First World War* (Cambridge, MA, 2012).

half a year's peacetime imports. Its wartime inflation was lower than that of the UK, France and Italy, and at the end of the war it still had a stock of about $535 million of gold, at pre-war rates of exchange.[19] Britain, whose financial system had a truly global reach, was more vulnerable to financial crisis, and the outbreak of war hit the City hard. But within a week the government had suspended debts and gold payments, and guaranteed outstanding bills, and finance went back to business.[20] A German lunge into France carried the risk that it might fail, with no fallback except for a defensive posture. If maritime encirclement impelled German planners into a short and decisive war, that was their inclination anyway – it had been the German style in warfare for decades. Maritime encirclement became critical only if the land campaign failed. Like its British counterpart, German planning took the denial of imports as given, but failed to consider the effect of losing so much of the rural labour force. British interdiction of German food supplies took some time to get going, but eventually played out more or less as expected.

Once the war broke out, maritime thinking moved down to the operational level. There were three such issues: (1) how to deploy naval units; (2) how to manage merchant shipping, or how to interdict it; (3) access and entitlement to overseas low-density renewable-energy supplies. Before the war, Britain was committed to naval superiority and was able, with some effort, to maintain it in home waters. But the country was falling behind in productive capacity, and its continued naval position could not rest on superior tonnage, speed and firepower alone. Smaller naval powers, Germany, France, Italy, Austria, Japan, Russia, the USA, constructed fleets for local dominance. British naval mobility could not deliver a decisive advantage on land, but with command of the sea, British forces could go anywhere, if ships were available (the British–French diversion at Salonika was held up and hampered by lack of shipping). Once landed, as in Gallipoli, they could hardly move beyond the beach. In narrow waters, shore batteries and naval mines dominated battleships. Eventually the dumb mine, laid out in sufficient quantities and in the right places, sank more tonnage than the big guns that embodied naval pride.[21]

In these circumstances, the prime mission of the Royal Navy was (to use a current American term) "force protection", i.e. to safeguard its primacy. Its mobility and firepower at sea could not contribute much to the decision on land. It kept most of its main fighting units ("capital ships") in the remote and fortified northerly redoubt of Scapa Flow, with some confidence that if the force was handled prudently, this "fleet in being" would remain in being. The escape of the battlecruiser *Goeben* to Turkey may have brought that country into the war, but was a fluke from an operational point of view. Clashes off South America

---

[19] HARDACH G., *The First World War, 1914-1918* (London, 1977), p. 172, table 22. OFFER, *Agrarian Interpretation*, p. 65.
[20] ROBERTS R., *Saving the City: The Great Financial Crisis of 1914* (Oxford, 2014).
[21] HALVORSEN P., 'The Development of Mines and Mine Warfare in the Fisher Era: 1900–1914' (M.Phil. thesis, Oxford University, 2000); FRIEDMAN, *Fighting the Great War at Sea*, ch. 15.

(Coronel and the Falklands) and even in the North Sea (Dogger Bank) made little operational difference, although they were useful for keeping the force on its mettle.

The German fleet followed the same strategy, with somewhat less justification. The ocean wave cannot be fortified. The scale of the distances and surfaces involved gave rise to difficulties in communication, coordination and deployment, and also opportunities for asymmetric warfare. The sea was contestable. Success also depended on doctrine, daring, management and skill, although for two societies at a similar level of development, capabilities largely cancelled out and a prior advantage (in the British case, in the stock of capital ships and geographic position) was not easy to overcome. But challenge was an option. Before the existence of radar and of effective aerial reconnaissance, a warship had to be seen in order to be detected. Visibility was often low in daylight, and non-existent at night: there were opportunities to evade contact or to find it, and also an incentive to do so, if only to discover whether German ships and seamanship had any tactical advantage, and to "learn by doing". The British Grand Fleet was a strategic asset, the German High Seas fleet only an operational one, which was more expendable. It carried out the occasional raid, and a substantial foray at Jutland, which suggested that the strategy of harassment might have been viable. On the other hand, it might be argued that naval skirmishing with Britain was unlikely to be decisive, and that keeping the High Seas fleet "in being" was the more prudent strategy. Whatever the options, that was what actually happened. A German "fleet in being" did have an operational purpose, mostly in denying the option of a landing in the North, of commanding the Baltic, and diverting British efforts into an expensive fleet. But the experience of Gallipoli suggests that opposed coastal landing was never a serious option, although supply lines from Sweden and Norway were important for Germany, and received adequate cover.

II

Merchant shipping was a distinctively British asset. Most merchant shipping was built in Britain, and about 40 per cent was owned there. Safeguarding passage was a precondition of Britain's oceanic economy. Three years before the war, Rudyard Kipling wrote,

> "But if anything happened to all you Big Steamers,
> And suppose you were wrecked up and down the salt sea?"
> "Why, you'd have no coffee or bacon for breakfast,
> And you'd have no muffins or toast for your tea."
> ...
> "Then what can I do for you, all you Big Steamers,
> Oh what can I do for your comfort and good?"

> "Send out your big warships to watch your big waters,
> That no one may stop us from bringing you food."[22]

Before the war it was envisaged in France and Germany (and feared in Britain) that they could threaten British supply chains by means of commerce-raiders, either naval cruisers or armed merchant ships; but the traffic was so vast that this method could not hope to dent it seriously so long as Britain had a powerful surface fleet. On the British side, a similar deployment using converted passenger liners as auxiliary cruisers (beyond the range of the German Fleet) was sufficient to interdict German imports.

If distance converts into time, this was much less of a barrier in 1914. Cable and wireless signals leapt over the oceans in an instant. Wireless appeared on fighting ships. But bandwith (the information transmitted per unit of time) was limited. Preparing and decrypting messages caused delay, and restricted communication to the point of incoherence at those times when it was needed most urgently. The Germans were ahead in systematic deployment of wireless, but this turned out to be a handicap, which gave them an excess of visibility. Radio chatter signalled to the Admiralty's Room 40 that something was afoot in Wilhelmshaven, and allowed the Grand Fleet to go to sea in good time.

The commerce-raiding submarine emerged rather suddenly as a potential game-changer. The story is well known: tactically, submarines were devastatingly effective against merchant ships. It took more than two years to bring them under control by the expedient of steaming in convoy, and by means of technical counter-measures. Sinkings were heavy, and reduced British food stocks at some times, but they did not seriously affect consumption of calories. Operationally, however, and in the absence of an overwhelming superiority, the submarine operation had not been adequately thought through in Germany and was ultimately self-defeating. It was a throw of the dice rather than a calculated choice, an expressive rather than an instrumental move, that inevitably challenged the United States and eventually drew that country into the conflict.

Importing in wartime raised the logistical problem of access, and the financial one of entitlement. Millions of tons of grain had to be carried for long distances. During the war, Britain also outsourced vital munitions production. Its pre-war assets provided it with substantial endurance, but as the war went on this maritime capital had to be maintained and extended, and so the issue of optimising its deployment became crucial. To minimise storage costs, before the war Britain maintained a "just in time" system in which most of the grain consumed in the country was stored in transit along the supply chain. Domestic reserves were small. In wartime, the mechanics of the supply chain presented novel but not decisive logistical problems. More than half the imported calories took the form of grain, and likewise with tonnage.[23] Over the previous five

---

[22] FLETCHER R.L. and KIPLING R., *A School History of England* (Oxford, 1911), pp. 235-6.
[23] Table 1 above, and BEVERIDGE W.H., *British Food Control* (London, 1928), table XX, facing p. 360.

decades or so, the cost of carriage had fallen sharply, and its regularity and predictability increased. Journeys were shortened in distance and time, and reliable timetables required smaller inventories. Steamers no longer depended on trade winds, and converged on the shortest routes.

The sea was also a social terrain. Wartime access to the ocean surface and to overseas granaries was governed by social conventions and institutions. In peacetime trans-oceanic exports from Britain took the form of manufactures, migration and services, the latter mostly as shipping and finance, but also intangibles like culture, institutional conventions and traditions, Imperial governance and sea power. Even in peacetime, the balance of trade was heavily against Britain: more imports than exports by value, with the difference made up in shipping, services and credit.

This daily mercantile interchange formed a web of familiarity and obligation, underpinned by a common language, conventions, routines, institutions and traditions. For sure, German shipping was everywhere, and its merchants competed keenly. But German and Austrian public awareness of the trans-oceanic realities was stifled by veils of language and imagination. Germany contributed little to the great flows of transatlantic emigration. In the late 19th century, it absorbed its own population growth and the migration from the countryside. The stream of migrants from the Habsburg empire to North America consisted of ethnic minorities either actively hostile to the crown or (like East European Jews) socially marginal. Had the Germans been able to steam unhindered in wartime, they might still have found it difficult to fill their holds for lack of finance, although the United States and Argentina might have continued to trade. Despite the influence of the Hamburg ship-owner Ballin at the imperial court, the landowners and generals who led Germany failed to perceive that commerce, not conquest, was the gateway to parity.

In wartime, the exchange of commodities and services which drove the international division of labour abated and Britain found it more difficult to balance its books. It could not fight a land war in Europe and keep industrial exports at pre-war levels. The contracts that underpinned British trade were of varying maturities, most of them no longer than the duration of an ocean voyage, but some of them, like the corporate bonds and sovereign debt held in London, on much longer terms. If imported grain could not be paid for with manufactures, it had to be paid for by promises, embodied in credit. But commercial trust was not a one-sided affair. Wartime opportunity was a powerful incentive on the supply side as well, in North America, Australasia and South America. Heavy prior investment (much of it British) had pre-committed their economies to staple exports.

Undersea cable had been in place for long enough to stimulate the development of the institutions and conventions that mediated payments by means of rolling contracts and short-term credits. With most of this trade taking place either in English-language jurisdictions or in a semi-dependent Argentina, exchange was carried out within the legal framework of English commercial law and analogues overseas. Another layer of governance was the gold-standard financial system (founded on the financial surplus of the City of London), which made it easy for money to flow across political boundaries even after settlement in gold was suspended. Within the empire, commitment to Britain was the rule in Canada, Australia and New Zealand. It was only controversial in South Africa, and to some extent in Quebec. The United States wavered: even if it wanted to avoid any military entanglements, it had a big stake in trade.

It is a testimony to the value of reputation that Britain continued to import for more than two years before it approached its financial limits. It converted its stock of overseas financial assets into commodity flows by the gradual surrender of ownership of the overseas export infrastructure, selling off securities to obtain supplies and taking on commercial debt to the limits regarded as prudent by North American bankers. Just as these lines of credit began to dry up (in the early months of 1917) the sea opened up again. German submarine attacks tipped the American government into war. Nothing else would have done so. And once governments entered war, the limits of private lending no longer held. Exports were financed by sovereign debt, with guaranteed prices for farmers and lending to the European allies.

As soon as the war ended, the sovereign lender (the United States) assumed the manner of a private banker, cut off credits and insisted on full repayment. It was able to do so because the oceanic moat appeared to insulate American society from the political consequences. This insistence on repayment can be seen as a preference for the interests of finance over those of everyone else, a policy trope long familiar in Britain, and much in evidence since. International debt, however, stood in the way of a viable peace. At Versailles, the Allies attempted to fill the financing gap with reparations from Germany. Australia had been prevented by the "tyranny of distance" from taking full advantage of wartime export opportunities, but had sacrificed its share of troops. With no claim for physical restitution, its insistence on including war pensions in the bill (always a large element in war expenditure) hardened the Allied position against Keynes's counsel for moderating the demands on Germany.

The twenty-year crisis which followed was dominated by the unrepayable debt of the European combatants and an excess of productive capacity beyond the ocean. This condemned the world economy to stagnation and depression, and eventually to another World War. That war also reached back across the ocean and pulled in the United States. Once again, American participation was triggered by the interdiction of ocean trade, this time in the Pacific rather the Atlantic, with the United States provoking and Japan provoked. The wartime boom which followed pulled the United States out of depression and underpinned its subsequent global hegemony – naval, military, financial, mercantile and political.

The Mediterranean and World War I

PAUL G. HALPERN is Professor Emeritus in Modern History at the Florida State University, United States

ABSTRACT. *The British, French and later Italian control of the Mediterranean was threatened by the surface fleets, and even more by the submarines of Austria-Hungary, Germany and Turkey. In the end these threats were contained, but the overall allied victory, and the survival of three overseas empires, depended on retaining control of the Mediterranean.*

RÉSUMÉ. *Le contrôle de la Méditerranée par les britanniques, les français puis les italiens risquait d'être mis à mal par les flottes de surface, voire même davantage par les forces sous-marines, austro-hongroises, allemandes et turques. Ces menaces furent au final écartées mais la victoire alliée dans son ensemble, ainsi que la survie de trois empires coloniaux, dépendirent du maintien de leur contrôle sur la Méditerranée.*

．•．

The Mediterranean on the outbreak of war was the scene of intense rivalries. The sea was a vital link for the British Empire as it was the route to the Suez Canal and onward communications with India, the Far East, Australia and the newly developed oil resources in Persia. The Mediterranean route was also the most important one for the export of British manufactured goods. The British also controlled two of the major entrances to the Mediterranean at Gibraltar and the Suez Canal and had a centrally located base at Malta. For the French the Mediterranean was a link with their North African possessions and colonies in Asia and the Indian Ocean. Furthermore, security in the Mediterranean was essential for the French mobilization scheme, which included the transfer of the XIXe army corps to metropolitan France to join the anticipated battles along France's eastern frontier with Germany. The Italians saw the Mediterranean as a link with their newly won footholds in Libya and the Dodecanese as well as the route to Gibraltar and the Atlantic. In 1914 Austria-Hungary had control of much of the eastern shores of the Adriatic and had traditional interests in trade with the Eastern Mediterranean and the Levant. Moreover, the Austro-Hungarian Navy – the *K.u.K. Kriegsmarine* – was a new and disturbing factor in the Mediterranean naval balance of power. In the first decade of the 20th century the Austrians began to build more modern and powerful warships, including

Dreadnought-class battleships, the standard of strength at the time. Austrian resources ensured that they would be small in number – only four in the first program – but their existence opened a disturbing possibility. Italy and Austria might have been traditional rivals in the Adriatic but they were also allied with Germany in the Triple Alliance. If they combined their fleets there was the possibility of achieving naval superiority over the French.

The Anglo-French Entente of 1904 reflected a rapprochement between these two historic rivals in the face of the perceived German menace and created a situation in which, without any formal agreement, the British would look after the North Sea and the French would handle affairs in the Mediterranean. This also implied that the British would prevent any German move against the northern French coast. But would the French fleet alone be strong enough to face a possible Austro-Italian combination? The British sought to ensure that it would by leaving enough strength in the Mediterranean so that when added to the French forces they would prevail.

The Austrian–Italian combination came close to reality in 1913 with the conclusion of a secret Triple Alliance naval convention, brokered by the Germans. The Italians, with a long exposed coastline and overseas possessions to protect, felt terribly exposed, and to induce the Austrians to risk their precious battle fleet outside of the Adriatic even agreed for the initial period to an Austrian admiral as commander-in-chief of the combined fleets which on the outbreak of war would concentrate in Sicilian waters at Augusta. The Austrians and Italians would be joined by whatever German warships might be in the Mediterranean. This added a complication, for, as a result of the Balkan Wars, 1912–1913, the Germans established the *Mittelmeerdivision*, a permanent naval force in the Mediterranean. This consisted of the new battle cruiser *Goeben* and the fast light cruiser *Breslau*. Of course combinations on paper are one thing and how well the Austrian and Italian fleets would have acted in concert without much mutual training is an open question. Nevertheless, on the eve of the World War there was every expectation that the Mediterranean might be the scene of a major clash at sea.

It all turned out very differently. The Triple Alliance naval convention became a dead issue with the decision of the Italian government to remain neutral on the outbreak of the war. The German cruisers might have constituted a threat to the French troop convoys, since the *Goeben* was faster than any of the French ships powerful enough to engage her. This meant that the primary concern of the French commander-in-chief was protection of the convoys, and pursuit of the Germans was initially left to the British forces, which included battle cruisers capable of matching the *Goeben*. It was anticipated that the Germans would attempt to join the Austrian fleet in the Adriatic, and the Austrian fleet sailed southwards in the Adriatic to facilitate the junction. The German commander elected to make for the Dardanelles instead and succeeded in eluding British forces. The arrival of the *Goeben* and *Breslau* in Turkish waters was followed by their ostensible transference to the Ottoman Navy and may have had important repercussions for Turkey's decision to enter the war on the side of the Central

Powers. The trade in grain and other Russian products from Black Sea ports was therefore cut off from the Mediterranean. This did not alter the fact that in the Mediterranean as a whole the British and French were not challenged. The Austrian fleet remained in a position of inferiority in the face of the British and French forces and was destined to remain bottled up in the Adriatic, carefully watching the Italians in a correct appreciation that Italy would eventually enter the war on the opposite side. Austria-Hungary's maritime trade with the Eastern Mediterranean and outlet to the remainder of the world was closed. The initial lack of a serious challenge in the Mediterranean meant that the British, with their primary concern the German fleet in the north or Germans surface raiders loose on the high seas, were content to conclude an agreement with the French giving the French naval command in the Mediterranean.

The creation of an Austrian battle fleet had been a matter of controversy in the Habsburg monarchy before the war. What did a land power like Austria-Hungary need with a battle fleet? The Hungarians were notably hard to convince. Yet it might be claimed that the small but relatively powerful Austrian navy justified its existence as a "fleet-in-being." It may have been hopelessly outclassed in the Mediterranean but within the narrow confines of the Adriatic it served to increase the potential costs to an aggressor. Anyone operating inside the Adriatic had to face a potential encounter with powerful ships. The technological advances available to the Austrians included a small force of submarines. Consequently, the French found it too dangerous to risk their own capital ships in the Adriatic. This meant that the potentially vulnerable Habsburg possessions along the Dalmatian coast on the eastern shores of the Adriatic were unmolested for most of the war. The situation did not really change when Italy entered the war on the Allied side, adding even more weight to the Anglo-French superiority. The Austrian and Italian naval forces tended to check each other, conducting their own unique naval war primarily with light forces, but one confined to the Adriatic. The Italians were reinforced in blocking the Otranto Straits by French and British light forces at Brindisi.

British and French trade flowed freely through the Mediterranean during the first half-year of the war. The vital British route to the Suez Canal and France's communications with its North African possessions were undisturbed and the Allies were also free to employ their sea power for military purposes. Naval forces helped to defeat a Turkish thrust through the Sinai Desert against the Suez Canal. The canal enabled the British to move forces into the Persian Gulf to secure the oil fields, although this would subsequently evolve into an expensive and controversial campaign in Mesopotamia. The most important Allied use of naval superiority was the attempt to force the Dardanelles and bring the Ottoman capital, Constantinople, under the guns of Allied warships, open maritime communications with southern Russia, and, it was hoped, knock Turkey out of the war. A purely naval assault failed in March 1915, turning the expedition into a combined operation which, after successfully establishing a beachhead, was ultimately checked. After several months the Allied forces were evacuated, notably after Bulgaria's entry into the war on the side of Germany and Austria led to the over-running of Serbia, the opening of direct rail communications between Germany and the Turks and the beginning of a new Anglo-French commitment in maintaining a perimeter around Salonika.

The Dardanelles expedition had unexpected but unfortunate consequences for the Allies in the Mediterranean. It was a major cause of the arrival of German submarines. The hard-pressed Turks had asked their Austrian and German allies for some form of naval assistance or diversion. The Austrians, aware that their former ally Italy was moving towards entry into the war on the Anglo-French side, had previously resisted proposals to send their battle fleet to Turkish waters, a move that would have created major and probably insoluble logistical difficulties. Their small submarine force also lacked the technical capabilities to respond to the Turkish request. It was left to the Germans to act. They initially sent small, partially assembled submarines by rail to the Austrian base at Pola and also sent a larger submarine through the Gibraltar Straits. Once the latter had been proven to be feasible other submarines followed. The Germans initially operated off the Dardanelles and scored major successes which greatly complicated Anglo-French activities. The Germans also realized that, just as in northern waters, submarines could cause major damage to merchant shipping. The German naval staff, in justifying, its arguments to transfer more submarines from operations around the British Isles to the Mediterranean, claimed that 99 percent of British imports of tea and jute, 75 percent of rice, 73 percent of hemp, 70 percent wool, 65 percent of gasoline, 52 percent of manganese, and 51 percent of rubber came via the Suez Canal. Furthermore, diversion of traffic around the Cape of Good Hope meant a considerable delay in voyages and subsequent reduction in carrying capacity. The Italians were also dependent on British shipping for their coal supplies once their sources in central Europe had been cut off.

During the war the Germans steadily increased the number of their submarines operating in the Mediterranean. By the late spring of 1917 there were close to thirty. They used the Austrian naval bases at Pola and in the Gulf of Cattaro, the latter conveniently located near the entrance to the Mediterranean through the Otranto Straits. The Austrians also built submarines of their own, mostly German designs built under license. Nevertheless it was difficult to create a submarine-building industry in the midst of the war and the number of Austrian submarines capable of operating outside of the Adriatic remained small. The Austrian submarines generally worked in the Eastern Mediterranean.

The Mediterranean proved an excellent area for submarines to operate. There were many targets, certain choke points through which traffic had to pass, the weather was on the whole better than in northern waters and the British, French and Italians tended to pursue their own interests. Italy initially did not declare war against Germany and German submarines as a result should not have been able to attack ships under the Italian flag. The Germans surmounted this problem by, in agreement with their Austrian allies, adopting a classic *ruse de guerre*. German submarines when attacking Italian ships operated under Austrian colors. To preserve the fiction in case disputes over shipping losses wound up in a prize court, the Austrians agreed that German submarines were entered into the Austrian naval list – retroactively if necessary – the moment they passed through the Gibraltar Straits into the Mediterranean. In 1915 and 1916 the Mediterranean had another advantage in that ships under the United States flag were less likely to be encountered and consequently there would be fewer diplomatic complications with a powerful neutral.

The Allied strategies for countering the submarine through hunting groups or patrols proved faulty. In March 1916 the Allies at a conference held at Malta agreed to divide the Mediterranean into zones, with each nation assigned specific zones of responsibility. Masters of merchant ships would be advised to follow secret patrolled routes, frequently changed, within those zones. Unfortunately, submarines continued to have little difficulty in discovering unprotected ships within the zones. The attempt by the British to block the Otranto Straits with trawler patrols and mine-net barrages proved equally unsuccessful. By mid-March 1916 the German submarine operations had also partially achieved one of the naval staff's goals. As of 15 March British traffic proceeding to and from Atlantic ports to the Far East or Australia would be diverted to the Cape route, although traffic to India would continue to use the Mediterranean.

The amount of tonnage sunk by submarines in the Mediterranean rose sharply in 1916. In July and August Kapitänleutnant von Arnauld de la Perière in *U.35* conducted the most successful patrol of the war, sinking a total of fifty-four steamers and sailing craft representing over 90,150 tons. The Mediterranean U-boat flotilla in August 1916 sank 129,368 tons out of a total of 156,918 tons sunk in all theaters. The continued high losses forced the British in December 1916 to divert more shipping to the Cape route, notably ships bound for Burma and the east coast of India. The British by the end of the year were understandably disillusioned by the system introduced at Malta and proposed abandonment of the fixed routes in favor of dispersion. There were some British officers who now looked to convoys, but the proposals at this stage were put aside, largely because of a perceived lack of suitable craft for convoy escorts. The French, however, insisted on retention of the fixed routes. The result was a compromise solution adopted by a naval conference in London in January 1917. The two systems would undergo a trial with fixed routes retained for traffic to and from Salonika and the Aegean and dispersion between Cap Bon and Port Said for all British ships and any others that cared to join them. In the western Mediterranean ships would use coastal waters as much as possible, with ships making for French and Italian ports using neutral Spanish waters. The compromise at least partially reflected France's major interest in sustaining its forces at Salonika.

The crisis of the submarine war began in February 1917 when the Germans elected to gamble that unrestricted submarine warfare could bring the Allies to their knees before potential American intervention could have any effect. The losses due to submarines or submarine-laid mines in the Mediterranean rose sharply and reached a record 254,911 tons in the month of April. The Italians, as the Germans had anticipated, were particularly vulnerable because of their reliance on shipping to ensure adequate coal supplies. As early as the beginning of 1917 the Italians were warning that a shortage of coal might curtail production of ammunition. The situation grew worse because coal shortages restricted the distribution of supplies by rail throughout the Italian peninsula. In September the Italian chief of naval staff claimed that three-quarters of Italian trains were no longer running and the Italians were growing increasingly dependent on coastal shipping to distribute supplies. The lack of coal also meant that Italian coastal shipping was dependent on sail, subject to the vagaries of wind and weather. The British were forced to shift some shipping back from the Cape route to meet the Italian crisis.

Anti-submarine warfare required large numbers of small craft. The numbers available to the French and Italians were relatively limited. They tried to remedy this by purchasing craft abroad, notably Japan. The French also had an entire class of twelve destroyers built in Japan. It was the British, however, who had the largest supply of suitable craft as well as relatively more of the men to man them. Their Allies did not. A survey of Allied resources for the protection of maritime traffic in May 1917 showed the number of ships suitable for escort and patrol to be: British, 179; French, 153; Italian, 47. The result was that while they were initially willing to concede command in the Mediterranean to the French, the British increasingly found that they had to take more and more responsibility for the anti-submarine war themselves. The French and Italians combined would have been quite able to handle threats from surface warships, notably the Austrian fleet. However, the danger was not from surface warships but, rather, from submarines. In the crisis, with both fixed routes and dispersion discredited, the Allies met at Corfu at the end of April and moved towards a convoy system. It was limited at first, with ships in convoy from Gibraltar to Oran, following patrolled coastal routes from Oran to Bizerte and then formed into convoys for the remainder of the voyage to the Eastern Mediterranean. Ships bound for Marseilles or Genoa would continue to use Spanish territorial waters. However, if the Germans decided not to respect the latter, the ships would be formed into convoys from Algiers or Bizerte for the voyage northwards across the Mediterranean. All traffic from the Atlantic to ports east of Aden would proceed via the Cape route, except for ships necessary to support the British expeditions in Egypt and Mesopotamia. Furthermore, a "Direction Générale" was established at Malta. This consisted of representatives of the Allied navies and would coordinate transport routes and their protection. The British, in turn, placed their scattered Mediterranean forces under a single commander. The result was that while the French remained nominally in command in the Mediterranean it was the British who really took charge of the anti-submarine war.

The introduction of the convoy system proved to be the method that eventually reduced losses to submarines to tolerable proportions. There continued to be spikes during certain months and there would be painful events for the remainder of the war. The trend, however, was down. The Germans and their Austrian allies would not win the submarine war. The convoy systems were steadily expanded, the British controlling the east–west convoys (except for a jointly controlled Milo–Alexandria convoy) and the French controlling north–south convoys from French North Africa to metropolitan ports. In October 1917 the British were able to begin through convoys between Great Britain and Port Said. This permitted trade with India being shifted back from the Cape to the Suez Canal, with a considerable savings in tonnage. The through-Mediterranean convoys required a high degree of coordination, for the sloops and escort vessels did not have the range to make the entire trip and reliefs from Malta had to take place mid-way.

The naval war in the Mediterranean became even more cosmopolitan after the United States entered the war. In 1918 the Americans joined the effort to bottle up German and Austrian submarines in the Adriatic. They had developed 110-foot wooden-hulled craft dubbed "submarine chasers" that were really too slow and small for work in the Atlantic. They were, however, well suited for work in the Straits of Otranto, where they hunted in groups of three, employing hydrophones to detect and fix submarines which would then be destroyed by depth charges. Despite high hopes, they were generally ineffective. The Americans also contributed to the anti-submarine forces working out of Gibraltar. Here there were a heterogeneous collection of older warships, unsuited for any major encounter but able to escort ships between Gibraltar and southern French or Italian ports. The other naval force not normally found in the Mediterranean was Japanese. The Japanese had entered the war in 1914 but seemed mainly concerned with gobbling up German possessions in Asia. They had refused to send major warships to European waters, but with the submarine crisis at its height agreed to contribute a flotilla of a dozen destroyers accompanied by an old cruiser as mother ship. They insisted, however, on working solely with the British, escorting convoys between Malta and Suez. Australian destroyers and Canadian motor launches also joined the Allies at the entrance to the Adriatic. After Greece entered the war on the Allied side Greek light forces joined in operations in the Aegean and Eastern Mediterranean. The Allied naval forces would have become even more cosmopolitan when Brazil decided to send a naval force to Gibraltar, although for a number of reasons these forces arrived only in the closing days of the war.

Could the Allied superiority in surface warships have been used offensively after the end of the Dardanelles campaign? The answer is not effectively. The narrow waters of the Adriatic remained too dangerous for large ships. The Austrians conducted a successful raid on the light forces maintaining the Otranto blockade in May 1917. It was the largest encounter between surface ships in the Mediterranean during the war, but it was just a raid. When the Austrians tried a more ambitious action with heavy warships in June 1918 they lost one of their precious dreadnoughts. There were occasional plans for French operations in the Adriatic but it was always a case that troops could be used more effectively elsewhere. The French high command preferred the Western Front. The British and French navies supported the overseas expeditions in Egypt, Palestine and Macedonia. In 1916 a miscellaneous collection of converted British small craft conducted cattle raids along the Anatolian coast, operations which had a minimal effect on the war. The Americans in 1918 had serous plans to seize the Sabbioncello peninsula on the Dalmatian coast. The great German offensive in the spring of 1918 meant the troops were diverted to the Western Front. The Americans also had proposals for extensive mine barrages, including one between Sicily and Cap Bon.

Given the large Allied superiority in surface warships, it is odd then to learn that in the winter and spring of 1918 the allies were actually worried about their naval position in the Eastern Mediterranean. The reason for this was the collapse of Russia and the advance by the Central Powers deep into Russian territory, which resulted in their occupation of the major Russian naval base in the Black Sea at Sevastopol. This raised fears that the Germans and their Turkish and Austrian allies would gain possession of the Russian Black Sea Fleet. The Russians had enjoyed naval superiority in the Black Sea for most of the war. Now their powerful fleet in whole or part might fall into German hands. There were fears that some of the most powerful units might be employed to break out of the Dardanelles, overwhelm the obsolete British and French warships in the Eastern Mediterranean and threaten Allied lines of communication. There was a warning of what might occur in January 1918 when the German-manned battle cruiser *Goeben* and light cruiser *Breslau* sortied from the Dardanelles and sank two British monitors. However, the *Breslau* was mined and sunk and the Germans were lucky not to lose the *Goeben*, which was badly damaged.

Were the Allied fears irrational? The French fleet alone should have sufficed to handle the situation. However, the major units of the French fleet were concentrated at Corfu, guarding against the possibility that the Austrians might seek to come out of the Adriatic. The combined French and Italian forces enjoyed considerable superiority but the Italians insisted on French assistance, since they did not have what they considered to be a sufficient margin of superiority over the Austrians. However, the Italians regarded the Adriatic as their sea and insisted on command of operations. The French, not surprisingly, were reluctant to put their larger force under Italian command. The result was a considerable waste of resources, two fleets watching for the unlikely circumstance that the Austrians would come out. This left seemingly weaker forces to face the potential threat in the Aegean. The Allies never achieved the unity of command in the Mediterranean that they did on the Western Front during the crisis caused by Ludendorff's offensive in 1918. The British made a serious attempt to do so and nominated Admiral Jellicoe, former commander of the Grand Fleet and former First Sea Lord to be a Mediterranean *admiralissimo* in a position analogous to that of Marshal Foch on the Western Front. The proposal failed, largely due to open Italian and covert French opposition. The French eventually sent a number of their older pre-dreadnoughts to the Aegean and this gave them a sufficient margin of superiority to claim command of the combined Allied squadron. It was one of the few instances in the war when British ships actually operated under French command, although preliminary maneuvers indicated that much practice would have been necessary to achieve efficiency.

The crisis in the Aegean and Eastern Mediterranean never materialized and demonstrated the folly of merely counting numbers of ships. The threat of the

Russian Black Sea Fleet proved to be a mirage. The Russians managed to get some of their ships away when the Germans advanced on the major naval base of Sevastopol and scuttled others, including a dreadnought. The Germans and their allies wound up with few ships in a condition to be used and even fewer potential crews. At this stage of the war it was hard for them to find the necessary men and difficult to restore ships to fighting condition under the circumstances prevailing at Sevastopol. In the end they put only a handful of ships into service, the largest a former Russian dreadnought, destined to serve as a floating battery at the Dardanelles.

In the last month of the war the Allied forces at Salonika under General Franchet d'Esperey began a successful offensive and forced the Bulgarians to conclude an armistice. While the French and Serbians concentrated on moving north, the British intended to move along the northern shores of the Aegean towards Constantinople. These forces had naval support on their seaward flank. They also dispatched two dreadnoughts to the scene, giving them sufficient naval force to justify reclaiming command in the Aegean. Once again they had been willing to leave command to the French, but when it really mattered found the strength to reclaim it for themselves. Furthermore, they concluded the armistice of Mudros with the Ottoman Empire largely to the exclusion of the French admiral in the Aegean. It was a British admiral who led the Allied naval forces through the Dardanelles to anchor off Constantinople.

The submarines remained a menace to the very end. After the Habsburg monarchy concluded an armistice the Germans evacuated their submarines from the Adriatic. They scuttled those not fit to sail but Allied efforts to block the Otranto and Gibraltar Straits were unsuccessful. It was, however, a hollow success, for Germany too was quickly forced to conclude an armistice, and under the peace terms her submarines were forfeit. With the dissolution of the Habsburg monarchy Austria ceased to be a maritime power. The brief moment when the Austro-Hungarian fleet was a potential naval factor was over. The major port of Trieste and naval base at Pola fell into Italian hands. The successor state on the eastern shores of the Adriatic, the Kingdom of Croats, Serbs and Slovenes, later Yugoslavia, would lack the means to develop a strong navy. The bulk of the surviving Austrian merchant marine came under the Italian flag.

The Mediterranean during the First World War was not the scene of major encounters between rival fleets as it had been in previous centuries. The action at sea was centered on the assault by submarines on trade routes and lines of communication. However, the successful defence of those routes was of crucial importance to the Allies; had they failed it could have cost them the war.

Germany in World War One: Naval Strategy and Warfare

WERNER RAHN is a Captain (ret.) of the German Navy and freelance researcher and lecturer in Military and Naval History, Germany

ABSTRACT. *German plans for the High Seas Fleet on the outbreak of war rested on highly unrealistic assumptions. When these proved false, the fleet did little or nothing. Neither army nor navy contemplated joint action. Only the unexpected success of submarines seemed to offer hope of victory at sea, but that chance was thrown away by confused and irrational decisions based on political and psychological rather than strategic factors.*

RÉSUMÉ. *Lorsque la guerre éclata, les plans de l'Allemagne pour sa flotte de guerre (NDLT « Hochseeflotte ») ne reposaient que sur des présomptions profondément irréalistes. Lorsque celles-ci s'avérèrent fausses, la flotte ne fit rien ou très peu. Ni la marine ni l'armée n'envisagèrent une action conjointe. Seul le succès inattendu des sous-marins souleva l'espoir d'une victoire en mer, mais cette opportunité fut anéantie par des décisions confuses et irrationnelles, basées sur des facteurs psychologiques et politiques plutôt que stratégiques.*

.•.

In October 1910 Tirpitz argued in an audience with Kaiser Wilhelm II that German naval policy had to aim at strengthening the German fleet to such an extent that

> an attack would mean a great risk for Great Britain. This risk constitutes the basis of the imperial position of the German Reich and the peace-securing effect of our fleet. If the British fleet can achieve and maintain a permanent and structural strength sufficient to attack the German Reich without risk, then the fleet development was a historical mistake and Your Majesty's naval policy [*Flottenpolitik*] a historical fiasco.[1]

This estimate became a reality almost four years later. During the July crisis of 1914 the anticipated deterrent effect of the High Seas Fleet (HSF) turned out to be a miscalculation, since Great Britain, relying on the superiority of its fleet and

---

[1] TIRPITZ, A. VON, *Der Aufbau der deutschen Weltmacht* (Stuttgart and Berlin, 1924), p. 182.

its worldwide strategic positions, did not regard the German fleet as an unpredictable risk for the security of its sea lines of communication.

The High Seas Fleet: from a failed deterrent to a fleet-in-being

In August 1914 the German Imperial Navy was under the spell of the great material superiority of the enemy. In the North Sea alone the Royal Navy had twenty-six modern capital ships (battleships and battle cruisers) compared to only eighteen equally modern units of the German Navy. The British superiority in older ships of the line as well as cruisers and torpedo boats was even more striking. Only with respect to ocean-going submarines did the German Navy with twenty-eight units outnumber the Royal Navy, which had only eighteen comparable units plus forty small coastal submarines. The force ratio of capital ships became even more unfavourable for Germany when four British battle cruisers changed station from the Mediterranean and/or overseas to their home sea territories and the Royal Navy commissioned seven more capital ships. In contrast, the HSF did not get more than five new capital ships until early 1915.

In view of this situation, the German Naval Command placed all its hopes on a reduction of enemy forces through offensive submarine and mine-laying operations. Then, the fleet was to be employed in a battle "under favourable conditions", still assuming that the opponent would seek battle as well.

The most important weapon in the intended guerilla war at sea was to be the mine. With this strategic concept, the Navy focused on a means of naval warfare for which those in the lead had so far not been adequately prepared. The information on the opponent's planned deployment was insufficient, and the available number of mines and the mine-laying capacities were inadequate for a far-reaching offensive. Most of the barriers did not have the operational effects hoped for. By the end of 1914 the Grand Fleet had lost only one capital ship to a mine. On the other hand, the far-reaching submarine offensive proved more successful and led to a new appreciation of this weapon system on both sides.

Only when it became clear that the balance of forces was not going to change in their favour did the Germans debate other operational possibilities for the fleet. Plans for longer-range and thus more dangerous sorties were opposed by the Kaiser, who was the Commander-in-Chief. He considered the HSF more and more a factor of political power that was to be kept combat-ready until peace had been achieved. These thoughts were undoubtedly based on the hope that the question of winner or loser would be resolved by the army before long. What was remarkable already in this first phase of the war was that Germany had no grand strategy for coordinating all its forces.

While the Army went for a decision in the west on the River Marne and was confronted by the strong British expeditionary corps, the HSF did nothing to support the Army by exercising pressure on the Allied lines of supply in the

English Channel. There were no synchronized Army and Navy operational plans, which would at least have taken the reciprocal relationship into account.

The concept of a decisive battle in the North Sea had inevitable consequences for the Baltic, which right from the beginning was rated a secondary theatre of war. The operation order of 31 July 1914 called for intercepting any Russian offensive, securing the Kiel Bight and damaging enemy trade. It is striking that this order contains no hint how to secure friendly lines of communication, especially since the German armaments industry relied on an undisturbed ore supply from Sweden.

Since the Kiel Canal allowed for a quick shift of naval units on internal lines, the HSF looked from the North Sea like a fleet-in-being, and thus constituted in the years to come a potential threat which was always present but difficult to estimate. To prevent British naval forces from penetrating into the Baltic, Denmark was requested to block the straits after the war had started. Denmark complied and installed the desired mine barriers, which were supplemented by German barriers. This precipitate closure of the straits was a strategic mistake, which in the long run had more disadvantages than advantages. By foregoing the use of the straits for raids Germany limited its naval opportunities and improved the situation of the enemy. The option of a HSF raid from the Kattegat/Skagerrak would always have kept the British Naval Command in suspense.

When it became evident at the turn of the year (1914/15) that England could not be defeated by a decisive battle in the North Sea, naval opinion could not agree whether to shift the centre of activities to the Baltic. Commander Wolfgang Wegener, the staff officer of HSF/First Squadron, attributed the German strategic dilemma primarily to the geographically unfavourable position and therefore pleaded for more naval activity in the Baltic. His squadron commander, Vice-Admiral Lans, took up this idea in February 1915 and emphasized that the main value of the HSF in the North Sea was as a "fleet in being", but in the Baltic it could maintain German supremacy, protecting supplies coming from Sweden, blocking Allied deliveries to Russia and preventing enemy landings anywhere on the German coast. Lans compared the strategic situation of Russia in the Baltic with the German situation in the North Sea, and therefore urged shifting the main assets of the fleet to the east, but the Naval Command continued to focus on the North Sea. The lack of a central naval command with authority over all naval forces in the various operational theatres made such a strategic shift very difficult.

The discussion on employment of the fleet was soon eclipsed by the controversy about the submarine war. Submarine warfare against the British sea lines of communication was a new naval strategy which logically had consequences for the employment and structure of the HSF. Instead, the Naval Command operated by a "system of half measures" and without clear focus: on the on hand, commerce raiding by U-boats, on the other, fleet activities in the North Sea under the motto "something must be done with the fleet, but nothing must happen to it".

After ports on the British east coast had been bombarded twice in November and December 1914, the British had to expect further offensive raids threatening their coasts and North Sea lines of communication. But, being in possession of the German radio code, they were able to intercept the German battle cruisers with superior forces at the Dogger Bank on 24 January 1915; in this action the armoured cruiser *Blücher* was lost. The commander-in-chief of the fleet, Admiral von Ingenohl, was relieved for inadequate preparation of the sortie. His successor, Admiral von Pohl, made a total of seven shorter sorties in 1915, which had no strategic impact and did not even make contact with the enemy.

When Vice Admiral Scheer took over command of the HSF in January 1916, he developed no new concept for employment of the fleet, since he wanted at all costs to avoid a battle with the Grand Fleet. The only difference from the former doctrine was that Scheer planned to make farther sorties towards the British coast to achieve partial success if possible.

Within reach of the HSF were the British homeland, the sea routes linking Scandinavia and Scotland, and the English Channel. Sporadic bombardments of the coasts were, however, nothing but pinpricks that could irritate the opponent but not seriously threaten it. This also applied to the interruption of the sea routes linking Scandinavia and Scotland, which had no vital importance for Britain. In the end, only the Channel in its function as supply line for the Allied powers was a strategic objective worth attacking; but that would have required common strategic planning and close cooperation with the Army on the basis of an overall strategy.

All war experience had shown that concentrating the forces and establishing points of main effort were the basic prerequisites to secure success. On the German side, operational thinking still focused on the battle of heavy units. This was the reason why the basic strategic questions of naval warfare against Great Britain never found a convincing solution.

After two HSF sorties in spring 1916, 31 May saw the Battle of Jutland, with the result of which neither Britain nor Germany could be satisfied. The British had not achieved the final victory they had hoped for. Germany had to realize that the battle had not even brought about the balance of forces hoped for as a partial success, for the strength ratio between the two fleets had remained unchanged. In his realistic assessment of the situation on 4 July 1916, Scheer came to realize

> that even the most successful outcome of a Fleet action in this war will not force England to make peace. The disadvantages of our military-geographical position in relation to that of the British Isles, and the enemy's great material superiority, cannot be compensated by our Fleet to the extent where we shall be able to overcome the blockade or the British Isles themselves ... A victorious end to the war within a reasonable time can only be achieved through the defeat of British economic life – that is, by using the U-boats against British trade.[2]

---

[2] MARDER, A.J., *From the Dreadnought to Scapa Flow. The Royal Navy in the Fisher Era, 1904-1919*, 5 vols (London, 1961–78), vol. III (2nd edn, 1978), p. 253.

After the Battle of Jutland the HSF made only two more sorties into the North Sea, namely towards the British east coast in August 1916 and towards the north off Bergen in April 1918, neither of which led to direct enemy contact.

The various operations of the HSF in the North Sea and the Baltic cannot detract from the fact that the Fleet primarily performed the function of a "fleet in being": protecting the coast of Germany, blocking the Baltic approaches and keeping submarine exit routes clear. A realistic cost-benefit analysis shows, however, that in the end the fleet did not achieve what was expected of it.

FIGHTING AGAINST ALLIED SHIPPING ROUTES: CRUISERS, RAIDERS AND U-BOATS

Since the German Naval Staff had concentrated on battle, the real goal of all naval warfare, i.e. securing one's own and attacking the enemy's sea lines of communication, had almost been neglected. Thus, naval thinking hardly took into account the fundamental fact that fighting against Britain would always have overseas and world-wide dimensions, and that there would consequently be interrelations between the different, frequently distant, operational theatres which would have to be exploited or reinforced. The inadequate preparation of a cruiser war against the enemy sea lines of communication was a sign of this miscalculation. Except for the conversion of a few fast liners into auxiliary cruisers, the only naval forces considered were the few already stationed overseas.

Although the few German cruisers stationed overseas achieved some notable successes in 1914, the Royal Navy soon neutralized them. The Indian Ocean was the theatre of operations of the light cruisers *Emden* and *Königsberg*. Apart from their success in sinking merchantmen, they down tied numerous Allied naval forces and sank two light cruisers. The Australian light cruiser *Sydney* destroyed the *Emden* in action on 9 November 1914. From October 1914 the *Königsberg* was blockaded in East Africa, and in July 1915 was attacked and destroyed.

At the outbreak of the war, the East Asiatic Cruiser Squadron with its two armoured cruisers *Scharnhorst* and *Gneisenau* under the command of Vice-Admiral Graf von Spee was in the South Pacific. Three light cruisers were widely scattered. After Japan entered the war against Germany, the German forces had to leave the Pacific region in order to have any chance of operating successfully. Consequently, Spee decided to move to South America, attempting a breakthrough to Germany. Thus he swept eastward across the entire Pacific and destroyed two British armoured cruisers at Coronel. This success made his squadron dangerous to British naval strategy, as the Royal Navy no longer had any equivalent forces around South America. In view of the loss of prestige and the threat to its own sea lines of communication, the British Admiralty sent two battle cruisers to the South Atlantic to search for, and destroy, the German squadron. Graf Spee's push to the Falkland Islands led him to his doom there on 8 December 1914. These operations reduced the Grand Fleet's strength by three battle cruisers, but the Imperial Navy did not recognize the opportunity for the HSF which had been won by its cruisers overseas.

However, one small but powerful German squadron was to influence the balance of forces and the overall course of the First World War. It was the Mediterranean Division under Rear Admiral Souchon, comprising the battle cruiser *Goeben* and the light cruiser *Breslau*. The breakthrough of the two vessels to Constantinople and their formal handover to Turkey in August 1914 so enhanced German influence on that country that it joined the war on the side of the Central Powers at the end of October 1914. Thus the Turkish Straits – Dardanelles and Bosphorus – became impassable to the Allies. All their attempts to penetrate the straits failed, with heavy losses. Thus, the second important line of communication to Russia after the Baltic was closed as well, and the routes via Siberia and Murmansk proved to be insufficient. It was hardly possible to supply Russia with war matériel, and the Allied Powers could not rely on her as an ally in 1917. After the war, Sir Julian S. Corbett appreciated this German strategic success in a fair commentary:

> When we consider that the Dardanelles was mined, that no permission to enter it had been ratified, and that everything depended on the German powers of cajolery at Constantinople, when we also recall the world wide results that ensued, it is not too much to say that few naval decisions more bold and well-judged were ever taken. So completely, indeed, did the risky venture turn a desperate situation into one of high moral and material advantage, that for the credit of German statesmanship it goes far to balance the cardinal blunder of attacking France through Belgium.[3]

In cruiser warfare three German light cruisers and ten auxiliary cruisers sank 149 merchant ships with a total of 598.730 GRT (gross register tons), two light cruisers, one destroyer and one auxiliary cruiser.

COMMERCE RAIDING BY U-BOATS, 1915–1918

The various arguments about commerce raiding by submarines conducted against Great Britain are a classic example of the civil–military struggle in a nation at war – a struggle greatly influenced by public opinion as a large segment the German population came to believe that the infallible "magic weapon" would bring victory.

In the first months of war, the "submarine weapon" did prove an effective means of naval warfare. However, thanks to a few spectacular successes (the U-9, Lieutenant Weddigen, sank three aged armoured cruisers in September 1914

---

[3] CORBETT, J.S., *History of the Great War: Naval Operations* (vols 1–3, London 1920–23), vol. 1, pp. 70 ff.

within one hour), the efficiency of this weapon was considerably over-estimated by both the naval leadership and the public.

Initial discussions within the navy regarding the employment of submarines against British trade had not yielded a clear conclusion when Tirpitz, without consulting Chancellor Theobald von Bethmann-Hollweg or the Chief of the Naval Staff, Admiral von Pohl, publicly spoke about this issue. In response to the British threat to "strangle the economy with the help of a blockade", as Churchill had put it in a speech on 9 November, Tirpitz hinted that Germany could "play the same game" by torpedoing all British ships. In Germany, this interview triggered passionate public debates that in turn had repercussions on the naval leadership.

The naval staff was encouraged to demand commerce warfare from the Reich leadership; however, the prospects of success could not be assessed, on account of the small number of major submarines available. Of the twenty-two submarines available in the North Sea in early 1915, only fourteen were technically reliable enough to operate west of the British Isles. The Chancellor now came under strong pressure from the public and the naval leadership. In making his decision he relied too much on the optimistic forecast made by the naval staff. Early in February 1915 he gave his permission to start submarine warfare – though the naval leadership had not thoroughly analysed the method, the international problems or the political risks associated with commerce raiding.

By employing commerce warfare Germany opened new questions of military and international law, as submarines could not adequately adhere to the classic prize rules, particularly not after the arming of British merchant vessels and, later, the creation of British disguised auxiliary cruisers (Q-ships), which jeopardized the safety of the U-boats.

Despite this, commanding officers, displaying caution and skill, managed to comply with the prize regulations, achieving remarkable results with their deck guns. For lack of space, the submarines were not able to embark survivors, but in many cases lifeboats were towed to nearby coasts. The German Declaration of 4 February 1915 announced that all British ships would be destroyed "and that, in doing so, it would not always be possible to avert the danger threatening the crews and passengers". Additionally, the declaration included a warning that neutral shipping was endangered by British shipping flying neutral flags. Without providing its commanding officers with clear instructions, the naval leadership obviously assumed that most ships would be sunk without warning by torpedoes, thus deterring neutral shipping.

When the US government raised concerns about the way the war was being waged and referred to the accepted international principles of naval warfare, the Chief of the General Staff, General von Falkenhayn, feared the USA might enter into the war. He wanted a guarantee that submarine warfare would force England "to give in" within six weeks. When the Kaiser enquired about the matter, Tirpitz and the new chief of the naval staff, Vice Admiral Bachmann, confirmed this amazing forecast without explaining what they meant by England's "giving in".

On 7 May 1915, U-20 sank the British liner *Lusitania* (30,396 GRT). This attack claimed the lives of 1,201 civilians, among them 128 US citizens. However, the

Lusitania had been carrying war matériel. That incident resulted in a severe diplomatic rift with the USA. President Wilson called on Germany to adhere to the accepted principles of naval warfare and to respect the safety of American citizens travelling in the war zone. Following a similar incident involving the *Arabic* in August 1915, the German government yielded. In September, over the objections of the naval leadership, commerce raiding was stopped west of the British Isles. Only in the North Sea and Mediterranean was commerce raiding continued in accordance with the prize regulations.

By early 1916, the number of operational U-boats had risen to fifty-one. Intensified submarine warfare, which had been demanded by the Chief of the General Staff, was resumed in February 1916. It was aimed at sinking British armed merchant vessels without warning, while sparing passenger liners. This led to another severe crisis between Germany and the United States after the French cross-Channel steamer *Sussex* was torpedoed on 24 March 1916. In a sharp note, virtually an ultimatum, on 18 April 1916 Washington threatened to sever diplomatic relations.

Chancellor Bethmann-Hollweg now saw his pessimistic assessment of the situation confirmed. From the beginning of this new stage of submarine warfare he had doubted the need for such a hazardous venture, "which would claim as a stake our existence as a great power and the future of our nation in its entirety, while the chance of winning, that is, the prospect of bringing England down by fall, is a rather uncertain one".[4]

Bethmann-Hollweg provided an assurance to the USA that merchant vessels "would not be sunk without warning or without saving people's lives". As a result, the operational commanders (i.e. HSF and Marine Corps in Flanders), acting on their own initiative, withdrew their submarines because they felt they were exposed to too great a danger by operating under the prize regulations. Commerce raiding under the prize regulations continued only in the Mediterranean. This reaction on the part of the naval leadership was inconsistent with the actual situation: of the thrity-five submarines that were lost by June 1916, only four had been destroyed by decoy vessels and none had been destroyed by armed merchant vessels.

The promising capabilities of the submarines employed in commerce raiding under the prize regulations became evident in the summer of 1916. In October the resumption of this type of submarine warfare provoked no political risks, while achieving considerable results: the monthly average between October 1916 and January 1917 was 189 merchant vessels of 324,742 GRT. This was not enough to force a decision in the war against Britain, but the Allies' war economy was damaged heavily enough to provide a chance of a negotiated peace.

Still, the naval leadership, in a rigid and dogmatic manner, repeatedly demanded "unrestricted submarine warfare". It was convinced that this would

---

[4] HERZFELD, H., *Der Erste Weltkrieg* (Munich 1968), p. 175.

gain a decisive victory. The navy deliberately disregarded the expected break with the United States.

The new General Headquarters under Hindenburg and Ludendorff realized that the campaign of attrition had failed and that victory in France was more and more unlikely. Unlike the military, the Chancellor intended to avoid the USA's entry into the war on the Allied side. He hoped that President Wilson would arrange a negotiated peace. However, when in December 1916 the British government harshly rejected a German peace offer, the response was a change of opinion among the German leadership. Now the military leaders, especially Hindenburg and Ludendorff, categorically demanded "unrestricted submarine warfare" as a last means to gain victory. At the conference of 9 January 1917, after controversial discussions, the Chancellor supported the demand, and the German High Command decided to commence unrestricted submarine warfare on 1 February. A few weeks later, at a meeting of the Main Parliament Committee, Admiral Capelle, the successor of Tirpitz, "went so far as to insist that the effect of American entry into war would be 'zero'! American troops would not even be able to cross the ocean for lack of transport".[5]

With the start of unrestricted warfare came the expected break with the United States, which for the time being announced "armed neutrality". On the other hand, the Entente desired the USA's entry into the war, so that it might take full advantage of that country's entire war economy. This goal was soon reached, thanks to extremely maladroit German diplomacy. The German leadership aimed at keeping the Americans militarily engaged on their continent and in the Pacific Ocean. To this end, an alliance, also inviting Japan, had been offered by cable to Mexico as early as 16 January 1917. With the aid of captured German codebooks the British Naval Intelligence managed to decrypt all the German diplomatic cables transmitted between Berlin, Washington and Mexico.

To expedite the United States' decision making-process in view of its entry into the war, the British government transmitted the pertinent cables to Washington, where President Wilson put them into the hands of the press on 28 February. The German offer to Mexico of an alliance inflamed public opinion against Germany. Early in April the USA entered into the war on the side of the Allies. There is no doubt that this step was not triggered by unrestricted submarine warfare alone, but the German stance toward that issue possibly contributed to the decision in a substantial way.

On 1 February 1917, Germany had 105 operational submarines available for "unrestricted submarine warfare". Up to June 1917 their number increased only to 129. Because of the intensive operations conducted between February and July 1917, refit periods had to be extended, leading to a decrease in the number of submarines on patrol. The great success of the submarines (in April 1917 alone,

---

[5] RITTER, G., *The Sword and the Scepter. The Problem of Militarism in Germany*, Vol. III: *The Tragedy of Statesmanship - Bethmann Hollweg as War Chancellor (1914-1917)*, Vol. IV: *The Reign of German Militarism and the Disaster of 1918* (Coral Gables, FL, 1972-73), Vol. III, p. 334.

458 ships of a total of 840,000 GRT were sunk) led to a severe crisis among the Allies.

The strategic objective – effective disruption of British sea communication – was not achieved, however, because far fewer ships were sunk after the convoy system was introduced in the summer of 1917. Between February and June 1917 the monthly average was 363 ships of 629,863 GRT, whereas in the last quarter of 1917 the number of ships sunk amounted to a monthly average of 159 ships of 365,489 GRT.

In 1918 the numbers of ships sunk decreased even further. The German naval leadership thus was not able to keep its promise; in autumn 1918, about 1.4 million American soldiers were in France. The USA's entry into the war finally proved to be a decisive factor in the German defeat. After the Allies introduced the convoy system German submarines faced serious operational and tactical problems.

The concentration of merchant ships in a convoy had to be countered with a concentration of submarines operating against the convoys. To this end, the convoys had to be detected, that is, the problem of reconnaissance needed to be solved. But the few boats available west of the British Isles were not able to cover the entire operating area. Many convoys thus reached Britain undetected. When a submarine sighted a convoy, it could attack with torpedoes only while submerged. The gun armament, which until that time had achieved most results, remained unused.

After introducing the convoy system, the Allies enhanced their anti-submarine defences by using more-efficient depth charges and developing the first locating devices. It was above all the intensive mining of the channels in the North Sea and in the Channel that caused many casualties. Of the 132 German submarines lost between the years 1917 and 1918, at least fifty sank after hitting mines.

At the end of September 1918, the Army's Supreme Command admitted military defeat and demanded an immediate armistice. The termination of unrestricted submarine warfare was a precondition for establishing contact with the United States. Now, the Naval Command prepared to send the fleet out for one final battle so that it could at least justify its existence. The ships' companies saw that the Naval Command was acting arbitrarily in the operation and refused to obey. Within a few days this developed into a revolt which led to the collapse and end of the Imperial Navy and accelerated the general uprising in Germany.

Conclusion

In spite of outstanding achievements and successes against a superior opponent in the various naval war theatres, the outcome of the operations of the Imperial Navy was negative at the end of World War I, not only because its strategic concepts for the employment of the HSF and for the merchant war with submarines had failed, but because it was the starting point of a revolt which overthrew the German regime. The various sorties of the HSF cannot obscure the fact that the fleet mostly operated like a "fleet in being". Its strong presence pinned down the British Grand Fleet in the North Sea. It protected the German coast, blocked the Baltic for Allied resupply shipments to Russia and to a certain extent backed up submarine warfare by keeping the departure and return routes clear. Contrary to the current appreciation of historians who entirely deny the fleet's strategic importance, it was an asset for the German war effort, but a realistic analysis shows that the fleet did not achieve what was expected of it.

One of the fundamental lessons learned during World War I was that the German war effort and economy, which heavily depended on the import of raw materials, could in the long run be so weakened by an effective blockade that not even defensive operations could be conducted. The German Naval Command had not realized that naval power is essentially the product of fleet strength and geographical position. If one factor was deficient, the other could not make up for it. This was one of the essential reasons why the HSF was not decisive in the overall conduct of war. Nor did it succeed in developing a strategy to integrate naval surface forces and submarines against the strategic weak points of the enemy alliance, i.e. the sea lines of communication in the Atlantic and the Russian part of the Baltic. In the trade war with submarines, the Naval Command rigidly relied on an inadequate concept which deliberately provoked the US entry into the war and consequently contributed to the defeat of Germany. During the operations against Russia, German superiority was hardly ever exploited. However, by blocking the Danish and Turkish straits the war power of the Russians was considerably diminished. This economic war, which the Germans had not foreseen, liberated Germany from the war on two fronts in spring 1918, but this success came too late for the overall war effort. Defeat was the result not only of insufficient means, but also of the strategic incompetence of the Naval Command, which was unable to recognize the geographical limits that no German naval strategy could escape.

Select Bibliography

BEESLY P., *Room 40, British Naval Intelligence 1914-1918* (London, 1982).
BIRNBAUM K.E., *Peace Moves and U-Boat Warfare. A Study of Imperial Germany's Policy towards the United States, 1916-17* (Stockholm, 1958).
CORBETT J.S., *History of the Great War: Naval Operations*, Vols 1-3 (London, 1920-23).
EPKENHANS M., *Tirpitz. Architect of the German High Seas Fleet* (Washington, DC, 2008).
HALPERN P.G., *A Naval History of World War I* (Annapolis, MD, 1994).
HERZFELD H., *Der erste Weltkrieg* (Munich, 1968).
HEZLET A., *The Submarine and Sea Power* (London, 1967).

HILLGRUBER A., *Germany and the Two World Wars* (Cambridge, MA and London, 1981).
HORN D., *The German Naval Mutinies of World War I* (New Brunswick, NJ, 1969).
JELLICOE ADMIRAL VISCOUNT, *The Grand Fleet, 1914-1916: Its Creation, Development and Work* (London, 1919).
KELLY P.J., *Tirpitz and the Imperial German Navy* (Bloomington and Indianapolis, 2011).
KENNEDY P.M., ed., *The War Plans of the Great Powers, 1880-1914* (London, 1979).
KOERVER H.J., ed., *German Submarine Warfare 1914-1918 in the Eyes of British Intelligence: Selected Sources from the British National Archives, Kew*, 2nd edn (Steinbach, 2012).
Der Krieg zur See 1914-1918, 22 vols, ed. Marine-Archiv und Arbeitskreis für Wehrforschung (Berlin and Frankfurt 1920-1966).
MARDER A.J., *From the Dreadnought to Scapa Flow. The Royal Navy in the Fisher Era, 1904-1919*, 5 vols (London, 1961-78).
PHILBIN T.R., *Admiral von Hipper: The Inconvenient Hero* (Amsterdam, 1982).
RAEDER E., *Der Kreuzerkrieg in ausländischen Gewässern*, Vol. 1 (rev. edn, Berlin, 1927).
RAHN W., 'The German Naval War 1814-18. Strategy and Experience', in *Facing Armageddon. The First World War Experienced*, ed. H. CECIL and P.H. LIDDLE (London, 1996), pp. 121-33.
RITTER G., *The Sword and the Scepter. The Problem of Militarism in Germany*, Vol. III: *The Tragedy of Statesmanship - Bethmann Hollweg as War Chancellor (1914-1917)*, Vol. IV: *The Reign of German Militarism and the Disaster of 1918* (Coral Gables, FL, 1972-73).
SCHEER R., *Germany's High Sea Fleet in the World War* (London, 1919).
TIRPITZ A. VON, *My Memoirs*, 2 vols (London, 1919).
TIRPITZ A. VON, *Der Aufbau der deutschen Weltmacht* (Stuttgart, Berlin, 1924).
WEGENER W., *The Naval Strategy of the World War*, trans. H.H. HERWIG (Annapolis, MD, 1989).

THE SEA IN GERMAN GRAND STRATEGY, 1919–1939/40

WERNER RAHN is a Captain (ret.) of the German Navy and freelance researcher and lecturer in Military and Naval History, Germany

ABSTRACT. *The navy was developed in the 1920s as a political rather than strategic instrument, to divide the victorious powers and upset the terms of the Versailles Treaty by "assymetric" ship designs. But the 1935 Anglo-German agreement tempted Germany into competing once more in a conventional naval arms race, which she lacked the resources and the time to pursue.*

RÉSUMÉ. *La marine fut développée dans les années 1920 comme un instrument politique plus que stratégique, pour diviser les puissances victorieuses et contrarier les termes du traité de Versailles par une conception « asymétrique » des navires. Mais l'accord germano-britannique de 1935 entraîna l'Allemagne dans une nouvelle course à l'armement naval qu'elle n'avait ni les ressources ni le temps nécessaires de mener.*

.•.

At the end of World War I, the German Imperial Navy was the starting point of a revolt which overthrew the German regime. Under such circumstances, the question would soon have to be asked, as to whether and how the continued existence of a navy could be justified. In the course of drafting the Versailles Peace Treaty, Great Britain was largely successful in gaining acceptance for her security interests: removal of the German colonies as possible naval bases, free use of the Kiel Canal, elimination of Heligoland as a naval base and the drastic limitation of German naval armament, reducing Germany to a status of a third-rate naval power.

Under Article 181 of the Peace Treaty, the active forces in the German Navy could not exceed the following size: six pre-dreadnought battleships, six light cruisers, twelve destroyers and twelve torpedo boats. Since the Treaty had not stipulated how many units Germany was to be allowed to keep in reserve, the Conference of Allied Ambassadors determined on 26 March 1920 the number of reserve units: two battleships, two light cruisers, four destroyers and four torpedo boats. Thus, the German Navy, in contrast to the curtailment of the Army, was reinforced by 33 per cent. Submarines and military aircraft were forbidden altogether. As a result, the German Navy lacked those weapons which modern naval warfare required. However, the attempt by Britain and the United States to abolish the submarine as a naval weapon was thwarted by the opposition of France, which made itself the champion of the minor naval powers by emphasizing the importance of the submarine as a naval weapon of weak nations.

Germany was allowed to replace the permitted naval forces after the units had reached the age of fifteen to twenty years. The new ships were not to exceed certain displacements: armoured ships ten thousand tons, after twenty years; light cruisers six thousand tons, after twenty years; destroyers eight hundred tons, after fifteen years; and torpedo boats two hundred tons, after fifteen years. The armament of the ships intended for replacement purposes was not specified, nor was there a precise definition of displacement.

Britain had originally demanded that Germany should disarm and destroy all her coastal fortifications. However, this demand was opposed by the United States, who wanted to leave Germany a minimum level of defensive capabilities. Both sides resigned themselves to the compromise that Germany should be allowed to retain her existing North Sea fortifications, with the exception of Heligoland.

The naval personnel were limited to fifteen thousand men, with the strength of officers and warrant officers not to exceed 1,500 men, without examining whether this figure made any sense in relation to the permitted naval forces and coastal fortifications.

The German government initially rejected the Allied demands to limit the Army to a hundred thousand men, but a mitigation of the terms relating to the Navy was never seriously discussed. The burdens imposed on Germany by the Peace Treaty were so great, and the small Navy was in such a weak position, that the government even wanted to renounce the core of the fleet it had been granted, i.e. six old battleships, in order to obtain concessions in other areas. However, the Allied and Associated Powers rejected this proposal, pointing out that Germany had to retain naval forces for her protection and for naval police services. Thus, Germany's former enemies helped to ensure that the German Navy remained in existence, albeit on a modest scale.

While fierce debate was raging in Germany as to whether the Peace Treaty should be accepted or rejected, the Navy, acting on its own authority, scuttled the interned fleet at Scapa Flow on 21 June 1919 as an act of defiance against the Allies. The Naval Command regarded the accomplished deed primarily as a moral success. The consequences of the scuttling were severe: the Allies demanded full compensation and claimed 80 per cent of Germany's entire port equipment. The Navy had to surrender its last five modern light cruisers.

The Navy and national defence

All military planning is normally based on the capabilities and not on the supposed intentions of the potential enemy. In Germany, the deliberations of the military after 1919 regarding national defence had to take into consideration its inferiority in terms of personnel and matériel as compared with the armed forces of the major neighbouring states. When it became apparent that the arms limitations of the other powers that had been announced at Versailles were not going to materialize, the German government consistently aspired to equal rights and national sovereignty in the military sphere, in order to be able to develop the armed forces into an effective instrument for national defence. However, it was not clear what government and *Reichswehr* (armed forces) Command actually meant by "security", and under what conditions German security could be guaranteed at all. In its national defence planning activities, the military took as its starting point the war potential of those states immediately adjacent to Germany.

German naval forces seemed superfluous, given the total military defeat of 1918, the domestic unrest of 1919 and the border conflicts with Poland. However, in order to secure its existence, the Navy required a plausible long-run mission to preserve its independence from the Army. The Naval Command argued that a Navy was necessary, due to the territorial changes in Eastern Europe after 1918, referring primarily to Poland and the related isolation of East Prussia. In 1920–21, a Polish–Russian border dispute had led to war. Future border conflicts could not be ruled out. If Germany did not have any naval forces at all, it would be impossible for her to defend East Prussia. Without naval protection, the Poles could cut the sea route across the Baltic, the only reliable line of supply for East Prussia.

The Navy's deliberations, unlike those of the Army, soon moved to consider other possible conflicts. As early as 1922, they took into account Poland's ties with France. Once again the German naval strategy focused its attention on the North Sea. Given the great dependence of the economy on seaborne supplies, the prerequisites for the conduct of defensive operations could be achieved only if German shipping in the North Sea and the Baltic continued unhindered.

In terms of material, gradually a new start was made by constructing some torpedo boats and light cruisers. However, developing a ten-thousand-ton armoured vessel, as permitted by the Peace Treaty, with sufficient combat power to survive an engagement with French capital ships was a tough nut to crack. Given the displacement limitation, it was not possible to meet the requirements for heavy armament and armour plating. When the Naval Command's hoped-for change of the armament limitations failed to materialise, the Navy was forced to concentrate on planning a ship which was in fact more like a cruiser than a battleship.

The decisive elements which influenced this change in planning lay on two levels: the tactical-operational and the political-military. In the tactical-operational sphere, exercises showed that heavy naval forces needed more speed. In the political-military sphere, the Naval Command thought it imperative that Germany should construct a ship which was always superior in one respect to the warship categories of the 1922 Washington Naval Agreement. It sought speed in the case of battleships and heavy guns in the case of cruisers. To replace the old battleships under the terms of the Peace Treaty, the Naval Command planned a ship carrying six 28cm guns and reaching a top speed of twenty-eight knots.

To understand the German line of reasoning, we need to take a look at the status of international naval armaments at the end of the 1920s. The countries which had signed the Washington Naval Agreement (United States, Great Britain, Japan, France and Italy) had navies which were dominated by capital ships with eight to twelve heavy guns (calibres between 30.5cm and 40.6cm) and a speed of twenty to twenty-three knots. Only Britain and Japan had battle-cruisers with six to eight heavy guns. Some of them were more lightly armoured than other capital ships, but they had a top speed between twenty-seven and thirty-one knots. The Washington Naval Treaty until 1930 limited the total tonnage and construction of battleships and aircraft carriers. For cruisers, on the other hand, the treaty established ceilings only for displacement and armament of the individual vessel, not total fleet size. Thus, cruisers with a standard displacement of ten thousand tons and light armour were built. Their main armament comprised six to ten 20.3cm guns, and they had a top speed of thirty-three knots. Although they could evade slower capital ships, they had to avoid contact with battle-cruisers, which were far superior to them in terms of armament and were capable of almost the same speed.

Since the core of the French fleet consisted of nine slow capital ships and five fast heavy cruisers, the German Naval Command deliberately endowed its then-thousand-ton vessel with the characteristics of a small battle-cruiser; thus it was at least superior to cruisers in gunnery and to capital ships in speed. With six heavy guns and a speed of twenty-six to twenty-eight knots, the *Panzerschiff* (also known as the "pocket-battleship") came very close to the concept of the battle-cruiser. Moreover, diesel engines would give the ship a maximum range up to twenty thousand miles, vastly exceeding that of any cruiser or capital ship. Due to its combat effectiveness and endurance, the *Panzerschiff* was suitable for both: long defensive operations in the North Sea and far-reaching offensive operations in the Atlantic. The construction of the ship immediately attracted the attention of foreign naval experts.

However, the Naval Command regarded the *Panzerschiff* not just as a military necessity, but also as a political-military lever with which to upset the system of international naval armament established without German participation at Washington in 1922. The Naval Command hoped that this step would give Germany the chance to be readmitted to the group of major naval powers. Of course, if Germany had been included in the Washington Naval Agreement this would have been tantamount to a wholesale abrogation of the naval arms limitations laid down by the Peace Treaty. The Washington agreement would have given Germany a tonnage of between 100,000 and 175,000 for capital ships and total freedom in designing individual vessels. Moreover, submarines and aircraft would have been permitted.

Change of Strategy and Operational Planning

Being aware of Germany's high degree of dependence on sea imports, the Naval Command had tried to bring home this overall strategic approach to the Army and to get it to take it into account when drawing up its own operational plans.

From 1928 onwards, the new Minister of the *Reichswehr*, Lieutenant General (ret.) Wilhelm Groener, set new standards for all operational planning by the Army and Navy. He stressed that, for the *Reichswehr*, the idea of a large-scale war had to be ruled out from the start, limiting military operations against foreign powers to two possible types of conflict: (1) repelling raids by neighbouring states into German territory; and (2) armed neutrality during a conflict between foreign powers.

Groener demanded that the *Reichswehr* should immediately be combat ready to oppose a sudden Polish invasion. For the Navy, this new concept meant that it had to be able, on seventy-two hours' notice, to begin operating to destroy the Polish Navy and neutralize the port of Gdynia as a naval base. Such a demonstrative strike was clearly intended to be part of a strategy of deterrence. With this concept of calculated escalation, the German government could react quickly to a possible invasion and refer the conflict to the League of Nations without delay. Thus, the government gave the Navy, for the first time, the role of an effective instrument of crisis management.

In spring 1929 Groener requested the Naval Command to review whether Germany would need for its maritime defence any surface units that would go beyond the ceiling of the Peace Treaty. In doing so, Groener undoubtedly got to the heart of the self-perception of the Navy's leadership, which saw its service not merely as an instrument of national defence but also, in the long run, as an indispensable prerequisite for a future German maritime position of power. Under no circumstances would a return to the status of a brown-water navy be acceptable; it was, rather, intended to build ocean-going units, thus proceeding in accordance with the traditional concept of naval prestige and expressing the hope for a better future. Naturally, it was not possible, nor was it intended, to explain this to a minister who, although he had pushed through the *Panzerschiff* in the Reichstag, had otherwise often expressed a critical attitude toward the build-up of the German High Seas Fleet before 1914.

In his reply to Groener's question "Does Germany need big warships?" the Chief of Naval Command, Admiral Erich Raeder, therefore argued in accordance with the former concept, which focused on the potential conflict with France and Poland, as follows: the attitude of the Navy must not be determined by wishful thinking to re-establish an outstanding naval power. Its most important task in war was to prevent at all costs enemy blockading forces from interdicting German sea lanes. The World War had proved the connection between German resistance on the home front and naval blockade:

> Cutting off our sea lanes is the simplest and safest way, without any bloodshed, of defeating us. Our enemies know this as well. England has the most powerful

fleet world-wide and its geographical position is disastrous for Germany. Therefore, any armed conflict has to be avoided that would turn England into one of our enemies. We would be doomed to failure right from the start.[1]

The memorandum concluded that the Navy – even without the limits set by the Peace Treaty – could fight only a fleet of a second-class sea power, such as France.

WAR LESSONS AND STRATEGY DISCUSSION

The year 1925 witnessed the beginning of a broader discussion on the fundamental problems of naval strategy. This discussion was initiated by Rear Admiral Wolfgang Wegener, who, in September 1925, submitted his treatise "Reflections Concerning the Concepts of Our War Games and War Studies" to the Chief of Naval Command.

Wegener criticized the navy for trying to solve its problems in purely tactical ways. His rationale defined the terms "sea power" and "strategy":

Two things are required for sea power and naval warfare:

1. The tactical fleet,
2. The strategic-geographical position, from which this fleet can operate, that is, control the sea lanes and thereby exercise sea control.

Strategy, therefore, is the doctrine of strategic-geographical positions, their changes, and their deterioration. Offensive strategy is the acquisition of a geographical position; defensive strategy is its deterioration.[2]

Wegener extended his study into a memorandum which he presented in 1926, entitled "The Naval Strategy of the World War". In it he explained in detail an alternative concept according to which Germany could have had a better chance in the naval war against Great Britain. His concept centred on the strategic-geographical position as the indispensable element of any sea power whose strategy would concentrate on the struggle for naval supremacy. In order to get a grip on the Atlantic sea lanes, Germany would have had to improve the geographic basis. According to Wegener, Denmark, Norway, the Faeroes and Iceland would have been the crucial positions on the way to the Atlantic Ocean, if Germany had been unable to gain the French Atlantic coast. He did not reject the battle fleet as a means of naval warfare, but he wanted to give it a clearly defined strategic aim. This aim, however, had been lacking because the political leadership had ignored geographic aims in terms of world politics and thus had

---

[1] Translation from RAHN W., *Reichsmarine und Landesverteidigung 1919-1928. Konzeption und Führung der Marine in der Weimarer Republik* (Munich, 1976), pp. 483 ff.
[2] WEGENER, W., *The Naval Strategy of the World War*, trans. H.H. Herwig (Annapolis, MD, 1989), p. 200.

not geared the fleet to a strategic offensive. Having analysed the war lessons, Wegener formulated the political demand that Germany

> had to re-explore the avenues to world and sea power, but this time with a mature instinct for sea power. Without sea power, Germany would be left at the mercy of Great Britain. But once our people and state are in good shape again, we will feel this drive to go out to sea and establish our position at sea where we will encounter the Anglo-Saxons as enemies.[3]

Wegener's far-reaching deliberations evidently assumed that Germany would regain its former posture in power politics. However, when he published his memorandum in 1929 he moderated these aggressive formulations. Wegener did not influence planning directly. The importance of his paper arose not so much from his critical analysis of naval warfare in World War I but, rather, from his theory of naval strategy dealing with the fundamental problems of naval warfare, which in Germany had not been deeply thought about.

However, as soon as it became apparent that it would be possible to overcome the limitations imposed by the Peace Treaty, the traditional principle of *"similia similibus"* came to the fore again. Naval officers wanted to build ships which were at least the equal of those of the potential enemy. The demand for equal rights overshadowed the obvious strategic and operational problem of what functions capital ships should and could assume in performing the Navy's most important wartime tasks of protecting supplies in large areas of the North Sea and attacking enemy sea lines of communication. The reasoning favouring the *Panzerschiff*-type also supported the Navy's power-policy calculation. The Navy did not want to be reduced to the status of a "coastal Navy" but, rather, to pursue a course which would take Germany to a position of power which, in the eyes of the Naval Command, was commensurate with the country's economic potential.

NAVAL ARMAMENT UNDER HITLER, 1933–1937

A few days after seizing power in January 1933, Adolf Hitler made it clear to military and naval commanders that he intended to develop the armed forces into an instrument of his power politics. As far as the translation of this objective into armament was concerned, however, Hitler was initially cautious as we know from his speech of 3 February 1933:

> The most dangerous period is that of rearmament. Then we shall see whether France has statesmen. If she does, she will not grant us time but will jump on us (presumably with eastern satellites).[4]

---

[3] RAHN, W., 'German Naval Strategy and Armament, 1919–39', in *Technology and Naval Combat in the Twentieth Century and Beyond*, ed. P.P. O'BRIEN (London 2001), pp. 109–127 (p. 117).

[4] HILLGRUBER A., *Germany and the Two World Wars* (Cambridge, MA and London, 1981), p. 57.

Therefore, the Navy had to make do with compromises regarding the displacement and armament of its future capital ships. However, in view of the long-term build-up of the fleet, these compromises seemed to be acceptable. The last of three *Panzerschiffe* was launched in June 1934 and completed eighteen months later. The next two units were upgraded to battle-cruisers (thirty-one thousand tons, thirty-one knots, nine 28cm guns) in response to the French battle-cruisers *Dunkerque* and *Strasbourg*.

The Anglo-German Naval Agreement of 18 June 1935 allowed Germany to have a surface fleet with a tonnage up to 35 per cent of the British Empire's. German naval leaders now believed that they had attained their goal of equal rights. The 35 per cent ceiling applied not just to the total tonnage but also to the individual categories of warships. Only in the case of U-boats, Germany was allowed to achieve first 45 per cent and later even 100 per cent of British submarine strength. In this context, Germany gave the assurance that her Navy would adhere to the "cruiser rules" regarding submarine warfare on merchant shipping.

The Navy's planning was thus based wholly on the structure of the other naval powers. Its motto was: what the other navies, with their rich traditions, consider proper, and what Germany is now permitted within the 35 per cent ceiling, is what Germany will now build. The Navy started to build a so-called "normal fleet": fast capital ships, heavy and light cruisers, aircraft carriers, destroyers – and for the first time in seventeen years, submarines. One week after the Anglo-German Naval Agreement was announced, the Navy commissioned the first small, 250-ton U-boat, thus uncovering the long-term secret activity in this matter. Even if the U-boat had not been basically improved since 1918, it had considerably developed in every direction, i.e. for example, better torpedoes, the ability to lay mines from all U-boats and to transmit and receive signals when both surfaced and submerged.

Nevertheless, a widespread opinion prevailed in all navies that the U-boat had lost the role it had achieved in World War I as one of the most effective naval weapons. The British Admiralty was convinced that the Asdic had reduced the submarine threat almost to extinction. Contrary to this opinion, the German U-boat Staff, centred on Captain Karl Dönitz, was convinced that anti-submarine warfare weapons were greatly overrated and had not made decisive progress since 1918.

From 1928 onwards, the Navy's thinking was determined by Admiral Erich Raeder. In his study of the cruiser campaign in the First World War, Raeder had come to the conclusion that there had been a strategic correlation between the operations of the cruiser squadron in the Pacific and South Atlantic and in the North Sea campaign in autumn 1914. Raeder based his concept of naval strategy on the realization that all naval theatres of war formed a homogeneous whole and that consequently any operation had to be viewed in its correlation with other areas. Accordingly, cruiser warfare overseas and operations by the battle fleet in home waters were integral components of a single naval strategy which, by exploiting the diversionary effect, sought to exhaust the enemy's forces and disrupt its supplies.

Raeder formulated his strategic thinking most clearly in a briefing he gave to Hitler on 3 February 1937. Analysing the war's experiences, he pointed out the correlation between strategy and a country's military-geographical situation. Raeder was aware of the totality of a future war, which would be a struggle not just between forces, but of "nation versus nation". He emphasized the negative consequences for Germany if she were unable continually to procure the raw materials she lacked. Thus, Raeder pointed out the glaring weaknesses in Germany's war potential, but without being able to influence Hitler's policy of confrontation.

BUILD-UP OF THE NAVY AGAINST BRITAIN 1938–39

A fundamental change in the Navy's strategic planning commenced in spring 1938. As it became apparent that the Western powers opposed German expansion, Hitler issued the directive that all German war preparations should consider not only France and Russia but also Great Britain as potential enemies. A second confrontation with Britain now influenced all further planning for the next naval war. Raeder followed Hitler's hazardous course of confrontation willingly and without protest, neglecting his strong statement on this matter to Groener in 1929 and erroneously assuming that the Navy would still have several years of peace to continue its build-up.

In summer 1938 the Naval Staff's strategic study concluded that, given a geographical starting position similar to that of 1914, only oceanic cruiser warfare with improved *Panzerschiffe* and U-boats could hold out any prospect of success. Despite this realization, a planning committee of senior officers busied itself with the question of what task battleships could perform in a cruiser war in the Atlantic. The result was paradoxical and revealing:

> [T]he chief of staff of the naval staff concluded at the end of the discussion that all participants agreed that battleships were necessary, but that no consensus regarding their use could be achieved for the time being.[5]

To the traditionalists, who considered capital ships to be the most important arm of a naval power, this meant that the concept of sea denial had been pushed into the background by the concept of sea control. Unlike Tirpitz, the Naval Staff had repeatedly proposed a sea-denial strategy in the 1930s. However, the new suggestion to develop a German strategy of sea control constituted a second approach to sea and world power in the 20th century, as the then Commander-in-Chief of the Fleet, Admiral Rolf Carls, noted in September 1938:

---

[5] DEIST, W., 'The Rearmament of the Wehrmacht', in *Germany and the Second World War*, vol. I: *The Build-up of German Aggression* (Oxford, 1990), pp. 372–540 (p. 474).

If, in accordance with the will of the *Führer*, Germany is to achieve a firm world-power position, it will need, in addition to sufficient colonies, secure sea routes and access to the high seas. ... A war against Britain means a war against the Empire, against France, probably also against Russia and a number of countries overseas, in other words against one-half or two-thirds of the whole world.[6]

Nevertheless, Raeder was more inclined towards a sea-denial strategy in an oceanic cruiser campaign with *Panzerschiffe*, and he intended to give this strategy priority in the future armament programme. In November 1938, however, he was unable to gain Hitler's support for his programme. Hitler did not accept the cruiser warfare strategy, and insisted instead that the Navy should step up the pace of its battleship construction so that he would have at his disposal an instrument of power which could be employed globally as soon as possible.

The Navy had to accept this decisive change and formulated a new concept, the so-called Z-Plan, which centred on the construction of six capital ships by 1944. As well, battle-cruisers, *Panzerschiffe*, aircraft carriers, fast light cruisers and 247 U-boats were to form the backbone of German naval forces for the future Battle of the Atlantic. On 27 January 1939, when Hitler ordered that the build-up of the Navy was to take precedence over all other tasks, including the rearmament of the Army and *Luftwaffe*, he heralded a gigantic build-up of naval forces. Within a few months the planning of a series of six newly designed diesel-driven battleships was completed; the construction of two units began in summer 1939. In the meantime, Hitler had denounced the Anglo-German Naval Agreement of 1935 on 27 April 1939.

Disillusionment came on 3 September 1939. Totally unexpectedly, Hitler ordered the Navy to launch a naval war against Great Britain. The Navy was in no way prepared. Raeder's initial estimate of the situation was very pessimistic and he resigned himself to the realization that neither the few U-boats nor the surface forces would have any decisive effect on the outcome of the war:

> They can do no more than show that they know how to die gallantly and thus are willing to create the foundations for later reconstruction.[7]

As at the end of the war in 1918, the Navy once again faced a hopeless situation. It seemed to believe that the only purpose of its actions was to go down fighting, thereby proving its *raison d'être*. However, the progress of the war soon demanded a new estimate of the situation.

Nine months later, Poland, Denmark, Norway, Belgium, Luxemburg and the Netherlands were occupied; by 22 June 1940 France had suffered a total defeat. German naval control extended from Norway to the Pyrenees. Therefore, the German Naval Staff concentrated on an offensive concept of naval warfare aimed

---

[6] *Ibid.*, p. 475.
[7] Reflections of the Commander-in-Chief Navy, on the outbreak of war, 3 September 1939, in 'Fuehrer Conferences on Naval Affairs, 1939–1945', in *Brassey's Naval Annual 1948*, ed. H.G. THURSFIELD (London 1948), pp. 25–496 (p. 38).

solely at destroying the maritime transport capacity of Britain. The surface force was insufficient for such warfare. To supplement it, the Navy concentrated on constructing and employing a means of naval warfare that had proved its worth during the First World War: the U-boat.

Conclusion

The small *Reichsmarine* considered itself to be an essential element of national defence against France and Poland. Therefore, the Baltic and the North Sea were the centre of German maritime strategy for nearly ten years. After 1933, the Navy became subject to Hitler's long-term ambitions for dominating the world, and the seas in particular. When the war came, the Navy was totally unprepared for it. To compensate, Germany attempted to force a strategic decision by destroying the superior Anglo-Saxon maritime powers' shipping capacity (sea denial) rather than fighting them for mastery of the Atlantic (sea control). From 1940 onwards, the German Navy possessed a good geographical basis for warfare in the Atlantic, but this basis could not be fully exploited, due to insufficient weaponry. In 1941, Germany turned the European war into an over-ambitious world war against the Soviet Union and the United States. There was no chance to win this war with a maritime strategy that was based on U-boats only. In October 1942, the Naval Staff wrote in a situation report that "no war in history ... has yet been won by the use of one method of warfare". With this statement the Naval Staff moved to a level of argument that was close to actual conditions.

Select Bibliography

DEIST W., 'The Rearmament of the Wehrmacht', in *Germany and the Second World War*, vol. I: *The Build-up of German Aggression* (Oxford, 1990), pp. 372–540.

DÜLFFER J., *Weimar, Hitler und die Marine. Reichspolitik und Flottenbau 1920-1939* (Düsseldorf, 1973).

'Fuehrer Conferences on Naval Affairs, 1939–1945', in *Brassey's Naval Annual 1948*, ed. H.G. THURSFIELD (London 1948), pp. 25–496.

GEMZELL C.A., *Raeder, Hitler und Skandinavien. Der Kampf für einen maritimen Operationsplan* (Lund, 1965).

GEYER M., *Aufrüstung oder Sicherheit. Die Reichswehr in der Krise der Machtpolitik 1924-1936* (Wiesbaden, 1980).

HILLGRUBER A., *Germany and the Two World Wars* (Cambridge, MA and London, 1981).

HOWARD M., 'A Thirty Years War? The Two World Wars in Historical Perspective', *Transactions of the Royal Historical Society*, Ser. 6. Vol. 3 (1993), 171–84.

MAIOLO J.A., *The Royal Navy and Nazi Germany, 1933-39. A Study in Appeasement and the Origins of the Second World War* (London, 1998).

Rahn W., 'German Naval Strategy and Armament, 1919-39', in *Technology and Naval Combat in the Twentieth Century and Beyond*, ed. P.B. O'Brien (London, 2001), pp. 109-27.

Rahn W., *Reichsmarine und Landesverteidigung 1919-1928. Konzeption und Führung der Marine in der Weimarer Republik* (Munich, 1976).

Rodger N.A.M., *Naval Power in the Twentieth Century* (Basingstoke, 1996).

Roskill S., *Naval Policy between the Wars*, Vol. 1: *The Period of Anglo-American Antagonism 1919-1929*, London 1968, Vol. 2: *The Period of Reluctant Rearmament 1930-1939* (London 1976).

Salewski M., *Die deutsche Seekriegsleitung 1935-1945*, Vol. 1 (Frankfurt, 1970).

Salewski M., 'Zur deutschen Sicherheitspolitik in der Spätzeit der Weimarer Republik', *Vierteljahreshefte für Zeitgeschichte* 22 (1974), 121-47.

Salewski M., 'Das maritime "Dritte Reich" - Ideologie und Wirklichkeit 1933 bis 1945', in *Deutsche Marinen im Wandel. Vom Symbol nationaler Einheit zum Instrument internationaler Sicherheit*, ed. W. Rahn (Munich, 2005), pp. 427-49.

Schreiber G., 'Thesen zur ideologischen Kontinuität in den machtpolitischen Zielsetzungen der deutschen Marineführung 1897 bis 1945 - Rückblick und Bilanz', in *Deutsche Marinen im Wandel*, ed. Rahn, pp. 451-84.

Wegener W., *The Naval Strategy of the World War*, trans. H.H. Herwig (Annapolis, MD, 1989).

THE CASE OF GERMANY IN THE FIRST PART OF WORLD WAR II, 1939–1942

JÖRG HILLMANN is a Captain in the German Navy attached to the European Defence Agency in Brussels

ABSTRACT. *Pre-war German naval strategy was more ideological than practical, and unrelated to the army's plans. In 1939 the Navy adopted a campaign against British and French trade, primarily with surface ships, for which it had scarcely prepared. In 1940 the invasion of Norway and France gave the Navy good access to the open Atlantic, but the losses incurred in Norway made a realistic plan for the invasion of Britain very difficult. In any case neither the Army nor Hitler wanted to invade. Even when it became clear that Britain was not going to accommodate herself to German dominance of Europe, they preferred to win the "real" war against the Soviet Union before considering naval plans. It was left to the incipient Anglo-American alliance to develop a sea-based world-war strategy which Germany largely ignored until it was too late.*

RÉSUMÉ. *La stratégie navale allemande d'avant-guerre était davantage d'ordre idéologique que pratique et sans rapport avec les plans de l'armée. En 1939, la marine se lança dans une campagne contre les échanges britanniques et français (pour laquelle elle était à peine préparée), en utilisant surtout des navires de surface. Les invasions de la Norvège et de la France en 1940 lui donnèrent le champ libre pour accéder à l'Atlantique mais les pertes subies en Norvège rendirent très difficile l'élaboration d'un plan d'attaque réaliste pour l'invasion de la Grande-Bretagne, ce que de toute façon ni Hitler ni l'armée ne souhaitaient. Même quand il devint clair que les britanniques ne s'accommoderaient pas de sa domination en Europe, l'Allemagne préféra gagner la guerre « véritable » contre l'Union Soviétique avant d'envisager des plans pour sa marine. Ceci laissa à l'alliance anglo-américaine naissante l'opportunité de développer une stratégie de combat mondial basée sur la mer dont l'Allemagne ne s'inquiéta pas avant qu'il ne soit trop tard.*

.•.

Germany never developed a maritime cast of mind at any stage in its history. Only the Emperor Wilhelm II tried to change this and fix Germany's future on the sea, but he failed in 1918. The German revolution of 1918, which started in the Navy, the restrictions of the Versailles settlement of 1919 and the scuttling of the fleet in Scapa Flow all reduced the maritime capabilities of the Weimar Republic and left the Navy in a miserable condition. In the 1920s it developed the strategic

Table 1. *Z Plan fleet, 1939 (SCHULZE-WEGENER G., Deutschland zur See (Hamburg etc, 2007), p. 145)*

Type	By end of 1943	By end of 1947
Battleships	6	10
"Armoured ships" (*Panzerschiffe*)	3	3
Cruisers	3	10
Aircraft carriers	2	4
Heavy cruisers	5	5
Light cruisers	2	12
Scouts (*Spähkreuzer*)	2	20
Destroyers	44	58
Torpedo boats	44	78
Submarines	161	249

Note: Fast patrol vessels, smaller mine-laying and mine-clearing capabilities, anti-submarine vessels omitted)

idea of diversion (*Diversionswirkung*)[1] and designed the "pocket battleships" to give it a few opportunities of visibility and strength.[2] The Navy, the Army and the infant Luftwaffe developed their own strategies without co-ordination. The Navy welcomed the political change of January 1933 as a unique opportunity to regain strength and influence, though the Navy and its commander-in-chief Admiral Raeder did not trust the Nazi Party or Hitler himself. All three services grew in strength from 1933, but lacked any joint strategy beyond a general priority for the Army, with the Navy and Luftwaffe in supporting roles. Raeder had been a staff officer during World War I and had then spent two years writing the official history of the "Cruiser War".[3] For the staff historians and the naval officers the Great War offered no hopeful model: no decisive battle because Jutland had not been fought to a finish; a "fleet-in-being" which had bred mutiny and revolution before sinking itself. They were backward oriented, trapped in their history, and all they had were hopes of revenge against the obvious and former enemy, Britain – but Hitler thought of Britain as a necessary ally. He foresaw Germany dominating the Continent in partnership with Britain, which would protect Germany's maritime flanks. Raeder and the Navy developed their own policy in

---

[1] During his education at the Naval Academy, Erich Raeder translated the study of the French Captain René Daveluy (later Admiral in the French Fleet) with the title 'Etude sur la tactique navale'. This study confessed that a country with fewer naval capabilities could survive only by deploying single assets in a wide range of the operational area in order to force the enemy to put all available capabilities in place to secure its own sea lines of communication. RAEDER E., *Mein Leben I* (Tübingen, 1956), p. 54.
[2] For German naval strategy see: *Deutsche Marinen im Wandel*, ed. W. RAHN (Munich 2005); *Seemacht und Seestrategie*, ed. J. DUPPLER (Hamburg, 1999); *Seestrategische Konzepte*, ed. E. OPITZ (Bremen, 2004).
[3] RAEDER E., *Der Kreuzerkrieg in ausländischen Gewässern*, 2 vols (Berlin, 1922 and 1923).

increasing isolation from Hitler. The Navy had low political visibility and gave the impression of being a submissive and subordinate service.[4]

The situation changed between 1936 and 1938 as Hitler became aware that Britain was not likely to adopt his preferred role of loyal partner, but he still expected her to remain a neutral observer of the coming war. The German Navy would now have a more important role during the war and after the German victory. The fleet of the "Z Plan" (27 January 1939) was intended for the post-war era, consequently the money and resources devoted to it remained limited, although Hitler proposed to give the Navy financial priority. Raeder was content with the new situation and looked forward to opportunities to defeat a weakened Royal Navy. None of these German plans took any account of what Britain might do: they were based on wishful thinking rather than analysis. There were no plans to invade Britain, since Hitler assumed she would remain neutral and passive until her position was so weak that she would be forced to co-operate. Raeder held to the Navy's long-standing plan to weaken the enemy by diversionary attacks on seaborne trade, followed eventually by a decisive battle. Both were wrong, since the enemy did not behave as they expected and desired.

The importance of the sea – or sea-blindness

Raeder was an experienced naval officer who well understood the importance of the sea, but he was unable to persuade Hitler. Instead of stressing the importance of the sea, he stressed the importance of the Navy. After 1945 the Navy explained that Hitler had never understood the sea, just as Tirpitz had blamed Wilhelm II and all Germans after 1918.[5] More accurately, it seems that the leaders of the Navy failed to explain to Hitler the importance of the sea, assuming that he would share their own maritime awareness. In inter-war Germany, however, maritime awareness did not extend beyond the Baltic and North Sea. Ever since Frederick the Great of Prussia had suppressed the infant colonial empire founded by the Great Elector of Brandenburg, anything beyond the English Channel had been outside the imagination of the German people.[6] This lack of long-term maritime awareness, and the loss of technical knowledge after World War I, made it very difficult to reconstruct a navy in the 1930s with insufficient resources and trained personnel.

---

[4] For the history of the Naval High Command (*Seekriegsleitung*) see M. SALEWSKI, *Die Deutsche Seekriegsleitung 1935-1945*, 3 vols (Frankfurt/M, 1973).

[5] VON PUTTKAMER K.J., *Die unheimliche See. Hitler und die Kriegsmarine* (Vienna and Munich, 1952); A. VON TIRPITZ, *Erinnerungen* (Leipzig, 1919), p. 203; W. WEGENER, *Die Seestrategie des Weltkrieges* (Berlin, 1929), p. 32; W. WEGENER, *The Naval Strategy of the World War*, trans. H.H. HERWIG (Annapolis, MD, 1989).

[6] HARTWIG D., 'Maritimes Denken und Handeln bei Friedrich II', in *Dieter Hartwig - Marinegeschichte und Sicherheitspolitik*, ed. J. GRAUL and M. KÄMPF (Bochum, 2003), pp. 17-26.

THE CASE OF GERMANY IN THE FIRST PART OF WORLD WAR II, 1939-1942

1 SEPTEMBER 1939: BEGINNING OF THE WAR

On the day that the Army and Luftwaffe attacked Poland, the old battleship *Schleswig-Holstein*, now a training ship, was visiting Gdansk. Her guns and the troops she had concealed aboard captured the fortress of the Westerplatte. A couple of smaller German vessels were also involved, aboard one of which was Friedrich Ruge, later the first head of the Federal German Navy after it was re-established in 1955-56.[7] According to the memories of the participants, it was either the Army or the Navy which won the battle single-handed. Neither conceded any important role to the other. When France and Britain declared war on 3 September it came as a surprise to Germany, which had expected the international community to acquiesce in Germany's aggression as it had at Munich in 1938. Raeder noted despairingly that the war had come too soon, that the Navy was unprepared and only one-tenth of British strength, and now it could not hope to do more than pave the way for a future reconstruction by showing how to die with honour.[8] Notwithstanding Raeder's expressed shock, however, on 21 and 24 August he had ordered the "pocket battleships" *Admiral Spee* and *Deutschland*, with the refuelling tankers *Altmark* and *Westerwald*, to waiting positions in the Atlantic. On 31 August his War Order No.1 declared the strategic objective of a "trade war against England". Raeder "slipped into the war"[9] with two battleships (*Scharnhorst* and *Gneisenau*), three "armoured ships" or "pocket battleships" (*Admiral Spee, Admiral Scheer, Deutschland*), one heavy cruiser (*Admiral Hipper*), six light cruisers (*Emden, Karlsruhe, Köln, Königsberg, Leipzig, Nürnberg*) and twenty-six submarines (not counting minelayers or mine-clearing vessels, patrol craft and supply vessels). Captain Karl Dönitz, commanding the submarines, had already argued the need of a force of three hundred boats, allowing one third to be at sea at any time, but Raeder intended the submarine force to be developed only after the battle-fleet.

Erich Raeder was definitely wrong to say that the Navy was unprepared for war, but it was unprepared for this kind of war. It lacked the capabilities for a war on British trade (or anyone else's); it lacked overseas bases, facilities, communications and supply arrangements. In distant waters the Navy was ineffective, but nearer home it was efficient. Minelaying and submarine warfare were highly successful. On 14 October Lt. Günther Prien of *U-47* demonstrated the vulnerability of the Home Fleet by sinking the battleship *Royal Oak* in Scapa Flow, becoming an instant hero and receiving the first award to a naval officer of the "Knight's Cross". The Nazi regime celebrated his courage and success as symbols of the Führer's leadership. Two months later, on 17 December 1939, when Captain Hans Langsdorff scuttled his ship the *Graf Spee* in the River Plate and committed

---

[7] RUGE F., *In vier Marinen* (Munich, 1979); F. RUGE, *Der Seekrieg 1939-1945* (Stuttgart, 1962).
[8] On the relationship between Hitler and Raeder, as well as Raeder's note of 3 September 1939, see *Lagevorträge des Oberbefehlshabers der Kriegsmarine vor Hitler 1939-1945*, ed. G. WAGNER (Munich, 1972).
[9] HILLMANN J., 'Slipping into the War. German Naval Strategy between 1920-1940', in *Northern European Overture to War, 1939-1941, From Memel to Barbarossa*, ed. M. CLEMMESEN and M. FAULKNER (Leiden and Boston, 2013), pp. 129-63.

suicide, Raeder forbade any ship to surrender again. It is notable that Raeder gave no thought to the fate of the ship's company and made no mention of their success in sinking fifty thousand tons of British shipping in the opening months of the war. In Britain the scuttling of the *Graf Spee* was treated as the first naval victory of the war, but Langsdorff's bravery and integrity were praised as well. These different reactions encapsulate the difference between British seafaring professionalism and German atavistic militarism overpowering strategic logic.

German strategy continued to concentrate on land warfare. The rapid success of the *Blitzkrieg* in the West aroused irresistible enthusiasm, strengthened the "Führer-cult" and overcame all misgivings. The conquest of Belgium, the Netherlands and France indicated the kind of war the *Wehrmacht* would fight, and for the first time in history Germany had direct access to the Atlantic. Raeder understood the possibilities, but unfortunately he lacked the resources to take advantage of them. Much the same applied to Denmark and Norway: for the first time Germany controlled the entrance to the Baltic, had free access to the North Sea and to the Atlantic beyond. Operation *Weserübung*, the Norwegian invasion starting on 9 April 1940, was the first joint operation based on full co-operation between the services. In post-war writings, however, the campaign is described as dominated by whichever single service the author belonged to. Its image was shaped by famous writers like Walther Hubatsch, who described the operation in detail but avoided its strategic purpose to gain access to the Atlantic.[10] The invasion of Norway, unlike that of Denmark, was difficult and costly. From a military perspective the object was to secure access to raw materials, but the Navy wanted to outflank any British mine barrage (similar to that laid in 1917-18) which might block its access to the open sea. Raeder regarded this as an object of the highest importance, planned it carefully and committed much of his strength to it. But the loss of the new heavy cruiser *Blücher*, sunk by Norwegian batteries in Oslo Fjord on morning of 9 April, was the result of trying to show off naval strength by entering Oslo with the biggest possible ship: propaganda rather than rational planning. The conduct of *Weserübung* showed the difference between Hitler's and Raeder's thinking on the use of the sea. Raeder wanted to use Norwegian harbours as bases for Atlantic operations, but Hitler preferred to use the Navy to defend the coast.[11] His focus was on raw materials from Sweden: another example of his blindness to maritime strategy.

At the beginning of June 1940 Raeder sent the battleships *Scharnhorst* and *Gneisenau*, the *Admiral Hipper* and four destroyers to sea for Operation *Juno*. Following Hitler's orders, the ostensible purpose was to protect communications on the Norwegian coast and attack the Allied shipping in northern Norway – but Raeder also wanted to demonstrate the value of the battleships, which

---

[10] HUBATSCH W., *Weserübung. Die deutsche Besetzung von Dänemark und Norwegen* (Göttingen, 1960).
[11] GEMZELL C-A., *Raeder, Hitler und Skandinavien. Der Kampf um einen maritimen Operationsplan* (Lund, 1965); C-A. GEMZELL, *Organisation, Conflict and Innovation. A Study of German Naval Strategic Planning 1888-1940* (Lund, 1973).

had contributed little to the war so far. The battleships succeeded in sinking the aircraft carrier *Glorious*, but *Scharnhorst* was torpedoed by the destroyer *Acasta*, and *Gneisenau* by the submarine *Clyde*, putting them both out of action till December. Admiral Marschall, the Commander-in-Chief of the Fleet, was personally blamed and was relieved by Admiral Lütjens. At the end of the Norwegian campaign the *Kriegsmarine* had one heavy cruiser, two light cruisers and four destroyers still operational. This weakened the position of Raeder and of the Navy, which could now contribute nothing to the Atlantic campaign but a submarine war on merchant shipping. At this stage of the war the U-boats observed international law, but as the convoy system and Allied anti-submarine warfare developed, the submarines became more ruthless.

In 1940–41 the campaign was fought across the whole Atlantic from Halifax to the Gulf of Guinea. With only a small number of submarines and no bases, success was limited, but the *Kriegsmarine* deployed supply ships and took advantage of the merchant raiders (*Hilfskreuzer*), which themselves were effective weapons against merchant shipping.

Besides its operations in the open sea, the Navy was also responsible for protecting the whole coastline of German-occupied Europe from North Norway via the Baltic to the German, Dutch, Belgian and French coasts. It was an enormous task for which the Navy had inadequate capabilities and experience. Protecting German shipping and seaborne communications was not mentioned by the political leadership, which gave thought only to lines of supply on land. They understood the sea as an offshore war zone rather than a means of transport; an opportunity for themselves as well as a vulnerability for Great Britain. Germany should have learnt from her operations on the high seas in former times how to use naval bases and to safeguard seaborne trade in a particular area, but she had always thought more of attacking enemy communications than of protecting her own. This explains Germany's regional and coastal approach to naval warfare, and may explain why the Naval Command were unable to convince their superiors of the importance of the sea: they had no real maritime mindset.

WHICH FIRST: *BARBAROSSA* OR *SEELÖWE*?

The Naval Command started planning for the invasion of Britain (codenamed *Seelöwe*, "Sealion") in the spring of 1940. Though it was expected to be difficult, the geographical situation had never been so favourable. The planning was excellent but unrealistic. The resources were not available to build the necessary shipping. The operation had to involve all three services, but the Army and Luftwaffe were not enthusiastic. The Navy would have to be in charge, but was neither told nor experienced enough to know what would happen after the troops were landed. The operation was postponed several times as Hitler lost interest and turned to *Barbarossa*, the plan to invade the Soviet Union. Despite his pact with Stalin, by which Germany and the Soviet Union had divided Poland, Hitler was driven by a sense of his racial duty to free Europe from Bolshevism and the Jews. Geography, and Germany's capabilities, made *Barbarossa* a land campaign. Repeating the formula of the *Blitzkrieg* won rapid successes, but was eventually stopped by the heroic resistance of the Red Army and the unexpectedly hard winter. In these campaigns Germany lost the men and material she needed to gain victory in the West. Raeder several times advised Hitler to deal with Britain before starting a war in the East, but he was increasingly excluded from the planning of *Barbarossa* and isolated from the high command. He worried about the increasing engagement of the USA, and Britain's commitment in the Mediterranean, which the Italians were not able to contain.

1941 ONWARDS

At the end of 1940 both *Gneisenau* and *Scharnhorst* were operational again and ready to take part in the Battle of the Atlantic. Once more Raeder tried to combine battleships and submarines, with considerable success, but British losses were only a small percentage of cargoes shipped, and German losses were heavy. Though Norwegian ports brought the Navy closer to the Atlantic, the lack of adequate bases, especially the French Atlantic ports, was a weakness. The Luftwaffe refused to provide sufficient air cover and support; the lack of common purpose, especially at the top of the two services, was a major reason for the defeats of 1941 and 1942.

In January 1941 *Gneisenau* and *Scharnhorst* took part in Operation *Berlin* against convoys from Halifax and Sierra Leone. In two months Lütjens sank twenty-two ships of 115,000 tons before returning safely to Brest. Other successes were achieved by the *Admiral Hipper* and *Admiral Scheer*, but the supply of the battleships, which needed seven tankers, was a major difficulty. The new battleships *Tirpitz* and *Bismarck* were expected to be operational in April 1941. The German battleships and cruisers worried the British Admiralty, but British aircraft carriers and radar worried the Germans. The Germans had concentrated on building more ships, but the British had improved their technology and their relations with the USA. Losses of U-boats mounted in the first half of 1941, and Raeder feared that the USA might join the war. He warned Hitler to prepare, but he was determined to avoid war with the US until he had won the war in the East. He was even prepared to suspend the Atlantic campaign in order not to provoke the Americans. When *U-552*, Lt. Erich Topp, sank the US destroyer *Reuben James* on 31 October 1941, US participation grew very close.

In May 1941 Admiral Lütjens, commanding the battleship *Bismarck* and the cruiser *Prinz Eugen* sailed from Gotenhafen (Gdynia) for the Atlantic. The plan of Operation *Rheinübung* was to maintain a German battleship presence in the Atlantic, but the British had detected the move and put a high priority on stopping it. *Bismarck* was intercepted in the Denmark Strait by *Hood*, *Prince of Wales* and the cruisers *Norfolk* and *Suffolk*. In the resulting action *Hood* was sunk with the loss of 1,400 lives, but the *Bismarck* also was damaged. Lütjens decided to send the *Prinz Eugen* to Brest and head for St Nazaire, where the *Bismarck* could be repaired. He skilfully evaded the pursuit, but then revealed his position by a long signal to the Naval Command. The British concentrated all available strength against the *Bismarck*, which was sunk on 27 May with the loss of all but 115 of the 2,106 men on board. Raeder's order to "fight to the last shell" had been obeyed; only after the war were questions asked about this tradition of blind obedience.[12] In his report Sir John Tovey, Commander-in-Chief of the Home Fleet, praised the *Bismarck*'s "most gallant fight against impossible odds, worthy of the old days of the Imperial German Navy, and she went down with her colours still flying". Hitler was personally affected by the loss of the *Bismarck*, his relationship with Raeder grew cooler and he set limits on the Navy's strategy. After the *Lützow* was torpedoed in June 1941 and put out of action for months, Hitler forbade the Navy to risk big ships in the Atlantic. The U-boats did their best to carry on the campaign alone, but could not do enough.

On 22 June 1941 three million German soldiers invaded the Soviet Union, opening the war on two fronts. The Naval High Command remained calm, as though it had given up coping with the overwhelming range of tasks before it. Adding another task, Germany declared war on the United States four days after Pearl Harbor, on 11 December 1941. Contemplating war against the Soviet Union, the Navy drafted plans for a future fleet, which far surpassed the then-available resources.[13] Actual operations were effectively handed over to the submarine force, the only part of the Navy still active at sea. Operation *Paukenschlag* ("Drumroll") in early 1942, submarine operations on the American coast, could be seen as an attempt to keep the U.S. Navy busy in home waters. Five hundred Allied ships were sunk but the U-boats suffered heavy losses: during the war thirty thousand out of forty thousand submariners died, but the operational control of the North Atlantic remained clearly in Allied hands. Fearing an Allied invasion, Hitler ordered the remaining heavy ships to Norwegian waters. The *Tirpitz* arrived in Trondheim on 16 January 1942, followed by *Admiral Scheer*, *Admiral Hipper* and *Lützow*, *Köln* and one destroyer squadron. *Scharnhorst*, *Gneisenau* and *Prinz Eugen*, escorted by six destroyers, fourteen torpedo boats and 250 aircraft, sailed from Brest on 11 February and succeeded in getting up the Channel with little damage. Operation *Cerberus* was a tactical masterpiece, but represented the abandonment of surface warfare in the open ocean. Now the Navy supported coastal convoys for *Barbarossa* and around the European coasts, mainly with minelayers and small craft, while the big ships served effectively as coastal anti-aircraft batteries and anti-invasion forces.

Taking all the events, changes and developments of the year 1941 into account, it is more than surprising that the German Naval Command started

---

[12] AFFLERBACH H., 'Untergang mit wehender Flagge', *Vierteljahrsheft für Zeitgeschichte* 49 (2001), 595–612.

[13] SALEWSKI M., *Die Deutschen und die See. Studien zur deutschen Marinegeschichte des 19. und 20. Jahrhunderts*, 2 vols, ed. J. ELVERT and S. LIPPERT (Stuttgart, 1998 and 2002).

planning for the future role and size of the German Fleet. This was contrary to the general focus of German warfare against the Soviet Union, as though the Naval Command was fully isolated from the rest of the *Wehrmacht*. Regarding the conduct of the Battle in the Atlantic, they left the decisions with the leader of the submarines. De facto the Naval Command became a shadow cabinet without any influence, working on utopia. This showed the command's – and especially Erich Raeder's – limited understanding of maritime and naval strategy.

Conclusion

The withdrawal of the German heavy ships to the North Sea marked the end of the Navy's short period of access to the open ocean. Allied technical and material superiority had defeated the German Atlantic campaign. Hitler's egocentricity and inability to understand the conduct of war at sea, as well as Raeder's reluctance to take an active part in the *Wehrmacht*, were further causes of mismanagement and failure. The French coast offered the best chances, but instead of taking time to develop the necessary bases and supplies, the Navy tried to command a huge area with a handful of ships inadequately supported. Finally, the *Kriegsmarine* abandoned its oceanic ambitions and reverted to being a coastal navy.

BRITAIN ON THE DEFENSIVE, 1939–1942

W.J.R. GARDNER is a Historian at the Naval Historical Branch of the Ministry of Defence, United Kingdom

ABSTRACT. *In a complex and fast-changing situation, Britain suffered repeated defeats and the loss of all her allies, but the flexibility and defensive depth offered by naval power allowed her to avoid the worst consequences, draw on support overseas and rebuild her strength. The German submarine force, which might have been a serious threat, was neglected by Germany until far too late.*

RÉSUMÉ. *Dans cette situation complexe et en perpétuel changement, la Grande-Bretagne essuya de nombreuses défaites et souffrit de la perte de tous ses alliés. La flexibilité et l'ampleur défensive que lui offrait son pouvoir maritime lui permirent cependant d'éviter des conséquences désastreuses en s'appuyant sur des soutiens outre-mer, et de retrouver sa puissance. La force sous-marine allemande, qui aurait pu constituer une menace sérieuse, fut jusqu'à bien trop tard négligée par l'Allemagne.*

.•.

INTRODUCTION

In the beginning it is necessary to define two terms: "Britain" and "defensive". Britain was, naturally, the focus of the Eurocentric war, but it was also at the centre of the British Empire, which took in nations in all significant continents and consequently brought huge resources of manpower, food and raw materials to bear on the conflict. To be sure these also implied commitments too, but these were not fully called in until late in 1941 with the entry of Japan into the war. Much, if not most, of this strength was accessed by the sea.

The main meaning given to "defensive" in the *Oxford English Dictionary* is "Having the quality of defending against attack or injury; serving for defence; protective". On land, its campaigns and warfare, this lends itself to easy comprehension. Broadly "I want to keep this piece of ground" (defensive): "my enemy wants to take it" (offensive). The fluid nature of the sea, both literally and conceptually, renders such easy definition diffuse at best. This is further muddied by the nature of maritime operations and warfare. One aspect of this is the differing outcomes of offensive and defensive events at different levels of warfare, and, indeed, the possibility of differing perceptions by the participants. Thus the German invasion of Norway in 1940 was fairly clearly offensive and the British (and French) reaction to it was obviously defensive at the strategic level. However, much of the British naval activity was extremely aggressive, leading to heavy German losses, and the British action is best considered as offensive – at least at the tactical level.[1] The withdrawal from Norway was tactically and strategically defensive. Thus it can be a complex matter to attribute offensive or defensive characteristics to specific campaigns or actions.

A further dimension of difficulty arises with the effects of the changing pattern of alliances during the whole World War, and this period in particular. From 1939 to the end of 1942 Britain (in the sense of the British Empire) spent approximately half of the period with at least one ally. This was principally the French until their capitulation in June 1940, and the Americans from December 1941 onwards.

The first important attribute of maritime-based warfare is the ability to accept or decline combat at least to some extent. This was moderated by the 20th century's own warfare innovations: submarines and aircraft. The former had made a significant impact during the First World War; the latter less so, but their growing inter-war potency made them impossible to ignore by the time of the Second. This was especially marked for navies operating within the vicinity of enemy-held coasts, which had to devote much material, tactical and training effort to countering enemy aircraft. This first became apparent in Norway, was continued in the Mediterranean and culminated in the loss of the capital ships *Prince of Wales* and *Repulse* in the South China Sea in December 1941.

The earliest period of the war, until mid-1940, offered a maritime war of relatively high activity, unlike the static "phoney war", *drôle de guerre* or *Sitzkrieg* on land. Examples were the early submarine campaign against shipping in the Atlantic and the River Plate action off South America. There was also the recurrent role of transporting, then maintaining, the British Expeditionary Force to France in 1939, another example of the utility of the options available to a maritime nation. It can be argued that these were all strategically defensive, but the first two were also offensive, if only tactically. Indeed it has been argued at some length that even the defence of convoys was an offensive measure.[2] But, however it is argued there was a clear capability of operating over a wide geographical spread in differing types of operations and warfare.

British maritime war from 1939 to the end of 1942 can be looked at from two perspectives: theatres of war and types of war. This analytical construct to some extent runs contrary to the kaleidoscopic pattern of activities as they would have been perceived by its participants. A relatively short account such as this

---

[1] The number of British and German losses was broadly similar, but the much lower numbers from which the Germans had started were proportionally much greater, an outcome which was to have an important effect later in the year.

[2] See particularly United Kingdom, The National Archive (hereafter TNA) ADM 234/578 *The Defeat of the Enemy Attack on Shipping: a Study of Policy and Operations*, Chapter 7.

also cannot take proper account of all activities. So, such significant activities as mine warfare and coastal forces receive little or no mention.

There were three main arenas of the maritime war: the Atlantic, Mediterranean and the Eastern theatre. All had different characteristics and they did not all immediately become active arenas of war. The Atlantic was active from the outset; the Mediterranean from the middle of 1940 with the simultaneous fall of France and the entry of Italy on the German side; and the East with the Japanese attacks on Pearl Harbor and other places in December 1941. But this apparent gradual progression from Western European conflict to worldwide conflagration did not mean that the initially unengaged regions could be ignored. They were still important generators of resource, both material and human, and thus they represented both opportunity and vulnerability.

In the Atlantic the war against shipping began from the outset with the sinking of the passenger liner *Athenia* by a German submarine on 3 September, emphasising the potential of the submarine for harming shipping. However, the Germans had a relatively small number of submarines, not all of which were suitable for oceanic warfare. The Admiralty initiated a convoy system from the outset, although this was nowhere near as extensive as it was to be later. Indeed the number of ships sailing outside of convoy supplied a sufficiency of targets for the relatively small number of submarines deployed. A further threat to shipping was posed by surface raiders. These took two forms – undisguised warships and vessels posing as merchant ships. The former were viewed as the greater threat because of their mobility and firepower, but both were more susceptible to reconnaissance – especially by aircraft – than the submarine, and thus they tended to operate in distant waters. The best-known was *Admiral Graf Spee*, a large cruiser with 11-inch guns and diesel engines. For several weeks she moved in the South Atlantic capturing ships. However, after a period in which she took up the efforts of many warships of greater size she was eventually intercepted by three smaller cruisers which inflicted sufficient damage on the German ship to force her to seek the shelter of a neutral port, prior to being scuttled.[3] This can be argued as a classic instance of *guerre de course* in which dealing with relatively minor forces occupies the efforts of much greater ones. However, it also gave a strong signal to the Germans that the British intended to counter such sorties. There were other German attempts to pursue this strategy. Effectively, this ended with the battleship *Bismarck*'s deployment in 1941, although it dripped on in the form of disguised raiders in ever more remote areas. Arguably, its greatest legacy was the British concern about the *Bismarck*'s sister-ship the *Tirpitz* until late in the war. Attacking surface raiders made it clear to the Germans that, whatever short-term gains might accrue from such expeditions, these ships were a declining asset. Further, the strategic location of Great Britain rendered deployment itself a risk. At another level, the nation with the greater experience of naval operations had an advantage even when confronted with a modern force.

---

[3] GROVE E., *The Price of Disobedience* (Annapolis, MD, 2001).

The submarine war against shipping continued during the period of this chapter and, indeed, for the duration of the European war: some further aspects of this will be considered below. Its effective prosecution and *de facto* victory just after the period discussed here owed much to the strategic imperatives, culture and experience of a nation which understood the importance of not just naval operations but maritime activity more generally. In this the effective use of the sea checked, then trumped, the dominant land power. It might be said that the relative lack of German maritime exploitation propelled it in the direction of *lebensraum*, although clearly other factors mattered too. Another way of looking at this might be to consider the flexibility that extensive maritime movement gives to those who use it. An important item of faith in land warfare is the superiority of internal lines of communication. This apparently works well on land although consideration of relatively straight geographical lines should always be factored with two further things: ease of movement and capacity of a given line of communication. Fewer such reasons tend to apply at sea.

In broad terms, the Atlantic war took a turn for the worse in April 1940 when German forces invaded Norway. British and French intervention was hasty and improvised. The naval battles were sometimes aggressively executed and although naval losses on both sides were broadly numerically similar, they fell proportionally harder on the Germans. This was to have important consequences later that year. The British losses included the aircraft-carrier *Glorious*. The net result was Norway in German hands, apparently a serious loss but one which, ironically, was to benefit the Allies strategically later, largely because of Hitler's pre-occupation with defence of that country.

Worse was to follow the following month with the German invasion, first of the Low Countries, then of France. The latter capitulated in June 1940. British seapower could not prevent these events but was able to rescue much of the British Army from Dunkirk and other French ports.[4] Again, this was an illustration of the utility of maritime strength. The succeeding autumn was to see the British fear of invasion. Although much of the conventional historiography concentrates on the subsequent air battles over Southeast England, it is now clear that the German Navy had been deterred from an amphibious invasion by the events in Norway earlier in the year.

The immediate consequences of the fall of France were serious, with profound consequences for the maritime war. Firstly, the Germans were given access to the Biscay ports, greatly increasing the potential for harm by German submarines. Secondly, despite the previously mentioned lack of appetite by the German Navy for cross-Channel operations, the dangers of invasion were not illusory, and required a significant allocation of naval forces for anti-invasion duties. Thirdly, the Italians joined the Axis, bringing the Mediterranean into play as an active theatre of war. Lastly, the residual French fleet, especially its capital units and submarines, if turned over to Germany, could have completely unbalanced the

---

[4] GARDNER W.J.R., *The Evacuation from Dunkirk: 'Operation Dynamo' 26 May–4 June 1940* (London, 2000).

distribution of naval power. This was resolved in July with naval attacks on Oran and elsewhere. Balance was restored, albeit at the cost of alienating much French opinion. If all these events had had a land analogue, then total downfall would have been likely to have eventuated, but the inherent strengths and flexibility of seapower prevented such an outcome.

Most significant events and developments in the Atlantic for the next year are described below. Mid-1941, however, saw the last of the large-scale surface ship sorties, with the *Bismarck*'s sinking of *Hood*, but her own demise followed in days. One feature of this operation was the involvement of Force H, a formation of battle units and supporting forces which operated predominantly in the Mediterranean but which was occasionally deployed to the Atlantic. The two most important events for the maritime war occurred far inland in Europe, and half a world away in the Pacific. The German invasion of Russia in June 1941 removed all realistic probability of a German invasion of Britain. The initial effect of this was positive, releasing more escorts for the Battle of the Atlantic. However, it generated an eventual demand for ships to support convoys to North Russia. Initially these were scheduled all year round, but after the disaster of convoy PQ17 in July 1942 they reverted to the winter months. However, their exposure to air, surface and sub-surface threats, as in the Mediterranean, with the addition of poor weather conditions, was considerable. In the Pacific the initial effect was setback after setback, but the entry of the USA into the war was a middle- and long-term benefit with access to almost limitless resources, both material and manpower. In Churchill's reported phrase, "So now we have won".

In the Mediterranean the war proper began with the entry of the Italians into the conflict in the summer of 1940 and the exit of the French. This piled problem on problem for the British. Although they were secure – at least for the moment – at the two ends of the Mediterranean, their central base of Malta was very vulnerable, being only a short distance from Italy. The Italian Navy was relatively strong in most types of ship except aircraft carriers, but this lack was more than offset by its strength in shore-based aircraft. The Italians had ambitions in Greece and North Africa. The British moving of land forces to Egypt and North Africa from Britain became much lengthier, as the Mediterranean became impassable and the convoys had to reach Egypt by way of the Cape of Good Hope. A successful operation to reduce the Italian battle fleet was carried out in November 1940. This was followed up by other victories such as Matapan the following year. Less successful was the attempt in 1941 by British land forces to take Crete in the face of German opposition. This operation and the subsequent evacuation led to the losses of several ships, including two cruisers. The Mediterranean as a largely closed body of water did not demonstrate the asymmetries that were evident in the uses of the sea in the Atlantic.

The key to British strategy was the retention of Malta. It would have been very difficult, if not impossible, for the British to have done anything of significance in the Mediterranean had Malta been lost. It was nothing new for the Mediterranean to be vital to British strategy, as had been evinced many times during the sail era, but rarely more critically than in the years 1940–1943.

Keeping Malta in existence as an entity, as a small island and as a base for limited offensive operations was never easy. As adduced earlier, Malta was within easy reach of Italian airbases, especially in Sicily. It was difficult but essential to maintain a fighter defence, which could be done only by reinforcing and resupply by sea. Further, the Maltese population needed supplying. Running convoys to Malta, from either east or west, involved an extremely hostile environment over, on and under the sea. It also meant a significant allocation of forces and a greater acceptance of loss than elsewhere in the maritime conflict. Over thrity convoys were run, some of which got only a few ships through.[5] The maintenance of Malta was also important in maintaining an offensive, when possible once the demands of defence had been met, against the supply of Axis forces in North Africa. This, ultimately, was extremely successful, throttling the efficacy of enemy land forces through air, submarine and surface warship actions. The culmination was the amphibious landings on the Atlantic and Mediterranean coasts of Africa, Operation TORCH in November 1942.

In the Far East the active war started in early December 1941 with Japanese near-simultaneous attacks on Pearl Harbor, the Malayan peninsula and other places. For the British, the Americans and many indigenous people a disastrous year followed. For the British particularly, their strategy in the East hinged on the retention and reinforcement of Singapore and the large naval base that had been built up there. An early blow was struck by the Japanese in December 1941 when Force Z – the capital ships *Prince of Wales* and *Repulse* – were sunk by Japanese shore-based aircraft. However, in practice, all that British maritime capability permitted was the ability to reinforce Malaya and Singapore and then conduct a limited and somewhat chaotic evacuation, leaving much of the military and all of the native populations behind. Later setbacks were to follow: the Battle of the Java Sea was another Allied defeat for the British, Americans and Dutch in February 1942. Later, in the Indian Ocean, the aircraft carrier *Hermes* was lost to air attack in April. This then led to a period of relatively long-range warfare around the Indian Ocean. The Japanese had made huge strategic strides and had further ambitions towards India and the Persian Gulf as well as the East African littoral, but they were reaching the point of over-extension. They still remained a potent threat to the exiguous residual British naval forces, however, which played a poor strategic hand, using weak and inadequate forces, as well as possible. They would use the base of Trincomalee in Ceylon except when it was threatened imminently. Then they would move to the East African coast. Tactically, they would often move in the direction of the enemy by night, then back in the day. For the rest of the period submarine operations were the only offensive action possible and, based on Ceylon, these were carried out by a small number of British and Dutch submarines. This again demonstrated the options open to an alliance which fully understood the sea and deployed a range of capabilities. By such means naval forces contained the threat as much as possible

---

[5] LLEWELLYN-JONES M., *The Royal Navy and the Mediterranean Convoys* (London, 2014).

until, in the following year – beyond the scope of this chapter – it became possible to take up a more offensive posture.

Turning to different types of warfare in the period 1939–1942, there are several taxonomies that could be considered. One might be to analyse the actual encounters that occurred; another might classify it by ship type and a third would be a combination of the two previous approaches. This last one, broadly, is what is followed here.

In 1939 the category of "capital ship" was still limited to battleships and the few remaining battlecruisers. The former type was approaching its ultimate form: well-armed, heavily armoured and fast, and the latter a throwback to the era of the earlier 20th century. What had changed radically was the size of battlefleets and the ways of deploying them. Instead of vast fleets, much smaller numbers of ships were manoeuvred more flexibly.[6] A further advance lay in the practice of night warfare. This was exercised extensively and a further dimension was added by the development of radar. This gave several benefits, particularly air warning, tactical picture compilation and accurate ranges, especially at distance, for gunnery fire control. Despite the judgement that the Second World War saw the eclipse of the battleship as the premier naval unit due to the speedy development of the aircraft carrier, it was still of use in the earlier part of the war. Its utility lay not just in combating its own kind but also in carrying out shore bombardments. The latter had hardly been done in the First World War, largely because of the perceived risks of taking such valuable ships into inshore waters. The second conflict saw bombardment become more prevalent in such places as Norway and North Africa. This was a potent capability, giving the British the ability to inflict massive firepower from the sea with almost no warning. Certainly, defences both mobile and static could be deployed against bombardment but this implied a considerable investment of resources by an enemy. At sea, there were several encounters between heavy ships, such as at Cape Matapan in the Mediterranean, where the British triumphed over a broadly equal Italian force. However, the pursuit and destruction of the *Bismarck* in the Atlantic in the spring of 1941 is perhaps the best example of battleship conflict. This takes in the difficulties of reconnaissance in the period, the British necessity of having to split forces in order to cover *Bismarck*'s courses of action and the vagaries of weather. After the initial setback of the loss of the battlecruiser *Hood* in the Denmark Strait, *Bismarck* was later relocated, and then dealt with by battleships. Two further matters arise from this series of actions. The first is the part played by aircraft carriers, both for reconnaissance and then for attack on the German battleship, the hobbling of which was very important for bringing it to its final end. Thus the aircraft carrier was growing in utility, not yet reaching the dominance it attained by the end of the war, but moving in that direction. Further, in the Mediterranean it developed a significant air-defence capability as well as being able to deliver much-needed

---

[6] BELL C.M., *The Royal Navy, Seapower and Strategy Between the Wars* (Stanford, CA, 2000), p. 132.

fighter aircraft to Malta. Thus was the ability to exploit seapower given another manifestation. The other point of note about the *Bismarck* campaign was that the system of trans-Atlantic shipping continued on its way. Certainly there were diversions and detachment of some escort forces, but the system continued without abnormal disruption or loss. The action as a whole indicates the options open to a nation when it understands the potential of the sea and reinforces this perception by a significant investment in associated equipment, personnel and expertise.

Mentioning trade shipping opens a huge area of warfare: the protection of that shipping against the war fought against it by Axis forces, principally German submarines. The classical way of looking at this war-long conflict is as one of convoy battles with multiple sinkings of merchant ships being only slowly overcome, and the central role of monocausal explanations such as signals intelligence and long-range maritime aircraft. There is an element of truth in this but, like the iceberg, much more lies below. Firstly, supply, whether it is for food, raw materials or munitions of war, has to be sourced, bought outright or otherwise financed, then brought to maritime loading points. Account has to be taken of the availability of suitable ship types and of appropriate cargo-handling facilities. Groups of ships then have to be marshalled into convoys and provided with escorting forces. In turn, these warships and aircraft will have to have been built, their crews trained, and organised. A convoy would then either receive submarine attention or not, and subsequently take damage or not. What is surprising is that most convoys were not attacked.[7] At the convoy's destination similar problems of unloading and distribution arose. The whole system of supply called on a vast panorama of resources and depended crucially on the ability to exploit the fundamental characteristics of the sea: ease of movement and carrying capacity. It also drew on merchant and naval ships and the ability to build and repair them. Manning was important both at sea and in support of these units, directly and indirectly. Science, technology and engineering were significant too. The ability to organise at different levels and the handling of information were critical factors as well. These facets, even when they did not impinge directly on the sea, came most readily to a nation whose human talents had an inbuilt understanding of how to use the asset of an ocean.

Turning to submarines, this was a sphere of warfare that had probably reached a degree of maturity in the First World War unmatched then by naval aviation. Whereas the latter had made significant progress in the interwar years, submarine improvement had been incremental, rather than revolutionary. Certainly the intensity of the First World War had resulted in a good deal of innovation, but much of this had been nugatory, or at least premature.[8] As a result, Britain began the Second World War with submarines that were qualitatively little different

---

[7] GARDNER W.J.R., *Decoding History: The Battle of the Atlantic and Ultra* (Basingstoke, 1999), pp. 185-8.
[8] EDMONDS M., ed., *100 Years of the Trade: Royal Navy Submarines Past, Present and Future* (Lancaster, 2001), Ch. 4.

from those of twenty years before. Although British submarines were never to enjoy the significance and prominence which those of the *Kriegsmarine* did, they were nevertheless of great utility. In the Atlantic theatre their main roles were reconnaissance, minelaying (especially in areas effectively inaccessible to surface minelayers) and even convoy escort, notably in the hard-fought convoys to North Russia. In the Eastern theatre a small number of submarines, after the low points of the falls of Singapore, Malaya and other possessions, were engaged in relatively low-level warfare against Japanese merchant shipping. Although the results were small by the standards of world war they represented almost the sole way in which offensive action could be taken against a rampant enemy. But it was in the Mediterranean that submarines were most effective. Here their greatest contribution to the war effort lay in interdicting Axis supply shipping to North Africa. Although this was an activity undertaken by aircraft and surface forces too, their availability and relative vulnerability when Malta was under the most intense air attack was often limited: under such circumstances submarines were often the only offensive forces operating from Malta. Nevertheless, when in harbour they might have to submerge with a minimum crew during the day to evade air attack.

So, what did the sea contribute to Britain's efforts in the years 1939–1942? Firstly, it provided the ability to transmit the substances of survival and war to the point of use. In general the military activities in the campaigns in the West, Mediterranean and East all occurred within short distances from the sea: it was different, clearly, in the land war between Germany and Russia. Here the sea had a role to play as an instrument of partial supply, but no more. Returning to Britain, sea supply was not always easy, perhaps most obviously in the sustenance and reinforcement of Malta, but it was nearly always possible. Secondly, the sea gave Britain a number of strategic choices not open to her enemies. Most of all, it enabled Britain to play a weak hand extraordinarily well. It is an aphorism, largely true, that seapower cannot win a war but can prevent defeat. Thus, the first duty of any war leadership is not to lose a war. This may seem self-evident, but disregard of this all-important principle generally leads to disaster. Looking back from the 20th century to the 19th, the Napoleonic Wars support this assertion. Although Napoleon's downfall began with his withdrawal from Moscow, his defeat was reinforced by both the blockade of the Continent and, even more so, the long campaign in the Iberian peninsula, only made possible by British seaborne supply and reinforcement. Returning to the next century, the sea provided both a barrier to an enemy's hostile intention and a many-branched highway for military and civil traffic. At the grand strategic level it allowed the movement of all types of resources between theatres. It is difficult to envisage the shift of a large German land formation, such as a division, from Eastern to Western fronts, from battle-readiness in the first location to the same state in the second, with anything like as little time and effort as would be used by Force H transferring from the Mediterranean to the Atlantic. At the strategic level, too, the inherent flexibility and mobility of naval forces was a key contributor to British efficacy. Consider a notional British destroyer which might have taken part in the Norwegian campaign bombarding land targets, then embarking and conveying troops at Dunkirk, before being engaged in battles with similar German ships in the North Sea before escorting Atlantic convoys, all of this in the period of the war under consideration.

These strengths combined enabled Britain to continue in a war which some calculations would have suggested that it had no right to continue with, far less have any expectation of winning, even in the longer term. Consider the situation in which the Britain and the British Empire was in from mid-1940 until the end of 1941. It had no full-scale national allies, minimal presence on the ground in Europe, was for most of this time under threat of invasion and suffered from significant air bombardment. For most participants in a modern war this would have been overwhelming, if not terminal. For Britain, however, the sea provided advantages which allowed it to hold its position against such odds: through supply and naval flexibility, a position could be held until the arrival of salvation from across the ocean.

BRITAIN AND THE SEA, 1943-1945

CHRISTOPHER BAXTER is an Honorary Lecturer at the Queen's University Belfast, United Kingdom

ABSTRACT. *Britain fought as part of an allied coalition which was completely dependent on the sea to connect its different components and to mount all its major military operations. The invasions of Sicily, Italy and France, the campaigns in the East Indies and the Pacific, were wholly dependent on the command of the sea, and on shipping to exploit it. The sea made possible military success, economic survival and political unity.*

RÉSUMÉ. *La Grande-Bretagne combattit au sein d'une coalition alliée qui dépendait exclusivement de la mer pour connecter ses différentes parties et monter ses principales opérations militaires. Les invasions de la Sicile, de l'Italie et de la France, les campagnes dans le Pacifique et les Indes orientales n'auraient pu être réalisées sans le contrôle de la mer, et son exploitation par le transport maritime. La mer a rendu possible succès militaires, survie économique et unité politique.*

∴

When Japan formally surrendered on 2 September 1945, drawing the Second World War to a close, Britain and its Allies were in secure control of all the oceans of the world. During that conflict the Royal Navy played a decisive part in executing a maritime strategy which took centre stage after Britain's withdrawal from the European continent following France's collapse in June 1940. Julian Corbett, the influential British naval historian, has explained that "by maritime strategy we mean the principles which govern a war in which the sea is a substantial factor".[1] Corbett was writing in 1911; during 1943–1945, Britain's maritime strategy had evolved to include amphibious and submarine warfare, escort-to-convoy systems, floating logistics organisations or "fleet trains", air power (both ship-borne and shore-based) and economic and naval blockade.

The ability to execute such a broad maritime strategy was based, in part, upon centuries of experience at sea. The Second World War was not the first time that Britain had fought successfully against a determined foe to control sea communications across the world's oceans and its own narrow coastal waters, while also bringing force to bear against its enemies by projecting power ashore. By

---

[1] CORBETT J., *Some Principles of Maritime Strategy* (London, 1972), p. 13.

securing command of the seas the latter were, concomitantly, also denied to the enemy to help support its war effort. Captain Stephen Roskill, the British official historian of the *War at Sea* volumes, has argued that maritime power depended upon three elements: strength, security and transport. The "Strength Element" rested upon sheer weight in numbers; the "Security Element" related to the possession and protection of bases; while the "Transport Element" was based on an industrial capacity to build and repair ships, and a strong merchant fleet to facilitate the safe passage of commercial and military traffic.[2]

Britain, however, could not execute a successful maritime strategy on its own. It drew support from the Empire and Dominions and had powerful Allies, such as the United States, to help gain command of the seas. The growing wartime maritime assets of the Dominions played a vital role in ensuring the safe movement of men, raw materials, food and munitions around the globe. For a significant period in 1943 and 1944, for example, over 80 per cent of North Atlantic convoy escort duties were the Royal Canadian Navy's responsibility, while South African shipyards were used to repair ships and service convoys.[3] The expansion of the United States Navy meant that by the end of war it became the world's leading naval power and was in possession of some 23 battleships, 99 carriers, 72 cruisers, 380 destroyers, 360 destroyer escorts and 235 submarines.[4]

Although the exploitation of the sea through a powerful maritime alliance allowed Britain to move men and trade around its Empire and multiple theatres of war, the British dependence upon imports delivered by the sea also proved a weakness. Britain relied on food, oil and raw materials for its industries to arrive every week: the minimum import requirement for 1943 was twenty-seven million tons. With European ports under German control, most of Britain's vital supplies now had to come across the Atlantic from Canada and the United States.[5] Admiral Karl Dönitz, the head of the *Kriegsmarine*'s U-boat command, knew that the Atlantic theatre was the key to Britain's survival and attempted to carry out a policy of "sea denial". In 1943 the outcome of that campaign remained uncertain. That March, British, Allied and neutral merchant shipping losses had risen to 693,389 tons a month, with 120 vessels sunk. The Admiralty remarked later that "the Germans never came so near to disrupting communications between the New World and the Old as in the first twenty days of March 1943".[6] Yet, within two months the Royal Navy (with the Canadians and Americans) had gained the upper hand in the Atlantic, the result of better air support (new escort carriers and long-range bombers), technological advances in weapons and location equipment, and intelligence breakthroughs, such as cracking the new Enigma key employed by the German *Kriegsmarine*. In May 1943, merchant

---

[2] ROSKILL S., *The War at Sea, 1939-1945* (London, 1954-63, 3 vols in 4), I, pp. 3-7.
[3] JOHNSTON I., 'The Dominions and British maritime power in World War II', *Global War Studies* 11 (2014), 103 and 113.
[4] BAER G., *One Hundred Years of Sea Power: The U.S. Navy, 1890-1990* (Stanford, 1994), p. 182.
[5] BARNETT C., *Engage the Enemy More Closely* (Harmondsworth, 2000), p. 576.
[6] ROSKILL, *The War at Sea 1939-1945*, II, pp. 367 and 485.

ship losses dropped dramatically, to 299,428 tons with fifty-eight ships sunk, and Dönitz withdrew his U-boats from the North Atlantic.[7]

The outcome was critical. The safe passage and support of land operations required command of the seas, not least for the all-important build-up of forces for the invasion of Europe. However, the U-boat threat and the potential for German warships to break out from their ports (most notably the *Tirpitz* and the *Scharnhorst*, stationed in Norway) remained a concern. The enemy occupied a large swathe of coastline and this led to a certain division of Britain's maritime forces to keep watch on ports from where attacks could be launched against merchant shipping. The amount of naval resources needed to devote to this task was alleviated somewhat by the fact that the enemy's lines of operations (particularly from northwest France to southern Norway) crossed British home waters. Reconnaissance and minelaying from the air, together with superior intelligence (from well-placed agents and the decryption of enemy signals), eased the strain on the Royal Navy even further.

Consequently, German and Italian surface vessels remained boxed up in their ports and worldwide U-boats losses mounted: 237 were sunk in 1943 and 242 in 1944. Britain, through its maritime alliance with other powers, was therefore able gradually to open up global sea communications, allowing for flexibility in deployment and the projection of power ashore. Global connectivity through control of the oceans saw Britain and its Allies join up the various theatres of war across the world, a feat that the Axis powers could never emulate. Finite resources (especially in shipping) and the Europe-first strategy, however, meant that a degree of sequencing took place in relation to which theatre took priority. The Allies were nevertheless enabled by their supremacy at sea to choose where to prosecute the war. Once North Africa had been cleared they chose to engage the enemy in Sicily and then on the Italian mainland. They fought initially in the Mediterranean because an invasion of Western Europe was unrealisable before 1944, as the *Bolero* build-up (the movement of American forces to the United Kingdom) was a long way from completion.[8]

The British preference for a Mediterranean strategy required substantial shipping and landing craft to support it while resources still had to be built up for an invasion of Europe. The Royal Navy expanded more slowly than the other services and in 1943 it was required to man a wave of new construction just when the Ministry of Labour was warning that less than half of the 912,000 additional men and women allocated to the services and industry for the last half of 1943 could actually be found.[9] The result was that the Royal Navy could devote few naval resources to the Far East, but some scholars have argued that the Mediterranean was also an unnecessary drain on resources (especially shipping), restricting Britain's options and diverting attention away from the

---

[7] *Ibid.*, p. 485; DOUGLAS W.A.B. et al, *A Blue Water Navy: The Official Operational History of the Royal Canadian Navy the Second in World War, 1943-1945* (St Catharines, ONT, 2007), p. 35.
[8] BAER, *Sea Power*, pp. 223 and 227-8.
[9] EHRMAN J., *Grand Strategy*, V, *August 1943-September 1944* (London, 1956), pp. 41-4.

main war effort.[10] There is no doubt that Britain's maritime ally, the United States, saw some merit in these arguments and did not want to get dragged into what it perceived to be a non-essential theatre before it successfully pushed for, and secured, an agreement to mount a cross-Channel invasion at the Cairo and Tehran conferences in November and December 1943.[11]

Nevertheless, the decision to attack Sicily and the Italian mainland was an Allied one, made by its political leaders at the Casablanca conference of January 1943 and based on the ability to project Anglo-American maritime (principally amphibious) power ashore. Its successful execution was the result of sea control in the Atlantic and Mediterranean and the ability to bring assault forces together across the oceans from Britain and the North American and African continents. By 8 July, a stream of convoys, comprising some 2,500 ships with over 130,000 British and Americans soldiers embarked, was moving towards Sicily and, two days later, landings were successfully carried out. The capture of Sicily in August 1943 and the subsequent invasion of the Italian mainland the following month delivered very real political and military benefits. They led to the surrender of Italy in September, control of the surrounding seas and the passing of the greater part of the Italian fleet into British and Allied hands.[12]

With Italy knocked out of the war, a key British objective since 1940, the Allies occupied valuable ports in southern Italy, while liberating Sardinia and Corsica. Britain and its maritime partners now secured an even tighter grip over the whole of the Mediterranean while reducing the amount of coastline available to the enemy for it to conduct attacks against Allied shipping.[13] Furthermore, command of the seas in these waters allowed Britain and its Allies to provide naval gunfire support, supplies and reinforcements to the landings at Salerno in September 1943 and to the Anzio beachhead four months later when the land armies encountered stiff enemy resistance. Sea power had enabled the Allies to launch an audacious amphibious assault against Anzio, just thirty miles south of Rome, in January 1944, in an attempt to draw off enemy forces from the main Italian front. The assault convoys, assembled in Naples Bay, achieved complete surprise with thirty-six thousand men and three thousand vehicles put ashore, but operational mistakes allowed the enemy to counter-attack with ferocity and stalemate ensued. The invading force was unable to link up with the main land armies until May, just days before Allied troops entered Rome on 6 June 1944.[14]

Throughout 1944, the Royal Navy gradually extended its maritime control northwards up both coasts of Italy, conducting successful attacks against German coastal traffic attempting to supply its forces in the Balkans. Prosecuting a maritime strategy in the Mediterranean after the Italian surrender, however, could still meet with failure if all the elements to pursue such a strategy were not

---

[10] See BARNETT, *Engage the Enemy*, ch.22.
[11] BAER, *Sea Power*, p. 227.
[12] ROSKILL S., *The Strategy of Sea Power: Its Development and Application* (London, 1962), pp. 202-6.
[13] *Ibid.*, p. 206.
[14] ROSKILL, *The War at Sea 1939-1945*, III, pp. 170-88, 297-309.

in place. The British decision to occupy Cos, Leros and a few smaller islands off the coast of Asia Minor in the Aegean during late 1943 ended in disaster. This was in part due to the fact that the British did not have enough resources to carry out a combined operation against German-held Rhodes, enabling the enemy to hold command of the air over those waters.[15] Indeed, chronic shortages of shipping continued to have an impact on the Royal Navy's ability to project force in strength in multiple theatres of war. The decision to launch an enlarged assault against Anzio could be realised only by withdrawing most of Southeast Asia Command's combined operation vessels, and abandoning an attack on Rhodes by which the British had hoped to re-establish the position lost in the Aegean.[16]

Meanwhile, nearly all the Mediterranean fleet's larger warships and many combined operation vessels had been recalled to Britain to prepare for operation *Neptune*, the naval component of the invasion of Normandy, operation *Overlord*. By 1944, the main conditions for the execution of successful maritime strategy across the channel were falling into place: command of the seas, command of the air, the necessary amphibious assault craft and the continued *Bolero* build-up of forces. Proof of British and Allied success was the fact that the German *Kriegsmarine* was unable to oppose the invasion of France. The peak year of 1944 saw the sailing of more than 380 convoys to the United Kingdom, including 18,856 merchant ships and 3,070 escorts.[17] The Normandy invasion took place on 6 June from an armada of over 6,900 vessels, including some 1,600 auxiliary and merchant ships required for the build-up phase, 1,213 naval vessels and more than 4,100 landing craft. Of the 444 major warships (from battleships to minesweepers), 316 were from the Royal Navy, 54 from the United States Navy and 63 from the Royal Canadian Navy. The massive operational orders for *Neptune* dealt with twenty-one separate activities, from minelaying to deception to loading schedules and underwater pipelines.[18]

Once the assault divisions were ashore and the follow-up convoys were running smoothly, the Royal Navy's main tasks were the speedy construction of artificial harbours, the security of crowded anchorages in Seine Bay against U-boats and torpedo craft and the provision of naval gunfire support for the army. Indeed, Field Marshal Erwin Rommel, the Commander Army Group B, reported to Adolf Hitler that Allied naval gunfire support was such "that no operation of any kind is possible in the area commanded by this rapid-fire artillery, by either infantry or tanks".[19] Within a month, despite a severe and disruptive storm, the combined build-up stood at 929,000 men, 586,000 tons of supplies and 177,000 vehicles.[20] Six weeks after D-Day, on 15 August, the Allies launched another large-scale maritime amphibious operation, against the south

---

[15] *Ibid.*, pp. 188–204.
[16] ROSKILL, *Sea Power*, p. 210.
[17] BAER, *Sea Power*, p. 228; DOUGLAS, *Blue Water Navy*, pp. 78 and 105.
[18] *Ibid.*, pp. 231 and 235.
[19] ROMMEL is quoted from *ibid.*, p. 230.
[20] *Ibid.*, p. 231.

of France, operation *Dragoon*. The flexibility of sea power allowed for the release of amphibious assault from the Normandy beachhead, to be deployed once again in the Mediterranean. British and American escort carriers provided close air support from the sea and the land forces encountered little resistance. *Dragoon* saw the capture of Marseilles, another major port on the French coast, Cherbourg having already been secured in the north during late June.[21]

In Western Europe the breakout of Allied armies from Normandy in August 1944 and the rapid advance across France and Belgium produced the need for new ports of supply, as the artificial harbours off the original assault area and Cherbourg were now too far from the front. Boulogne, Calais, Dunkirk, Ostend and Le Havre were captured in September 1944 but they were so blocked and wrecked that many weeks elapsed before appreciable quantities of stores could be unloaded in them. On 4 September the deep-water port of Antwerp fell to the British Army virtually intact. The Germans, however, held both banks of the River Scheldt and the Allies could make no use of it whatsoever. It took three months before the port could be opened (28 November), the result of focusing instead on operation *Market Garden*, the failed attempt to drive across the Maas and Lower Rhine at Arnhem. Here, Roskill has argued that the banks of the Scheldt should have been cleared earlier as "the navies could not restore the armies' mobility until they had gained the use of Antwerp".[22] Some figures for April 1945 illustrate Antwerp's importance. In that month 1,341,610 tons of stores were delivered for the land armies through the port (triple the amount discharged through Le Havre and Rouen combined), together with 288,809 tons of petrol, oil and lubricants.[23]

As Allied armies fought their way across Europe, the Royal Navy and its coalition partners remained busy on the seas. They patrolled the Atlantic, tackled a new inshore threat from U-boats operating from Norway and continued Arctic convoys to their ally, the Soviet Union, delivering 450,000 tons of supplies in 1943 (without loss), over one million tons in 1944 and just under 650,000 tons in 1945. In 1944, the Royal Navy seized the initiative in the Arctic, sending ships ahead to attack U-boats, while aircraft aboard escort carriers kept U-boats submerged ahead of convoys.[24] The U-boats, however, were never concentrated in sufficient numbers to cause more than slight damage and sixty-six were destroyed around British coastal waters in the littoral campaigns between August 1944 and May 1945.[25] Furthermore, the sinking of the *Scharnhorst* in December 1943 by the Royal Navy (aided once again by vital signals intelligence) and the destruction of the *Tirpitz* at Tromsö by the Royal Air Force in November 1944 allowed the British finally to contemplate a projection of force into the Far Eastern theatre.[26] Events

---

[21] See EHRMAN, *Grand Strategy*, V, pp. 377-78 and ROSKILL, *Sea Power*, p. 216.
[22] *Ibid.*, p. 225 and BARNETT, *Engage the Enemy*, pp. 845-7.
[23] *Ibid.*, p. 851.
[24] *Ibid.*, p. 748 and LAMBERT A., 'Seizing the Initiative: The Arctic Convoys 1944-45', in *Naval Power in the Twentieth Century*, ed. N.A.M. RODGER (London, 1996), pp. 151-62.
[25] DOUGLAS et al., *Blue Water Navy*, pp. 218-21 and 407.
[26] BARNETT, *Engage the Enemy*, pp. 739-47.

in Mediterranean and European waters continually thwarted bold plans for any type of amphibious operation across the Bay of Bengal, with the result that the reconquest of Burma had to be carried out by means of a long and gruelling land campaign.

Nevertheless, by the spring of 1944 the British Eastern Fleet in command of the Bay of Bengal was able to launch carrier air attacks, firstly on targets in Sumatra and then against the important naval base of Soerabaya in eastern Java. Control of the Indian Ocean and the Bay of Bengal having been re-established, supplies and reinforcements for the land army in Burma flowed in almost unhindered. Britain's reasserted maritime supremacy also prevented Japanese reinforcements and supplies from reaching Rangoon by sea. The most fundamental question, however, revolved around where Britain's maritime assets should be concentrated: should they be deployed to Southeast Asia, where most of Britain's imperial interests lay, or in the Central Pacific. After prolonged debate, it was decided to form a British fleet to serve with the United States Navy in the Pacific, which the Americans accepted at the Quebec conference in September 1944. The British Pacific Fleet (BPF) would become the single most powerful strike force assembled by the Royal Navy during the Second World War.[27]

Raised from the British Eastern Fleet and additional units sent from the European theatre, the BPF comprised four battleships, five fleet, four light fleet and eight escort carriers, ten cruisers, forty destroyers and over 170 minesweepers and support vessels, together with some thirty submarines. The BPF attacked Sumatra as part of operation *Outbreak* while on passage to Australia. After reaching the Dominion it sailed north to support the American landings at Okinawa, operation *Iceberg*. Following replenishment and a brief sortie against Truk, the BPF operated with the US Sixth Fleet off the coast of Japan until the Japanese surrender ended its activities. Before the ships came home they helped to repatriate thousands of British prisoners-of-war. While even the most vehement supporter of the BPF might find it difficult to argue that this British naval force was essential to the defeat of Japan (it participated in four operations amounting to 140 carrier strike days), the Royal Navy learnt valuable maritime lessons from working with the Americans in a new, highly specialised type of warfare.[28]

The major challenge for the BPF was the sheer scale of its operational setting, especially as the British had promised the Americans that their ships would be self-supporting. During the war, the Royal Navy had never fought so far from its bases for so long. During *Iceberg*, the BPF's advanced base was at Leyte in the Philippines, some 800 miles from its theatre of operations in Okinawa, while Leyte itself was some 3,500 miles from its forward base in Australia and that was 12,000 miles from its rear base in the United Kingdom. Ships designed to be at

---

[27] BAXTER C., *The Great Power Struggle in East Asia, 1944-50: Britain, America and Post-War Rivalry* (Basingstoke, 2009), Ch. 1; ROBB-WEBB J., *The British Pacific Fleet Experience and Legacy, 1944-1950* (Farnham, 2013), p. 52.
[28] *Ibid.*, pp. 13-14.

sea for days were now expected to be at sea for weeks.[29] Due to the vast distances in the Pacific and the lack of developed bases, the Americans had begun to perfect the art of operating their mobile "Fleet Train". British fleets, however, had always relied to a greater extent on fixed bases and Britain's "Fleet Train" of some sixty ships of varying types and nationalities only just met the requirements of the Royal Navy's warships and relied on a very liberal American interpretation of self-sufficiency.[30]

While the long-term regional political benefits of the BPF's deploying to the Pacific have been questioned with regard to Britain's post-war position in Far East,[31] its presence nevertheless showed the Americans a British determination to fight to the last enemy, while the flexibility, adaptability, courage and determination of the Royal Navy's sailors won admiration from the Allies. Operating in the Pacific gave the Royal Navy a chance to work closely with the most powerful navy in the world and to learn valuable lessons in carrying out power-projection operations at great distances over long periods against a capable and dogged enemy.[32] And it was the destruction of the Japanese main fleets off Midway Island, in the Solomons Campaign, in the battles of the Philippine Sea and of Leyte Gulf that made the Allies' offensive strategy possible, while the complete destruction of Japan's merchant navy brought it to the brink of collapse.

Allied command of the seas in the Far East and the Pacific played a crucial role in the defeat of Japan. Like Britain, merchant shipping was of immense importance to Japan, its armies, its population and outlying Empire, but the Japanese made a disastrous strategic mistake in not taking steps to protect it. By August 1945 Japan had in service only 12 per cent of its pre-war merchant fleet and because of fuel losses only half of that, some 312,000 tons, was in operation. In comparison, the Allies at the same time had eighty-eight million tons in operation.[33] The result was a population left starving, an economy in chaos, trade at a standstill and Japanese armies unable to be supplied. Fittingly, it was aboard a battleship the USS *Missouri* that the final proceedings of the Second World War were concluded on 2 September 1945 with Japan's formal surrender, perhaps illustrating that it was sea power and a maritime strategy that had largely brought about the downfall of the Axis powers.

During the period under study British sea power provided the key to Britain's national security and the means to deliver crushing blows to Britain's enemies. The sea helped to bond together a materially superior coalition of states and to connect the entire world of friendly and unfriendly shore lines. The former comprised a maritime network of economic strength and the latter were potential targets for the projection of military power from the sea. The inherent mobility of sea power allowed Britain and its Allies to express a large degree of

---

[29] DOUGLAS et al., *Blue Water Navy*, p. 538.
[30] ROSKILL, *Sea Power*, p. 227.
[31] See BAXTER, *Great Power Struggle*.
[32] ROBB-WEBB, *British Pacific Fleet*, pp. 51 and 77.
[33] BAER, *Sea Power*, p. 235.

strategic and operational agility, creating the conditions to achieve surprise, perhaps best illustrated by the assaults on Sicily and Normandy.[34] For Britain, the sea became a multifaceted enabler and its maritime strategy – one that by definition is joint but rests on an ability to operate on, over, under and from the sea – remained one of the nation's most useful and powerful assets. Britain's use of the sea could even alleviate inland transport problems by moving large blocks of traffic (such as coal, iron, steel and iron ore) over long distances by coasters instead of by rail.[35]

Like every other part of Britain's war effort, the Royal Navy had grown substantially from just under two hundred thousand men at the outbreak of war to over eight hundred thousand men and seventy-four thousand women in 1945. In 1943 some nine hundred thousand workers were also committed to maritime industrial resources, including shipbuilding. Modern warships required greater numbers of electrical and radar personnel in ships' companies too, while the Fleet Air Arm grew as new escort carriers came off the production line. This meant that more resource had to be poured into training, putting further pressure on the Navy's manpower requirements.[36] Indeed, the clear divide between what did and did not constitute "suitable" work for women became increasingly irrelevant. As well as writers, messengers, stewards and cooks, Wrens (Women's Royal Naval Service) became wireless telegraphists, bomb-range markers and radio mechanics. There was also a group of Special Duties (Linguist) Wrens, often with language degrees, who were drafted to Stations around the coast, intercepting signals, not to mention those posted to Bletchley Park.[37]

Even after the Royal Navy decided to scrap old battleships, cruisers and destroyers in an attempt to alleviate the manpower situation, a shortfall of personnel, however, remained. But, as part of a maritime coalition, the Royal Navy could turn to Allies to help meet its operational objectives; witness, for example, the American decision to send extra battleships, cruisers and destroyers for *Neptune*.[38] Before the war, the Dominions maintained separate navies but they were small and relied significantly on the Royal Navy for training, shipbuilding and security. Yet, by the war's end, all the Dominions had developed substantial maritime resources and contributed to the overall British and Allied maritime strategy for defeating the Axis powers. The Canadians played a critical role, not just with regard to Allied maritime strategy, but in Britain's survival, escorting over twenty-five thousand ships to the United Kingdom and building some 3.6 million tons of shipping. Canadian personnel dedicated to shipping repairs had risen from four thousand workers in 1939 to some seventy-five thousand at its

---

[34] GRAY C., 'The Leverage of Sea Power', in *Dimensions of Sea Power: Strategic Choice in the Modern World*, ed. E. GROVE and P. HORE (Hull, 1998), pp. 36, 38–40, 42.
[35] SAVAGE C.I., *Inland Transport* (London, 1957), pp. 449–53, 614–18.
[36] BARNETT, *Engage*, pp. 54, 589, 770–1.
[37] See www.wrens.org.uk.
[38] BARNETT, *Engage the Enemy*, pp. 771–2.

peak. The South Africans increased their workforce in this area by thirty-fold to three thousand personnel in 1942.[39]

Although the Royal Australian and New Zealand Navies worked in the American zone of operations, their maritime strength grew too. The Royal New Zealand Navy's personnel rose five-fold from 2,009 at the start of the war to 10,649 in July 1945. The Royal Australian Navy quadrupled its size in the same period to 39,650 personnel and possessed a force of 337 vessels in June 1945. Nevertheless, by 1943 Australia and New Zealand still relied on British merchant vessels for overseas trade,[40] and when the BPF started to operate in the Pacific it comprised ships from the Royal Canadian, Australian and New Zealand Navies. The Royal Indian Navy, too, participated in operations across the globe in the Atlantic and the Mediterranean, but principally in the Arakan coast where a maze of inland waterways flanked so much of the terrain over which the army fought.[41] Furthermore, the exchange of personnel between these navies and the Royal Navy illustrated that British sea power sat truly at the heart of a maritime Commonwealth.

War, meanwhile, led to innovation at sea. The Landing Ship Tank (LST) had allowed for "shore to shore" assaults to be carried out, in which the troops would land directly from the vessels in which they had embarked at the assembly ports, instead of transferring from troopships to landing craft on arriving in the assault area. First designed by the British, they were mass produced by the Americans after 1942. The Merchant Navy was also transformed. By May 1945, Britain and the Dominions had armed 9,500 ships, of which 5,600 were ocean-going vessels.[42] Furthermore, armed merchant cruisers had become sophisticated vessels by 1942–43, equipped with radar. Highlighting British adaptability and flexibility at sea, these vessels were turned into depot/repair and assault ships.[43] The British also devoted much effort into operational research, working out, for example, the optimum size of convoys and the theoretical number of escorts necessary for their best protection. In the Pacific, analyses of strike operations were carried out to improve performance.[44]

A final word should be reserved for individuals. Britain is a seafaring nation and its history is littered with famous naval commanders such as Drake and Nelson. During the period under study, figures such as Winston Churchill, the British Prime Minister who had twice been First Lord of the Admiralty, recognised the war-winning potential of the sea, while Admiral Sir Andrew Cunningham oversaw stunning victories against the enemy at Taranto in 1940 and Cape Matapan in 1941, before becoming First Sea Lord in 1943. Furthermore, Admiral Sir Bertram Ramsay not only orchestrated the British evacuation at Dunkirk in

---

[39] JOHNSTON, 'The Dominions and British maritime power', pp. 96, 104,.
[40] Ibid., pp. 96, 113–15.
[41] COLLINS D.J.E., *The Royal Indian Navy, 1939–1945* (India and Pakistan, 1964).
[42] ROSKILL, *War at Sea*, I, p. 22.
[43] OSBORNE R., SPONG H. and GROVER T., *Armed Merchant Cruisers 1878–1945* (Windsor, 2007), p. 222.
[44] ROBB-WEBB, *British Pacific Fleet*, p. 81.

1940 but also oversaw operation *Neptune* in 1944, a stunning feat of operational planning. But it was perhaps the ordinary British sailor recruited from society and his determination to fight the enemy that not only contributed to British victory but changed the fabric of the Royal Navy itself. The Royal Navy had to be part of an evolving society, by 1943 anxiously waiting for the Welfare State, and "Citizen Sailors" would change the old Victorian way of life at sea. They brought new ideas and values with them, civilianised the service and demanded better conditions, transporting the Royal Navy into the modern world.[45]

---

[45] See LAMBERT A., review article in the *Independent*, 19 August 2011; PRYSOR G., *Citizen Sailors: The Royal Navy in the Second World War* (London, 2012).

THE WASHINGTON TREATY ERA, 1919–1936: NAVAL ARMS LIMITATION

PHILLIPS PAYSON O'BRIEN is Emeritus Professor of Economic History at the London School of Economics, London, United Kingdom

ABSTRACT. *Hailed at the time as a new era in peaceful international diplomacy, the interwar naval treaties have since been blamed for encouraging the rise of the dictators and the Second World War. In reality they were useful, if limited, exercises in arms restraint which established important precedents for the future, but were incapable of resisting aggression by themselves.*

RÉSUMÉ. *Saluée à l'époque comme une nouvelle ère de paix dans la diplomatie internationale, les traités sur les forces navales de l'entre-deux-guerres ont depuis été rendus responsables de la montée des dictateurs et de la seconde guerre mondiale. En réalité, ils furent - et ce même en étant restreints - des exercices utiles à la limitation des armes et établirent d'importants précédents pour l'avenir, quoiqu'ils ne purent par eux-mêmes empêcher les agressions.*

. • .

At the moment of its birth the interwar-period naval arms limitation process was considered one of the most important events in global diplomatic history. To many, it seemed to hold out the possibility of major powers reshaping their behavior in a more liberal, more rational, and less confrontational manner. When the Washington Conference concluded in 1922 its host, the US President Warren Harding, described the agreement as representing a "new and better epoch in human affairs". The head of the British delegation, Arthur Balfour, claimed that the Washington treaties were "absolute unmixed blessing to mankind".

History has been much less kind to the process. Its demise in 1936, followed shortly by the outbreak of the Second World War, has colored the view of many. Often this has led to the naval arms limitation process being labeled as idealistic on the part of the British and the Americans, one which led them to neglect their naval defenses in the Asia-Pacific region and delay their naval build-ups until too late in the day - resulting in catastrophe during the early stages of the conflict.

The process itself centered on four major conferences. These were the Washington Conference of 1921–22, the Geneva (or Coolidge) Conference of 1927, the First London Conference of 1930, and finally the Second London Conference of 1935–36. Philosophically, the naval arms limitation process aimed to prevent future conflict, using a multi-layered process. In the short term it was directed at averting a potential naval building race between the United States, the British Empire, and Japan. In that sense it was an attempt to deal with the legacy of the First World War.

The results of the First World War had confirmed to many the idea that sea power was the decisive element in world power. The Allies controlled the world's oceans throughout, sweeping the Germans from most of their overseas empires with relative ease. Trade between Germany and the world outside central Europe was throttled, leading to significant food shortages such as the famous "Turnip Winter" of 1916–17, events which many believe led to a collapse in German morale in 1918. On the other hand, when the Germans threatened to sunder British maritime trade with their submarine offensive of 1917 it led some in the British government to contemplate that they might lose the war.

If the overriding importance of sea power had been reinforced by the lessons of 1914–1918, the future balance of that sea power remained uncertain. In 1918, the naval balance between the great powers was strangely constructed. Britain's Royal Navy was by far the world's largest, with significant numerical advantages in completed warships of almost all types. The British had also seen their greatest naval rival of the previous decade, the German High Seas Fleet, swept from the world's oceans. And yet, there was some real worry about the future of British naval supremacy. Before the United States even entered the war, America had approved the construction of the most modern and powerful capital ship fleet in the world, as part of the 1916 Naval Program.[1] Though building this enormous striking force was delayed when the United States entered the war, the ships remained on the slips and construction could be re-started at any time. If they were completed, the Royal Navy believed that the United States would then possess the most powerful fleet in the world, and the Admiralty pressed for the construction of massive new British battleships in response.

The wild-card in this equation was the Japanese. The Japanese fleet had been slowly and steadily built up for decades. Its supposed main enemy was the United States. As European powers actually reduced their naval presence in the Pacific in the run-up to the First Word War, the Japanese and Americans became the two largest powers in the region. The Japanese plan, never realized, was to possess a substantial sixteen capital ship fleet (eight battleships and eight battlecruisers), which would have necessitated an even larger American fleet if the two forces were to fight in the Western Pacific. The Japanese–American balance was further complicated by the existence of the Anglo-Japanese Alliance. First signed in 1902 and then renewed twice, the Alliance had provided security to both British and

---

[1] Capital ships were both battleships and battlecruisers and were considered the greatest indicator of national naval strength during the First World War. Ships of both types displace approximately the same tonnage, but battlecruisers were much less heavily protected than battleships, and therefore had a much higher top speed. Unfortunately, the lack of protection could be a major handicap in combat, as was shown during the Battle of Jutland.

Japanese imperial possessions in the Pacific. It was, however, deeply resented in the United States.

This naval instability was, however, tempered by domestic considerations in all three countries. British, American, and Japanese political leaders all wanted to control military spending after the war, and looked on with skepticism as their navies pressed for new, large, expensive shipbuilding programs. This must always be remembered. Even though much of the rhetoric of the interwar naval arms limitation process stressed the idealistic, its roots were also extremely practical.

In fact it was the desire not to continue funding the very expensive 1916 naval program that led President Harding to issue an invitation to the world's greatest naval powers to come to a conference in Washington in November 1921. It was at the opening of this conference that a great piece of political theater was etched in the history of diplomatic relations. The US Secretary of State, Charles Evans Hughes, began by laying out a comprehensive plan to stop the construction of all new capital ships while at the same time establishing formal ratios which would control all future building. He offered to scrap every American capital ship then under construction if the Japanese did the same and the British promised to start no new ones. From that point the capital-ship strength of the three powers was to be kept to a 5 (US)–5 (UK)–3 (Japan) ratio. The French and Italians were then added with a ratio of 1.75. Hughes' opening address provided unstoppable momentum to the process and the final settlement was almost exactly as he had hoped. The 5–5–3 ratio was accepted and most capital ship construction stopped (the Japanese were allowed to keep one capital ship that was nearing completion, the United States two, and the British were given the right to build two new ones). The same approximate ratio was extended to the different nations' aircraft carrier tonnage.

While this was the most dramatic decision reached at Washington, the treaties in their entirety offered change throughout the world's seas. Politically, and controversially, the Anglo-Japanese Alliance was ended. This was a non-negotiable demand of the United States, and in its place a new Four-Power Treaty (including France) was agreed to regulate behavior in the Pacific. There was also a restriction on any new fortification construction in the Western Pacific, providing Japan some measure of security against forward deployments of the US Navy. On the other hand, the Washington conference was unable to reach settlements in other areas. Auxiliary warships such as cruisers and destroyers were regulated only by size, not numerically. Moreover, submarines, which had shown themselves to be so dangerous, were left uncontrolled.

As a whole the agreements reached were remarkable. Never before had sea power between the dominant naval powers in the world been so regulated. Indeed in many cases the politicians were so eager to reach agreement that they over-ruled their more hawkish naval personnel. Of course the great question was not how the process started, but was whether the process could continue.

When the delegates returned to their home countries they were usually greeted enthusiastically – in Japan as much as in Great Britain and the United States. In the short term the country that reacted most dramatically to the agreements was America. The Americans, having been guaranteed the public relations satisfaction of equality in capital ship strength with the Royal Navy, stopped almost all naval construction entirely. The political support for US shipbuilding had been almost entirely due to the enormity of the First World War, and with that over and agreement reached at Washington, there was no support to build warships of any kind.

The British and Japanese, on the other hand, continued to press ahead with modest plans for cruiser construction. By 1925 the Americans, partially embarrassed, partially outraged, started pressing for an extension of the 5-5-3 ratio to smaller warships such as cruisers and destroyers. The British government, however, led by Winston Churchill, the Chancellor of the Exchequer, believed that the American demand was selfish, and was content to leave things as they were, with its significant advantages in this class of vessel. It argued that the United Kingdom, because of its reliance on trade to eat and produce, and because of the scattered nature of the British Empire, was rightfully entitled to a larger number of cruisers than the happily self-sufficient United States.

When the next naval arms control conference met in Geneva in 1927 this Anglo-American dispute ended up dominating proceedings. The American delegation pressed the British to formally accept the American right to parity in all classes of naval vessel, while the British delegation sought to have such a high limit applied to cruisers that the US would never build up to it – allowing the British to maintain their supremacy in this class of vessel. This dispute ended up triggering the greatest Anglo-American confrontation of the 20th century. To the Coolidge administration, the British were attempting to undo the whole premise of the Washington agreements, the notion that the United States and Britain should base their naval power on parity. The President was personally furious at what he saw as British perfidy and, not long after the conference ended, called for the construction of twenty-five modern cruisers of ten thousand tons, ships that would have qualitatively dwarfed the Royal Navy's. The American Congress was not quite so incensed, but did end up approving a plan for the construction of fifteen large cruisers, which was still enough to threaten British supremacy in the class.

The British government was stuck in a quandary. The Prime Minister, Stanley Baldwin, did not realize that in endorsing Churchill's position he was about to precipitate such a dramatic American reaction. Things were compounded when Lord Robert Cecil, one of the lead British delegates to Geneva, resigned afterwards and published a letter condemning the government's position. This Anglo-American confrontation boiled down to a conflict between the symbolic message of the naval arms control process, which was very real, and the hard calculus of political will. The British argument about the need for a large number of cruisers and destroyers was certainly defensible in the abstract, but it struck a discordant note in the 1920s as societal perceptions of militarism and the First World War were turning more skeptical.

In the end the British government was forced to fully accept the United States as an equal in all classes of warship. The final concession was not made by the Baldwin government, as it was replaced by Ramsay MacDonald's Labour Party in the 1929 elections. MacDonald saw no reason for any kind of unnecessary and wasteful confrontation with the United States and set about finding a compromise solution. He was helped by a change in the American administration. In 1929 Calvin Coolidge, still bitter, was replaced by Herbert Hoover. Hoover, born a Quaker, was perhaps the least military-minded president in American history. He also, particularly after the economic crisis set off by the collapse of the New York Stock Exchange in 1929, which came to be known as the Great Depression, wanted to keep the American naval budget to as small a figure as possible.

With willingness to compromise apparent on both sides, it was clear that the next naval arms conference, which was to be held in London in 1930, would be far less contentious for Anglo-American relations. What it did do, however, was return much of the focus onto the position of the Japanese government. The Japanese had almost been forgotten during the Geneva conference as the American and British delegations battled. However, during preparations for London it became apparent that certain elements in both the Japanese government and navy were increasingly unhappy with the Washington ratios. In the early 1920s certain powerful Japanese politicians, such as the eventual Prime Minister Kato Tomosabura, were far from dogmatic about issues surrounding naval power and were willing to make significant concessions to reach agreement with the United States and United Kingdom. However, by the second half of the 1920s the willingness to compromise seems to have weakened and was replaced by a desire to improve Japan's naval position. For instance, at Geneva the Japanese had begun to press for a cruiser and destroyer ratio of 70% with the USA and UK. As Anglo-American animosity ended up dominating proceedings, the importance of this demand was obscured. However, going into the London conference, the Imperial Japanese Navy's General Staff was determined to get the 70% ratio.

The different tensions that existed going into the 1930 meeting, sometimes referred to as the "First" London Conference, makes it, in historical terms, perhaps the most controversial of all the naval arms control meetings. The controversy was possible because the delegates actually ended up reaching a compromise on a number of the most difficult issues. The Anglo-American cruiser issue was finessed cleverly. The British were given an overall larger tonnage allowance in cruisers than the United States, which meant that the Royal Navy would maintain numerically the largest force in the world. The United States, on the other hand, was allowed to build a greater number of the large ten-thousand-ton cruisers, which would make its force (once constructed) superior on a unit-by-unit basis. The exact cruiser tonnages were 339,000 tons for the British and 323,500 tons for the Americans. When it came to other classes, they were given exactly the same tonnages, 150,000 tons for destroyers and 52,700 tons for submarines.

The Japanese situation was handled with great delicacy. Though the Japanese right to a 70% ratio was not endorsed, and in fact the Japanese were forced to accept 60% in the case of heavy cruisers, overall the Japanese were allowed to maintain a force of cruisers with approximately 70% of the striking power of the British. There were also, for the first time, agreements to control the size and armaments of individual submarines. This situation would hold only until the next conference, scheduled for 1935–36, but in the meanwhile the naval arms control process endured.

Not every issue could be settled at London, however. In particular, the continuing issue of French and Italian naval power remained insuperable. Though the French had accepted at Washington, grudgingly, the notion of parity with the Italians in capital ships, the decision still rankled. France was a global power with a large overseas empire and many in the French state and navy believed it was only right for the French fleet to be considerably larger than the Italian. As it was, they also chafed at the notion that the Japanese were allowed a force of capital ships almost twice as large as their own. On the other hand, the Italians had a very simple position, parity with the French in all classes of warship. This basic contradiction made any agreement on a Franco-Italian auxiliary ship ratio impossible.

Taken together, the wheeling and dealing in London leaves a somewhat confusing picture. One view is that the Anglo-American powers, particularly the British, made concessions that endangered their global security. The Japanese, with their de facto larger ratio, were now secure in the Western Pacific. On the other hand, to appease the United States, the British gave up any notion of supremacy in cruisers and destroyers, which the British Empire needed if it were to defend itself. Finally, the agreements were seen as a sign that the British and Americans were still hoping to reduce military spending, which eventually left them unprepared when the international situations deteriorated in the late 1930s.

On the other hand, there were also some real positives that came out of London. The Anglo-American relationship, which was seriously damaged because of the fallout from the Geneva Conference, was significantly strengthened and the way was set for the very close cooperation that would emerge during the Second World War. Moreover, the naval arms control system itself had shown some resilience. The whole process could have collapsed at London, particularly over the Japanese demand for a 70% ratio. However, a workable compromise was reached and the process was actually expanded to cover new classes of warship.

Ultimately the vision of the naval arms control process to this point must be subsumed within the discussion of the origins of the Second World War. If one views the war as practically inevitable, a conflict whose seeds were sown during the First World War, then it must be seen as a doomed and perhaps dangerous series of agreements that reached its high point during the First London Conference, during which the United Kingdom and United States sacrificed their security in a vain struggle for an idealistic international structure. If, on the other hand, the demise of the system, which occurred over the next six years, was not preordained but came about because of the development of events after

1930, then the decisions made were considerably more logical and reasonable than it might seem on the surface.

Of course the system did unravel during the next six years. The foundational reason for this was a hardening of the Japanese position. What stands out up until 1930, surprisingly to some who view Japanese behavior through a prism of the 1930s and Second World War, is how the Japanese were actually integrated into the naval arms control system. Though elements within the Japanese navy were always skeptical of the process (as were elements within the American and British navies) the Japanese government and people still seemed determined to keep the naval arms control system going. Japanese society also had significant democratic impulses throughout the 1920s, and had a full national debate over foreign affairs.

However, in the 1930s the political power of the Japanese armed services, due partly to vagaries of the Japanese political system, but also due to the constant threat of assassination of those who were seen to be opposing the military and nationalist goals of the aggressive factions, strengthened. The Japanese Army and Navy gained great control over government policy and started pushing aggressive action. For instance, the Japanese government withdrew from the League of Nations in 1933, in reaction to criticism about the Japanese invasion of Manchuria. Specifically, within the navy those who had argued for constructive engagement with the United States and Great Britain within the Washington system were almost entirely marginalized. In their place a dominant consensus arose which rejected any inferior ratio, undermining the whole rationale behind the naval arms control system. Amongst these critics was Japan's most revered and well-known naval officer, Admiral Togo Heihachiro, the victor who had destroyed the Russian Fleet at Tsushima in 1905. No longer was it allowable for Japan to have even 70% of the naval power of the Anglo-American powers; now the Japanese started calling for complete parity, or a "common upper limit" between the three nations. They were willing to press for this parity even if it spelled the end of the Washington system.

While the Japanese started hardening their view towards the process, some important developments also occurred within the USA and UK which also ended up weakening their attachment to it. The combined international outlook of MacDonald and Hoover, which was grounded in the notion of smaller military budgets and international cooperation, weakened as the global situation appeared to become far more unstable. The Japanese invasion of Manchuria in 1931, followed in January 1933 by the election of Adolf Hitler as chancellor of Germany, led the British government to end the famous ten-year rule which had governed its strategic thinking in the 1920s. This rule, which stated that Britain could plan on not being involved in a major war for at least a decade, was scrapped, and in its place serious discussions took place about just how the British state should plan its rearmament. Finally, Italian expansionist aspirations seemed to be growing as Mussolini's fascist state continued with its naval build-up. Though the British were not, at first, particularly concerned with Italy in the way that they were by Germany, it was an additional unsettling factor that supported moves towards planning for rearmament.

For the United States, the most interesting change was one of personality, the election of Franklin Roosevelt in 1932. Whilst Hoover, much to the dismay of many in the United States Navy, remained committed to small naval budgets for the entirety of his term, Roosevelt was not only instinctively supportive of larger naval budgets but believed that they were economically beneficial as well. Roosevelt was an avid sailor and had served as Assistant Secretary of the Navy during the presidency of Woodrow Wilson. He often casually referred to the United States Navy as "we" and the United States Army as "them". Moreover, Roosevelt was given almost *carte blanche* by the US Congress to try to bring the United States out of the Great Depression. One way he chose to do this was by increasing government spending hugely – and the United States Navy (USN) benefited. In particular, Roosevelt gave the USN enough money that it could now build its full treaty allowance for all types of warship. It was a remarkable change, and it should always be kept in mind that between the First and Second London Conferences the United Kingdom and the United States actually started the construction of considerably more warships than the Japanese, so it is hard to argue that the treaties somehow led to their neglecting their defenses. Between 1930 and 1935 the United States laid down three aircraft carriers, seventeen cruisers and forty-six destroyers, and the British one aircraft carrier, seventeen cruisers and forty-five destroyers. The Japanese built approximately half as many warships, laying down one aircraft carrier, six cruisers and twenty-four destroyers. Accusing the naval disarmament process of being too idealistic and leading the US and UK to neglect their naval defenses is not straightforward when one looks at such figures.

At the same time, the British ended up using the naval arms control system to shape their relationship with a potentially threatening Nazi Germany. The Hitler regime made great play of the Versailles Treaty limiting Germany to a small number of new surface vessels with a maximum tonnage of ten thousand, and no submarines. Not long after Hitler took power in 1933, the Germans started pressing the British to negotiate a different relationship, one using ratios which would allow the German fleet to reach a specific size vis-à-vis the Royal Navy. In May 1935 Hitler made a public offer to limit a future German Navy to 35% of the British fleet if the British government would renounce the Versailles Treaty restrictions. It was a clever move by the German dictator, offering the British a ratio of strength far larger than they enjoyed before the First World War, but at the same time forcing them to publicly repudiate the Versailles system. Faced with this dilemma, the British government made the deal and in June 1935 the Anglo-German naval agreement was signed. It was easily one of the most controversial moments of the interwar naval arms control process. On the one hand, it showed that the ratio system had become a new international norm which could be extended in important, if unlikely, directions. On the other hand, for those who call the system a futile exercise in idealism, it seemed like a textbook example of appeasing an aggressive and dangerous dictatorship.

The Anglo-German naval agreement also marked the last significant "achievement" of the process. By the time the delegates convened in London in December 1935 for the next and final meeting of the naval arms control process, the system was poised to collapse. The Japanese delegation this time stuck firmly to the position that it would accept only parity with the United States and United Kingdom, and when this demand was rejected it withdrew from the talks. To make matters worse, it was actually while the conference was in session that the Italians invaded Ethiopia. This further clouded the hopes of trust and cooperation in the naval sphere. If the ratio system was now dead and buried, there was some hope that naval arms control could be prolonged through the maintenance of certain size and caliber limits of different classes of warship. In particular the British, who on the whole had opted for a larger number of smaller warships, wanted to maintain the long-term viability of their present fleet by pre-empting any future naval race, particularly in capital ships. With this in mind, the US and UK agreed to limit future capital ships to thirty-five thousand tons – with the proviso that this limit could be instantly scrapped if it was discovered that other powers were exceeding it.

The end of the naval arms control process sometimes leads people to argue that it failed, a question that is worthy of real reflection. If judged by the lofty, idealistic standards of some of the rhetoric that it produced, particularly during the Washington Conference, then it clearly fell short. The system lasted only fourteen years and did little or nothing to halt the global slide into a Second World War. It did not bring about a new international order. On the other hand, the main national delegations that brought it into existence, in particular the British, American and Japanese, were motivated by two very practical desires. The first was to head off a potentially catastrophically expensive naval race just after the First World War. The other was to provide greater security for each. The first was certainly achieved for at least a decade.

The second question remains, however, and the answer to this is considerably more complex. To some, the process made the Second World War more dangerous and costly for the Western democracies, in particular the British. It meant that they entered the war with much smaller forces than they would have otherwise maintained, and moreover that in retarding their naval construction so dramatically in the 1920s, they had weakened their domestic shipbuilding capacity to such a degree that they were no longer the world's naval leader. Combining this with the symbolic concession of Britain's long-standing claim to rule the seas, the entire process can be seen as a body-blow to British power, one from which it never recovered.

Some of these criticisms, particularly about the impact on Britain's shipbuilding industry, have merit. However, others seem based on a very naval-centric understanding of what the British would otherwise have actually built in the interwar period. The 1920s were not like the decade before the First World War – and it is very unlikely that the Admiralty would have received large naval building programs if the naval arms control process had not come about.

Between 1930 and 1939, the British built more warships than any other power in the world.

The United States, on the other hand, probably achieved more from the naval arms control process than any other country. This had relatively little to do with the symbolic fact that for the first time it was accepted as a naval equal of Great Britain. The great advantage for the United States was how it eventually influenced the Second World War in the Pacific. Of all the great powers, the United States had probably the shakiest political support for naval building. The American Congress, which liked to support large and extensive shore installations, often significantly reduced the building programs put forward by the Navy Department and the White House. With the end of the First World War, much of the domestic pressure to support naval building evaporated. On the other hand, the United States had the industrial capability to build many more warships much more quickly than any other country in the world – far more than Japan, as would be shown between 1942 and 1945. It therefore was in the American interest to restrain all naval building in the interwar period for as long as possible. Also, the naval arms control process played a part in the crucial process of bringing the British and Americans together. The relationship between the two, once their differences were settled in 1930, became closer than ever before. Many of the officers who served at this time in both navies would play crucial roles during the war.

The Japanese experience of naval arms control is quite uneven, and it might even have been detrimental. By giving the Japanese a naval ratio 60% as large as the US and UK's, the process fed Japanese vanity. In industrial terms the Japanese were still minnows in the 1920s, with an industrial economy closer to Belgium's than Britain's, to say nothing of the Americans'. And yet, the process fed resentment within the Japanese Navy that its ratio was too small. Had the system remained in operation, it would have provided Japan a with great deal of security in the Eastern Pacific; however, once it ended and naval building limits were lifted, the Japanese position actually became considerably more precarious.

In the end the naval arms control process leaves us with more questions than answers. Its controversial nature, then as now, emphasizes that sea power was one of the key definitions of global power in the interwar period. Neither land nor air armaments caused such tension or resulted in such famous agreements. Looking back at the process from almost a century later, the process has left one obvious legacy. Its method of controlling armaments through adjustable ratios, which take into account different national needs and force structures to provide both security and international peace, has endured. The nuclear relationship between the USA and the USSR (now Russia), for instance, is regulated in similar ways to naval power in the interwar years. In that sense the naval arms control process left behind a template with real value.

THE WASHINGTON TREATY ERA: NEUTRALISING THE PACIFIC

CHRISTOPHER M. BELL is Professor of History at Dalhousie University, Canada

ABSTRACT. *The 1922 Washington Treaty and its associated agreements "froze" the battlefleet strengths of Britain, the United States and Japan in the ratio 5:5:3. They also forbade the "fortification" of naval bases in the Western Pacific. The intention was to prevent a naval race such as seemed to have encouraged the First World War, and to keep potential enemies too far apart to attack one another. Initially it worked, but in the 1930s it kept Britain and the United States too far away to hamper Japanese aggression in China. Increasingly preoccupied with aggression in Europe, the Western powers attempted to deter Japan with inadequate forces, and long-range Japanese strikes inflicted heavy losses on both at the beginning of the Pacific War.*

RÉSUMÉ. *Le traité naval de Washington de 1922 et les termes en découlant « gelèrent » les forces des flottes de guerre de la Grande-Bretagne, des États-Unis et du Japon selon le ratio 5:3:3. Ils interdirent également la « fortification » des bases navales dans le Pacifique occidental. Visant à prévenir une course à la puissance maritime comme celle semblant avoir conduit à la première guerre mondiale, le traité avait également pour intention de garder des ennemis potentiels trop éloignés géographiquement pour pouvoir s'attaquer. Initialement, le plan fonctionna mais dans les années 30, la Grande-Bretagne et les États-Unis se retrouvèrent trop loin pour empêcher l'invasion japonaise en Chine. De plus en plus préoccupés par les conflits en Europe, les puissances occidentales tentèrent d'enrayer la menace de l'Empire du Japon avec des forces inadaptées et les frappes de longue portée japonaises infligèrent aux deux côtés de lourdes pertes au début de la guerre du Pacifique.*

. • .

Japan's emergence as a first-class naval power around the beginning of the 20th century created serious, and increasingly complex, challenges for both Great Britain and the United States. The most dangerous maritime threats to Britain's extensive imperial and economic interests in the Far East had traditionally come from other European powers. Any immediate danger from a rising Japan was effectively neutralized by the Anglo-Japanese Alliance, concluded in 1902 and renewed in 1905 and 1911. The steady growth of Japan's power and suspicions of its long-term ambitions nevertheless fuelled concerns about its reliability as an ally. By 1918 British naval leaders believed that Japan hoped to exclude western powers from China and, in time, to obtain regional hegemony, goals that would eventually lead to war. With the destruction of German naval power at the end of the First World War, the British Admiralty identified Japan as the most likely threat to Britain's global interests.[1] Similar concerns had also emerged by this time in the United States, where Japan's aggressive policies towards China were viewed with alarm. American naval leaders, like their British counterparts, identified Japan as their most likely postwar adversary.[2] By 1920, the Pacific Ocean had become the focus of great-power naval rivalry.

British and Dominion decision makers were forced to address this problem in mid-1921 when the renewal of the Anglo-Japanese Alliance came up for discussion. There were compelling reasons for the British to extend the Alliance: it had provided strategic benefits in the past, and some hoped that its continuation would give Britain a measure of influence over Japanese policies in the future. Failure to continue the Alliance also ran the risk of antagonizing Japan, something Britain and its Australasian Dominions were naturally eager to avoid. However, renewal would be unpopular in the United States. As long as a formal alliance continued, American strategists could not rule out the possibility of conflict with Britain and Japan simultaneously, even if the prospect seemed unlikely. But the main American objection to the Alliance was that it seemed to provide tacit support and encouragement for Japan's expansionist proclivities. The British hoped to avoid inflaming opinion in the United States, especially at a time when an expensive naval arms race seemed to be developing. The Canadian government's strenuous objections to the renewal of the Alliance at the 1921 Imperial Conference provided the final push London needed to begin looking for an opportunity to jettison its ally. The arms-limitation conference that convened in Washington in late 1921 provided an ideal venue for the three leading naval powers to consider the future of the Anglo-Japanese Alliance and other unresolved Far Eastern issues.

The Washington Conference (November 1921–January 1922) was not intended to provide a comprehensive settlement of Pacific questions, although the three major naval powers recognized from the outset that a successful arms control agreement would require some alleviation of the deepening rivalry in the Far East.[3] The connection between arms limitation and the naval balance in the Pacific is best illustrated by the negotiations over relative naval strength. Japanese delegates hoped to secure a 10:7 ratio against Britain and the United States, but the two English-speaking powers were determined that the Japanese ratio should be limited to 10:6. The British calculated that this would enable them to despatch a large fleet to the Far East while simultaneously retaining enough capital ships in home waters to neutralize the largest European fleet. Similarly, the United States Navy believed a large margin was necessary to ensure victory in a fleet action fought near Japan's home waters and far from American naval bases. The Japanese accepted the 10:6 ratio in return for an agreement by which Britain, Japan and the United States maintained the status quo with

---

[1] BELL C.M., *The Royal Navy, Seapower and Strategy between the Wars* (Stanford, CA, 2000), Ch. 3.
[2] BRAISTED W.R., *The United States Navy in the Pacific, 1909–1922* (Austin, TX, 1971), pp. 473–90.
[3] BUCKLEY T.H., *The United States and the Washington Conference, 1921–1922* (Knoxville, TN, 1970).

respect to fortifications and naval bases in the Western Pacific. Article XIX of the five-power naval treaty prevented the United States from building new fortifications or bases in its territories and possessions west of Hawaii, while the British were similarly restricted with respect to their possessions east of 110°. Japan, in turn, agreed to the same terms for its possessions, including the Kurile Islands, the Bonin Islands, the Ryukyu Islands, Formosa and the Pescadores. By depriving the British and American navies of forward bases at Hong Kong, Guam or the Philippines, Japan would be assured of regional naval superiority, even at the lower ratio of naval strength. At the time, this concession seemed advantageous to American leaders, who recognized that Congress was unlikely to provide funds for fortified bases at either Guam or the Philippines. As Theodore Roosevelt, Jr., the Assistant Secretary of the Navy, observed during the conference, "We trade certain fortifications, which we would never have completed, for fortifications which they [the Japanese] would unquestionably have completed."[4]

The Americans were also able to secure the abrogation of the Anglo-Japanese Alliance, which was replaced with a new four-power treaty in which Britain, the United States, Japan and France agreed to respect each other's "insular possessions and insular dominions in the region of the Pacific Ocean".[5] From Britain's perspective, the new agreement was a poor substitute for the alliance. The Americans, however, were determined to avoid any formal military obligations, and the four-power treaty contained no provisions for enforcement. In the event of a dispute arising, the signatory powers agreed only to seek a resolution through consultation. The Americans also took a leading role in shaping the nine-power treaty on the future of China, which was the most persistent cause of tension with Japan. This agreement committed the signatories to "respect the sovereignty, the independence, and the territorial and administrative integrity of China".[6] At American insistence the treaty also recognised the "open door" policy, which ensured all nations equal access to Chinese markets. However, like the four-power treaty, this agreement lacked any mechanisms for enforcement.

The relative success of the agreements reached at Washington is usually attributed to the decision to blend disarmament measures with political agreements designed to resolve specific disputes and reduce underlying tensions. But even though many hailed the treaty as a promising step towards global disarmament and world peace, naval leaders in both Britain and the United States continued to believe that Japan posed a long-term threat to their nations' interests in the Far East. Moreover, both were determined to defend these interests in the event of Japanese aggression. The Washington Treaty did not dramatically alter the relative naval strength of the three major Pacific naval powers, but the non-fortification provisions ensured that the potential adversaries' bases would remain so far apart that neither the United States nor Britain could easily challenge Japan's dominance in the Western Pacific. Both

---

[4] BRAISTED, *United States Navy in the Pacific*, p. 646.
[5] BUELL R.L., *The Washington Conference* (New York, 1970), pp. 399-400.
[6] *Ibid.*, 407.

navies would nevertheless struggle throughout the interwar period to develop plans and acquire resources that would enable them to wage a protracted naval campaign in the Pacific.

GREAT BRITAIN

Britain's postwar leaders were unwilling to contemplate the heavy costs associated with the permanent stationing of a large battle fleet in the Far East, but they were not prepared to leave British interests in the region entirely at Japan's mercy. Lloyd George's postwar coalition government decided that the bulk of the British navy would normally be stationed in European waters and a large force would be transferred to the Far East only in the event of a crisis. In June 1921 the decision was therefore taken to begin the construction of a major naval base at Singapore to provide the docking and repair facilities that a fleet would require for extended operations in the Pacific.[7] Naval planners hoped that by maintaining the *ability* to dispatch a large fleet to Singapore, Japan could be deterred from attacking Britain's eastern interests. But if the Japanese did embark on war, the Admiralty was determined to meet the challenge. It assumed from the outset that an Anglo-Japanese war would be fought for high stakes, since Japan was unlikely to resort to force unless it intended to overthrow Britain's entire position in the Far East. British planners therefore concluded that they would have to inflict a crushing defeat on Japan in order to bring the war to a successful conclusion.

The navy's plans for war in the Pacific were embodied in the series of War Memoranda (Eastern) prepared by the Admiralty's Plans Division.[8] During the 1920s, when the Royal Navy still possessed a comfortable numerical superiority over Japan in capital ships, the Admiralty was confident that Britain could promptly despatch a powerful fleet to Singapore and maintain it there for an extended period without running unacceptable risks in European waters. Planners expected that the arrival of the fleet at Singapore would be followed immediately by offensive operations. The best means to inflict decisive pressure on Japan was to destroy the main Japanese fleet, which would enable the Royal Navy to impose an economic blockade that would eventually cripple the Japanese economy and force the enemy to seek terms. However, it was assumed that the Japanese, like the Germans before them, would be reluctant to accept battle with superior British forces. Consequently, the Admiralty planned for a protracted war. The main British fleet would provide cover for the detached cruiser squadrons protecting British trade, and operations would be launched into the Western Pacific to interfere with Japan's maritime communications.

---

[7] On the Singapore Naval Base, see NEIDPATH J., *The Singapore Naval Base and the Defence of Britain's Eastern Empire, 1919-1941* (Oxford, 1981); and MCINTYRE D.W., *The Rise and Fall of the Singapore Naval Base, 1919-1942* (London, 1979).
[8] BELL, *Royal Navy, Seapower and Strategy*, Ch. 3.

By gradually increasing the economic pressure on Japan, it was hoped that the enemy would be compelled to risk a fleet action. The elimination of the Japanese fleet would enable British forces to operate close to the Japanese home islands and impose decisive economic pressure by cutting Japan's access to resources in East Asia.

While the docking and repair facilities planned for Singapore made it essential for the effective projection of British power into the Pacific, their distance from Japan – over 2,500 miles – made it unsuitable as a forward fleet base from which to stage offensive operations. When the Admiralty began to develop its first eastern war plans, it was assumed that Hong Kong would serve as the navy's main advance base, and that it would probably be necessary to establish other bases even closer to Japan, probably along the Chinese coast. During the late 1920s and early 1930s, the main problem British naval planners had to grapple with was that Hong Kong, unlike Singapore, was subject to the non-fortification clauses of the Washington Treaty. Consequently, the colony would be exposed to capture or investment at the beginning of hostilities. War plans during this period emphasized the importance of rapidly moving the British fleet north from Singapore in order to eliminate any threat to Hong Kong, or to recapture it in the event that it had fallen. Once established at its forward base, the Admiralty hoped to begin a step-by-step campaign northward.

The navy's ambitious plans for a forward strategy in the Pacific were consistently out of step with the views of successive British governments. The cornerstone of any British strategy, the Singapore Naval Base, was cancelled outright by the Labour government in 1924, and work on the base was suspended when the Labour Party returned to power in 1929. The project was restored by a more sympathetic Conservative government in 1924–1929, but this did not translate into support for all aspects of the navy's proposed strategy. The Admiralty's leading critic during this period was Winston Churchill, the Chancellor of the Exchequer. Churchill did not believe that Japan was in a position to threaten any truly vital British interests; he doubted that a Pacific war was likely; and he questioned whether Britain could hope to inflict a decisive defeat on Japan, except at a ruinous cost. He therefore supported the eventual completion of the naval base at Singapore, but only as the basis for an essentially defensive strategy. During this period, Churchill and his colleagues regularly opposed expenditure on the new naval base, the accumulation of oil fuel reserves to support the eastward movement of a British fleet, and many of the warships which the Admiralty insisted were essential for an Anglo-Japanese war.[9] Even after the Japanese embarked on overtly expansionist policies in the 1930s, and the possibility of war became more likely, British leaders were still reluctant to provide the navy with the resources it wanted. The precarious state of the British economy during the early years of the Great Depression destroyed any chance that the Admiralty's lavish demands would be met during the early 1930s,

---

[9] BELL C.M., *Churchill and Sea Power* (Oxford, 2012), Ch. 4.

while the rise of Nazi Germany forced leaders to think carefully about defence priorities. When the decision was finally taken to begin rearmament, the mortal threat posed by Germany consistently received the highest priority.[10]

The reluctance of successive governments to support the Admiralty's ambitious war plans and the emergence of serious threats close to home forced naval planners to develop less-ambitious strategies. By 1934 it was clear that Hong Kong would probably not be available as a naval base; that there would be few troops available for combined operations; and, most alarmingly, that the need to counter German and Italian naval forces might preclude the dispatch of a numerically superior fleet to the Far East. In 1937 the Admiralty largely abandoned its plans for a progressive advance northward from Singapore. However, it remained hopeful that Britain might be able to exert decisive economic pressure on Japan even if the fleet remained based at Singapore. This was based on an overly optimistic interpretation of intelligence on the Japanese economy, which suggested that Japan would have trouble securing all its essential raw materials from the Asian mainland. Hence, even if Japan's communications with China remained relatively secure, it might still be starved into submission if its trans-Pacific trade could be severed.[11] By 1939 the deteriorating situation in Europe forced the Admiralty to consider a worst-case scenario in which Britain could dispatch only modest naval forces to Singapore and, rather than projecting naval power into the Pacific, the Admiralty would be hard pressed to protect its base at Singapore and prevent Japanese incursions into the Indian Ocean or the South Pacific.

The United States

Like their British counterparts, American naval planners generally assumed that a war between the United States and Japan would be an unlimited conflict whose outcome would be decided by the ability to project superior naval force into the Western Pacific and inflict decisive economic pressure on Japan. Prior to the Washington Conference, the United States Navy's (USN) "War Plan Orange" envisaged the immediate dispatch of a large fleet from Hawaii to fortified advance bases, ideally at Guam and Manila.[12] The non-fortification provisions of the five-power treaty meant that after 1922 the USN had to face the possibility that the forward bases it needed to carry the war into Japanese waters would be weakly defended at the beginning of the conflict and might need to be recaptured before offensive operations could be launched. The 1924 Orange war plan nevertheless assumed that the Philippines could be held by American forces

---

[10] BELL, *Royal Navy, Seapower and Strategy*, pp. 99–111.
[11] BELL C.M., 'The Royal Navy, War Planning and Intelligence Assessments of Japan between the Wars', in *Intelligence and Statecraft: The Use and Limits of Intelligence in International Society*, ed. JACKSON P. and SIEGEL J. (Westport, CN, 2005), pp. 139–55.
[12] On American war plans, see in particular MILLER E.S., *War Plan Orange* (Annapolis, MD, 1997).

at the start of the war. The fleet, accompanied by a large "fleet train" to provide logistical support, would therefore be rushed immediately to the Philippines to prevent it falling to the Japanese. Once safely in American hands, Manila would be converted into a fully functioning naval base. Confidence in this aspect of the plan gradually diminished, however. By 1934, naval planners accepted that there was little possibility that the Philippines could be held or that an American fleet could expect to reach it quickly without suffering heavy losses. Naval war plans were therefore modified on the assumption that the navy would have to fight its way across the central Pacific. This would involve an extended island-hopping campaign designed to seize a series of bases from which American forces could project their power with growing effectiveness into Japanese waters.

The various iterations of the USN's War Plan Orange assumed that the steadily mounting pressure on Japan's maritime communications would eventually force the Japanese navy to accept a fleet action with superior American forces. The destruction of the Japanese fleet – the only outcome contemplated – would expedite the American advance and eventually permit the establishment of advance bases near the Japanese home islands. The navy's plans envisioned a large contribution from US land and air forces, which would support fleet and amphibious operations as American forces crossed the central Pacific. From 1928 onwards, the navy also called for the establishment of air bases from which industrial and military targets in Japan could be bombed.[13] Ultimately, it would not be necessary to invade Japan, as the bombing campaign, in conjunction with the maritime blockade, would eventually bring victory. However, the process was expected to be a slow one. American planners believed that Japan could obtain virtually all of its essential raw materials from its relatively secure sea routes to Asia. These supplies could be cut off only from an advance base at Tsushima Island, and even then Japan might be able to continue fighting for a year or more.[14]

War Plan Orange provided a reasonable forecast of the requirements for prosecuting a Pacific war to a successful conclusion, but American naval leaders were unable to secure explicit political backing for their ambitious strategy. It was uncertain after the First World War what interests in the Far East the United States would fight to defend, or whether the American people would even be willing to support a lengthy war in the Pacific. During the Washington Conference, most American leaders doubted that the United States would ever fight to maintain the "open door" in China, or that Congress would pay for the warships and fortified bases necessary for an offensive strategy in the Pacific. The wholesale scrapping of American capital ships at the Washington Conference and the non-fortification restrictions in the treaty ensured that the United States could not immediately project its power into the Western Pacific in the event of war. "Never before", William Braisted observes, "had naval men

---

[13] MILLER, *War Plan Orange*, Ch. 14.
[14] Ibid., pp. 162–4.

found their views so overwhelmingly rejected by public opinion."[15] The situation changed little over the next fifteen years. Navy planners remained committed to the offensive strategy embodied in War Plan Orange, but the resources to implement it were not provided. The US Army had little interest in preparing to support an advance through the central Pacific, and Congress failed to build up to treaty levels in warships. As historian George Baer has noted, during the 1930s War Plan Orange was unworkable and the United States possessed no national strategy for protecting its interests in the Far East.[16]

The Second World War, 1939–1941

The liberal worldview underpinning the Washington Treaty began to break down in the early 1930s as the Japanese government became dominated by nationalist and militarist factions with far-reaching expansionist goals. Neither Britain nor the United States was able or willing to oppose Japan's conquest of Manchuria in 1931 or its war in China after July 1937. The outbreak of the European war in September 1939 further strengthened Japan's regional dominance and encouraged Tokyo to pursue a more aggressive foreign policy. British leaders had no intention of risking defeat at the hands of Nazi Germany in order to strengthen their position in the Far East. Australia and New Zealand were assured that Britain would sacrifice its interests in the Mediterranean in the event that Japan mounted a major attack on either Dominion, although Churchill doubted that this was ever likely to happen. The fall of France further altered the strategic balance in the Pacific in Japan's favour. With Britain itself in danger of invasion throughout the summer of 1940, the British Chiefs of Staff accepted that there was no possibility of dispatching significant naval forces to Singapore in the immediate future.[17] Japan, its regional dominance more secure than ever, demanded and received the right to station forces in French Indo-China in September 1940.

The United States was only slightly better positioned than the British to restrain Japanese aggression. Congress authorized a modest expansion of the USN in 1938, and provided for even larger increases in 1940 after the fall of France, but the goal of creating a "two ocean navy" would take years to achieve. In the short term, the United States' interests in the Western Pacific could not be successfully defended from a determined Japanese attack, and the navy lacked the resources to take the offensive in the early stages of a war. Moreover, political backing for a forward strategy in the Pacific was still not forthcoming. The prospect of a German–Italian triumph in Europe forced American leaders to shift their attention to the Atlantic. A Nazi-dominated Europe was rightly regarded as a greater threat to American security than was Japanese hegemony in East

---

[15] BRAISTED, *United States Navy in the Pacific*, p. 670.
[16] BAER G.W., *One Hundred Years of Sea Power* (Stanford, CA, 1994), pp. 127–9.
[17] On British naval planning and grand strategy, see BELL, *Churchill and Sea Power*, Ch. 8.

Asia and the Western Pacific. However, Hitler's victories in Europe made it more likely that Japan would resort to arms against Britain and, possibly, the United States. American strategists were therefore confronted with the real possibility of fighting a two-ocean war. The USN's Chief of Naval Operations, Admiral Harold R. Stark, took a leading role in the development of the United States' "Germany first" strategy. In November 1940, Stark drafted his famous "Plan Dog" memorandum, which would become the basis of American wartime grand strategy. This document laid down the principle that in the event of a war with both Germany and Japan, the United States would give priority to the defeat of Germany. As British resources would never be sufficient to bring Germany down, and nothing less would ensure American security, planners began to prepare for the all-out mobilization of American resources and the transfer of land, sea and air forces on a massive scale to fight in the European theatre alongside the British. This would leave little for the Pacific, where the United States would be forced to adopt a defensive strategy.

The British were eager to secure American entry into the European war and enthusiastically endorsed the "Germany First" strategy, which closely mirrored Britain's own priorities. American–British–Canadian staff talks in the spring of 1941 envisaged the US Pacific fleet maintaining a defensive posture in the Pacific along the line Alaska–Hawaii–Panama. However, war in the Pacific was not regarded as inevitable. British and American leaders still had reason to believe that Japan's leaders would not embark on war with both Britain and the United States. To deter Japanese aggression, President Franklin Roosevelt moved the main US fleet to Hawaii in May 1940. The President's main concern was the war in Europe, and by early 1941 his administration was committed to channelling as much aid as possible to support the British war effort. Over the course of the year, the US Navy also became increasingly involved in protecting Britain's north Atlantic supply routes against German submarines. By November, the United States was effectively fighting an undeclared naval war against Germany. But as Roosevelt edged closer to belligerency in Europe, his deterrent strategy in the Pacific was beginning to break down. American economic sanctions against Japan following its occupation of southern French Indo-China in July 1941 threatened to undermine Japan's ongoing war in China, and eventually convinced Japanese leaders to embark on war with the United States and Great Britain in order to seize resource-rich territories in South East Asia.

As the likelihood of Japanese aggression increased during the latter half of 1941, the British also pinned their hopes on a deterrent strategy. The British Chiefs of Staff hoped to strengthen the forces allocated to the defence of Malaya and Singapore, but their efforts were consistently vetoed by Churchill, who had no desire to send men or equipment to an inactive theatre when they were desperately needed to defend Britain's position in the Middle East and, after June 1941, to strengthen the hard-pressed Soviet Union. With the naval balance in European waters starting to tilt back in Britain's favour, the Admiralty began planning to build up a small but balanced fleet at Singapore in early 1942. Naval leaders believed this would be the best deterrent to an attack on British interests, but Churchill was eager to send an immediate signal to Japanese decision makers as they weighed their decision between peace and war. He therefore secured the dispatch of two fast capital ships – the new battleship HMS *Prince of Wales* and the older battlecruiser HMS *Repulse* – to Singapore. It was hoped that this movement, together with reinforcements for the garrison at Hong Kong, would convince Japanese leaders that Britain's position in the Far East was strengthening and, more importantly, that Britain and the United States were acting in concert. In the event that deterrence failed and Japan did attack British territories, Churchill was optimistic that American support would be forthcoming. With the United States as an ally, the prime minister was confident that any British losses would eventually be made good.[18]

As the Pacific war approached, British and American naval leaders refined their war plans in light of changing conditions. The US Pacific fleet continued to prepare for a defensive strategy from its base at Pearl Harbor, and there were no plans for reinforcing the Philippines after hostilities began. The Pacific fleet would not remain inactive, however. American naval leaders hoped to draw Japanese forces away from the Malay barrier by launching the fleet into the central Pacific and threatening the Marshall Islands.[19] The promise of American co-belligerency encouraged British naval planners to revive aspects of their pre-war offensive strategy. Naval leaders initially hoped that the USN would agree to base its Pacific fleet at Singapore, but this was never a realistic option. The presence of a powerful American fleet at Pearl Harbor was still expected to restrict Japan's southward movements and relieve the pressure on British territories. The decision to begin building up a British fleet at Singapore in early 1942 raised hopes that the Royal Navy could launch offensive operations against Japanese communication north of the Malay barrier, ideally from an advance base at Manila.[20]

Conclusion

The main feature shared by British and American war plans in late 1941 was an under-estimation of Japanese strength and capabilities. For two decades, Japan had enjoyed a dominant position in the Western Pacific by virtue of the Washington settlement. However, British and American leaders at Washington were only acknowledging the fundamental weakness of their respective positions. Neither country was willing to pay a high price during the interwar period to be able to defend their interests in the Far East. Even if there had been no treaty restrictions on bases and fortifications, British and American leaders would not have invested heavily in defended bases in the Western Pacific, nor in the warships needed to wage a protracted and unlimited war against Japan

---

[18] *Ibid.*
[19] MILLER, *War Plan Orange*, pp. 302–12.
[20] BELL, *Royal Navy, Seapower and Strategy*, pp. 90–3.

to defend interests regarded as important but not vital. The patent inability of the USN and the Royal Navy to project their power effectively into the Western Pacific allowed Japan to pursue an expansionist policy in China during the 1930s, and encouraged it to strike against the French, Dutch, British and Americans in 1941. The presence of an American fleet at Pearl Harbor and British capital ships at Singapore failed to deter, because Japanese leaders knew they could still inflict a devastating blow against the Western powers at the beginning of a war. Japanese Admiral Isoroku Yamamoto, Commander-in-Chief of the Japanese Combined Fleet, correctly predicted that "In the first six to twelve months of a war with the United States and Great Britain I will run wild and win victory upon victory." In the first months of the Pacific conflict, Japanese forces did just that: they seized Guam, the Philippines, Hong Kong, Malaya and Singapore; they destroyed Britain's two capital ships; and they devastated the US Pacific fleet in a surprise attack on Pearl Harbor. But Yamamoto had also acknowledged that in a prolonged war with the United States, "I have no expectation of success".[21] This, too, was prophetic. The real deterrent to Japanese aggression was always the United States' industrial might and latent naval power. In December 1941, Japanese leaders gambled that their early victories would lead to a favourable peace rather than a prolonged war of attrition that they could not hope to win. However, it soon became clear that they had miscalculated. After the attack on Pearl Harbor the United States possessed both the political will and, in time, the resources to fight the unlimited war in the Pacific that American naval planners had spent decades planning for.

---

[21] BEEVOR A., *The Second World War* (New York, 2012), p. 248.

The United States and the Second World War

Nicholas Evan Sarantakes is an Associate Professor of Strategy at the US Naval War College, United States

Abstract. *Distance from the threat, always the prime advantage of an island situation, was no longer sufficient in 1941 to save the U.S. from involvement in a world war, but it still provided the luxury of the strategic initiative, and the ability to develop campaigns when and where it suited the allies.*

Résumé. *Leur distance face à la menace, qui constitue depuis toujours le principal avantage d'une situation insulaire, ne suffit plus en 1941 à empêcher les États-Unis de s'engager dans un conflit mondial. Elle leur offrit cependant toujours le luxe de l'initiative stratégique et la capacité de développer des campagnes aux endroits et au moment qui convenaient le mieux aux alliés.*

•

The United States of America is a land power – actually, to be more accurate, a continental power – that has had its development and commerce shaped fundamentally by water even if most Americans were unaware of this fact. There was, however, a small group of political and military leaders who understood both the importance of the sea and its flexibility as a medium of power. These two factors – the importance of water and a general adaptability of the U.S. military services that fought on and near it – are major considerations in explaining U.S. strategies and experiences in the Second World War.

Throughout American history, natural bodies of water had been highways for commerce and migration, and, to a much lesser extent, defensive barriers. That changed on 7 December 1941. While maritime factors had led the United States to war against France in the undeclared Quasi War of the 1790s, against Great Britain in the War of 1812, and against Germany in the First World War, the Second World War was different. The Imperial Japanese Navy had shown that weapons technology now made it possible for foreign powers to threaten the security of the American homeland. (The last foreign power to do so – the United Kingdom in 1812 – had bases in Canada that negated the barrier of the Atlantic even before the war started.) It was also within the resources of Nazi Germany and Imperial Japan to damage in a systematic way the commerce of the United States.

When the United States entered the war, it faced a strategic situation that several peacetime decisions had shaped. Acquisitions policies often shape the capabilities of military forces; none more so than navies, where it takes years to produce new weapons platforms. The U.S. Navy was unique among the major naval services of that era in that it required its officers to obtain a strategic education at its war college if they wanted to command at flag rank. The courses offered at the U.S. Naval War College focused on fleet-on-fleet actions similar to the Battle of Jutland, which U.S. naval officers refought in war games. The most likely opponent in a future naval war was Japan. This emphasis led Fleet Admiral Chester Nimitz to return to the campus many years later and explain: "I regard the course I had here in 1922 to the middle '23, an 11 months course as best training I could conceive for command at sea – responsible command at sea. We were engaged then in a problem of the war across the Pacific both strategical games and tactical games, and the course was so complete that when the war in the Pacific actually started, nothing that happened surprised us at all except the kamikaze attacks, the suicidal attacks, the Japanese fired towards the end of the war. Everything was just about as we thought it would be."

This statement is not entirely correct. In December 1941, the United States faced a two-front war for which it had little preparation. Both theaters required naval assets and tradeoffs between one another. Another complication was the presence of General Douglas MacArthur and the strategic role of the U.S. Army in this conflict. Prewar thinking had focused on a one-front naval war.

In 1941 President Franklin D. Roosevelt committed the United States to a "Europe-first" strategy. The exact details of that commitment remained fuzzy. The thinking among the general staff of the U.S. Army was that the fastest way to defeat Germany was to initiate a cross-channel invasion, liberate France, breach the Rhine River, and drive into the heart of Germany. Maritime and naval assets played important supporting roles in providing troop transport from the United States to the United Kingdom and amphibious lift across the English Channel, but had little voice in the decisive engagements that determined the final fate of the conflict.

While this strategy was basically correct, it had several significant problems. First, the United States Army was neither big enough nor good enough to conduct the operation early in the war. It would take months and months and months to build up the Army. Another problem was that the allies lacked both the lift and experience to conduct amphibious assaults. The British had more experience, dating back to the First World War, and had learned that these operations required a good deal more specialized training than operations on the land. A third problem was that German Kriegsmarine was conducting offensive operations in the Atlantic, which made troop transport risky. Finally, the idea of simply waiting for a year or two, while the U.S. Army expanded, before taking any offensive operations against the Germans was politically unrealistic. President Roosevelt understood the political necessity of committing his people to the fight before they reconsidered their commitment or demanded action against the Japanese in a region of peripheral importance to world affairs.

The United States had certain advantages in trying to implement this strategy. First, it had a cooperative enemy. The German Navy had learned very little from the First World War. The German attempt to starve the British out of the First World War with U-boat attacks against merchant shipping had scored some early success in that conflict, but had failed in its overall strategic mission. In fact, the effort was strategically counterproductive because that campaign ended up bringing the United States into the war. When hostilities ended, German naval officers studied their campaign against British commerce and decided that the only change they needed to make was to use different tactics. When the Americans entered the Second World War, the Germans initiated Operation "Drumbeat," an improvised plan to take unrestricted submarine warfare into North American waters. Despite lacking submarines with sufficient size and range and logistics to support them in enemy waters, the hunting was good for the Germans early on and well into the summer of 1942, since U.S. cities made few efforts to impose light discipline and the U.S. Navy took little action to protect merchant shipping. The Germans sunk ships from Galveston, Texas to Portland, Maine. Although these actions were impressive, the Germans made no effort to differentiate between ship types, and that was a problem. Cargo ships were just as important as troop transports and oil tankers. The goal was tonnage sunk; the higher the better. "The strategic task of the German Navy was to wage war on trade; its objective was therefore to sink as many enemy merchant ships as it could. The *sinking of ships* was the only thing that mattered," Grand Admiral Karl Dönitz, the head of the U-boat force and later head of the German Navy explained.

Anti-submarine operations were not the type of warfare that the U.S. Navy had prepared to fight. There was also a professional and nationalistic resistance in the early months of the war to taking cues from the Royal Navy and Royal Canadian Navy. Admiral Ernest J. King, the Chief of Naval Operations and Commander-in-Chief of the U.S. Fleet, wanted to use convoys as bait to destroy the U-boats. The British objected; the objective was to get merchant ships across the Atlantic, not to wage a campaign of attrition against the Kriegsmarine. After suffering months of German success, American admirals decided to reassess and adapt. In May of 1942 the U.S. Navy conceded convoy operations along the east coast to it allies. Although the Germans enjoyed their best month in June of 1942, the course of this campaign was turning. As 1942 turned into 1943, a series of events worked to the advantage of the allies. Good weather combined with additional air assets, improvements in radar and radio detection technology, and command arrangements between the Americans, Canadians, and British ended the limited success the Germans had enjoyed. In May 1943 the U-boats had been clearly bested. Over a two-week period, the Kriegsmarine lost 25 percent of its submarines while sinking only 2.54 percent of the merchant ships it was targeting. German efforts to attack the seaborne commerce of the United Kingdom and the United States had failed.

A second factor that worked to the advantage of the United States in the strategic realm was that, as a sea power, it had far more control in picking the place and time of its operations. Both Roosevelt and British Prime Minister Winston Churchill understood this advantage. In this approach, the allies were leaning on the ideas of Sir Julian Corbett, a British naval theorist from the early 20th century. Corbett had been interested in developing theories on what are now called joint operations. He argued that the ultimate mission of a navy was to help an army to project power inland to achieve the political interests of the state. He wrote before the creation of air power, but he simply would have added air forces to the mix, giving them similar missions to a fleet. Although Churchill and Roosevelt had differences regarding timing and location, these were issues more about ways. They generally agreed on both ends and means, including the utility of sea power.

Churchill wanted to attack along the periphery of Europe, softening up the Germans before a direct attack on the enemy homeland itself. Since this approach promised action sooner than the strategy that General George C. Marshall was advocating on the part of the U.S. Army, Roosevelt agreed to invade North Africa. Operation TORCH leveraged the naval assets of both the Americans and British against the air and land resources of the Axis powers. The initial operations in North Africa also showed that the U.S. Army still needed experience. A close look at these battles shows that the U.S. Army – like the U.S. Navy – had a good institutional ability to adapt rapidly. Success in North Africa led to the invasion of Sicily. The taking of this island was the natural strategic progression following North Africa. The real issue became what to do next. Should the allies attack Italy, Sardinia, Corsica, or launch an invasion of southern France?

Invading Italy required the least amount of resources, and that was the action the allies took. The resolve of the Italian government to continue the war faded as a result of the invasion of Sicily and the landings on the Italian mainland itself, but in September German defenders were still more than capable. The initial landing by the British Eighth Army fell behind schedule after German combat engineers destroyed key bridges on roads leading north. Marching up the Italian peninsula did not strike allied leadership as an effective way to seize control of the country. Given their preponderance of naval assets, the allies attempted to flank the German defenders a week later – by this time the Italian government had signed an armistice – with the U.S. Fifth Army. This effort was less than a success. As a result, a significant gap existed between the Fifth U.S. Army and the British Eighth Army. The Germans attempted to exploit this opening, but allied air, sea, and ground firepower forced them to retreat. The Germans conceded the southern third of the peninsula to the allies, pulled back north of Naples, and established the Gustav Line.

Italy was a secondary theater in this conflict and the allies could have easily stopped where they were. The allies had knocked Italy out of the war, and turned it into a drag on the German war effort. Hitler had his army fill the void of the Italians left behind both on the peninsula and in the Balkans. The problem he faced, though, was that the units he sent to southern and southeastern Europe could have been used to much more advantage on the eastern and western fronts. Given the nature of the terrain of northern Italy – the Alps were a natural defensive barrier protecting Austria and southern Germany – control of the peninsula was a strategic cul-de-sac. A way around this barrier – to a degree – was air power. The southern third of Italy gave the allies the air fields around Foggia, which were closer to Germany than air bases in England and allowed the U.S. Army Air Forces to ravage the German economy in 1944 and 1945.

Under the prodding of British Prime Minister Winston Churchill, however, the allies tried again to circumvent the German defenses and seize more of the peninsula. On 22 January 1944 a U.S.–British task force arrived off the western coast of Italy at Anzio and landed the U.S. VI Corps and the British 1st Infantry Division. Despite a promising beginning – the allies got thirty-six thousand troops ashore on the first day and had an open road to Rome – this advance stalled and the Germans managed to contain the beachhead. The German Air Force sunk nine ships and damaged another five, but their efforts to drive the allies back into the sea failed, due to the weight of allied firepower. Efforts to link up the units around Anzio and those on the Gustav line would have to wait until May, and the liberation of Rome would not take place until June.

The advantages that the allies enjoyed in mobility because of sea power allowed them to reduce the strategic priority of the Italian campaign. As the campaign in Italy stalled, preparations for Operation OVERLORD moved to the forefront. The Royal Navy took the lead in planning for this operation. An amphibious invasion required different skill sets than simply driving a ship across an ocean or firing on a hostile enemy. The British simply had more experienced personnel than the U.S. Navy had in the theater in areas such as mine sweeping, and supplying a ground force included the creation of the "Mulberry Harbours" – artificial harbors on the landing beaches composed of large concrete caissons that were towed across the English Channel and sunk into position – and thy laying of oil pipelines that started in England, traversed the Channel and terminated on the beachheads. The planes of RAF Costal Command thrashed the U-boat packs before they even entered open waters. After the landings of 6 June the German Navy made an effort to interdict the supply trains with flotillas of surface ships and submarines. The allied navies were prepared for this response and in a series of nasty night engagements dueled the Germans to a draw, which at the strategic level was a victory. German naval attempts to stop or strangle the invasion had failed.

The ability of the allies to pick the time and location of amphibious assaults was less than absolute, more because of their own limitations than due to the actions of the Axis powers. The allied invasion of France was originally projected to be a two-pronged offensive, one coming across the English Channel, the other coming out of the Mediterranean and landing in southern France. This second assault was postponed for six weeks, rather than cancelled, due to a shortage of landing craft. When the allies did launch Operation DRAGOON on 15 August it was a pointless operation. They landed against little opposition from by-passed German units in what was essentially a strategic dead end. The lack of landing craft in the Indian Ocean, though, prevented allied operations from taking place in Burma and Malaya, which allowed the Japanese to threaten India even this late in the war.

Someone forgot to tell the Germans they were defeated. They continued to fight until the very end. The command of Dwight D. Eisenhower was facing enormous logistical problems and needed the port of Antwerp. British troops captured the port city in undamaged condition in September of 1944, but the allies could not make use of it because the Germans still held the banks of the Scheldt estuary and the island of Walcheren, which allowed them to interdict shipping. Part of Field-Marshal Sir Bernard Montgomery's failure to take this territory was a deliberate effort on his part to force Eisenhower to support his plan to drive into northern Germany. It was only after Eisenhower gave direct orders to Montgomery that a joint British task force with Canadian and Polish units attacked. The Royal Marines suffered heavy casualties landing on Walcheren, and only after working in tandem with the RAF were the Marine and Canadian units able to take the island. It was eighty-five days after the capture of Antwerp before the allies could begin to use its port facilities.

While the war in Europe represented two types of naval warfare, the war in the Pacific was far more complicated in an operational sense. The U.S. Navy fought three different forms of naval warfare in overlapping fashion. In a political and diplomatic sense, though, this part of the war was much simpler than the one in Europe. Japan, not Germany, had attacked the United States at Pearl Harbor, and the American public demanded action against the Japanese. This mandate was one the U.S. Navy was willing and even eager to meet. At the same time, the contribution from allies in this naval war would be minimal, freeing the American admirals from burdensome diplomatic concerns and restrictions – for the most part.

Both the Imperial Japanese Navy and the U.S. Navy depended heavily on the writings of Alfred Thayer Mahan for their ideas on facing one another. Mahan emphasized fleet-on-fleet actions and saw the secondary effects of sea power as less important. In keeping with these theories, both navies during the interwar period built battleships. They developed carriers and naval aviation slowly. There were sound reasons for doing so at the time. Only battleships had the endurance to cross the Pacific under fire from smaller ships and their big guns had greater range than torpedoes and more accuracy than bombs. It took literally over a thousand planes to equal the firepower of one battleship. Admirals in both navies had limited funds with which to build and maintain their fleets, and the offensive power of naval aviation was still an open question. It was clear that naval aviation was an important asset in spotting approaching enemy forces beyond the limits of the horizon. It was, however, only in the late 1930s that the Americans developed dive-bombers that were capable of delivering accurate strikes at greater range than the battleship.

Pearl Harbor was a key event in the Pacific conflict. It obviously brought the United States into the conflict. Less obvious is that on a strategic level it incapacitated U.S. naval power on a temporary basis. Many observers also argue that it ended the era when Mahan's views dominated strategic thinking among navies, and ushered in a new period in which carriers moved to the forefront.

This last view is only partially correct. While carriers became the major platform for power projection in the Pacific theater, they did so in a distinctly Mahanian manner. Japanese carriers in the first half of 1942 isolated the colonies and territories of the British, Dutch, and United States, allowing smaller but better trained Japanese ground forces to defeat the armies of the allies. Raids into the Indian Ocean forced the Royal Navy to retreat to the eastern coast of Africa. In all these operations, carriers were performing the same missions that battleships and men-of-war had performed in earlier eras. The major difference was that the distances from which the ships could operate were much greater and the projectiles they fired were manned by pilots and could return to their ships and be used again and again. Admiral Chester W. Nimitz did much the same thing in a series of hit-and-run operations that centered on carrier task forces. The Battle of the Coral Sea was really a Mahanian battle fought by aircraft carriers, the major difference from previous battles being that the two opposing forces never actually saw one another. The Battle of Midway, which followed a month later, was another Mahanian battle.

Historians generally consider Midway a major turning point in the war. It was not. Midway was an upset victory, where a smaller force defeated a superior opponent with better technology. The Americans had better doctrine on the release and recovery of planes off carrier decks and an information advantage due to the cracking of Japanese naval codes. These two factors were the critical difference in the victory. Coral Sea and Midway were strategic gambles, since Nimitz had little depth if he lost his ships. The two together represented a one-two punch in which the U.S. Navy blunted the Japanese advance. Japan, however, still had the ability to conduct offensive operations and push further to the south and east if it wished, which it did.

After Midway, the Japanese began building a base on Guadalcanal. Despite the strategy to focus on the defeat of Germany first, Guadalcanal was the early manifestation of what became a two-front war. After MacArthur's futile defense of the Philippines he arrived in Australia, courtesy of the U.S. Navy, and began to leverage against the "Europe first" strategy the Australians' fear of the Japanese as a fundamental threat to their homeland. In 1942 and early 1943 the majority of troops under MacArthur's command were Australians. Admiral King also worked against the exclusive focus on Germany. The war in Europe would be determined on the ground and the U.S. Navy would never be able to provide anything more than a supporting role, and a minor one at that. The American public wanted revenge against the Japanese, not the Germans.

All these factors led the United States to contest Japanese control of Guadalcanal and represented a different form of naval warfare that often overlapped with a Mahanian approach. Guadalcanal was a series of interrelated air, land, and sea battles over six months in 1942 and 1943. During these six months the U.S. Navy – along with small units of the Royal Australian Navy, and the Royal Navy – took on the Imperial Japanese Navy in seven battles: Savo

Island, Eastern Solomons, Santa Cruz Islands, Cape Esperance, Naval Battle of Guadalcanal, Tassafaronga, and Rennell Island. These battles were surface engagements, carrier battles, and air-sea battles. In between, the United States and Japan landed troops on Guadalcanal and used naval gunfire to shell units on the island. Although several of these naval engagements were Japanese victories, particularly those fought at night, collectively they did significant damage to the Imperial Navy, which had less recuperative power than the U.S. Navy. These battles failed to dislodge the Americans from the island or destroy U.S.-based land airpower. In the end, Guadalcanal was a strategic U.S. victory, but it was extremely close. The U.S. Marine Corps – the naval infantry of the U.S. Navy – was making plans to evacuate from the island when the Japanese withdrew first.

Despite the tightness of this victory, the United States began driving north using the twin commands of MacArthur and Nimitz. There was a good deal of learning as the U.S. seized a small series of islands with odd names. The two commands and services worked well together, despite a few well-publicized exceptions. The real problem was the failure of the political leadership in the United States to set priorities in the war against Japan and create a unified strategy. This divided approach worked, but there were several instances where the Japanese accidentally came close to exploiting these uncoordinated approaches.

The growing naval amphibious lift of the United States allowed it to circumvent well-fortified Japanese positions, leaving them in logistical isolation. Although these battles are well remembered – and rightly so – for the bravery and tenacity of U.S. Army soldiers and U.S. Marines, they also show the adaptability of American admirals. The Battle of the Philippine Sea in June of 1944 was another battle in which the carrier played the role of the Mahanian capital ship. This engagement had significant results in that U.S. naval aviation destroyed what remained of Japan's pilot force in what has often been referred to as the "Marianas Turkey Shoot," given the lopsided nature of the battle. A total of 445 Japanese pilots were lost to only about twenty Americans. Admiral Raymond Spruance then called off the battle, allowing the Japanese carriers – without their planes – and their surface fleet to escape destruction. Although staring at the possibility of a Trafalgar-like victory, he decided that his primary assignment was to protect the amphibious force invading Saipan. His mission was to be part of a joint force and help ground forces to establish a firm presence on land, rather than to fight for Mahanian control of the sea.

Later in the year, Admiral William Halsey showed the wisdom of Spruance's prudence. From 24 to 26 October the Imperial Japanese Navy and the U.S. Navy – with some assistance from the Royal Australian Navy – fought the largest naval battle in history, the Battle of Leyte Gulf. The Japanese had sent out four task forces and were trying to catch the landing force in between a giant pincer of two or more of these prongs. Carrier-based aviation turned back the center force. The two southern forces were next. The Japanese faced the U.S. and Australian battleships and cruisers of the Seventh Fleet at night in the Surigao Straits. The allies performed the classic naval maneuver of "crossing the T" and with their radar-controlled guns devastated their opponent. Halsey then went after the Northern force in the hopes of destroying Japan's carrier, scoring the decisive victory that had eluded Spruance. The hitch in this action was that the carriers had no planes and were nothing more than a decoy force. The Japanese center force had turned around, and without Halsey's Third Fleet guarding the entrance to the San Bernardino Strait fell upon the small ships protecting the landing force. These small ships were outgunned, but over the course of four hours fought with such tenacity that they convinced Vice Admiral Kurita Takeo that he was up against a much larger force. Even though he had not lost a ship, he turned back. Had he continued on, he would have been able to do serious and significant damage to the invasion force.

While the U.S. Navy was fighting Mahanian- and Corbettian-style naval battles, it was also waging a war against Japanese commerce with its submarines along the lines that *Jeune Ecole* had recommended a century earlier. The Imperial Japanese Navy had studied the U-boat campaign of the First World War and had decided that it had failed. This assessment was basically correct, but the lesson the Japanese took from this analysis was that commerce raiding was a type of warfare that they would neither practice nor prepare against. This decision gave the Americans an advantage. Ships could travel behind the lines of battle without protection. The sinking of the USS *Indianapolis* by a Japanese submarine late in the war was the exception rather the rule. Nor did the Japanese make any effort to coordinate strikes against the U.S. homeland with their German counterparts. They clearly ignored the indirect impact of sea power.

The Americans, on the other hand, started pursuing these types of operation at the very beginning of the conflict. Admiral Thomas C. Hart, the commanding officer of the Asiatic Fleet based in Manila, authorized unrestricted submarine warfare on 8 December 1941. He gave this order on his own authority, but Admiral Harold Stark, the chief of naval operations, issued similar orders a few minutes later following consultations with Roosevelt. Although the U.S. Navy entered the war with better submarines than the Germans or the Japanese, the service faced serious shortcomings. First, the submarine service had trained to a conservative doctrine that required attack using sound or sonar to find its targets, rather than the more risky but more accurate use of a periscope. The ship captains commanding submarines that used this type of approach early in the war were regular officers and, as they failed to achieve results, they were replaced with more audacious commanders who were generally younger, had commissions in the reserves, and had less training in and familiarity with conservative pre-war methods. Second, the torpedoes that U.S. submarines used were ineffective and failed to denote on a regular basis. It took even longer for ship crews to convince higher command that there were design flaws in these weapons. In 1944 after the U.S. Navy solved all these problems, submarines sunk 2.7 million tons of Japanese shipping, more than the combined totals from 1941 to 1943. At the end of the year, half of the Japanese merchant fleet had been sunk. In fact, half of all the Japanese merchant ships lost in the war were lost to submarines. The loss of these ships – oil tankers in particular – had a cascading effect, reducing the efficiency of Japanese naval aviation, since pilots could not fly as many sorties in flight school or on regular missions. The destruction of the merchant fleet also reduced the voyages of surface-fleet ships and the foodstuffs that were available to the army and navy, much more so to the Japanese public. The end result was that carrier battles like the Philippine Sea were much easier for the U.S. Navy than they had been in 1942. The same was also true for surface engagements.

Service in the submarine force, however, was extremely risky. Fifty-two ships, or one-fifth of the submarines in the U.S. Navy, never returned to port, suggesting that the Japanese Navy was not entirely wrong in its attitudes.

The importance of water as a transportation medium in shaping U.S. history cannot be overstated. Those that understood its significance were small in number, but they did more with it than their opponents, which included – ironically enough – an island nation. It was the ability to adapt and reassess that proved so crucial. The most important adjustment was their ability to use three different forms of sea power in an overlapping, mutually supportive manner.

THE SEA AS A DECISIVE FACTOR IN THE SECOND WORLD WAR

EVAN MAWDSLEY is Professor of International History at the University of Glasgow, United Kingdom

ABSTRACT. *The Second World War began as two wars of continental domination, in China and then in Europe. Some of the major campaigns were fought partly or entirely at sea, but the real importance of the sea was that it permitted the Western alliance to unify its efforts, shipping supplies and armies around the world, and to choose its targets, while at the same time dividing and isolating its enemies.*

RÉSUMÉ. *La seconde guerre mondiale commença par deux guerres de domination continentale, en Chine puis en Europe. Certaines des principales campagnes s'exécutèrent partiellement ou intégralement en mer. Cependant, le véritable rôle de la mer fut de permettre à l'alliance occidentale d'unifier ses efforts, de transporter des armées et des stocks d'approvisionnement à travers le monde et de choisir ses cibles tout en divisant et isolant ses ennemis.*

. • .

"Because World War II was in truth worldwide, it was basically a naval war." Chester Nimitz set out this assessment in his foreword to a 1961 history.[1] Nimitz had been the most successful admiral of that war, as Commander-in-Chief of the American Pacific Fleet; in a long and distinguished career he also served as Chief of Naval Operations.

The statement that 1939–1945 was "basically a naval war" is an extreme one. To evaluate it we need to bear in mind that the conflict was indeed "in truth worldwide" and that it was an extremely complex event. Few simple generalisations can be made, and the war needs to be considered from multiple national perspectives. And in enumerating "basic" features, the *causes* of the Second World War, and the *conduct* and *results* of that struggle must be treated as distinct entities.

---

[1] NIMITZ C. and POTTER E., eds, *The Great Sea War: The Story of Naval Action in World War II* (London, 1961), p. v. My chapter should certainly not be taken as wholesale negative criticism of Admiral Nimitz. If not a profound strategic thinker, he was a very capable administrator.

The Causes of the Second World War

Nimitz's use of the word "naval" is narrow for present purposes; "maritime" is better – for discussion of the role of "the sea". But even so, it is hard to argue that the Second World War was essentially *caused* by maritime issues. It might be there were "deep" causes related to the sea: challenges by regional "revisionist" ("new-order") powers – Germany, Italy and Japan – to the existing overseas empires of the European powers, especially Britain. But that is really too general to be helpful.

This is not the place to detail the origins of the war. But in very general terms the eventual "worldwide" conflagration had two distinct sites of ignition. One was in East Asia in 1937, the other in Central and Western Europe in 1939. Both sites involved "continental" issues rather than maritime ones.[2] The war of 1937/1939 was caused by attempts to achieve *regional* hegemony, in particular the attempts by Japan, Germany and Italy to gain control of regional resource bases. For Hitler's Third Reich the medium-term vision of expansionism was away from the sea and into *Mitteleuropa* (and this contrasted with the situation before 1914, when Wilhemine Germany possessed a global empire in Africa, Asia and Oceania). In the pre-war Japanese and Italian visions maritime factors did exist, but they focused on adjacent territories which, if not accessible overland, could be reached by relatively short sea crossings (e.g. to Manchuria or Libya).

The Second World War was also not caused by a naval arms race. Wilhemine Germany and Britain competed in dreadnought construction in the first decade of the 1900s, and this influenced the British decision to go to war in 1914. In the late 1930s, however, Nazi Germany concentrated on developing its ground and air forces, and it did not have the time or resources necessary to develop as a naval power. France and Italy did compete in a limited Mediterranean naval arms race from the 1920s, but this was not the major cause of conflict between them.

The situation in the Far East was somewhat different. Japan's war with China in 1937 had nothing to do with any naval construction competition between the two states – there being almost no Chinese navy. However, naval competition with the West, especially with the USA, had been a significant issue for Japanese nationalists in the 1930s, especially with the negotiations for the London Naval Treaty in 1930. The international resumption of large-scale warship construction following the expiry of the 1922 Washington and 1930 London treaties was accompanied by a spurt of Japanese activity. This was matched by American ship-building programmes – the Congressional Naval Acts of 1938 and 1940 – which threatened to consign Japan to a position of permanent disadvantage. As a result of this, some members of the Japanese elite – including a number of leaders of the Imperial Navy – saw a closing "window of opportunity" before

---

[2] The word 'continental' is put in quotation marks to signal that this relates to British usage of a strategy based on fighting on 'the continent' (inland in Europe) as opposed to fighting a maritime war. There is a potential confusion with war 'between' continents, which is how some (European) observers portrayed the situation after December 1941.

December 1941. Non-naval factors were, however, more important in pushing Japan into another war in December 1941. One underlying cause was American opposition to Japan's adventures in China. A more important cause was a miscalculated Japanese attempt to exploit a rapidly changing global power system: France and the Netherlands, both of them Asiatic imperial powers, had been defeated in 1940, and Britain and Russia were weakened and preoccupied with war in Europe.

The conduct of the Second World War

If the causes of the Second World War were not essentially maritime, what can be said about the *conduct* of the war? From one point of view, the suggestion that the operations of the Second World War were "basically" naval – or maritime – is easily challenged. Two of the most important theatres of the war, the Chinese-Japanese and the German-Soviet, were far inland. Nimitz was a navalist and an American, and he was writing at a time when the Soviet Union and the People's Republic of China were apparently mortal enemies of the United States; it is not surprising that he made little of the contributions of those two states.[3]

However, although the campaigns in China and Russia have to be regarded as essentially "continental", the maritime dimension was certainly not absent. In its war against China control of the sea gave Imperial Japan an overwhelming advantage. China had virtually no navy or maritime air force in 1937, indeed no significant coastal defences; Japan possessed one of the world's three most powerful navies, and a large merchant marine. Japanese control over the East and South China Seas made it possible to reinforce troops already stationed in China and to send large new expeditionary forces there from 1937 onwards. The amphibious-war techniques of the Japanese Army and Navy – building on the experience of the 1904–5 war with Russia – were at the time more advanced than those of Britain or the USA. After 1937 the Chinese government lost control of almost the entire coastline and was unable to block Japanese shipment of troops and supplies. Maritime factors also played a part in the "escalation" of Japan's war effort in December 1941. A desire to force the capitulation of Chiang Kai-shek's Chongqing government by blocking all channels of supply from overseas, including French Indochina, the Burma Road (from the Indian Ocean into south China) and Hong Kong, contributed to growing tension with Britain and the United States.

The Soviet-German campaign was "basically" a vast land war between giant mechanised armies. The wartime USSR had difficult access to the world ocean. It possessed only a small navy and merchant marine, split into four locations – in the Baltic, the Black Sea, northern European Russia, and eastern Siberia. The

---

[3] For the context of the admiral's remarks see POTTER E.B., *Nimitz* (Annapolis, MD, 1976), pp. 413–72.

Soviet surface fleet was destroyed, damaged or immobilised in 1941–1942, and many seamen were transferred to the Red Army. The Germans deployed naval forces in the Baltic only from time to time and in small quantities, and they could send only coastal craft and small submarines to the Black Sea.

But, as in China, the maritime element was not insignificant. Hitler had concerns in 1941 about Soviet naval interference with iron ore supplies from Sweden, and he detoured forces to the Crimea to eliminate the Black Sea naval base of Sevastopol. More important, the overall German plans in 1941 and 1942 included sealing off maritime supply routes to the west by capturing the north Russian ports and Vladivostok (the latter with expected Japanese participation). From late 1941 the surviving major ships of the Kriegsmarine, along with U-boats and a considerable number of anti-shipping aircraft, were concentrated in northern Norway in an attempt to block the inter-Allied sea route. Fortunately, the Red Army kept control of Murmansk, Arkhangelsk, Vladivostok and the lower Volga (at Stalingrad), enabling the flow of Allied Lend-Lease aid. In 1941 and 1942 this assistance arrived in too small quantities to be a factor in the initial survival of the USSR (which was supported largely by domestic Soviet production). But the sea-borne imports of 1943–1945 – especially through the Persian Gulf – certainly increased the weight and pace of the Red Army's grand counter-offensive.

The great American and British land campaigns fought in northwestern Europe, from the Normandy invasion of June 1944 to May 1945, brought about the liberation of Western Europe and played a major part in the destruction of Nazi Germany. The British–American strategic bombing campaign also contributed to the final victory. Neither of these was "basically" a naval campaign. Admiral Nimitz took a different view in 1961: "[I]n the European theatre [by which the admiral meant the *western* European theatre] ... it was the navies that brought the armies to the beaches, landed them, and kept them supplied. And it was the navies that brought in, or protected the ships that brought in, most of the aircraft and bombs and all of the aviation fuel for land-based air operations."[4] He was, of course, correct that the delivery of American troops and their supplies to northwest Europe, and of all supplies to the British – including fuel for RAF Bomber Command – depended on trans-oceanic shipping. That does not mean that the maritime effort was *the* essential feature of the war. In particular, Nazi Germany could be defeated only by the arrival of ground troops and military occupation.

The situation regarding northwestern Europe seems different if the years 1939–1943 – before D-Day – are considered. Prior to the outbreak of war in 1939 the British government had been, broadly speaking, in favour of a national "maritime" strategy for a European war. Economic warfare would defeat the Third Reich, and the French (and perhaps the Soviets) would tie up the German Army. This would avoid a British "continental" strategy involving a repetition of

---

[4] POTTER, *Great Sea War*, p. v.

the hugely costly trench warfare of 1914–1918 by British forces on the European mainland. This maritime strategy was understood as a return to the successful "British way of war" of the 18th and 19th centuries.[5] The French in 1939–1940 also hoped to avoid excessive losses by engaging the Germans on the periphery of Europe, cutting their access to resources in Scandinavia, the Balkans and the USSR, while in the short term holding German troops at arm's length in front of the Maginot Line.

It was, to be sure, basic to the successful Allied outcome, in northwestern Europe and elsewhere, that Britain was an island and possessed strong defences. The Royal Air Force often receives credit for victory in the "Battle of Britain", but the great numerical superiority of the Royal Navy over the small Kriegsmarine (smaller still, having lost warships sunk and damaged by the British in Norway) meant that the German preparations for invasion were largely bluff. Britain is often portrayed as outnumbered and cornered in the summer of 1940, but the situation was more of a stalemate. Hitler's Germany essentially controlled two-thirds of the continent, but Britain had access to its Empire and to the good will of the United States. The impracticality of a direct attack on Britain pushed Hitler and his generals toward other – fatal – strategies, notably in the Soviet Union.

But while sea power could protect Britain, it certainly could not, in 1940–1942, allow effective *offensive* measures by Britain on its own to break German hegemony on the continent. Both in 1939–1940 and in 1943–1945 Britain's allies (in the first period the French, and in the second the Americans and the Soviets) forced the British to commit troops and resources to ground war. The leaders of the US Army, for their part, with greater potential manpower than Britain (and less experience), were interested in the quick establishment of a lodgement on the continent, which would be followed by a flow of army divisions from the United States and the rapid defeat of Germany – in the steam-roller style of Ulysses S. Grant. The navies would have the auxiliary task of ferrying troops across the Atlantic.

Even the campaign in the Mediterranean – including North Africa in 1940–1942 and Italy in 1943–1944 – was not "basically" a naval one. The Mediterranean ceased to function as a normal shipping route from the time of the fall of France in June 1940. The overstretched British were also unable completely to block Axis north–south shipping until the early spring of 1943, when the land campaign in North Africa was almost over. Although the operations of the Italian Navy are sometimes underrated by historians, the main Axis forces contesting control the Mediterranean were the land-based aircraft of the Luftwaffe and (from late 1941) the U-boats. By the end of 1941 most of the big British ships operating in the Mediterranean had been lost or disabled in a war of attrition. Admiral Raeder, the Commander-in-Chief of Hitler's navy, did in late 1940 and early 1941 strongly urge the development of the Mediterranean as Germany's major war theatre (as

---

[5] This view was popularised in LIDDELL HART B.H., *The British Way in Warfare* (London, 1932).

an alternative to the invasion of Russia), but such aspirations came to an end with Operation Barbarossa. But even so, Allied sea power on its own could not knock even Italy out of the war. A land campaign was needed to eject the Germans and Italians from North Africa, and a land-based Allied air campaign was needed to gain control of the central Mediterranean and the approaches to Sicily, Italy and (in 1944) the south of France.

Maritime factors were, however, important in the Allied victory in the Mediterranean. The first factor was logistics; the central Mediterranean was blocked from 1940 to 1943, but an oceanic transport capability allowed the transfer of troops and supplies to Egypt around the Cape of Good Hope. The second factor was the newly developed Allied amphibious forces. Operation Overlord/Neptune in June 1944 was huge and decisive, but it involved a relatively short crossing of the English Channel and was predictable (except for timing and the precise location of the landing). The situation in the south, in contrast, allowed a larger element of surprise, from the time of Operation Torch in Morocco and Algeria in November 1942. The invasion of Sicily in July 1943 demonstrated the coming of age of British–American amphibious technology with the deployment of a large number of landing craft, specialised tank/vehicle ro-ro transport vessels (LSTs) and long range "amphibious" ships. Remarkably, Operation Torch involved the passage of some of the attack convoys right across the Atlantic; for Sicily one division was moved all the way from Scotland.[6] Amphibious warfare would thereafter prove a much more successful feature of the conduct of war than in 1914-1918 – where the landings in the Dardanelles had ultimately been unsuccessful; the triumph on the Normandy beaches in 1944 was aided greatly by experience gained in the Mediterranean.

The American war with Japan might seem the classic case. As Admiral Nimitz put it, "The basically naval nature of World War II was obvious in the Pacific Ocean Areas [POA, the formal name of Nimitz's command] where the United States Navy controlled every man and every weapon of all Allied services and nationalities ..."[7] It was certainly true that Japan achieved regional superiority in the Pacific after inflicting heavy losses on the American and British navies in the first days of the war, and then lost it after a decisive defeat at the Battle of Midway in June 1942 – inflicted mainly by the what had become the new capital ships, the aircraft carriers of the US Navy.

And yet there are some obvious problems even here with Nimitz's view. First of all, the POA were only half the "Pacific" theatre, the other half being the Southwest Pacific Area (SWPA) of 1942-1945. This latter area fought under General MacArthur, and the main forces came from the US Army (including

---

[6] The first successful Allied long-range amphibious operation was Operation Ironclad, directed against Vichy-held Madagascar in May 1942. This was, however, on a much smaller scale than Operation Torch six months later. The very first successful Allied amphibious attack, the Soviet Kerch-Feodosiia operation of January 1942, involved a relatively short sea crossing.

[7] POTTER, *Great Sea War*, p. v. Nimitz did admit that his command did not include the B-29 bombers based in the Marianas, which came directly under the U.S. Joint Chiefs of Staff.

the land-based Army Air Forces [USAAF]) and from the land and air forces of Australia and New Zealand. Second, although crucial events certainly included the advance of the US Navy across the Pacific to the Marianas, the Philippines and Okinawa, the *immediate* causes of the surrender of Japan in 1945 were the late-war strategic bombing campaign by the USAAF (including the use of the atomic bombs) and the entry into the war of the USSR, with its powerful ground forces.[8]

Without doubt, *for the Japanese* the sea was crucial. The South China Sea, which they had gained control of in the winter of 1941-1942, was the route to the fuel and other raw materials of Southeast Asia. This route was interrupted in 1943-1944 by an American submarine campaign and then blocked in 1945 by the capture of Luzon in the Philippines and Okinawa. Even the East China Sea and the route to the Empire's 1930s gains in China (including Manchuria) was now imperilled. Worse than that, in 1944-1945 the great ocean to the south and east was, for the home islands of Japan, the most vulnerable wartime front, one from which the enemy could mount bombing raids and even invasions.

But for the overall *Allied* cause the Pacific Ocean was a subordinate theatre – and this was a case made during the war not only by the leaders of the British and American armies. Japan could not threaten, after the winter of 1941-1942, any further vital Allied interests. Compared to the danger that would have been posed by secure German control over Europe, Japan was of only secondary concern. Control of Allied shipping routes had only a limited significance in the Pacific war, although up to the time of the Battle for Guadalcanal in late 1942 both sides were concerned about the trans-Pacific route to Australia. Fortunately, the Japanese made little attempt, even in 1942, to interfere with the long US supply lines, partly due to lack of resources and partly due to their preoccupation with winning another decisive battle – they were true followers of Mahan here. It is hard altogether to avoid the sense that some of the wholesale American commitment to the Pacific war stemmed from bureaucratic factors. Of these the most important was the desire of the leaders of the US Navy – notably Admiral Nimitz's superior, Admiral Ernest J. King – to have the fleet play a part in the global war effort comparable to that of the US Army.[9] The Pacific theatre demanded an enormous American productive effort in terms of ship construction, and it tied up manpower, aircraft, escort vessels and troop-transport and supply ships; all this involved high opportunity costs.

However, in defence of Washington's grand strategy it must be noted that the

---

[8] While the Soviet factor should not be exaggerated, it had a significant influence on the Japanese Army high command. Like the atomic bombs, it provided a face-saving moment for the Shōwa era elite. On this see HASEGAWA T., *Racing the Enemy: Stalin, Truman, and the Surrender of Japan* (Cambridge, MA, 2005).

[9] In contrast, King's predecessor as professional head of the U.S. Navy, Admiral Harold Stark, had stressed the importance of the European – rather than the Pacific – theatre in his prescient 'Plan Dog' memorandum of November 1940. That memorandum was, however, written before the Japanese navy attacked Pearl Harbor, before the collapse of British power in the Far East, and before the entry of the Soviet Union into the war.

United States' war effort had only limited flexibility. The country had embarked in 1938 and 1940 on long-term shipbuilding programmes. The long lead-time required in naval construction, especially for large ships, came into play here. Hitler's small surface navy had been largely neutralised by the time American forces actively entered the war in the spring of 1942; the Italian fleet was also no longer a threat, even on paper. A year later, when the US Navy's new heavy ships began to enter the fleet en masse, both of the European Axis navies had been defeated by the British. The "two-ocean navy" of capital ships (including fleet carriers) which the American government had embarked upon in the summer of 1940 – in response to the fall of France – was no longer required for a one-ocean war with the Axis. Modern American "fleet" carriers almost never operated in European waters after the spring of 1942.[10] The same was true of the new battleships, the great majority of the many new cruisers, almost the entire American submarine force and all elements of the Marine Corps. More escort carriers, destroyers, destroyer escorts and amphibious ships operated in the Atlantic and in European waters in an anti-submarine warfare (ASW) role, but it was still the case that most of these types were used only in the Pacific.

The North Atlantic was the most vital maritime theatre for the Allies. In grand strategic terms the conduct of war in the Atlantic was indeed "basic" to victory. The survival of Britain as the early core of the coalition was essential at several moments in the war (especially in 1940). Because the United Kingdom had become isolated from the continental economies, the maintenance of the Atlantic link, first to the British Empire and then to the United States, was essential. Given the technical realities of the first half of the 1940s (as opposed to the Cold War era), American power could be brought to bear by only control of forward bases on the European periphery, above all in the United Kingdom. This was crucial, too, to eventual Soviet victory, as a successful counter-offensive by the Red Army depended on the existence of a fighting front in the West.

The Atlantic sea route was never as seriously threatened by Hitler's U-boat fleet as is sometimes suggested. Only a small number of submarines were available in the first two years. Fortunately the Germans made limited use maritime patrol aircraft, and their development of anti-ship missiles came late. The conservative Kriegsmarine leadership was not air-minded, and the Luftwaffe gave commerce raiding a low priority. To defeat the U-boats the British (and Canadians) were eventually able to deploy a large number of ASW ships and long-range maritime aircraft, and they developed superior electronics and radio intelligence; the Americans played a major but secondary operational role. The Atlantic was also, compared to the other theatres of war, more of a purely "naval" one – especially if RAF Coastal Command is included as a naval force. Ground forces played little direct role. The 1940 occupation of Norwegian ports by the Germans and of Icelandic ones by the British were related to the Battle of the

---

[10] The second-rate fleet carrier *Ranger* did briefly serve in European waters. A number of escort carriers supported Operation Torch and the invasion of southern France in August 1944.

Atlantic, but those incursions were not directly opposed; there was in 1941–1942 some thought of occupying the Azores, the Canaries and the Cape Verde islands but neither side actually mounted such operations.[11]

From the spring of 1942 it is difficult to envisage Britain being forced to surrender. The United States was now committed to the war. The Soviet Union had survived the first terrible shocks. As the global counter-offensive began, the oceanic (not just Atlantic) supply lines became in many respects the backbone of the war. This was a war in which rapid victory – and perhaps even avoidance of a stalemate – depended on the industrial might of the United States, a country which was three thousand miles from the western European battle front, and five thousand miles from the Pacific one. In this respect the conduct of the Second World War was quite different from that of the First.

Allied grand-strategic use of global shipping lanes in 1942–1945 rarely involved fighting against Axis surface units, and only limited resistance was latterly met from enemy aircraft and submarines. British and American shipping shortages from the autumn of 1942 onwards were less the result of attrition than of the competing demands of general shipping and the provision of extensive "lift" for amphibious offensives (not to mention the commitment of resources to the "luxury" Pacific war). Nevertheless, the effort required to create, patrol and exploit these lines of communications was not always appreciated; Stalin frequently noted – both in speeches and in secret correspondence – the disparity in the number of active ground-force divisions deployed on "his" front and those of his allies. While such criticisms had some justification, Stalin thought in terms of tank armies and battlefield aircraft, rather than Liberty ships, LSTs, "combat loaders" and escort vessels fighting a war at oceanic ranges. It is worth remembering, too, that the reason why Britain and the United States could achieve rapid success in the Second World War with *relatively* limited losses was because sea power allowed them to choose when and where to fight. The Russians and Germans were in a less happy position, as were the Japanese after the spring of 1942.

Outcome of the Second World War

The *outcome* of the Second World War – Allied victory – resulted from different factors; these were not exclusively maritime. Three of the Allied countries (Britain, the USSR and the USA) possessed strong industrial economies. They had relatively free access to a spectrum of resources (especially petroleum and foodstuffs). Some Allied advantages were technological; of the Axis powers, only Germany was as advanced as the USA and Britain. Some were demographic; the population of the Soviet Union was over twice that of Germany, and China was

---

[11] I am not treating the invasion of Morocco ('Torch') or the 1944 Normandy landings as part of the 'Atlantic' war.

four or five times the size of Japan. Victory was also related to geography and climate – the expanse of Russia and China and the insularity of Britain and the United States. The authoritarian and super-nationalist governments of the Axis states alienated the populations of the areas they occupied, and they conducted the war in a dysfunctional manner.

The outcome for Britain and the United States did, however, also come about because they had bigger navies. Thanks to their insularity they did not need to raise large standing armies in peacetime. Already when the war began in 1939 they possessed much larger fleets of warships and merchant vessels (and much greater shipbuilding capacity) than did their potential opponents. Britain's network of colonies and bases made it possible to support ships all over the globe. Japan commanded a navy less than a third the size of the combined "Anglo-Saxon" navies, and had a weak industrial and raw-material base; for various historical and bureaucratic reasons the Imperial Navy needed to share limited funds with a large standing army. Germany and Italy were – for different reasons – in the naval third or fourth rank in 1939.

Stephen Roskill argued that the Allies sought victory through "exploiting maritime power; and we may be thankful that among the weaknesses of the enemy's camp ... was his inability to grasp the nature of such a strategy".[12] It is neither accurate nor helpful to suggest that the Axis powers did not "understand" sea power. The strategy of each of the fighting powers was determined by geography, level of economic development, historical situation and other factors. On the German side, Admiral Raeder's grasp of the nature of sea power was in many respects subtle, and not any more out of touch with technical naval and aviation developments than that of officers of his generation in Britain, France and the United States. It is true that Admirals Raeder and Dönitz were relatively minor players at Hitler's court. (And it is also true that the Vichy French and Italian Fascist governments had a better grasp of extra-continental strategy.) But the real problem was that the Third Reich lacked both naval assets (due to late beginning of rearmament) and overseas bases (due to the outcome of the 1914–1918 war). The leaders of the Japanese Navy certainly grasped the importance of maritime power, although they stressed the battle fleet and decisive battle at the expense of commerce protection and sea denial.

Another way of evaluating the place of sea power in the war's outcome – although it involves a high degree of generalisation – is through the competing interpretations of Alfred Thayer Mahan and the geographer Halford Mackinder. The war might be seen as a competition between two approaches or strategies, one of which was continental, the other oceanic.[13] Mahan had argued that the possession of powerful navies was the key to world power. The attitude of the British and American naval leadership in 1939 was one which stressed that sea

---

[12] ROSKILL S.W., *The War at Sea 1939-45*, 3 vols (London, 1954–61), vol. 3, p. 389.
[13] The contrast is used differently in KENNEDY P., 'Mahan versus Mackinder: Two Interpretations of British Sea Power', in his *Strategy and Diplomacy, 1870-1945: Eight Studies* (London, 1983), pp. 127–60.

power and blockade were – as they been in the 17th and 18th centuries, which Mahan wrote about – the best way to achieve victory. Mackinder believed that in the 20th century the Eurasian "heartland" had become crucial. His argument was partly technological. For him there had been a "Columbian" age from the 15th century in which movement by sea was a central feature of world history; the late 19th century, however, saw the development of means of land communication – notably the railways – that superseded merchant ships. Mackinder influenced – albeit indirectly – the geopolitical views of Hitler and many of his advisors. Hitler grasped the geopolitical concept of Mitteleuropa and believed its possession could make the Third Reich a world power comparable to the United States or the British Empire. Germany needed to gain control of the (inland) food and mineral resources of a large part of Eurasia – including the grain of the Ukraine and the oil of Romania and the Caucasus – as well as an area for settler colonisation. This Mackinder/Mahan duality does not map directly onto the realities of the Second World War, not least because of the special cases of Russia and Japan. Nevertheless, looking just at the European case, and everything else being equal, control of the oceanic communications (which Britain and the United States possessed) did indeed turn out to be more valuable than control of western and central Europe (which was the advantage of Hitler's Third Reich).

To return finally to Admiral Nimitz. It is no easy task to determine what the Second World War "basically" was. A more subtle interpretation of the outcome of the war was that made by the British naval historian Admiral Herbert Richmond in the published version of his Oxford University Ford Lectures: "Sea power did not win the war itself; it enabled the war to be won."[14] Control of the seas – maritime power, not just naval power – was *an* (not *the*) underlying reason for Allied victory. It was *a* (not *the*) decisive factor.

---

[14] RICHMOND H.W., *Statesmen and Sea Power* (Oxford, 1946), p. 336.

THE SEA AND THE RISE OF THE DICTATORS: ITALY, 1919–1940

MACGREGOR KNOX is Stevenson Professor of International History Emeritus at the London School of Economics and Political Science, United Kingdom

ABSTRACT. Poets and visionaries had lamented that Italy was "the prisoner of the Mediterranean"; Mussolini took the phrase as a guide to strategy and built up a modern navy "to gain free access to the oceans." In practice, command of the central Mediterranean proved to be excessively ambitious without aircraft carriers or air force cooperation, and Italy lacked the oil to fuel its new battlefleet.

RÉSUMÉ. Les poètes et les visionnaires ont déploré que l'Italie fût « la prisonnière de la Méditerranée ». Mussolini reprit cette phrase dans l'élaboration de sa stratégie et construisit une nouvelle marine pour « gagner un accès libre aux océans ». En pratique, la maîtrise de la Méditerranée centrale s'avérait excessivement ambitieuse en l'absence de porte-avions ou de coopération avec les forces aériennes, et l'Italie ne disposait pas du carburant nécessaire au fonctionnement de sa nouvelle flotte de combat.

.•.

In the Mediterranean Italy will either founder or dominate.
– Mussolini, 8 November 1929

Half-way prophetic words, which the Duce of Fascism and *Capo del Governo* prefaced with an abiding geopolitical fixation: "We are locked in the Mediterranean, and cannot willingly remain imprisoned."[1] Mastery of Italy's sea was a longstanding obsession of the Fascist movement, of Fascism's Nationalist allies, of much of literate, urban Italian opinion, and of Mussolini himself. His proposed extra-Mediterranean jail-break was yet more ambitions. It derived from the speculations of poets and nationalist sages, the Royal Italian Navy's reflections on the Great War, Italy's painful dependence on seaborne imports, and Mussolini's enduring resentment after Britain blocked his attempted annexation of Corfù in 1923.

Yet these objectives remained far beyond Italy's limited strength. The French

---

[1] Minutes of 8 December 1929, Archivio Centrale dello Stato, Rome (henceforth ACS), Verbali del Consiglio dei Ministri, vol. 18, p. 79.

navy alone retained superiority over the *Regia Marina Italiana* until June 1940, while Britain's positions at Gibraltar and Suez, its Mediterranean and Home Fleets, and its naval airpower promised a dramatic end not merely to Italy's claims to Mediterranean domination and world power, but even to national independence.

ASPIRAZIONI

United Italy's purported entitlement to Mediterranean hegemony had a long and illustrious pedigree: Fascist Italy did not "turn to the sea" by chance. Mazzini had invoked imperial Rome's domination of "mare nostro" and had claimed Tunisia, Malta, and Corsica – the last "assigned to Italy by God." Successors such as the poet Giovanni Pascoli had lamented the alleged martyrdom of "proletarian" Italy, and proclaimed its "right not to be thwarted and choked in its [own] sea." Gabriele D'Annunzio had played numerous variations on the theme of mechanized violence and its corollary, Italian naval supremacy: "Ship of steel, straight swift vibrant / splendid as a naked sword [...] Fearsome prow, steering toward the domination of the world." The luminaries of the Italian Nationalist Association, particularly after the frustration of Italy's extravagant war aims in 1919, had railed incessantly against Italy's encirclement by France's "chain of formidable strongholds that surround and can blockade Italy" and Britain's hold on the decisive choke-points at Gibraltar and Suez.[2] The nascent Fascist movement likewise proclaimed the sovereign right of United Italy, reborn through war, to reassert primacy in the face of the "feebleness and decadence of the other [powers]." And the black-shirted warlord of Trieste, Francesco Giunta, with the strategic myopia characteristic of the entire Italian ruling class, insisted that Mediterranean primacy meant world domination.[3]

The *Regia Marina*, in the person of its wartime chief, Admiral Paolo Thaon di Revel, likewise contributed mightily to the Fascist regime's maritime aspirations. In the Great War's aftermath, Revel inveighed at length in parliament against the failure of Liberal Italy's final governments to secure "a maritime situation in the Adriatic that was strategically Italian." He dwelt in detail on Italy's dependence on maritime imports of food and raw materials, recalled British blockade measures against Italian shipping during Italy's 1914–1915 neutrality, and proclaimed with all the authority and vehemence at his command that "with Suez and Gibraltar barred, Italy would soon be at the mercy of its adversary, even before the latter deployed the full violence of his armaments."[4] As navy minister in Mussolini's first government, the admiral repeatedly stressed Italy's helplessness in the face

---

[2] See KNOX M., *To the Threshold of Power*, vol 1 (Cambridge, 2008), pp. 117, 113, 297.
[3] RUMI G., *Alle origini della politica estera fascista* (Bari, 1968), pp. 113–28 (quotation: p. 119).
[4] Italy, *Atti parlamentari*, Rome, various dates (henceforth AP, chamber, session date, volume:page), Senato, 1921–22, 3:3833–34 (14 August 1922); see also AP, Senato, 1919–20, 1:754, 1154–58; 2:2285–88. For the naval staff's similar assessment of Italy's resource

of distant blockade at Gibraltar and Suez. The Corfù crisis of September 1923 drove the lesson home. Italy's economy and coastal cities were at Britain's mercy; when Mussolini asked his ministers how long the navy could hold off its British counterpart, the admiral's reputed reply was a laconic "forty-eight hours."[5] That depressing insight dominated the extensive discussions about the *Regia Marina*'s budget and organization in the Senate and the Chamber of Deputies in winter-spring 1924-25.[6] Revel summed up at the end of March 1925 with a phrase with a long future: without adequate naval forces, Italy, "instead of being the dominating power [*dominatrice*] would remain a prisoner in the Mediterranean."[7]

The dictator himself had long since taken that metaphor to heart. From his conversion to war in 1914 onward he demanded with increasing vehemence that Italy dominate not merely the Adriatic – a central component of Italy's war aims – but also the Mediterranean, "sea of Rome, sea of the expansion of Italy in its entirety."[8] That expansion might as yet involve mere shipping and commerce, "carrying Italy's *tricolore* across every ocean to the shores of the entire world." But by 1920 Mussolini had adopted – perhaps from the Nationalists – the notion of a "chain of hostility that surrounds Italy in the Mediterranean."[9] In March 1925 the dictator, fresh from decisive victory over his domestic opponents, returned to the theme with inimitable ferocity. To the alarm and horror of his foreign ministry advisers, Mussolini, sporting a "fixed stare ... that resembled that of a lunatic [*esaltato*]," injected into a policy discussion of Anglo-Italian rivalry in Albania the following "stupefying phrases":

> Gibraltar, Malta, Suez, Cyprus represent a chain that gives England license to encircle, to imprison Italy in the Mediterranean. If another link, Albania, were welded to [that chain], we would have had to break it with a war. A short war; it would not have lasted more than a few weeks, for Italy today is no longer the Italy of the days of Giolitti ...[10]

The dictator noted a month later, in an inevitably more demure public speech to the Senate, the vulnerability to blockade of Italy's food supply, much of which had

---

dependence and maritime strategic situation (October 1921), see BERNARDI G., *Il disarmo navale fra le due guerre mondiali (1919-1939)* (Rome, 1975), pp. 45-8.

[5] FERRANTE E., *Il grande ammiraglio Paolo Thaon di Revel* (Rome, Rivista Marittima, 1989), p. 106; see also *I documenti diplomatici italiani*, Rome, Libreria della Stato, 1952- (henceforth DDI series/volume/document), 7/2/348.

[6] AP, Camera, 1924-25, 2:123-37, 1247-48, 1284-1309, 1347-54 (6, 9, 10 December 1924); AP, Senato, 1924, 1:898-917; AP, Camera, 1924-25, 3: 3106-37, 3142-74.

[7] AP, Camera, 1924-25, 3:3151 and 3171 (28 and 30 March 1925); also Revel to Mussolini, 28 March 1925, in BERNARDI, *Disarmo*, p. 217.

[8] *Opera omnia di Benito Mussolini*, 44 vols, ed. E. and D. SUSMEL (Florence and Rome, 1951-80) (henceforth OO volume:page), 7:233-4, 8:177, 9:117, 11:86, 290; quotation: 12:77.

[9] OO 14:206, 15:37.

[10] Quotations: Ugo Sola memoirs (typescript ms., copy in the author's possession), p. 184, 188-9; also quoted (but omitting the role of 'England') in CAROCCI G., *La politica estera dell'Italia fascista (1925-1928)* (Bari, 1969), p. 265 note 18.

to pass through the three "well-guarded" gates to the Mediterranean.[11] And in October 1926, in addressing a private gathering of high officers, he transformed his previous insights and those of the navy into a geopolitical dogma, valid for all nations at all times, that fastened upon Fascist Italy a stern duty far beyond its strength: "A nation that has no free access to the sea cannot be considered a free nation; a nation that has no free access to the oceans cannot be considered a great power. Italy must become a great power."[12] The dictator returned to this theme at intervals, most notably in his secret policy speech of 4 February 1939 to the Grand Council of Fascism proclaiming Italy's duty to "march to the ocean," his March 1940 war memorandum for his principal subordinates and King Victor Emmanuel III, and his 10 June 1940 war speech to the Italian people.[13]

Geopolitical freedom was thinkable only if Italy could secure an ally of overwhelming power with aims and enthusiasms complementary to its own. Not coincidentally, Mussolini was aware virtually from Fascism's very beginnings – as he put it in early 1922 – that "the axis of European history passes through Berlin."[14] He all too presciently pronounced Weimar Germany neither republican nor pacifist; "an overwhelming thirst for a rematch and for revenge" permeated the German Reich. That abiding and entirely correct conviction remained a guiding principle of Mussolini's policy, despite German reticence and capriciousness, until its consummation in the Rome–Berlin Axis of 1936–1937 and the Pact of Steel war alliance of 1939–1943.[15]

IMPLEMENTATION

Mediterranean domination, much less a "march to the ocean," nevertheless remained wholly utopian unless the mighty ally the dictator sought could magically neutralize French and British seapower. As of 1923 four-fifths of Italy's twenty million tons of annual imports arrived by sea – the oil, coal, iron ore, pig iron, iron and steel scrap, and grain that stood between Mussolini's regime and economic collapse and social chaos. The Fascist "battle of grain" of the 1920s largely achieved autarky in bread and pasta; urban Italy would not automatically erupt in food riots if imports ceased. Domestic low-quality coal and hydroelectric power slightly lessened Italy's energy dependence. And the Great Depression freed Fascist Italy from the nannying of Paris, London, and New York bankers. Yet except when Italy's foreign trade contracted drastically (1930–31, 1936, 1941–41), the peninsula ran an irremediable – structural – balance of payments deficit. The mighty fleet and air force intrinsic to the regime's aims, however,

---

[11] OO 21:273.
[12] Mussolini, quoted in CANEVARI E., *La guerra italiana* (Rome, 1948–49), vol. 1, p. 212; PIERI P. and ROCHAT G., *Pietro Badoglio* (Milan, 2002), pp. 365–6, place the speech in autumn 1926.
[13] OO 37:151–2, 29:365, 29:404.
[14] OO 18:120, 122–3 ('Maschere e volto della Germania,' 25 March 1922).
[15] See KNOX M., *Common Destiny* (Cambridge, 2000), Ch. 3.

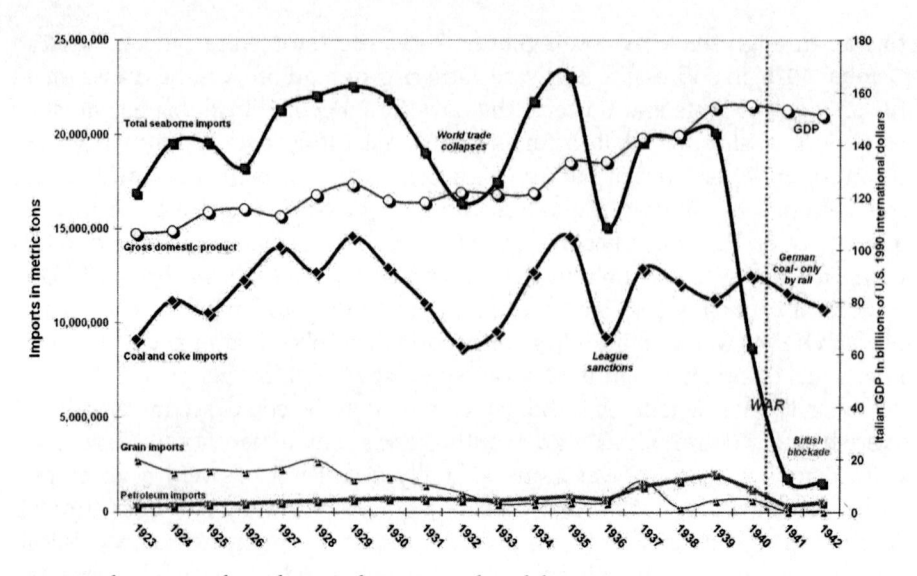

Fig. 1. *Italian import dependence and strategic vulnerability 1923-1942*

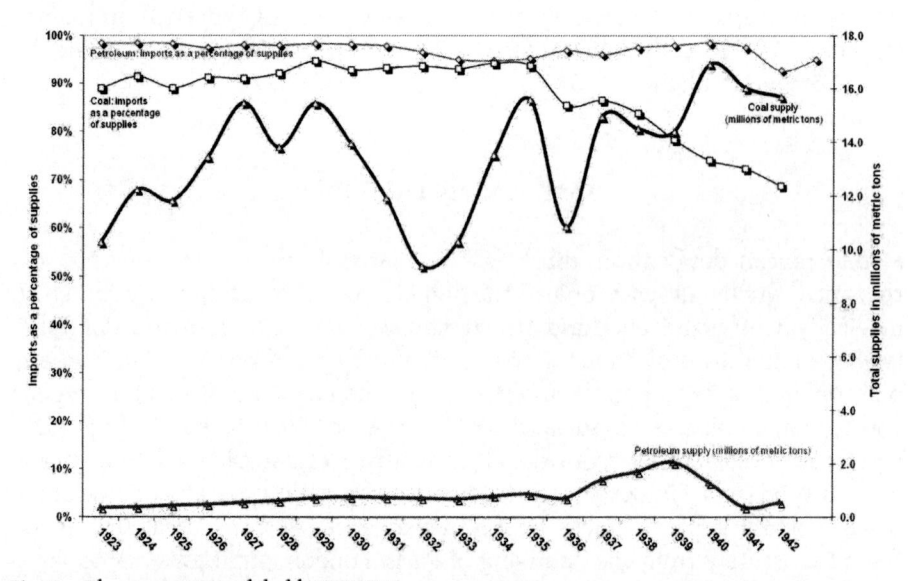

Fig. 2. *The energy stranglehold, 1923-1942*
Source: Base data (both charts): MADDISON A., *The World Economy*, 2 vols (Paris, 2006), vol. 2, p. 428; *Sommario di statistiche storiche italiane 1861-1955* (Rome, 1958), pp. 123, 139, 146, 159, 160.

demanded oil, steel, copper, rubber, machine tools, electronic devices, and a host of lesser strategic imports in quantities both far beyond Italy's ability to pay and wholly unobtainable if Italy sought war with France and Britain.

Neither the inherited machinery of the Italian state, nor dictator and regime, nor – above all – the *Regia Marina* had ready solutions. Fascist Italy's persistently ineffectual interwar efforts at autarky impeded rearmament by inhibiting the import of vital raw materials and advanced technologies such as modern machine tools.[16] Mussolini contributed – grandiose objectives apart – through his dramatic failure to provide the strategic guidance and interservice coordination required to accomplish even modest aims through military force. In his role as minister of each of the three services from 1925 to 1929 and from 1933 to the regime's destruction in 1943, he ensured that no organization emerged capable of assessing, controlling, or coordinating the force structures, technological choices, and strategic and operational concepts of the services.

The dictator's obsessive mistrust of his subordinates, the mutual hostility of the services, and their underlying loyalty to the monarchy precluded the creation of a genuine interservice general staff. Italy's "Chief of General Staff" from 1927 to 1940, Pietro Badoglio, remained in constitutional terms a mere "consultant" to Mussolini, with a diminutive office staff and vague and inconclusive coordinating functions. Nor did the Duce, unlike his German counterpart and ally, create a personal high command with genuine expertise and command prerogatives. The monarchy stood in the way and the dictator feared and resented expert advice, lacked the necessary military and naval expertise, and was often too busy micromanaging virtually every other aspect of Italian government to attend closely to military affairs. He controlled the armed forces politically, as minister and head of government, by manipulating senior appointments, promotions, and budgetary allocations.

The army, as the traditional senior service of the House of Savoy, asserted and maintained a primacy based on its fundamental if often inglorious role in United Italy's many wars, its tacit sponsorship of Mussolini in 1922, its firm support thereafter, and its commanding position as the one institution that could destroy the regime – should the king ever nerve himself to give the order. The air force, founded in 1923 from the debris of the wartime army and navy air arms, enjoyed the preeminent favor of the dictator – a flying enthusiast since 1915-1918 – as the "mythic representation of fascism." It was intolerant of military aircraft that it did not control, and sought fiercely to avoid cooperation with the other services. The army normally commanded between 50 and 60 percent of Italy's armed forces budget from 1922 to 1940; only in 1938-1939 did it fall short, as the air force share rose to roughly 28 percent. And the *Regia Marina*, after securing over a quarter of the budget through 1936, fell behind both army and air force as wars in Ethiopia and Spain and air rearmament unrelated to the navy's needs drained the funds potentially available for Mediterranean domination.[17]

The navy's initial understanding of its strategic tasks scarcely reflected the full measure of Mussolini's objectives. The naval leadership happily forgot Italy's

---

[16] RISTUCCIA C.A., 'The Italian Economy under Fascism, 1934-1943: The Rearmament Paradox,' (PhD thesis, University of Oxford, 1998), particularly pp. 60-121.

[17] Quotation: LEHMANN E., *Le ali del potere, La propaganda aeronautica nell'Italia fascista* (Turin, 2010), p. xii; SANTONI A., 'I rapporti tra la Regia Aeronautica e la Regia Marina', in *Italo Balbo: aviazione e potere aereo*, ed. C.M. SANTORO (Rome, 1998, pp. 331-40; percentages calculated from ZAMAGNI V., *Come perdere la guerra e vincere la pace* (Bologna, 1997), pp. 48-9 and REPACI F.A., *La finanza italiana nel ventennio 1913-1932* (Turin, 1934), p. 109.

1923 confrontation with Great Britain, and ignored the strategic demands that a recurrence would entail. Mussolini for his part sought from 1925 to 1933 to conciliate London while attempting to destroy Yugoslavia, Italy's nearest vulnerable neighbor, by subversion if possible and by war if necessary. France countered with a 1927 security treaty with Belgrade, and fostered its rearmament thereafter, placing Fascist Italy in a strategic vise by land.[18] The naval correlative was war in the central and western Mediterranean against far superior French forces.

When Thaon di Revel resigned in May 1925 over army domination of a projected reform of the high command, Mussolini took his place – as with the other services – as minister. But in practice the dictator delegated the navy's management to his undersecretary, a pliable and very junior admiral, Giuseppe Sirianni, and elevated him to ministerial rank in 1929 when relinquishing the three service ministries until 1933. Sirianni presided over a gradual renewal of Italy's cruisers, destroyers, light units, and submarines that increased Italy's war fleet from roughly four hundred thousand tons in 1926 to six hundred thousand in 1934. The aim was a force that could command the central Mediterranean and protect Italy's supply lines to its Libyan colony, to the grain and oil of the Black Sea, and to the wider world through Suez. Counteroffensive cruiser raids on French bases and amphibious operations against the Dalmatian islands would keep the enemy off balance.

That design rested, however, on two perilous assumptions. At the strategic level, the navy assumed Britain's neutrality in a Franco-Yugoslav war with Italy. Yet by 1928-1929 London had already developed palpable misgivings about Mussolini's pacific intentions. A Mediterranean war would force Britain to choose between Italy and France – a choice not in doubt, especially if Mussolini's Balkan machinations triggered the conflict. At the operational level, the navy was well aware that command of the central Mediterranean and the protection of convoy traffic to Libya and from the Levant depended upon timely, closely coordinated, and effective air reconnaissance and anti-shipping strikes.

Yet the *Regia Aeronautica*, with Mussolini's tacit and sometimes overt backing, persistently and cavalierly ignored its ostensible responsibilities. As early as the mid-1920s, naval exercises demonstrated both the virtual absence of communication links between supporting air units and the fleet at sea, and the ineptitude of air force flight crews lacking specific training in maritime operations and ship recognition. The 1927 exercises rested on a scenario that resembled the February 1941 bombardment of Genoa by the Royal Navy's Force H; the Italian fleet commander in 1941 ably summed up the result: "aerial reconnaissance failed totally, and throughout the entire day reports of the position and movements of the enemy were extremely sparse, imprecise, and worsened by lengthy delays."[19]

---

[18] KNOX M., *Common Destiny*, p. 122-39; idem, 'Fascist Italy and strategic terrorism, 1922-1941: the quest for success', forthcoming, Institut für Zeitgeschichte, Munich.

[19] GIORGERINI G., *Da Matapan al golfo persico* (Milan, 1989), p. 192; FIORAVANZO G., *Le azioni navali in Mediterraneo dal 10 giugno 1940 al 31 marzo 1941* (Rome, 1970), p. 379.

The *Regia Aeronautica* also perennially resisted navy requests for a maritime strike force built around torpedo-bombers. Even a solemn interservice treaty of September 1935 failed to settle the issue; the air force immediately raised the specious objection that the navy's torpedo was unsuited to the high speeds and preferred attack altitudes of its future – but not current – aircraft.[20] In the end, Badoglio made one of his few recorded contributions to Italian military effectiveness by forcefully overruling the air force in November 1939. But the weapons system, once installed on the quasi-obsolete Savoia-Marchetti S79 trimotor bomber, did not become fully effective until 1941–1942.[21] The air force also insisted on the efficacy against moving warships of high-altitude level bombardment with small-caliber bombs, despite numerous trials that showed otherwise. Dive-bombers were a discovery so belated that in late summer 1940 the German Reich had to supply a hundred of the already venerable Junkers Ju. 87.

The navy was nevertheless itself largely responsible for a further fundamental deficiency in its air cover. Alone of the five Washington Treaty naval powers, Italy failed to commission a single aircraft carrier, although the Treaty assigned Italy sixty thousand to sixty-six thousand tons in that category – three or four small fleet carriers or two large ones. Revel and a few of the navy's brighter mid-level officers urged the development of an experimental carrier. But shortly after the admiral's resignation in 1925, a meeting in Mussolini's presence of the service's supreme consultative body, the Committee of Admirals, overwhelmingly approved the proposition that "for us an aircraft carrier would neither be useful nor necessary." Land-based airpower could allegedly cover Italy's home waters with ease.[22] Carrier designs occasionally made the rounds of the naval authorities in subsequent years. But by the mid-1930s the navy had missed its prewar window of opportunity. An effective carrier force equipped with reconnaissance, maritime strike, and fighter aircraft would presumably have required a decade or so to emerge, given Italy's limited technological base, the navy's inexperience, and air force recalcitrance.

Instead, with the advent in 1933 of Sirianni's successor, the single-minded and politically astute Domenico Cavagnari, the navy turned decisively toward a force organized around heavy units. Navy and dictator had already reacted to France's 1931 decision to build the *Dunkerque* – designed to hunt the new German "pocket battleships" – by ordering the extensive and lengthy modernization of two pre-1914 dreadnoughts. Cavagnari followed up in 1934 by persuading Mussolini to authorize two entirely new and formidable vessels, ostensibly adherent to the

---

[20] Ministero della Marina, Gabinetto (henceforth MMG), ACS, b. 338, Naval staff memorandum, 'Traccia delle pratiche svolte con lo Stato maggiore della Regia Aeronautica sui siluri per aerei,' 1 June 1937; and FIORAVANZO G., *L'organizzazione della marina durante il conflitto*, vol. 1 (Rome, 1972), pp. 40–51.

[21] DDI 9/2, Appendix VII, p. 634.

[22] SANTONI A., 'La mancata risposta della Regia Marina alle teorie del Douhet', in *La figura e l'opera di Giulio Douhet* (Caserta, 1988), pp. 257–69 (quotation: p. 259).

Treaty limit of thirty-five thousand tons, but actually over forty-five thousand tons combat-loaded: *Littorio* and *Vittorio Veneto*.

When confrontation with Britain inevitably recurred in August–September 1935 on the eve of Mussolini's invasion of Ethiopia, Cavagnari took the initiative from a position of strength, as the service chief most supportive of the dictator's East African war. The British, he declared forcefully, were now the main enemy. Only battleships would impress them, but the navy as yet had no modern capital ships in service. In December 1935 the admiral duly presented to the dictator a draft five-year proposal for two additional *Littorio*-class super-battleships, the modernization of two further pre-1914 ships, and three fourteen-thousand-ton aircraft carriers; Mussolini's markup of the document suggests dictatorial qualms about the carriers. The naval staff then confected a prolix memorandum packed with charts and graphs, setting forth as "minimum program" Cavagnari's December proposals less the aircraft carriers, and suggesting as alternative an oceanic "escape fleet" [*flotta d'evasione*] named in apparent celebration of Mussolini's – and the navy's – geopolitics. That utopian option included nine to ten battleships, three to four aircraft carriers, and a lavish provision of escorts.[23] Mussolini's eventual choice resembled the minimum program: two further *Littorio*-class behemoths, the modernization of two additional pre-1914 dreadnoughts, and an assortment of light units. The naval staff estimated that the second two super-battleships, *Roma* and *Impero*, would consume 41 percent of the entire construction budget from 1938 to 1944.[24]

Only a few relatively junior figures in the naval commands and staffs seem to have harbored doubts about this allocation of Italy's limited resources, or about the fuel-efficiency of the *Littorio*-class solution to Italy's naval requirements. Not until the eve of war did Mussolini himself belatedly recognize that the new battleships would drink up "rivers of bunker oil" that Italy entirely lacked.[25] Nor was Cavagnari's ostensible vision of a Mediterranean Jutland an appealing precedent. The 1916 battle had been tactically indecisive and strategically unnecessary, given Britain's command of the North Sea exits; the same was clearly true of the Mediterranean. Nor had the admiral or his predecessors given adequate consideration to the effectiveness of the weapons system at the core of the great ships: their main guns. The navy accepted from industry an amazing 1 percent tolerance in shell weight and a similar lack of uniformity in propellant charges, and failed to correct severe rangefinder, loading system, firing circuit, and shell fuse defects revealed in practice shoots. The naval staff was fully aware

---

[23] KNOX M., *Mussolini Unleashed, 1939-1941* (Cambridge, 1982), p. 20; MMG ACS, b. 295, especially the undated, unsigned memorandum requesting a 'first orientation for the study of a program of new naval constructions,' marked 'V' ('*visto*') and marked up by the dictator, and naval staff, 'Studio sul programma navale' and supporting documents, 13 January 1936.

[24] MMG ACS, b. 338, naval staff memoranda, 'Nuove construzioni navali,' responding to Mussolini's guidance, 25 January, 26 August, and September 1937; percentage calculated from Archivio dell'Ufficio Storico della Marina Militare, Rome, b. 2703, 'Rateazione del nuovo programma navale,' 20 March 1938.

[25] KNOX, *Mussolini Unleashed*, p. 77.

before 1939 that Italian battleship and cruiser salvos grouped so loosely that hitting the enemy was supremely problematic.[26] Night combat by battleships was thought unfeasible or inadvisable – although practiced extensively by British and Japanese. And as late as November 1940 the naval staff dismissed as "futuristic" – and refused to deploy – an effective Italian-built radar system.[27]

The battle fleet was not unique in its deficiencies. Many lighter units, from light cruisers down, were unseaworthy in heavy weather – throughout the interwar era the navy had scheduled sea training only in spring and summer. The fleet command system Cavagnari imposed reflected both the admiral's own intolerant authoritarianism and the control-mania characteristic of Italian military culture. Naval headquarters in central Rome was empowered to micro-manage fleet movements up to contact with the enemy – without reliable or timely communications with the fleet or with the air units detailed to support the fleet. And with the exception of the navy's large submarine force, Cavagnari and his staff took up asymmetric remedies only grudgingly, when Italy's back was to the wall in 1935–1936 and 1940–1943. Doctrinal autism crippled the submarine fleet: other navies had long moved on from the submerged daylight ambush of 1915–1917, and the *Regia Marina* had learned virtually nothing from its clandestine piratical attacks on the Spanish Republic's supply lines in 1937. Its boats suffered from unreliable radio communications, rudimentary attack computers, a submersion rate three times slower than German boats, lethally shallow maximum operating depths, a surface speed of only eleven to twelve knots, inadequate torpedo capacity, too-short periscopes, and outsized superstructures that fatally attracted enemy escorts and aircraft.

Cavagnari's battleships also siphoned off funds better spent both on anti-submarine warfare and convoy escorts, and on mine warfare, which had the vital strategic task of blocking the Sicily channel to east–west British traffic; the mines Italy deployed in 1940 were mostly Great War surplus. The one major naval weapon of the Second World War that Italy developed first – the *"maiale"* [hog], the frogman-guided "slow-running torpedo" that sank the battleships *Valiant* and *Queen Elizabeth* at Alexandria in December 1941 – was anything but a navy staff product. Only the emergency of 1935–1936 gave the devoted band of diving enthusiasts at the La Spezia submarine flotilla their chance to develop the *maiali*, explosive speedboats, and frogman-delivered limpet mines. Navy staff indifference then starved the program from 1936 to the Munich crisis of 1938.[28] Like the torpedo-bombers, these systems thus only reached initial operational effectiveness in 1941, long past their potentially most telling use – in surprise attacks at the very instant Italy went to war.

---

[26] CEVA L., 'Gli ultimi anni dell'Ansaldo "privata",' *Nuova antologia* 2122 (1999), 91–131.
[27] KNOX M., *Hitler's Italian Allies* (Cambridge, 2000), pp. 61–3.
[28] *Ibid.*, p. 61.

CONSEQUENCES

Cavagnari's sporadic public bluster that the *Regia Marina* had no need for aircraft carriers and that gunnery was the essence of "that great naval battle for which the soul of every sailor yearns" ceased abruptly in 1939-1940. Mussolini's war memorandum of 31 March 1940 demanded a naval "offensive all along the line in the Mediterranean and outside it." The admiral predicted despairingly at the follow-up chiefs-of-staff meeting that "one [enemy] fleet will place itself at Gibraltar and another at Suez, [and] we shall asphyxiate inside the Mediterranean." With notable audacity he even prophesied directly to his master that "Italy could arrive at the peace negotiations not only without territorial bargaining counters, but also without a fleet and possibly without an air force."

Yet once Fascist Italy's mighty ally had swept France from the board and threatened Britain with invasion, the situation seemed less desperate. By late September 1940 Badoglio could happily surmise that Italy's invasion of Egypt and a German thrust into Spain would checkmate the Royal Navy; Italy "will dominate the Mediterranean, and nothing more can stop us."[29] But the British resolutely stayed put, despite the demands of home defense and control of the Atlantic, forceful German intervention in the Mediterranean and North Africa, and Japan's eventual war against the West. Revel had been wrong: the *Regia Marina* fought – often creditably at the tactical level – not for forty-eight hours but for thirty-nine months, despite the manifold galling mismatches between its doctrine, training, procedures, and ships on the one hand and its wartime operational and tactical tasks on the other. Yet the outcome was no more in doubt than in 1923. Fascist Italy's bid for the domination of "its own sea" led inexorably to the destruction of its armed forces by both Allies and Germans, and the September 1943 surrender at Malta of what remained of its fleet.

---

[29] Quotations: CAVAGNARI D., 'La dottrina – lo spirito', in *Le forze armate dell'Italia fascista*, ed. T. SILLANI (Rome, 1939), p. 211; KNOX, *Mussolini Unleashed*, pp. 90, 93-4; *Verbali delle riunioni tenute dal Capo di Stato Maggiore Generale*, vol. 1 (Rome, 1982), p. 84.

The Italian offensive, 1940–1941

SIMON BALL is Professor of International History and Politics at the University of Leeds, United Kingdom

ABSTRACT. *Fascist Italy had a second-class navy but an outstanding strategic position astride Britain's most essential imperial line of communication. It built an impressive fleet to express its great-power aspirations, though its real advantage lay in the asymmetric "stealth weapons" with which it achieved several triumphs to make up for the disappointments of orthodox warfare. The Italian-German alliance supported its army in North Africa and went a long way to neutralizing British naval strength, but by 1942 it had run out of fuel to send the Italian battleships to sea.*

RÉSUMÉ. *L'Italie fasciste n'avait qu'une marine de seconde catégorie mais une position stratégique exceptionnelle, à cheval sur la voie de communication la plus importante de l'empire britannique. Le pays construisit une flotte impressionnante qui reflétait ses aspirations de grande puissance. Mais son réel avantage consistait en la possession d'armes furtives asymétriques. Grâce à elles, l'Italie parvint à remporter plusieurs triomphes qui compensèrent les déceptions engendrées par la guerre traditionnelle. L'alliance germano-italienne soutint l'armée en Afrique du Nord et parvint même à neutraliser la force navale britannique. Mais en 1942, à court de pétrole, l'alliance ne put plus envoyer les cuirassés italiens en mer.*

.•.

The irony of Italian sea power

There were three ironies for Italian sea power in the Mediterranean during its brief efflorescence in 1940 and 1941. The first was that Italy itself was a second-class power in naval terms, but Italy's geographical position, and its choice of Britain as an enemy, gave it an enormously strong operational position in the Central Mediterranean.

In particular Italy dominated west–east passage of the Mediterranean via the Sicilian Narrows, the point at which the gap between Europe and North Africa was at its shortest. Its bases in southern Italy, Sicily and Sardinia could not be replicated by any other power. By the same measure, the route between Italy and its "fourth shore", its colonies in Libya, was short and relatively secure. The Italians had prepared for a naval war against Britain and France. But the Germans had defeated France before Italy entered the war, yielding an even more advantageous operational position.

The second irony was that Italy's naval leaders well understood how to maximize the strength of their operational position – through the deployment of *mezzi insidiosi*, "insidious methods" of asymmetric warfare – yet only episodically held to such methods. Italy built a surface fleet that could act as the anvil to the hammer of *mezzi insidiosi*; but the very glamour of that "luxury fleet" meant that the avoidance of direct fleet actions, required by *mezzi insidiosi*, caused loss of face, and was thus hard to sustain politically.

The third irony, flowing from the first two, was that Italian sea power, a central weapon for Fascist aggrandizement in time of peace, played little part in the calculations that guided Italy's prosecution of a Mediterranean war from June 1940. The combination of geographical advantage and asymmetric methods meant that the Italians waged the naval war with some success, whilst at each step becoming less able to set their own strategy. The result was tactical defeat for Italian squadrons, partial operational victory in the Central Mediterranean for the *Regia Marina*, and catastrophic strategic failure for the nation.

THE COMPROMISE POLICY

Strategic commentators recognised Italy's geo-operational strength from the outset. The British writer on naval intelligence Hector Bywater, subsequently famous as "the man who predicted Pearl Harbor", wrote of "what an appalling liability the Mediterranean was". The best that could be achieved, in Bywater's view, was a "compromise policy" by which Britain attempted to maintain some "strategic grip" on the Mediterranean "while declaring that route out of bounds for all non-combatant traffic".[1] Before 1939 British navalists rejected such new thinking on Mediterranean strategy. In 1939, however, the Royal Navy accepted the "compromise policy".

In Italy, the Fascist elite was divided on how best to take operational advantage of its geo-strategic position. There were two main schools of thought. On one side were those who advocated *mezzi insidiosi*, "insidious methods". The driving force behind Mediterranean expansion would be political warfare. If naval force was to be used, it should be limited and aimed at weak opponents. The most useful type of naval power was provided by light ships – such as minelayers and submarines – and special forces. Such forces could engage in asymmetric warfare, using a few men armed with innovative weapons to cause disproportionate amounts of damage to the enemy. Capital ships were a luxury fleet, cowing and deterring potential enemies whilst the *mezzi insidiosi* took their toll, a "guerrilla warfare at sea" as it was described. With such methods a "system of defence" that would force Britain to adopt the "compromise policy" was plausible.

This cannot be true Fascism, others objected. The road to world power was

---

[1] BYWATER H., 'The changing balance of forces in the Mediterranean', *International Affairs* 16 (1937), pp. 361–87.

paved by catalytic battles. The battleship was not for show. In August 1936 Admiral Domenico Cavagnari, the professional head of the Italian navy, declared that *mezzi insidiosi* lacked ambition. He ordered his officers to concentrate on building a battle fleet capable of attacking the British in conjunction with the German *Kriegsmarine*. The predicted date for such a war was 1942. The fleet would redeploy to a new base at Taranto to prepare for such an eventuality.

The modernization of the fleet and its new base at Taranto went ahead, but the real prospect of war in 1939 prompted a more realistic appreciation of Italy's naval position. In late May 1939 Mussolini and Hitler consummated their formal alliance in the Pact of Steel. Cavagnari was dispatched to meet his German opposite number, Admiral Raeder. Although the *Kriegsmarine* was by far the most "Mediterranean-minded" of the German services, Cavagnari found little support for Italian ambitions. The German naval staff agreed that the *Kriegsmarine* and the *Regia Marina* would fight in alliance. But the German sailors regarded Italy's struggle for the Mediterranean as merely a means to an end. If the Italians managed to close the Mediterranean, the British would have to use other "oceanic" routes and by so doing leave themselves vulnerable to sinking by German raiders. The Germans had little aid to offer the Italians, they merely wished to use them as bait to draw out the British.

The *Regia Marina* abandoned grandiose plans for Mediterranean naval dominance before the war in the Mediterranean had begun. The *Regia Marina* believed it could force the "compromise policy" on the Royal Navy by dividing the Mediterranean into Eastern and Western basins. The linch-pin of its system was the Central Mediterranean, and in particular the Sicilian Narrows. The first naval mission of the war was mining in the Sicilian Narrows.

The *Regia Marina* identified and achieved the "compromise policy". The Royal Navy was properly respectful of its capabilities. The "compromise policy", adopted by both sides, resulted in an operational naval conflict of curious symmetry. There were four significant naval engagements in 1940, two in the east, two in the west. There was one eastern and one western battle in July 1940, another eastern and another western battle in November 1940. None of the naval battles was a decisive fleet engagement. Two – Mers el-Kébir on 3 July 1940 and Taranto on 11 November 1940 – comprised attacks by one fleet at sea upon another riding at anchor. Both fleets at anchor suffered significant damage, but neither was destroyed. In both cases battleships were able to leave the port under attack and sail to safer ports. In the two battles at sea – Punta Stilo on 9 July 1940 and Cape Spartivento on 27 November 1940 – the two fleets followed engagement with evasion, privileging the survival of their ships. As a result, in neither battle were there heavy casualties. The fleets performed a delicate quadrille, living up to their own expectation that – barring disaster – the Mediterranean could be neither completely closed nor fully opened.

The biggest surprise for Mediterranean strategists lay in who was fighting whom. There were undoubtedly tensions between the British and the French in the Mediterranean, but few, on either side, had believed before June 1940 that their navies would fight one another. As it happened, the bitterest naval conflict in the Mediterranean turned out to be Anglo-French, rather than Anglo-Italian. Because that conflict did not fit into the grand narrative of "total war" it tended to be underplayed – Britain and France never declared war on each other – its main event, the British attack on the French fleet at Mers el-Kébir, becoming an incident rather than a battle. After Mers el-Kébir the French fleet demonstrated that it could move in and out of the Mediterranean. In particular the British feared that whilst they were engaged with the Italians, the French would run the Straits of Gibraltar. On 11 September 1940 their fears were realized when a French cruiser force sailed through the Straits heading for Casablanca. The French cruiser force turned a British attempt to seize Dakar in West Africa into a fiasco.

Mussolini's gamble, that Italy would be able to land a spectacular blow on Britain in the Mediterranean, however, failed. The British and Italian fleets clashed at Punta Stilo, off the southeast coast of Italy, on 9 July 1940. Punta Stilo proved to be the classic Mediterranean battle, based on movement around the basins. The British Mediterranean Fleet was at sea to rendezvous with Force H so that it could pass a naval convoy from west to east. The Italian fleet, under Admiral Campioni, was at sea to prevent the Mediterranean Fleet from intercepting a convoy sailing from Naples to Benghazi. The British conceded that the Italians may have had the better of the engagement. The Italian convoy reached Benghazi unscathed, whereas the British convoy suffered constant attack.

On the other side of the coin the imperial cruiser HMAS *Sydney* intercepted an Italian cruiser on its way from Tripoli to Leros later in the month and sank her with an outstanding display of gunnery. Although the battle of Cape Spada, as the sinking of the *Colleoni* was called, was a much smaller engagement than Punta Stilo, it made more of an impression. Mussolini was "depressed on account of the loss of the *Colleoni*, not so much because of the sinking itself as because he feels the Italians did not fight well".[2]

THE COMPROMISE POLICY: THE AXIS ADAPTATION

The basis of Italian naval strategy altered after the initial naval engagements. Mussolini was determined to make land conquests on the Mediterranean littoral. In October 1940 he ordered the Italian army to invade first Egypt, and then Greece. As a result, Germany became more involved in Italian naval affairs.

Mussolini and Hitler met twice in October 1940, on the Brenner at the beginning of the month, and in Florence at the end. Commentators on these meetings divide into two schools of thought. Some believe that Hitler wanted Mussolini to fight an effective "parallel war" in the Mediterranean. Others prefer the image of a "brutal friendship" in which Hitler intended to exploit the Italians. The Germans certainly explored both options. The best that can be said

---

[2] *Ciano's Diary, 1937–1943*, ed. L. MILLER and S. PUGLIESE (London, 2002), 22 July 1940, p. 372.

is that Hitler himself had not made up his mind. As it was, the Greek campaign set in motion changes around the Mediterranean basin.

Marshal Badoglio, Italy's senior military leader, pointed out that if the British could operate from Greek waters then the Fleet at Taranto "would no longer be safe".[3] Taranto had hummed with activity throughout 1940 as, one by one, *Caio Duilio*, *Vittorio Veneto* and *Andrea Doria* were completed or underwent modernization there. Along with the *Littorio*, the *Cavour* and the *Giulio Cesare* they comprised Italy's entire battleship fleet. Mussolini himself travelled to Taranto to inspect that fleet on 1 November 1940. It was a shining symbol of Italian power and modernity.

The British attack on Taranto surprised the Italians, not least because it somewhat surprised the British too. The British had long harboured plans to attack Taranto but it barely seemed practicable. Several factors improved the chances of success in the autumn of 1940: the post-invasion availability of the Greek anchorage at Suda Bay on Crete to the Royal Navy; the arrival of the modern aircraft carrier *Illustrious* via the Suez Canal, the effectiveness of reconnaissance aircraft on Malta, and unseasonably good weather. The operation was still a long shot: it was also a sideshow. The main operation was a combined Mediterranean Fleet and Force H "compromise policy" operation to pass a battleship, *Barham*, from west to east. The *Illustrious* and her escorts left the fleet after the main mission was completed on the evening of 11 November 1940 to launch torpedo bombers. They sank the battleship *Cavour*, and three more torpedoes hit the *Littorio*. No one knew what effect Taranto would have. The Italians had lost two battleships – but it was unclear for how long. Despite the three holes in its hull, the *Littorio* did not sink; indeed it was rapidly repaired. The remaining battleships fled Taranto for Naples.

One immediate consequence of Taranto was the adoption of Churchill's wish to send a convoy, not only of warships but also of military reinforcements, all the way through the Mediterranean. The obvious strategy for the Italians was to strike back against their setback in the eastern basin with an attack in the west. A convoy wallowing around south of Sardinia with a battleship, an aircraft carrier, useless at short range, a few light cruisers and a convoy of slow supply ships was vulnerable to an ambush by battleships and heavy cruisers. The resulting battle of Cape Spartivento on 28 November 1940, however, resolved little.

It was close-run thing. Force H rendezvoused with the convoy on the morning of 27 November 1940 south of Sardinia. Spotter aircraft reported that the Italian fleet was nearby. Force H was facing Admiral Campioni with the battleships *Vittorio Veneto* and *Giulio Cesare*, escorted by a powerful cruiser force. For one-and-a-quarter hours, it seemed that a desperate capital-ship battle was in the offing until the British battleship *Ramillies*, heading west as part of the operation, evened the odds to two battleships per side. Campioni was unwilling

---

[3] CIANO, *Diary*, 12 November 1940, p. 395.

to gamble on those odds: he turned his battleships round and withdrew up the east coast of Sardinia. The British did not pursue an engagement either.

Although Cape Spartivento was inconclusive as a naval engagement it had major political reverberations in Italy. Mussolini dismissed Admiral Cavagnari, Admiral Campioni and Marshal Badoglio: in order to protect its leader, the Fascist revolution began to eat itself. British propaganda targeted Mussolini in person. Churchill's Christmas 1940, "Appeal to the Italian People" declared that "one man and one man alone has ranged the Italian people in deadly struggle against the British Empire". Churchill called for a military coup to topple Mussolini. Mussolini reluctantly admitted to his confederates that he needed Germany's help. The idea that Mussolini must be "saved" from the Italians entered the *Führer*'s table talk. Hitler ordered *Luftwaffe* units to deploy to the Mediterranean in December 1940.

At the beginning of January 1941 the first major Italo-German mission was launched from western Sicily. The victor of Taranto, HMS *Illustrious*, had been sent through the Sicilian Narrows to cover a convoy from Gibraltar to Malta. Even though they had but a few days to prepare, the two air forces choreographed a complex aerial attack. Italian torpedo bombers flew a decoy mission to draw off the *Illustrious*'s fighters. Once she was denuded of protection the dive bombers attacked, hitting the aircraft carrier with six bombs.

The shift from a purely Italian to an Italo-German "system of defence" did not re-invent the "compromise policy", it merely made it more potent. The potency of the "system of defence" forced the British to seek more radical means of breaking their shackles. Against naval objections, Force H was ordered to attack Genoa. Although the bombardment of Genoa had little military significance it reinforced the view of the Axis formed in Berlin in December 1940. The general whom Hitler had dispatched to assist the Italians in Libya, Erwin Rommel, arrived in Rome as the British shells hit Genoa.

The German decision to "assist" Italy militarily in Libya and Greece – whatever its motivation – weakened Italy in the naval sphere. British monitoring of German signals revealed clues about Italian naval deployments. It located an Italian squadron south of Crete. Italian intelligence, on the other hand, reported to Admiral Iachino that the British had sent cruisers, not battleships, to Crete. On 28 March 1941 the two fleets fought an encounter battle off Cape Matapan. Although the fast Italian battleships were able to outrun the obsolescent British capital ships with ease, the unwary Italian cruiser division blundered into the British pursuit to be destroyed by the heavy guns of the British battleships. Not only did the Italian fleet suffer severe losses at Cape Matapan, the battle strengthened the hand of those who argued that the Royal Navy should make more effort to break the Italo-German "system of defence" by using Malta as an offensive base. On 16 April 1941 British destroyers from Malta were guided to a convoy off the Tunisian port of Sfax by signals intelligence. In May 1941 the British sent a major convoy through the Sicilian Narrows.

Any successes in the Sicilian Narrows, however, were overborne by the failure of the Royal Navy to prevent the German conquest of Crete. Crete was the perfect arena for short-range air strikes. Short-range aircraft could operate with comfort to the east of Crete from a base on Scarpanto. Another base in the Peloponnese was equally well placed for the sea lanes to the west of the island. Even dive bombers from Italian Cyrenaica could reach ships to the south of Crete. Effectively, Crete was a killing zone. British cruisers and destroyers proved frighteningly vulnerable to attack within this zone. After three days the commander of the Mediterranean Fleet made the unilateral decision to recall his Fleet to prevent its slaughter by the *Luftwaffe*. There had been nothing short of a trial of strength between Mediterranean Fleet and the German air force: the German air force had won.

At first sight the fall of Greece and Crete heavily favoured the Axis. It now had the advantage of two major north–south routes across the Mediterranean. The more direct, but more dangerous, western route saw ships depart from Naples for Cape Bon. From there the ships would sail along the Libyan coast to unload at either Tripoli or Benghazi. Ships on the eastern, or Ionian, route sailed from Naples to Corfu and then turned for North Africa, docking at either Benghazi or Derna. The Royal Navy could no longer enforce a blockade between Europe and North Africa.

Conversely, British options for travel around the Mediterranean had been severely limited. The only route they had left was the western Mediterranean run from Gibraltar to Malta. They could proceed no further than Malta, and no ships could reach Malta from the east. The balance was redressed only by some outstanding signals intelligence in the summer of 1941. The offensive potential of submarines, pre-warned of Mediterranean sailings, was significantly enhanced. The number of British submarines operating in the Mediterranean doubled.

It is often argued too that the *Luftwaffe* and the *Regia Aeronautica* played into British hands. In mid-1941 the two air forces struck a deal whereby the Germans would continue to concentrate their forces in the eastern Mediterranean, operating from Crete and Greece, against the Suez Canal. The Italians were to operate from their Sicilian and Sardinian bases against British forces on the Gibraltar–Malta route. Some *Luftwaffe* and *Kriegsmarine* officers were unhappy with the deal, and argued in vain that the Italians should concentrate their naval and air forces in the eastern Mediterranean, whilst the Germans moved back to Sicily. The German fliers, it was later claimed, had got a raw deal because only long-range aircraft could reach Egypt from Greece: they were never able to mount an attack of sufficient weight to choke off the Red Sea supply route. If they had gone to Sicily, they would have been able to erect an impermeable "system of defence".

These arguments were based upon the assumption that the *Luftwaffe* was bound to be more effective than the *Regia Aeronautica* in air-sea operations. This is not what British naval leaders believed at the time. In the narrow seaways around Crete, German dive-bombing had proved a particularly effective tactic. In the more open seas to the south of Sardinia, torpedoes were the most effective form of attack. It was unlikely that the Germans would have been any better at the all-important torpedo-bomber attacks than the Italians. The Germans began to improvise training for torpedo attacks only in the autumn of 1941. A Mediterranean training centre at Grosseto was not established until 1942. Neither was a German air-dropped torpedo that could be used against moving ships produced in large numbers until 1942. In the interim the German units borrowed such torpedoes from the Italians.

Neither, when the British were attacking and the Italians defending, was it immediately clear that the intelligence advantage was leading to overwhelming success. In their first few months back in control of the Libyan convoy route, the Italians held down the number of sinkings the British were able to achieve. The great British successes against the Libyan route had to wait until the autumn of 1941. In the summer of 1941 the Italians decided that the best ships to transport troops were ocean-going liners. The problem was that the loss of such ships caused enormous casualties. The Malta-based submarine *Upholder* sank the liners *Neptunia* and *Oceania* in September 1941. It was these attacks that led the Italians to doubt seriously, for the first time, the security of their "system of defence" and thus "the fate of Libya". The loss of the liners also convinced Hitler that the Germans had to move into the Mediterranean in more force in order to shore up the "system of defence".

Later commentators saw these decisions as yet more proof of Hitler's fatuity as a strategist; he was dispersing his efforts, guaranteeing failure everywhere. *Luftwaffe* units were transferred from Russia to the Mediterranean. The *Kriegsmarine* was ordered to send the U-boats from the Atlantic into the Mediterranean. In the short term, however, British offensive naval action against the "system of defence" played into Italo-German hands. Success at sea was even more spectacular than the effort in the air. The second group of U-boats to sail through the Straits of Gibraltar ran into Force H. On 13 November 1941 Force H's aircraft carrier, *Ark Royal*, was torpedoed by a U-boat. The shock was immense.

The outbreak of "world war" on 7 December 1941 had an impact on the Mediterranean inasmuch as it prevented Britain from sending any major naval reinforcements into the sea to offset its losses. Plans for replacing the carriers sunk earlier in the year were abandoned. The immediate problem was not outside the Mediterranean, however, but within. In December 1941 Britain's Mediterranean Fleet lost the naval war. The Mediterranean's own "day of infamy" was not 7 December but 19 December 1941. Early in December 1941 one of the Mediterranean Fleet's three battleships, *Barham*, was sunk by a U-boat. Faced with the dual threat of German submarines and Italian battleships, the capital ships of the Mediterranean Fleet and Force H were confined to harbour.

The Italians recovered their own confidence. "Today the entire fleet is at sea," Count Ciano recorded in hope and trepidation on 17 December 1941. The commanders of the *Regia Marina* believed "a clash with the British is inevitable". They claimed "that we are definitely superior in quantity and quality" and promised success. "Can it be our luck will change?" Ciano recorded.[4] Italian naval

---

[4] CIANO, *Diary*, 17 December 1941, p. 475.

expectations were tolerably accurate. The British had only cruisers at sea. When they collided with the Italian battleships in the Gulf of Sirte the British squadrons were hopelessly outmatched. Faced with the big guns of the Italian fleet, they had little choice other than to flee. Avoiding destruction in the Gulf of Sirte did not save the British, however. *Mezzi insidiosi* finished off what the battleships had started. The British had no idea that the Italians had developed a method of tethering mines in very deep water. On 19 December 1941 the British Malta cruiser force ran at full tilt into an unsuspected minefield and was destroyed as a fighting squadron within minutes.

If British cruisers were destroyed by one kind of *mezzi insidiosi*, then the capital ships fell victim to an even more spectacular version at the same time. Over the course of 1941 *Decima Mas*, Italy's underwater special forces, had attacked the British in each major harbour in which they had anchored: Suda Bay, Malta and Gibraltar. Their masterpiece, however, was the attack on Alexandria, where the Mediterranean Fleet's two remaining capital ships were supposedly wrapped in cotton wool. The Italian assault force sailed from the submarine base on Leros. A mother submarine carried three "pigs", two-man human torpedoes. The "pigs" attached charges to the *Queen Elizabeth* and the *Valiant*. The charges sank the *Queen Elizabeth* and crippled the *Valiant*. British naval power in the Mediterranean was thus humbled in two separate *Regia Marina* operations in the space of hours.

All sides realized the enormity of what had been achieved. "The most significant factor at this time is that not a single heavy British ship in the Mediterranean is fully seaworthy," Admiral Raeder crowed in Berlin, "the Axis rules both the sea and the air in the Central Mediterranean."[5] The Royal Navy abandoned Malta: all its ships left, the submarines the last to go. The *Upholder* was sunk by an Italian sub-hunter on its last mission. When a small flotilla of destroyers tried to return a symbolic naval presence, the result was disaster. Three of the four destroyers were sunk by German aircraft. The Mediterranean Fleet had been stripped of each of its ship classes in turn: it had started with aircraft carriers but they had been lost; there were no more battleships; the cruisers had been sunk or were overmatched; even the destroyers could not evade their hunters. The Axis route from Italy to Libya was indeed open; east–west passage by sea was impossible.

Of course, the Axis air–sea victory in the Mediterranean in 1941 was utterly hollow. The British could call on the United States Navy for aid, and did so in order to re-supply Malta and Egypt. On the other side, the Axis was just as ill-equipped to fight a long drawn-out war as had been predicted in the 1930s. In particular the long-predicted fuel crisis of the Third Reich arrived in the summer of 1942. In 1940 and 1941 fuel problems in the Mediterranean had meant the difficulty of shipping petrol from Italy to North Africa. From June 1942 onwards, the Axis suffered not only a crisis of transportation but a crisis of supply. The most obvious manifestation of this crisis was that the *Regia Marina* ran out of fuel for its battleships. The Germans cancelled supplies, pleading more pressing

---

[5] Report by the Commander-in-Chief, Navy, to the Fuehrer, 13 February 1942, *Fuehrer Conferences on Naval Affairs, IV, 1942* (London, 1947).

commitments. The Mediterranean Fleet was still devoid of battleships, but so too now was the Italian fleet. The Italian failure in the Second World War was a failure of national power rather than naval power. No amount of operational success at sea could ever make up for the flawed bases of Italian war-making.

Further Reading

BRAGADIN M., *The Italian Navy in World War II* (Annapolis, MD, 1957).
CORUM J., 'The *Luftwaffe* and its allied air forces in World War II: parallel war and the failure of strategic and economic co-operation', *Air Power History* 51 (2004), 4–20.
GREENE J. and MASSIGNANI A., *The Naval War in the Mediterranean, 1940-43* (London, 1998).
HINSLEY F., *British Intelligence in the Second World War: Its Influence on Strategy and Operations*, 5 vols (Vols I and II, London, 1979 and 1981).
KNOX M., 'Fascist Italy Assesses its Enemies, 1935-1940', in *Knowing One's Enemies: Intelligence Assessment Before the Two World Wars*, ed. E. MAY (Princeton, 1986), pp. 347–72.
MALLETT R., *The Italian Navy and Fascist Expansionism, 1935-1940* (London, 1998).
NEITZEL S., '*Kriegsmarine* and *Luftwaffe* co-operation in the war against Britain, 1939-1945', *War in History* 10 (2003), 448–63.
PATERSON L., *U-Boats in the Mediterranean* (London, 2007).
PRATT L., *East of Malta, West of Suez: Britain's Mediterranean Crisis, 1936-1939* (Cambridge, 1975).
RASPIN A., *The Italian War Economy, 1940-1943* (New York, 1986).
SALERNO R., *Vital Crossroads: Mediterranean Origins of the Second World War, 1935-1940* (Ithaca, NY, 2002).
SCHREIBER G., 'Italy and the Mediterranean in the Power-Political Calculations of German Naval Leaders, 1919-1945', in *Naval Policy and Strategy in the Mediterranean: Past, Present and Future*, ed. J.B. HATTENDORF (London, 2000), pp. 108–43.
SIMPSON M., 'Superhighway to the World Wide Web: The Mediterranean in British Imperial Strategy', in *Naval Policy and Strategy in the Mediterranean: Past, Present and Future*, ed. J.B. HATTENDORF (London, 2000), pp. 51–76.
SULLIVAN B., 'A fleet in being: the rise and fall of Italian sea power, 1861-1943', *International History Review* 10 (1988), 106–24.
THOMAS M., 'After Mers-el-Kébir: the armed neutrality of the Vichy French navy, 1940-43', *English Historical Review* 112 (1997), 643–70.
TITTERTON G.A., *The Royal Navy and the Mediterranean, September 1939-October 1940* and *The Royal Navy and the Mediterranean, November 1940-December 1941* (London, 2002 and 2001) [reprint of 1952 Naval Staff History].

The Sea and the Cold War

Norman Friedman is an American author associated with the U.S. Naval Institute, United States

Abstract. *In cold war as in world war, the sea united a western coalition and allowed it to bring strength to bear against the long open frontiers of the Soviet empire. It also insulated different countries against the spread of subversion, so that the West, even when defeated abroad (for example in Vietnam), was not vulnerable to the sort of progressive collapse which brought down the Soviet system.*

Résumé. *Pendant la guerre froide comme pendant la guerre mondiale, la mer unifia la coalition occidentale et servit à apporter du renfort pour lutter contre les longues frontières ouvertes de l'empire soviétique. Elle protégea également de nombreux pays contre la propagation de la subversion, ce qui permit à l'Occident, même en cas de défaite à l'étranger (comme au Vietnam), d'échapper à l'effondrement progressif qui perdit le système soviétique.*

．•．

The geography of the Cold War closely resembled that of the two World Wars; like them, it can be seen as a contest between a maritime coalition and one centered on the Eurasian land mass. In both cases, the sea offered the maritime coalition what turned out to be decisive advantages, though they were little appreciated in the cases of World War I and the Cold War. The Cold War differed from the other two in important ways, however. It never escalated to full-scale central war, although it included several bitter, costly wars. In addition, the Cold War was partly ideological, and ideology was never bound by geography, maritime or otherwise. This essay is primarily about the role of the sea in the war, more than about the role of naval forces.

The central role of the sea is reflected in the name of the Western Alliance: it is the *North Atlantic* Treaty Organization (NATO) because the North Atlantic links North America with Western Europe.

Ultimately the Cold War remained cold because both sides came to realize that nuclear weapons made a central war mutually suicidal. They therefore faced the paradox that much of their military investment, and indeed much of the shape of their forces and their policies, was in weapons and strategies which had only limited impact on the outcome.

When World War II ended, Stalin's Soviet Union occupied much of Central Europe. Despite objections voiced by some of the victorious Western Allies, there was no serious prospect of ejecting him. The question was whether, and how far, his empire would expand beyond the line won by Soviet troops. For the Western powers, the Cold War meant resistance against further growth of Stalin's empire. Soviet ideology did not envisage Western acceptance of the postwar accessions. It justified its own militarized system on the ground that ultimately the West would have to attack to avoid its own collapse. Although this ideology was modified after Stalin's death, almost to the end of the Soviet Union its leaders assumed that either they or their Western competitors would be destroyed. That in turn justified heavy expenditure on the military, ultimately perhaps as much as half the economic output of the Soviet Union.

The sea mattered in this calculation. The Soviets saw their and other Communist coastlines as a long-threatened perimeter which had to be defended at every point Western navies could reach. During the last decade of the struggle, the sense of vulnerability along that coastline had important consequences. Conversely, Western navies did not have to attack everywhere; by their existence they imposed a broad threat. This threat helped to force the Soviets to spend heavily on what amounted to coast defenses. Also, Soviet geography did not favor naval operations, because the Soviet Union was separated from the world ocean by a variety of choke points accessible to its Western enemies.

At the outset, ideology trumped geography or military capability in Stalin's mind. During the first few years after World War II Communist parties, particularly in France and Italy, enjoyed considerable popular support. It helped enormously that the capitalist governments which had come to power in the wake of German occupation had generally failed to revive the economies of Western Europe. Many voters imagined that the Soviets had solved the crucial economic problems in the 1930s, while capitalist economies suffered from the "great depression." For a few years it seemed possible that prewar-type Popular Front governments would bring Communists to power in much of Western Europe. A similar Popular Front had won in Czechoslovakia, without the support of a Soviet occupying force.

The sea mattered. In 1947 the United States announced the European Recovery Program (Marshall Plan) as a specific attempt to restart the European economies. This was a political gesture, but its key was inexpensive movement of goods over the North Atlantic, between the prosperous economies of North America and the badly damaged ones of Western Europe. Only the sea offered this possibility. Although World War II had badly damaged Western merchant fleets, the United States had built vast numbers of new freighters, mainly Liberty Ships, which were available to carry goods in both directions. Many Europeans alive at that time remember seeing Liberty Ships in their ports, carrying vital U.S. aid. Their economies revived because the same ships carried their new products in the opposite direction (U.S. funding also helped to revive trade inside Europe).

Without the sea, goods would have moved by rail. World War II sank ships and damaged ports, but it could not destroy the sea, the highway along which the goods moved postwar. The war also destroyed railroads' rolling stock (equivalent to ships), marshalling yards (like ports) – and the rail networks themselves. It took considerable investment to rebuild the prewar European rail network. Had there been a North America connected to Europe by rail, infinitely more investment would have been needed (and a land connection with North America would probably have meant devastation there, too).

Stalin had no equivalent of an undamaged North America to revive either his country or those his army had conquered. Despite Western fantasies, the Soviet Union had never solved the crucial economic questions, and it had no magic formula for recovery. In the 1930s it had crushed the countryside to support industrial investment; overall growth had not been anything like what was imagined. The best Stalin could do after the war was to rebuild his own country by taking what he could from those he conquered. That applied particularly to occupied East Germany, which rebelled soon after Stalin's death.

For Stalin and his heirs, geography carried a frightening implication. Because the empire was entirely contiguous to the Soviet Union, anything which happened in it could spread by land. Any part of the empire which managed to break away might inspire the neighboring populations, and ultimately the population of the Soviet Union itself. Thus the need to crush rebellion in Hungary in 1956 (and the fear that a similar attack on Poland might have repercussions) and the need to crush the "Prague Spring" in 1968. History proved the Soviet leadership correct: East Germany began to collapse when the governments of other Soviet satellite states allowed East Germans in their countries to emigrate freely. Once East Germany had collapsed, the Soviet Union itself began to disintegrate, albeit under further pressures.

By way of contrast, the West could survive numerous reversals overseas without collapse. The sea united Western Europe and North America, and it provided relatively easy access to the rest of the world, but it also provided a degree of insulation. Easy access made it possible for Western countries to wage war far from home and to limit the cost of such warfare. That was never an option for the Soviet Union. In the 1980s, for example, as Poland became more and more rebellious, the Soviet leadership had to decide whether to stage a Hungarian-style invasion. The crucial argument against such an operation was that if the Poles fought back (as they were expected to) the invasion could become an intolerable protracted war with direct consequences for the Soviet Union itself. Moreover, by that time the chief lever the Soviets had was the threat of a land assault against Western Europe. Many in Western Europe took it very seriously, but the Soviets had to contend with the reality that their line of communications stretched back through Poland. Soviet reliance on the land, rather than the sea, made Poland crucial in a way no single European member of the Western Alliance was.

By this time the Western Alliance had already experienced exactly this reality. When the Alliance was formed, its three strongest European military members were Britain, France, and West Germany. France offered valuable strategic depth behind the front line of the Alliance on the inter-German border. In 1965,

French President Charles de Gaulle announced that he was withdrawing from the military arm of the Alliance, although he did not withdraw from the Alliance as a whole. The massive Alliance presence in France had to be withdrawn to Germany. Now that French ports were no longer available, the NATO supply lines were shifted East, to German ports. This new arrangement would have been more exposed in wartime, but it was acceptable.

The shift was possible because transport by sea was infinitely flexible. A ship could steam from North America to, say, Brest, but equally well it could steam to Hamburg or Bremerhaven in West Germany. The wartime problem of securing its passage (the major NATO preoccupation throughout the Cold War) would be roughly the same in each case. The main change would be the need to keep the port intact, even though it was closer to the border of the Soviet Union. There was real fear that the change would make sea supply difficult at first, so the U.S. Army stockpiled equipment in Germany, planning to fly troops in to use it. However, in the event of a protracted European war – if the troops staved off initial defeat – there was no alternative to seaborne supply. The sea route would also have remained vital in a period of prewar tension.

Perhaps the most important difference between the Cold War and its hot predecessors was the global impact of ideology. World War II ignited nationalism throughout the former European empires, all of which lay overseas from their mother countries. In the Far East, the victorious Japanese proclaimed an ideology of "Asia for the Asians," although they often made themselves thoroughly unpopular by the way they exploited the territories they conquered. The British had to promise India independence as the price of wartime service. Without India, their position further East was not very secure (they left Burma, too), and the main financial props of the empire were lost. At the same time the British found it difficult to afford empire, given the financial disaster of World War II. French defeat in 1940 led to nationalist unrest in the Levant, and the Allied occupation of North Africa further reduced French power there, at least during the war. That the United States fought the war as an anti-colonial power had further effects.

In 1945 only the Soviet Union and the United States could present themselves as non-colonial powers. Many nationalists saw the Soviet Union as their natural ally. In Latin America the United States was widely seen as a semi-colonial power, even though it had pursued an anti-colonial policy during World War II. As the United States sought to revive Western Europe, U.S. policy shifted to some extent because many of the prostrate West Europeans hoped to use their intact colonial resources to help revive themselves. There was an important caveat: in some places nationalism seemed too dominant to reject. That is why the United States supported France in Vietnam, but refused to do so in Algeria. In neither case was the sea a key issue for the United States (although access by sea was the reason the French considered Vietnam an asset, and it was also why the French could maintain themselves in Algeria). Initially the Soviets did not enjoy overseas access by sea; only with Khruschev in the 1960s did they begin to build the sort of merchant fleet which offered it to them.

The first big Third World conflict of the Cold War fight was over China, which was not a colony but which had been exploited by several European powers over the past century. In China Stalin had two major advantages. The obvious one, which is typically emphasized, was the land connection between China and Manchuria, the territory the Soviet army seized in a quick 1945 campaign. Manchuria was the industrial heartland built up by the Japanese. The Soviets looted its factories, as they looted German and other European factories in areas they controlled, but they also provided Mao Tse-tung's Communist Army with sanctuary and with masses of captured weapons.

The second advantage was subtler. The Russians controlled the North Chinese ports. When the war ended, Chiang Kai-Shek's Nationalists expected to reoccupy their country. Travel by land, particularly through devastated areas, would have been slow and difficult, and might well be opposed by Mao's army. Chiang expected to enter North China by sea. Had he been able to do so, he might have been able to defeat Mao's army at the outset, when it was weakest. The U.S. Navy was willing to lift Chiang's army, but not if the movement was opposed in any way. Simply by shutting the North Chinese ports, the Soviets precluded any such movement, and condemned Chiang to a lengthy and ultimately unsuccessful land campaign in a protracted Civil War.

After Mao defeated him on the mainland, the sea saved Chiang; he was able to withdraw to Formosa (Taiwan) and Mao did not have the means to follow. The end of the Chinese Civil War cut Taiwan off from its natural hinterland in China. However, the sea offered an open commercial connection to the rest of the world. Taiwan prospered.

Chiang's defeat had further consequences. In 1945 the Soviets and their Western Allies agreed to split occupation of Korea, a country Japan had seized after the Russo-Japanese War of 1904–5. That placed Korea in the same divided category as Germany and Austria. Stalin knew that any military move in Germany or Austria would have ignited a much larger war, which he wanted to avoid. Because Korea was separated by sea from other Western areas, he could imagine that nothing which happened there would have large consequences (it helped that U.S. Secretary of State Dean Acheson declared Korea outside the U.S. vital perimeter in the Far East). Korea bordered the Soviet Union, but most of its land border was with China.

The difference between land and sea access determined what happened next. Stalin's North Korean allies invaded South Korea in June 1950. Initially they were victorious; the South Koreans and their U.S. Allies were driven back into a toehold around Pusan. Access by sea transformed the situation. Aircraft carriers acted as local U.S. and Allied air bases; without them, the closest air support would have come from relatively distant Japan, and it would have been far less effective. Free use of the sea made possible an amphibious operation at Inchon, in the North Koreans' rear, which routed them.

On the other hand, the open land border between China and North Korea made it possible for the Chinese to insert massive ground forces, pushing the Western force back. The war stalemated near the original border between the two Koreas, and it has remained stalemated ever since: the inter-Korean border is now the main remnant of the Cold War. The great irony of Korea was that, whether or not Stalin considered it a limited operation in an obscure place, its outbreak convinced the U.S. government that a major war was imminent. The resulting build-up financed many of the key U.S. Cold War military and naval programs, and it permanently changed the balance of military power.

The sea offered South Korea access to the world economy; South Korea's is now one of the largest economies in the world. The logic of contagion by land is also still alive and well. The failure of the North Korean regime is now a constant problem for the Chinese. Among their fears is that collapse of North Korea would place a capitalist regime on their border, perhaps raising questions about the wisdom of their own Communist Party.

Mao's triumph on the mainland of China affected a nearby anti-Western war. During World War II, the Japanese occupied French Indo-China (Vietnam, Laos, and Cambodia). In 1945 the French began to reoccupy it. They had much greater success in the south of Vietnam than in the north, but defeat in the north became inevitable once the Communists fighting them there enjoyed support and sanctuary across the border in China. Seaborne access to the South made it possible for the French, and later the Americans, to keep South Vietnam intact, until U.S. support was cut off through war-weariness in 1974.

Even then the sea mattered. The U.S. public was badly demoralized by defeat in Vietnam, but the insulating effect of distance limited the consequences. That was not the case with a somewhat analogous Soviet defeat in Afghanistan a decade later.

The Cold War offered a good illustration of what would have happened had Mao *not* triumphed to offer the North Vietnamese sanctuary. Roughly in parallel with the war in Vietnam, a Communist insurgency broke out in British-ruled Malaya. The rebels had no contiguous sanctuary. As in Vietnam, the British had free access by sea. It took time, but they defeated the rebels.

Perhaps the most interesting case of ideology trumping seaborne access was Cuba. Like many other Latin American countries, in the 1950s Cuba was run by a dictator enjoying limited U.S. support. Many Americans were glad to see his downfall in 1959 at the hands of populist rebel Fidel Castro. Over the next two years they learned that Castro was a committed Communist, hence a Soviet ally, and there was considerable domestic support for a U.S. effort to overthrown Castro. When the attempt came in 1961, it was half-hearted and it failed miserably. If anything, it brought Castro closer to his Soviet allies.

At this time the Soviets were trying and failing to build effective intercontinental missiles, which they saw as vital equalizers to U.S. strategic bombers ranged around their borders. The Soviets did have shorter-range missiles, sufficient to threaten anything in Western Europe. Soviet dictator Nikita Khrushchev realized that, based in Cuba, such missiles would be as effective, as deterrents, as the longer-range weapons his experts were failing to build. He sold the idea to Castro on the ground that, with such missiles in place, the Americans would not dare to attack him again.

Now the sea came into play. Ideology like Castro's might leap continents and seas, but missiles and supplies had to travel by sea – which the U.S. Navy controlled. After rejecting proposals to attack the missiles directly, U.S. President John F. Kennedy imposed an embargo. Khrushchev could not fight a naval war around Cuba. He withdrew the missiles. He did not consult Castro; he saw Cuba as a Soviet dependency just like the puppet states of Eastern Europe. He did not reckon with the difference: Cuba was not contiguous to the Soviet Union. Castro enjoyed considerable independence, tempered only by his need for Soviet support. The sea could carry weapons and goods, but it was ill-adapted to the sort of massive, sudden cross-border incursions (as in Hungary in 1956) which maintained the colonial status of Eastern Europe.

The lesson Castro drew from the withdrawal of the missiles was that the Soviets would treat him, and any other Soviet ally, as expendable. By this time the Soviets had split from their Chinese allies. Castro did not have the option of siding with the Chinese because only the Soviets could supply the resources that he needed to stay alive. Castro understood that Khrushchev was the first Soviet leader to realize that nuclear weapons might well deter the West from any attempt to crush the Soviet Union and its revolution. By the same token, he did not want to risk a nuclear holocaust in his country. Castro knew that the Soviets might easily sell him out to the Americans. He knew that the Soviets derived much of their influence from their claim that they, not the Chinese, led the world revolution. Castro apparently decided to make himself so prominent in the world revolution that the Soviets could never dare drop him. That perception seems to have led to Cuban involvement in colonial wars in Africa, using, as it happened, the sea to get there.

From 1957 on, Mao increasingly attacked Khruschev as a reactionary, claiming leadership of the world revolution. In 1959 the North Vietnamese Communists exploited the tension between the two main Communist powers to extract initial support for their war against South Vietnam. Through that war the Soviets supplied the weapons but the Chinese dominated the North Vietnamese. The Soviets supplied the North Vietnamese largely by sea, not least because weapons shipped through China often stayed there, to be copied by the Chinese. U.S. unwillingness to risk escalation left this supply route unmolested until 1972, when U.S. attacks on the key North Vietnamese harbor of Haiphong made it obvious that the North Vietnamese could not function without it. That the United States had access to South Vietnam by sea made it possible for it to fight a protracted war against the North Vietnamese. It happened that there were long-standing cultural and ethnic tensions between China and the Vietnamese, so that the North Vietnamese later sided with the Soviets against the Chinese.

It took the U.S. government a long time to accept that the Soviets and the Chinese were mutual enemies. The evidence gradually mounted. In 1965, when the Chinese exploded their first atomic bomb, the Soviets apparently approached the Americans to mount a joint attack on Chinese nuclear facilities. In 1969 armies of the two countries fought on the Amur River. U.S. intelligence received inside information describing utterly failed attempts to heal the rift. Finally, in 1973

American President Richard Nixon went to China to mend relations with Mao. In doing so he had to break relations with the Nationalist government on Taiwan, which the United States had recognized as the legitimate Chinese government. Nixon's hope was that Mao would restrain the North Vietnamese, allowing South Vietnam to survive after U.S. forces left. Mao did try, but by this time the Soviets were willing to provide the North Vietnamese whatever they needed. South Vietnam collapsed after a North Vietnamese blitzkrieg. Its access to the sea did not matter, because the United States was no longer willing to supply weapons and other resources. The sea did allow millions of South Vietnamese to flee as "boat people."

The U.S. rapprochement with China turned out to have important maritime consequences. Enmity with China forced the Soviets to maintain a large military force in the Far East, supplied via the slender capacity of the Trans-Siberian Railway. Moving that force back into European Russia (for example to fight a NATO war) would be a slow, laborious process. It would not have been anything like Stalin's 1941 shift of his Siberian troops back into Russia to face the invading Germans. These troops were further west, and they did not have to carry nearly as much heavy equipment with them.

Conversely, every Soviet soldier in the Far East cost a lot more to maintain than a soldier in the West, because whatever fed and equipped him had to come much further at much greater expense. It does not cost much more to move a lot further by sea, but on land every mile can be painful. Nor was there any easy way to increase the capacity of the one line of supply on which the Soviet East Asian army depended (the Soviets did add a new main line). Soviet aircraft based in East Asia could move West quickly, as could submarines based in Siberia. Both the aircraft and the submarines would have been available to fight a European war.

Western access to the sea played an important part in the downfall of the Soviet Union. By the late 1970s, the Soviets still feared overland ideological contamination. They faced a new version of it in the south, where they had large Muslim populations ethnically connected to those in Afghanistan and further south. Afghanistan had long been a semi-client state. A coup deposed the Afghan king and brought a more radical regime to power. Although in theory the new regime was exactly what the Soviets wanted, in reality it enraged religious elements of the population and hence had the potential to spread unrest into the southern Soviet Union. The Soviets felt compelled to support the new regime with troops. When the regime faltered, they staged a coup to bring in what they hoped would be a competent one. The coup was supported by a massive increase in Soviet troop strength in Afghanistan.

Western governments did not see the Soviet move as essentially defensive. It looked like the beginning of the long-feared thrust to the Persian Gulf and thus to the oil route, which was the jugular of the Western world. No one realized that a land power like the Soviet Union did not see the world that way. It did not help the Soviets that the Cubans' war in Africa, which they had felt compelled to back, also looked like a break-out to seize key Western resources and even to threaten the tanker route around Africa.

Afghanistan turned out to be a valuable opportunity for the West because it was accessible by sea through Pakistan. The Soviets were well aware of Pakistan's key role, and under other circumstances they might well have attacked it. This time they were painfully aware that the West, particularly the United States, had a seaborne option of supporting Pakistan directly. They certainly did not want to fight a major war in Southwest Asia, which was particularly badly served by land transportation out of the Soviet Union. Readers may remember the single tunnel through which Soviet forces eventually left Afghanistan.

Afghanistan was the Soviet Union's Vietnam. In both cases, the superpower left undefeated militarily. It withdrew because the cost of continued war was grossly disproportionate to what seemed to be at stake. In the Soviet case, the consequences were far worse. The Soviet army was the bulwark of the regime; defeat in Afghanistan showed that it was far less effective than might have been imagined. Defeat in one place suggested to others, for example in Poland, that the threat of armed force might not be quite as significant as it had seemed. Also, the Soviet defeat in Afghanistan at the hands of fundamentalist Muslims caused serious problems in Soviet Central Asia, previously a safe area.

In the 1980s the Soviet Union was in serious economic trouble. Its only remaining means of imposing its will on, for example, Western Europe was its military power. Most Westerners did not realize how badly that power was being crippled by the developing Polish problem. The U.S. Navy offered a seaborne strategy which might finally demonstrate to Europeans that the Soviets could be beaten.

The Europeans were impressed by the sheer size and power of Soviet ground forces, which might roll irreversibly west. NATO had never been able to build powerful enough ground forces to stop the Soviet force at or near the inter-German border, the "Central Front" geographically and, in many NATO minds, metaphorically. What could a vast NATO investment in seapower do to retrieve the situation?

The U.S. Navy argued that the flanks of a Soviet advance, and its strategic flank in the Far East, were all accessible from the sea. Credible threats to these flanks would tie down so much of the Soviet ground force that the balance on the Central Front might even tip. In the Far East, naval pressure could tie down the Soviet airplanes and naval forces there. It might arouse in Soviet planners' minds the fear of a Chinese attack to recover the Siberian provinces lost in the 19th century. Had the West tried to rely on ground-based forces in China, the Chinese would have had a veto over such pressures, and they might well have preferred not to risk war. Naval forces offshore were free to mount whatever attacks they might, implying to the Soviets a Chinese agreement which might well not exist – but which could not be disproven.

In Europe itself, the navy argued that the threat of flanking attacks – including a direct amphibious threat to Leningrad (St. Petersburg) – would force the Soviets to dedicate substantial ground forces to areas away from the main battle front. Movement on land was always more restricted than at sea, so that it would take many times the strength of U.S. and other amphibious forces to deal with this threat. The U.S. Navy called this "virtual attrition."

The flanking attacks would probably have been costly. Making them possible required, as a prerequisite, that the main forces of the Soviet Navy be defeated. That focussed U.S. attention on the Soviet naval aircraft and submarines based in the northern Soviet Union, hence on the need to fight a decisive battle in the Norwegian Sea. In this vision of a future war, Norway became a key NATO position.

The U.S. Navy's maritime strategy never became formal U.S. strategy; it was bitterly resisted by the U.S. Army, which was building up to fight a battle on the Central Front. However, the Soviets certainly took it seriously; they pulled back from the open seas. That alone would have much improved NATO's chance of moving necessary supplies across the North Atlantic in wartime.

When Mikhail Gorbachev took power in the Soviet Union in 1985, the developing NATO maritime threat and the deteriorating position in Afghanistan were both severely damaging his position. He was also acutely aware that the outgoing Chief of his General Staff, Marshal Ogarkov, had written that unless the Soviet Union solved the problem of mass computer production it could not hope to win any future war on an acceptable non-nuclear basis. Gorbachev told the Politburo that he could solve that problem, and thus rebuild Soviet military superiority – the single key to power outside the Soviet empire. He thought he could do so by unleashing the productivity of his people, which meant freeing them to speak far more freely than in the past. He discovered that when restraints were lifted, most of the free speech was about how the regime should be destroyed. The attempt to solve the computer problem failed, and Gorbachev discovered that liberalization of his empire could not be limited.

How important in all of this was Western access to – and effective use of – the world ocean? Access created a unified Western economy embracing not only Western Europe and North America but also Japan, Korea, Taiwan, and large parts of Asia. The Chinese also joined this system, but their main leap into prosperity came after the fall of the Soviet Union. The unified Western economy was wealthy enough to support enough military power to checkmate a Soviet Union which was carrying a crushing military burden. Western wealth supported, among many other things, the computer revolution which Marshal Ogarkov envied and feared. By the time that Gorbachev was in power, this particular revolution had gone so far that most Westerners accepted its fruits casually, and assumed that the Soviets had comparable assets. Even Marshal Ogarkov's plaintive tone made little or no impression. In retrospect, by enticing Gorbachev to tear up his own system in order to remain militarily competitive, the significance of the computers changes dramatically. Western wealth, generated by seaborne trade, becomes more of a strength than the flabbiness many saw during the Cold War.

The Soviet Union had peacetime access to the same seas, and by the end of the Cold War it had a huge merchant fleet. It did not, however, gain the same sort of economic advantages that the West accrued, because it did not have anything other than raw materials worth trading, and at home it did not have an economy which could have taken advantage of world trade. Militarization saw to that.

The sea made it possible for the West to deal with crises around the periphery of the Soviet Union, and ultimately to make such a crisis, in Afghanistan, extremely destructive of the Soviet Union. Conversely, the Soviets found it difficult to support overseas operations in the face of Western hostility. The long-running U.S. failure to seize Cuba had only the most limited political ramifications in the United States, whereas the more remote crisis in Afghanistan had devastating consequences. That was partly due to the very different character of the U.S. political system, which was more adaptable to change because it did not face devastating cross-border threats. In a larger sense, the sea and seaborne trade shaped the West. The land shaped the Soviet Union. The difference defeated the Soviets.

Bibliography

BARLOW J., *From Hot War to Cold: The U.S. Navy and National Security Affairs, 1946-1955* (Stanford, CA, 2009).

ELLEMAN B.A. and PAINE S.C.M., *Naval Coalition Warfare from the Napoleonic War to Operation Iraqi Freedom* (London, 2007).

FRIEDMAN N., *The Fifty-Year War: Conflict and Strategy in the Cold War* (Annapolis, MD, 2001).

FRIEDMAN N., *The U.S. Maritime Strategy* (London, 1988).

GIELIJESES P., *Conflicting Missions: Havana, Washington, and Africa 1959-1976* (Chapel Hill, NC, 2002).

GORSHKOV S.G., *The Seapower of the State* (London, 1979).

PALMER M.A., *Origins of the Maritime Strategy: American Naval Strategy in the First Postwar Decade* (Washington, DC, 1988).

POOLE W.S., *Rearming for the Cold War* (Washington, DC, 2012).

ZALOGA S.J., *The Kremlin's Nuclear Sword: The Rise and Fall of Russia's Strategic Nuclear Forces, 1945-2000* (Washington, DC, 2002).

NATO AS A MARITIME ALLIANCE IN THE COLD WAR

Eric Grove is Professor, Naval Historian and Maritime Strategist, First Sea Lord's Fellow and Fellow of the Society for Nautical Research and the Royal Historical Society, United Kingdom

ABSTRACT. *The essence of NATO was that it was an Atlantic alliance, binding U.S. power to the defence of Western Europe against a Soviet attack, and therefore guarding the free use of the Atlantic. It was intended to make a quick Soviet victory impossible and protect the maritime flanks of Europe. Its credibility in this role contributed essentially to the eventual collapse of the Soviet system.*

RÉSUMÉ. *Le principe de l'OTAN était de constituer une alliance atlantique, engageant la puissance américaine à défendre l'Europe occidentale contre une attaque soviétique, et par là même de préserver la libre exploitation de l'Atlantique. Elle avait pour but de rendre impossible une victoire soviétique rapide et de protéger les bords maritimes européens. Sa crédibilité en la matière contribua grandement à l'effondrement du système soviétique.*

. • .

The North Atlantic Treaty, signed in Washington on 4 April 1949, was always a fundamentally maritime arrangement. Although at first it seemed that the major strategic priority was tying US long-range strategic nuclear air power to a more credible defence of Western Europe, the title of the organisation it set up, the North Atlantic Treaty Organisation (NATO), demonstrated that the foundation of the alliance was the ability of the USA – and Canada – to project their military power across a major maritime space, the Atlantic Ocean. The Alliance also contained the other main Western European naval powers, Britain, France and the Netherlands.

The Medium Term Defence Plan adopted by the Alliance's Military Committee in 1949 stressed successful defence against any Soviet attack and then moving forward to offensive operations that would eventually achieve war termination on the Alliance's terms. This campaign would be supported by control of North Atlantic sea and air lines of communication. In October the North Atlantic Regional Planning Group with representatives from the USA, Britain, France, Canada, Denmark, the Netherlands, Norway, Belgium, Portugal and Iceland was tasked with drafting plans for a unified defence of the North Atlantic area.

There were five planning sub-groups, the first on offensive operations. This sub-group was formed only of US and British representatives although there was a permanent French observer. Its task was: "To prepare broad plans for offensive action against enemy armed forces and shipping, their bases and port facilities, including attack at source, amphibious and airborne operations and offensive mining." A major component of this role was the use of carrier air power. This was the origin of NATO's Atlantic Striking Fleet. Another two groups with wider membership were concerned with sea lines of communication over the Atlantic as well as their continuation to Western Europe and French West Africa. These planned for the organisation and protection of convoys and independent shipping against air, surface and submarine attack, including counter-offensive anti-submarine operations. A fourth group was concerned with the defence of the Atlantic islands and Portugal, which the Americans in particular saw as vital to the control of the Atlantic region.[1] This set out the overall pattern that would shape NATO maritime strategy in the Atlantic for the rest of the Cold War, a powerful forward-deployed battle fleet supporting the direct defence of shipping considered vital for the maintenance of resistance on land and in the air against Soviet attack. The following month, in November 1949, representatives of the Alliance members with significant merchant fleets agreed to pool their ships under NATO authority if war broke out. It was also decided to combine the British and American naval control of shipping publications into a single Alliance document.

In the early days the priority was the creation of a NATO European command under Supreme Allied Commander Europe (SACEUR). This was achieved in 1951, with General Eisenhower taking up the role at his headquarters in Paris. SACEUR had considerable maritime responsibilities around his northern and western maritime flanks with a naval component in all his subordinate commands in the North in Norway and in Central Europe at Fontainebleu. NATO's CINCNORTH was a British admiral, a reflection of the maritime nature of the whole theatre.

Already it had been decided in 1950 that an equivalent Atlantic command should be set up under a Supreme Allied Commander Atlantic (SACLANT). It was hoped that this could be done as soon after the creation of Allied Command Europe as possible, but inter-allied wrangling delayed matters. Winston Churchill, back in power in Britain in 1951, strongly opposed the plans to make an American admiral SACLANT. In the end, with extreme reluctance, he had to accept the situation and Admiral Lynde McCormick USN became the first SACLANT, with his headquarters at Norfolk, Virginia. The Royal Navy (RN) provided a deputy at Norfolk while its Commander-in-Chief Home Fleet Admiral Sir George Creasey became NATO Commander-in-Chief Eastern Atlantic, subordinated to McCormick. In compensation for this, the British Commander-in-Chief Portsmouth was given a separate NATO command, Commander-in-Chief Channel, notionally the equal of the two Supreme Commanders. Channel Command looked after the English Channel and

---

[1] SOKOLSKY J.J., *Sea Power and the Nuclear Age: The United States Navy and NATO* (London and Annapolis, 1991), pp. 13–14.

Southern North Sea and, largely to please the French, who were understandably worried about too much British control of waters also vital to them, he was made subordinate to a Channel Committee made up of the heads of the British, French, Dutch and Belgian Navies. Effectively, this meant the major Western European navies were primarily responsible for the eastern extremity of the Atlantic line of communication; mine countermeasures (MCM) were its major priority.

The first major NATO maritime exercise, "Main Brace", was held in 1952. The scenario was that the Soviets had taken Germany and were attacking Denmark and Northern Norway. The aim was to demonstrate SACLANT's ability to provide Northern Flank support for SACEUR and to reassure Denmark and Norway of NATO's ability to defend them. At the exercise press conference it was stressed by NATO spokesmen that the Alliance needed to demonstrate a capacity to operate on its northern flanks and it could not be restricted to small areas (such as the Central Front).

The "Blue" forces were commanded by CINCEASTLANT. The "battle fleet" had been allocated to him on this occasion for the exercise. Later the "Striking Fleet", as it became known, usually operated directly subordinate to SACLANT. The main carrier striking force was of two Groups; the first was composed of three American fleet carriers and the second of two British carriers with an American light carrier. One of the British carriers was carrying a primarily Dutch air group. The role of this Group Two was to give Group One air anti-submarine warfare (ASW) and air cover. There was also a "Heavy Support Unit" of two battleships, one American, the other HMS *Vanguard*, with five cruisers – three American, one British and one Canadian. The Striking Fleet screen was composed of thirteen American, twelve British, two Dutch and two Norwegian destroyers.

Other SACLANT/CINCEASTLANT forces included an American amphibious force, an ASW carrier support force of three light fleet carriers (one each from Canada, Britain and the USA) with a British cruiser. There were also a heavy support force of two cruisers (one British and one working with the RN from New Zealand) with eight US destroyers; a hunter-killer anti-submarine warfare force of Britain's two latest specialised ASW fast frigates, an American escort carrier and five US ASW destroyers; a logistic support force (with its own British light fleet carrier); a convoy escort group of two French and two Dutch destroyers, two British destroyers and a British frigate; and a minesweeping group of twenty-four vessels provided by France, the UK and the Netherlands.

Other ships taking part were under SACEUR's overall command. Subordinated to CINCNORTH were a Scandinavian–British Task Force of frigates, destroyers and submarines and a Norwegian minesweeper group. Separately under Flag Officer Denmark was another mixed task force of nineteen Danish units including submarines and fast patrol boats.

The size and combined diversity of this force are noteworthy (well over a hundred major surface combatants), a sign of the scale of maritime effort that the Alliance could deploy in its early days. The limited capabilities of the Soviet naval threat expected at the time were demonstrated by the size of the "Orange" forces, under the control of the British Flag Officer Submarines. The main hostile assets were fourteen submarines, eight British and two each from Denmark, Netherlands and Norway. There was an Atlantic single surface raider played by the second Canadian cruiser HMCS *Quebec*. A hostile squadron in the Baltic was provided by the fast minelayer HMS *Apollo* (playing another surface raider), three British frigates, seven Scandinavian destroyers and a Danish submarine. Land-based Orange striking air forces were provided by the Royal Air Forces of Britain, the Netherlands, Norway and Denmark. Land-based aircraft from seven countries provided the maritime support to "Blue".

As the "Orange" submarines were engaged, the Striking Fleet provided air and gunfire support for the NATO ground forces in Norway and amphibious landings in Denmark. Small Allied convoys were run to and from Bergen with carrier and land-based air support. Both "enemy" major surface ships were duly sunk. Despite difficulties caused by bad weather, the first large NATO maritime exercise seems to have been a success and a major step forward.

The year 1952 saw the appearance of the NATO "Allied Control of Shipping Manual" and various exercises were carried out to test Alliance defence of shipping practices. Plans were drawn up for a convoy schedule from the USA to Britain, France or Mediterranean/North African ports depending on the course of the land war. Convoys would leave the USA every fifteen days. An Emergency Defence Plan, EDP1-52, was drawn up for the first six months of war. In the words of Joel Sokolsky:

> The plan envisioned that SACLANT would simultaneously have to seek to secure the North Atlantic lines of communication, provide convoy protection and use his striking fleet to support SACEUR in Europe. Sea control and ASW operations would be centralized. All contributing navies would be aware of the location to which to send their earmarked[2] forces in the event of war. American and Canadian escort forces, including some carriers would not be sent immediately into the open sea. Rather, these ships would move to selected North American ports in order to "support early heavy convoys" of American reinforcements to Europe.[3]

The year 1952 also saw Greece and Turkey join NATO. This put greater stress on the Southern Flank of the Alliance. Eisenhower had already created a Commander-in-Chief Allied Forces South (CINCSOUTH), an American admiral, no less an officer than Admiral Robert C. Kearney – the national US Commander-in-Chief Eastern Atlantic and Mediterranean. Kearney also occupied the position of Commander Allied Naval Forces South. He initially commanded the US Sixth Fleet along with French and Italian forces. The arrival of Greece and Turkey caused some changes to these arrangements with the creation at the end of 1952 of an Allied Forces Mediterranean Command, the first CINCAFMED being Admiral Lord Louis

---

[2] 'Earmarked' forces were those allocated in peacetime to NATO command on a contingency basis.
[3] SOKOLSKY, *Sea Power and the Nuclear Age*, pp. 23-4.

Mountbatten, Commander-in-Chief of the British Mediterranean Fleet. He took over the European allied assets and COMNAVSOUTH was abolished but CINCSOUTH retained control of the Sixth Fleet and its carriers as STRIKFORSOUTH.

Mountbatten's command was concerned with the Mediterranean sea lines of communication. The Sixth Fleet was concerned with the support of forces ashore, increasingly with nuclear weapons. The "nuclearisation" of the US carrier force was a major development of the 1950s. The carriers became in Mountbatten's words "an extension of the strategic air force".[4] This also had implications in the Atlantic, where the nuclear armed Striking Fleet had to be kept under national American control directly responsible to SACLANT.

The year 1953 saw an even larger exercise in the Atlantic, "Mariner", but it was spoiled by more bad weather, which allowed HMS *Vanguard* to prove her superior sea keeping to the USS *Iowa* (the last time battleships took part in NATO exercises for some time); *Vanguard* duly "sank" the Soviet cruiser raider played by HMS *Swiftsure*. Sadly, the latter ship was shortly after so badly damaged by a collision in the bad weather that her career came to a genuinely premature end. Nevertheless, the strategic point had been made again. The NATO Secretary General made it clear the following year that the Striking Fleet would "undertake offensive and support operations rather than direct defence of Atlantic Trade Routes".[5] A key role remained support of SACEUR.

By the late 1950s, with "massive retaliation" adopted as Alliance strategy the nuclear strike role of both the Striking Fleets in the Atlantic and Mediterranean had become an important factor in NATO's deterrent strategy. The US carriers, soon to be joined by nuclear-armed British ships, would mount an offensive to destroy the Soviet Navy "at source" as well as cover other strategic targets. These attacks were eventually more or less coordinated with those by land-based forces in the "Single Integrated Operational Plan", the only problem with which from the naval point of view was that American carriers were constrained in deployment flexibility to make sure their strike aircraft could always "service" their assigned targets. The carriers were supplemented with ballistic missile-firing submarines when in the early 1960s the latter replaced the land-based intermediate-range ballistic missiles allocated to SACEUR. This meant the carriers could concentrate away from deep targets to more regional strike plans with both conventional and tactical nuclear weapons. Late in the decade the British Polaris submarine-launched ballistic missile force was also declared to SACEUR. The advantages of covert sea basing made these ballistic-missile carrying nuclear submarines a much more secure long-range nuclear striking force.

The imponderable factor of the length of a future war, however, meant that SACLANT still had to plan for reinforcement with ships defending themselves by nuclear ASW and anti-air warfare weapons. Even at this stage what I later called "Long War Uncertainty" played a significant role in overall deterrence.

---

[4] *Ibid.*, p. 30.
[5] GROVE E., *Battle for the Fiords: The Forward Maritime Strategy in Action* (Shepperton and Annapolis, 1991), p. 9.

NATO's capacity to use the sea for reinforcement meant that the Soviets could not calculate with certainty that their offensive would succeed in sufficient time before Western thermonuclear power made the USSR a "smoking radiating ruin".

From the arrival of the Kennedy Administration in 1961, the West began a major strategic revision that led to a transformation of Alliance strategy in a direction that made maritime forces even more important. The Americans argued that in a situation of increasing nuclear parity, it was incredible that the NATO alliance would immediately mount a nuclear counter-offensive. This did not go down well with some allies, notably France, which was developing its own nuclear capability and wished to keep nuclear weapons in the foreground of deterrent strategy. The desire of France for strategic independence and the withdrawal first of its fleet from NATO command, and then in 1966 France's withdrawal from the whole military side of NATO, allowed the Alliance to come to a compromise that made a great deal of strategic sense.

At the end of 1967, the Alliance adopted a new strategy of "Flexible Response" that emphasised the role of conventional forces, both in crisis management and in taking a much larger share of the deterrent burden, especially on the Northern and Southern Flanks. This confirmed a trend that was already clear earlier in the 1960s. In 1964 the first "Teamwork" Exercise had been carried out by SACLANT with 160 ships to rehearse the maritime reinforcement of Norway. In the year of the official adoption of "Flexible Response" the Deputy Chief of Staff to SACLANT, Rear Admiral Richard Colbert, called for a reconceptualisation of the Alliance's whole maritime strategy. This would improve NATO's ability to respond rapidly and collectively at sea and would provide clearer recognition of the importance of the sea to the Alliance's overall strategy. In order to respond early to a crisis, the concept of Maritime Contingency Forces (MCF) was evolved with earmarked units that could be mobilised at short notice in "specially tailored multinational task forces"[6] at an early point in a crisis.

In order to provide SACLANT with his own contingency force, the same NATO Council meeting that approved "Flexible Response" also approved the setting up of a permanent multinational "Standing Naval Force Atlantic" (STANAVFORLANT). Such a force had been suggested by Admiral Sir Charles Madden when he had been CINCEASTLANT and it had been exercised as "Matchmaker" in 1965 with four ships, the RN frigate *Leander*, Canadian destroyer escort *Columbia*, Dutch ASW destroyer *Overijssel* and the USN escort ship *Hammerberg*. After further Matchmakers in 1966 and 1967, "Matchmaker IV" duly became the first STANAVFORLANT. It had four functions: to provide training experience in combined operations, to prove by its existence Alliance solidarity, to provide SACLANT with an immediately available surveillance capability and to provide a combined force to be dispatched "to the scene of any possible contingency to reaffirm the solidarity of the NATO Alliance and to provide a visible deterrent". The force was intended to move "quietly to a threatened area, or just

---

[6] SOKOLSKY, *Sea Power and the Nuclear Age*, p. 109.

out of sight over the horizon", and would provide a core for "a more powerful and versatile" MCF.[7] An attempt by Colbert to commission the nuclear-powered transport *Savannah* as a mixed-manned NATO command ship was, however, turned down in Washington. A multinational but non-permanent "Naval On Call Force Mediterranean" (NAVOCFORMED) was formed in 1970. Three years later a Standing Naval Force Channel (STANAVFORCHAN) of MCM vessels was set up under CINCHAN's command.

NATO's command structure was also revised in the 1960s in response to France's departure from the Alliance's military structure, the reductions in the Royal Navy of the period and the move to more flexibility in strategic response. The process of French disengagement had begun in 1959 when President De Gaulle withdrew the French Mediterranean Fleet from AFMED, claiming that it required to concentrate on protecting north-south shipping to North Africa rather than east-west sea lines of communication. NATO retained access to the base facilities at Mers-el Kebir and French officers continued to serve with AFMED, including in the post of commander of the western Mediterranean basin (COMEDOC). France then suggested that a new IBERLANT command be set up under a French flag officer covering the western approaches to the Straits of Gibraltar. The NATO Council would do this only if the French Mediterranean Fleet was restored to NATO earmarking. No agreement was reached and when IBERLANT was eventually set up in 1966 it was under an American admiral based in Lisbon. This was also something of a defeat for the British, as they had always opposed the creation of such a command coequal with CINCEASTLANT. The initial compromise had been IBERLANT being placed as part of EASTLANT with a small integrated staff at Gibraltar.

In 1963 France had withdrawn its sixteen destroyers from allocation to SACLANT and its officers from CINCHAN's and AFMED's staff. With the final French departure from the integrated command structure in 1966, the post of COMEDOC ceased to be held by a French flag officer. The whole Mediterranean command system was shaken up in 1967 with the abolition of AFMED, and a new Allied Naval Forces Southern Europe Command was set up under an Italian COMNAVSOUTH, initially at the old AFMED headquarters in Malta but later moving to Naples. He was subordinate to CINCSOUTH and through him to SACEUR at his new headquarters at Mons. The Sixth Fleet's carriers, STRIKFORSOUTH, remained directly subordinate to CINCSOUTH, given their role in the new strategy of providing air support to Italy, Greece and Turkey. COMNAVSOUTH's primary role was the neutralisation of the maritime threat to the carrier Striking Force.

By the late 1960s, the increasing quality and longer reach of the Soviet Navy were beginning to create concerns, especially in the context of the new Flexible Response strategy. A special study by the SACLANT staff was commissioned by the Alliance's Secretary General Manlio Brosio of how NATO would deal with a crisis,

---

[7] Colbert Papers, quoted in SOKOLSKY, *Sea Power and the Nuclear Age*, p. 105.

both in the short term and in the late 1970s. It was presented to Brosio in March 1969. It argued that Flexible Response "expanded the contribution of maritime forces to NATO's overall deterrent posture and war fighting capability". Now, however, NATO would look to its forces at sea to fulfil these tasks throughout the conflict spectrum, from normal peacetime conditions, through limited war to major conventional and nuclear war. The study emphasised the importance of early pre-hostilities deployment of maritime forces and the need to be able to oppose Soviet actions at sea under conditions of limited war. To the overall strategy of flexible response, the allied maritime forces would bring the flexibility and mobility of maritime forces.[8]

In crisis, the MCF would be created, their purpose being "to compel the Soviets to choose between withdrawal and escalation". They "would also seek to deter, and in the case of failure of deterrence, prevent the Soviets from achieving any quick, limited *fait accompli*". In limited war the study "suggested that in support of NATO's flexible strategy maritime forces might respond to Soviet pressures on land and in the air by applying pressures at sea against the Soviet Bloc as a deterrent against further escalation". In major war NATO "would seek to maintain or re-establish overall supremacy at sea and employ its maritime forces in various capacities to support the land and air battle".[9]

The study played through a Norwegian scenario, postulating an invasion of northern Norway with amphibious and airborne forces. NATO had used warning time to bring carrier task forces into the Norwegian Sea, while ASW barriers were set up in the Greenland–Iceland–UK gap (GIUK), with further carrier and convoy escort units in deeper field in the Atlantic. When war broke out the carrier air groups attacked the Soviets ashore and fought air combat with Soviet Naval Aviation. The Soviets were deemed to have held back most of their submarines for defensive purposes and the barriers and convoy escorts defeated the attack on NATO shipping. The Alliance was able to rotate sufficient carriers into the Norwegian Sea to ensure both the defeat of the attacks on the Striking Fleet and the defeat of the Soviet invasion of Norway. The study assessed that after a three-month battle using conventional weapons alone, the war would be won and the Soviets' only option would be an attack on the Central Front in Germany.

The Brosio Study was much less optimistic about the 1977 scenario. On contemporary trends as Western maritime strength declined and Soviet strength increased, sea control in vital areas could no longer be assured. This was the way things turned out. In Exercise Strong Express in 1972, a combination of the air-deployed Allied Command Europe Mobile Force and amphibious forces defended Norway. In 1973 "Swift Move" saw the Striking Fleet exercising its air power and power-projection capabilities in the Norwegian Sea. By 1978, however, things had changed. In that year's exercise "Northern Wedding" the Striking Fleet operated not in the Norwegian Sea but against the Shetlands that were "playing" Southern Norway, *already occupied* by "Orange" forces.

---

[8] SOKOLSKY, *Sea Power and the Nuclear Age*, p. 113.
[9] Ibid., pp. 113–14.

The Norwegians were far from happy with this scenario. They had reason to be concerned. Much greater emphasis was now being placed on the "Maginot Line" of the GIUK gap, where sea-bed sonar sensors of the expanded SOSUS system could detect Soviet submarines passing into the Atlantic. There was also evidence that the Americans were moving to a more defensive "Sea Control" strategy and there was much talk of "pre-inforcement" in crisis rather than making amphibious landings in war. The late 1970s saw a real crisis of confidence in NATO's capacity to prevail in the maritime campaign that had to be won if NATO could survive before catastrophic nuclear escalation – or defeat – became inevitable.

In 1977, NATO's Defence Ministers became so concerned that they ordered a major reassessment of NATO's position at sea. They ordered the Alliance's military commanders to draw up a new "Concept of Maritime Operations", a statement of principles as to how maritime forces might contribute to deterrence, forward defence and flexible response. The three major NATO commands duly drew up CONMAROPS in 1980 that was approved by the Alliance's Defence Planning Committee in 1981. CONMAROPS was an assessment of NATO's maritime interests, the threats to those interests and the types of confrontation to be expected. Allied priorities in those confrontations were defined, along with the roles of various kinds of forces in five "campaigns": Atlantic Lifelines, Norwegian Sea, Shallow Seas (CINCHAN), Mediterranean Lifelines and Eastern Mediterranean.

The deputy SACLANT tried to reassure a Norwegian Conference in 1987 thus: "CONMAROPS establishes three operational principles: first – containment, keeping the Soviet Fleet from reaching the open ocean either undetected in tension or unopposed in war; second – defence in depth, being ready to fight the Soviets at the forward edge of the NATO area, along their exit routes and in defence of Allied war and merchant shipping; and third – the most important – keeping the initiative."[10]

CONMAROPS chimed in well with American national maritime strategic developments. The Reagan Administration's adoption of a proactive "Maritime Strategy" tied in to improvements in US Naval capabilities as part of the "600 Ship Navy" programme. There were also technological developments, the development of long-range towed-array sonars for surface ships that could detect Soviet submarines at very long ranges and the development of layered anti-air defences with F-14 fighters with Phoenix missiles and the combination of the Aegis system and Standard missiles in "Aegis cruisers".

As a US national statement, the Maritime Strategy was a clear expression that it would have been hard for the Alliance to have explored publicly. Nevertheless, much of the concept expressed in the American strategy was fully congruent with the thought in CONMAROPS. US Maritime Strategy and NATO Maritime Strategy were in full agreement with reference to the NATO area. When the NATO Concept was revised in 1985 and 1998 the American work confirmed the

---

[10] Quoted in GROVE, *Battle for the Fiords*, pp. 19–20.

emphasis on forward defence and seizing and maintaining the initiative. In the mid-1980s the Striking Fleet Commander, Vice Admiral Harry C. Mustin, set about a major reorganisation of the Striking Fleet with a carrier Striking Force, an ASW Striking Force commanded by a British Admiral in one or more of the *Invincible*-class ASW carriers, the Amphibious Striking Force and the combined US–British–Dutch Marine Force it carried. US organisation was brought into line with NATO's to allow better training and easier transition to war.

These concepts were demonstrated in a series of exercises. In "Ocean Safari" in 1985 Mustin took part of the Striking Fleet into the Norwegian Sea, led by RN Rear Admiral Julian Oswald commanding the ASW Striking Force in HMS *Illustrious*. The American carrier USS *America* was placed in Vestfiord, a "bastion" to help protect it from Soviet air attack. This created a pattern exercised over the next few years: deployment of the Striking Fleet in the fiords after a successful battle in the GIUK between the ASW Striking Force and Soviet submarines, the defeat of Soviet land-based naval air power and the successful use of maritime forces to defeat a Soviet invasion of Norway and threaten the Soviet maritime periphery. Most of the Soviet Fleet would have to be held back to defend Soviet ballistic-missile submarines threatened primarily by Western attack submarines in the Soviet "defended bastions" relatively close to the Kola Peninsula.

NATO's maritime strategy was a key factor in exerting the decisive strategic pressure on the Soviet Union that caused the implosion that ended the Cold War with Western victory. Not only did it promise a flexible response to attack on the Central Front and around the Alliance's flanks but, from what we now know of Soviet plans, it is likely that Britain and France would have been sanctuaries from nuclear attack in the preferred Soviet scenario for limited nuclear war. This would have required maritime reinforcement and the Alliance, with its CONMAROPS and the forces available in the 1980s, could have provided this. The Atlantic Alliance won the Cold War because it could control the seas around and leading to Western Europe. This allowed NATO to offer a credible conventional and nuclear response to potential Soviet aggression, reinforcing deterrence and thus making war unlikely, while exerting the pressure on the Soviet Union that led to its eventual demise. For the third time in the 20th century, on an oceanic planet, the maritime alliance had prevailed against the continental.

BIBLIOGRAPHY

GROVE E., *Maritime Strategy and European Security* (London and McLean, VA, 1990).
GROVE E., *Vanguard to Trident: British Naval Policy since the Second World War* (Annapolis MD and London, 1987).
GROVE E. with THOMPSON G., *Battle for the Fiords: The Forward Maritime Strategy in Action* (Shepperton and Annapolis MD, 1991).
SOKOLSKY J.J., *Sea Power and the Nuclear Age: The United States Navy and NATO* (London and Annapolis MD, 1991).

The Sea and the Soviet Empire

COLIN S. GRAY is Professor at the Department of Politics and International Relations, University of Reading, United Kingdom

ABSTRACT. *Growing naval power was an essential component of the Soviet challenge to the West, but Western perception of it was badly distorted by the assumption that the Soviets were building an American-style "battle-fleet" – which in fact was well beyond its economy and technology. In the 1970s the Soviet merchant fleet was built up to carry food imports and to earn hard currency. In both cases, however, investment in the sea was part of a defensive strategy and strictly subordinate to the land.*

RÉSUMÉ. *Former une puissance navale était une composante essentielle du défi soviétique face à l'Occident. Mais la perception qu'en avaient les pays occidentaux fut largement faussée par leur supposition que les soviétiques construisaient une « flotte de guerre » à l'américaine, ce qui s'avéra être bien au-delà de leur économie et de leur technologie. Dans les années 1970, la flotte marchande soviétique fut construite pour permettre l'importation de nourriture et rapporter une devise forte. Dans les deux cas, cependant, l'investissement dans le domaine maritime fit partie d'une stratégie de défense et fut toujours subordonnée à la terre.*

. ● .

The Soviet empire found itself compelled to compete strategically at sea with its Western foes, yet systemically constrained by factors which it could not change. A major difficulty in assessing the value of sea power to the Soviet empire is uncertainty as to the proper standard of measurement. What might that sea power have achieved, and how well or poorly did it perform? These are the core concerns requiring answer here. Two leading Western commentators observed in 1989 as follows:

> Over the last thirty years the Soviet Union has developed from a minor naval power with largely coastal capabilities and has become a major sea power able to challenge the supremacy of the US Navy throughout the world.[1]

These observers of the Soviet Navy in the Cold War were well informed about their subject, yet the assessment proved seriously flawed. Soviet sea power was

---

[1] RANFT B. and TILL G., *The Sea in Soviet Strategy* (Annapolis, 1983), p. 206.

not really embarked upon a global expansion of presence and influence, even though its technical capabilities assuredly improved to a remarkable degree through the 1960s, 1970s and well into the 1980s. It is now quite apparent that the Soviet Navy in the Cold War was insolubly limited by contextual constraints. The picture painted by Western commentators in the mid- to late 1980s was soon shown to be at least partially illusory. The Soviet Navy of the 1980s was technically impressive, quantitatively huge and potentially troublesome to Western interests. However, peril to the West was easily exaggerated.

Contexts

To understand the challenges to Soviet sea power in the Cold War, it is necessary to comprehend the changing situation which faced the Soviet leadership. The approach employed here is to consider the context, in terms of history, geography, politics and strategy, of the Soviet endeavour to develop and exploit sea power.

History

The strategic context of Soviet sea power was one of bilateral competition between two superpowers. The geostrategic and strategic cultural differences between the United States and the Soviet Union were enormous, but ultimately not defining. What was most compelling and enduring about their strategic relationship was their pre-eminence as powerful polities. The sea power of the United States was, and long has remained, in a superior class all its own, while from a fairly humble entry in the 1940s the Soviet bid for sea power began, and long continued, to be worthy of serious strategic note. The grand narrative of the Cold War certainly was partially fuelled by a political antagonism that owed something to ideological hostility.[2] But, when we endeavour to understand the rivalry between the superpowers and their allies, we can appreciate that the superpower rivalry was not caused primarily by ideology. The Cold War was a consequence of a bilateral balance of world power. Moscow needed sea power to contribute to its global statecraft and strategy. Soviet sea power in the Cold War performed as it did for reasons largely of historical circumstance and geography. The Soviet Empire, victorious but notably damaged in the Great Patriotic War of 1941-1945 against Germany, was obliged to co-habit with the other principal victor of 1945, the new superpower United States. The Soviet Union found itself obliged to compete for relative security against the post-war world's premier maritime power which, all but inevitably, came to lead an effectively maritime alliance hostile to Soviet interests. Of course, the novel nuclear dimension to the

---

[2] The most insightful recent treatment of the Cold War is BARRASS G.S., *The Great Cold War: A Journey Through the Hall of Mirrors* (Stanford, CA, 2009).

East–West antagonism was a complicating constraint for both good and ill, but the historical context for Soviet sea power in the decades of Cold War should be viewed as fundamentally the product of the bilateral distribution of national power.

Geography

Physical geography is by far the most constraining element in the narrative of Soviet sea power. Russian, then Soviet, and now Russian again, access to the world's oceans has been persistently hindered by geography. Soviet sea power was constrained both by climate/weather and by the relative ease with which hostile military power could contest maritime passage.

In descending order of strategic importance, the Soviet Union developed and maintained four fleets and several flotillas: the Northern fleet (based in Murmansk); the Baltic Sea fleet (based in Baltiysk, near Kaliningrad – the former Königsberg); the Pacific fleet (based in Vladivostok); and the Black Sea fleet (based in Sevastopol). Also there were naval flotillas on the Danube, the Dnieper, the Amur and the Caspian Sea. This extreme dispersion meant that each fleet would have to face combat in operational isolation from the others. Not only were the principal fleet bases enormously far apart, but in addition each could face serious opposition in attempts to reach the open ocean in time of war. Ice either was or could be a constraint of importance for all four fleet bases, while even the relatively warm sea approaches to the Kola peninsula and Murmansk called for ice-breakers to negotiate the floating Arctic ice pack. The Soviet Northern fleet was based a long way from main trans-Atlantic shipping routes, while the Pacific fleet, and even more its submarine force (based at Petropavlovsk on the Kamchatka peninsula), was not close to important trade routes.

The Soviet Navy in the Cold War faced serious maritime opposition at every point of access to the open ocean. The Northern fleet might need to shoot its way out into the North Atlantic through hostile waters dominated by NATO sea and air power. The Baltic fleet would have to pass through the Danish straits and then a North Sea owned strategically by NATO. The Black Sea fleet would need to pass through the Dardanelles, only to reach a Mediterranean that NATO all but controlled from bases in Greece, Italy, France and Gibraltar. Even the remote Pacific fleet at Vladivostok could be denied access to sea lanes in the Pacific by maritime blockades.

Political and strategic navigation

In its size and technological quality the Soviet Navy was indeed impressive. However, it is necessary to remember that it was the product of a highly inefficient economy. Even more to the point, that navy was challenging NATO, one of the greatest maritime alliances in all of strategic history. The Soviet fleet in the

Cold War decades was engaged in a competition that it could not possibly win.[3] Despite its many technological accomplishments, it was never clear what the Soviet fleet was about, politically or strategically. Major warships long have been the most complex machines mankind has constructed and operated. Given that complexity and very high costs have been enduring truths about naval power for millennia, it is not hard to see why a hugely disadvantaged economy would be well advised not to compete at sea with the navies of far stronger economies. Soviet sea power could perform impressively (e.g., in the welding of titanium submarine hulls), but it could never really be successful against a United States that chose to be alert.

The Soviet Union could not afford the human and technological costs of serious maritime competition in the Cold War. Whatever maritime advance the Soviet Union achieved, the United States would be certain to offset. For several decades the Soviet Union appeared to be capable of staying in touch with the naval technology of the West, but by the mid-1980s it was plain that it could not continue to compete effectively. And what did the Soviet Union need to ask of its navy? What was it for?

Soviet/Russian strategic culture is continental in character. Physical (fuelling psychological) geography has been a dominant factor influencing political and strategic choices. The narrative here is one of relative success in the face of much adversity. The Soviet/Russian Navy before 1945 did not have a glorious record of success, provided one is allowed to be restrained in enthusiasm over the major contribution of the sailors of the Baltic fleet in Kronstadt to the revolution in 1917. There is nothing remotely comparable to the British Royal Navy's victory at Trafalgar (1805) or the US Navy's great success with ambush at Midway (1942). The Soviet Navy did not disgrace itself after the fashion of the Imperial Navy's comprehensive defeat in the Strait of Tsushima (1905), but neither did it save a properly grateful nation. Given that Nazi Germany could not be defeated through action at sea, it is scarcely surprising that little worthy of much note was done by the Soviet Navy in the Great Patriotic War of 1941–1945.

Stalin's eventual successor, Nikita Khrushchev, did not share his predecessor's respect for large surface vessels. Under his political direction the Soviet Navy renewed and even strengthened its liking for submarines, in part in hope of posing a potential threat of maritime blockade upon NATO, but rather more in order to invest in a missile-firing threat deliverable in some safety from the sea. Also, the Soviet Navy devoted much effort to anti-submarine warfare. The US Navy deployed its first nuclear-powered ballistic missile-firing submarine (SSBN) in 1960. Khrushchev's exciting tenure of power was concluded abruptly in 1964 through a political coup. What followed for the better part of twenty years can be characterized as a "golden age" for Soviet sea power. Led extraordinarily for thirty years (1956–1985) by Admiral Sergei Gorshkov, the Soviet Navy was enabled politically to make a historic bid for global respect. From

---

[3] For a superior terse analysis see TILL G., 'Luxury Fleet? The Sea Power of (Soviet) Russia', in *Naval Power in the Twentieth Century*, ed. N.A.M. RODGER (Annapolis, MD, 1996), pp. 14–26.

the early 1960s until the mid-1980s it seemed as if the Russians were coming. Gorshkov was careful to avoid giving offence to the continentalist mainstream in Soviet opinion and culture. Nonetheless, many people were convinced that anything the US Navy could do, the Soviet Navy either could do also, or at least would do soon. However, pride and high ambition tend to fall victims of their own imprudence. In the late 1980s the Soviet fleet was crippled by the state's poverty.

THE SOVIET NAVY, 1945-1991: OVERVIEW

The Soviet Navy in the post-war years was hampered by the lack of a strong shipbuilding industry. Whilst the Soviets had a large fleet (which included some 175 submarines in 1945), much of it was technically outdated and many of the warships requisitioned from conquered Germany were worn down mechanically and lacked spare parts.[4] While the Soviet leadership was keen on building a large navy in order to confirm their status as a world power, they were aware that the country could ill afford to do so. The bulk of the navy's post-war reduction came from the naval infantry; bases were closed and many men discharged, all in an effort to leave the fleet substantially intact.[5] Growth in the Soviet Navy and its strategy were also limited by the country's defensive doctrine: no true aircraft carriers were constructed until the 1970s. The lack of seaborne air cover meant that the navy and its large (if ageing) submarine fleet were limited by their need to operate within the air-defence umbrella provided by land-based units. By the time Khrushchev became premier the Soviet economy had made a significant recovery, and the Soviet shipbuilding industry could begin to meet the demands of a navy that was no longer merely ancillary to the army, or a coastal defence force. During the late 1950s and early 1960s Khrushchev and Admiral Gorshkov expanded the navy to a point where it had a substantial submarine fleet which could support the strategy of trade interdiction proposed by Khrushchev and Marshal Zhukov in 1955.[6]

The operations of the Soviet Navy were still hindered by a persistent belief that war with the United States would be nuclear. The naval infantry were neglected in the 1950s and 1960s, and did not experience anything like a revival until the late 1990s. It was decided that if the need for a large naval infantry force arose, then it could be filled by mechanized and armoured divisions from the army, seconded to the navy's coastal command.[7] Soviet naval expansion occurred at a time when the USSR was experiencing a huge increase in imports

---

[4] YEGOROVA N.I., 'Stalin's conception of maritime power: revelations from the Russian archives', *Journal of Strategic Studies* 28 (2005), 157-86.
[5] Ibid.
[6] KUZIN V.P. and NIKOLSKII V.I., *Voenno-morskoi flot SSSR, 1945-1991* [The USSR Navy 1945-1995] (St Petersburg, 1996), p. 16.
[7] YEGOROVA, 'Stalin's conception of maritime power'.

and exports.[8] The Soviet reliance on imported grain meant that a strong seagoing navy was required in order to ensure that in the event of hostilities the grain should continue to flow.

After the Cuban missile crisis in 1962, Soviet political leaders perceived that their navy was weak. The lack of large surface units, especially aircraft carriers to project Soviet air power overseas, plainly hampered Soviet efforts to confront the United States. Khrushchev was removed from office in 1964 and superseded by Leonid Brezhnev: his period in power (until 1982) would be the one in which the Soviet Navy would grow more than previously or subsequently. Brezhnev's premiership saw the introduction of aircraft carriers into the navy, the expansion of the SSBN fleet and its SSNs (nuclear-powered attack submarines). The expansion of the surface fleet during Brezhnev's tenure ran parallel to his measures to boost the trade and cargo carried by Soviet ships, and also to his efforts to expand Soviet influence and diplomacy in third world countries.[9] This was helped by the use of impressive-looking large cruisers and aircraft carriers to make port calls.

After Brezhnev's death in 1982 the Soviet Navy suffered as a result of political infighting in Moscow. Whilst Brezhnev's two successors, Andropov and Chernenko, largely continued with expansion of the surface fleet and strategic submarine fleets, these leaders were in power only for very short periods. During this period the Soviet Navy was engaged in a constant struggle to remain integral to the political establishment and maintain influence in Moscow. Once Gorbachev came to power this battle clearly was lost. He oversaw massive reductions in the surface fleet, with destroyers, escorts, amphibious ships and naval air power all suffering cuts in numbers. In parallel with these reductions naval manpower plummeted to one of its lowest levels by the end of the 1980s, and the submarine fleet, both ballistic and attack, was reduced.

Gorbachev generally was opposed to the idea of an ocean-going Soviet fleet. So much is visible in the sudden contraction of Soviet naval strength and capabilities in the period that he was in charge. His approach to the navy was in keeping with his approach to the Soviet military as a whole. That military is and has been a powerful, indeed often key, social and political force in Soviet and Russian history. During the Brezhnev years the military had been granted top priority in resource and budgetary allocation, with the result that much policy in defence had been driven by military technical considerations and not by political process. Gorbachev was determined to bring military spending into line with that of the wider economy. This affected all branches of the military establishment, but the navy in particular was hit hard and suffered setbacks which severely limited its capabilities. It was in many ways relegated to its older role in support of the army.

The Soviet Navy suffered a great deal as a consequence of changes in political

---

[8] SHRIVENER D., 'The merchant marine in Soviet naval strategy', *Marine Policy* 7.2 (1983), 118–21.
[9] Ibid.

leadership and the dominance of the army in politics. During the immediate post-war years, under Stalin's leadership, the navy suffered heavily from the extreme lack of resources and the post-war reduction of manpower. Although Stalin wished to construct a blue-water navy, the economic difficulties, lack of shipbuilding expertise and a defensive strategy precluded a large-scale naval build-up. Under Khrushchev matters improved only partially. While he was determined to expand the fleet, mainly he was obsessed with constructing submarines. He believed the construction of large cruisers and aircraft carriers to be a waste of time and resources. "To put forth a goal of strengthening the surface fleet is unreasonable ... It is not needed to build aircraft carriers in the near term ... The construction of landing vessels ought not to be developed ..."[10] After Khrushchev's removal from power in 1964, Brezhnev pursued a much more proactive programme of expansion and modernization of the navy. In part this was because Brezhnev's ascension to power largely was attributable to military backing. Under the Brezhnev regime Gorshkov succeeded in developing a modern navy with a more modern doctrine. Brezhnev's successors, resentful of the political strength of the military, reversed much of his policy course. As a consequence, by the time of the fall of the Soviet Union the navy was languishing in harbour, much reduced in size. A large proportion of the defence budget had been spent on such dubious programmes as the gigantic *Typhoon*-class submarine of twenty-five thousand tons, carrying twenty SS-NX-2 SLBMs, which first became operational in 1983: production ceased after six were constructed.

As the range of Soviet submarine-launched ballistic missiles (SLBMs) increased, so the tactical need for their parent submarines to approach Western shorelines diminished markedly. As a result, the primary military function of the Soviet fleet gradually became the preservation of its missile-firing nuclear submarines, operating principally from Arctic Sea bastions. The US Navy and its NATO allies demonstrated to the Soviet Union that they were not overly impressed by the security of its Arctic Sea retreats. For a telling example, in August 1982 a NATO battle group comprising more than eighty warships "passed through the Greenland-Iceland-UK Gap in radio silence and came close to Soviet territory before they were detected".[11]

Trade and the economy

Soviet trade during the Stalin era was weak at best and in many cases non-existent. By 1945 the Soviet Union is estimated to have lost almost 50% of its industrial base in the war and, as a consequence, was in very serious economic trouble. This situation was worsened by Stalin's refusal to participate in the Marshall Plan (1947), mainly to avoid the USSR's becoming reliant on American finance. The Fourth and Fifth Five Year plans of the USSR concentrated almost entirely on reconstruction, heavy industry and transport. The damage to all

---

[10] KUZIN and NIKOLSKII, *Voenno-morskoi flot SSSR, 1945–1991* [The USSR Navy 1945–1995], p. 16.
[11] BARRASS, *The Great Cold War*, p. 279.

areas of Russian industry and manpower during the war meant that a long period of rebuilding was required. During this period the USSR seized factories, workers and machines from occupied territories and extracted large sums in reparations. Because Stalin refused to accept playing any part in the Marshall Plan, the United Kingdom and the United States would not trade with the USSR.

During Stalin's post-war years the Soviet Union experienced several crises with grain supplies and suffered from massive food shortages in some regions, especially the Ukraine. After his death in 1953, when the Soviet Union decided to open up to certain kinds of trade, its biggest import was grain. For several decades Soviet agriculture was heavily reliant upon Western imports.

The post-Stalin era began with a surge in trade. Stalin had been generally anti-trade because he saw trade as being in essence anti-socialist. Khrushchev did not suffer from this belief. He persuaded the collective leadership that trade with the outside world was necessary for the overall benefit of the state and socialism. As a result the USSR began to expand its trade with third world states and other socialist states. To catch up with Western powers, competitors were undercut, using state funding. A near-total Soviet focus on hard-cash gains allowed low prices to be offered.[12] The growth in trade led to the creation and rapid growth of MORFLOT (Ministry of the Merchant Marine). Initially the bulk of MORFLOT cross-trading was directed towards socialist states and LDCs (Lesser Developed Countries); its longest period of growth in size and capacity took place between 1965 and 1981.

> In the period 1965–1981 the Soviet Merchant Marine increased numerically by 75% – from 1,741 vessels to 3,046 and in tonnage by 154% – from 6.5 million to 16.5 millions GRT.[13]

These statistics are impressive. Much of the growth is explained by the fact that MORFLOT and Soviet seaborne trade benefited heavily from state backing which, combined with MORFLOT's focus on hard-currency earnings, allowed it to undercut Western companies by 15–30%. These Soviet merchant shipping policies in the 1970s and 1980s contributed to a sharp contraction in the Western share of seaborne carriage in bilateral Soviet–Western trade. The Soviets achieved a growing penetration of lucrative international cross-trading, further aggravating the decline in West European shipbuilding and promoting import substitution by carrying a growing proportion of Soviet imports and exports in Soviet ships. This also reduced the political vulnerability of reliance on Western shipping lines. In 1981 Soviet vessels carried 42% of export tonnage and 70% of import tonnage, which translates into 53% of total seaborne foreign trade. However, these efforts were hampered by the lack of high-quality modern port facilities in Soviet home waters, a practical logistical matter which contributed

---

[12] SMALLEY G., 'The role of the merchant fleet in Soviet global strategy', *Marine Policy* 11.2 (1984), 65–8.
[13] SHRIVENER, 'The merchant marine in Soviet naval strategy'.

to a high share of annual tonnage being carried by coastal transports until the late 1980s.[14]

The expansion in Soviet trade post-Stalin shows much deliberate state planning in the undercutting of Western companies, and a concerted effort to trade with third world polities to expand the Soviet sphere of influence. This increase in trade coincided with an expansion of the Soviet Navy as a whole, with efforts during the 1970s and 1980s to create effective power-projection capabilities, including destroyers, cruisers and other ships required for the protection of Soviet overseas trade. In addition, such ships could help keep the Dardanelles, Bosporus and Danish straits open for trade in the case of tension occasioned by protracted crises.

Understanding Soviet sea power

Western observers frequently have allowed themselves to be confused about enduring Soviet/Russian realities. Although the Soviet Navy was a serious enterprise, it was always regarded officially as the fifth and last in order of relative importance among the armed services. The descending rank order during the Cold War (and beyond) was as follows: (1) strategic rocket forces; (2) army; (3) air defence forces; (4) air force; and (5) last and least, navy. The Russians were not confused about this. The Soviet Navy was understood to have value for its versatility and ability to be employed to be "present" near the scene of Western crimes, hopefully to complicate the political and military choices of antagonists around the world. As Soviet seaborne trade expanded greatly through the 1960s and 1970s, a navy with a global reach was appreciated as a useful policy tool that could register political interest fairly convincingly.

However, by far the most important role of the Soviet Navy in the Cold War was its potential contribution to the defence of the homeland. To advance this primary state policy goal the navy provided a growing proportion of the nuclear deterrent with its SLBMs. These were deployed at ever-longer range, eventually largely from Arctic Sea bastion areas protected by the whole array of the Soviet fleet, surface and sub-surface. No less important was the contribution of the navy to the defence of the homeland from Western air and missile attack. Through the 1950s certainly, the US Navy posed a large threat from its growing carrier aviation strength. Towards the close of the Cold War, partly thanks to assistance from espionage, Soviet SSNs were becoming a notable menace to Western SSBNs. Nonetheless, in time of crisis the Soviet Navy could not neutralize the submarine-borne nuclear threat to the Soviet empire.

The navy was a strategically useful complement to the more senior services. Soviet leaders understood that an ocean-going navy was a desirable instrument

---

[14] ELLIS J., 'Expansion of the Soviet merchant fleet – implications for the West', *NATO Review* 3 (1979), 21.

of state, especially given that the enemy was a maritime alliance headed by a global maritime superpower. The Soviet Navy, however, was not and could not become a strategically decisive force except, eventually, as a bastion-guarding holder of the state's strategic nuclear reserve force (of SLBMs). It should never be forgotten that the Soviet Union/Russia was, and remains, truly a deeply continental power.

THE SEA AND THE ECONOMIC SLUMP, 1919-1939

MARTIN DAUNTON is Emeritus Professor of Economic History, University of Cambridge, United Kingdom

ABSTRACT. *Before the First World War most of the advanced economies were at last partly committed to free trade and free exchange. After the war protectionism, tariffs and financial controls threw international trade into disarray, and some countries subsidized shipping for strategic reasons. Ships and ship-owners were both victims and instruments of economic nationalism, but international trade fell as a proportion of economic activity.*

RÉSUMÉ. *Avant la première guerre mondiale, la plupart des économies avancées étaient au moins en partie attachées au libre-échange et au commerce libre. Avec le protectionnisme découlant de la guerre, les droits de douane et les contrôles financiers ont jeté le commerce international dans le chaos et certains pays ont dû, pour raisons stratégiques, subventionner la navigation. Les navires et leurs propriétaires se retrouvèrent à la fois les victimes et les instruments du nationalisme économique mais le commerce international ne devint plus qu'un pourcentage de l'activité économique.*

. • .

In 1919, John Maynard Keynes reflected, with a sense of nostalgia for a lost era, on the world economy as it existed in the last days of peace:

> The inhabitant of London could order by telephone, sipping his morning tea in bed, the various products of the whole earth, in such quantity as he might see fit, and reasonably expect their early delivery upon his doorstep; he could at the same moment and by the same means adventure his wealth in the natural resources and new enterprises of any quarter of the world, and share, without exertion or even trouble in their prospective fruits and advantages.[1]

It was a time of free movement of labour - a world in which the wealthy inhabitant of London could take a Cunard liner from Liverpool to New York, or a poor immigrant from southern Italy could travel steerage to Ellis Island for a

[1] KEYNES J.M., *The Economic Consequences of the Peace, Collected Writings of John Maynard Keynes*, vol. II (London, 1971), pp. 6-7.

new life. It was a world economy in which most prosperous areas accepted the gold standard, so reducing the uncertainties of trade and capital investment.

Tensions were already appearing before the war, for the obverse of an open, cosmopolitan economy was the difficulty of adopting domestic economic policies to protect industries from foreign competition, to maintain wage rates from being undercut by cheap migrant labour or to pursue an activist monetary policy. By 1914, American workers were demanding controls on immigration from southern Europe. Even in Britain, the home of free trade, voices were demanding tariff reform. After the First World War, these pressures grew in intensity, and cosmopolitanism gave way to economic nationalism – a world of "beggar my neighbour" economic policies as each country tried to look after its own interests by protection, competitive devaluation or subsidies. What was the point of the gold standard if it forced countries to cut wage rates to compete for trade? What was the point of free movement of capital if it starved domestic industry of investment? Why maintain free trade if it destroyed domestic industries and agriculture?

Even Keynes, a supporter of the pre-war cosmopolitan economy, changed his mind. He no longer held to the faith of Richard Cobden that trade led to prosperity and peace – rather, the attempt to capture trade led to susceptibility to economic fluctuations, neglect of domestic prosperity and a loss of identity resting on local trades. In 1933 he argued that it was preferable to "minimise rather than ... maximise economic entanglements between nations. Ideas, knowledge, art, hospitality, travel – these are the things which should of their nature be international. But let goods be homespun whenever it is reasonably and conveniently possible; and above all let finance be primarily national."[2]

Britain abandoned the gold standard in 1931, allowing sterling to depreciate, so increasing the price of imports and making exports more competitive. It turned away from free trade to imperial preference in 1932. In America, controls were imposed on migration in 1922, and swingeing tariff increases were introduced in 1930. Other countries soon followed: in fifteen European countries, the average increase in tariffs between 1927 and 1931 was 50 per cent. Japan abandoned gold in 1931, devalued the yen and invaded Manchuria to secure raw materials. Other countries such as France and Germany stayed on gold much longer, losing markets as a result of their high export prices. Trade and money were in disarray, and in 1933 the World Monetary and Economic Conference met in London to attempt to solve the problems of currency instability and trade restrictions. The chances of success were not high, for participants lacked a common understanding of the problem. Europeans wanted a settlement of war debts, requiring concessions from the US that were not on the agenda. The British saw no need to return to gold; by contrast, the French and Germans saw gold as the basis of order and stability. Any prospect of agreement failed when Franklin Delano Roosevelt abandoned the gold standard and looked for economic recovery at

---

[2] KEYNES, 'National self-sufficiency', *Collected Works of John Maynard Keynes*, vol. XXI, pp. 236–7.

home. The same year, Hitler came to power in Germany and clung to gold, with the result that exports collapsed and his economic minister, Hjalmar Schacht, turned to a policy of self-contained trade blocs and bilateral exchange of goods. The US Secretary of State, Cordell Hull, feared that the outcome would be war. He clung to the Cobdenite faith that "unhampered trade dovetailed with peace; high tariffs, trade barriers and unfair competition, with war".[3] Schachtianism collided with Hullism in the 1930s – and it seemed that Schacht was winning, with trade war leading inexorably to real conflict.

The maritime history of the interwar period was deeply implicated in these changes in economic policy, in ways that were complicated and ambivalent. Ship-owners were both the victims and proponents of economic nationalism. The economic difficulties of the interwar period affected the demand for shipping space and led to serious problems for shipping firms that lost their markets in immigration or the free movement of goods. In some cases, they were able to adapt to new opportunities. The encouragement of domestic economic growth and a marked fall in prices meant that many people in work in the 1930s had more disposable income – with a consequent rise in demand for petrol for their motor cars, or the possibility of foreign travel. In other cases, they responded to the economic problems of declining trade by forming cartels that cut across national boundaries. Paradoxically, economic nationalism could lead to an international response, with firms from different countries striking deals to contain destructive competition. But economic nationalism could also seize upon shipping as countries sought to build up their merchant marines to win trade wars and prepare for real war. The First World War indicated that flows of men and munitions, oil and food across the sea were central to success: the merchant marines were drawn into preparation for future conflict.

Returning to peace

During the war, about fifteen million tons of shipping were lost to enemy action and normal risks of the sea, but there was no *absolute* shortage of shipping on the return to peace. Although the British fleet was down by three million tons, the world fleet *increased* by four million tons, largely as a result of the expansion of the American fleet, which increased from two million gross registered tons in 1914 to ten million in 1919. Much of the new construction came into operation after the war, so that the world fleet was up by ten million tons by 1921. However, there was an *apparent* shortage of effective capacity, in large part because of serious congestion in ports. In Britain, dockers, railwaymen and miners mounted strikes in 1919 which disrupted trade, and they secured reduced hours of work that slowed down trade. Ships were in the wrong place and there was a massive, short-term restocking boom. Freight rates and the price of both

[3] Hull C., *Memoirs Vol. 1* (New York, 1948), p. 81.

new and second-hand ships soared to unprecedented levels. The index number of charter rates on British cargo ships was 100 in 1913, rising to 2,492 in 1918. The building cost of a 7,500 deadweight ton ship in December 1919 was £195,000, but the price of a ready ship was £232,500, and soon rose to a peak of £258,750 in March 1920, reflecting a premium to take advantage of high freight rates. In some cases, owners with experience of booms and slumps in shipping wisely sold their fleets at inflated prices to gullible newcomers; other owners decided to purchase new vessels from ship-builders at high prices. The situation was exacerbated by banks, which were involved to an unprecedented degree, leaving many ship-owners and ship-builders trapped into indebtedness when charter rates on British cargo ships fell to 561 in 1919 and 330 in 1920. By December 1920, the building cost of a 7,500 deadweight ton ship had risen to £225,000 and the price of a ready ship had fallen to £105,000; by the end of 1922 both were down to £70,000. Enough tonnage had been built to last a decade, and by 1921 five million tons of shipping were laid up, of which two million tons were British.[4]

The results of the post-war boom were disastrous for British shipping. Reserves were dissipated, and when the boom broke many companies were bankrupt or used profits to write down the value of their ships. Before the war, British ship-owners used modern ships with lower costs of operation and maintenance, selling off second-hand ships to other countries with lower wages which allowed them to cover the higher costs of fuel and repair. Until the First World War, British owners were generally successful in competing with foreign owners, buying the most efficient ships from British builders on easy terms. This ceased to be the case after the war, for British owners were less able to buy new ships and were obliged to operate older ships, at the same time as their rivals were able to buy new ships with lower costs. British owners lost much of their pre-war advantage, and were tardy in moving to motor ships that were faster and carried more cargo in relation to their gross tonnage, with lower engine-room costs.

The situation in Britain was particularly serious because of the decline in the coal export trade, which had been a major component of demand for shipping before the war, employing about 25 per cent of all British shipping and 40 per cent of British tramp ships – that is, vessels hired to carry bulk cargoes according to need. Coal was a central element in British shipping, for it was the only bulk export providing a return cargo for ships that brought imports of food and raw materials into British ports. This relationship changed after the war, for coal exports from Britain fell from 73.4 million tons in 1913 to around forty million tons a year in the 1930s.[5] The coal trade was also the main reason why tramp ships accounted for about two-thirds of the British fleet in 1913. By contrast,

---

[4] STURMEY S., *British Shipping and World Competition* (London, 1962), pp. 36, 59; ALDCROFT D., 'Port congestion and the shipping boom of 1919–20', *Business History* 3 (1961), 98, 101, 106; GREGG E., 'Vicissitudes in the shipping trade, 1870–1920', *Quarterly Journal of Economics* 35 (1921), 615.

[5] MITCHELL B., *Abstract of British Historical Statistics* (Cambridge, 1962), p. 121.

liners operating on regular routes with a fixed timetable were as much as 90 per cent of the fleets of Greece and Norway.

Although Britain remained the largest ship-owner in the world throughout the interwar period, its share of world tonnage was in decline, from 41.6 per cent in 1914 to 33.6 per cent in 1920 and 27.5 per cent in 1939. New owners were emerging, better able to take advantage of the changed circumstances of the interwar years. The German fleet was redistributed to the allies, so that its share fell sharply from being the second-largest fleet in 1914 (11.2 per cent) to 0.7 per cent in 1920. However, Germany then made a comeback with a new, modern fleet: it had the fifth-largest fleet in 1939, with 6.8 per cent of world tonnage. The main winners were the Japanese (3.7 per cent of tonnage in 1914 and 8.8 per cent in 1939), Norwegians (rising from 4.4 per cent to 7.6 per cent) and, above all, the Americans. The American fleet rose from 4.4 per cent of world tonnage in 1914 to be the second-largest between the wars, with 23.0 per cent in 1920 and 14.2 per cent in 1939.[6] The Americans adopted a conscious policy of encouraging the growth of their merchant fleet. Although the ships built and owned by the American government in the war were sold off to private owners in 1920, the Shipping Board that handled war-time construction and post-war sales had a loan fund to assist in building ships for trades that were considered desirable. As the Merchant Marine Act of 1920 put it, "It is necessary for national defense and for the proper growth of its foreign and domestic commerce that the United States shall have a merchant marine of the best-equipped and most suitable types of vessels sufficient to carry the greater proportion of its commerce and serve as a naval or military auxiliary in time of war or national emergency."[7] On their entry into the war in 1916, the Americans had been forced to rely on the British to move troops and supplies, and they wished to avoid this situation in the future.

The economic experience of the 1920s was mixed. Britain experienced slow recovery because of deflationary policies needed to return to gold; the United States experienced a boom. Seaborne trade recovered to reach a new peak in 1929 at 35 per cent above pre-war levels (see Table 1). Even so, there were serious problems for the shipping industry. Total tonnage was 45 per cent above pre-war levels, and this figure understates the growth in capacity, for the switch from coal to oil meant that ships were faster and could carry more cargo. Despite the growth in world trade in the 1920s, about four million tons of shipping were laid up in 1929 and, not surprisingly, freight rates were lower than before the war. The situation was soon to be far worse with the onset of the Great Depression. By 1932, world seaborne trade had fallen back steeply from the peak of 1929, by almost 30 per cent, with shipping tonnage now up 48 per cent and twenty-six million tons of shipping laid up and freight rates down by 25 per cent from pre-war levels. The world's shipping industry was facing a serious crisis: how would it respond?

---

[6] STURMEY, *British Shipping*, pp. 37, 139.
[7] GREGG E., 'The failure of the Merchant Marine Act of 1920', *American Economic Review* 11 (1921), 601.

Table 1. *Indices of world trade, shipping and freight rates (1913 = 100)*

	World seaborne trade	Shipping tonnage Total	Shipping tonnage Active	Freight rates (Economist)
1920	83	122	n.a.	438.7
1921	82	132	n.a.	158.4
1929	135	145	141	96.8
1932	101	148	122	75.4
1938	135	144	142	97.6

Source: STURMEY S.G., *British Shipping and World Competition* (London, 1962), p. 65.

THE WORLD DEPRESSION

A major explanation for the slow recovery of trade in the 1930s was the pursuit of nationalist commercial policies, the collapse of multilateral trade and a shift to trade blocs. By 1938 the volume of world seaborne trade had returned only to the peak of 1929, despite world primary and industrial production being respectively 7 and 11 per cent above 1929 levels. The discrepancy between seaborne trade and production was the result of countries turning to policies of self-sufficiency and import-substituting industrialisation such as in Latin America. Before the First World War, much of that continent depended on export-led growth, with massive inflows of foreign capital leading to the development of export sectors such as coffee in Brazil or livestock in Argentina or copper and nitrates in Chile. After the slump of 1929, commodity prices collapsed at a much faster rate than prices of manufactured imports, forcing these countries to reduce their purchases from Europe and to default on their debts. They turned away from export-led growth to import-substituting industrialization. At the same time, many countries in Europe turned to self-sufficiency in foodstuffs, reducing their purchases of grain from the new world and Australia, so that these countries were less able to buy European manufactures. Trade spiralled downwards.

Despite this gloomy picture, there were some areas of growth. As the trade in coal declined, so the movement of oil increased with the construction of tankers. British ship-owners suffered from the collapse of coal exports and did not gain as much from the growth of oil, where Norway was more successful. Oil was under 5 per cent of world sea-borne trade in 1913, accounting for a world tanker fleet of 1.5 million tons, rising to 25 per cent of trade and a fleet of 10.7 million tons in 1938. Consumption of oil rose six-fold between 1913 and 1937, with a geographic spread to Latin America, the Gulf and south-east Asia which meant the construction of specialist port and storage facilities. Oil companies owned between 25 and 40 per cent of the tonnage needed to move their output. The remainder was obtained from independent fleets through time charters of up to ten years and by voyage charters. British ship-owners held 50 per cent of the world tanker fleet in 1913, but only 25.2 per cent in 1938; their share of independent tankers was very modest, amounting to only 0.5 million tons out of 4.9 million tons in 1938. British oil companies preferred not to build tankers and instead kept capital for exploration. Neither did British owners of liners move into the trade, preferring to replace their liner fleets. Tramp owners were constrained by the purchase of expensive ships for the coal trade after the war. By contrast, Norwegian owners were able to exploit this new business, building fast and efficient tankers with borrowed money to charter to American and British oil companies. By 1938, Norwegian owners had 1.75 million tons of independent tankers, moving swiftly into a growing sector of the world economy without subsidy.[8]

American closure of mass migration seriously hit passenger traffic on the north Atlantic which fell from 2,578,000 in 1913 to 785,000 in 1924; it recovered to over a million in 1929. However, there were still buoyant passenger movements on other routes, with pilgrim ships to Mecca, Chinese moving to south-east Asia, and British migration to Australia. In 1927, for example, there were 1.25 million migrants to south-east Asia. On the crowded north Atlantic routes, companies vied with each other to build new, fast liners to attract customers by their prestige, modernity and speed – great ships that were commenced in the 1920s and completed in the 1930s, such as Norddeutscher Lloyd's *Bremen*, Compagnie Generale Transatlantique (CGT)'s *Normandie* and Cunard's *Queen Mary*. These liners were more efficient, for two fast and large ships could do the work of three, and they replaced migrant accommodation with tourist or third-class cabins. Indeed, one way that passenger liners could regain customers was by catering for a new form of tourism. Cruising was more attractive than laying up or scrapping a ship, provided that the receipts were higher than the voyage costs less the cost of laying up. The companies used agents and canvassers to attract business, showed films about exotic locations and drew on their networks to acquire information on local visits. The CGT even owned a chain of hotels in north Africa with motor cars for touring. As yet, very few ships were built specifically for cruising with on-board facilities for entertainment and recreation, it was rather a way of finding a use for passenger liners.

These new trades were not enough to compensate for falling volumes, and another response was to form cartels in order to prevent competition leading to mutual destruction, above all in the liner trades. Liners were owned by highly capitalised joint stock companies; most of their costs were overheads in providing expensive ships and port facilities for a regular service. The cost of carrying an extra ton of cargo was mainly loading and discharging the ship, so that a liner company would take any rate above this marginal cost as a contribution to overheads. Unrestrained competition would mean that rates would fall to this level – a case of "beggar my neighbour" that would drive everyone to financial ruin. There was therefore an incentive to enter into agreements or

---

[8] STURMEY, *British Shipping*, pp. 73-5, 77-81; MILLER M., *Europe and the Maritime World: A Twentieth-Century History* (Cambridge, 2012), p. 250.

"conferences" to fix freight and passenger rates in order to minimise competition and protect investments.

Did the conference system keep rates at a higher level than would otherwise have been the case? Conference rates could be challenged in a number of ways. Different regions of the world were in competition with each other, so too high a rate in one area could lead to a switch to another area. Aggressive outsiders with modern, fast ships, such as the Scandinavians, could make a profit by undercutting conference rates, and tramp ships could enter the market. In some cases, the abuse of market power led to new entrants. The conferences tried to limit competition from outsiders by offering customers deferred rebates on condition that shippers used only conference ships for a defined period. In some countries, deferred rebates were illegal as a limit on competition – as in the United States in 1916. A way around this limitation was the use of loyalty contracts: a shipper agreed to use the conference for all cargoes, with any breach of the contract leading to a penalty charge. The overall results are difficult to assess. The conferences might have kept rates more stable and at a somewhat higher level. On the other hand, keeping surplus tonnage in operation meant more part cargoes and hence lower returns.

Increasingly, the merchant marine was drawn into economic nationalism as a weapon in commercial warfare and in preparation for possible conflict. Clearly, the economic and political policy failures in 1933 were crucial to the rise of dictators and the slide into conflict – and shipping was both a victim and an actor. Subsidies and bounties were needed to compensate shipping for the damage caused by economic policies. In Germany, subsidies were used to offset the overvalued mark: in 1932 German ship-owners were given interest-free loans to scrap and rebuild, and in 1933 they were given an operating bounty. But trade and shipping were also part of the trade war and strategic preparation for war. The Germans realised that they needed access to raw materials for any future war, and offered bilateral trade deals to countries in Latin America that were in desperate need of export markets. The Americans saw a threat to the Monroe Doctrine with the incursion of Germany, leading Hull to offer tariff reductions and President Roosevelt to develop the "good neighbor policy". Maritime and trade policy were inexorably drawn into strategic thinking.

Nowhere was the link between shipping, trade and strategic preparation for war clearer than in the Far East. In the 19th century, major European trading companies combined trading, shipping and industrial operations. John Swire and Sons, a merchant house in Liverpool, had a major interest in Alfred Holt's Blue Funnel Line, the dominant company on routes to the Far East. Swire had trading interests in China and owned the China Navigation Co that linked the river and coastal trades with the trans-oceanic Blue Funnel Line. Swires and Holts moved into sugar refining, and they penetrated markets in China through a network of local agents or *hongs*. These integrated companies faced difficulties between the wars. They were hit on all sides by the end of free trade, constraints on capital mobility, a fall in freight rates, the collapse in commodity prices and the outbreak of war with the Japanese invasion of Manchuria and civil war in China.

The difficulties of these western concerns created opportunities for Japanese trading houses and ship-owners to take over markets, selling their manufactures in Asia and making links with indigenous networks of Chinese and Indian merchants. New trading and shipping concerns were challenging western domination. Lee Kong Chian, a Singaporean Chinese businessman, created a major rubber firm, using Western banks but also credit from Japanese trading and shipping companies. Already in the 1930s, the Japanese had the third-largest fleet in the world, and great *zaibatsu* business conglomerates such as Mitsubishi had large interests in banking, industry and shipping, with strong links with the Japanese navy and imperialism. The Japanese government was pursuing a policy of militaristic expansion into China and the creation of a yen bloc to combat the protectionist dollar and sterling zones. These developments were portrayed as a sort of Japanese Monroe Doctrine, freeing the region from Western colonialism and creating prosperity for Asia. The implications were obvious to British strategists, who realised that they might soon be fighting a maritime war in both Europe and the Far East. The Japanese were challenging British trade – and if war ensued, it was vital for Britain to have sufficient ships to supply men, oil and materials.

The United States was expanding into the Pacific, and its maritime policies both helped and hindered British interests in the Far East. American shipping was supported by grants and general postal subsidies in the 1920s, and the election of Roosevelt gave a new emphasis to shipping as a central element in American commercial and naval strategy. He served as Assistant Secretary of the Navy from 1913 to 1920, had close personal links to merchant shipping and adhered to Mahan's concept of sea power. The British complained that the Americans were subsidising their fleet and "dumping" shipping space; the Americans countered that the British had lower costs and were not scrapping ships. Relations were seriously strained in the Far East with the incursion of the Matson Line, which received very generous support, and Secretary of State Hull worried that conflict over shipping would undermine the creation of peace through trade. However, Roosevelt decided to expand the American merchant marine to ensure that it had sufficient shipping and naval auxiliaries for a war against Japan in the Far East. In 1936, the Shipping Board was replaced by the Maritime Commission, staffed by former naval officers, who used support of the merchant marine – including firms such as Matson – as a tool of strategic policy.

The British were in a dilemma, caught between dislike of American subsidies and the need for American oil and tankers in the event of war in the Far East. A fine line needed to be drawn. One solution was subsidies to British ships, but these were relatively modest. Unlike in the United States, there was little state support in the 1920s. The Trade Facilities Acts of 1921–1926 guaranteed loans by private lenders to companies with high unemployment, including in shipbuilding. Although the facility was used by some British owners to buy new ships, it was opposed by the Chamber of Shipping on the grounds that it would increase surplus tonnage. The government offered support for building two Cunard liners, the *Queen Mary* and *Queen Elizabeth*, on condition that Cunard and White Star merged. In 1935, the British Shipping (Assistance) Act gave modest support to tramp ships, but it was little used and did not apply to liner trades. The subsidy was conditional on the creation of a Tramp Shipping Administrative Committee to prevent any subsidy being wasted in competition. Of course, competition was international, so agreement was needed to control rates for all ships on major trade routes, such as the River Plate agreement of 1935 for Argentinian grain.

Sea routes and access to food and raw materials were crucial strategic considerations in the 1930s and the Second World War. Hull was right to fear that commercial warfare would lead to real warfare. His naivety was in assuming that peace could be restored by the simple expedient of reducing trade barriers and creating peaceful commerce. As another American politician, said it was "like hunting an elephant with a fly-swatter".[9] Much more was needed to remove the pursuit of Schachtian beggar-my-neighbour policies. It entailed a shift from Roosevelt's pursuit of sea power as propounded by Mahan to the adoption of a new form of internationalism that imposed commitments on nations to balance their own domestic interests with a concern for the world economy.

Conclusion

The years between the outbreaks of the two world wars were difficult ones for the world's shipping industry. It flourished before 1914 on the basis of multilateral, open trade that went into retreat between the wars. During and after the Second World War, attention turned to international rules and institutions, balancing the needs of the international economy with domestic prosperity and sovereignty, creating commitment mechanisms to prevent the pursuit of "beggar my neighbour" policies. Roosevelt now realised the need for a more outward-looking approach. Keynes and other officials and economists embarked on the difficult task of creating a new set of rules and institutions that would allow a smoother transition to peace than was achieved after the First World War, and that would start the task of reconstructing an open, multilateral economy.

Bibliography

ALDCROFT D., 'Port congestion and the shipping boom of 1919–20', *Business History* 3 (1961).

COONS L. and VARIAS A., *Tourist Third Cabin: Steamship Travel in the Interwar Years* (Basingstoke, 2003).

---

[9] ICKES H., *The Secret Diary of Harold L. Ickes, II: The Inside Struggle 1936–1939* (New York, 1953), p. 211.

FALKUS M., *The Blue Funnel Legend: A History of the Ocean Steamship Company, 1865-1973* (London, 1990).
GREEN E. and MOSS M., *A Business of National Importance: The Royal Mail Shipping Group, 1902-37* (London, 1982).
GREGG E., 'The decline of tramp shipping', *Quarterly Journal of Economics* 40 (1926).
GREGG E., 'The failure of the Merchant Marine Act of 1920', *American Economic Review* 11 (1921).
GREGG E., 'Vicissitudes in the shipping trade, 1870-1920', *Quarterly Journal of Economics* 35 (1921).
HYDE F., *Cunard and the North Atlantic, 1840-1973: A History of Shipping and Financial Management* (London, 1975).
JONES G., *Merchants to Multinationals: British Trading Companies in the Nineteenth and Twentieth Centuries* (Oxford, 2000).
KENNEDY G., 'American and British Merchant Shipping: Competition and Preparation, 1933-39', in *The Merchant Marine in International Affairs, 1850-1940*, ed. G. KENNEDY (London, 2000).
MILLER M., *Europe and the Maritime World: A Twentieth-Century History* (Cambridge, 2012).
MILLER M., 'Pilgrim's progress: the business of the Hajj', *Past and Present* 191 (2006).
POST P., 'Chinese Business Networks and Japanese Capital in South-East Asia, 1880-1940', in *Chinese Business Enterprise in Asia*, ed. R. BROWN (London, 1995).
STURMEY S., *British Shipping and World Competition* (London, 1962).

Océans et globalisation depuis 1945

Hubert Bonin is professor of economic history at Sciences Po Bordeaux and at the UMR CNRS 5113 GRETHA-University of Bordeaux, France

Résumé. L'essor d'une économie mondiale « globalisée », fondée sur le commerce en mer, a de lui-même transformé toutes les composantes de l'économie maritime, pas seulement au niveau du transport, mais aussi des ports, de la finance, des « chaînes d'approvisionnement » et de la logistique. Bien que de nombreux pays et quelques régions restent, par choix ou par nécessité, plus ou moins exclus de cette économie mondiale en pleine expansion, le commerce international n'a eu de cesse de prouver sa capacité à détruire les obstacles artificiels.

Abstract. The rise of a 'global' world economy, founded on seaborne trade, has itself transformed all aspects of the maritime economy; not only shipping but ports, finance, 'supply chains' and logistics. Though many countries and some regions remain more or less excluded from the rise of the world economy by choice or necessity, world trade has repeatedly demonstrated its power to break down artificial barriers.

• • •

Par 'globalisation', nous entendons le déploiement mondialisé des activités des acteurs de l'économie maritime, sur terre (ports, logisticiens, chargeurs) et sur mer (armements maritimes, gestionnaires des flux), et la gestion des institutions publiques et des firmes (publiques ou privées) à l'échelle internationalisée puis mondiale, donc au-delà des simples intérêts nationaux des entreprises concernées. Un décideur globalisé prend en considération les marchés et les flux mondiaux et gère l'entité dont il a la responsabilité en fonction de ces données et des enjeux géo-économiques: il dispose d'informations, d'une vision et de mentalités, d'objectifs stratégiques, d'un modèle économique (*business model*) à l'échelle de cette mondialisation. La globalisation est bien plus large que l'internationalisation; l'économie-monde maritime a évolué de l'internationalisation à la globalisation, en fonction des mutations de l'environnement géopolitique, des systèmes productifs et des technologies, ainsi que de la configuration du commerce mondial.

Une internationalisation soumise aux aléas géopolitiques

Le transit maritime est contraint à une relative contraction de son extension internationale à cause des retombées géopolitiques de la Seconde Guerre mondiale. Les ports chinois se ferment, là où les compagnies maritimes participaient à l'économie des concessions. Le Japon vaincu doit replier ses flux orientés vers son 'aire asiatique de co-prospérité.' Le démantèlement progressif des empires coloniaux sape parfois les bases des liaisons privilégiées entre les métropoles et les colonies: entre les Pays-Bas et la nouvelle Indonésie d'abord, entre la France et l'Indochine ou entre le Royaume-Uni et l'Égypte; la force des relations commerciales fait prévaloir ces flux classiques, dans le cadre dorénavant d'une certaine mise en concurrence des prestataires maritimes. Le déploiement de la puissance américaine devient tel que les flux reliant l'Amérique latine et les États-Unis deviennent prépondérants, au détriment de la thalassocratie anglaise; le transit par le canal de Panama en profite. La constitution d'une vaste aire économique européenne contrôlée par l'URSS impose une recomposition dans la vie portuaire en mer Noire ou en mer Baltique et mer du Nord. Les secousses du Proche-Orient ont perturbé les flux, que ce soit le sort des oléoducs reliant l'Irak à la Méditerranée, les deux fermetures du canal de Suez en 1956/57 et 1973/77, la guerre entre l'Irak et l'Iran, voire les deux Guerres du Golfe. Des tactiques de blocus commercial et bancaire ont tenté de briser l'ouverture maritime de l'Afrique du Sud, puis de l'Iran.

La relance continuelle de l'insertion des économies dans l'internationalisation

Sur le long terme, le mouvement d'internationalisation aura surmonté ces obstacles récurrents; l'histoire du commerce est celle de la recomposition incessante de ses flux internationalisés. Il aura profité de la réinsertion successive des pays 'fermés' dans le système économique mondial. Cela fut le cas du Japon, devenu l'une des locomotives de la croissance à partir des années 1960, avec ses besoins en matières premières et hydrocarbures et ses exportations – d'où la percée de ses compagnies de transport et transit à l'échelle interocéanique. La Chine communiste a recouru à la colonie britannique de Hong Kong pour maintenir des flux orientés vers le monde capitaliste, surtout après la rupture avec l'URSS en 1960; son retour au sein du système productif mondial depuis les années 1980/90 a bouleversé la donne, grâce aux importations de produits manufacturés, de pétrole ou de minerais (Australie, Afrique) et au tsunami de ses exportations de produits de consommation. Depuis les années 1960/80, les pays 'sous-développés' ont brisé le carcan colonial en diversifiant leurs ventes de produits de base et leurs achats de produits manufacturés. Ceux d'entre eux qui sont devenus des 'pays émergents' ont rejoint les grands utilisateurs des services maritimes. La percée déterminante de la façade Pacifique nord-américaine a stimulé les flux par le canal de Panama et les importations d'Asie.

Les ports de ces régions ont accueilli hydrocarbures, denrées et minéraux destinés à nourrir cette croissance. L'économie minière et celle des hydrocarbures, sans cesse renouvelées sur tous les continents grâce à l'exploitation de nouveaux gisements et au boum de la demande des pays en forte croissance (Japon et, depuis les années 1990/2000, la Chine), ont stimulé la navigation intercontinentale. Cela explique la conception de navires de grande dimension, de pétroliers (*tankers*, puis *supertankers*), soit en direct depuis les gisements, soit en relais d'oléoducs ou gazoducs (à travers l'isthme de Suez, par exemple), de minéraliers géants (*capesize*) et vraquiers, cargos aptes à répandre à travers le monde les produits semi-finis (produits chimiques, ciment) élaborés dans les nouveaux pôles de production ou orientés vers les pôles de consommation.

Un phénomène de compensation commerciale entre les 'sous-régions' du système économique globalisé caractérise la troisième révolution industrielle depuis le tournant des années 1980, dans le cadre d'un nouveau système productif mondial. Les firmes multinationales puis transnationales ont dessiné des espaces de production et d'échanges à l'échelle de grands groupes de pays: ils constituent des nœuds de relations maritimes intégrés, reliant des pôles de production complémentaires, entre lesquels circulent les composants et pièces à assembler en autant de flux intermédiaires. La recomposition incessante de la division internationale du travail et des processus de production au sein de chaque branche d'activité redessine souvent les routes maritimes. L'essaimage de l'industrie automobile américaine puis japonaise a nourri des flux de voitures achevées et de composants, tandis que les fabricants ont exporté des véhicules en pièces détachées à assembler sur le lieu d'importation. Le transfert du raffinage du pétrole au plus près des sites de production, depuis les années 1970/80, a suscité des inversions de flux, en ajoutant au pétrole brut de plus en plus de produits raffinés, comme le prouve le transit par le canal de Suez. La puissance du raffinage et de la pétrochimie des États-Unis (sur le golfe du Mexique) nourrit des exportations vers l'Amérique latine, notamment le Mexique. Le boum de l'industrie aéronautique suscite des flux maritimes pour le transport de pièces et blocs d'avions, de moteurs et d'équipements intérieurs entre les diverses usines spécialisées dans l'élaboration de tel ou tel bloc (au sein d'Airbus en Europe; pour Boeing, entre le Japon et les États-Unis).

Le remodelage des processus productifs s'intensifie avec la troisième révolution industrielle. Le 'toyotisme' (théorisé par William Edwards Deming) prône le 'zéro stock' et le 'juste à temps', une externalisation maximale des composants auprès des équipementiers et sous-ensembliers, d'où l'optimisation de la chaîne d'approvisionnement (*supply chain management*) au nom du 'sans délai' et de la 'flexibilité' dans la chaîne logistique maritime, puis des ports aux zones d'entreposage et de production, en monde d'industries et de services intégré, où les secteurs secondaire et tertiaire sont en osmose. Nombre d'usines ne se contentent plus de vendre dans leur aire de proximité puisqu'elles sont des pivots d'une diffusion transocéane, insérées dans un mouvement d'échanges intercontinentaux de produits, sans plus de rapport avec le pays d'origine de la marque: des modèles BMW fabriqués aux États-Unis sont exportés dans le monde entier; les usines britanniques Nissan font embarquer les 4/5 de leur production vers des outre-mers; les usines de Toyota à Valenciennes (France) et en Tchéquie envoient leurs voitures sur Zeebrugge pour rejoindre Halifax (Canada), Porto Rico, New York, Jacksonville (Floride) et Long Beach.

La Chine, l'Asie du Sud-Est, avec une compétition interne pour attirer telle ou telle spécialité manufacturière, Singapour et Hong Kong (et ses zones franches), et le Japon constituent ce que F. Gipouloux appelle 'la Méditerranée asiatique;'[1] le trafic intra-asiatique constitue un système maritime ample. Le Moyen Orient, avec ses émirats et royaumes, la Turquie et ses 'marches' en Asie centrale et caucasienne, diverses façades latino-américaines ou nord-américaines, le Maghreb, sont aussi essentiels à la globalisation que les sous-ensembles européens. Cet entrecroisement des mini-systèmes de production avec l'animation d'une économie de marché globalisée a déclenché la révolution d'une intensification des échanges, un nouveau mode de gestion du transport et de logistique et des firmes d'armement maritime.

VERS LA GLOBALISATION DE LA GESTION DU COMMERCE

L'économie maritime a longtemps reposé sur des maisons de négoce, souvent familiales, ancrées dans leur pays d'origine et en liaison avec un petit nombre de ports, de chargeurs et de sociétés publiques (pays communistes, puis aussi pays du Tiers-Monde socialisants) ou privées d'exportation de denrées ou de minéraux. Une révolution a entraîné ce secteur à partir des années 1970: la taille géographique, quantitative et financière des marchés est devenue telle que nombre de négociants ont disparu ou ont dû fusionner. De grands groupes ont émergé, en Occident, au Japon, puis en Russie et en Chine: Archer Daniels Midland-ADM (USA), Bunge (Argentine), Cargill (USA), Glencore et Trafigura (Suisse), *Louis Dreyfus Commodities* (France) – avec 230 000 salariés à eux cinq en 2013 –, Marubeni (Japon). Ces acteurs (depuis Genève ou Chicago, pour beaucoup) de la globalisation de l'économie de marché exercent une influence certaine sur la vie des flux maritimes. Les Bourses de denrées (Chicago, New York, Londres, etc., avec leurs marchés à terme) et leurs courtiers et, en amont de la chaîne, le financement du négoce (*trade finance*) par les firmes bancaires déterminent la vie des flux maritimes tout en aval.

Chaque cargo est un pion sur la carte du négoce mondial. Le jeu des cours détermine plus ou moins le rythme des échanges internationaux, selon le prix du fret au jour le jour ('prix *spot*'). Nombre de navires sont réorientés en cours de navigation vers tel ou tel port en fonction de l'évolution soudaine de la demande

---

[1] GIPOULOUX F., *La Méditerranée asiatique. Villes portuaires et réseaux marchands en Chine, au Japon et en Asie du Sud-Est, XVIe-XXIe siècles*, Paris: CNRS Éditions (2009).

et des prix. Cargill affrète 500 navires en 2012, puisque les négociants supervisent toute la chaîne logistique, quasiment du silo de collecte au silo du port de destination. Certaines possèdent une filiale de vraquiers et cargos, comme Louis Dreyfus Armateurs qui, en 2012, possède une soixantaine de navires et en affrète une seconde soixantaine. Parfois, ces maisons gèrent en sus des entrepôts et des ports de transit des pondéreux, comme *GrainCorp* (gestionnaire en 2013 de sept des huit ports céréaliers de la côte Est de l'Australie).

Vers la globalisation du transit maritime

Plusieurs étapes ont marqué l'intensification du transit maritime. Le bloc de compétences classique a prospéré pendant les Trente Glorieuses, dans les années 1945-1975: courtiers maritimes, spécialistes du transit au sein des chargeurs, multiples transitaires dans les anciens empires coloniaux et les ports métropolitains, consignataires. Tous ont accompagné l'expansion commerciale à l'échelle du monde capitaliste et notamment les flux concernant les États-Unis, l'Europe de l'Ouest, avec ses sites portuaires modernisés (équipement des quais en grues, entrepôts frigorifiés, nœuds ferroviaires, grandes zones et entrepôts pour le fret routier), puis aussi le Japon.

Depuis les années 1980, la performance du système toyotiste repose sur l'efficacité de la chaîne logistique, des lieux de production aux lieux de stockage et de redistribution, pour la masse des produits élaborés dans les sous-régions à bon prix de main-d'œuvre. Depuis le tournant du XXIe siècle, la filière logistique est devenue l'axe majeur de la révolution commerciale causée par le système Internet. Malgré la concurrence des 'intégrateurs' utilisant le fret aérien puis le transport routier, l'alimentation en amont des énormes entrepôts gérant les flux à l'échelle d'une sous-région globalisée s'effectue massivement par mer (produits électroniques et électroménagers, habillement; jouets du groupe Mattel, avec un entrepôt à Marseille-Fos pour toute l'Europe du Sud, réceptionnant 3 000 conteneurs en 2012). L'exigence du transport multimodal s'impose de, ou vers, l'hinterland, dans le cadre d'une gestion verticale intégrée: des câbles d'acier ArcelorMittal quittent l'usine de Bourg-en-Bresse par route, puis joignent Marseille-Fos sur la Saône et le Rhône par barges, puis Shenzhen en Chine par cargo, sous l'égide du commissionnaire de transport Geodis-Wilson.

La filière logisticienne s'érige en levier de la troisième révolution industrielle de l'amont à l'aval (transport, entreposage, transit/*freight forwarding*). Cela explique le processus d'intégration au sein de groupes transnationaux, comme la Suisse Panalpina, passée depuis 1954 des flux rhénans à la mondialisation (15 000 salariés en 2007, avec 500 agences en direct dans 90 pays). La Française SDV-Bolloré, qui a réuni SCAC, SAGA et Transcap dans les années 1990, traite 700 000 conteneurs par an au tournant des années 2010: elle est spécialiste du transit Nord-Sud (entre l'Europe et l'Afrique), face aux concurrents nord-américains et asiatiques orientés le Nord-Nord (entre pays développés de tous continents), tandis qu'a percé le Sud-Sud (de l'Asie ou du Brésil émergents vers les pays en voie développement). Plusieurs grands armements maritimes disposent d'une maison sœur de logistique, dans une stratégie d'intégration verticale (comme Mitsui-MOL ou Maersk). Des intermédiaires spécialisés résistent: les Bourses de fret traitent les appels d'offres des chargeurs. Ils proposent à ces derniers, devenus adeptes de l'externalisation dans les années 1980/90 – en perdant une partie de leur savoir-faire historique –, une gestion complète (*total solutions providers* avec des progiciels de gestion et d'optimisation du transport) du processus de transport de port à port et également en-deçà ou au-delà pour le transport terrestre (avec des licences de *non vessel operating common carriers*).

Le financement bancaire des armateurs ou des sociétés d'investissement et de location de navires s'est affûté au sein des départements spécialisés de la 'banque d'entreprise', bien au-delà par conséquent des opérations historiques de crédit documentaire, pourtant encore élargies. Le marché des navires est devenu une sorte de marché à terme, qui facilite le progrès technique grâce aux ventes d'unités défraîchies et au financement des achats. Les marchés du fret sont devenus de vastes bourses mondiales, à l'échelle de l'énormité des tonnages, avec des index synthétiques par types de bateaux (*Baltic Dry Index*, sur le *Baltic Exchange*, pour les produits secs: céréales, minerais, charbon, avec son sous-indice *Baltic Capesize*, pour les minéraliers et vraquiers au format du passage au large de l'Afrique australe). Tandis que l'agence mutualiste de notation et de quasi-réassurance *Lloyd's Register*, à Londres, conserve sa mission, malgré les aléas subis dans les années 1980 pendant une grave récession économique, et les soubresauts liés aux catastrophes, l'assurance maritime s'est reconfigurée en fonction de l'économie maritime globalisée: ses courtiers portuaires renouvellent leur gamme, en fonction des types de navires mis en service, des risques d'obsolescence rapide dus à leur rotation intense, aux risques de piraterie qui ont surgi dans les passages du globe proches de zones de moindre contrôle géomilitaire (au large de certaines côtes d'Asie du Sud-Est, océan Indien-mer Rouge-golfe d'Aden, côte occidentale d'Afrique, Caraïbes–isthme de Panama).

Vers la globalisation de la gestion de l'armement maritime

Des groupes intégrés et diversifiés se sont constitués à partir des années 1960. Les sociétés classiques des pays ayant animé la thalassocratie depuis le tournant du XXe siècle ont généralement manqué les révolutions stratégiques imposées par la restructuration des flux. Par ailleurs, les gestionnaires du transport de passagers se sont effondrés à cause de la disparition des paquebots transocéaniques. Seules de grandes firmes sont devenues capables de faire face aux bouleversements des techniques et donc à la rapidité des investissements nécessaires pour accompagner les mutations des minéraliers, pétroliers, méthaniers, cargos pour automobiles, notamment. La révolution du conteneur a bouleversé les armements maritimes: les premières 'boîtes' apparaissent entre 1956 (*Pan-Atlantic Steamship Co*, qui devient *Sealand* en 1960) et 1968, selon les types; P&O lance en 1965 *Overseas Containers* (premier navire en 1969). La capacité de la flotte de conteneurs bondit de 200 000 EVP (équivalents vingt pieds) en 1970 à 2,2 millions en 1985 et 9,4 millions en 2005; 5 900 porte-conteneurs naviguent en 2010 (14 millions EVP et 186 millions de tonnes de capacité).

Ces facteurs ont convergé vers une globalisation du transport maritime, doublement articulée. La gestion de l'armement s'effectue en fonction des cours du fret avec une affectation des navires au mieux de la demande, y compris avec des affrètements en location en période de boum. Pour les marchandises, aux lignes essaimant des pôles européens ou nord-américains se sont substituées des lignes globalisées de porte-conteneurs (ou cargos de biens d'équipement), faisant le tour du monde de port-relais (*sea hub*) en port-relais: la première en 1984, de la société Evergreen; CMA-CGM anime la *French Asia Line* entre l'Europe et l'Asie avec trente navires de haute capacité gérant la rotation de 110 000 conteneurs par semaine en 2013. Selon la conception de 'port d'éclatement' (*hub and spokes*), chaque pôle-relais alimente des lignes (*feeders*) desservant les ports secondaires des sous-régions, en un cabotage globalisé et modernisé, dépendant de l'implantation des sites de production ou d'entreposage insérés dans la chaîne d'approvisionnement mondialisée.

Le cabotage a évolué, de services locaux à des prestations intégrées dans la globalisation, à l'échelle de sous-régions. Les armateurs du cabotage classique (grecs, indiens, sud-américains, européens) ont effectué un intense effort d'adaptation technique. Les niches procurées par le cabotage spécialisé au sein des sous-régions (redistribution des produits pétroliers raffinés ou du ciment, mini-porte-conteneurs, gestion des navires aux normes *Panamax* entre les deux versants maritimes des États-Unis) permettent à des armements modestes de résister. Des 'autoroutes de la mer' relient ainsi l'Europe du Nord-Ouest et l'Europe du Sud au sein des sous-régions. La fragmentation du système productif a créé un marché pour le transport de pièces d'équipement, à l'échelle des sous-régions, pour Airbus, entre l'Europe du Nord et la Gironde en France; pour les fabricants de grosses pièces élaborées par les industries électrotechnique (installations éoliennes) ou métallique (plates-formes pétrolières, tubes, ponts). Les grands armements maritimes effectuent un arbitrage permanent pour leurs investissements et leurs activités stratégiques entre les grands navires, les super-caboteurs et les cargos, spécialisés ou non, capables de passer par les canaux de Suez ou de Panama; cela explique que les autorités gérant ceux-ci procèdent à des travaux d'élargissement et approfondissement, avec des tronçons dédoublés dans l'isthme de Suez (7% du commerce mondial y transitant en 2001 grâce aux *Suez-Max* de 150 000 tonnes en pleine charge à partir de 1981 au lieu de 70 000) et l'immense chantier de doublement des écluses dans l'isthme de Panama, car 4% du commerce mondial transitent par ses 80km en 2009 (dont 68% en provenance ou à destination de l'une des côtes des États-Unis): à partir de 2016 y passeront des vraquiers ou pétroliers de 150 à 170 000 tonneaux (au lieu de 80 à 85 000) et des cargos de 12 000 conteneurs EVP (au lieu de 5 000).

Tableau 1. *La restructuration mondiale des flottes maritimes: classement en 2005 (millions de tonnes brutes; sans tenir compte des 'pavillons de complaisance')*

Extrême-Orient et Inde	
Japon	98,7
Chine	48,7
Hong Kong	35,7
Singapour	28,6
Corée du Sud	25,7
Taiwan	18,9
Inde	11,9
Malaisie	6,5
Pays pétroliers	
Arabie saoudite	10,5
Iran	7,2
Pays émergents (autres que ceux cités plus haut)	
Russie	16,1
Turquie	8,8
Brésil	7,8
Pays 'classiques'	
Grèce	143,1
États-Unis	44,7
Allemagne	32,9
Norvège	30,3
Royaume-Uni	19,3
Danemark	18,1
Italie	13,2
Suède	10,3
[...] France	5,5

Source: Institut français de la mer, *Marine*, n°202, premier trimestre 2004, p. 11

L'armature des thalassocraties européennes héritée du XIXe siècle et préservée jusqu'aux années 1950 s'est disloquée. Les flottes marchandes des 'vieux pays' ont résisté; mais le patriotisme économique européen doit admettre la fin des armements nationaux, symbolisant la puissance maritime des pays; un processus de concentration a fait disparaître les grands armements au profit d'un leader unique, comme Hapag Lloyd en Allemagne; CMA-CGM est le fruit du rassemblement de presque toutes les compagnies maritimes françaises de bonne taille dans les années 1970–2000, notamment Compagnie générale transatlantique, Messageries maritimes, Delmas-Vieljeux, etc.); sept sociétés hollandaises fusionnent en 1970 dans Nedloyd, qui s'unit à l'Anglaise P&O en 1997; PO Nedloyd finit rachetée par Maersk en 2005, qui la rapproche de l'Américaine

Tableau 2. *Les grands armateurs en 2008 (en capacité)*

Maersk Line	Danemark
MSC (Mediterranean Shipping Co)	Suisse et Italie
CMA-CGM	France
Evergreen Line	Taiwan
Hapag-Lloyd	Allemagne
Cosco Container	Chine
APL	Singapour
China Shipping Container Lines (CSCL)	Chine
NYK Lines	Japon
Mitsui OSK	Japon
Orient Overseas Container Line (OOCL)	Hong Kong
Hanjin Shipping	Corée du Sud
K Line (Kawasaki Kisen Kaisha)	Japon
Yang Ming	Taiwan
Hamburg-Sud	Allemagne

Sealand, passée sous son emprise en 1999. À part celles des États-Unis et de rares européennes, elles sont dépassées par les flottes des pays émergents (Brésil, Turquie, Inde), des pays producteurs d'hydrocarbures et de l'aire maritime de l'Extrême-Orient. La pression de la compétitivité favorise la propriété de flottes massives dans le cadre du statut de 'pavillon de complaisance' accordé par divers pays (Panama, Liberia, Bahamas, Antigua & Barbuda, îles Marshall, Malte, Chypre, île de Man) en une forme de globalisation de l'optimisation des coûts sociaux et fiscaux.

Des firmes transnationalisées (les japonaises NYK, *K Lines* (depuis 1919) ou *Mitsui OSK Lines*, (depuis 1964), la Danoise Maersk (groupe AP Moeller Maersk), CMA-CGM se sont dotées d'immenses flottes de navires commandés souvent en séries par souci d'économies d'échelle aux chantiers de construction navale à moindre coût, d'où la disparition des chantiers historiques européens. *K Lines* dispose en 2012 de 449 navires traitant 344 000 conteneurs. Des sociétés de haut de gamme, filiales des groupes ou non, participent à la mondialisation des investissements en assurant des transports à la fois lourds et pointus à l'échelle intercontinentale (plates-formes pour hydrocarbures, usines à assembler) et en gérant des navires spécialisés (câbliers).

La globalisation a plutôt tendu à disloquer les 'conférences' et les 'alliances' qui formaient autant de cartels pour fixer des barèmes de prix et se répartir des tranches de clientèle. Nées de la mondialisation, elles n'ont pas résisté au choc d'une compétition farouche, animée par des francs-tireurs des pays émergents; l'alliance TRIO (Japon, Allemagne, Royaume-Uni) a tenu vingt ans (1971/91), par exemple. De nouvelles associations se sont cristallisées, tenant compte des nouveaux rapports de force (*Grand Alliance, New World Alliance*, CKYH).

Vers la globalisation de la gestion des ports maritimes

Les cités-ports historiques ont subi le choc de la décolonisation, de l'industrialisation de certains pays sous-développés et de la remise en cause de leur industrie classique (agro-alimentaire, textile) par la reconfiguration de la division internationale du travail. Pendant des décennies, elles ont bénéficié de l'apport de nouvelles branches dans les industries de base notamment (pétrochimie, 'sidérurgie sur l'eau', aluminium) au contact direct avec les matières premières importées, au fur et à mesure de la désindustrialisation relative des 'pays noirs' de l'intérieur situés sur les gisements de charbon et de fer. Elles aussi ont tiré parti des formes de mondialisation qui se sont esquissées dans les années 1950/70, en 'terminus' de flux intercontinentaux (comme pour le charbon d'Afrique du Sud ou américain et le fer brésilien et canadien (grâce à l'aménagement du Saint-Laurent, en particulier) pour les aciéries de l'Europe portuaire du Nord-Ouest). Le Japon est devenu un immense havre d'importation de matériaux et denrées, pour les industries lourdes et semi-lourdes, tout autant qu'un pôle d'exportation de produits manufacturés: le boum des chantiers navals nippons en a été une conséquence, avant le relais pris par la Corée du Sud.

L'ouverture des continents industrialisés a été autant le fait du fort abaissement des droits de douane dans le cadre des Accords généraux sur le commerce et les tarifs douaniers (GATT) que des mutations techniques et de l'offre de matières premières par les pays en développement. Les ports les plus en pointe dans cette mondialisation sont des pôles de redistribution vers l'hinterland, puis aussi, sauf exception, des plates-formes industrielles, avec comme symboles Dunkerque, Le Havre, Rotterdam-Europort, Anvers, Hambourg/Bremerhaven, Baltimore (et d'autres ports de la façade atlantique: Philadelphie, Norfolk, Boston; les ports du Texas; Miami), Yokohama, Kobe ou Nagoya. Le tournant du XXIe siècle voit cette double fonction prendre corps également au Moyen-Orient (Dubaï-Jebel Ali) ou en Asie du Sud-Est (Pusan, en Corée, Kaohsiung à Taiwan, Singapour, Port Klang en Malaisie, etc.) et en Chine (Shanghai, Hong Kong/Shenzhen, Ningbo, Guangzhou, Qingdao).

La globalisation du transport maritime bouleverse la vie portuaire. Le 'juste à temps' impose ses règles de compétitivité aux 'ports-relais', qui s'imposent des investissements d'envergure pour s'équiper en matériels de manutention des conteneurs, d'accueil du gaz liquide, en plates-formes logisticiennes (entrepôts, zones de tri pour wagons et camions), en maintenance des bateaux; les grands armateurs mettent la pression sur les ports. Cette course à la performance bouscule le mode de relations sociales dans ces ports et les statuts des dockers, car, érigés en leviers du progrès dans les années 1940/70, ils sont souvent devenus des facteurs d'immobilisme et de corporatisme, inadaptés aux changements technologiques, à la reconfiguration des sociétés de logistique et aux contraintes de délai fixées par les lignes maritimes mondialisées. Des sociétés se sont affirmées par leur excellence dans le management portuaire, et ont essaimé leur portefeuille de savoir-faire à l'échelle du monde maritime.

À partir des années 1990, l'intégration verticale par le biais des systèmes de multimodalité exprime la quête de l'abaissement des coûts de transaction sur les plates-formes portuaires. Les sociétés régionales ou les filiales des grands groupes mondiaux se concurrencent pour animer une chaîne amont-aval, mêlant transport continental (routier, ferroviaire et fluvial) et relais maritime en une économie de proximité mêlant fret globalisé et territorialisation marchande. Les ports du Havre, de Rouen et Paris scellent en 2012 l'alliance Haropa pour valoriser le nouveau port à conteneurs du Havre (2007) grâce au 'corridor' en amont, l'ensemble (90 millions de tonnes en 2013) pesant plus que Marseille (80), mais loin derrière Rotterdam (442) et Anvers (191). Plusieurs gros armateurs ont créé des filiales communes en Europe du Nord-Ouest (*European Rail Shuttle*, 1994) en levier de leurs opérations de transit maritime sur l'axe Nord-Europe (*North-Europe Range*). *Bolloré Africa Logistics* (entité créée en 2008; 25 000 salariés) gère des concessions portuaires, des entrepôts (ports secs), des voies ferrées et des barges fluviales en Afrique de l'Ouest, avec des 'corridors' logistiques reliant hinterland et ports, puis le transport maritime mondialisé. Mais SDV Asie-Pacifique perce, par exemple en Australie et en Chine: les sociétés issues de la 'Françafrique' historique s'insèrent peu à peu dans l'économie globalisée.

Conclusion

Les fonctions de 'l'économie bleue' ont été sublimées par la troisième révolution industrielle, la globalisation et l'émergence de l'Asie (en sus du Japon): les réseaux maritimes sont des rouages de la nouvelle division mondialisée du travail; les cités-ports ont dû adopter une nouvelle culture de la productivité et de la flexibilité, au nom du 'flux tendu' du fret maritime; les révolutions technologiques (porte-conteneurs) ont une fois de plus accéléré la croissance; et même les canaux historiques ont dû se moderniser. Le plus marquant aura été le relais pris par de nouveaux acteurs (pays, ports, compagnies de transport et de transit, chantiers navals) aux dépens des puissances maritimes ouest-européennes, où seuls quelques champions ont réussi à s'imposer au terme de processus de consolidation capitalistique. Les exigences d'investissement ont été gigantesques chez les parties prenantes de la vie maritime à cause de la course à la compétitivité (prix, techniques) imposée par la pression concurrentielle, à cause du déplacement intercontinental des pôles énergétiques, miniers et productifs et à cause de la remise en cause fréquente des chaînes d'approvisionnement logistique.

America's Pacific power in a global age

ANDREW PRESTON is Professor of American History at the University of Cambridge, and a Fellow of Clare College, Cambridge, United Kingdom

ABSTRACT. *The U.S.A. had long believed that China was the key to the markets of the world. Defeat of Japan in the Second World War made the U.S. the dominant power in the Pacific, but not China as it expected. Instead the U.S. found itself confronting Chinese communism, and trading around the Pacific with coastal states outside communist control. Confrontation was only a limited success, but trade overcame communism and opened the door to China at last.*

RÉSUMÉ. *Les États-Unis considéraient depuis longtemps la Chine comme la clé d'accès aux marchés mondiaux. La défaite du Japon pendant la seconde guerre mondiale fit des État-Unis la puissance dominante sur le Pacifique, mais non sur la Chine comme ils l'espéraient. Ils se retrouvèrent au contraire à faire face au communisme chinois et ne purent établir d'échanges commerciaux qu'avec les États côtiers du Pacifique non contrôlés par le communisme. La confrontation n'eut qu'un succès limité mais le commerce finit par dominer le communisme et ouvrit enfin les portes de la Chine.*

. • .

The country now known and constituted as the United States began life as a series of transplanted colonies of Europeans. They forged new societies along the Atlantic coastline of North America, and they maintained constant contact with their home countries across the ocean. Thus it is little surprise that, for several centuries, the American worldview held Europe as its main ideological and cultural reference point. This Eurocentric perspective has been reflected in the historiography, most recently in the influential Atlantic World school of early modern history which sees the Atlantic coastlands of the Americas, Europe and Africa as an integrated, systemic whole.[1]

Yet the continental United States borders another ocean, the Pacific, that has played an equally important role in the nation's political and economic

---

[1] For overviews of the Atlantic World approach, see BAILYN B., *Atlantic History: Concept and Contours* (Cambridge, MA, 2005); GREENE J.P. and MORGAN P.D., eds, *Atlantic History: A Critical Appraisal* (New York, 2008); and ARMITAGE D. and BRADDICK M.J., eds, *The British Atlantic World, 1500-1800*, 2nd edn (New York, 2009). For a brilliant analysis of the field's evolution, see O'REILLY W., 'Genealogies of Atlantic history', *Atlantic Studies* 1 (2004), 66-84.

development.[2] The Atlantic World may have been important, but so too were what Matt K. Matsuda has called the "Pacific worlds".[3] From the earliest days of the republic, statesmen like John Quincy Adams believed that the United States must expand westward or perish. If the Atlantic marked the natural beginnings of the nation, the Pacific coast was its logical, indeed necessary, conclusion. So important was the Pacific terminus that Adams pursued westward expansion even though it exacerbated sectional tensions over slavery between the North and the South.[4] The Pacific coast was secured in three stages: the settlement of the Oregon Country dispute with Britain in 1846, which ceded the Pacific Northwest up to the 49th parallel; the end of the Mexican War in 1848, which ceded California to the United States; and the admission to the union of the states of California (1850), Oregon (1859) and Washington (1889). By the end of the 19th century, when Americans coveted access to China and seized the Philippines from Spain, the United States had become a transpacific power of the first rank.

Yet, until the 1940s the United States remained one of several Pacific powers. Ironically, it took one of the nation's single greatest military disasters to turn it into a transpacific hegemon. When the Japanese attacked the U.S. naval base at Pearl Harbor in December 1941, they put in motion a chain of events that was the exact opposite of what they had intended. Japan's military never sought the occupation of Hawaii, at least not in the short term. Instead, Japanese strategists intended their pre-emptive strike to be a blow that would knock the U.S. Navy down long enough for Japan to become the hegemonic power in the Pacific and control the entire maritime space between the Hawaiian Islands and the Japanese home islands. But, while partially successful in the short term, the attack on Pearl Harbor was wholly unsuccessful in the medium and long terms. Instead of smoothing the way for a Japanese empire in East Asia and the western Pacific, the attack created the conditions for America's near-total dominance of the Pacific Ocean, from Alaska in the north to Australasia in the south, and from the shores of California to the waters just off the coast of mainland China. In the Atlantic and Arctic oceans, and in many of the world's great seas, the Americans played a cat-and-mouse game with their Soviet counterparts. But in the Pacific, from 1945 until very recently, the U.S. Navy patrolled what was essentially an American lake.

Japan unwittingly facilitated the completion of a process that American strategists, missionaries and merchants had begun half a century earlier. Towards the

---

[2] A theme advanced most thoroughly by CUMINGS B., *Dominion from Sea to Sea: Pacific Ascendancy and American Power* (New Haven, 2009).
[3] MATSUDA M.K., *Pacific Worlds: A History of Seas, Peoples, and Cultures* (Cambridge, 2012). See also THOMAS N., *Islanders: The Pacific in the Age of Empire* (New Haven, 2010); FOJAS C. and GUEVARRA R.P. Jr., eds, *Transnational Crossroads: Remapping the Americas and the Pacific* (Lincoln, NE, 2012); IGLER D., *The Great Ocean: Pacific Worlds from Captain Cook to the Gold Rush* (Oxford, 2013); and ARMITAGE D. and BASHFORD A., eds, *Pacific Histories: Ocean, Land, People* (New York, 2014).
[4] See EDEL C.N., *Nation Builder: John Quincy Adams and the Grand Strategy of the Republic* (Cambridge, MA, 2014).

end of the 19th century, when the United States decided to become a great power and an active participant in geopolitics, Americans looked west, to the Pacific, as the world's future centre of gravity. Control over the territory of East Asia and the maritime space of the western Pacific would afford a large measure of control of the modern, increasingly interconnected, globalizing world. "The storm center of the world has shifted ... to China," Secretary of State John Hay observed in 1899. "Whoever understands that mighty Empire ... has a key to world politics for the next five centuries."[5] President Theodore Roosevelt reinforced Hay's message a few years later. "In the century that is opening, the commerce and the command of the Pacific will be factors of incalculable moment in the world's history," he declared in a 1903 speech. "America's geographical position on the Pacific is such as to insure our peaceful domination of its waters in the future if only we grasp with sufficient resolution the advantages of that position."[6]

With both China and Japan independent, eastern Asia seemed to be the last place in the world not already claimed by either the United States or one of the European powers. But China was weak, and Americans feared that a rival power (or consortium of powers) would come to dominate it, and thus dominate the region and from there possibly the entire world. In 1899 and 1900, Hay responded with two missives to the great powers, known as the Open Door Notes, which demanded that China remain open to trade with all countries and free from foreign colonization or annexation. Historians have for the most part interpreted the principle of the Open Door through a narrowly commercial lens, but Hay intended to do much more than simply protect American access to the China market.

Though Hay did not live to see it, the Second World War provided Americans with the opportunity to seize the Pacific as their "ocean of destiny".[7] This was not the first opportunity to come along, but the settlement after the Great War, enshrined in the Pacific in the three naval Washington Treaties of 1921-22, had proved to be too fleeting and fragile. In Washington, a reluctant Japan had agreed to be shackled to a lower amount (60 percent) of naval shipping tonnage in relation to Britain and the United States. Naval arms limitations worked in the 1920s, when the global economy surged and the Japanese were content to work within the confines of the post-war order. But with the onset of the Depression in 1929, which hit Japanese exporters hard, and the subsequent rise of militarism and expansionism in Japanese politics, control of the Pacific was once again a source of contention between Tokyo and Washington. Strategists in Japan and the United States both realized that control of the western Pacific facilitated control of the East Asian mainland, and so when Japanese expansionist ambitions

---

[5] Quoted in ZIMMERMANN W., *First Great Triumph: How Five Americans Made Their Country a World Power* (New York, 2002), p. 446.

[6] ROOSEVELT T., 'Address at Mechanics' Pavilion in San Francisco, California,' 13 May 1903, *The American Presidency Project*, http://www.presidency.ucsb.edu/ws/?pid=97733.

[7] O'CONNOR R., *Pacific Destiny: An Informal History of the U.S. in the Far East, 1776-1968* (Boston, MA, 1969).

turned first against Manchuria in 1931, then against China in 1937 and then against French Indochina in 1940, it was inevitable that their gaze would turn to the vast maritime spaces that enveloped the Asian continent. The result was the attack on Pearl Harbor, which was supposed to knock the U.S. Pacific fleet out of action long enough for Japan to consolidate its territorial gains in East Asia and Southeast Asia.

America's strategy for victory in the Second World War was global, and underpinning that global framework was a transoceanic vision. Although it is a large continental nation, geopolitically the United States has more in common with offshore island nations like Britain and Japan: with several long coastlines, it is bordered on the east and west by two vast oceans, and much of its southern border is formed by the coastline along the Gulf of Mexico. To the north and south, it is bordered by Canada and Mexico, two militarily weak and mostly friendly neighbours. This is a very different condition than those which have faced powers such as Germany, France, Russia, India and China, which all had extensive maritime interests but were all rendered vulnerable by territorial considerations. Amphibious warfare became central to U.S. military doctrine, just as it did for the British, out of geographical necessity.

In projecting its economic and military power through relatively small standing armies, large permanent navies and diverse merchant marines, the United States behaved much like the Dutch in the 17th century or the British in the 19th century. For the most part, the United States avoided acquiring foreign territories apart from in North America. Those territories the Americans did colonize before 1945 – the Philippines, Guam, Hawaii, Alaska – were key exceptions in that they acted as stepping stones on the maritime route across the Pacific to Asia. Not coincidentally, this policy of island-hopping became the basis for the assault against Japan in the Second World War. Once the Japanese were stopped at the Battle of Midway in June 1942, the Americans slowly pushed them back across the Pacific, culminating in the final air campaigns of 1944–45 and the atomic bombings of Hiroshima and Nagasaki.

On 2 September 1945, when Japan's political and military leaders stepped aboard the USS *Missouri* to sign their terms of surrender to the United States, they effectively ceded indefinite control of the Pacific. Americans had never lost their grip on key choke points for transpacific travel, especially Hawaii but also the islands of Guam, American Samoa and Midway. But victory over Japan left Washington the dominant power in Japan, Taiwan, South Korea, the Philippines and, through its allies France and the Netherlands, Indochina and Indonesia. Americans now presided over a vast maritime space that afforded them virtually total control of the Pacific and its approaches to the Asian mainland, and two of the main rivals to American liberal internationalism – Japanese expansionism and European imperialism – had been battered and broken by the Second World War. In 1947, Harry Truman authorized the creation of the United States Pacific Command, a unified military command that would oversee the entire Pacific ocean from its headquarters in Honolulu. The most optimistic hopes of John Hay's Open Door had been realized.

Keeping that door ajar became one of the driving forces of U.S. foreign policy over the ensuing decades. At first, in the few years after the Japanese surrender on the deck of the *Missouri*, the task seemed straightforward. America's only adversary, the Soviet Union, seemed to pose a threat in 1946–47 to Europe's security, but not to Asia's; indeed, by initially spurning the Chinese Communist Party (CCP) under the leadership of Mao Zedong and instead giving tacit encouragement to Chiang Kai-shek's Nationalists, Moscow seemed to acknowledge that its sphere of influence extended east only as far as the borders of the Soviet Union itself. Yet, in October 1949 the CCP's victory in the Chinese Civil War turned the politics of Asian security on their head. Now there was a new threat to American liberal hegemony: Chinese revolutionary communism. In the eyes of Americans, particularly those in Congress, communist China posed a threat every bit as acute as the Soviet Union did in Europe. The two communist powers appeared to act in tandem, promoting individual designs to conquer their part of the world which could then link up into an unstoppable global force, much as Nazi Germany and imperial Japan had done a decade before. The facts that Mao distrusted Stalin, and that the Sino-Soviet alliance signed in 1950 was more a marriage of convenience than true love, were lost on most Americans. After a premature glimmer of hope in 1945, then, U.S. officials quickly realized that keeping the door to Asia open would require a robust military strategy.

Containment, initially devised in 1947–1949 to keep the Soviets from conquering western Europe, was thus applied to East Asia in 1950 with the communist invasion of South Korea; it was then extended to Southeast Asia in 1954, when the Geneva Conference failed to reverse communist gains in Vietnam resulting from the First Indochina War (1946–1954) between France and the Vietminh. Both American wars that resulted – the Korean War of 1950–1953 and the Vietnam War (or Second Indochina War) of 1964–1975 – should be considered wars of the Open Door, for they were conflicts with objectives that had little to do with the fates of Korea and Vietnam themselves. Neither South Korea nor South Vietnam held any intrinsic political, cultural, historical or economic value to Americans; they were instead important for what they represented within the larger realm of Asian geopolitics. Both wars were about preventing communist China from dominating East Asia and preventing U.S. access to the continent. Should the CCP control Asia and implant pliant revolutionary regimes in Seoul, Pyongyang, Hanoi, Saigon and elsewhere, it would, as Hay had once prophesied, hold the key to world politics. This prospect was doubly fearful if Beijing combined its Asian power with Moscow's European power. The United States had gone to war in 1941 to prevent a similar scenario from unfolding. Faced with a seemingly similar threat in the Cold War, the United States would do so twice again, in 1950 and 1964–65, for much the same reason.

In January 1950, only five months before the outbreak of war, Secretary of State Dean Acheson deliberately excluded Korea from America's offshore defensive perimeter in East Asia. Yet, when Kim Il-sung's communist forces invaded South Korea in June 1950, the United States quickly intervened. After a series of stunning defeats, in September General Douglas MacArthur, the architect of the island-hopping campaign in the Second World War, launched an amphibious landing far behind enemy lines, at Inchon near the capital, Seoul. This bold move divided communist forces and enabled U.S. troops, in tandem with various nations fighting under the United Nations flag, to begin a successful counter-offensive. Within two months, U.S. and UN forces were pushing north, towards the Chinese border, with the intention of eradicating communism from the Korean peninsula. Worried by the spectre of an American-client regime on its border, the People's Republic of China (PRC) dramatically entered the war in November 1950. U.S./UN troops were pushed back south, and by the spring of 1951 the front line stabilized along the 38th parallel – precisely where the war had begun nearly a year before.

The imposition of Cold War geopolitics and ideological conflict onto East Asia led to the division of Korea and China into communist and non-communist sections. In Korea, North and South continued to glower at each other across the 38th parallel, with each claiming to be the sole voice of Korean nationalism. In China, the communist mainland was unable to seize the island of Taiwan (then known as Formosa), where Chiang Kai-shek and the Nationalists had fled after losing the civil war. The division of these countries stimulated and perpetuated the Cold War in Asia, but, along with Japan, South Korea and Taiwan also gave the United States an important foothold at various strategic points along the western half of the Pacific Rim. For a nation that relied on its military prowess in the air and at sea, possessing a chain of strategic allies, from Japan to Korea to Taiwan, was vital. Moreover, to the east, behind this advance chain of offshore islands and peninsulas, Americans dominated the rest of the Pacific, including the Philippine, Hawaiian and Aleutian island chains, and behind them lay the continental bedrocks of Alaska, Washington, Oregon and California, with their large naval bases and commercial ports. All this enabled the United States to play a dominant role in Asian security, more dominant than that of Japan, China, Russia and all the traditional European great powers – a remarkable feat, considering that America's west coast is six thousand miles away from the eastern shore of the Asian mainland.

This commanding position across the entire breadth of the Pacific afforded several benefits to the United States. The first was geopolitical: no matter what happened on the mainland, American power was the dominant feature everywhere along the Pacific Rim, from Southeast Asia up to the Arctic and back down again to the cone of South America. This did not mean that the United States was all-powerful: its ally in China was thoroughly defeated in 1949, its advance into North Korea was checked and reversed in 1950–51, and its war to preserve South Vietnam resulted in the greatest national humiliation in American history. However, these setbacks did little to alter the trajectory of U.S. power; indeed, America's ability to survive stalemate in Korea and defeat in Vietnam relatively unscathed simply confirmed that any rival would have to deal with the U.S. military to achieve its goals, usually at great cost. This gave the United States a determining position in security matters throughout the Pacific world.

Second, and related, this commanding position enabled the United States to implant its economic and political systems at key points, with the potential to spread further afield. After 1950, Japan became an important industrial powerhouse; South Korea and Taiwan followed suit in the 1980s, but even in the decades before, they stood as imperfect capitalist bastions in the face of revolutionary command economies in the PRC and North Korea. By the late 1970s, the tide of political economy was beginning to turn decisively against communism and towards an American-inflected prioritization of the market. Other U.S. allies in the region, from Thailand and the Philippines in Southeast Asia to Chile in South America, followed suit. Liberal democracy did not always follow economic liberalization, as the examples of the Philippines and Chile illustrate, but it was nonetheless clear that the United States had in large part shaped the economic climate of the Pacific Rim. Even the People's Republic of China, under the leadership of Deng Xiaoping, defected from a centralized command economy to the market in the late 1970s.

Much of the growth in transpacific economic ties stemmed from private and public forces working in tandem. The advent of containerized shipping in the 1960s and the explosive growth of oceanic trade both reflected and drove an increase in consumerism in the United States. Consumer demand surged with each passing decade after 1945, and Asian economies, particularly in Japan, Taiwan and South Korea, were adept at supplying this booming market. These private commercial incentives were then given further boosts by Washington's efforts to liberalize trade, predominantly through sponsorship of successive free trade initiatives, or "rounds", under the aegis of the World Trade Organization. The Tokyo Round, a series of ongoing negotiations during the 1970s, nearly doubled the number of participating countries and stimulated trade between the West and the rest of the world. In practice, container shipping enabled this trade to function on a much larger scale, and ports in both the United States and Asia converted their infrastructures to be able to handle containers and the ever-larger merchant vessels that carried them across the Pacific. The boom in American consumerism in turn stimulated the development of major industries, predominantly in financial services and information technology, along the west coast, in and around cities such as Seattle, Portland, San Francisco, San Jose and Los Angeles – which in turn stimulated their commercial exchanges with like-minded cities in Asia from Tokyo and Seoul to Singapore and Manila. Today, nearly all of the world's busiest ports are in mainland China (Busan and Hong Kong are the exceptions), but they've been able to build upon a U.S.-led system established between the 1960s and 1980s in Japan, South Korea, Taiwan and Southeast Asia.

However, the maintenance of this transpacific American imperium was not always so smooth and profitable. The most intractable problem, epitomized by the struggle for Vietnam from the 1950s to the 1970s, was equal parts geopolitical and ideological. If the Korean War provided a difficult challenge that ended in stalemate, the conflict in Vietnam a decade later offered one that was insurmountable. After the Second World War, Washington reluctantly supported the French drive to re-establish its hegemony in Indochina only because the alternative, Chinese-backed communism, seemed much worse. When the Vietminh defeated the French at the battle of Dienbienphu in the spring of 1954, thus bringing the war to a close and signalling the end of the French empire in Indochina, President Dwight Eisenhower was confronted with a choice either to abandon Vietnam to its fate or to inherit the French role. Eisenhower chose the latter course. At the Geneva Conference on Vietnam, which convened just as the fighting at Dienbienphu was ending, Secretary of State John Foster Dulles encouraged the division of Vietnam into northern and southern halves at the 17th parallel. The Eisenhower administration then supported the leadership claim of Ngo Ding Diem, a fiercely anti-communist Roman Catholic, and pumped billions of dollars of aid (mostly military) into building South Vietnam into a viable, independent nation-state. When this project appeared to be succeeding, the Vietminh, which governed North Vietnam, began to support an insurgency in the South, first by helping to found the National Liberation Front (NLF, also known as the Vietcong) and then by sending regular North Vietnamese troops and huge quantities of supplies southward down the Ho Chi Minh Trail. With the South Vietnamese unable to check communist advances, the United States assumed control of the war effort in 1965, first with a massive bombing known as Operation Rolling Thunder and then with the deployment of over half a million U.S. soldiers. Either ineffective or insufficient, or both, the application of American power to Vietnam did nothing to forestall a communist victory, and U.S. troops left Vietnam in 1973. The country was reunified under communist rule in April 1975, when North Vietnamese tanks stormed onto the grounds of the presidential palace in Saigon.

Never had the strategy of containment been dealt such a comprehensive and decisive defeat, yet the effects on America's standing as a Pacific hegemon were surprisingly limited. In large part, this had to do with the changes in political economy that were transforming the Pacific Rim. While the U.S. military was bogged down in the jungles, mountains and rice paddies of Vietnam, the rest of Southeast Asia, from Indonesia to Thailand, was following the example of Japan, South Korea and Taiwan by liberalizing its trading relations and stimulating its manufacturing base. This new outlook, pioneered in Southeast Asia in the 1970s and not in China in the 2000s, in which authoritarian rule was wedded to free-market capitalism, became codified and embedded throughout the region with the founding of the Association of Southeast Asian Nations (ASEAN) in 1967. Some observers, mostly former policymakers responsible for the debacle in Vietnam, later argued that the war contained communism within Indochina and kept it from spreading further, thus "buying time" for the rest of Southeast Asia to stabilize politically and prosper economically, but these developments were entirely coincidental.[8] However, as the historian Robert J. McMahon has pointed out, if there was a link between the Vietnam War and the emergence of ASEAN, it

---

[8] See, for example, ROSTOW W.W., 'Vietnam and Asia,' *Diplomatic History* 20 (July 1996), pp. 467–71.

was because America's allies in the region worried that it was being weakened by the war and would not be able to contain communism elsewhere. ASEAN formed in spite of American power, then, not because of it.[9]

Still, whatever the ultimate effect, it is clear that the war in Vietnam did not deflect the growth of U.S. power in eastern Asia or the western Pacific. In fact, the war should be seen as the last vestige of an old system, grounded in the history of European imperialism and driven by suddenly obsolescent ideological contestation, at precisely the moment when deindustrialization and globalization were transforming the Pacific Rim. It is probably not a coincidence that after five major imperial/ideological/geopolitical wars in four decades – the Sino-Japanese War, the Pacific War, the Chinese Civil War, the Korean War and the Second Indochina War – East and Southeast Asia began an era of relative peace in the mid-1970s, stimulated mainly by the transformation in the region's political economy and its compatibility with the burgeoning consumer market in the United States. It was a partnership based on the most elemental laws of supply and demand: America demanded, and Asia supplied.

Nonetheless, structural difficulties accompanied the growth of international trade and commerce. Economically, the deregulation and deindustrialization of the U.S. economy in the 1970s brought with it profound economic distress as industrial manufacturing emigrated overseas. Latin American nations benefitted by providing unskilled or semi-skilled labour at much cheaper wages than American workers were willing to accept. But the economic boon to East Asia was much greater because Japan, South Korea and other countries were able to combine much lower labour costs with high-quality, high-tech consumer goods, such as automobiles and cameras. With governments encouraging the free flow of international trade and shipping companies making it easier and cheaper to do so, Asian economies imported jobs from America, causing resentment to rise alongside unemployment, and exported consumer products in return.

As a result, by the late 1980s Americans were perceiving Japan as their main rival for hegemony in the Pacific. Japanese auto manufacturers, such as Toyota and Honda, made a better product at a lower cost; the same was true for electronics manufacturers like Sony and Panasonic and games companies such as Nintendo. In a process that essentially used U.S. dollars to augment Japanese prestige, Japanese companies used their profits from selling their products to American consumers to invest in landmark U.S. properties (such as Mitsubishi's purchase of the Rockefeller Center in New York in 1989) and major corporations (Sony's acquisition of Columbia Pictures in Los Angeles that same year). For some Americans, this was a humiliating state of affairs, particularly when the cost of Japan's external defence was paid for by the U.S. taxpayer and the burden of protecting Japanese national security was borne by the U.S. military – which in turn gave Japanese companies an artificial advantage in the global marketplace.

---

[9] MCMAHON R.J., 'What Difference Did It Make? Assessing the Vietnam War's Impact on Southeast Asia', in *International Perspectives on Vietnam*, ed. L.C. GARDNER and T. GITTINGER (College Station, TX, 2000), pp. 189–203.

Yet capitalism is not always a zero-sum game, and the new trading relationship provided benefits on both sides of the Pacific. After enduring roughly a decade of economic distress, the U.S. economy transitioned in the 1980s to a tertiary, services-based foundation that was ideally suited to prospering in a globalized economy powered by transpacific trade. American leadership of the Pacific Rim, then, has survived economic distress just as it had survived defeat in Vietnam. U.S. power has not, however, remained uncontested. More worrying than the rise of Japan in the 1980s has been the rise of China since the 1990s. The PRC's decision to join the global economy was initially greeted in the United States as an unparalleled opportunity. "China is very important to Disney – it will be the No. 1 market for our growth going forward," the company's head, Michael Eisner, predicted in 2003. "We talk to Beijing about a lot of things – motion pictures, television, consumer products, even theme parks."[10] Eisner's comments were a direct echo of American industrialists of the late 19th century, when John Hay's Open Door demanded equal foreign access to a fabled, limitless China market. Beijing followed a path, blazed originally by Tokyo in the 1960s and Seoul in the 1980s, of encouraging rapid economic growth through exporting low-cost goods to American consumers, and then recycling the profits back into the American economy by investing in U.S. assets. In the Chinese case, the investments were mainly Treasury bills – in other words, U.S. government debt – which kept U.S. interest rates low and therefore enabled a transpacific trading relationship not only to continue but to flourish at previously unimaginable levels.

However, China's rise has not been welcomed by all Americans. Where corporations see profits and consumers find savings, the national-security bureaucracy perceives danger. China is unlike any previous American great-power rival: it is an economic partner on such an extensive and intimate basis that observers have referred to the tightly intertwined bilateral relationship as "Chimerica".[11] But its economic power can also appear ominous. China is also America's geopolitical competitor – indeed, one that is increasingly adversarial and confrontational. As China expands its influence by investing vast amounts of capital not only in East and Southeast Asia but also in Africa, Latin America and Canada, it is raising anxiety levels in Washington. The Chinese military may still be far behind its American counterpart in its technological sophistication and ability to project power overseas, but it is now a genuine regional rival. The potential great-power conflict which analysts in Washington fear most is not with Russia, but with China. Economically, Sino-American relations are mutually profitable; geopolitically, however, they amount to what Aaron L. Friedberg has called the 21st century's "contest for supremacy".[12]

---

[10] 'Disney Stepping Up Efforts to Increase Presence in China', *Los Angeles Times*, 13 January 2003.
[11] FERGUSON N., 'Team Chimerica', *Washington Post*, 17 November 2008; FERGUSON N., 'The trillion dollar question: China or America?' *Daily Telegraph*, 1 June 2009.
[12] FRIEDBERG A.L., *A Contest for Supremacy: China, America, and the Struggle for Mastery in Asia* (New York, 2011). For other recent books in this genre, see JACQUES M., *When China Rules the World: The End of the Western World and the Birth of a New Global Order* (New York, 2009); KAPLAN

China's ambitions are also raising anxiety levels in Asian capitals from Tokyo and Seoul to Hanoi and Manila. Chinese ships have clashed with Vietnamese vessels in disputed waters in the South China Sea, while nearby the Chinese air force and navy have created a new atoll which can host an airstrip and docking stations out of landfill. As China tries to exert control over contested maritime spaces in the western Pacific, it is stoking fear among other Asian states, thus forcing them to turn to the only plausible check to Chinese power in the Pacific: the United States.

Nothing illustrates the changing geopolitical landscape – and the endurance of American power in the region – more than the Socialist Republic of Vietnam's overtures to the Pentagon about the possibility of sharing the naval facilities at one of Asia's best natural harbours, Cam Ranh Bay.[13] In his 1966 tour of wartime South Vietnam, President Lyndon B. Johnson made a point of visiting the massive naval and air base at Cam Ranh Bay, one of the war's most indomitable symbols of American military strength. This "wonderful harbor", Johnson said to the troops, "built here by you, will become a source of strength to the economic life of Vietnam, Asia, and this part of the world".[14] Johnson was prescient, but not for the reasons he envisioned: Cam Ranh Bay has indeed become a symbol of Vietnam's economic growth and strategic ambitions, but under a communist government that defeated U.S. forces in the Second Indochina War. After the United States ignominiously fled Vietnam in 1975, Cam Ranh Bay became an important port for the Soviet navy. But the Vietnam–Soviet alliance frayed after the end of the Cold War, and the rapid rise of China, a traditional adversary, has worried the Vietnamese so much that they have begun to look to a new ally to replace the Soviet Union – the United States, the very superpower they evicted in one of the 20th century's longest and bloodiest conflicts.

This remarkable turn of events should in fact be considered wholly unremarkable. America's presence in the Pacific is irrepressible and unavoidable, a geopolitical but also cultural reality acknowledged by leaders from John Hay in 1899 to Barack Obama more than a century later. In a November 2011 speech to the Australian parliament in Canberra, as he was winding down direct U.S. military intervention in Afghanistan and Iraq, Obama announced that American grand strategy would henceforth "pivot" to Asia. "Our new focus on this region reflects a fundamental truth: The United States has been, and always will be, a

---

R.D., *Asia's Cauldron: The South China Sea and the End of a Stable Pacific* (New York, 2014); and PILLSBURY M., *The Hundred-Year Marathon: China's Secret Strategy to Replace America as the Global Superpower* (New York, 2015). However, for a sober and insightful historical overview of Chinese foreign policy and strategic ambitions, see WESTAD O.A., *Restless Empire: China and the World Since 1750* (New York, 2012).

[13] 'Vietnam's Cam Ranh base to welcome foreign navies', *Washington Post*, 2 November 2010; 'Defense Secretary Panetta seeks closer U.S. ties to Vietnam during visit', *Washington Post*, 3 June 2012; 'Changing times: door may open to US military at former Vietnam War hub', *Stars and Stripes*, 18 June 2014.

[14] JOHNSON L.B., 'Remarks to Members of the Armed Forces at Cam Ranh Bay, Vietnam,' 26 October 1966, *The American Presidency Project*, http://www.presidency.ucsb.edu/ws/?pid=27962.

Pacific nation," declared a man who had been born in Hawaii and partly raised in Indonesia. "Here, we see the future. As the world's fastest growing region, and home to more than half the global economy, the Asia-Pacific is critical to achieving my highest priority, and that's creating jobs and opportunity for the American people. ... Asia will largely define whether the century ahead will be marked by conflict or cooperation, needless suffering or human progress."[15]

Obama recognized a fact of international life first identified by Hay: in terms of its domestic culture and public life, its economic development and its national security and geostrategic ambitions, the Pacific has shaped the United States in profound and enduring ways.

---

[15] OBAMA B., 'Remarks to the Parliament in Canberra, Australia,' 17 November 2011, *The American Presidency Project*, http://www.presidency.ucsb.edu/ws/?pid=97064.

Les nouvelles ressources océaniques

Alain Beltran is professor in history and a research director at the CNRS, France

Résumé. *Le pétrole et le gaz constituent le plus célèbre exemple continu de l'exploitation des « nouvelles ressources océaniques ». Rétablie par le forage en milieu marin depuis les années 1920, leur extraction est aujourd'hui possible à des profondeurs pouvant dépasser les 3000 mètres. Ceci implique néanmoins de surmonter des difficultés techniques et écologiques considérables, et n'est rendu rentable que par un coût élevé du pétrole à l'échelle mondiale. Plus récemment, l'exploitation de la mer s'est tournée vers les énergies renouvelables, notamment par l'implantation d'éoliennes en eaux peu profondes et la récupération directe par des turbines sous-marines de l'énergie des marées et des courants. Les projets d'exploitation de l'énergie marémotrice, des gradients thermiques et des différences de salinité restent aujourd'hui au stade expérimental. En outre, réside la possible exploitation des riches gisements minéraux, couchés dans les grands fonds marins, si les problèmes considérables d'ingénierie et d'écologie en découlant peuvent être dépassés.*

Abstract. *The best-known and longest exploited of the 'new oceanic resources' are oil and gas, which have been recovered by underwater drilling since the 1920s, and are now being exploited at depths of up to 3,000 metres. To achieve this requires overcoming formidable technical and ecological difficulties, and is economical only with a sustained high world oil price. More recently the sea has been exploited for renewable energy, with wind turbines planted at sea in shallow water, and underwater turbines directly exploiting the energy of tides or currents. Projects to exploit wave energy, thermal gradients and differences of salinity remain at the experimental stage. Beyond them lie rich mineral deposits on the deep sea bed, potentially exploitable if the various engineering and ecological problems can be overcome.*

.•.

Désormais, le 8 juin est devenu Journée mondiale de l'Océan. Cette célébration n'en est pas moins ambiguë: une consécration mais aussi un appel à la vigilance. L'exploitation des mers et des océans dans un but commercial n'est pas nouvelle. Outre la pêche, les fonds les plus accessibles ont livré des perles, des coraux et d'autres biens précieux. Puis, les techniques de pointe ont permis de répondre aux besoins croissants des économies développées. Dans le domaine de l'énergie et des matières premières, de vastes possibilités s'ouvrent aujourd'hui non sans poser de redoutables problèmes juridiques, technologiques et environnementaux. La mer n'est pas la simple prolongation des questions terrestres:

elle offre des opportunités tout autant que de nouveaux défis dans un milieu différent. De la résolution de ces contradictions dépend pour partie l'avenir de l'Humanité.

Si on jette un œil sur la première grande encyclopédie moderne, celle de Diderot et d'Alembert, on trouve dès le début de l'article 'mer' un historique autour de la question de la propriété des océans. Depuis longtemps, les puissances riveraines ont essayé d'obtenir un accès réservé aux possibilités des profondeurs maritimes. Avec les recherches d'hydrocarbures 'offshore' (au-delà des côtes), les conflits entre puissances voisines ont amené à envisager des règlements internationaux. Le droit de la mer est actuellement régi par la convention des Nations Unies de Montego Bay entrée en vigueur en 1994, douze ans après sa signature en 1982 et après environ trente ans de négociations. À peu près unanimement reconnue, elle a abouti à ce que les océans soient désormais découpés entre une bande côtière qui dépend d'un État et des eaux internationales. La bande côtière est divisée entre la zone économique exclusive (ZEE) et le plateau continental (fond de mer et sous-sol). Dans la zone économique exclusive de 200 milles, les états disposent de droits souverains sur l'exploitation des ressources minérales du sol et du sous-sol. Cette limite des 200 milles marins peut être modifiée dans le cas d'états voisins mais de nouveaux horizons ont pu entraîner des conflits récents comme les contestations dans la zone arctique. Dans ce cas, plusieurs états côtiers aimeraient étendre leur plateau continental officiel. Les eaux internationales sont quant à elles ouvertes à tous mais on peut souligner le rôle d'organisations comme l'Autorité Internationale des Fonds Marins (elle a commencé depuis 2010 à organiser l'exploitation des métaux dans les grands fonds marins). Des phénomènes récents comme la fonte de la banquise arctique viennent ajouter de nouveaux problèmes comme la définition juridique des zones dites de transit.

Les hydrocarbures offshore

'Les réserves d'hydrocarbures en mer représentent en 2010 près de 650 milliards de barils d'équivalent pétrole, soit 20% des réserves mondiales de pétrole découvertes et restantes. Les gisements offshore de gaz en représentent quant à eux 53% (25% des réserves découvertes et 28% des réserves restantes). Les mers et les océans constituent donc pour les compagnies pétrolières un enjeu de première importance.'[1] Dans le domaine énergétique, s'il y a au moins depuis les années 1970 une prise de conscience de la finitude des énergies fossiles, d'un autre côté, la pression de la demande en pétrole et en gaz naturel émanant en particulier des pays émergents ouvre le champ vers des explorations repoussant sans cesse les limites techniques.

---

[1] CHABAUD C., 'Quels moyens et quelle gouvernance pour une gestion durable des océans ?', *Avis du conseil économique, social et environnemental*, 31 juillet, Paris: La Documentation française (2013), p. 64.

Dès l'entre-deux-guerres, sur de faibles profondeurs (Azerbaïdjan et Venezuela), puis à partir des années 1950 dans le Golfe du Mexique, la recherche d'hydrocarbures offshore est devenue une réalité. La mer du Nord (les explorations ont été accélérées dans cette zone après le premier choc pétrolier pour trouver du pétrole en zone non-OPEP) a imposé de nouveaux défis à la fois en termes de profondeur mais aussi de capacité de résistance face à des mers souvent très difficiles. Dès l'an 2000, les deux kilomètres de profondeur d'eau étaient dépassés, puis au-delà de 3000 mètres en 2013 (le record de 3000 mètres a été atteint dans le Golfe du Mexique). Chaque champ pétrolier en mer a sa physionomie et le nombre et la nature des plates-formes varient d'un site à un autre tout en prenant en compte évidemment les questions de coût. Les principales zones offshore sont le Moyen-Orient, en général à des profondeurs assez faibles, et le Golfe de Guinée où de grandes profondeurs sont atteintes (Nigeria, Angola). L'Europe avec la mer du nord et l'Amérique du sud avec les grands champs brésiliens sub-salifères présentent également des réalisations notables.

Les plates-formes appartiennent à plusieurs types selon la configuration des fonds:

- les plates-formes auto-élévatrices ('jack-up'), apparues dans les années 1950, qui supposent une bonne connaissance des fonds d'ancrage et conviennent à des hauteurs d'eau inférieures à 100 mètres;
- pour des profondeurs supérieures, des navires de forage (ancrés ou à positionnement dynamique) et des plates-formes semi-submersibles assurent une meilleure stabilité même par gros temps;
- les plates-formes fixes ('jackets') restent les plus fréquentes mais sont en général limitées à des hauteurs d'eau inférieures à 400 mètres;
- les structures gravitaires en béton: il est à noter que ce sont sans doute les plus importantes constructions jamais construites et déplacées par les hommes (certaines dépassent 800 000 tonnes). On les trouve en particulier en mer du Nord, par exemple sur le champ de Troll;
- au-delà de 300 mètres de profondeur, les structures souples et les plates-formes à lignes tendues permettent de réduire les coûts;
- en très grande profondeur, les supports flottants de production sont de plusieurs types: les plus fréquents étant les FPU (Floating Production Unit) ou FPSO (Floating Production, Storage and Off Loading).

Les différents ouvrages rapidement évoqués sont soumis à des conditions environnementales extrêmement difficiles. La puissance de la houle et l'usure des matériels doivent être étudiés de près. La hauteur des vagues est cruciale (la puissance varie avec le carré de la hauteur). Les têtes de puits sous-marines peuvent être utilisées pour des champs satellites qui ne sont pas trop éloignés des plates-formes de production mais elles peuvent aussi relier plusieurs champs qui dépendent d'une seule structure flottante ce qui permet de baisser les coûts d'exploitation. Fin 2011, on comptait plus de 1300 appareils de forage dans le monde avec une baisse d'activité due à la crise de 2008/9 tandis que la production relevait de 17 000 plates-formes (il s'en construit 400 chaque année).

Il convient désormais de distinguer l'offshore profond (plus de 1000 mètres de profondeur) et l'ultraprofond ('ultradeep') au-delà de 1500 mètres. Les progrès technologiques les plus récents ont permis cette course aux profondeurs de même qu'une meilleure imagerie des abysses et la connaissance des conditions maritimes. Ces avancées datent des années 1970 pour les puits d'exploration et plutôt des années 1990 pour les puits d'exploitation. Quatre cents cinquante nouveaux champs ont été découverts dans le monde par plus de 1000 mètres de profondeur. Si le pourcentage est encore modeste, les découvertes se multiplient à grande profondeur[2] malgré le coût (plusieurs dizaines de millions de dollars) et la tendance récente montre un rythme de découverte deux fois plus important pour l'ultraprofond par rapport à l'offshore.

La France a le deuxième espace maritime au monde avec une superficie de 11 millions de km^2 (zone économique exclusive) et des possibilités de découverte importantes en Guyane, à Saint-Pierre et Miquelon, en terre Adélie (pour le moment aucune exploration n'est possible au vu des traités internationaux), en Nouvelle-Calédonie et dans les parties profondes du Golfe du Lion en Méditerranée. Une découverte fin 2011 à 150km de Cayenne à une profondeur de 2000 mètres d'eau a montré l'intérêt de la zone (tout en provoquant des décisions politiques contradictoires). Les permis et les explorations concernent en particulier l'Afrique de l'ouest, au large du Brésil et le golfe du Mexique. Il n'est donc pas étonnant de voir des compagnies comme Petrobras, Total, Chevron, BP ... concentrer une grande part des investissements offshore actuels et à venir. Toutefois, l'accident de la plate-forme Deepwater Horizon en 2010 a provoqué une très importante fuite et une nappe de pétrole de 20 000km^2. Cette catastrophe a incontestablement ralenti certains projets et revu les conditions de sécurité à la hausse. Shell de son côté a dû faire face à une importante contestation de la part de Greenpeace quand l'entreprise pétrolière a voulu couler au fond de l'Océan atlantique une plate-forme désuète. L'occupation du site et les protestations ont amené Shell à déplacer la plate-forme vers la côte pour en assurer le démantèlement.

'L'exploitation des ressources énergétiques des océans est liée à deux facteurs principaux: la fluctuation des prix des hydrocarbures et l'existence de tensions politiques dans les zones de production traditionnelles.'[3] Les variations du prix du baril de pétrole ont en effet des conséquences directes sur l'exploitation des hydrocarbures: récemment, le développement des gaz et pétrole de schistes ainsi que la baisse rapide du baril de pétrole ont rendu peu rentables de nombreuses recherches offshore, surtout dans l'offshore profond et très profond. Sans

---

[2] IFP Énergies nouvelles, 'Les hydrocarbures offshore', *Panorama* (2012). Disponible en ligne: http://www.ifpenergiesnouvelles.fr/Publications/Analyses-technico-economiques/Notes-de-synthese-Panorama/Panorama-2012.

[3] SALIOU V., 'Mers et océans, nouveaux eldorados énergétiques ?', *Revue internationale et stratégique*, 3.95 (2014) 122.

compter certains gisements en fin d'exploitation: 'malgré des technologies de plus en plus performantes, certaines exploitations en offshore profonds connaissent déjà une rentabilité déclinante (cas du gisement d'Elgin-Franklin en mer du Nord) et coûtent 40 fois plus chers que ceux du golfe arabo-persique.'[4] Enfin, les zones arctiques intéressent les prospecteurs au moins depuis les années 1920 (régions du Yukon et d'Alaska). Les ressources énergétiques de la mer du Nord ont conduit progressivement vers les zones arctiques: Snohvit ou Stochman par exemple. Des pays comme le Canada ou la Russie ont une large part de leurs ressources en zone arctique y compris dans les eaux polaires. Toutefois les conflits de frontières sont aigus dans cette région très prometteuse: 'l'Arctique recélerait 22% des ressources énergétiques non découvertes mais techniquement exploitables de la planète.'[5]

Les énergies marines[6]

En dehors des gisements d'hydrocarbures, les étendues marines permettent d'envisager l'exploitation d'énergies renouvelables dont les capacités, assez difficiles à jauger, sont très importantes (Tableau 1). Cependant, la plupart de ces énergies marines n'ont pas atteint un stade commercial, restent largement expérimentales sauf quelques exemples comme l'usine marémotrice de la Rance (entre Saint-Malo et Dinard, en Bretagne) dont la création relativement ancienne en 1966 permet déjà de tirer des leçons sur cette filière de production.

On peut obtenir de l'énergie à partir des mers et des océans de nombreuses manières dont certaines ont déjà une longue histoire:

- L'énergie des marées à partir d'un barrage ou de différentes constructions sur un estuaire. L'exemple le plus ancien – sans compter les moulins à marée encore visibles – est le barrage de la Rance en France (1966) entre Dinard et Saint-Malo, utilisé commercialement pour ses 240MW de capacité. Le potentiel énergétique reste faible du fait du petit nombre de sites possibles dans le monde. Les sites d'Annapolis aux États-Unis et Jingxia en Chine peuvent également être cités. En Grande-Bretagne, la Severn est un lieu souvent évoqué pour une installation marémotrice majeure: en effet l'amplitude des marées peut y atteindre 11 mètres. Récemment, en Écosse, des rapports plutôt critiques ont freiné le zèle des partisans de cette technique. L'énergie marémotrice est plutôt chère à installer, peut avoir des conséquences écologiques mais sa production est parfaitement prévisible et l'entretien est relativement facile. Longtemps le barrage de la Rance a été le plus important au monde: il est désormais dépassé par des projets coréens et chinois.

---

[4] Ibid., 127.
[5] BUCHET C., Cap sur l'avenir, France Info, 18 février 2014.
[6] Voir les dossiers de Planètes Énergies: 'les différentes catégories d'énergies marines', 'l'énergie houlomotrice', 'l'énergie des courants marins' …

Tableau 1. *Les énergies maritimes*

	Capacité énergétique en GW
Énergie des marées ou des courants	50
Énergie des vagues	2700
Usines marémotrices	30
Énergie thermique des mers	2000
Gradient de salinité	2600
Total des ressources océaniques	7380

Source: *Marine Technology Society Journal* cité dans l'Ocean Energy Report, 2009.

- L'énergie des courants marins utilise aussi les marées mais son potentiel reste assez faible. Les installations reprennent en fait le principe d'un moulin à vent. La première turbine de 1,2MW (SeaGen) a été installée en 2008 en Irlande du Nord. Une utilisation assez habituelle pourrait consister en l'alimentation des îles ou des lieux isolés. Cette technique peut s'appuyer sur les progrès des éoliennes, des turbines électriques. Les turbines sous-marines ont une taille moitié moindre de leurs homologues terrestres à puissance fournie égale.
- L'énergie des vagues (ou énergie houlomotrice) utilise l'énergie cinétique de la houle. En théorie, vu la surface des océans, elle représenterait une source d'énergie de l'ordre de la puissance électrique mondiale déjà installée. Certains pays seraient plus avantagés que d'autres comme dans l'Atlantique nord. Toutefois, comme pour d'autres technologies marines les questions de corrosion, de stabilité et d'environnement viennent quelque peu freiner les espoirs mis dans ce mode de production. En fait, de nombreuses techniques sont possibles pour recueillir cette énergie sans cesse recommencée: des colonnes d'eau oscillantes, une plateforme à déferlement, des caissons flottants, etc. Les projets concernant l'énergie des vagues sont les plus avancés en Grande-Bretagne et au Portugal. On peut citer le projet Pelamis (commencé en 1998) qui est un ensemble articulé de plusieurs cylindres semi-submergés soumis à l'action des vagues. Des vérins agissent sur un fluide qui entraîne des turbo-alternateurs. Le courant est ensuite envoyé vers la côte. En 2004, le système Pelamis a été raccordé au réseau britannique au niveau des îles Orkney. D'autres essais concluants ont eu lieu au large du New Jersey aux États-Unis. Une plus large coopération internationale permettrait sans doute d'avancer plus vite en évitant les doublons. On peut aussi citer les projets nantais Searev, Wave Dragon au Pays de Galles ...
- L'énergie thermique des mers utilise les différences de température entre la surface et la profondeur des eaux (en anglais: OTEC, Ocean Thermal Energy Conversion). Les conditions idéales seraient une différence de température de 20°C et une différence de niveau de 1000 mètres (pour profiter des courants froids venus des pôles). La production d'électricité ne serait qu'un des

avantages de cette technique: on peut penser aussi à de l'aquaculture ou à la production d'eau potable. De très nombreux pays ont fait des essais comme la Côte d'Ivoire, Cuba, la Polynésie française, le Japon, l'Indonésie ...
- L'énergie des gradients de salinité des eaux peut être captée en particulier dans les zones où les fleuves se jettent dans la mer (on parle aussi d'énergie osmotique). À cet endroit, une grande partie de l'énergie est libérée en raison de la différence de concentration en sel. Cette énergie peut être récupérée avec des membranes semi-perméables: soit par osmose (utilisation de la surpression créée) soit par électrodialyse inversée (les ions salins génèrent un courant électrique). La Norvège et les Pays-Bas ont lancé des prototypes. Cette technique en est encore à un stade expérimental et n'est pas rentable pour le moment. L'Inde et le Japon sont parmi les pays les plus avancés dans ce domaine et ont construit des installations de 1MW. En théorie, tout moyen pour dessaler de l'eau de mer peut être inversé pour produire de l'énergie.

En termes de potentiel, l'énergie des vagues ou celle des gradients de salinité pourraient procurer d'énormes quantités d'énergie à l'inverse de l'énergie des marées. Parmi les pays concernés, il faut noter le rôle de leader de l'Écosse et d'une façon plus générale du Royaume-Uni qui peut être considéré comme ayant une forte avance dans le domaine.

ÉOLIENNES ET HYDROLIENNES

Les éoliennes ou aérogénérateurs utilisent la force cinétique du vent pour la transformer en courant électrique. Dégagées des reliefs qui peuvent arrêter les vents, les éoliennes en mer ont une productivité supérieure à celles qui sont à terre, quelquefois dans une proportion de un à deux. En théorie, les espaces marins offrent une certaine latitude d'implantation (toutefois les passages maritimes, les zones de pêche, les pollutions visuelles doivent malgré tout être pris en compte). Les éoliennes en mer ne peuvent être assimilées à une extension de celles qui sont installées sur terre. En effet, l'environnement marin suppose des installations spécifiques et en général la taille des éoliennes offshore est supérieure à celle des éoliennes terrestres. La base doit être solidement fixée sous les eaux. Les éoliennes doivent être conçues pour résister à la corrosion marine et les nacelles sont équipées de grues pour permettre les réparations en quelque point que ce soit.

Les premières éoliennes installées au milieu des années 1980 avaient un diamètre de 15 mètres et une puissance d'un demi MW; les plus récentes ont des diamètres supérieurs à 120 mètres pour des puissances devant atteindre progressivement 10MW.[7] Les progrès ont donc été considérables. Les éoliennes sont en

---

[7] 'L'énergie éolienne en mer', *France Énergies Marines* (Institut pour la transition énergétique dédié aux énergies marines renouvelables), http//www.connaissancedesenergies.org.

général regroupées en parc (on parle aussi de 'ferme éolienne') dans des zones à faible profondeur. On peut citer le premier parc d'éoliennes au Danemark en 2001 (20 éoliennes de 2MW), celui au large d'Ostende en Belgique (éoliennes de 5MW), au Royaume-Uni (7,5MW) ... Ces parcs devraient augmenter de taille pour atteindre d'ici quelques années de 50 à 100 éoliennes de puissance unitaire comprise entre 5 et 10MW. Des éoliennes plus éloignées de la côte sur des bases flottantes ('farshore') sont aussi à l'étude car elles permettraient de s'affranchir des faibles profondeurs jusqu'à présent nécessaires. Un ancrage au moyen de câbles permettrait en outre de faire des économies de matériaux.

Malgré tout, les éoliennes en mer coûtent nettement plus cher que les installations à terre, ne serait-ce que parce que leurs structures sont soumises aux effets des courants. Fatalement, la maintenance est également plus complexe puisqu'il faut se déplacer en mer, avec des navires adaptés et souvent dans conditions maritimes difficiles. De même, la connexion électrique entre l'éolienne et la côte demande des installations complexes (par exemple un acheminement en courant continu avec conversion à l'arrivée). Le secteur des éoliennes est relativement concentré sur le plan industriel: la société allemande Siemens est largement leader en Europe tandis que chez les opérateurs, l'allemand EON, le suédois Vattenfall et le danois DONG représentent à eux trois près de 50% de la capacité éolienne offshore (2012). Cette répartition souligne le rôle pionnier de ces trois pays, en y ajoutant la Grande-Bretagne qui est un leader mondial en termes de capacité installée, mais on peut aussi souligner les conditions optimales que présentent les pays du nord de l'Europe (fortes densités, vents puissants et réguliers). En dehors de l'Europe (environ 5000MW de capacité en 2012), la Chine se plaçait en 2012 en troisième position toujours en termes de capacité installée. La France s'est lancée plus tardivement dans les grands parcs éoliens: un certain nombre de sites sont concernés par des appels d'offres pour une capacité de 2000MW qui devrait être portée à 6000MW d'éoliennes offshore en 2020.

Les hydroliennes sont des turbines sous-marines qui génèrent de l'électricité. La masse de l'eau étant très largement supérieure à celle de l'air, une hydrolienne plongée en mer doit fournir plus d'énergie qu'une éolienne terrestre. Les courants étant prévisibles, il est assez facile de calculer les puissances et les productions d'électricité. En conséquence, l'Europe posséderait un potentiel énergétique très important que les hydroliennes pourraient capter. C'est une énergie renouvelable mais qui doit s'adapter à des conditions assez spécifiques. Les études d'impact en cours étudient les possibles conséquences sur la flore et la faune sans compter les inquiétudes des pêcheurs au chalut. Cependant, une des questions majeures à résoudre semble être celle de la maintenance car l'érosion des pales (à cause du sable) ou l'action des algues demandent un entretien régulier. La question de l'arrivée du courant sur la côte n'est pas non plus très simple d'un point de vue environnemental. Britanniques et Français ont les projets les plus avancés. On peut citer les essais faits par EDF dans la zone de Paimpol-Bréhat avec le soutien de l'ADEME et du fonds européen FEDER. Un câble de 15 kilomètres joint l'hydrolienne à la côte. Une mise en service du parc de démonstration était prévue pour 2015 ('les Bretons seront les premiers à s'éclairer aux courants marins' écrit fièrement un quotidien régional).[8] On peut encore citer des prototypes en Norvège et en Floride (dans ce dernier cas, les premières expériences datent des années 1980: un parc de turbines de 20kW avec des hélices à trois pales est essayé depuis 2006). Les hydroliennes restent pour le moment d'un coût élevé mais les essais en cours permettent d'espérer des progrès sensibles. En effet, hydroliennes et énergie houlomotrice sont en phase de développement mais à un meilleur niveau que l'éolien à ses débuts.

Les richesses nouvelles des abysses

L'eau de mer elle-même contient de nombreuses ressources mais en quantités en général très faibles. Par exemple l'uranium dissous dans l'eau de mer représente une source très importante, bien plus importante en théorie que les mines terrestres recélant ce matériau indispensable à l'énergie nucléaire. Reste à trouver le moyen d'absorber et de concentrer l'uranium dissous en très faible quantité. Après les premiers résultats des laboratoires japonais, récemment, l'Oak Ridge National Laboratory américain a mis au point un matériau adsorbant (qui retient les matières en suspension dans un liquide) assez efficace et réutilisable. Lors d'un symposium (2012), les carapaces de crevettes ont été évoquées comme matériau adsorbant biodégradable.[9]

La connaissance des grands fonds quant à elle reste encore largement lacunaire. La plongée dans les abysses relève d'exploits technologiques au moins aussi spectaculaires que la conquête de la lune (plutôt bien cartographiée) ou celle de Mars. Dans un monde sans cesse plus anxieux face à la pénurie possible en ressources finies, les océans peuvent-ils apporter une réponse ou tout au moins quelques espoirs ? Les grands fonds sont désormais mieux connus et on sait que d'importants gisements de métaux (cobalt, fer, platine, nickel, cuivre, terres rares ...) existent entre quelques centaines de mètres de profondeur et plusieurs milliers de mètres. Certes les ressources sont importantes mais deux écueils majeurs viennent tempérer les optimismes: d'une part, technologiquement, il faudra travailler à des profondeurs importantes; d'autres part, les écosystèmes découverts dans l'ultra-profond sont riches et fragiles à la fois. Plusieurs ressources majeures intéressent tout particulièrement les compagnies internationales: les dépôts placériens, les nodules polymétalliques, les encroûtements et les sulfures hydrothermaux.

- Les dépôts placériens: issus des alluvions, ils se rencontrant à faible profondeur sur le plateau continental mais aussi dans les grands fonds. Ils sont riches en métaux lourds et en éléments non métalliques. Les exploitations sont liées aux cours internationaux mais on peut citer l'exemple de l'or

---

[8] 'Hydrolien, l'Europe pousse à la consommation', *Ouest France*, 2 octobre 2014.
[9] http://www.enerzine.com/2/14337+extraire-de-luranium-a-partir-de-leau-de-mer-bientot-une-realite+.html.

au large de l'Alaska, l'étain au large de la Thaïlande, les diamants au large de la Namibie, mais le cas le plus fréquent est l'exploitation des sables et graviers pour la construction.
- Les nodules polymétalliques sont des boules d'une dizaine de centimètres de diamètre composés de cristaux d'oxyde de fer et de manganèse dans lesquels on peut trouver du cuivre, du cobalt, du nickel et même des terres et métaux rares (lithium, thallium, molybdène, tellure ...). Ces nodules se trouvent en général à une profondeur comprise entre 3 et 5000 mètres. 'La région d'exploration la plus intéressante actuellement connue est la zone Clarion-Clipperton, dans le Pacifique nord. Dans ce secteur plusieurs permis d'exploration ont été accordés par l'autorité internationale des fonds marins (AIFM). Les nodules y sont particulièrement concentrés en cuivre, en nickel et en manganèse.'[10] Il est délicat de faire des prévisions mais l'ESCO (expertise scientifique collective) demandée au CNRS et à l'IFREMER[11] conclut que dans la région de l'océan Pacifique la plus riche en nodules (Clarion-Clipperton), soit 15% de la surface de cet océan, le poids total des nodules est estimé à 34 milliards de tonnes, soit 6000 fois plus de thallium, trois plus de cobalt, plus de manganèse et de nickel que la totalité des ressources connues hors des océans et des mers. Ayant dépassé la recherche fondamentale, les organismes spécialisés comme l'IFREMER en France sont désormais sollicités dans une perspective d'exploitation des nodules polymétalliques.
- Les encroûtements sont également composés d'oxyde de fer et de manganèse avec une forte teneur en cobalt, platine et tellure. On peut aussi en extraire des métaux comme le titane, le vanadium, le cérium, le zirconium, le phosphore. Les dépôts riches essentiellement en cobalt et platine se trouvent en particulier en Polynésie. Les encroûtements ont une épaisseur qui peut atteindre 25 centimètres mais sur des surfaces importantes, sur les reliefs sous-marins et près des volcans immergés, entre 400 et 4000 mètres de profondeur. Des estimations donnent comme surface des encroûtements sous-marins plus de 6 millions de km^2 (douze fois la superficie de la France) soit près de 2% de la surface des océans.
- Les sulfures hydrothermaux ont été découverts plus récemment mais constituent un des grands espoirs pour l'avenir. Car ces sulfures apportent aussi bien des métaux de base (cuivre, zinc, plomb), des métaux précieux (argent et or) que des éléments rares (indium, sélénium, germanium). Selon le contexte (volcanique, sédimentaire, continental) et la localisation, les métaux sont différents. On trouve plus de chrome dans les fosses océaniques, plus de cuivre et de zinc sur la dorsale. Les gisements hydrothermaux se trouvent le long des 60 000km des dorsales océaniques

---

[10] FOUQUET Y., 'Les ressources minérales marines. État des connaissances sur l'importance des dépôts', *Annales des mines. Responsabilité et environnement*, 70.2 Paris: Éditions Eska (2013), p. 51.
[11] PIGENET Y., 'Exploiter les profondeurs des océans', *Le Journal du CNRS*, 277 (2014), 45.

Les ressources marines ne s'arrêtent pas là. De grands espoirs sont placés dans les hydrates de méthane qui se situent à des profondeurs variables mais constitueraient une source de carbone de très grande taille. Toutefois les difficultés techniques de récupération ne semblent pas encore résolues, sans compter que ce sont évidemment des sources de gaz à effet de serre. Les possibilités de récupérer de l'hydrogène en profondeur sont également étudiées ainsi que l'utilisation des algues en tant que biocarburants.

Une telle richesse attire bien évidemment les grandes sociétés. Déjà près de 2 millions de km² aux fonds des océans ont fait l'objet de demandes de permis d'exploration. Le stade actuel en est encore à la connaissance des gisements avant de passer à une phase d'exploitation. Les sociétés intéressées communiquent assez peu sur les moyens à mettre en œuvre. Il y a encore peu d'études par exemple sur les conséquences environnementales de l'exploitation des grandes profondeurs. Des questions comme celles du rejet dans la mer des déchets miniers doivent encore largement être étudiées car elles peuvent avoir de lourdes conséquences comme la dissémination de métaux lourds ou l'ensevelissement des espèces existantes dans les grands fonds. Les animaux qui vivent à ces profondeurs ont des métabolismes lents et une résilience éventuelle peu rapide. Les fonds marins sont à cette profondeur fragiles et les cicatrices causées par des prélèvements de nodules restent, semble-t-il, longtemps visibles. Il y a dans les grandes profondeurs un équilibre qui a mis longtemps à s'établir qui peut être vite déstabilisé. Certaines questions sont mal connues comme la responsabilité des milieux marins profonds dans les échanges avec les zones supérieures. Éviter une exploitation 'sauvage' mais aller vers une maîtrise de l'exploitation des grands fonds, tel est le défi d'aujourd'hui et de demain.

La mer offre donc des ressources importantes – mais non infinies – sur le plan énergétique. Le défi n'est pas seulement technologique: il faudra accéder à des possibilités en milieu complexe sinon hostile. Le challenge est aussi de ne pas détruire des écosystèmes fragiles, lents à se reconstituer mais sans doute essentiels aux grands équilibres naturels. Pour l'énergie comme pour les matières premières, il faudra trouver un équilibre entre les ressources exploitables, le degré d'intensité de leur exploitation et la modération dans les besoins mondiaux en énergie et matières premières. L'exploitation des océans et des mers suppose en conséquence une prise de conscience, une nouvelle solidarité internationale donc un certain volontarisme: 'Constituer une société de l'océan mondial, affirmer une citoyenneté de l'océan, impulser une appartenance au monde de la mer.'[12]

---

[12] LEFEBVRE C., 'Pour une gouvernance effective et durable des océans', *Annales des Mines. Responsabilité et environnement*, 70.2, Paris: Éditions Eska (2013), p. 80.

Hiérarchies portuaires dans le monde et changements régionaux de connectivité maritime, 1890–2010

César Ducruet is a researcher at the CNRS, Paris, France and Bruno Marnot is a professor of contemporary history at the University of La Rochelle, France

Résumé. *Les statistiques souvent incomplètes et faussées du commerce maritime international peuvent être remplacées par une analyse de la circulation entre les ports, telle que mesurée par le « Lloyd's Shipping Index ». Jusqu'à la seconde guerre mondiale, les ports britanniques et d'Europe occidentale demeurèrent les centres névralgiques du commerce international mais par la suite, la puissance économique et politique des États-Unis s'exprima à travers la densité de leur commerce extérieur. À la fin du XXe siècle, le commerce international devint multipolaire, sans qu'aucun pays dominant ne se détache.*

Abstract. *Incomplete and distorted statistics of international seaborne trade can be replaced by an analysis of flows from port to port drawn from Lloyd's Shipping Index. Up until the Second World War, British and Western European ports remained the centres of international trade. After it, the political and economic power of the U.S.A. was expressed by the density of its overseas trade. By the end of the 20th century world trade was multipolar, with no one dominant country.*

.•.

Introduction

Le rôle du fait maritime dans l'évolution des sociétés humaines est difficile à évaluer faute d'informations précises sur l'importance même de l'activité maritime à l'échelle mondiale. Les statistiques de tonnage portuaire ne couvrent que partiellement le globe ou la période contemporaine. Le recours aux pavillons pour comparer la taille de la flotte des pays reste un pis-aller eu égard aux immatriculations échappant aux contraintes fiscales. Les nombreux travaux faisant le point sur une région et/ou une période donnée sont difficilement synthétisables tant les sources utilisées diffèrent. L'une des rares solutions restantes est de considérer la façon dont ports, régions, ou nations sont reliés les uns aux autres par les flux du commerce maritime. Ceci est possible grâce à la redécouverte d'archives jusqu'ici inexploitées, celles de l'assureur maritime Lloyd's sur les mouvements de navires dans le monde, publiées depuis l'année 1696 de façon quotidienne ou hebdomadaire.

Présentation de la source et résultats préliminaires

La présente analyse propose ainsi de mesurer le nombre d'escales de navires par pays et couple de pays au niveau mondial à cinq dates-clé de la période contemporaine (1890, 1925, 1960, 1985 et 2008). Même si une part d'arbitraire peut apparaître dans leur choix et pourrait donner l'impression d'orienter l'étude, elles ont été choisies selon trois critères complémentaires: une certaine régularité de la fréquence, l'exclusion des séquences de grands conflits internationaux ou des crises économiques internationales et surtout des moments qui apparaissent historiquement signifiants: 1890 correspond au cœur de la mondialisation de la deuxième moitié du XIXe siècle, 1925 à une année 'normale' d'échanges internationaux dans l'entre-deux-guerres, 1960 au cœur de la période de croissance mondiale des trente années d'après-guerre, 1985 au début de la mondialisation de la fin du XXe siècle et à la déstabilisation du bloc soviétique, enfin 2008 à la situation de la mondialisation au début du XXIe siècle, avant la crise financière des subprimes.

Le *Shipping Index* recense le dernier mouvement connu de chaque navire répertorié par Lloyd's, soit environ 80% de la flotte mondiale actuelle (Ducruet et al., 2015). Le nombre d'escales par pays et couple de pays est l'indicateur le plus comparable sur la période, même s'il a l'inconvénient de ne pas tenir compte de la taille des navires. En revanche, il exprime bien la *fréquence* de l'activité maritime et constitue par-là un bon indicateur de puissance économique et logistique des états. Le découpage actuel des frontières étatiques permet de retracer l'évolution des pays sur la base d'un même territoire, en dépit des remodelages plus ou moins profonds ayant eu lieu.

Tout d'abord l'on s'intéresse au réseau maritime mondial des flux entre pays et à sa structure d'ensemble, qui par le recours à quelques indicateurs synthétiques nous renseigne beaucoup sur la logique globale des échanges (Tableau 1). De façon logique, le nombre de pays et de navires a cru très régulièrement sur toute la période, reflétant ainsi l'augmentation continuelle des partenaires commerciaux et de la flotte mondiale, tous trafics confondus. Le nombre total d'escales dans le monde reflète avant tout des périodes de croissance et de crise. Or si les impacts respectifs de la Seconde Guerre Mondiale (1946–1951) ou des chocs pétroliers (1973 et 1979) étaient attendus, le déclin du nombre d'escales à partir de 1995 (on retrouve en 2008 un niveau inférieur à 1925), lui, s'explique davantage par la rationalisation des escales par les compagnies maritimes. En effet, le nombre moyen d'escales par navire a considérablement chuté dans la période récente, passant d'environ 1 en 1890 à 0,5 en 2008.

D'autres tendances opposent nettement les périodes d'avant et après 1970, comme la baisse de la concentration du nombre d'escales entre les pays (Gini, HHI), ce qui est dû à l'expansion géographique du commerce maritime. En revanche, si le réseau se consolide, eu égard à l'augmentation du nombre de liens inter-pays jusque vers 1990, on observe comme pour les escales une baisse récente depuis 1995, elle aussi due à la rationalisation des escales, ce qui se reflète aussi dans la baisse récente du nombre maximum et moyen de liaisons dont un pays peut

Tableau 1. *Evolution du réseau maritime mondial, 1890-2008*

Year	No. countries	No. vessels	No. vessel calls	Calls/vessels	Gini coefficient	HHI index	No. links	Clustering coefficient	Eccentricity	Max. degree	Avg. degree	Power-law exponent
1890	122	8,781	17,950	1.023	**0.823**	**0.080**	749	0.621	0.472	94	12.3	**0.753**
1925	150	12,460	40,704	**1.621**	**0.832**	**0.075**	1,333	**0.676**	0.481	114	17.8	**0.627**
1930	150	12,144	**42,154**	**1.730**	**0.825**	**0.075**	1,417	**0.671**	0.535	108	18.9	**0.601**
1935	146	11,236	38,836	**1.772**	**0.809**	**0.072**	1,468	**0.650**	0.574	104	20.1	**0.579**
1940	145	11,651	39,162	**1.767**	**0.811**	**0.080**	1,454	**0.758**	0.500	102	20.0	**0.577**
1946	152	14,736	32,448	1.118	**0.801**	**0.077**	1,291	0.602	0.481	109	17.0	**0.677**
1951	149	11,815	32,088	**1.390**	0.779	**0.054**	1,557	**0.663**	0.533	107	20.9	**0.562**
1960	**168**	14,317	**42,698**	**1.525**	0.770	0.046	**2,101**	**0.665**	0.632	**122**	25.0	**0.553**
1965	166	16,265	**58,044**	**1.830**	0.784	**0.058**	**2,364**	**0.667**	0.596	**129**	28.5	0.492
1970	**169**	15,948	**45,412**	**1.412**	0.741	0.039	**2,568**	0.642	0.612	**129**	30.4	0.442
1975	164	**20,115**	**43,848**	1.068	0.735	0.034	**2,474**	**0.660**	0.615	**123**	30.2	0.437
1980	166	**21,066**	40,446	0.953	0.731	0.031	**2,505**	**0.660**	0.647	**126**	30.2	0.441
1985	**173**	**22,942**	**44,034**	0.927	0.741	0.030	**2,632**	0.619	0.651	**125**	30.4	0.460
1990	**173**	**23,806**	**57,456**	1.142	0.753	0.031	**3,091**	**0.662**	0.637	**136**	35.7	0.341
1995	**175**	**21,423**	**46,482**	1.022	0.743	0.028	**2,864**	**0.651**	0.642	**127**	32.7	0.388
2000	**182**	**22,162**	**42,552**	0.875	0.764	0.030	**2,325**	0.580	**0.670**	113	25.6	**0.561**
2008	**177**	**25,212**	28,564	0.518	0.752	0.027	1,680	0.522	**0.595**	92	19.0	**0.695**

N.B. Les chiffres en caractères gras sont plus élevés que la moyenne de la période

bénéficier (degré). Le maillage du réseau (excentricité) s'est renforcé, permettant des liens plus directs entre pays, tandis que la hiérarchisation du réseau (loi de puissance) a augmenté fortement et très rapidement en fin de période (1995-2008), retrouvant alors un niveau initial. Ainsi, face à la croissance des échanges, le réseau maritime s'est densifié mais en même temps a connu une centralisation et rationalisation récente qui rappelle la configuration d'il y a plus d'un siècle.

La cartographie du nombre d'escales par pays montre bien en quoi l'évolution du réseau fut également marquée par d'importants changements géographiques (Figure 1). Ce glissement de l'Atlantique au Pacifique est bien l'une des causes des tendances lourdes observées: l'allongement des distances parcourues a accentué la nécessité de centraliser les trafics en certains points stratégiques du globe. L'une des stratégies des acteurs maritimes mais aussi des Etats a donc été de se spécialiser dans le trafic de transit, une façon pour ces derniers de garder la mainmise sur l'architecture mondiale des flux non seulement physiques mais informationnels.

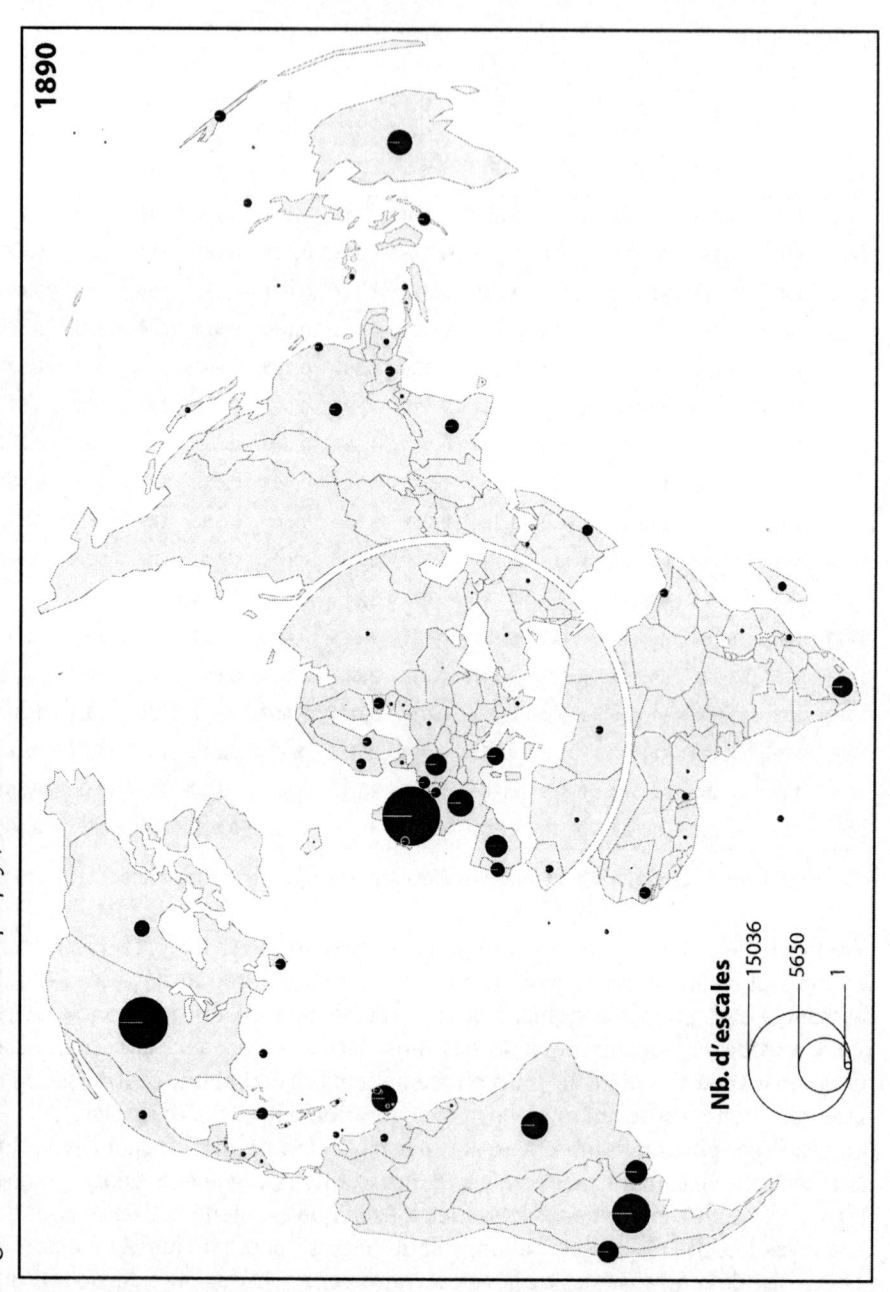

Fig. 1. *Nombre d'escales de navires par pays, 1890–2008*

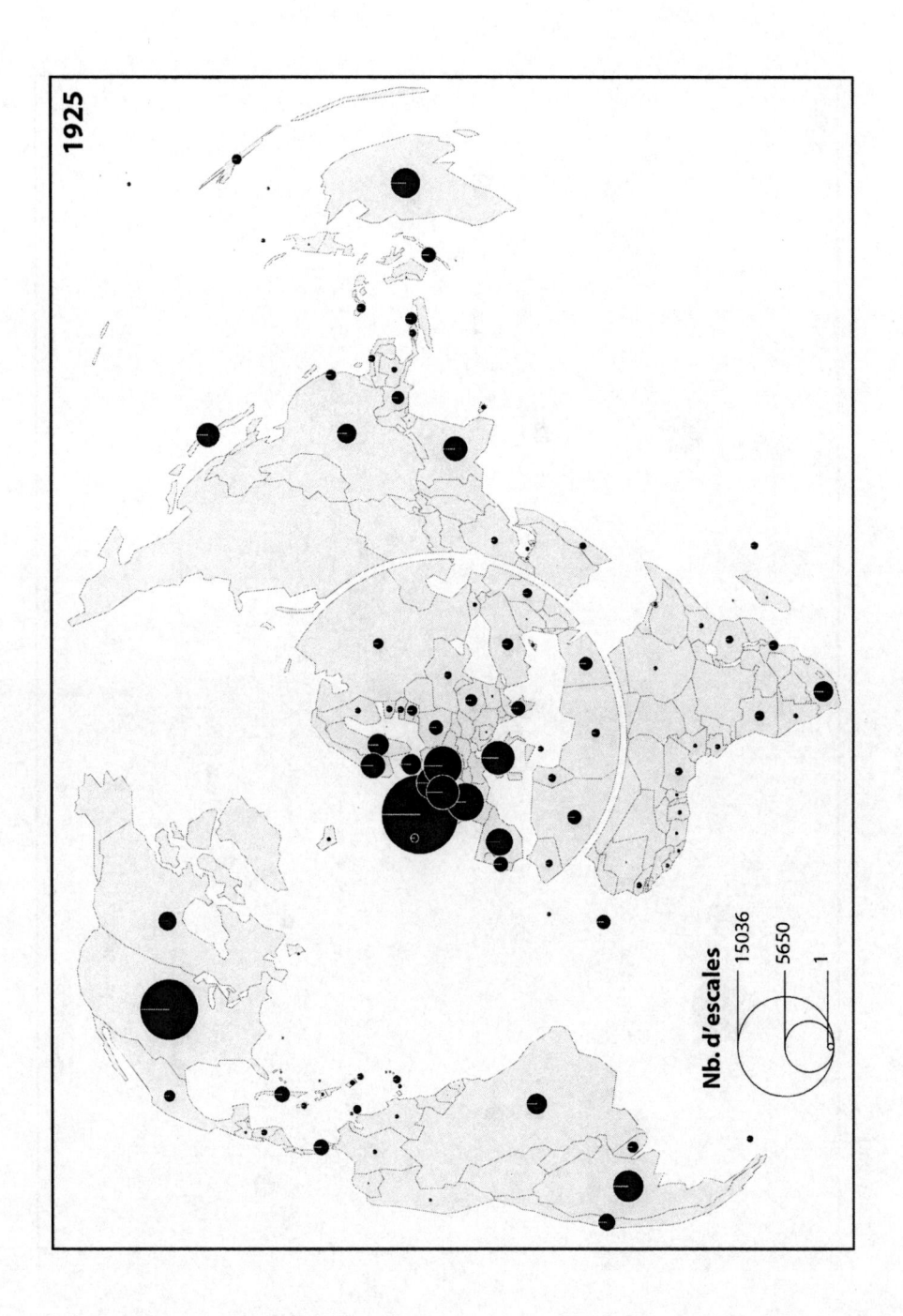

Hiérarchies portuaires dans le monde, 1890–2010

Fig. 1. *(cont)*

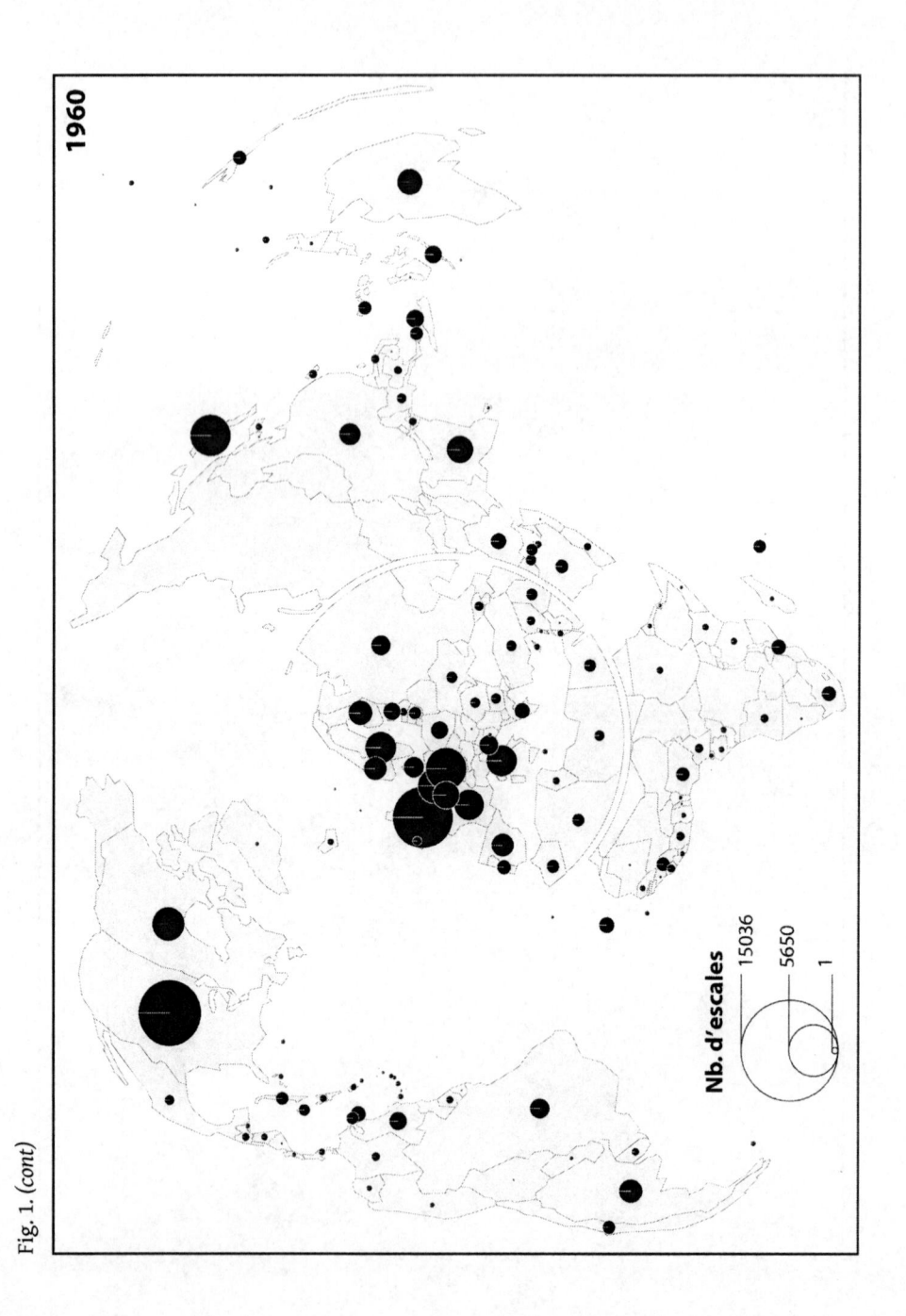

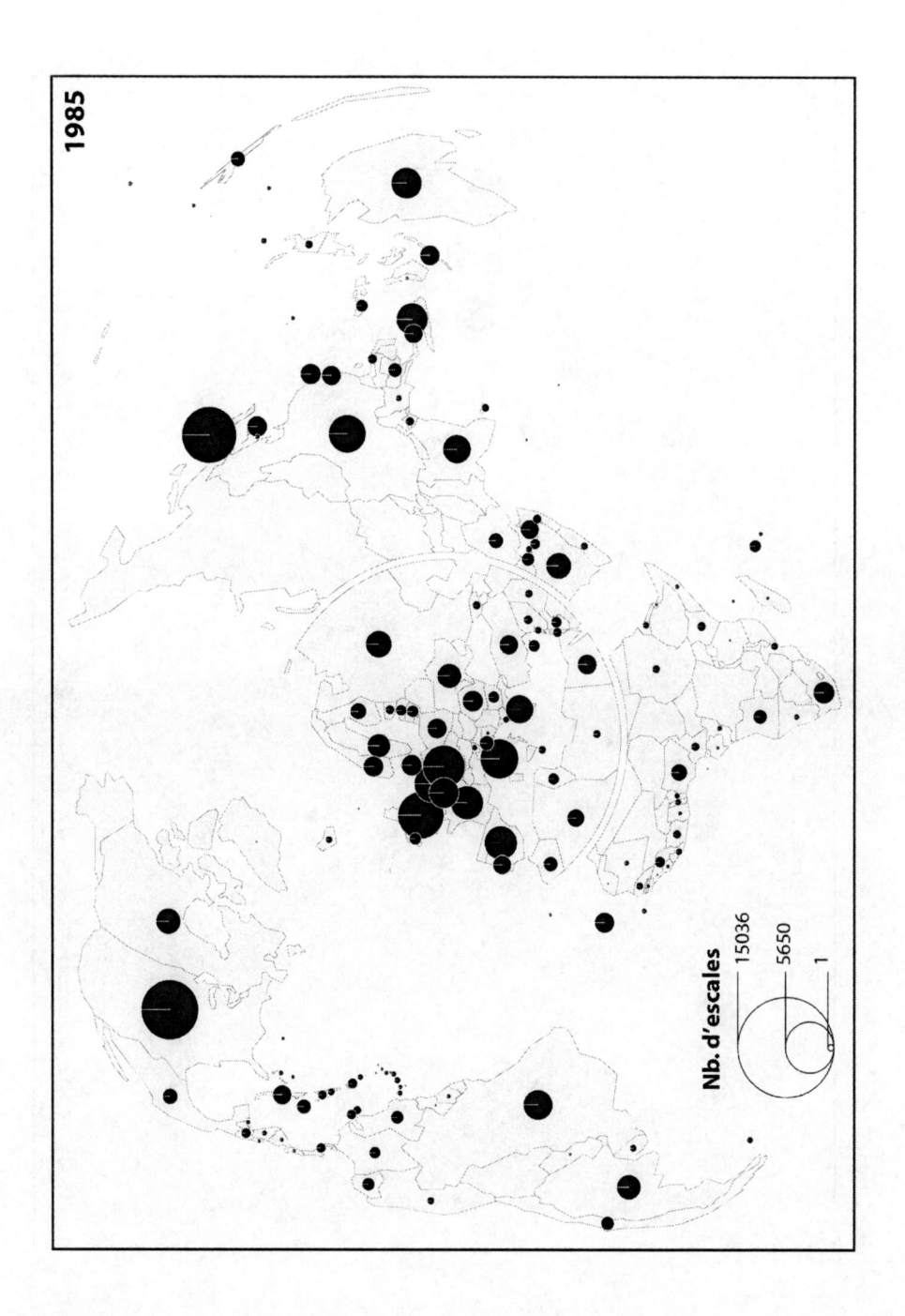

HIÉRARCHIES PORTUAIRES DANS LE MONDE, 1890–2010

1985

Nb. d'escales
15036
5650
1

Fig. 1. (cont)

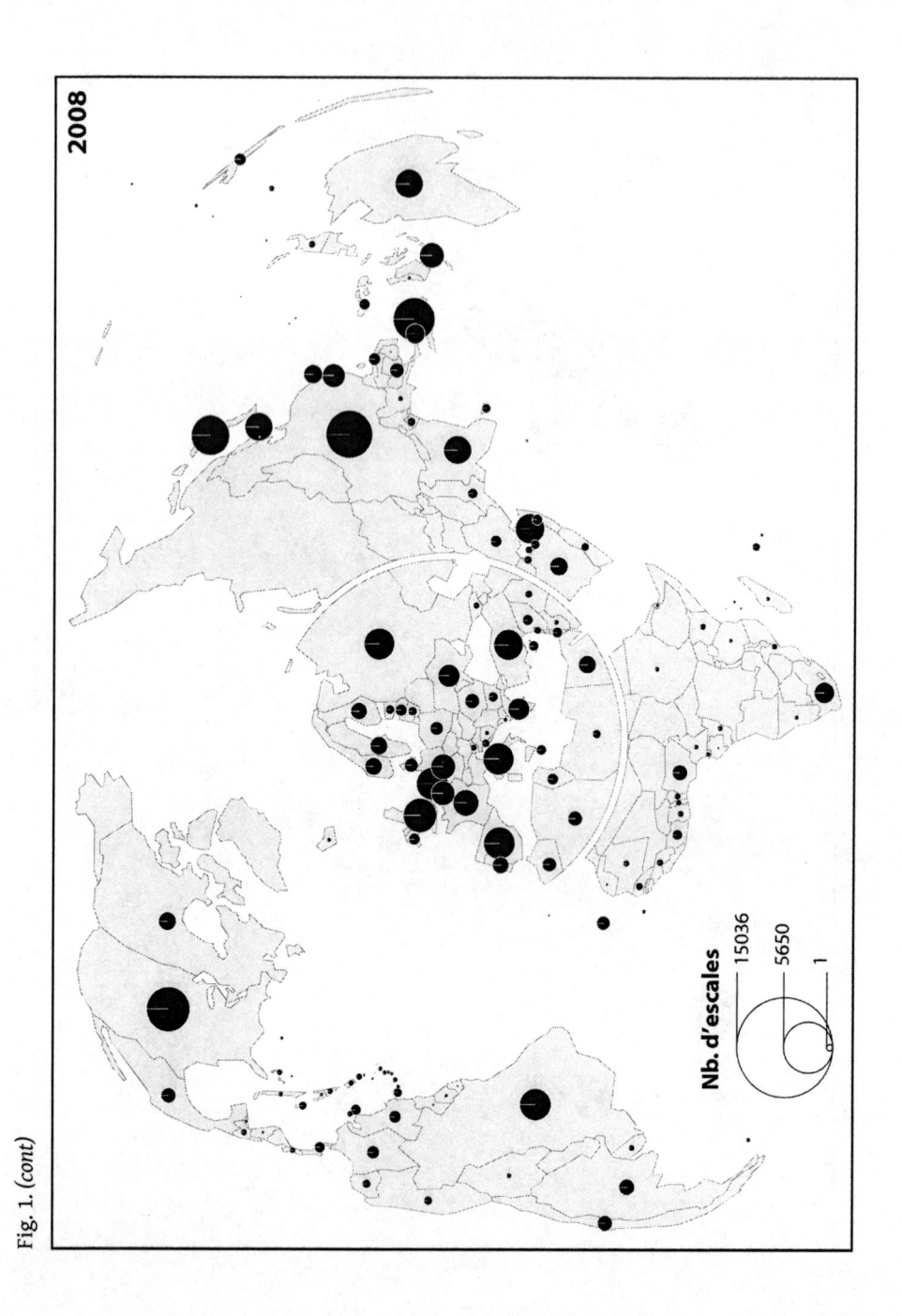

Evolution diachronique générale (1890-2008)

L'analyse qui suit fournit tout d'abord un regard nouveau sur l'évolution de la hiérarchie maritime mondiale (Tableau 2), à partir des vingt premiers pays par le nombre d'escale. Ensuite, le réseau maritime simplifié (*flux dominants*) révèle le niveau de centralisation des flux maritimes entre pays du monde (Figure 2).

L'analyse en première approximation du tableau 2 montre que la part des vingt premiers pays régresse de façon substantielle sur un peu plus d'un siècle, passant de presque 82% du nombre d'escales mondiales en 1890 à presque 62% en 2008. Cette évolution peut être interprétée comme l'approfondissement du processus séculaire de multilatéralisation des échanges, mais aussi par le nombre croissant de pays dont les ports participent au processus de mondialisation (multiplication des escales, des hubs et des spokes). Sur la longue durée, la multilatéralisation des échanges prend la configuration d'une structure réticulaire de plus en plus éclatée et complexe en raison de la multiplication et de la ramification des sous-réseaux qui s'articulent aux flux dominants. En outre, multilatéralisation et tendance à l'éclatement du schéma réticulaire s'accompagnent d'un rééquilibrage Nord-Sud au sommet de la hiérarchie des pays comptabilisant le plus grand nombre d'escales mondiales. De l'analyse combinée du tableau et des graphes décrivant les liens de dépendances des flux majeurs se dégagent trois séquences chronologiques majeures.

Domination britannique et 'bipôle atlantique'

La première séquence (années 1890 et 1925) se caractérise par la domination du Royaume-Uni comme centre des échanges maritimes mondiaux à un moment, du reste, où elle a cessé d'être la première puissance industrielle. Toutefois, elle demeure durant cette période la première puissance commerciale, la première flotte marchande et se trouve à la tête d'un empire colonial qui atteint son apogée dans l'entre-deux-guerres. La suprématie commerciale de la Grande-Bretagne apparaît en l'occurrence par le nombre et la diversité géographique de ses liens, ce qui confirme le degré d'extraversion et de mondialisation de son économie (Saul, 1960). Les neuf premiers ports britanniques se caractérisent par leurs horizons mondiaux, à commencer par les deux plus puissants d'entre eux, Londres et Liverpool (Starkey, 1999). En 1890, trois directions majeures s'articulent autour du centre britannique. Des États d'Amérique du Sud, comme l'Argentine, le Brésil, voire le Chili, avec prolongement vers les îles caribéennes, apparaissent comme des sous-pôles importants. Leur forte intégration commerciale – et financière – à la Grande-Bretagne a servi d'argument pour considérer ces pays comme faisant partie de 'l'empire informel' britannique. La deuxième catégorie de liens commerciaux majeurs est constituée par les 'colonies de peuplement' britannique, en premier lieu l'Australie, et, à moindre titre, le Canada, exportateurs essentiels, au même titre que les pays d'Amérique du Sud, de matières premières et de produits agricoles en direction de la métropole britannique.

Tableau 2. *Vingt premiers pays par le nombre d'escales, 1890–2008*

Rank	1890 Country	1890 Calls	1925 Country	1925 Calls	1960 Country	1960 Calls	1985 Country	1985 Calls	2008 Country	2008 Calls
1	U.K.	7483	U.K.	15036	U.S.A.	10231	U.S.A.	8542	China	5401
2	U.S.A.	5654	U.S.A.	8799	U.K.	8890	Japan	7597	U.S.A.	4742
3	Argentina	3317	Germany	3796	Japan	4232	U.K.	5172	Singapore	4448
4	Brazil	1721	France	3408	Germany	4170	Germany	4348	Japan	3852
5	France	1594	Italy	2803	Netherlands	2992	Italy	3757	U.K.	2780
6	Barbados	1588	Belgium	2758	Canada	2747	Netherlands	3434	Netherlands	2528
7	Australia	1464	Netherlands	2467	Sweden	2398	China	3417	Spain	2479
8	Uruguay	1154	Argentina	2456	Italy	2328	Spain	2774	Italy	2454
9	Spain	1144	Australia	2270	France	2263	France	2633	Brazil	2400
10	Germany	1059	Spain	1888	India	1868	Singapore	2480	Russia	2359
11	Chile	1052	India	1588	Belgium	1801	Australia	2337	Turkey	2216
12	South Africa	1019	Norway	1548	Australia	1671	Brazil	2189	U.A.E.	2140
13	Italy	706	Japan	1461	Finland	1482	Belgium	2158	Australia	2037
14	Canada	613	Sweden	1245	Argentina	1372	India	1964	India	1986
15	Portugal	478	Brazil	1116	Norway	1319	Greece	1948	South Korea	1935
16	India	471	South Africa	1050	Spain	1302	Russia	1706	France	1611
17	China	391	Denmark	1049	China	1198	Saudi Arabia	1655	Indonesia	1508
18	Indonesia	375	China	996	Denmark	1023	Canada	1577	Germany	1483
19	Netherlands	340	Canada	904	Brazil	995	Argentina	1508	Belgium	1412
20	Trinidad	334	Chile	764	Russia	968	Ukraine	1442	Hong Kong	1329
World share (%)		81.8		78.5		67.3		61.6		61.8

Hiérarchies portuaires dans le monde, 1890-2010

Fig. 2. *Flux maritimes dominants entre pays du monde, 1890-2008*

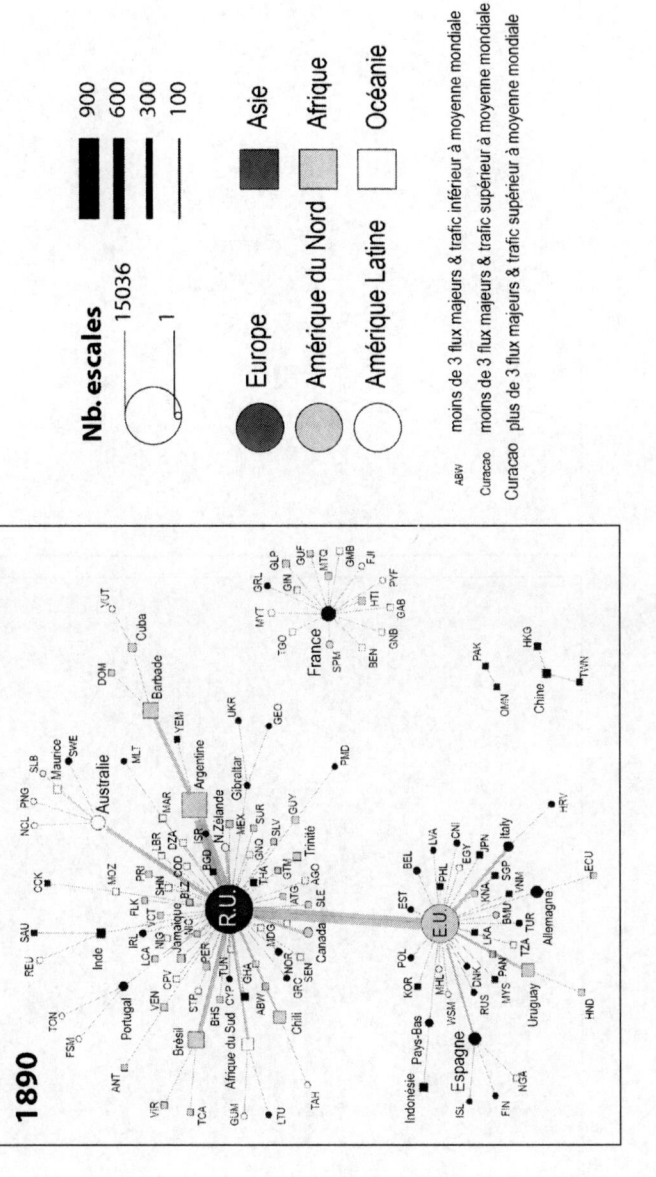

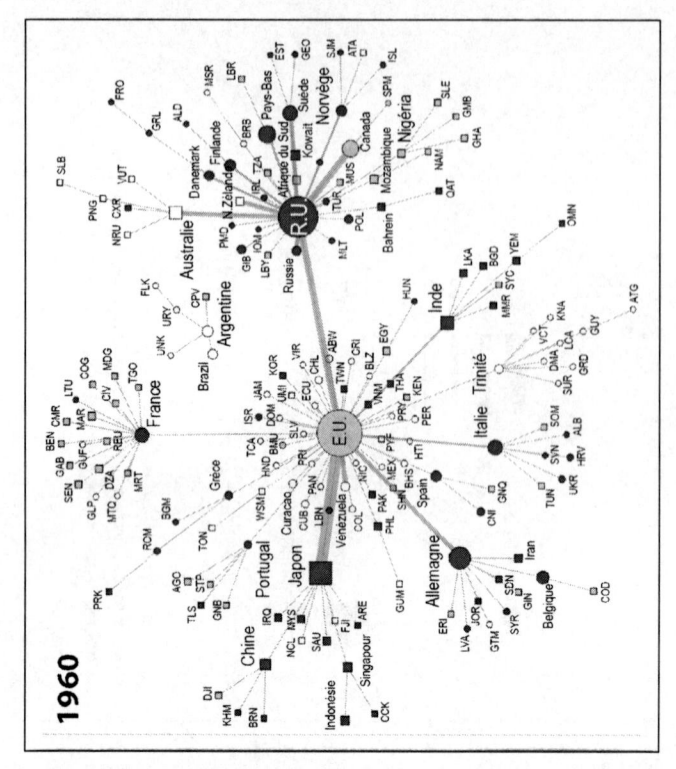

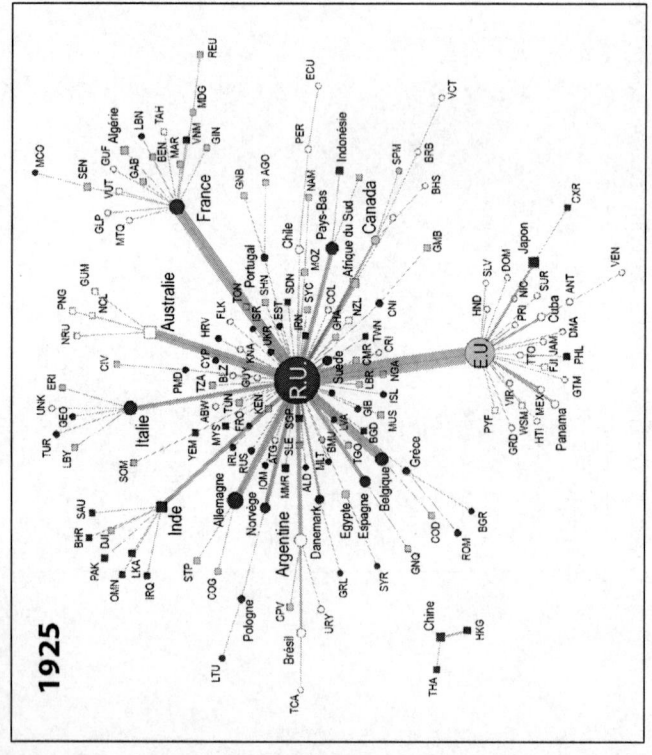

Fig. 2. (cont)

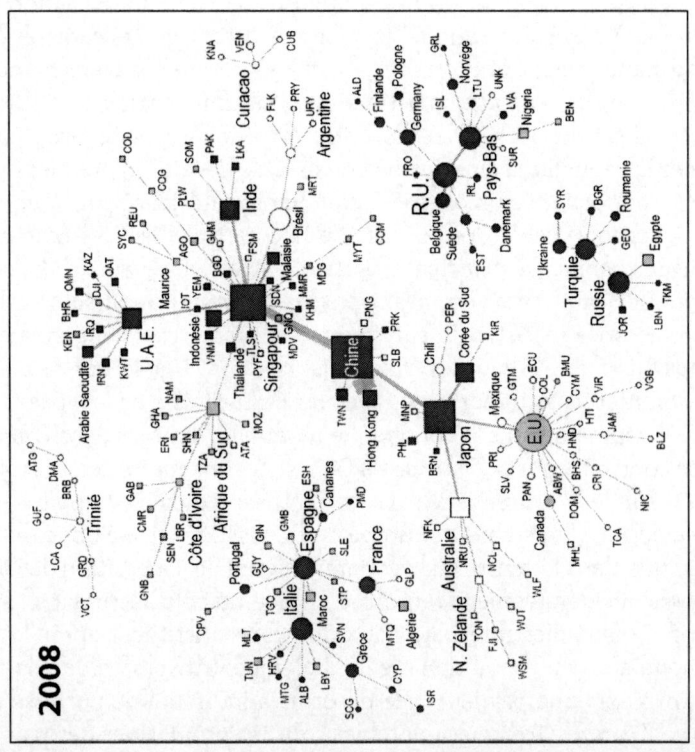

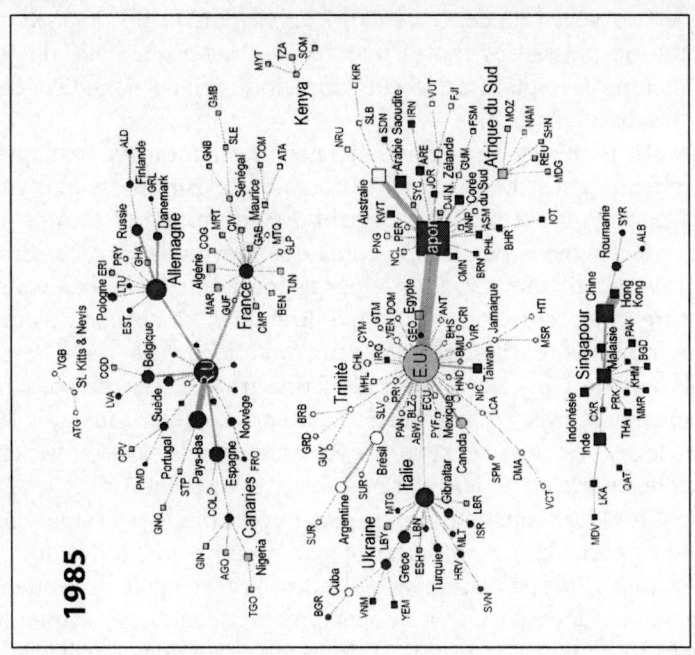

Hiérarchies portuaires dans le monde, 1890-2010

Cependant, le troisième lien commercial majeur entre le Royaume-Uni et les États-Unis est de loin le plus intense. La figure 1 est la matérialisation cartographique du 'bipôle nord-atlantique' (Guillaume, 1998), qui se caractérise par un volume d'échanges élevé et diversifiés (matières premières, biens manufacturés, migrants) le long de la route maritime qui s'est imposée comme l'axe majeur de la mondialisation du XIXe siècle entre la première puissance économique mondiale et la république américaine en passe de devenir la première puissance industrielle mondiale. Ce bipôle est notamment matérialisé par la ligne transatlantique Liverpool–New York. Le port de la côte Nord-Est des États-Unis s'est alors affirmé comme la principale porte d'entrée et de sortie du commerce extérieur américain avec un avant-pays de niveau mondial. L'Allemagne, première puissance industrielle européenne et puissance commerciale grandissante, appartient au réseau des flux majeurs de ce bipôle par le biais de ses relations commerciales importantes avec les États-Unis. Ce n'est pas le cas de la France, quatrième puissance économique mondiale, dont les liens commerciaux majeurs se concentrent sur l'Europe de l'Ouest et son empire colonial africain.

En 1925, sur les 20 premiers pays en matière d'escales 7 appartiennent au monde occidental (États-Unis et Europe de l'Ouest). S'affirme donc une concentration des flux dans le centre de l'économie mondiale. La position de l'Europe de l'Ouest s'est considérablement renforcée et joue un rôle accru dans l'animation des échanges maritimes internationaux qui se reconstituent après la Première Guerre mondiale. La promotion de la Belgique (Anvers) et de la Hollande (Rotterdam) s'explique par leur rôle désormais indiscuté de portes d'entrée et de sortie de l'Europe. Tout aussi notables sont les promotions des pays du Nord de l'Europe (Norvège, Suède, Danemark) qui depuis la fin du XIXe siècle ont (re)constitué de puissantes flottes marchandes, ainsi que celle du Japon, qui s'affirme comme la seule grande puissance industrielle non-européenne, aux visées impérialistes régionales.

La reconstitution des liens commerciaux internationaux de l'après-guerre révèle la prééminence du Royaume-Uni, dont la position est plus que jamais centrale. Les ports britanniques totalisent 20% du total des escales mondiales et la Grande-Bretagne apparaît bien comme le moyeu d'une roue composée de plusieurs rayons saillants. On assiste, par rapport à 1890, à une évolution vers une structure monocentrée sur la Grande-Bretagne, tandis que les connections du pôle américain se réorientent dans deux directions majeures: l' 'arrière-cour' des Caraïbes et de l'Amérique centrale, d'une part, et les relations transpacifiques, d'autre part, avec l'intensification des liens commerciaux avec le Japon. À la jonction de ces deux espaces se trouve Panama, dont le canal ouvert en 1914 est sous contrôle américain. Si les relations entre le Royaume-Uni et les États-Unis apparaissent toujours comme le lien le plus important, le pôle américain a donc relativement perdu de son importance par rapport aux connexions entre le Royaume-Uni et l'Europe, d'une part, et entre la métropole britannique et son empire colonial, d'autre part. L'interdépendance croissante de l'économie britannique avec son empire annonce le système de préférence impériale formalisé dans les années 1930 (accords d'Ottawa en 1932). Il repose notamment sur les liens accrus avec les dominions, notamment l'Australie et l'Afrique du Sud, et l'Inde, qui joue toujours le rôle de clé de voûte du système de la balance des paiements britanniques.

La polarisation américaine

L'émergence de la nouvelle superpuissance dominant le bloc occidental et libéral dans les quarante années qui suivent la fin de la Deuxième Guerre mondiale se traduit par la substitution des États-Unis au Royaume-Uni comme centre nerveux des échanges internationaux où la maritimisation s'amplifie constamment. Comme pour le Royaume-Uni, il existe une corrélation apparente entre puissance politique / rayonnement international / puissance commerciale. Les relations transatlantiques entre les États-Unis et l'Europe se matérialisent par la multiplication de sous-pôles (France, Allemagne, Italie), dont la Grande-Bretagne n'est que la composante la plus importante. Ces liens décrivent le rôle des États-Unis dans le relèvement économique de l'Europe de l'Ouest et les partenariats commerciaux étroits entre les deux composantes de l'OTAN. Quant au Royaume-Uni, la disparition de son empire réduit ses connexions majeures à ses anciennes colonies de peuplement dans le cadre du Commonwealth (Australie, Nouvelle-Zélande, Canada). En revanche, les États-Unis se sont substitués à l'Angleterre dans les flux majeurs avec l'Inde indépendante, qui est entrée dans l'orbite stratégique américaine. Malgré son déclassement économique dans la hiérarchie mondiale, la Grande-Bretagne se caractérise toujours comme un pôle majeur, avec un nombre et une intensité des relations commerciales majeures très élevés.

La montée en puissance des liens entre États-Unis et Japon constatée en 1925 est confirmée en 1960. Elle s'inscrit désormais dans le cadre d'un partenariat étroit entre les deux pays au sein duquel la superpuissance américaine joue le rôle de tuteur économique et de protecteur militaire de son ancien adversaire vaincu en 1945. L'intensité de ces liens commerciaux témoigne du rôle joué par les États-Unis dans le relèvement économique de leur ancien ennemi du Pacifique. La puissance commerciale et industrielle nippone s'affirme par l'édification d'une mégalopole portuaire constituée des trois ensembles Tokyo-Yokohama, Osaka-Kobé et Kitakyushu. Elle est le produit d'une politique ambitieuse de poldérisation et de construction d'îles-ports artificielles loties de vastes zones industrialo-portuaires qui s'imposent comme les poumons économiques du pays. Pays le plus développé d'Extrême-Orient, le Japon s'affirme d'ailleurs comme le noyau d'un sous-pôle régional avec des liens majeurs avec la Chine communiste et Singapour. Au faîte de leur puissance, les États-Unis se trouvent au cœur des relations transpacifiques et transatlantiques. Si le graphe rappelle à certains égards la configuration de la fameuse 'triade' (Amérique du Nord–Europe de l'Ouest–Japon), l'intérêt d'une telle représentation est de substituer à la neutralité géo-commerciale de cette notion sa réalité géopolitique, à savoir une structure tripolaire centrée sur le leader du monde occidental et libéral, qui inonde les marchés de consommation de ses alliés en biens manufacturés et culturels.

Cependant le tableau et le graphe de l'année 1960 révèlent d'autres évolutions non moins significatives. Le rôle des pays fournisseurs de matières premières (Inde, Chine, Australie, Argentine, Brésil) de la mondialisation du XIXe siècle n'a pas disparu mais a relativement diminué. Si la route par l'Afrique du Sud a perdu de son importance, le nombre de ports touchés sur la route Golfe d'Oman–mer Rouge–Suez–Méditerranée a sensiblement augmenté en raison de l'essor du trafic des hydrocarbures. L'apparition de l'URSS parmi les 20 pays comptant le plus d'escales mérite également d'être signalée. Elle correspond à l'essor de ses relations maritimes avec les pays extra-européens relevant de sa sphère d'influence politique et économique. C'est le tournant décrit par A. Vigarié (1995) sous l'expression de 'maritimisation des socialismes' où le commerce maritime devient un moyen d'intervention extérieure, auprès des pays du tiers-monde notamment; sans oublier le développement d'échanges avec les pays capitalistes même s'il demeure marginal dans le commerce extérieur de l'URSS.

Vers la dispersion multipolaire

L'actuelle mondialisation qui s'est esquissée à partir des années 1980 et s'est renforcée avec l'implosion du bloc communiste au début des années 1990 ne se traduit pas par un renforcement de la centralité américaine. Les graphes relatifs aux 1985 et 2008 se caractérisent par une tendance croissante à l'éclatement multipolaire de la structure des échanges maritimes. Contrairement aux phases antérieures, il n'apparaît plus d'état dominant dans le nombre et la diversité géographique des relations.

Le tableau montre que si les États-Unis demeurent, comme en 1960, le premier pays au monde pour le nombre d'escales, celui-ci a déjà diminué en valeur absolue de 20% en 1985. Le Japon se hisse à la deuxième place pour le nombre d'escales, ce qui confirme son statut d'économie la plus dynamique du monde dans les années 1980 et de modèle pour les 'dragons asiatiques'. De surcroît, la Chine et le port franc de Singapour – ce dernier étant depuis le XIXe siècle la porte d'entrée et de sortie de toute l'Asie du Sud-Est – se hissent aux premières places des États concentrant le plus d'escales. La nouvelle hiérarchie traduit un processus de déplacement des courants d'échanges internationaux et du centre de gravité du commerce mondial. En contrepoint, le poids de l'Europe de l'Ouest diminue relativement dans l'animation du commerce maritime, au profit des pays de l'Europe méditerranéenne (Espagne, Italie, Grèce), tandis que se confirme la place nouvelle de l'URSS – en l'occurrence Russie et Ukraine avec son grand complexe portuaire polyfonctionnel d'Odessa – et le rôle croissant de l'Arabie Saoudite et des monarchies pétrolières.

La représentation graphique des liens de dépendance majeurs révèle l'existence d'une structure tripolaire avec un bipôle États-Unis–Japon, un axe asiatique centré sur Singapour et un troisième sur l'Europe de l'Ouest. Le premier ensemble témoigne d'une évolution historiquement très significative, à savoir la disparition de la connexion séculaire majeure entre les États-Unis et le Royaume-Uni. Elle confirme une évolution en germe dans la représentation graphique de 1960. En 1985, les liens majeurs États-Unis–Europe de l'Ouest s'effectuent par l'Italie qui s'affirme comme le centre d'un pôle régional Méditerranée–Mer Noire et l'espace de mise en contact commercial du monde libéral avec certains pays du giron communiste (Cuba, Vietnam, Ukraine, Bulgarie). La distension des liens entre les États-Unis et les principales puissances économiques de l'Europe de l'Ouest est contrebalancée par la prépondérance des escales avec le Japon, ce qui confirme le tropisme asiatique et pacifique de la puissance américaine. Le rayonnement du pôle nippon s'élargit de l'Extrême-Orient – où il perd certaines connexions majeures comme la Chine et Singapour – à l'Océanie et à l'Océan Indien.

Par rapport à 1960, un ensemble extrême-oriental s'est individualisé, centré sur le hub singapourien qui rayonne sur le sud-est asiatique, le monde indien et la Chine. Pour contrarier l'influence de l'URSS sur l'aire d'obédience communiste, la Chine entre dans un processus de maritimisation active en développant notamment des flux avec deux pays européens communistes, la Roumanie et l'Albanie, ce dernier état étant dissident du bloc soviétique depuis 1960 pour se rapprocher de la République populaire de Chine.

L'ensemble européen s'organise autour des trois premières puissances économiques de la CEE que sont le Royaume-Uni, la République Fédérale d'Allemagne et, à moindre niveau, la France. Cet ensemble montre le rôle d'intégration intra-européen du Marché Commun. Le premier constat significatif est la régression britannique dont les flux majeurs se sont géographiquement réduits et '(ré)européanisés' après une très longue séquence mondiale. Le port de Rotterdam, alors considéré comme le premier port mondial en termes de tonnage manutentionné, représente la principale porte d'entrée de la Grande-Bretagne en Europe. Cependant, malgré la suprématie de leurs établissements portuaires, ni la Hollande ni la Belgique ne constituent des sous-pôles maritimes, en raison de l'importance de leur fonction de redistribution continentale. Le sous-pôle allemand se caractérise par l'importance des flux avec le nord de l'Europe et l'Europe de l'Est soviétique (URSS qui inclut les pays Baltes, Pologne). On peut y voir la traduction commerciale de l'Ostpolitik, c'est-à-dire de la politique de normalisation des relations avec l'Europe de l'Est lancée par le chancelier Willy Brandt. Du côté français, se vérifie la constance historique du flux avec les pays de son ancien domaine colonial et avec le Benelux, porte d'entrée de produits vers la France, d'un côté, et de sortie des produits français, de l'autre.

En 2008, le bipôle États-Unis–Japon et l'ensemble Extrême-Orient se sont rassemblés par la liaison Chine–Japon. Mais le nouvel axe nerveux relie la Chine à Singapour. La Chine occupe la première place pour le nombre d'escale, reflet de son nouveau statut d' 'atelier du monde': les plus grands armements mondiaux viennent y remplir leurs porte-conteneurs, mais la Chine affiche aussi l'ambition politique de se doter d'une puissante marine marchande, doublée d'une volonté d'influence politique régionale non moins évidente. Du reste, la nouvelle hiérarchie des 20 pays cumulant le plus grand nombre d'escales révèle un bouleversement historique majeur de l'époque contemporaine: 3 pays d'Extrême-Orient figurent dans les 5 premiers (et 6 dans le top 20) contre un seul pays Européen, le Royaume-Uni, en raison de son rang économique et de son caractère insulaire. Le tableau souligne également le nouveau rang occupé par les économies émergentes dans la structuration du commerce maritime international (Brésil, Russie, Inde, Chine).

La Chine s'affirme comme le centre d'un quadripôle qui confirme la dimension nouvelle des relations commerciales Amérique du Nord–Asie-Pacifique. La Chine ne constitue toutefois pas le hub d'un pôle étoffé de rayonnement mondial, comme ce fut le cas pour le Royaume-Uni et les États-Unis au temps de leur hégémonie. C'est en fait Singapour qui joue davantage ce rôle, mais sans bénéficier de la puissance politique. La cité-état de la péninsule malaise constitue le grand carrefour sud-asiatique autour duquel rayonnent des connexions majeures avec l'Inde, l'Amérique du Sud, le continent africain via l'Afrique du Sud – sous-pôle régional qui s'étoffe – et les Émirats Arabes Unis se sont substitués à l'Arabie Saoudite comme plaque tournante de l'économie du golfe persique. Ils ont tiré le meilleur parti de la déstabilisation politique de l'Irak depuis le début des années 1990. Au sein de cette structure, les États-Unis se trouvent en position excentrée. De façon paradoxale, ils n'ont plus la densité spatiale des liens commerciaux correspondant à leur rôle d'hyperpuissance.

L'Europe se trouve à l'écart des flux majeurs de la structure centrale et se dédouble même en trois ensembles très distincts: l'un méditerranéen centré sur l'Espagne, avec la France, l'Italie et la Grèce; l'autre nord-européen (Royaume-Uni, Hollande, Belgique, Allemagne) et un ensemble oriental Russie-Turquie qui structure un ensemble composé de partenaires commerciaux historiques (Ukraine, Égypte, Jordanie, Syrie, Bulgarie).

Conclusion

L'évolution contemporaine du réseau maritime mondial fournit de nombreuses réponses quant au rôle changeant des états dans l'articulation physique des échanges internationaux. A l'échelle des états, l'un des enseignements majeurs réside dans le découplage entre capacité géopolitique d'affirmation mondiale et polarisation des flux maritimo-commerciaux internationaux. Cette forme de puissance globale développée par la Grande-Bretagne et relayée par les États-Unis après 1945 a disparu dans les années 1980, au moment même où se forge la mondialisation contemporaine. La dispersion multipolaire est l'expression de formes de puissances spécifiques selon les états ou les régions du globe. Si, à la fin du XIXe siècle, le niveau de trafic reflète bel et bien la puissance commerciale et donc le volume des échanges, la fin du XXe siècle est animée de logiques plus complexes. D'un côté, la rationalisation et la concentration des escales de navires en certains points stratégiques pour le trafic de transit ont donné à certains pays un niveau de trafic bien supérieur à la demande commerciale. De l'autre, de grands partenaires comme la Chine restent finalement peu centraux dans le réseau malgré le volume de leurs échanges. Dans ce cas précis, le facteur politique joue bien plus que le facteur économique et technique, le réseau asiatique restant centralisé par la Corée du Sud, Hong Kong, Taiwan et Singapour, même si la Chine joue commercialement un rôle qui va en s'amplifiant. En Europe, les pays du Benelux s'imposent comme portes d'entrée et de sortie principales du continent. Cette spécialisation accompagne et accentue la mainmise sur l'information logistique (et par-là sécuritaire, géostratégique) par quelques grandes plates-formes mondiales toujours plus en avance sur le plan technologique de la manutention et des échanges de données informatisées.

Remerciements

The research leading to these results has received funding from the European Research Council under the European Union's Seventh Framework Programme (FP/2007-2013) / ERC Grant Agreement n. [313847] "World Seastems".

La recherche menant à ces résultats est financée par le Conseil Européen de la Recherche dans le cadre du Septième Programme Cadre de l'Union Européenne (FP/2007-2013) / ERC Grant Agreement n. [313847] « World Seastems ».

Bibliographie

DUCRUET, C., HAULE, S., AIT-MOHAND, K., MARNOT, B., KOSOWSKA-STAMIROWSKA, Z., DIDIER, L., COCHE, M.A., 'Maritime shifts in the contemporary world economy: Evidence from the Lloyd's List corpus, 18-21 c.', *Maritime Networks: Spatial Structures and Time Dynamics*, ed. C. Ducruet (Abingdon, 2015), pp. 134-60.

GUILLAUME, Jacques, 'Les ports de commerce entre ambiance atlantique et mondialisation', *Historiens et Géographes*, 363, 'L'Atlantique, un regard géographique', août-septembre (1998), 199-205.

MILLER, Michael B., *Europe and the Maritime World. A Twentieth-Century History* (Cambridge, 2012).

SAUL, Samuel B., *Studies in British Overseas Trade, 1870-1914* (Liverpool, 1960).

STARKEY, David J. (éd.), *Shipping Movements in the Ports of the United Kingdom, 1871-1913. A Statistical Profile* (Exeter, 1999).

VIGARIÉ, André, *La mer et la géostratégie des nations* (Paris, 1995).

Between Empires and Institutions: Non-State Actors and the Sea since 1945

Martin N. Murphy is a Visiting Fellow at the Corbett Centre for Maritime Policy Studies, Kings' College London

Abstract. *Piracy has revived since 1945 with the failure of new international legal regimes to replace the former imperial naval power. Crime at sea is technically harder than terrorism or smuggling, but similar forces and capabilities make it possible and profitable.*

Résumé. *La piraterie a connu une recrudescence depuis 1945 de par l'échec des nouveaux régimes juridiques internationaux à remplacer les anciennes puissances maritimes impériales. La criminalité en mer est techniquement plus complexe que le terrorisme ou la contrebande mais des forces et capacités similaires la rendent possible et lucrative.*

. • .

Piracy declined at the end of the 19th century, thanks to technology and empires, but it never went away. Steam power revolutionized the operation of both warships and merchant vessels but was too expensive for pirates to adopt. Like other colonial peoples, they had little access to modern arms. The British Empire in particular had the naval wherewithal, but also the political will and legal justification of *hostes humani generis* ("enemies of all mankind"), to hunt them down, including putting an end to the coastal raiding that had always been part, often the largest part, of pirate practice. Off the coast of China, a geographical expanse wracked by internal discord and foreign intervention where Western imperial power was applied with less certainty, maritime depredation continued to be troublesome.

Brief history

In Asia piracy almost certainly continued during and after World War II, albeit at a low level. Amongst the coastal peoples of Southeast Asia, around the Straits of Malacca and Singapore ("the Straits"), the Sulu Sea and southern Thailand,

Table 1. *Categories of piracy*

Type	Category	Description	Example
1	Inland water assault	Small bands in harbors, etc. akin to petty thieving; rarely violent	Chittagong; Santos; Indonesian ports; Lagos
2	Local vessel assault	Can be violent; fishing common cause; often persistent	Ganges Delta; Malacca Strait; Indonesia; Sulu Sea; Nigeria
3	Coastal shipping; fixed installation assault	Perpetrators can use or threaten violence; primary objective is theft of crew valuables or ship's equipment; kidnap and ransom (K&R) in some locations	Southeast Asia; Nigeria and parts of Gulf of Guinea
4	Major ship assaults	Theft of ship and cargo; selective K&R; highly organized	Malacca and Singapore Straits; South China Sea; Nigeria and parts of Gulf of Guinea
5	Major hostage taking	K&R over-riding objective; highly organized	Somalia
6	Coastal raiding	Historically common; currently rare	Philippines; Sabah; Gulf of Guinea

activity that is regarded by outsiders as piracy remained widely accepted.[1] In addition, groups affiliated to the nationalist Kuomintang regime, after its defeat by the Communists in 1949 and its retreat to Taiwan, attacked shipping along the southern Chinese coast as far south as the South China Sea well into the 1950s.[2]

Six categories of piracy have been observed around the globe since 1945 (Table 1).

Records prior to 1992 are patchy and confused because at the time neither states nor international institutions saw piracy and its territorial sea equivalent, armed robbery at sea, as a problem, largely because international shipping was unaffected.[3] The International Maritime Organization (IMO), the UN body responsible for maritime issues, made its disquiet known in only 1983 when it passed a resolution expressing its "great concern", although it had been receiving reports of incidents against commercial ships waiting to berth in Lagos starting in the early 1970s. These had begun following the 1973 OPEC oil price rise – when a construction boom sucked in large volumes of cement and other goods that Lagos harbour was unable to cope with, leaving ships waiting offshore vulnerable to attack – and continued until 1983, when the oil price fell sharply.[4]

Far worse followed the imposition of Communist rule on South Vietnam after 1975. People poured out of the country by boat. The southern route across the

---

[1] BATEMAN S., 'Confronting Maritime Crime in Southeast Asian Waters', in *Piracy and Maritime Crime*, ed. B.A. ELLEMAN et al. (Newport, RI, 2010), pp. 137–40.
[2] MENEFEE S.P., *Trends in Maritime Violence* (Coulsdon, 1996), p. 55.
[3] MURPHY M., *Small Boats, Weak States, Dirty Money* (London, 2009), pp. 59–72.
[4] *Ibid.*, pp. 112–13.

Gulf of Thailand to Thailand and Malaysia became notorious until 1989 for theft, rape and death perpetrated by fishermen. For many years Thailand appeared to turn a blind eye to this mass migration before it eventually attracted international humanitarian relief.[5] States have exploited piracy throughout history, and the period since World War II has been no exception.

Elsewhere in Asia three changes fed the sharp upturn in Straits piracy between the early 1990s and 2005. In 1978 Deng Xiaoping came to power in China and transformed its economy from Communism to authoritarian capitalism, in the process unleashing a wave of corruption across the southern provinces. Second, and quite separately, a series of ship frauds took place in the 1980s organized by gangs based in China and around Southeast Asia. Tracked down by insurance investigators but never prosecuted by any state, these highly sophisticated criminal operations, which benefitted from high-level political protection, later went on to organize so-called "phantom ship" hijackings in which ships were boarded by pirates in the Strait of Malacca and sailed to ports in China. There the cargoes were sold to corrupt Chinese buyers before the ships were renamed and re-registered and sent out in search of new cargoes that could be diverted fraudulently.[6] Third was the rise of coastal piracy against commercial shipping transiting the Straits and the southern part of the South China Sea. The gangs involved quickly developed links to corrupt figures in shipping and local law enforcement. They provided the labour for the organized criminal groups behind the "phantom-ship" heists, and others later who were in the market for tugs and the occasional ship's cargo.[7]

The number of attacks in the Straits increased significantly in the mid-1990s. They peaked in 2000, then declined without being eliminated entirely. In addition to the coastal piracy gangs two other actors were involved. The first were members of the TNI, the Indonesian armed forces, where corruption is rife, taking advantage of a criminal opportunity that played to their skills. Reports of pirates in uniform were too common to be ignored. The second group was the Aceh separatist organization, GAM, which took hostages at the northern end of the Straits before it made peace with the Indonesian government after the 2004 Indian Ocean tsunami devastated the province's coastal areas.[8] Organized piracy remains a low-level problem in the southern South China Sea and Sulu Sea.[9]

Piracy numbers were collected systematically for the first time starting in 1992, when a private industry body, the International Maritime Bureau (IMB), established its Piracy Reporting Centre (PRC) in Kuala Lumpur, Malaysia. It advertised a telephone number seafarers could call to report attacks. Its figures were inflated

---

[5] ELLEMAN B., 'The Looting and Rape of Vietnamese Boat People', in *Piracy and Maritime Crime*, ed. Elleman et al., pp. 97–108.
[6] MURPHY, *Small Boats*, pp. 146–50 and 164–77; LISS C., *Oceans of Crime* (Singapore, 2011), pp. 22–3 and 41–2.
[7] MURPHY, *Small Boats*, pp. 80–93; LISS, *Oceans of Crime*, pp. 26–40, 58–65.
[8] MURPHY, *Small Boats*, pp. 305–10; LISS, *Oceans of Crime*, pp. 237–40.
[9] 'Indonesia, Malaysia and Philippines to conduct coordinated anti-piracy patrols in South China Sea', *The Straits Times*, 5 May 2016.

by the inclusion of thefts from ships in harbours, which became a contentious issue with coastal states because attacks that occur in territorial waters are not classified as piracy under the governing treaty law, the United Nations Convention on the Law of the Sea (UNCLOS). The IMB, however, saw harbour attacks, while less dangerous, as a more general indicator of poor maritime law enforcement by the port state. If the objective was (and continues to be) to name-and-shame rather than to arrive at a strictly accurate assessment of piracy, as opposed to maritime depredation more widely, then they were right. It was undeniable that states with poor port security such as Indonesia, the Philippines, Bangladesh and Nigeria also suffered the highest numbers of offshore incidents.

Whatever their provenance, piracy statistics are unreliable. They depend upon self-reporting, which is always questionable: is an approach by a skiff an attempted attack or fishermen trying to protect their nets? Masters are reluctant to report incidents for a variety of reasons, including liability fears, reputational risks and delay costs. Also, as with any crime, people will report only what they believe will be acted upon; if official action is unlikely, or if the only action will be another visit by pirates seeking revenge after being tipped off by their friends in the police, reports are unlikely to be filed. Related to this is the question of regional imbalance. Does the presence of an observer affect the outcome? Because Southeast Asia was seen as the locus of pirate activity when the IMB established the PRC, more reports of pirate activity were received from that region than elsewhere. This may not have been a true reflection of pirate activity globally.

Furthermore, it is suspected that on average only half of all pirate activity is actually reported, with the figures for large commercial carriers off Somalia from about 2005 onwards being considerably more accurate than average, and figures for incidents off Nigeria being substantially less so. Most attacks on coastal fishing craft and local shipping such as dhows are believed to go unrecorded. Attempts have been taken to rectify the regional imbalance with the creation of an inter-governmental centre in Southeast Asia, a centre focused on Somali piracy and a new centre covering the Gulf of Guinea all established as part of broader counter-piracy measures. None, however, is in any position to overcome the self-reporting problem

Straits piracy demonstrated that to operate on a scale large enough to reap substantial profits, pirates had to master three essential elements: markets, organization and skilled labour. The market in China was driven by demand from newly liberated industries for commodities, including refined petroleum products, palm oil and minerals. Organization was provided by existing criminal gangs that had experience of maritime crime, which meshed with the new centres of corruption in China's southern provinces. The skilled labour was provided by coastal pirates, many of whom had been fishermen, but also others who, while they had little or no experience of the sea, served as "muscle". Large-scale piracy stopped when Beijing finally saw that corruption fuelled fissiparous political tendencies and cracked down in 1998. No other regional market, which included the Philippines and Singapore on one occasion that is known about publicly, proved large enough to replace it.

Piracy off Somalia began shortly after the government of Mohammed Siad Barre fell from power in 1991.[10] Isolated incidents of ship and yacht hijackings took place alongside more frequent attacks on fishermen, several perpetrated by groups linked to clan-based warlords. Somali fishermen attacked other Somalis, but also large trawlers owned by East Asian and European deep-water fishing companies exploiting the country's unprotected fishing grounds. Warlords, recognizing the potential profit, cooperated in licensing these outsiders in return for protection from attacks by local fishermen. Puntland, the break-away state in the country's north-east, hired a British company to set up a coast guard. When political turmoil inside Puntland made the company's position untenable it left, leaving behind a cadre of men trained in ship-boarding. The suspicion is that these men formed part of the labour pool that pirate organizers later exploited for their own ends.[11]

It was Mohammed Abdi Hassan, better known as "Afweyne", who in 2003 had the vision to exploit the ability of Somalis to stop and board ships at sea and the willingness of foreigners to pay for the release of hostages. Although they never thought in these terms, he and the Somali pirate bosses who followed him showed that the formula that had worked so well for the Barbary corsairs for three hundred years, beginning in the early sixteenth century, could be updated for modern conditions.[12]

Unlike the pirates of Southeast Asia who had sailed stolen goods to buyers, the Somali pirates forced buyers to come to them. Organizers who had honed their skills in the deadly environment of Somali state failure bought protection from local clans. Previous contact with the foreign governments and international organizations that had been active in Somalia ever since Barre's departure meant they knew the mentality of their Western customers. Even key elements in the labour force had been trained to Western professional standards. When these men retired, started their own pirate groups or were lost at sea an endless stream of aspiring pirates, motivated by the prospect of wealth unimaginable in a country where the average income amounted to less than $2 per day, emerged from the interior, eager to take their place in the boats.

For the moment at least, large-scale Somali piracy has abated. Some estimates suggest the pirates extracted over $400 million in ransom payments between 2005 and 2013. To change pirate incentives towards risk and away from reward, the states that committed navy ships and aircraft, diplomatic effort and law-enforcement resources invested many times this amount. The World Bank has estimated that Somali piracy cost the world economy $18 billion annually, much of it accounted by trade distortions and counter-measures.[13] If true, then it took a monstrous hammer to crack a nut.

---

[10] MURPHY M., *Somalia the New Barbary?* (London, 2011), pp. 11–16; HANSEN S.J., *Piracy in the Greater Gulf of Aden* (Oslo, 2009).
[11] MURPHY, *Somalia the New Barbary?*, pp. 17–27; HANSEN S.J., 'Debunking the piracy myth', *RUSI Journal* (December 2011), 28–31.
[12] MURPHY, *Somalia the New Barbary?*, pp. 55–9, 111–22.
[13] 'The Pirates of Somalia' (Washington, DC, 2013), pp. 22–7.

When piracy returned to Nigerian waters in the 1990s it took place off the Niger Delta, not Lagos, and was both more complex and more violent. Its cause, and its continuing motivation, is access to the country's oil wealth. Pirates have attacked Nigeria's fishing industry, which for a time in 2008 refused to put to sea in protest at the federal government's failure to address the problem. Even though fishing is Nigeria's second-largest industry after energy extraction, it has little leverage against the fortunes that can be made from oil theft.

The attacks off the Niger Delta are the seaward extension of the battle between the federal authorities – and Nigeria's political and economic elite more generally – and the region's inhabitants.[14] Some observers are divided as to whether the attacks are politically or criminally motivated when in fact they are both; as are the responses of the authorities that oppose them. Nigeria is a country blessed with natural resources but cursed by corruption, a problem with a long history that appears now to be ingrained in its social fabric. Its effects are felt at all levels of the government, from the presidential palace down to individual police, army and naval units.

The Delta's inhabitants believe they have gained little or nothing from the billions of dollars paid for the oil extracted from beneath their feet and off their coast. The violence and theft that has taken place is a reaction to the rapacity of international oil companies (IOCs) and the Nigerian politicians who have colluded with them over decades. The resulting resentment has made victims out of foreign oil workers who have been kidnapped, fishermen who have been attacked and killed, seafarers who have been murdered and held hostage and the inhabitants of neighbouring states whose coastlines have been raided, all acts that pirates and corsairs have engaged in throughout history. Some acts may be more overtly political than others, such as the attack on the Shell-owned *Bonga* floating offshore storage facility by the Movement for the Emancipation of the Niger Delta (MEND) in 2008, but such groups were never cohesive and engaged freely in criminal activity.[15]

These piratical acts are an extension of the theft, kidnapping and murder that has taken place on land, connected, in many cases, to the theft of crude oil directly from pipelines. All oil theft in the region is referred to as "illegal bunkering". It has proven links to international criminal networks, some of which are in turn linked to Hezbollah and Hamas. Nigeria has a severe shortage of domestic refining capacity. Most stolen crude is either refined in illegal refineries dotted throughout the region or sold abroad. At sea the focus has shifted to refined-oil carriers, some taken at distances of over a thousand nautical miles from the Delta. In most cases a significant portion of the cargo is transferred to a smaller tanker. Like stolen crude, an unknown quantity of stolen refined oil is recycled back into the domestic Nigerian market while the rest is disposed of in other counties in the region.

---

[14] NODLAND A., 'Guns, Oil, and "Cake"', in *Piracy and Maritime Crime*, ed. Elleman et al., pp. 191–206.
[15] MURPHY M., 'Petro-Piracy', in *Modern Piracy*, ed. D. GUILFOYLE (Cheltenham, 2013), pp. 61–90.

Conditions

Looked at on a case-by-case basis, seven factors encourage piracy. They vary in importance and although one may predominate in one case and not another, they are all usually present to some degree.

1. Reward
2. Favorable geography
3. Permissive political environment
4. Inadequate security
5. Conflict and disorder
6. Legal and jurisdictional opportunities
7. Maritime tradition/cultural acceptability

The causes of piracy are on land, not at sea. What occurs on the water is merely its most visible manifestation. It cannot occur just anywhere. Pirates need access to markets (or to people who will dispose of goods on their behalf), to secure locations where operations can be planned and organized and to a labour pool. Ships carrying items whose value, relative to the risk, exceeds whatever is available to the perpetrators on land must pass by at an acceptable range from the coast. The shape of the coast must provide safe anchorages and launching points, ideally ones that require detailed local knowledge to navigate safely. Political authority on land must be incapable or unwilling to take suppressive action, either because it is absent or because it connives in what is taking place. The enforcement arms of the state – the police and the military – must therefore be limited in their ability to respond effectively. Conflict and disorder can be conducive – ports handling stolen cargoes and ships sprang up along the Lebanese coast, for example, during the 1975–90 civil war – but not if it forces pirates to take disproportionately expensive security measures to defend their activities. Legal and jurisdictional opportunities can include poorly demarcated or contested maritime borders that allow pirates to slip between competing jurisdictions; failure to enact adequate domestic legislation; and the unwillingness of states to assert jurisdiction when they are entitled to, thereby allowing pirates to escape justice for administrative reasons. The existence of an experienced maritime community – usually fishermen – is generally essential, but, as the Somali example has demonstrated, this base can be relatively small provided it can be supplemented by recruits with other skills who are willing or desperate enough to go to sea. Wherever the recruits come from, the communities which host the pirates must either find their behaviour acceptable, or be bribed or cowed into doing so.

Piracy does not stand alone. It is inseparable from other maritime crimes including illegal fishing and all forms of smuggling. This is a *milieu* which can extend to maritime insurgency and terrorism. The factors that facilitate both are similar to piracy, with targets judged according to political, not economic criteria.

That only 2 percent of all terrorist and insurgent groups have used the sea demonstrates the difficulty of maritime operations.[16] The sea is an unforgiving environment and few groups have succeeded unless they emerge from areas with strong maritime traditions, as the Sri Lankan Liberation Tigers of Tamil Eelam (LTTE) and the Philippine "Moro" groups did, or received state-sponsored training and support like the Palestinian groups, Hezbollah and Lashkar-e-Taiba (LeT). Insurgent and terrorist organizations have relatively limited resources; it is hard to justify expenditure on maritime targets, rather than targets on land where the impact will be greater.[17] Consequently, the number that has persisted is small. Those that have used the sea extensively – such as the Moro insurgent groups in the southern Philippines and the formidable LTTE in Sri Lanka – have done so mainly as a medium to move men and matériel because their operating areas were bounded by water. If they were to fight they had no alternative but to master maritime logistics. In the LTTE's case they built what was, in effect, the 20th century's only non-state navy primarily to defend their supply routes as they approached the Sri Lankan coast.

Palestinian groups were forced to use the sea once Israel was able to close its land borders, leaving the coast as its only vulnerable flank. This changed when Israel invaded Lebanon in 1982. Now with targets they could attack outside Israel's borders, Palestinian coastal raiding declined almost to zero. The onset of the suicide bomber and the almost limitless supply of Katyusha rockets available to Hezbollah and Hamas have shifted the balance away from the maritime option still further.

The pattern appears to be that if terrorists view the maritime medium as their only viable option, then, providing they can assemble the necessary skills and equipment, they will use it. LeT's attack on Mumbai in 2008, for example, was conducted with military precision that suggested training and support from elements within Pakistan's military and intelligence services.[18] But unless exploitation of the maritime domain is essential to their entire operation, they will abandon it as soon as less risky options present themselves.

LEVELLING UP: THE EFFECTS OF TECHNOLOGY PROLIFERATION ON MARITIME DISORDER

The seven factors, when looked at globally, can be distilled down to three: reward disproportionate to risk; favourable geography; and permissive security and political environments. But another overarching factor is also important: the technological advantages that gave piracy hunters the edge for nearly three-quarters of a century have narrowed on three fronts since 1945.

The first was reliable and increasingly inexpensive internal combustion

---

[16] CHALK P., 'Maritime Terrorism in the Contemporary Era', in *The MIPT Terrorism Annual, 2006*.
[17] MURPHY, *Small Boats*, pp. 369–75.
[18] KILCULLEN D., *Out of the Mountains* (London, 2013), pp. 52–4.

engines. Initially these were probably war surplus, but as Japan re-emerged as an industrial power it began to manufacture low-cost marine and outboard motors in large numbers. Many were sold to fishermen, some of whom, as result of overfishing, turned to piracy. The all-weather mobility advantage that counter-piracy forces had first acquired thanks to the steamship revolution at the end of the 19th century was eroded significantly.

The second was the proliferation of small arms and light weapons such as rocket-propelled grenades. Supplies of both expanded exponentially across Southeast Asia following the Indo-China wars and across Africa as a result of the colonial and post-colonial conflicts. Once they had them, organized pirate gangs showed they were prepared to use them.

The final leveller was the advent of cell phones, satellite phones and Global Positioning System (GPS) devices enabling pirates to coordinate their attacks and operate further out to sea. Without modern communications it is hard to see how Somali hostage negotiations and payments could have proceeded as efficiently as they did.

Significance: from empire to institutions

Violent non-state criminally or politically motivated maritime actors have affected our world since 1945 by creating a *milieu* in which each other can operate. Different forms of depredation can mutate into another; so, for example, smugglers can become pirates and terrorists can exploit the known presence of smugglers to cover their own actions.

However, the impact of piracy on the global economy since 1945 has been insignificant. Even when a figure such as $18 billion dollars per annum is attributed to Somali piracy alone, agglomerating ransom payments, higher insurance rates, additional fuel for faster and longer steaming, private armed teams, naval protection and a host of other direct and indirect costs, it is of no consequence when compared to the total of global trade, or even the value of what passes through the northern Arabian Sea. Some individual ship-owners, of course, have been devastated and weak economies have suffered. For individual seafarers (including yachtsmen), whose experiences have all too often been lost in the debate about piracy's economic costs, it can be a matter of life or death. This risk extends to fishermen in many areas of the developing world, a problem that is often ignored.

Maritime terrorism is rare. Some attacks have been immensely successful: MEND's attack on the *Bonga* platform succeeded in raising world oil prices if only fleetingly, the Mumbai attack exposed the vulnerability of coastal cities, while the al-Qaeda attack on the USS *Cole* in Aden harbour in 2000 led to a permanent change in the security arrangements for naval visits everywhere. In general, however, it is insurgents, not terrorists, that use the sea, and only when they have no other alternative.

Piracy that targets international shipping is significant because it challenges the free and uninterrupted use of the sea and therefore the balance between commercial liberty and state interference. Because it occurs on the high seas beyond the territorial jurisdiction of any state, it asks questions about sovereignty and international law. In a very practical sense, those questions were answered by the Anglo-American hegemony of the last two hundred years and for most of that time by the maritime preponderance of the British Empire and its navy. This Anglo-American maritime preponderance is now passing and maritime security has moved into a period of transition from a domain ordered by an essentially imperial paradigm to one rooted in international institutions, although this too is being challenged by some states who seek greater control over their neighbouring seas.[19]

Britain asserted its maritime preponderance strongly from 1815 to about 1943. America has asserted its preponderance more selectively since then. Britain could justify its investment in its navy not just by the need to maintain communications with distant colonies but because for much of the time over 60 percent of shipping was British owned and insured. Maritime law was largely British law. The idea of *hostes humani generis*, a concept more medieval than Roman, was turned into a workable legal concept mainly by British courts. Britain also had the means to suppress piracy; it possessed the world's strongest navy and controlled the landward side of critical straits. While the United States has an immense indirect interest in the security of seaborne commerce, it has always been less dependent on trade than Great Britain. Its merchant marine shrunk drastically during the US Civil War, never recovered and is now insignificant. It was never a serious imperial power and lacked Britain's experience of international maritime security. Its navy, which after 1945 focused successively on the Soviet Union, Iran and China, has taken only limited steps to acquire it.

Even after Britain folded its imperial tent and went home its influence over vulnerable straits such as Malacca, Singapore and the Gulf of Aden, where pirates now operate, lingered until 1971. Although the successor states guarded their maritime territorial rights jealously, protecting international shipping passing close to their coasts from pirates, even if they were based on their territory, was not a priority. Moreover, they lacked the resources to do so.

Greater wealth and growing inter-state tensions have changed that. Piracy is mobile and spreads when suitably organized, transforming it into an international problem. Access to satellite phones and GPS enabled the Somali pirates to operate at ranges in excess of two thousand nautical miles, drawing in regional powers and enabling international powers, such as China and Russia, to extend their influence into a region where previously it had been limited. State exploitation of piracy to achieve larger foreign policy objectives is as old as history. Modern states have acted no differently than their predecessors.

The United States is what may be described a hybrid or "transitional" imperial

---

[19] KRASKA J., *Maritime Power and the Law of the Sea* (Oxford, 2011), pp. 1–27.

power. It often acts in an imperial manner and maintains overwhelming means to impose its will militarily if it chooses. Yet it has also worked to shape an international system based on consent and mutual cooperation. It has supported independence and national self-determination while promoting collective security and rule-based international order to restrain unilateral state action.

The 1982 UNCLOS treaty was a "grand bargain" between the maritime powers wishing to uphold traditional navigational freedoms and resist creeping territorialization of the seas, and coastal states wanting greater control of their waters primarily for economic and, subsequently, security reasons. Combined with membership of the IMO, the SUA convention, human rights legislation and regional bodies such as ASEAN, the African Union, NATO and the EU, plus UN Security Resolutions, it has enmeshed states in multiple layers of obligation over the global maritime space. The very intricacy of this framework, however, allows states to avoid their obligations if they diverge from an over-riding national policy imperative, and to ignore them selectively if, like China, they view coastal waters as territory. While piracy is a crime of universal jurisdiction, for instance, many states have failed to reflect that in their domestic legislation.

Piracy off Somalia has accelerated the trend amongst states, led by the United States, to institutionalize the governance of the world's oceans. The UN Security Council has been involved with and overseen the creation of new regional bodies to address the problem, which remains vulnerable to states' willingness to act. Legal discourse has played the crucial role in framing institutional responses to piracy issues, arguably at the expense of economic and political measures that could help to stabilize fragile states, increase pirate risk and decrease pirate rewards. Instead states have pursued a law enforcement approach, which has inevitably brought with it human rights considerations that have made prosecutions harder to obtain, using navies which are disproportionately costly compared to the economic damage pirates inflict and ill-suited to the law enforcement mission.

Pirates, smugglers and insurgents have exploited the gaps that have emerged in international maritime governance and enforcement since 1945 as the international community has struggled to replace the imperial security model with one based on international institutions. Pirates and others have taken advantage of similar power shifts in the past. What hubris to think our age is any different. What hubris, too, to imagine that the spread of international security institutions will be uncontroversial and remain limited to the suppression of piracy and maritime crime alone.

The narcotics trade and the sea

Peter Chalk is a Senior Maritime Security Contractor, Naval Postgraduate School, Monterey, California, United States

ABSTRACT. *Weakly governed and policed, the world's seas offer ample opportunities for the international trade in illegal narcotics. The bulk of Afghan heroin is exported at least partly by sea, as are the opiates produced in Burma. Eighty percent of the drugs produced in South America are carried to their markets in North America by sea. In most cases the drugs are concealed aboard apparently law-abiding container ships or fishing vessels, with or without the connivance of their crews, but in the Caribbean high-speed motor launches ("go-fasts") are used, and on the Pacific coast cocaine is sometimes shipped in powered semi-submersibles. With twelve to fifteen million containers at sea at any time, and more than 6,500 ports in use around the world, it is impossible to exercise any close control over a world trading system which is both highly complex and infinitely dispersed. Neither legal nor practical means suffice to make more than a small impact on a highly profitable trade with ample supply and demand.*

RÉSUMÉ. *Les mers du monde entier offrent de vastes opportunités au trafic international de stupéfiants, du fait du faible contrôle et du manque de surveillance dont elles bénéficient. L'essentiel de la production afghane d'héroïne et des opiacés fabriqués en Birmanie est exporté, du moins en partie, par la mer et 80% des drogues produites en Amérique du Sud sont expédiées par voie maritime vers leurs marchés nord-américains. Dans la plupart des cas, les drogues sont dissimulées à bord de porte-conteneurs ou de bateaux de pêche d'apparence respectueux des lois, et dont les équipages peuvent, ou pas, être complices du trafic. Dans les Caraïbes, des vedettes à grande vitesse (les « go-fasts ») sont utilisées et sur la côte Pacifique, la cocaïne est parfois transportée dans des semi-submersibles à propulsion. Entre 12 et 15 millions de conteneurs en mer au même moment et plus de 6500 ports en fonctionnement à travers le monde rendent impossible le contrôle rapproché d'un système commercial international à la fois extrêmement complexe et infiniment épars. Les moyens pratiques et juridiques à disposition ne suffisent pas à générer plus qu'un faible impact sur un marché hautement lucratif et bénéficiant d'une offre et d'une demande importantes.*

.•.

Introduction

The maritime "commons" remain particularly vulnerable to many of the transnational criminal designs that have come to typify international security in the contemporary era. A vast area covering 139,768,200 square miles, most of this environment takes the form of high seas that lie beyond the strict control of any single state – meaning they are, by definition, devoid of any form of sovereign jurisdiction. These "over the horizon" oceans are fringed and linked by a complex lattice of territorial waters, estuaries, riverine systems and ports that, due to a lack of resources or will (and in some cases both), are frequently un-policed.[1] Combined, these attributes and practices have served to ingrain the planet's aquatic expanse with the same type of unpredictable and lawless qualities that Thomas Hobbes once famously wrote ensured life as "nasty, brutish and short."

One particular maritime sea-based threat that occupies a prominent place on the contemporary international security agenda is drug trafficking. The trade is conservatively estimated to generate annual revenues of between US$2 and US$4 billion; has impacted most countries around the world as either source, transit, or consumption states; and has had highly deleterious effects for national, regional, and global security. This essay will briefly discuss the scope and dimension of the contemporary drug industry and the manner by which the maritime environment has been exploited to facilitate its operation. It will also detail key pillars of the emergent global drug prohibition regime and provide an overview of the main maritime mitigation measures that have been brought to bear by the United States Coast Guard (USCG) to blunt the trade.

Scope and Dimensions

Although an international scourge, the most addictive and socially harmful narcotics derive from only a handful of states: Afghanistan (which accounts for 80 percent of the global heroin supply), Myanmar (the world's second largest-producer of opiates and one of the main manufacturers of amphetamine-type stimulants/ATS), Colombia (the source for 90 percent of all refined cocaine), and Peru (the principal origin for coca leaf). The proliferation of these drugs in what is now an entrenched global market reflects a distribution network that is overwhelmingly maritime based.

Heroin

The majority of Afghan heroin trafficked by sea is bound for consumers in Western Europe, although important secondary markets exist in the Middle East and the Balkans.[2] Shipments are typically smuggled from Pakistan's eastern

---

[1] See, for instance, HERBERT-BURNS R., 'Terrorism in the Early 21st Century Maritime Domain', in J. HO and C.Z. RAYMOND, *The Best of Times, the Worst of Times: Maritime Security in the Asia Pacific* (Singapore, 2005), pp. 157–8.
[2] Russia and the former Central Asian republics of the Soviet Union are the main markets for Afghan heroin that is trafficked overland. The main corridor appears to run via the Tajik districts of Gorno-Badakshan, Shurobod, Moskovski and Panj to the Ferghana valley in Uzbekistan. From here opiates are redistributed and shipped through Kyrgyzstan and Kazakhstan to Russia.

seaboard, passing through one of three corridors: (1) the Gulf of Oman to Iran, Turkey, and southeastern Europe; (2) across the Arabian Sea to Yemen, Saudi Arabia, Jordan, Israel, and the Mediterranean; and (3) via the Horn of Africa to the Red Sea and Suez Canal. An increasingly important secondary route transits Turkmenistan and the Caspian Sea for onward delivery to southeastern Europe through Azerbaijan, Armenia and Turkey. Pakistani traffickers based in Quetta are thought to organize most of these shipments, coordinating with Kurdish brokers and sub-contractors in Iran and Turkey.[3]

A significant proportion of opiates produced in Myanmar similarly use maritime routes to "feed" regional demand in Thailand, Vietnam, Cambodia, and the Philippines as well as consumers in more distant markets such as Japan, South Korea, China, Taiwan, Hong Kong, and Australia. In this case, the Gulf of Thailand constitutes the main transshipment zone. A large area covering 117,000 square miles, this body of water is situated near the strategic Malacca Strait that connects North and Southeast Asia, lies close to other important chokepoints that bisect the South China Sea and is located near to major shipping lanes serviced by established road and rail infrastructure.

Cocaine

Around 80 percent of the drugs produced in Latin America are exported by sea. Shipments bound for the United States and Canada – historically the main consumers of Colombian cocaine – either travel up the Central American Pacific coast or pass through the Caribbean Island chain, with Mexico acting as the main gateway to the American market. Intensive interception campaigns by the USCG as well as higher street prices and rising demand for derivatives such as crack have seen increased consignments now being dispatched to Europe, and, again, maritime conveyance is the preferred means for delivery. Drugs are normally concealed on freighters berthed in Venezuelan waters that then sail direct to ports such as Lisbon, Antwerp, Rotterdam, and Barcelona or travel via hubs in the Gulf of Guinea (GoG), where the cocaine is offloaded and moved by truck to North Africa and the adjoining southern Mediterranean coast.[4]

In the latter case, vessels follow what has colloquially become known as "Highway 10" – a reference to the 10th degree of Northern latitude that connects the northern part of Latin America with its closest point on the African continent across the Atlantic. Within the GoG, Guinea-Bissau forms the apex of smuggling activity – so much so that the country is now generally considered to be the world's first genuine narco-state. The value of drugs that pass through this West African nation rivals that of its official economy, while complicity in the trade extends to the very highest levels of the military and governing

---

[3] See, generally, U.S. DEPARTMENT OF STATE, *International Narcotics Control Strategy Report, 2016*, available online at http://www.state.gov/j/inl/rls/nrcrpt/2016/vol1/253221.htm.
[4] CHALK P., *The Latin American Drug Trade: Scope, Dimensions, Impact, and Response* (Santa Monica, CA, 2011), pp. 3–13.

civil bureaucracy.[5] In 2013, the head of Guinea-Bissau's armed forces, General Antonio Injai, was indicted in absentia by a New York court on cocaine and weapons trafficking charges that directly tied him to the criminal enterprises of the Fuerzas Armadas Revolucionárias de Colombia (FARC, or Revolutionary Armed Forces of Colombia).[6] Two weeks earlier the former chief of the Navy, Rear Admiral José Américo Bubo Na Tchuto, was arrested in a Drug Enforcement Agency (DEA) sting operation during which he admitted to undercover agents that he could arrange for the storage and transfer of Colombian cocaine at a rate of $1 million for every one thousand kilograms brought into the country.[7]

ATS

Several countries have emerged as important ATS centers, including Myanmar, China, the Philippines, North Korea, the Netherlands, Mexico, and Poland. These source countries supply national markets as distinct and distant as Costa Rica, Iceland, South Africa, and the United Kingdom. It is within Southeast Asia, however, that the problem of ATS has been most apparent. As with opiates, the main regional producer is Myanmar, where ethnic militias have increasingly turned to the trafficking of synthetic drugs as a cost-effective way of augmenting profits from the heroin trade. Again, the Gulf of Thailand constitutes a prominent transit hub, acting as an export gateway to maritime Southeast Asian states as well as countries/territories in the wider Asia-Pacific.[8]

Trafficking vessels

Container vessels and deep-water fishing trawlers

Container ships and deep-water fishing trawlers (usually tuna boats) are the preferred means for smuggling large intercontinental drug consignments. The attraction of these vessels stems from their sophisticated navigation and communication technology, capacity to travel over long distances, and ability to carry large payloads – all of which negate the need to retrofit the vessel in a manner that could indicate its role in trafficking activities. In addition, the circuitous routes that most freighters take provide numerous drop-off and pick-up points for illicit consignments.[9]

---

[5] ANYIMADU A., *Maritime Security in the Gulf of Guinea: Lessons Learned from the Indian Ocean*, Chatham House, Africa Paper 2013/02, July (London, 2013), p. 6.
[6] NOSSITER A., 'U.S. Indicts Guinea-Bissau's Military Chief in Drug Case', *New York Times*, 19 April 2013.
[7] NOSSITER A., 'U.S. Sting That Snared African Ex-Admiral Shines a Light on the Drug Trade', *New York Times*, 16 April 2013.
[8] U.S. DEPARTMENT OF STATE, *International Narcotics Control Strategy Report, 2016*.
[9] RUSSEL D., 'Smugglers are using tuna boats to transport cocaine,' *Defenders of Wildlife* (Summer 2002).

In most cases, drugs are concealed in legitimate cargoes, packed in metal containers welded to the ship's hull, hidden in false bulkheads or stored in secret engine compartments. Cocaine traffickers have also increasingly moved to liquefy their product so that it can be stored in fuel and ballast tanks.[10] In May 2014, one particularly large such consignment was seized off the Yucatan peninsula in Mexico. The drug, which was subsequently traced back to Argentina, had been mixed with insulating oil and had an estimated street value of $40 million.[11]

Self-propelled semi-submersibles

Self-propelled semi-submersibles (SPSSs) have also been used to transport large quantities of drugs, particularly for cocaine runs in the eastern Pacific. These vessels can carry loads of between six and ten metric tons (MT), although for buoyancy reasons they generally operate at only 75 percent capacity. A standard semi-submersible would be constructed out of wood overlaid with roughly five MT of lead ballast, one to two diesel engines, air-intake valves, and electronic navigation systems.[12] They offer no radar return and effectively eliminate infrared signatures by dissipating engine heat through keel coolers. A typical semi-submersible would be crewed by four to six persons and used for a single journey of up to one thousand nautical miles.[13]

Many SPSSs are also equipped with a scuttling valve, which is designed to rapidly sink the vessel in the event that it is spotted by a coastal patrol boat. As it goes down – a process that may take little more than twelve minutes – the traffickers jump overboard, forcing the interdiction team to perform an immediate search and rescue mission. By the time this is completed, the semi – together with its cargo of drugs – is in all probability lost, leaving authorities little option but to release the apprehended crew. In an effort to overcome this particular problem, the U.S. government passed legislation in November 2008 (in congruence with the Colombian National Parliament) making it a criminal offence to operate a semi-submersible, irrespective of whether evidence existed that it was being used to traffic drugs.[14]

---

[10] Interviews, Bogotá, March 2009 and Cartagena, November 2009.
[11] "Argentina Finds Liquid Cocaine Inside Transformers' Oil," *BBC News*, 16 May 2014, available online at http://www.bbc.com/news/world-latin-america-27451782.
[12] Officials with the U.S. Joint Interagency Task Force South (JIATF-S) estimate that between 50 and 80 SSPPs are produced each year in Colombia at a unit cost of $1 million to $2 million each.
[13] Interviews, Bogotá, March 2009 and Cartagena, November 2009; OFFICE OF NATIONAL DRUG CONTROL POLICY (ONDCP), 'Transit Zone Operations', The White House, available online at www.whitehouse.gov/ondcp/transit-zone-operations/.
[14] Interviews, Cartagena, November 2008 and Key West, March 2009.

Go-fasts

For smaller consignments moved over short distances, so-called "go-fasts" are normally used. These boats are capable of carrying up to two metric tons of drugs at a time, lie low in the water and are powered by at least four 200hp outboard engines that give them a top speed approaching 70mph. Go-fasts are usually painted a dark color or covered with aquamarine plastic sheets to disguise their configuration. In one noteworthy case that occurred in the summer of 2008, for instance, a British and two American coast guard cutters failed to detect a go-fast that was lying stationary between them, even though they had coordinates of its position and were separated by just half a mile. The vessel was eventually spotted only when the airflow from a low-flying surveillance plane disturbed the tarpaulin that was draped over the boat.[15]

Go-fasts typically "hop-scotch" up the Central American/eastern Caribbean coast, hugging the shoreline and mixing with legitimate littoral patrols to avoid patrols by the USCG and international navies. According to U.S. authorities, they account for the movement of over 50 percent of the drugs that are currently exported from Colombia and will, in all likelihood, continue to be the favored means for transporting cocaine over the short to medium term.[16]

DRUG TRAFFICKING AND THE MARITIME REALM

The maritime realm remains conducive to narcotics trafficking for several reasons. First is the sheer volume of trade that is transported across the world's oceans. Today roughly 80–90 percent of all commercial freight moves by sea, with an estimated twelve to fifteen million containers sailing at any one time.[17] This highly intensive throughput of traffic provides drug lords with a ready-made vector for the intercontinental transshipment of their products – frequently to markets that may be tens of thousands of miles from production locations.

Second is the near impossibility of instituting comprehensive container checks at some 6,591 global ports currently in operation. Indeed, even for terminals equipped with highly advanced X-ray and scanning technology, inspection rates typically amount to no more than 5–10 percent of all incoming cargo.[18] The statistical probability of successfully trafficking a drug shipment is, as a result, far greater than the risk of its being intercepted, something that obviously works to the direct advantage of the smuggler.

---

[15] Interviews, Cartagena, November 2009 and Washington, DC, February 2009.
[16] Interviews, Bogotá, March 2009 and Cartagena, November 2009; ONDCP, 'Transit Zone Operations'.
[17] RICHARDSON M., *A Time Bomb for Global Trade* (Singapore, 2004), p. 3. See also ORGANISATION FOR ECONOMIC COOPERATION and DEVELOPMENT (OECD), *Security in Maritime Transport: Risk Factors and Economic Impacts* (Paris, July 2003), p. 3.
[18] RAYMOND C.Z., 'Maritime Terrorism: A Risk Assessment', in HO and RAYMOND eds, *The Best of Times, the Worst of Times*, p. 187.

Third is the deregulated nature of the international maritime trading system, which in order to maximize turnover and minimize costs is deliberately designed to be as open and accessible as possible. While this trait may encourage greater efficiency and freer trade, it also necessarily creates numerous openings for narco-syndicates to exploit marine conveyance for their own nefarious designs.[19]

Fourth is the complex nature of the containerized supply chain, which is highly prone to criminal infiltration. Unlike other cargo vessels that normally handle payloads for a single customer loaded at dock, container ships deal with commodities from hundreds of companies and individuals that, in most cases, are received and transported from inland warehouses. For even a standard consignment numerous parties and agents would be involved, including the exporter, the importer, the freight forwarder, the customs broker, excise inspectors, commercial trucking/railroad firms, harbor workers, feeder craft, and the ocean carrier itself. Each transfer along this spectrum of movement represents a potential source of vulnerability for the overall integrity of the cargo and affords cartels with a plethora of opportunities to "stuff" or otherwise tamper with boxed crates.[20]

Fifth – and directly compounding the general susceptibility of the containerized supply chain – is the highly rudimentary nature of the locks that are used to fasten boxed crates. Most consist of little more than plastic ties or bolts that can be quickly cut and then reattached by using a combination of superglue and heat. Commercial shipping companies have generally been reluctant to develop more robust seals, given the costs involved,[21] and certainly so-called "smart containers" that emit warnings if they are tampered with have yet to be embraced with any real degree of enthusiasm.[22]

Last is the ineffectiveness of point-of-origin inspections. Many littoral states fail to routinely vet port employees, frequently do not require those entering an offloading facility to present valid identification, and often overlook the need to ensure that all cargo is accompanied by an accurate manifest.[23] Although many of these problems find their clearest expression in the developing world, they are certainly not unique to these ports. Privacy regulations in the Netherlands, for instance, preclude the option of comprehensive security vetting for workers at major terminals such as Rotterdam without first gaining their permission.[24] Equally, some 11,000 truck drivers arrive at or depart from the Port of Los Angeles

---

[19] See, for instance, RICHARDSON, *A Time Bomb for Global Trade*, p. 7.
[20] FRITELLI J., *Port and Maritime Security: Background and Issues for Congress* (Washington, DC, 30 December, 2004), p. 9.
[21] A standard (plastic) lock can be purchased for a few cents if ordered in bulk, whereas more resistant versions might cost several hundred dollars.
[22] Interviews, London and Singapore, September 2005. Smart containers are equipped with GPS transponders and radio-frequency identification devices.
[23] See, for instance, BLOCK R., 'Security Gaps Already Plague Ports', *Wall Street Journal*, 23 February 2006.
[24] Interviews, Amsterdam, September 2005.

and Long Beach with only a standard motorist's license,[25] while Singapore (which runs arguably one of the world's most sophisticated and well-protected ports) does not require shipping companies to declare goods on their vessels if they are only transiting the city-state's territorial waters.[26] This type of uneven portside security directly benefits drug trafficking, both because it is virtually impossible to open a container once it is on the high seas and due to the aforementioned fact that only a tiny fraction of boxed freight is actually checked on arrival at its destination.

THE GLOBAL DRUG PROHIBITION REGIME

For most of the 19th century, the international drug trade was not subjected to any form of regulatory control. During the early 1800s Great Britain actively sponsored the opium industry, fostering a thriving and highly lucrative trade between India and China. Indeed so great was the financial interest in maintaining the sanctity of this export market that when the Imperial Chinese government tried to ban the import of Indian opiates, London responded with full-scale "gun boat diplomacy," which played at least a partial role in triggering the so-called "Opium War" of 1839–1840.[27] The actual consumption of drugs was also viewed as benign in many countries, particularly in England and America, where cocaine and morphine were hailed both for their presumed health benefits and on account of their ability to effectively numb local and regional pain.[28]

By the end of the 20th century, however, increased opposition to the drug trade had begun to emerge. On one level, this reflected a growing appreciation of the harmful side-effects that could result from the unregulated ingestion of addictive substances as well as anger at the unscrupulous manufacture of medicines and popular drinks that often contained large amounts of cocaine, opiate derivatives, and other potentially dangerous products. On another level, it was indicative of the growing influence of moral activists in Britain and, especially, the United States. Of particular importance was their advocacy of sobriety, which struck a

---

[25] BLOCK, 'Security Gaps Already Plague Ports'.
[26] Interviews, Singapore, September 2005. Singapore does not require transiting vessels to declare the goods they are transporting, largely due to the fear that if this were made mandatory the resulting red tape would deflect trade north to Malaysia.
[27] The fundamental cause of the Opium War stemmed from a dispute between the (British) Indian government and the Viceroy of the Two Kwangs, with local officials and commanders on both sides operating independently. For more on this episode see FAIRBANK J., *Trade and Diplomacy on the China Coast* (Cambridge, MA, 1953) and INGLIS B., *The Opium War* (London, 1976).
[28] NADLEMAN E., 'Global Prohibition Regimes: The Evolution of Norms in International Society', available online at www.criminology.fsu.edu/transcrime/articles/GlobalProhibition Regimes.htm, pp. 13–14.

Table 1. *Major international counter-narcotic conventions*

Convention	Year enacted	Purpose	Protocol (if relevant)
Single Convention on Narcotic Drugs	1961	Aims to control the provision of supplies of narcotic drugs for medical and scientific purposes and to prevent their diversion into the illicit market.	The 1972 Protocol to the convention calls for increased efforts to prevent illicit production of, traffic in, and use of narcotics
Convention on Psychotropic Substances	1971	Extends the provisions of the 1961 convention to include synthetic drugs, covering hallucinogens (such as lysergic saueure [acid] diethylamide/LSD), stimulants (such as amphetamines and barbiturates), euphorics (such as ecstasy and Prozac), hypnotics, sedatives, and anxiolytics	None
Convention Against Illicit Traffic in Narcotic Drugs and Psychotropic Substances	1988	Intensifies efforts against the illicit production and manufacture of narcotic and psychotropic substances by calling for strict monitoring of the chemicals most often used in their production. Also aims to provide for strengthened mechanisms for extradition, mutual legal assistance, the transfer of criminal proceedings and tracing, freezing, and confiscating the proceeds of crime	None

Source: CHALK P., *Non-Military Security and Global Order* (London, 2000), pp. 152-3.

responsive chord among millions whose own religious convictions led them to view any form of inebriation as wholly abhorrent.[29]

The combined efforts of these health, economic, political, and missionary interest groups proved to be highly successful in stimulating anti-drug legislation in the U.S. They were also a key factor in laying the foundation for what, during the 20th century, was to emerge as a global narcotics prohibition regime vested on three main conventions: the Single Convention on Narcotic Drugs, the Convention on Psychotropic Substances and the Convention Against Illicit Traffic in Narcotic Drugs and Psychotropic Substances (Table 1).[30]

Problematically, however, the international regulatory framework for combating the global drug trade has largely not progressed beyond these accords. Moreover the conventions themselves suffer from four major weaknesses. First, they have not been universally ratified. Second, they address only certain aspects

---

[29] NADLEMAN, 'Global Prohibition Regimes,' p. 14. See also YOUNG J.H., *The Toadstool Missionaries: A Social History of Patent Medicines in America Before Federal Regulation* (Princeton, 1961).

[30] 'Drug Enforcement Administration', available online at http://www.dea.gov/index.shtml.

of the issues they were intended to counter. Third, they are non-self-executing in nature (leaving interpretation of offenses and penalties to the particular state concerned). Fourth, they have no enforcement mechanism per se (meaning that compliance is fully dependent on the individual commitment of signatories to the respective agreements).[31] As a result, the real fulcrum of counter-narcotic activity has necessarily defaulted to the national level, and in terms of maritime interdiction it is the United States that is generally recognized to have instituted the most developed strategies.

U.S. MARITIME DRUG INTERDICTION

Measured in dollar value, about 90 percent of all illicit drugs consumed in the United States arrive by sea, passing through a six million square mile transit zone (TZ) that embraces the Caribbean, the Gulf of Mexico, and the eastern Pacific Ocean. An integral component of Washington's national counter-narcotics strategy therefore focuses on instituting effective maritime interception and supply disruption in this wider expanse. The interdiction goal as set forth in the National Drug Control Strategy is to achieve a removal rate of 40 percent of the documented flow of cocaine to the United States by 2015.[32]

At the forefront of these efforts is the USCG, which runs a dedicated, multi-layered Drug Interdiction Program (DIP) directed toward the tracking, monitoring, and apprehension of suspected trafficking vessels approaching the U.S. coastline. In conducting this mission, the agency relies on specific or general information derived either from its own intelligence capabilities or from those of foreign law enforcement agencies (LEAs). Approximately 50 percent of all illicit narcotics seizures occur as a direct result of this support data.[33]

To give added force and direction to its DIP, the USCG concentrates its maritime surveillance and apprehension assets in high-threat TZ areas. Known as Campaign STEEL WEB, this strategy emphasizes the use of cutters, specially outfitted patrol-pursuit boats, and armed helicopters that are designed to interdict, stop, and board "go-fast" vessels. Operations are carried out both independently as well as in conjunction with other U.S. law enforcement agencies, including Customs, the DEA, the Federal Bureau of Investigation/FBI, and local LEAs. The USCG also frequently cooperates with foreign military, naval, and police counterparts (collaboration with the British, Dutch, and Colombians has been particularly evident), which has been highly useful in allowing for a

---

[31] See, for instance, CHALK, *Non-Military Security and Global Order*, p. 145; and BEWLEY-TAYLOR D. and JELSMA M., 'Fifty years of the 1961 Single Convention on Narcotics Drugs: a reinterpretation,' *Transnational Institute* (March 2011), 9.
[32] ONDCP, 'Transit Zone Operations'.
[33] U.S. Coast Guard, 'Drug Interdiction Program', available online at www.ncjrs.org/htm/uscg.htm.

degree of "force projection" in areas that exist beyond U.S. territorial waters but which nevertheless lie contiguous to high-volume TZ transit points.[34]

In addition to using its own vessels for interdiction operations, the USCG is able to draw on maritime resources belonging to the U.S. Navy. Since 1981, Coast Guard Law Enforcement Detachments (LEDETs) have routinely deployed from US warships in accordance with the provisions of the Military Appropriations Act (Public Law 97–86), which specifically permits the employment of defense assets in the role of law enforcement.[35]

The planned introduction of ScanEagle unmanned aerial vehicles (UAVs) in 2017 should further augment the overall interdiction and monitoring capabilities of the USCG. The low-cost drones have a cruising speed of sixty to eighty knots and are able to operate for up to 24 hours; the platforms are part of a five-year effort aimed at equipping the agency's national security cutter (NSC) fleet with advanced surveillance craft. The UAVs are equipped to transmit video and infrared images to a NSC command center where they are assessed and used to direct interdiction operations.[36]

The USCG has recorded some notable successes in terms of maritime narcotics interdiction. Simultaneous operations instituted under the auspices of Campaign STEEL WEB, for instance, resulted in the interception of more than twenty-three thousand pounds of illicit drugs in 2000, one of the highest hauls since the agency was set up.[37] The pace of seizures has remained intense, reducing cocaine availability in the United States to historic lows for the past four years. In 2015 the agency disrupted 228 smuggling attempts, which included the appropriation of 145 vessels, the detection of 503 suspected narco-traffickers and the removal of 143MT of cocaine.[38]

Despite these figures and successes, large quantities of cocaine continue to be shipped to the United States, which remains the world's largest consumer of the drug. The inability to decisively stem the flow reflects not only the dynamic and "hydra-like" quality of the contemporary South American narcotics trade but also the inherent difficulty of effectively monitoring and securing a vast maritime expanse that is well suited to the designs of transnational criminal organizations.

---

[34] The Subcommittee on Coast Guard and Maritime Transportation Hearing on Drug Interdiction, p. 6.

[35] SALONIA M., 'The U.S. Navy's Future in Drug Interdiction,' available online at www.globalsecurity.org/military/library/report/1990/SMJ.htm, p. 5. LEDETs have also deployed on partner-nation vessels and in 2015 they spent a total of 1,100 days on board American, British, Dutch and Canadian warships. See U.S. DEPARTMENT OF STATE, International Narcotics Control and Strategy Report, 2016.

[36] 'UAVs in the U.S. Coastguard', Defense Update, 13 August 2013, available online at http://defense-update.com/20130813_uavs-in-the-u-s-coast-guard.html#.VJHHC744SS0; INSITU, 'ScanEagle System', available online at http://www.insitu.com/systems/scaneagle.

[37] ONDCP, 'Fact Sheet: Interdiction Operations', available online at www.whitehouse.drugpolicy.gov/publications/international/factsht/interdiction.html. See also The Subcommittee on Coast Guard and Maritime Transportation, p. 7.

[38] U.S. DEPARTMENT OF STATE, International Narcotics Control Strategy Report, 2016.

Climate change and world trade

Mark Maslin is Professor of Climatology at the Department of Geography, University College London, United Kingdom

ABSTRACT. *There is now no doubt that human activity has increased and is increasing the temperature of the earth and the violence of the weather. Agriculture, fisheries and the supply of fresh water are all being affected. The falling cost of transport has driven a steep increase in world trade, now more than a quarter of world GDP. This has spread prosperity but increased the burning of fossil fuels. Technical remedies for climate change are available; the real difficulty is political solutions.*

RÉSUMÉ. *Il ne fait plus aucun doute aujourd'hui quant à la responsabilité de l'activité humaine de l'augmentation passée et actuelle de la température terrestre et de la violence météorologique. L'agriculture, la pêche et l'approvisionnement en eau douce en sont tous affectés. La baisse des coûts de transport a provoqué une augmentation considérable du commerce international qui représente aujourd'hui plus d'un quart du PNB mondial. La prospérité s'est par conséquent répandue mais la combustion des carburants fossiles a, de même, fortement augmentée. Il existe des remèdes techniques au changement climatique mais la difficulté principale réside dans les solutions politiques.*

.•.

Introduction

Climate change is one of the few scientific theories that makes us examine the whole basis of modern society including globalisation and the expansion of world trade. It is a challenge that has politicians arguing, sets nations against each other, queries modes of economic development and ultimately asks questions about humanity's relationship with the rest of the planet. The Fifth Assessment Reports of the Intergovernmental Panel on Climate Change (IPCC) published in 2013 and 2014 state that the evidence for climate change is unequivocal; with evidence over the last one hundred years of a 0.8°C rise in global temperatures and a 22cm rise in sea level. Depending on how much we control future greenhouse gas (GHG) emissions the global mean surface temperature could rise between 2.8°C and 5.4°C by the end of the 21st century. In addition, global sea level could rise by between 52cm and 98cm and there will be significant changes in weather patterns, with more extreme climate events. Significant changes in world trade will be needed if both the causes and impacts of climate change are to be addressed. For example, world trade through transport of goods is a major contributor to global GHG emissions. World trade could also be used to counter the predicted increased food, water, resource and energy insecurity due to the effects of climate change. Climate change is not the end of the world as envisaged by many environmentalists in the late 1980s and early 1990s, but it does mean the possible increase in misery for billions of people, and world trade could exacerbate or ameliorate these impacts.

THE CAUSES OF CLIMATE CHANGE

Greenhouse gases absorb and re-emit some of the heat radiation given off by the Earth's surface and warm the lower atmosphere (Figure 1). The most important greenhouse gas is water vapour, followed by carbon dioxide and methane, and without their warming presence in the atmosphere the Earth's average surface temperature would be approximately −20°C (Maslin, 2014). While many of these gases occur naturally in the atmosphere, humans are responsible for increasing their concentration through burning fossil fuels, deforestation and other land-use changes. Although carbon dioxide is released naturally by volcanoes, ecosystems and some parts of the oceans, this release is more than compensated for through the carbon absorbed by the biosphere and the oceans. Had these natural carbon sinks not existed, atmospheric CO_2 would have built up twice as

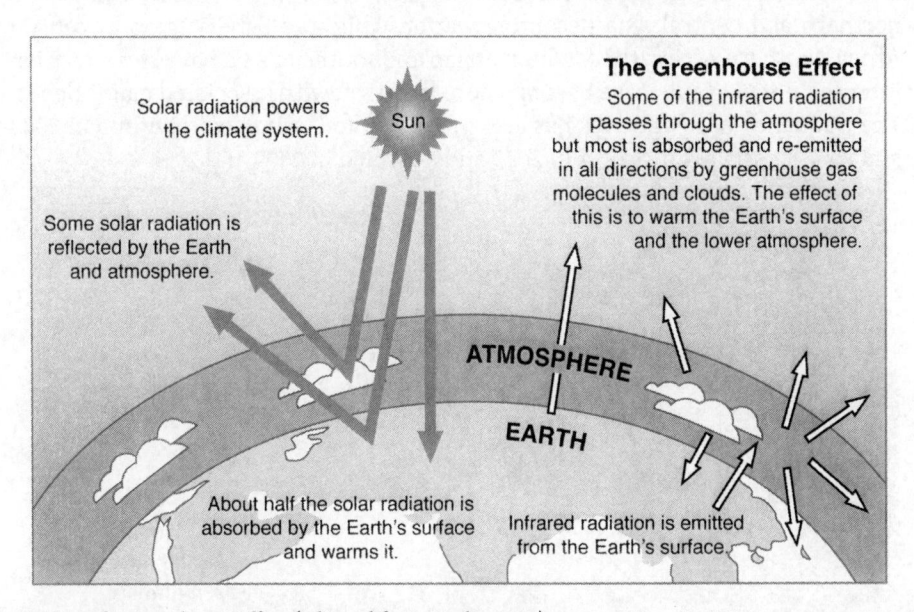

Fig. 1. *The greenhouse effect (adapted from Maslin, 2014)*

fast as it has done. Records of air bubbles in ancient ice show us that carbon dioxide and other GHG are now at their highest concentrations for more than 800,000 years (Maslin, 2014).

Evidence for climate change

There are six main lines of evidence for climate change. First, we have tracked the unprecedented recent rise in atmospheric carbon dioxide and other GHG since the beginning of the Industrial Revolution (IPCC, 2013). Second, we know from laboratory and atmospheric measurements that GHG do indeed absorb heat when they are present in the atmosphere. Third, we have tracked significant changes in global temperatures and sea level rise over the last century. Average global temperatures rose by 0.8°C over the last 100 years (Figure 2); while sea level rose by approximately 20cm over the last 100 years, partly due to thermal expansion of the ocean as it warms up and partly due to the melting of ice on land. Fourth, we have analysed the effects of natural changes on climate, including sun-spots and volcanic eruptions, and though these are essential to understand the pattern of temperature changes over the last 150 years, they cannot explain the overall warming trend. Fifth, we have observed significant changes in the Earth's climate system, including reduced snowfall in the northern hemisphere, retreat of sea ice in the Arctic, retreating mountain glaciers on all continents and shrinking of the area covered by permafrost and the increasing depth of its active layer. Sixth, we continually track global weather and have seen significant shifts in weather patterns and an increase in extreme events. Patterns of precipitation (rainfall and snowfall) have changed, with parts of North and South America, Europe and northern and central Asia becoming wetter, while the Sahel region of central Africa, southern Africa, the Mediterranean and southern Asia have become drier. Intense rainfall events have become more frequent, with associated major floods. The frequency of heat waves has also increased, for example, in Europe in 2003 and 2007, Russia in 2010, USA in 2012 and Australia in 2009 and 2014.

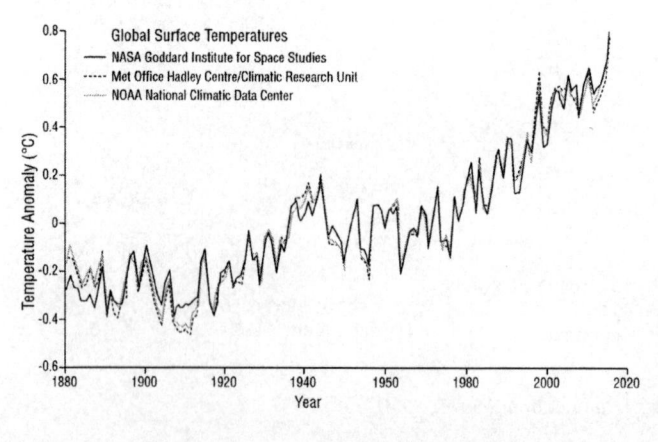

Fig. 2. *Variation of the Earth's surface temperature over the last 150 years*

FUTURE CHANGES IN CLIMATE

Continued burning of fossil fuels will inevitably lead to a further warming of our climate. The complexity of the climate system is such that the extent of such warming is difficult to predict, particularly as the largest unknown is how much GHG we as a global society will emit over the next eighty-five years (Maslin, 2013). The IPCC developed a range of emissions scenarios or Representative Concentration Pathways (RCPs) to examine the possible range of future climate change (Figure 3). These include key assumptions about the increase in the amount and type of world trade and the growth of the world's population (van Vuuren et al., 2011). Three RCPs are realistic scenarios, including a "business as usual" one (RCP 8.5) and one that examines what needs to be done in terms of greenhouse gas emissions to keep climate change beneath 2°C (RCP 2.6). Using the three main realistic RCPs over the next eighty-five years, the climate model projections suggest the global mean surface temperature could rise by

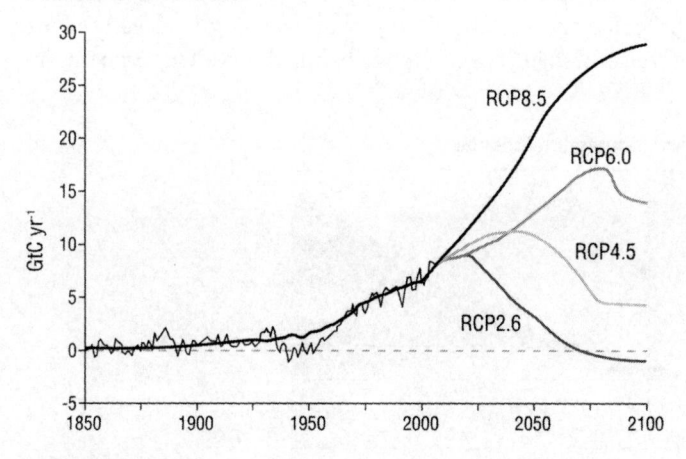

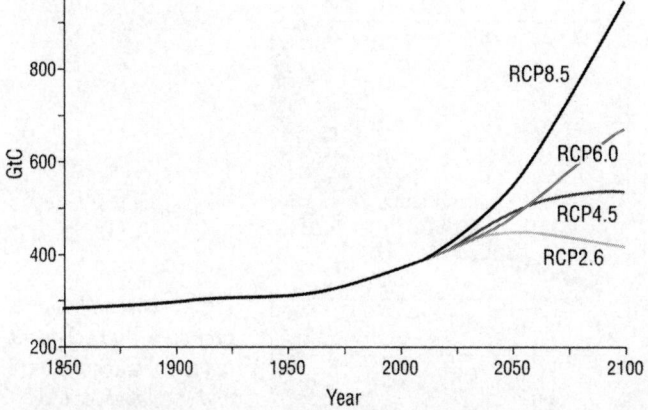

Fig. 3. *Representative concentration pathways (a) Giga tonnes of carbon emitted per year and (b) Giga tonnes of carbon emitted in total (IPCC 2013; 2014)*

between 2.8°C and 5.4°C by the end of the 21st century (Figure 4a). Sea level is projected to rise by between 52cm and 98cm by 2100, threatening coastal cities, low-lying deltas and small islands (Figure 4b). Extents of snow cover and sea ice are projected to continue to reduce, and some models suggest that the Arctic could be ice free in late summer by the latter part of the 21st century. This could threaten species that rely on cold habitats, such as the polar bear. Heat waves, extreme rainfall events and flash-flood risks are projected to increase, posing potential threats to health, ecosystems and human settlements and security (Costello et al., 2009; Watts et al., 2015). Even if global GHG emissions were to be cut immediately, there would still be some level of ongoing warming for decades and some sea level rise continuing for centuries, because the climate system is slow to respond fully to imposed changes.

These changes will not be spread uniformly around the world. Some regions will warm faster than the global average, while others will warm more slowly. Faster warming is expected near the poles as the melting snow and sea ice exposes the darker underlying land and ocean surfaces which then absorb more of the sun's radiation instead of reflecting it back to space in the way that brighter ice and snow do. Indeed, such "polar amplification" of global warming is already being seen. The expansion of tree and shrub cover already being observed in some tundra

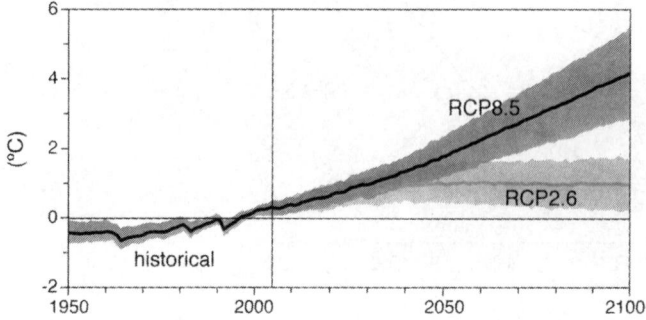

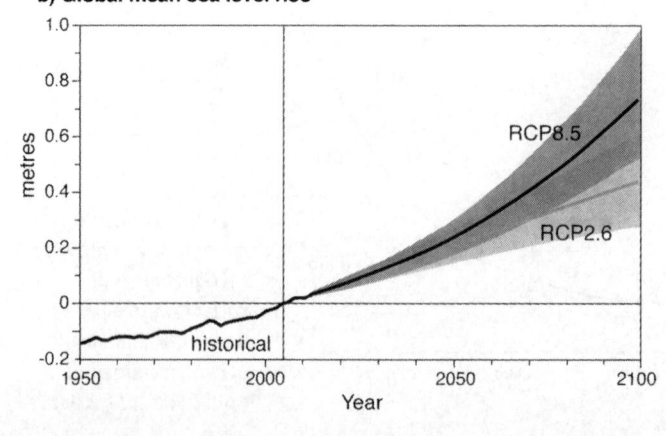

Fig. 4. Past and projected future changes in (a) global temperature and (b) global sea level

regions is expected to continue as the climate warms further, and permafrost is projected to continue to thaw. Changes in precipitation are also expected to vary from place to place. In the high-latitude regions (central and northern regions of Europe, Asia and North America) the year-round average precipitation is projected to increase, while in most sub-tropical land regions it is projected to decrease by as much as 20%. This would increase the risk of drought and, in combination with higher temperatures, threaten agricultural productivity. However, this may be offset to some extent by the effects of rising carbon dioxide on plants, which can enhance growth and also reduce their water requirements. In many other regions of the world, species and ecosystems may experience climatic conditions at the limits of their optimal or tolerable ranges or beyond. They may also be subject to competition from invasive species becoming established in newly favourable climates. Human land-use conversion for food, fuel, fibre and fodder, combined with targeted hunting and harvesting, has resulted in species extinctions some one hundred to one thousand times higher than background rates. Climate change will exacerbate this changing ecosystem composition and the accelerating extinction rates (Garcia et al., 2014). As well as impacting on biodiversity, such ecological changes may feed back into the processes of climate change by reducing the strength of the natural carbon sink, which is currently offsetting some of the human emissions of carbon dioxide (IPCC, 2014).

Marine Changes

Sea-level rise is usually considered the main effect on the marine system due to climate change, but direct measurements of the ocean's chemistry have shown that climate change is also causing ocean acidification (Barker and Ridgwell, 2012). This is because carbon dioxide in the atmosphere dissolves in the water of the surface ocean. This is controlled by two main factors, the amount of carbon dioxide in the atmosphere and the temperature of the ocean. The oceans have already absorbed about a third of the carbon dioxide resulting from human activities, which has led to a steady decrease in ocean pH levels. With increasing atmospheric carbon dioxide in the future the amount of dissolved carbon dioxide in the ocean will continue to increase. Some marine organisms, such as corals, foraminifera, coccoliths and shellfish, have shells composed of calcium carbonate, which dissolves more readily in acid. Laboratory and field experiments show that under high carbon dioxide the more acidic waters cause some marine species to have misshapen shells and lower growth rates, although the effect varies among species. Acidification also alters the cycling of nutrients and many other elements and compounds in the ocean, and it is likely to shift the competitive advantage among species and to have impacts on marine ecosystems and the food web. This is a major worry, as fishing is still a major source food, with about ninety-five million (metric) tonnes caught by commercial fishing and another fifty million tonnes produced by fish farms per year.

Human Impact of Climate Change

The potential health impacts of climate change are immense and managing those impacts will be an enormous challenge (Watts et al., 2015). Climate change will increase deaths from heat waves, droughts, storms and floods. However, higher global temperatures will also be a challenge for many societies, particularly those that rely heavily on subsistence agriculture. Higher air temperatures will make working outside more difficult and increase the likelihood of hyperthermia. This will also impact on the health of anyone who has to work outside regularly, including construction workers and farm workers (Watts et al., 2015).

The major effect of climate change in terms of global health is the potential increase in water and food insecurity that could impact on billions of people (Costello et al., 2009; Watts et al., 2015). The most important threat to human health is access to fresh drinking water. At present there are still one billion people who do not have regular access to clean, safe drinking water (Papworth et al., 2014). Not only does the lack of water cause major health problems from dehydration but a large number of diseases and parasites are present in dirty water. Rising human populations, particularly growing concentrations in urban areas, are putting great stress on water resources. The impacts of climate change – including changes in temperature, precipitation and sea levels – are expected to have varying consequences for the availability of fresh water around the world. For example, changes in river run-off will affect the yields of rivers and reservoirs and thus the recharging of groundwater supplies. An increase in the rate of evaporation will also affect water supplies and contribute to the salinization of irrigated agricultural lands. Rising sea levels may result in saline intrusion in coastal aquifers. Currently, approximately 1.7 billion people, one-quarter of the world's population, live in countries that are water stressed.

Human health is threatened by the lack of access to affordable basic food. Future changes in temperatures, precipitation and length of growing season will all affect the production of food and other agricultural goods. Extreme weather events must also be considered. For example, the 2010 Russian heat wave led to severe droughts that reduced grain production so much that Russia banned its export to ensure there was enough for home consumption. Between 2007 and 2011 drought affected much of Syria, resulting in the loss of 75% of crops and 85% of livestock. With an increasingly globalized economy very few countries are self-sufficient in basic food and hence food imports are very important. However, access to basic food is also about cost, and food prices have increased by 80% since 2004. The expansion of meat eating in developing countries such as India and China is an important forcing factor, because beef cattle require 8kg of grain or meal for every kilogram of flesh they produce. Moreover, much of the meat they consume is shipped or flown in as part of world trade. The cost of food is also influenced by the world's commodity markets. In 2008–9 there was a 60% rise in the price of food and in 2011–12 there was a 40% jump in price (Figure 5). The New England Institute of Complex Systems study into these price rises shows that the underlying trend in rising prices is due to the price of oil, increased overall

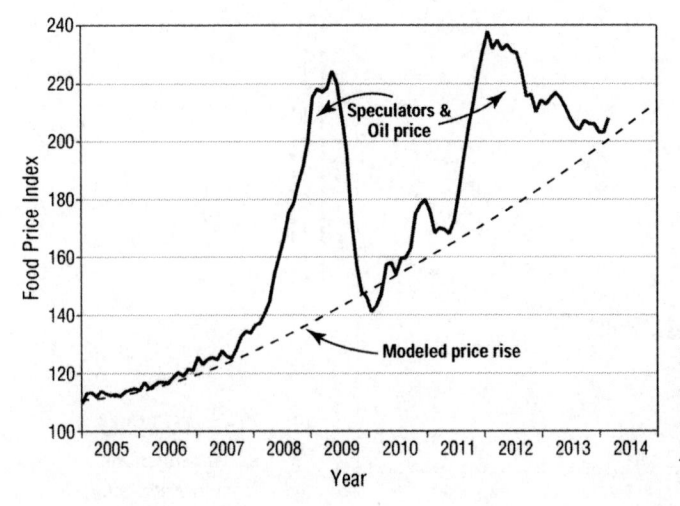

Fig. 5. Modelled and actual food prices since 2005 (adapted from Lagi et al., 2012 and Maslin 2014)

demand, biofuel production and natural disasters, but the price spikes were due to food speculation on the global markets (Lagi et al., 2012). So, the inability of many people to afford basic food, which leads to malnutrition and starvation, can be linked directly to speculation on food prices on the global markets. In India, to counter these huge changes in food prices driven by international trading, the National Food Security Act (otherwise known as the Right to Food Act) was enacted in 2013, a $12 billion annual programme to provide subsidized grain to approximately two-thirds of India's 1.2 billion people. However, this has created controversy with the World Trade Organization (WTO) as it limits international trade and is anti-competitive. So world trade agreements could either increase or decrease regional or country-specific water and food security in the future, depending on how they are structured.

WORLD TRADE

The second half of the 20th century and the start of the 21st century have been marked by an unprecedented expansion of international trade. Since 1950, world trade has grown by more than twenty-seven times in terms of volume. In the same period world GDP rose eight times (WTO, 2015). Hence the share of international trade within world GDP has risen from ~5% in 1950 to ~28% in 2015. This expansion has been driven by the considerably reduced cost of transportation and communications. The introduction of the jet engine and containerization in the last 60 years has significantly reduced the cost of air and maritime transportation, expanding both the range and volume of goods that are traded. The information technology revolution has made it easier to trade and to coordinate production of parts and components, and thus the final assembly of goods, all in different countries.

Through international organization and agreements, trade and investment policies have opened up. Driven by the neoliberal dream, countries have been

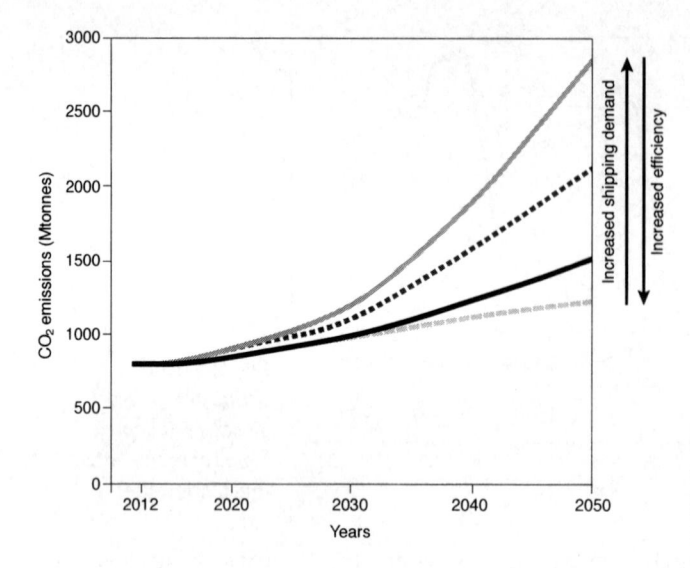

Fig. 6. Modelled carbon emissions from international shipping (IMO, 2014)

pushed to open up their trade regimes unilaterally, bilaterally, regionally and/or multilaterally. Measures that taxed, restricted or prohibited trade have either been eliminated or reduced significantly. These changes in economic policies have not only facilitated trade, they have also broadened the number of countries participating in global trade expansion. For example, developing countries now account for 36% of world exports, about double their share in the early 1960s. This expansion in world trade has had a significant effect on GHG emissions. For example, the International Maritime Organization GHG study estimated that the average emissions from shipping between 2007 and 2012 were over nine thousand million tonnes of carbon per year (IMO, 2014). This represents 3.1% of global emissions. With world trade predicted to continue to rise rapidly in the first half of the 21st century the total emissions are likely to increase at a time when countries are trying to reduce overall GHG emissions (Bows-Larkin et al., 2015). Depending on what assumptions are made about world trade expansion and efficiency gains from transport there could be a between 50% and 250% increase in international shipping carbon emissions (Figure 6). World trade is also responsible for the distribution of fossil fuels (oil, coal, natural gas) around the world, mainly via shipping. Hence not only does world trade have a large carbon footprint itself but it is also responsible for delivering most of the energy-based global carbon emissions.

Perfect Storm

World trade is also at the centre of what Professor Sir John Beddington (previous UK Government Chief Scientific Adviser) calls the "perfect storm" (Figure 7). By 2030 global food and energy demand will have increased by 50% and water

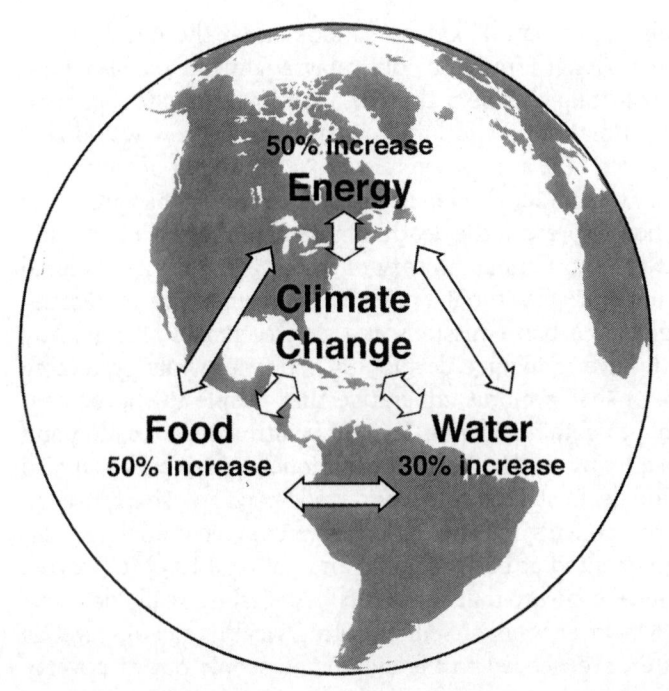

Fig. 7. *The perfect storm*

requirement will have increased by 30%. This will be partly due to the rise in global population but will also be caused by the rapid development of lower-income countries and a huge increase in consumption. According to the UN predictions, global population will grow to nine billion people by 2050 and then it will stabilise and may even drop slightly. However, that means there will be another two billion people on the planet in the next thirty-five years. This is because as countries develop they go through the demographic transition. The demographic transition refers to the transition from high birth and death rates to low birth and death rates as a country develops from a pre-industrial to an industrialized economic system (Stephenson et al., 2013).

SOLUTIONS

Reducing GHG emissions is a major challenge for our global society. This should not be underestimated because, despite thirty years of climate change negotiations, there has been no deviation in GHG emissions from the "business as usual" pathway. The failure of the international climate negotiations, most notably at Copenhagen in 2009, set back meaningful global cuts in GHG emissions by at least a decade. Anticipation and hope is building for future negotiations and there are some glimmers of hope. China, now the largest GHG polluter in the world, has started discussing a national carbon-trading scheme. The USA, which has emitted a third of all the carbon pollution in the atmosphere, has placed the responsibility for regulating carbon dioxide emissions under the Environment Protection Agency, at arm's length from the political wrangling in Washington.

Despite this lack of political agreement there is a strong economic argument for taking action. It is estimated that tackling climate change now would cost between 2% and 3% of world GDP, as opposed to over 20% if we put off action till the middle of the century (Stern, 2007). Even if the benefits were not so great, the ethical case for paying now to prevent the deaths of tens of millions of people and to avoid a significant increase in human misery must be clear. An international political solution is an imperative: without a post-2015 agreement we are looking at huge increases in global carbon emissions and severe climate change. Any political agreement will have to include developing countries while protecting their right to develop, as it is a moral imperative that people in the poorest countries should be able to obtain a similar level of health care, education and life expectancy to those living in the West. International agreements will also have to acknowledge and deal with the role world trade plays in driving carbon emissions. Climate change policies and laws based around international negotiations must also be implemented at both regional and national level to provide multi-levels of governance to ensure that these cuts in emissions really do occur (Maslin and Scott, 2011). Novel ways of redistributing wealth, globally and as well within nation-states, are needed to lift billions of people out of poverty without huge increases in consumption, resource depletion and GHG emissions. Support and money is also needed to help developing countries to adapt to the climate changes that will inevitably happen. World trade has been instrumental in the rapid expansion of global wealth but more focus is required on its negative impacts, both in terms of driving carbon emission and exacerbating food, water and resource insecurity.

Conclusions

To avoid extreme climate change cheap and clean energy production is required, as all economic development is based on increasing energy usage. Countries need to focus on localized renewable energy production to cut down on both the use and transport of fossil fuels. Fossil fuel subsidies should be made illegal and sanctions applied to countries which continue to skew the world's energy markets. The International Monetary Fund report estimated that direct fossil fuel subsidies are £1.3 trillion per year and if the cost of air pollution and climate change are added this rises to £5.3 trillion per year which is ~6.5% of global GDP (Coady et al., 2015). The International Energy Agency estimates $20 trillion will be invested in energy over the next fifteen years – what we must do is to ensure that it is not in fossil fuels. We must not pin all our hopes on global politics and clean energy technology, so we must prepare for the worst and adapt. If the right policies are implemented now, a lot of the costs and damage that could be caused by changing climate can be mitigated (Watts et al., 2015).

Climate change, therefore, challenges the very way we organize our society. It challenges not only the concept of the nation-state versus global responsibility, but the perceived advantages of ever-increasing world trade. Climate change also needs to be seen within the context of the other great challenges of the 21st century: global poverty, population growth, environmental degradation and global security. To meet these twenty-first-century challenges we must change some of the basic rules of our society to allow us to adopt a much more global and long-term approach, and in doing so develop solutions that benefit everyone.

References

Bows-Larkin et al., 'Shipping charts a high carbon course', *Nature Climate Change* 5 (2015), 293–95.

Coady D., Parry I.W.H., Sears L., Shang B., 'How Large Are Global Energy Subsidies?' (International Monetary Fund working paper, 2015), http://www.imf.org/external/pubs/cat/longres.aspx?sk=42940.0.

Costello A. et al., 'Managing the health effects of climate change', *The Lancet* 373 (2009), 1693–733.

Garcia R.A. et al., 'Multiple dimensions of climate change and their implications for biodiversity', *Science* 344 (2014), 486–96.

IMO, 'International Maritime Organization Greenhouse Gas Study 2014', http://www.imo.org/en/OurWork/Environment/PollutionPrevention/AirPollution/Pages/Greenhouse-Gas-Studies-2014.aspx.

IPCC, Climate Change 2014, *Impacts, Adaptation, and Vulnerability, Contribution of Working Group II to the Fifth Assessment Report of the Intergovernmental Panel on Climate Change* (Cambridge, 2014).

IPCC, Climate Change 2013, *The Physical Science Basis Contribution of Working Group I to the Fifth Assessment Report of the Intergovernmental Panel on Climate Change* (Cambridge 2014).

Lagi M., Bar-Yam Y., Bertrand K.Z. and Bar-Yam Y., UPDATE February 2012, 'The food crises: predictive validation of a quantitative model of food prices including speculators and ethanol conversion', arXiv:1203.1313 (2012).

Maslin M.A., 'Cascading uncertainty in climate change models and its implications for policy', *Geographical Journal* 179 (2013), 264–71.

Maslin M., *Climate Change, A Very Short Introduction* (Oxford, 2014), p. 160.

Papworth A., Randalls S. and Maslin M.A., 'Is climate change the greatest threat to global health?', *Geographical Journal*, doi:10.1111/geoj.12127 (2014).

Stephenson J., Crane S., Levy C. and Maslin M.A., 'Population, development and climate change: links and effects on human health?' *Lancet Online* 11 July 2013, http://dx.doi.org/10.1016/S0140-6736(13)61460-9.

Stern N., *The Economics of Climate Change: The Stern Review* (Cambridge, 2007), p. 692.

VAN VUUREN D.P. et al., 'The representative concentration pathways: an overview', *Climatic Change* 109 (2011), 5-31.

WATTS N. et al. (including MASLIN M.A.), 'Lancet Commission on Health and Climate Change: Policy Responses to Protect Public Health' *The Lancet* 23 (2015), http://dx.doi.org/10.1016/S0140-6736(15)60854-6.

WTO, 'World Trade Organization Assessment of Impacts of World Trade on Climate Change', https://www.wto.org/english/tratop_e/envir_e/climate_impact_e.htm.

LA FRANCE ET LA MER DEPUIS 1945 : UNE MUTATION INACHEVÉE

PHILIPPE VIAL is Research Director of the Centre d'Etudes d'Histoire de la Défense, France

RÉSUMÉ. *En 1945, le monde maritime français sort ruiné de la guerre. Sa reconstruction est menée tambour battant, dans le cadre d'un volontarisme d'État hérité de la tradition colbertienne. Ce redémarrage va de pair avec une ouverture nouvelle à la mer, qui passe à la fois par le développement rapide de la civilisation des loisirs et la maritimisation croissante de l'économie. Parallèlement, les accords de Montego Bay dotent en 1982 le pays d'un domaine maritime d'une importance inédite, tandis que l'État confie l'essentiel de sa force nucléaire de dissuasion à la Marine. Pourtant, si au début du XXIe siècle la France est à bien des égards plus maritime que jamais, le pays tarde à en tirer toutes les conséquences.*

ABSTRACT. *In 1945 the French maritime world was in ruins, but the powerful centralized state inherited from the era of Colbert immediately set about reconstructing it. At the same time a new vision of the national significance of the sea embraced seaside leisure activities, yachting and boating as well as the growth of seaborne trade. The 1982 Montego Bay agreements endowed the country with a vast new coastal territory, and the state entrusted the greater part of its nuclear deterrence to the Navy. Still, if France is more maritime than ever at the dawn of the 21st century, the country is far from having understood all the consequences of this evolution.*

.•.

Alors que s'achève la Seconde Guerre mondiale, Charles Trenet, compose « La mer », une chanson qui s'impose rapidement comme un grand succès et le restera jusqu'à nos jours. Mais la mer chantée par l'enfant de Narbonne est celle « que l'on voit danser le long des golfes clairs », non le grand large. C'est la mer d'une France d'abord continentale, qui découvre ses rivages depuis que la généralisation des congés payés, en 1936, a commencé à les rendre accessibles au plus grand nombre. Le rapport que le pays entretient depuis plus d'un demi-siècle avec l'élément marin ne serait-il pas à l'image de ce succès, un rapport décalé ? La mer devenue proche, désormais familière, mais dont les enjeux réels demeurent pour une part méconnus.

L'hypothèse demande à être rapportée à ce que la mer représente objectivement pour la puissance nationale, dans la diversité de ses déclinaisons. Or, indubitablement, les choses changent durant la période. Profonde, diversifiée, la mutation reste néanmoins incomplète. Au début du XXIe siècle, si rapports et initiatives se multiplient pour que la nouvelle maritimisation du monde soit prise en compte, le pays et ses élites peinent à prendre la pleine mesure de cette transformation. La France et la mer depuis 1945, une mutation inachevée ?

Une importance inédite de la dimension maritime à la Libération

Le 13 septembre 1944, quand la flotte française rentre à Toulon, c'est un spectacle de désolation qu'elle découvre. Les épaves du sabordage encombrent la rade et se combinent aux destructions opérées depuis par les bombardements alliés. Les autres bases navales sortent également ruinées du conflit, comme nombre de grands ports marchands. Par ailleurs, l'occupation allemande a transformé le visage des côtes, des « murs » censés les défendre (*Atlantikwall*, *Südwall*) aux abris construits pour les U-Boat à l'ouest. Des centaines de milliers de mines infestent le littoral à terre et en mer, rendant périlleuse toute forme d'activité.

Si on compte toujours environ 20 000 bateaux de pêche, à 99% en bois, les deux tiers des chalutiers en acier ont disparu et les prises ne sont plus que de 130 000t. en 1945 (contre près de 350 000t. en 1938). La marine marchande a vu son tonnage divisé par trois, passant de 2,75 à 0,9 millions de *tonneaux de jauge brute* (tjb). Le tonnage de la Marine nationale a, lui, diminué de moitié pour tomber à 350 000t. de bâtiments hétérogènes. Jamais, dans son histoire, la France maritime n'a été aussi éprouvée.

Jamais pourtant, la mer n'a été aussi présente dans l'horizon mental des Français. À la différence du précédent conflit mondial, batailles navales et opérations combinées d'une importance sans précédent ont rythmé la guerre. Si la maîtrise des mers et l'arrivée des Américains avaient déjà joué un rôle décisif dans la victoire de 1918, la dimension maritime a pris cette fois une importance encore supérieure. En Afrique du Nord comme en métropole, ce sont des débarquements qui ont initié la libération des territoires. Après quatre ans d'un blocus qui a largement contribué aux pénuries, le salut est venu d'outre-mer et par la mer. C'est une première dans l'histoire nationale.

Un retour volontariste à la normale

Dès leur libération, la remise en route des grands ports commence. C'est le début d'un processus qui va durer jusqu'à la fin de la décennie et mobiliser des moyens considérables, spécialement pour le déminage des littoraux et le dragage de leurs eaux. Le redressement de l'économie maritime associe efficacement les acteurs privés, comme le Comité central des armateurs de France, et les pouvoirs publics, en premier lieu le nouveau Commissariat général au Plan. Signe qui ne trompe pas, un compromis historique est trouvé en 1947, qui dote les dockers d'un statut remarquablement protecteur. Dès 1950, la marine de commerce retrouve sa capacité d'avant-guerre. La même année, le tonnage de la flotte de pêche a pratiquement doublé, atteignant 220 000tjb, bien que le nombre des navires ne soit plus que de 17 000. Cette expansion bénéficie de la reconversion temporaire des arsenaux et chantiers de la Marine nationale, que la faiblesse des crédits militaires prive pratiquement de toute commande de bâtiment neuf.

Un état de fait qui perdure jusqu'au début des années 1950, quand l'aggravation des tensions Est/Ouest conduit à un effort de réarmement national qui va dépasser ceux des deux avant-guerres. Il bénéficie d'aides alliées massives, essentiellement américaines. L'ensemble va permettre la reconstitution d'une marine moderne, où l'aéronavale tient désormais une place centrale. L'objectif est de disposer d'ici vingt ans d'une force de 540 000t. Lors de la crise de Suez, en 1956, la marine rassemble une flotte d'une cinquantaine de bâtiments, la plus grande du XXe siècle. Mais l'ensemble souffre encore de nombreuses carences, en particulier sur le plan logistique. Or, le redressement naval marque le pas les années suivantes compte tenu du coût croissant de la guerre d'Algérie. Plus généralement, la marine conserve une place secondaire dans l'équation stratégique française. Si l'Allemagne et l'Italie ont cédé la place à l'URSS et ses satellites, la menace demeure à l'Est. Sa nature aéroterrestre condamne la flotte à un rôle d'appoint, d'autant qu'au sein de l'OTAN, Américains et Britanniques disposent déjà de moyens navals surabondants.

Les débuts d'un nouveau monde

La défense du domaine colonial demeure la raison d'être première de la marine, spécialement dans sa dimension eurafricaine. En témoigne, après-guerre, un ambitieux programme de développement des bases outre-mer, d'une ampleur inédite. La décolonisation sonne le glas de cette ambition, que sapent d'autre part les progrès de l'arme atomique. Ils dessinent également une nouvelle échelle de la puissance. À la fin des années 1950, la marine entreprend la construction de son premier sous-marin à propulsion nucléaire, le *Q-244*. Ce sera un échec, mais la dynamique est lancée, à laquelle le général de Gaulle va donner une nouvelle dimension. D'autant qu'à son retour au pouvoir, la reconstitution d'une flotte moderne est acquise, malgré les difficultés rencontrées. En témoigne la multiplication des grandes revues navales (1958, 1959, 1964), les premières depuis l'entre-deux-guerres.

Au même moment, pourtant, la France perd l'essentiel de son espace maritime. À l'issue de la décolonisation, les littoraux qu'elle contrôlait auront diminué des deux tiers par rapport à 1939, passant d'environ 35 000km à 13 000km. La disparition du domaine colonial sape les bases du commerce qui lui était lié et sur lequel reposait la prospérité de la marine marchande. Une marine depuis le départ instrument de souveraineté autant que de profit, à ce titre protégée par la puissance publique et largement entretenue dans une situation de rente. Or, le développement rapide de la construction européenne s'accompagne d'une croissance soutenue des échanges extérieurs français et de leur réorientation géographique. La zone franc, qui représentait 38% des exportations françaises en 1951, ne compte plus que pour 26% en 1961, une évolution quasi inverse de celles vers la CEE et le Royaume-Uni. Dix ans plus tard, le déséquilibre sera devenu vertigineux (10% contre plus de 53%), quand le montant des exportations vers le reste du monde n'aura que peu varié entre 1951 et 1971.

Les débuts de la Ve République sont marqués par un autre effacement des cadres traditionnels de la puissance maritime. Réduit au rang de secrétariat d'État depuis 1948, temporairement supprimé à plusieurs reprises, le ministère de la marine (de guerre) est intégré en juin 1958 au sein du ministère des armées, qui deviendra celui de la défense en 1974. C'est la fin d'une tradition tricentenaire, établie par Colbert ... D'autant que la marine marchande, dotée d'un ministre à part entière en 1929, mais qui avait connu une existence à éclipses depuis la Libération, est elle aussi intégrée au sein d'un ensemble plus vaste, rejoignant le ministère des transports. Enfin, en avril 1961, les chantiers et arsenaux de la marine sont incorporés au sein de la nouvelle délégation ministérielle pour l'armement qui prendra, en 1977, le nom de délégation générale pour l'armement (DGA).

Un ministère du tourisme a, lui, été créé pour la première fois en 1948. L'année précédente a été fondé en Bretagne le futur Centre nautique des Glénans, où des centaines de milliers de Français vont apprendre la voile. En 1946, l'invention du bikini – une création française ! – annonce la relance du tourisme balnéaire. La fin de la reconstruction, les débuts de l'expansion, en créent les conditions dans la décennie suivante. Qu'ils séjournent sur le littoral atlantique comme dans « Les vacances de Monsieur Hulot » (Jacques Tati, 1953) ou prennent la « Route nationale 7 » (Charles Trenet, 1955) vers « les rivages du Midi », les Français se tournent de plus en nombreux vers la mer. D'autant qu'ils disposent d'une troisième semaine de congés payés à partir de 1956 ... La mer attire, en témoigne le succès du documentaire « Le monde du silence » la même année. Récompensé par une palme d'or et un oscar, le film consacre le commandant Cousteau comme l'une des nouvelles icônes de la mer en France et dans le monde.

Expansion et mutation

Cette dynamique prend toute son ampleur dans les deux décennies suivantes. En particulier parce que l'État la met au service du développement régional, spécialement en Languedoc et en Aquitaine. Créée en 1963, la Délégation à l'aménagement du territoire et à l'action régionale (DATAR) est son bras armé. Il ne s'agit pas seulement de répondre à la demande nationale, mais aussi de détourner les touristes d'Europe du Nord en route vers les littoraux espagnols. Le tourisme de masse conduit au développement *ex nihilo* de nouvelles stations balnéaires. Lancée en 1968, la Grande Motte, à proximité de Montpellier, va en être le symbole par ses dimensions et son originalité architecturale. L'État cherche à éviter la « bétonisation » du littoral, à l'instar de ce qui menace la Côte d'Azur.

Une nouvelle étape est franchie, en 1975, avec la création du Conservatoire de l'espace littoral et des rivages lacustres. Établissement public sans équivalent en Europe, il va mener avec succès une politique d'acquisitions foncières visant à la protection définitive des espaces naturels et des paysages. Cette préoccupation environnementale anime la première émission de télévision dédiée au monde de la mer, « Thalassa », lancée également en 1975. Son développement régulier jusqu'à nos jours est un autre témoignage de l'engouement croissant des Français pour l'univers maritime dans la diversité de ses déclinaisons.

Le succès du salon du nautisme et de la plaisance, fondé en 1962, en est une illustration supplémentaire. Trois ans plus tard, on y présente au général de Gaulle, venu l'inaugurer, le vainqueur surprise de la Transat anglaise, Éric Tabarly, un jeune officier de marine. Lui aussi va devenir l'une des nouvelles figures de la mer en France et dans le monde. Avec son voilier *Pen Duick II*, il va faire découvrir les courses au large à ses compatriotes. Elles ne vont cesser de se développer et rencontrer un succès populaire croissant, d'autant que les navigateurs français s'y illustrent. Dans leur sillage, la plaisance va rapidement se démocratiser et connaître un essor jamais démenti. Alors que la flotte pouvait être estimée à 30 000 bateaux au milieu des années 1960, elle en compte près de 600 000 en 1980 !

Le développement parallèle des infrastructures littorales et portuaires facilite, à partir de la seconde moitié des années 1970, l'essor spectaculaire d'un nouveau sport nautique, la planche à voile. Dès la fin de la décennie le parc national atteint les 100 000 unités, faisant de la France la nation leader dans le monde sur le plan de la pratique comme de la production (Bic Sports). Cet essor des sports nautiques est indissociable du développement parallèle de la natation, que permet le développement volontariste des piscines publiques. Alors qu'elles étaient à peine plus de 400 en France en 1960, elles approchent les 4 000 vingt ans plus tard... Parallèlement, le marché des piscines privées prend son essor.

Le boom touristique va de pair avec le développement de l'économie maritime traditionnelle. La disparition du marché colonial révélant le manque de compétitivité de la flotte marchande, l'État met en place dans le cadre du Plan une politique de soutien ambitieuse, qui concerne également les chantiers navals. Présidé par le général de Gaulle, le lancement du *France* à Saint-Nazaire, le 11 mai 1960, devant 100 000 personnes, symbolise ce volontarisme étatique. Avec ses 66 500tjb, ce transatlantique va être pendant longtemps l'un des plus grands paquebots du monde. Une quinzaine d'années plus tard, les Chantiers de l'Atlantique se distinguent de nouveau avec une série de quatre supertankers géants de plus de 270 000tjb, dont le *Pierre Guillaumat* qui restera comme le navire le plus gros jamais construit. Accompagnant, la croissance continue du commerce mondial, le tonnage de la marine de commerce triple entre 1958 et 1978, atteignant presque les 12 millions de tjb. Restructurés après le livre blanc de 1959, les chantiers navals privés emploient encore plus de 30 000 salariés à l'issue des « trente glorieuses », guère moins que leur niveau d'avant-guerre.

Le développement des grands ports marchands est le corollaire de cette expansion. En 1965, la plupart d'entre eux reçoivent un statut d'autonomie qui va favoriser leur développement. Le bilan n'est pas moins positif en ce qui concerne la flotte de pêche. Le nombre de navires continue de diminuer lentement entre 1950 et 1970, passant de 17 000 à un peu moins de 15 000, mais le tonnage global augmente de 220 000 à 270 000tjb. Une évolution qui témoigne de la logique productiviste à l'œuvre, dont atteste également l'augmentation du total des prises. Après avoir retrouvé ses niveaux d'avant-guerre à l'orée des années 1950 (350 000t. annuelles), ce total passe le cap des 450 000t. dix ans plus tard et atteint un maximum historique de 560 000t. en 1973.

De nouvelles formes de souveraineté en mer

Le domaine naval est l'autre domaine où s'exprime le volontarisme étatique. Au moment où le *France* commence son exploitation (1962), entrent successivement en service les porte-avions *Clemenceau* (1961) et *Foch* (1963), ainsi que le croiseur porte-hélicoptères et navire-école *Jeanne d'Arc* (1964), sur lequel vont se former des générations d'officiers. Si tous ces bâtiments sont des « enfants » de la Quatrième République, il n'en va pas de même du premier sous-marin nucléaire lanceur d'engins (SNLE), le *Redoutable*, dont la construction est décidée en 1963 par le général de Gaulle.

Le lancement du submersible intervient en 1967, l'année même où est créé le Centre national pour l'exploitation des océans (CNEXO). Ses travaux scientifiques, en particulier en matière de bathymétrie, vont être indispensables au développement de la Force océanique stratégique (FOSt). Il en va de même pour ceux du Service hydrographique de la marine, qui ajoute à son nom, en 1971, le qualificatif d'océanographique, pour devenir le SHOM. Parallèlement, a été établi le Centre d'expérimentation du Pacifique (CEP), où le premier essai nucléaire a lieu en 1966, à Mururoa, sous la protection d'une puissante escadre, la force Alfa. Pendant plusieurs années, cette mission va constituer le principal déploiement opérationnel de la marine hors de l'Hexagone. Aboutissement de tous ces efforts, la première patrouille du *Redoutable* intervient en 1972. Une veille permanente est désormais assurée, performance que seuls les États-Unis, le Royaume-Uni et l'URSS sont également capables d'assurer.

C'est une rupture majeure. Pour la première fois de son histoire, le vieux pays continental qu'est la France confie à la mer les clés ultimes de sa sécurité: les six SNLE vont à terme embarquer l'essentiel de l'armement atomique français. La création de la Force aéronavale nucléaire (FANu), en 1978, complète le dispositif. Son activation, en tant que de besoin, donnera aux appareils des porte-avions la mission de délivrer l'arme atomique. L'entrée en service des sous-marins nucléaires d'attaque (SNA) à partir de 1983 parachève la mutation. Quarante ans après le sabordage de Toulon, la page est tournée: la flotte française est redevenue l'une des premières au monde. Un succès qui va de pair avec la fin d'une certaine marine, dont le réalisateur Pierre Schoendoerffer livre une évocation nostalgique en 1977 avec « Le crabe-tambour ». Surtout, le renouveau n'est pas sans limites. L'annulation de l'ambitieux « plan bleu », pourtant adopté par décret en 1972, compromet le renouvellement de la flotte conventionnelle.

La révolution de la dissuasion intervient alors que se cristallise une autre mutation considérable pour la souveraineté nationale. La troisième conférence des Nations Unies sur le droit de la mer aboutit le 10 décembre 1982 à la signature de la convention de Montego Bay, en Jamaïque. Avec la reconnaissance d'une zone économique exclusive (ZEE) de 200 milles marins, la France se retrouve à la tête du deuxième domaine maritime mondial. Sa ZEE compte en effet 11 millions de km^2, soit vingt fois la superficie de l'Hexagone (550 000km^2): mieux, beaucoup mieux, que les conquêtes de Charlemagne, Louis XIV et Napoléon réunis ... Mieux que la France coloniale à son apogée (8 millions de km^2 en 1939) ... Et sans coup férir !!

Si la France ne ratifie la Convention de Montego Bay qu'en 1996, elle a en fait créé sa propre ZEE vingt ans plus tôt. La loi du 16 juillet 1976 est votée pour lui permettre de se prémunir contre les agissements unilatéraux d'autres États en la matière. Cette loi est l'aboutissement d'une série de mesures législatives visant à adapter le cadre juridique national à l'émergence du droit international de la mer. Parallèlement, l'État réorganise son dispositif en matière maritime. Pour la première fois depuis la fin des années 1950, des séries de navires militaires dédiés spécialement à l'outre-mer sont lancées (patrouilleurs Trident, puis P400, bâtiments de transports légers ou BATRAL, frégates de surveillance). L'ensemble doit permettre à la France d'assumer les nouvelles missions de contrôle induites par la création de la ZEE.

DE NOUVELLES FORMES D'ACTION DE L'ÉTAT DANS LE DOMAINE MARITIME

D'autre part, la fonction de préfet maritime est réformée par le décret du 9 mars 1978. « L'officier général, placé dans ce cadre sous la responsabilité interministérielle du Premier ministre », se voit confier un pouvoir de coordination des administrations intervenant en mer, la responsabilité d'y assurer la défense des droits souverains et des intérêts de la nation, la sauvegarde des personnes et des biens, la lutte contre la pollution et le maintien de l'ordre public. La catastrophe de l'*Amoco Cadiz*, une semaine plus tard, confirme la nécessité de cette réforme. Enfin, le 2 août 1978, après vingt ans de désert institutionnel au niveau gouvernemental, sont créés le Comité interministériel de la mer (CIMer) et la Mission interministérielle de la mer (MISMer), placés sous l'autorité du Premier ministre.

Le travail de sensibilisation mené par l'Institut de la mer, fondé en 1971 par Jean Morin, n'est sans doute pas étranger à cette évolution. Devenu l'Institut français de la mer quatre ans plus tard, après avoir fédéré l'ensemble des acteurs du lobby maritime, il va accompagner la mutation de ces années charnières par le biais de la *Revue maritime* et, surtout, des Journées nationales de la Mer, créées en 1983.

Structure légère de coordination préparant les décisions d'arbitrage entre administrations centrales, la MISmer apparaît dès le départ comme insuffisante. Le 22 mai 1981, l'alternance conduit à la création d'un « ministère de la Mer » – appellation inédite dans l'histoire de l'État français – confié à Louis Le Pensec. Ce nouveau ministre exerce les attributions relatives à la marine marchande, aux ports maritimes et aux pêches. Il dispose de la MISMer et préside le CIMer. Inversement, le Premier ministre conserve la tutelle de la recherche scientifique maritime. Il faudra attendre le 8 juin 1984 pour que cette dernière passe sous l'autorité partagée des ministres de la Mer et de la Recherche à l'occasion de la création de l'Institut français de recherche pour l'exploitation de la mer (IFREMER). Celui-ci naît du rapprochement de l'Institut scientifique et technique des pêches maritimes et du Centre national pour l'exploitation des océans (CNEXO).

La mise en place du ministère de la Mer intervient à un moment charnière. Non seulement les négociations qui vont conduire à Montego Bay entrent dans leur phase finale, mais « l'Europe bleue » émerge avec la définition en 1983, pour la première fois, d'une « politique commune de la pêche ». Dix ans plus tôt, l'adhésion à la CEE du Danemark, de l'Irlande et du Royaume-Uni, pays à forte activité halieutique, avait en effet modifié profondément la donne. En conséquence, la décision avait été prise de suspendre pour dix ans la liberté d'accès aux eaux côtières d'un autre État membre. La fin de cette décennie de transition conduit à l'ouverture de négociations pour fixer des quotas de pêche. Leur négociation, âpre, va être au cœur des activités du nouveau ministère de la Mer.

La fin des années 1970 et le début des années 1980 sont ainsi marqués par une série de ruptures qui, à des degrés divers, renouvellent les rapports de la France et de la mer. Il faut y ajouter l'émergence du patrimoine maritime, qu'il soit naturel ou culturel. La préservation du premier passe par l'adoption de la loi sur le littoral le 3 janvier 1986, votée à l'unanimité par les députés. Le développement du second se manifeste en particulier à travers la multiplication des fêtes maritimes et la préservation de vieux gréements, dont le plus emblématique sera le *Belem*. Lancé en 1981, le magazine *Le Chasse-Marée* va accompagner cette dynamique. Ces ruptures interviennent au terme de « trente glorieuses » qui ont vu à la fois la modernisation des piliers traditionnels de l'économie maritime et une croissance spectaculaire des activités touristiques. Cette *success story* n'est pourtant pas sans ombres, qui se sont accumulées depuis le milieu de la décennie précédente.

AVIS DE GROS TEMPS

Dès cette époque, le premier choc pétrolier change la donne. Il porte ainsi le coup de grâce à l'exploitation des grands transatlantiques, dont la rentabilité est concurrencée depuis les années 1960 par l'explosion du trafic aérien. Le

France, dont le désarmement est annoncé en 1974, est la victime emblématique de ce retournement. Avec sa célèbre chanson au titre éponyme, Michel Sardou se fait l'écho de l'amertume populaire. À la veille du second choc pétrolier, le naufrage de l'*Amoco Cadiz* au large du Finistère, le 16 mars 1978, constitue un autre tournant. Si une « marée noire » avait frappé dès 1967, conséquence de l'échouement du *Torrey Canyon* au large des côtes anglaises, c'est la première fois que le littoral français est touché directement. Les 220 000 tonnes de brut déversées par le tanker provoquent une catastrophe écologique majeure.

À une autre échelle, la disparition du navigateur Alain Colas, en novembre 1978, lors de la première Route du Rhum, bouleverse également l'opinion publique. En témoigne le succès, un an plus tard, de la chanson hommage qu'Alain Chamfort consacre à *Manureva*, le voilier d'Alain Colas. En novembre 1984, la mort d'Arnaud de Rosnay, lors de sa tentative de traversée en planche en voile du détroit de Formose, est un nouveau signal. Chacun à leur manière, ces drames disent la fin d'une certaine époque: les nouvelles formes d'appropriation de la mer ne sont pas sans risques, la collectivité nationale en prend brutalement conscience. Et si les piliers traditionnels de la puissance maritime ont résisté au premier choc pétrolier, en particulier grâce aux aides publiques, le suivant va emporter les digues, obligeant les pouvoirs publics à un aggiornamento sans précédent de leur politique de soutien.

« Les chênes qu'on abat ... » (Malraux)

Entre le milieu des années 1970 et celui des années 1990, le tonnage des navires marchands mis annuellement en chantier est réduit de 65%. Les emplois directs dans la construction navale passent, eux, de 32 500 à 5 800 personnes, soit une diminution de 80%. La flotte marchande connaît, elle aussi, un véritable effondrement: entre 1980 et 1990, son tonnage est divisé par trois. La création en 1987 du registre des terres australes et antarctiques françaises (TAAF), dit aussi « registre Kerguelen », qui améliore la compétitivité du pavillon marchand français, ne parviendra pas à stopper l'hémorragie. À terre, la réforme du statut des dockers, menée par le secrétaire d'État à la Mer, Jean-Yves Le Drian, constitue en 1992 un succès inespéré. Mais elle ne permet pas d'inverser le déclin des grands ports français à l'échelle européenne, en particulier compte tenu de leur retard à prendre le virage de la conteneurisation.

La flotte de pêche est, elle, divisée par deux entre le début des années 1980 et le milieu des années 1990, passant de 13 000 à 6 500 navires environ. Durant la même période, les effectifs tombent à 17 500 marins, soit une baisse de 40%. La flambée du prix du pétrole est un catalyseur évident. Elle accélère la concentration de la flotte au profit de navires usines beaucoup moins nombreux, mais bien plus productifs. Si cette logique permet de limiter l'érosion du volume des prises, la crise de la morue en montre au même moment les limites structurelles. À partir de la fin des années 1970, la ressource dans les eaux de Terre Neuve se raréfie, ce qui conduit à y interdire la pêche en 1992. Une décision aujourd'hui toujours en vigueur ...

Seule la plaisance continue son expansion, avec une augmentation de plus de 45% du nombre d'unités entre 1980 et 1995: on en compte désormais 850 000. À l'exemple des sociétés Bénéteau et Jeanneau, qui fusionnent en 1995, les chantiers français font la course en tête sur le plan international. Ils ne sont pas les seuls: en 1985, la société Informatique et Mer lance le logiciel de navigation qui deviendra MaxSea, leader mondial de la cartographie électronique trente ans plus tard. La France demeure en première position sur le marché de la planche à voile, avec un demi-million de planches en service et 3,5 millions de pratiquants. Mais cet engouement s'essouffle à partir de la fin des années 1980, sans que le surf prenne le relai.

Pour autant, la mer continue de fasciner, en témoigne le succès phénoménal du film « Le Grand bleu » (1988), que Luc Besson consacre au monde de la plongée en apnée. Ce succès fait écho à celui, croissant, des nouvelles fêtes maritimes, qui se multiplient à partir des exemples de Douarnenez, Brest et Rouen. Elles rassemblent en particulier de nombreux vieux gréements, comme ceux labellisés par la Fondation du Patrimoine maritime et fluvial, créée en 1992. Il faut y ajouter le développement réussi de nouveaux complexes scientifiques et ludiques, qu'ils soient installés dans d'anciennes institutions maritimes (Corderie royale de Rochefort, 1986; ancienne gare transatlantique de Cherbourg, devenue la Cité de la Mer, 2002) ou créés *ex nihilo* (Océanopolis à Brest, en 1989; Nausicaà à Boulogne, en 1991).

LES HÉSITATIONS DE LA PUISSANCE PUBLIQUE

Face à cette mutation profonde du monde maritime, la puissance publique peine à s'organiser. Les nouvelles instances apparues au début de la période (CIMer, MISMer, ministère de la Mer) n'arrivent pas à se stabiliser, alors même que s'amorce le déclin du Commissariat général au Plan. Qu'il soit simple secrétaire d'État, ministre délégué ou ministre de plein exercice, un ministre dédié à la mer existe certes de manière continue entre mai 1981 et mars 1993. Mais, la plupart du temps, il est rattaché au ministre des Transports, dont le portefeuille est rapidement élargi à la Ville, à l'Urbanisme ... La situation s'aggrave par la suite: entre mars 1993 et mai 2002, plus aucun ministre n'est spécifiquement en charge de la mer.

Cette valse-hésitation peut être mise en parallèle avec l'évolution de la puissance navale française. Celle-ci continue en apparence son développement. Le dernier SNLE de la classe *Redoutable*, entré en service en 1985, emporte désormais des missiles à têtes multiples. Un an plus tard est mis sur cale le premier SNLE de nouvelle génération, le *Triomphant*. En 1986, également, est commandé un premier porte-avions à propulsion nucléaire, alors que l'opération Prométhée, face à l'Iran, confirme l'année suivante tout l'intérêt d'un groupe aéronaval. Mais la fin de la guerre froide conduit à différer la commande d'un second porte-avions. Plus généralement, le renouvellement de la flotte se fait désormais au ralenti, amenant à parler d'un « désarmement silencieux ». Le nombre de bâtiments diminue en effet d'un tiers (189 en 1980, contre 123 en 1996), même si le tonnage ne régresse que de 360 000 à 325 000 tonnes.

Cette érosion s'accélère avec la professionnalisation des armées. Le nombre de bâtiments baisse seulement d'un quart (92 en 2012) et le tonnage total ne recule que faiblement (305 000t. en 2012). Mais la flotte de combat passe de 240 000t. en 1996 à 160 000t. en 2012. Cet affaiblissement quantitatif est partiellement compensé sur le plan qualitatif: en 2001, l'opération Héraklès, qui voit l'engagement du porte-avions *Charles de Gaulle* dans l'océan Indien, en soutien des opérations en Afghanistan, marque un tournant. Pour la première fois, tous les nouveaux systèmes d'armes développés depuis la fin des années 1970 (SNA et porte-avions en particulier) sont mis en œuvre de façon intégrée.

Mais l'entrée en service de nouvelles générations de grandes unités (SNLE de type le *Triomphant* à partir de 1997, bâtiments de projection et de commandement entre 2005 et 2012, frégates de défense aérienne en 2010-2012) ne peut masquer l'évidence. Les « dividendes de la paix » ont été tirés également au détriment de la puissance navale, alors même que la menace à l'Est avait disparu et que les opérations extérieures se multipliaient pour la marine (Adriatique, 1992-1999; Afghanistan, 2001-2002, puis 2010; Liban, 2006-2008; Libye, 2011; Golfe, 2013-2015). Il en résulte des affaiblissements inquiétants, mettant en cause la capacité de la marine à se projeter dans la durée ou à contrôler les espaces maritimes nationaux.

Le nouveau volontarisme des années 2000

Inversement, la mondialisation nourrit au même moment une nouvelle prise de conscience. À partir de la fin des années 1990, se multiplient les rapports publics sur les différents aspects de la politique maritime française. En juin 2006, la Commission européenne publie, elle, un livre vert: il va servir de base, l'année suivante, au lancement de la « politique maritime intégrée » de l'UE. Fin 2006, un deuxième rapport fait date, porté par le « groupe Poséidon » qui associe le SGMer et le Centre d'analyse stratégique – successeur du Commissariat général au Plan. Préparé dans le cadre d'une démarche fédératrice, *Une ambition maritime pour la France* ouvre le chemin vers le Grenelle de la mer.

Débuté en 2009, celui-ci marque une rupture. À l'opposé du dirigisme étatique traditionnel, il s'agit d'une démarche publique de réflexion et de négociation entre l'État, les collectivités territoriales, les acteurs économiques et la société civile. L'objectif est de « *définir une feuille de route en faveur de la mer, du littoral et de la promotion des activités maritimes dans une perspective de développement durable* ». Totalement inédite, cette démarche est menée par le ministre de l'Écologie, de l'Énergie, du Développement durable et de l'Aménagement du territoire,

Jean-Louis Borloo, sur le modèle du Grenelle de l'environnement tenu deux ans plus tôt. Validées au Havre, le 16 juillet 2009, par le Président de la République, Nicolas Sarkozy, les propositions de ce nouveau Grenelle sont détaillées dans le livre bleu *Stratégie nationale pour la mer et les océans*, adopté le 8 décembre par le CIMer. Celui-ci décide par ailleurs que la France va s'engager dans l'élaboration d'une « politique maritime intégrée », selon le modèle validé par l'UE.

Enfin, le CIMer consacre la création de la fonction « garde-côtes », qui doit permettre d'améliorer la cohérence de l'action des parties prenantes. Placée sous l'autorité du Premier ministre, mise en œuvre par le SGMer, cette nouvelle fonction est instituée l'année suivante. Il s'agit de la dernière d'une série de mesures prises depuis 2004 pour réorganiser « l'action de l'État en mer ». Plusieurs naufrages de grande ampleur (*Erika*, 1999; *Levoli Sun*, 2000; *Prestige*, 2002), ont en effet provoqué une prise de conscience. Ils contribuent à l'adoption de la « posture permanente de sauvegarde maritime », qui modernise la participation de la marine aux missions de service publique. Ces naufrages amènent également la France, aux côtés de l'UE et de l'Organisation maritime internationale, à renforcer sa politique en matière de sécurité maritime et de lutte contre la pollution.

Le 12 juillet 2010 est votée la loi « portant engagement national pour l'environnement », qui intègre les engagements pris dans le cadre du Grenelle de la mer. Cette loi donne une base juridique à la Stratégie nationale pour la mer et le littoral (SNML), dont l'élaboration incombe au ministre chargé de la mer, dans le cadre des orientations arrêtées par le CIMer. Une concertation nationale est par ailleurs assurée dans le cadre du Conseil national de la mer et des littoraux, installé le 18 janvier 2013.

En écho, le monde maritime multiplie les initiatives pour s'organiser, se rencontrer et rayonner. À partir de 2005, se tiennent chaque année les Assises de l'économie maritime et du littoral, à l'initiative du quotidien *Les Échos* et de l'hebdomadaire *Le marin*. Elles fusionnent en 2007 avec les Journées de la mer, organisées depuis 1983 par l'Institut français de la Mer (IFM), et deviennent rapidement le premier événement de ce genre en Europe. Entretemps, a été lancé le Cluster maritime français (CMF), qui entend jouer le rôle d'un véritable lobby économique, dans une logique de complémentarité avec l'IFM, dont l'action est plus politique. Le Groupement des industries de construction et activités navales (GICAN) est, lui, créé en 2009, pour rassembler les acteurs civils et militaires du secteur. Enfin, en 2013, a lieu à Paris la première édition du salon Euromaritime, organisé par l'hebdomadaire *Le marin* et le GICAN, en partenariat avec le CMF.

Le début du XXIe siècle est ainsi marqué par une prise en compte inédite du fait maritime en France. Au dirigisme d'État, hérité de la tradition colbertienne, succède un volontarisme collectif où la puissance publique conserve un rôle prépondérant, sans être exclusif. Cette dynamique repose sur la prise de conscience de l'importance nouvelle du fait maritime pour la collectivité nationale. Au-delà d'un discours désormais bien rodé, et qui peut à l'occasion agacer, qu'en est-il réellement ?

Une économie maritime en renouvellement

Globalement, le nombre d'emplois liés aux secteurs traditionnels de l'économie maritime a fortement régressé depuis la Libération. Les effectifs cumulés des marins pêcheurs, de leurs camarades de la marine marchande et des salariés des chantiers navals ont été divisés par deux et demi, passant de près de 180 000 à 75 000 environ. La tendance ne semble pas foncièrement différente pour les salariés des ports de commerce ou ceux du transport maritime. Cette évolution est d'autant plus significative que la France a vu dans le même temps sa population active passer de 19,3 millions, en 1945, à 28,6 en 2012.

Aujourd'hui, dans leur définition la plus restrictive, les emplois directement liés à l'économie maritime sont chiffrés à un peu plus de 100 000 (baromètre 2014 AGEFOS PME et Odyssée Développement). Avec un périmètre élargi, le Cluster maritime français les estime à 250 000, quand l'IFREMER n'en recense que 175 000. De son côté, le secteur public non marchand est évalué de manière concordante aux alentours de 50 000 emplois. Lui aussi a vu ses effectifs baisser: les personnels de la Marine nationale sont moins de 40 000 en 2015, alors qu'ils étaient près de 70 000 en 1980.

Cette évolution des effectifs est à l'unisson des autres indicateurs. Ainsi, la marine marchande n'émarge plus qu'en vingt-neuvième position dans le classement mondial, alors qu'elle pointait au cinquième rang au milieu des années 1950. La création du « registre international français », en 2005, qui rassemble désormais l'essentiel de la flotte de navires de commerce au long cours, a seulement permis de stabiliser la situation. Et alors que la France demeure la cinquième puissance exportatrice mondiale, elle ne disposait plus en 2005 que de deux ports parmi les cent premiers, avec Le Havre à la trente-sixième place et Marseille à la soixante-dixième. Le secteur de la pêche, lui, semble plongé dans une crise continue, qui fait écho aux difficultés de l'UE en ce domaine.

Ce tableau déprimant a son revers positif. Basé à Marseille, le groupe CMA-CGM pointe au troisième rang mondial dans le secteur du transport maritime. La réforme portuaire de 2008, qui a remplacé le statut des ports autonomes par celui de « grand port maritime », a donné une impulsion nouvelle à leur modernisation. Les chantiers de l'Atlantique continuent de construire des navires parmi les plus importants au monde en tonnage, cette fois dans le domaine de la croisière. Longtemps différée, la privatisation réussie des arsenaux a donné naissance, avec DCNS, à un acteur reconnu du secteur naval militaire mondial. Et dans celui de la construction de plaisance, les chantiers français occupent la deuxième place sur le plan international.

Surtout, depuis l'après-guerre, le tourisme littoral est devenu un phénomène de masse. Les emplois qu'il génère sont aujourd'hui évalués entre 190 000 (Cluster) et 235 000 (IFREMER). Il faut y ajouter ceux du secteur parapétrolier offshore (24 000 emplois selon l'IFREMER, 32 000 pour le Cluster). L'ensemble a fait plus que compenser le recul des emplois engendrés par les activités traditionnelles du monde maritime. Pour autant, il est difficile d'apprécier précisément le gain en raison des limites de l'appareil statistique existant.

Au total, les emplois liés à la mer peuvent être évalués entre 460 000 (IFREMER) et 490 000 (Cluster). Il faut y ajouter un certain nombre d'emplois induits – indépendamment de ceux liés au tourisme – mais il est difficile d'être précis, faute là encore de données suffisamment détaillées. À s'en tenir à ce qui est établi, les emplois issus des activités liées à la mer concernent, au mieux, à peine 2% des 25 millions d'actifs effectivement au travail, en France, en 2015.

Un nouveau rapport à la mer pour la société française ?

Pourtant, la mer tient une place nouvelle dans la vie nationale. En particulier parce que les différentes formes d'activité touristique ont renouvelé la problématique des espaces littoraux, qui n'ont jamais été autant occupés par l'homme. En 2005, ils accueillaient un peu plus de 10% de la population métropolitaine permanente sur seulement 4% du territoire. Il faut y ajouter la foule des touristes et des occupants des résidences secondaires.

Si la plupart des Français n'ont qu'une connaissance incomplète ou fragmentaire de la mer, elle fait désormais partie de leur univers. La célèbre définition d'Éric Tabarly – « La mer, c'est ce que les Français ont dans le dos quand ils regardent la plage ... » – traduit plus l'orgueil du navigateur qu'une exacte appréciation de la situation. Les Français viennent sur les littoraux pour la mer: pour l'admirer, en profiter et, à leur échelle, même modeste, l'apprivoiser. Ils s'en donnent les moyens: la natation est ainsi la deuxième activité sportive la plus prisée des Français, avec 12,7 millions de pratiquants. Et la flotte de plaisance atteint désormais le million d'unités en métropole.

Ce changement de paradigme n'est pas isolé. Jusqu'à la décolonisation, la mer comptait moins que l'outre-mer à bien des égards. Elle était d'abord ce qui permettait de contrôler l'Empire, dont les eaux territoriales ne représentaient que peu de choses, au contraire des terres. Désormais, la souveraineté nationale passe largement par la mer, en premier lieu via la FOSt qui déporte loin du sanctuaire national sa garantie ultime. Tournant majeur, s'il en est, inscrit dans la durée, et qui singularise la France dans le monde. De même, la création de la ZEE a conduit à une dilatation inédite et pacifique de l'espace national, qui a fait plus que compenser la disparition du domaine colonial. Même si les promesses des fonds marins restent à concrétiser, c'est une « nouvelle frontière » qui s'offre au pays ... alors que l'épée de Damoclès d'une invasion terrestre a disparu, rupture inédite au regard de l'histoire des derniers siècles.

Enfin, jamais l'économie nationale n'a été aussi dépendante de la mer, par laquelle transitent 90% des flux du commerce mondial. L'approvisionnement énergétique du pays se fait essentiellement par voie maritime, tout comme pour les minerais. Il en va de même des conteneurs, qui transportent la masse des produits manufacturés, des biens de consommation courante aux composants électroniques. Seul le domaine agro-alimentaire fait exception. Mais la voie maritime est indispensable à ses exportations, comme pour les autres secteurs de l'économie nationale: Rouen est ainsi le premier port céréalier d'Europe.

Pour la France aussi, la mondialisation est une maritimisation. La mer de Chine voit passer plus des deux tiers du trafic conteneurisé concernant le pays. Et le grand large n'est pas seul concerné: près de 40% du transport de fret intérieur à l'UE est assuré par le mode maritime. Que s'interrompent ces flux qui, quotidiennement, alimentent les entreprises françaises et c'est l'économie comme la société qui seraient rapidement asphyxiées.

Cependant, la mer n'est pas encore perçue comme un espace prioritaire à protéger, ni à contrôler. De fait, la France n'a pas eu à se battre d'abord pour cela: au Panthéon, aux Invalides, sur les murs de l'Arc de Triomphe, les noms de marins sont rares. Pendant la Seconde Guerre mondiale, la bataille de l'Atlantique a été gagnée sans participation française autre que symbolique. Et, depuis, la *pax americana* paraît garantir la liberté des mers de manière absolue. Si, depuis 1958, les chefs de l'État ont tous présidé au moins une revue navale, une spécificité qui n'a pas d'équivalent en Europe sauf outre-Manche, les crédits pour la marine sont toujours restés comptés, la FOSt mise à part.

La mutation, réelle, demeure donc inachevée. À cette limite doit être opposée la prise de conscience inédite des enjeux liés à la mer enregistrée depuis quinze ans, d'autant plus remarquable qu'elle conduit à un dépassement inédit de l'héritage colbertien. Largement portée par les collectivités locales et la société civile, cette prise de conscience constitue sans doute la meilleure chance pour la France d'aller, cette fois, plus loin dans la réalisation de sa vocation maritime.

Changes in naval power and seaborne trade in postwar Asian waters

GEOFFREY TILL is Professor of Maritime Studies at King's College London, United Kingdom

ABSTRACT. *The Cold War, the arrival of nuclear weapons and the decline of European empires were among the factors which made Asian waters unstable and dangerous. Western navies faced few real enemies at sea until the growth of the Soviet navy in the 1970s, but were heavily involved in supporting war on land. By the end of the century local navies, merchant and fishing fleets were growing fast. The booming Pacific economies depend heavily on the sea, and are vulnerable to any interruption of trade.*

RÉSUMÉ. *La guerre froide, l'arrivée des armes nucléaires et le déclin des empires européens firent partie des facteurs qui rendirent les eaux asiatiques instables et dangereuses. Les marines occidentales n'eurent que peu de réels adversaires en mer jusqu'à l'expansion de la marine soviétique dans les années 1970, mais furent lourdement engagées en renfort des combats au sol. Vers la fin du siècle, les marines locales ainsi que les flottes marchandes et de pêche se développèrent rapidement. Les économies florissantes du Pacifique s'appuient aujourd'hui lourdement sur la mer et sont vulnérables à la moindre interruption commerciale.*

.•.

INTRODUCTION

In 1947 the US Navy's Admiral Chester Nimitz produced a report that dramatically proclaimed that the Second World War, especially in the Pacific, had been won essentially by seapower.[1] Its successful outcome seemed to demonstrate that the traditional strategic verities enunciated by the likes of Mahan and Corbett were as true, and as critical, now as they had ever been. The capacity to control the sea had led apparently inexorably to the capacity to control the land. This seemed particularly to apply to the waters of the Indo-Pacific region. Given the eventual triumph of Western seapower, it seemed reasonable to conclude that with the war now over, things would go back to normal.

Almost immediately, though, these comforting conclusions were challenged

---

[1] NIMITZ C., ADMIRAL, *Report to the Secretary of the Navy, 1947*, in *Brassey's Naval Annual 1948*.

by a number of radical developments. Most dramatically, the concept and shape of war seemed to be transformed by the consequences of the technological advances made during the Second World War. The arrival of atomic and nuclear weapons and ballistic missiles, for example, produced what the Soviet Navy's Admiral Sergei Gorshkov called "the atomic shock". This reflected concern that future wars would be so short – if their truly devastating consequences allowed them to be fought in the first place – that seapower would be much less influential in determining their outcome than it had been in the past. In due course, however, navies absorbed the new technology and either developed new roles (such as maintaining the nuclear deterrent at sea) or refined old ones (such as the conduct of amphibious operations and the defence of trade) accordingly.

Less obviously, there were legal movements afoot that seemed likely eventually to change the way that people and their nations would think about the sea and could well limit what navies could do upon it. Starting in the 1950s, the nations came together with the long-term objective of agreeing a new legal regime for the sea, designed to help preserve the peace, to assure prosperity and to provide a more equitable distribution of marine resources that would reflect the notion that the sea was indeed "the common heritage of mankind".

This process ended with the UN Convention on the Law of the Sea (UNCLOS), which was ratified and finally came into effect in 1996. UNCLOS widened the territorial sea to twelve miles, introduced a "contiguous zone" of a further twelve miles in which some of the laws of the coastal state could be applied in certain circumstances, and introduced the new concept of the Exclusive Economic Zone of two hundred miles (from the coastal "baseline") in which the coastal state had sole rights over marine resources. This provided navies with new duties (most importantly to monitor and, if necessary, guard their nation's now greatly expanded maritime domain). Alongside this, though, the regime also seemed likely to introduce new complexities into the concept of the unconstrained freedom of navigation that was, firstly, so central a part of Mahan's thinking about the "maritime commons",[2] and secondly, one of the main strategic advantages of naval power.

Although UNCLOS was intended to ease international relationships, it has had precisely the reverse effect, in the short term at least. Like most international treaties it is a compromise between competing views and there are sometimes ambiguities which constructively paper over the cracks. Accordingly, there is plenty of scope for international argument about what was actually agreed (especially over a warship's freedom of navigation within another country's EEZ) and its detailed implementation in terms of defining critical baselines and the jurisdictional entitlements of land features at sea. Moreover, many of these complex issues have still to be worked out in practice. In the meantime, there is huge scope for potentially violent disagreement between the nations of the Indo-Pacific, confronted as they are by a skein of complex disputes over maritime

---

[2] MAHAN A.T., *The Influence of Sea Power Upon History 1660–1783* (London, 1890), p. 25.

boundaries and the ownership of islands, rocks and reefs that start with the South Kuriles north of Japan and sweep down through the bitterly contested waters of the East and South China Seas, swing round through the Straits of Malacca and the Indonesian archipelago and wriggle their divisive way deep into the Indian Ocean. What was intended as an act of international consensus has become, it would seem, something to fight over.

Little of this was foreseen when maritime lawyers first convened in the 1950s, for they, like the rest of the world, had much more in mind that other great contextual shift to which the world's navies would need to respond. This was a dramatic shift in the shape of the international environment. The old wartime alliance splintered into the new and threatening international configuration of the Cold War, which made healing the wounds caused by the Second World War so much more difficult. Since it almost immediately harnessed the new technologies of the nuclear age, this new rivalry seemed immensely dangerous. Perhaps for that reason, much of the competition was fought out globally in areas remote from its European epicentre. The pressures and the preoccupations of the Cold War therefore leached into the Indo-Pacific region and helped to determine events there.

For instance, the consequences of the Cold War intermingled with, and often exacerbated, the decolonisation process that was going on throughout the region at the same time. After the shattering experience of the Second World War, the European empires all rapidly dissolved in varying degrees of conflict. Western navies were active in all of this. Sometimes this required Europe's navies to engage in supporting counter-insurgency campaigns as in the Dutch East Indies and French Indo-China. In other places they became involved in operations designed to manage the process of transition or to shape its future direction as the British did in defeating Malayan communists during the "Emergency" insurgency and in fending off Indonesian threats in the "Confrontation" period shortly afterward, or as the Americans sought to do with far less success in Vietnam. The new navies of the region also had important roles to play in managing the consequences of decolonisation, as exemplified by the three wars between India and Pakistan of 1947, 1965 and 1971.[3]

NAVIES AND THE CONTROL OF LAND IN ASIA

The consequences for the role and function of navies of these three radical contextual shifts – which in the Cold War period were mainly in technology and strategic circumstance – were many and varied, but one thing that they had in common was that their preoccupation was with the control of land, rather than with the struggle to control the sea. In this they mirrored the observations of a

---

[3] HIRANDANI G.M., VICE ADMIRAL, *Transition to Triumph: Indian Navy 1965-1975* (New Dehli, 2000).

deservedly famous article by Samuel Huntington in 1952.[4] In this he observed that in the circumstances of the time, Western navies faced no real opposition at sea, a situation very different from that faced in the Second World War, and so could concentrate principally on the projection of military power ashore. This was naval power *from* the sea, rather than *at* sea. It was Corbett rather than Mahan. Although the developing capacity of the Soviet Navy made European navies more hesitant about this proposition, it certainly made sense in the Indo-Pacific region in a variety of ways.

First, some navies, especially the Dutch and the French, became embroiled in the campaigns to restore their authority in their respective colonies. The Royal Navy did likewise in the rather less malign circumstances of the Malayan "Emergency" and the subsequent "Confrontation" with President Sukarno's Indonesia. In such messy unconventional land wars, the navy's role was less to struggle for superiority at sea than to transport soldiers, their equipment and their supplies to and around the operational area, and to support their forces ashore as much as they could, given the often meagre resources at their disposal, with naval air and gunfire support. On a much larger scale, this was also the role of the US Navy in the long drawn-out Vietnam war, where hugely greater and more varied naval resources were thrown into the battle in an attempt to beat back the Viet Cong and the North Vietnamese army. With the exception of the still controversial Bay of Tonkin incident of 1964, when North Vietnamese fast-attack craft are alleged to have threatened a US battle group, the Americans faced no significant opposition at sea. Instead, under the guidance of people like Admiral Elmo Zumwalt, they had to develop the specialist and equally demanding skills of littoral and riverine operations in support of the troops on the ground, while seeking once again to deploy naval air against a variety of military and civilian targets ashore that were frequently a good deal more ambiguous than they had seemed during the Second World War.[5] Political circumstances, rather than military effectiveness, made this a thankless task. In the Indian Ocean the Pakistan and Indian navies were engaged in three wars, but once again, despite the occasional clash and loss at sea, their strategic effect was mainly on operations ashore. The 1971 war, for example ended with an Indian sea-based missile attack on Karachi which reminded the Pakistanis of the vulnerability of their coast, given the superiority of the Indian navy.[6]

One of the reasons why there was external engagement in the local conflicts of the Indo-Pacific region was the widespread belief that they were inspired by the aggressive aspirations of the Communist bloc and flowed naturally from the central East/West confrontation in Europe. Accordingly, when the North Koreans attacked the South in 1950, the American and other Western navies intervened

---

[4] HUNTINGTON S., 'National policy and the transoceanic navy', *Proceedings of the US Naval Institute*, May 1954.
[5] See http://www.history.navy.mil/docs/vietnam/high5.htm and MOISE E.E., *Tonkin Gulf and the Escalation of the Vietnam War* (Chapel Hill, NC, 1996).
[6] NANDA S.M., ADMIRAL (retd), *The Man who Bombed Karachi* (New Delhi, 2004).

and rehearsed once more all the capabilities in the projection of power ashore that they had demonstrated during the Second World War. This even extended to a large-scale amphibious operation at Inchon in September 1950. This was intended by General MacArthur to make the most of the strategic outflanking potential offered by superiority at sea. Thereafter Western navies shuttled up and down both sides of the Korean peninsula supporting South Korean and allied forces ashore in their battle to keep the North Korean and Chinese armies at bay. It incidentally demonstrated that in some circumstances at least, the traditional functions of seapower *were* still valid in the nuclear era. In just the same way and for the same reason, the US Navy successfully interposed itself between the Chinese mainland and Taiwan and the offshore islands, in an effort to save the now demoralised Kuomintang from strategic extinction.

All of this was possible because allied fleets faced no, or at least very little, serious opposition at sea, with the exception of North Korean sea-mines and Chinese coastal artillery in the 1950s, and the very limited possibility of North Vietnamese fast-attack craft attack in the 1970s. This was even largely true of the confrontation with the Soviet Far East Fleet for much of this period, for American commanders were reasonably confident that they could protect Japan and South Korea by at least containing and neutralising Soviet forces in the region.

But as Soviet naval power developed under the auspices of Admiral Sergei Gorshkov, America's confidence in its capacity to do this wavered. It began to appear that America's capacity to control the sea might be under increasingly significant threat. This loss of confidence was reinforced by the service demoralisation that resulted from the loss of the Vietnam war. The developing problem was addressed by the US Pacific Fleet, which in 1978–79 sparked a series of studies that resulted in the celebrated "The Maritime Strategy" of 1986.[7] This was a Mahanian philosophy which envisaged the US Navy and Marine Corps and their allies determinedly developing the technological and operational capacity to take on the Soviet Navy and Air Forces at both ends of the Eurasian landmass, defeat them and then project power ashore against military and industrial targets both in coastal regions and deep inside the Soviet homeland. Since the strategy had a most depressing effect on the Soviet Union and may well have played a significant role in ending the Cold War, it certainly appeared as a triumphant vindication of a sea power's capacity to help shape events ashore. But what was significant about this was the quite explicit recognition of the fact that by the mid to late 1970s the growth of the Soviet Navy meant that sea control would have to be secured first.

---

[7] A public version of this appeared as a special report of the *US Naval Institute Proceedings* in January 1986.

The Control of Asian Waters

Carving time into distinct periods is always a risky and difficult business. It is true that during the latter stages of the Cold War there was a growing acceptance of the need to secure sea control, and afterwards there were occasions when seapower could be projected ashore without fear of significant opposition at sea (such as the Adriatic operations of the 1990s, the second Iraq war and Afghanistan). All the same, with the end of the Cold War came a new emphasis, especially in the Indo-Pacific region, on the need to contest and, hopefully, control the sea for the benefits it offered.

This was manifested by the extraordinary growth in capability and aspiration of most of the navies of the Indo-Pacific region. This is particularly true of the main Asian navies, those of China, Japan and India and the medium navies of South Korea and Australia, but it applies to the rest of them too. Until the 1980s, most navies of the region, especially the smaller ones, largely consisted of old ships passed on to them by foreign sponsors, and their aspirations were accordingly modest. Increasingly necessary naval modernisation plans were, however, stalled by the Asian currency crisis of 1997–98, and further interrupted by the global credit crisis a decade later; only recently has fleet rebuilding resumed with a vengeance. The US-based naval consultancy firm AMI International anticipateed naval spending in the Asia-Pacific of some US$170 billion by 2030; the Asia-Pacific naval market as a whole is expected to overtake NATO European countries to become the second-largest source of future naval spending after the United States. For the first time in perhaps four hundred years, in a truly historic shift, maritime Asia now spends more on its navies than does Europe.[8]

In general, the region's navies are seeking much more advanced, first-class ships, weapons and systems, rather than the re-conditioned, second-hand or new but modest equipment they generally received in the past. Whether it is Korea's *Aegis* destroyers, Malaysia's *Scorpene*-class submarines or Indonesia's *Sigma*-class corvettes, there is now a new insistence on high quality, which inevitably means larger and more expensive ships. This approach tends to produce navies that, while not necessarily larger are certainly more powerful. With the completion of the KDX programme, for example, the South Korean navy's current force of 120 small and medium surface combatants will be replaced by about seventy much larger and more capable ones. The acquisition of modern submarines even by the smaller navies of Southeast Asia illustrates the same point. Submarine numbers in the Asia-Pacific are expected to increase markedly over the next couple of decades, not least amongst the lesser naval powers, where they are seen as a force equaliser.[9] With this can be expected significant improvements

---

[8] KARNIOL R., 'Boom time ahead for Asia-pacific navies', *Straits Times*, 9 November 2009. I am extremely grateful to Bob Nugent, Vice President of Advisory Services of AMI International (see http://aminter.com) for these figures.

[9] DAVIES A., 'Up periscope: the expansion of submarine capabilities in the Asia-Pacific region', *Journal of the RUSI* (October 2007), 64–9.

in local anti-submarine warfare capacities. The growth of the region's interest in so-called network-enabled operations may in the end prove even more significant in enhancing its naval power.

To add to this increasing panoply of power, the larger Asian navies are developing aircraft carriers, amphibious capabilities, the capability for ballistic missile defence and, in the case of India and China, ballistic missile-carrying nuclear submarines.

Not the least important aspect of the region's naval advance has been a determination to build up national capacities for indigenous production and so to reduce their reliance on others. With all this new operational and industrial capacity comes an expanding operational reach and a plethora of more ambitious capabilities in the battle for sea control (in the anti-submarine, anti-aircraft and -missile and anti-surface ship areas) and in the capacity to project power ashore and to defend or attack shipping at increasing range from the home base.

The reasons for this very significant tectonic shift in the balance of the naval world are not hard to find. Firstly, it reflected a growing awareness of the value of the economic resources that the sea had to offer, especially in the light of the extended maritime domains provided by UNCLOS. Fish, oil, gas, gas hydrates and eventually who knows what else offered much higher levels of food and energy security to those countries able to secure them. The fact that China alone operates 695,000 fishing boats of various kinds illustrates both the extent of its investment in the fishing industry and the challenge posed by the need to keep the Asian fish take sustainable.

For this reason, the maritime element became, through the 1990s and into the 21st century, an increasingly important part of the national economies of most countries in the region. Marine resources seemed sure to provide government revenue, employment, access to accelerated industrialisation and a degree of strategic independence. Consequent talk of the "blue economy" inevitably included reference to the growing importance of the global shipping industry, which in the post-Cold War period has been going through a remarkable transformation.

The growth in the extent, scale and relative importance of Asia's sea-based trade also readily explains the growth of its naval power. The 1944 Bretton Woods meeting ushered in a postwar era of free trade in which sea trade expanded from half a billion tonnes of sea imports in 1950 to ten billion in 2010, growing at an annual rate of 4.3 per cent.[10] An increasing proportion of this was, and remains, Asia based, for trade around and across the Pacific now greatly

---

[10] This was higher than the annual growth in GDP at 3.6%. Presentation by Martin Stopford, President Clarkson Research to RUSI, 1 July 2014. Presentation by Rajiv Biswas, Asia Pacific Chief Economist, HIS Global Insight, Singapore Dec 2013. I am grateful to both for permission to use these figures. Detailed analysis may be found in BISWAS, R., *Future Asia: The New Gold Rush in the East* (London, 2013); STOPFORD, M., *Maritime Economics* (London, 2009); and the UNCTAD *Review of Maritime Trade 2013*.

exceeds that across the Atlantic.[11] China, Japan and Korea also trade extensively across the Indian Ocean, taking manufactured goods to Europe, bringing back commodities from Africa and oil and gas, especially from the Gulf. The countries of APEC (the Asia Pacific Economic Cooperation group) account for nearly half the world's trade and their economies are growing three times faster than Europe's.[12] Dry and liquid bulk and general cargo totals are expected to rise from nine thousand million tonnes in 2012 to fifteen thousand million tonnes by 2025. Most of these increases in trade were Asian in origin and increasingly fuelled by a dramatic growth in sea imports in the non-OECD countries of the region. This has encouraged intra-Asian and so-called South-South trade. Although much of this is driven by the current major countries of the Indo-Pacific region (and so can be expected to moderate somewhat) smaller countries are developing fast in this regard. ASEAN, for example, is expected to have a $10 trillion economy by 2030. Ominously for Europe, Asian countries, now strong in ship-building and operation, are already moving into the shipping service industries: finance, insurance, brokerage and so forth.[13]

Even with the growth of pipelines, and rail and road routes across the Eurasian land-mass, the relative cost and safety advantages of sea transport will persist. While there may be strategic advantages in diversifying supply routes so that countries are not wholly dependent on the security of their shipping, and while there may be time advantages in getting "fast fashion" products from China to Europe, it remains twice as expensive to transport a container of them by rail as it does to send it by sea. Sea freight costs are now an insignificant element of the cost of a manufactured product when it arrives in Europe, but the greater time taken may be critical in some cases.[14] Totally predictable arrival times are crucial too, hence the importance of investment in efficient port infrastructure and inter-modal supply chains. Hence, too, the current implausibility of major changes to existing shipping arrangements resulting from the opening of the "Northern Sea Route".[15]

Challenges

If Asian countries are now wholly dependent on the maritime system, they seem well aware of the vulnerabilities this brings. As Mahan remarked over a century ago, the maritime system has its fragilities and shows that a dependence on the

---

[11] Transpacific trade with the Americas in 2013 totaled $1.8 trillion compared to $0.12 trillion worth of trade going over the Atlantic. 'Special Report: the Pacific', *The Economist*, 15 November 2014. STOPFORD presentation.

[12] *Ibid*. In 2013 APEC's economies grew at 5.4%, Europe's at 1.7%.

[13] 'Europe Reacts as Ship Finances Moves East', *Fairplay*, 7 October 2010.

[14] It takes just 14 days to send a container from Chonqing in Southwest China to Duisburg in Germany and costs approximately £9,000, compared to 60 days and £4,000 by ship. *Ibid*. See also STOPFORD, Presentation.

[15] QUASEM H., 'Arctic Route Not "Big Concern" for Singapore', *Straits Times*, 8 November 2012.

sea can be a source of strategic weakness, if not properly attended to, as well as of strategic strength. He warned:

> This, with the vast increase in rapidity of communication, has multiplied and strengthened the bonds knitting together the interests of nations to one another, till the whole now forms an articulated system not only of prodigious size and activity, but of excessive sensitiveness, unequalled in former ages.[16]

For the sea-dependent countries of the Indo-Pacific region any disruption of international shipping could indeed have devastating consequences. With their continuing heavy reliance on oil and gas from the Gulf, China, Japan and South Korea for example are much more vulnerable to, say, the closure of the Straits of Hormuz than either the United States or Western Europe.[17] The security of shipping could be threatened from a host of sources, including piracy and other forms of maritime crime, political instability ashore that endangers the conditions for trade, inter-state conflict and even direct attack from hostile states or terrorist organisations, as exemplified by Al-Qaeda's attack on New York's World Trade Towers in 9/11. Less dramatically, global recessions and depressions can threaten the system too.[18]

TURNING BLUE

For all these reasons many of the countries of the Indo-Pacific region have recently adopted very maritime policies at the highest level. In 2014 both China's President Xi Jinping and Indonesia's President Joko Widowo (Jokowi) have established the development of their country's maritime attributes as a very high and public national priority. Xi Jinping has talked of establishing a "21st century maritime silk road" from China to Africa and beyond, by extensive investment in the maritime infrastructure of countries in Southeast Asia and across the Indian Ocean. Likewise appealing to the inspiration of past maritime glories, President Jokowi has vowed to make his archipelagic country once more the "global maritime axis" it used to be in the days of the Srivijaya empire. India, South Korea, Vietnam, Malaysia and even the Philippines are following suit. Singapore, of course, set off on this enterprise decades ago.

In their grand strategic plans, all these countries include a substantial investment in naval power as a natural corollary of their maritime growth. As the well-known Chinese scholar Ni Lexiong put it back in 2005, "when a nation embarks upon a process of shifting from an 'inward-leaning economy' to an 'outward-leaning economy,' the arena of national security concerns begins to

---

[16] MAHAN A.T., CAPT., *Retrospect and Prospect* (London, 1902), p. 144.
[17] MITCHELL J., 'Asia's Oil Supply: Risks and Pragmatic Remedies', Chatham House Report, May 2014.
[18] CHU J., 'Shipping Lines Battle Slump', *(Asian) Wall Street Journal*, 31 October 2014.

move to the oceans. Consequently, people start paying attention to sea power. This is a phenomenon of history that occurs so frequently that it has almost become a rule rather than an exception. Therefore it is inevitable that such a shift is taking place in today's China."[19] This helps to explain why the Indo-Pacific region is investing so heavily in the dramatic recapitalisation of its navies, in consequence of its ever-increasing dependence on the sea.

CONSEQUENCES, BOTH GOOD AND BAD

Two kinds of naval preoccupations and behaviour in regard to the control of the sea are emerging from all this. The first is essentially conflictual, suggesting that Asian states will most likely follow the historic patterns of competition set by their European predecessors over the past several centuries.

Disputed jurisdiction over large sections of the South and East China seas has led to the expansion of navies and coastguards in the region and to the development of capabilities (most notably small diesel submarines and coastal missiles) plainly intended to deter intrusions into the claimed areas and has led to a string of dangerous and confrontational incidents. Inspired by a mix of growing nationalism and an appreciation of the potential commercial importance of these waters, these incidents do much to justify Robert Kaplan's view that the South China Sea is a "simmering pot of potential conflict" which could well have profound "implications for global peace and security ... a corner of the globe that will affect all our lives for decades to come".[20] Given the historic baggage that comes with it, the China–Japan–Taiwan dispute over the East China Sea could be even more dangerous.

Running alongside this and inevitably intermingled with it are a number of national rivalries which are also finding expression in naval competition. The most obvious of these is the strategic wariness of a rising China and an allegedly declining United States. It is hard not to believe that competition between these two is driving both their naval policy, especially given the fact that so much of it boils down to an attempt on the part of China to deny the waters of the first and second island chains to the US Navy (through its "counter-interventionary" anti-access/area-denial strategy), and a corresponding response on the part of the United States to build up its "Air/Sea battle" capabilities to defend its capacity to control and use the waters of the Western Pacific.[21]

Lower-scale versions of the same developing tensions between the control and

---

[19] NI L. 'Sea Power and China's Development', *People's Liberation Daily*, 17 April 2005.
[20] KAPLAN R.D., *Asia's Cauldron: The South China Sea and the End of a Stable Pacific* (New York, 2014). See also RAINE S. and LE MIERE C., *Regional Disorder: The South China Sea Disputes* (London, 2013); and HAYTON B., *The South China Sea: The Struggle for Power in Asia* (New Haven, 2014).
[21] See FRIEDBERG A.L., *Beyond Air-Sea Battle: The Debate over US Military Strategy in Asia* (Abingdon, 2014).

denial of the sea are evident in the relationship between China and Japan, China and the various Southeast Asian claimants to the South China Sea, and China and India, over Xi Jinping's project for a maritime silk route across the Indian Ocean. The fact that China seems to be the common denominator in all this doubtless reinforces the sense of imminent containment in Beijing, but conceals the fact that throughout the area there are many other edgy bilateral relationships that either have degenerated or easily could degenerate into the use of lethal force at sea. Of these, the sinking in 2010 of the South Korean corvette *Cheonan* by a North Korean submarine with the loss of forty-six lives is only the most obvious example. This naval competition for control of the sea is usually bolstered by wider political, legal and economic activity too.

Compensating to some extent for this depressing catalogue of actual or potential competition for the control of Asian waters, however, there are many indications of regional cooperation to moderate and manage such tensions and disputes and to come together to defend the sea-based trading system on which the countries of the Indo-Pacific region nearly all depend. These include multinational naval cooperation to defend trade against piracy in the Straits of Malacca and off Somalia, to control international terrorism and various forms of maritime crime and to come together to relieve distress in the wake of the catastrophic weather events to which the region is unfortunately prone. All of these cooperative activities are facilitated by a veritable host of multinational exercises at sea that are distinguished by the fact that they are not generally aimed against anyone.

The common element in all these cooperative activities is that they proceed from a different conception of sea control, not one that is aimed at securing strategic dominance, but one that is instead intended to make the seas safe for all to use and enjoy in common security – less sea control in the English sense, more supervision, monitoring and protection as the French *contrôle* would have it.

Conclusion

How this mixture of competition and cooperation for the control of the sea in Asian waters turns out in the years to come will be of huge significance for Europe and the rest of the world, given the evident truth of the warning William H. Seward, US Secretary of State gave to Congress in 1852 when he predicted that "the Pacific ocean, its shores, its islands and the vast regions beyond will become the chief theatre of events in the world's great hereafter".[22] Maritime developments in Asian waters could indeed determine our future.

---

[22] BAKER G.E., ed., *The Works of William H. Seward Vol. 5* (Boston, 1884), pp. 51, 236 ff.

Looking to the Future

Jeremy Black is Professor in History at the University of Exeter, United Kingdom

ABSTRACT. *The early 21st century has been marked by growing instability at sea even as the value and economic significance of seaborne trade has continued to increase. The relative decline of both US and NATO naval power, and the rise of challengers, notably China, are one factor. These in turn have provoked the growth of other navies such as Japan, India and Australia. New weapons such as drones and anti-ship missiles, whose effects it is too soon to evaluate fully, introduce another element of uncertainty. All these are aspects of the naval situation, but that in turn is not self-contained but bound up with land-based aircraft and missiles.*

RÉSUMÉ. *Le début du XXIe siècle a été marqué par une instabilité croissante en mer bien que la valeur et l'importance économique du commerce maritime n'aient cessé d'augmenter. Le déclin respectif de la puissance navale des États-Unis et de l'OTAN et la montée de pays concurrents comme la Chine en est un des facteurs. Cela a provoqué le développement d'autres marines nationales telles que celles du Japon, de l'Inde et de l'Australie. L'arrivée de nouvelles armes comme les drones et les missiles antinavires, dont on ne peut aujourd'hui mesurer entièrement les conséquences, introduit un autre élément d'incertitude mais ne constitue qu'un aspect de la situation navale, ces armes ne fonctionnant pas de manière autonome mais étant liées à des missiles et avions basés au sol.*

. • .

The significance of naval power to the 21st century can be seen in the range of uses that are pursued and planned.[1] That states have different assessments of what naval power can offer them and how it might threaten them is scarcely new, but these differences have become more prominent due to political, economic and technological developments over the last decade. These developments will be considered first, and then attention will be devoted to the different strategies of individual states. This topic will be linked to the salience of sea power, and not only for major states but also for weaker counterparts. Last, there will be consideration of possible scenarios and changes in the future. Perhaps far more than developments on land or in the air, the future of navies is difficult to predict. There have been more changes in weapon systems and platforms at sea

---

[1] I have benefited repeatedly from the sage advice of Nicholas Rodger on successive drafts. I have also profited from that of Stanley Carpenter, Mike Duffy and Mark Stanhope on individual drafts.

than on land or in the air. This is likely to continue, and not least, given the cost of present ship types, at all levels of strategic influence and operational activity.

A CHANGING MARITIME ENVIRONMENT

The key developments over the last decade relate to political and economic power and interest. The two have combined to suggest a move from the allegedly "unipolar" situation that followed the Cold War. This American hegemony, which lasted from the collapse of Soviet power in Eastern Europe in 1989 until the aftermath of the rapid and total conquest of Iraq in 2003, was particularly apparent at sea, where America was clearly the dominant power. Moreover, America was readily able to use the sea for power projection. Indeed, it appeared best placed to use the sea for strategic and operational purposes, notably for protecting allies and threatening opponents at both the strategic and the operational levels. Sea power offered a forward presence as a deterrent action. Moreover, American naval power was presented as the key guarantor of what was discussed as the "global commons", namely the idea that free movement by sea, particularly of trade, was a general good that was essential to the world system.

America's strength appeared, and was, more apparent due to the rapid decline of the world's second naval power, the Soviet Union. Indeed, naval strength became distinctly marginal to the Soviet military system in the 1990s. The navy was affected not only by a lack of funds and investment, leading to obsolescence, but also by a more corrosive lack of political interest. Russia, the successor to the Soviet Union, focused on acting as a regional naval power, although small squadrons were dispatched further afield, for example to the Caribbean.

Moreover, there was no other challenger in the 1990s to the USA. It might encounter resistance in military commitments, notably with Iran in 1987–88 at the close of the Iran–Iraq war and in Somalia in 1993, or opposition to pressure, especially from Serbia in 1995 and 1999, and Iraq and Sudan in the late 1990s. However, none of this opposition was seen at sea or represented a challenge to America's unrivalled maritime position and naval power-projection. This capability was demonstrated most clearly with the huge *Nimitz*-class nuclear-powered super carriers, each of which was the centre of a carrier group including jet fighters and ground-attack aircraft, as well as escorting warships armed with Tomahawk cruise missiles.

In the mid-2000s, however, the distribution and nature of power appeared to change considerably. The great and costly difficulty America encountered in overcoming sustained resistance in Iraq encouraged a sense that technological capability was not a reliable measure of effectiveness. America's military difficulties were accentuated by grave economic and fiscal problems which led to growing talk of decline, and to associated discussion of the likely future effectiveness of American military power.

This talk was given direction by a perception of new or rising threats. The most significant appeared to arise from the massive growth in the Chinese economy, the strength of its public finances and its growing interest in military, especially naval, expansion. Moreover, the alignment between China and Russia from the 2000s constituted a geopolitical revolution, as it reversed the animosity between the two powers that had prevailed from the early 1960s, and made the USA relatively weaker. There were no immediate manifestations of this alignment at sea, but the general military and political context was thereby transformed.

Other developments were linked to this transformation. The relative weakness of the USA, combined with divisions in NATO and an unwillingness to spend on the military, notably by Germany, NATO's second-wealthiest power, ensured that the West appeared less potent. Another once-prominent NATO naval power, Canada, failed to maintain its naval strength. A similar failure was seen elsewhere. For example, after the Cold War ended, Sweden did not maintain an anti-submarine helicopter capability. In 2014, when it was spending 1.2% of GDP on defence, Sweden was unable to detain a probable Russian submarine operating close to Stockholm. Indeed, the Baltic appears to be the sea where Russia can most easily display its naval power unmolested, and it may be tempted to, for example by putting pressure on Estonia, Latvia, Lithuania and Poland.

The apparent weakness of the West encouraged both political opposition on the part of some powers, especially Russia, and a conviction on the part of threatened Western states, notably Japan and Israel, that they needed to be able to defend their own interests without relying on the USA. The issue posed by Russian naval power projection was demonstrated in 2014 when Russian warships were deployed near Australia prior to the holding there of the G-20 summit and at a time of poor relations between Russia and Australia. Deficiencies in amphibious capability when Australia intervened in support of East Timorese independence in 1999 led to a new emphasis on seaborne forward defence, with the formation of an Amphibious Ready Group, and adoption by the army of the doctrine of MOLE (Manoeuvre Operations in the Littoral Environment), and the emphasis on a "strategic" amphibious capability. The latter was in accord with the American emphasis, under the 2014 Quadrennial Defence Review, on the contribution by America's allies.

Linked to concern about power politics came opportunities and pressures arising from global developments in political economy. The two crucial ones were, first, the increase in long-distance maritime trade, which, by its very nature, meant trade exposed to the vagaries of international stability and security; and second, the rapid and unprecedented growth in the world's population, as well as the certainty that this would continue into an uncharted demographic future, which led to increased sensitivity about resource possibilities, sensitivity linked to a determination to affirm and protect maritime territorial claims. The availability of maritime strength was made even more of an issue by the use of intimidation and violence in certain areas. This was notably so with China in the East and South China Seas, and also with piracy based in Somalia and, increasingly,

Nigeria. This situation created a more general anxiety based on the increase of risk and the danger of new norms in behaviour.

Volatility was further increased by developments in military technology and by the resulting uncertainty over what this might mean in terms of effectiveness at sea, and thus the measure of naval power. In particular, the likely relationship between major warships and less-expensive anti-ship weaponry created a sense that the age of the big ship was possibly passing. Although the enhanced weaponry and control systems of the latter were highly impressive, there were also questions of the vulnerability of warships. This situation was exacerbated by the extent to which the procurement structure of naval power was driving leading navies toward fewer, and more expensive, vessels. The maintenance in service of each thus becomes more significant, and this enhances vulnerability, irrespective of specific weapons characteristics.

That there are fewer, larger and more expensive warships reduces their individual vulnerability, but makes the ships harder to risk – a situation also seen with aircraft. This risk-adverse orientation is a phenomenon known in some circles as the "lumpy capital dynamic" where, based on the cost and restricted number of major capital assets, navies are reluctant to put their warships into harm's way, thus negating their power-projection capability and, ultimately, their utility. This situation has been witnessed before, notably in the German navy's reticence to commit the High Sea Fleet to a general action with the British Royal Navy's Grand Fleet in World War One.

THE USA

Despite these points, the USA clearly remains the leading naval power and is likely to continue to do so. However, the American navy faced serious problems. American military spending fell with the end of the military commitment in Iraq and its run-down in Afghanistan. The unprecedented size of the accumulated federal debt and of the annual deficit, and the pressure to cut them, had an impact, as did the political preference, notably under the Obama administration (2009–2017), for welfare expenditure and economic "pump priming". While the army and marines were scheduled for significant cuts in the 2010s, there were even more substantial ones in the navy. It is planned that the navy will be reduced to 280 vessels, of which only about 90 will be at sea at any one time. Partly as a result, the ability of the USA to inflict a rapid defeat on Iran was called into question in 2013, as was its capability when confronted in 2014–15 by concurrent crises in relations with China and Russia and in the Middle East. Moreover, the reduction in American naval strength created acute concern among regional allies worried about Chinese naval plans and expansionism.

At the same time, the USA continued to employ its carriers as a key element of its foreign policy and strategic effectiveness. A political reluctance to commit troops encourages maritime solutions, which offer engagement in that embroilment. An operational crisis at sea can have fewer political consequences than similar events on land. In 2014, when the USA still had ten carriers, it used them to deploy strength around the world. This policy meant keeping three on operations and one usually en route to a patrol area, while the remainder were in deep maintenance, or on training, or having major refurbishment. In 2014, repeated airstrikes on ISIS (the so-called Islamic State of Iraq and Syria) targets in Iraq and Syria were launched from the USS *George H.W. Bush* in the Gulf and the USS *Carl Vinson* in the Red Sea. In turn, $13 billion is being spent on the USS *Gerald R. Ford*, the first of a new class of American carriers.

The USA therefore continued the pattern of activity seen since the 1940s. In doing so, however, it is, and will be, confronted by other states that are acting in an unaccustomed (to the Americans) fashion, and will have to shape planning, doctrine and procurement accordingly. This is separate to, but linked with, the other changes arising from developments in naval technology, and the opportunities and problems these pose.

CHINA

The most important novelty is that of Chinese naval power, which has not been a significant factor, even regionally, since major defeat at the hands of Japan in the Sino-Japanese War of 1894–95. The opportunities brought to China by economic growth have been matched by a geopolitical commitment to naval expansion. The traditional land-based focus on "interior strategies" – the development of expanding rings of security around a state's territory – has been applied to the maritime domain. In part, this is in response to a reading of Chinese history in which it is argued that, from the 1830s, the ability of foreign powers to apply pressure from the sea has greatly compromised Chinese interests and integrity. "Near China" has therefore been extended as a concept to cover the nearby seas. This gives both an enhancement of security and a sense of historical validity, one that apparently provides purpose to Communist rule of China. Chinese naval strategists now think in terms of naval operations in the "far seas", or those areas beyond the First Island and even Second Island Chain out from the Chinese mainland.

However, the definition and implementation by China of the relevant attitudes and policies ensure both considerable problems and significant mission creep. This is because the security of what may seem to be the near seas apparently requires regional hegemony and an ability to repel any potential oceanic-based power, which means at present the USA. The Chinese desire may be motivated by security, but it challenges that of all others and, crucially, does not adopt or advance a definition of security that is readily capable to compromise or, indeed, negotiation. In part, this is a reflection of the Chinese focus on "hard power", a power very much presented by the presence and use of warships for purposes of coercion. The Chinese navy offers force to support the application of psychological and political pressure. Unilateralism is a key element.

A willingness to resort to force creates for others a key element of uncertainty. The Chinese emphasis on naval strength as a key aspect of national destiny, and the rapid build-up of the Chinese navy, have helped drive the pace for other states. They have led Japan and India, in particular, to put greater emphasis on a naval build-up, while also ensuring that the USA focuses more of its attention on the Asia-Pacific region. In 2014, the Australians considered turning to Japan in order to provide a new generation of submarines that are clearly designed to provide security against China. Japan has considerable experience in the building of effective submarines. Talk in 2014 that conflict over the East China Sea might lead to a broader international struggle, with the USA backing Japan, underlined the significance of maritime issues and power.

The previous October, the USA agreed to base surveillance drones and reconnaissance planes in Japan so as to patrol waters in the region. The development of anti-ship missiles by China, able to challenge American carriers, notably the BF-21F intermediate-range ballistic missile fitted with a manoeuvring re-entry head containing an anti-ship seeker, poses a major problem. As a result, the carriers may have to operate well to the east of Taiwan, in other words beyond the range of the Navy's F-35s. Access-denial operations directed against the USA are seen by Chinese planners as crucial for conflict over Taiwan. Indeed, the doctrine of sea denial provides the weaker navy with an opportunity to thwart the stronger. This entails asymmetric capabilities such as saturation missile strikes against carrier battle groups. Asymmetric warfare at sea will create particular requirements for both sides, on the pattern of asymmetric warfare on land and in the air. Chinese missiles also threaten American bases, such as Guam in the western Pacific, as well as the use of allied bases, for example in Japan.

The likely future trajectory of Chinese naval ambitions and power is currently a, if not the, foremost question for commentators focused on power politics, and that itself is a clear instance of the continuing relevance of naval strength. At present, attention is on Chinese sea power in the China seas, but the weapon systems it is presently developing, including carriers, will give it a global reach. This may be used to support friendly regimes and states, for example in Africa.

The ready willingness of Chinese internet users to identify with these issues reflected their salience in terms of national identity and interests. Moreover, this willingness suggested a pattern that would also be adopted in other conflicts over maritime rights. They proved readily graspable. The Chinese government is struggling to ride the tiger of popular xenophobia. In China, as earlier with Tirpitz and the *Flottenverein* in Germany, popular support for naval expansion has proved easier to arouse than to calm. Thus, the utility of naval power was symbolic, ideological and cultural as much as it was based on "realist" criteria of military, political and economic party. It has been ever thus, but became more so in an age of democratisation when ideas of national interest and identity had to be reconceptualised for domestic and international publics.

Other Leading Powers

While no other navy can match that of the USA, China is not alone in seeking to be a leading naval power. Focusing on carriers as an index of naval strength may adopt an outdated criterion, due to the deployment of drones, which can be launched from smaller platforms, and of more effective anti-ship missiles. Ships carrying drones may soon be more important and far cheaper than carrier-based fleets. Nevertheless, carrier numbers are indicative, at least of legacy issues, and with particular reference to naval air power and the prestige of naval power. In 2014, aside from the ten American carriers, India had two and a third under construction, Italy had two, Britain had two under construction and Brazil, China, France, Russia, Spain and Thailand each had one. The sea trials in 2011 of China's first aircraft carrier intensified speculation about strategic rivalry with the USA, as did tensions when it was deployed in 2013, although there is no comparison between American and Chinese carrier power.

Sea-based air power, however, appeared to offer less in terms of sea denial than submarines and missiles, while the delivery of force against land targets could be provided in more cost-effective terms by sea-based missiles and, very differently, by warships designed to support amphibious operations, such as two *Mistral*-class helicopter carriers Russia wished to purchase from France, but of which France blocked the sale in 2014. More states sought to commission submarines and missile-firing surface ships than carriers. For example, once the Russians gained control of Crimea and its key naval base of Sevastopol in 2014, they announced an expansion and modernisation of their Black Sea fleet, with new warships and submarines. The sense of naval power as inherently competitive was captured with Russian claims in 2014, notably by President Putin, that it was necessary to gain control in order to prevent Ukraine from giving anchorage to American warships.

The specific configurations of regional geography, and related tasking requirements, ensured that naval powers with regional ambitions focused on nearby waters, such as Iran and Israel, did not seek to develop a carrier force. In most cases, the development of naval capacity was primarily linked to regional goals and concerns, rather than to a desire to project power at a greater distance. Thus, both Japan and the powers of South-East Asia sought to counter the build-up of Chinese naval strength, while Indian naval plans, for long directed against Pakistan, were increasingly focused on concern about Chinese intentions in the Indian Ocean, an issue at a very different scale. Replacing its earlier calls for a neutral, in other words Indian-dominated, Indian Ocean, Indian support for the USA is relevant in the Indian Ocean as India may be able to block, or at least challenge, Chinese naval moves beyond the Straits of Malacca. India's role thus supplements the American base in Diego Garcia and the major presence in Singapore.

There is a separate naval arms race in the Middle East, albeit one that is distinctly secondary to that in land-based air power. The Iranians and Israelis are particularly active in developing naval power, although for different reasons, each of which exemplifies the role of tasking. The Iranians seek an asymmetrical capability able to challenge the deployment of American naval power in the Gulf, while the Israelis seek to be able to blockade opponents in Lebanon and Gaza and to support ground operations against them. The Iranian goal, but not that of Israel, clashes with American policy. In 2012, the carrier *Abraham Lincoln*, supported by five other American warships, sailed through the Strait of Hormuz into the Gulf in order to underline the right of passage under international law, and thus demonstrate that the USA was not deterred by Iran. Naval power offered a strategic capability, notably with the Iranian ability to threaten oil movements through the Gulf and with Israel's submarine-borne nuclear weapons. The latter weapon type is the best instance of a hitherto untested naval strategic potential.

Indeed, the extent to which many ambitious medium powers, such as Iran, Israel and Brazil, devoted significant resources to building up effective naval power was notable. Brazil agreed in 2009 to purchase four enlarged French *Scorpène*-class submarines, which were to be in service by 2021, and to develop a nuclear-powered submarine. In 2010, Brazil agreed to purchase six patrol vessels and five or six frigates from Britain's BAE Systems.

The determination of would-be great powers, namely China and India, to be able to wield naval power, including, if necessary, in conflict, is also notable. Indeed, the variety of national policies that sea power can be taken as furthering is notable. In part, this reflects the extent to which the sea as a space is now more securely part of the strategic culture of states that have a coastline than was the case a century ago.

That does not mean that all states have an equal interest. Moreover, the topic of strategic culture has to be handled with care, as major changes can be noted with individual states. Whereas the Japanese navy of the late 1930s supported intervention in China and planned for war with the USA and Britain, now the focus has shifted from access-denial aimed at the Soviet Union to access-denial aimed at China, and, in each case, in co-operation with the USA. Similarly, the German navy has not only broken with the naval tradition and tasks of the first half of the 20th century but has also not responded to Germany's economic growth and territorial reunification by pursuing additional naval power. Thus, while Britain, a medium-sized power, maintained an oceanic navy capable of intervention everywhere, not least with amphibious and submarine capability, Germany, a state with a larger economy and generally higher growth rate, had a weak navy that has no strategic impact and only limited operational potential notably in the Baltic. However, it is unclear whether Britain will replace its Trident submarines and whether it can afford to maintain two carriers and necessary task forces to support and protect them. The costs of maintaining sea power have long been one of the most potent factors in great-power league tables, and that is equally, indeed especially, applicable to medium powers.

A VARIETY OF TASKS

The variety of tasks that navies might have to discharge ensured that a range of states sought to deploy naval vessels with a more modest capability. Indeed, while some of these vessels were organised as part of navies, others were under coastguard services. Initially, the expansion of piracy suggested a multi-layered need for naval power. For most of the 20th century, this had very much been a form of power dominated by the major states, while most states, instead, focused on their armies, not least for internal control and policing. In the early 21st century such control and policing, however, increasingly also encompassed maritime tasks. Control over refugee flows, the maintenance of fishing rights and the prevention of drug smuggling proved prime instances. Thus, Australia employed its navy to try to ensure control over refugee flows, and thus to address strong domestic concerns. Piracy has proved a major challenge, both in economic terms and as a type of asymmetric warfare. Aside from practical problems on both heads, there are also questions about the necessary international agreement and the legal framework.

As a consequence of these requirements, naval capability became as much a matter of the patrol boat, as of the guided missile destroyer. Naval power became essential even to small states. The reasons varied. Thus, fishery protection was more significant for more states, while for others protecting territorial waters and claims therein related more to oil and natural gas for drilling. For example, in the eastern Mediterranean, Cyprus and Israel were concerned to protect claims to a natural gas field between the two. This resource raised fears about terrorism as well as ambitions on the part of others with territorial claims. Brazil's attempt to extend control over its continental shelf is linked to the exploitation and security of oil and gas reserves. The "National Strategy of Defense" published by Brazil in 2008 declared that the "national strategy of defense is inseparable from the national strategy of development".

Drug money is a threat in particular to the stability of Caribbean states. These, however, have tiny navies. As a result, alongside local navies such as that of Colombia, it is the navies of major powers that have a Caribbean presence, the USA, Britain and France, each of which also have colonies there, that play a key role, one that is greatly facilitated by aerial surveillance and interception capabilities. These powers also transfer warships that they deem redundant to local states. That states such as St Lucia need to be able to maintain force at sea indicates the extent to which it has become a key aspect of strength and law enforcement for all maritime powers.

THE FUTURE

Population growth will bring far greater and much more frequent competition over resources and access to resources, and may make trade more vulnerable to interruption. This will increase the need for maritime security. Already, production facilities and shipping need to be protected, whether oil platforms off the Nigerian coast, oil-survey ships off the Somali coast or shipping in the Indian Ocean.

Climate change brings more change. The melting of the Arctic ice cap is leading to new commitments, for example, by Canada, as new trade routes and mining opportunities are opened up, and contested. In 2014, Canada and Russia quarrelled over the situation in the Arctic. In turn, future climate change may well accentuate the issues.

As a separate issue, rivalry between major powers is likely to be played out in large part in terms of naval power projection and with new warships and related technologies. As a result of this focus on rivalry at sea, the apparent equations of naval effectiveness between competing powers will command great attention. The sea, in short, continues to make a great difference to the strength or weakness of states and to the stability or instability of the global system, whether understood primarily as political or economic, and in terms of blunt force or of international law. The significance of maritime commerce and security represents both positive and negative (or preventive) reasons why so many states are pursuing maritime interests.

At the same time, power at and over the sea is not simply a matter of naval activity. Indeed, the very significance of the sea as a space encourages a variety of strategies for dominance, control or denial: goals and doctrines vary significantly. In addition, this variety of goals, strategies and doctrines is linked to a range in weapons procurement, institutional structure and operational planning. This range includes much of what would classically be termed naval. However, the extent to which shore-based air and missile capability is also involved underlines the difficulty of thinking of the future of sea power solely in terms of navies. Land-based weaponry that is explicitly aimed against naval forces, for example that deployed along the Chinese coast or threatening the Straits of Hormuz from the Iranian coast, is a central part of the equation of sea power. This is notably so at the regional level, but, to an extent, the global levels of naval capability and potential owe much to the regional levels, or, at least, those of prominent regions.

Thus, the very significance of the maritime sphere can in part be understood in terms of a focus of attention that is not solely naval, or, at least, naval as conventionally understood. The concept of joint-service operations is pertinent, although it is overly apt to be employed to take an institutional and doctrinal focus that does not capture the shifting character of the force environment. The latter is at once distinctive to particular elements, yet also overlapping and interacting. The sea is, and will continue to be, a crucial element, but of a greater whole. To think in terms of maritime and naval histories is therefore to think not of a restricted range but of particular approaches to the human experience, past, present and future.

Conclusion

There are many dimensions to the sea, and even a work of this size cannot possibly deal with them all. We have here the sea as a means of trade and communication, of the movement of people and ideas. We have the sea as a theatre of war, a sea fought-over itself, and the means of projecting force to distant lands. The sea unites, but it also divides; it may be an instrument of stability or of disorder. Different nations and societies, with different historical experiences, have seen the sea as a threat or an opportunity, and it is clear that either view may be correct. The sea has been the means of constructing empires, and of subverting them. The sea has opened opportunities for individuals to work and travel in remote parts of the world, and for whole populations to migrate to other continents. Fishing and whaling have provided rich sources of nutrition and industrial raw materials to peoples not otherwise endowed with them. Inland seas, navigable rivers and ship canals carry the sea into the interior of continents, but the influence and jurisdiction of coastal states may extend the control of the land far out to sea. Seaborne trade connects places on shore, often places remote from the coast; people and enterprises who have never seen the sea may still be deeply involved in the use of it. Nevertheless there have always been, and there remain, countries and regions which from choice or necessity have been little involved with the use of the sea. As a result they have avoided both the risks and the opportunities it brings.

In war the sea allows forces to be moved swiftly, economically and secretly to parts of the world which could not otherwise have been reached; it allows distant countries to unite their forces in empires or alliances, but it also parts friends and separates enemies, improving defence by distance and strategic depth. The free use of the sea invariably increases strategic options, but an uncommanded sea multiplies risks and dangers. For those who have failed to master it, the sea can be a destructive factor, dividing forces and exposing them to defeat in detail [Kennedy].

Because the sea means so much, it has a powerful symbolic force. A fleet of warships is both an instrument of power and an expression of wealth and might, of industrial strength and technical supremacy. States as diverse as Wilhelmine Germany, Meiji Japan, the twentieth-century United States and Soviet Russia built fleets as symbols of the great-power status they claimed, as much or more than as instruments of strategy and foreign policy [Epkenhans, Frank, Hagan, Åselius]. Sometimes naval development has signified different things at home and abroad; sometimes a fleet has successfully projected the intended image in one direction while failing altogether in another. As mobile concentrations of power, able to approach potential enemies without trespassing on foreign soil or even necessarily revealing their presence, fleets are versatile instruments of deterrence and diplomacy – but deterrence is always vulnerable to mistranslation. What is meant as a warning may be construed as a threat, what is meant as a threat may be construed as an attack, and what is meant as moderation may be construed as weakness.

Legally as well as physically, the sea is quite unlike the land. Human societies on land are everywhere regulated by law, and the laws divide and distinguish different societies. There are traditionally two ways in which law may be applied to the sea. One is to extend the land, so to speak, to claim a 'territorial' jurisdiction over coastal, adjacent or enclosed seas as though they were really dry land. The latest and most ambitious examples of this approach are the UNCLOS agreements (from the 'United Nations Conference on the Law of the Sea' which drew them up). These markedly restrict the traditional 'freedom of the seas' by extending the jurisdiction of coastal states. The other approach is to improve and solidify the limited and indefinite forms of customary international law, providing a kind of substitute law by tacit or formal international agreement. The first formal agreement setting international law at sea was the Declaration of Paris of 1856, regulating the legitimacy of blockade and capture of private property at sea. During the 19th and 20th centuries the reach of both kinds of international law was greatly extended, but the problem of enforcement still remains the major weakness of the law of the sea. Powerful states do not seem constrained to observe it when it does not suit them, and it is an open question how many of these new legal structures would survive a major war [Frei, Bateman, Haines].

The weakness of law is very relevant to the environmental value of the sea. In the late 20th century mankind has become more and more aware of the sea as the indispensable common component of the human environment, as the engine which drives climate and weather, and consequently makes it possible (or impossible) to feed and sustain its human and animal populations. In very many cases the activities of one country or group degrade the sea and threaten the life or livelihood of others. Supranational organisations are painfully ineffective, and in some parts of the world even nation states are disintegrating. The weakness of international law and international politics leave few effective instruments to resolve disputes and promote beneficial policies. In too many cases, the urgent need of agreement and common action only promotes disagreement and obstacles to action. The sea is at the heart of the world's problems as well as of its solutions, and it can only be understood through its history.

The 1815 peace settlement of the Congress of Vienna expressed the desire of the European powers to forget more than a quarter century of war and destruction, and return to the world they had known before the French Revolution. In Britain Parliament and government shared the objective of shrinking the state and its expenditure to its pre-war size by abolishing wartime taxes. Abroad they looked for economic influence with no repeat of their eighteenth-century imperial fiasco [Lambert]. They expected to preserve their social and economic systems by maintaining the Corn Laws (which kept up the price of grain, and therefore the income of landowners), and the Navigation Laws (which kept British foreign trade in British ships manned by British seamen). In the event both had been abandoned by the middle of the century. Free trade and industrialization opened up a new world of massive trade flows, as the working classes of the new industrial cities were fed by cheap imported food, paid for by the exported products of the new industries. By sacrificing income, or potential income, and consenting to successive increases in the electorate, landowners were able to preserve much of their political influence into the 20th century. British shipowners lost their protection, but the expanding demand for shipping massively increased their market [O'Rourke]. British coal not only fuelled the new steamships, but answered the rapidly growing world-wide demand for steam coal. This meant that tramp shipping in particular (most of it under sail until late in the century) could always rely on an outward freight of coal to balance the bulk imports of raw materials [Palmer]. British shipbuilding dominated the world market and added another successful element to trade and industry [Lemmers]. The new prosperity was vastly greater than the old, and it was not immediately obvious that Britain's economic gain had been bought with strategic risk. Shipping and shipbuilding was at the heart of the new economic system and a great access of wealth and strength – but dependence on seaborne trade for both exports and imports vital to the life of the country gradually exposed her to a grave new vulnerability which had not been present when she had been largely self-sufficient in both food and raw materials. In 1889 Britain reacted by the Naval Defence Act, financing a larger Navy, and in particular a larger cruiser force for the defence of trade. In retrospect it can be seen that this began a twenty-five year naval arms race which preserved British naval supremacy but helped to transform the strategic landscape of the whole world [Beeler, Sumida].

One of the reasons why Britain was slow to appreciate the risks of her new dependence on overseas trade was her renewed enthusiasm for empire in the later 19th century. Free trade led to British investment and activity in many corners of the world, free movement of people rapidly expanded the colonies of settlement, and both of them generated political demands and commitments which home governments had to answer even if they were opposed to new colonies in principle. Colonial officials and colonial garrisons demonstrated a capacity for unilateral action which repeatedly drew the home government further than it meant to go, and steadily increased the areas under British direct rule or influence. As the colonies of settlements grew into self-governing Dominions they built up their own navies and armies, strengthening the empire as a whole, but weakening its political unity [Stevens].

Most other countries took only so much of the nineteenth-century liberal revolution as suited their purposes. Imperial powers like the Netherlands helped themselves into the industrial age by protecting imperial trade (implicitly relying on British protection), and only reached for the benefits of free trade when their industries and merchant fleet were strong enough to face competition. France and Germany re-imposed agricultural tariffs when the interests of landowners were threatened by imported food [van Dissel, O'Rourke]. Austria-Hungary strengthened its empire by building a powerful fleet in the central Mediterranean, and a major international seaport (Trieste), but the Ottoman empire's attempts to do something similar failed [Sondhaus, Heywood]. Newly-united Italy's geographic situation as a peninsula in the central Mediterranean seemed to offer large opportunities to link overseas and overland trade, but in practice underdeveloped industries, ports and railways, and dependence on imported fuel, left Italy behind its neighbours until well into the 20th century. Nevertheless the navy was one of the most modern and efficient agencies in a backward state, and in the 20th century did help Italy to an empire in North and East Africa [Zampieri]. Spain was an unqualified failure as a naval and imperial power, losing its South American colonies to internal revolt and nearly all the rest to foreign aggression in the Spanish-American War, but though the state failed, private enterprise allied to the new industrial economy of the Basque Country revived a flourishing merchant fleet which Spain had not seen since the 16th century [Valdaliso]. Denmark, a remnant empire of islands scattered from the Baltic to the Arctic, depended entirely on sea communications and prospered without protection in tramp shipping, the most competitive of all sea trades [Møller]. Sweden, having lost its overseas empire to Russia in 1809, built up shipping and overseas trade in the later 19th century as an aspect of the imports and exports of a newly-industrial economy [Müller].

In all these cases the engagement of different countries with the sea can be understood in terms of national policies interacting with the facts of geography. The relations of the South American states with each other and with the outside world were dominated by the difficulty of inland and overland communications. These states faced outwards, and both their friendly connections and their rivalries were conducted by sea and along the great rivers [Vale]. The same was true of the U.S.A., much of whose Civil War was fought at sea, between blockaders and blockade-runners, and along the rivers of the interior [Symonds]. In Central America and the Caribbean Basin, the sea commands communications between North and South America, the Atlantic and the Pacific, but the land is composed of small and weak states connected only by sea and easily dominated by outside maritime powers. The Spanish-American War and the building of the Panama Canal by the United States offers a striking example of a new power relationship, simultaneously replacing one imperial power by another, while brutally altering the facts of geography. Something similar had happened in the Eastern Mediterranean forty years before, when the building of the Suez Canal transformed the home waters of the Ottoman Empire into a key link in Britain's imperial maritime system [von Grafenstein, Milne].

The new transcontinental ship canals, favouring low over high latitudes and steam over sail, changed the trade flows of the world. They also had strategic functions, allowing Britain to maintain control of its Eastern empire, and the

United States of its Western empire. The Suez Canal very much promoted, though it did not create, the important new international trade in oil. Thanks to the development of a new type of ship, the tanker, it allowed the new fuel to dominate the shipping, industrial and domestic markets of the world, largely supplanting coal in the first half of the 20th century. This had massive economic effects, bringing huge wealth to a small number of hitherto impoverished and underdeveloped countries, magnifying the strategic significance of what had been an obscure corner of the Ottoman world, and making many more countries than before economically dependent on shipping. The Second World War illustrates the strategic effects of oil, the indispensable fuel for which Britain, Japan and Italy depended wholly on seaborne imports, and Germany largely. Of the four oil-importing belligerents Britain alone obtained enough, because only she had sufficient command of the seas [Alderton].

It is so easy to demonstrate the advantages of access to the sea, that it is easy to overlook the fact that not all countries and societies have understood them. China in the 19th century was still a self-sufficient world in which the sea was of little importance either economically or militarily. Provincial officials had some responsibilities for trade and naval defence, but they did not attract the interest of the imperial government until China had already suffered grave damage from a combination of internal revolt and outside interference. When China did finally attempt fundamental reform in the early 20th century, it was too late to avert collapse into half a century of civil war. A navy became associated with internal and foreign threats, and is not entirely trusted in China even today [Paine, Elleman]. India, ideally situated by geography and history to engage with the sea, still shows itself reluctant to embrace free trade and profit from easy access to world trade, and slow to appreciate the risks of not controlling its own waters [Goldrick].

All these contributions consider primarily the uses of the sea by nation-states and governments, although none ever had any monopoly over the sea. The sea is available to anyone within reach of it, and usable in many ways which require little or no capital or organisation. The existence of long-distance sea trades opens to coastal populations the possibility of working at sea. Well before the 19th century some European shipowners were manning their ships partly or mainly with foreign, mainly Asian, seafarers. When the Europeans came to the Pacific they accorded a high status to the Polynesians and incorporated some of their kingdoms into the new colonial order partly because, as natural seamen and members of hierarchical and even aristocratic societies, they fitted the British or French ideal. Poor seamen like the Melanesians were more likely to be dismissed as 'savages' and subject to direct rule [Laux]. Nowadays merchant shipping offers numerous unskilled or semi-skilled jobs, attractive to those in parts of the world with few better alternatives. This provides many livelihoods, but it also operates at a cultural level, allowing people to travel and see the world who would not otherwise have been able to do so. Countries like India or the Philippines whose people have a tradition of seafaring are more open to the world than those who travel little. There is a dark side to all this, however. The weakness of the law of the sea, and especially the widespread use of flags of convenience, allows shipowners to exploit their crews. In deep-sea fishing, in particular, many crews work in conditions scarcely short of slavery, in which the people and the environment are equally abused [Couper].

Fishing is another means of earning a livelihood afloat, and of tapping a rich source of protein for societies without sources of meat. Coastal subsistence fishing needs only small capital, but deep-sea fishing demands much more capital and technology, not only to build and operate the fishing vessels, but to preserve and transport the fish to market. The first essential for commercial fishery was salt, but later canning, drying and freezing widened the fisheries' range. Steam and later motor fishing vessels extended the possibilities of trawling, and delivered the fish to port faster, while railways opened new inland markets [Heidbrink]. This triumph of industrial fishing, as it seemed, has turned out to presage ecological disaster as overfishing has destroyed many fishing-grounds and caused grave damage to the underwater environment.

Whaling is an even clearer example of the same process. From the beginning of the modern whaling trade in the early 19th century it was a long-range, highly-capitalized business supplying raw materials and lubricants to industry as well as meat and domestic oil for lighting and cooking. Here, too, steam and other new technologies increased productivity and rapidly exceeded the capacity of the whale stocks to regenerate. By the mid-twentieth century whaling was both a commercial and an ecological catastrophe, but a modestly successful example of international law has since allowed some recovery of the whale population [Dyer].

Britain's nineteenth-century economic supremacy depended on free trade and the free use of the sea. Neither economic nor military threats to Britain could come any way but by sea. At first intermittent public concern (the 'panics', as Cobden contemptuously called them) were generated by anxieties about French intentions, and the supposed possibilities for a great military power equipped with steam vessels to mount a sudden surprise invasion. These ideas were never taken very seriously in France, but various projects did exist to overturn British material and industrial supremacy by French genius and originality [Battesti]. Notably the *Jeune École* of the 1880s proposed a ruthless attack on merchant shipping by cruisers and torpedo-boats. This had much more to do with Radical politics in France than with rational naval strategy, and political confusion contributed to the decline of French power, which in turn led to the rapprochement with Britain in 1904 known as the *Entente Cordiale*. Britain and France composed their colonial differences and France abandoned serious naval competition, stimulated by the rise of Germany as a dangerous rival. Russia spent most of the 19th century trying to build up a modern navy as part of its engagement with the industrial age, but the sea divided Russia's fleets, which rested on a weak industrial foundation, and exposed them to defeats in detail of which by far the worst was the Russo-Japanese War of 1904–05. This was the high point of the Anglo-Japanese alliance, an eloquent example of the power of the sea to annihilate distance and link states on opposite sides of the world in a common purpose [Saul, Hirama].

The new navy promoted by Wilhelm II was an obvious challenge to British naval supremacy, but it was also a challenge to contemporary modes of thinking about naval power. The British had so firmly established seapower's natural home in a liberal, free-trading international order and a Parliamentary system of government, that contemporaries were unsure what to make of a navy representing the militarist and illiberal German regime. The Germans themselves were equally unclear whether their new fleet was intended for a naval strategy in wartime, a diplomatic strategy in peacetime, a political campaign against the enemies of Hohenzollern autocracy, or a psychological campaign to embody and enforce all that was noble and characteristic in the German character. In practice the Wilhelmine naval expansion provoked an arms race which German industry and public finances could not sustain, and made enemies of her natural friends, starting with Britain [Epkenhans]. At the same period a new navy was being built in the United States with a very similar mixture of motives and not dissimilar results [Hagan].

All the navies were to find the experience of the First World War baffling and disappointing. The great battle-fleets from which so much had been expected, so quickly, proved to be apparently impotent. The war became a drawn-out contest of production, manpower and harvests. Britain and her allies could win such a war so long as they had access to the food and raw materials of the overseas world. In particular the alliance needed freedom to use the Atlantic and the Mediterranean if Britain, France and Italy were to be able to sustain and apply their war effort. Against all expectations, the obstacle proved to be the submarine. Given the weakness of the British response, a rational submarine campaign might have won Germany the war, but what Germany actually did only made things worse, crippling the effectiveness of the U-Boats while provoking a new and formidable enemy [Offer, Halpern, Rahn].

Between the wars Germany once again began on a naval policy based on political or psychological rather than strategic logic. With the 1935 Anglo-German Naval Agreement Britain successfully tempted Germany into another battleship-building competition which she lacked the resources to carry through, neglecting the submarine force which was a potential instrument of victory [Rahn]. When the war broke out in Europe in 1939 Germany had several disconnected strategies, each as much ideological as practical. The few big ships lacked numbers and opportunities for effective action; an easy invasion of Denmark and Norway was improvised, but the army was not interested in tackling the difficult target of Britain. The U-Boats were not taken seriously until it was at least four years too late to win the war [Hillmann, Gardner]. The army and air force could and did win campaigns, but Germany never developed a unified strategy to fight a world war. Germany's enemies depended entirely on the sea to connect the components of their alliance and exploit their scattered resources. Only a sea-based strategy, as advocated by Germany's ally Italy (and would-be ally Vichy France) could have defeated the Western powers [Gardner, Baxter].

In the Pacific the Washington Treaties of 1921-22 imposed an arms-limitation settlement on the potential naval enemies around the rim of the Pacific, and kept them far apart by demilitarizing the Western Pacific [O'Brien]. This useful exercise in arms limitation did not prevent the Japanese invasion of China and arguably assisted it by keeping the U.S. Navy far away from the China Seas [Bell]. Japan's Pacific War was probably unnecessary and certainly disastrous, but it made the sea an even more critical factor. In the long run the great distances of the Pacific conferred on the U.S.A. the luxury of invulnerability, of strategic initiative and the choice of campaign. In the short run Japan and Germany neglected a brief but promising opportunity to link their war efforts in 1942, and allowed the Western alliance to control the sea, divide its enemies and dictate the strategy of the world war [Frank, Sarantakes, Mawdsley]. This depended on the possession and good management of a sufficiently large merchant fleet [Baxter]. Only Italy of the Axis powers understood that command of the sea was the key to the command of the world, but found it sufficiently difficult to command the central Mediterranean. Both Mussolini and the admirals preferred battleships (which in the event were crippled by lack of oil among other essentials), to the 'stealth weapons' (*mezzi insidiosi*) which achieved the Italian navy's greatest success [Knox, Ball].

The Cold War can be regarded in strategic terms as repeating the pattern of the Second World War, mercifully with much less fighting. NATO was another maritime alliance whose scattered components were bound together by seaborne communications, surrounding and checking a central Continental power. The sea linked the western alliance, providing strategic depth and the time to react to a sudden attack. It also isolated the individual states, limiting the effects of subversion. Soviet attempts to develop sea power and shipping were never as ambitious or dangerous as NATO feared [Friedman, Grove, Gray]. But the most important story of the Cold War was not the containment of Soviet aggression, but the reconstruction of the world economy. In the 19th century free trade, plus the free movement of capital and expertise, had generated the conditions for a rapid increase in wealth throughout the world – to the extent that countries permitted themselves to participate. Britain, which went first and farthest, was the greatest beneficiary of all, though by the beginning of the 20th century it was becoming clear that free trade brought pains and penalties as well as prosperity. The First World War broke up the world trading system. Afterwards unpaid debts, tariffs and exchange controls depressed international trade, hitherto the engine of growth, and massive unemployment of people and capital opened the way for the rise of the dictators and the Second World War [Daunton]. In the post-war years, as a conscious policy of the Western Powers and especially the United States, a free-trading international order was slowly reconstructed, bringing prosperity to many (though by no means all) countries outside the Communist block [Bonin]. The U.S. had gone to war in 1941 still wedded to her traditional belief that China was the great untapped market which would be the key to the economic future. It was half a century early, but eventually the attractions of the free-market economy opened even China's doors [Preston].

Conclusion (English)

To-day the world has been transformed by sixty years of growing trade and prosperity. Virtually all countries with functioning governments and direct or indirect access to seaborne trade have profited from it. New technological opportunities to extract oil and minerals from the seabed, and to generate electricity from winds and tides, have opened completely new ways of exploiting the sea, to the enormous profit of coastal states in many parts of the world [Beltran, Ducruet & Marnot]. Nevertheless the situation does not justify unqualified optimism. In many parts of the world the political situation is unstable and dangerous. Law and government are weak or failing in many places, at sea and on land. Terrorism, smuggling and the revival of piracy reflect the modern world's inability to provide the basic good government at sea which nineteenth-century empires assured. The narcotics trade, one of the most successful of all international seaborne trades, further weakens law and society. Flags of convenience, however effective as lubricants of free trade, make it much harder to enforce regulations and standards on international shipping in a world in which it is unusual for a merchant ship to fly the flag of her country of ownership or operation [Murphy, Chalk, Couper]. This is particularly relevant to ecological standards. The massive increase in world trade has been made possible by the falling cost of transport, but that cost does not account for the cost to the environment of a huge increase in the burning of fossil fuels, mostly oil, which are heavily implicated in climate change. Here again the blessings of freedom are easier to identify at sea than the blessings of good government [Maslin].

The navies of the world have spent recent years mainly engaged in 'constabulary' functions, but they could be called upon to fight at short notice. The booming economies of the Pacific region, in particular, are vulnerable to any disruption of sea trade, but lack strong alliance structures like NATO to deter aggression [Haines, Till]. New weapons such as drones and anti-ship missiles, some of them accessible to non-state actors like terrorist groups, seem to have the capacity to upset the strategic situation [Black]. There is no shortage of threats to peace. The conditions for prosperity and economic growth can be preserved, given wisdom and prudence, but the supply of these good qualities has always been scanty.

Of one thing we can be sure. Whatever the problems and opportunities, the risks and benefits which the future may offer, the sea will remain the most important factor in handling and exploiting them. Whether large or small, strong or weak, rich or poor, states and societies which have learnt to use the sea will be the best equipped to survive and prosper.

Conclusion

Le monde maritime revêt de nombreux aspects qui ne peuvent être abordés de manière exhaustive, même par un travail de cette envergure. La mer est par exemple un moyen d'échange commercial et de communication, elle permet la circulation des peuples et des idées. Elle est également le théâtre de la guerre; c'est un bien âprement disputé par lequel on peut envoyer des forces armées sur des terres lointaines. La mer unit autant qu'elle divise, c'est un instrument utilisé à des fins de stabilité ou de troubles.

Elle a été considérée comme un objet de menace ou comme une source d'opportunité par des nations et des sociétés diverses, avec des expériences historiques différentes. A l'évidence, ces deux opinions sont justes. La mer a été le moyen de construire des empires et de les détruire. Elle a offert la possibilité à chacun de travailler et de voyager dans des parties reculées du monde; et pour des peuples entiers de migrer vers d'autres continents. Des populations qui sans quoi auraient été démunis, ont pu profiter de la pêche et de la chasse à la baleine comme sources importantes d'alimentation et de matières premières industrielles. Les mers intérieures, les rivières navigables et les canaux maritimes ont transporté la mer au sein même des continents. Mais l'influence et la compétence territoriale des pays côtiers peuvent accroître le contrôle opéré par la terre sur la mer. Le commerce maritime relie entre eux des territoires terrestres qui sont souvent éloignés de la côte; des populations et des entreprises qui n'ont jamais vu la mer peuvent tout de même être profondément impliquées dans son utilisation. Néanmoins, il y a toujours eu et il existe encore des pays et des régions qui, par choix ou par nécessité, n'ont que peu de liens avec la mer. En conséquence, ils ont certes échappé aux risques qu'elle présente mais se sont également privés des opportunités qu'elle offre.

En temps de guerre, la mer permet aux troupes d'être déplacées rapidement, discrètement et à peu de frais dans des parties du monde qui n'auraient pu être atteintes autrement. Elle offre à des pays éloignés les uns des autres l'opportunité d'unir leur force et de créer des empires ou des alliances, mais elle éloigne également les alliés et sépare les ennemis, améliorant par là même la défense et par la distance et par la profondeur stratégique. Le libre accès à la mer démultiplie sans aucun doute les options stratégiques, mais sans maîtrise, cela augmente les risques et les dangers. La mer peut devenir une force destructrice pour ceux qui ont échoué à la contrôler; elle les oblige à diviser leurs troupes et à les exposer à des défaites cuisantes [Kennedy].

Conclusion (français)

Par tout ce qu'elle représente, la mer possède une force symbolique formidable. Une flotte de navires de guerre est un instrument de pouvoir, mais également un moyen de montrer sa richesse et sa puissance, sa force industrielle et sa suprématie technique. Des pays aussi différents que l'Allemagne wilhelmienne, le Japon sous l'ère Meiji, les États-Unis du XXe siècle et la Russie soviétique ont édifié leurs flottes comme symboles de leur statut autoproclamé de grande puissance, autant voire plus que comme outils stratégiques et de politique internationale [Epkenhans, Frank, Hagan, Åselius]. Le perfectionnement de la marine s'est parfois manifesté de manière différente à l'intérieur des frontières ou dans les pays étrangers; une flotte a pu être vue de la façon souhaitée dans un pays, mais pas dans d'autres. En qualité de concentration de puissance mobile, capable d'approcher des ennemis potentiels sans pour autant violer les limites territoriales ou même sans forcément révéler sa présence, les flottes sont des outils polyvalents de diplomatie et de dissuasion – même si celle-ci court toujours le risque d'être mal interprétée. Ce qui doit constituer une mise en garde peut être interprété comme une menace, ce qui se veut une menace peut s'entendre comme une attaque, et ce qui s'exprime comme une preuve de modération peut apparaître comme un signe de faiblesse.

Tant sur le plan légal que physique, la mer est bien différente de la terre. Les sociétés humaines terrestres sont réglementées par le droit, et les lois les divisent et les distinguent entre elles. Il existe traditionnellement deux manières par lesquelles le droit peut être appliqué au monde maritime. La première est d'étendre le territoire et d'y revendiquer, pour ainsi dire, une juridiction « territoriale » sur des mers intérieures, côtières et contiguës, comme s'il s'agissait vraiment de terre ferme. Les accords CNUDM (pour la « Convention des Nations unies sur le droit de la mer » qui a établi le traité) constituent l'illustration la plus récente et la plus ambitieuse de cette méthode. Ces accords ont nettement restreint la classique « liberté des mers » en augmentant la portée des juridictions des pays littoraux. La deuxième manière est d'améliorer et de solidifier les formes limitées et vagues du droit international coutumier, afin d'élaborer une forme de droit de substitution fondé sur un accord international tacite ou formel. Le premier accord officiel à mettre en place un droit international maritime fut le Traité de Paris de 1856 qui permet de réglementer la légitimité des blocus et des saisies de biens en mer. Pendant les XIXe et XXe siècles, la portée de ces deux types de droit international fut grandement accrue mais le problème de son application demeure la plus grande faiblesse du droit maritime. Les grandes puissances ne semblent pas forcées de l'observer quand cela ne leur convient pas, et la question reste ouverte de savoir combien de ces nouvelles structures juridiques réchapperaient d'une guerre de grande ampleur [Frei, Bateman, Haines].

La faiblesse du droit se répercute surtout sur la valeur environnementale de la mer. À la fin du XXe siècle, l'être humain prit de plus en plus conscience de la mer comme élément intrinsèque et indispensable à son environnement. Il comprit qu'elle était le moteur du climat et du temps, et par conséquent responsable de la possibilité (ou impossibilité) de se nourrir et de subvenir aux besoins des populations humaines et animales. Très souvent, les agissements d'un seul pays ou d'un seul groupe dégradent la mer et menacent la vie et les moyens de subsistance des autres. Les organisations internationales ont malheureusement peu d'effets, et dans certaines parties du monde on voit même des États-nations se désintégrer. La fragilité du droit international et des dirigeants politiques internationaux ne laisse que peu d'outils réellement efficaces pour résoudre les conflits et pour encourager des mesures bénéfiques. Dans de trop nombreux cas, le nécessité immédiate d'un accord et d'une action commune ne fait que créer des différends et des obstacles à l'action. La mer est à la base des problèmes du monde mais aussi au cœur de ses solutions, et cela ne peut être appréhendé que par l'intermédiaire de son histoire.

L'accord de paix signé en 1815 lors du Congrès de Vienne manifesta le désir des puissances européennes de mettre derrière elles une période de guerre et de destruction de plus d'un quart de siècle, et de revenir au monde tel qu'il était avant la Révolution française. En Grande-Bretagne, le Parlement et le gouvernement eurent pour objectif commun de diminuer l'importance de l'État et de ses dépenses en supprimant les impôts liés à l'effort de guerre, pour revenir à sa taille d'avant-guerre. À l'international, leur vue était d'accroître leur influence économique en évitant de répéter le désastre entraîné par leur velléité impériale au XVIIIe siècle [Lambert]. Ils espéraient préserver leurs systèmes socio-économiques en maintenant les Corn Laws (qui encadraient le prix des céréales et donc le revenu des propriétaires terriens), ainsi que les Actes de Navigation (qui réservaient le commerce extérieur britannique aux navires anglais à l'équipage britannique). Au final, les deux lois furent abandonnées avant 1850. Le libre-échange et le processus d'industrialisation ont ouvert un nouveau monde avec des flux d'échanges considérables. Ainsi, les classes ouvrières des nouvelles villes industrielles se nourrirent d'aliments importés bon marché, payés grâce à l'exportation des produits des nouvelles industries. En sacrifiant leur revenu, ou leur revenu potentiel, et en permettant l'augmentation progressive du nombre d'électeurs, les propriétaires terriens furent à même de conserver la plupart de leur influence politique jusqu'au XXe siècle. Les armateurs britanniques perdirent leur protection, mais la demande grandissante en navires étendit grandement leur marché [O'Rourke]. Le charbon anglais n'a pas seulement servi à alimenter les nouveaux bateaux à vapeur, il a également permis de répondre à la demande mondiale de charbon à vapeur en pleine croissance. Cela signifie que le *tramping* (qui s'effectuait la plupart du temps à la voile avant la fin du siècle) put notamment toujours s'appuyer sur l'exportation d'une cargaison de charbon pour compenser les importations de matières premières en gros [Palmer]. L'industrie navale britannique domina le marché mondial et vint s'ajouter aux autres succès qu'étaient l'échange et l'industrie [Lemmers]. La nouvelle prospérité fut grandement supérieure à l'ancienne, et le fait que le profit économique de la Grande-Bretagne se soit construit sur des risques stratégiques n'était alors pas flagrant. Le transport maritime et l'industrie navale devinrent le cœur du nouveau système économique et une manière facile de s'enrichir et de se renforcer. Mais dépendre du commerce maritime tant pour l'importation que pour l'exportation, vitales à la survie du pays, l'exposa peu à peu à une grande vulnérabilité nouvelle, qui n'existait pas lorsque la Grande-Bretagne était auto-suffisante du point de vue alimentaire et des matières premières. En 1889, le pays réagit par l'intermédiaire du Naval Defence Act, qui finança une plus grande marine de guerre et notamment une plus grande force de croiseurs pour protéger les échanges commerciaux. Rétrospectivement, on peut considérer que cette date marque le début d'une course à l'armement naval qui s'étala sur vingt-cinq ans. Cela préserva la suprématie navale britannique mais participa à la transformation du paysage stratégique du monde entier [Beeler, Sumida].

Une des raisons pour laquelle la Grande-Bretagne mit du temps à mesurer les risques de sa dépendance nouvelle au commerce extérieur fut son enthousiasme renouvelé pour l'expansion de son empire à la fin du XIXe siècle. Le libre-échange permit de développer l'investissement et l'activité dans de nombreuses parties du monde et la libre circulation des populations produisit un accroissement rapide des colonies de peuplement. Cela suscita des revendications et des engagements politiques auxquels les gouvernements centraux furent obligés de répondre et ce, même s'ils étaient en théorie opposés à l'implantation de nouvelles colonies. Les autorités coloniales et les garnisons sur place prouvèrent qu'ils pouvaient agir de manière unilatérale, ce qui força le gouvernement central à s'engager plus que prévu. Petit à petit, le nombre de régions sous contrôle direct ou sous influence britannique augmentèrent. En se développant au point de devenir des dominions autonomes, les colonies de peuplement formèrent leurs propres armées et édifièrent leurs propres flottes, solidifiant de ce fait l'empire dans son ensemble tout en affaiblissant son unité politique [Stevens].

La plupart des autres pays ne retint de la révolution libérale du XIXe siècle que ce qui servaient leurs intérêts. Les puissances impériales telles que les Pays-Bas entrèrent par leurs propres moyens dans l'âge industriel en protégeant le commerce impérial (qui s'appuyait néanmoins tacitement sur une protection britannique). Ils ne virent l'intérêt que pouvait leur offrir le libre-échange que lorsque leurs industries et leur flotte marchande furent assez importantes pour affronter la compétition. La France et l'Allemagne imposèrent de nouveau des droits de douane sur les produits agricoles lorsque les intérêts des propriétaires terriens furent menacés par les aliments importés [van Dissel, O'Rourke]. L'Autriche-Hongrie renforça son empire en déployant une flotte puissante sur la Méditerranée centrale, et en créant un port maritime d'envergure internationale (Trieste). Mais l'entreprise semblable de l'empire Ottoman se solda, elle, par un échec [Sondhaus, Heywood]. L'Italie nouvellement unifiée présentait une situation géographique particulière; sa forme de péninsule au cœur de la Méditerranée centrale semblait lui offrir de grandes opportunités pour articuler le commerce intérieur et le commerce extérieur. Mais en réalité, le sous-développement des industries, des ports et du réseau ferroviaire auquel vient s'ajouter la dépendance en carburant importé, firent de l'Italie un pays distancé par ses voisins jusqu'au beau milieu du XXe siècle. Néanmoins, sa marine militaire était des plus modernes et des plus efficaces qui soit pour un État en retard sur les autres, et lui fut d'une grande aide, au XXe siècle, pour bâtir un empire en Afrique du Nord et en Afrique de l'Est [Zampieri]. Les velléités navales et impériales de l'Espagne furent un échec complet; le pays perdit en effet ses colonies sud-américaines à la suite de révoltes intérieures, et la quasi-totalité des autres lors d'agressions extérieures pendant la guerre hispano-américaine. Mais malgré la défaillance de l'État, les entreprises privées s'associèrent à la nouvelle économie industrielle du Pays Basque pour faire renaître une flotte marchande florissante que l'Espagne n'avait plus connue depuis le XVIe siècle [Valdaliso]. Le Danemark, un empire résiduel composé de plusieurs îles éparpillées entre la mer Baltique et l'Arctique, était entièrement tributaire des communications maritimes et prospéra, sans bénéficier de protection, dans le secteur du *tramping*, le commerce maritime le plus compétitif [Møller]. La Suède, qui avait perdu son empire colonial au profit de la Russie en 1809, développa un commerce maritime extérieur à la fin du XIXe siècle en l'intégrant au système d'import–export d'une économie nouvellement industrialisée [Müller].

Dans tous ces exemples, le rapport qu'entretiennent les différents pays au monde de la mer peut se comprendre par le croisement des politiques nationales et des caractéristiques géographiques. Les relations existant entre les différents pays d'Amérique du Sud et leurs rapports avec le monde extérieur ont été dominés par la difficulté des communications intérieures et par voie terrestre. Ils étaient tournés vers l'extérieur, et c'est la mer et les grands fleuves qui déterminèrent aussi bien les relations amicales que les rivalités entre pays [Vale]. Il en fut de même pour les États-Unis d'Amérique; une bonne partie de la guerre de Sécession s'est ainsi jouée en mer, entre les vaisseaux bloquant l'accès aux ports et les navires briseurs de blocus, et le long des fleuves à l'intérieur des terres [Symonds]. En Amérique centrale et dans le Bassin des Caraïbes, la mer régulait les communications entre l'Amérique du Nord et l'Amérique du Sud et entre l'Atlantique et le Pacifique. Mais la terre ferme était composée de petits États faibles uniquement connectés par la mer et facilement dominés par les puissances maritimes extérieures. La guerre hispano-américaine et la construction du Canal de Panama par les États-Unis constituent un exemple frappant de l'établissement d'un nouveau rapport de force, mettant simultanément fin à un impérialisme au profit d'un autre et modifiant brutalement les caractéristiques géographiques de la région. Un événement similaire s'était produit en Méditerranée orientale quarante ans plus tôt, lorsque la construction du canal de Suez fit des eaux territoriales de l'Empire Ottoman une liaison cruciale pour le système maritime impérial du Royaume-Uni [von Grafenstein, Milne].

Les nouvelles voies maritimes transcontinentales, qui privilégiaient les latitudes basses sur les hautes et la vapeur sur la voile, ont transformé les flux commerciaux dans le monde. Elles eurent également des fonctions stratégiques, permettant ainsi à la Grande-Bretagne de rester maîtresse de son empire oriental, et aux États-Unis de garder la main mise sur ses terres occidentales. Même s'il existait avant l'existence du canal de Suez, le récent commerce du pétrole profita grandement de sa construction pour gagner en importance.

Le développement d'une nouvelle sorte de bateau – les pétroliers – permit au nouveau carburant de dominer les marchés intérieurs, les marchés industriels et le marché du transport maritime dans le monde, et de largement supplanter le charbon pendant la première moitié du XXe siècle. Cela eut des effets gigantesques sur l'économie, en apportant une grande richesse à un petit nombre de pays qui restaient jusque-là pauvres et en situation de sous-développement – amplifiant l'importance stratégique de ce qui avait toujours été un recoin obscur du monde Ottoman – et en rendant de plus en plus de pays dépendants économiquement du commerce maritime. La Seconde Guerre mondiale illustre parfaitement les effets stratégiques du pétrole. La Grande-Bretagne, le Japon et l'Italie étaient complètement dépendants des importations par voie de mer pour s'approvisionner, l'Allemagne dépendait également en grande partie de ce carburant indispensable qu'elle ne produisait pas, et sur ces quatre belligérants importateurs de pétrole, seule l'Angleterre parvint à en avoir assez, grâce notamment à son emprise suffisante sur les mers [Alderton].

Il est tellement aisé de percevoir les avantages qu'offre l'accès à la mer, qu'on oublie souvent le fait que tous les pays et toutes les sociétés ne les avaient pas envisagés. La Chine du XIXe siècle était encore un pays auto-suffisant, pour qui la mer ne revêtait qu'une importance minime, que ce soit économiquement ou militairement parlant. Les responsables provinciaux avaient certes quelques responsabilités concernant le commerce et la marine militaire, mais cela ne suscita l'intérêt du gouvernement impérial qu'une fois que le pays eût subi de graves dommages du fait de révoltes intérieures et d'interférences extérieures conjuguées. Lorsque la Chine se résolut enfin à entreprendre une réforme plus que nécessaire au début du XXe siècle, il était déjà trop tard pour éviter l'éclatement d'une guerre civile de près d'un demi-siècle. La marine devint synonyme de menaces internes et extérieures, et même aujourd'hui, la Chine s'en méfie encore [Paine, Elleman]. L'Inde, bénéficiant pourtant d'une situation géographique et historique idéale à une interaction avec la mer, se montre encore réservée quant à l'adoption du libre-échange et du profit venant d'un accès simplifié au marché mondial. Elle s'avère également lente à mesurer les risques qu'engendre le fait de laisser le contrôle de ses eaux territoriales à d'autres [Goldrick].

Toutes ces contributions étudient avant tout les formes d'utilisation de la mer par les États-nations et les gouvernements, bien qu'aucun n'ait pourtant jamais eu le monopole des mers. La mer est un bien accessible à tous ceux qui sont à sa portée, et elle peut être utilisée de manière multiple, sans pour autant nécessiter un grand investissement en capital ou en organisation. L'existence d'un commerce maritime de longue distance a permis aux populations des côtes de pouvoir vivre de la mer. Bien avant le XIXe siècle, certains armateurs composaient leurs équipages en partie ou en totalité de marins étrangers, et notamment de marins asiatiques. Lorsque les Européens investirent le Pacifique, ils accordèrent un statut supérieur aux Polynésiens et intégrèrent certains de leurs royaumes dans le nouvel ordre colonial, du fait entre autres de leur qualité de marins et en tant que membres de sociétés hiérarchisées, voire aristocratiques, qui correspondaient à l'idéal français et britannique. Les marins pauvres comme les Mélanésiens étaient plus susceptibles d'être qualifiés de « sauvages » et d'être soumis à un contrôle direct [Laux]. Aujourd'hui, le transport maritime offre de nombreux emplois sans qualification ou peu qualifiés, attractifs dans des parties du monde qui proposent peu d'alternatives meilleures. C'est pour beaucoup un gagne-pain, mais qui revêt également un intérêt culturel puisqu'il permet à ces personnes de voyager et de voir le monde, ce qu'elles n'auraient jamais pu faire autrement. Des pays comme l'Inde ou les Philippines, dont les populations ont toujours été constituées de navigateurs, sont plus ouverts sur le monde que d'autres pays sans véritable tradition maritime. Il existe cependant un revers de la médaille. La faiblesse du droit maritime, et en particulier le recours généralisé aux pavillons de complaisance, permettent aux armateurs d'exploiter leurs équipages. La pêche en haute mer, notamment, présente des conditions de travail proches de l'esclavage pour beaucoup d'équipages. L'homme et l'environnement sont alors tous les deux pareillement maltraités [Couper].

La pêche est un autre moyen de gagner sa vie grâce à la mer, et d'en tirer une source riche de protéines pour des sociétés qui n'ont pas accès à la viande. La pêche de subsistance côtière ne nécessite qu'un faible apport en capital. La pêche en haute mer, en revanche, en exige beaucoup plus; d'une part afin de construire et de faire naviguer les bateaux de pêche, mais également afin de conserver et de transporter le poisson jusqu'au marché. Le sel fut tout d'abord l'élément essentiel pour la pêche commerciale, mais la mise en conserve, le séchage et la congélation permirent d'augmenter la portée de la pêche. Les bateaux de pêche, qui étaient à vapeur avant le passage au moteur, accrurent les possibilités de chalutage et permirent d'apporter plus rapidement le poisson jusqu'au port, alors que le chemin de fer ouvrait de nouveaux marchés intérieurs [Heidbrink]. Le triomphe de la pêche industrielle s'est avéré être un présage de la catastrophe écologique que constituerait la pêche intensive, qui détruisit de nombreuses zones de pêche et qui provoqua d'énormes dommages au milieu sous-marin.

La chasse à la baleine témoigne encore plus clairement de ce même processus. Dès son entrée dans le marché moderne au tout début du XIXe siècle, la pêche à la baleine fut une activité de longue distance fortement capitalisée, qui approvisionna l'industrie en matières premières et lubrifiants, tout comme en viande et en huile à consommation domestique pour l'éclairage et pour cuisiner. Là encore, la vapeur et d'autres technologies plus récentes permirent d'augmenter la productivité et provoquèrent un dépassement du seuil de renouvellement des stocks de baleine. Dès le milieu du XXe siècle, la chasse à la baleine devint une catastrophe écologique et commerciale. Mais un exemple de succès modeste de loi internationale a depuis permis un rétablissement partiel de l'effectif des baleines [Dyer].

La supériorité économique du Royaume-Uni au XIXe siècle reposait sur le libre-échange et la libre exploitation de la mer. Les menaces qu'auraient pu subir l'Angleterre, qu'elles soient d'ordre militaires ou économiques, ne pouvaient venir que par la mer. Les inquiétudes occasionnelles de la population (que

Cobden qualifia avec mépris de « paniques ») furent d'abord liées aux craintes concernant les intentions françaises, et les risques supposés d'une invasion surprise et soudaine portée par une grande puissance militaire équipée de bateaux à vapeur. Ces idées n'ont jamais vraiment été prises en considération en France, mais différents projets pour renverser la supériorité matérielle et industrielle de la Grande-Bretagne grâce au génie et à l'originalité française ont bel et bien existé [Battesti]. La *Jeune École* de 1880, en particulier, proposa une attaque impitoyable des croiseurs et des torpilleurs sur le commerce maritime. Ces initiatives étaient moins liées à une stratégie navale rationnelle, qu'à l'arrivée au pouvoir des Radicaux en France. La confusion politique contribua au déclin de la puissance française, qui par la suite conduisit, en 1904, au rapprochement avec l'Angleterre connu sous le nom d'*Entente Cordiale*. Le Royaume-Uni et la France s'entendirent sur leurs divergences coloniales, et la France renonça à rivaliser de manière sérieuse sur le plan naval, menacée qu'elle était par l'essor de l'Allemagne comme dangereuse concurrente. La Russie passa la majeure partie du XIXe siècle à tenter de moderniser sa flotte pour lui faire intégrer l'ère industrielle. Mais la mer divisa les navires russes, conçus sur un socle industriel fragile, et exposa le pays à de cuisantes défaites dont la guerre russo-japonaise de 1904-1905 représente de loin la plus importante. Cela constitua l'apogée de l'alliance anglo-japonaise: un exemple éloquent du pouvoir de la mer pour rayer la distance et connecter entre eux des États de part et d'autre du globe dans un projet commun [Saul, Hirama].

La nouvelle flotte construite par Wilhelm II était une manière évidente de défier la supériorité navale britannique mais bouscula également les modes de pensée de l'époque concernant la puissance navale. Du fait du précédent britannique qui inscrivit le fondement naturel de la puissance maritime dans un ordre libéral et libre-échangiste international et un système de gouvernance parlementaire, leurs contemporains sont restés dubitatifs face à la naissance d'une flotte dans le régime militariste et autoritaire allemand. Les allemands étaient de la même manière assez ambigus sur la constitution de leur nouvelle flotte et son édification comme l'outil d'une stratégie militaire en temps de guerre, d'une stratégie diplomatique en temps de paix, d'une campagne politique contre les ennemies de l'autocratie d'Hohenzollern, ou d'une campagne psychologique pour personnifier et souligner la noblesse propre au caractère allemand. En réalité, l'expansion navale sous Wilhelm provoqua une course à l'armement que l'industrie et les finances publiques allemandes ne pouvaient pas supporter, et le pays fit de ses alliés traditionnels de nouveaux ennemis, la Grande-Bretagne en tête [Epkenhans]. Au même moment, une nouvelle marine était en cours de construction aux États-Unis selon un mélange d'intentions très proches et des résultats loin d'être dissimulés [Hagan].

Les événements de la Première Guerre mondiale furent pour le moins déconcertants et décevants pour toutes les flottes. Les grandes marines de guerres dont les pays espéraient tant, et vite, s'avérèrent à première vue impuissantes. La guerre se transforma en une course interminable à la production, à la main-d'œuvre et aux ressources agricoles. La Grande-Bretagne et ses alliés pouvaient gagner la guerre tant que l'accès à la nourriture et aux matières premières en outre-mer leur était possible. Pour se maintenir et continuer à employer l'effort de guerre, l'alliance menée par l'Angleterre, la France et l'Italie nécessitait notamment de garder les routes de l'Atlantique et de la Méditerranée ouverte. Contre toute attente, l'obstacle vint des sous-marins. Étant donné la faiblesse de la riposte britannique, les Allemands auraient légitimement pu gagner la guerre si seulement ils avaient mis en place une campagne sous-marine rationnelle. Mais en paralysant l'efficacité des U-Boats tout en provoquant un nouvel ennemi redoutable, l'Allemagne ne fit qu'empirer la situation [Offer, Halpern, Rahn].

L'entre-deux guerre a vu l'Allemagne se lancer une nouvelle fois dans une politique navale fondée sur des aspects politiques et psychologiques plutôt que sur une logique stratégique. Avec le traité naval germano-britannique de 1935, la Grande-Bretagne parvint à inciter l'Allemagne à entrer dans une nouvelle compétition de construction de cuirassés. Le pays n'en avait pourtant pas les moyens, et a par ailleurs négligé une force sous-marine qui aurait potentiellement pu le mener à la victoire [Rahn]. Lorsque la guerre éclata en Europe en 1939, l'Allemagne présentait des stratégies décousues, qui reposaient autant sur l'idéologie que sur la pratique. Les quelques grands bateaux qui existaient étaient trop peu nombreux et n'avaient pas assez d'opportunités pour avoir un réel impact. L'invasion aisée du Danemark et de la Norvège fut improvisée, alors que l'armée ne voulait pas s'attaquer à la cible compliquée que représentait la Grande-Bretagne. Les U-Boats ne furent considérés sérieusement qu'au moins quatre ans trop tard pour gagner la guerre [Hillmann, Gardner]. L'armée et l'aviation pouvaient et ont bel et bien remporté des campagnes, mais l'Allemagne n'a jamais développé une stratégie assez unifiée pour mener une guerre mondiale. Ses ennemis dépendaient complètement de la mer pour connecter les éléments de leur alliance et d'exploiter leurs ressources éparpillées. Seule une stratégie fondée sur la mer, telle que prônée par leur allié italien (et par la suite leur nouvel allié français du régime de Vichy) aurait pu vaincre les puissances occidentales [Gardner, Baxter].

Dans le Pacifique, les Traités de Washington de 1921–1922 imposèrent un accord sur la limitation des armements des flottes des belligérants éventuels du pourtour pacifique, et les isola en démilitarisant le Pacifique occidental [O'Brien]. Cette démarche utile pour limiter l'armement n'empêcha pas l'invasion japonaise de la Chine, et voire même, la facilita vraisemblablement en tenant la marine américaine éloignée de la mer de Chine [Bell]. La guerre du Pacifique menée par le Japon était vraisemblablement inutile et sans nul doute désastreuse, mais fit de la mer un facteur encore plus déterminant. Sur le long terme, les grandes distances du Pacifique ont offert aux États-Unis le luxe de l'invulnérabilité, de l'initiative stratégique et le choix des campagnes à mener. Sur le court terme, le Japon et l'Allemagne n'ont pas saisi la brève opportunité de joindre leurs efforts de guerre en 1942, ce qui aurait pu pourtant s'avérer gagnant. Ils ont de ce fait permis à l'alliance de l'Ouest de contrôler la mer, de diviser ses ennemis, et plus généralement de dicter la stratégie de l'ensemble de la guerre [Frank, Sarantakes,

Mawdsley]. Les pays de l'alliance avaient besoin pour cela de posséder et de gérer convenablement une flotte marchande suffisamment grande [Baxter]. Parmi les puissances de l'Axe, seule l'Italie s'est rendue compte que le contrôle de la mer était essentiel à la maîtrise du monde. Mais il lui était déjà bien assez difficile de commander la Méditerranée centrale. Mussolini et ses amiraux ont préféré l'utilisation de cuirassés (qui dans ce contexte étaient handicapés par les pénuries de carburant entre autres nécessités), aux « armes furtives » (*mezzi insidiosi*) alors qu'elles avaient permis les grands succès de la marine italienne [Knox, Ball].

En termes de stratégie, la guerre froide peut être considérée comme une redite du scénario de la Seconde Guerre mondiale, avec heureusement beaucoup moins d'affrontements. L'OTAN représenta une nouvelle alliance maritime, dont les membres étaient dispersés mais reliés entre eux par voies maritimes, encerclant et empêchant de ce fait l'expansion d'un pouvoir continental central. La mer unit l'alliance occidentale et lui apporta une immense profondeur stratégique et assez de temps pour réagir à une attaque inattendue. Elle isola également les États individuels et limita les risques de subversion. Les tentatives des Soviétiques de développer une puissance navale et un commerce maritime n'eurent jamais le degré d'ambition ou de danger que craignait l'OTAN [Friedman, Grove, Gray]. Mais le point le plus important à retenir de la guerre froide a moins été l'endiguement de l'agression soviétique que le redressement de l'économie mondiale. Au XIXe siècle, le libre-échange et la libre circulation du capital et du savoir-faire ont provoqué des conditions favorables pour la croissance rapide de la richesse dans le monde – dans les limites établies par chaque pays. La Grande-Bretagne, qui mena en premier et le plus loin cette transition, en fut ainsi la principale bénéficiaire, même s'il devint clair, dès le début du XXe siècle, que le libre-échange était source aussi bien de peines et de dommages que de prospérité. La Première Guerre mondiale détruisit le système commercial international. Par la suite, les dettes impayées, les tarifs et le contrôle des changes ont diminué le commerce international qui était jusqu'alors le moteur de la croissance. Le fort taux de chômage et d'oisiveté des fonds capitaux ouvrirent la voie à l'émergence des dictateurs et par la suite à l'éclatement de la Seconde Guerre mondiale [Daunton]. Dans les années d'après-guerre, par la politique délibérée des puissances de l'Ouest et notamment des États-Unis, un système international de libre-échange fut lentement rebâti et fit prospérer un grand nombre de pays – mais en aucun cas tous – en dehors du bloc communiste [Bonin]. Les États-Unis étaient entrés en guerre en 1941, depuis toujours persuadés que la Chine restait le grand marché encore inexploité et serait le futur de l'économie. Ce n'est qu'un demi-siècle plus tard que la Chine ouvrit finalement ses portes, attirée par l'économie de libre-marché [Preston].

Le monde est aujourd'hui transformé par soixante ans de prospérité et de commerce grandissant. Quasiment tous les pays possédant un gouvernement en état de fonctionner et un accès direct ou indirect au commerce maritime ont pu en profiter. De nouvelles possibilités techniques ont ouvert la voie à une autre exploitation de la mer – de l'extraction de pétrole et de minéraux dans les fonds marins à la production d'électricité grâce au vent et aux marées – et ont apporté un profit énorme aux États côtiers dans de nombreuses parties du monde [Beltran, Ducruet & Marnot]. Pour autant, la situation ne doit pas mener à un optimisme sans réserve. Dans bien des régions du monde, la situation politique reste instable et dangereuse. À bien des endroits, le droit et les gouvernements sont faibles ou défaillants, que ce soit en mer ou sur terre. Le terrorisme, la contrebande et le retour de la piraterie démontrent l'impuissance du monde moderne à assurer un gouvernement en mer fondamental et efficace que garantissaient les empires du XIXe siècle. Le trafic de stupéfiants, un des commerces maritimes mondiaux les plus fructueux, a affaibli encore plus le droit et la société. Les pavillons de complaisance, même s'ils sont efficaces en termes de fluidification du libre-échange, ont rendu l'application des règles et des normes sur le commerce maritime international moins aisée, dans un monde où il est fort inhabituel qu'un navire marchand porte le pavillon de son pays d'origine ou d'exploitation [Murphy, Chalk, Couper]. Ce problème s'applique d'autant plus aux normes écologiques. La progression immense du commerce mondial a été rendue possible par la baisse du coût du transport. Mais ce prix ne prend pas en compte le coût environnemental de l'augmentation de la combustion des carburants fossiles qui, pétrole en tête, sont lourdement responsables du changement climatique. Là encore, les bienfaits de la liberté sont plus facilement identifiables en mer que ceux d'une bonne gouvernance [Maslin].

Les flottes de guerre du monde entier ont été réduites ces dernières années à des fonctions avant tout policières, mais elles pourraient être mobilisées au pied levé pour le combat. Les économies florissantes de la zone pacifique, notamment, sont exposées à la moindre perturbation du commerce maritime mais ne bénéficient pas des structures solides apportées par une coalition comme celle de l'OTAN pour décourager les agressions extérieures [Haines, Till]. De nouvelles armes telles que les drones et les missiles antinavires – dont certaines sont accessibles à des acteurs non étatiques comme les groupes terroristes – semblent avoir les moyens de bouleverser le contexte stratégique [Black]. Les menaces contre la paix ne manquent pas. Les conditions de la prospérité et de la croissance économique peuvent être préservées avec de la prudence et de la clairvoyance. Mais ces qualités n'ont jamais été en grand nombre.

On peut être sûr d'une chose. Quels que soient les problèmes et les opportunités, quels que soient les risques et les avantages que le futur pourrait réserver, la mer restera le facteur le plus important pour y faire face et les exploiter. Qu'ils soient grands ou petits, forts ou faibles, riches ou pauvres, les États et les sociétés qui ont appris à exploiter la mer seront les mieux équipés pour survivre et prospérer.

General conclusion[*]

Three compelling conclusions emerge from the contributions brought together in these four volumes, offering a clear response to our questions. Indeed, engaging in maritime activities, anywhere and in any age, is the single most powerful impetus to create a positive impact on historical trajectories. This is so because the sea acts as (1) the accelerator of political and economic development; (2) the driver of predominance and expansion; (3) the driver of History.

1. The sea: driving force of political and economic development

The archaeological sites at Pinnacle Point in South Africa, Haida Gwaii in British Columbia and On Your Knees Cave on Prince of Wales Island, which offer the oldest known evidence of a subsistence economy based on marine mammals, seals, sea lions, cetaceans, as well as fish, some of them quite large, and shellfish such as mussels and sea snails, illustrate that the sea has always provided coastal populations with a significant source of additional resources. Isotopic remains of a 20-year-old man, dating from 10,300 years ago show a diet made up mainly of food taken from the sea.[1]

The sea is thus a source of food, clothing and primitive currency based on shells, as well as functional and artistic objects. Very early on, through the dynamism of maritime activities, the sea provided a structure for economic sociability among coastal populations, whether in Asia, Europe, Africa or the Americas.[2]

Even more significantly, the sea was the principal vector of trade because it offered an easy means of transport. Indeed, propelling a vessel on the water requires infinitely less energy than land transport.[3] People turned increasingly

---

[*] References to chapters in the *Sea in History* volumes are given by author name and volume. The volume titles (the Ancient World, The Medieval World, The Early Modern World and the Modern World) are shortened to Ancient, Medieval, Early Modern and Modern respectively.
[1] See Pascal Picq (Ancient).
[2] See Jorge Ortiz Sotelo (Medieval), Alioune Dème (Ancient), Benoit Bérard (Ancient), Barry Cunliffe (Ancient), Richard T. Callaghan (Ancient).
[3] See for example Benoit Bérard (Ancient) for the Caribbean, Carla Antonaccio (Ancient) and Graciela Gestoso Singer (Ancient) for the connected nature of trade in the Mediterranean, Félix Chami (Ancient) for the Indian Ocean.

to the sea, travelling ever further from the coast, to find supplementary food and other necessary products.

Mesopotamian civilisation offers a perfect example of this phenomenon, as far back as the third millennium BC Located in the Fertile Crescent, Mesopotamia – literally, the land between rivers – was rich in agricultural foodstuffs. However, it was painfully lacking in natural resources. Consequently, populations exploited waterways – rivers and the sea – to find wood for construction, copper and other metals for metalworking, diorite and gabbro for royal statues, lapis lazuli, gold, ivory and more. This rapidly growing trade, controlled by rich and powerful sovereigns, thus enabled the development of irrigation systems and other defences against the floods that threatened cultivated land. An impressive transport fleet was built in an effort to secure trade. Dockyards were established at Gu'aba and Nigin in Girsu province, Apisal and Guedena in Umma province and Drehem and Nibru in the Ur region. Between the years 900 and 1000, these dockyards employed as many as 900 or 1,000 men, under the direction of a dedicated administration, the Marsa. All the magnificence of Mesopotamian civilisation emerged from this network of waterways, as shown by the significant role of ships and marine navigation in mythological compositions, hymns, prayers and proverbs.[4]

Asia provides a similar illustration. From the first millennium BC, a veritable marine network linked South China to the Moluccas and India. Cloves, nutmeg and other spices and perfumes were the main merchandise of a very active trade system, whereby goods travelled up through the seas of Celebes and Java to the Strait of Malacca, some being distributed to China, others through the Indian Ocean and beyond, all the way to the Red Sea.[5] From the 4th century BC, the Egyptians tended to pay their tribute to Rome in cloves from the Moluccas.[6] In the 1st century BC, the opening of the Bahrain Pearl Road, better known as the Maritime Silk Road, which linked China to the Persian Gulf and the Red Sea, created unprecedented prosperity.

In time, valuable commodities like lapis lazuli, rhinoceros horns, ivory, precious woods and precious metals (copper, gold, silver and iron) began circulating on Asian seas, bestowing unprecedented splendour on cities or states which participated in or controlled trade. Such was the case, for example, of Funan on the Mekong Delta, one of the most important kingdoms in Southeast Asia. Similarly, Srivijaya, today Palembang, on the island of Sumatra, was a true Venice of Asia. Between the 7th and 11th centuries, Srivijaya successfully made itself the hub of trade links between the Indian Ocean, the South China Sea and the Java Sea, dazzling contemporaries with the brilliance of a thalassocratic city of unparalleled wealth and artistic development. This power was seized by the Chola kingdom in the south of the Indian peninsula, which conquered Srivijava in 1025 with an eye to controlling the most significant naval resources. The kingdom

---

[4] See Ariel M. Bagg (Ancient), Grégory Chambon (Ancient).
[5] See John Miksic (Ancient).
[6] WARMINGTON E.H., *The Commerce between the Roman Empire and India*, Cambridge: Cambridge University Press (1928).

of Majapahit in East Sumatra, followed by Malacca and then Guangzhou, gateway to a vast Chinese hinterland, succeeded to spectacular prestige. These were nerve centres before their time in this vast trade network.[7]

With the momentum of coastal and urban population growth, hinterlands were soon unable to produce sufficient quantities of food. Indeed, crop yields were poor due to a lack of draught animals capable of adequately ploughing the soil (part of a vicious cycle: insufficient yields made it impossible to feed the animals that could have increased production). This was combined with crops that in many cases were ill suited to the local soil. Farmers nonetheless continued to plant such crops due to the urgent need for the main staples of the local diet.

From this point of view, maritime transport clearly seems to have been the catalyst and driving force of a gradual trend in agricultural specialisation that made it possible to adapt crops to the local climate and thereby escape the fundamental deadlock outlined above. This food input enabled population settlements on or near the coast to grow steadily and continuously. Athens imported more than half of its wheat from the Black Sea, Thrace, Sicily and even Egypt. By the height of the Roman Empire, one million people were concentrated in Rome and Alexandria. Feeding such urban densities required the progressive development of increasingly substantial port infrastructures. The Roman Empire is the prime example, with a network of maritime innovations which remind us of the revolution in marine transport taking place today, at the start of the third millennium.

From this perspective, the work of Pascal Arnaud (Ancient) on the ports of Antiquity is particularly enlightening. Perhaps as early as the 2nd millennium BC, entrepôt ports started to arise next to commercial ports, making for permanent spaces designed to facilitate the exchange of local surpluses for necessary goods. This was a new model for trade based on a concentration of goods of different origins, only part of which would be absorbed by the local market, the remainder being sent on to other destinations. Entrepôt ports were part of specialised networks of direct trade and redistribution that are far removed from the primitive picture which is sometimes painted of trade in Antiquity. Indeed, seaborne trade, a key driver of transformation, was already moving full speed ahead on a regional scale. As early as the Hellenistic period, there existed an entire network made up of main ports, intended for international trade (*emporia*), and 'secondary' structures.

Trade made the sea a strategic factor. Control of the sea and coast became essential, leading to unprecedented levels of military pressure. Piracy flourished, often with the discreet support of states, with port cities becoming a choice target for raids, a pirate specialty.

In this highly unstable context, war fleets became the strategic instrument of wars fought for mastery of the sea. The sea became the primary means of carrying troops and supplies over long distances. Cutting these communications

---

[7] See Tansen Sen (Ancient), Pierre-Yves Manguin (Medieval), Paul Wormser (Medieval).

or depriving the enemy of needed supplies was a major step towards victory. An arms race thus began among states, in terms of the number and tonnage of ships and the required infrastructure. Highly specialised military ports appeared as of the Hellenistic period, like the *naustathmos* of the Thalamegos or the 'aviso arsenal' in Schedia, outside Alexandria.[8] This progress drove economic development, as Vincent Gabrielsen (Ancient) has illustrated in the case of Athens.

During Antiquity, the Roman Empire brought this development to its most complete form.[9] The imperial age was characterised by several key innovations: political unification of the Mediterranean, the 'inland' sea around which all of the empire's possessions were spread (the Roman Empire could not survive without controlling the *mare nostrum*); universal development of an urban civilisation engendering new needs and consumer hubs; finally – a consequence of the first two phenomena – safeguarded and income-generating maritime traffic on an unprecedented scale.[10]

The new economic, social and cultural model that developed with the Roman Empire created unprecedented needs among consumers. The development of megacities with populations of over one million inhabitants called for massive volumes of supplies. Considering only consumer needs for the basic necessities of wine and wheat, Rome required 2,000 round voyages per year for ships with a load capacity of 400 tonnes, or 8,000 for ships with the more usual load capacity of 100 tonnes...

Nonetheless, conceptualising maritime traffic as revolving exclusively around megacities would lead to a severely distorted image of this phenomenon in Roman times. The development of widespread urban culture and massive consumer communities at the borders, where soldiers with high purchasing power were stationed, attracted substantial inflows of goods. Imports were mainly sent to transhipment ports at the intersections of major shipping routes and Mediterranean basins, or at sites where inland waterways converged with maritime routes.

New needs triggered the development of new infrastructures, which in turn led to profound changes to the art and techniques of construction, making it possible to create artificial ports. Two inventions seen as Roman 'signatures', hydraulic concrete capable of setting under water, and the arch, made it possible to go ever further from the shore without having to manage the transport, handling and positioning of hewn blocks of stone. They made building moles in submerged areas a commonplace practice, thereby facilitating access for vessels with greater draught. Increasing depths (5 to 7 meters in Ostia) led in turn to the development of quays and pontoons. Not only did this new design provide for greater security, it also facilitated hauling operations and allowed for new containers. No more the 30-kilogram bags and amphorae, with the slow and delicate handling they required: these delicate containers were supplanted by

---

[8] See Pascal Arnaud (Ancient).
[9] See Catherine Virlouvet (Ancient).
[10] See Phyllis Culham (Ancient), Nicholas Purcell (Ancient).

barrels. This development stands out as a prime example of continuous action and feedback leading to clusters of innovation. Rome drew its power from its trade flows and maritime connectivity in the 'blue blood' of the sea.

History tends to repeat itself. Development of maritime links, a key feature of European modernity in the 16th and 17th centuries, sparked an agricultural revolution based on specialisation, making it possible to concentrate on crops suited to the local soil and climate. From this point of view, comparing England and France provides profound insight into a nation's choice to turn to the sea and the ensuing commercial and industrial rewards.

Contrary to popular belief, England's increasing maritime activity was not motivated by relatively infertile soil, particularly compared to France, driving Englishmen to turn to the sea as fishermen at best, pirates at worst. The truth is quite the opposite. England took to the sea thanks to an early agricultural revolution that increased yields from the 16th century, gradually allowing the country to feed its population without putting the entire active population in the fields. Freed from the shackles of subsistence agriculture, the country focused on industrial development, buoyed by the intensification of maritime trade, which this newly available workforce had made possible. This was the start of a virtuous cycle from which England, the Dutch Republic and Portugal all benefited. How? Simply because by offering a channel to market agricultural products, sea/river shipping made it possible, year after year, to match crops better with local soil and climate. With trade among these three maritime pioneers growing, each country embraced a national specialisation: sheep farming for England, leading to a booming textile industry; dairy products for the Dutch Republic, where rich meadowlands are better suited to cattle than to grain; wine for Portugal. All of these products offered high added value, allowing the three countries to procure the grain they needed at a lower cost than if they had cultivated it themselves. Amsterdam's development in the wheat trade in the 16th century was a crucial step in the central role the Dutch Republic was to play in European commerce. The wheat trade, universally considered the mother of all trades (*moedernegotie*) at the time, became the main branch of Dutch foreign commerce in the 17th and 18th centuries.[11]

Likewise, around the Vistula, as Jean-Pierre Poussou (Early Modern) has highlighted, Polish grain exports continued to grow, with rye figuring prominently. In Poland, exports accounted for only a very small share of production, around 10%. Nonetheless, it was a lucrative trade that provided the kingdom as a whole with additional resources. Meanwhile, France was at an utter standstill. No region was entitled to sell grain, the main component in the local diet, for fear of creating widespread famine. Thus, every region was required to be self-sufficient, making it virtually impossible to improve yields. While trading grain was the rule in other countries, in France the practice was still in its infancy in the late 18th century. Louis XVI's successive governments attempted to liberalise trade,

---

[11] See SICKING L. and DE VRIES J., *The Dutch Rural Economy in the Golden Age, 1500-1700*, New Haven: Yale University Press (1974).

provoking great discontent in the country. Some pointed to a 'Pact of Famine' which contributed significantly to the French Revolution of 1789.

The mutually beneficial dynamism between the sea and agriculture continued well after its initial appearance, constantly marking the continuum of value creation. Trade grew more vigorous, going beyond local exchanges and becoming part of a worldwide system. This phenomenon was particularly pronounced in the 19th century, with unprecedented increase in volume due not only to a proliferation of vessels on the sea, but also to the ability of so-called 'new-world' countries to meet demand. The rise of Argentine, Australian and New Zealand crop and livestock farming was spectacular, and soon became even more so with the use of cold storage systems on ships based on the invention of French engineer Charles Tellier. Throughout the world, Great Britain took advantage of the dominant positions it enjoyed thanks to its economic leadership and the primacy of the Royal Navy. For example, with respect to Argentina, Great Britain held a dominant economic and financial position that it initially leveraged starting in the 1850s to obtain increasing quantities of wool; imports of mutton subsequently followed from the 1870s. Toward the end of the century, trade began in beef, as well as wheat and corn.[12] Argentina thus developed a very substantial export-based agricultural economy: nearly two-thirds of national grain production was sold abroad. Initiatives abounded to optimise the quality of Argentine meat, particularly with the introduction of British breeds of sheep (such as Lincoln and Romney Marsh) and cattle (such as Hereford and Aberdeen Angus). An export-based agricultural economy thus emerged, dominated by the consumer, Great Britain, which absorbed 90% of Argentine agricultural exports.

The consequences of this 'maritimisation' of agriculture were impressive: lower prices for imported products led to the collapse of the British farming population, notwithstanding great increases in the productivity of grain production thanks to imported fertilisers (guano and nitrates from Chile and Peru) brought to British shores by the powerful British merchant marine.[13] But these developments also had positive effects for the population as a whole, reducing the cost of living just as the momentum of industrial development was putting upward pressure on wages: between 1860 and 1900, real wages rose by 60% in Great Britain.

By driving the agricultural revolution and consolidating trade, maritime development also contributed to the industrial revolution both through the conditions it created and the considerable impact of shipbuilding on innovation and growth of the metalworking industry, which was the foundation of industrial transformation. The example of England, which had experienced its first industrial revolution in the first half of the 17th century, is once again enlightening. Shipbuilding activities led to increasing price pressure for wood and to rising demand for metal to meet the Navy's massive demand for cannons (about 10 times greater than the Army's). These challenges contributed greatly

---

[12] See Jean-Pierre Poussou (Early Modern).
[13] Indeed, British grain yields were the highest in Europe: 26 hectolitres of wheat per hectare in 1876, compared to 15 in France.

to the increasing in the use of coal as a substitute for wood, as well as to the technological development of foundries. The reverberatory furnace thus gained in popularity during the Nine Years' War (1689-1697), while production of blast furnaces increased sharply during the War of the Spanish Succession (1701-1713). Throughout the following decades, the Royal Navy continued stimulating development of the copper industry.[14]

Likewise, we often do not recognise the extent to which construction of naval bases contributed to integrating isolated lands into the economy. The very notion of hinterlands was beginning to take shape back in the 18th century. Thus it was that A.J. Templeton noted the simultaneous rise of shipyards in Kent at the beginning of the Seven Years' War (1756-1763), and the significant extension of the regional road network.[15]

Such momentum naturally implies sustained underlying financial capacity to provide the market with the necessary liquidity. Once again, this achievement was due in large part to the initial progress-inducing impact of maritime activities on the agricultural revolution. The resulting rural exodus made it much easier to attract savings by concentrating populations in cities. Indeed, rural isolation and unsafe roads hardly motivated people to deposit their savings in banks. The development of local 'country banks' in England accelerated the trend even further, while abundant cash made for easy credit and low interest rates. It should be remembered that the Dutch Republic, the foremost merchant marine power in the first half of the 17th century, was at the same time the first country to have a majority of its population living in cities. England followed suit in the mid-19th century, whereas in France the urban population exceeded the rural one only in 1931.

The growing appeal of London as a financial market for Dutch investors, analysed by C.H. Wilson, further augmented England's ability, thanks to its financial capacity, to rule the waves and assimilate the wealth and power offered by the sea. During the War of the Austrian Succession, (1744-1748), the government was able to finance the war effort by borrowing at 3 to 4% interest rates, a 50% drop compared to rates at the beginning of the century. For the Seven Years' War, England, which as Paul Butel and Michel Morineau have shown, devoted the same amount overall to the war effort as France – 1.8 billion pounds between 1756 and 1763 – was able to cover 81% of these expenditures through borrowings (compared to 65% for France) with no effect on the extremely low interest rates. As for the American Revolution and the disastrous consequences that ensued for the French crown, Paul Kennedy (Modern) has calculated that the national debt stood at similar levels in France and England, but annual interest payments for France were twice as high as for its neighbour.

---

[14] See BUCHET C., 'Le maritime, moteur du développement économique ?', in *La Puissance Maritime*, ed. C. BUCHET, J. MEYER and J.-P. POUSSOU, Paris: PUPS (2004), pp. 509-514.

[15] See the following sources for the Dutch Republic: DE VRIES J., 'Barges and Capitalism: Passenger Transportation in the Dutch Economy, 1632-1839', *A.A.G. Bijdragen*, n°21 (1978) and DE VRIES J. and VAN DER WOUDE A., *The first Modern Economy. Success, Failure, and Perseverance of the Dutch Economy, 1500-1815*, Cambridge: Cambridge University Press (1997).

The work of Pierre-François Tuel (Early Modern), following that of Paul Bairoch, shows that when a country's capital is connected to the sea, it catalyses an infinitely more pronounced demographic and economic concentration than land-based capitals. Focusing on eight modern capital cities, one can see that the land-based capitals Paris, Madrid, Moscow and Beijing accounted for no more than 3% of the total population of their respective countries, a rate that rises to 8 to 12% for maritime capitals (London, Amsterdam, Naples, capital of the kingdom of the Two Sicilies, and Lisbon). By combining the power of a political capital with the wealth of a maritime and therefore commercial city, throughout modern times maritime capitals have enjoyed a supremacy arising from a commercial spirit that no land-based capital or simple port city could hope to attain. The blend of political and economic power makes for extraordinary dynamism thanks to the appeal of these cities for both men and money.

How could a city gain commercial momentum if it is not located at the epicentre of trade flows?

London was truly the country's economic nerve centre. At the end of the 18th century, it was already twice as large as Paris in terms of population with nearly one million inhabitants; the population of the British capital doubled in a century while Paris gained a mere 150,000 to 180,000 new inhabitants. It is essential to note that the concentration of activity in London in no way hindered the development of other cities such as Glasgow, Hull, Bristol and Liverpool, as they were port cities and the lion's share of domestic traffic in England was carried by water. London, the heart of the country, relied on the sea for supplies. Moreover, the trade flows generated by this tentacular city in turn attracted capital that benefited investment and the stock exchange. London's immensity provided the fundamental means of expansion for large-scale English maritime trade. Everything naturally converged in London, located at the centre of all national networks. And this centripetal force, precisely because it was a natural phenomenon, required no outside intervention to speak of. In other words, the most centralised country from an official point of view, France, has always been in the grip of centrifugal forces. Whereas, in the most organically liberal country, England, everything has always flocked to the centre before heading back out to supply the provinces. In England, liberalism found its home. In France, power operated through institutions. In Great Britain, it operated through the economy.

There is little doubt that History would have been different had Spain's capital been Seville instead of Madrid, if the sea port of Rouen had played the role of Paris, Shanghai instead of Beijing, Saint Petersburg instead of Moscow, Budapest instead of Vienna, Mumbai instead of Delhi, São Paulo instead of Brasilia...

The lesson is clear: political entities that turn towards the sea think in terms of flows, exchanges and openness, all drivers of economic development. Through taxes and supply-based income, this dynamic contributed to the emergence of increasingly strong and structured political entities. Indeed, in addition to being a source of wealth, trade is also a source of conflict, and merchant marines require protection by navies, which are extremely costly to build and maintain. Navies everywhere have served as spearheads of modernity, with the construction and development of arsenals being the perfect example of the simultaneous technological and organisational development they engendered.[16] The creation of specialised warships, the birth and perennial renewal of permanent navies, as well as the growing, and today even exponential cost of technical innovations, made this financial challenge all the greater. Only sufficiently structured powers with an efficient system of administration and a citizenry capable of bearing a significant tax burden have been and will in the future be able to sustain a navy. With his concept of 'fiscal-naval state', Patrick O'Brien (Early Modern) set the stage for an approach that seems to apply to all maritime and naval powers. The case of Great Britain was the textbook example: English economic growth, stimulated by international trade, provided resources for the state budget, enabling the country to build and maintain the Royal Navy, which could in turn impose the *pax britannica* in international waters, thereby promoting increased trade. The links between economic development, taxation and the navy seem obvious, but it should be noted that nearly 50% of public expenditure in recent times has gone to the navy rather than the army, an English particularity that has clearly proved effective.

One could go even further by pointing to interactions between the nature of society, the nature of the political system and that of military pursuits. Societies with a commercial spirit, founded on a spirit of political and social openness with strong participation by the middle class have enjoyed a virtuous cycle of growth grounded in the development of maritime trade and a strong navy; the opposite has proven true for states governed by autocratic institutions, relying on land-based military power, a rural economy, etc.[17]

2. The Sea: Driving Force of Predominance and Leadership

For all political entities, regardless of kind (city, state, alliance, etc.), period or location, the most prominent always seems to be that with the greatest number of ships. Warships, merchant vessels and fishing vessels spring to mind, but why not also scientific vessels?

Egypt in the age of the Pharaohs managed to supplant its adversaries thanks to the sea, initiating a vigorous tradition of trade.[18] In the first naval battle in recorded history, around 1191 BC, Ramses III used his fleet to push back invaders from the north, known as 'peoples of the sea'. Moreover, the decline of ancient Egypt resulted from the Pharaohs' decision to rely on a Greek and Phoenician fleet for defence from the 4th century onwards.

---

[16] See Jean Meyer (Early Modern), Daniel Baugh (Early Modern), Jakob Seerup (Early Modern).
[17] See Nicholas Rodger (Early Modern).
[18] See Graciela Gestoso Singer (Ancient), Sydney Hervé Aufrère (Ancient).

So too did the Greek city-states incorporate the sea as a factor of power. In the case of ancient Greece, it would surely be premature to speak of thalassocracy, a form of outside domination in which states base their power essentially on control of the sea.[19] Nonetheless, certain states had already implemented large-scale maritime policies. Such was the case for Miletus, Naxos, Phocaea, Corinth and Samos, Aegina and others. According to Herodotus, Miletus had sailing vessels and controlled the sea right from the late 7th century BC, and continued to do so until it was conquered by Darius. Likewise, it was thanks to the sea that Aegina was able to break away from Epidaurus and pursue a violent policy of plundering coastal populations.

For a true thalassocracy to exist, a state must have external support, permanent facilities and a fleet that is not only large but well maintained and constantly renewed, unlike certain fleets of Antiquity that were built for a specific purpose and soon forgotten. For a fleet to be maintained, it must be indispensable. As such, a state's foreign policy must require extensive mastery of the sea, either to underpin dominance on land or to contribute to territorial expansion. Such was the case of the Persian Empire, the first maritime power in history, which continually expanded from the final third of the 6th century to the beginning of the 5th century BC, controlling the entire coastline from Asia Minor to Syria. Control later extended as far as Egypt following the conquest by Cambyses, who boasted of having completed his father's empire by adding an empire of the sea. The Persians initially relied on Phoenician expertise to build their powerful fleet, but were forced to go further. It was then that, thanks to contact with Egypt during the fight against Amasis, the trireme came into being.

The Persian maritime juggernaut culminated with Darius (522–486 BC) who conquered Samos in 517BC, ventured into the Cyclades, starting with Naxos, and attacked the Scythians with an armada of 600 ships. He also succeeded in placing Cyrenaica under Persian influence, retaking control of Cyprus and strengthening his hold over the Hellespont. The Battle of Lade (494 BC), where the first stirrings of the art of naval tactics can be seen, brought together a total of 600 Phoenician, Cilician, Cypriot and Egyptian warships fighting for the Persians. The armada vanquished the 353 Greek triremes (80 from Miletus, 12 from Priene, 3 from Myus, 17 from Teos, 100 from Chios, 8 from Erythraea, 3 from Phocaea, 70 from Lesbos, 60 from Samos).

These expeditions and those that followed, targeting the Cyclades, Euboea and Aegina, reflect the thalassocratic rationale of control of the land from the sea. In 490 BC, thanks to the technical effect of its victory of Lade, the undertaking was quite reasonable. The ultimate defeat, at Salamis and Plataea, was due to the creation in Athens, at the initiative of Themistocles, of the first standing war fleet capable of measuring up to the Persian armada. Moreover, this new force was perfectly suited to a specific vessel, the trireme. Although it was not an Athenian invention, the Athenians nonetheless recognised the true worth of this design. Twenty-three centuries before Alfred Mahan, conceptualisation of naval power

---

[19] See Jean-Nicolas Corvisier (Ancient).

had been achieved.[20] It would seem that the only way to triumph over maritime predominance is with maritime predominance itself.

But Poseidon is capricious, and the slightest technology gap can be fatal.[21] The superiority of its triremes led Athens to victory in the Greco-Persian Wars, but her disregard for new forms of combat which favoured large-size vessels and boarding enemy ships rather than mobility and ramming, resulted in defeat, first in the Bay of Syracuse and later at the Battle of Aegospotami.

Carthage, thanks to its maritime strength, took the place of Athens as the dominant power, reigning over the western Mediterranean from the 6th century BC until the first Punic War in 241 BC, when it fell to the single greatest naval power of Antiquity: Rome.

Yes, Rome. Well before the fabled military supremacy of the legions under Caesar and other illustrious generals, Rome was first and foremost a naval power. If Hannibal, Rome's mortal enemy, chose to skirt the Mediterranean by land, enduring the painful ordeal of crossing the Pyrenees and Alps with his elephants, it was simply because his age-old adversary ruled the waves; reaching Italy by sea would have been impossible. This same maritime dominance made it possible for Scipio to land in Africa, where he definitively crushed Hannibal at Zama (202 BC), thereby ending the second Punic War. The Roman navy was everywhere, contributing to combined operations with what today is called force projection: a portion of the troops reached the battlefield by land, while the others travelled by sea (or an inland waterway) to surround the enemy. Ships were also mobilised specifically to observe and report on enemy movements. Thanks to the *pax maritima*, Rome had control over maritime traffic, which then continued by land as far as the regions around the Indian Ocean.[22] Only piracy – the poor man's warfare – occasionally succeeded in disrupting delivery of supplies to the Empire's constellation of urban centres. However, any act of piracy elicited a strong and determined response: in 67 BC, General Pompey was entrusted with 500 vessels and 120,000 men, i.e. the equivalent of 20 legions, to eradicate pirates. His success elevated him to the highest rank of the imperial podium.

But the time came when Roman stability fell victim to acerbic ambitions throughout the excessively large empire. The sea continued to take centre stage in these conflicts. The naval Battle of Actium (31 BC) brought Octavian victory over Mark Antony and Cleopatra; the equally decisive battle of Eleous (324 A.D.) brought Constantine victory over Licinius, a follower of highly combative polytheism, and ensured continuing adherence to monotheistic Christianity. Under Julian, the Roman war fleet once again provided strong support to land operations as it had for centuries. However, funds were lacking and the navy would soon become impossible to maintain. The weight and precious metal content of Roman currency was decreasing. The Roman navy fell into decline and

---

[20] See Jean-Nicolas Corvisier (Ancient), Vincent Gabrielsen (Ancient).
[21] See for example the role of innovation in conflicts between Athens and Sparta in Daniel Battesti and Laurène Leclercq (Ancient).
[22] See Phyllis Culham (Ancient).

soon became incapable of taking effective action against the ever more numerous – and better organised – barbarians at its borders.[23]

The Vandal King Genseric was able to dominate the entire western Mediterranean for nearly half a century thanks to the naval force he established. Sea power was also the key to his conquest of Rome in 455. Likewise, maritime development lies behind Neustria's turning the scales to dominate Burgundy and Austrasia in the late 6th century.[24]

In the south, Byzantium, a direct successor of the empire, replaced Rome. It endured from the founding of its arsenal following the Battle of the Dardanelles in 324 until the 10th–11th centuries, some 700 years. From the 4th to the 10th centuries, the imperial city relied on the main fleet based in the Bosphorus, as well as provincial fleets. It remained impregnable until the assault and sack of the Fourth Crusade (1202–1204). The Byzantine phenomenon represents the mirror image of the paradoxically maritime domination of the Roman Empire. Rome rose to supremacy through successive conquests of the shores of the Mediterranean, which ultimately became a Roman lake. Having inherited Rome's naval power, Byzantium disintegrated due to the loss of its coastlines, as the core of Byzantine resistance consisted of the city–navy relationship. Technological superiority, manifested principally by Greek fire, played a fundamental role until the secret behind this weapon was revealed, making it available to all. The Byzantine fleet made extensive use of surprise tactics in the form of sophisticated assaults. The fleet served simultaneously as a weapon of combat, a logistical tool, a strike force and a means of force projection. Our knowledge of the Byzantine merchant marine remains largely uncertain. It would seem that in comparison with Italian cities, the decline of this institution was much less clear-cut than traditionally thought. The Middle East became a Muslim territory following the Arab conquest of the 7th to 10th centuries, with the final blows to Byzantium delivered by the Seljuk dynasty and later the Ottoman Empire. Byzantium, already crumbling in the wake of betrayal by Venice, Genoa and the crusaders, endured the final stages of a very slow decline.

The coast was thus clear for the Italian cities, radiating with opulence and splendour taken directly from the sea. The Doges of Venice officially recognised the Adriatic as their benefactor every year at the feast of the Ascension, celebrating the marriage between the Serenissima and the sea. 'We wed thee, O sea, as a sign of true and everlasting domination', they would say, throwing a ring into the water from the state barge, the *Bucentaur*.

Indeed, the notion of maritime predominance seems to be the key to geopolitical oscillations. Henri Legohérel (Medieval) arrives at the same conclusions in his remarkable contribution, 'Capetians and Plantagenets: the Struggle for Maritime Supremacy', which radically upsets the traditional, land-focused understanding of this period. Maritime struggles in fact play the role of kingmaker over the

---

[23] See Yann Le Bohec (Ancient).
[24] See Régine Le Jan (Medieval).

250-year period in question. The sea divides the period into different segments, bestowing predominance on the side with the most proactive maritime policy.

From this perspective, the business of Aquitaine is enlightening. Triggered by disputes between seamen from Bayonne and Normandy, it ultimately led to the confiscation of the fiefdom of Aquitaine in 1294, followed by a counter-attack by England, unwilling to abandon one of its foremost possessions: an English fleet devastated the French Atlantic coast, sailed up the Gironde to La Réole, well past Bordeaux, and liberated Bayonne. Philip IV rose to England's challenge by establishing the Clos des Galées in Rouen, France's first dockyard, and building a fleet that outnumbered Edward I Plantagenet's 500 ships. The result was spectacular: the Capetian navy gained control of the sea. Philip IV attempted a sort of blockade of England, while the French navy engaged in ever more attacks on a terrorised English coast. The sea took the day: the peace of 1299 led Edward I to evacuate Flanders and accept French occupation of Bordeaux.

Likewise, the predominance of the Capetian navy over the following 30 years contributed to consolidating and strengthening the reign of Philip IV by protecting the salt convoys from the Bay of Bourgneuf and providing security for areas with significant merchant marine activity (the Seine estuary, the area around the Channel Islands, tidal passages in Brittany, the Saintonge Narrows).

The same is true for the Hundred Years' War. Each of the conflict's three phases was fought at sea.

The first (1337-1360) was marked by English preponderance. England's mastery of the sea brought wealth through development of trade, while making it possible to transport English troops. Such factors serve to explain England's successes and France's setbacks (Poitiers in 1356 and the capture of King John II).

During the second phase of the war (1360-1413), France took the necessary steps: Charles V reorganised and strengthened the Clos des Galées, put the Admiral of France at the same rank as the Constable and found the right man for the job, Jean de Vienne. In 1377, France took back the initiative at sea, and the waves were once again under Capetian control. English ports were neutralised, supply routes towards the continent were cut off and the morale of the English maritime community hard hit. French control of the sea created excellent conditions for the land-based campaign of Du Guesclin and Clisson. France held sway until 1386, when dissent within the government composed of the uncles of Charles VI led the French to abandon the plan for a land invasion of England. Faced with the decline of French naval forces, Jean de Vienne left to join the Crusade.

The third and final phase witnessed a dual victory thanks once again to the sea. Henry V, the most brilliant of the Lancasters, was the first Plantagenet since Richard the Lionheart to understand how to use naval might as a tool of war. He rebuilt a powerful fleet with ships of up to 800 tons, such as the *Grace-Dieu* and the *Trinity*. England's only hope against a wealthier enemy motivated by defending its own land was to use the mobility offered by the sea to take the strategic initiative, choosing the time and place of the decisive encounter. The English victory was absolute. Henry V had shown military superiority and would become heir to the French crown on the death of Charles VI a few weeks later. The enemy fleet had disappeared and the English Channel was once again *mare britannicum*. Why then continue to maintain a costly and seemingly useless English fleet that had unquestionably grown too large? Thus it was that in 1423, the government of the young King Henry VI, presided by his uncle, the Duke of Bedford, took the peculiar decision to sell most of England's ships. This was a sensible decision from a purely financial standpoint, but scorning such a beneficial ally as the sea turned out to be a major strategic error. History abounds with lessons...

The tide soon turned. The Plantagenet government no longer had the means to convey reinforcements to the continent: there is no other explanation for England's weak reaction to the campaigns of Joan of Arc and her successors, as well as the decisive French victories at the final battles of Formigny (1450) and Castillon (1453).

We tend not to realise that a second Hundred Years' War opposed France and England, starting in 1689 with the beginning of the penultimate war waged by Louis XIV, and continuing until the end of the Napoleonic Wars. Despite what one reads in history books, this was no simple string of conflicts, but indeed a Hundred Years' War fought not for eastern territorial expansion, but rather for maritime predominance in the west and access to American markets. In the age-old struggle between land and sea, the sea took the day as it always has. England, umbilically connected to the sea, took the mantle of worldwide supremacy that continental France had temporarily achieved due to its excessive centralisation and strong population growth. Great Britain would display this manifestation of power throughout the seven seas, with an empire upon which the sun never set, until the 1922 Washington Conference at which England graciously agreed to share its supremacy with its protective big brother on the other side of the Atlantic.[25] England's brilliance lies in its having been the first to realise that the sea is the world's largest free-trade zone.

As we have seen, history repeats itself. The 'Continental Blockade' decreed by Napoleon did much more harm to France's empire than to England. Thanks to the mobility of its fleets, the latter was always able to obtain the resources it needed and to maintain its trade, even if that meant expanding over the world to develop its economy and meet its needs. Ultimately, he who controls the sea controls the land: this is one of the primary lessons of this study of the role and place of maritime activities in the march of History.

By addressing human history through the lens of the sea for the first time, the research conducted by Océanides utterly revises our approach to History, and thus to geopolitics, which has hitherto focused on land-based history in its search for structural components. Sir Halford Mackinder, in the famed lecture of 25 January 1904 that established him as the founding father of twentieth-century geopolitics, defined his notion of 'Heartland', the geographical pivot of history and 'Citadel of the World Empire'. 'Who rules the Heartland commands the World-Island', he wrote, 'who rules the World-Island commands the world'.

---

[25] Cf. Phillips Payson O'Brien (Modern).

General Conclusion

This is far from the 1595 quote by Sir Walter Raleigh, beautifully expressing the British ideal from the depths of the Tower of London where he was held prisoner: 'For whosoever commands the sea commands the trade; whosoever commands the trade of the world commands the riches of the world, and consequently the world itself'. Taken in its full depth, History favours Raleigh over Mackinder.[26] Do we fully realise this fact? Geopolitics remains an eminently land-based science despite the work of Alfred Thayer Mahan at the end of the 19th century and John Spykman's adaptation of Mackinder's thoughts at the turning point of World War II, introducing the particularly central notion of 'Rimland'.

War after war, the same conclusion stands out. It only becomes perceptible by reading between the lines of history to understand the importance of mobility and connectivity of flows, the very quintessence of maritime activities. Following the imperial epic, in World War I, World War II and even in the Cold War, victory went to the country or alliance that has mastered these flows.

From this point of view, it may be interesting to focus on World War I, a conflict for which historians have come to the overly hasty conclusion that navies had little impact on the military events that brought the war to an end. After Norman Friedman,[27] Avner Offer (Modern) of Oxford demonstrates precisely the contrary for Océanides.

Indeed, unable to procure foodstuffs on the world market for lack of a strong navy, Germany and Austria-Hungary needed men in the fields and could therefore not mobilise as many soldiers as would have been necessary. Russia's choice of ensuring a strong military by sacrificing agricultural production soon led to a famine that precipitated the October Revolution. Conversely, England and France enjoyed communications thanks to mastery of the sea, thus guaranteeing supplies of food and energy, especially coal. In the long run, this advantage inevitably led to victory.

In order for the Central Powers to prevail, the war would have to be short. Only sufficient destruction of allied trade by U-boats could have made the difference. However, such a turn of events would hardly have been a realistic ambition so long as the German Empire could not command the sea. Moreover, merciless undersea warfare precipitated American participation in the conflict in 1917, transforming the Atlantic into a bridgehead that forced Germany to accept unconditional surrender.

Like Napoleon, Germany in the First and Second World Wars attempted to overcome this food and energy shortage by advancing ever further into the continent, as far as Russia, serving only to prolong the war without changing the final outcome.[28]

---

[26] BUCHET C., 'Du Heartland à Océanides', *Revue de Défense Nationale* (April 2016), 49–53.
[27] FRIEDMAN N., *Fighting the Great War at Sea: Strategy, Tactics and Technology*, Barnsley: Seaforth Publishing (2014).
[28] OFFER A., *The First World War: An agrarian Interpretation*, Oxford: Clarendon Press (1989), p. 317. See also: LAMBERT N.A., *Planning Armageddon: British Economic Warfare and the First World War*, Cambridge, MA : Harvard University Press (2012).

Later in the century, another war was fought on the Atlantic – but this time against the submarines of Admiral Dönitz – together with the construction of some 8 million tonnes of merchant ships, made it possible to liberate Europe and guarantee the Allied victory during World War II.[29] Mastery of the sea makes for primacy in trade and therefore economic predominance, enhancing military capacity and inevitably overcoming the adversary. This is precisely what Charles de Gaulle conveyed, with such vision and grandeur, in his famous Appeal of 18 June. France had lost a battle, but not the war, he wrote, because the country was 'overwhelmed by the mechanical, ground and air forces of the enemy'. But France was not alone. She was not alone because she had a vast Empire behind her and could 'align with the British Empire that *holds the sea* and continues the fight' and 'like England, use without limit the immense industry of the United States'.

Thanks to the work of C. Baxter (Modern) and G. Baer, we also discover how the collapse of Japanese trade, by stifling the national economy, prevented Japan from maintaining its operational capacity and allowed American and British forces to win the war in the Pacific. By August of 1945, Japan's foreign trade had dropped to 312,000 tonnes (less than 12% of pre-war traffic), while the Allies enjoyed 88 million tonnes in trade.

Likewise, throughout the Cold War, Soviet inability to develop maritime trade, and thus its economy as a whole, ultimately undermined the willpower of Russian leaders to contain American hegemony. Today, we are conscious that the Soviet navy would have been powerless to contest U.S. supremacy.[30] The Reagan administration's considerable efforts to strengthen naval capacity, aiming for 600 warships that also surpassed the Soviet fleet in terms of quality, was the key factor in the collapse of the Soviet Union, marking the end of the Cold War and Western victory.[31] For the third time in the 20th century, on an ever more oceanic planet, a maritime alliance eclipsed a land-based alliance...

All things considered, developing, and in particular maintaining, a navy requires wealth that cannot exist without powerful trade. Control of international trade is thus an indispensable factor for the long-term conservation of naval power. However, one must also keep in mind that, by the same token, a powerful navy is essential for a strong maritime economy. The counterexample for the Soviet navy is the French merchant fleet, which grew spectacularly under Louis XV and was poised to overtake British trade. However, England deliberately undertook to destroy French maritime trade through periodic wars. Indeed, for lack of a sufficiently powerful French navy, war served to shatter French trade while benefiting the English merchant marine.

In this regard, Patrick Villiers (Early Modern) has beautifully demonstrated that maritime trade can only be maintained or strengthened when it enjoys the

---

[29] See Christopher Baxter (Modern) and W. J. R. Gardner (Modern).
[30] See Colin S. Gray (Modern).
[31] See Eric Grove (Modern): 'NATO's maritime strategy was a key factor in exerting the decisive strategic pressure on the Soviet Union that caused the implosion that ended the Cold war with Western victory'.

support of a modern and powerful navy. From this perspective, the British model brilliantly illustrates the paradigm of naval policy contributing to a maritime economy. In 1815, England achieved the long-standing dream of Portugal, Spain and the Dutch Republic: a virtual monopoly in maritime trade, a powerful driver of economic development.

The example of Russia is even more enlightening, magnificently illustrating the impact of the sea on the development or decline of nations. As long as Denmark, Sweden and the Hanseatic League denied Russia access to trade in the Baltic Sea, the country was unable to develop economically. Thus, contrary to the classic pattern according to which fishing is the first to develop, followed by trade, and finally a naval force to protect the rest, Russia started by instituting a navy under Tsar Aleksey Mikhailovich (1645-1676) and especially Peter the Great (1682-1725), who established a maritime capital in the country. The navy allowed Russia to enjoy economic development engendered by trade, while gaining the military and diplomatic status of a major power.[32]

Much further south, the lesson was the same. Cyrille Poirier-Coutansais (Early Modern) shows a gap between Persia under the Safavid dynasty (1501-1736) and its Ottoman neighbour. The former, having failed to look to the sea, gradually found itself excluded from trade circuits and was soon faced with a critical situation in its struggle against the Ottoman Empire of Selim I. Yet, a different policy would certainly have been possible.

The Mayan Empire offers the perfect demonstration of this phenomenon, having established and maintained its supremacy through maritime connectivity based on substantial trade in salt, obsidian, precious stones, gold and copper. This activity brought power and wealth, creating and expanding a territorial unit through an internal market. Nonetheless, this sea-based predominance fell victim to the superior technology of Spanish ships, which were able to bring the empire to a rapid collapse by severing its maritime links.[33]

The same conclusion applies in Asia. In China, the prohibition of deep-sea shipping following the death of the eunuch Zheng He in 1434, and the decision to favour inland waterways, particularly the Grand Canal, impeded the development of commercial capitalism, the system that brought glory to Japan during the Meiji era in the late 19th century. Note that today all G8 and even G20 countries are maritime states.

The question arises, in contrast to these converging examples, whether political entities can develop and achieve predominance without turning to the sea. From this perspective, the Mongol Empire serves as the perfect counter-example. Indeed, the Mongols created the most extensive empire of all time, all the while completely neglecting the Pacific and Indian Oceans to which they enjoyed potential access. Their world was the world of steppes, forests, deserts,

---

[32] See Pavel Krotov (Early Modern), Jakob Seerup (Early Modern).
[33] See Heather McKillop (Early Modern) and Emiliano Melgar (Early Modern). See also the contribution of Sebastian Kolditz (Medieval) on this issue of Mediterranean connectivity in the medieval period.

lakes and rivers, and they never entertained even symbolic ties with the great maritime spaces. They aimed to conquer land.

The work of Didier Gazagnadou (Medieval) is particularly helpful in understanding the factors that made it possible to establish and maintain this empire without being affected by the sea. The Mongols owed their success to a typically maritime feature: fluidity. By creating a dense network of post houses and caravanserais, they managed to develop a veritable hinterland, while the gravitational motion of caravans made for trade flows similar to those of the *voltas* of vessels operated by maritime powers. The Mongol Empire employed tens of thousands of men, no fewer than 200,000 horses and even more camels and dromedaries, from the Pacific coast to the shores of the Black Sea, from the borders of Indochina to the heart of Tibet, from China to the borders of the Iranian world and Iraq, over a vast network covering at least 50 to 60,000 kilometres. 'These great nomads opened up Eurasian societies thanks to the fluidity of the traffic they established. Metaphorically speaking, they treated the land as an ocean'.[34] Goods were transported by camel and dromedary caravans, 'ships of the steppes and the desert' (Bactrian camels travel some 60 kilometres per day carrying between 150 and 200 kilogrammes on average, and dromedaries between 100 and 150 kilogrammes).

It remains to be seen whether the failure to develop and control the Indian and Pacific Oceans contributed to the collapse of the Mongol Empire. Perhaps, says Didier Gazagnadou, and despite the fluidity of the land networks along the silk roads that conveyed substantial flows of goods, especially from east to west. Land transport is always slower and more expensive, and requires many more intermediaries and transhipments than maritime transport... If the Mongols in Iran and China had built fleets and had undertaken to conquer the oceans, the history of Africa, America and the world as a whole might have been very different. The Indian Ocean provides access to Africa and the Indies; the Pacific provides access to the Americas. Unknown to the Mongols, these links allowed many European businessmen and religious leaders to discover little-known lands in Asia, encouraging them to circumvent this immense empire, taking to the seas to establish direct contact with the rich wonders of China and the Indies. And thus it was that from the late 15th century European mariners struck out on sea expeditions, financed by powerful settled states, to make direct contact with Asian worlds and, by chance, discover the Americas.

In the same vein, India under the Great Moghul deserves to be studied, considering its conventional reputation as a hopelessly land-based geographic area unable to turn to the sea, except at rare and short-lived intervals. Hindu society, and particularly elite castes, are said to have felt not only indifference for the sea, but actual repugnance at the idea of leaving the shore due to religious prohibitions. Historical realities are in fact infinitely more complex.

---

[34] See Didier Gazagnadou (Medieval).

GENERAL CONCLUSION

Close examination of the facts over several centuries shows that here as well, the success or failure of the various sovereigns hinged on the sea.[35]

Indeed, Sher Shah Suri's disregard for the sea and maritime trade contributed greatly to his ultimate failure. In contrast, Akbar (1566-1605) broke down barriers within his empire by linking production centres to the coast in Bengal and Gujarat, and implemented a mercantile policy grounded in the notion of hinterland. By doing so, he brought about the development of prosperous towns at the crossroads of trade routes connected with seaborne trade and earned the title of 'Great Moghul'. This initiative was suspended by his successors Jahangir (1605-1627) and Shah Jahan (1628-1657), only to be renewed under Aurangzeb (1659-1707), who went so far as to transfer the capital south to Aurangabad, a choice geopolitical and economic location at the junction of the two maritime regions of Golkonda and Vijayapur. This increased tax revenue, making it possible to consolidate the empire and resist the Maratha uprisings.

It is also interesting to consider the role and place of the sea for groups whose epicentre is distant from the sea. Olivier Chaline's study of Central Europe and the sea in modern times (Early Modern) shows how far inland maritime shock waves stirred the continent. Indeed, at first glance the sea may have had virtually nothing to do with the successes or failures of Central European states. Nonetheless, at certain key moments, maritime factors played a decisive role. Central Europe was largely deprived of access to the sea by coastal states. Such was the case of Sweden, which thanks to its navy was able to project power well into Central Europe.[36] The Holy Roman Empire and Poland both paid a high price, the former for its inability to develop naval power in time, and the latter for its inability to maintain its influence on the seas. At the height of their power in 1629, the Habsburgs were unable to prevent the seaborne landing by Gustavus Adolphus the following year and the establishment of lasting Swedish influence in the northern part of the Empire. Likewise, Austria and Prussia would have met with defeat in any number of conflicts without the support of maritime allies.

By definition, the notion of predominance concerns but one political entity at any given time, two or three at the very most. However, in addition to generating virtuous economic cycles, as shown in the first part of our study, the turn to the sea provides groups with greater dynamism and positions of leadership, impelling historical trajectories in a favourable direction for institutions, populations and intellectual and cultural life.

The example of Portugal likewise reveals the benefits of maritime dynamics. Indeed, the sea forged the country's destiny and independence at the same time. Portugal's geographic location on the Atlantic Ocean and proactive openness to the sea were the two factors that shaped the character of this 'maritime nation', as well as its ability, thanks to the sea, to play an infinitely greater role in History than its demographic weight would otherwise have allowed.[37]

---

[35] See Michel Vergé-Franceschi (Early Modern).
[36] See Jakob Seerup (Early Modern).
[37] See Jorge Semedo de Matos (Ancient).

The existence, independence and wealth of the Dutch Republic can also be understood only through the sea. The country's control of the seaports was the factor that allowed it to break away from Spain.[38] Thanks to fishing, trade and the ensuing agricultural specialisation, as well as the resulting industrial innovations, the Dutch population enjoyed the highest standard of living in Europe, and thus in the world, during the first half of the 17th century.[39] The Dutch Republic was known at the time as the ultimate 'enlightened power', the country with the greatest respect for the values of freedom and tolerance. Newspapers enjoyed extraordinary editorial freedom for the time, and printers revelled in dissent. The country offered refuge to scholars and philosophers, not least among whom Descartes and Spinoza. Urban concentration, wealth and an entrepreneurial spirit gave rise to the greatest commercial entities of the age, including the VOC, the famous Dutch East India Company, founded in 1602 as the first joint-stock company. It was in the Dutch Republic as well that many decisive inventions came into being: the telescope, microscope, chronometer, optical lenses, the first spectacles, etc.[40]

The sea also proved to be a decisive factor in Korean history, as control of the coasts ensured not only the kingdom's rise to power, but its very survival, independence and sovereignty for nearly a millennium.[41] In the same way, but over a much shorter period, the development of a navy profoundly modified the course of history for some 60 years in the small Indian kingdom of Maratha, located in the north-west of the Indian subcontinent. The existence of a navy resulted in economic and commercial development, each strengthening the other. Furthermore, this maritime development offered the small kingdom unprecedented political influence, even for a certain time preventing European navies from taking advantage of the resulting economic benefits.[42]

On a different scale, the sea made it possible for military orders, including the Knights Hospitaller, the Templars and the Teutonic Order, to assert their supranationality and derive substantial revenues from trade. It was thus no coincidence that fighting orders gave rise to illustrious seafarers of modern times, such as the Portuguese explorers Vasco de Gama and Pedro Alvares Cabral who explored the coasts of India and Brazil under the flag of the Order of Christ.[43]

---

[38] See Louis Sicking (Early Modern).
[39] Throughout the 17th and 18th centuries, maritime activities served as the foundation for economic development of the Dutch Republic. In the 17th century, more than 25% of the active male population worked on ships' crews, and 1/6 continued to be employed at sea at the end of the 18th century. This demand for seafarers required significant foreign labour and spectacular investments in human capital in terms of training, generating substantial economic benefits. See Jelle Van Lottum (Early Modern).
[40] Jean-Pierre Poussou, *Les Iles Britanniques, les Provinces-Unies, la guerre et la paix au XVIIe siècle*, Paris: Economica (1991).
[41] See Alexandre Le Bouteiller (Early Modern).
[42] See Sachin Pendse (Early Modern).
[43] See Pierre-Vincent Claverie (Medieval) and Juhan Kreem (Medieval).

Furthermore, if the Order of Malta continues to exist to the present day, it is thanks to a greater focus on maritime activities than other orders.[44]

Likewise, do we truly realise that not only was the sea the stage for the greatest human migrations, as we have mentioned, but also for the global transfer of ideas and beliefs? This is true for all three major monotheistic religions, as well as for Hinduism and Buddhism. [45] In Europe, caricatures of the work of Max Weber have sometimes led to the conclusion that the protestant work ethic is more conducive to the development of a capitalist spirit, although perfect counter-examples undermine this hypothesis.[46] It is true that the relationship to money often differs considerably between countries with Catholic or Protestant majorities, but is not this fact more a corollary than a root cause? It is interesting to note that Protestantism spread very quickly through maritime communities, and that the sea carried the Reformation over a large part of the European coast. Rather than the cause of this famous protestant work ethic, the Reformation seems to have been adopted on the basis of a pre-existing attitude towards trade, an attitude developed through contact with the sea. In our opinion, the true division lies rather between rural and maritime traditions, between a spirit of openness and one of inland isolationism. There is a striking contrast between eighteenth-century France, where Physiocrats, particularly François Quesnay, saw the land as the sole source of wealth, and England, where the first optimistic portrayal of industrial philosophy appeared in 1776: Adam Smith's *The Wealth of Nations*.[47]

Along the same lines, utopian socialist theories like those of Fourier, Saint-Simon and Cabet are based on the establishment of rural communities of craftsmen with one common characteristic: a location far from the sea, unlike Thomas More's island of Utopia. The same trend stands out in Spain with the *Proyectistas*, as well as in Russia, where the countryside continued to be of enormous significance, and where industrialisation had hardly begun at the end of the 19th century, despite the efforts of the state.

Perhaps more than any other, the Polynesian people, a veritable 'Ocean People', as Emmanuel Desclèves (Early Modern) elegantly describes them, achieved exceptional influence thanks to the sea. The Polynesian character is connected at its very core with the sea, at one with the ocean from which it derives strength and prestige, and which profoundly forged its originality. Spread along the coasts of Southeast Asia and the Americas, the maritime peoples of the Oceania lived with a single point of reference: the sea, a source of both knowledge and power. Their gods and founding myths took shape in the Ocean. From this perspective, discovery appears as an act of creation. Chiefs were the descendants of the gods, enlightened leaders and guardians of the ancestral *mana*. They were the masters of discoveries and relations with the other islands, their power granted by their

---

[44] See Alain Blondy (Early Modern).
[45] See in particular Chantal Reynier (Ancient), Tansen Sen (Ancient).
[46] See Klaus Malettke in *La Puissance Maritime*, ed. C. BUCHET, J. MEYER and J.-P. POUSSOU, Paris: PUPS (2004); MASSON P., *De la Mer et de sa Stratégie*, Paris: Taillandier (1986).
[47] BUCHET C., *Une Autre Histoire des Océans et de l'Homme*, preface by President Jacques Chirac, Paris: Robert Laffont (2004).

people's incomparable ability to navigate freely across this empty space open to inter-island communications. Communing with the ocean and the sky overhead, Polynesians are at home everywhere in this vast area. That is why they conceive the universe very differently from sedentary peoples whose horizon ends at the coast. Claire Laux (Modern) shows that Polynesian maritime societies appear as dynamic and hierarchical, while land-based Melanesian societies remained much more split up, as if unable to produce organised and hierarchical structures. Once again, we see the influence of a connection with the sea – or lack thereof – even on social attitudes. Claire Laux goes further, considering that within the Polynesian population 'the most dynamic individuals were "people of contact", particularly those of mixed race whose very existence was the fruit of maritime contact'.[48] 'Our ancestors saw the world as a "sea of islands" rather than as "islands in the sea"', said the Polynesian anthropologist Epeli Hau'ofa.

In certain parts of the African continent one sees this same close connection between the ability to govern and the ability to navigate at sea, the foundation and legitimisation of power and a factor of prestige and political influence. Myths collected in the Congo in the 20th century portray seaborne expeditions, a ritual carried out under the watchful eye of a benevolent rainmaking goddess, as a sign of blessedness or a test used to choose a new king, particularly when there is no natural successor. A century ago on the coast of southern Somalia or northern Kenya, a Persian folk tale rich in maritime imagery recounted the long journey of a young man across the Indian Ocean. Upon his return, he is recognised by his people as their king, and by travelling merchants as a Muslim. Such practices also seem to have existed in the Malian Empire in the 14th century.[49] These rituals indicate that the sea, as Bishop François-Xavier Fauvelle-Aymar (Medieval) rightly states, serves as a political horizon, the matrix or mirror of a sovereign and occult afterlife: unfathomable, apt to provide answers to the mysteries of power, apt to bring forth dynastic legitimacy.

The sea is not only a means of discovery and exchange, but also a powerful driver of literary and artistic creation and inspiration.[50] Indeed, mankind's view of the world and other cultures has long been seen through the eyes of seafarers. Maritime history has left a profound mark upon literary traditions and the history of ideas. This close correlation deserves a book in itself. For example, the maritime orientation of Indonesian ports in the Middle Ages gave rise to the country's assimilation of cultural influences, with Indian-style art mixing with the Muslim religion. The Indonesian language itself features words from the four corners of the Indian Ocean.[51]

Maritime contacts have inspired and driven original artistic developments such as Manueline architecture, as well as interior design. Thus the Indo-

---

[48] Cf. Emmanuel Desclèves (Early Modern).
[49] Cf. François-Xavier Fauvelle-Aymar (Medieval).
[50] See Sydney Hervé Aufrere (Ancient) for ancient Egypt.
[51] See Paul Wormser (Medieval), see also Fabrizia Baldissera (Ancient) for India.

Portuguese style, encouraged by the Jesuits, combined ivory, exotic woods and Indian aesthetics for sculpture and furnishings.

As another example, the rise of Holland as a maritime power led to the birth of bourgeois art. In Genoa a long-established community of people from Antwerp accounts for the proliferation of Flemish workshops in the city in the early 17th century, at the same time that artists in Haarlem were producing the first paintings to portray the sea. Mansions on Via Balbi were hung with the work of Dutch and Flemish masters, as well as paintings by the emerging school of Genoese painters. As François Bellec (Early Modern) has demonstrated, the Ligurian school of painting developed a passion for decorative compositions – *Vedute di Marina*, *Bataglie Navali* and *Fortuna di Mare* – while Dutch and Flemish painters glorified the Dutch Republic by emphasising the fruitfulness of the sea. Freed from the obligation to produce hagiography and biblical scenes, and stirred by patriotic enthusiasm, the first school of marine painting was established in Haarlem, born from the convergence of a brilliant artistic tradition, the maritime vocation of a nation intimately connected with the sea, and a new clientele of wealthy art patrons. Andries van Eertvelt was the first to immortalise *The Return to Amsterdam of the Second Expedition to the East Indies* in 1599.[52] Three years later, the founding of the VOC, the famous Dutch East India Company, marked the emergence of a maritime and economic world power.

Starting in the 1620s, Amsterdam developed a new school founded on atmospheric painting in muted tones, more impressionist than documentary. Aelbert Cuyp's *A Senior Merchant of the Dutch East India Company, Jacob Mathieusen and his Wife* presented as an established reality Holland's quiet power, prosperity, and industrial, commercial and maritime competence. England called upon Dutch artists, who appeared as useful as the carpenters in Amsterdam shipyards, to understand and appropriate the sea. They worked for England with no misgivings, even settling in the country despite the ongoing wars. Vroom, Bakhuizen and the Van de Veldes were soon as famous in London as in their home country. Furthermore, as had been the case in Portugal, the East Indies brought a touch of exoticism to European furnishings. This was particularly true for Jingdezhen porcelain, imported by the million and inspiring enduring aesthetic tastes.[53]

3. THE SEA: DRIVER OF HISTORY

Scholars almost everywhere divide History into four periods: Antiquity, the Middle Ages, the Early Modern era (16th, 17th and 18th centuries) and the Modern world. This breakdown reflects a reality. Each of these eras forms a coherent, characteristic whole, defined by a certain way of thinking, behaving, producing and consuming, and even its own way of using the five senses. Distinguishing each period from the others, these aspects are what build our mindset and therefore

---

[52] See François Bellec (Early Modern).
[53] *Ibid.*

our way of understanding the world. And this goes as far as shaping our methods for problem-solving.

Each period perished as a new era came to birth. The fall of the Western Roman Empire, which re-emerged transformed and extended in the Holy Roman Empire, laid the groundwork for the Middle Ages. The deadly spasms of the Black Death in the 14th century, the shortage of precious metals – an early form of monetary crisis – and the decadence of the old scholastic philosophy led to the collapse of the Middle Ages and sparked the powerful and explosive revolution that became the Renaissance. And in turn the Renaissance set the stage for the modern era, before the defeat of the Ancien Régime, in a France incapable of controlling its debts, brought us in 1789 – or at the end of the French Revolutionary and Napoleonic Wars in various countries – into the modern era.

Four periods. Four historical eras, each fascinating and unique, all reflect a Western division of history which very imperfectly fits the history of other regions in the world, especially Asia and Oceania.

However, there is a different way of understanding, approaching and presenting History, which was the whole point of the Océanides Programme. The work conducted by the 260 contributors has led me to suggest a different structure which more adequately reflects history, the history specific to each geographical region, providing a framework that makes the time dynamic much more intelligible and powerful. What if we used the sea as the instrument through which to analyse and understand major geopolitical shifts?

Instead of considering the land as the space used for marking out history, we could change our attitude completely by considering the sea, shifting focus away from studying our subjects of research within a regional, national or political framework to studying that which unites these different entities. This approach considers the sea not as a separation but as a bridge. It is the quintessential domain of all forms of exchange – commercial, cultural, scientific, etc. This viewpoint involves no longer studying political entities in isolation and in rivalry with their neighbours, but understanding them in their participation in the overall synergy created by these flow dynamics called History.

This synergy, these dynamics, this connectivity are the very essence of the sea. I have always believed that studying a people from the point of view of their relationship with the sea would be valuable and revealing of their overall mindset. The sea offers us an exceptional lens through which to observe both the general history of a people and History itself, because the sea is the common denominator, the shared space of all. It is the sea that, when we look closer, sets the pace of the ups and downs of history.

From this perspective, we can define not four eras but two which have presided over human destiny: the era of 'the Mediterraneans', and the era of the Atlantic. This approach, this universal framework in no way invalidates our division into four periods, but in fact confirms it and specifies their relevance. The ancient and medieval periods fall into the era of 'the Mediterraneans', while the early modern and modern periods belong to the Atlantic era. But even the Atlantic era is already over. Without fully realising it, we have left the modern period and moved into a new, third era in History, in which anything is possible. We will call it the Age of the Global Ocean.

When seen from the point of view of the sea, the ancient and medieval periods actually form a whole: the era of 'the Mediterraneans'.

By putting the word 'Mediterranean' in the plural, we refer to the history of several regions, of several spaces in which History unfolded at the same time. History unfolded everywhere, of course, where large human communities lived. But in Western societies, we have too often neglected the history of Asia, spread around what François Gipouloux, in line with the work of Jacob Van Leur, Georges Coedès and Fernand Braudel, referred to as the 'Asian Mediterranean'.[54] In other words, this sea corridor articulated around several interconnected basins: the Yellow Sea, the South and East China Seas, the Sulu Sea, the Celebes Sea, flowing into the Indian Ocean. We have barely begun to discover all the strength and wealth of this History built on encounters, exchange and conflicts. On one side of it stands the great Chinese space, which has continuously swayed between continental power and openness to this maritime space, which lies at its heart and drives its flows. It is the same dynamic as that inspired by *Mare Nostrum*, the sea in the middle of lands, along the shores of which the most brilliant civilisations were founded and developed, such as Assyria, the Egypt of the pharaohs, Greece, Byzantium, Rome, Venice, Genoa...

One of the strong points of the Océanides Programme is the special importance given to the Indian Ocean, the 'great sea' as it was called in Antiquity. The Indian Ocean connected these two Mediterranean waters much more than it separated them. Much historical and archaeological research is needed to assess the position and role played by the Indian Ocean in human History. The Indian Ocean could in fact be the heart, the epicentre of all the upheavals in the world, as it was the point where the roads linking the three continents of the ancient world converged: the Malacca road, linking the Malacca, or Malay, peninsula and the island of Sumatra to China and Japan, the Persian Gulf road, the Red Sea road and soon, after 1488, the Cape of Good Hope road.

We could even say, to paraphrase Walter Raleigh, that whoever commands the Indian Ocean commands most of trade of the world. More than the heartland (Eurasia), which Mackinder believed to be the key to world domination, the Indian Ocean could actually be what we would like to call by analogy the *Heartsea*. And control over this space brought world predominance.[55] All of world History would benefit from being reinterpreted through this prism, to understand the order of geopolitical balance from the ancient world to the world today.

May we consider, for example, that the decline of the Roman Empire could be closely linked to losing control of trade in the Indian Ocean? From 242, warfare

---

[54] GIPOULOUX F., *La Méditerranée asiatique*, Paris: CNRS Éditions (2009). See also GUILLERM A., *Géopolitique des mers, les Méditerranées d'Europe et d'Asie*, Paris: Cirpés, 1999, and the contribution by Pierre-Yves Manguin (Medieval).

[55] See the outstanding book on this subject by KEARNEY M., *The Indian Ocean in World History*, New York: Routledge (2004).

weakened the Roman Empire, while the Goths from Ukraine settled on its lands. The Sassanids, rising after the fall of the Parthians, invaded Mesopotamia, while Queen Zenobia of Palmyra proclaimed independence and seized Antioch. The Ethiopian kingdom of Aksum crossed the Gulf of Aden and seized Yemen, gaining control over access to the Red Sea. As a result, the silk trade slipped through the hands of the Romans into those of the Ethiopians and the Persians. The steady devaluation of the Roman currency could therefore result from the continuous drain towards India and rising prices due to the loss of trade routes. These events did not directly cause the fall of the Roman Empire, but marked its gradual collapse, while the Sassanid Persians took control of trade in the Indian Ocean.[56]

As we gain knowledge through further study, might we be able to add other Mediterraneans, viewed as trade hubs within a given maritime boundary, shaping regional history in a melting pot of fluidity? From this point of view, François Gipouloux argues that the Baltic Sea and North Sea resemble a northern Mediterranean. And Polynesia could also, perhaps, be viewed as a Mediterranean.

What defines this first era is the relative separation of these maritime spaces and their individual history, even though, as we showed above, we may distinguish the same lines of force and the same lessons varying as each political or trade entity was able to turn towards the epicentre of this space, the sea.

But then a geographic big bang occurred – a genuine Copernican Revolution within an extraordinarily short period of time – four years! All of human History was turned upside down by the events that took place between 1488 and 1492, opening the second era of History, a History that became universal. It was the beginning of the Atlantic era, named after the ocean that fuelled the movement.

1488: The Portuguese explorer Bartholomeu Dias sailed around the tip of Africa, the Cape of Good Hope. This was the discovery of the sea route to the Orient, and this new passage would shake up the economic powers of the world as it had existed up to that point. Spices, fragrances and other goods brought from Asia since Early Antiquity via land routes to the ports of Beirut and Alexandria, would now come directly by the Atlantic, which connects the Indian Ocean to Europe. In 1498, barely ten years after the discovery of the route used to reach the Cape of Good Hope, Vasco de Gama reached India, landing in Calicut.

The time of the economic supremacy of the Atlantic, or Western, world had come. That meant the end of the countless intermediaries, who, by the strength of camels, from caravan to caravan, slowly carried spices and fragrances to the shores of the Mediterranean. From now on, European ship-owners in Atlantic countries would lay claim to all the gains from this trade, taking it over from end to end. The wealth that had been dispersed along the land routes was now pooled in Europe. Profits exploded, as Europeans did not limit themselves to this global trade. They soon got involved in, and at times dominated, regional trade in India and Indonesia, referred to at the time as 'country trade'. For the first time in

---

[56] See Arthur Landon, Master's thesis under the supervision of Christian Buchet, Institut catholique de Paris, 2015–2016.

History, the world economy was controlled by a single geographic area, and the West experienced tremendous economic and technological growth which gave the region the predominance it has to this day.

Within less than a century, all Mediterranean trade collapsed, replaced by Atlantic trade. Merchants in Italian cities, which maintained ties with Asia by shipping these goods overland, were unable to hold on to the era of 'the Mediterraneans', now part of the past. The number of ships used in Mediterranean trade fell inexorably, year after year in the 16th century. Now it was the Portuguese and soon the Dutch and British who would be bringing the goods from overseas. The sun rose on the Atlantic world. Venice was better than Genoa at developing in other areas, as night does not fall on those who can adapt, innovate and optimize their strengths. As it could not maintain its trade links, La Serenissima specialized in manufacturing luxury goods, such as glass, and in banking, the heritage of its expertise gained in the sea trade.

1492: Christopher Columbus discovered, or rediscovered, America. Have we adequately measured the upheaval that this represented for England, until then the nation lying at the outermost tip of the known world? All of a sudden, it was thrust into the centre of the New World. Before that point, England had been restricted with the only possibility for expansion being to the east, towards the continent. This explains the Hundred Years' War from 1337 to 1453, as the country could now focus on the west, not so much to conquer land as to control trade. And rightly so. Due to wind and ocean currents, the return routes from America pass precisely off Lizard Point, its westernmost tip. Spain's ban on all other countries from trading with its new possessions, its American territories, did not stop England, at the nerve centre of Atlantic trade, from answering its calling.

1488 to 1492, the dice are cast! The game is now being played by the new rules of the Atlantic era, the 'great opening up of the planet', to paraphrase the French historian Pierre Chaunu.

The full impact of this revolution was not understood, especially in France and Spain, countries each with one foot in the Mediterranean and the other in the Atlantic. The situation was different for England, as we have seen, as well as Portugal and the Dutch Republic, which emerged from their peripheral backwater and found themselves repositioned in the centre. Back in the saddle, as horsemen say.

This period coincides with the modern and contemporary eras of history. They flow without a break, but are distinguishable by the increasing rate of breaking down of barriers.

The 16th, 17th and 18th centuries in fact began maritime globalisation. European powers pushed their networks to the outermost corners of the globe in a ruthless competition, but trade volumes were still limited. From this point of view, the 19th century is when things truly accelerated with the industrial revolution, which was driven by two factors: the sea revolution (with the development of steam shipping, marine technology, copper sheathing used on hulls, etc.), the development of ironclad ships and railways which extended sea trade in an increasingly massive shift inland.

The major discoveries of the modern era had already enabled Europeans to increase the area of available land per inhabitant six-fold. From the 19th century, with the exponential growth of shipbuilding, the cost of sea transport plummeted as sea trade continued to rise in volume, taking on an entirely different magnitude.[57] The era of planetary de-isolation was being supplanted by the era of globalisation. Sea trade grew by some 1% per year between 1500 and 1800, not a bad performance in a world where growth rates generally stood at about 0.1% or 0.2% per year. After 1815, the annual growth rate of the sea trade rose to 3.7%. And that rate remained relatively stable, except in periods of war or crisis, until 1992.

The flow of goods from one continent to another continued to flatten price differentials, gradually giving rise to a genuine global market. Farmers in the American Mid-West, the Argentine pampas, the Punjab, Burma, Russia and Australia increasingly competed with farmers in Western Europe and Japan. This had considerable consequences for countries with the most open markets, such as England and Germany, which were then able to lead their people towards industrial transformation, encouraging more profitable, high value-added goods over agricultural production, relying for the latter on cheap imports. It is worth noting that without this explosion in sea links, in terms of both imports of agricultural products in exchange for manufactured goods and of emigration (60 million people left Europe between 1815 and 1914), Europe would not have been able to support its tremendous population growth.[58] Africa, having left sea travel largely undeveloped, missed out on these opportunities in the 20th century.

This Atlantic era has dissipated, even though we still refer to the Atlantic Alliance, the last phase for a community which became aware of its shared values and worked to protect them. Since the early 1990s, we have experienced a geographic, economic and cultural revolution of at least the same magnitude as the revolution, with the Renaissance at the turn of the 15th and 16th centuries, which brought us into the Atlantic era.

While many, still seeing the world through the lens of bygone times, talk of crisis, we are actually living in a period of extraordinary, ever-accelerating changes. And this has caused us to lose our bearings, precisely because this third era in History before us, the 'New Oceanic' era, is more than ever founded on flexibility and connections, or, basically, a relationship with the sea. We have chosen the term, 'New Oceanic' era, as it is the ocean, the global ocean, that has brought the modern world to life.

The absolute supremacy of the powers of the Atlantic powers is over, and the Asian space has taken back control of its economic destiny. The Chinese example

---

[57] See Kevin O'Rourke (Modern).
[58] See John Beeler (Modern).

is an amazing reflection of this. The Middle Kingdom has left its centre of gravity and wholeheartedly embraced the sea.

More than any other country, China has too often turned its back on the sea, which has outlined and shaped the course of History. The remarkable expeditions led by Zheng He between 1405 and 1433 cannot overshadow the fact that China had, over extremely long periods, deliberately isolated itself, closed off to the north by the Great Wall and to the east by the sea. The sea was thought of as an enclosure, sometimes even a border not to be crossed. In certain periods, the authorities went as far as banning ocean navigation and, to avoid it completely, building an artificial river, the Grand Canal. Recall that the country developed a printing press long before Gutenberg, and paper money as early as the 12th century. Building on these inventions, along with the sternpost rudder, gunpowder, the compass and a population of some 250 million – compared with France's population of only 20 million under Louis XIV, and England's 7 million – China undeniably could have rewritten History as we know it. In fact, it is China that logically should have sent its ships out to travel the seas in the 12th and 13th centuries, opening up world-wide communication. Through China, Asia would have been the epicentre of a geopolitical upheaval that would have robbed the West of its geographic 'big bang' of 1488 to 1492. History would have been reversed, and the Pacific Era would have replaced the Atlantic era. But it was not to be, for what were essentially ideological reasons.

The country is no longer closed off now. It has finally awakened from its torpor, its complacent world view of being the Centre, the Middle Kingdom. It has now learnt from the lessons of History. And it is no accident that the country once again honours Zheng He today. He instilled the mental image that he had of the sea, which, far from being considered a wall, would from now on be seen as the most powerful communication channel of all. And all of China is taking giant steps forward in its maritime development.

What holds true for China also applies to most of the countries in the region, starting with Indonesia. In 2014 President Joko Widowo, following the example of his Chinese counterpart, decided to invest in maritime industry, and making it a top priority, to ensure his country's economic development. Maritime investment has been growing steadily since the 1990s, creating an ever-accelerating growth dynamic. Revenue from maritime development is increasing, boosting government budgets, creating jobs and stimulating industrialisation. The trade flows across the Pacific are already higher than those crossing the Atlantic. China, Japan and South Korea are also moving into the Indian Ocean to trade with Europe, Africa and the Middle East. Trade from member economies of the Asia Pacific Economic Cooperation (APEC) accounts for nearly half of global trade and their economies are experiencing growth three times higher than that of European countries, driving global trade, which is expected to rise from 9 billion tonnes in 2012 to about 15 billion tonnes before 2025.[59]

---

[59] See Geoffrey Till (Modern).

And of course, these countries' investment in naval defence is following the same exponential growth and, through a knock-on effect, fuelling technological, industrial and commercial development. American experts believe that in 2030, investment in naval defence by Asian countries should reach some US$170 billion. For the first time in over 400 years, their investments would exceed the budgets allocated by all European countries to their navies.

The frenetic development of the Asian Mediterranean is not the only factor that has moved us from the Atlantic era into the 'New Oceanic' era. Three other profound structural changes are also simultaneously and lastingly affecting the geopolitics and geo-economics of the old order: overpopulation and the concentration of people along coastlines, the new law of the sea upsetting the balance of powers, and the geographical revolution opened by the northern sea routes.

Demographic growth is guiding this shift, both by its extent and its makeup. Growth of this magnitude is unprecedented in the History of humanity. In 1804, under Napoleon, only 1 billion people lived on Earth. In October 2011, the world population was 7 billion. And there will be 8 billion of us in 2025. The world population is expected to reach about 9.1 billion in 2050, i.e. an increase of over two billion people on the planet in just 35 years. And more and more of these people will be living by the sea. In 2025, 75% of the world population of eight billion people will be concentrated within 75 kilometres of the coast, and 80% of the nine or so billion people will be living on that same strip of land by 2050. This suggests how much we will be increasingly counting on the sea which, as the 327 experts who worked on the Grenelle Maritime Forum debate in France put it, holds 'virtually all the solutions' for a future that is not just sustainable but desirable.[60]

Today, the sea is not simply driving economic development, planetary de-isolation and globalisation. It is the very heart of the world economy.[61] The 'New Oceanic' era is when humans will push back and break through the last frontier. Under the glittering surface of the sea, humans are on the edge of a new world. The sea bed is the shoreline separating them from their future, the sixth and last continent to be explored.[62]

Political entities are, unsurprisingly, joining this movement by turning to the sea.[63] The Law of the Sea signed in Montego Bay, Jamaica in 1982 and in effect since 1994 has thrown political geo-economics off course by establishing exclusive economic zones (EEZ).[64] In addition to sovereignty over their territorial sea extending up to 12 nautical miles off their coast, coastal states now have

---

[60] BUCHET C., *Cap sur l'Avenir, A contre-courant les raisons d'être optimistes,* Paris: Éditions du Moment (2014).
[61] See Hubert Bonin (Modern).
[62] *Sous la Mer, le Sixième Continent,* ed. C. BUCHET, Paris: Presses de l'université de Paris-Sorbonne (2001).
[63] See Jeremy Black (Modern).
[64] See Sam Bateman (Modern).

sovereign rights over the economic activities from surface to sea bed in a zone stretching out at least 200 nautical miles (372 kilometres) from their baseline.

This EEZ can reach a maximum of 350 nautical miles if the country can establish that as the outer limit of its continental shelf. Bearing in mind that most of the raw materials and fishing resources are found in the waters closest to dry land, we can easily understand why the most well-informed countries, such as the United States, Canada, Russia and China, are so eager to expand their maritime boundaries as far as possible. China's claims to islands that belong to Japan, Korea, the Philippines and Vietnam have no other explanation, as the giant currently has only the tenth largest maritime area behind the United States, France, Australia, New Zealand, Indonesia, Canada, the United Kingdom and Japan.

With the enlargement of the Panama Canal and the Suez Canal and plans to build new canals to establish further maritime connections, the northern routes, like the 1488–1492 geographic 'big bang', will completely revolutionise the world economy.

The Northwest Passage along the Canadian coast and the Northeast Passage along the Russian coast which, due to global warming, can be used 365 days a year using icebreakers – a feat accomplished by LNG tankers in the middle of winter for the past three years – are altering the entire geopolitical landscape. Whichever route is taken, the distance between the West and Asia has been reduced to 15,700 kilometres from 21,000 kilometres via the Suez Canal and 23,000 kilometres via Panama. That means 25% to 30% fewer kilometres to be covered and nearly 40% less travelling time by doing away with the administrative procedures and inevitable ship manoeuvring required to get through the canals. It also means the end of problems due to draught, which will no longer limit the size of ships. Furthermore, these two routes have another major advantage as they offer safer waterways located far from high-risk regions.

If we look at the situation realistically, without in any way advocating global warming, nothing will stop the development of traffic through these passages, which will gradually become the highways of the sea. They not only represent safe, extraordinary shortcuts for Europe–Asia trade routes, but they will also open up the two richest areas on the planet, which have until now been inaccessible dead ends: northern Canada and Siberia. Both the land and sea in these regions are abundant in oil, natural gas, iron ore, nickel, diamonds and more. But these raw materials cannot be exploited without routes to reach them. And now they will be very soon within reach of the most frequently travelled sea lanes.

In the 'New Oceanic' era, the global ocean, having broken through all geographic barriers and with its coastlines soon being home to 80% of the world's population, is what truly sets the pace of the planet. This global ocean offers a fertile pool, from which we will increasingly draw the materials and chemicals that dry land can no longer provide in adequate amounts. As such, it is under such pressure that its development brings threats that are as serious as the hopes it is fuelling. Experts agree that this development is at the core of many of the challenges we face today: climate change, collapsing sedimentary rock and coastal erosion, exhaustion of certain species of fish,[65] pollution and threats to marine ecosystems that are home to 80% of the planet's biodiversity.

One of the biggest challenges of this nascent 'New Oceanic' era will be to find a new approach to the old concept of the 'common good'.[66] Seas and oceans fall under *res communis*, a new form of *mare nostrum* on a global scale in which the traditional power relationships between nations must leave more latitude for the necessary new understanding. The sea, understood as a unique, global and physically unified space, where the expressions of sovereignty – in regions currently fragmented by legislation – could fade before the manifestation of a new collective responsibility managed by governments and civil society together, with shared governance concerned with keeping exploitation at reasonable levels. In the end, the sea is the future of the Earth, and we have no spare oceans.

At the conclusion of this lengthy academic and editorial process that brought together 260 researchers from around the world, making Océanides the most extensive programme in the Human Sciences since the first Encyclopaedia of 1751–72, it is clear that maritime pursuits stand out as the most defining component of History. The sea bestows military, economic and cultural predominance and spurs competitiveness, with visible consequences for society. By turning towards the sea, any political entity improves its chances of success, whether in demographic, geographic, economic or political terms. May this new vision of history enlighten decision makers and show one and all that the sea is the key of history and, more than ever, the catalyst of our future.

CHRISTIAN BUCHET
from the Académie de Marine,
Professor of Maritime History, Catholic University of Paris,
Océanides Scientific Director

---

[65] See Ingo Heidbrink (Modern).
[66] See Sam Bateman (Modern).

Conclusion générale*

De l'ensemble des contributions regroupées dans ces quatre volumes, trois puissantes vagues de fond se dégagent et répondent clairement à notre questionnement. Oui, le fait de se tourner vers la mer quel que soit le temps, le lieu, est le moteur le plus puissant qui soit pour impacter positivement les trajectoires historiques. C'est que la mer est l'accélérateur du développement économique et politique (1) ; le moteur de la prédominance et du rayonnement (2) ; le moteur de l'Histoire (3).

1. La mer, moteur du développement économique et politique

Les sites archéologiques de Pinnacle Point en Afrique du sud, des îles de Haida Gwaï et de On Your Knees sur l'île du Prince de Galles, qui recèlent les plus anciens témoignages d'une économie de subsistance exploitant les mammifères marins, phoques, otaries, cétacés, ainsi que des poissons, parfois de grande taille, de coquillages comme des moules et des escargots de mer, montrent combien la mer a toujours été pour les populations littorales un important complément de ressources. Les traces isotopiques d'un homme de vingt ans daté de 10 300 ans, révèlent un régime alimentaire composé principalement de nourritures venues de la mer[1].

Apport alimentaire, mais aussi apport vestimentaire, et utilisation monétaire avant l'heure par le biais des coquillages, objets utilitaires et artistiques. Très tôt la mer a été par la dynamique des activités, des échanges, un élément structurant de la sociabilité économique des populations littorales que ce soit en Asie, en Europe, en Afrique, aux Amériques[2].

Plus que cela, la mer, par la facilité du mode de transport qu'elle offre, le flottement d'une coque sur l'eau nécessitant infiniment moins de débours

---

* Les références aux chapitres publiés dans *The Sea in History* sont données par nom d'auteur et titre de volume (The Ancient World, The Medieval World, The Early Modern World et The Modern World qui ont été abrégés en Antiquité, Moderne, Moyen Âge et Contemporaine).
[1] Cf. Pascal Picq (Antiquité).
[2] Cf. Jorge Ortiz Sotelo (Moyen Âge), Alioune Dème (Antiquité), Benoit Bérard (Antiquité), Barry Cunliffe (Antiquité), Richard T. Callaghan (Antiquité).

énergétiques que l'acheminement par voie terrestre, a été le principal vecteur des échanges[3]. C'est par voie de mer que l'on est allé chercher, de plus en plus, et de plus en plus loin, les compléments alimentaires et autres produits dont on avait besoin.

La civilisation mésopotamienne en offre déjà, dès le troisième millénaire avant notre ère, un parfait exemple. La Mésopotamie, littéralement terre du milieu des fleuves, riche en denrées agricoles pour être située sur le croissant fertile, manquait, par contre, cruellement de ressources naturelles. C'est donc par voie fluviale et maritime que l'on allait chercher les bois pour la construction, le cuivre et autres métaux nécessaires à la métallurgie, la diorite et le gabbro pour les statues royales, le lapis-lazuli, l'or et l'ivoire... C'est ce commerce en expansion croissante, contrôlé par de riches et puissants souverains, qui permit de développer les réseaux d'irrigation et autres défenses contre les inondations qui menaçaient les cultures. Pour assurer ce commerce, on développa une imposante flotte de transport. On établit des arsenaux à Gu'aba et Nigin dans la province de Girsu, à Apisal et Guedena dans la province d'Umma, à Drehem et Nibru dans la région d'Ur. Des arsenaux où pouvait travailler jusqu'à 1 000 hommes, sous la direction d'une administration spécifique, la *Marsa*. C'est à cette connectivité fluvio-maritime que la civilisation mésopotamienne doit tout son éclat, ce dont témoigne encore la place importante des navires, de la navigation maritime dans les compositions mythologiques, les hymnes, les prières et les proverbes[4].

Le monde asiatique en offre une pareille démonstration. Dès le premier millénaire avant notre ère, une véritable connectivité maritime relie le sud de la Chine aux Moluques et à l'Inde. Les clous de girofle, les noix de muscade et autres épices et parfums sont à la base d'un commerce très actif, qui les voit remonter à travers les mers de Sulawesi et de Java jusqu'à la hauteur du détroit de Malacca où les cargaisons sont ventilées, les unes vers le monde chinois, les autres vers l'océan Indien et au-delà, jusqu'à la mer Rouge[5]. Il était fréquent, dès le 4e siècle av. J.C., que les Égyptiens s'acquittent de leurs redevances à Rome en clous de girofle venant des Moluques[6]. Au 1er siècle av. J.C., l'ouverture de la route des Perles, davantage connue sous le nom de la route de la soie maritime, qui relie la Chine au golfe persique et à la mer Rouge, génère une prospérité sans précédent.

Au fil du temps, lapis-lazuli, cornes de rhinocéros, ivoire, bois précieux, mais aussi métaux précieux : cuivre, or, argent, fer, circulent sur les mers asiatiques, conférant aux villes ou aux États qui pratiquent ou contrôlent ce commerce, un éclat sans précédent. Tel fut par exemple le cas de Funan, sur le delta du Mékong, l'un des plus importants royaumes de l'Asie du Sud-est. Celui de Srivijaya, l'actuelle Palembang, sur l'île de Sumatra, véritable Venise asiatique pour être parvenue

---

[3] Cf. par exemple Benoit Bérard (Antiquité) pour l'espace caraïbe, Carla Antonaccio (Antiquité) et Graciela Gestoso Singer (Antiquité) pour la connectivité des échanges en Mediterranée, Félix Chami (Antiquité) pour l'océan Indien.

[4] Cf. Ariel M. Bagg (Antiquité), Grégory Chambon (Antiquité).

[5] Cf. John Miksic (Antiquité).

[6] WARMINGTON E.H., *The Commerce between the Roman Empire and India*, Cambridge: Cambridge University Press (1928).

à s'ériger entre le VIIe et XIe siècles comme la plaque tournante des liaisons commerciales entre l'océan Indien, le sud de la mer de Chine et la mer de Java, et qui offre aux contemporains l'éclat d'une cité thalassocratique à la richesse et au développement artistique sans pareil. Une puissance dont va s'emparer le royaume Chola au sud de la péninsule indienne qui, pour être à la tête de moyens navals plus conséquent, se rend maître de Srivijaya en 1025. Le royaume de Majapahit, à l'est de Sumatra, puis Malacca et Guangzhou, tête de pont sur le littoral chinois d'un vaste hinterland, connaîtront également de spectaculaires rayonnements, hubs avant l'heure sur ce vaste réseau d'échanges[7].

La concentration littorale et urbaine aidant, les arrière-pays ne furent bientôt plus suffisants à l'ère d'une économie agricole aux faibles rendements, faute d'animaux de trait capables d'entailler suffisamment le sol (animaux que l'on ne peut avoir pour ne pas être précisément en mesure de les nourrir par insuffisance de rendements...), mais aussi en raison de l'inadaptation d'une bonne partie de la production aux terres et au climat résultant de l'impérieuse nécessité de devoir disposer des principaux produits de subsistance.

Le transport maritime apparaît clairement, de ce point de vue, avoir été le catalyseur, puis le moteur d'une progressive spécialisation agricole permettant d'adapter la production à la latitude et sortir ainsi du blocage intrinsèque que nous venons de souligner. C'est cet apport vivrier qui permet aux implantations humaines sur le littoral ou à proximité de celui-ci de croître, de ne cesser de croître. Athènes faisait venir plus de la moitié de son blé du Pont-Euxin, de la Thrace, de la Sicile ou même de l'Égypte. Ce sont bientôt un million de personnes qui se trouvent concentrées à Rome et à Alexandrie à l'apogée de l'Empire romain. Nourrir de telles concentrations urbaines a nécessité le développement progressif d'infrastructures portuaires de plus en plus conséquentes. L'Empire romain en offre le plus parfait exemple avec un maillage et des innovations dans le domaine maritime qui ne sont pas sans faire penser à la révolution du transport maritime que nous connaissons en ce début de troisième millénaire.

Les travaux de Pascal Arnaud (Antiquité) sur les ports antiques sont, de ce point de vue, particulièrement éclairants. Très tôt apparaissent à côté des ports de commerce, des ports entrepôts, peut-être dès le IIe millénaire, définissant un espace irréductible à l'écoulement de surplus locaux en échange de produits nécessaires, et un modèle original de l'échange fondé sur la concentration de produits d'origine multiples dont seule une partie sera absorbée par le marché local, le reste étant échangé pour repartir vers d'autres destinations. Le port-entrepôt s'inscrit alors dans des réseaux spécialisés de navigation en droiture et de redistribution très éloignés de l'image primitiviste que l'on se fait parfois du commerce antique. Oui le grand commerce, le commerce maritime, vecteur de transformation bat déjà son plein à des échelles régionales. A l'époque hellénistique déjà c'est tout un réseau de ports principaux dévolus au commerce international (les *emporia*), et de ports « secondaires » qui est en place.

---

[7] Cf. Tansen Sen (Antiquité), Pierre-Yves Manguin (Moyen Âge), Paul Wormser (Moyen Âge).

Cette dynamique d'échange confère à l'espace maritime une dimension stratégique. Le contrôle des mers et des littoraux constitue un enjeu essentiel. Elles deviennent l'objet d'une pression militaire inconnue jusque-là. La piraterie, souvent encouragée en sous-main par les États, prospère et fait des agglomérations portuaires une cible attractive pour les opérations de razzia dont les pirates s'étaient fait une spécialité.

Dans ce contexte hautement instable, les flottes de guerre deviennent l'outil le plus stratégique des guerres qui se déroulent de plus en plus loin et passent nécessairement par la maîtrise de la mer. La mer est devenue le vecteur par excellence du transport des troupes et celui du ravitaillement à grande distance. Couper ces lignes ou priver l'État adverse de son propre ravitaillement, c'est prendre une sérieuse option sur la victoire. Les États sont dès lors confrontés à une véritable course à la fois au nombre d'unités, et au tonnage, qui n'est pas sans impact sur les infrastructures. C'est ainsi que l'on voit apparaître dès l'époque hellénistique des ports militaires hautement spécialisés, comme le *naustathmos* des thalamèges, ou l'« arsenal des avisos », à Schedia dans les faubourgs d'Alexandrie[8]. Un essor qui constitue le moteur du développement économique, comme l'a montré, pour Athènes, Vincent Gabrielsen (Antiquité).

Mais lors de l'Antiquité, c'est sous l'Empire romain que cette évolution atteint sa forme la plus poussée[9]. La période impériale se caractérise par plusieurs nouveautés majeures : l'unification politique de la Méditerranée, cette mer du milieu des terres, qui relie toutes les possessions de l'empire réparties sur son pourtour. L'Empire ne saurait donc tenir sans la maîtrise de cette *mare nostrum* ; le développement universel d'une civilisation urbaine, ensuite, génératrice de besoins nouveaux et de pôles de consommation nouveaux ; enfin, un trafic, par voie de conséquence, inégalé en volume, générateur de revenus et protégé[10].

Le modèle économique social et culturel nouveau qui se développe avec l'empire romain a créé des besoins jusque-là inconnus en matière de consommation. Le développement de mégapoles d'un million d'habitants ou plus suppose un volume de ravitaillement colossal. Si l'on s'en tient aux stricts besoins de consommation des deux denrées de premières nécessités que sont le vin et le blé, il faut imaginer à Rome chaque année 2 000 rotations de navires d'une capacité de charge unitaire de 400 tonnes, ou de 8 000 si cette capacité se réduit à celle, plus commune de 100 tonnes...

Se limiter à l'image d'un trafic entièrement centré sur les mégapoles donnerait néanmoins une image très déformée du trafic maritime à l'époque romaine. Le développement d'une culture urbaine généralisée et de pôles de consommation énorme aux frontières, du fait de la présence de militaires au pouvoir d'achat significatif, a attiré des flux considérables de marchandises, notamment vers quelques ports de rupture de charge à l'articulation entre les grandes routes

---

[8] Cf. Pascal Arnaud (Antiquité).
[9] Cf. Catherine Virlouvet (Antiquité).
[10] Cf. Phyllis Culham, Nicholas Purcell (Antiquité).

maritimes et les bassins de la Méditerranée, ou à l'interface entre les voies fluviales et les voies maritimes.

Ces besoins nouveaux ont générés le développement d'infrastructures nouvelles, qui elles-mêmes ont induits de profondes mutations dans l'art et les techniques de construction permettant la construction de ports artificiels. L'invention du béton hydraulique capable de prendre sous l'eau et la voûte, qui sont deux « signatures » romaines ont, en effet, permis d'intervenir de plus en plus loin en mer et de ne plus dépendre du transport, de la manutention et de l'ajustement de blocs taillés. Elles ont banalisé la construction de môles dans des secteurs immergés facilitant l'utilisation de navires dotés de besoins en tirant d'eau plus conséquent. L'accroissement de la colonne d'eau (5 à 7m à Ostie) a induit à son tour le développement des quais et des pontons. Cette conception nouvelle ne permettait pas seulement d'accroître la sécurité, elle allait faciliter les opérations de halage et de changer de conteneurs. Finis les sacs et les amphores d'une trentaine de kilos à la manutention lente et délicate, voici venir le tonneau. Bel exemple d'action et de rétroaction en boucle aboutissant à des grappes d'innovations. C'est dans ses flux et sa connectivité maritime, dans ce sang bleu, que Rome a tiré toute sa puissance.

L'Histoire aime se répéter. Au cœur de la modernité européenne des XVI et XVIIe siècles, le développement des liaisons maritimes fut de la même manière l'aiguillon de la révolution agricole fondée sur la spécialisation permettant d'adapter la production aux terres et au climat. L'exemple comparé de l'Angleterre et de la France est de ce point de vue éclairant sur l'orientation maritime d'une Nation et de ses retombées aux plans commercial et industriel.

Contrairement à des idées reçues, si l'Angleterre se tourna de plus en plus intensément vers la mer, ce n'est pas parce que ses ressortissants, dotés de sols peu fertiles, comparés à ceux de la France notamment, auraient été contraints de moissonner les mers en s'adonnant à la pêche pour le meilleur, à la piraterie pour le pire. C'est tout le contraire qui est vrai. C'est parce que l'Angleterre a connu une révolution agricole précoce, dès le XVIe siècle, que le pays a pu améliorer ses rendements et réussir progressivement à nourrir sa population sans avoir besoin de toute sa force de travail. Les bras ainsi dégagés l'ont autorisée à se lancer dans le développement industriel, lequel a été soutenu par la multiplication des échanges, c'est-à-dire par le négoce maritime, lui-même rendu possible par cette main-d'œuvre disponible. C'est ainsi qu'a été engendré un cercle vertueux tel qu'en ont connu l'Angleterre, les Provinces-Unies et le Portugal. Comment ? Tout simplement parce que les liaisons maritimo-fluviales ont permis, d'année en année, en commercialisant les produits agricoles, de les adapter au mieux à la nature du sol et au climat. Avec l'accroissement des échanges entre eux, ces trois pays, fers de lance du maritime, ont abouti à une spécialisation nationale : l'élevage du mouton pour l'Angleterre, avec pour finalité l'industrie textile ; les produits laitiers pour les Provinces-Unies, dont les grasses prairies sont davantage adaptées à l'élevage bovin qu'à la culture des céréales ; le vin pour le Portugal. Tous produits à haute valeur ajoutée, cédés pour obtenir à meilleur marché que chez soi les indispensables céréales. Le développement d'Amsterdam dans le commerce de blé au XVIe siècle fut d'ailleurs une étape cruciale dans la place centrale que prendra la République des Provinces-Unies dans le commerce européen. Le commerce du blé, considéré par tous les contemporains comme la mère de tous les commerces (« commerce-mère » ou « moedernegotie »), devint la branche principale du commerce international de la Hollande aux XVII et XVIIIe siècles[11].

De la même manière, autour de la Vistule comme l'a souligné Jean-Pierre Poussou (Moderne), les espaces polonais exportent de manière toujours croissante des céréales dans lesquelles le seigle tient une grande place. Là, les exportations ne représentent qu'une partie très minoritaire de la production – autour de 10% –, mais elles sont plus lucratives, et apportent là encore des ressources qui profitent à l'ensemble du royaume de Pologne. En France, en revanche, c'est l'immobilisme le plus total. Aucune région n'a le droit de vendre à une autre les céréales qui constituent l'essentiel de l'alimentation, par peur que cela ne génère une famine généralisée. Chaque contrée se doit donc de produire tout ce dont elle a besoin, rendant les rendements quasi-impossible à améliorer. Alors que la circulation des céréales est dans les autres pays la règle commune, elle n'en est encore qu'à ses balbutiements en France à la fin du XVIIIe siècle. Les gouvernements successifs de Louis XVI s'y essayèrent, ce qui provoqua un vif mécontentement dans le pays, certains dénonçant un « pacte de famine », qui contribua grandement à la Révolution de 1789.

Cette dynamique croisée entre mer et agriculture ne s'arrête pas à ce développement initial et continue sa course, imprimant toujours sa marque dans un continuum de création de valeurs. Les échanges s'intensifient, le temps n'est plus aux seuls échanges de proximité, mais se situent dans un système-monde. Un phénomène particulièrement marqué au XIXe siècle avec un accroissement quantitatif sans précédent lié à celui des navires de transport mais aussi à la capacité des pays que l'on a qualifiés de « neufs », à répondre à la demande. Spectaculaire a été la montée des agricultures et élevages argentin, australien et néo-zélandais dont les possibilités ont été davantage encore accrues par l'utilisation des cales frigorifiques, à partir de l'invention du français Charles Tellier. Dans l'ensemble du monde, la Grande-Bretagne tira profit des positions dominantes qu'elle s'était assurée grâce à son avance économique et à la primauté de la Royal Navy. Par exemple, dans le cas de l'Argentine, il s'agit d'une position économique et financière dominante, dont elle a d'abord tiré parti pour se procurer des quantités croissantes de laine à partir des années 1850 ; puis les ventes de viande ovine se sont accrues à partir des années 1870, avant que ne viennent s'y ajouter, à la fin du siècle, les envois de viande bovine, mais aussi de blé et de maïs[12]. L'Argentine développa ainsi une économie agricole d'exportation à un niveau tout à fait considérable : près des deux tiers de la production du pays pour les céréales étaient vendus au loin. Tout fut fait pour accroître la qualité de

---

[11] Cf. SICKING L. et DE VRIES J., *The Dutch Rural Economy in the Golden Age, 1500-1700*, New Haven: Yale University Press (1974).
[12] Cf. Jean-Pierre Poussou (Moderne).

la viande produite avec notamment l'introduction de races anglaises ovines (par exemple les *Lincoln* ou les *Romney Marsh*) et bovines (telles les *Hereford* ou *Aberdeen Angus*). Ainsi se met en place une économie agricole d'exportation dominée par le pays consommateur, la Grande-Bretagne, absorbant les neuf dixièmes des exportations agricoles argentines.

Les conséquences de cette maritimisation de l'agriculture sont impressionnantes : la population agricole britannique s'effondre devant les prix meilleur marché des produits importés, et cela malgré une augmentation très forte de la productivité dans la production céréalière grâce aux importations d'engrais (guano et nitrates du Chili et du Pérou) qu'apporte la puissante flotte de commerce britannique[13]. Mais cette évolution n'est pas sans effet positif pour l'ensemble de la population du Royaume-Uni qui voit le coût de la vie diminuer au moment où s'accroissait les salaires sous l'emprise du développement industriel : entre 1860 et 1900, les salaires réels se sont accrus de 60% en Grande-Bretagne...

Moteur de la révolution agricole, catalyseur des échanges et du commerce, le développement maritime contribue également à la révolution industrielle par les conditions qu'il crée mais aussi par l'impact considérable de la construction navale au plan de l'innovation et du développement de l'industrie métallique, moteur de la révolution industrielle. L'exemple anglais, qui connaît une première révolution industrielle dans la première moitié du XVIIe siècle, est encore à cet égard probant. La tension au niveau des prix du bois, que cette construction navale provoqua, jointe à la demande croissante de métal, pour satisfaire aux besoins en canons tellement supérieurs de la Marine sur l'Armée de Terre (de l'ordre de 1 à 10), contribuèrent très largement à l'utilisation croissante du charbon comme ersatz au bois et au développement technologique de la fonderie. C'est ainsi que le four à réverbère prit son essor durant la guerre de la Ligue d'Augsbourg (1689–1697), que la production des hauts-fourneaux augmenta fortement lors de la guerre de Succession d'Espagne (1701–1713) et que la Royal Navy stimula encore au cours des décades suivantes le développement de l'industrie du cuivre[14].

De même, mesure-t-on encore suffisamment que l'édification des bases navales contribua au désenclavement des terres ? C'est toute la notion d'hinterland, avant l'heure, qui commence déjà, au XVIIIe siècle, à prendre corps. Ainsi A.J. Templeton a-t-il pu constater une concomitance parfaite entre le développement de la construction navale dans le Kent, au début de la guerre de Sept Ans (1756–1763), et l'extension considérable du réseau routier dans cette région[15].

Une telle dynamique suppose bien évidemment d'être sous-tendue par une capacité financière sans faille, insufflant dans l'économie les liquidités

---

[13] C'est là, en effet, que les rendements céréaliers sont les plus élevés d'Europe : en 1876, 26 hectolitres de blé à l'hectare contre 15 en France.

[14] Cf. BUCHET C., 'Le maritime, moteur du développement économique ?', in *La Puissance Maritime*, ed. C. BUCHET, J. MEYER et J.-P. POUSSOU, Paris: PUPS (2004), pp. 509–14.

[15] Cf. pour les Provinces-Unies les travaux suivants : DE VRIES J., *Barges and Capitalism: Passenger Transportation in the Dutch Economy, 1632-1839*, A.A.G.Bijdragen n°21, Wageningen UR (1978) et DE VRIES J. et VAN DER WOUDE A., *The first Modern Economy. Success, Failure, and Perseverance of the Dutch Economy, 1500-1815*, Cambridge: Cambridge University Press (1997).

nécessaires. Là encore cette aptitude procède dans une large mesure de l'impact initial probant du maritime au plan de la révolution agricole. L'exode rural qui en résulta, en concentrant les populations dans des villes, permit de drainer beaucoup plus facilement l'épargne. L'éloignement dans les campagnes, l'insécurité régnant sur les voies de communication n'étaient, en effet, guère propices au dépôt de l'argent dans des institutions bancaires. Le développement des *country banks*, ces banques de proximité, accélérèrent encore le mouvement en Angleterre et permirent, abondance monétaire aidant, une maîtrise des taux d'intérêt et une capacité à recourir aisément aux emprunts. Faut-il rappeler que les Provinces-Unies, première puissance maritime au plan commercial dans la première moitié du XVIIe siècle est au même moment le premier pays à avoir une majorité de citadins, rejointe par l'Angleterre au milieu du XIXe siècle, alors qu'il faut attendre 1931 en France, pour que le nombre de citadins dépasse celui des ruraux ?

Le caractère de plus en plus attractif de Londres comme marché financier parmi les détenteurs de capitaux aux Provinces-Unies, analysé par C.H. Wilson, majorera encore la capacité financière à se donner les moyens de maîtriser la mer, cette mer qui donne richesse et puissance. Au temps de la guerre de Succession d'Autriche (1744-1748), le gouvernement peut financer celle-ci avec des emprunts dont les taux n'étaient que de 3 à 4%, soit inférieurs de moitié comparé à ceux du début du siècle. Lors de la guerre de Sept Ans, l'Angleterre qui, dans le cadre d'une pesée globale, consacre les mêmes sommes que la France pour la guerre comme l'ont montré Paul Butel et Michel Morineau, soit 1,8 milliard de livres entre 1756 et 1763, parvint à couvrir ces dépenses à 81% par l'emprunt (contre 65% pour la France), sans que cela n'altère l'extrême modération des taux pratiqués. Quant à la guerre d'Amérique, dont les conséquences seront désastreuses pour la monarchie française, Paul Kennedy (Contemporaine) a calculé que la dette nationale sera du même ordre en France et en Angleterre mais les paiements d'intérêts annuels furent doubles du côté français...

Les travaux de Pierre-François Tuel (Moderne), à la suite de ceux de Paul Bairoch, montrent combien lorsque la capitale d'un pays est maritime, elle catalyse une concentration démographique et économique infiniment plus poussée que les capitales terrestres. En focalisant notre attention sur huit capitales de l'époque moderne, on constate que les capitales terrestres que sont Paris, Madrid, Moscou et Pékin, ne dépassent pas 3% de la population de leur pays respectif contre 8 à 12% pour les capitales maritimes (Londres, Amsterdam, Naples, capitale du royaume du même nom, et Lisbonne). En combinant le pouvoir d'une ville politique avec les richesses d'une cité maritime et donc marchande, les capitales maritimes ont pu imposer tout au long de la période moderne une redoutable suprématie induite par un souffle, un esprit commercial qui ne pouvait nullement être atteinte par une capitale terrestre ou par une simple ville portuaire. La combinaison du politique et de l'économie permet une dynamique inédite due à la capacité attractive de ces villes pour les capitaux comme pour les hommes.

Conclusion générale

Comment insuffler une dynamique commerciale quand on n'est pas à l'épicentre des flux commerciaux ?

Londres aura vraiment été le poumon économique du pays. La ville, à la fin du XVIIIe siècle, fait déjà en nombre d'habitants près de deux fois Paris : près d'un million d'habitants en 1800 – la capitale anglaise a doublé sa population en un siècle, pendant que la capitale française ne gagnait que 150 à 180 000 nouveaux parisiens. Il est essentiel de souligner que la centralisation londonienne n'empêche pas, bien au contraire, d'autres villes de se développer comme Glasgow, Hull, Bristol ou Liverpool, car ce sont des ports et que l'essentiel du trafic intérieur de l'Angleterre passe par voie d'eau. Le ravitaillement du poumon londonien passe par voie maritime. Et le commerce généré par cette ville tentaculaire crée à son tour un afflux de capitaux qui profitent à la bourse et aux investissements. Le grand commerce maritime anglais trouve dans le gigantisme de sa capitale l'aliment premier de son expansion. Au centre de la toile anglaise, Londres est naturellement l'endroit vers lequel tout converge. Et cette force centripète, justement parce qu'elle est naturelle, ne nécessite aucun interventionnisme, sauf à doses homéopathiques. Si l'on préfère, le pays le plus officiellement centralisé, la France, est celui dans lequel, de tout temps, ont joué des forces centrifuges. Et le pays le plus organiquement libéral, l'Angleterre, est celui dans lequel tout revient au centre, en permanence, pour en repartir alimenter les régions. Le libéralisme a trouvé en Angleterre un terrain d'élection. Le pouvoir, en France, passe par l'institution. En Grande-Bretagne, il passe par l'économie.

Parions que l'Histoire eût pu être différente, si Séville au lieu de Madrid eût été la capitale de l'Espagne, Rouen au lieu de Paris pour être port maritime, Shanghai au lieu de Pékin, Saint-Pétersbourg au lieu de Moscou, Budapest au lieu de Vienne, Mumbai au lieu de Delhi, Sao Paulo au lieu de Brasilia...

La leçon est claire : les entités politiques qui se tournent vers la mer, s'inscrivent dans une logique de flux, d'échanges et d'ouverture, moteur du développement économique. Cette dynamique par le biais des taxes, des revenus annonaires, a contribué à l'émergence d'entités politiques de plus en plus fortes et structurées car pour être source de richesse, le commerce est source de conflits et les flottes de commerce se doivent d'être protégées par des flottes de guerre ô combien coûteuses à édifier et à entretenir. Partout la marine se fait le fer de lance de la modernité dont l'édification et le développement d'arsenaux en est la parfaite illustration au double plan du développement technologique et organisationnel[16]. L'apparition de navires de guerre spécialisés, la naissance et renaissances récurrentes au cours du temps de marines de guerre permanentes, le coût croissant, voire aujourd'hui exponentiel, des innovations techniques ont considérablement accru ce défi financier. Seules les puissances suffisamment structurées, dotées d'une administration performante et adossées à un réservoir de population susceptible de répondre à d'importantes sollicitations fiscales, furent et seront à-même d'y parvenir. Par son concept d'« État navalo-fiscal » Patrick O'Brien (Moderne) a posé les jalons d'une approche qui semble bien se

---

[16] Cf. Jean Meyer (Moderne), Daniel Baugh (Moderne), Jakob Seerup (Moderne).

vérifier pour toutes les puissances maritimes et navales. Le cas britannique fut le modèle du genre : la croissance économique anglaise, stimulée par le commerce international a nourri le budget de la couronne qui a pu ainsi faire face à la construction et à l'entretien de la Royal Navy, qui elle-même pouvait imposer la *pax britannica* sur les eaux internationales et ainsi permettre la poursuite des échanges commerciaux. Les liens entre développement économique, fiscalité et marine de guerre apparaissent évidents mais encore convient-il de souligner que presque la moitié de la dépense publique au cours de la période moderne allait à la marine plutôt qu'à l'armée, une originalité anglaise aux résultats patents.

Il est même possible d'aller plus loin en considérant qu'il y a interaction entre la nature de la société, la nature du système politique, et la nature des activités militaires. Les sociétés s'inscrivant dans une dynamique commerciale, fondée sur un système social et politique ouvert, avec une forte implication des classes moyennes, ont été en mesure de profiter d'un cercle vertueux de croissance fondé sur le développement maritime et l'édification d'une puissance marine ; à la différence des États fermés reposant sur des institutions de nature autocratique, une puissante armée de terre et une économie rurale[17].

2. La mer, moteur de prédominance et de rayonnement

La prédominance d'une entité politique, quels que soient sa nature (Ville, État, Alliance...), le temps ou l'espace, semble toujours aller à celle qui dispose du plus grand nombre de navires. On pense aux bâtiments de guerre, de commerce, de pêche, mais pourquoi pas aussi aujourd'hui aux navires scientifiques ?

L'Égypte des pharaons a su supplanter ses adversaires par voie maritime et s'adonner à un puissant commerce[18]. La première bataille navale dont nous gardons le souvenir, vers 1191 avant J.C., voit Ramsès III utiliser des navires pour repousser des envahisseurs venus du nord, qualifiés de « peuples de la mer » et le déclin de l'Égypte antique procède de ce que les pharaons, à partir du VIe siècle, ont préféré s'en remettre aux services d'une flotte grecque et phénicienne.

Puis c'est au tour des cités grecques d'intégrer la mer comme un élément de puissance. Parler de thalassocratie, forme de domination extérieure qui fait reposer la puissance d'un État essentiellement sur sa maîtrise des mers, est sans doute prématuré pour le monde grec de l'époque archaïque[19]. Il n'empêche que certains États y ont déjà mené une politique maritime d'envergure. Ce fut au moins le cas de Milet, de Naxos, de Phocée, de Corinthe, de Samos, et de l'Égine... Selon Hérodote, Milet, par exemple, possédait des vaisseaux et la maîtrise de la mer dès la fin du VIIe siècle av. J.C., et son rôle se maintint jusqu'à sa prise par Darius. De la même manière, c'est dans la mer qu'Égine trouva le moyen de se

---

[17] Cf. Nicholas Rodger (Moderne).
[18] Cf. Graciela Gestoso Singer (Antiquité), Sydney Hervé Aufrère (Antiquité).
[19] Cf. Jean-Nicolas Corvisier (Antiquité).

séparer d'Épidaure et de mener une politique de rapines à l'égard des peuples littoraux.

Pour constituer une véritable thalassocratie, il faut des points d'appuis extérieurs, des installations à demeure, une flotte dont les vaisseaux ne soient pas seulement nombreux mais entretenus, renouvelés sans cesse, à la différence de certaines flottes archaïques construites pour une occasion précise mais qui tombent ensuite dans l'oubli. Il faut surtout en avoir besoin, et donc qu'une politique extérieure suivie exige la maîtrise de la mer sur un vaste espace, pour appuyer le contrôle de la terre ou pour appuyer sa prise de possession. Ce fut le cas de l'Empire perse, qui fut à cet égard la première puissance maritime de l'Histoire, dont l'expansion est continue dans le dernier tiers du VIe et au tout début du Ve siècle av. J.C. et qui devait contrôler toute la côte depuis l'Asie Mineure jusqu'en Syrie, puis, à partir de sa conquête par Cambyse qui se vantait d'avoir ajouté à l'empire de son père celui de la mer, jusqu'en Égypte. Les Perses s'appuyèrent d'abord sur le savoir-faire phénicien pour constituer leur puissante flotte, mais durent aller plus loin. C'est alors que, en marge de leur lutte contre Amasis, mais par le contact avec l'Égypte se serait répandue la trière.

Le rouleau compresseur maritime perse devait culminer avec Darius (522-486 av. J.C.) qui s'empara de Samos en 517 av. J.C., s'intéressa aux Cyclades en commençant par Naxos et attaqua les Scythes en utilisant les services de 600 navires. Il lui permit également de placer la Cyrénaïque sous influence perse, de reprendre le contrôle de Chypre et de renforcer sa puissance sur l'Hellespont. La bataille de Ladé (494 av. J.C.), dans laquelle il est permis de percevoir les premiers débuts dans l'art de la tactique navale, opposa côté perse des navires phéniciens, ciliciens, chypriotes et égyptiens, au total encore 600 navires, qui firent ployer les 353 trières grecques (80 de Milet, 12 de Priène, 3 de Myonte, 17 de Téos, 100 de Chios, 8 d'Érythrée, 3 de Phocée, 70 de Lesbos, 60 de Samos).

Ces expéditions, comme celles qui suivirent encore vers les Cyclades, l'Eubée et Égine, rentrent donc dans une logique thalassocratique, une logique de contrôle de la terre à partir de la mer. Encore en 490 av. J.C., et en bénéficiant de l'effet technique de sa victoire de Ladé, l'entreprise était plus que raisonnable. L'échec final, celui de Salamine et de Platées, vient de ce que, pour la première fois, avait été créé en Grèce, à Athènes, par l'entremise de Thémistocle, une véritable flotte de guerre permanente, susceptible de rivaliser avec la flotte perse, et adaptée à un navire précis, la trière, dont les Athéniens, s'ils n'en sont pas les inventeurs, ont su percevoir les qualités. Vingt-quatre siècles avant Mahan, la conceptualisation du pouvoir maritime fut alors réalisée[20]. A croire que seul au total une prédominance maritime peut venir à bout d'une prédominance maritime.

Mais Poséidon n'est pas facile à satisfaire ; le moindre décalage technologique est fatal[21]. La supériorité de ses trières permit à Athènes de triompher lors des guerres médiques, mais pour avoir négligé les nouvelles formes de combat qui

---

[20] Cf. Jean-Nicolas Corvisier (Antiquité), Vincent Gabrielsen (Antiquité).
[21] Cf., par exemple, le rôle de l'innovation dans les conflits qui opposèrent Athènes à Sparte in Daniel Battesti et Laurène Leclercq (Antiquité).

apparaissent alors, privilégiant la taille des vaisseaux et l'abordage à la mobilité et à l'éperonnage, elle fut vaincue dans la rade de Syracuse puis à Aigos Potamos.

Et Carthage de lui succéder comme puissance dominante parce que maritime, de régner sur la Méditerranée occidentale, du VIe siècle av. J.C. jusqu'à la fin de la Première Guerre punique, en 241 avant notre ère, où elle fut terrassée par la grande puissance maritime de l'Antiquité : Rome.

Rome, oui Rome, bien avant la suprématie militaire des légions de César et autres augustes chefs de guerre, est avant tout une puissance maritime. Si Hannibal, ennemi mortel de Rome, a contourné la Méditerranée par voie terrestre et enduré la terrible épreuve de franchir les Pyrénées et les Alpes avec ses éléphants, c'est tout simplement parce son adversaire séculaire maîtrisait la mer – le Carthaginois ne pouvait atteindre l'Italie par cette voie. Et c'est cette même maîtrise qui permit à Rome de faire aborder Scipion en Afrique, où il écrasa définitivement Hannibal à Zama (202 av. J.C.), mettant ainsi un terme à la Deuxième Guerre punique. La marine romaine est partout, participant à ce que l'on appelle aujourd'hui la projection de forces ou de puissance dans le cadre d'opérations combinées : une partie des troupes gagnait le champ de bataille par voie de terre, l'autre par voie de mer (ou par un fleuve), de façon à prendre l'ennemi en tenaille. Des navires sont également spécialement affectés à la quête des informations sur les mouvements ennemis. La *pax maritima* permet à Rome de maîtriser des flux maritimes qui vont s'étendre ensuite par voie terrestre jusque dans les contrées de l'océan Indien[22]. Seules les actions de piraterie, la guerre du pauvre, purent sporadiquement inquiéter les approvisionnements de la constellation urbaine de l'Empire. Mais à chaque fois la réaction est forte et musclée, ce sont 500 navires et 120 000 hommes, soit l'équivalent de vingt légions, que l'on confie au général Pompée en 67 av. J.C. pour l'éradiquer. Un succès qui lui permet de monter sur la plus haute marche du podium impérial.

Mais voici que l'empire commence à se déchirer sous l'effet d'ambitions acerbes ventilées sur un empire trop large. La mer continuera à jouer les premiers rôles dans ces conflits. La bataille navale d'Actium (31 av. J.C.) permit à Octave de l'emporter sur Marc-Antoine et Cléopâtre ; la bataille tout aussi décisive d'Éleous (324 ap. J.C.) permit à Constantin de l'emporter sur Licinius, adepte d'un polythéisme très combatif, et de continuer à favoriser le monothéisme chrétien. Sous Julien la marine de guerre romaine va encore fortement épauler les opérations terrestres, comme elle le faisait depuis des siècles mais voici qu'elle n'a bientôt plus les moyens financiers de sa survie. Les monnaies diminuent en poids et en taux de métaux précieux. La marine de guerre romaine décline, s'étiole et n'est bientôt plus en mesure d'agir efficacement contre les peuples barbares de plus en plus nombreux sur sa périphérie terrestre et, de surcroît, mieux organisés[23].

Et c'est aussi parce que le roi Vandale Genseric édifia une puissance navale qu'il domina durant près d'un demi-siècle toute la méditerranée occidentale et put s'emparer, en 455, de Rome. De la même manière le développement maritime

---

[22] Cf. Phyllis Culham (Antiquité).
[23] Cf. Yann Le Bohec (Antiquité).

explique, à la fin du VIe siècle, le basculement et la prédominance de la Neustrie sur la Burgondie et l'Austrasie[24].

Byzance, au Sud, a remplacé Rome, dont elle est une émanation directe. Elle dure depuis la fondation de son arsenal suite à la bataille des Dardanelles de 324 jusqu'aux X–XIe siècles, soit quelque sept siècles. Du IVe au Xe siècles, la ville impériale imprenable jusqu'à l'assaut et le pillage par la quatrième croisade (1202-1204) s'appuie sur la flotte principale centrée dans le Bosphore, et les flottes provinciales. Le phénomène byzantin représente l'image inverse de la domination paradoxalement maritime de l'empire romain. Celui-ci s'est constitué par conquêtes successives des rives de la Méditerranée, devenue lac romain. Byzance, héritière de la force navale romaine, se déstructure par la perte de ses rivages, le noyau de la résistance byzantine étant formé par le couple ville-marine. La supériorité technologique, concrétisée, notamment, par le feu grégeois a joué un rôle capital, jusqu'au moment où ce secret s'évente, donc s'imite. Cette flotte utilise largement la stratégie de la prise à revers sous forme de débarquements sophistiqués. La flotte est à la fois arme de combat, instrument logistique et puissance de frappe et de projection. Notre connaissance de la flotte de commerce byzantine demeure largement incertaine. Il semblerait que son déclin ait été, par rapport aux villes italiennes, beaucoup moins net qu'on ne l'a longtemps cru. La perte du Moyen-Orient devenu musulman sous les coups de boutoir de la conquête arabe des VII au Xe siècles, le coup de grâce final perpétré par les Seldjoukides, puis par l'empire ottoman sur un moribond pour être atteint en ses œuvres vives par la trahison de Venise, de Gênes, comme des croisés, constituent les étapes d'un déclin finalement très lent.

Le champ est donc libre pour les villes italiennes dont l'éclat de leur splendeur leur vient de la mer. Et les doges de Venise de le reconnaître officiellement en célébrant chaque année, le jour de l'ascension, les « épousailles » de la cité de saint Marc avec la mer. « Nous t'épousons, Ô Mer, en signe de véritable et perpétuelle domination », disaient-ils en jetant un anneau dans l'eau, depuis la galère d'apparat, le *Bucentaure*.

Oui, la notion de prédominance maritime semble bien être le facteur clef des basculements géopolitiques. Le Recteur Legohérel (Moyen Âge) en arrive aux mêmes conclusions dans sa remarquable contribution « Capétiens et Plantagenets à l'épreuve de la suprématie maritime » qui bouscule radicalement la manière classique, parce qu'essentiellement terrienne, d'appréhender cette période. C'est la mer qui est la maîtresse du jeu sur les deux siècles et demi étudiés. C'est la mer qui segmente ce temps en différentes phases conférant la prédominance à celui des deux camps qui est le plus volontariste en matière maritime.

L'Affaire d'Aquitaine est de ce point de vue éclairant. Née de querelles entre marins bayonnais et normands, elle débouche sur la confiscation du fief aquitain en 1294 et la riposte de l'Angleterre qui ne pouvait pas abandonner l'un des fleurons de sa puissance : une flotte anglaise dévaste la côte française de l'Atlantique, pénètre dans la Gironde bien en amont de Bordeaux jusqu'à La

---

[24] Cf. Régine Le Jan (Moyen Âge).

Réole et délivre Bayonne. La réponse de Philippe le Bel est à la mesure du défi anglais : la construction du Clos des Galées à Rouen, premier arsenal français et la construction d'une flotte supérieure en nombre aux 500 navires attribués au Plantagenêt, Edouard Ier. Le résultat est spectaculaire : la maîtrise de la mer passe à la marine capétienne. Philipe le Bel tente une sorte de blocus de l'Angleterre, et les coups de main de la marine française se multiplient sur une côte anglaise terrorisée. La mer emporte la décision, la paix de 1299 conduit Edouard Ier à évacuer la Flandre et à accepter une occupation française à Bordeaux.

De la même manière la prédominance de la marine capétienne durant les trente années qui suivent en protégeant les convois de sel de la baie de Bourgneuf, en assurant la sécurité des zones où se concentre la navigation commerciale (estuaire de la Seine, passage des îles anglo-normandes, raz bretons, pertuis saintongeais), contribue à asseoir et à donner toute sa force au règne de Philippe le Bel.

Le constat est identique pour la guerre de Cent Ans. C'est sur mer qu'elle s'est joué, à chacune de ses trois phases.

La première (1337-1360) est marquée par la prépondérance anglaise. Sa maîtrise de la mer lui confère richesse par le développement commercial, lui permet d'assurer l'acheminement de ses troupes et explique les succès anglais et les revers français (Poitiers en 1356 et la capture du roi Jean le Bon).

La France en tire les conséquences, c'est la seconde phase (1360-1413), Charles V relance et réorganise le Clos des Galées, fait de l'Amiral l'égal du Connétable, avec la chance de trouver l'homme de la situation, Jean de Vienne. En 1377, l'initiative sur mer est redevenue française, la mer est de nouveau capétienne. Les ports anglais sont neutralisés, les routes des renforts vers le continent coupées et le moral de la communauté maritime anglaise durement touché. Cette maîtrise française de la mer allait grandement favoriser les opérations terrestres de du Guesclin et de Clisson et se prolonger jusqu'en 1386 lorsque des dissensions au sein du gouvernement des oncles de Charles VI conduisent à l'abandon du projet de débarquement en Angleterre et au départ de Jean de Vienne.

La troisième et dernière phase voit la mer signer la victoire en deux temps. Henri V, le plus brillant des Lancastre, est le premier Plantagenêt depuis Richard Cœur de Lion à avoir compris l'usage de la puissance navale comme arme de guerre. Il reconstitue une flotte puissante avec des navires atteignant, telles la *Grace-Dieu* ou la *Trinity*, 800 tonneaux. Le seul espoir de l'Angleterre, contre un adversaire plus riche qu'elle et qui se battait pour défendre son sol, était de profiter de la mobilité offerte par la mer pour avoir l'initiative stratégique et pouvoir choisir le moment et le lieu de l'engagement décisif. Le triomphe anglais est alors total. La couronne de France va échoir au Plantagenêt quelques semaines plus tard à la mort de Charles VI et le sort des armes lui est favorable. Il n'y a plus alors de flotte adverse et la Manche est devenue, ou redevenue, *mare britannicum*. Pourquoi, dès lors, continuer d'entretenir une flotte anglaise coûteuse, apparemment devenue inutile, et en tous cas beaucoup trop nombreuse ? C'est ainsi que le gouvernement du jeune Henri VI, présidé par son oncle, le duc de Bedford, prit, en 1423, l'étrange décision de vendre la plus grande partie de ses navires, décision logique en termes

Conclusion générale

de stricte gestion financière, mais erreur majeure que de dédaigner la maîtrise de la mer dont on tirait tant d'avantages. L'Histoire est riche en leçons...

Très vite, le vent tourne. Le gouvernement du Plantagenêt n'a plus les moyens de faire passer des renforts sur le continent : la faiblesse des réactions anglaises face aux campagnes de Jeanne d'Arc et de ses successeurs, puis lors des ultimes combats de Formigny (1450) et de Castillon (1453), n'a pas d'autre explication.

Et sait-on suffisamment qu'une seconde guerre de Cent Ans opposa encore la France à l'Angleterre là où nous ne décryptons qu'une kyrielle de conflits successifs, de 1689, début de l'avant-dernière guerre de Louis XIV, jusqu'au terme des guerres napoléoniennes ? Une seconde guerre de Cent Ans non pas, cette fois, pour une expansion territoriale vers l'est, mais pour la prédominance maritime de l'ouest et des marchés américains. Dans le bras de fer terre contre mer, c'est la mer qui, comme toujours l'a emporté. L'Angleterre, viscéralement tournée vers la mer, a ravi à la France continentale le sceptre de la prédominance mondiale, que sa centralisation exagérée et sa forte démographie lui avaient un moment permis de s'arroger. Ce signe de puissance, la Grande-Bretagne le promènera sur toutes les mers du globe, à travers un empire sur lequel le soleil ne se couchait jamais, jusqu'à ce qu'elle accepte de partager à l'amiable, lors de la Conférence de Washington de 1922, sa suprématie avec le grand frère américain[25]. Le génie anglais, c'est d'avoir compris, avant les autres, que la mer constitue la plus vaste zone de libre-échange au monde.

L'histoire, on le sait, se répète. Le blocus continental décrété par Napoléon asphyxia bien plus l'Empire sous l'égide de la France, qu'il n'handicapa l'Angleterre, toujours à même d'obtenir par la mobilité de ses navires ce qui lui était nécessaire et de maintenir son commerce quitte à l'élargir à l'échelle du globe pour satisfaire ses besoins et développer son économie. Qui tient la Mer, tient à terme la Terre, telle est l'une des principales leçons qui se dégagent de cette pesée du rôle et de la place du maritime dans l'Histoire.

En abordant pour la première fois l'histoire humaine sous le prisme de la mer, les travaux d'Océanides renouvellent complètement notre approche de l'Histoire et donc de la géopolitique qui s'est jusqu'ici toujours focalisée sur l'histoire terrienne pour y déceler des éléments structurants. C'est ainsi que dans la célèbre conférence du 25 janvier 1904, qui l'établit comme le fondateur de la pensée géopolitique du XXe siècle, Sir Halford Mackinder définit sa notion du *Heartland*, cet espace pivot « citadelle de la puissance terrestre ». « Qui contrôle le cœur du monde », écrit-il, « commande à l'île du monde ; qui contrôle l'île du monde commande au monde ». Nous sommes bien loin de la citation de Sir Walter Raleigh, du fin fond de la Tour de Londres où il est alors reclus en 1595, résumant magnifiquement l'idéal britannique : « Qui contrôle la mer commande le commerce ; qui contrôle le commerce commande le monde ». L'Histoire prise dans son épaisseur donne raison à Raleigh contre Mackinder[26]. En avons-nous bien conscience, alors que la géopolitique reste toujours éminemment terrienne,

---

[25] Cf. Phillips Payson O'Brien (Contemporaine).
[26] BUCHET C., 'Du Heartland à Océanides', *Revue de Défense Nationale*, (avril 2016), pp. 49–53.

malgré les travaux d'Alfred Thayer Mahan à l'extrême fin du XIXe siècle ainsi que les aménagements apportés à la pensée de Mackinder par John Spykman au tournant de la Seconde Guerre mondiale avec sa notion de *Rimland*, conférant une importance particulière aux « terres du bord » ?

Guerre après guerre, le même constat s'impose, imperceptible si l'on n'analyse pas l'Histoire dans ce qui est le plus difficile à saisir, à savoir la mobilité et la connectivité des flux, qu'incarne précisément le maritime. Après l'épopée impériale, la Première Guerre mondiale, la Seconde Guerre mondiale, comme pour la Guerre froide, c'est le pays ou l'alliance qui dispose de cette maîtrise des flux qui l'emporte.

Il peut être intéressant de ce point de vue de s'arrêter sur la Première Guerre mondiale dont on a jugé trop rapidement que les marines n'ont guère eu d'impact sur les événements militaires dont découlent l'issue du conflit. Après Norman Friedman[27], Avner Offer (Contemporaine), d'Oxford, pour Océanides, montre précisément le contraire.

Faute, en effet, de pouvoir s'approvisionner en vivres en ayant recours au marché mondial, pour ne pas disposer de la maîtrise navale, l'Allemagne et l'Autriche-Hongrie ne purent mobiliser autant d'hommes que nécessaires pour devoir laisser dans les campagnes une population agricole importante. La Russie qui privilégia la mobilisation au détriment de la production agricole, connut bientôt une pénurie alimentaire qui précipita les événements révolutionnaires. A l'inverse, l'Angleterre et la France bénéficièrent tant pour les vivres que pour les apports énergétiques, avec en premier lieu le charbon, d'une connectivité de par la maîtrise de la mer, qui ne pouvait que leur conférer la victoire dans la durée.

Pour être gagnée par les Puissances centrales, le conflit se devait d'être court. Seule une destruction suffisante du commerce allié par les U-boot aurait pu modifier la donne. Mais n'était-il pas illusoire de penser que cet objectif était atteignable alors que l'Empire allemand ne disposait pas de la maîtrise navale ? Une guerre sous-marine sans merci qui, au demeurant, devait précipiter, en 1917, l'entrée des États-Unis dans le conflit, et transformer l'atlantique en tête de pont pour imposer une capitulation sans condition à l'Allemagne.

Les Allemands, comme Napoléon, au cours de la Première comme de la Deuxième Guerre mondiales tentèrent de pallier à ce déficit alimentaire et énergétique en s'enfonçant dans le continent, jusqu'en Russie, « ce qui pouvait prolonger la guerre mais non en modifier l'issue finale[28] ».

C'est encore une bataille de l'Atlantique, gagnée cette fois contre les sous-marins de l'amiral Dönitz qui, conjuguée à la construction, notamment, de quelque huit millions de tonnes de navires marchands, permit de libérer l'Europe et d'assurer la victoire finale des Alliés lors de la Seconde Guerre mondiale[29].

---

[27] FRIEDMAN N., *Fighting the Great war at Sea : Strategy, Tactics and Technology*, Barnsley: Seaforth Publishing, 2014.

[28] OFFER A., *The First World War: An agrarian Interpretation*, Oxford: Clarendon Press (1989), p. 317. Voir également : Lambert N.A., *Planning Armageddon : British Economic Warfare and the First World War*, Cambridge, MA: Harvard University Press (2012).

[29] Cf. Christopher Baxter (Contemporaine) et W.J.R. Gardner (Contemporaine).

Maîtriser la mer confère une primauté commerciale et donc économique, permettant d'augmenter ses capacités militaires qui ne peut conduire qu'à surclasser l'adversaire terrestre. C'est précisément ce qu'exprimait avec tant de hauteur de vue et de grandeur le Général de Gaulle dans son appel du 18 juin 1940. La France a perdu une bataille mais non pas la guerre, peut-il écrire parce que le pays a été « submergé par la force mécanique, terrestre et aérienne de l'ennemi ». Mais la France n'est pas seule. Elle n'est pas seule parce qu'elle a un vaste empire maritime derrière elle et qu' « elle peut faire bloc avec l'Empire britannique qui tient la mer » et qu' « elle peut, comme l'Angleterre, utiliser sans limite l'immense industrie des États-Unis ».

On découvre également, grâce aux travaux de C. Baxter (Contemporaine) et de G. Baer, combien c'est l'effondrement des flux commerciaux japonais, asphyxiant son économie, qui empêche bientôt le Japon de maintenir sa capacité opérationnelle et permet aux forces américaines, mais aussi anglaises, de l'emporter dans la guerre du Pacifique. En août 1945, les flux commerciaux du Japon ne sont plus que de 312 000 tonnes (moins de 12% de leurs flux commerciaux d'avant-guerre) alors que ceux des alliés sont de 88 millions de tonnes...

De la même manière, durant toute la Guerre froide, c'est l'incapacité soviétique à développer son commerce maritime et à travers celui-ci son économie qui greva au final la volonté des dirigeants russes de contenir l'hégémonie américaine, dont on sait aujourd'hui qu'elle n'a jamais pu être contestée par l'imposante marine de guerre soviétique[30]. Le renforcement considérable de la capacité navale américaine sous l'Administration Reagan, avec un objectif de 600 navires de combat, supérieurs qualitativement de surcroît à la flotte soviétique, fut le facteur clef qui aboutit à l'implosion de l'Union Soviétique qui marqua la fin de la Guerre froide et la victoire des Occidentaux[31]. Pour la troisième fois au cours du XXe siècle, sur une planète devenue océanique, l'alliance maritime surclassait l'alliance terrestre...

C'est qu'à tout bien considérer, le développement et plus encore le maintien d'une marine de guerre nécessite une capacité financière qui ne peut exister sans de puissantes positions commerciales. La maîtrise des flux commerciaux est donc une donnée indispensable au maintien dans la durée d'une flotte de guerre. Mais il est tout aussi important de souligner qu'une économie maritime conséquente ne saurait, à l'inverse, durer sans être protégée par une puissante capacité navale. L'exemple opposé à celui de la marine soviétique est la flotte de commerce française qui progresse de façon spectaculaire sous Louis XV et qui est bientôt en passe de rattraper le commerce britannique mais que l'Angleterre s'emploie à détruire à dessein en nous faisant régulièrement la guerre parce que, faute d'une flotte de guerre suffisante du côté français, la guerre casse notre commerce et augmente le sien.

---

[30] Cf. Colin S. Gray (Contemporaine).
[31] Cf. Eric Grove (Contemporaine) : 'Nato's maritime strategy was a key factor in exerting the decisive strategic pressure on the Soviet Union that caused the implosion that ended the Cold war with Western victory'.

Patrick Villiers (Moderne) a, à cet égard, magnifiquement montré que le commerce maritime se maintient ou n'augmente que lorsqu'il est soutenu par une marine de guerre puissante et moderne. De ce point de vue, le modèle britannique illustre brillamment le cas d'une politique navale au service d'une économie maritime. L'Angleterre en 1815 a réalisé le rêve du Portugal, de l'Espagne et des Provinces-Unies : avoir le quasi monopole du commerce maritime, puissant moteur du développement économique.

L'exemple russe est peut-être encore plus probant et illustre magnifiquement l'impact de la mer dans le développement ou le déclin d'une puissance. Tant que le Danemark, la Suède et la Ligue hanséatique empêchèrent la Russie d'avoir accès au commerce de la mer Baltique, le pays ne fut pas en mesure de se développer économiquement. Ainsi, contrairement au schéma classique, qui voit successivement apparaître un développement de la pêche, puis du commerce et, enfin, une marine de guerre pour protéger l'ensemble de ces flux ; en Russie, c'est l'instauration en premier d'une marine de guerre, avec le tsar Aleksey Mikhailovitch (1645-1676) et surtout Pierre le Grand (1682-1725), fort de sa capitale maritime, qui permit à la Russie de connaître le développement économique généré par le commerce, et d'atteindre au plan militaire comme diplomatique le statut de grande puissance[32].

La leçon est la même beaucoup plus au sud. Cyrille Poirier-Coutansais (Moderne) montre que faute de s'être tournée vers la mer, la Perse Séfévide (1501-1736), contrairement à son voisin ottoman, s'est progressivement trouvée exclue des circuits commerciaux, et bientôt dans une situation critique dans ses combats contre les Ottomans de Sélim Ier, alors qu'une autre politique aurait pu être assurément possible.

Et l'Empire maya, d'en offrir déjà la parfaite démonstration pour avoir pu s'établir et se maintenir par une connectivité maritime fondée sur un important commerce de sel, d'obsidienne, de pierres rares, d'or et de cuivre lui donnant richesse et puissance, créant et développant une unité territoriale par l'existence d'un marché intérieur. Une prédominance, parce que maritime, brisée par la technologie supérieure des navires espagnols qui purent précisément en cassant ces liaisons maritimes provoquer l'effondrement brusque de cet empire[33].

Du côté asiatique, le même constat s'impose. En Chine, l'interdiction de la navigation hauturière après la mort, en 1434, de l'eunuque Zheng He, le choix de lui substituer la voie d'eau intérieure, avec le canal impérial, empêchèrent le développement du capitalisme commercial qui fonda, avec l'ère Meiji, à la fin du XIXe siècle, la grandeur japonaise. A-t-on suffisamment noté aujourd'hui que tous les États du G8 comme du G20 sont des pays maritimes ?

En contrepoint à ce faisceau de convergences, il convenait de se poser la question de la capacité d'entités politiques à prédominer et à se développer sans

---

[32] Cf. Pavel Krotov (Moderne), Jakob Seerup (Moderne).
[33] Cf. Heather McKillop (Moyen Âge) et Emiliano Melgar (Moyen Âge). Voir également sur cette question de la connectivité en Méditerranée pour la période médiévale la contribution de Sebastian Kolditz (Moyen Âge).

Conclusion générale

être tourné vers la mer. De ce point de vue, l'Empire mongol peut apparaître comme le parfait contre-exemple. En effet, les Mongols ont créé le plus vaste empire de tous les temps, en négligeant totalement les océans Pacifique et Indien auxquels ils avaient potentiellement accès. Leur univers était celui des steppes, des forêts, des déserts, des lacs et des rivières et ils n'ont jamais entretenus de rapports, fut-ce symboliques, avec les grands espaces maritimes. Leur objectif majeur était la conquête d'espaces terrestres.

Les travaux de Didier Gazagnadou (Moyen Âge) sont particulièrement intéressants pour comprendre ce qui a permis à cet empire de se constituer et de se maintenir sans être impacté par la dynamique de la maritimité. Leurs succès, les Mongols le doivent à ce qui est l'essence propre du maritime : la fluidité. Ils ont su créer, par le maillage serré de relais de poste et de caravansérails, un véritable hinterland avant l'heure, et par le mouvement gravitationnel des caravanes un développement des échanges commerciaux analogues à celui des *voltas* de navires opérées par les puissances maritimes. Ce sont des dizaines de milliers d'hommes mobilisant pas moins de 200 000 chevaux et plus encore de chameaux et de dromadaires qui étaient ventilés des bords du Pacifique aux rivages de la mer Noire, des frontières indochinoises au cœur du Tibet en passant par la Chine jusqu'aux frontières du monde iranien et de l'Irak, sur ce gigantesque réseau d'au moins 50 à 60 000 kilomètres. « Ces grands nomades, par la fluidité des circulations qu'ils permirent, désenclavèrent les sociétés eurasiatiques et ont traité, pourrait-on dire métaphoriquement, l'espace terrestre comme un espace maritime[34] ». Le transport des marchandises se faisait par caravanes de chameaux et de dromadaires « vaisseaux des steppes et des déserts » (le chameau de Bactriane porte en moyenne entre 150 et 200 kilos et le dromadaire entre 100 et 150 kilos pour des parcours d'environ 60 kilomètres par jour).

Reste à savoir si l'absence de développement et de contrôle des océans Indien et Pacifique a contribué à l'effondrement de l'empire mongol ? Peut-être, répond Didier Gazagnadou, et ce malgré la fluidité des réseaux terrestres des routes de la soie qui transportèrent d'importants tonnages de marchandises, surtout d'est en ouest. Le transport terrestre est toujours plus lent, plus cher et nécessite tellement plus d'intermédiaires, de ruptures de charge comparé au transport maritime... Si les Mongols d'Iran et de Chine avaient construits des flottes et s'étaient lancés à la conquête des océans, l'histoire de l'Afrique, de l'Amérique et du monde aurait été toute autre. L'océan Indien, c'est l'accès à l'Afrique et aux Indes ; l'océan Pacifique, c'est l'accès aux Amériques. À leur insu par ces liaisons les Mongols permirent à de nombreux hommes d'affaires et de religieux européens de découvrir les mondes jusque-là presque inconnus de l'Asie et susciter le désir de contourner cet immense empire afin de rentrer directement en contact par les mers avec cette Chine et ces Indes et leurs richesses. Et c'est ainsi qu'à partir de la fin du XVe siècle, les marines européennes, financés par de puissants États sédentaires, allaient se lancer dans une tribulation d'expéditions pour venir, par voie de mer, au contact direct des mondes asiatiques et découvrir par hasard... les Amériques.

---

[34] Cf. Didier Gazagnadou (Moyen Âge).

L'Inde du Grand Moghol méritait dans la même veine d'être étudiée pour être bien souvent considérée comme une zone géographique « irrémédiablement terrienne » dont la continentalité aurait toujours été incapable, sinon à de rares et éphémères moments, de se tourner vers la mer. La société hindoue, et notamment ses élites, aurait éprouvé pas seulement de l'indifférence pour la mer mais même une véritable répugnance au service de la mer en raison d'interdits religieux. La réalité historique est infiniment plus complexe. À y regarder de près les faits, ici aussi la mer fut l'élément essentiel présidant à la réussite ou aux échecs des différents souverains sur plusieurs siècles[35].

Le non-intérêt de Sher Shâh Sûri pour la mer et ses flux explique, en effet, dans une large mesure son échec final. À l'inverse, Akbar (1566-1605), en désenclavant son empire avec la connexion des centres de production aux bandes littorales du Bengale et du Gujarat, en insufflant une politique mercantiliste fondée sur la notion d'hinterland, aboutit à la création de villes prospères nées aux carrefours des routes marchandes sur une connectivité maritime, et se vit attribuer le titre de « Grand Mogol ». Une œuvre interrompue par ses successeurs Jahangir (1605-1627) et Chah-Jahan (1628-1657), mais reprise avec Aurengzeb (1659-1707) qui alla jusqu'à déplacer la capitale au sud, à Aurangabad, emplacement géoéconomique pour être située au carrefour des deux régions maritimes de Golconde et de Bijapur. Ce qui lui permit, par les effets induits au plan fiscal, de consolider son Empire et de maîtriser les soulèvements marathes.

Il était également intéressant de s'interroger sur la place et le rôle de la mer pour des ensembles dont l'épicentre est décalé par rapport à la maritimité. L'étude d'Olivier Chaline (Moderne) sur l'Europe centrale et la mer à l'époque moderne montre combien les ondes de choc maritimes rentrent très à l'intérieur des terres. En effet, si, à première vue, la mer n'est à peu près pour rien dans les succès ou échecs des États d'Europe centrale, pourtant, à certains moments essentiels, le facteur maritime a joué un rôle décisif. L'Europe centrale s'est vue largement écartée de la mer par des États aux territoires dispersés sur différents rivages et qui ont entendu s'approprier les flots. Il en va ainsi, par exemple, de la Suède qui forte de sa marine a bénéficié d'une capacité de projection de puissance très à l'intérieur de cette Europe centrale[36]. Impériaux et Polonais ont payé cher, les uns, de n'avoir pu développer à temps leur instrument naval, les autres de n'avoir su le maintenir. Les Habsbourg, au faîte de leur puissance en 1629, n'ont pu empêcher le débarquement de Gustave-Adolphe l'année suivante et l'installation durable de la Suède dans le nord de l'Empire. Et dans bien des conflits l'Autriche et la Prusse n'auraient pu tenir sans alliés maritimes...

Si la notion de prédominance ne peut concerner par définition qu'une ou tout au plus deux ou trois entités politiques à la fois, le fait de se tourner vers la mer, outre les enchaînements vertueux au plan économique développés dans notre première partie, confère donc aux ensembles qui s'y adonnent un rayonnement,

---

[35] Cf. Michel Vergé-Franceschi (Moderne).
[36] Cf. Jakob Seerup (Moderne).

un surplus d'énergie, impulsant la trajectoire historique dans un sens positif que ce soit sur les institutions, les populations, ou la vie culturelle et intellectuelle.

L'exemple du Portugal est à cet égard également révélateur des bienfaits générés par la maritimité. C'est la mer qui a, en effet, forgé tout à la fois la destinée et l'indépendance du Portugal. Sa position géographique face à l'océan Atlantique et son ouverture volontariste vers la mer ont été les deux éléments ayant forgé l'âme de cette « Nation maritime » qui, grâce à la mer, a pu tenir dans l'Histoire une place et un rôle sans commune mesure avec son poids démographique[37].

L'existence, l'indépendance et la richesse des Provinces-Unies sont également incompréhensibles sans la mer. C'est grâce à sa maîtrise des ports que le pays a pu arracher son indépendance à l'Espagne[38]. C'est grâce à la pêche, à son commerce et à la spécialisation qui en résulte au plan agricole et aux innovations que cela induit au plan industriel que sa population avait le niveau de vie le plus élevé d'Europe, et donc du monde, au cours de la première moitié du XVIIe siècle[39]. Les Provinces-Unies sont alors considérées comme la « puissance éclairée » par excellence, le pays dans le monde où les valeurs de liberté et de tolérance sont les plus respectées. Les gazettes pullulent avec une liberté de ton étonnante pour l'époque, des imprimeurs volontiers contestataires. C'est le pays où les savants et philosophes, Descartes et Spinoza en tête, indésirables dans leur propre pays trouvent refuge. Concentration urbaine, richesse et esprit entrepreneurial donnent le jour aux plus grandes compagnies commerciales du temps dont la VOC, la célèbre compagnie hollandaise des Indes fondée en 1602, qui est la première société par actions. C'est là aussi que surgissent de multiples inventions décisives : télescope, microscope, chronomètres, les lentilles optiques, les premières lunettes...[40]

La mer fut également un facteur tout à fait décisif dans l'histoire de la Corée car c'est en maîtrisant ses côtes que le royaume put non seulement devenir puissant mais assurer sa survie, son indépendance et sa souveraineté pendant presque un millénaire[41]. De la même manière, mais sur une durée infiniment plus courte, l'édification d'une marine a totalement modifié, sur une soixantaine d'années, la trajectoire historique du petit royaume indien de Maratha, situé au nord-ouest du sous-continent indien. Cette édification a induit un développement économique et commercial qui se sont mis en interaction. Et ce développement maritime a eu pour effet un rayonnement sans précédent pour ce petit royaume qui est même

---

[37] Cf. Jorge Semedo de Matos (Moderne).
[38] Cf. Louis Sicking (Moderne)
[39] Les activités maritimes constituèrent à travers tout le XVIIe comme au XVIIIe siècles le pilier du développement économique des Provinces-Unies. Au XVIIe siècle, c'est près du quart de la population active masculine qui sert à bord des seuls navires, et encore un sixième de celle-ci à la fin du XVIIIe siècle, nécessitant le recours à une importante main d'œuvre étrangère et un spectaculaire investissement dans le capital humain en terme de formation qui eut également d'importantes retombées au plan économique. Cf. Jelle Van Lottum (Moderne).
[40] Poussou J.-P., , *Les îles Britanniques, les Provinces-Unies, la guerre et la paix au XVIIe siècle*, Paris: Economica (1991).
[41] Cf. Alexandre Le Bouteiller (Moderne).

parvenu, un temps, à empêcher les marines européennes de bénéficier de ces retombées économiques[42].

À une autre échelle, c'est la mer qui permit aux ordres militaires, qu'ils soient hospitaliers, templiers ou teutoniques d'affirmer leur supranationalité et de tirer des revenus substantiels du commerce. Cela n'est donc pas un hasard si de grands navigateurs de l'époque moderne émanèrent d'ordres combattants comme les portugais Vasco de Gama et Pedro Alvares Cabral, qui explorèrent les côtes de l'Inde et du Brésil sous le pavillon de l'ordre du Christ[43]. Et c'est de s'être adossé plus que les autres ordres sur des activités maritimes que l'Ordre de Malte fut le seul ordre à avoir pu se maintenir et traverser le temps jusqu'à nous[44].

Mesure-t-on également que c'est par la mer qu'ont été opérées non seulement les plus grandes migrations humaines, nous l'avons dit, mais aussi que les idées, les croyances se sont diffusées de par le monde, et cela est vrai pour l'ensemble des trois grandes religions monothéistes, comme pour l'hindouisme, le bouddhisme ? [45] Au sein de l'Europe, en caricaturant les travaux de Max Weber, on en est parfois arrivé à considérer que l'éthique protestante était plus propice au développement de l'esprit capitaliste, thèse qui souffre de parfaits contre-exemples[46]. Il est vrai que le rapport à l'argent est souvent très différent entre pays majoritairement protestant ou catholique mais ne serait-ce pas plutôt un corollaire que la cause première ? Il peut être intéressant de constater que ce sont très rapidement les communautés maritimes qui furent gagnées par le protestantisme et par le biais de la mer que la Réforme put se répandre sur une bonne partie du littoral européen. La Réforme nous apparaît plus qu'une cause, une adoption conséquente à une attitude commerçante et donc maritime préexistante. C'est, pour notre part, bien plus dans l'atavisme rural ou maritime, dans l'esprit d'ouverture ou terrien au sens isolationniste du terme, que nous entrevoyions la véritable zone de fracture. Quel contraste en effet saisissant entre la France du XVIIIe siècle où, avec les Physiocrates, Docteur Quesnay en tête, la terre apparaît comme la seule source de richesse, et l'Angleterre où est publié, en 1776, sous la plume d'Adam Smith, le premier ouvrage optimiste à philosophie industrielle, *La Prospérité des Nations*[47].

Dans le même esprit, les théories des socialistes utopiques, comme celles de Fourier, Saint-Simon, Cabet reposent sur la constitution de communautés artisanales et rurales présentant toutes un point commun : d'être éloignées de la mer, à la différence de l'île d'*Utopia* de Thomas More. La même tendance se retrouve en Espagne avec les *Proyectistas*, ainsi qu'en Russie où l'empreinte rurale

---

[42] Cf. Sachin Pendse (Moderne).
[43] Cf. Pierre-Vincent Claverie (Moyen Âge) et Juhan Kreem (Moyen Âge).
[44] Cf. Alain Blondy (Moderne).
[45] Cf. notamment Chantal Reynier (Antiquité), Tansen Sen (Antiquité).
[46] Cf. MALETTKE K. in *La Puissance Maritime*, ed. C BUCHET., J. MEYER et J.-P.POUSSOU, Paris: PUPS (2004) ; MASSON P., *De la Mer et de sa Stratégie*, Paris: Taillandier (1986).
[47] BUCHET C., *Une Autre Histoire des Océans et de l'Homme*, préface du Président Jacques Chirac, Paris: Robert Laffont (2004).

pèse d'un poids énorme et où le démarrage industriel s'amorce à peine en dépit des efforts de l'État, à la fin du XIXe siècle.

S'il est aussi un peuple qui doit un rayonnement tout particulier à la mer, c'est bien le peuple polynésien, véritable « Peuple de l'océan » pour reprendre la belle expression d'Emmanuel Desclèves (Moderne). C'est dans son essence la plus profonde à la mer, à cet océan dont il est à l'unisson, avec lequel il fait corps, qui lui donne force, prestige et fonde profondément son originalité. Dispersé des côtes du Sud-est asiatique à celles de l'Amérique, le peuple maritime de l'océan n'avait qu'une seule référence : la mer, à la fois source du savoir et de la puissance. Les dieux et leurs mythes fondateurs sont conçus à partir de l'océan. La découverte apparaît à cet égard comme un acte de création. Le chef est le descendant des dieux, l'initié, le gardien du *mana* des ancêtres. C'est le maître des découvertes et des relations avec les autres îles, pouvoir que lui confère son incomparable aptitude à naviguer librement dans cet espace vierge ouvert sur les communications interinsulaires. Il est en communion avec l'océan et le ciel qui le surplombe, il est partout chez lui dans ces vastes espaces. C'est pourquoi il conçoit l'univers d'une façon très différente de celle du sédentaire, dont l'horizon se borne à la terre. Claire Laux (Contemporaine) montre que les sociétés maritimes de Polynésie apparaissent comme des sociétés dynamiques et hiérarchisées, alors que les sociétés terriennes mélanésiennes demeuraient bien plus émiettées, comme incapables de produire des structures organisées et hiérarchisées. Une fois encore, on voit combien le rapport ou non à la mer est important jusqu'à la structuration mentale. Et Claire Laux d'aller plus loin en considérant qu'au sein même de la population polynésienne « les individus les plus dynamiques, étaient alors les « gens de contact », en particulier les métis dont l'existence même est fruit de la rencontre maritime...[48] ». « Nos ancêtres voyaient leur monde comme une « mer d'îles » plutôt que comme des « îles dans la mer » » nous dit l'anthropologue océanien Epeli Hau'ofoa.

On trouve également dans certaines parties du continent africain ce même rapport étroit entre l'aptitude à gouverner et l'aptitude à naviguer, comme fondement et légitimation du pouvoir, comme élément de prestige et de rayonnement. Des mythes recueillis au XXe siècle dans la région du Congo font du détour en mer, rituel accompli sous l'égide d'une divinité faiseuse de pluie et dispensatrice de bienfaits, le signe d'élection ou l'épreuve permettant d'investir un nouveau roi, particulièrement en cas de vide dynastique. Déjà un millénaire plus tôt, sur la côte du sud somalien ou du nord du Kenya, un récit persan pénétré de folklore maritime évoque le long périple par-delà l'océan Indien d'un jeune homme qui, à son retour, se voit doublement confirmé, comme roi, pour son peuple, et comme musulman par les marchands de passage. Pareilles pratiques semblent aussi avoir été le cas pour l'Empire malien au XIVe siècle[49]. C'est que, comme l'évoque François-Xavier Fauvelle-Aymar (Moyen Âge), la mer est un horizon politique pour être la matrice ou le miroir d'un au-delà souverain et

---

[48] Cf. Emmanuel Desclèves (Moderne).
[49] Cf. François-Xavier Fauvelle-Aymar (Moyen Âge).

occulte, insondable, propre à apporter des réponses au mystère des fondements du pouvoir, propre à engendrer une légitimité dynastique.

La mer, vecteur de découvertes, d'échanges, est également un puissant moteur de création et d'inspiration au niveau littéraire et artistique[50]. C'est, en effet, par navigateurs interposés que l'on a longtemps vu le monde et considéré l'Autre. L'histoire littéraire et l'histoire des idées ont été profondément marquées par l'histoire maritime. C'est un ouvrage entier qui mériterait d'être consacré à cette étroite corrélation. Ainsi, par exemple, l'orientation maritime des ports indonésiens au Moyen Âge est-elle à l'origine de la culture métisse de l'Indonésie, dans laquelle l'art indianisé se mélange à la religion musulmane et où la langue indonésienne elle-même porte la marque de vocables venus des quatre coins de l'océan Indien[51].

Les contacts opérés par le biais du maritime ont été source et vecteurs de développements artistiques originaux comme le style manuélin en architecture, ou encore dans l'aménagement intérieur. C'est ainsi que le style indo-portugais, encouragé par les jésuites, introduisit l'ivoire, les bois exotiques et l'esthétique indienne dans la sculpture et l'ameublement.

Autre exemple, l'essor maritime hollandais eut pour conséquence la naissance d'un art bourgeois. Une communauté anversoise fixée durablement à Gênes explique que des ateliers flamands s'ouvrirent dans le port ligure dans les premières années du XVIIe siècle, au moment où naissait simultanément à Haarlem une peinture qui donnait à la mer son premier emploi dans l'histoire de l'art. Les hôtels de la Via Balbi s'ornèrent d'œuvres des maîtres hollandais et flamands, mais aussi de la jeune école génoise de peinture. Si comme l'a montré François Bellec (Moderne), l'école ligure se passionna pour des compositions décoratives, *Vedute di Marina, Bataglie Navali* ou *Fortuna di Mare*, les peintres hollandais et flamands rendirent à la mer fructueuse, l'hommage des Provinces-Unies. Affranchie de l'obligation de traiter l'hagiographie et le récit biblique, portée par un enthousiasme national, la première école de peinture de marine naquit à Haarlem, de la rencontre d'une école artistique brillante, de la vocation maritime d'une nation au contact immédiat avec la mer, et d'une nouvelle clientèle de riches amateurs d'art. Andries van Eertvelt immortalisa le premier *Retour de la flotte hollandaise des Indes Orientales* en 1599[52]. Trois ans plus tard, la fondation de la célèbre VOC, la compagnie hollandaise des Indes, annonça l'émergence d'une puissance économique et maritime mondiale.

A partir des années 1620, Amsterdam imposa une nouvelle école fondée sur une peinture d'atmosphère aux tonalités sourdes, impressionniste plutôt que documentaire. *Le Marchand Jacob Mathieusen et sa femme devant Batavia* d'Aelbert Cuyp affirmait comme une évidence la puissance tranquille, la prospérité, la compétence industrielle, commerciale et maritime de la Hollande. L'Angleterre invita des artistes hollandais, qui lui semblaient aussi utiles que les maîtres de

---

[50] Cf. pour l'Égypte antique Sydney Hervé Aufrere (Antiquité).
[51] Cf. Paul Wormser (Moyen Âge), voir également pour l'Inde Fabrizia Baldissera (Antiquité).
[52] Cf. François Bellec (Moderne).

hache des chantiers d'Amsterdam pour comprendre la mer et se l'approprier. Ils travaillèrent sans états d'âme pour l'Angleterre jusqu'à s'y installer, malgré les guerres en cours. Vroom, Bakhuizen, les Van de Velde furent bientôt aussi célèbres à Londres qu'aux Provinces-Unies. Et comme au Portugal, les Indes orientales apportèrent un exotisme dans l'ameublement européen, avec notamment la porcelaine de Jingdezhen, importée par millions de pièces, qui imposa une esthétique durable[53].

3. La mer moteur de l'histoire

Pour ainsi dire partout dans le monde, l'Université a découpé l'Histoire en quatre périodes : l'Antiquité, le Moyen Âge, l'époque moderne (XVI, XVII et XVIIIe siècles), et l'époque contemporaine. Cette segmentation découle d'une réalité. Chacun de ces temps forme un ensemble cohérent, caractérisé, notamment, par une certaine manière de penser, d'agir, de produire, de consommer... jusqu'à une utilisation spécifique des cinq sens, lesquels édifient de façon dissemblable d'un âge à l'autre notre structuration mentale et, partant, notre manière d'appréhender le monde, ce qui va modifier jusqu'aux méthodes de résolution des problèmes.

Chacune des périodes meurt dans les soubresauts d'un profond traumatisme, qui sont autant de ferments de l'avènement d'un monde nouveau. C'est la chute de l'empire romain d'occident, qui ressurgit transformé, rehaussé géographiquement dans le cadre du Saint Empire romain germanique, lequel pose les fondements de la période médiévale. Ce sont les spasmes mortifères de la peste noire du XIVe siècle, la pénurie de métaux précieux – crise monétaire avant l'heure – et la décadence de la vieille philosophie scolastique qui mènent à l'effondrement du Moyen Âge et à la révolution formidable et détonante qu'est la Renaissance. Et c'est celle-ci qui pose les fondements de la modernité, avant que la défaite de l'Ancien Régime dans une France incapable de maîtriser son endettement ne nous fasse entrer, avec 1789 ou, selon les pays, au terme des guerres de la Révolution et de l'Empire, dans l'époque contemporaine.

Quatre temps, quatre ères historiques, aussi riches que variées, mais dont l'enchaînement est occidentalo-centré, et dont la découpe ne convient que très imparfaitement aux réalités historiques des autres zones géographiques. Nous pensons, en particulier, à l'Asie, à l'Océanie...

Il est cependant une manière différente de voir, d'aborder, de présenter l'Histoire et cela a été toute la quête du Programme Océanides. Les travaux menés par les 260 contributeurs m'amènent à proposer une autre segmentation, une structuration bien plus en adéquation avec l'Histoire, les Histoires particulières des différentes aires géographiques, un cadre rendant bien plus intelligible et parlante la dynamique du temps. Et si la mer nous donnait des instruments d'analyse nous permettant de comprendre les grands basculements géopolitiques ?

---

[53] *Ibid.*

Prendre non plus la terre comme espace de référencement historique mais la mer est un renversement complet d'attitude qui ne centre plus l'étude de nos objets de recherche dans le seul cadre territorial, national ou politique, mais sur ce qui précisément unit les différents ensembles. C'est considérer l'espace marin non pas comme une séparation mais comme un trait d'union. L'espace par excellence des échanges qu'ils soient d'ordre commercial, culturel, scientifique... C'est ne plus se contenter d'étudier les ensembles politiques en eux-mêmes et dans les rivalités qu'ils ont eu avec leurs voisins mais les appréhender dans leur participation à la synergie générale qui se dégage de cette dynamique de flux et qui s'appelle l'Histoire.

Cette synergie, cette dynamique, cette connectivité est le propre du maritime. Et il m'a d'ailleurs toujours semblé intéressant et révélateur de l'esprit général d'un peuple, de considérer son rapport à la mer. La mer nous offre un exceptionnel télescope d'observation tant de l'histoire générale d'un peuple que de l'Histoire universelle, puisque dénominateur, espace commun ; c'est elle qui, à bien y regarder, en rythme les soubresauts.

Dans cette perspective, on peut distinguer non plus quatre temps, mais seulement deux, qui nous semblent avoir présidés aux destinées humaines. Il y eut d'abord le Temps des Méditerranées, au pluriel, auquel succéda le Temps de l'Atlantique. Loin de totalement contredire la segmentation en quatre périodes, cette vision, ce cadre universel en confirme et en précise la pertinence puisque, aux périodes antique et médiévale, nous pouvons faire correspondre le Temps des Méditerranées, tandis que les périodes moderne et contemporaine coïncident avec le Temps de l'Atlantique. Mais celui-ci n'est déjà plus ; sans même en avoir pleinement conscience, nous avons quitté la période contemporaine, pour rentrer dans un nouveau troisième Temps de l'Histoire qui ouvre à tous les possibles et que nous appellerons : l'océanotemporain, le Temps de l'océan mondial.

Les périodes antique et médiévale forment, en effet, un tout sous l'emprise de la maritimité : le Temps des Méditerranées. Par Méditerranées au pluriel, nous voulons signifier qu'il y eut en parallèle plusieurs histoires, plusieurs espaces où l'Histoire s'est déployée. Elle s'est déployé partout, bien sûr, où vivaient d'importantes communautés humaines, et l'on n'a que trop négligé en occident l'histoire du monde asiatique, répartie sur le pourtour de ce que François Gipouloux a qualifié dans la veine des travaux de Jacob Van Leur, de Georges Coedès et de Fernand Braudel, de « Méditerranée asiatique[54] ». C'est-à-dire ce corridor maritime articulé sur plusieurs bassins interconnectés : mer du Japon, mer Jaune, mer de Chine, mer de Sulu, mer des Célèbes et débouchant sur l'Inde. Nous commençons à peine à découvrir toute la force et la richesse de cette Histoire faite de rencontres, d'échanges, de conflits, avec sur l'un de ses contours le grand espace chinois qui n'a cessé d'osciller entre assise continentale et ouverture sur cet espace maritime, qui en est le cœur et impulse ses flux. Une

---

[54] GIPOULOUX F., *La Mediterranée asiatique*, Paris: CNRS Éditions (2009). Voir également l'ouvrage de GUILLERM A., *Géopolitique des mers, les Mediterranées d'Europe et d'Asie,* Paris: Cirpés, 1999, et la contribution de Pierre-Yves Manguin (Moyen Âge).

dynamique identique à celle qu'insuffla la *Mare Nostrum*, cette mer du milieu des terres sur les rives de laquelle les civilisations les plus éclatantes prirent naissance et se développèrent, que l'on pense à Assur, à l'Égypte des pharaons, à la Grèce, à Byzance, Rome, Venise, Gênes.

Et ce n'est pas l'un des moindres mérites du Programme Océanides que d'avoir mis un accent particulier sur l'océan Indien, cette « grande Mer » comme on l'appelait lors de l'Antiquité, qui, bien plus qu'il ne séparait, mettait en connexion ces deux Méditerranées. Bien des travaux historiques et archéologiques doivent être menés pour évaluer la place et le rôle de l'océan Indien dans l'Histoire humaine. L'océan Indien pourrait bien être le cœur, l'épicentre de tous les bouleversements du monde pour être le lieu de convergence des routes qui reliaient déjà les trois continents de l'Ancien monde entre eux : la route de Malacca, qui relie la péninsule de Malacca et l'île de Sumatra à la Chine et au Japon ; la route du golfe Persique ; la route de la mer Rouge ; et bientôt, après 1488, la route du Cap de Bonne Espérance.

Qui tient l'océan Indien, tient l'essentiel du commerce mondial pourrait-on dire en paraphrasant Walter Raleigh. Bien plus que le *heartland* (l'Eurasie) dans lequel McKidder voyait l'élément pivot de la domination mondiale, l'océan Indien pourrait bien être ce qu'il nous plaît d'appeler par analogie le *heartsea*, dont la maîtrise des flux confère la prédominance[55]. C'est toute l'Histoire universelle qui gagnerait à être revisitée sous ce prisme pour comprendre le cadencement des équilibres géopolitiques, de l'Ancien monde jusqu'à aujourd'hui.

N'est-il pas possible de considérer, par exemple, que le déclin de l'empire romain serait étroitement lié à la perte du contrôle du commerce indien ? A partir de 242, les guerres fragilisent, en effet, l'Empire romain tandis que fondent sur lui les Goths venus d'Ukraine. Les Sassanides, successeurs des Parthes, envahissent la Mésopotamie tandis que la reine Zénobie de Palmyre proclame son indépendance et s'empare d'Antioche. Le royaume éthiopien d'Axoum franchit le détroit d'Aden et s'empare du Yémen, contrôlant l'accès à la mer Rouge. Le commerce de la soie échappe donc aux mains des Romains pour passer dans celles des Éthiopiens et des Perses. La constante dévaluation de la monnaie romaine pourrait donc venir du drainage constant vers l'Inde et l'accroissement de ses prix dû à une perte des voies marchandes. Ces événements ne signifient pas la fin de l'empire romain, mais marque son lent effondrement, pendant que les Perses sassanides s'imposent dans le commerce de l'océan Indien[56].

Peut-être pourrons-nous, au fil des avancées de nos connaissances rajouter d'autres Méditerranées, considérées toujours comme un hub d'échanges dans un espace maritime donné, façonnant dans le creuset de la fluidité une histoire régionale ? De ce point de vue la mer Baltique et la mer du Nord apparaissent à

---

[55] Voir à cet égard le remarquable ouvrage de KEARNEY M., *The Indian Ocean in World History*, New York: Routledge (2004).
[56] Cf. Arthur Landon, mémoire de M2 sous la direction de Christian Buchet, Institut catholique de Paris, 2015-2016.

François Gipouloux comme une Méditerranée du nord. Et le monde polynésien peut, peut-être, être considéré déjà de la sorte...

Ce qui définit ce premier Temps, c'est le cloisonnement relatif de ces espaces maritimes dotés de leurs histoires particulières, même si, comme nous l'avons montré, se déclinent les mêmes lignes de force, les mêmes enseignements, à partir de la plus ou moins grande aptitude des ensembles, qu'ils soient politiques ou marchands, à se tourner vers l'épicentre de l'espace considéré : la mer.

Mais voici que survient un big bang géographique, une véritable révolution copernicienne dans un temps extraordinairement court : quatre ans ! Par ce qui se produit en 1488 et 1492 toute l'Histoire humaine est bouleversée, nous entrons dans le second Temps de l'Histoire, une Histoire qui devient universelle, c'est le Temps de l'Atlantique, du nom de cet océan qui va en impulser la dynamique.

1488 : le portugais Bartholomeu Dias double la pointe de l'Afrique, le cap de Bonne-espérance. La route maritime vers l'Orient venait d'être découverte, et cette voie nouvelle allait ébranler les assises économiques du monde tel qu'il tournait alors. Les épices, les parfums et autres produits que l'on faisait venir d'Asie depuis la plus haute Antiquité, par voie terrestre, jusqu'aux ports de Beyrouth et d'Alexandrie, vont désormais arriver directement par l'Atlantique qui connecte jusqu'en Europe l'océan Indien... Dès 1498, dix années tout juste après la découverte de la route permettant d'atteindre le cap de Bonne-espérance, Vasco de Gama atteint l'Inde, à Calicut.

L'heure de la primauté économique du monde atlantique, ou de l'Occident, est venue. Fini les innombrables et incalculables intermédiaires qui, à force de chameaux, de caravane en caravane, acheminaient lentement épices et parfums jusqu'aux rives de la Méditerranée. Ce sont désormais les armateurs européens des pays atlantiques qui vont s'arroger tous les fruits de ce négoce pour l'assurer de bout en bout. Les richesses jusqu'alors disséminées le long des routes traversées se concentrent en Europe. Les bénéfices explosent d'autant que les armateurs européens ne se limitent pas à ce commerce mondial mais parviennent bientôt à s'immiscer voire même, par moments à dominer, le commerce régional que ce soit en Inde, en Indonésie, alors qualifié de « commerce d'Inde en Inde ». Pour la première fois dans l'Histoire, l'économie mondiale est tenue par une seule aire géographique, et l'Occident connaît un formidable essor économique, en même temps que technologique, qui va lui conférer jusqu'à aujourd'hui la prédominance que l'on sait.

En moins d'un siècle, tous les échanges méditerranéens s'effondrent, supplantés par ceux de l'Atlantique. Les marchands des villes italiennes qui, en acheminant ces marchandises, assuraient le trait d'union avec l'Asie, ne peuvent retenir ce Temps des Méditerranées révolu. Année après année, inexorablement, au XVIe siècle, le nombre de navires assurant ce commerce décroît. Au tour des Portugais, bientôt des Hollandais et Britanniques, d'aller chercher les produits ultramarins. Le soleil se lève sur le monde atlantique. Venise mieux que Gênes saura trouver de nouvelles aubes, car la nuit ne s'éternise pas pour qui sait s'adapter, innover, optimiser ses atouts. Ne pouvant maintenir ses liaisons commerciales, La Sérénissime se spécialise dans la fabrication de produits de luxe, la verrerie notamment, et la banque, héritage de sa capacité maritime.

1492 : Christophe Colomb découvre, ou plutôt redécouvre, l'Amérique. A-t-on suffisamment mesuré le cataclysme que ce fut pour certains pays, tout particulièrement pour l'Angleterre, jusqu'alors la nation la plus excentrée de l'univers connu ? D'un coup, la voilà projetée au cœur du Nouveau Monde. Limitée jusqu'alors à la seule expansion possible vers l'est, vers le continent, ce qui explique la guerre de Cent ans de 1337 à 1453, elle va pouvoir désormais tourner ses regards vers l'ouest, non pas tant pour conquérir des terres que pour maîtriser les flux commerciaux. D'autant que les routes de retour d'Amérique, compte-tenu de la conjonction des vents et des courants, passent très précisément au large du cap Lizard, son extrémité la plus occidentale. Que l'Espagne interdise à tous les autres pays les échanges avec ses nouvelles possessions, ces territoires américains, n'empêchera pas l'Angleterre, au centre névralgique du dispositif atlantique, de répondre à sa vocation.

1488... 1492, les dés sont jetés ! Une partie s'engage sur des règles inédites, réinventées. Voici venu le Temps de l'Atlantique, du « grand désenclavement planétaire », pour reprendre l'expression de Pierre Chaunu. Cette véritable révolution n'a pas été perçue dans toute sa force, notamment en France et en Espagne, pays qui ont chacun un pied en Méditerranée, un autre dans l'Atlantique. Il en va différemment pour l'Angleterre, nous l'avons vu, mais aussi pour le Portugal et les Provinces-Unies, qui sortent de leur impasse périphérique et se trouvent recentrés, remis en selle comme disent les cavaliers.

Ce temps va donc coïncider avec les périodes moderne et contemporaine, deux périodes qui s'inscrivent dans une parfaite continuité même s'il convient de les différencier dans l'intensité du décloisonnement auquel elles donnent lieu.

Les XVI, XVII et XVIIIe siècles voient la mise en place, en effet, de cette première mondialisation maritime de bout en bout. Les puissances européennes poussent jusqu'aux extrémités du globe leurs réseaux dans un affrontement sans merci, mais le volume des échanges est encore limité. Le XIXe siècle va de ce point de vue marquer une forte accélération sous l'effet de la révolution industrielle dont les deux moteurs sont la révolution nautique (avec le développement de la navigation à vapeur, celui de la technologie nautique, du revêtement des coques avec du cuivre...), le développement de cuirassés et le réseau ferroviaire qui va bientôt permettre de prolonger les échanges océaniques toujours plus massivement à l'intérieur des terres.

Les grandes découvertes de l'époque moderne avaient déjà permis aux Européens d'augmenter de six fois le volume de terre disponible par habitant. À partir du XIXe siècle, sous l'effet d'un développement exponentiel de la construction navale, le coût du transport maritime baisse fortement et le commerce océanique ne cesse de croître en volume, et va prendre une toute autre ampleur[57]. Le temps du désenclavement planétaire est en passe de laisser la place au temps de la globalisation. Entre 1500 et 1800, le commerce maritime

---

[57] Cf. Kevin O'Rourke (Contemporaine).

a crû de quelque 1% par an, un résultat déjà très respectable dans un monde où le taux de croissance était de l'ordre de 0,1 à 0,2 % par an. Après 1815, le taux de croissance annuelle du commerce maritime monte à 3,7% par an. Un taux à peu près stable, hormis les périodes de guerre ou de crises, jusqu'en 1992.

La fluidité d'un continent à l'autre estompe de plus en plus les différences de prix, donnant progressivement naissance à un véritable marché mondial. Les agriculteurs de l'Amérique du middle west, de la pampa en Argentine, du Punjab, du Burma, de Russie ou d'Australie... sont de plus en plus en compétition avec ceux de l'Europe de l'ouest ou du Japon. Les conséquences vont être considérables en permettant aux pays les plus ouverts, comme l'Angleterre ou l'Allemagne, d'orienter leur population vers la transformation industrielle à haute valeur ajoutée et à haute rentabilité, préférant s'en remettre, au plan agricole, aux importations bon marché. Il est important de souligner que sans cette explosion des liaisons maritimes tant au niveau des importations de produits agricoles contre des produits manufacturés, qu'au niveau de l'émigration (c'est 60 millions de personnes qui quittent l'Europe entre 1815 et 1914), l'Europe n'aurait pas été en mesure de digérer la formidable croissance démographique qui fut la sienne[58]. Pareille chance manquera, pour être encore si peu maritime, à l'Afrique au XXe siècle.

Mais ce Temps de l'Atlantique s'est dissipé, même si l'on parle toujours de l'Alliance atlantique, ultime étape pour une communauté qui a pris conscience de ses valeurs communes pour en assurer la défense. Nous vivons depuis le début des années 1990 une révolution géographique, économique et culturelle, qui a pour le moins l'ampleur de celle qui, avec la Renaissance au tournant des XV-XVIe siècles, nous a fait rentrer dans le Temps de l'Atlantique.

Alors que beaucoup, encore chaussés du prisme des lunettes du Temps révolu, parlent de crises, nous vivons plutôt une période d'extraordinaires mutations qui ne cessent de s'accélérer, nous faisant perdre nos repères parce que précisément ce troisième Temps de l'Histoire qui s'ouvre à nous, le Temps de l'Océanotemporain, est plus que jamais fondé sur la fluidité, la connectivité, en un mot : la maritimité. Le terme que nous avons choisi d'océanotemporain veut signifier tout à la fois que nous ne sommes plus dans la période contemporaine et que c'est l'océan, l'océan mondial qui en est la matrice.

Finie la primauté absolue des puissances de l'espace atlantique, voici que l'espace asiatique a repris en main sa destinée économique. L'exemple chinois est de ce point de vue éclatant. L'empire du Milieu quitte son métacentre et se projette résolument sur les mers.

Plus qu'aucun autre pays, la Chine a, en effet, trop souvent tourné le dos à la mer, dessinant ainsi le cours et les contours de l'Histoire. Les étonnantes expéditions conduites par Zheng He entre 1405 et 1433, ne sauraient occulter que la Chine a été, sur de très longues périodes, le pays de l'enfermement voulu, ceinturé côté nord par la Grande Muraille et, côté est, par la mer. Une mer perçue comme une enceinte, une enceinte parfois même interdite puisqu'à

---

[58] Cf. John Beeler (Contemporaine).

certaines époques les autorités allèrent jusqu'à prohiber la navigation hauturière et, pour s'en affranchir totalement, à construire un canal intérieur, le canal impérial. Si l'on se souvient que c'est la Chine qui a découvert l'imprimerie bien avant Gutenberg, la monnaie fiduciaire dès le XIIe siècle, forte de ces inventions, mais aussi du gouvernail d'étambot, de la poudre noire, de la boussole et d'une démographie de quelque 250 millions d'habitants – la France de Louis XIV n'en comptait que 20 millions, l'Angleterre 7 – elle aurait pu modeler autrement et sans conteste l'Histoire du monde. C'est elle qui, logiquement, aurait dû, dès les XII et XIIIe siècles, envoyer ses navires sillonner les espaces maritimes, procéder au désenclavement planétaire. À travers elle, l'Asie aurait été l'épicentre d'un séisme géopolitique qui aurait raflé à l'Occident son big bang géographique de 1488-1492. L'Histoire en eût été inversée, et le Temps du Pacifique eût supplanté le Temps de l'Atlantique... mais tel ne fut pas le cours des choses pour des raisons d'ordre essentiellement idéologiques.

L'enfermement n'est plus. Le pays sort enfin de sa léthargie, de sa vision complaisante du Centre, d'Empire du Milieu. Il tient compte désormais des leçons de l'Histoire, et ce n'est pas un hasard s'il remet aujourd'hui à l'honneur Zheng He. Il a enfoncé l'image mentale qu'il avait de la mer pour considérer dorénavant que, loin d'être un mur, elle est la plus formidable voie de communication qui soit. Et toute la Chine court à pas de géant vers sa maritimisation.

Ce qui est vrai pour la Chine, l'est également pour la plupart des pays de la région, à commencer par l'Indonésie où, en 2014, le Président Joko Widowo, à l'exemple de son homologue chinois, a décidé d'investir dans le secteur maritime, et d'en faire la priorité absolue, pour assurer le développement économique de son pays. Partout, les investissements maritimes ne cessent de croître depuis les années 1990, créant une dynamique de croissance qui ne cesse de s'accélérer. Les revenus issus de la mer augmentent, dopant les budgets des États, créent de l'emploi, et stimulent l'industrialisation. Les flux commerciaux traversant le Pacifique sont d'ores et déjà supérieurs à ceux traversant l'Atlantique. La Chine, le Japon, la Corée du Sud... se projettent tout autant dans l'océan Indien pour des échanges avec l'Europe, l'Afrique, le Moyen-Orient. Le commerce émanant des pays de l'APEC (Asia Pacific Economic Cooperation group), représente près de la moitié des échanges mondiaux et leurs économies connaissent une croissance trois fois supérieure à celle des pays européens, dopant un commerce mondial qui de 9 000 millions de tonnes en 2012, devrait avoisiner, selon les prévisions, 15 000 millions de tonnes avant 2025[59].

Bien évidemment, les investissements de ces pays dans le naval de défense suivent les mêmes courbes exponentielles, contribuant également, par leurs effets induits, à stimuler tout à la fois le développement technologique, industriel et commercial. Les experts américains considèrent qu'en 2030, les investissements dans le naval de défense des pays de la zone devraient atteindre quelque 170 billions de dollars américains, dépassant pour la première fois depuis plus de 400 ans les crédits affectés par l'ensemble des pays européens pour leurs marines.

---

[59] Cf. Geoffrey Till (Contemporaine).

Ce n'est pas uniquement ce rattrapage forcené de la Méditerranée asiatique qui nous fait quitter le Temps de l'Atlantique pour entrer dans le Temps de l'Océanotemporain, mais également, et concomitamment, trois autres facteurs éminemment structurants en passe de modifier durablement la géopolitique et la géoéconomie de l'ordre ancien : l'explosion démographique et sa concentration sur le littoral, le nouveau droit de la mer bouleversant les équilibres entre puissances, et la révolution géographique impulsée par les routes du nord.

La croissance démographique aiguillonne ce basculement tout à la fois par son ampleur et sa ventilation. Une croissance, en effet, sans précédent par son ampleur dans l'Histoire de l'humanité. Alors que la planète ne comptait qu'un milliard de Terriens sous Napoléon Ier, en 1804 exactement, nous sommes 7 milliards depuis octobre 2011, nous serons 8 milliards en 2025, et la population mondiale devrait culminer à quelque 9,1 milliards en 2050... Soit une augmentation de plus de 2 milliards de terriens en seulement 35 ans. Une population qui va se concentrer de plus en plus en bordure de mer. En 2025, 75% de la population mondiale – sur la base de 8 milliards donc – va se concentrer sur une bande littorale de 75 kilomètres de large, et ce seront même 80% des quelque 9 milliards de terriens qui vivront en 2050 sur cette même bande littorale... C'est dire combien nous allons avoir de plus en plus recours à la mer qui contient, pour reprendre l'expression des 327 experts qui ont travaillé en France dans le cadre du Grenelle de la mer « la quasi-totalité des solutions » pour un avenir que nous pouvons plus que durable qualifier de désirable[60].

Le maritime n'est plus seulement aujourd'hui l'aiguillon, le moteur du développement économique, le vecteur du désenclavement planétaire et de la globalisation, il est le cœur même de l'économie-monde[61]. Le Temps de l'Océanotemporain voit l'homme repousser, transpercer la dernière frontière : sous le voile miroitant de la mer qui matérialisait l'obstacle cruel aux amours du pêcheur et de la sirène, l'homme est à l'orée d'un monde nouveau. Les fonds marins sont les rivages de son avenir, le sixième et dernier continent à découvrir[62].

Dans le même mouvement, mais qui s'en étonnera, les ensembles politiques se tournent de plus en plus vers la mer[63]. Le nouveau Droit de la mer conclu en 1982 à Montego Bay, à la Jamaïque, et appliqué depuis 1994 bouscule la géoéconomie politique en créant des ZEE – zones économiques exclusives[64]. Tout pays bordier de l'océan dispose, en plus de ses eaux territoriales s'étendant jusqu'à 12 miles marins, d'une bande minimale de 200 miles marins – soit 372 kilomètres – dont il est, en surface comme dans ses fonds, pleinement souverain au plan économique. Une approche pouvant aller jusqu'à 350 milles marins si le pays peut prouver que son plateau continental s'étend jusqu'à cette limite. Quand on sait que ce sont dans ces terres marines proches des terres émergées que se trouve l'essentiel

---

[60] BUCHET C., *Cap sur l'Avenir, A contre-courant les raisons d'être optimistes,* Paris: Éditions du Moment (2014).
[61] Cf. Hubert Bonin (Contemporaine).
[62] BUCHET C. (dir.), *Sous la Mer, le Sixième Continent,* Paris: PUPS (2001).
[63] Cf. Jeremy Black (Contemporaine).
[64] Cf. Sam Bateman (Contemporaine).

des matières premières et des ressources halieutiques, on comprend aisément la détermination des pays les plus avertis (États-Unis, Canada, Russie, Chine...) à se doter du plus grand domaine maritime possible. Les revendications de la Chine sur des îles appartenant au Japon, à la Corée, aux Philippines, au Vietnam, n'ont pas d'autres explications pour ce géant qui ne bénéficie pour l'heure que du dixième domaine maritime derrière respectivement les États-Unis, la France, l'Australie, la Russie, la Nouvelle-Zélande, l'Indonésie, le Canada, le Royaume-Uni et le Japon.

Avec l'élargissement du canal de Panama, de Suez, les créations envisagés d'autres canaux afin de rendre toujours plus percutante la connectivité maritime, les routes du Nord, à l'instar du big bang géographique des années 1488-1492 fondé sur la découverte de nouvelles routes maritimes, vont profondément bouleverser l'économie-monde.

Le passage du Nord-ouest, en longeant les côtes canadiennes, ou du Nord-est, en longeant celles de la Russie, qu'il est possible d'emprunter sous l'effet du réchauffement climatique et avec des brise-glace 365 jours par an comme le montre plusieurs passages de méthaniers en plein hiver ces trois dernières années, modifie toute la donne géopolitique. Que l'on emprunte l'un ou l'autre, la distance de l'occident à l'Asie se réduit à 15 700 kilomètres contre 21 000 kilomètres par le canal de Suez, et 23 000 kilomètres par Panama. Soit 25 à 30% de kilomètres en moins et un gain de temps de près de 40%, du fait que l'on s'affranchit des formalités administratives et manœuvres nautiques inévitables sur ces deux canaux. Finies les difficultés liées au tirant d'eau, ce qui ne limitera plus le gabarit des navires, et ces deux passages présentent, de surcroît, un autre atout majeur, celui de la sécurité pour être éloignés des zones à risques.

On l'imagine avec réalisme, même s'il ne s'agit nullement de faire l'apologie du réchauffement climatique qui en imprime la marque, rien n'arrêtera le développement du trafic dans ces passages, qui vont progressivement devenir de véritables autoroutes de la mer. Non seulement ils représentent d'extraordinaires raccourcis sécurisés pour les liaisons Europe–Asie, mais ils vont aussi désenclaver les deux zones à la fois les plus riches de la planète, véritables cul de sac jusque-là inaccessibles : le nord du Canada et la Sibérie. Ces régions du globe, dans leur composante maritime comme dans leur espace terrestre, regorgent de pétrole, de gaz, de fer, de nickel, de diamants... Mais, faute de routes, ces matières premières ne peuvent être exploitées. Or voici qu'elles vont incessamment se trouver à portée des artères maritimes les plus fréquentées.

Avec l'océanotemporain l'océan mondial, pour être venu à bout de tous les cloisonnements géographiques et pour accueillir sur son pourtour bientôt 80% de la population mondiale, est vraiment le pouls du monde. Véritable creuset où l'on va aller chercher de plus en plus les matériaux et les molécules que le sol terrestre émergé ne peut plus fournir en quantité suffisante, l'océan mondial est en passe de connaître une pression telle que son exploitation fait peser des menaces tout aussi importantes que les espoirs qu'il permet de nourrir. Les scientifiques s'accordent, en effet, à penser qu'il est au cœur des défis d'aujourd'hui : changement climatique, effondrement du capital sédimentaire et érosion du littoral, effondrement de certaines espèces de ressources halieutiques[65], pollution et menaces sur les écosystèmes marins qui abritent 80% de la biodiversité de la planète...

Aussi l'un des plus grands enjeux de la période océanotemporaine qui s'ouvre sera-t-il de parvenir à une nouvelle réflexion sur le concept, ancien, de « bien commun[66] ». Mers et océans, « *rex communis* », une nouvelle sorte de *mare nostrum* à l'échelle du globe dans laquelle les rapports traditionnels de puissance entre les nations doivent laisser une place plus large aux nécessités d'une nouvelle entente. La mer comprise comme un espace unique, global et physiquement solidaire, où l'expression de la souveraineté – dans des zones aujourd'hui morcelées par le droit –, pourrait s'effacer devant l'expression d'une nouvelle responsabilité collective, animée par les États comme par la société civile dans une gouvernance partagée et soucieuse d'en maîtriser l'exploitation raisonnable... Car si la mer est l'avenir de la terre, nous n'aurons pas d'océan de rechange.

Au terme de ce long travail qui a réuni 260 chercheurs du monde entier, et qui fait d'Océanides le plus vaste Programme en sciences humaines depuis l'Encyclopédie, il ressort clairement que le maritime est l'élément le plus structurant de l'Histoire pour conférer tout à la fois une prédominance militaire, économique, culturelle et être le moteur de la compétitivité, avec, à l'évidence, des conséquences sociales et sociétales. Toute entité politique qui se tourne vers la mer optimise ses paramètres constitutifs, qu'ils soient d'ordre démographique, géographique, politique, pour entrer dans une dynamique de développement, de rayonnement, dans laquelle puissance se conjugue avec croissance, emplois, pouvoir d'achat et bien-être. Non avons là non plus une réflexion mais un constat, bien plus une vision nouvelle de l'Histoire. Puisse-t-elle être éclairante pour tout décideur et montrer, à tout un chacun, que la mer est la clef de l'Histoire, et partant de ce constat, plus que jamais le catalyseur de notre avenir.

CHRISTIAN BUCHET
de l'Académie de Marine,
Professeur d'Histoire maritime, Institut catholique de Paris
Directeur scientifique d'Océanides

---

[65] Cf. Ingo Heidbrink (Contemporaine).
[66] Cf. Sam Bateman (Contemporaine).

Océanides

UNDERSTANDING THE ROLE THE SEA HAS PLAYED IN OUR PAST IN ORDER TO SHED LIGHT ON OUR FUTURE!

"Globalisation has made it more necessary than ever before to take account of maritime issues, on a geopolitical, economic and ecological level, something that the companies and institutions which support us know and understand well. Our long term objective is to raise awareness of today's maritime challenges and development opportunities as well as to convince our societies of the sea's crucial role in our future. Readers will be fascinated by the diverse subjects explored by our researchers: natural resources, military technologies, trade, and political and social organisations, among others."

ANNE-MARIE IDRAC
former minister, Chairwoman of the Board of Océanides

Founded in March 2012, Océanides is a five-year, international research project which aims to provide scientific evidence of the key role seas and oceans have played in human evolution, culture and history.

Its primary objective is to provide the most global overview of maritime history to date, spanning five millennia and five continents. It aims to give policy makers the necessary tools with which to understand the close connection between humans and the sea, to appreciate the evidence of its crucial role in our future and to improve worldwide maritime policy.

MEMBERS OF THE BOARD OF DIRECTORS

ANNE-MARIE IDRAC, Public Company Director and Chairwoman of Océanides
PATRICK BOISSIER, former Chairman-CEO of DCNS, Chairman of GICAN
MICHEL BENEZIT, Special Counsel to the Chairman-CEO of TOTAL
CHRISTOPHE BARNINI, Senior Vice President, Communication, of CGG
FRANÇOIS JACQ, Chairman-CEO of IFREMER
FRÉDÉRIC MONCANY DE SAINT-AIGNAN, Chairman of Cluster Maritime Français
SABINE MARIE DECUP-PROVOST, Managing Director of Océanides
MAXIME PETIET, Public Company Director and Treasurer of Océanides

Océanides has set up an independent Scientific Committee, chaired by Professor CHRISTIAN BUCHET, Director of the CETMER Maritime Studies Center (*Centre d'Étude de la Mer*), Catholic University of Paris, and member of the Académie de Marine. The members of the committee are:

PASCAL ARNAUD, Professor of Classical Studies, University of Lyon II, Co-editor of *The Sea in History – The Ancient World*

MICHEL BALARD, Emeritus Professor, University Paris I-Sorbonne, Editor of *The Sea in History – The Medieval World*

CHRISTIAN BUCHET, Co-editor of *The Sea in History – The Early Modern World*

OLIVIER CHALINE, Director of the Archaeology and Maritime History Laboratory, University Paris IV–Sorbonne, Advisor

PHILIP DE SOUZA, PhD, Professor of Classical Studies, Dublin University, Co-editor of *The Sea in History – The Ancient World*

MASASHI HANEDA, Vice-President of Tokyo University, Asian Advisor

JOHN HATTENDORF, Professor of Maritime History, US Naval War College of Rhode Island, Advisor

GÉRARD LE BOUEDEC, Director of the Scientific Interest Group of Maritime History, Co-editor of *The Sea in History – The Early Modern World*

JORGE ORTIZ-SOTELO, Director of the Peruvian Institute of Politics and Economics, Advisor for South America

NICHOLAS RODGER, Senior Research Fellow at All Souls College, Oxford, Editor of *The Sea in History – The Modern World*

DONORS

We are very grateful to DCNS, TOTAL, and CGG, which have supported our adventure from the outset as major contributors, and to the French Navy, GICAN, the Grand Port Maritime du Havre, STX France and Automatic Sea Vision and DCI-NAVFCO for their continuing support.

We also wish to thank the following sponsors: Alcen, Banque Transatlantique, Bureau Veritas, Gonzague de Blignières intuitu personae, Ilago, Safran, Socatra, Thales and Vallourec.

INSTITUTIONAL SPONSORS

The French Ministry of Transportation, Oceans, and Fisheries has sponsored the association from the start. Other institutional sponsors include the CCI of Le Havre, Cluster Maritime Français, GICAN, Ifremer, and the City of Saint Pierre and Miquelon.

The Committee of Honour, which comprises leading figures from the maritime, scientific and political sectors, is headed by CLAUDIE HAIGNERÉ, astronaut, former French Minister and currently special advisor to the Managing Director of the European Space Agency.

www.oceanides-association.org, @ProjetOceanides, FB: Association Oceanides

Océanides

COMPRENDRE LE RÔLE DE LA MER DANS L'HISTOIRE
POUR ÉCLAIRER NOTRE AVENIR

« La mondialisation rend plus que jamais nécessaire une meilleure prise en considération des questions maritimes, aux plans géopolitique, économique, écologique, comme le savent bien les entreprises et institutions qui nous soutiennent. Notre ambition de fond est de faire connaître ces enjeux maritimes et opportunités de développement, et convaincre de leur importance cruciale pour l'avenir de nos sociétés. Vous ne serez pas déçus, je pense même que vous allez être passionnés par la variété des aspects de l'histoire humaine étudiés : des ressources naturelles aux technologies, des guerres au commerce, des idées aux organisations politiques et sociales. »

ANNE-MARIE IDRAC
ancien ministre, présidente du Conseil d'administration

Lancé en mars 2012, Océanides est un projet de recherche international, programmé sur cinq années et ayant pour objectif d'apporter la preuve scientifique de l'importance de la mer dans les grandes étapes de l'évolution des peuples.

L'objectif premier d'Océanides est de combler une lacune en disposant d'une vision d'ensemble de l'histoire maritime de notre planète s'étendant sur cinq millénaires et cinq continents. Ainsi, les décideurs, politiques en particulier, disposeront des éléments nécessaires pour fonder leur vision dans le domaine maritime et pourront y puiser des arguments pour voir dans la mer l'avenir de la Terre.

MEMBRES DU CONSEIL D'ADMINISTRATION

ANNE-MARIE IDRAC, administrateur de sociétés, présidente d'Océanides
PATRICK BOISSIER, ancien PDG de DCNS, président du GICAN
MICHEL BENEZIT, conseiller spécial du PDG de TOTAL
CHRISTOPHE BARNINI, directeur de la communication du groupe CGG
FRANÇOIS JACQ, PDG de l'IFREMER
FRÉDÉRIC MONCANY DE SAINT-AIGNAN, président du Cluster Maritime Français
SABINE MARIE DECUP-PROVOST, déléguée générale d'Océanides
MAXIME PETIET, administrateur de sociétés, trésorier d'Océanides

Océanides possède un Conseil scientifique parfaitement indépendant, dirigé par le Professeur Christian Buchet, directeur du Centre d'Etude de la Mer de la Faculté Catholique de Paris et membre de l'Académie de Marine. Il regroupe :